HISTORY OF PSYCHOLOGY

A Source Book in Systematic Psychology

HISTORY OF PSYCHOLOGY

A Source Book in Systematic Psychology

EDITED BY

William S. Sahakian, Ph. D.

SUFFOLK UNIVERSITY

F. E. PEACOCK PUBLISHERS, INC.

ITASCA, ILLINOIS

Printed in U.S.A. by F. E. Peacock Publishers, Inc.
Library of Congress Catalog Card Number 68–21871

DEDICATED TO MY WIFE

MABEL LEWIS SAHAKIAN

THE ACTUALIZATION OF ALL
THAT IS BEAUTIFUL IN WOMANHOOD

Preface

The paucity of books of readings in the field of the history of psychology is sufficient warrant for a new one. In fact, strictly speaking, to date there is none which encompasses the field, rather than a specialized area within it as the few source books in the history of psychology available today are wont to do. If one knew no better, a reading of the leading current source books devoted to the history of psychology would imply the absence of important areas in psychology, such as, personality theory, abnormal psychology, psychotherapy, and social psychology, to cite a few.

Another feature characterizing the present volume is its departure from the traditional approach, its chronological and typological arrangement of men and subject matter so that men are not ordered according to their chronological categories only, but as to their nationality and area of specialty as well.

The variety of men and subjects herein treated spans more than merely two millennia of time; it covers 133 different men, and schools as diverse as behaviorism and existentialism.

A psychological history would tend to define the scope of psychology, but this is not exactly the case with a source book whose contents comprise only the most outstanding of the pioneers who were responsible for original material. Accordingly, a source book (without the aid of an instructor to complement the material found in such a book) may give to a person unversed in the history of psychology, the impression that psychological study is absent in countries such as: Japan, the Philippines, or even Spain and the countries of South America. To remedy the possibility of gaining any such erroneous idea, a chapter on the "Landmarks in the History of Psychology" is appended to the source material. Although this chapter contains an adequate bibliography, there is a further bibliography containing books in English treating the history of psychology ordered alphabetically by author, whereas the former is chronologically arranged.

WILLIAM S. SAHAKIAN

Beacon Hill
Boston, Massachusetts
August 28, 1967

Contents

1

Ancient Greek and Latin Psychology

ANAXAGORAS
(500–428),

EMPEDOCLES
(490–430),

DEMOCRITUS
(460–370),

LEUCIPPUS
(5th century B.C.),

and other

PRE-SOCRATIC PSYCHOLOGISTS

The Psyche [1]

Animate nature is thought to be different from the inanimate mainly in two particulars, viz. in movement and sense perception. And these, I may say, are the two traditional characteristics of the soul which we have received from earlier writers. Some of these writers, indeed, affirm that motion is the first and foremost characteristic of the soul, and in the belief that what is itself unmoved cannot impart motion to anything else, they suppose that the soul is a moving entity. This is the reason why Democritus declares the soul to be a sort of fire or warm element. He asserts that, although atomic structures are infinite in variety, both fire and soul are composed of spherical atoms, similar to the particles, as we call them, seen in the air when sunbeams stream through a doorway, and these atoms, as collective seed-particles, he calls the elements of the universe. Leucippus also holds a similar view. It is the spherical atoms, he says, that constitute the soul, because such forms can most easily penetrate through everything, and, being themselves in motion, can move everything else, the theory of these philosophers being that the soul is the principle which imparts motion to animals. It is for this reason too that they regard respiration

as the function that fixes life's limit. They think that the surrounding air presses together and expels the atomic bodies, which, because they are themselves never at rest, impart motion to animals, but that relief comes through respiration, because similar particles thereby enter into the body from without. These latter, by restraining the contracting and condensing element, prevent the spherical atoms which are already in animals from being entirely expelled. So long as they can do this, life continues. The theory which has been handed down from the Pythagoreans appears to have the same import. For some members of this school maintain that the sun-motes in the air are the soul; others declare that the soul is the principle which sets these in motion. They refer to these particles in their theory, because the particles appear to be in constant motion, even when there is a complete calm. The philosophers who regard the soul as a self-moved principle come to the same conclusion. For they all seem to regard motion as the most characteristic attribute of the soul, and while everything else is moved by the soul, the soul is self-moved. They came to this conclusion because they observed that nothing sets anything else in motion without being itself in motion. In a similar spirit Anaxagoras also declares the soul to be the principle of motion, and this view is held by such others, if there are any, as assert that Reason sets the All in motion.

---

[1] Aristotle, *De Anima*, trans. William Alexander Hammond (New York: Macmillan, 1902), bk. 1, ch. 2, *steph*. 403b–405b.

Anaxagoras does not, however, quite agree with Democritus. For Democritus absolutely identifies soul with reason, and considers truth to be that which appears to the senses. Consequently, Homer is right in singing of Hector that he lay "thinking awry." Democritus does not employ reason as a specific faculty for the apprehension of truth, but asserts that soul and reason are identical. Anaxagoras, however, is less clear on this point. For although he says in many passages that reason is the cause of the beautiful and the true, in other passages he says that reason is the same as the soul, for it is found in all animals, great and small, high and low. Reason, however, in the sense of intelligence, is not found equally in all animals, nor even in all men.

Such philosophers as fix their attention on movement as the main fact in animate creation conceive of the soul as the most mobile principle. On the other hand, such philosophers as emphasize the knowledge and perception of reality, define the soul as the principle of things, some holding there are several such principles, others that this psychical principle is the only one. Empedocles, for instance, regards the soul as composed of all the elements, and he asserts that each of these elements is a soul. He says:

"Earth we apprehend by earth, water by water,
  And air divine by air, destructive fire by fire,
  And love we know by love, sad hate by hate."

In this way, too, Plato in his *Timaeus* constructs the soul out of the elements; for we know like by like, and things are composed of elemental principles. A similar theory is given in his *Discourses on Philosophy*, where he defines an animal, regarded absolutely, as a structure derived from the idea of unity and the primary elements length, breadth, and thickness; other things are similarly fashioned. Again, in a different way, Plato defines reason as unity, and science as two; for the latter moves towards unity in a single course. He also defines opinion as the number of a plane surface and sense-perception as the number of a solid. Numbers were declared to be the actual forms and first principles of things and to be composed of the elements. But things are discerned partly by reason, partly by science, partly by opinion, and partly by sense-perception. Numbers, however, are the

forms of things. Since the soul was regarded by these Platonists as at once the principle of motion and the principle of knowledge, some of them included both these ideas in their definition, and explained the soul as a self-moving number. These philosophers differ, however, in regard to the kind and number of their principles. The most far-reaching difference is that between the philosophers who regard the elements as corporeal and those who regard them as incorporeal. There are others who define the elements as a composite of corporeal and incorporeal. They differ also in regard to the number of the elements, some believing there is one only, and others that there are several, and their definitions of the soul vary with their theories of the elements. Amongst the primal elements they classified, not unreasonably, the principle of inherent movement. And so some philosophers held the soul to be fire; for fire is the finest and most nearly incorporeal of all the elements, and furthermore, it most readily receives and imparts motion. Democritus has explained in a very neat way the cause of these phenomena. Soul and reason, he says, are identical, and belong to the primary and indivisible bodies, and are, furthermore, the principle of motion by virtue of their particles and atomic forms. Amongst these atomic forms, he regards the spherical as the most easily moved, and says that reason and fire are of this sort. Anaxagoras, on the other hand, appears to say that the soul and reason are different, as we remarked above, and yet he employs them as essentially one, except that he regards reason as more than anything else the initial principle of the world. At any rate he asserts that reason is the only entity which is absolute, unmixed, and pure. But he ascribes both attributes of knowledge and motion to the same principle, affirming that reason sets the universe in motion. Thales also, according to the traditional stories of him, appears to have conceived of the soul as a sort of kinetic principle, if it be true that he said the loadstone has a soul because it moves iron. Diogenes, however, and certain others say that the soul is air, in the belief that it is the finest element and the ultimate principle. It is for this reason, also, that the soul knows and produces motion. On the one hand, it knows by virtue of the fact that it is primary and other things are derivatives from it. On the other hand, it is the principle of motion by virtue of its being the first element. Heraclitus, also, says the soul is the first principle, since it is fiery vapor from which everything else is derived. It is also the most incorporeal of all the elements and is in constant flux. We apprehend that which is moved by what is in motion, and he believed, as did most others, that the real world is in motion. Alcmaeon, too, appears to have held views of the soul very similar to these. For he says the soul is immortal because it is like the Immortals, and this property of immortality belongs to it by virtue of its perpetual motion. Now, all divine things are in perpetual motion,—moon, sun, stars, and all the heavens. Certain cruder thinkers, like Hippo, asserted that the soul is water. They appear to have based their belief on the nature of animal seed, which in all cases is moist. Hippo confutes those who say the soul is blood by the argument that the seed is not blood, and seed is the elemental soul. Others, like Critias, regard the blood as the soul, on the supposition that the most characteristic attribute of the soul is sense-perception, and sense-perception is due to the blood. So all the elements, with the exception of earth, have received a vote. No one has represented earth as the principle of soul, unless it were certain philosophers who regarded the soul as composed of all the elements, or as identical with them all. They all define the soul, one may say, in terms of three things: motion, sensation, and incorporeality, and each of these is referred back to the ultimate elements. Therefore, with one exception, those who define the soul in terms of knowledge, make it an element or a derivative of the elements. For they say that we know like by like, and inasmuch as it is the soul that knows all things, it must consist of all the elements. Those philosophers, who maintain there is only one cause and one element, regard the soul as a unit, like fire or air. On the other hand, the philosophers who maintain that there are several elements, make the soul a plurality. Anaxagoras alone declares that the soul is affected by nothing and has nothing in common with anything else. But, if this is its nature, he did not explain, nor is it evident from his writings, how the soul is to acquire knowledge and virtue. The philosophers who include contraries amongst their first principles regard the soul as composed of contraries. On the other hand, those who include in their principles only particular contraries, such as heat and cold or similar opposites, likewise regard the soul as one of these. And so there are some who take into consideration the derivation of the words, certain of them claiming that the soul is heat because the verb "to live" is derived from this, others claiming the soul is cold, because the name "soul" is derived from respiration and refrigeration. These, then, are the traditional views of the soul, and these are the grounds on which they have been advanced.

SOCRATES
(470–399)

and PLATO
(427–347)

Psychology of Perception [2]

SOC.: I think that you have delivered yourself of a very important doctrine about knowledge, which is indeed that of Protagoras, who has another way of expressing the same thing when he says that man is the measure of all things, of the existence of things that are, and of the non-existence of things that are not: You have read that?

[2] Plato, *Theatetus*, trans. Benjamin Jowett (Oxford: Clarendon Press, 1888), *steph.* 152–164.

THEAET.: Yes, I have read that, again and again.

SOC.: Does he not mean to say that things are to you such as they appear to you, and are to me such as they appear to me, for you and I are men?

THEAET.: Yes, that is what he says.

SOC.: Such a wise man has doubtless a meaning: let us try to understand him; the same wind is blowing, and yet one of us may be cold and the other not, or one may be slightly and the other very cold?

THEAET.: Very true.

SOC.: Now is the wind, regarded not in relation to us but absolutely, cold or not; or are we to say, with Protagoras, that the wind is cold to him who is cold, and not to him who is not?

THEAET.: I suppose the last.

SOC.: This is what appears to each of them?

THEAET.: Yes.

SOC.: And "appears to him" means the same as "he perceives?"

THEAET.: True.

SOC.: Then appearance and perception coincide in this instance of hot and cold, and in similar instances; for things appear, or may be supposed to be, to each one such as he perceives them?

THEAET.: Yes.

SOC.: Then perception is always of existence, and being the same as knowledge is unerring?

THEAET.: That is clear.

SOC.: Now, I verily and indeed suspect that Protagoras, who was an almighty wise man, spoke these things in a parable to the common herd, like you and me, but he told the truth, "his truth," in secret to his own disciples.

THEAET.: What do you mean, Socrates?

SOC.: I am about to speak of an illustrious philosophy, in which all things are said to be relative; you cannot rightly call anything by any name, such as great or small, or heavy or light, for the great will be small and the heavy light.

* * * * *

SOC.: And is not the bodily habit spoiled by rest and idleness, but preserved for a long time by motion and exercise?

THEAET.: True.

SOC.: And is not this true of the mental habit also? Is not the soul informed, and improved, and preserved by thought and attention, which are motions; but when at rest, which in the soul means only want of thought and attention, is uninformed, and speedily forgets whatever she has learned?

THEAET.: True.

* * * * *

SOC.: Then apply this to perception, my good friend, and first of all to vision; that which you call white color is not in your eyes, and is not a distinct thing which exists out of them, having no assignable place; for

that would imply order and rest, and there would be no process of generation.

THEAET.: Then what is color?

SOC.: Let us carry out the principle which has just been affirmed, that nothing is self-existent, and then we shall see that every color, white, black, and every other color, arises out of the eye meeting the appropriate motion, and that what we term the substance of each color is neither the active nor the passive element, but something which passes between them, and is peculiar to each percipient; are you certain that the several colors appear to every animal—say to a dog—as they appear to you?

THEAET.: Indeed I am not.

SOC.: Or that anything appears the same to you as to another man? Would you not rather question whether you yourself see the same thing at different times, because you are never exactly the same?

THEAET.: I should.

SOC.: And if that with which I compare myself in size or which I apprehend, were great or white or hot, it could not without actually changing become different by mere contact with another; nor again, if the apprehending or comparing subject were great or white or hot, could this, when unchanged from within, become changed by any approximation or affection of any other thing. For already, my friend, we see that there are most ridiculous and wonderful contradictions into which we are only too readily falling, as Protagoras and all who take his line of argument would remark.

* * * * *

Their principle is, that all is motion, and upon this all the affections of which we were just now speaking are supposed to depend; there is nothing but motion, which has two forms, one active and the other passive, both in endless number, and out of the union and friction of them there is generated a progeny in endless number, having two forms, sense and the object of sense, which are ever breaking forth at the same moment and coming to the birth. The senses are variously named hearing, seeing, smelling; there is the sense of heat, cold, pleasure, pain, desire, fear, and many more which are named, and there are innumerable others which have no name; and there are all sorts of colors of a nature akin to the sight, and of sounds akin to the hearing, and other objects of sense which are akin to the several senses. Do you see, Theaetetus, the bearing of this tale on the preceding argument?

THEAET.: Indeed I do not.

SOC.: Then attend, in the hope that there may be an end. The meaning is that all these things are in motion, as I was saying, and that this motion has degrees of swiftness or slowness; and the slower elements have their motions in the same place and about things near them, and thus beget, but the things begotten are quicker, for their motions are from place to place. Apply this to sense: When the eye and the appropriate object meet together and give birth to whiteness and the sensation of white, which could not have been given by either of them going to any other object, then, while the sight is flowing from the eye and whiteness from the color-producing element, the eye becomes fulfilled with sight, and sees, and becomes, not sight, but a seeing eye; the object which combines in forming the color is fulfilled with whiteness, and becomes not whiteness but white, whether wood or stone, or whatever the object may be which happens to be colored white. And this is true of all sensations, hard, warm, and the like, which are similarly to be regarded, as I was saying before, not as having any absolute existence, but as being all of them generated by motion in their intercourse with one another, according to their kinds; for of the agent and patient, taken singly, as they say, no fixed idea can be framed, for the agent has no existence until united with the patient, and the patient has no existence until united with the agent; and that which unites with anything and is an agent, when meeting with another thing, is converted into a patient. And out of all this, as I said at first, there arises a general reflection, which is, that there is no one or self-existent thing, but everything is becoming and in relation; and being has to be altogether abolished, although custom and ignorance may compel us to retain the use of the word. But philosophers tell us that we are not to allow either the word "something," or "belonging to something," or "to me," or "this" or "that," or any other detaining name to be used; in the language of nature all things are being created and destroyed, coming into being and passing into

new forms; nor can any name fix or detain them he who attempts to fix them is easily refuted. And this should be the way of speaking, not only of particulars but of aggregates; such aggregates as are expressed in the word "man" or "stone," or any name of an animal or of a class.

* * * * *

SOC.: Let us not leave the argument unfinished, then; as there still remains to be considered an objection which may be raised about dreams and diseases, in particular about madness, and the various illusions of hearing and sight, or any other misapprehension. For you know that in all these cases the theory of the truth of perception appears to be unmistakably refuted, as in dreams and illusions we certainly have false perceptions; and far from saying that everything is which appears, we should rather say that nothing is which appears.

THEAET.: That is very true, Socrates.

SOC.: But then, my boy, how can any one assert that knowledge is perception, or that things are to each one as they appear?

THEAET.: I am afraid to say, Socrates, that I have nothing to answer, because you rebuked me just now for saying that; but I certainly cannot undertake to argue that madmen or dreamers think truly, when they imagine some of them that they are gods, and others that they can fly, and are flying in their sleep.

SOC.: Do you know that there is a question which is raised about all these errors, and especially about waking and sleeping?

THEAET.: What question?

SOC.: A question which I think that you must often have heard persons ask: How can you prove whether at this moment we are sleeping, and all our thoughts are a dream; or whether we are awake, and talking to one another in the waking state?

THEAET.: Indeed, Socrates, I do not know how you can prove that the one is any more true than the other, for all the phenomena correspond; and there is no difficulty in supposing that we have now been talking to one another in our sleep; and when in a dream we seem to be telling thoughts which are only dreams, the resemblance of the two states is quite astonishing.

SOC.: You see, then, that there is no difficulty in raising a doubt, since there may even be a doubt whether we are awake in or a dream. And as the time is equally divided in which we are asleep or awake, in either sphere of existence the soul contends that the thoughts which are present to our minds at the time are true; and during one half of our lives we affirm the truth of the one, and during the other half, of the other; and are equally confident of both.

THEAET.: Certainly.

* * * * *

SOC.: There is no other object of which I shall ever have the same perception, for another object would imply another perception, and would make the percipient other and different; nor can that object which affects me meeting another subject, produce the same or become similar, for that too will produce another result from another subject, and become different.

THEAET.: True.

SOC.: Neither can I for myself have this sensation, nor the object by or for itself, this quality.

THEAET.: Certainly not.

SOC.: When I perceive I must become percipient of something; there can be no such thing as perceiving and perceiving nothing; the quality of the object, whether sweet, bitter, or any other quality, must have relation to a perception; there cannot be anything sweet which is sweet to no one.

THEAET.: Certainly not.

SOC.: Then the inference is, that we [the agent and patient] are or become in relation to one another; there is a law which binds us one to the other, but not to any other existence, nor yet to ourselves; and therefore we can only be bound to one another; so that whether a person says that a thing is or becomes, he must say that it is or becomes to or of or in relation to something else; but he must not say that anything is or becomes absolutely, or allow any one else to say this: that is the conclusion.

THEAET.: Very true, Socrates.

SOC.: Then, if that which acts upon me has relation to me and to no other, I and no other am the percipient of it?

THEAET.: Of course.

SOC.: Then my perception is true to me, and is always a part of my being; and as Protagoras says, to myself I am judge of what is and what is not to me.

THEAET.: That seems to be true.

SOC.: How then, if I never err, and if my mind never trips in the conception of being or becoming, can I fail of knowing that which I perceive?

THEAET.: You cannot.

SOC.: Then you are quite right in affirming that knowledge is only perception; and the meaning turns out to be the same, whether with Homer and Heracleitus, and all that company, you say that all is motion and flux, or with the great sage Protagoras, that man is the measure of all things; or with Theaetetus, that, supposing all this, perception is knowledge. Am I not right, Theaetetus, and may I not say that this is your newborn child, of which I have delivered you—what say you?

THEAET.: I cannot but agree, Socrates.

* * * * *

SOC.: I say nothing against his doctrine, that what appears is to each one, but I wonder that he did not begin his great work on Truth with a declaration that a pig or a dog-faced baboon, or some other stranger monster which has sensation, is the measure of all things; then, when we were reverencing him as a god, he might have condescended to inform us that he was no wiser than a tadpole and did not even aspire to be a man—would not this have produced an overpowering effect? For if truth is only sensation, and one man's discernment is as good as another's, and no man has any superior right to determine whether the opinion of any other is true or false, but each man, as we have several times repeated, is to himself the sole judge, and everything that he judges is true and right, why should Protagoras be preferred to the place of wisdom and instruction, and deserve to be well paid, and we poor ignoramuses have to go to him, if each one is the measure of his own wisdom? Must he not be talking "ad captandum" in all this? I say nothing of the ridiculous predicament in which my own midwifery and the whole art of dialectic is placed; for the attempt to supervise or refute the notions or opinions of others would be a tedious and enormous piece of folly, if to each man they are equally right; and this must be the case if Protagoras' Truth is the real truth, and the philosopher is not merely amusing himself by giving oracles out of the shrine of his book.

* * * * *

SOC.: And the way will be to ask whether sensation is or is not the same as knowledge; for this was the real point of our argument, and with a view to this we raised (did we not?) those many strange questions.

THEAET.: Certainly.

SOC.: Shall we say that we know all that which we see and hear? for example, shall we say that not having learned, we do not know the language of foreigners when they speak to us? or shall we say that hearing them, we also know what they are saying? or suppose that we see letters which we do not understand, shall we say that we do not see them? or shall we maintain that, seeing them, we must know them?

THEAET.: We shall say, Socrates, that we know that which we actually see and hear of them—that is to say, we see and know the figure and color of the letters, and we hear and know the elevation or depression of the sound of them; but we do not perceive by sight and hearing, or know, that which grammarians and interpreters teach about them.

SOC.: Capital, Theaetetus; I shall not dispute that, as I want you to grow; but there is another difficulty coming, which you will also have to repulse.

THEAET.: What is that?

SOC.: Some will say.—Can a man who has ever known anything, and still has and preserves a memory of that which he knows, not know that which he remembers at the time when he remembers? I have, I fear, a tedious way of putting a simple question, which is only, whether a man who has learned, and remembers, can fail to know?

THEAET.: That, Socrates, would be impossible and absurd.

SOC.: Am I dreaming, then? Think: is not seeing perceiving, and is not sight perception?

THEAET.: True.

SOC.: And if our recent definition holds, every man knows that which he has seen?

THEAET.: Yes.

SOC.: And you would admit that there is such a thing as memory?

THEAET.: Yes.

SOC.: And is memory of something or of nothing?

THEAET.: Of something, surely.

SOC.: Of things learned and perceived, that is?

THEAET.: Certainly.

SOC.: Often a man remembers that which he has seen?

THEAET.: True.

SOC.: And if he closed his eyes, would he forget?

THEAET.: That, Socrates, would indeed be an absurd thing to affirm.

SOC.: And yet that must be affirmed, if the previous argument is to be maintained.

THEAET.: How is that? I am not quite sure that I see your meaning, though I have a strong suspicion that you are right. Will you explain how this is?

SOC.: As thus: he who sees knows, as we say, that which he sees; for perception and sight and knowledge are supposed to be all the same.

THEAET.: Certainly.

SOC.: But he who saw, and has knowledge of that which he saw, remembers, when he closes his eyes, that which he no longer sees.

THEAET.: True.

SOC.: And seeing is knowing, and therefore not seeing is not knowing?

THEAET.: That is true.

SOC.: Then the inference is, that a man may have attained the knowledge of something, which he may remember and yet not know, because he does not see; and this has been affirmed by us to be an absurdity.

THEAET.: That is very true.

SOC.: Thus, then, the assertion that knowledge and perception are one, involves a manifest impossibility?

THEAET.: Yes.

SOC.: Then they must be distinguished?

THEAET.: I suppose that they must.

SOC.: Once more we shall have to begin, and ask, "What is knowledge?" and yet, Theaetetus, what are we going to do?

THEAET.: About what? . . .

SOC.: Then I will try to explain myself: just now we asked the question, whether a man who had learned and remembered could fail to know, and we showed that a person who had seen might remember when he had his eyes shut and could not see, and then he would at the same time remember and not know. But this was an impossibility, and so the Protagorean fable came to nought, and yours also, who maintain that knowledge is the same as perception.

THEAET.: True.

Interpretation of Dreams and Unconscious Motivation [3]

Certain of the unnecessary pleasures and appetites I conceive to be unlawful; every one appears to have them, but in some persons they are controlled by the laws and by reason, and the better desires prevail over them—either they are wholly banished or they become few and weak; while in the case of others they are stronger, and there are more of them.

Which appetites do you mean?

I mean those which are awake when the reasoning and human and ruling power is asleep; then the wild beast within us, gorged with meat or drink, starts up and having shaken off sleep, goes forth to satisfy his desires; and there is no conceivable folly or crime—not excepting incest or any other unnatural union, or parricide, or the eating of forbidden food—which at such a time, when he has parted company with all shame and sense, a man may not be ready to commit.

Most true, he said.

But when a man's pulse is healthy and temperate, and when before going to sleep he has awakened his rational powers, and fed them on noble thoughts and enquiries, collecting himself in meditation; after having first indulged his appetites neither too much nor too little, but just enough to lay them to sleep, and prevent them and their enjoyments and pains from interfering with the higher principle—which he leaves in the solitude of pure abstraction, free to contemplate and aspire to the knowledge of the unknown, whether in past, present, or future: when again he has allayed the passionate element, if he has a quarrel against any one—I say, when, after pacifying the two irrational principles, he rouses up the third, which is

reason, before he takes his rest, then, as you know, he attains truth most nearly, and is least likely to be the sport of fantastic and lawless visions.

* * * * *

Tell him, Cebes, he replied, what is the truth—that I had no idea of rivalling him or his poems; to do so, as I knew, would be no easy task. But I wanted to see whether I could purge away a scruple which I felt about the meaning of certain dreams. In the course of my life I have often had intimations in dreams "that I should compose music." The same dream came to me sometimes in one form, and sometimes in another, but always saying the same or nearly the same words: "Cultivate and make music," said the dream. And hitherto I had imagined that this was only intended to exhort and encourage me in the study of philosophy, which has been the pursuit of my life, and is the noblest and best of music. The dream was bidding me do what I was already doing, in the same way that the competitor in a race is bidden by the spectators to run when he is already running. But I was not certain of this; for the dream might have meant music in the popular sense of the word, and being under sentence of death, and the festival giving me a respite, I thought that it would be safer for me to satisfy the scruple, and, in obedience to the dream, to compose a few verses before I departed.

The Association of Ideas [4]

This is what I would say, he replied:—We should agree, if I am not mistaken, that what a man recollects he must have known at some previous time.

Very true.

And what is the nature of this knowledge or recollection? I mean to ask, Whether a person who, having seen or heard or in any way perceived anything, knows not only that, but has a conception of something else which is the subject, not of the same but of some other kind of knowledge, may not be fairly said to recollect that of which he has the conception?

What do you mean?

---

[3] Plato, *Republic*, trans. Benjamin Jowett (New York: Charles Scribner's Sons, 1895), bk. 9, *steph.* 571–572, conversation transpiring between Socrates and Adeimantus; also from Plato, *Phaedo*, trans. Benjamin Jowett (New York: Macmillan, 1892), *steph.* 60–61, conversation transpiring among Socrates, Simmias, and Cebes.

[4] Plato, *Phaedo*, *op. cit.*, conversation transpiring between Socrates and Simmias.

I mean what I may illustrate by the following instance:—The knowledge of a lyre is not the same as the knowledge of a man?

True.

And yet what is the feeling of lovers when they recognize a lyre, or a garment, or anything else which the beloved has been in the habit of using? Do not they, from knowing the lyre, form in the mind's eye an image of the youth to whom the lyre belongs? And this is recollection. In like manner any who sees Simmias may remember Cebes; and there are endless examples of the same thing.

Endless, indeed, replied Simmias.

And recollection is most commonly a process of recovering that which has been already forgotten through time and inattention.

Very true, he said.

Well; and may you not also from seeing the picture of a house or a lyre remember a man? and from the picture of Simmias, you may be led to remember Cebes;

True.

Or you may also be led to the recollection of Simmias himself?

Quite so.

And in all these cases, the recollection may be derived from things either like or unlike?

It may be.

And when the recollection is derived from like things, then another consideration is sure to arise, which is—whether the likeness in any degree falls short or not of that which is recollected?

Very true, he said.

And shall we proceed a step further, and affirm that there is such a thing as equality, not of one piece of wood or stone with another, but that, over and above this, there is absolute equality? Shall we say so?

Say so, yes, replied Simmias, and swear to it, with all the confidence in life.

And do we know the nature of this absolute essence?

To be sure, he said.

ARISTOTLE
(384–322)

The Senses [5]

In discussing any form of sense-perception we must begin with the sensible object. The "object of sense" is used in three meanings, two of which touch the essential nature of sensation and one its accidents. Of the two first-named, one applies specially to each particular sense, the other is common to them all. By "peculiar object of sense" I mean a sense-quality which cannot be apprehended by a sense different from that to which it belongs, and concerning which that sense cannot be deceived, e.g. colour is the peculiar object of vision, sound of hearing, flavour of taste. Touch, however, discriminates several sense-qualities. The other particular senses, on the contrary, distinguish only their peculiar objects, and the senses are not deceived in the fact that a quality is colour or sound, although they may be deceived as to what or where the coloured or sonorous object may be. Such qualities are called the peculiar objects of particular senses, whereas common objects are motion, rest, number, form,

magnitude. Properties of the latter kind are not the peculiar objects of any sense, but are common to them all. Motion is apprehended by touch and by sight. A thing is an object of sense accidentally, e.g. when a white object proves to be the son of Diares. The latter is perceived accidentally, for the person whom one perceives is an accident of the white object. Therefore, the sense as such is not affected by the sensible object ([as a person]). To the objects of sense, strictly regarded, belong such properties as are peculiarly and properly sense-qualities, and it is with these that the essential nature of each sense is naturally concerned.

Vision

The object of vision is the visible. The visible is colour and something whose notion is expressible, but for which there is no single definite name. What I mean will be best explained as we proceed. The visible, then, is colour, and this is diffused upon that which is in itself visible, and by visible "in itself," I do not mean notionally visible, but something which has in itself the cause of the visible.

---

[5] Aristotle, *De Anima, op. cit.*, bk. 2, ch. 5–12.

All colour has the power to move the actually diaphanous and herein consists its nature. Therefore colour is not visible without light, but every particular colour is seen in the light. For this reason we must first explain what light is. Light is something diaphanous. By diaphanous I mean that which is visible, though not in itself and absolutely, but only by means of an agent, namely colour. Of such nature is air and water and many other bodies. Water and air are not diaphanous as water and air, but because there is in both these elements the same property that is found in the eternal empyrean. The activity of this diaphanous, as such, is light. But where the diaphanous exists only potentially, there is darkness. Light is the colour, as it were, of the diaphanous, when the diaphanous is made really so by fire or by some such agent as the supernal body, for in the supernal body there is something which is identical with fire. The nature of the diaphanous, therefore, and of light has been explained. Light is, namely, neither fire nor in a word any body nor the efflux of any body (for this would then also be a body), but it is the presence of fire or some such agent in a diaphanous medium.

Sense of Sound

The medium for sound is the atmosphere; the medium for smell has no name. It is an element that is common to air and water, and as the diaphanous is related to colour, so there is a something in water and air similarly related to an odorous body. For aquatic animals appear to be capable of the sensation of smell. But man and the respiring landanimals smell only in so far as they employ inspiration.... Light is constantly reflected (otherwise light would not be found everywhere, but there would be darkness outside the region illuminated by the sun), but the reflection is not similar to that which is caused by water or bronze or any other polished solid, where a shadow is cast whereby the light-area is delimited. A void is correctly regarded as a chief factor in hearing. Now, the air appears to be a void, and this, when it is moved as a single and continuous element, is what produces hearing. But, because of the swift dissipation of the air, no sound arises unless the object struck be smooth. In this case, however, the air by reason of the even surface, is made one throughout, for the

surface of a smooth body is one throughout.

A body is sonorous when it is capable of setting in motion up to the organ of hearing the single and continuous air. Hearing is naturally related to the air, and owing to the fact that sound is in the air, the inner air is set in motion by the moving outside air. Therefore, an animal does not hear in all parts of its body, neither does the air penetrate everywhere. And the psychical organ that is to be stimulated does not contain air in all its parts. The air in and for itself is, by reason of its facile dispersion, non-sonorous. But when it is restrained from dispersion, its motion produces sound. The air within the ears is so deeply immured as to be in itself immovable, in order that it may detect all distinctions in communicated motions.

Sense of Smell

Smell and its object are less easy to define than the foregoing senses, for the nature of smell is not so clear to us as is that of sound and colour. The reason for this is the fact that this sense with us is inaccurate and less perfect than in many animals. Man has a poor sense of smell, and smells no odorous object without painful or pleasant association, because the sense-organ does not sharply discriminate qualities. It is probable that the hard-eyed animals discriminate colours in the same way, and that distinctions in colour are not clear to them except as they have the feeling of fear or not. So it is with smell in the human race. Smell has apparently some analogy to taste, and the species of flavours correspond to those of odours; but our sense of taste is more accurate because it is a sort of touch, and the sense of touch is the most accurately developed of all the senses in man. In the case of the other senses, man is inferior to many animals, but in discriminations of touch he is far superior to the others....

As one flavour is sweet, another bitter, so it is with smells. Although in some cases smell and flavour correspond to each other, —I mean, for example, where we have a sweet smell and a sweet flavour,—in other cases they are contraries.

* * * * *

Smell is transmitted through a medium, such as air or water. For aquatic animals appear to smell; so, too, sanguineous and bloodless animals, and the birds of the air, have this sense. . . . Man smells while inhaling, but without inhaling and while exhaling or holding his breath, he does not smell, whether the object be remote or near, not even if it be placed in the nose itself. That an object when placed upon the sense-organ itself is not perceived, is a fact common to all the animals. But not to perceive odours without inhaling is peculiar to man, as may be proven by experiment. Were it not so, the bloodless animals, inasmuch as they have no respiration, would have to possess a sense beyond those already named.

Sense of Touch

If touch is not a single sense but several, then tangible objects must also be manifold. There is some doubt whether touch is manifold or unitary, and it is uncertain what the sense-organ is which apprehends the tangible.

* * * * *

Another question is whether the sense-organ is internal or not, or whether the flesh immediately senses touch-qualities.

* * * * *

However, as a matter of fact, since the media through which sense-movements are transmitted are different, the sense-organs themselves are different. In the case of touch this is not clear. . . . Consequently, the body [i.e. the flesh] must be the natural medium for the sense of touch, by which the several sensations are mediated.

Memory [6]

There is no memory of the present in the present moment, as we have said, but there is perception of the present, expectation of the future, and memory of the past. Consequently, all memory is associated with time. Therefore, only those creatures that have perception of time, have memory, and memory attaches to that organ whereby time is perceived. Now we have already discussed imagination in the treatise On the Soul and we concluded there that thought is impossible without an image. For we find in thought the same conditions as in drawing figures. In the latter without

needing a triangle of a definite magnitude, we nevertheless draw a triangle of definite size. So, too, the thinking mind, even if it does not think a magnitude, still places a quantitative body before its eyes, although it does not think it as such. If it is the nature of the quantitative in an indefinite sense with which the mind is concerned, then thought represents it under the form of a definite quantity, but thinks it merely as quantity. The reason why it is impossible to think anything apart from continuity (even things that are not subject to the laws of time cannot be thought without time) is a problem that belongs elsewhere. We must be conscious of magnitude and motion by the same faculty whereby we are conscious of time. An image is a product of sensation in general. Evidently, therefore, the cognition of these things is to be ascribed to the primary power of sense. Memory, even the memory of concepts, does not take place without an image.

The question arises whether one remembers the impression or the thing from which the impression was derived. For if it is this impression of ours which is the object of memory, then we do not remember what is absent. On the other hand, if it is the thing that we remember, how does it come that while we perceive this impression we remember what we do not perceive, viz. the absent thing? And if memory is analogous to an imprint or picture within us, why should the perception of precisely this thing be the memory of something else, and not the memory of just this picture? For it is this impression which one contemplates and perceives in actual memory. In what sense then does one remember what is not present? It would then be possible to see and to hear what is not present. Or is there a sense in which this is possible and in which it actually occurs?

Recollection [7]

Recollection is effected, when one suggestion succeeds another in natural order. If the succession is a necessary one, it is plain that when the antecedent suggestion is given, it will excite the succeeding one. If, however, the succession is not a necessary one, but only customary, the recollection will be stirred generally. But it is a fact that some persons

---

[6] Aristotle, Parva Naturalia, trans. William Alexander Hammond (New York: Macmillan, 1902), bk. 2, ch. 1.

[7] Ibid., ch. 2.

by being impressed only once are trained in a given way more than others after frequent impressions. And so there are some things which after we have seen once, we remember better than others do who have seen them frequently. When, therefore, we recollect, we awaken certain antecedent processes and continue this until we call up that particular experience, after which the desired one is wont to appear. That is the reason why we hunt through a series in thought, beginning with an object presently before us, or with something else, or with an object that is similar, or opposite, or contiguous. In this way, recollection is awakened. For mental movements in these instances are identical in some cases, in others simultaneous with, the desired experience, and in other cases they involve a portion of it, so that there is a small remainder whose stimulation ensues. . . . One does not at all need to look at the remote and ask how we remember it, but at what lies near before us. For the same method applies to both cases,—I mean the method of sequences, without any prior effort to find this sequence and without recalling it. For mental movements follow one another, this one after that, by habituation. When a person wants to recall a thing, he will do the following: he will try to gain a starting-point in the process, in sequence to which the desired experience was had. Consequently, recollections which are awakened from the starting-point are most quickly and best effected. For just as things are mutually related in their order of succession, so also are the mental processes. And such things as have a fixed order are easily remembered, as e.g. mathematical truths. Other things are remembered poorly and with difficulty. Recollection differs from re-learning in this, that there can be in the former case a sort of self-movement back to that which follows upon the original experience. When this is not done, but the recollection is prompted by another person, then it is no longer memory. Often-times one is unable to recollect a thing, but after searching succeeds in finding it. This seeking and finding is what happens when one awakens a number of experiences and continues to do so until one sets that particular experience in motion upon which the desired thing is attendant. . . . One must, however, have a starting-point. And so persons appear some-

times to recall things from local suggestions. The reason is that one passes rapidly from one thing to another, e.g. from milk to the suggested idea of white, from white to air, from air to the moist, and from this one recalls the late autumn, which is the season one was trying to think of. In general, it is the middle, too, of the entire series that seems to be the starting-point for memory. For when a person does not remember earlier, then he does so when he comes to the middle point, or when he does not remember here, then at no other point at all, as is the case e.g. when one passes through the series ABCDEFGH. If one does not remember at H, one remembers when one comes to E, provided one is in quest of F or G. For from that point the movement of suggestion is possible in both directions, towards the point D as well as towards the point F. If, however, a person is not in quest of one of these, he will remember on reaching C, and if not then, he will remember on reaching A, and this is the case always. But from the same point of suggestion one sometimes remembers and sometimes does not, the reason for which lies in the possibility of movement in more than one direction from the initial point, e.g. from E to F or from E to D. If the movement is influenced by an old suggestion, it takes place in the direction of the more fixed habit. For habit is second nature. Consequently, we remember easily what we often ponder. For as one definite thing succeeds another in nature, so it is also in our activity. Frequent repetition produces nature. Since we find in the realm of nature occurrences that violate her laws and are due to chance, much more do we find this in the realm of custom, to which the term nature cannot be applied in the same sense. The consequence is that a movement here sometimes takes place in one direction and sometimes in another, especially when the mind is distracted from a particular point to something else. Therefore, when one has to remember a name, and remembers one like it, one commits a solecism in regard to it. This then is the way in which recollection takes place.

Dreams [8]

It is evident that we have no sensation in

[8] *Ibid.*, bk. 4, ch. 1.

sleep, and so it is not by means of sensation that we experience dreaming. Neither are dreams mediated by opinion. For we not only say that an approaching object is a man or a horse, but also that it is white or beautiful, as to which qualities opinion apart from sensation makes no deliverances, whether true or false. However, this is just what the soul does in sleep. For, as in waking, so in sleep, we believe we see that the approaching object is a man, and that it is white. Again, we think of other things along with the dream, just as is the case with perception in our waking state. For we also often think about what we perceive. So in sleep along with our imaginings we sometimes have different thoughts. This would become apparent to anyone who would give attention on rising and try to remember. There have been persons who have in this way observed their dreams, as *e.g.* those who try to arrange their deliverances in accordance with the precepts of the mnemonic art. For it often happens in their case that along with the dream they put something else, an image before their eyes, in the place in question. And so it is clear that not every image seen in sleep is a dream, and what we think conceptually we regard as true or false through the organ of opinion. So much is clear on this subject that the same agency which in disease produces illusion while we are awake, also produces the condition of illusion in sleep. Even when we are in sound health and know the truth, still the sun appears to us to be only a foot in diameter. But whether the soul's powers of imagination and sensation are the same or different, in any case dreams do not take place independently of seeing and some sort of sensation. For illusions of sight and hearing occur when a person really sees and hears something, although not the thing that he thinks he sees

or hears. In sleep, however, there is according to the foregoing hypothesis no seeing, no hearing, no sensation at all. The hypothesis that there is no vision is, therefore, untrue, and that sensation experiences no excitation is untrue; on the other hand, it is possible for sight and the other senses to undergo some change and things impinge on each of them to a certain extent, as in the sensation belonging to the waking state, though with a certain difference. Sometimes opinion declares that the seen object is false, as in the waking state; sometimes it is held in check and conforms to the imagination.

After-Images [9]

Actual sensation is a kind of qualitative change. Consequently, this condition is found in the sense-organs not only during the process of sensation, but also after the process has ceased, and in their inner depths as well as on the surface. This becomes evident when we have a sensation that continues over some time. For when we turn our senses to something else, the original sensation persists, as *e.g.* when we turn from the sun to a dark object. The result is that one sees nothing owing to the fact that the sense-process, stimulated by the light, still lurks in the eyes. And if one looks a long time at a single colour, whether it be white or green, things appear to be similarly coloured wherever we turn our eyes. Again, if we look at the sun or some bright object, and then shut our eyes, there appears to sharp observation, in the direct line which vision employs, first of all a colour like the actual one, which then changes to scarlet, then to purple, until it passes into blackness and vanishes.

---

[9] *Ibid.*

ZENO
(356–264)

Stoical Psychology [10]

The Stoics have chosen to treat, in the first place, of perception and sensation, because

[10] Diogenes Laertius, *Lives and Opinions of Eminent Philosophers*, trans. Charles D. Yonge (London, 1853), bk. 7.

the criterion by which the truth of facts is ascertained is a kind of perception, and because the judgment which expresses the belief, and the comprehension, and the understanding of a thing, a judgment which precedes all others, cannot exist without perception. For perception leads the way; and then thought, finding vent in expressions, explains in words the feelings which it derives from perception.

... According to their ideas of the φαντασίαι, some are sensible, and some are not. Those they call sensible, which are derived by us from some one or more senses; and those they call not sensible, which emanate directly from the thought, as for instance, those which relate to incorporeal objects, or any others which are embraced by reason. Again, those which are sensible, are produced by a real object, which imposes itself on the intelligence, and compels its acquiescence; and there are also some others, which are simply apparent, mere shadows, which resemble those which are produced by real objects.

Again, these φαντασίαι are divided into rational and irrational; those which are rational belong to animals capable of reason; those which are irrational to animals destitute of reason.

* * * * *

By sensation, the Stoics understand a species of breath which proceeds from the dominant portion of the soul to the senses, whether it be a sensible perception, or an organic disposition, which, according to the notions of some of them, is crippled and vicious. They also call sensation the energy, or active exercise, of the sense. According to them, it is to sensation that we owe our comprehension of white and black, and rough and smooth: from reason, that we derive the notions which result from a demonstration, those for instance which have for their object the existence of Gods, and of Divine Providence. For all our thoughts are formed either by indirect perception, or by similarity, or analogy, or transposition, or combination, or opposition. By a direct perception, we perceive those things which are the objects of sense; by similarity, those which start from some point present to our senses; as, for instance, we form an idea of Socrates from his likeness.

* * * * *

The Stoics also say that the mind is divisible into eight parts; for that the five organs of sensation, and the vocal power, and the intellectual power, which is the mind itself, and the generative power, are all parts of the mind. But by error, there is produced a perversion which operates on the intellect, from which many perturbations arise, and many causes of inconstancy. And all perturbation is itself, according to Zeno, a movement of the mind, or superfluous inclination, which is irrational, and contrary to nature. Moreover, of the superior class of perturbations, as Hecaton says, in the second book of his treatise on the Passions, and as Zeno also says in his work on the Passions, there are four kinds, grief, fear, desire, and pleasure. And they consider that these perturbations are judgments, as Chrysippus contends in his work on the Passions; for covetousness is an opinion that money is a beautiful object, and in like manner drunkenness and intemperance, and other things of the sort, are judgments. And grief they define to be an irrational contraction of the mind, and it is divided into the following species, pity, envy, emulation, jealousy, pain, perturbation, sorrow, anguish, confusion. Pity is a grief over some one, on the ground of his being in undeserved distress. Envy is a grief, at the good fortune of another. Emulation is a grief at that belonging to some one else, which one desires one's self. Jealousy is a grief at another also having what one has one's self. Pain is a grief which weighs one down. Perturbation is grief which narrows one, and causes one to feel in a strait. Sorrow is a grief arising from deliberate thought, which endures for some time, and gradually increases. Anguish is a grief with acute pain. Confusion is an irrational grief, which frets one, and prevents one from clearly discerning present circumstances. But fear is the expectation of evil; and the following feelings are all classed under the head of fear: apprehension, hesitation, shame, perplexity, trepidation, and anxiety. Apprehension is a fear which produces alarm. Shame is a fear of discredit. Hesitation is a fear of coming activity. Perplexity is a fear, from the imagination of some unusual thing. Trepidation is a fear accompanied with an oppression of the voice. Anxiety is a fear of some uncertain event.

Again, desire is an irrational appetite; to which head, the following feelings are referable: want, hatred, contentiousness, anger, love, enmity, rage. Want is a desire arising from our not having something or other, and is, as it were, separated from the thing, but is still stretching, and attracted towards it in vain. And hatred is a desire that it should be ill with some one, accompanied with a certain continual increase and extension. Contentiousness is a certain desire accompanied with deliberate choice. Anger is a desire of revenge, on a person who appears to have injured one in an unbecoming way. Love is a desire not conversant about a virtuous object, for it is an attempt to conciliate affection, because of some beauty, which is seen. Enmity is a certain anger of long duration, and full of hatred, and it is a watchful passion, as is shown in the following lines:—

For though we deem the short-liv'd fury past,
'T is sure the mighty will revenge at last.

But rage is anger at its commencement.

Again, pleasure is an irrational elation of the mind over something which appears to be desirable; and its different species are enjoyment, rejoicing at evil, delight, and extravagant joy. Enjoyment, now, is a pleasure which charms the mind through the ears. Rejoicing at evil is a pleasure which arises at the misfortunes of others. Delight . . . that is to say turning is a certain turning of the soul to softness. Extravagant joy is the dissolution of virtue. And as there are said to be some sicknesses in the body, as, for instance, gout and arthritic disorders; so too are those diseases of the soul, such as a fondness for glory, or for pleasure, and other feelings of that sort. For an ἀῤῥώστημα [Arhrostema] is a disease accompanied with weakness; and a disease is an opinion of something which appears exceedingly desirable. And, as in the case of the body, there are illnesses to which people are especially liable, such as colds or diarrhœa; so also are there propensities which the mind is under the influence of, such as enviousness, pitifulness, quarrelsomeness, and so on.

There are also three good dispositions of the mind; joy, caution, and will. And joy they say is the opposite of pleasure, since it is a rational elation of the mind; so caution is the opposite of fear, being a rational avoidance of anything, for the wise man will never be afraid, but he will act with caution; and will, they define as the opposite of desire, since it is a rational wish. As therefore some things fall under the class of the first perturbations, in the same manner do some things fall under the class of the first good dispositions. And accordingly, under the head of will, are classed goodwill, placidity, salutation, affection; and under the head of caution are ranged reverence and modesty; under the head of joy, we speak of delight, mirth, and good spirits.

EPICURUS
(341–270)

Epicurean Psychology [11]

Sense Perception

Moreover, there are images resembling, as far as their form goes, the solid bodies which we see, but which differ materially from them in the thinness of their substance. In fact it is not impossible but that there may be in space some secretions of this kind, and an aptitude to form surfaces without depth, and of an extreme thinness; or else that from the solids there may emanate some particles which preserve the connection, the disposition, and the motion which they had in the body. I give the name of images to these representations.

* * * * *

It is useful, also, to retain this principle, and to know that the images have an incomparable thinness; which fact indeed is in no respect contradicted by sensible appearances. From which it follows that their rapidity also is incomparable; for they find everywhere an easy passage, and besides, their infinite smallness causes them to experience no shock, or at all events to experience but a very slight one, while an infinite multitude of elements very soon encounter some resistance.

One must not forget that the production of images is simultaneous with the thought; for from the surface of the bodies images of this kind are continually flowing off in an insensible manner indeed, because they are immediately replaced. They preserve for a long time the same disposition, and the same

---

[11] *Ibid.*, bk. 10.

arrangement that the atoms do in the solid body, although, notwithstanding, their form may be sometimes altered. The direct production of images in space is equally instantaneous, because these images are only light substances destitute of depth.

But there are other manners in which natures of this kind are produced; for there is nothing in all this which at all contradicts the senses, if one only considers in what way the senses are exercised, and if one is inclined to explain the relation which is established between external objects and ourselves. Also, one must admit that something passes from external objects into us in order to produce in us sight and the knowledge of forms; for it is difficult to conceive that external objects can affect us through the medium of the air which is between us and them, or by means of rays, whatever emissions proceed from us to them, so as to give us an impression of their form and colour. This phenomenon, on the contrary, is perfectly explained, if we admit that certain images of the same colour, of the same shape, and of a proportionate magnitude pass from these objects to us, and so arrive at being seen and comprehended. These images are animated by an exceeding rapidity, and, as on the other side, the solid object forming a compact mass, and comprising a vast quantity of atoms, emits always the same quantity of particles, the vision is continued, and only produces in us one single perception which preserves always the same relation to the object. Every conception, every sensible perception which bears upon the form or the other attributes of these images, is only the same form of the solid perceived directly, either in virtue of a sort of actual and continued condensation of the image, or in consequence of the traces which it has left in us.

* * * * *

The Psyche

Let us now return to the study of the affections, and of the sensations; for this will be the best method of proving that the soul is a bodily substance composed of slight particles, diffused over all the members of the body, and presenting a great analogy to a sort of spirit, having an admixture of heat,

resembling at one time one, and at another time the other of those two principles. There exists in it a special part, endowed with an extreme mobility, in consequence of the exceeding slightness of the elements which compose it, and also in reference to its more immediate sympathy with the rest of the body. That it is which the faculties of the soul sufficiently prove, and the passions, and the mobility of its nature, and the thoughts, and, in a word, everything, the privation of which is death. We must admit that it is in the soul most especially that the principle of sensation resides. At the same time, it would not possess this power if it were not enveloped by the rest of the body which communicates it to it, and in its turn receives it from it; but only in a certain measure; for there are certain affections of the soul of which it is not capable.

It is on that account that, when the soul departs, the body is no longer possessed of sensation; for it has not this power, (that of sensation namely) in itself; but, on the other hand, this power can only manifest itself in the soul through the medium of the body. The soul, reflecting the manifestations which are accomplished in the substance which environs it, realises in itself, in a virtue or power which belongs to it, the sensible affections, and immediately communicates them to the body in virtue of the reciprocal bonds of sympathy which unite it to the body; that is the reason why the destruction of a part of the body does not draw after it a cessation of all feeling in the soul while it resides in the body, provided that the senses still preserve some energy; although, nevertheless, the dissolution of the corporeal covering, or even of any one of its portions, may sometimes bring on with it the destruction of the soul.

The rest of the body, on the other hand, even when it remains, either as a whole, or in any part, loses all feeling by the dispersion of that aggregate of atoms, whatever it may be, that forms the soul. When the entire combination of the body is dissolved, then the soul too is dissolved, and ceases to retain those faculties which were previously inherent in it, and especially the power of motion; so that sensation perishes equally as far as the soul is concerned.

can will who is not and who does not live; and they also refer that will itself to something which they will with that will. They know also that they remember; and they know at the same time that nobody could remember, unless he both was and lived; but we refer memory itself also to something, in that we remember those things. Therefore the knowledge and science of many things are contained in two of these three, memory and understanding; but will must be present, that we may enjoy or use them. For we enjoy things known, in which things themselves the will finds delight for their own sake, and so reposes; but we use those things, which we refer to some other thing which we are to enjoy. Neither is the life of man vicious and culpable in any other way, than as wrongly using and wrongly enjoying. But it is no place here to discuss this.

But since we treat of the nature of the mind, let us remove from our consideration all knowledge which is received from without, through the senses of the body; and attend more carefully to the position which we have laid down, that all minds know and are certain concerning themselves. For men certainly have doubted whether the power of living, of remembering, of understanding, of willing, of thinking, of knowing, of judging, be of air, or of fire, or of the brain, or of the blood, or of atoms, or besides the usual four elements of a fifth kind of body, I know not what; or whether the combining or tempering together of this our flesh itself has power to accomplish these things. And one has attempted to establish this, and another to establish that. Yet who ever doubts that he himself lives, and remembers, and understands, and wills, and thinks, and knows, and judges? Seeing that even if he doubts, he lives; if he doubts, he remembers why he doubts; if he doubts, he understands that he doubts; if he doubts, he wishes to be certain; if he doubts, he thinks; if he doubts, he knows that he does not know; if he doubts, he judges that he ought not to assent rashly. Whosoever therefore doubts about anything else, ought not to doubt of all these things; which if they were not, he would not be able to doubt of anything.

They who think the mind to be either a body or the combination or tempering of the body, will have all these things to seem to be in a subject, so that the substance is air, or fire, or some other corporeal thing, which they think to be the mind; but that the understanding is in this corporeal thing as its quality, so that this corporeal thing is the subject, but the understanding is in the subject, viz. that the mind is the subject, which they rule to be a corporeal thing, but the understanding, or any other of those things which we have mentioned as certain to us, is in that subject. They also hold nearly the same opinion who deny the mind itself to be body, but think it to be the combination or tempering together of the body; for there is this difference, that the former say that the mind itself is the substance, in which the understanding is, as in a subject; but the latter say that the mind itself is in a subject, viz. in the body, of which it is the combination or tempering together. And hence, by consequence, what else can they think, except that the understanding also is in the same body as in a subject?

And all these do not perceive that the mind knows itself, even when it seeks for itself, as we have already shown. But nothing is at all rightly said to be known while its substance is not known. And therefore, when the mind knows itself, it knows its own substance; and when it is certain about itself, it is certain about its own substance. But it is certain about itself, as those things which are said above prove convincingly; although it is not at all certain whether itself is air, or fire, or some body, or some function of body. Therefore it is not any of these. And that whole which is bidden to know itself, belongs to this, that it is certain that it is not any of those things of which it is uncertain, and is certain that it is that only, which only it is certain that it is. For it thinks in this way of fire, or air, and whatever else of the body it thinks of. Neither can it in any way be brought to pass that it should so think that which itself is, as it thinks that which itself is not. Since it thinks all these things through an imaginary phantasy, whether fire, or air, or this or that body, or that part or combination and tempering together of the body: nor assuredly is it said to be all those things, but some one of them. But if it were any one of them, it would think this one in a different manner from the rest, viz. not through an imaginary phantasy, as absent things are thought, which either themselves or some of like kind have been touched by the bodily sense; but by some inward, not feigned, but true presence (for nothing is more present to it than itself); just as it thinks that itself lives, and remembers, and understands, and wills. For it knows these things in itself, and does not imagine them as though it had touched them by the sense outside itself, as corporeal things are touched. And if it attaches nothing to itself from the thought of these things, so as to think itself to be something of the kind, then whatsoever remains to it from itself, that alone is itself.

Memory, Understanding, and Will [2]

Putting aside, then, for a little while all other things, of which the mind is certain concerning itself, let us especially consider and discuss these three—memory, understanding, will. For we may commonly discern in these three the character of the abilities of the young also; since the more tenaciously and easily a boy remembers, and the more acutely he understands, and the more ardently he studies, the more praiseworthy is he in point of ability. But when the question is about any one's learning, then we ask not how solidly and easily he remembers, or how shrewdly he understands; but what it is that he remembers, and what it is that he understands. And because the mind is regarded as praiseworthy, not only as being learned, but also as being good, one gives heed not only to what he remembers and what he understands, but also to what he wishes; not how ardently he wishes, but first what it is he wishes, and then how greatly he wishes it. For the mind that loves eagerly is then to be praised, when it loves that which ought to be loved eagerly. Since, then, we speak of these three—ability, knowledge, use—the first of these is to be considered under the three heads, of what a man can do in memory, and understanding, and will. The second of them is to be considered in regard to that which any one has in his memory and in his understanding, whither he has attained by a studious will. But the third, viz. use, lies in the will, which handles those things that are contained in the memory and understanding, whether it refer them to anything

further, or rest satisfied with them as an end. For to use, is to take up something into the power of the will; and to enjoy, is to use with joy, not any longer of hope, but of the actual thing. Accordingly, every one who enjoys, uses; for he takes up something into the power of the will, wherein he also is satisfied as with an end. But not every one who uses, enjoys, if he has sought after that, which he takes up into the power of the will, not on account of the thing itself, but on account of something else.

Since, then, these three, memory, understanding, will, are not three lives, but one life; nor three minds, but one mind; it follows certainly that neither are they three substances, but one substance. Since memory, which is called life, and mind, and substance, is so called in respect to itself; but it is called memory, relatively to something. And I should say the same also of understanding and of will, since they are called understanding and will relatively to something; but each in respect to itself is life, and mind, and essence. And hence these three are one, in that they are one life, one mind, one essence; and whatever else they are severally called in respect to themselves, they are called also together, not plurally, but in the singular number. But they are three, in that wherein they are mutually referred to each other; and if they were not equal, and this not only each to each, but also each to all, they certainly could not mutually contain each other; for not only is each contained by each, but also all by each. For I remember that I have memory, and understanding, and will; and I understand that I understand, and will, and remember; and I will that I will, and remember, and understand; and I remember together my whole memory, and understanding, and will. For that of my memory which I do not remember, is not in my memory; and nothing is so much in the memory as memory itself. Therefore I remember the whole memory. Also, whatever I understand I know that I understand, and I know that I will whatever I will; but whatever I know I remember. Therefore I remember the whole of my understanding, and the whole of my will. Likewise, when I understand these three things, I understand them together as whole. For there is none of things intelligible which I do not understand, except what I do not know; but what I do not know,

² *Ibid.*, ch. 11, sect. 17–18.

I neither remember, nor will. Therefore, whatever of things intelligible I do not understand, it follows also that I neither remember nor will. And whatever of things intelligible I remember and will, it follows that I understand. My will also embraces my whole understanding and my whole memory, whilst I use the whole that I understand and remember. And, therefore, while all are mutually comprehended by each, and as wholes, each as a whole is equal to each as a whole, and each as a whole at the same time to all as wholes; and these three are one, one life, one mind, one essence.

ST. THOMAS AQUINAS
(1225–1274)

The Soul as an Intellective Principle [3]

The principle of intellectual activity, which we term the human soul, is a bodiless and completely substantial principle.

This principle, also termed the mind or intellect, can act without the body having an intrinsic part in the activity. Nothing can act independently unless it be independent.

Psychophysical Unity [4]

Having shown that an intellective substance is neither a body nor a power dependent on the body, we now have to investigate whether it can be united to a body.

In the first place the union obviously cannot come about in the manner of a mixture nor by touching properly so called, for contact is between bodies. Neither by merging nor by being fastened together can one perfectly single thing be constituted from intellectual and from bodily substance. There is, nevertheless, a mode of contact by which spirit can be joined to body, not by a mutual joining of quantities, but by the touching implied in the action of one thing on another: thus we say that we are touched by another's grief. This is the touch of power, not of quantity; it is feasible between spirits and bodies: intellectual substances can act on bodies and set them in motion. Yet though spirit and body are united as regards action and reaction, they do not thereby make up one thing simply so called.

Consequently we find ourselves inquiring

whether one thing simply speaking can be constituted from spirit and body. Now a natural unity cannot be constituted from two permanent realities unless they be related as substantial form and matter. Hence, we are faced with the problem how an intellective substance can be the substantial form of a body.

* * * * *

But this is impossible, for animals and men are natural and sensible things, which would not be the case were bodies and bodily organs not part of their essence, in other words, were they wholly souls. Moreover, it is impossible to have one single operation issuing from things which are diverse in being—I say one single operation, not as regards the term or effect, but as regards the going out from the principle, for when many haul at a boat, though one effect is produced, there are many efforts and different heaves from the haulers. Now there are actions common to soul and body; for sensing and feeling are functions of soul and body simultaneously, which are here at one, and not diverse in their being.

Sensation [5]

Some wish to base the distinction and number of the external senses on the difference of their organs; others on the diverse natures of sensible qualities in the medium of sensation. But neither attempt really meets the bill. For faculties are not for organs, but conversely; there are not diverse senses because there are different organs, instead nature provides diverse organs to match the diversity of powers. Similarly as regards the media of sensation. Moreover, it is for the mind to

[3] St. Thomas Aquinas, *Summa Theologica*, Ia. lxxv. 3; from *St. Thomas Aquinas: Philosophical Texts*, trans. Thomas Gilby (New York: Oxford University Press, 1951). Reprinted by permission.
[4] St. Thomas Aquinas, *Contra Gentes*, 56, 57; trans. Thomas Gilby, *op. cit*. Reprinted by permission.
[5] St. Thomas Aquinas, *Summa Theologica. op. cit*., Ia. lxxviii. 3–4 & *ad* 2. Reprinted by permission.

judge about the nature of sensible qualities.

The basis for the distinction and number of the external senses should be grounded on what is direct and proper to sense. Sense is a receptive power, the subject of change by an external sensible object. This external principle of action is what is directly perceived by sense, and the senses are diversified according to the diversity found here.

* * * * *

The proper external senses are appointed to receive sensible forms, and so also is a common internal sense, which is like a joint root and principle for the external senses. The proper senses judge of their proper sensible objects, discerning one object from another within their proper field; for instance the sight distinguishes white from black or green. But to tell white from sweet cannot be done by the sight or taste, for to discern between two things implies knowing them both. This discrimination is the work of a common sense, to which are referred as in a joint clearing-house the perceptions of the other senses. This sense is also able to sense sensation itself, as when somebody sees that he is seeing. This cannot be done by the proper senses, which merely know the sensible forms that alter them.

Then to hold and keep these images, the phantasy or sense-imagination is appointed; it may be described as the storehouse of sense-impressions. In addition, and in order to perceive connexions that are not apparent in the immediate environment perceived by the external senses, there is appointed the estimative sense. Lastly, to retain what has been discovered the memory is appointed—that animals remember what has been beneficial or harmful is a sign of this faculty, to which any sense of the past also belongs.

As regards sensible forms there is little difference between men and animals, for they are similarly worked on by external sense-objects. But there is a difference as regards the implications in the sense situation. For while animals perceive these purposes by a kind of natural instinct, men need to make comparisons. What is called the natural estimative power in animals is called the cogitative power in men, for these purposes are discovered by drawing comparisons: it is also called the particular reason. Then, as regards memory, man does not merely have the sudden recognition of the past, as in the sense-memory of animals, but also the power of reminiscence, which reproduces preceding individual consequences by an effort of recollection.

3

Renaissance Continental Psychology

RENÉ DESCARTES
(1596–1650)

Interaction of Mind and Body [1]

Article II

In order to understand the passions of the soul, it is necessary to distinguish its functions from those of the body.

---

[1] René Descartes, *Passions of the Soul*, trans. Henry A. P. Torrey (New York: Henry Holt, 1892), pt. 1, pp. 292–305. Original French, *Les passions de l'âme* (Amsterdam, 1650).

Next I take into consideration that we know of no subject which acts more immediately upon our soul than the body to which it is joined, and that consequently we must think that what in the one is a passion is commonly in the other an action; so that there is no better path to the knowledge of our passions than to examine into the difference between the soul and the body, in order to know to which of them is to be attributed each of our functions.

Article III

The rule to be observed to this end.

No great difficulty will be found in this, if it be borne in mind that all that which we experience in ourselves which we see can also take place in bodies entirely inanimate is to be attributed only to our body; and, on the contrary, all that which is in us and which we cannot conceive in any manner possible to pertain to a body is to be attributed to our soul.

Article IV

That heat and the movement of the limbs proceed from the body, thoughts from the mind.

Thus, because we cannot conceive that the body thinks in any manner whatever, we have no reason but to think that all forms of thought which are in us belong to the mind; and because we cannot doubt that there are inanimate bodies which can move in as many or more different ways than ours, and which have as much or more heat (as experience teaches us in the case of flame, which alone has more heat and motion than any of our members), we must believe that all the heat and all the motions which are in us, in so far as they do not depend at all on thought, belong only to the body.

* * * * *

Article XVI

How all the limbs can be moved by the objects of the senses and by the spirits without the aid of the soul.

Finally, it is to be observed that the machine of our body is so constructed that all the changes which occur in the motion of the spirits may cause them to open certain pores of the brain rather than others, and, reciprocally, that when any one of these pores is opened in the least degree more or less than is usual by the action of the nerves which serve the senses, this changes somewhat the motion of the spirits, and causes them to be conducted into the muscles which serve to move the body in the way in which it is commonly moved on occasion of such action; so that all the movements which we make without our will contributing thereto (as frequently happens when we breathe, or walk, or eat, and, in fine, perform all those actions which are common to us and the brutes) depend only on the conformation of our limbs and the course which the spirits, excited by the heat of the heart, naturally follow in the brain, in the nerves, and in the muscles, in the same way that the movement of a watch is produced by the force solely of its mainspring and the form of its wheels....

Article XXX

That the soul is united to all parts of the body conjointly.

But, in order to understand all these things more perfectly, it is necessary to know that the soul is truly joined to the entire body, and that it cannot properly be said to be in any one of its parts to the exclusion of the rest, because the body is one, and in a manner indivisible, on account of the arrangement of its organs, which are so related to one another, that when any one of them is taken away, that makes the whole body defective: and because the soul is of a nature which has no relation to extension, or to dimensions, or other properties of the matter of which the body is composed, but solely to the whole collection of its organs, as appears from the fact that we cannot at all conceive of the half or the third of a soul, nor what space it occupies, and that it does not become any smaller when any part of the body is cut off, but that it separates itself entirely from it when the combination of its organs is broken up.

Pineal Gland

Article XXXI

That there is a small gland in the brain in which the soul exercises its functions more particularly than in the other parts.

It is, also, necessary to know that, although the soul is joined to the entire body, there is, nevertheless, a certain part of the body in which it exercises its functions more particularly than in all the rest; and it is commonly thought that this part is the brain, or, perhaps, the heart: the brain, because to it the organs of sense are related; and the heart, because it is as if there the passions are felt. But, after careful examination, it seems to me quite evident that the part of the body in which the soul immediately exercises its functions is neither the heart, nor even the brain as a whole, but solely the most interior part of it, which is a certain very small gland, situated in the middle of its substance, and so suspended above the passage by which the spirits of its anterior cavities communicate with those of the posterior, that the slightest motions in it may greatly affect the course of these spirits, and, reciprocally, that the slightest changes which take place in the course of the spirits may greatly affect the motions of this gland.

Article XXXII

How this gland is known to be the principal seat of the soul.

The reason which convinces me that the soul cannot have in the whole body any other place than this gland where it exercises its functions immediately, is the consideration that the other parts of our brain are all double, just as also we have two eyes, two hands, two ears, and in fine, all the organs of our external senses are double; and inasmuch as we have but one single and simple thought of the same thing at the same time, there must necessarily be some place where the two images which by means of the two eyes, or the two other impressions which come from a single object by means of the double organs of the other senses, may unite in one before they reach the mind, in order that they may not present to it two objects in place of one; and it may easily be conceived that these images or other impressions unite in this gland, through the medium of the spirits which fill the cavities of the brain; but there is no other place whatever in the whole body, where they can thus be united, except as they have first been united in this gland.

Passions

Article XXXIII

That the seat of the passions is not in the heart.

As for the opinion of those who think that the soul experiences its passions in the heart, it is of no great account, because it is founded only on the fact that the passions cause some stir to be felt there; and it is easy to see that this change is felt, as if in the heart, only through the medium of a small nerve, which descends to it from the brain, just as pain is felt as if in the foot through the medium of the nerves of the foot, and the stars are perceived as in the heavens by the medium of their light and the optic nerves; so that it is no more necessary that our soul exercise

its functions immediately in the heart in order to feel there its passions, than it is necessary that it should be in the heavens in order to see the stars there.

Article XXXIV

How the soul and the body act one upon the other.

Let us conceive, then, that the soul has its principal seat in this little gland in the middle of the brain, whence it radiates to all the rest of the body by means of the spirits, the nerves, and even of the blood, which, participating in the impressions of the mind, can carry them by means of the arteries into all the members, and; bearing in mind what has been said above concerning the machine of our body, to wit, that the minute filaments of our nerves are so distributed throughout all its parts that, on occasion of the different motions which are excited there by means of sensible objects, they open in divers manners the pores of the brain, which causes the animal spirits contained in these cavities to enter in various ways into the muscles, by means of which they can move the limbs in all the different ways of which they are capable, and, also, that all the other causes, which in other ways can set the spirits in motion, have the effect to turn them upon various muscles [keeping all this in mind], let us add here that the little gland which is the principal seat of the soul is so suspended between the cavities which contain the spirits, that it can be affected by them in all the different ways that there are sensible differences in objects; but that it can also be variously affected by the soul, which is of such a nature that it receives as many different impressions—that is to say, that it has as many different perceptions— as there occur different motions in this gland; as also, reciprocally, the machine of the body is so composed that from the simple fact that this gland is variously affected by the soul, or by whatever other cause, it impels the spirits which surround it toward the pores of the brain, which discharge them by means of the nerves upon the muscles, whereby it causes them to move the limbs. . . .

Article XL

The principal effect of the passions.

It is to be noted that the principal effect of all the passions in man is that they incite and dispose the mind to will the things to which they prepare the body, so that the sentiment of fear incites it to will to fly; that of courage, to will to fight; and so of the rest.

Will, Memory, and Imagination

Article XLI

The power of the mind over the body.

But the will is so free in its nature that it can never be constrained; and of the two kinds of thoughts which I have distinguished in the mind—of which one is its actions, that is, its volitions; the other its passions, taking this word in its most general signification, comprehending all sorts of perceptions—the first of these are absolutely in its power, and can be changed only indirectly by the body, while, on the contrary, the last depend absolutely on the movements which give rise to them, and they can be affected only indirectly by the mind, except when it is itself the cause of them. And the whole action of the mind consists in this, that by the simple fact of its willing anything it causes the little gland, to which it is closely joined, to produce the result appropriate to the volition.

Article XLII

How the things we wish to recall are found in the memory.

Thus, when the mind wills to recall anything, this volition causes the gland, by inclining successively to different sides, to impel the spirits toward different parts of the brain, until they come upon that where the traces are left of the thing it wills to remember; for these traces are due to nothing else than the circumstance that the pores of the brain, through which the spirits have already taken their course, on presentation of that object, have thereby acquired a greater facility than the rest to be opened again in the same way by the spirits which come to them; so that these spirits coming upon these pores, enter therein more readily than into the others, by which means they excite a particular motion in the gland, which represents to the mind the same object, and causes it to recognize that it is that which is willed to remember.

Article XLIII

How the mind can imagine, attend, and move the body.

Thus, when it is desired to imagine something which has never been seen, the will has the power to cause the gland to move in the manner requisite to impel the spirits toward the pores of the brain by the opening of which that thing can be represented; so, when one wills to keep his attention fixed for some time upon the same object, this volition keeps the gland inclined during that time in the same direction; so, finally, when one wills to walk or to move his body in any way, this volition causes the gland to impel the spirits toward the muscles which serve that purpose.

Article XLIV

That each volition is naturally connected with some motion of the gland, but that, by intention or by habit, the will may be connected with others.

Nevertheless, it is not always the volition to excite within us a certain motion, or other effect, which is the cause of its being excited; but this varies according as nature or habit has variously united each motion of the gland to each thought. Thus, for example, if one desires to adjust his eyes to look at a very distant object, this volition causes the pupil of the eye to expand, and if he desires to adjust them so as to see an object very near, this volition makes it contract; but if he simply thinks of expanding the pupil, he wills in vain—the pupil will not expand for that, inasmuch as nature has not connected the motion of the gland, which serves to impel the spirits toward the optic nerve in the manner requisite for expanding or contracting the pupil, with the volition to expand or contract, but with that of looking at objects distant or near. And when, in talking, we think only of the meaning of what we wish to say, that makes us move the tongue and lips much more rapidly and better than if we thought to move them in all ways requisite for the utterance of the same words, inasmuch as the habit we have acquired in learning to talk has made us join the action of the mind—which, through the medium of the gland, can move the tongue and the lips—with the meaning of the words which follow these motions rather than with the motions themselves. . . .

Article XLVII

Wherein consist the conflicts which are im-

agined to exist between the inferior and the superior parts of the soul.

It is only in the opposition between the motions that the body through the spirits, and the soul through the will, tend to excite at the same time in the gland, that all the conflicts consist which are commonly imagined to arise between the inferior part of the soul, which is called sensitive, and the superior part, which is rational, or rather between the natural appetites and the will; for there is but one soul within us, and that soul has in it no diversity of parts whatever; the same which is sensitive is rational, and all its appetites are volitions.

Visual Perception [2]

All the qualities which we perceive in the objects of our vision may be divided into six main groups which are: light, color, position, distance, size, and shape. First, concerning light and color, which are the only qualities that belong specially to the sense of sight, one must believe that the soul is of such a nature that the strength of the movements which occur in the parts of the brain from which the optic nerve fibers come, produces the sensations of light, and the type of movement produces that of color. In the same way, the movements of the nerves connected with the ears determine the hearing of sounds and those of the nerves connected with the tongue determine the tasting of flavors, and, in general, nerve movements in any part of the body produce a titillation when they are moderate and pain when they are too violent.

However, in all this, there need not be any resemblance between the ideas which are conceived by the soul and the movements which produce these ideas. You can easily believe this if you observe that those who receive a blow in the eye believe that they see an infinite number of lights and flashes in front of them, even if they shut their eyes or if they are in a very dark place. Thus the sensation can only be attributed to the force of the blow, which moves the optic nerve fibers in the same way that a bright light would do. A similar force, touching the ears, could

make one hear a sound, and touching other parts of the body, could make one feel pain in that place. Another confirmation of this is that, if at some time you force your eyes to look at the sun or some other very strong light, they retain the sensation of it after some time has passed, in such a way that even if you keep them closed, you seem to see various colors which change and pass from one to another as they fade. This can only be caused by the fact that the optic nerve ends, having been moved with extraordinary force, cannot come to rest as quickly as usual, but the agitation which remains in them after the eyes are closed not being great enough to represent this strong light which caused it, represents less brilliant colors, and these colors change as they fade, thus showing that their nature only consists of the diversity of movement, just as I supposed above. Finally, this is also shown by the fact that colors often appear in transparent bodies, where it is certain that they can only be caused by the different ways in which light rays are received, as when a rainbow appears in the clouds, and, even more clearly, as when one sees the likeness of a rainbow in a glass cut with several facets.

But we must consider here especially the makeup of the quantity of light which we see, that is to say, with what force each optic nerve fiber is moved, for that force is not always equal to the light which is in objects, but is varied according to the distance and the size of the pupil, and also according to the space which the light rays which come from each part of the object occupy at the back of the eye. For example, it is obvious that point X (Figure 17) would send more rays into eye B than it does if the pupil FF were open as far as G; and that it sends as many rays into eye B, which is close to it and whose pupil is very narrow, than it does into eye A whose pupil is much larger but which is proportionally farther away. And although there are not more light rays from the different points of object VXY, considered all together, reaching the back of eye A than that of eye B, nevertheless, since these rays only extend over the space TR, which is smaller than HI, in which they extend to the back of eye B, they must strike there with greater force against the end of each optic nerve-fiber which they touch. This is easy to calculate; for if, for

² René Descartes, *The Dioptrics*, discourse 6. Translated from the French, *La dioptrique* (Leiden, 1637), for the present volume by Catherine Fehrer.

example, space HI is four times TR and contains the extremities of 4,000 optic nerve fibers, TR will only contain those of 1,000, and therefore each nerve fiber at the back of eye A will be moved by one-thousandth of the sum total of forces of light rays entering the eye and the back of eye B, by only a quarter of one-thousandth.

We must also consider that one can only distinguish the parts of bodies one looks at insofar as they somehow differ in color, and that distinct vision of these colors depends not only on the reassembling of all the rays coming from each point of the object at corresponding points at the back of the eye and the absence of rays reaching these same points from other sources, as I clearly explained previously, but also on the many optic nerve fibers which are in the space occupied by the image at the back of the eye. If, for example, the object VXY is composed of 10,000 parts, so arranged as to send rays towards the back of eye RST in 10,000 different ways, and therefore to make 10,000 colors visible at the same time, nevertheless they will not be able to make the soul perceive more than 1,000, if we suppose that there are only 1,000 optic nerve fibers in the space RST. Ten parts of the object, activity together on each one of these fibers, can only affect it in one way, composed of all the movements of all the parts, so that the space occupied by each fiber must be considered as only one point. This is why a field which is painted with an infinite number of different colors will often appear from a distance all white or blue. Generally all bodies are seen less distinctly from afar than close at hand. Finally the more space an object occupies at the back of the eye, the more distinctly it can be seen as we will notice especially further on.

With regard to position, that is, the direction in which each part of the object lies with respect to our body, we perceive it by means of our eyes in the same way as by means of our hands. Our knowledge of it does not depend on any image or any action which comes from the object, but only on the location of the small points of the brain where the nerves originate. For this position, changes, no matter how slightly, each time that there is a change in the position of the members into which these nerves are inserted, and this is ordered by nature not only as a

means by which the soul may know the location of each part of the body which it is considering, in relation to all the others, but also as a way to transfer attention to all the places located on the straight lines one can imagine as drawn from the extremity of each of these parts and prolonged to infinity. In the same way, when the blind man . . . turns his hand A towards E or his hand C (Figure 18) also towards E, the nerves located in that hand cause a certain change in his brain which permit his soul to know not only the locations A or C, but also all the others which are on the straight line AE or CE, so that the soul may transfer its attention to objects B and D and determine their locations without in any way knowing or thinking of the positions of his two hands. And thus, when our eye or our head turns in some direction, our soul is informed of this by change which the nerve located in the muscles which execute these movements produce in our brain. For example, in eye RST (Figure 16) it must be remarked that the position of the optic nerve fiber which is at points R or S or T corresponds to another fixed location in the parts of the brain 7 or 8 or 9, which causes the soul to be able to know all the places on the lines RV or SX or TY. So you must not be surprised that objects may be seen in their true position, although the picture which they imprint in the eye is inverted. Thus our blind man may feel at the same time the object B, which is on the right with his left hand and D, which is on the left, with his right hand. And just as this blind man does not judge that an object is double even when he touches it with his two hands, in the same way when our eyes are both disposed in such a way as to bring our attention to one place, they need not make us see more than one object, even though a picture of it is formed in each of them.

Vision of distance does not depend, any more than that of position, on images sent by objects, but principally on the figuration of the eye. For, as we have said, this figuration must be somewhat different to permit us to see what is close to our eyes and what is farther off. As we adjust this figuration to the distance of objects we also modify a certain part of our brain in a way which is ordained by nature to make our soul perceive this distance. This ordinarily happens without our thinking about it. In the same way, when we squeeze some body with our hand, we adapt our hand to the size and shape of the body and feel it by this means without having to be aware of the movements of the hands. Secondly, we know distance by the relation of the eyes to one another. For our blind man, holding his two sticks AE, CE, of whose length I assume he is unaware, and knowing only the distance between his two hands A and C and the size of the angles ACE, CAE, can deduce from these, as by a natural geometry, where the point E lies. In the same way, when our two eyes RST (Figure 16) and rst are turned towards X, the length of the line Ss and the size of the two angles XSs and XsS permit us to know where the point X is. We can do the same thing with the aid of a single eye by making it change place; if, for example, keeping it turned towards X, we direct it first to the point S and immediately afterwards to the points, this will be sufficient to ensure the coexistence in our imagination of the length of the line Ss and the size of the two angles XSs and XsS and make us perceive the distance of point X. This will be accomplished by an operation of the mind which, although it is only a simple act of imagination, nevertheless involves a calculation very similar to that made by surveyors when, by means of two different vantage points, they measure inaccessible places. We have still another way of perceiving distance; that is by the distinctness or confusion of the shape seen and by both the strength and weakness of the light. Thus, while we keep our gaze fixed on X (Figure 14), the rays which come from the objects 10 and 12 are not focused so exactly on R and T at the back of our eye as if these objects were at points V and Y. From this we see that they are more or less distant from us than X. Then because the light coming from object 10 towards our eye is stronger than if this object were near V, we judge that it is nearer, and because the light coming from object 12 is weaker than if it were near Y, we judge that it is more distant. Finally, when we have already imagined because of some other reason the size of an object or its position or the distinctness of its shape and colors or merely the strength of the light which comes from it, this can serve, not strictly speaking to see but to imagine its distance. Thus

when we look from afar at somebody which we are accustomed to see close at hand, we judge its distance far better than we should if its size were less well known to us. Also when looking at a mountain exposed to the sun, lying beyond a forest which is in shadow, it is only the location of this forest which makes us judge it to be closer. Again, when we look at two ships at sea, of which one is smaller than the other but proportionately closer, so that they appear equal, we can judge by the difference of their shapes and colors and the light which they send towards us, which is farther away.

Finally, I need not say anything in particular about the way in which we see the size and shape of objects since it is determined by the way we see the distance and location of its parts; that is to say, their size is judged by the knowledge or opinion we have as to their distance, compared with the size of the images which they impress on the back of the eye, and not by the absolute size of these images. This is close enough since, although the images are 100 times larger when the objects are very close to us than when they are 10 times farther away, nevertheless they do not make us see the objects 100 times larger, but almost equal, at least when their distance does not deceive us. And it is also clear that shape is judged by the knowledge and opinion we have of the position of the different parts of the object and not by any resemblance with the pictures in the eye. For these pictures ordinarily contain only ovals and diamonds when they make us see circles and squares.

But, in order that you may not doubt that vision occurs as I have explained, I now wish to have you consider further the reasons why sight sometimes deceives us. The first reason is that it is not the eye but the soul that sees, and it is only through the intermediary of the brain that immediate sight takes place. This is why demented persons and those who sleep often see or think they see various objects which are not actually before their eyes, that is to say, when certain vapors disturbing their brain act upon those of its parts which are accustomed to serve for vision in the same way as these objects would if they were present. Then, since the impressions which come from outside move toward the brain through the intermediary of the nerves, if the location of these nerves is modified by some extraordinary cause, it may make one see objects in other places than where they are. Thus if eye rst (Figure 16) being disposed to look at X, is obliged by the finger N to turn towards M the parts of the brain from which its nerves come will not be disposed in exactly the same way as if its own muscles turned it towards M, nor even in the same way as if it were truly looking at X, but midway between the two, that is, as if it were looking at Y. Thus the object M will appear in the place where Y is through the intermediary of this eye, and Y in the place where X is, and X where V is. Since these objects also appear at the same time in their true position through the intermediary of the other eye RST, they will appear double. In the same way, while touching the little ball G (Figure 19) with one's two fingers A and D crossed one over the other, one imagines one as touching two balls because, while these fingers are thus crossed, the muscles of each tend to separate them, pushing A towards C and D towards F, and by this means the points of the brain where the nerves inserted in these muscles originate are disposed in the manner required to make them appear to be pushing A towards B and D towards E and therefore seem to touch two different balls H and I.

Moreover, we are accustomed to judge that the impressions which affect our sight come from the places towards which we must look to be aware of them. When it happens that they come from another place, we can easily be deceived. For example, those whose eyes are affected by jaundice or who look through a yellow glass or who are shut in a room where the only light comes through such glass, attribute this color to all the bodies they look at. And a man who is in the dark room I described a little while ago attributes the colors of objects VXY to the white body RST (Figure 14) since he only gazes at that. The eyes A, B, C, D, E, F (Figures 20, 21, 22, 23, 24, 25) seeing the objects T, V, X, Y, Z, U through the lenses N, O, P and in the mirrors Q, R, S judge them to be points G, H, I, K, L, M, and believe that V, Z are smaller and X, U larger than they really are. Or else they judge X, U smaller and inverted, as when they are at some distance from the eyes C, F, all the more because these lenses and mirrors deflect the rays which come from these

objects in such a way that the eyes can only see them distinctly by placing themselves in a position to look towards the points G, H, I, K, L, M as those who take the trouble to examine the question will easily see. By the same means they will see how mistaken the ancients were in their catoptrics when they tried to determine the place of the images in concave and convex mirrors.

One must also remark that all the means we have of knowing distance are very unreliable. The shape of the eye scarcely varies significantly when the object is more than 4 or 5 feet away; moreover it changes so little when the object is closer that one cannot gain any very precise knowledge from it. As for the angles between the lines drawn between the two eyes and extended from them to the object or two positions of the same object, they also scarcely vary when one looks at all far away. Consequently our reason seems in effect incapable of conceiving the idea of a distance greater than about 100 or 200 feet, as can be verified by the case of the moon or the sun, which are among the most distant bodies that we can see, and whose diameters are to their distances roughly as 1 to 100. They usually appear to be at most 1 or 2 feet in diameter although we know by reasoning that they are extremely large and far away. This does not happen because we cannot conceive them to be larger, since we imagine many towers and mountains that are far bigger. But since we cannot imagine them as being more than 100 or 200 feet away, their diameter cannot appear to be more than 1 or 2 feet across. Their position also helps to deceive us, for usually these heavenly bodies seem smaller when they are very high up in the heavens towards noon than when, upon rising or setting, there are various objects between them and our eyes which allow us better to estimate their distance. Upon measuring them with their instruments, astronomers have shown clearly that the fact that they thus appear larger at certain times than others does not result from their being seen (under) (to subtend) a wider angle but from their being judged farther away. Hence, it follows that the axiom of the ancient optics which states that the apparent size of objects is proportional to the angle of vision is not always true.

One is also deceived by the fact that white

Fig. 14.

Fig. 18.

Fig. 16.

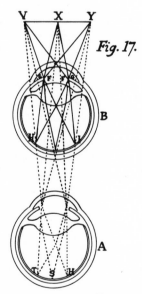

Fig. 17.

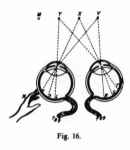

Fig. 19.

Fig. 26.

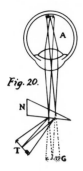

Fig. 20.

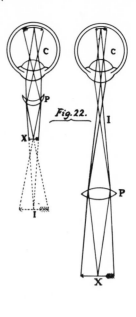

Fig. 22.

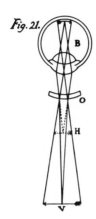

Fig. 21.

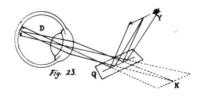

Fig. 23.

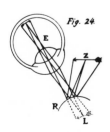

Fig. 24

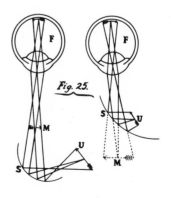

Fig. 25.

or luminous bodies and in general all those which have great power to affect the sense of sight, always seems somewhat closer and larger than they would if they were less powerful. The reason that they appear closer is that the movement by which the pupil contracts to avoid their strong light is so connected with that which brings the whole eye to adjust to close vision and by which one judges their distance, that one movement can scarcely occur without the other's being carried out to some extent. In the same way one cannot entirely close the first two fingers of the hand without the third bending somewhat as if to close with them. The reason why these white, luminous bodies seem larger is not only that the estimate of their size depends on their distance, but also that they impress larger images on the back of the eye. For it must be remarked that the ends of the optic nerve fibers which cover it, although very small, nevertheless have some size. Thus each one of them can be touched in one of its parts by one object and by different objects in others. Nevertheless it is capable of being moved each time in only one way, so when the least of its parts is touched by some very brilliant object, and the others by less brilliant objects. The entire nerve end follows the stimulus of the most brilliant one and represents its image, and not that of the others.

For example, if the nerve endings are 1, 2, 3 (Figure 26) and the rays which come to trace the image of a star on the back of the eye extend over the one marked 1, and slightly beyond all around the extremities of the six others marked 2 on which, as I suppose, fall only very weak rays from the parts of the sky surrounding this star, the image of the star will extend over the whole space occupied by these six marked 2. Perhaps it may even extend over all the space occupied by the 12 marked 3, if the force of the impulse is sufficiently great to be communicated to them. Thus you see that the stars, although they appear quite small, nevertheless seem much larger than they should, by reason of their extreme remoteness, and even if they were not entirely round. They must appear to be. In the same way a square tower seen from afar, appears round, and all bodies that form only very small images in the eye are unable to form the image of their angles there.

Finally, with regard to the judgment of distance by size, shape, color or light, paintings in perspective show us how easy it is to be deceived in these matters. For often, because things which are painted in them are smaller than we imagine they should be, and their outlines are more indistinct, and their colors darker or fainter, they appear to us to be farther off than they are.

BENEDICT SPINOZA
(1632–1677)

Psychophysical Parallelism [3]

Prop. VII

The order and connection of ideas is the same as the order and connection of things.

Proof. This proposition is evident from Part i., Ax. iv. For the idea of everything that is caused depends on a knowledge of the cause, whereof it is an effect.

Corollary. Hence God's power of thinking is equal to his realized power of action—that is, whatsoever follows from the infinite nature of God in the world of extension (*formaliter*) follows without exception in the same order

and connection from the idea of God in the world of thought (*objective*).

Note. Before going any further, I wish to recall to mind what has been pointed out above—namely, that whatsoever can be perceived by the infinite intellect as constituting the essence of substance, belongs altogether only to one substance: consequently, substance thinking and substance extended are one and the same substance, comprehended now through one attribute, now through the other. So, also, a mode of extension and the idea of that mode are one and the same thing, though expressed in two ways. This truth seems to have been dimly recognized by those Jews who maintained that God, God's intellect, and the things understood by God are identical. For instance, a circle existing in

---

[3] Benedict Spinoza, *The Ethics*, trans. R. H. M. Elwes (London: George Bell & Sons, 1888) pt. 2, prop. 7, 21. Original Latin, *Ethica More Geometrico Demonstrata* (Amsterdam, 1677).

nature, and the idea of a circle existing, which is also in God, are one and the same thing displayed through different attributes. Thus, whether we conceive nature under the attribute of extension, or under the attribute of thought, or under any other attribute, we shall find the same order, or one and the same chain of causes—that is, the same things following in either case.

I said that God is the cause of an idea—for instance, of the idea of a circle,—in so far as he is a thinking thing; and of a circle, in so far as he is an extended thing, simply because the actual being of the idea of a circle can only be perceived as a proximate cause through another mode of thinking, and that again through another, and so on to infinity; so that, so long as we consider things as modes of thinking, we must explain the order of the whole of nature, or the whole chain of causes, through the attribute of thought only. And, in so far as we consider things as modes of extension, we must explain the order of the whole of nature through the attribute of extension only; and so on, in the case of other attributes. Wherefore of things as they are in themselves God is really the cause, inasmuch as he consists of infinite attributes. I cannot for the present explain my meaning more clearly.

* * * * *

Prop. XXI

We there showed that the idea of body and body, that is, mind and body . . . are one and the same individual conceived now under the attribute of thought, now under the attribute of extension; wherefore the idea of the mind and the mind itself are one and the same thing, which is conceived under one and the same attribute, namely, thought. The idea of the mind, I repeat, and the mind itself are in God by the same necessity and follow from him from the same power of thinking. Strictly speaking, the idea of the mind, that is, the idea of an idea, is nothing but the distinctive quality (*forma*) of the idea in so far as it is conceived as a mode of thought without reference to the object; if a man knows anything, he, by that very fact, knows that he knows it, and at the same time knows that he knows that he knows it, and so on to infinity. But I will treat of this hereafter.

Determinism and Critique of Mental Faculties [4]

Prop. XLVIII

In the mind there is no absolute or free will; but the mind is determined to wish this or that by a cause, which has also been determined by another cause, and this last by another cause, and so on to infinity.

Proof. The mind is a fixed and definite mode of thought . . . therefore it cannot be the free cause of its actions; . . . in other words it cannot have an absolute faculty of positive or negative volition; but . . . it must be determined by a cause, which has also been determined by another cause, and this last by another, etc. Q.E.D.

Note. In the same way it is proved, that there is in the mind no absolute faculty of understanding, desiring, loving, etc. Whence it follows that these and similar faculties are either entirely fictitious, or are merely abstract or general terms, such as we are accustomed to put together from particular things.

Emotions: Love and Hate [5]

Prop. XXXVIII

If a man has begun to hate an object of his love, so that love is thoroughly destroyed, he will, causes being equal, regard it with more hatred than if he had never loved it, and his hatred will be in proportion to the strength of his former love.

Proof. If a man begins to hate that which he had loved, more of his appetites are put under restraint than if he had never loved it. For love is a pleasure . . . which a man endeavors as far as he can to render permanent; . . . he does so by regarding the object of his love as present, and by affecting it as far as he can pleasurably; this endeavor is greater in proportion as the love is greater, and so also is the endeavor to bring about that the beloved should return his affection. . . . Now these endeavors are constrained by hatred toward the object of love; . . . wherefore the lover . . . will for this cause also be affected with pain, the more so in proportion as his love has been greater; that is, in addition to the pain caused by hatred, there is a pain

---

[4] *Ibid.*, pt. 2, prop. 48.
[5] *Ibid.*, pt. 3, prop. 38, 43, 57, and pt. 5, prop. 3.

caused by the fact that he has loved the object; wherefore the lover will regard the beloved with greater pain, or in other words, will hate it more than if he had never loved it, and with the more intensity in proportion as his former love was greater. Q.E.D.

* * * * *

Prop. XLIII

Hatred is increased by being reciprocated, and can on the other hand be destroyed by love.

Proof. He who conceives, that an object of his hate hates him in return, will thereupon feel a new hatred, while the former hatred (by hypothesis) still remains. . . . But if on the other hand, he conceives that the object of hate loves him, he will to this extent . . . regard himself with pleasure, and . . . will endeavor to please the cause of his emotion. In other words, he will endeavor not to hate him, . . . and not to affect him painfully; this endeavor . . . will be greater or less in proportion to the emotion from which it arises. Therefore, if it be greater than that which arises from hatred, and through which the man endeavors to affect painfully the thing which he hates, it will get the better of it and banish the hatred from his mind. Q.E.D.

* * * * *

Prop. LVII

Any emotion of a given individual differs from the emotion of another individual, only in so far as the essence of the one individual differs from the essence of the other.

* * * * *

Emotion, which is called a passivity of the soul, is a confused idea, whereby the mind affirms concerning its body, or any part thereof, a force for existence . . . greater or less than before, and by the presence of which the mind is determined to think of one thing rather than another.

* * * * *

Prop. VII

An emotion can only be controlled or destroyed by another emotion contrary thereto, and with more power for controlling emotion.

Proof. Emotion, in so far as it is referred to the mind, is an idea, whereby the mind affirms of its body a greater or less force of

existence than before. . . . When, therefore, the mind is assailed by any emotion, the body is at the same time affected with a modification whereby its power of activity is increased or diminished. Now, this modification of the body . . . receives from its cause the force for persistence in its being; which force can only be checked or destroyed by a bodily cause . . . , in virtue of the body being affected with a modification contrary to . . . and stronger than itself; . . . wherefore . . . the mind is affected by the idea of a modification contrary to and stronger than the former modification, in other words . . . the mind will be affected by an emotion contrary to and stronger than the former emotion, which will exclude or destroy the existence of the former emotion; thus an emotion cannot be destroyed nor controlled except by a contrary and stronger emotion. Q.E.D.

* * * * *

Prop. III

An emotion, which is a passion, ceases to be a passion, as soon as we form a clear and distinct idea thereof.

Proof. An emotion, which is a passion, is a confused idea. . . . If, therefore, we form a clear and distinct idea of a given emotion, that idea will only be distinguished from the emotion, in so far as it is referred to the mind only, by reason; . . . therefore . . . the emotion will cease to be a passion. Q.E.D.

Corollary. An emotion therefore, becomes more under our control, and the mind is less passive in respect to it, in proportion as it is more known to us.

Perception [6]

Reflection shows that all modes of perception or knowledge may be reduced to four:

I. Perception arising from hearsay or from some sign which everyone may name as he pleases.

II. Perception arising from mere experience —that is, from experience not yet classified

---

[6]   Benedict Spinoza, *On the Improvement of the Understanding*, trans. R. H. M. Elwes (London: George Bell & Sons, 1888), from the section entitled: "Of the Four Modes of Perception." Original Latin, *De Intellectus Emendatione* (Amsterdam, 1677).

by the intellect, and only so called because the given event has happened to take place, and we have no contradictory fact to set against it, so that it therefore remains unassailed in our mind.

III. Perception arising when the essence of one thing is inferred from another thing, but not adequately; this comes when from some effect we gather its cause, or when it is inferred from some general proposition that some property is always present.

IV. Lastly, there is the perception arising when a thing is perceived solely through its essence, or through the knowledge of its proximate cause.

All these kinds of perception I will illustrate by examples. By hearsay I know the day of my birth, my parentage, and other matters about which I have never felt any doubt. By mere experience I know that I shall die, for this I can affirm from having seen that others like myself have died, though all did not live for the same period, or die by the same disease. I know by mere experience that oil has the property of feeding fire, and water of extinguishing it. In the same way I know that a dog is a barking animal, man a rational animal, and in fact nearly all the practical knowledge of life.

We deduce one thing from another as follows: when we clearly perceive that we feel a certain body and no other, we thence clearly infer that the mind is united to the body, and that their union is the cause of the given sensation; but we cannot thence absolutely understand the nature of the sensation and the union. Or, after I have become acquainted with the nature of vision, and know that it has the property of making one and the same thing appear smaller when far off than when near, I can infer that the sun is larger than it appears, and can draw other conclusions of the same kind.

Lastly, a thing may be perceived solely through its essence; when, from the fact of knowing something, I know what it is to know that thing, or when, from knowing the essence of the mind, I know that it is united to the body. By the same kind of knowledge we know that two and three make five, or that two lines each parallel to a third, are parallel to one another, etc. The things which I have been able to know by this kind of knowledge are as yet very few.

Memory [7]

The point most worthy of attention is, that memory is strengthened both with and without the aid of the understanding. For the more intelligible a thing is, the more easily it is remembered, and the less intelligible it is, the more easily do we forget it. For instance, a number of unconnected words is much more difficult to remember than the same number in the form of a narration. The memory is also strengthened without the aid of the understanding by means of the power wherewith the imagination or the sense called common is affected by some particular physical object. I say PARTICULAR, for the imagination is only affected by particular objects. If we read, for instance, a single romantic comedy, we shall remember it very well, so long as we do not read many others of the same kind, for it will reign alone in the memory. If, however, we read several others of the same kind, we shall think of them altogether, and easily confuse one with another. I say, also PHYSICAL. For the imagination is only affected by physical objects. As, then, the memory is strengthened both with and without the aid of the understanding, we may conclude that it is different from the understanding, and that in the matter considered in itself there is neither memory nor forgetfulness. What, then, is memory? It is nothing else than the actual sensation of impressions on the brain, accompanied with the thought of a definite duration of the sensation. This is also shown by reminiscence. For then we think of the sensation, but without the notion of continuous duration; thus the idea of that sensation is not the actual duration of the sensation or actual memory. Whether ideas are or are not subject to corruption will be seen in my philosophy. If this seems too absurd to any one, it will be sufficient for our purpose, if he reflect on the fact that a thing is more easily remembered in proportion to its singularity, as appears from the example of the comedy just cited. Further, a thing is remembered more easily in proportion to its intelligibility; therefore we cannot help remembering that which is extremely singular and sufficiently intelligible.

Thus, then, we have distinguished between

[7] *Ibid.*, from the section entitled: "Of Memory and Forgetfulness."

a true idea and other perceptions, and shown that ideas fictitious, false, and the rest, originate in the imagination—that is, in certain sensations fortuitous (so to speak) and disconnected, arising not from the power of the mind, but from external causes, according as the body, sleeping or waking, receives various motions.

GOTTFRIED WILHELM LEIBNIZ
(1646–1716)

The Human Mind as an Activity, Psychophysical Parallelism, and the Subconscious [8]

The *Essay on the Understanding*, by a distinguished Englishman, being one of the most beautiful and esteemed works of this period, I have resolved to make some remarks upon it, because having sufficiently meditated for a long time upon the same subject and upon the greater part of the matters therein touched upon, I have thought that it would be a favorable opportunity to publish something under the title of "New Essays on the Understanding," and to procure a favorable reception to my thoughts, by putting them in so good company.

* * * * *

Our differences are upon subjects of some importance. The question is to know whether the soul in itself is entirely empty as the tablets upon which as yet nothing has been written (*tabula rasa*) according to Aristotle, and the author of the Essay, and whether all that is traced thereon comes solely from the senses and from experience; or whether the soul contains originally the principles of many ideas and doctrines which external objects merely call up on occasion, as I believe with Plato, and even with the schoolmen, and with all those who interpret in this way the passage of St. Paul (Rom 2:15) where he states that the law of God is written in the heart. The Stoics call these principles *prolepses*, *i.e.* fundamental assumptions, or what is taken for granted in advance. The Mathematicians call them *general notions* (κοιναὶ ἔννοιαι).

* * * * *

8 Gottfried Wilhelm Leibniz, *New Essays concerning the Understanding*, trans. Alfred Gideon Langley (New York: Macmillan, 1896), from the preface and bk. 1–2. Conversation transpiring between Philalethes and Theophilus. Original French, *Nouveaux essais sur l'entendement humain* (1765).

Whence it appears that necessary truths such as are found in pure mathematics, and particularly in arithmetic and in geometry, must have principles whose proof does not depend upon examples, nor consequently upon the testimony of the senses, although without the senses it would never have occurred to us to think of them.

* * * * *

Herein, also, human knowledge differs from that of the brutes: the brutes are purely empirics and only guide themselves by examples; for, so far as we can judge of them, they never attain to the formation of necessary propositions; while men are capable of demonstrative sciences. It is also for this reason that the faculty the brutes have for making *consecutions* is something inferior to the reason of man. The consecutions of the brutes are merely like those of simple empirics, who claim that what has sometimes happened will happen again in a case where something strikes them as similar, without being able to judge whether the same reasons hold good. This is why it is so easy for men to entrap the brutes, and so easy for simple empirics to make mistakes.

* * * * *

The consecutions of the brutes are only a shadow of reasoning, *i.e.* are only connections of the imagination and passages from one image to another, because in a new juncture which appears similar to the preceding they expect anew that connection which they formerly met with, as if things were united in fact because their images are united in the memory.

* * * * *

Now reflection is nothing else than attention to what is in us, and the senses do not give us what we already carry with us. That being so, can it be denied that there is much that is innate in our mind, since we are innate, so to speak, in ourselves? and that there is in us: being, unity, substance, duration, change, action, perception, pleasure, and a thousand other objects of our intellectual ideas? And these objects being immediate to our understanding and always present (although they cannot always be perceived by reason of our distractions and needs), what wonder that we say that these ideas with all depending upon them are innate in us? I have made use also of the comparison of a block of marble which has veins, rather than of a block of marble wholly even, or of blank tablets, *i.e.* of what is called among philosophers a *tabula rasa*. For if the soul resembled these blank tablets, truths would be in us as the figure of Hercules is in the marble, when the marble is wholly indifferent to the reception of this figure or some other. But if there were veins in the block which should indicate the figure of Hercules rather than other figures, this block would be more determined thereto, and Hercules would be in it as in some sense innate, although it would be needful to labor to discover these veins, to clear them by polishing, and by cutting away what prevents them from appearing. Thus it is that ideas and truths are for us innate, as inclinations, dispositions, habits, or natural potentialities, and not as actions; although these potentialities are always accompanied by some actions, often insensible, which correspond to them.

* * * * *

I do not know whether it will be so easy to harmonize him with us and with the Cartesians, when he maintains that the mind does not always think, and particularly that it is without perception when we sleep without dreaming; and he objects that since bodies can exist without motion, souls can also exist without thought. But here I make a somewhat different reply than is customary, for I hold that naturally a substance cannot exist without action, and that there is indeed never a body without movement. Experience already favors me, and you have only to consult the book of the distinguished Mr. Boyle against absolute rest, to be convinced of it; but I believe reason favors it also, and this is one of the proofs I have for doing away with atoms.

Moreover, there are a thousand indications which make us think that there are at every moment an infinite number of *perceptions* in us, but without apperception and reflection, *i.e.* changes in the soul itself of which we are not conscious, because the impressions are either too slight and too great in number, or too even, so that they have nothing sufficiently distinguishing them from each other; but joined to others, they do not fail to produce their effect and to make themselves felt at least confusedly in the mass.

* * * * *

For all attention requires memory, and often when we are not admonished, so to speak, and warned to take note of some of our own present perceptions, we allow them to pass without reflection, and even without being noticed; but if any one directs our attention to them immediately after, and makes us notice, for example, some noise which was just heard, we remember it, and are conscious of having had at the time some feeling of it. Thus there were perceptions of which we were not conscious at once, consciousness arising in this case only from the warning after some interval, however small it may be. And to judge still better of the minute perceptions which we cannot distinguish in the crowd, I am wont to make use of the example of the roar or noise of the sea which strikes one when on its shore. To understand this noise as it is made, it would be necessary to hear the parts which compose this whole, *i.e.* the noise of each wave, although each of these little noises makes itself known only in the confused collection of all the others, *i.e.* in the roar itself, and would not be noticed if the wave which makes it were alone. For it must be that we are affected a little by the motion of this wave, and that we have some perception of each one of these noises, small as they are; otherwise we would not have that of a hundred thousand waves, since a hundred thousand nothings cannot make something. One never sleeps so soundly as not to have some feeble and confused sensation, and one would never be awakened by the greatest noise in the world if he did not have some perception of its small beginning; just as one would never break a rope by the greatest effort in the world if it were not stretched and lengthened a little by smaller efforts, although the slight extension they produce is not apparent.

* * * * *

It is also by means of the insensible perceptions that this admirable pre-established harmony of the soul and the body, and indeed of all the nomads or simple substances, is explained; which supplies the place of the unmaintainable influence of one upon the others, and which in the judgment of the author of the most excellent of dictionaries exalts the grandeur of the divine perceptions beyond what has ever been conceived. After this I would add little if I should say that it is these minute perceptions which *determine* us in many junctures without being thought of, and which deceive the vulgar by the appearance of an *indifference of equilibrium*, as if we were entirely indifferent whether we turned (for example) to the right or to the left. It is not needful also that I notice here, as I have done in the book itself, that they cause that *uneasiness* which I show to consist in something which differs from pain only as the small from the great, and which, however, often constitutes our desire and even our pleasure by giving to it an exciting flavor. It is also the insensible parts of our sensible perceptions, which produce a relation between the perceptions of colors, heat, and other sensible qualities, and between the motions in bodies which correspond to them; while the Cartesians together with our author, penetrating as he is, conceive the perceptions which we have of these qualities as arbitrary, *i.e.* as if God had given them to the soul according to his good pleasure, without any regard to any essential relation between these perceptions and their objects: a view which surprises me and which appears to me little worthy of the wisdom of the Author of things, who does nothing without harmony and without reason.

In a word, *the insensible perceptions* are as eminently useful in Pneumatology [9] as are the insensible corpuscles in Physics, and it is equally unreasonable to reject the one or the other under the pretext that they are out of reach of our senses. Nothing is accomplished all at once, and it is one of my great maxims, and one of the most verified, that *nature makes no leaps:* a maxim which I called the *Law of Continuity*, . . . and the use of this

---

[9] Pneumatology is the term for psychology.

law is very considerable in Physics. This law declares that we pass always from the small to the great, and the reverse, through the medium, in degree as in parts, and that motion never springs immediately from rest, nor is reduced thereto save by a smaller motion, as one never completes the survey of any line or length until he has completed a smaller line, although hitherto those who have set forth the laws of motion have not observed this law, believing that a body can receive in a moment a motion contrary to the preceding. And all this makes one indeed think that the *noticeable perceptions* also arise by degrees from those which are too minute to be observed. To think otherwise, is to have little knowledge of the immense subtilty of things which always and everywhere surrounds an actual infinite.

* * * * *

Critique of Locke's Tabula Rasa Mind

§ 2. PH.: We who suppose that at the beginning the soul is a *tabula rasa*, void of all characters and without an idea, ask how it comes to receive ideas, and by what means it acquires this prodigious quantity of them? To that question the reply in a word is: From experience.

TH.: This *tabula rasa*, of which so much is said, is in my opinion only a fiction which nature does not admit, and which is based only upon the imperfect notions of philosophers, like the vacuum, atoms, and rest, absolute or relative, of two parts of a whole, or like the primary matter which is conceived as without form. Uniform things and those which contain no variety are never anything but abstractions, like time, space, and the other entities of pure mathematics. There is no body whatever whose parts are at rest, and there is no substance whatever that has nothing by which to distinguish it from every other. Human souls differ, not only from other souls, but also among themselves, although the difference is not at all of the kind called specific. And, according to the proofs which I believe we have, every substantial thing, be it soul or body, has its own characteristic relation to every other; and the one must always differ from the other by *intrinsic connotations*. Not to mention the fact that those who speak so frequently of this *tabula rasa* after having taken away the ideas cannot say what remains, like the scholastic philosophers, who leave nothing in their primary matter. You may perhaps reply that this *tabula rasa* of the philosophers means that the soul has by nature and originally only bare faculties. But faculties without some act, in a word the pure powers of the school, are also only fictions, which nature knows not, and which are obtained only by the process of abstraction. For where in the world will you ever find a faculty which shuts itself up in the power alone without performing any act? There is always a particular disposition to action, and to one action rather than to another. And besides the disposition there is a tendency to action, of which tendencies there is always an infinity in each subject at once; and these tendencies are never without some effect. Experience is necessary, I admit, in order that the soul be determined to such or such thoughts, and in order that it take notice of the ideas which are in us; but by what means can experience and the senses give ideas? Has the soul windows, does it resemble tablets, is it like wax? It is plain that all who so regard the soul, represent it as at bottom corporeal. You oppose to me this axiom received by the philosophers, *that there is nothing in the soul which does not come from the senses.* But you must except the soul itself and its affections. *Nihil est in intellectu, quod non fuerit in sensu, exipe: nisi ipse intellectus.*[10] Now the soul comprises being, substance, unity, identity, cause, perception, reason, and many other notions which the senses cannot give.

Psychophysical Parallelism [11]

TH.: All impressions have their effect, but all the effects are not always perceptible; when I turn to one side rather than to the other, it is very often through a series of minute impressions of which I am not conscious, and which render one movement a little more uncomfortable than the other. All our unpremeditated actions are the results of a concurrence of minute perceptions, and even our customs and passions, which influence so much our deliberations, come therefrom; for

these habits grow little by little, and, consequently, without the minute perceptions, we should not arrive at these noticeable dispositions. I have already remarked that he who would deny these effects in the sphere of morals, would imitate the poorly taught class who deny insensible corpuscles in physics; and yet I see that among those who speak of liberty are some who, taking no notice of these unperceived impressions, capable of inclining the balance, imagine an entire indifference in moral actions, like that of the ass of Buridan equally divided between two meadows. . . .

PH.: Perhaps we might say that in the case of a man awake who thinks, his body counts for something and that memory is preserved by means of marks in the brain, but when he is asleep the soul thinks apart by itself.

TH.: I am very far from saying that, since I believe there is always an exact correspondence between the body and the soul, and since I employ the impressions of the body of which we are not conscious, whether awake or asleep, in order to prove that the soul has in itself similar ones. I maintain even that something goes on in the soul which corresponds to the circulation of the blood and to all the internal movements of the viscera, of which we are never conscious however, just as those who live near a water-mill do not perceive the noise it makes. In fact, if there were impressions in the body during sleep or waking hours, by which the soul was not touched or in any wise affected, limits would be given to the union of the soul and of the body, as if corporeal impressions required a certain form and size in order for the soul to perceive them; which is not at all tenable if the soul is incorporeal, for there is no relation between an incorporeal substance and this or that modification of matter. In a word, it is a great source of error to believe that there is no perception in the soul besides those of which it is conscious.

* * * * *

TH.: The soul's perceptions correspond always naturally to the constitution of the body, and when there are a multitude of movements confused and little distinguished in the brain, as happens in the case of those who have little experience, the soul's thoughts

---

[10] There is nothing in the intellect which was not previously in the senses, except the intellect itself.

[11] Gottfried Wilhelm Leibniz, *New Essays concerning the Understanding, op. cit.*

(following the order of the things) cannot be more distinct. Yet the soul is never deprived of the help of *sensation*, because it always expresses its body, and this body is always impressed by its surroundings in an infinite number of ways, but which often give only a confused impression.

* * * * *

§ 19. PH.: I do not remember that those who tell us that the soul always thinks ever say that man always thinks.

TH.: I think that is because they understand their statement of the separated soul, and yet they voluntarily admit that man always thinks during the union. For myself, who have reasons for holding that the soul is never separated from the entire body, I believe that we can state absolutely that man always does and will think.

Perception and Apperception [12]

§ 1. PH.: Come we now to the ideas of reflection in particular. *Perception* is the first faculty of the soul which is occupied with our ideas. It is also the first and simplest idea which we receive by reflection. *Thought* signifies often the mind's working upon its own ideas, when it acts and considers a thing with a certain degree of voluntary attention: but in what we call *perception* the mind is

[12] *Ibid.*, bk. 2, ch. 9.

ordinarily purely passive, not being able to avoid perceiving what it actually perceives.

TH.: We might perhaps add that the animals have perception, and that it is not necessary that they have thought, that is to say, that they have reflection or what may be its object. We ourselves also have minute *perceptions* of which we are not conscious in our present state. It is true that we might very well perceive them ourselves, and reflect upon them, if we were not turned aside by their multitude, which distracts our mind, or if they were not effaced, or rather obscured, by greater ones.

§ 4. PH.: I admit that when the mind is strongly occupied in contemplating certain objects it does not perceive in any way the impression which certain bodies make upon the organ of hearing, although the impression may be quite strong; but no perception arises therefrom if the soul takes no cognizance thereof.

TH.: I should prefer to distinguish between *perception* and *consciousness* (*s'appercevoir*). The perception of light and color, for example, of which we are conscious, is composed of many minute perceptions, of which we are not conscious; and a noise which we perceive, but of which we take no notice, becomes *apperceptible* by a little addition or increase; for if what precedes make no impression upon the soul, this little addition would also make none, and the whole would make no more.

4

British Empiricism during the Renaissance and Enlightenment

THOMAS HOBBES
(1588–1679)

Sense [1]

The Originall of them all, is that which we

[1] Thomas Hobbes, *Leviathan, or the Matter, Form and Power of a Commonwealth Ecclesiastical and Civil* (London, 1651), ch. 1.

call SENSE; (For there is no conception in a man's mind, which hath not at first, totally, or by parts, been begotten upon the organs of Sense.) The rest are derived from that originall. . . .

The cause of Sense, is the Externall Body,

or Object, which presseth the organ proper to each Sense. . . . All which qualities called *Sensible*, are in the object that causeth them, but so many several motions of the matter, by which it presseth our organs diversly. Neither in us that are pressed, are they any thing else, but divers motions; (for motion, produceth nothing but motion.) But their apparence to us is Fancy, the same waking, that dreaming. And as pressing, rubbing, or striking the Eye, makes us fancy a light; and pressing the Eare, produceth a dinne; so do the bodies also we see, or hear, produce the same by their strong, though unobserved action.

Memory, Imagination, and Retroactive Inhibition [2]

For after the object is removed, or the eye shut, wee still retain an image of the thing seen, though more obscure than when we see it. And this is it, the Latines call *Imagination*, from the image made in seeing; and apply the same, though improperly, to all the other senses. But the Greeks call it *Fancy;* which signifies *apparence*, and is as proper to one sense, as to another. IMAGINATION therefore is nothing but *decaying sense;* and is found in men, and many other living Creatures, as well sleeping, as waking.

The decay of Sense in men waking, is not the decay of the motion made in sense; but an obscuring of it, in such manner, as the light of the Sun obscureth the light of the Starres; which starrs do no less exercise their vertue by which they are visible, in the day, than in the night. But because amongst many stroaks, which our eyes, eares, and other organs receive from externall bodies, the predominant onely is sensible; therefore the light of the Sun being predominant, we are not affected with the action of the starrs. And any object being removed from our eyes, though the impression it made in us remain; yet other objects more present succeeding, and working on us, the Imagination of the past is obscured, and made weak; as the voyce of a man is in the noyse of the day. From whence it followeth, that the longer the time is, after the sight, or Sense of any object, the weaker is the Imagination. For the

continuall change of mans body, destroyes in time the parts which in sense were moved: So that distance of time, and of place, hath one and the same effect in us. For as at a great distance of place, that which wee look at, appears dimme, and without distinction of the smaller parts; and as Voyces grow weak, and inarticulate: so also after great distance of time, our imagination of the Past is weak; and wee lose (for example) of Cities wee have seen, many particular Streets; and of Actions, many particular Circumstances. This *decaying sense*, when wee would express the thing it self, (I mean *fancy* it selfe), wee call *Imagination*, as I said before: But when we would express the *decay*, and signifie that the Sense is fading, old, and past, it is called *Memory*. So that *Imagination* and *Memory*, are but one thing, which for divers considerations hath divers names.

Causation and the Association of Ideas [3]

The *remembrance* of succession of one thing to another, that is, of what was *antecedent*, and what *consequent*, and what *concomitant*, is called an *experiment;* whether the same be made by us *voluntarily*, as when a man putteth any thing into the fire, to see what effect the fire will produce upon it: or *not* made by us, as when we remember a fair morning after a red evening. To have had many *experiments*, is that we call *experience*, which is nothing else but *remembrance* of what antecedents have been followed by what consequents.

No man can have in his mind a conception of the *future*, for the future is *not yet:* but of our conceptions of the *past*, we make a *future;* or rather, call *past*, *future* relatively. Thus after a man hath been accustomed to see like antecedents followed by like consequents, whensoever he seeth the like come to pass to any thing he had seen before, he looks there should follow it the same that followed then: as for example, because a man hath often seen offences followed by punishment, when he seeth an offence in present, he thinketh punishment to be consequent thereunto; but consequent unto that which is

³ Thomas Hobbes, *Human Nature, or the Fundamental Elements of Policy* (London, 1651), ch. 1, 2.

present, men call future; and thus we make *remembrance* to be the *prevision* of things to come, or *expectation* or presumption of the future.

In the same manner, if a man seeth in present that which he hath seen before, he thinks that that which was antecedent to that which he saw before, is also antecedent to that he presently seeth: as for example, he that hath seen the ashes remain after the fire, and now again seeth ashes, concludeth again there hath been fire: and this is called again *conjecture* of the past, or presumption of the fact.

When a man hath *so often* observed like antecedents to be followed by like consequents, that *whensoever* he seeth the antecedent, he looketh again for the consequent; or when he seeth the consequent, maketh account there hath been the like antecedent; then he calleth both the antecedent and the consequent, signs one of another, as clouds are signs of rain to come, and rain of clouds past.

JOHN LOCKE
(1632–1704)

Tabula Rasa Mind [4]

Let us then suppose the mind to be, as we say, white paper void of all characters, without any *ideas*. How comes it to be furnished? Whence comes it by that vast store which the busy and boundless fancy of man has painted on it with an almost endless variety? Whence has it all the materials of reason and knowledge? To this I answer, in one word, from *experience;* in that all our knowledge is founded, and from that it ultimately derives itself. Our observation, employed either about *external sensible objects, or about the internal operations of our minds perceived and reflected on by ourselves, is that which supplies our understandings with all the materials of thinking.* These two are the fountains of knowledge, from whence all the *ideas* we have, or can naturally have, do spring.

First, *our senses*, conversant about particular sensible objects, do *convey into the mind* several distinct *perceptions* of things, according to those various ways wherein those objects do affect them. And thus we come by those *ideas* we have of *yellow, white, heat, cold, soft, hard, bitter, sweet,* and all those which we call sensible qualities; which when I say the senses convey into the mind, I mean, they from external objects convey into the mind what produces there those *perceptions*. This great source of most of the *ideas* we have, depending wholly upon our senses, and derived by them to the understanding, I call SENSATION.

Secondly, the other fountain from which experience furnisheth the understanding with *ideas* is the *perception of the operations of our own minds* within us, as it is employed about the *ideas* it has got; which operations, when the soul comes to reflect on and consider, do furnish the understanding with another set of *ideas*, which could not be had from things without. And such are *perception, thinking, doubting, believing, reasoning, knowing, willing,* and all the different actings of our own minds; which we, being conscious of and observing in ourselves, do from these receive into our understandings as distinct *ideas* as we do from bodies affecting our senses. This source of *ideas* every man has wholly in himself; and though it be not sense, as having nothing to do with external objects, yet it is very like it, and might properly enough be called internal sense. But as I call the other *sensation*, so I call this REFLECTION, the *ideas* it affords being such only as the mind gets by reflecting on its own operations within itself. By REFLECTION then, in the following part of this discourse, I would be understood to mean that notice which the mind takes of its own operations, and the manner of them, by reason whereof there come to be *ideas* of these operations in the understanding. These two, I say, viz. external material things as the objects of SENSATION, and the operations of our own minds within as the objects of REFLECTION, are to me the only originals from whence all our *ideas* take their beginnings. The term *operations* here I use in a large sense, as comprehending not barely the actions of the mind about its *ideas*, but some sort of

---

[4] John Locke, *An Essay concerning Human Understanding* (London, 1690), bk. 2, ch. 1, 2.

passions arising sometimes from them, such as is the satisfaction or uneasiness arising from any thought.

The understanding seems to me not to have the least glimmering of any *ideas* which it doth not receive from one of these two. *External objects furnish the mind with the* ideas *of sensible qualities*, which are all those different perceptions they produce in us; and the *mind furnishes the understanding with* ideas *of its own operations*.

* * * * *

The better to understand the nature, manner, and extent of our knowledge, one thing is carefully to be observed concerning the *ideas* we have, and that is that *some* of them are *simple* and *some complex*.

* * * * *

These simple *ideas*, the materials of all our knowledge, are suggested and furnished to the mind only by those two ways above mentioned, viz. *sensation* and *reflection*. When the understanding is once stored with these simple *ideas*, it has the power to repeat, compare, and unite them, even to an almost infinite variety, and so can make at pleasure new complex *ideas*. But it is not in the power of the most exalted wit or enlarged understanding, by any quickness or variety of thought, to *invent or frame one new simple* idea in the mind, not taken in by the ways before mentioned; nor can any force of the understanding *destroy* those that are there.

Sense Perceptions [5]

The better to conceive the *ideas* we receive from sensation, it may not be amiss for us to consider them in reference to the different ways whereby they make their approaches to our minds and make themselves perceivable by us.

First, then, There are some which come into our minds *by one sense* only.

Secondly, There are others that convey themselves into the mind *by more senses than one*.

Thirdly, Others that are had from *reflection* only.

Fourthly, There are some that make themselves way and are suggested to the mind *by all the ways of sensation and reflection*.

* * * * *

To discover the nature of our *ideas* the better, and to discourse of them intelligibly, it will be convenient to distinguish them as they are *ideas* or perceptions in our minds, and as they are modifications of matter in the bodies that cause such perceptions in us: that so we *may not* think (as perhaps usually is done) that they are exactly the images and *resemblances* of something inherent in the subject: most of those of sensation being in the mind no more the likeness of something existing without us, than the names that stand for them are the likeness of our *ideas*, which yet upon hearing they are apt to excite in us.

Whatsoever the mind perceives in itself, or is the immediate object of perception, thought, or understanding, that I call *idea*; and the power to produce any *idea* in our mind, I call *quality* of the subject wherein that power is. Thus a snowball having the power to produce in us the *ideas* of *white*, *cold*, and *round*, the power to produce those *ideas* in us as they are in the snowball I call *qualities*; and as they are sensations or perceptions in our understandings, I call them *ideas*; which *ideas*, if I speak of sometimes as in the things themselves, I would be understood to mean those qualities in the objects which produce them in us.

Qualities thus considered in bodies are:

First, such as are utterly inseparable from the body, in what state soever it be; such as in all the alterations and changes it suffers, all the force can be used upon it, it constantly keeps; and such as sense constantly finds in every particle of matter which has bulk enough to be perceived; and the mind finds inseparable from every particle of matter, though less than to make itself singly be perceived by our senses. V.g., take a grain of wheat, divide it into two parts, each part has still *solidity, extension, figure*, and *mobility*; divide it again, and it retains still the same qualities; and so divide it on, till the parts become insensible: they must retain still each of them all those qualities. For division (which is all that a mill or pestle or any other body does upon another in reducing it to insensible parts) can never take away

[5] *Ibid.*, bk. 2, ch. 3.

either solidity, extension, figure, or mobility from any body, but only makes two or more distinct separate masses of matter, of that which was but one before; all which distinct masses, reckoned as so many distinct bodies, after division make a certain number. These I call *original* or *primary qualities* of body; which I think we may observe to produce simple *ideas* in us, viz. solidity, extension, figure, motion or rest, and number.

Secondly, such *qualities* which in truth are nothing in the objects themselves but powers to produce various sensations in us by their *primary qualities*, i.e. by the bulk, figure, texture, and motion of their insensible parts,

as colours, sounds, tastes, etc. These I call *secondary qualities*. To these might be added a third sort, which are allowed to be barely powers, though they are as much real qualities in the subject as those which I, to comply with the common way of speaking, call *qualities*, but for distinction, *secondary qualities*. For the power in fire to produce a new colour, or consistency in wax or clay, by its primary qualities, is as much a quality in fire as the power it has to produce in me a new *idea* or sensation of warmth or burning, which I felt not before, by the same primary qualities, viz. the bulk, texture, and motion of its insensible parts.

GEORGE BERKELEY
(1685–1753)

Theory of Vision [6]

I.   My design is to show the manner wherein we perceive by sight, the distance, magnitude, and situation of *objects*. . . .

II.   It is, I think, agreed by all, that *distance* of itself, and immediately, cannot be seen. For *distance* being a line directed end-wise to the eye, it projects only one point in the fund of the eye. Which point remains invariably the same, whether the distance be longer or shorter.

III.   I find it also acknowledged, that the estimate we make of the distance of *objects* considerably remote, is rather an act of judgment grounded on *experience* than of *sense*. For example, when I perceive a great number of intermediate *objects*, such as houses, fields, rivers, and the like, which I have experienced to take up a considerable space; I thence form a judgment or conclusion, that the *object* I see beyond them is at a great distance. Again, when an *object* appears faint and small, which, at a near distance, I have experienced to make a vigorous and large appearance; I instantly conclude it to be far off. . . .

IV.   But when an *object* is placed at so near a distance, as that the interval between the eyes bears any sensible proportion to it, it is the received opinion that the two *optic axes* (the fancy that we see only with one eye

at once being exploded) concurring at the *object*, do there make an *angle*, by means of which, according as it is greater or lesser, the *object* is perceived to be nearer or further off.

V.   Betwixt which, and the foregoing manner of estimating distance, there is this remarkable difference. That whereas there was no apparent, necessary connexion between small distance and a large and strong appearance, or between great distance, and a little and faint appearance. Yet there appears a very necessary connexion between an obtuse angle and near distance, and an acute angle and further distance. It does not in the least depend upon experience, but may be evidently known by any one before he had experienced it, that the nearer the concurrence of the *optic axes*, the greater the *angle*, and the remoter their concurrence is, the lesser will be the *angle* comprehended by them.

VI.   There is another way, mentioned by the optic writers, whereby they will have us judge of those distances, in respect of which, the breadth of the *pupil* hath any sensible bigness. And that is the greater or lesser divergency of the rays, which, issuing from the visible point, do fall on the *pupil;* that point being judged nearest, which is seen by most diverging rays; and that remoter, which is seen by less diverging rays. And so on, the apparent distance still increasing, as the divergency of the rays decreases, till at length it becomes infinite, when the rays that fall on the *pupil* are to sense parallel. And after

---

[6]   George Berkeley, *An Essay towards a New Theory of Vision* (Doublin, 1709), sect. 1–28.

this manner it is said we perceive distances when we look only with one eye.

VII. In this case also, it is plain we are not beholding to experience: it being a certain, necessary truth, that the nearer the direct rays falling on the eye approach to a *parallelism*, the further off is the point of their intersection, or the visible point from whence they flow.

VIII. I have here set down the common, current accounts that are given of our perceiving near distances by sight. . . .

IX. *First*, It is evident, that when the mind perceives any *idea*, not immediately and of itself, it must be by the means of some other *idea*. Thus, for instance, the passions which are in the mind of another, are of themselves to me invisible. I may nevertheless perceive them by sight, though not immediately, yet by means of the colours they produce in the countenance. We do often see shame or fear in the looks of a man, by perceiving the changes of his countenance to red or pale.

X. Moreover it is evident, that no *idea* which is not itself perceived, can be to me the means of perceiving any other *idea*. If I do not perceive the redness or paleness of a man's face themselves, it is impossible I should perceive by them the passions which are in his mind.

XI. Now from Sect. II., it is plain that distance is in its own nature imperceivable, and yet it is perceived by sight. It remains, therefore, that it be brought into view by means of some other *idea* that is itself immediately perceived in the act of *vision*.

XII. But those *lines* and *angles*, by means whereof *mathematicians* pretend to explain the perception of distance, are themselves not at all perceived, nor are they, in truth, ever thought of by those unskilful in optics. I appeal to any one's experience, whether, upon sight of an *object*, he compute its distance by the bigness of the *angle* made by the meeting of the two *optic axes?* Or whether he ever think of the greater or lesser divergency of the rays, which arrive from any point to his *pupil?* Nay, whether it be not perfectly impossible for him to perceive by sense the various angles wherewith the rays, according to their greater or lesser divergence, do fall on his eye. Every one is himself the best judge of what he perceives, and what not. In vain shall all the *mathematicians* in the world tell me, that I perceive certain *lines* and *angles* which introduce into my mind the various *ideas* of *distance;* so long as I myself am conscious of no such thing.

XIII. Since, therefore, those *angles* and *lines* are not themselves perceived by sight, it follows from Sect. X., that the mind does not by them judge of the distance of *objects*.

XIV. Secondly, the truth of this assertion will be yet further evident to any one that considers those *lines* and *angles* have no real existence in nature, being only an *hypothesis* framed by *mathematicians*, and by them introduced into *optics*, that they might treat of that science in a *geometrical* way.

XV. The third and last reason I shall give for my rejecting that doctrine is, that though we should grant the real existence of those *optic angles*, &c., and that it was possible for the mind to perceive them; yet these principles would not be found sufficient to explain the phenomena of *distance*. As shall be shown hereafter.

XVI. Now, it being already shown that distance is suggested to the mind by the mediation of some other *idea* which is itself perceived in the act of seeing. It remains that we inquire what *ideas* or *sensations* there be that attend *vision*, unto which we may suppose the *ideas* of distance are connected, and by which they are introduced into the mind. And first, it is certain by experience, that when we look at a near *object* with both eyes, according as it approaches or recedes from us, we alter the disposition of our eyes, by lessening or widening the interval between the *pupils*. This disposition or turn of the eyes is attended with a sensation, which seems to me, to be that which in this case brings the *idea* of greater or lesser distance into the mind.

XVII. Not that there is any natural or necessary connexion between the sensation we perceive by the turn of the eyes, and greater or lesser distance. But because the mind has by constant *experience* found the different sensations corresponding to the different dispositions of the eyes, to be attended each with a different degree of distance in the *object:* there has grown an habitual or customary connexion, between those two sorts of *ideas*. So that the mind no sooner perceives the sensation arising from the different turn it gives the eyes, in order to bring the *pupils* nearer or further asunder, but it withal perceives the different *idea* of distance which was wont to be connected with that sensation. Just as upon hearing a certain sound, the *idea* is immediately suggested to the understanding, which custom had united with it.

XVIII. Nor do I see, how I can easily be mistaken in this matter. I know evidently that distance is not perceived of itself. That by consequence, it must be perceived by means of some other *idea* which is immediately perceived, and varies with the different degrees of distance. I know also that the sensation arising from the turn of the eyes is of itself immediately perceived, and various degrees thereof are connected with different distances: which never fail to accompany them into my mind, when I view an *object* distinctly with both eyes, whose distance is so small, that in respect of it the interval between the eyes has any considerable magnitude.

XIX. I know it is a received opinion, that by altering the disposition of the eyes, the mind perceives whether the angle of the *optic axes* is made greater or lesser. And that accordingly by a kind of *natural geometry*, it judges the point of their intersection to be nearer, or further off. But that this is not true, I am convinced by my own experience. Since I am not conscious that I make any such use of the perception I have by the turn of my eyes. And for me to make those judgments, and draw those conclusions from it, without knowing that I do so, seems altogether incomprehensible.

XX. From all which it plainly follows, that the judgment we make of the distance of an *object*, viewed with both eyes, is entirely the *result of experience*. If we had not constantly found certain sensations arising from the various disposition of the eyes, attended with certain degrees of distance, we should never make those sudden judgments from them, concerning the distance of *objects;* no more than we would pretend to judge of a man's thoughts, by his pronouncing words we had never heard before.

XXI. Secondly, an *object* placed at a certain distance from the eye, to which the breadth of the *pupil* bears a considerable proportion, being made to approach, is seen more confusedly. And the nearer it is brought, the more confused appearance it makes. And this being found constantly to be so, there

arises in the mind an *habitual* connexion between the several degrees of confusion and distance. The greater confusion still implying the lesser distance, and the lesser confusion, the greater distance of the *object*.

XXII. This confused appearance of the *object*, doth therefore seem to me to be the *medium*, whereby the mind judges of distance in those cases, wherein the most approved writers of optics will have it judge, by the different divergency with which the rays flowing from the radiating point fall on the *pupil*. No man, I believe, will pretend to see or feel those imaginary angles, that the rays are supposed to form according to their various inclinations on his eye. But he cannot choose seeing whether the *object* appear more or less confused. It is therefore a manifest consequence from what has been demonstrated, that instead of the greater or less divergency of the rays, the mind makes use of the greater or less confusedness of the appearance, thereby to determine the apparent place of an *object*.

XXIII. Nor doth it avail to say, there is not any necessary connexion between confused *vision*, and distance, great or small. For I ask any man, what necessary connexion he sees between the redness of a blush and shame? and yet no sooner shall he behold that colour to arise in the face of another, but it brings into his mind the *idea* of that passion which has been observed to accompany it.

XXIV. What seems to have misled the writers of optics in this matter is, that they imagine men judge of distance, as they do of a conclusion in mathematics: betwixt which and the premises, it is indeed absolutely requisite there be an apparent, necessary connexion. But it is far otherwise, in the sudden judgments men make of distance. We are not to think that brutes and children, or even grown reasonable men, whenever they perceive an *object* to approach, or depart from them, do it by virtue of *geometry* and *demonstration*.

XXV. That one *idea* may suggest another to the mind, it will suffice that they have been observed to go together: without any demonstration of the necessity of their coexistence, or without so much as knowing what it is that makes them so to coexist. Of this there are innumerable instances, of which no one can be ignorant.

XXVI. Thus greater confusion having been constantly attended with nearer distance, no sooner is the former *idea* perceived, but it suggests the latter to our thoughts. And if it had been the ordinary course of nature, that the further off an *object* were placed, the more confused it should appear; it is certain, the very same perception that now makes us think an *object* approaches, would then have made us imagine it went further off. That perception, abstracting from *custom* and *experience*, being equally fitted to produce the *idea* of great distance, or small distance, or no distance at all.

XXVII. Thirdly, an *object* being placed at the distance above specified, and brought nearer to the eye, we may nevertheless prevent, at least for some time, the appearance's growing more confused, by straining the eye. In which case, that sensation supplies the place of confused *vision*, in aiding the mind to judge of the distance of the *object*. It being esteemed so much the nearer, by how much the effort, or straining of the eye in order to distinct *vision*, is greater.

XXVIII. I have here set down those sensations or *ideas* that seem to me to be the constant and general occasions of introducing into the mind the different *ideas* of near distance. It is true in most cases, that divers other circumstances contribute to frame our *idea* of distance, viz., the particular number, size, kind, &c., of the things seen. Concerning which, as well as all other the forementioned occasions which suggest distance, I shall only observe, they have none of them, in their own nature, any relation or connexion with it: nor is it possible they should ever signify the various degrees thereof, otherwise than as by *experience* they have been found to be connected with them.

Conscious Context Theory of Meaning [7]

XLV. In these and the like instances, the truth of the matter stands thus: having of a long time experienced certain ideas, perceivable by touch, as distance, tangible figure, and solidity, to have been connected with certain ideas of sight, I do, upon perceiving these ideas of sight, forthwith conclude what tangible ideas are, by the wonted ordinary course of nature, like to follow. Looking at an object, I perceive a certain visible figure and colour, with some degree of faintness and other circumstances, which from what I have formerly observed, determine me to think, that if I advance forward so many paces or miles, I shall be affected with such and such ideas of touch: so that in truth and strictness of speech, I neither see distance itself nor any thing that I take to be at a distance. I say, neither distance nor things placed at a distance are themselves, or their ideas, truly perceived by sight. This I am persuaded of, as to what concerns myself; and I believe whoever will look narrowly into his own thoughts, and examine what he means by saying, he sees this or that thing at a distance, will agree with me, that what he sees only suggests to his understanding, that after having passed a certain distance, to be measured by the motion of his body, which is perceivable by touch, he shall come to perceive such and such tangible ideas which have been usually connected with such and such visible ideas. But that one might be deceived by these suggestions of sense, and that there is no necessary connexion between visible and tangible ideas suggested by them, we need go no further than the next lookingglass or picture to be convinced. Note, that when I speak of tangible ideas, I take the word idea for any the immediate object of sense, or understanding, in which large signification it is commonly used by the moderns.

XLVI. From what we have shown it is a manifest consequence, that the ideas of space, outness, and things placed at a distance, are not, strictly speaking, the object of sight; they are not otherwise perceived by the eye than by the ear. Sitting in my study I hear a coach drive along the street; I look through the casement and see it; I walk out and enter into it; thus, common speech would incline one to think, I heard, saw, and touched the same thing, to wit, the coach. It is nevertheless certain, the ideas intromitted by each sense are widely different, and distinct from each other; but having been observed constantly to go together, they are spoken of as one and the same thing. By the variation of the noise I perceive the different distances of the coach, and know that it approaches before I look out. Thus by the ear I perceive distance, just after the same manner as I do by the eye.

---

[7] *Ibid.*, sect. 45–58.

XLVII. I do not nevertheless say, I hear distance in like manner as I say that I see it, the ideas perceived by hearing not being so apt to be confounded with the ideas of touch, as those of sight are; so likewise a man is easily convinced that bodies and external things are not properly the object of hearing, but only sounds, by the mediation whereof the idea of this or that body or distance is suggested to his thoughts. But then one is with more difficulty brought to discern the difference there is betwixt the ideas of sight and touch: though it be certain, a man no more sees or feels the same thing, than he hears and feels the same thing.

XLVIII. One reason of which seems to be this: It is thought a great absurdity to imagine, that one and the same thing should have any more than one extension, and one figure. But the extension and figure of a body, being let into the mind two ways, and that indifferently, either by sight or touch, it seems to follow that we see the same extension, and the same figure which we feel.

XLIX. But if we take a close and accurate view of things, it must be acknowledged that we never see and feel one and the same object. That which is seen is one thing, and that which is felt is another; if the visible figure and extension be not the same with the tangible figure and extension, we are not to infer that one and the same thing has divers extensions. The true consequence is, that the objects of sight and touch are two distinct things. It may perhaps require some thought rightly to conceive this distinction. And the difficulty seems not a little increased, because the combination of visible ideas hath constantly the same name as the combination of tangible ideas wherewith it is connected: which doth of necessity arise from the use and end of language.

L. In order therefore to treat accurately and unconfusedly of vision, we must bear in mind that there are two sorts of objects apprehended by the eye, the one primarily and immediately, the other secondarily and by intervention of the former. Those of the first sort neither are, nor appear to be, without the mind, or at any distance off; they may indeed grow greater or smaller, more confused, or more clear, or more faint, but they do not, cannot approach or recede from us. Whenever we say an object is at a distance, whenever we say it draws near, or goes further off, we must always mean it of the latter sort, which properly belong to the touch, and are not so truly perceived, as suggested by the eye in like manner as thoughts by the ear.

LI. No sooner do we hear the words of a familiar language pronounced in our ears, but the ideas corresponding thereto present themselves to our minds; in the very same instant the sound and the meaning enter the understanding: so closely are they united, that it is not in our power to keep out the one, except we exclude the other also. We even act in all respects as if we heard the very thoughts themselves. So likewise the secondary objects, or those which are only suggested by sight, do often more strongly affect us, and are more regarded than the proper objects of that sense, along with which they enter into the mind, and with which they have a far more strict connexion, than ideas have with words. Hence it is, we find it so difficult to discriminate between the immediate and mediate objects of sight, and are so prone to attribute to the former, what belongs only to the latter. They are, as it were, most closely twisted, blended, and incorporated together. And the prejudice is confirmed and riveted in our thoughts by a long tract of time, by the use of language and want of reflection. However, I believe any one that shall attentively consider what we have already said, and shall say upon this subject before we have done (especially if he pursue it in his own thoughts) may be able to deliver himself from that prejudice. Sure I am, it is worth some attention to whoever would understand the true nature of vision.

LII. I have now done with distance, and proceed to show how it is, that we perceive by sight the magnitude of objects. It is the opinion of some that we do it by angles, or by angles in conjunction with distance. But neither angles nor distance being perceivable by sight, and the things we see being in truth at no distance from us, it follows, that as we have shown lines and angles not to be the medium the mind makes use of in apprehending the apparent place, so neither are they the medium whereby it apprehends the apparent magnitude of objects.

LIII. It is well known, that the same extension at a near distance shall subtend a greater angle, and at a further distance a lesser angle. And by this principle, we are told, the mind estimates the magnitude of an object, comparing the angle under which it is seen with its distance, and thence inferring the magnitude thereof. What inclines men to this mistake (beside the humour of making one see by geometry) is, that the same perceptions or ideas which suggest distance, do also suggest magnitude. But if we examine it, we shall find they suggest the latter, as immediately as the former. I say they do not first suggest distance, and then leave it to the judgment to use that as a medium, whereby to collect the magnitude; but they have as close and immediate a connexion with the magnitude, as with the distance; and suggest magnitude as independently of distance, as they do distance independently of magnitude. All which will be evident to whoever considers what hath been already said.

Doctrine of Divine Arbitrariness [8]

XXXIX. Ideas, which are observed to be connected with other Ideas, come to be considered as Signs, by means whereof Things, not actually perceived by Sense, are signified or suggested to the Imagination, whose Objects they are, and which alone perceives them. And as Sounds suggest other things, so Characters suggest those Sounds; and, in general, all Signs suggest the things signified, there being no Idea which may not offer to the Mind another Idea, which hath been frequently joined with it. In certain Cases, a Sign may suggest its Correlate as an Image, in others as an Effect, in others as a Cause. But where there is no such Relation of Similitude or Causality, nor any necessary Connexion whatsoever, two things by their mere Coexistence, or two Ideas, merely by being perceived together may suggest or signify one the other, their Connexion being all the while arbitrary; for it is the Connexion only, as such, that causeth this Effect.

XL. A great Number of arbitrary Signs, various and apposite, do constitute a Language. If such arbitrary Connexion be instituted by Men, it is an artificial Language; if by the Author of Nature, it is a Natural Language. Infinitely various are the Modifications of Light and Sound, whence they are each capable of supplying an endless Variety of Signs, and, accordingly, have been each employed to form Languages; the one by the arbitrary Appointment of Mankind, the other by that of God himself. A Connexion established by the Author of Nature, in the ordinary course of things, may surely be called Natural; as that made by Men will be named Artificial. And yet this doth not hinder but the one may be as arbitrary as the other. And, in Fact, there is no more Likeness to exhibit, or Necessity to infer, things tangible from the Modifications of Light, than there is in Language, to collect the Meaning from the Sound. But, such as the Connexion is of the various Tones and Articulations of Voice with their several Meanings, the same is it between the various Modes of Light and their respective Correlates; or in other Words, between the Ideas of Sight and Touch.

XLI. As to Light, and its several Modes or Colours, all thinking Men are agreed, that they are Ideas peculiar only to Sight; neither common to the Touch, nor of the same Kind with any that are perceived by that Sense. But herein lies the Mistake, that beside these, there are supposed other Ideas common to both Senses, being equally perceived by Sight and Touch, such as Extension, Size, Figure, and Motion. But that there are in reality no such common Ideas, and that the Objects of Sight, marked by those Words, are intirely different and heterogeneous from whatever is the Object of Feeling, marked by the same Names, hath been proved in the *Theory*, and seems by you admitted. Though I cannot conceive how you should in reason admit this, and at the same time contend for the received Theories, which are as much ruined, as mine is established, by this main Part and Pillar thereof.

XLII. To perceive is one thing; to judge is another. So likewise to be suggested is one thing, and to be inferred another. Things are suggested and perceived by Sense. We make Judgments and Inferences by the Understanding. What we immediately and properly perceive by Sight, is its primary Object, Light and Colours. What is suggested or perceived by Mediation thereof, are tangible Ideas, which may be considered as secondary and improper Objects of Sight. We infer Causes

---

[8] George Berkeley, *The Theory of Vision, or Visual Language, Shewing the Immediate Presence and Providence of a Deity, Vindicated and Explained* (London, 1733), sect. 39–43.

from Effects, Effects from Causes, and Properties one from another, where the Connection is necessary. But, how comes it to pass, that we apprehend by the Ideas of Sight certain other Ideas, which neither resemble them, nor cause them, nor are caused by them, nor have any necessary Connexion with them? The Solution of this Problem, in its full Extent, doth comprehend the whole Theory of Vision. Thus stating of the Matter placeth it on a new Foot, and in a different Light from all preceding Theories.

XLIII. To explain how the Mind or Soul of Man simply sees, is one thing, and belongs to Philosophy. To consider Particles as moving in certain Lines, Rays of Light as refracted, or reflected, or crossing, or including Angles, is quite another thing, and appertaineth to Geometry. To account for the Sense of Vision by the Mechanism of the Eye, is a third thing, which appertaineth to Anatomy and Experiments. These two latter Speculations are of use in Practice, to assist the Defects, and remedy the Distempers of Sight, agreeably to the natural Laws obtaining in this mundane System. But the former Theory is that which makes us understand the true Nature of Vision, considered as a Faculty of the Soul. Which Theory, as I have already observed, may be reduced to this simple Question, to wit, How comes it to pass, that a Set of Ideas, altogether different from tangible Ideas, should nevertheless suggest them to us, there being no necessary Connexion between them? To which the proper Answer is, That this is done in virtue of an arbitrary Connexion, instituted by the Author of Nature.

Psychologism [9]

It is evident to any one who takes a survey of the objects of human knowledge, that they are either ideas actually imprinted on the senses; or else such as are perceived by attending to the passions and operations of the mind; or lastly, ideas formed by help of memory and imagination—either compounding, dividing, or barely representing those originally perceived in the aforesaid ways. By sight I have the ideas of light and colours, with their several degrees and variations. By

[9] George Berkeley, *A Treatise concerning the Principles of Human Knowledge* (Doublin, 1710), ch. 1.

touch I perceive hard and soft, heat and cold, motion and resistance, and of all these more and less either as to quantity or degree. Smelling furnishes me with odours; the palate with tastes; and hearing conveys sounds to the mind in all their variety of tone and composition. And as several of these are observed to accompany each other, they come to be marked by one name, and so to be reputed as one thing. Thus, for example, a certain colour, taste, smell, figure and consistence having been observed to go together, are accounted one distinct thing, signified by the name *apple;* other collections of ideas constitute a stone, a tree, a book, and the like sensible things—which as they are pleasing or disagreeable excite the passions of love, hatred, joy, grief, and so forth.

2. But, besides all that endless variety of ideas or objects of knowledge, there is likewise something which knows or perceives them, and exercises divers operations, as willing, imagining, remembering, about them. This perceiving, active being is what I call *mind*, *spirit*, *soul*, or *myself*. By which words I do not denote any one of my ideas, but a thing entirely distinct from them, wherein they exist, or, which is the same thing, whereby they are perceived—for the existence of an idea consists in being perceived.

3. That neither our thoughts, nor passions, nor ideas formed by the imagination, exist without the mind, is what everybody will allow. And it seems no less evident that the various sensations or ideas imprinted on the sense, however blended or combined together (that is, whatever objects they compose), cannot exist otherwise than in a mind perceiving them.—I think an intuitive knowledge may be obtained of this by any one that shall attend to what is meant by the term *exist*, when applied to sensible things. The table I write on I say exists, that is, I see and feel it; and if I were out of my study I should say it existed—meaning thereby that if I was in my study I might perceive it, or that some other spirit actually does perceive it. There was an odour, that is, it was smelt; there was a sound, that is, it was heard; a colour or figure, and it was perceived by sight or touch. This is all that I can understand by these and the like expressions. For as to what is said of the absolute existence of unthinking things without any relation to their being perceived,

that seems perfectly unintelligible. Their *esse* is *percipi*, nor is it possible they should have any existence out of the minds or thinking things which perceive them.

4. It is indeed an opinion strangely prevailing amongst men, that houses, mountains, rivers, and in a word all sensible objects, have an existence, natural or real, distinct from their being perceived by the understanding.

DAVID HUME
(1711–1776)

Association of Ideas [10]

All the perceptions of the human mind resolve themselves into two distinct kinds, which I shall call IMPRESSIONS and IDEAS. The difference betwixt these consists in the degrees of force and liveliness with which they strike upon the mind, and make their way into our thought or consciousness. Those perceptions, which enter with most force and violence, we may name *impressions;* and under this name I comprehend all our sensations, passions and emotions, as they make their first appearance in the soul. By *ideas*, I mean the faint images of these in thinking and reasoning; such as, for instance, are all the perceptions excited by the present discourse, excepting only, those which arise from the sight and touch, and excepting the immediate pleasure or uneasiness it may occasion.

* * * * *

There is another division of our perceptions, which it will be convenient to observe, and which extends itself both to our impressions and ideas. This division is into SIMPLE and COMPLEX. Simple perceptions or impressions and ideas are such as admit of no distinction nor separation. The complex are the contrary to these, and may be distinguished into parts. Tho' a particular colour, taste, and smell are qualities all united together in this apple, 'tis easy to perceive they are not the same, but are at least distinguishable from each other.

* * * * *

Upon a more accurate survey I find I have been carried away too far by the first appearance, and that I must make use of the distinction of perceptions into *simple and complex*, to limit this general decision, *that all our ideas and impressions are resembling.* I observe,

that many of our complex ideas never had impressions, that corresponded to them, and that many of our complex impressions never are exactly copied in ideas. I can imagine to myself such a city as the *New Jerusalem*, whose pavement is gold and walls are rubies, tho' I never saw any such. I have seen *Paris;* but shall I affirm I can form such an idea of that city, as will perfectly represent all its streets and houses in their real and just proportions?

Thus we find, that all simple ideas and impressions resemble each other; and as the complex are formed from them, we may affirm in general, that these two species of perception are exactly correspondent.

* * * * *

We shall here content ourselves with establishing one general proposition, *That all our simple ideas in their first appearance are deriv'd from simple impressions, which are correspondent to them, and which they exactly represent.*

In seeking for phænomena to prove this proposition, I find only those of two kinds; but in each kind the phænomena are obvious, numerous, and conclusive. I first make myself certain, by a new review, of what I have already asserted, that every simple impression is attended with a correspondent idea, and every simple idea with a correspondent impression. From this constant conjunction of resembling perceptions I immediately conclude, that there is a great connexion betwixt our correspondent impressions and ideas, and that the existence of the one has a considerable influence upon that of the other. Such a constant conjunction, in such an infinite number of instances, can never arise from chance; but clearly proves a dependence of the impressions on the ideas, or of the ideas on the impressions. That I may know on which side this dependence lies, I consider

---

[10] David Hume, *A Treatise of Human Nature* (London, 1739), bk. 1, pt. 1–3.

the order of their *first appearance;* and find by constant experience, that the simple impressions always take the precedence of their correspondent ideas, but never appear in the contrary order. To give a child an idea of scarlet or orange, of sweet or bitter, I present the objects, or in other words, convey to him these impressions; but proceed not so absurdly, as to endeavour to produce the impressions by exciting the ideas. Our ideas upon their appearance produce not their correspondent impressions, nor do we perceive any colour, or feel any sensation merely upon thinking of them. On the other hand we find, that any impressions either of the mind or body is constantly followed by an idea, which resembles it, and is only different in the degrees of force and liveliness. The constant conjunction of our resembling perceptions, is a convincing proof, that the one are the causes of the other; and this priority of the impressions is an equal proof, that our impressions are the causes of our ideas, not our ideas of our impressions.

* * * * *

It may not be amiss to remark on this head, that the principle of the priority of impressions to ideas must be understood with another limitation, *viz.* that as our ideas are images of our impressions, so we can form secondary ideas, which are images of the primary; as appears from this very reasoning concerning them. This is not, properly speaking, an exception to the rule so much as an explanation of it. Ideas produce the images of themselves in new ideas; but as the first ideas are supposed to be derived from impressions, it still remains true, that all our simple ideas proceed either mediately or immediately from their correspondent impressions.

Memory and Imagination

We find by experience, that when any impression has been present with the mind, it again makes its appearance there as an idea; and this it may do after two different ways: either when in its new appearance it retains a considerable degree of its first vivacity, and is somewhat intermediate betwixt an impression and an idea; or when it entirely loses that vivacity, and is a perfect idea. The faculty, by which we repeat our impressions in the first manner, is called the MEMORY, and

the other the IMAGINATION. 'Tis evident at first sight, that the ideas of the memory are much more lively and strong than those of the imagination, and that the former faculty paints its objects in more distinct colours, than any which are employ'd by the latter. When we remember any past event, the idea of it flows in upon the mind in a forcible manner; whereas in the imagination the perception is faint and languid, and cannot without difficulty be preserv'd by the mind steddy and uniform for any considerable time. Here then is a sensible difference betwixt one species of ideas and another. . . .

There is another difference betwixt these two kinds of ideas, which is no less evident, namely that tho' neither the ideas of the memory nor imagination, neither the lively nor faint ideas can make their appearance in the mind, unless their correspondent impressions have gone before to prepare the way for them, yet the imagination is not restrain'd to the same order and form with the original impressions; while the memory is in a manner ty'd down in that respect, without any power of variation.

* * * * *

Association of Ideas (Resemblance, Contiguity, Cause and Effect)

As all simple ideas may be separated by the imagination, and may be united again in what form it pleases, nothing wou'd be more unaccountable than the operations of that faculty, were it not guided by some universal principles, which render it, in some measure, uniform with itself in all times and places. Were ideas entirely loose and unconnected, chance alone wou'd join them; and 'tis impossible the same simple ideas should fall regularly into complex ones (as they commonly do) without some bond of union among them, some associating quality, by which one idea naturally introduces another. This uniting principle among ideas is not to be consider'd as an inseparable connexion; for that has been already excluded from the imagination: nor yet are we to conclude, that without it the mind cannot join two ideas; for nothing is more free than that faculty: but we are only to regard it as a gentle force, which commonly prevails, and is the cause why, among other things, languages so nearly correspond to each other; nature in a manner pointing out to every one those simple ideas, which are most proper to be united into a complex one. The qualities, from which this association arises, and by which the mind is after his manner convey'd from one idea to another, are three, *viz.* RESEMBLANCE, CONTIGUITY in time or place, and CAUSE and EFFECT.

I believe it will not be very necessary to prove, that these qualities produce an association among ideas, and upon the appearance of one idea naturally introduce another. 'Tis plain, that in the course of our thinking, and in the constant revolution of our ideas, our imagination runs easily from one idea to any other that *resembles* it, and that this quality alone is to the fancy a sufficient bond and association. 'Tis likewise evident, that as the senses, in changing their objects, are necessitated to change them regularly, and take them as they lie *contiguous* to each other, the imagination must by long custom acquire the same method of thinking, and run along the parts of space and time in conceiving its objects. As to the connexion, that is made by the relation of *cause and effect*, we shall have occasion afterwards to examine it to the bottom, and therefore shall not at present insist upon it. 'Tis sufficient to observe, that there is no relation, which produces a stronger connexion in the fancy, and makes one idea more readily recall another, than the relation of cause and effect betwixt their objects.

That we may understand the full extent of these relations, we must consider, that two objects are connected together in the imagination, not only when the one is immediately resembling, contiguous to, or the cause of the other, but also when there is interposed betwixt them a third object, which bears to both of them any of these relations. This may be carried on to a great length; tho' at the same time we may observe, that each remove considerably weakens the relation.

* * * * *

Of the three relations above-mention'd this of causation is the most extensive. Two objects may be consider'd as plac'd in this relation, as well when one is the cause of any of the actions or motions of the other, as when the former is the cause of the existence of the latter. For as that action or motion

is nothing but the object itself, consider'd in a certain light, and as the object continues the same in all its different situations, 'tis easy to imagine how such an influence of objects upon one another may connect them in the imagination.

We may carry this farther, and remark, not only that two objects are connected by the relation of cause and effect, when the one produces a motion or any action in the other, but also when it has a power of producing it.

* * * * *

These are therefore the principles of union or cohesion among our simple ideas, and in the imagination supply the place of that inseparable connexion, by which they are united in our memory. Here is a kind of ATTRACTION, which in the mental world will be found to have as extra-ordinary effects as in the natural, and to shew itself in as many and as various forms. Its effects are every where conspicuous; but as to its causes, they are mostly unknown, and must be resolv'd into *original* qualities of human nature, which I pretend not to explain.

Causation and Association [11]

What is our idea of necessity, when we say that two objects are necessarily connected together. Upon this head I repeat what I have often had occasion to observe, that as we have no idea, that is not deriv'd from an impression, we must find some impression, that gives rise to this idea of necessity, if we assert we have really such an idea. In order to this I consider, in what objects necessity is commonly suppos'd to lie; and finding that it is always ascrib'd to causes and effects, I turn my eye to two objects suppos'd to be plac'd in that relation; and examine them in all the situations, of which they are susceptible. I immediately perceive, that they are *contiguous* in time and place, and that the object we call cause *precedes* the other we call effect. In no one instance can I go any farther, nor is it possible for me to discover any third relation betwixt these objects. I therefore enlarge my view to comprehend several instances; where I find like objects always existing in like relations of contiguity and succession. At first sight this seems to serve but little to my

[11] *Ibid.*, bk. 1, pt. 3, sect. 14.

purpose. The reflection on several instances only repeats the same objects; and therefore can never give rise to a new idea. But upon farther enquiry I find, that the repetition is not in every particular the same, but produces a new impression, and by that means the idea, which I at present examine. For after a frequent repetition, I find, that upon the appearance of one of the objects, the mind is *determin'd* by custom to consider its usual attendant, and to consider it in a stronger light upon account of its relation to the first object. 'Tis this impression, then, or *determination*, which affords me the idea of necessity.

* * * * *

I begin with observing that the terms of *efficacy, agency, power, force, energy, necessity, connexion,* and *productive quality,* are all nearly synonimous; and therefore 'tis an absurdity to employ any of them in defining the rest. By this observation we reject at once all the vulgar definitions, which philosophers have given of power and efficacy; and instead of searching for the idea in these definitions, must look for it in the impressions, from which it is originally deriv'd. If it be a compound idea, it must arise from compound impressions. If simple, from simple impressions.

I believe the most general and most popular explication of this matter, is to say, that finding from experience, that there are several new productions in matter, such as the motions and variations of body, and concluding that there must somewhere be a power capable of producing them, we arrive at last by this reasoning at the idea of power and efficacy. But to be convinc'd that this explication is more popular than philosophical, we need but reflect on two very obvious principles. *First,* That reason alone can never give rise to any original idea, and *secondly,* that reason, as distinguish'd from experience, can never make us conclude, that a cause or productive quality is absolutely requisite to every beginning of existence. . . .

I shall only infer from them, that since reason can never give rise to the idea of efficacy, that idea must be deriv'd from experience, and from some particular instances of this efficacy, which make their passage into the mind by the common channels of sensation or reflection. Ideas always represent their objects or impressions; and *vice versa,* there are some objects necessary to give rise to every idea. If we pretend, therefore, to have any just idea of this efficacy, we must produce some instance, wherein the efficacy is plainly discoverable to the mind, and its operations obvious to our consciousness or sensation. By the refusal of this, we acknowledge, that the idea is impossible and imaginary; since the principle of innate ideas, which alone can save us from this dilemma, has been already refuted.

* * * * *

The necessary connexion betwixt causes and effects is the foundation of our inference from one to the other. The foundation of our inference is the transition arising from the accustom'd union. These are, therefore, the same.

The idea of necessity arises from some impression. There is no impression convey'd by our senses, which can give rise to that idea. It must, therefore, be deriv'd from some internal impression, or impression of reflexion. There is no internal impression, which has any relation to the present business, but that propensity, which custom produces, to pass from an object to the idea of its usual attendant. This therefore is the essence of necessity. Upon the whole, necessity is something, that exists in the mind, not in objects; nor is it possible for us ever to form the most distant idea of it, consider'd as a quality in bodies. Either we have no idea of necessity, or necessity is nothing but that determination of the thought to pass from causes to effects and from effects to causes, according to their experienc'd union.

Thus as the necessity, which makes two times two equal to four, or three angles of a triangle equal to two right ones, lies only in the act of the understanding, by which we consider and compare these ideas; in like manner the necessity or power, which unites causes and effects, lies in the determination of the mind to pass from the one to the other. The efficacy or energy of causes is neither plac'd in the causes themselves, nor in the deity, nor in the concurrence of these two principles; but belongs entirely to the soul, which considers the union of two or more objects in all past instances. 'Tis here that the real power of causes is plac'd, along with their connexion and necessity. . . . How often must we repeat to ourselves, *that* the simple view of any two objects or actions, however related, can never give us any idea of power, or of a connexion betwixt them: *that* this idea arises from the repetition of their union: *that* the repetition neither discovers nor causes any thing in the objects, but has an influence only on the mind, by that customary transition it produces: *that* this customary transition is, therefore, the same with the power and necessity; which are consequently qualities of perceptions, not of objects, and are internally felt by the soul, and not perceiv'd externally in bodies? There is commonly an astonishment attending every thing extraordinary; and this astonishment changes immediately into the highest degree of esteem or contempt, according as we approve or disapprove of the subject. I am much afraid.

If we define a cause to be *an object precedent and contiguous to another, and where all the objects resembling the former are plac'd in a like relation of priority and contiguity to those objects, that resemble the latter;* we may easily conceive, that there is no absolute nor metaphysical necessity, that every beginning of existence shou'd be attended with such an object. If we define a cause to be, *An object precedent and contiguous to another, and so united with it in the imagination, that the idea of the one determines the mind to form the idea of the other, and the impression of the one to form a more lively idea of the other;* we shall make still less difficulty of assenting to this opinion. Such an influence on the mind is in itself perfectly extraordinary and incomprehensible; nor can we be certain of its reality, but from experience and observation.

5

French Behaviorism and Sensationalism during the Enlightenment

JULIEN OFFRAY DE LA METTRIE
(1709–1751)

Early French Behaviorism [1]

The soul and the body fall asleep together. As the movement of the blood slows, a gentle feeling of peace and tranquility spreads through the entire machine. The soul feels itself slowly growing heavy as the eyelids droop, and its tensions relax as the fibers of the brain become lax. Little by little in this fashion the soul becomes as though paralyzed, and with it all the muscles of the body. The latter can no longer sustain the weight of the

head; the former is not able to carry the burden of thought. The soul finally sleeps, as though it did not exist.

Is the circulation too rapid? Then the soul cannot sleep. Is the soul restless? Then the blood cannot be calmed, but rather it rushes through the veins with an audible pounding. Such are the two reciprocal causes of insomnia. A single fright experienced in a dream sets the heart to beating at double speed, and snatches us from sweet and necessary sleep, just as a real pain or other urgent need would do. Lastly, as the mere cessation of the functions of the soul brings on sleep, there are even in wakefulness (or more precisely halfwakefulness) various kinds of short naps

---

[1] Julien Offray de La Mettrie, *Man a Machine* (Leiden, 1748). Translated for the present volume by Cleophas W. Boudreau from the French, *L'homme machine* (Leiden, 1748).

of the soul, daydreams and the like, which prove that the soul doesn't always wait for the body, if it wishes to sleep. In such states of semi-wakefulness, if the soul is not entirely asleep it is indeed not far from that condition, for its reacts to no objects toward which its attention appears to be directed. The soul is lost, as it were, among a countless multitude of confused ideas which, like clouds, fill the atmosphere of the brain.

Opium stands in such close relationship to the matter we are discussing that it cannot be omitted here. It is a drug that intoxicates, like wine, coffee, etc., each in its own way and according to the amount taken. Opium produces a happy state, which seemingly is the very tomb of feeling, or the image of death itself. What sweet lethargy! The soul longs never to leave it. Where previously it may have been racked by the greatest of pain and sorrow, the soul in an opium dream feels only a pleasure of no longer suffering, and enjoys the sweetest tranquility. Opium has its effect also upon the will, for the soul is forced to sleep even though it wishes to remain awake and enjoy life. I shall omit

any discussion of the effect of the poisons of this drug.

Coffee, the well-known antidote for wine, dispels our cares and cures our headaches by stimulating the imagination. Unlike wine it does not produce in us ill effects on the following day.

Let us consider the soul with regard to its other needs.

The human body is a machine which winds its own springs. It is the living image of perpetual movement. It is the function of nourishment to continue those bodily functions originally produced by heat. Without nourishment for the body, the soul also languishes, goes mad, or dies through exhaustion. The soul is not unlike a taper, which flares up briefly a moment before it goes out. But nourish the body, pour into its veins vigorous juices and strong liquors and the soul becomes strong again, and the soldier who would have been put to flight by water becomes fierce, and gallantly rushes forward to his death to the sound of drums. It is in this fashion that a hot drink excites the blood, where a cold drink calms it.

ÉTIENNE BONNOT
DE CONDILLAC
(1715–1780)

French Sensationalism [2]

The Mind of a Man Limited to the Sense of Smell

The notions of our statue being limited to the sense of smell, can include odours only. It cannot have any conception of extent, of form, of anything external to itself, or to its sensations, any more than it can have of colour, sound or taste.

If we offer the statue a rose, it will be, in its relation to us, a statue which smells a rose; but in relation to itself, it will be merely the scent itself of the flower.

Therefore, according to the objects which act upon its organ, it will be scent of rose, of carnation, of jasmine, of violet. In a word,

odours are, in this respect, merely modifications of the statue itself or modes of being; it is not capable of believing itself aught else, since these are the only sensations it can feel.

Let those philosophers to whom it is so evident that everything is material, put themselves for a moment in the place of the statue, and let them reflect how they could suspect that there exists anything resembling what we call *matter*.

We may then already be convinced that it is sufficient to increase or to diminish the number of the senses to cause us to come to conclusions wholly different from those which are at present so natural to us, and our statue, limited to the sense of smell, may thus enable us to comprehend somewhat the class of beings whose notions are the most restricted.

With the first odour the capacity for feeling of our statue is wholly taken up by the impression made upon its organ. I call this attention.

---

[2] Étienne Bonnot de Condillac, *Treatise on Sensations*, trans. Frederick C. de Sumichrast, in Benjamin Rand, *Modern Classical Philosophers* (Boston: Houghton Mifflin, 1908). Original French, *Traité des sensations* (Paris, 1754), ch. 1, 2, 6, 7.

From that moment it begins to enjoy or to suffer: for if the power of feeling is wholly devoted to a pleasant odour, enjoyment is the result; and if it be wholly devoted to an unpleasant odour, suffering results.

But our statue has yet no idea of the different changes it may experience. Therefore it is well; or is not well, without the desire to be better. Suffering is no more capable of exciting in the statue a longing for an enjoyment of which it has no knowledge, than enjoyment is capable of making it fear an ill of which it is equally ignorant. Consequently, no matter how disagreeable the first sensation may be, even to the point of wounding the organ and of being a violent pain, it cannot cause desire.

While suffering with us is always accompanied by the desire not to suffer, it cannot be so with the statue. Pain creates that desire in us only because the condition of non-suffering is already known to us. The habit we have contracted of looking upon pain as a thing we have been without and of which we may be freed, is the cause that the moment we suffer we immediately desire not to suffer, and this condition is inseparable from a state of suffering.

But the statue which, at the first moment, is conscious of its feeling only through the very pain it experiences, does not know whether it can cease to be a statue and become something else, or cease to exist. It has, as yet, no conception of change, of succession or of duration. Therefore it exists without having the power to form a desire.

Once it has observed that it is capable of ceasing to be what it is, in order to become once more what it was before, we shall see its desires spring from a condition of pain, which it will compare with a condition of pleasure recalled to it by memory. Thus it is that pleasure and pain are the sole principle which, determining all the operations of its soul, will gradually raise it to all the knowledge of which it is capable; and in order to determine the progress of which it is susceptible, it will suffice to observe the pleasure it will have to desire, the pains it will have to fear, and the influence of either according to circumstances.

Supposing the statue to have no remembrance of the changes it has undergone, then on every occasion of a change it would believe itself to be conscious of sensation for the first time: whole years would be swallowed up in each present moment. Therefore by ever confining its attention to a single mode of being, it would never reckon two together, and would never note their relations to each other: it would enjoy or suffer, without yet knowing desire or fear.

But the odour it smells does not, so soon as the odoriferous object ceases to act upon its organ, become wholly lost to the statue. The attention it bestowed upon it still retains the odour, and there remains a more or less strong impression of that odour in proportion as the attention itself has been more or less active. That is memory.

When, therefore, our statue is a new odour, there is still present to it the odour that it was the moment before. Its power of feeling is divided between memory and the sense of smell, the former of these faculties being attentive to the past sensation, while the latter is attentive to the present sensation.

Thus there are in the statue two modes of feeling, differing only in this, that the one is concerned with a present sensation and the other with a sensation no longer existent, but the impression of which still remains. Unaware of the fact that there are objects which act upon it, unaware even of the fact that it possesses an organ, the statue ordinarily distinguishes between the remembrance of a sensation and a present sensation merely by dimly feeling what it has been and feeling strongly what it is at the moment.

I say *ordinarily*, because remembrance will not always be a faint sentiment, nor sensation a lively one. For every time that memory recalls very strongly these states of being, while, on the contrary, the organ itself receives but slight impressions, the consciousness of a present sensation will be much less vivid than the remembrance of a sensation which has ceased to be.

As, therefore, one odour is present to be the sense of smell through the impression made by an odoriferous body upon the organ itself, so is another odour present in the memory, because the impression made by another odoriferous body continues in the brain, to which the organ of smell has transmitted it. Passing thus through two states of being, the statue feels that it is no longer what it has been: the knowledge of this change causes it to refer the first state to a different moment from that in which it experiences the second state, and this it is which causes the statue to make a distinction between existing in one way and having existed in another way.

The statue is active in relation to one of its two modes of feeling, and passive in relation to the other. It is active when it remembers a sensation, because it has within itself the cause which brings about that recollection, that is memory. It is passive at the moment when it experiences a sensation, because the cause which produces it is external to the statue itself, that is, it lies in the odoriferous bodies which act upon its sense of smell.

But, unable even to suspect the action upon itself of objects external to it, it cannot distinguish between a cause within itself and a cause outside of itself. As far as the statue is concerned all the modifications of its state of being appear to it due to itself, and whether it experiences a sensation or merely recalls one, it is never aware of aught save that it is or has been in such and such a state of being. It cannot, therefore, observe any difference between the condition in which it is itself active or that in which it is wholly passive.

Nevertheless the more numerous the occasions for the exercise of the memory the more readily will the memory act. And it is in this way that the statue will acquire the habit of recalling without an effort the changes through which it has passed, and of dividing its attention between what it has been and what it is. For habit is merely the facility of repeating what one has done, and that facility is acquired by the reiteration of the actions.

If, after having repeatedly smelled a rose and a carnation, the statue once more smells a rose, the passive attention, acting by the sense of smell, will be wholly given up to the present odour of the rose, and the active attention, which acts through the memory, will be divided between the remains of the scents of the rose and of the carnation. Now these two states of being cannot share the capacity for feeling without comparing themselves one with the other, for comparing is nothing else than bestowing one's attention upon two ideas at the same time.

From the moment that comparison exists,

judgment exists. Our statue cannot at one and the same time be attentive to the scent of the rose and that of the carnation, without perceiving that the one is not the same as the other, and it cannot be attentive to the odour of a rose which it smells and to that of a rose which it has previously smelled without perceiving that they are a similar modification. Judgment, therefore, is simply the perception of the relation between two ideas which are being compared.

As the comparisons and conclusions become more frequent the statue acquires greater facility in making them. It contracts therefore the habit of comparing and judging. Consequently it will be sufficient to make it smell other odours in order to cause it to make additional comparisons, come to additional conclusions and contract new habits.

The first sensation it experiences causes no surprise to the statue, for it is as yet unaccustomed to form any kind of judgment, nor is it surprised when, on smelling successively different odours, it perceives each but for a moment. Under these conditions it does not abide by any conclusion it has formed, and the more the statue changes the more it feels itself naturally inclined to change.

Nor will it feel any more surprise if we lead it, by unnoticeable gradations, from the habit of believing itself one odour to the conclusion that it is another odour, for the statue changes without having the power of noticing the change.

But it cannot fail to be surprised if it passes suddenly from a condition to which it was accustomed to a totally different state of which it had no previous conception.

This amazement causes it to feel more distinctly the differences between its modes of being. The more abrupt the change from one to the other the greater the astonishment of the statue, and the more is it struck by the contrast between the pleasures and the pains which mark these changes. Its attention, excited by pains which are more keenly felt, applies itself with greater acuteness to the sensations which succeed each other. It therefore compares them more carefully; it judges more accurately their relations to each other. Amazement consequently increases the activity of the operations of its mind. But, because it is by bringing out a more marked opposition between feelings of pleasure and feelings of pain that amazement thus increases activity of mind, it follows that it is always pleasure and pain which are the primary motive cause of its faculties.

If each successive odour acts with equal force upon the statue's attention, the memory will remember them in the order in which they followed each other, and they will by this means become connected one with another.

If the series is numerous, the impression made by the most recent odours, being the most recent, will be the strongest; the impression made by the first in order will be imperceptibly weakened, then disappear altogether, and these sensations will be as if they had never been.

But if there be any which have acted but slightly upon the attention, they will leave no impression behind them and will be forgotten as soon as they have been perceived.

Finally the impressions which will have more vividly struck the attention, will be more vividly recalled, and will so strongly engage it that they will be capable of making it forget the others.

Memory therefore is a series of ideas forming a sort of chain. It is this connection which enables us to pass from one idea to another, and to recall the most distant. Therefore we remember an idea that we had some time since only because we recall, more or less rapidly, the intermediary ideas.

In the case of the second sensation our statue experiences, it has not to make any selection: it can remember but the first sensation. It will merely act more or less vigorously, according as it is inclined thereto by the intensity of the pleasure or the pain.

But when there has been a succession of changes, the statue, having a great number in remembrance, will be inclined to recall preferably those which can best contribute to its happiness, passing rapidly over the others or dwelling on them only in spite of itself.

To make this truth fully plain it is necessary to know the different degrees of pain and of pleasure of which we are susceptible, and the comparisons which may be drawn between them.

* * * * *

Whenever it is ill or less well, it recalls its past sensations, compares them with its actual condition, and feels that it is important that it should become once more what it was formerly. Hence springs the need or knowledge of a state of well-being, which it concludes that it needs to enjoy.

Therefore it knows that it has wants only because it compares the pain from which it is suffering with the pleasures it has enjoyed.

* * * * *

The want experienced by the statue may be caused by a genuine pain, by a disagreeable sensation, by a sensation less agreeable than those which have preceded it, or, finally, by a state of languor, in which it is reduced to one of those states of being which it has become accustomed to consider indifferent.

* * * * *

There are then two principles which determine the degree of action of its faculties: on the one hand, the lively remembrance of a well-being it has lost; on the other, the small amount of pleasure in the sensation actually felt, or else the pain by which it is accompanied.

* * * * *

But if its actual condition is the happiest it knows, then pleasure induces it to enjoy it by preference. There no longer exists any cause capable of inducing the mind to act strongly enough to overbear the sense of smell to the extent of destroying the feeling in it. Pleasure, on the contrary, concentrates at least the greater part of the attention or of the capacity for feeling upon the present sensation; and if the statue even yet recalls what it has been, it is because the comparison with its present state causes it to enjoy its happiness still more.

Here then are two of the effects of memory: the one is a sensation which is recalled as strongly as if it were acting upon the organ itself; the other is a sensation of which naught remains but a faint recollection.

* * * * *

Nevertheless when the statue imagines a sensation which it no longer is experiencing, and when it recalls it in as lively a manner as if it were still experiencing it, it is not aware that there exists in itself a cause which produces the same effect as would be produced by an odoriferous body acting upon its organ of smell. It cannot therefore distinguish, as we do so, between imagination and feeling.

* * * * *

Association of Ideas in a Man Limited to the Sense of Smell

Our statue cannot pass successively through various states of being, some pleasant and some unpleasant to it, without observing that it passes alternately from a condition of pleasure to a condition of pain, or vice versa. In the former are content and enjoyment; in the latter, discontent and suffering. Therefore it preserves in its memory the notions of content and discontent common to several modes of being; and it need then only consider its sensations in these two connections in order to divide them into two classes, in each of which it will learn to distinguish degrees, in proportion as it practices the habit of distinguishing.

To abstract, is to separate one idea from another to which it appears to be naturally united. Now when the statue observes that the notions of content and discontent are common to several of the modifications of its state of being, it acquires the habit of separating them from some particular modification, from which it had not at first distinguished them. It therefore forms abstract notions of them, and these notions become general, because they are common to several of its states of being.

But when it smells in succession several flowers of the same species, it will always experience one and the same sensation, and will have but one particular notion of the subject. For instance, the perfume of the violet cannot be, for the statue, an abstract notion, common to several flowers, since the statue is not aware of the existence of violets. Therefore it is only the particular notion of a state of being which is proper to the statue. Consequently, all its abstractions are confined to more or less agreeable modifications, and to others more or less disagreeable.

Personality of a Man Limited to a Sense of Smell

Our statue being capable of remembering, it is no sooner one odour than it remembers that it has been another. That is its personality,

for it could say *I*, it would say it at every instant of its own duration, and each time its *I* would comprise all the moments it remembered.

True, it would not say it at the first odour. What is meant by that term seems to me to suit only a being which notes in the present moment, that it is no longer what it has been. So long as it does not change, it exists without thought of itself; but as soon as it changes, it concludes that it is the selfsame which was formerly in such another state, and it says *I*.

This observation confirms the fact that in the first instant of its existence the statue cannot form desires, for before being able to say *I wish*, one must have said *I*.

The odours which the statue does not remember do not therefore enter into the notion it has of its own person. Being as foreign to its *Ego* as are colours and sounds, of which it has no knowledge, they are, in respect of the statue, as if the statue had never smelled them. Its *Ego* is but the sum of the sensations it experiences and of those which memory recalls to it. In a word, it is at one the consciousness of what it is and the remembrance of what it has been.

Conclusions

Having proved that the statue is capable of being attentive, of remembering, of comparing, of judging, of discerning, of imagining; that it possesses abstract notions, notions of number and duration; that it is acquainted with general and particular truths; that desires are formed by it, that it has the power of passions, loves, hates, wills; and finally that it contracts habits, we must conclude that the mind is endowed with as many faculties when it has but a single organ as when it has five. We shall see that the faculties which appear to be peculiar to us are nothing else than the same faculties which, applied to a greater number of objects, develop more fully.

If we consider that to remember, compare, judge, discern, imagine, be astonished, have abstract notions, have notions of duration and number, know general and particular truths, are but different modes of attention; that to have passions, to love, to hate, to hope, to fear and to will are but different modes of desire, and that, finally, attention and desire are in their essence but sensation, we shall conclude that sensation calls out all the faculties of the soul.

* * * * *

The fact is that our earliest notions are pain or pleasure only. Many others soon follow these, and give rise to comparisons, whence spring our earliest needs and our earliest desires. . . .

Nearly all that I have said about the faculties of the soul, while treating of the sense of smell, I might have said if I had taken any other sense; it is easy to apply all to each of the senses.

6

British Associationism and Empiricism

DAVID HARTLEY
(1705–1757)

1. The Doctrine of Vibrations [1]

The doctrine of *vibrations* may appear at first sight to have no connexion with that of *association;* however, if these doctrines be found in fact to contain the laws of the bodily and mental powers respectively, they must be related to each other, since the body and mind are. One may expect, that *vibrations* should infer *association* as their effect, and *association* point to *vibrations* as its cause. I will endeavour, in the present chapter, to trace out this mutual relation.

* * * * *

PROP. I. *The white medullary Substance of the Brain, spinal Marrow, and the Nerves proceeding from them, is the immediate Instrument of Sensation and Motion.*

Under the word *brain*, in these observations, I comprehend all that lies within the cavity of the skull, *i.e.* the *cerebrum*, or *brain* properly so called, the *cerebellum*, and the *medulla oblongata.*

This proposition seems to be sufficiently proved in the writings of physicians and anatomists; from the structure and functions of the several organs of the human body; from experiments on living animals; from the symptoms of diseases, and from dissections of morbid bodies. Sensibility, and the power of motion, seem to be conveyed to all the parts, in their natural state, from the brain and spinal marrow, along the nerves. These arise from the medullary, not the cortical part, every where, and are themselves of a white medullary substance. When the nerves of any part are cut, tied, or compressed in any considerable degree, the functions of that part are either entirely destroyed, or much impaired. When the spinal marrow is compressed by a dislocation of the *vertebræ* of the back, all the parts, whose nerves arise below the place of dislocation, become paralytic. When any considerable injury is done to the medullary substance of the brain, sensation, voluntary motion, memory, and intellect, are either entirely lost, or much impaired; and if the injury be very great, this extends immediately to the vital motions also, *viz.* to those of the heart, and organs of respiration, so as to occasion death. But this does not hold equally in respect of the cortical substance of the brain; perhaps not at all, unless as far as injuries done to it extend themselves to the medullary substance. In dissections after apoplexies, palsies, epilepsies, and other distempers affecting the sensations and motions, it is usual to find some great disorder in the brain, from preternatural tumours, from blood, matter, or serum, lying upon the brain, or in its ventricles, &c. This may suffice as general

---

[1] David Hartley, *Observations on Man, His Frame, His Duty, and His Expectations* (London, 1749), ch. 1, 3.

evidence for the present. The particular reasons of some of these phænomena, with more definite evidences, will offer themselves in the course of these observations.

* * * * *

After-Images

PROP. III.—*The Sensations remain in the Mind for a short time after the sensible Objects are removed.*

This is very evident in the sensations impressed on the eye.

* * * * *

When a person has had a candle, a window, or any other lucid and well-defined object, before his eyes for a considerable time, he may perceive a very clear and precise image thereof to be left in the *sensorium*, fancy, or mind (for these I consider as equivalent expressions in our entrance upon these disquisitions,) for some time after he has closed his eyes. At least this will happen frequently to persons who are attentive to these things in a gentle way; for, as this appearance escapes the notice of those who are entirely inattentive, so too earnest a desire and attention prevents it, by introducing another state of mind or fancy.

* * * * *

Association of Ideas [2]

PROP. X.—*Any Sensations* A, B, C, *&c. by being associated with one another a sufficient Number of Times, get such a Power over the corresponding Ideas* a, b, c, *&c. that any one of the Sensations* A, *when impressed alone, shall be able to excite in the Mind,* b, c, *&c. the Ideas of the rest.*

Sensations may be said to be associated together, when their impressions are either made precisely at the same instant of time, or in the contiguous successive instants. We may therefore distinguish association into two sorts, the synchronous, and the successive.

The influence of association over our ideas, opinions, and affections, is so great and obvious, as scarcely to have escaped the notice of any writer who has treated of these, though the word *association*, in the particular sense here affixed to it, was first brought into use

by Mr. Locke. But all that has been delivered by the ancients and moderns, concerning the power of habit, custom, example, education, authority, party prejudice, the manner of learning the manual and liberal arts, &c. goes upon this doctrine as its foundation, and may be considered as the detail of it, in various circumstances. I here begin with the simplest case, and shall proceed to more and more complex ones continually, till I have exhausted what has occurred to me upon this subject.

This proposition, or first and simplest case of association, is manifest from innumerable common observations. Thus, the names, smells, tastes, and tangible qualities of natural bodies, suggest their visible appearances to the fancy, *i.e.* excite their visible ideas; and *vice versâ*, their visible appearances impressed on the eye raise up those powers of reconnoitring their names, smells, tastes, and tangible qualities, which may not improperly be called their ideas, as above noted; and in some cases raise up ideas, which may be compared with visible ones, in respect of vividness. All which is plainly owing to the association of the several sensible qualities of bodies with their names, and with each other. It is remarkable, however, as being agreeable to the superior vividness of visible and audible ideas, before taken notice of, that the suggestion of the visible appearance from the name is the most ready of any other; and, next to this, that of the name from the visible appearance; in which last case, the reality of the audible idea, when not evident to the fancy, may be inferred from the ready pronunciation of the name. For it will be shewn hereafter, that the audible idea is most commonly a previous requisite to pronunciation. Other instances of the power of association may be taken from compound visible and audible impressions. Thus the sight of part of a large building suggests the idea of the rest instantaneously; and the sound of the words which begin a familiar sentence, brings the remaining part to our memories in order, the association of the parts being synchronous in the first case, and successive in the last.

It is to be observed, that, in successive associations, the power of raising the ideas is only exerted according to the order in which the association is made. Thus, if the

---

[2]   *Ibid.*

impressions *A, B, C,* be always made in the order of the alphabet, *B* impressed alone will not raise *a,* but *c* only. Agreeably to which it is easy to repeat familiar sentences in the order in which they always occur, but impossible to do it readily in an inverted one. The reason of this is, that the compound idea, *c, b, a,* corresponds to the compound sensation *C, B, A;* and therefore requires the impression of *C, B, A,* in the same manner as *a, b, c,* does that of *A, B, C.*

* * * * *

PROP. XI.—*Any Vibrations,* A, B, C, *&c. by being associated together a sufficient Number of Times, get such a Power over* a, b, c, *&c. the corresponding Miniature Vibrations, that any of the Vibrations* A, *when impressed alone, shall be able to excite* b, c, *&c. the Miniatures of the rest.*

This proposition may be deduced from the foregoing, in the same manner as the ninth has been from the eighth.

But it seems also deducible from the nature of vibrations, and of an animal body. Let *A* and *B* be two vibrations, associated synchronically. Now, it is evident, that the vibration *A* (for I will, in this proposition, speak of *A* and *B* in the singular number, for the sake of greater clearness) will, by endeavouring to diffuse itself into those parts of the medullary substance which are affected primarily by the vibration *B,* in some measure modify and change *B,* so as to make *B* a little different from what it would be, if impressed alone. For the same reasons the vibration *A* will be a little affected, even in its primary seat, by the endeavour of *B* to diffuse itself all over the medullary substance. Suppose now the vibrations *A* and *B* to be impressed at the same instant, for a thousand times; it follows, from the ninth proposition, that they will first overcome the disposition to the natural vibrations *N,* and then leave a tendency to themselves, which will now occupy the place of the original natural tendency to vibrations. When therefore the vibration *A* is impressed alone, it cannot be entirely such as the object would excite of itself, but must lean, even in its primary seat, to the modifications and changes induced by *B,* during their thousand joint impressions; and therefore much more, in receding from this primary seat, will it lean that way; and

when it comes to the seat of *B,* it will excite *B*'s miniature a little modified and changed by itself.

Memory [3]

Memory was defined in the introduction to be that faculty by which traces of sensations and ideas recur, or are recalled, in the same order and proportion, accurately or nearly, as they were once presented.

Now here we may observe,

First, that memory depends entirely or chiefly on the state of the brain. For diseases, concussions of the brain, spirituous liquors, and some poisons, impair or destroy it; and it generally returns again with the return of health, from the use of proper medicines and methods. And all this is peculiarly suitable to the notion of vibrations. If sensations and ideas arise from peculiar vibrations, and dispositions to vibrate, in the medullary substance of the brain, it is easy to conceive, that the causes above alleged may so confound the sensations and ideas, as that the usual order and proportion of the ideas shall be destroyed.

Secondly, the rudiments of memory are laid in the perpetual recurrency of the same impressions, and clusters of impressions.

* * * * *

Thirdly, suppose now a person so far advanced in life, as that he has learnt all these rudiments, *i.e.* that he has ideas of the common appearances and occurrences of life, under a considerable variety of subordinate circumstances, which recur to his imagination from the slightest causes, and with the most perfect facility; and let us ask, how he can be able to remember or recollect a past fact, consisting of one thousand single particulars, or of one hundred such clusters as are called the rudiments of memory; ten single particulars being supposed to constitute a rudiment? First, then, we may observe, that there are only one hundred links wanting in the chain; for he has already learnt considerable exactness in the subordinate circumstances of the one hundred clusters; and perfect exactness is not to be supposed or required. Secondly the one hundred clusters recur again and

---

[3] *Ibid.,* sect. 4, prop. 90.

again to the imagination for some time after the fact, in a quick and transient manner, as those who attend sufficiently to what passes in their own minds may perceive; and this both makes the impression a little deeper, and also serves to preserve the order. If the person attempts to recollect soon after the impression, the effect remaining in the brain is sufficient to enable him to do this with the accuracy required and experienced; if a longer time intervenes, before he attempts to recollect, still the number of involuntary recurrencies makes up in some measure for the want of this voluntary recollection. However, the power of recollection declines in general, and is entirely lost by degrees. It confirms this reasoning, that a new set of strong impressions destroys this power of recollection. For this must both obliterate the effects of the foregoing impressions, and prevent the recurrency of the ideas. (Thirdly) as the single impressions, which make the small clusters, are not combined together at hazard, but according to a general tenor in nature, so the clusters which make facts succeed each other according to some general tenor likewise. Now this both lessens the number of varieties, and shows that the association between many of the clusters, or rudiments, or one hundred links supposed to be wanting, is cemented already. This may be both illustrated and exemplified by the observation, that it is difficult to remember even well-known words that have no connection with each other, and more so to remember collections of barbarous terms; whereas adepts in any science remember the things of that science with a surprising exactness and facility. (Fourthly) some clusters are excluded from succeeding others, by ideas of inconsistency, impossibility, and by the methods of reasoning, of which we become masters as we advance in life. (Fifthly) the visible impressions which concur in the past fact, by being vivid, and preserving the order of place, often contribute greatly to preserve the order of time, and to suggest the clusters which may be wanting. (Sixthly) it is to be observed, that as we think in words both the impressions and the recurrencies of ideas will be attended with words; and these words, from the great use and familiarity of language, will fix themselves strongly in the fancy, and by so doing bring up the associated trains of ideas in the proper order, accurately or nearly. And thus, when a person relates a past fact, the ideas do in some cases suggest the words, while in others the words suggest the ideas.

THOMAS REID
(1710–1796)

Sensation and Perception [4]

In speaking of the impressions made on our organs in perception, we build upon facts borrowed from anatomy and physiology, for which we have the testimony of our senses. But, being now to speak of perception itself, which is solely an act of the mind, we must appeal to another authority. The operations of our minds are known, not by sense, but by consciousness, the authority of which is as certain and as irresistible as that of sense.

* * * * *

If, therefore, we attend to that act of our mind which we call the perception of an external object of sense, we shall find in it these three things:—*First*, Some conception or notion of the object perceived; *Secondly*, A strong and irresistible conviction and belief of its present existence; and, *Thirdly*, That this conviction and belief are immediate, and not the effect of reasoning.

First, It is impossible to perceive an object without having some notion or conception of that which we perceive. We may, indeed, conceive an object which we do not perceive; but, when we perceive the object, we must have some conception of it at the same time; and we have commonly a more clear and steady notion of the object while we perceive it, than we have from memory or imagination when it is not perceived. Yet, even in perception, the notion which our senses give of the object may be more or less clear, more or less distinct, in all possible degrees.

Thus we see more distinctly an object at a small than at a great distance. An object

---

[4] Thomas Reid, *Essays on the Intellectual Powers of Man* (Edinburgh, 1785), ch. 5, 16.

at a great distance is seen more distinctly in a clear than in a foggy day. An object seen indistinctly with the naked eye, on account of its smallness, may be seen distinctly with a microscope. The objects in this room will be seen by a person in the room less and less distinctly as the light of the day fails; they pass through all the various degrees of distinctness according to the degrees of the light, and, at last, in total darkness they are not seen at all. What has been said of the objects of sight is so easily applied to the objects of the other senses, that the application may be left to the reader.

* * * * *

Secondly, In perception we not only have a notion more or less distinct of the object perceived, but also an irresistible conviction and belief of its existence. This is always the case when we are certain that we perceive it. There may be a perception so faint and indistinct as to leave us in doubt whether we perceive the object or not. Thus, when a star begins to twinkle as the light of the sun withdraws, one may, for a short time, think he sees it without being certain, until the perception acquire some strength and steadiness. When a ship just begins to appear in the utmost verge of the horizon, we may at first be dubious whether we perceive it or not; but when the perception is in any degree clear and steady, there remains no doubt of its reality; and when the reality of the perception is ascertained, the existence of the object perceived can no longer be doubted.

* * * * *

It appears, therefore, that the clear and distinct testimony of our senses carries irresistible conviction along with it to every man in his right judgment.

I observed, *Thirdly,* That this conviction is not only irresistible, but it is immediate; that is, it is not by a train of reasoning and argumentation that we come to be convinced of the existence of what we perceive; we ask no argument for the existence of the object, but that we perceive it; perception commands our belief upon its own authority, and disdains to rest its authority upon any reasoning whatsoever.

* * * * *

Having finished what I intend, with regard

to that act of mind which we call the perception of an external object, I proceed to consider another, which, by our constitution, is conjoined with perception, and not with perception only, but with many other acts of our minds; and that is sensation.

Almost all our perceptions have corresponding sensations which constantly accompany them, and, on that account, are very apt to be confounded with them. Neither ought we to expect that the sensation, and its corresponding perception, should be distinguished in common language, because the purposes of common life do not require it. Language is made to serve the purposes of ordinary conversation; and we have no reason to expect that it should make distinctions that are not of common use. Hence it happens, that a quality perceived, and the sensation corresponding to that perception, often go under the same name.

This makes the names of most of our sensations ambiguous, and this ambiguity hath very much perplexed philosophers. It will be necessary to give some instances, to illustrate the distinction between our sensations and the objects of perception.

When I smell a rose, there is in this operation both sensation and perception. The agreeable odour I feel, considered by itself, without relation to any external object, is merely a sensation. It affects the mind in a certain way; and this affection of the mind may be conceived, without a thought of the rose, or any other object. This sensation can be nothing else than it is felt to be. Its very essence consists in being felt; and, when it is not felt, it is not. There is no difference between the sensation and the feeling of it— they are one and the same thing. It is for this reason that we before observed that, in sensation, there is no object distinct from that act of the mind by which it is felt—and this holds true with regard to all sensations.

Let us next attend to the perception which we have in smelling a rose. Perception has always an external object; and the object of my perception, in this case, is that quality in the rose which I discern by the sense of smell. Observing that the agreeable sensation is raised when the rose is near, and ceases when it is removed, I am led, by my nature, to conclude some quality to be in the rose, which is the cause of this sensation. This quality in the rose is the object perceived; and that act of my mind by which I have the conviction and belief of this quality, is what in this case I call perception.

But it is here to be observed, that the sensation I feel, and the quality in the rose which I perceive, are both called by the same name. The smell of a rose is the name given to both: so that this name hath two meanings; and the distinguishing its different meanings removes all perplexity, and enables us to give clear and distinct answers to questions about which philosophers have held much dispute.

Thus, if it is asked, whether the smell be in the rose, or in the mind that feels it, the answer is obvious: That there are two different things signified by the smell of a rose; one of which is in the mind, and can

be in nothing but in a sentient being; the other is truly and properly in the rose. The sensation which I feel is in my mind. The mind is the sentient being; and, as the rose is insentient, there can be no sensation, nor anything resembling sensation in it. But this sensation in my mind is occasioned by a certain quality in the rose, which is called by the same name with the sensation, not on account of any similitude, but because of their constant concomitancy.

All the names we have for smells, tastes, sounds, and for the various degrees of heat and cold, have a like ambiguity; and what has been said of the smell of a rose may be applied to them. They signify both a sensation, and a quality perceived by means of that sensation. The first is the sign, the last the thing signified.

THOMAS BROWN
(1778–1820)

Primary Laws of Suggestion (Association): Resemblance and Contiguity [5]

To the threefold division, which Mr. Hume has made, of the principles of association in the trains of our ideas, as consisting in resemblance, contiguity, and causation, there is an obvious objection. . . . Causation, far from being opposed to contiguity, so as to form a separate class, is, in truth, the most exquisite species of proximity in time, and in most cases of contiguity in place also.

* * * * *

Resemblance and contiguity in place and time,—to which, on his own principles, Mr Hume's arrangement must be reduced,—may be allowed, indeed, to hold a prominent rank, in whatever classification there may be formed, if any be to be formed, of the principles that regulate our trains of thought.

* * * * *

To begin, then, with resemblance, no one can be ignorant of the effect of strong similarity, in recalling objects, as when a pictured

landscape recalls a familiar scene, or a portrait a familiar countenance. There are many cases of this kind, indeed, which, strictly speaking, cannot be said to be instances of suggestion, from resemblance, but to be reducible to the simple laws of perception, or, at least, to associations, which may be considered almost as involved in every repeated perception of the same object.

* * * * *

I proceed to consider the force of contrast as a suggesting principle. I consider it at present as forming a class apart, for the same reason which has led me, in these illustrations of the general principle, to class separately the suggestions of resemblance, though I conceive that all, or at least the greater number of them, on a more subtle analysis, might be reduced to the more comprehensive influence of former proximity.

* * * * *

In the use of antithesis, then, as much as in the use of the other rhetorical forms of thought and expression before considered by us, it is in the general nature of spontaneous suggestion that we have to find the principle which is to direct us. Contrast is one of the forms of this suggestion.

[5] Thomas Brown, *Lectures on the Philosophy of the Human Mind* (Edinburgh, 1820), lectures 35–37, vol. 2.

Secondary Laws of Suggestion (Association) [6]

I proceed now to the consideration of nearness in place or time—the next general circumstance which I pointed out as modifying suggestion.

Of all the general principles of connexion in the trains of our thought, this is evidently the most frequent and extensive in its operation; even when we confine our attention to its grosser and more obvious forms, without attempting, by any very refined analysis, to reduce to it any of the other tribes of our suggestions. The gross and obvious nearness in place or time, of which alone I speak when I use Mr. Hume's phrase of contiguity, forms the whole calendar of the great multitude of mankind, who pay little attention to the arbitrary eras of chronology, but date events by each other, and speak of what happened in the time of some persecution, or rebellion, or great war, or frost, or famine. Even with those who are more accustomed to use, on great occasions, the stricter dates of months and years, this association of events, as near to each other, forms the great bond for uniting in the memory those multitudes of scattered facts which form the whole history of domestic life, and which it would have been impossible to remember by their separate relation to some insulated point of time.

* * * * *

After the remarks which I have already frequently made on this subject, I trust it is now unnecessary for me to repeat, that the term *laws*, as employed in the physics, whether of matter or of mind, is not used to denote any thing different from the phenomena themselves,—that, in short, it means nothing more than certain circumstances of general agreement in any number of phenomena. When Mr. Hume reduced, to the three orders of resemblance, contiguity, and causation, the relations on which he believed association to depend, he considered himself as stating only facts which were before familiar to every one, and did state only facts that were perfectly familiar. In like manner, when I reduce under a few heads those modifying circumstances, which seem to me as secondary laws, to guide, in every

[6] *Ibid.*

particular case, the momentary direction of the primary, my object is not to discover facts that are new, or little observed, but to arrange facts that, separately, are well known.

The first circumstance which presents itself, as modifying the influence of the primary laws, in inducing one associate conception rather than another, is the length of time during which the original feelings from which they flowed, continued, when they co-existed, or succeeded each other. Every one must be conscious, that innumerable objects pass before him, which are slightly observed at the time, but which form no permanent associations in the mind. The longer we dwell on objects, the more fully do we rely on our future remembrance of them.

In the second place, the parts of a train appear to be more closely and firmly associated, as the original feelings have been more lively. We remember brilliant objects more than those which are faint and obscure. We remember, for our whole lifetime, the occasions of great joy or sorrow; we forget the occasions of innumerable slight pleasures or pains, which occur to us every hour. That strong feeling of interest and curiosity, which we call attention, not only leads us to dwell longer on the consideration of certain objects, but also gives more vivacity to the objects on which we dwell,—and in both these ways tends, as we have seen, to fix them more strongly in the mind.

In the third place, the parts of any train are more readily suggested, in proportion as they have been more frequently renewed. It is thus we remember, after reading them three or four times over, the verses which we could not repeat when we had read them only once.

In the fourth place, the feelings are connected more strongly, in proportion as they are more or less recent. Immediately after reading any single line of poetry, we are able to repeat it, though we may have paid no particular attention to it; in a very few minutes, unless when we have paid particular attention to it, we are no longer able to repeat it accurately, and in a very short time we forget it altogether. There is, indeed, one very striking exception to this law, in the case of old age: for, events which happened in youth, are then remembered, when events of the year preceding are forgotten. Yet, even in the case of extreme age, when the time is not extended so far back, the general law still holds; and events which happened a few hours before are remembered, when there is total forgetfulness of what happened a few days before.

In the fifth place, our successive feelings are associated more closely, as each has co-existed less with other feelings. The song, which we have never heard but from one person, can scarcely be heard again by us, without recalling that person to our memory; but there is obviously much less chance of this particular suggestion, if we have heard the same air and words frequently sung by others.

In the sixth place, the influence of the primary laws of suggestion is greatly modified by original constitutional differences, whether these are to be referred to the mind itself, or to varieties of bodily temperament. Such constitutional differences affect the primary laws in two ways,—first, by augmenting and extending the influence of all of them, as in the varieties of the general power of remembering, so observable in different individuals. Secondly, they modify the influence of the primary laws, by giving greater proportional vigour to one set of tendencies of suggestion than to another. It is in this modification of the suggesting principle, and the peculiar suggestions to which it gives rise, that I conceive the chief part, or, I may say, the whole of what is truly called genius, to consist.

* * * * *

The next secondary law of suggestion to which I proceed, is one akin to the last which we have considered. The primary laws are modified, not by constitutional and permanent differences only, but by differences which occur in the same individual, according to the varying emotion of the hour. As there are persons whose general character is gloomy or cheerful, we have, in like manner, our peculiar days or moments in which we pass from one of these characters to the other, and in which our trains of thought are tinctured with the corresponding varieties. A mere change of fortune is often sufficient to alter the whole cast of sentiment.

* * * * *

The temporary diversities of state that give rise to varieties of suggestion are not mental only, but corporeal; and this difference of bodily state furnishes another secondary law, in modification of the primary. I need not refer to the extreme cases of intoxication or actual delirium,—to the copious flow of follies which a little wine, or a few grains of opium, may extract from the proudest reasoner. In circumstances less striking, how different are the trains of thought in health and in sickness, after a temperate meal and after a luxurious excess! It is not to the animal powers only that the burthen of digestion may become oppressive, but to the intellectual also; and often to the intellectual powers even more than to the animal. In that most delightful of all states, when the bodily frame has recovered from disease, and when, in the first walk beneath the open sunshine, amid the blossoms and balmy air of summer, there is a mixture of corporeal and mental enjoyment, in which it is not easy to discriminate what images of pleasure arise from every object, that, in other states of health, might have excited no thought or emotion whatever.

* * * * *

There is yet another principle which modifies the primary laws of suggestion with very powerful influence. This is the principle of habit. I do not speak of its influence in suggesting images which have been already frequently suggested in a certain order,—for it would then be simpler to reduce the habit itself to the mere power of association. I speak of cases in which the images suggested may have been of recent acquisition, but are suggested more readily in consequence of general tendencies produced by prior habits.

* * * * *

In addition, then, to the primary laws of suggestion, which are founded on the mere relations of the objects or feelings to each other, it appears that there is another set of laws, the operation of which is indispensable to account for the variety in the effects of the former. To these I have given the name of *secondary laws of suggestion;* and we have seen, accordingly, that the suggestions are various as the original feelings have been: 1st, Of longer or shorter continuance; 2dly, More or less lively; 3dly, More or less frequently present; 4thly, More or less recent;

5thly, More or less pure, if I may so express it, from the mixture of other feelings; 6thly, That they vary according to differences of original constitution; 7thly, According to differences of temporary emotion; 8thly, According to changes produced in the state of the body; and, 9thly, According to general tendencies produced by prior habits.

JAMES MILL
(1773–1836)

Association of Ideas [7]

Thought succeeds thought; idea follows idea, incessantly. If our senses are awake, we are continually receiving sensations, of the eye, the ear, the touch, and so forth; but not sensations alone. After sensations, ideas are perpetually excited of sensations formerly received; after those ideas, other ideas: and during the whole of our lives, a series of those two states of consciousness, called sensations, and ideas, is constantly going on. I see a horse: that is a sensation. Immediately I think of his master: that is an idea. The idea of his master makes me think of his office; he is a minister of state: that is another idea. The idea of a minister of state makes me think of public affairs; and I am led into a train of political ideas; when I am summoned to dinner. This is a new sensation, followed by the idea of dinner, and of the company with whom I am to partake it. The sight of the company and of the food are other sensations; these suggest ideas without end; other sensations perpetually intervene, suggesting other ideas: and so the process goes on.

* * * * *

Of the order established among the objects of nature, by which we mean the objects of our senses, two remarkable cases are all which here we are called upon to notice; the SYNCHRONOUS ORDER and the SUCCESSIVE ORDER. The synchronous order, or order of simultaneous existence, is the order in space; the successive order, or order of antecedent and consequent existence, is the order in time. Thus the various objects in my room, the chairs, the tables, the books, have the synchronous order, or order in space. The falling of the spark, and the explosion of the gun-

powder, have the successive order, or order in time.

According to this order, in the objects of sense, there is a synchronous, and a successive, order of our sensations. I have SYNCHRONICALLY, or at the same instant, the sight of a great variety of objects; touch of all the objects with which my body is in contact; hearing of all the sounds which are reaching my ears; smelling of all the smells which are reaching my nostrils; taste of the apple which I am eating; the sensation of resistance both from the apple which is in my mouth, and the ground on which I stand; with the sensation of motion from the act of walking. I have SUCCESSIVELY the sight of the flash from the mortar fired at a distance, the hearing of the report, the sight of the bomb, and of its motion in the air, the sight of its fall, the sight and hearing of its explosion, and lastly, the sight of all the effects of that explosion.

* * * * *

As ideas are not derived from objects, we should not expect their order to be derived from the order of objects; but as they are derived from sensations, we might by analogy expect, that they would derive their order from that of the sensations; and this to a great extent is the case.

Our ideas spring up, or exist, in the order in which the sensations existed, of which they are the copies.

This is the general law of the "Association of Ideas"; by which term, let it be remembered, nothing is here meant to be expressed, but the order of occurrence.

In this law, the following things are to be carefully observed.

1. Of those sensations which occurred synchronically, the ideas also spring up synchronically. I have seen a violin, and heard the tones of the violin, synchronically. If I think of the tones of the violin, the visible appear-

---

[7] James Mill, *Analysis of the Phenomena of the Human Mind* (London, 1829), ch. 3.

ance of the violin at the same time occurs to me. I have seen the sun, and the sky in which it is placed, synchronically. If I think of the one, I think of the other at the same time.

* * * * *

2. As the ideas of the sensations which occurred synchronically, rise synchronically, so the ideas of the sensations which occurred successively, rise successively.

Of this important case of association, or of the successive order of our ideas, many remarkable instances might be adduced. Of these none seems better adapted to the learner than the repetition of any passage, or words; the Lord's Prayer, for example, committed to memory. In learning the passage, we repeat it; that is, we pronounce the words, in successive order, from the beginning to the end. The order of the sensations is successive. When we proceed to repeat the passage, the ideas of the words also rise in succession, the preceding always suggesting the succeeding, and no other. *Our* suggests *Father*, *Father* suggests *which*, *which* suggests *art;* and so on, to the end. How remarkably this is the case, any one may convince himself, by trying to repeat backwards, even a passage with which he is as familiar as the Lord's Prayer. The case is the same with numbers. A man can go on with the numbers in the progressive order, one, two, three, &c. scarcely thinking of his act; and though it is possible for him to repeat them backward, because he is accustomed to subtraction of numbers, he cannot do so without an effort.

* * * * *

3. A far greater number of our sensations are received in the successive, than in the synchronical order. Of our ideas, also, the number is infinitely greater that rise in the successive than the synchronical order.

4. In the successive order of ideas, that which precedes, is sometimes called the suggesting, that which succeeds, the suggested idea; not that any power is supposed to reside in the antecedent over the consequent; suggesting, and suggested, mean only antecedent and consequent, with the additional idea, that such order is not casual, but, to a certain degree, permanent.

5. Of the antecedent and consequent feelings, or the suggesting, and suggested; the antecedent may be either sensations or ideas; the consequent are always ideas. An idea may be excited either by a sensation or an idea. The sight of the dog of my friend is a sensation, and it excites the idea of my friend. The idea of Professor Dugald Stewart delivering a lecture, recalls the idea of the delight with which I heard him; that, the idea of the studies in which it engaged me; that, the trains of thought which succeeded; and each epoch of my mental history, the succeeding one, till the present moment; in which I am endeavouring to present to others what appears to me valuable among the innumerable ideas of which this lengthened train has been composed.

6. As there are degrees in sensations, and degrees in ideas; for one sensation is more vivid than another sensation, one idea more vivid than another idea; so there are degrees in association. One association, we say, is stronger than another: First, when it is more permanent than another: Secondly, when it is performed with more certainty: Thirdly, when it is performed with more facility.

It is well known, that some associations are very transient, others very permanent. The case which we formerly mentioned, that of repeating words committed to memory, affords an apt illustration. In some cases, we can perform the repetition, when a few hours, or a few days have elapsed; but not after a longer period. In others, we can perform it after the lapse of many years. There are few children in whose minds some association has not been formed between darkness and ghosts. In some this association is soon dissolved; in some it continues for life.

* * * * *

7. The causes of strength in association seem all to be resolvable into two; the vividness of the associated feelings; and the frequency of the association.

In general, we convey not a very precise meaning, when we speak of the vividness of sensations and ideas. We may be understood when we say that, generally speaking, the sensation is more vivid than the idea.

* * * * *

In calling one IDEA more vivid than another, if we confine the appellation to the ideas of such SENSATIONS as may with precision be called more or less vivid; the sensations of pleasure and pain, in their various degrees, compared with sensations which we do not call either pleasurable or painful; our language will still have a certain degree of precision.

* * * * *

Next, we have to consider frequency or repetition; which is the most remarkable and important cause of the strength of our associations.

Of any two sensations, frequently perceived together, the ideas are associated. Thus, at least, in the minds of Englishmen, the idea of a soldier, and the idea of a red coat are associated; the idea of a clergyman, and the idea of a black coat; the idea of a quaker, and of a broad-brimmed hat; the idea of a woman and the idea of petticoats. A peculiar taste suggests the idea of an apple; a peculiar smell the idea of a rose. If I have heard a particular air frequently sung by a particular person, the hearing of the air suggests the idea of the person.

The most remarkable exemplification of the effect of degrees of frequency, in producing degrees of strength in the associations, is to be found in the cases in which the association is purposely and studiously contracted; the cases in which we learn something; the use of words, for example.

* * * * *

8. Where two or more ideas have been often repeated together, and the association has become very strong, they sometimes spring up in such close combination as not to be distinguishable. Some cases of sensation are analogous. For example; when a wheel, on the seven parts of which the seven prismatic colours are respectively painted, is made to revolve rapidly, it appears not of seven colours, but of one uniform colour, white. By the rapidity of the succession, the several sensations cease to be distinguishable; they run, as it were, together, and a new sensation, compounded of all the seven, but apparently a simple one, is the result. Ideas, also, which have been so often conjoined, than whenever one exists in the mind, the others immediately exist along with it, seem to run into one another, to coalesce, as it were, and out of

many to form one idea; which idea, however in reality complex, appears to be no less simple, than any one of those of which it is compounded.

* * * * *

To this case of high association, this blending together of many ideas, in so close a combination that they appear not many ideas, but one idea, we owe, as I shall afterwards more fully explain, the power of classification, and all the advantages of language. It is obviously, therefore, of the greatest moment, that this important phenomenon should be well understood.

9. Some ideas are by frequency and strength of association so closely combined, that they cannot be separated. If one exists, the others exist along with it, in spite of whatever effort we make to disjoin them.

For example; it is not in our power to think of colour, without thinking of extension; or of solidity, without figure. We have seen colour constantly in combination with extension, spread as it were, upon a surface. We have never seen it except in this connection. Colour and extension have been invariably conjoined. The idea of colour, therefore, uniformly comes into the mind, bringing that of extension along with it; and so close is the association, that it is not in our power to dissolve it. We cannot, if we will, think of colour, but in combination with extension. The one idea calls up the other, and retains it, so long as the other is retained.

* * * * *

The following of one idea after another idea, or after a sensation, so certainly that we cannot prevent the combination, nor avoid having the *consequent* feeling as often as we have the *antecedent*, is a law of association, the operation of which we shall afterwards find to be extensive, and bearing a principal part in some of the most important phenomena of the human mind.

* * * * *

10. It not unfrequently happens in our associated feelings, that the antecedent is of no importance farther than it introduces the

consequent. In these cases, the consequent absorbs all the attention, and the antecedent is instantly forgotten. Of this a very intelligible illustration is afforded by what happens in ordinary discourse. A friend arrives from a distant country, and brings me the first intelligence of the last illness, the last words, the last acts, and death of my son. The sound of the voice, the articulation of every word, makes its sensation in my ear; but it is to the ideas that my attention flies. It is my son that is before me, suffering, acting, speaking, dying. The words which have introduced the ideas, and kindled the affections, have been as little heeded, as the respiration which has been accelerated, while the ideas were received.

It is important in respect to this case of association to remark, that there are large classes of our sensations, such as many of those in the alimentary duct, and many in the nervous and vascular systems, which serve, as antecedents, to introduce ideas, as consequents; but as the consequents are far more interesting than themselves, and immediately absorb the attention, the antecedents are habitually overlooked; and though they exercise, by the trains which they introduce, a great influence on our happiness or misery, they themselves are generally wholly unknown.

That there are connections between our ideas and certain states of the internal organs, is proved by many familiar instances. Thus, anxiety, in most people, disorders the digestion.

* * * * *

11. Mr. Hume, and after him other philosophers, have said that our ideas are associated according to three principles; Contiguity in time and place, Causation, and Resemblance. The Contiguity in time and place, must mean, that of the sensations; and so far it is affirmed, that the order of the ideas follows that of the sensations. Contiguity of two sensations in time, means the successive order. Contiguity of two sensations in place, means the synchronous order. We have explained the mode in which ideas are associated, in the synchronous, as well as the successive order, and have traced the principle of contiguity to its proper source.

Causation, the second of Mr. Hume's principles, is the same with contiguity in time, or the order of succession. Causation is only a name for the order established

between an antecedent and a consequent; that is, the established or constant antecedence of the one, and consequence of the other. Resemblance only remains, as an alleged principle of association, and it is necessary to inquire whether it is included in the laws which have been above expounded. I believe it will be found that we are accustomed to see like things together. When we see a tree, we generally see more trees than one; when we see an ox, we generally see more oxen than one; a sheep, more sheep than one; a man, more men than one. From this observation, I think, we may refer resemblance to the law of frequency, of which it seems to form only a particular case.

* * * * *

12. Not only do simple ideas, by strong association, run together, and form complex ideas: but a complex idea, when the simple ideas which compose it have become so consolidated that it always appears as one, is capable of entering into combinations with other ideas, both simple and complex. Thus two complex ideas may be united together, by a strong association, and coalesce into one, in the same manner as two or more simple ideas coalesce into one. This union of two complex ideas into one, Dr. Hartley has called a duplex idea. Two also of these duplex, or doubly compounded ideas, may unite into one; and these again into other compounds, without end.

* * * * *

Brick is one complex idea, mortar is another complex idea; these ideas, with ideas of position and quantity, compose my idea of a wall. My idea of a plank is a complex idea, my idea of a rafter is a complex idea, my idea of a nail is a complex idea.

These, united with the same ideas of position and quantity, compose my duplex idea of a floor. In the same manner my complex idea of glass, and wood, and others, compose my duplex idea of a window; and these duplex ideas, united together, compose my idea of a house, which is made up of various duplex ideas. How many complex, or duplex ideas, are all united in the idea of furniture? How many more in the idea of merchandise? How many more in the idea called Every Thing?

WILLIAM HAMILTON
(1788–1856)

Law of Redintegration [8]

I have now, I think, gone through all the circumstances which philosophers have constituted into separate laws of Association; and shown that they easily resolve themselves into the two laws of Simultaneity and Affinity. I now proceed to show you, that these two laws themselves are reducible to that one law, which I would call the law of Redintegration or Totality, which, as I already stated, I have found incidentally expressed by St. Augustin. This law may be thus enounced,—*Those thoughts suggest each other which had previously constituted parts of the same entire or total act of cognition.* Now to the same entire or total act belong, as integral or constituent parts, in the first place, those thoughts which arose at the same time, or in immediate consecution; and in the second, those thoughts which are bound up into one by their mutual affinity. Thus, therefore, the two laws of Simultaneity and Affinity are carried up into unity, in the higher law of Redintegration or Totality; and by this one law the whole phænomena of Association may be easily explained.

The Law of Redintegration explained. But this law being established by induction and generalization, and affording an explanation of the various phænomena of Association, it may be asked, How is this law itself explained? On what principle of our intellectual nature is it founded? To this no answer can be legitimately demanded. It is enough for the natural philosopher, to reduce the special laws of the attraction of distant bodies to the one principle of gravitation; and his theory is not invalidated, because he can give no account of how gravitation is itself determined. In all our explanations of the phænomena of mind and matter, we must always arrive at an ultimate fact or law, of which we are wholly unable to afford an ulterior explanation. We are, therefore, entitled to decline attempting any illustration

of the ground on which the supreme fact or law of Association reposes; and if we do attempt such illustration, and fail in the endeavor, no presumption is, therefore, justly to be raised against the truth of the fact or principle itself.

But an illustration of this great law is involved in the principle of the unity of the mental energies, as the activities of the subject one and indivisible, to which I have had occasion to refer. "The various acts of mind," [says Schmid,] "must not be viewed as single, —as isolated, manifestations; they all belong to the one activity of the Ego: and, consequently, if our various mental energies are only partial modifications of the same general activity, they must all be associated among themselves. Every mental energy,—every thought, feeling, desire that is excited, excites at the same time all other previously existent activities, in a certain degree; it spreads its excitation over the whole activities of the mind, as the agitation of one place of a sheet of water expands itself, in wider and wider circles, over the whole surface of the fluid, although, in proportion to its eccentricity, it is always becoming fainter, until it is at last not to be perceived. The force of every internal activity exists only in a certain limited degree; consequently, the excitation it determines has only likewise a certain limited power of expansion, and is continually losing in vigor in proportion to its eccentricity. Thus there are formed particular centres, particular spheres, of internal unity, within which the activities stand to each other in a closer relation of action and reaction; and this, in proportion as they more or less belong already to a single energy,—in proportion as they gravitate more or less proximately to the same centre of action. A plurality, a complement, of several activities forms, in a stricter sense, one whole activity for itself; an invigoration of any of its several activities is, therefore, an invigoration of the part of a whole activity; and as a part cannot be active for itself alone, there, consequently, results an invigoration of the whole, that is, of all the other parts of which it is composed. Thus the supreme law of association,—that activities excite each other in proportion as they have previously

---

[8] William Hamilton, *Lectures on Metaphysics* (Boston, 1861), ch. 23, entitled "The reproductive faculty: laws of association: suggestion and reminiscence." Originally published in 1859, posthumously.

belonged, as parts, to one whole activity,—is explained from the still more universal principle of the unity of all our mental energies in general.

"But *on the same principle, we can also explain the two subaltern laws of Simultaneity and Affinity.* The phænomena of mind are manifested under a twofold condition or form; for they are only revealed, 1°, As occurrences in time; and, 2°, As the energies or modifications of the Ego, as their cause and subject. Time and Self are thus the two forms of the internal world. By these two forms, therefore, every particular, every limited, unity of operation, must be controlled; —on them it must depend. And it is precisely these two forms that lie at the root of the two laws of Simultaneity and Affinity. Thus acts which are exerted at the same time belong, by that very circumstance, to the same particular unity,—to the same definite sphere of mental energy; in other words, constitute through their simultaneity a single activity. Thus energies, however heterogeneous in themselves, if developed at once, belong to the same activity,—constitute a particular unity; and they will operate with a greater suggestive influence on each other, in proportion as they are more closely connected by the bond of time. On the other hand, the affinity of mental acts or modifications will be determined by their particular relations to the Ego, as their cause or subject. As all the activities of mind obtain a unity in being all the energies of the same soul or active principle in general, so they are bound up into particular unities, inasmuch as they belong to some particular faculty,—resemble each other in the common ground of their manifestation. Thus cognitions, feelings, and volitions severally awaken cognitions, feelings, and volitions; for they severally belong to the same faculty, and, through that identity, are themselves constituted into distinct unities: or again, a thought of the cause suggests a thought of the effect, a thought of the mean suggests a thought of the end, a thought of the part suggests a thought of the whole; for cause and effect, end and mean, whole and parts, have subjectively an indissoluble affinity, as they are all so many forms or organizations of thought. In like manner, the notions of all resembling objects suggest each other, for they possess some common quality, through which they are in thought bound up in a single act of thought. Even the notions of opposite and contrasted objects mutually excite each other upon the same principle; for these are logically associated, inasmuch as, by the laws of thought, the notion of one opposite necessarily involves the notions of the other; and it is also a psychological law, that contrasted objects relieve each other. *Opposita, juxta posita, se invicem collustrant.* When the operations of different faculties are mutually suggestive, they are, likewise, internally connected by the nature of their action; for they are either conversant with the same object, and have thus been originally determined by the same affection from without, or they have originally been associated through some form of the mind itself; thus moral cognitions, moral feelings, and moral volitions, may suggest each other, through the common bond of morality; the moral principle in this case uniting the operations of the three fundamental powers into one general activity."

ALEXANDER BAIN
(1818–1903)

Retentiveness—Law of Contiguity [9]

This principle is the basis of Memory, Habit, and the Acquired Powers in general. Writers on Mental Science have described it under various names. Sir William Hamilton terms it the law of "Redintegration," regarding it as the principle whereby one part of a whole brings up the other parts, as when the first words of a quotation recall the remainder, or one house in a street suggests the succeeding ones. The associating links called Order in Time, Order in Place, and Cause and Effect, are all included under it. We might also name it the law of Association proper, of Adhesion, Mental Adhesiveness, or Acquisition.

The following is a general statement of this mode of mental reproduction.

[9] Alexander Bain, *The Senses and the Intellect* (New York: D. Appleton, 1868, 3rd ed.), p. 327. (1st ed.: London, 1855).

Actions, Sensations, and States of Feeling, occurring together or in close succession, tend to grow together, or cohere, in such a way that, when any one of them is afterwards presented to the mind, the others are apt to be brought up in idea.

There are various circumstances or conditions that regulate and modify the operation of this principle, so as to render the adhesive growth more or less rapid and secure. These will be best brought out by degrees in the course of the exposition. As a general rule, Repetition is necessary in order to render coherent in the mind a train or aggregate of images, as, for example, the successive aspects of a panorama, with a sufficient degree of force to make one suggest the others at an after period. The precise degree of repetition needed depends on a variety of causes, the quality of the individual mind being one.

* * * * *

Agreement—Law of Similarity [10]

Contiguity joins together things that occur together, or that are, by any circumstance, presented to the mind at *the same time;* as when we associate heat with light, a falling body with a concussion. But, in addition to this link of reproductive connexion, we find that one thing will, by virtue of Similarity, recall another *separated from it in time,* as when a portrait recalls the original.

The second fundamental property of Intellect, termed Consciousness of Agreement, or Similarity, is a great power of mental reproduction, or a means of recovering past mental states.

* * * * *

Some preliminary explanation of the kind of relationship subsisting between the two principles of Contiguity and Similarity, is requisite in order to guard against mistakes, and especially to prevent misapprehension, as to the separate existence of the two modes of action in the mental framework. When the cohesive link between any two contiguous actions, or images, is confirmed by a new occurrence or repetition, obviously the present impression must revive the sum total of the past impressions, or reinstate the whole

mental condition left on the occasion immediately preceding. Thus, if I am disciplining myself in the act of drawing a round figure with my hand, any one present effort must recall the state of the muscular and nervous action, or the precise bent acquired at the end of the previous effort, while that effort had to reinstate the condition at the end of the one preceding, and so on. It is only in this way that repetition can be of any avail in confirming a physical habit, or in forming an intellectual aggregate. But this reinstatement of a former condition by a present act of the same kind, is really and truly a case of the operation of the associating principle of similarity, or of like recalling like; and we here plainly see, that without such recall, the adhesion of contiguous things would be impossible. Hence it would appear, that all through the exposition of Contiguity, the principle of Similarity has been tacitly assumed; we have everywhere taken for granted, that a present occurrence of any object to the view, recalls the total impression made by all the previous occurrences, and adds its own effect to that total.

Compound Association [11]

Associations that are individually too weak, to operate the revival of a past idea, may succeed by acting together; and there is thus opened up to our view a means of aiding our recollection, or invention, when the one thread in hand is too feeble to effect a desired recall. It happens, in fact, that, in a very large number of our mental transitions, there is present a multiple bond of association.

The combinations may be made up of Contiguities alone, of Similarities alone, or of Contiguity and Similarity mixed. Moreover, we shall find that in Emotion and in Volition there are influences either assisting or obstructing the proper intellectual forces. In the reviving of a past image or idea, it is never unimportant, that the revival gratifies a favourite emotion, or is strongly willed in the pursuit of an end. We must endeavour to appreciate, as far as we are able, the influence of these extra-intellectual energies within the sphere of intellect; but, as they would rarely suffice for the reproduction of

[10]   *Ibid.*, pp. 457–458.

[11]   *Ibid.*, pp. 544–545.

thought, if acting apart and alone, we are led to look at them chiefly as modifying the effects of the strictly intellectual forces, or as combining elements in the composition of associations.

The general law may be stated as follows:—

Past actions, sensations, thoughts, or emotions, are recalled more easily, when associated either through contiguity or through similarity, with *more than one* present object or impression.

JOHN STUART MILL
(1806–1873)

The Permanent Possibilities of Sensation [12]

We have seen Sir W. Hamilton at work on the question of the reality of Matter, by the introspective method, and, as it seems, with little result. Let us now approach the same subject by the psychological. I proceed, therefore, to state the case of those who hold that the belief in an external world is not intuitive, but an acquired product.

This theory postulates the following psychological truths, all of which are proved by experience. . . .

It postulates, first, that the human mind is capable of Expectation. In other words, that after having had actual sensations, we are capable of forming the conception of Possible sensations; sensations which we are not feeling at the present moment, but which we might feel, and should feel if certain conditions were present, the nature of which conditions we have, in many cases, learnt by experience.

It postulates, secondly, the laws of the Association of Ideas. So far as we are here concerned, these laws are the following: 1st. Similar phænomena tend to be thought of together. 2nd. Phænomena which have either been experienced or conceived in close contiguity to one another, tend to be thought of together. The contiguity is of two kinds; simultaneity, and immediate succession. Facts which have been experienced or thought of simultaneously, recall the thought of one another. Of facts which have been experienced or thought of in immediate succession, the antecedent, or the thought of it, recalls the thought of the consequent, but not conversely. 3rd. Associations produced by contiguity become more certain and rapid by

repetition. When two phænomena have been very often experienced in conjunction, and have not, in any single instance, occurred separately either in experience or in thought, there is produced between them what has been called Inseparable, or less correctly, Indissoluble Association: by which is not meant that the association must inevitably last to the end of life—that no subsequent experience or process of thought can possibly avail to dissolve it; but only that as long as no such experience or process of thought has taken place, the association is irresistible; it is impossible for us to think the one thing disjoined from the other. 4th. When an association has acquired this character of inseparability—when the bond between the two ideas has been thus firmly riveted, not only does the idea called up by association become, in our consciousness, inseparable from the idea which suggested it, but the facts or phænomena answering to those ideas, come at last to seem inseparable in existence: things which we are unable to conceive apart, appear incapable of existing apart; and the belief we have in their coexistence, though really a product of experience, seems intuitive.

* * * * *

Setting out from these premises, the Psychological Theory maintains, that there are associations naturally and even necessarily generated by the order of our sensations and of our reminiscences of sensation, which, supposing no intuition of an external world to have existed in consciousness, would inevitably generate the belief, and would cause it to be regarded as an intuition.

What is it we mean when we say that the object we perceive is external to us, and not a part of our own thoughts? We mean, that there is in our perceptions something which exists when we are not thinking of it; which existed before we had ever thought of it, and

---

[12] John Stuart Mill, *An Examination of Sir William Hamilton's Philosophy* (London, 1865), ch. 11.

would exist if we were annihilated; and further, that there exist things which we never saw, touched, or otherwise perceived, and things which never have been perceived by man. This idea of something which is distinguished from our fleeting impressions by what, in Kantian language, is called Perdurability; something which is fixed and the same, while our impressions vary; something which exists whether we are aware of it or not, and which is always square (or of some other given figure) whether it appears to us square or round, constitutes altogether our idea of external substance. Whoever can assign an origin to this complex conception, has accounted for what we mean by the belief in matter. Now all this, according to the Psychological Theory, is but the form impressed by the known laws of association, upon the conception or notion, obtained by experience, of Contingent Sensations; by which are meant, sensations that are not in our present consciousness, and perhaps never were in our consciousness at all, but which in virtue of the laws to which we have learnt by the experience that our sensations are subject, we know that we should have felt under given supposable circumstances, and under these same circumstances, might still feel.

I see a piece of white paper on a table. I go into another room, and though I have ceased to see it, I am persuaded that the paper is still there. I no longer have the sensations which it gave me; but I believe that when I again place myself in the circumstances in which I had those sensations, that is, when I go again into the room, I shall again have them; and further, that there has been no intervening moment at which this would not have been the case. Owing to this law of my mind, my conception of the world at any given instant consists, in only a small proportion, of present sensations. Of these I may at the time have none at all, and they are in any case a most insignificant portion of the whole which I apprehend. The conception I form of the world existing at any moment, comprises, along with the sensations I am feeling, a countless variety of possibilities of sensation: namely, the whole of those which past observation tells me that I could, under any supposable circumstances, experience at this moment, together with an indefinite and illimitable multitude of others which though I do not know that I could, yet it is possible that I might, experience in circumstances not known to me. These various possibilities are the important thing to me in the world. My present sensations are generally of little importance, and are moreover fugitive: the possibilities, on the contrary, are permanent, which is the character that mainly distinguishes our idea of Substance or Matter from our notion of sensation. These possibilities, which are conditional certainties, need a special name to distinguish them from mere vague possibilities, which experience gives no warrant for reckoning upon. Now, as soon as a distinguishing name is given, though it be only to the same thing regarded in a different aspect, one of the most familiar experiences of our mental nature teaches us, that the different name comes to be considered as the name of a different thing.

There is another important peculiarity of these certified or guaranteed possibilities of sensation; namely, that they have reference, not to single sensations, but to sensations joined together in groups. When we think of anything as a material substance, or body, we either have had, or we think that on some given supposition we should have, not some *one* sensation, but a great and even an indefinite number and variety of sensations, generally belonging to different senses, but so linked together, that the presence of one announces the possible presence at the very same instant of any or all of the rest. In our mind, therefore, not only is this particular Possibility of sensation invested with the quality of permanence when we are not actually feeling any of the sensations at all; but when we are feeling some of them, the remaining sensations of the group are conceived by us in the form of Present Possibilities, which might be realized at the very moment. And as this happens in turn to all of them, the group as a whole presents itself to the mind as permanent, in contrast not solely with the temporariness of my bodily presence, but also with the temporary character of each of the sensations composing the group; in other words, as a kind of permanent substratum, under a set of passing experiences or manifestations: which is another leading character of our idea of substance or matter, as distinguished from sensation.

Let us now take into consideration another of the general characters of our experience, namely, that in addition to fixed groups, we also recognise, a fixed Order in our sensations; an Order of succession, which, when ascertained by observation, gives rise to the ideas of Cause and Effect, according to what I hold to be the true theory of that relation, and is in any case the source of all our knowledge *what* causes produce what effects. Now, of what nature is this fixed order among our sensations? It is a constancy of antecedence and sequence. But the constant antecedence and sequence do not generally exist between one actual sensation and another. Very few such sequences are presented to us by experience. In almost all the constant sequences which occur in Nature, the antecedence and consequence do not obtain between sensations, but between the groups we have been speaking about, of which a very small portion is actual sensation, the greater part being permanent possibilities of sensation, evidenced to us by a small and variable number of sensations actually present. Hence, our ideas of causation, power, activity, do not become connected in thought with our sensations as *actual* at all, save in the few physiological cases where these figure by themselves as the antecedents in some uniform sequence. Those ideas become connected, not with sensations, but with groups of possibilities of sensation. The sensations conceived do not, to our habitual thoughts, present themselves as sensations actually experienced, inasmuch as not only any one or any number of them may be supposed absent, but none of them need be present. We find that the modifications which are taking place more or less regularly in our possibilities of sensation, are mostly quite independent of our consciousness, and of our presence or absence. Whether we are asleep or awake the fire goes out, and puts an end to one particular possibility of warmth and light. Whether we are present or absent the corn ripens, and brings a new possibility of food. Hence we speedily learn to think of Nature as made up solely of these groups of possibilities, and the active force in Nature as manifested in the modification of some of these by others. The sensations, though the original foundation of the whole, come to be looked upon as a sort of accident depending on us, and the possibilities as much more real than the actual sensations, nay, as the very realities of which these are only the representations, appearances, or effects. When this state of mind has been arrived at, then, and from that time forward, we are never conscious of a present sensation without instantaneously referring it to some one of the groups of possibilities into which a sensation of that particular description enters; and if we do not yet know to what group to refer it, we at least feel an irresistible conviction that it must belong to some group or other; *i.e.* that its presence proves the existence, here and now, of a great number and variety of possibilities of sensation, without which it would not have been. The whole set of sensations as possible, form a permanent background to any one or more of them that are, at a given moment, actual; and the possibilities are conceived as standing to the actual sensations in the relation of a cause to its effects, or of canvas to the figures painted on it, or of a root to the trunk, leaves, and flowers, or of a substratum to that which is spread over it, or, in transcendental language, of Matter to Form.

When this point has been reached, the Permanent Possibilities in question have assumed such unlikeness of aspect, and such difference of position relatively to us, from any sensations, that it would be contrary to all we know of the constitution of human nature that they should not be conceived as, and believed to be, at least as different from sensations as sensations are from one another. Their groundwork in sensation is forgotten, and they are supposed to be something intrinsically distinct from it. We can withdraw ourselves from any of our (external) sensations, or we can be withdrawn from them by some other agency. But though the sensations cease, the possibilities remain in existence; they are independent of our will, our presence, and everything which belongs to us. We find, too, that they belong as much to other human or sentient beings as to ourselves. We find other people grounding their expectations and conduct upon the same permanent possibilities on which we ground ours. But we do not find them experiencing the same actual sensations. Other people do not have our sensations exactly when and as we have them: but they have our possibilities of sensation;

whatever indicates a present possibility of sensations to ourselves, indicates a present possibility of similar sensations to them, except so far as their organs of sensation may vary from the type of ours. This puts the final seal to our conception of the groups of possibilities as the fundamental reality in Nature. The permanent possibilities are common to us and to our fellow-creatures; the actual sensations are not. That which other people become aware of when, and on the same grounds, as I do, seems more real to me than that which they do not know of unless I tell them. The world of Possible Sensations succeeding one another according to laws, is as much in other beings as it is in me; it has therefore an existence outside me; it is an External World.

* * * * *

Matter, then, may be defined, a Permanent Possibility of Sensation. If I am asked, whether I believe in matter, I ask whether the questioner accepts this definition of it. If he does, I believe in matter: and so do all Berkeleians. In any other sense than this, I do not. But I affirm with confidence, that this conception of Matter includes the whole meaning attached to it by the common world, apart from philosophical, and sometimes from theological, theories. The reliance of mankind on the real existence of visible and tangible objects, means reliance on the reality and permanence of Possibilities of visual and tactual sensations, when no such sensations are actually experienced. We are warranted in believing that this is the meaning of Matter.

Laws of the Mind [13]

The subject . . .of Psychology, is the uniformities of succession, the laws, whether ultimate or derivative, according to which one mental state succeeds another; is caused by, or at the least, is caused to follow, another. Of these laws, some are general, others more special. The following are examples of the most general laws.

---

[13] John Stuart Mill, *A System of Logic, Ratiocinative and Inductive, Being a Connected View of the Principles of Evidence, and the Methods of Scientific Investigation* (London, 1843), bk. 6, ch. 4, sect. 3, entitled "The principle investigations of psychology characterized."

First: Whenever any state of consciousness has once been excited in us, no matter by what cause; an inferior degree of the same state of consciousness, a state of consciousness resembling the former, but inferior in intensity, is capable of being reproduced in us, without the presence of any such cause as excited it at first. Thus, if we have once seen or touched an object, we can afterwards think of the object although it be absent from our sight or from our touch. If we have been joyful or grieved at some event, we can think of, or remember, our past joy or grief, although no new event of a happy or a painful nature has taken place. When a poet has put together a mental picture of an imaginary object, a Castle of Indolence, a Una, or a Juliet, he can afterwards think of the ideal object he has created, without any fresh act of intellectual combination. This law is expressed by saying, in the language of Hume, that every mental *impression* has its *idea*.

Secondly: These Ideas, or secondary mental states, are excited by our impressions, or by other ideas, according to certain laws which are called Laws of Association. Of these laws the first is, that similar ideas tend to excite one another. The second is, that when two impressions have been frequently experienced (or even thought of) either simultaneously or in immediate succession, then whenever either of these impressions or the idea of it recurs, it tends to excite the idea of the other. The third law is, that greater intensity, in either or both of the impressions, is equivalent, in rendering them excitable by one another, to a greater frequency of conjunction. These are the laws of Ideas: upon which I shall not enlarge in this place, but refer the reader to works professedly psychological, in particular to Mr. Mill's *Analysis of the Phenomena of the Human Mind*, where the principal laws of association, both in themselves and in many of their applications, are copiously exemplified, and with a masterly hand.

These simple or elementary Laws of Mind have long been ascertained by the ordinary methods of experimental inquiry; nor could they have been ascertained in any other manner. But a certain number of elementary laws having thus been obtained, it is a fair subject of scientific inquiry how far those laws can be made to go in explaining the actual phenomena. It is obvious that complex laws of thought and feeling not only may, but must, be generated from these simple laws. And it is to be remarked, that the case is not always one of Composition of Causes: the effect of concurring causes is not always precisely the sum of the effects of those causes when separate, nor even always an effect of the same kind with them. Reverting to the distinction which occupies so prominent a place in the theory of induction; the laws of the phenomena of mind are sometimes analogous to mechanical, but sometimes also to chemical laws. When many impressions or ideas are operating in the mind together, there sometimes takes place a process of a similar kind to chemical combination. When impressions have been so often experienced in conjunction, that each of them calls up readily and instantaneously the ideas of the whole group, those ideas sometimes melt and coalesce into one another, and appear not several ideas but one; in the same manner as when the seven prismatic colors are presented to the eye in rapid succession, the sensation produced is that of white. But as in this last case it is correct to say that the seven colors when they rapidly follow one another *generate* white, but not that they actually *are* white; so it appears to me that the Complex Idea, formed by the blending together of several simpler ones, should, when it really appears simple, (that is when the separate elements are not consciously distinguishable in it,) be said to *result from*, or be *generated by*, the simple ideas, not to *consist* of them. Our idea of an orange really *consists* of the simple ideas of a certain color, a certain form, a certain taste and smell, &c., because we can by interrogating our consciousness, perceive all these elements in the idea. But we cannot perceive, in so apparently simple a feeling as our perception of the shape of an object by the eye, all that multitude of ideas derived from other senses, without which it is well ascertained that no such visual perception would ever have had existence;

nor, in our idea of Extension, can we discover those elementary ideas of resistance, derived from our muscular frame, in which Dr. Brown has rendered it highly probable that the idea originates. These therefore are cases of mental chemistry: in which it is proper to say that the simple ideas generate, rather than that they compose, the complex ones.

* * * * *

The generation of one class of mental phenomena from another, whenever it can be made out, is a highly interesting fact in psychological chemistry; but it no more supersedes the necessity of an experimental study of the generated phenomenon, than a knowledge of the properties of oxygen and sulphur enables us to deduce those of sulphuric acid without specific observation and experiment. Whatever, therefore, may be the final issue of the attempt to account for the origin of our judgments, our desires, or our volitions, from simpler mental phenomena, it is not the less imperative to ascertain the sequences of the complex phenomena themselves, by special study in conformity to the canons of Induction. Thus, in respect of Belief, the psychologist will always have to inquire, what beliefs we have intuitively, and according to what laws one belief produces another; what are the laws in virtue of which one thing is recognized by the mind, either rightly or erroneously, as evidence of another thing. In regard to Desire, he will examine what objects we desire naturally, and by what causes we are made to desire things originally indifferent or even disagreeable to us; and so forth. It may be remarked, that the general laws of association prevail among these more intricate states of mind, in the same manner as among the simpler ones. A desire, an emotion, an idea of the higher order of abstraction, even our judgments and volitions when they have become habitual, are called up by association, according to precisely the same laws as our simple ideas.

7

German Philosophical Psychology

IMMANUEL KANT
(1724–1804)

The A Priori Intuition of Space [1]

By means of our external sense, a property of our mind we represent to ourselves objects as external or outside ourselves, and all of these in space. It is within space that their form, size, and relative position are fixed or can be fixed. The internal sense by means of which the mind perceives itself or its internal state, does not give an intuition of the soul itself, as an object, but it is nevertheless a fixed form under which alone an intuition of its internal state is possible, so that whatever belongs to its internal determinations must be represented in relations of time. Time cannot be perceived externally, as little as space can be perceived as something within us.

What then are space and time? Are they real beings? Or, if not that, are they determinations or relations of things, but such as would belong to them even if they were not perceived? Or lastly, are they determinations and relations which are inherent in the form of intuition only, and therefore in the subjective nature of our mind, without which such predicates as space and time would never be ascribed to anything?

In order to understand this more clearly, let us first consider space.

1. Space is not an empirical concept which has been derived from external experience. For in order that certain sensations should be referred to something outside myself, i.e. to something in a different part of space from that where I am; again, in order that I may be able to represent them as side by side, that is, not only as different, but as in different

places, the representation of space must already be there. Therefore the representation of space cannot be borrowed through experience from relations of external phenomena, but, on the contrary, this external experience becomes possible only by means of the representation of space.

2. Space is a necessary representation *a priori*, forming the very foundation of all external intuitions. It is impossible to imagine that there should be no space, though one might very well imagine that there should be space without objects to fill it. Space is therefore regarded as a condition of the possibility of phenomena, not as a determination produced by them; it is a representation *a priori* which necessarily precedes all external phenomena.

3. On this necessity of an *a priori* representation of space rests the apodictic certainty of all geometrical principles, and the possibility of their construction *a priori*. For if the intuition of space were a concept gained *a posteriori*, borrowed from general external experience, the first principles of mathematical definition would be nothing but perceptions. They would be exposed to all the accidents of perception, and there being but one straight line between two points would not be a necessity, but only something taught in each case by experience. Whatever is derived from experience possesses a relative generality only, based on induction. We should therefore not be able to say more than that, so far as hitherto observed, no space has yet been found having more than three dimensions.

4. Space is not a discursive or so-called general concept of the relations of things in general, but a pure intuition. For, first of all, we can imagine one space only and if we speak of many spaces, we mean parts only of one and the same space. Nor can these

[1] Immanuel Kant, *Critique of Pure Reason*, trans. F. Max Muller (New York: Macmillan, 1896), pt. 1, sect. 1; original German, *Kritik der reinen Vernunft* (Riga, 1781).

parts be considered as antecedent to the one and all-embracing space and, as it were, its component parts out of which an aggregate is formed, but they can be thought of as existing within it only. Space is essentially one; its multiplicity, and therefore the general concept of spaces in general, arises entirely from limitations. Hence it follows that, with respect to space, an intuition *a priori*, which is not empirical, must form the foundation of all conceptions of space. In the same manner all geometrical principles, e.g. "that in every triangle two sides together are greater than the third," are never to be derived from the general concepts of side and triangle, but from an intuition, and that *a priori*, with apodictic certainty.

5. Space is represented as an infinite quantity. Now a general concept of space, which is found in a foot as well as in an ell, could tell us nothing in respect to the quantity of the space. If there were not infinity in the progression of intuition, no concept of relations of space could ever contain a principle of infinity.

Conclusions from the Foregoing Concepts

a. Space does not represent any quality of objects by themselves, or objects in their relation to one another; i.e. space does not represent any determination which is inherent in the objects themselves, and would remain, even if all subjective conditions of intuition were removed. For no determinations of objects, whether belonging to them absolutely or in relation to others, can enter into our intuition before the actual existence of the objects themselves, that is to say, they can never be intuitions *a priori*.

b. Space is nothing but the form of all phenomena of the external senses; it is the subjective condition of our sensibility, without which no external intuition is possible for us. If then we consider that the receptivity of the subject, its capacity of being affected by objects, must necessarily precede all intuition of objects, we shall understand how the form of all phenomena may be given before all real perceptions, may be, in fact, *a priori* in the soul, and may, as a pure intuition, by which all objects must be determined, contain, prior to all experience, principles regulating their relations.

* * * * *

The A Priori Intuition of Time [2]

I. Time is not an empirical concept deduced from any experience, for neither coexistence nor succession would enter into our perception, if the representation of time were not given *a priori*. Only when this representation *a priori* is given, can we imagine that certain things happen at the same time (simultaneously) or at different times (successively).

II. Time is a necessary representation on which all intuitions depend. We cannot take away time from phenomena in general, though we can well take away phenomena out of time. Time therefore is given *a priori*. In time alone is reality of phenomena possible. All phenomena may vanish, but time itself (as the general condition of their possibility) cannot be done away with.

III. On this *a priori* necessity depends also the possibility of apodictic principles of the relations of time, or of axions of time in general. Time has one dimension only; different times are not simultaneous, but successive, while different spaces are never successive, but simultaneous. Such principles cannot be derived from experience, because experience could not impart to them absolute universality nor apodictic certainty. We should only be able to say that common experience teaches us that it is so, but not that it must be so. These principles are valid as rules under which alone experience is possible; they teach us before experience, not by means of experience.

IV. Time is not a discursive, or what is called a general concept, but a pure form of sensuous intuition. Different times are parts only of one and the same time. Representation, which can be produced by a single object only, is called an intuition. The proposition that different times cannot exist at the same time cannot be deduced from any general concept. Such a proposition is synthetical, and cannot be deduced from concepts only. It is contained immediately in the intuition and representation of time.

V. To say that time is infinite means no more than that every definite quantity of time is possible only by limitations of one time which forms the foundation of all times. The original representation of time must

2 *Ibid.*, sect. 2.

therefore be given as unlimited. But when the parts themselves and every quantity of an object can be represented as determined by limitation only, the whole representation cannot be given by concepts (for in that case the partial representations come first), but it must be founded on immediate intuition.

Conclusions

a. Time is not something existing by itself, or inherent in things as an objective determination of them, something therefore that might remain when abstraction is made of all subjective conditions of intuition. For in the former case it would be something real, without being a real object. In the latter it could not, as a determination or order inherent in things themselves, be antecedent to things as their condition, and be known and perceived by means of synthetical propositions *a priori.* All this is perfectly possible if time is nothing but a subjective condition under which alone intuitions take place within us. For in that case this form of internal intuition can be represented prior to the objects themselves, that is, *a priori.*

b. Time is nothing but the form of the internal sense, that is, of our intuition of ourselves, and of our internal state. Time cannot be a determination peculiar to external phenomena. It refers neither to their shape, nor their position, etc., it only determines the relation of representations in our internal state. And exactly because this internal intuition supplies no shape, we try to make good this deficiency by means of analogies, and represent to ourselves the succession of time by a line progressing to infinity, in which the manifold constitutes a series of one dimension only; and we conclude from the properties of this line as to all the properties of time, with one exception, i.e. that the parts of the former are simultaneous, those of the latter successive. From this it becomes clear also, that the representation of time is itself an intuition, because all its relations can be expressed by means of an external intuition.

c. Time is the formal condition, *a priori,* of all phenomena whatsoever. Space, as the pure form of all external intuition, is a condition, *a priori,* of external phenomena only. But, as all representations, whether they have for their objects external things or not, belong by themselves, as determinations of the mind, to our inner state, and as this inner state falls under the formal conditions of internal intuition, and therefore of time, time is a condition, *a priori,* of all phenomena whatsoever, and is so directly as a condition of internal phenomena (of our mind) and thereby indirectly of external phenomena also. If I am able to say, *a priori,* that all external phenomena are in space, and are determined, *a priori,* according to the relations of space, I can, according to the principle of the internal sense, make the general assertion that all phenomena, that is, all objects of the senses, are in time, and stand necessarily in relations of time.

If we drop our manner of looking at ourselves internally, and of comprehending by means of that intuition all external intuitions also within our power of representation, and thus take objects as they may be by themselves, then time is nothing. Time has objective validity with reference to phenomena only, because these are themselves things which we accept as objects of our senses; but time is no longer objective, if we remove the sensuous character of our intuitions, that is to say, that mode of representation which is peculiar to ourselves, and speak of things in general. Time is therefore simply a subjective condition of our (human) intuition (which is always sensuous, that is so far as we are affected by objects), but by itself, apart from the subject, nothing. Nevertheless, with respect to all phenomena, that is, all things which can come within our experience, time is necessarily objective. We cannot say that all things are in time, because, if we speak of things in general, nothing is said about the manner of intuition, which is the real condition under which time enters into our representation of things. If therefore this condition is added to the concept, and if we say that all things as phenomena (as objects of sensuous intuition) are in time, then such a proposition has its full objective validity and *a priori* universality.

What we insist on therefore is the empirical reality of time, that is, its objective validity, with reference to all objects which can ever come before our senses. And as our intuition must at all times be sensuous, no object can ever fall under our experience that does not come under the conditions of time. What we deny is, that time has any claim on absolute reality, so that, without taking into account the form of our sensuous condition, it should by itself be a condition or quality inherent in things; for such qualities which belong to things by themselves can never be given to us through the senses. This is what constitutes the transcendental ideality of time, so that, if we take no account of the subjective conditions of our sensuous intuitions, time is nothing, and cannot be added to the objects by themselves (without their relation to our intuition) whether as subsisting or inherent.

* * * * *

Time certainly is something real, namely, the real form of our internal intuition. Time therefore has subjective reality with regard to internal experience: that is, I really have the representation of time and of my determinations in it. Time therefore is to be considered as real, not so far as it is an object, but so far as it is the representation of myself as an object. . . . There remains therefore the empirical reality of time only, as the condition of all our experience, while absolute reality cannot, according to what has just been shown, be conceded to it. Time is nothing but the form of our own internal intuition. Take away the peculiar condition of our sensibility, and the idea of time vanishes, because it is not inherent in the objects, but in the subject only that perceives them.

* * * * *

Space and time are pure forms of our intuition, while sensation forms its matter. What we can know *a priori*—before all real intuition, are the forms of space and time, which are therefore called pure intuition, while sensation is that which causes our knowledge to be called *a posteriori* knowledge, i.e. empirical intuition.

JOHANN FRIEDRICH HERBART
(1776–1841)

Mathematical Psychology [3]

16. Here the expression "threshold of consciousness" must be explained, as we shall have occasion to use it. A concept is in consciousness in so far as it is not suppressed, but is an actual representation. When it rises out of a condition of complete suppression, it enters into consciousness. Here, then, it is on the threshold of consciousness. It is very important to determine by calculation the degree of strength which a concept must attain in order to be able to stand beside two or more stronger ones exactly on the threshold of consciousness, so that, at the slightest yielding of the hindrance, it would begin to rise into consciousness.

* * * * *

17. Among the many, and, for the most part, very complicated laws underlying the

movement of concepts, the following is the simplest:

While the arrested portion (*Hemmungssumme*) of the concept sinks, the sinking part is at every moment proportional to the part unsuppressed.

By this it is possible to calculate the whole course of the sinking even to the statical point.

NOTE.—Mathematically, the above law may be expressed: $\sigma = S(1 - e^{-t})$ in which $S =$ the aggregate amount suppressed, $t =$ the time elapsed during the encounter, $\sigma =$ the suppressed portion of all the concepts in the time indicated by t. As the latter quantity is apportioned among the individual concepts, it is found that those which fall directly beneath the statical threshold (16) are very quickly driven thence, while the rest do not reach exactly their statical point in any given finite time. On account of this latter circumstance, the concepts in the mind of a man of most equable temperament are, while he is awake, always in a state of gentle motion. This is also the primary reason why the inner perception never meets an object which holds it quite motionless.

18. When to several concepts already near equilibrium a new one comes, a movement arises which causes them to sink for a short

[3] Johann Friedrich Herbart, *A Text-Book in Psychology: An Attempt to Found the Science of Psychology on Experience, Metaphysics, and Mathematics*, trans. Margaret K. Smith (New York: D. Appleton, 1891), pp. 11–15; original German, *Lehrbuch der Psychologie* (Leipzig, 1816).

time beneath their statical point, after which they quickly and entirely of themselves rise again—something as a liquid, when an object is thrown into it, first sinks and then rises. In this connection several remarkable circumstances occur:

19. First, upon an occasion of this kind, one of the older concepts may be removed entirely out of consciousness even by a new concept that is much weaker than itself. In this case, however, the striving of the suppressed concept is not to be considered wholly ineffective, as shown above (see 16); it works with all its force against the concepts in consciousness. Although its object is not conceived, it produces a certain condition of consciousness. The way in which these concepts are removed out of consciousness and yet are effective therein may be indicated by the expression, "They are on the mechanical threshold." The threshold mentioned above (16) is called for the sake of distinction the statical threshold.

NOTE.—If the concepts on the statical threshold acted in the same way as on the mechanical threshold we should find ourselves in a state of the most intolerable uneasiness, or rather the body would be subjected to a condition of tension that must in a few moments prove fatal, even as under present conditions sudden fright will sometimes cause death; for all the concepts which, as we are accustomed to say, the memory preserves, and which we well know can upon the slightest occasion be reproduced, are in a state of incessant striving to rise, although the condition of consciousness is not at all affected by them.

20. Second, the time during which one or more concepts linger upon the mechanical threshold can be extended if a series of new, although weaker, concepts come in succession to them.

Every employment to which we are unaccustomed puts us in this condition. The earlier concepts are pressed back of the later ones. The former, however, because they are the stronger, remain tense, affect the physical organism more and more, and finally make it necessary that the employment cease, when the old concepts immediately rise, and we experience what is called a feeling of relief which depends in part upon the physical organism, although the first cause is purely psychological.

21. Third, when several concepts are driven in succession to the mechanical threshold, several sudden successive changes in the laws of reciprocal movements arise.

In this way is to be explained the fact that the course of our thoughts is so often inconsequent, abrupt, and apparently irregular. This appearance deceives in the same way as the wandering of the planets. The conformity to law in the human mind resembles exactly that in the firmament.

NOTE.—As a counterpart to the concepts which sink simultaneously are to be observed those which rise simultaneously, especially when they rise free—i.e., when a restricting environment or a general pressure suddenly disappears. With the rising the amount of suppression increases. Hence, in the case of three, one may be, as it were, bent back, and under certain conditions may sink quite to the threshold. Their elevation is greater than the depression to which, sinking together, they would have pressed one another, because in sinking the sum of their mutual limitation depends upon the total strength, which in the gradual rising is not the case.

Fusion and Blending [4]

22. The easily conceivable metaphysical reason why opposed concepts resist one another is the unity of the soul, of which they are the self-preservations. This reason explains without difficulty the combination of our concepts (which combination is known to exist). If, on account of their opposition, they did not suppress one another, all concepts would compose but one act of one soul; and, indeed, in so far as they are not divided into a manifold by any kind of arrests whatever, they really constitute but one act. Concepts that are on the threshold of consciousness can not enter into combination with others, as they are completely transformed into effort directed against other definite concepts, and are thereby, as it were, isolated. In consciousness, however, concepts combine in two ways: First, concepts which are not opposed or contrasted with one another (as a tone and a color) so far as they meet unhindered, form a complex; second, contrasted concepts [e.g., red and yellow], in so far as they are affected neither by accidental foreign concepts nor by unavoidable opposition, become blended (fused).

[4] *Ibid.*, pp. 16–23.

Complexes may be complete; blendings (fusions) from their nature must always be (more or less) incomplete.

* * * * *

23. That which is complicated or blended out of several concepts furnishes an aggregate of force, and for this reason works according to quite other statical and mechanical laws than those according to which the individual concepts would have acted. Also the thresholds of consciousness change according to the complex or blending (fusion), so that on account of a combination a concept of the very weakest kind may be able to remain and exert an influence in consciousness.

* * * * *

24. *Problem:* After an encounter between two concepts, P and Π, the remainders, r and ϱ, are blended (or incompletely united). The problem is to indicate what help one of the two concepts, in case it should be still more suppressed, would receive from the other.

NOTE.—*Solution:* Let P be the helping concept; it helps with a force equal to r, but Π can only appropriate this force in the ratio of $\varrho : \Pi$. Hence through P, Π receives the help $r\varrho/\Pi$, and in the same way P receives from Π the help $r\varrho/P$.

The proof lies immediately in the analysis of the ideas. It is plain that the two remainders, r and ϱ, taken together, determine the degree of union between the two concepts. One of them is the helping force; the other, compared with the concept to which it belongs, is to be considered as a fraction of the whole; and, of the totality of help which could be rendered by the first remainder, it yields that portion which here attains efficient activity.

25. The following principles may be observed here:

a. Beyond the point of union no help extends its influence.

If the concept Π has more clearness in consciousness than the remainder ϱ indicates, then by the striving of the concept P, which might come to the help of the former, already more than enough has been done; hence for the present it exerts no more influence.

b. The farther the one of the concepts is below the point of union, so much the more effectively does the other help.

NOTE.—This gives the following differential equation:

$$\frac{r\varrho}{\Pi} \frac{\varrho - \omega}{\varrho} \, dt = d\omega,$$

whence by integration $\omega = \varrho\{1 - e(- rt/\Pi)\}$.

This equation contains the germ of manifold investigations which penetrate the whole of psychology. It is indeed so simple that it can never really occur in the human soul, but all investigations into applied mathematics begin with such simple presuppositions as only exist in abstraction—e.g., the mathematical lever, or the laws of bodies falling in a vacuum. Here merely the influence of the help is considered, which, if everything depended upon it alone, would bring into consciousness during the time t a quantity ω from Π. Besides, if we take into consideration the single circumstance that Π meets with an unavoidable arrest from other concepts, then the calculation becomes so complicated that it can be only approximately solved by an integration of the following form:

$$d^3\omega = ad^2\omega dt + bd\omega dt^2 + c\omega dt^3.$$

It is self-evident that it much more nearly expresses the facts which are to be observed experimentally.

26. The foregoing contains the foundation of the theory of mediate reproduction, which, according to ordinary language, is derived from the association of ideas or concepts. Before pursuing this further we must mention immediate reproduction—i.e., that reproduction which by its own force follows upon the yielding of the hindrances. The ordinary case is that a concept gained by a new act of perception causes the old concept of the same or of a similar object to rise into consciousness. This occurs when the concept furnished by the new act of perception presses back everything present in consciousness opposed to the old concept, which is similar to the new one. Then, without further difficulty, the old concept rises of itself. From this are to be observed the following conditions, which are to be found by calculation, of which, however, no idea can be given here:

a. In the beginning the rising is in proportion to the square of the time, if the new act of perception occurs suddenly; but to the cube of the time, if the latter (as is usual) is formed by a gradual and lingering act of apprehension.

b. The course of the rising is adjusted principally to the strength of the concept furnished by the new act of perception in proportion to the opposing one which it has pressed back; but the individual strength of the rising concept only has influence under special conditions. It can, as it were, only use this strength in the free space which is given to it.

c. The rising concept blends as such with the concept, similar to it, furnished by the new act of perception. Since it does not rise entirely, however, the blending is incomplete.

d. The fact that immediate reproduction is not limited entirely to the old concept of exactly the same kind, but extends to the more or less similar so far as to receive partial freedom from the new act of perception, is of special importance. The whole reproduction may be indicated by the name of vaulting (or arching). In the case of a long duration, or of a frequent repetition of a new act of perception, a second important process, which we call tapering (or pointing), follows. The peculiarity of this latter consists in the fact that the concepts which are less similar are again arrested by the concepts received through the new act of perception, as the old concepts bring with them into consciousness others which are opposed to the new, so that finally the concept that is entirely homogeneous finds itself alone favored, and forms, as it were, a tapering summit where the highest point of the vault (or arch) was heretofore.

27. Where the circumstances allow, with this immediate reproduction is united that mediate reproduction mentioned in 25. The concept P, mentioned above, is reproduced immediately (i.e., without the mediation of others), then the free space allowed it may be regarded as that r (spoken of in 25) or as a force which strives to raise the Π blended with it to its point of blending ϱ.

NOTE.—As the free space gradually increasing (and again decreasing) is given, we must for the present observation regard r in the formula $\omega = \varrho\{1 - e(-rt/\Pi)\}$ as a variable quantity, and indeed as a function of that quantity upon which the propositions in 26 depend.

28. The most important applications of the previous theories are, if with different remainders r, r', r'', etc., of one and the same concept P several Π, Π', Π'', etc., are united, by which, for the sake of brevity, we may assume the remainders of the latter, viz.,

ϱ, ϱ', ϱ'', to be equal; also, Π, Π', etc., may be equal.

A concept acts upon several united with it in the same series according to the time in which its remainders (by which it is united with those others according to quantity) stand.

NOTE.—In order to avoid diffuseness, this most important law is here only very incompletely expressed in words. We recognize it better and more clearly in the formula given:

$$\omega = \varrho\{1 - e(-rt/\Pi)\},$$

if instead of one r we substitute different smaller and greater, r, r', r'', etc. But the more exact calculation mentioned in 25 shows that the Π, Π', Π'', etc., blended with them, not only rise, but sink again, as it were, to make place for each other, and in the order of r, r', r'', etc.

29. Here is discovered the ground of the genuine reproduction or of memory so far as it brings to us a series of concepts in the same order in which they were first received. In order to comprehend this, we must consider what union arises among several concepts that are successively given.

Let a series, a, b, c, d, be given by perception; then, from the first movement of the perception and during its continuance, a is exposed to an arrest from other concepts already in consciousness. In the meantime, a, already partially sunken in consciousness, became more and more obscured when b came to it. This b at first, unobscured, blended with the sinking a; then followed c, which itself unobscured, united with b, which was becoming obscured, and also with a, which was still more obscured. Similarly followed d, to become united in different degrees with a, b, c. From this arises a law for each of these concepts that states how, after the whole series has been, for a time, removed out of consciousness, upon the re-emergence of one of the concepts of such a series into consciousness, every other concept of the same series is called up. Let it be assumed that a rises first, then it is united more with b, less with c, and still less with d; backward, however, b, c, and d are blended collectively in an unobscured condition with the remainders of a; hence a seeks to bring them all again into an unobscured condition [i.e., into full consciousness]. But a acts the most quickly and strongly upon b, more slowly upon c, still more slowly upon *d*, etc., by which close investigation shows that *b* sinks again, while *c* rises, even as *c* sinks when *d* rises; in short, the series follows in the same order as first given. On the contrary, let us assume that *c* is originally reproduced, then *c* acts upon *d* and the following members of the series exactly in the same way as was indicated in the case of *a*—i.e., the series *c*, *d*, etc., unfolds gradually in the order of its succession. On the contrary, *b* and *a* experience quite another influence. The unobscured *c* was blended with their different remainders. Then *c* acts upon them with its whole strength, and without delay, but only to call back the remainders of *a* and *b* united with it, to bring a part of *b* and a smaller part of *a* into consciousness. Thus it happens that when we remember something in the middle of a known series, the preceding part of the series presents itself all at once in a lessened degree of clearness, while the portion following comes before the mind in the same order as the series it brings with it. But the series never runs backward; an anagram from a well-comprehended word never originates without intentional effort.

Apperception Mass [5]

39. From the foregoing, it may, in a way, be perceived that after a considerable number of concepts in all kinds of combinations is present, every new act of perception must work as an excitant by which some will be arrested, others called forward and strengthened, progressing series interrupted or set again in motion, and this or that mental state occasioned. These manifestations must become more complex if, as is usual, the concept received by the new act of perception contains in itself a multiplicity or variety, that at the same time enables it to hold its place in several combinations and series, and gives them a fresh impulse which brings them into new relations of opposition or blending with one another. By this, the concepts brought by the new act of perception are assimilated to the older concepts in such a way as to suffer somewhat after the first excitation has worked to the extent of its power, because the old concepts—on account of their combinations

with one another—are much stronger than the new individuals which are added.

40. If, however, already very strong complexes and blendings with many members have been formed, then the same relation which existed between the old and the new concepts may be repeated within between the old concepts. Weaker concepts, which, according to any kind of law, enter into consciousness, act as excitants upon those masses before mentioned, and are received and appropriated by them (apperceived) just as in the case of a new sense-impression; hence *the inner perception* is analogous to the outer. Self-consciousness is not the subject of discussion here, although it is very often combined with the above.

41. In what has been said, lies that which experience confirms, viz., that the inner perception is never a passive apprehension, but always (even against the will) active. The apperceived concepts do not continue rising or sinking according to their own laws, but they are interrupted in their movements by the more powerful masses which drive back whatever is opposed to them although it is inclined to rise; and in the case of that which is similar to them although it is on the point of sinking, they take hold of it and blend it with themselves.

42. It is worth the trouble to indicate how far this difference among concepts—which we might be inclined to divide into dead and living—may be carried.

Let us recall the concepts on the statical threshold (16). These are, indeed, in effect nothing less than dead; for, in the condition of arrest in which they stand, they are not able by their own effort to effect anything whatever [toward rising into consciousness]. Nevertheless, through the combination in which they stand, they may be reproduced, and, besides, they will often be driven back in whole heaps and series by those more powerful masses, as when the leaves of a book are turned hurriedly.

43. If the apperceived concepts—or at least some of them—are not on the statical threshold, then the apperceiving concepts suffer some violence from them; also the latter may be subject to arrest from another side, in which case the inner perception is interrupted; through this, uncertainty and irresolution may be explained.

[5] *Ibid.*, pp. 30–32.

The apperceiving mass may be, in its turn apperceived by another mass; but for this to occur, there must be present several concept masses of distinctly different degrees of strength. Hence it is somewhat seldom that the inner perception rises to this second power [the apperception of apperception], and only in the case of philosophical ideas is this series considered as one which might be prolonged into infinity.

RUDOLF HERMANN LOTZE
(1817–1881)

The Intuition of Space and the Theory of Local Signs [6]

§ 27. Metaphysic raises the doubt, whether space is actually extended and we, together with "Things," are contained in it; whether— just the reverse—the whole spatial world is not rather only a form of intuition in us.

... But since Things in space can never become the object of our perception by virtue of their bare existence, and, on the contrary, become such solely through the effects which they exercise upon us, the question arises: How do the Things by their influence upon us bring it to pass, that we are compelled mentally to represent them in the same reciprocal position in space, in which they actually exist outside of us?

§ 28. In the case of the eye, nature has devised a painstaking structure, such that the rays of light which come from a luminous point are collected again at one point on the retina, and that the different points of the image, which originate here, assume the same reciprocal relation toward one another as the points of the object outside of us, to which they correspond. Without doubt, this so-called "image of the object," so carefully prepared, is an indispensable condition of our being able mentally to present the object in its true form and position. But it is the source of all the errors in this matter, to believe that the bare existence of this image, without anything else, explains our idea of the position of its parts. The entire image is essentially nothing but a representative of the external object, transposed into the interior of the organ of sense; and how we know and experience aught of it, is now just as much the question as the question previously was,— How can we perceive the external object?

§ 29. If one wished to conceive of the soul itself as an extended being, then the impressions on the retina would, of course, be able to transplant themselves, with all their geometrical regularity, to the soul. One point of the soul would be excited as green, the other red, a third yellow; and these three would lie at the corners of a triangle precisely in the same way as the three corresponding excitations on the retina.

It is also obvious, however, that there is no real gain in all this. The bare fact that three different points of the soul are excited is, primarily, a disconnected three-fold fact. A knowledge thereof, however, and therefore a knowledge of this three-foldness, and of the reciprocal positions of the three points, is, nevertheless, by no means given in this way: but such knowledge could be brought about only by means of a uniting and relating activity; and this itself, like every activity, would be perfectly foreign to all predicates of extension and magnitudes in space.

§ 30. The same thought is more immediately obvious if we surrender this useless notion of the soul being extended, and consider it as a supersensible essence, which, in case we wish to bring it at all into connection with spatial determinations, could be represented only as an indivisible point.

On making the transition into this indivisible point, the manifold impressions must obviously lose all the geometrical relations which they might still have upon the extended retina,—just in the same way as the rays of light, which converge at the single focus of a lens, are not side by side with one another, but only all together, in this point. Beyond the focus, the rays diverge in the same order

[6] Rudolf Hermann Lotze, *Outlines of Psychology*, trans. George T. Ladd (Boston: Ginn, 1886), ch. 4; original German, *Grundzüge der Psychologie: Dictate aus den Vorlesungen* (Leipzig, 1881).

as that in which they entered it. Nothing analogous to this, however, happens in our consciousness; that is to say, the many impressions, which were previously side by side with one another, do not actually again separate from each other; but, instead of this, the aforesaid activity of mental presentation simply occurs, and it transposes their images to different places in the space that is only "intuited" by it.

Here, too, the previous observation holds good: The mental presentation *is* not that which it presents; and the idea of a point on the left does not lie on the left of the idea of a point on the right; but of one mental presentation, which in itself has no spatial properties whatever, both points are merely themselves so presented before the mind, as though one lay to the left, the other to the right.

§ *31.* The following result now stands before us: Many impressions exist conjointly in the soul, although not spatially side by side with one another; but they are merely together in the same way as the synchronous tones of a chord; that is to say, qualitatively different, but not side by side with, above or below, one another. Notwithstanding, the mental presentation of a spatial order must be produced again from these impressions. The question is, therefore, in the first place, to be raised: How in general does the soul come to apprehend these impressions, not in the form in which they actually are,—to wit, non-spatial,—but as they are not, in a spatial juxtaposition?

The satisfactory reason obviously cannot lie in the impressions themselves, but must lie solely in the nature of the soul in which they appear, and upon which they themselves act simply as stimuli.

On this account, it is customary to ascribe to the soul this tendency to form an intuition of space, as an originally inborn capacity. And indeed we are compelled to rest satisfied with this. All the "deductions" of space, hitherto attempted, which have tried to show on what ground it is necessary to the nature of the soul to develop this intuition of space, have utterly failed of success. Nor is there any reason to complain over this matter; for the simplest modes of the experience of the soul must always merely be recognized as given facts,—just as, for example, no one

seriously asks why we only hear, and do not rather taste, the waves of air.

§ *32.* The second question is much more important. Let it be assumed that the soul once for all lies under the necessity of mentally presenting a certain manifold as in juxtaposition in space; How does it come to localize every individual impression at a definite place in the space intuited by it, in such manner that the entire image thus intuited is similar to the external object which acted on the eye?

Obviously, such a clue must lie in the impressions themselves. The simple quality of the sensation "green" or "red" does not, however, contain it; for every such color can in turn appear at every point in space, and on this account does not, of itself, require always to be referred to the one definite point.

We now remind ourselves, however, that the carefulness with which the regular position on the retina of the particular excitations is secured, cannot be without a purpose. To be sure, an impression is not *seen* at a definite point on account of its *being situated* at such point; but it may perhaps by means of this definite situation *act* on the soul otherwise than if it were elsewhere situated.

Accordingly we conceive of this in the following way: Every impression of color **r**—for example, red—produces on all places of the retina, which it reaches, the same sensation of redness. In addition to this, however, it produces on each of these different places, **a, b, c,** a certain accessory impression, $\alpha, \beta, \gamma,$ which is independent of the nature of the color seen, and dependent merely on the nature of the place excited. This second local impression would therefore be associated with every impression of color **r,** in such manner that rα signifies a red that acts on the point **a,** rβ signifies the same red in case it acts on the point **b.** These associated accessory impressions would, accordingly, render for the soul the clue, by following which it transposes the same red, now to one, now to another spot, or simultaneously to different spots in the space intuited by it.

In order, however, that this may take place in a methodical way, these accessory impressions must be completely different from the main impressions, the colors, and must not disturb the latter. They must be, however, not merely of the same kind among themselves, but wholly definite members of a series or a system of series; so that for every impression r there may be assigned, by the aid of this adjoined "local sign," not merely a particular, but a quite definite spot among all the rest of the impressions.

§ 33. The foregoing is the theory of "*Local Signs.*" Their fundamental thought consists in this, that all spatial differences and relations among the impressions on the retina must be compensated for by corresponding non-spatial and merely intensive relations among the impressions which exist together without space-form in the soul; and that from them in reverse order there must arise, not a new actual arrangement of these impressions in extension, but only the mental presentation of such an arrangement in us. To such an extent do we hold this principle to be a necessary one.

ARTHUR SCHOPENHAUER
(1788–1860)

Psychology of Will [7]

Psychologism: The Phenomenal World as Idea

§ 1. "The world is my idea:"—this is a truth which holds good for everything that lives and knows, though man alone can bring it into reflective and abstract consciousness. ... It then becomes clear and certain to him what he knows is not a sun and an earth, but only an eye that sees a sun, a hand that feels an earth; that the world which surrounds him is there only as idea, *i.e.*, only in relation to something else, the consciousness, which is himself. ... No truth therefore is more certain, more independent of all others, and less in need of proof than this, that all that exists for knowledge, and therefore this whole world, is only object in relation to subject, perception of a perceiver, in a word, idea. ... All that in any way belongs or can belong to the world is inevitably thus conditioned through the subject, and exists only for the subject. The world is idea.

* * * * *

The World as Will

§ 21. Whoever has now gained from all these expositions a knowledge *in abstracto*, and therefore clear and certain, of what every one knows directly *in concreto*, *i.e.*, as feeling, a knowledge that his will is the real inner nature of his phenomenal being, which manifests itself to him as idea, both in his actions and in their permanent substratum, his body, and that his will is that which is most immediate in his consciousness.

* * * * *

He will recognise this will of which we are speaking not only in those phenomenal existences which exactly resemble his own, in men and animals as their inmost nature, but the course of reflection will lead him to recognise the force which germinates and vegetates in the plant, and indeed the force through which the crystal is formed, that by which the magnet turns to the north pole, the force whose shock he experiences from the contact of two different kinds of metals, the force which appears in the elective affinities of matter as repulsion and attraction, decomposition and combination, and, lastly, even gravitation, which acts so powerfully throughout matter, draws the stone to the earth and the earth to the sun,—all these, I say, he will recognise as different only in their phenomenal existence, but in their inner nature as identical, as that which is directly known to him so intimately and so much better than anything else, and which in its most distinct manifestation is called *will*. It is this application of reflection alone that prevents us from remaining any longer at the phenomenon, and leads us to the *thing in itself*. Phenomenal existence is idea and nothing more. All idea, of whatever kind it may be, all *object*, is *phenomenal* existence, but the *will* alone is a *thing in itself*. ... It is the inmost nature, the kernel, of every particular

[7] Arthur Schopenhauer, *The World as Will and Idea*, trans. R. B. Haldane and J. Kemp (London: Kegan Paul, Trench, Trubner, 1896), ch. 1, 21, 38, 52, 54, 56, 57, 58, 66, 67; original German, *Die Welt als Wille und Vorstellung* (Leipzig, 1819).

thing, and also of the whole. It appears in every blind force of nature and also in the preconsidered action of man; and the great difference between these two is merely in the degree of the manifestation, not in the nature of what manifests itself.

* * * * *

Man's Nature as Will, Force, and Desire

Now the nature of man consists in this, that his will strives, is satisfied and strives anew, and so on for ever. Indeed, his happiness and well-being consist simply in the quick transition from wish to satisfaction, and from satisfaction to a new wish. For the absence of satisfaction is suffering, the empty longing for a new wish, languor, *ennui*.

* * * * *

The will, which, considered purely in itself, is without knowledge, and is merely a blind incessant impulse, as we see it appear in unorganised and vegetable nature and their laws, and also in the vegetative part of our own life, receives through the addition of the world as idea, which is developed in subjection to it, the knowledge of its own willing and of what it is that it wills. And this is nothing else than the world as idea, life, precisely as it exists. Therefore we called the phenomenal world the mirror of the will, its objectivity. And since what the will wills is always life, just because life is nothing but the representation of that willing for the idea, it is all one and a mere pleonism if, instead of simply saying "the will," we say "the will to live."

Will is the thing-in-itself, the inner content, the essence of the world. Life, the visible world, the phenomenon, is only the mirror of the will. Therefore life accompanies the will as inseparably as the shadow accompanies the body; and if will exists, so will life, the world, exist. Life is, therefore, assured to the will to live; and so long as we are filled with the will to live we need have no fear for our existence, even in the presence of death.

* * * * *

In all the grades of its manifestation, from the lowest to the highest, the will dispenses altogether with a final goal and aim. It always strives, for striving is its sole nature, which no attained goal can put an end to. Therefore it is not susceptible of any final satisfaction, but can only be restrained by hindrances, while in itself it goes on for ever. We see this in the simplest of all natural phenomena, gravity, which does not cease to strive and press towards a mathematical centre to reach which would be the annihilation both of itself and matter, and would not cease even if the whole universe were already rolled into one ball. We see it in the other simple natural phenomena.

* * * * *

All *willing* arises from want, therefore from deficiency, and therefore from suffering. The satisfaction of a wish ends it; yet for one wish that is satisfied there remain at least ten which are denied. Further, the desire lasts long, the demands are infinite; the satisfaction is short and scantily measured out. But even the final satisfaction is itself only apparent; every satisfied wish at once makes room for a new one; both are illusions; the one is known to be so, the other not yet. No attained object of desire can give lasting satisfaction, but merely a fleeting gratification; it is like the alms thrown to the beggar, that keeps him alive to-day that his misery may be prolonged till the morrow. Therefore, so long as our consciousness is filled by our will, so long as we are given up to the throng of desires with their constant hopes and fears, so long as we are the subject of willing, we can never have lasting happiness nor peace. It is essentially all the same whether we pursue or flee, fear injury or seek enjoyment; the care for the constant demands of the will, in whatever form it may be, continually occupies and sways the consciousness; but without peace no true well-being is possible.

* * * * *

We have long since recognised this striving, which constitutes the kernel and in-itself of everything, as identical with that which in us, where it manifests itself most distinctly in the light of the fullest consciousness, is called *will*. Its hindrance through an obstacle which places itself between it and its temporary aim we call *suffering*, and, on the other hand, its attainment of the end satisfaction, wellbeing, happiness. We may also transfer this terminology to the phenomena of the unconscious world, for though weaker in degree, they are identical in nature. Then we see them involved in constant suffering, and without any continuing happiness. For all effort springs from defect—from discontent with one's estate—is thus suffering so long as it is not satisfied; but no satisfaction is lasting, rather it is always merely the starting-point of a new effort. The striving we see everywhere hindered in many ways, everywhere in conflict, and therefore always under the form of suffering. Thus, if there is no final end of striving, there is no measure and end of suffering.

But what we only discover in unconscious Nature by sharpened observation, and with an effort, presents itself distinctly to us in the intelligent world in the life of animals, whose constant suffering is easily proved. But without lingering over these intermediate grades, we shall turn to the life of man, in which all this appears with the greatest distinctness, illuminated by the clearest knowledge; for as the phenomenon of will becomes more complete, the suffering also becomes more and more apparent. In the plant there is as yet no sensibility, and therefore no pain. A certain very small degree of suffering is experienced by the lowest species of animal life—infusoria and radiata; even in insects the capacity to feel and suffer is still limited. It first appears in a high degree with the complete nervous system of vertebrate animals, and always in a higher degree the more intelligence develops. Thus, in proportion as knowledge attains to distinctness, as consciousness ascends, pain also increases, and therefore reaches its highest degree in man. And then, again, the more distinctly a man knows, the more intelligent he is, the more pain he has; the man who is gifted with genius suffers most of all.

* * * * *

We desire to consider in this way, in *human existence*, the inner and essential destiny of will. Every one will easily recognise that same destiny expressed in various degrees in the life of the brutes, only more weakly, and may also convince himself to his own satisfaction, from the suffering animal world, *how essential to all life is suffering.*

* * * * *

Existence, even when we consider only its formal side, is a constant hurrying of the present into the dead past, a constant dying. But if we look at it from the physical side; it is clear that, as our walking is admittedly merely a constantly prevented falling, the life of our body is only a constantly prevented dying, an ever-postponed death: finally, in the same way, the activity of our mind is a constantly deferred ennui. Every breath we draw wards off the death that is constantly intruding upon us. In this way we fight with it every moment, and again, at longer intervals, through every meal we eat, every sleep we take, every time we warm ourselves, &c. In the end, death must conquer, for we became subject to him through birth, and he only plays for a little while with his prey before he swallows it up. We pursue our life, however, with great interest and much solicitude as long as possible, as we blow out a soap-bubble as long and as large as possible, although we know perfectly well that it will burst.

We saw that the inner being of unconscious nature is a constant striving without end and without rest. And this appears to us much more distinctly when we consider the nature of brutes and man. Willing and striving is its whole being, which may be very well compared to an unquenchable thirst. But the basis of all willing is need, deficiency, and thus pain. Consequently, the nature of brutes and man is subject to pain originally and through its very being. If, on the other hand, it lacks objects of desire, because it is at once deprived of them by a too easy satisfaction, a terrible void and ennui comes over it, *i.e.*, its being and existence itself becomes an unbearable burden to it. Thus its life swings like a pendulum backwards and forwards between pain and ennui.

* * * * *

Man, as the most complete objectification of that will, is in like measure also the most necessitous of all beings: he is through and through concrete willing and needing; he is a concretion of a thousand necessities. With these he stands upon the earth, left to himself, uncertain about everything except his own need and misery. Consequently the care for the maintenance of that existence under exacting demands, which are renewed every day, occupies, as a rule, the whole of human life. To this is directly related the second claim, that of the propagation of the species. At the same time he is threatened from all sides by the most different kinds of dangers, from which it requires constant watchfulness to escape. With cautious steps and casting anxious glances round him he pursues his path, for a thousand accidents and a thousand enemies lie in wait for him. Thus he went while yet a savage, thus he goes in civilised life; there is no security for him. . . . The life of the great majority is only a constant struggle for this existence itself, with the certainty of losing it at last. But what enables them to endure this wearisome battle is not so much the love of life as the fear of death, which yet stands in the background as inevitable, and may come upon them at any moment.

* * * * *

Sex as the Blind Force of Will

As man is at once impetuous and blind striving of will (whose pole or focus lies in the genital organs), and eternal, free, serene subject of pure knowing (whose pole is the brain).

* * * * *

The Negative Character of Happiness

§ 58. All satisfaction, or what is commonly called happiness, is always really and essentially only *negative*, and never positive. It is not an original gratification coming to us of itself, but must always be the satisfaction of a wish. The wish, *i.e.*, some want, is the condition which precedes every pleasure. But with the satisfaction the wish and therefore the pleasure cease. Thus the satisfaction or the pleasing can never be more than the deliverance from a pain, from a want; for such is not only every actual, open sorrow, but every desire, the importunity of which disturbs our peace, and, indeed, the deadening ennui also that makes life a burden to us. It is, however, so hard to attain or achieve anything; difficulties and troubles without end are opposed to every purpose, and at every step hindrances accumulate. But when finally everything is overcome and attained, nothing can ever be gained but deliverance from some sorrow or desire, so that we find ourselves just in the same position as we occupied

before this sorrow or desire appeared. All that is even directly given us is merely the want, *i.e.*, the pain. The satisfaction and the pleasure we can only know indirectly through the remembrance of the preceding suffering and want, which ceases with its appearance. Hence it arises that we are not properly conscious of the blessings and advantages we actually possess, nor do we prize them, but think of them merely as a matter of course, for they gratify us only negatively by restraining suffering. Only when we have lost them do we become sensible of their value; for the want, the privation, the sorrow, is the positive, communicating itself directly to us. Thus also we are pleased by the remembrance of past need, sickness, want, and such like, because this is the only means of enjoying the present blessings. And, further, it cannot be denied that in this respect, and from this standpoint of egoism, which is the form of the will to live, the sight or the description of the sufferings of others affords us satisfaction and pleasure.

* * * * *

All that we intend to bring out clearly through these investigations, the impossibility of attaining lasting satisfaction and the negative nature of all happiness, finds its explanation in what is shown at the conclusion of the Second Book: that the will, of which human life, like every phenomenon, is the objectification, is a striving without aim or end.

* * * * *

Sublimation and Psychological Salvation

§ 39. All these reflections are intended to bring out the subjective part of æsthetic pleasure; that is to say, that pleasure so far as it consists simply of delight in perceptive knowledge as such, in opposition to will. And as directly connected with this, there naturally follows the explanation of that disposition or frame of mind which has been called the sense of the *sublime*.

* * * * *

The (Platonic) Ideas are the adequate objectification of will. To excite or suggest the knowledge of these by means of the representation of particular things (for works of art themselves are always representations of particular things) is the end of all the other arts, which can only be attained by a corresponding change in the knowing subject. Thus all these arts objectify the will indirectly only by means of the Ideas; and since our world is nothing but the manifestation of the Ideas in multiplicity, though their entrance into the *principium individuationis* (the form of the knowledge possible for the individual as such), music also, since it passes over the Ideas, is entirely independent of the phenomenal world, ignores it altogether, could to a certain extent exist if there was no world at all, which cannot be said of the other arts. Music is as *direct* an objectification and copy of the whole *will* as the world itself, nay, even as the Ideas, whose multiplied manifestation constitutes the world of individual things. Music is thus by no means like the other arts, the copy of the Ideas, but the *copy of the will itself*, whose objectivity the Ideas are. This is why the effect of music is so much more powerful and penetrating than that of the other arts, for they speak only of shadows, but it speaks of the thing itself. Since, however, it is the same will which objectifies itself both in the Ideas and in music, though in quite different ways, there must be, not indeed a direct likeness, but yet a parallel, an analogy, between music and the Ideas whose manifestation in multiplicity and incompleteness is the visible world. The establishing of this analogy will facilitate, as an illustration, the understanding of this exposition, which is so difficult on account of the obscurity of the subject.

I recognise in the deepest tones of harmony, in the bass, the lowest grades of the objectification of will, unorganised nature, the mass of the planet. It is well known that all the high notes which are easily sounded, and die away more quickly, are produced by the vibration in their vicinity of the deep bass-notes. When, also, the low notes sound, the high notes always sound faintly, and it is a law of harmony that only those high notes may accompany a bass-note which actually already sound along with it of themselves (its *sons harmoniques*) on account of its vibration.

* * * * *

If the whole world as idea is only the visibility of will, the work of art is to render this visibility more distinct. It is the *camera obscura* which shows the objects more purely, and enables us to survey them and comprehend them better. It is the play within the play, the stage upon the stage in "Hamlet."

The pleasure we receive from all beauty, the consolation which art affords, the enthusiasm of the artist, which enables him to forget the cares of life,—the latter an advantage of the man of genius over other men, which alone repays him for the suffering that increases in proportion to the clearness of consciousness, and for the desert loneliness among men of a different race,—all this rests on the fact that the in-itself of life, the will, existence itself, is, as we shall see farther on, a constant sorrow, partly miserable, partly terrible; while, on the contrary, as idea alone, purely contemplated, or copied by art, free from pain, it presents to us a drama full of significance. . . .

But before I go further, and, as the conclusion of my exposition, show how love, the origin and nature of which we recognised as the penetration of the *principium individuationis*, leads to salvation, to the entire surrender of the will to live, *i.e.*, of all volition, and also how another path, less soft but more frequented, leads men to the same goal, a paradoxical proposition must first be stated and explained; not because it is paradoxical, but because it is true, and is necessary to the completeness of the thought I have present. It is this: "All love (αγαπη, *caritas*) is sympathy."

* * * * *

All true and pure love is sympathy, and all love which is not sympathy is selfishness. Εϱως [Eros] is selfishness, αγαπη [agape] is sympathy. Combinations of the two frequently occur. Indeed genuine friendship is always a mixture of selfishness and sympathy; the former lies in the pleasure experienced in the presence of the friend, whose individuality corresponds to our own, and this almost always constitutes the greatest part; sympathy shows itself in the sincere participation in his joy and grief, and the disinterested sacrifices made in respect of the latter.

FRIEDRICH NIETZSCHE
(1844–1900)

The Will to Power [8]

What is *common* to all: the ruling instincts *wish to be regarded* as *the highest values in general*, even as the *creative* and *ruling powers*. It is understood that these instincts either oppose or overcome each other (join up synthetically, or alternate in power). Their profound antagonism is, however, so great, that in those cases in which they *all* insist upon being gratified, a man of very thorough *mediocrity* is the outcome.

* * * * *

The excessive importance which he attaches to the *sexual instinct* is not the *result* of the latter's importance to the species; for procreation is the actual performance of the individual, it is his greatest interest, and therefore it is his *highest expression of power* (not judged from the standpoint of consciousness, but from the very centre of the individual).

* * * * *

The will to power is the primitive motive force out of which all other motives have been derived;

That it is exceedingly illuminating to substitute *power* for individual "happiness" (after which every living organism is said to strive): "It strives after power, after *more* power";—happiness is only a symptom of the feeling of power attained, a consciousness of difference (it does not strive after happiness: but happiness steps in when the object is attained, after which the organism has striven: happiness is an accompanying, not an actuating factor);

That all motive force is the will to power; that there is no other force, either physical, dynamic, or psychic.

* * * * *

The will to *accumulate force* is confined to the phenomenon of life, to nourishment, to procreation, to inheritance, to society, states,

    [8] Friedrich Nietzsche, *The Will to Power*, trans. Anthony M. Ludovici (London: T. N. Foulis, 1910), pp. 161–165, 185; from the German, *Der Wille zur Macht* (posthumously published).

customs, authority.   Should we not be allowed to assume that this will is the motive power also of chemistry?—and of the cosmic order?

Not only conservation of energy, but the minimum amount of waste; so that the only reality is this: *the will of every centre of power to become stronger*—not self-preservation, but the desire to appropriate, to become master, to become more, to become stronger.

* * * * *

Life, which is our best known form of being, is altogether "will to the accumulation of strength"—all the processes of life hinge on this: everything aims, not at preservation, but at accretion and accumulation. Life as an individual case (a hypothesis which may be applied to existence in general) strives after the maximum feeling of power; life is essentially a striving after more power; striving itself is only a straining after more power; the most fundamental and innermost thing of all is this will.

* * * * *

It is not the satisfaction of the will which is the cause of happiness (to this superficial theory I am more particularly opposed—this absurd psychological forgery in regard to the most simple things), but it is that the will is always striving to overcome that which stands in its way. The feeling of happiness lies precisely in the discontentedness of the will, in the fact that without opponents and obstacles it is never satisfied.

The normal discontent of our instincts—for instance, of the instinct of hunger, of sex, of movement—contains nothing which is in itself depressing; it rather provokes the feeling of life, and, whatever the pessimists may say to us, like all the rhythms of small and irritating stimuli, it strengthens.   Instead of this discontent making us sick of life, it is rather the great stimulus to life.

(Pleasure might even perhaps be characterised as the rhythm of small and painful stimuli.)

* * * * *

Man has one terrible and fundamental wish;

he desires power, and this impulse, which is called freedom, must be the longest restrained.

* * * * *

There is a universal need to exercise some kind of power, or to create for one's self the appearance of some power, if only temporarily, in the form of intoxication.

There are men who desire power simply for the sake of the happiness it will bring; these belong chiefly to political parties. Other men have the same yearning, even when power means visible disadvantages, the sacrifice of their happiness, and well-being; they are the ambitious. Other men, again, are only like dogs in a manger, and will have power only to prevent its falling into the hands of others on whom they would then be dependent.

* * * * *

Ressentiment, Repression, Conscience, and Defense Mechanisms [9]

The slave-revolt in morality begins by *resentment* itself becoming creative and giving birth to values—the *resentment* of such beings, as real reaction, the reaction of deeds, is impossible to, and as nothing but an imaginary vengeance will serve to indemnify. Whereas, on the one hand, all noble morality takes its rise from a triumphant Yea-saying to one's self, slave-morality will, on the other hand, from the very beginning, say No to something "exterior," "different," "not-self;" *this* No being its creative deed. This reversion of the value-positing eye—this *necessary* glance outwards instead of backwards upon itself—is part of *resentment*. Slave-morality, in order to arise, needs, in the first place, an opposite and outer world; it needs, physiologically speaking, external irritants, in order to act at all;—its action is, throughout, reaction. The reverse is true in the case of noble valuation. It acts and grows spontaneously. It only seeks for its antithesis in order to say, still more thankfully, still more rejoicing- ly, Yea to itself.

* * * * *

[9] Friedrich Nietzsche, *A Genealogy of Morals*, trans. William A. Hausemann (New York: The Macmillan Co., 1897), vol. 2, pp. 35–39, 63–65, 77–78, 90, 110; original German, *Zur Genealogie der Moral* (1887).

Whereas, on the one hand, the life of the noble man is self-confident and self-sincere (γενναῖος "nobleborn" underscores the nuance "sincere" and perhaps also "naïve"), the man of resentment, on the other hand, is neither sincere, nor naïve, neither honest nor straightforward against himself. His soul *squints;* his mind loves hiding-places, alleys and back-doors; everything hidden appeals to him as *his* world, *his* shelter, *his* comfort; he is master in the art of keeping silence, of forgetting nothing, of waiting, of provisional self-diminution, of self-humiliation. A race of such men of resentment will at least, of necessity, be more *prudent* than any noble race; it will also learn to appreciate prudence in quite different measure: namely as a primary condition of existence; whereas prudence in the case of noble men is very apt to have about it a dainty tang of luxury and *raffinement*. For in their case prudence is far less essential than the perfect reliableness of function of the regulating, *unconscious* instincts or even a certain imprudence, such as readiness to encounter things—whether danger or an enemy—or that eccentric suddenness of anger, love, reverence, gratitude and revenge by which noble souls at all times have recognised themselves as such. Even the resentment of superior man, when it appears in him, acts and exhausts itself in the reaction which follows at once, and hence it does not *poison*. And again, it will not manifest itself at all in countless cases, in which with the poor and the feeble it is inevitable. Not to be able to take seriously, for a long time, an enemy, or a misfortune or even one's own *misdeeds*—is the characteristic of strong and full natures, abundantly endowed with plastic, formative, restorative, also obliterative force (a good example of this, in recent times, is Mirabeau, who had no memory for insults and affronts received, and who could not forgive for the sole reason that—he forgot). Such a man, with a single jerk, shakes off much vermin which burrows in others. Only here is also possible, if on earth it be possible at all, true *"love"* for one's enemies. How much veneration for his enemy has not superior man!—and such veneration is already a bridge to love. . . . He demands an enemy for himself, as his distinction, he will only suffer an enemy in whom he finds nothing to despise and *very much* to honour! On the other hand, let us figure to ourselves the enemy as conceived by the man of resentment —just therein, we shall have his deed, his creation: he has conceived the "foul fiend," "*the Evil* one," as his fundamental concept, proceeding from which he now conceives also a complementary image and counterpart, a "Good one" himself! . . .

* * * * *

Certain it is on the average that, even in the case of the most honest persons, a small dose of offence, malice and insinuation will suffice to force their blood to, and fairness *from* the brow. The active, aggressive, and transgressive man is, in any case, yet a hundred degrees nearer to justice than the re-active man; for the active one is not forced to a false and biased estimation of his object as the re-active is. And hence, as a matter of fact, the aggressive man, being also the stronger, braver, nobler man, has, at all times, had the *freer* eye and *better* conscience for his party. Reversely we see at once whose conscience must be held responsible for the invention of "bad conscience." It is the man of resentment.

* * * * *

This *instinct of freedom*, suppressed, drawn back and imprisoned in consciousness and finally discharging and venting itself only inwards, against self: only this is the beginning of *bad conscience*.

* * * * *

To rear an animal, which *may promise*,—is not even this that paradoxical task which nature has set herself, as regards man? Is not even this the true problem *of* man? . . . That this problem has, to a considerable extent, been solved, must seem all the more astonishing to any one capable of duly appreciating the reversely operative force,—that of *forgetfulness*. Forgetfulness is not merely a *vis inertiæ*, as superficial people believe; on the contrary, it is an active, and, in the strictest sense, a positive faculty of check, to which must be attributed the fact that whatever we live to see, whatever we experience and receive into ourselves, does not rise into consciousness during the state of digestion

(which state we might call inanimation); no more so, than the entire, thousandfold process, by which the nourishment of our body—so-called "incorporation"—is carried on. To close, for certain times, the doors and windows of our consciousness; to remain undisturbed by the noise and feud, with which the serving organs of our nether-world operate for and against one another; a little silence, a little *tabula rasa* of consciousness, in order to make room for something new, especially for the nobler functions and functionaries, for governing, fore-seeing, predetermining (for our organism is constituted oligarchically)—such is the advantage of—as we called it—active forgetfulness, comparable to a door-keeper and preserver of the order of soul, of peace and etiquette; which fact makes apparent at once the reason why there can be no happiness, no cheerfulness, no hope, no pride, no *presence*—without forgetfulness. The man, in whom this apparatus of checking is injured and stops may be compared (and not only be compared) to one suffering from dyspepsia —he never gets beyond things. . . . Even this of necessity forgetful animal, in which the forgetting represents a force, a form of *vigorous* health, has reared and acquired for itself a counter-faculty, a memory by the aid of which, in certain cases, forgetfulness is unhinged—for those cases, to wit, in which a promise is to be made. Hence this is not merely a passive not-to-be-able-to-get-rid-of an impression once imprinted; not merely the indigestion caused by a word pledged at some former time with which one cannot settle accounts; but an active not-to-*will*-to-get-rid-of, a continuous willing of that which once has been willed, a specific *memory of will;* so that between the original "I will," "I shall do" and the actual discharge of will, its *act*, we may unhesitatingly interpose a world of new and foreign things, circumstances and even acts of will, without causing this long chain of willing to break.

* * * * *

Sadism

In reading Don Quixote we modern readers experience a bitter sensation upon our tongues, almost a torture, and hence we should, for this very reason, appear very unintelligible and unfathomable to the author of it and his contemporaries. They read it with the very best conscience, as the most cheerful of books; they would almost—split with laughter. To see another suffer is pleasant; to make another suffer is still more pleasant—a stern dictum this is, but also a fundamental proposition, old, mighty, human, all-too-human, which, perhaps, even the apes would sign. For we are told that, in the devising of bizarre cruelties, the apes abundantly announce and, as it were, "prelude" man. No festival without cruelty: thus the oldest and longest history of man teaches us— and in punishment, also, there is so much that is *festival!*

8

Czechoslovakian Physiological Psychology

JAN EVANGELISTA PURKINJE
[PURKYNE]
(1787–1869)

Visual Phenomena [1]

1. The question which comes first to one's attention is the one regarding myopia and hypermetropia. If we wish to settle this question with mathematical precision, we can best use the apparatus of any optician, the usual one being the apparatus of Tauber in Leipzig. On a horizontal beam which is marked off by lines and sub-lines, resting on the ground on a well-fixed stand, the length of which should be 30 to 40 inches, attach in a vertical position a pedestal with several clamps, to which can be attached cardboards on which there are letters. This stand should be arranged so that it can be moved slowly on the horizontal beam forwards or backwards, permitting one to measure the slightest variation on the scale. On the front end of the beam place a cardboard with a proper opening in it which can be followed by the eye of the individual whose head must remain motionless. This arrangement for observation, together with the horizontal beam, must rest on a support which can be slowly raised or lowered and fixed to a position by means of a thumbscrew on a level, depending upon the position of the individual, whether standing or sitting. The greatest precision is necessary in order that the distance between the eye and the object it sees on the board can be expressed precisely by exact numbers, and it will be necessary at the side of the eye to place a small board which can be moved horizontally and which has a small opening, through which one can see the profile of the cornea; thus, on the scale, the exact measurement of the beginning of the distance of visual acuity can be determined. In addition, have several cardboards handy on which there are marked points and lines of various sizes measured by means of a micrometer and let these points and lines be white on a black background or black on a white background or, for various purposes, marked in some other colors. At the stand have handy a pointer which can be used to point on the board, according to various purposes, this or that marking. By means of this kind of apparatus, hypermetropia or myopia can be determined with the greatest precision and at the same time one can arrange experiments to find out how the appearance of the points and the lines are changing when the board

[1] Jan Evangelista Purkyne, *Memoirs of the American Philosophical Society Held at Philadelphia for Promoting Useful Knowledge*, Volume 49, trans. Henry J. John (Philadelphia: American Philosophical Society, 1959), pp. 56–62. Delivered by Purkinje as an inaugural address as Professor of Physiology and Pathology, Breslau University, on December 22, 1823. Original in Latin; translated from the Latin into Czech by Ritter von Lhoták, and from the Czech into English by H. J. John. Reprinted by permission.

is moved away from or toward distinct vision or when it is moved closer to the eye. Where this exactness is not necessary, as is usually the case, in order to decide visual discrimination or the lack of it, it will serve the purpose only to use the board with the written or printed letters on it, placed on the stand for the purpose of reading.

2. The same apparatus can be used to measure the distance for clear vision, the size of that part of the visual axis on which the objects which are moved toward or away from the eye can be recognized with the same acuity. By this we determine that ability of the eye which, by its inner composition and the construction of its optical mechanism, permits rays either from distant or from near objects to pass through the pupil and to form a focus on the retina itself.

3. Usually when the objects are moved beyond the distance of clear vision they become more or less widened, in fact, they may become a double or more than double picture, which nearly everyone has experienced at night if he has looked from a distance into the light of a candle. This refraction in the light depends undoubtedly upon the varying strength of the refraction of the cornea and the rest of the ocular media, and in some people it can lead to a diseased state, if they see any bright or a clearly white object spread out here and there, appearing hair-like or whisker-like. For a good observation of this deficiency the described apparatus can be used equally well when, in place of the cardboards, one places on the stand a tin sheet perforated by holes and lines, through which the light penetrates. Back of the stand a knitted wick produces a broad light which illuminates the holes and the lines. One must be careful to encase the flame to prevent the slightest part of the light from penetrating into the eye from some other side beyond the openings and the lines. After this is arranged, then by the movement of the tin together with the lamp toward or away from the eye, there appears a dispersion of the light; its direction and, according to various distances, its extent enable one in this manner to decide indirectly the manner of refraction because of the irregularity of the cornea and the rest of the mid-eye.

4. The same apparatus can serve for photometric experiments when there appear marked changes permitting one to obtain the various measurable degrees of either darkening or illuminating or full lighting and when certain objects which can be used for comparison are handy. By these experiments one can recognize either the degree of brightness of some object, for instance, the sky, the moon, or the stars, of various white bodies, or the degree of sensitivity of the eye for light.

5. By similar means one can determine the sensitivity of sight toward the quality of color at various distances and by various degrees of illumination. For it is known that the quality of colors of small objects at certain distances disappears and that the color surfaces, when illumination is gradually diminished, pass from gray or brown into complete indistinctness.

6. To determine the ability of the eye to follow moving objects and to determine the strength by which it can be fixed on these objects as well as the firmness and the rapidity with which it passes from one object to another, let us mark a point, barely visible, white, drawn on a black background or the reverse, on which the observing eye can be fixed. At the same time it is necessary to use a watch to record the minutes and seconds it takes from the beginning of the perception to the time when the image becomes indistinct or when the fatigued eye begins to blink and can no longer be fixed on the given point. If we wish to determine the strength of the free and voluntary movement of the eye, let us arrange a whole series of very small points between each of which a known small distance should be divided by either straight or crooked lines. When the eye enumerates these points in the shortest possible measurable time without hesitation or repetition of the execution and without error or with a minimal error, its strength is shown. Simultaneously with this experiment the eye must watch closely; its firmness of fixation or the strength and speed of its movement will show the same thing we judged from the quick count of the points.

7. In the visual field there is a point in the line of vision where the vision is more distinct than elsewhere. If the visual line terminates in this point we call it direct vision. Indirect vision is the viewing of all other points in the visual field which are outside the visual axis and are seen indistinctly and obliquely. The extent of direct vision then

is defined when the visual line leads to the surrounding objects when the eye turns in the socket. The extent of direct vision is greater the more the eye protrudes and the greater ability it has to turn in all directions. Thus the visual line describes a cone, the base of which is greater the more obtuse the angle of the tip, which rests in the eye. To observe the extent of direct vision more precisely, compose a segment of three-quarters of a circle divided into degrees, from the center of which the eye, without the movement of the head, can look at a picture which is distinctly seen when moved on the circle's circumference. Let the observer report how far he sees it clearly, that is, until the limitation of the eyeball's movement is reached, when it will be necessary to stop the picture on the periphery and to note the angle in degrees through which the eye moved when the picture was moved to the side.

The same can be tried for the other directions of movements when the segment is moved from its horizontal position around its axis into other positions.

8. The extension of indirect vision is given by the space which is less clearly seen when the eye is fixed on one point in the visual field. To determine the range of the extension of indirect vision the apparatus of the preceding experiment can be used, a target being added on which the eye is fixed, while a second, well-illuminated target is moved in or out from the side.

9. The same cut-out can be used to determine the relationship between the point in the retina through which the line of vision penetrates and the place where the optic nerve enters. It is peculiar that the picture, which on the rest of the retina is seen more or less clearly, is completely gone at this place in the retina. After the visual line is fixated on the target, which for this purpose can be raised or lowered, the line to the side of the horizontal circle is moved to and fro until it disappears. When we mark this place and note its relation to the intersection of the visual line on the retina by erecting an imaginary straight line through the lens, we can figure out the entrance of the optic nerve, which may vary in different individuals in the horizontal or the vertical direction from the point of the clearest vision.

* * * * *

13. The organic condition of the connective tissue, especially its larger and smaller blood vessels, can be studied by the use of an ordinary lens. This is particularly the case when the branching of the vessels becomes more distinct in the stage of a beginning inflammation.

In delicate subjects we see most often after a night's sleep a protruding streak leading from the corners of the eye toward the cornea and arising from the pressure of the corners of the lids.

14. The sensitivity of the conjunctiva can be determined from the length of time an open eye will tolerate the air before it closes. In this experiment one must consider, besides the chemical nature of the air, the temperature of the air in order to show how differently the warm air affects the eye as compared with the cold air in the same subject.

Where the sensitivity is less, the effect of the air can be emphasized by blowing on the eye. In this manner, however, one frequently proves the psychic influence rather than the degree of sensitivity.

15. This governing force of the mind over the body can be noticed when we suddenly approach the open eye with an outstretched finger. If a person's eye can tolerate it without movement we can consider him to be phlegmatic, one who can master his feelings. All this, which may appear as a plaything for children, a physiologist will not scorn to use as diagnostic means.

* * * * *

20.[2] The thickness and the transparency of the cornea can best be observed by the use of a lighted candle placed at the side of the eye. Then one will see a double image of the light which is reflected from the outer and at the same time the inner wall of the cornea.... One must observe further the edge of the cornea, which appears either diffuse or more definitely circumscribed or it is surrounded by an arcus senilis either beginning or well developed, all of which one must consider in the semeiotics of the various stages of human life.

21. The sclera is a connective tissue membrane and from its appearance one can judge the composition of the entire connective tissue system of the body according to the patho-

[2] The "Purkinje's image."

logical or physiological nature of the individual.

Its whiteness in children, where it enters the chorionic membrane, appears bluish. In adults it is yellowish because of the blood vessels. In some individuals it is of a peculiar whiteness like chalk and in various human races it takes on other coloring. The transparency of the sclera can best be observed if, on the nasal side of the eye, we place a lighted candle so that its light penetrates into the eyeball slantingly and on penetrating the cornea and the aqueous humor it centers on the edge of the cornea toward its nasal side. Being reflected from the inner substance of the sclera and from the outer surface of the cornea, it gives us a figure of a cone whose base rests on the cornea with its peak directed to the corner of the eye. . . . With an incipient, but not yet fully developed, varicosity of the eye, which for the most part takes place in the choroid, the sclera becomes partly or completely greyish when its wall is thinned or when the varicose blood vessels penetrate the inner substance. There also appear various kinds and degrees and places of redness caused by different inflammatory conditions. In an extreme degree of xerophthalmia the sclera together with the cornea takes on the appearance of a hardened epidermis.

22. Investigation of the aqueous humor is difficult. Its quantity one could judge from the curvature and the hardness of the cornea, were it not difficult to measure with precision this curvature and to feel the hardness. When the clearness of the aqueous humor and the transparency of the cornea is disturbed they will not remain hidden at the lateral view of the anterior chamber when they reach the diseased stage, but if one tries to determine the lesser degrees of damage, because of the small quantity of this liquid, we shall hardly see anything unless a strong microscope be placed in a position to permit the intermediary liquid to be examined by means of light reflected from the inner part of the eye, from the lens or the retina, as from an illuminated mirror which is placed in the microscope under the object studied. All this would require a special optical apparatus which could be firmly placed close to the eye.[3]

---

[3] Anticipating tonometry.

Subjectively one can see the turbidity of the aqueous humor by observing the colored halos which appear to surround the light of the candle in the reflection on the eye. How to differentiate the degree of turbidity, according to this criterion, is difficult to state, because in the majority of people it is not easy to correlate sensitivities. I am convinced, however, that if in the periphery of the subjective visual field one can see some sort of bodies, tendrils or balls, these cannot be in front of the lens, for the picture will be completely obliterated on the retina by the rays which penetrate from the side unless their strength and magnitude in relation to the weakness of the light within, is great enough to form a clear shadow of its own on the retinal nerve elements, where they will be seen as spots in the image of the external light. One will, however, not learn their special nature easily, because interference in the cornea, the lens, and the vitreous humor can have a similar effect.

23. The external examination of the iris shows a great variety of color and connective tissue. We must especially notice three circles differing from each other in color as well as in structure. Of these the outer one is usually a bit darker than the rest and its circumference is marked by parallel fibrils and ridges. The middle one is clearer with radiating fibrils and ridges. The inner one is darker and has fibrils and ridges far more numerous than the others, converging to the center of the pupil. In some individuals the inner canal has the shape of a funnel or a crater by which it surrounds the pupil. The notches, the crypts, the ridges and the corners of the iris we can best study when we throw light from the smallest possible source on it from the side. As we move the light slowly here and there, the shadowed and the lighted surface will change and the welltrained eye will see a very clear picture of the crypts and the ridges of the iris. Here also we will clearly see the funnel-like shape of the iris toward the pupil, which is striking in some individuals.

One can also see the various dimensions of the iris between the pupil and its inner edge where the circle of the pupil appears either contracted in this or that manner or dilated or where the outer circumference of the iris, together with the circumference of the cornea, deviates from the regular circular appearance, which in the upper part is usually a bit depressed. The iris of our own eye is best studied by placing the light at the side and adding a lens whose focus is half an inch. In this manner the front surface of the iris is clearly lighted and in the opposite mirror we can see even the smallest fibrils and bends. The problem can be more closely examined by studying the eye of another person with a microscope which has a lighted lens closely attached to it.

24. The response of the iris to stimulation and the degree of its constriction is studied in another way: by changing the light and shadow, either by covering the other eye or by looking at a near point or a distant one, or finally by means of certain narcotics, such as a solution of henbane, etc., which cause the pupil either to dilate or to contract. A rough examination of the effect of narcotics on the iris, sufficient for the use of ophthalmo-metrists, has been in use for a long time. However, for the physiological study of this subject one needs to use more precise ways. The various solutions, which have been concentrated to a definite point, one must apply in a carefully measured quantity to different individuals to find the exact relation between the irritability of the organ and the intensity of the effect. One has to observe also the iris of both far- and near-sighted individuals when they look afar and nearby, for this is accompanied by dilatation and contraction of the pupil. The variation of the iris is great according to sex, age, and individual and if someone wishes to describe all its forms and to establish a certain system, his task would not be a useless one.

25. Study of the inner chorion is almost impossible. In infants it can be seen through the sclera as a fine, uniformly greyish color whereas in adults it is varying in greyness. I suspect that in the subjective spheres of vision the composition of the choriodea offers a picture of the branching and pulsating vessels, which can be seen after a quick movement of the body or by pressure on the side of the eye. Here also should be placed the dark spots which can often be seen by subjective vision in summertime after a marked physical effort like going up a series of steps. I think that these spots are caused by the swelling of the vessels of the choriodea, which press on the retina.

26. The pigment, its color or its degree of paleness, can be seen by subjective vision by different individuals as a varied sensation of darkened colors. What influence the color of the pigment has on the light and the dark parts of the picture appearing in the retina, can be safely judged from the analogy with a camera obscura. If we spread behind this camera a translucent thin cloth which is colored, then the picture on the cloth will be colored differently. The outside colors, by this added color (of the cloth) will either be neutralized, the red by the green, weakened, or enhanced to a great degree of intensity, whereas the neutralized colors will take on the receding colors. Although this is purely a physical phenomenon, I do not hesitate to use it for the explanation of the perception changes and I do not doubt that the image is colored differently by the substratum of the pigment below the retina and that it appears differently colored to the observer.

It is true that the image in the case of albinos, where the pigment is light, will also be diminished in its intensity and there is no doubt that the phenomenon which is called acyanoblepsis depends mostly on the color of the pigment; this will be confirmed by anatomical observation.

Here also I place the observation that the black of printed letters appears to us purple when we turn our back to a setting sun and place the printed paper in front of partly closed eyes; the rays then penetrate slantwise through the skin and the membranes of the eyes and redden the retina and the pigment.

It does not seem correct to me that the black appears different to various individuals according to the kind of eyes they have, whether grey-green or black. But what we approach merely by introspection cannot be subjected to an objective measurement and comparison. Perhaps, just as we use a cyanometer for the study of the blue color in the sky, we could in the same manner construct a certain melanometer, where, for the basic measurement, we could study the black which appears to the eye when it is completely covered. This measure, however, will be hard to use, because it is easily disturbed by various optical illusions and foggings.

27. Since the lens capsule is fine and adheres to the lens, except in a diseased state, one could hardly differentiate between its

external surface and the surface of the lens. We must therefore understand, in what follows, the general surface of the two. If we place the candlelight about six inches from someone's eye in order that we can see the flame on the cornea when we are sitting to the side of the visual axis of the eye, within the circle of the pupil nearer the periphery, we will see in the back of the pupil a blinking flame, still smaller in its diameter but reversed and of feeble illumination, which we can easily judge, by comparing it with the one on the artificial lens, that it is reflected from the posterior wall of the lens....

The front surface of the lens, and partly its inner matter, under the conditions of full transparency we can make accessible for observation if, by looking into the pupil from the side and by placing the light on the opposite side of the eye, the straight lines from the eye of the observer and from the light of the candle shining into the pupil form an obtuse angle. Here one will see an elongated image of the flame, which, because it is straight, shows that it is reflected from the convex surface of the lens.... If the lens substance is somewhat cloudy, then the picture of the image of the flame coming from within the eye by repeated reflections is surrounded from one or the other side by a whitish light which is very diffused.

Both of these methods for the observation of the surfaces of the lens will not be without use, I think, in therapeutic investigation, especially where one wants to differentiate precisely whether only the capsule of the lens is involved, the lens itself, its posterior surface, or the vitreous humor. From the exact measurement of the flame reflections on the lens of a living human subject one can determine with considerable labor its shape and its relation to the acuity of vision, but, at the same time, not permanently, though it be done with mathematical precision.

The distance of the lens from the surface of the iris one can judge from the shadow which forms on it from the iris and from the speed of change which the image of the flame undergoes when the candle is brought closer or moved away....

28.[4] The transparency of the opaqueness of the vitreous humor can be noted from the

outside from the blackness of the pupil, either damaged or turbid. It can be studied more exactly by looking from one side and lighting, according to methods previously mentioned, which are similar for the study of the aqueous humor or of the lens.

I succeeded in a safe method of examining the hollow of the eyeball when, with glasses which the nearsighted use, I examined the eye of a dog by candlelight placed at the rear of the eye, throwing light from a distance, and thus learned about the manner of lighting which frequently illuminates the eye of the dog or the cat in a peculiar manner. The many times I looked into the eye of a dog that penetrating light appeared until I found its source in the light from the vitreous humor, which was being reflected within and from there it reflected back again. I repeated this experiment on man and I found the same phenomenon, for the sound pupil lighted up with a merry golden color. Being still in doubt about the source of the reflected light, I obtained an artificial eye, whose hollow I filled either with clear water or water made muddy by various means, which showed by the reflected light the back wall and at the same time the substance of the liquid.

Thus by a light properly reflected and the careful eye of the observer looking into the eye, no eye membrane or the liquid within the eye will remain hidden. The practitioners who reject the investigations of the physiologist will not refuse to accept this, nor will they be afraid to do it, for they shall find this useful in the diagnose of eye conditions.

In subjective vision I am convinced that the organic basis of many things rests in the vitreous humor.

I. The dots and the strands are marked by the edges and are parallel, changing from light to dark, having various curvatures and knottings. One can see them when one looks through a small opening placed opposite by means of a lighted and broad surface or through a lens as near to the eye as possible and focused on some small, lighted object like the distant light of the candle. These dots and tendrils, which appear during quick ocular movement when one moves the head up and down rapidly or turns it to the side, in changing the place and the likeness until one returns to the stage of calm, must certainly rest in the vitreous humor.

---

[4] The first ophthalmoscope and visualization of the eyeground.

The appearances which are concerned in all this are nothing more than shadows formed by the fibrils and the vessels, either dead or having grown up as parasites which are free in the cavity of the vitreous humor; the finer ones, according to the law of optics, are situated closer to the retina and the larger ones are farther removed from it.

If they are to be seen, it is very necessary that the rays originate only from one spot as far as possible in order that the insignificant shadows, not illuminated by the smallest side light, should not pale out. Thus an apparatus is needed which will neither cut out the light nor disperse it. The further these objects are situated from the surface of the retina, no matter what they are, whether blood vessels or fibrils, a softer light is needed and one must take care to prevent all the light from penetrating from a side; in addition, the opening must be as small as possible. The reverse applies to the objects which are placed near the retina, because the light can hardly penetrate into the eye in a lateral position, for then the shadow would completely disappear; hence, when we look on a surface which does not shine much, like the sky covered with clouds, we can notice the dots and lines mentioned.

II. These dots which Steinbuch noticed first, and described as due to the shadows of blood corpuscles, according to my views, originate in the vitreous humor near to the retina; though these bodies are very small, they reflect an image by their shadows and their focus which is illuminated by a small light on the near wall of the retina. One can best observe these floating bodies during wintertime, when we look longer either on a field covered by snow or on the sky covered by snow clouds.

For good results of these visual experiments one needs first of all a large, mildly illuminated, reflecting background; then he must look into the flame of the candle through a larger lens, the focus of which is two or three inches and at a distance from which the light can be seen the more dispersed, the more subdued. Here in a short time the whole visual field will be filled with spots, fibrils, and knotted threads and it will seem peculiar that the external objects can find place there and that they can reach the retina through the interrupted light.

III. It is not easy to decide whether the halos and the rainbows which we frequently find at certain distances as they surround the light of the candle are in the aqueous humor or in the vitreous or somewhere in the lens. That they are entirely subjective is shown by their immediate disappearance when the image of the flame is covered by a finger raised in the axis of vision. This, however, does not happen with the halos surrounding the moon or the sun, where the reason for their occurrence must be sought in the atmospheric vapors.

29. The study of the retina, besides the illumination of the vitreous humor, offers no objective signs. However, the greater number of signs present can be recognized subjectively. It would be necessary to study this large number of subjective appearances in a great number of individuals. It seems that the majority of people do not have the ability to observe or to describe correctly these phenomena or a love for science sufficient to subject their organs to difficult, though harmless experiments.

It would be necessary to investigate:

a. The sensitivity of the retina in the presence of brighter or more subdued light. One would need to investigate in what degree of light and in what degree of darkness the individual can recognize certain objects of a fixed size and how bright a light the eye can bear without causing tears.

b. In different people the ability to observe the picture varies, since, after a view of colors, there arises in the eye in an opposite and polar-like manner an afterimage, which in a measurable time persists.

c. The illumination appearances in the eye stimulated by the effect of galvanic current can be exhibited the more readily and with lessened effort in people who have a more sensitive nervous system. The great difficulty here is to have a constant and fixed measure of galvanic current, which would show as a measurement the variations in individuals.

d. Easily accessible are the appearances caused by pressure on the eyeball, which can be done without doing any harm to the inner eye vision unless there be prejudices against it or fear.

e. There will be but few people who, superficially and by chance, have not noticed sparks and a fiery circle, noticeable in the dark, especially toward morning, after a sudden turn of the eye toward the nose.

f. The study of the vessels requires finer and more ingenious observations and practice. According to my views, this study should be of the central artery of the retina, which can best be located for observation when we slowly move the candlelight in the circle of the visual field.

g. The ability of direct and indirect vision by various individuals should also be investigated, because from this the connection of the psyche with the sense organs becomes evident.

30. These and similar appearances, all of which one should enumerate completely and should be left to another place, one cannot leave out in a physiological study.

The main one shows the relationship of the eye to the central strength of the brain or the soul. The eye, by its uninterrupted relation to the brain, appears to be a special organ of fantasy.

The greater the energy with which the eye is permeated by the soul, the more the inner attention of the mind is illuminated and filled with the light of consciousness; the quicker and clearer the various intuitions which appear to the eye; the sooner this sense shall rise in some manner to the organ of thought. This noble character of the eye, which ap-

proaches the nobility of the spirit, does show itself when we observe it and when we concentrate our attention on the eye, its free and planned motility in the correct and penetrating direction toward its goal, whereby we can easily differentiate a glance which is sharp, firm, and conscious from a dull, roving, and unclear one. How remarkable is the harmony between the movement of the eyes and the rest of the bodily movements we notice often and not without wonderment in the case of musicians, actors, or artists. Nor must we overlook the skill of the gymnasts, the hunters, and those in the different trades, where the most varied association between the eyes and the hands is considered a very rich and abundant source of skill and dexterity in performing a difficult task.

Those who possess a store of medical experiences will readily add to the physiological moments of semiology those from pathology, for nature is a unit and from it there arise the appearances of life, healthy or ill; similarly let us make experiments in a unified manner about its existence. As we look on light objects where we can differentiate more easily the parts near the shadow, in the same manner, the pathological is illuminated by the physiological and in reverse, being illuminated, it forms in the mind a pleasant and a brilliant picture of its own.

9

German Experimental Psychology

ERNST HEINRICH WEBER
(1795–1878)

Weber's Law [1]

In comparing objects and observing the distinction between them, we perceive not the difference between the objects, but the ratio

of this difference to the magnitude of the objects compared. If we are comparing by touch two weights, the one of 30 and the other of 29 half-ounces, the difference is not more easily perceived than that between weights of 30 and 29 drachms.... Since the distinction is not perceived more easily in the former case than in the latter, it is clear that not the weights of the differences but their

---

[1] Ernst Heinrich Weber, *De Tactu* (Leipzig, 1834), trans. E. B. Titchener in *Experimental Psychology* (New York: Macmillan, 1905), vol. 2, pt. 2, p. xvi.

ratios are perceived. . . . Experience has taught us that apt and practised 0's sense the difference between weights, if it is not less than the thirtieth part of the heavier weight, and that the same 0's perceive the difference not less easily, if drachms are put in the place of half-ounces.

That which I have set forth with regard to weights compared by touch holds also of lines to be compared by sight. For, whether you compare longer or shorter lines, you will find that the difference is not sensed by most 0's if the second line is less by a hundredth part. . . . The length in which the distinction resides, therefore, although [in the case of lines of 50 and 50.5 mm.] it is twice as small [as it is in the case of lines of 100 and 101 mm.], is nevertheless no less easily apprehended, for the reason that in both cases the difference of the compared lines is one hundredth of the longer line.

I have made no experiments upon comparison of tones by the ear. [Delezenne, however, determined the j. n. d. of the b of 240 vs.] As this author does not say that this difference is discriminated less easily in deeper, more easily in higher tones, and as I have never heard that a difference is more easily perceived in higher tones, . . . I imagine that in audition also not the absolute difference between the vibrations of two tones, but the relative compared with the number of vibrations of the tones is discriminated.

The observation, confirmed in several departments of sense, that in observing the distinction between objects we perceive not the absolute but the relative differences, has again and again impelled me to investigate the cause of this phenomenon; and I hope that when this cause is sufficiently understood, we shall be able to judge more correctly regarding the nature of the senses.

* * * * *

The [2] smallest perceptible difference between two weights, which we can distinguish by the feeling of muscular exertion, appears according to my experiments to be that between weights which stand approximately in the

relation of 39 to 40: that is to say, of which one is about 1–40 heavier than the other. By means of the feeling of pressure, which two weights make upon our skin, all we are able to distinguish is a difference of weight that amounts to only 1–30, so that the weights accordingly stand in the relation of 29 to 30.

If we look at one line after another, any one who possesses a very exceptional visual discrimination can according to my experiments discover a difference between two lines whose lengths are related as 50 : 51, or even as 100 : 101. Those who have a less delicate visual discrimination distinguish lines, which are separated from one another by 1–25 of their length. The smallest perceptible difference of the pitch of two tones, (which are really in unison), that a musician perceives, if he hears two tones successively, is according to Delezenne 1–4 *Komma* (81–80) 1–4. A lover of music according to him distinguishes only about 1–2 *Komma* (81–80) 1–2. If the tones are heard simultaneously we cannot, according to Delezenne's experiments, perceive such small tonal differences. 1–4 *Komma* is nearly the relation of 321 : 322, but 1–2 *Komma* is nearly the relation of 160 : 161.

I have shown that the result in the determinations of weight is the same, whether one takes ounces or half ounces; for it does not depend upon the number of grains that form the increment of weight, but depends on the fact that this increment makes up the thirtieth of fiftieth [should be fortieth] part of the weight which we are comparing with the second weight. This likewise holds true of the comparison of the length of two lines and of the pitch of two tones. It makes no difference whether we compare lines that are, say, two inches or one inch long, if we examine them successively, and can see them lying parallel to each other; and yet the extent by which the one line exceeds the other is in the former case twice as great as in the latter. To be sure, if both lines lie close together and parallel, we compare only the ends of the lines to discover how much the one line exceeds the other; and in this test the question is only how great that length of line which overlaps the other really is, and how near the two lines lie to one another.

So too in the comparison of the pitch of two tones, it does not matter whether the two tones are seven tonal stops [i.e. an octave]

[2] Ernst Heinrich Weber, *The Sense of Touch and the Common Feeling*, trans. Benjamin Rand, ed., in *The Classical Psychologists* (Boston: Houghton Mifflin, 1912), pp. 557–561; original German, *Der Tastsinn und das Gemeingefühl* (Braunschweig, 1846).

higher or lower, provided only they do not lie at the end of the tonal series, where the exact discrimination of small tonal differences becomes more difficult. Here again, therefore, it is not a question of the number of vibrations, by which the one tone exceeds the other, but of the relation of the numbers of the vibrations of the two tones which we are comparing. If we counted the vibrations of the two tones it would be conceivable, that we should pay attention only to the number of vibrations by which one tone exceeds the other. If we fix the eyes first upon one line and afterwards upon a second, and thus permit both to be pictured successively upon the most sensitive parts of the retina, we should be inclined to suppose, that we compared the traces of the impression which the first image left, with the impression which the second image made upon the same parts of the retina, and that we thereby perceived how much the second image exceeds the first, and conversely. For this is the way we compare two scale-units: we place one upon the other, so that they coincide, and thus perceive how much the one exceeds the other. From the fact, that we do not employ this method which is so very advantageous, it seems to follow, that we are unable to employ it, and that therefore the preceding impression left behind no such trace upon the retina, or in the brain, as would permit of comparison in the manner mentioned with succeeding impressions. That it is possible for us to proceed otherwise in the comparison of the length of two lines appears from the fact, that we can compare two lines, which are longer than we can picture at once in their entirety on the most sensitive part of the retina. In this case we must move the eye and thereby cause the different parts of the same line to be pictured successively upon the same parts of the retina. Under these circumstances we must take account of the movement of the eye, and only thus do we form an idea of the length of the lines. Were the impressions of visible things, which we preserve in memory, traces, which the sensuous impressions left behind in the brain, and whose spatial relations corresponded to the spatial relations of the sensuous impressions, and

were thus so to speak photographs of the same, it would be difficult to remember a figure, which is larger than could be pictured at once wholly upon the sensitive part of the retina. It appears to me, indeed, as if a figure, which we can survey at a single glance, impressed itself better upon our memory and our imagination, than a figure, which we can survey only successively by moving the eyes; but we can nevertheless represent also the former by means of the imagination. But in this case the representation of the whole figure seems to be composed by us of the parts which we perceive all at once.

If we compare two lines, which are 20 and 21 *Linien* [i.e. 1–10 of an inch] long, the latter is 1–20 longer, but the absolute difference of length amounts to 1 *Linie*. If, on the other hand, we compare two lines, which are 1 *Linie* and 1.05 *Linie* long, the difference amounts also to 1–20, but the line is only 1–20 longer than the other. Consequently in the latter case the absolute difference is 20 times smaller. But 1–20 *Linie* is a size like a fine pinhole which lies at the very threshold of vision. The smallest possible point that we are able to see, is one whose diameter amounts to 1–20 *Linie*, and yet one who has a very good visual discrimination can distinguish in respect to their length two lines of which one is 1–20 *Linie* longer than the other. Two observers, before whom I placed such lines, both distinguished the longer from the shorter, and their visual discrimination extended even farther. I myself distinguished two lines, whose relative difference of length amounted to 1–20, and of which the one was between 1–17 and 1–18 longer than the other. The apprehension of the relations of whole magnitudes, without our having measured the magnitudes by a smaller scale-unit, and without our having ascertained the absolute difference between them, is a most interesting psychological phenomenon. In music we apprehend the relations of tone, without knowing their rate of vibration [i.e., their absolute pitch]; in architecture, the relation of spatial magnitudes, without having determined them by inches; and in the same way we apprehend the magnitudes of sensation or of force in the comparison of weights.

GUSTAV THEODOR FECHNER
(1801–1887)

Weber-Fechner Law [3]

Weber's law, that equal relative increments of stimuli are proportional to equal increments of sensation, is, in consideration of its generality and the wide limits within which it is absolutely or approximately valid, to be considered fundamental for psychic measurement.

* * * * *

Although not as yet having a measurement for sensation, still one can combine in an exact formula the relation expressed in Weber's law,—that the sensation difference remains constant when the relative stimulus difference remains constant,—with the law, established by the mathematical auxiliary principle, that small sensation increments are proportional to stimulus increments. Let us suppose, as has generally been done in the attempts to preserve Weber's law, that the difference between two stimuli, or, what is the same, the increase in one stimulus, is very small in proportion to the stimulus itself. Let the stimulus which is increased be called β, the small increase $d\beta$, where the letter d is to be considered not as a special magnitude, but simply as a sign that $d\beta$ is the small increment of β. This already suggests the differential sign. The relative stimulus increase therefore is $d\beta/\beta$. On the other hand, let the sensation which is dependent upon the stimulus β be called γ, and let the small increment of the sensation which results from the increase of the stimulus by $d\beta$ be called $d\gamma$, where d again simply expresses the small increment. The terms $d\beta$ and $d\gamma$ are each to be considered as referring to an arbitrary unit of their own nature.

According to the empirical Weber's law, $d\gamma$ remains constant when $d\beta/\beta$ remains constant, no matter what absolute values $d\beta$ and β take; and according to the *a priori* mathematical auxiliary principle the changes $d\gamma$ and $d\beta$ remain proportional to one another

so long as they remain very small. The two relations may be expressed together in the following equation:

$$d\gamma = \mathrm{K}d\beta/\beta \qquad (1)$$

where $\varkappa$ is a constant (dependent upon the units selected for γ and β). In fact, if one multiplies βd and β by any number, so long as it is the same number for both, the proportion remains constant, and with it also the sensation difference $d\gamma$. This is Weber's law. If one doubles or triples the value of the variation $d\beta$ without changing the initial value β, then the value of the change $d\gamma$ is also doubled or tripled. This is the mathematical principle. The equation $d\gamma = \mathrm{K}d\beta/\beta$ therefore entirely satisfies both Weber's law and this principle; and no other equation satisfies both together. This is to be called the *fundamental formula*, in that the deduction of all consequent formulas will be based upon it.

The fundamental formula does not presuppose the measurement of sensation, nor does it establish any; it simply expresses the relation holding between small relative stimulus increments and sensation increments. In short, it is nothing more than Weber's law and the mathematical auxiliary principle united and expressed in mathematical symbols.

There is, however, another formula connected with this formula by infinitesimal calculus, which expresses a general quantitative relation between the stimulus magnitude as a summation of stimulus increments, and the sensation magnitude as a summation of sensation increments, in such a way, that with the validity of the first formula, together with the assumption of the fact of limen, the validity of this latter formula is also given. . . .

One can readily see, that the relation between the increments $d\gamma$ and $d\beta$ in the fundamental formula corresponds to the relation between the increments of a logarithm and the increments of the corresponding number. For as one can easily convince oneself, either from theory or from the table, the logarithm does not increase by equal increments when the corresponding number increases by equal increments, but rather when the latter increases by equal relative amounts; in other

[3] Gustav Theodor Fechner, *Elements of Psychophysics*, trans. Herbert Sidney Langfeld in Benjamin Rand, ed., *The Classical Psychologists, op. cit.;* original German, *Elemente der Psychophysik* (Leipzig, 1860).

words, the increases in the logarithms remain equal, when the relative increases of the numbers remain equal. Thus, for example, the following numbers and logarithms belong together:

Number	Logarithm
10	1.000000
11	1.0413927
100	2.000000
110	2.0413927
1000	3.000000
1100	3.0413927

where an increase of the number 10 by 1 brings with it just as great an increase in the corresponding logarithm, as the increase of the number 100 by 10 or 1000 by 100. In each instance the increase in the logarithm is 0.0413927. Further, as was already shown in explaining the mathematical auxiliary principle, the increases in the logarithms are proportional to the increases of the numbers, so long as they remain very small. Therefore one can say, that Weber's law and the mathematical auxiliary principle are just as valid for the increases of logarithms and numbers in their relation to one another, as they are for the increases of sensation and stimulus.

The fact of the threshold appears just as much in the relation of a logarithm to its number as in the relation of sensation to stimulus. The sensation begins with values above zero, not with zero, but with a finite value of the stimulus—the threshold; and so does the logarithm begin with values above zero, not with a zero value of the number, but with a finite value of the number, the value 1, inasmuch as the logarithm of 1 is equal to zero.

If now, as was shown above, the increase of sensation and stimulus stands in a relation similar to that of the increase of logarithm and number, and, the point at which the sensation begins to assume a noticeable value stands in a relation to the stimulus similar to that which the point at which the logarithm attains positive value stands to the number, then one may also expect that sensation and stimulus themselves stand in a relation to one another similar to that of logarithm to number, which, just as the former (sensation and stimulus) may be regarded as made up of a sum of successive increments.

Accordingly the simplest relation between the two that we can write is $\gamma = \log \beta$.

In fact it will soon be shown that, provided suitable units of sensation and stimulus are chosen, the functional relation between both reduces to this very simple formula. Meanwhile it is not the most general formula that can be derived, but one which is only valid under the supposition of particular units of sensation and stimulus, and we still need a direct and absolute deduction instead of the indirect and approximate one.

The specialist sees at once how this may be attained, namely, by treating the fundamental formula as a differential formula and integrating it. In the following chapter one will find this done. Here it must be supposed already carried out, and those who are not able to follow the simple infinitesimal deduction, must be asked to consider the result as a mathematical fact. This result is the following functional formula between stimulus and sensation, which goes by the name of the measurement formula and which will now be further discussed:

$$\gamma = \varkappa (\log \beta - \log b) \qquad (2)$$

In this formula $\varkappa$ again stands for a constant, dependent upon the unit selected and also the logarithmic system, and b a second constant which stands for the threshold value of the stimulus, at which the sensation γ begins and disappears.

According to the rule, that the logarithm of a quotient of two numbers may be substituted for the difference of their logarithms, ... one can substitute for the above form of the measurement formula the following, which is more convenient for making deductions.

$$\gamma = \varkappa \log \beta/b \qquad (3)$$

From this equation it follows that the sensation magnitude γ is not to be considered as a simple function of the stimulus value β, but of its relation to the threshold value b, where the sensation begins and disappears. This relative stimulus value, β/b is for the future to be called the fundamental stimulus value, or the fundamental value of the stimulus.

Translated in words, the measurement formula reads:

The magnitude of the sensation (γ) is not

proportional to the absolute value of the stimulus (β), but rather to the logarithm of the magnitude of the stimulus, when this last is expressed in terms of its threshold value (b), i.e. that magnitude considered as unit at which the sensation begins and disappears. In short, it is proportional to the logarithm of the fundamental stimulus value.

Before we proceed further, let us hasten to show that that relation between stimulus and sensation, from which the measurement formula is derived, may be correctly deduced in turn from it, and that this latter thus finds its verification in so far as these relations are found empirically. We have here at the same time the simplest examples of the application of the measurement formula.

The measurement formula is founded upon Weber's law and the fact of the stimulus threshold; and both must follow in turn from it.

Now as to Weber's law. In the form that equal increments of sensation are proportional to relative stimulus increments, it may be obtained by differentiating the measurement formula, inasmuch as in this way one returns to the fundamental formula, which contains the expression of the law in this form.

In the form, that equal sensation differences correspond to equal relations of stimulus, the law may be deduced in quite an elementary manner as follows.

Let two sensations, whose difference is to be considered, be called γ and γ', and the corresponding stimuli β and β'. Then according to the measurement formula

$$\gamma = \varkappa \,(\log \beta - \log b)$$
$$\gamma' = \varkappa \,(\log \beta' - \log b)$$

and likewise for the sensation difference

$$\gamma - \gamma' = \varkappa \,(\log \beta - \log \beta')$$

or, since $\log \beta - \log \beta' = \log \beta/\beta'$

$$\gamma - \gamma' = \varkappa \log \beta/\beta'.$$

From this formula it follows, that the sensation difference $\gamma - \gamma'$ is a function of the stimulus relation β/β', and remains the same no matter what values β, β' may take, so long as the relation remains unchanged, which is the statement of Weber's law.

In a later chapter we shall return to the above formula under the name of the difference formula, as one of the simplest consequences of the measurement formula.

As for the fact of the threshold, which i- caused by the sensation having zero value not at zero but at a finite value of the stimulus, from which point it first begins to obtain noticeable values with increasing values of stimulus, it is so far contained in the measurement formula as γ does not, according to this formula, have the value zero when $\beta = o$, but when β is equal to a finite value b. This follows as well from equation (2) as (3) of the measurement formula, directly from (2), and from (3) with the additional consideration of the fact, that when β equals b, $\log \beta/b$ equals $\log 1$, and $\log 1 = 0$.

Naturally all deduction from Weber's law and the fact of the threshold will also be deductions from our measurement formula.

It follows from the former law, that every given increment of stimulus causes an ever decreasing increment in sensation in proportion as the stimulus grows larger, and that at high values of the stimulus it is no longer sensed, while on the other hand, at low values it may appear exceptionally strong.

In fact the increase of a large number β by a given amount is accompanied by a considerably smaller increase in the corresponding logarithm γ, than the increase of a small number β by the same amount. When the number 10 is increased by 10, (that is, reaches 20), the logarithm corresponding to 10, which is 1, is increased to 1.3010. When, however, the number 1000 is increased by 10, the logarithm corresponding to 1000, namely 3, is only increased to 3.0043. In the first case the logarithm is increased by 1–3 of its amount, in the latter case by about 1–700.

In connection with the fact of the threshold belongs the deduction, that a sensation is further from the perception threshold the more the stimulus sinks under its threshold value. This distance of a sensation from the threshold, is represented in the same manner by the negative values of γ, according to our measurement formula, as the increase above the threshold is represented by the positive values.

In fact one sees directly from equation (2), that when β is smaller than b and with it $\log \beta$ smaller than $\log b$, the sensation takes on negative values, and the same deduction follows in equation (3), in that β/b' becomes a proper fraction when $\beta < b$, and the logarithm of a proper fraction is negative.

In so far as sensations, which are caused by a stimulus which is not sufficient to raise them to consciousness, are called unconscious, and those which affect consciousness are called conscious, we may say that the unconscious sensations are represented in our formula by negative, the conscious by positive values. We will return to this statement in a special chapter . . . since it is of great importance, and perhaps not directly evident to everyone. For the present I shall not let it detain me longer.

According to the foregoing our measurement formula corresponds to experience:

1. In the cases of equality, where a sensation difference remains the same when the absolute intensity of the stimulus is altered (Weber's law).

2. In the cases of the thresholds, where the sensation itself ceases, and where its change becomes either imperceptible or barely perceptible. In the former case, when the sensation reaches its lower threshold; in the latter case, when it becomes so great that a given stimulus increase is barely noticed.

3. In the contrasting cases, between sensations which rise above the threshold of consciousness and those that do not reach it,—in short, conscious and unconscious sensations. From the above measurement formula may be considered well founded.

In the measurement formula one has a general dependent relation between the size of the fundamental stimulus and the size of the corresponding sensation and not one which is valid only for the cases of equal sensations. This permits the amount of sensation to be calculated from the relative amounts of the fundamental stimulus and thus we have a measurement of sensation.

HERMANN VON HELMHOLTZ
(1821–1894)

Young-Helmholtz Three Color Theory [4]

Every difference of impression made by light, as we have seen, may be regarded as a function of three independent variables; and the three variables which have been chosen thus far were (1) the luminosity, (2) the hue, and (3) the saturation, or (1) the quantity of white, (2) the quantity of some colour of the spectrum, and (3) the wave-length of this colour. However, instead of these variables, three others may also be employed; and in fact this is what it amounts to, when all colours are regarded as being mixtures of variable amounts of *three so-called fundamental colours*, which are generally taken to be *red, yellow* and *blue*. To conceive this theory objectively, and to assert that there are simple colours in the spectrum which can be combined to produce a visual impression

that will be the same as that produced by any other simple or compound light, would not be correct. There are no such three simple colours that can be combined to match the other colours of the spectrum even fairly well, because the colours of the spectrum invariably appear to be more saturated than the composite colours. Least suited for this purpose are red, yellow and blue; for if we take for blue a colour like the hue of the sky, and not a more greenish blue, it will be impossible to get green at all by mixing these colours. By taking a greenish yellow and a greenish blue, the best we can get is a very pale green. These three colours would not have been selected, had it not been that most persons, relying on the mixture of pigments, made the mistake of thinking that a mixture of yellow and blue light gives green. It would be rather better to take *violet, green* and *red* for fundamental colours. Blue can be obtained by mixing violet and green, but it is not the saturated blue of the spectrum; and a dead yellow can be made with green and red, which is not at all like the brilliant yellow in the spectrum.

[4] Hermann von Helmholtz, *Treatise on Physiological Optics*, trans. J. P. C. Southall (Rochester, N.Y.: Optical Society of America, 1924, 1925), vol. 2, pp. 141–145; original German edition, *Handbuch der physiologischen Optik* (Leipzig, 1860). Reprinted by permission.

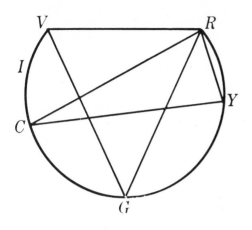

FIG. 20

If we think of the colours as plotted on a colour-chart by the method sketched above, it is evident from the rules given for the construction that all colours that are to be made by mixing three colours must be contained within the triangle whose vertices are the places in the chart where the three fundamental colours are. Thus, in the adjoining colour circle (Fig. 20), where the positions of the colours are indicated by the initial letters of their names ($I =$ indigo-blue, $C =$ cyan-blue, $Y =$ yellow, $G =$ green, etc.), all the colours that can be made by mixing red, cyan-blue and yellow are comprised within the triangle *RCY*. Thus, as we see, two large pieces of the circle are missing, and all that could be obtained would be a very pale violet and a very pale green. But if, instead of cyan-blue, the colour of the blue sky, indigo-blue, were taken, green would be missing entirely. The triangle *VRG* comprises the colours obtained by mixing violet, red and green, and a larger number of the existing colours would indeed be represented. But, as the diagram shows, large portions of the circle are still missing, as must always be the case according to the results of experiments on the mixture of the colours of the spectrum. The conclusion is that the boundary of the colour chart must be a curved line which differs considerably from the perimeter of the triangle.

Brewster, endeavouring to defend the objective nature of three fundamental colours,

maintained that for every wave-length there were three different kinds of light, red, yellow and blue, mixed merely in different proportions so as to give the different colours of the spectrum. Thus, the colours of the spectrum were considered as being compound colours consisting of three kinds of light of different quality; although the degree of refrangibility of the rays was the same for each individual simple colour. Brewster's idea was that light of all three fundamental colours could be proved to exist in the different simple colours by the absorption of light by coloured media. His entire theory is based on this conception, which was shown in the preceding chapter to be erroneous.

Apart from Brewster's hypothesis, the notion of three fundamental colours as having any objective significance has no meaning anyhow. For as long as it is simply a question of physical relations, and the human eye is left out of the game, the properties of the compound light are dependent only on the relative amounts of light of all the separate wave-lengths it contains. When we speak of reducing the colours to three fundamental colours, this must be understood in a subjective sense and as being an attempt to trace the *colour sensations* to three *fundamental sensations*. This was the way that Young regarded the problem; and, in fact, his theory affords an exceedingly simple and clear explanation of all the phenomena of the physiological colour theory. He supposes that:

1. The eye is provided with three distinct sets of nervous fibres. Stimulation of the first excites the sensation of red, stimulation of the second the sensation of green, and stimulation of the third the sensation of violet.

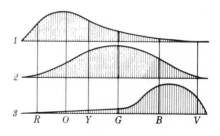

FIG. 21

2. Objective homogeneous light excites these three kinds of fibres in various degrees, depending on its wave-length. The red-sensitive fibres are stimulated most by light of longest wave-length, and the violet-sensitive fibres by light of shortest wave-length. But this does not mean that each colour of the spectrum does not stimulate all three kinds of fibres, some feebly and others strongly; on the contrary, in order to explain a series of phenomena, it is necessary to assume that that is exactly what does happen. Suppose that the colours of the spectrum are plotted horizontally in Fig. 21 in their natural sequence, from red to violet, the three curves may be taken to indicate something like the degree of excitation of the three kinds of fibres, No. 1 for the red-sensitive fibres, No. 2 for the green-sensitive fibres, and No. 3 for the violet-sensitive fibres.

Pure *red* light stimulates the red-sensitive fibres strongly and the two other kinds of fibres feebly; giving the sensation red.

Pure *yellow* light stimulates the red-sensitive and green-sensitive fibres moderately and the violet-sensitive fibres feebly; giving the sensation yellow.

Pure *green* light stimulates the green-sensitive fibres strongly, and the two other kinds much more feebly; giving the sensation green.

Pure *blue* light stimulates the green-sensitive and violet-sensitive fibres moderately, and the red-sensitive fibres feebly; giving the sensation blue.

Pure *violet* light stimulates the violet-sensitive fibres strongly, and the other fibres feebly; giving the sensation violet.

When all the fibres are stimulated about equally, the sensation is that of *white* or pale hues.

It might be natural to suppose that on this hypothesis the number of nervous fibres and nerve-endings would have to be trebled, as compared with the number ordinarily assumed when each single fibre is made to conduct all possible colour stimulations. However, in the writer's opinion there is nothing in Young's hypothesis that is opposed to the anatomical facts in this respect; because we are entirely ignorant as to the number of conducting fibres, and there are also quantities of other microscopical elements (cells, nuclei, rods) to which hitherto no spe-

cific functions could be ascribed. But this is not the essential thing in Young's hypothesis. That appears to the writer to consist rather in the idea of the colour sensations being composed of three processes in the nervous substance that are perfectly independent of one another. This independence is manifested not merely in the phenomena which are being considered at present but also in those of fatigue of the nervous mechanism of vision. It would not be absolutely necessary to assume different nervous fibres for these different sensations. So far as mere explanation is concerned, the same advantages that are afforded by Young's hypothesis could be gained by supposing that within each individual fibre there might occur three activities all different from and independent of one another. But the form of this hypothesis as originally proposed by Young is clearer in both conception and expression than it would be if it were modified as suggested, and hence it will be retained in its original concrete form, for the sake of exposition if for nothing else. Nowhere in the physical (electrical) phenomena of nervous stimulation either in the sensory or motor nerves can there be detected any such differentiation of activity as must exist if each fibre of the optic nerve has to transmit all the colour sensations. By Young's hypothesis it is possible even in this connection to transfer directly to the optic nerve the simple conceptions as to the mechanism of the stimulation and its conduction which we were led to form at first by studying the phenomena in the motor nerves. This would not be the case on the assumption that each fibre of the optic nerve has to sustain three different kinds of states of stimulation which do not mutually interfere with one another. Young's hypothesis is only a more special application of the law of specific sense energies. Just as tactile sensation and visual sensation in the eye are demonstrably affairs of different nervous fibres, the same thing is assumed here too with respect to the various sensations of the fundamental colours.

Resonance Theory of Hearing [5]

Now we cannot precisely ascertain what

---

[5] Hermann von Helmholtz, *Sensations of Tone*, trans. A. J. Ellis (London, 1885), ch. 6; original German, *Die Lehre von den Tonempfindungen* (Brunswick, 1863).

parts of the ear actually vibrate sympathetically with individual tones. We can only conjecture what they are at present in the case of human beings and mammals. The whole construction of the partition of the cochlea, and of Corti's arches which rest upon it, appears most suited for executing independent vibrations. We do not need to require of them the power of continuing their vibrations for a long time without assistance.

But if these formations are to serve for distinguishing tones of different pitch, and if tones of different pitch are to be equally well perceived in all parts of the scale, the elastic formations in the cochlea, which are connected with different nerve fibres, must be differently tuned, and their proper tones must form a regularly progressive series of degrees through the whole extent of the musical scale.

According to the recent anatomical researches of V. Hensen and C. Hasse, it is probably the breadth of the membrana basilaris in the cochlea, which determines the tuning. At its commencement opposite the oval window, it is comparatively narrow, and it continually increases in width as it approaches the apex of the cochlea. The following measurements of the membrane in a newly born child, from the line where the nerves pass through on the inner edge, to the attachment to the ligamentum spirale on the outer edge, are given by V. Hensen:—

Place of Section	Breadth of Membrane or Length of Transverse Fibres	
	Millimetres	Inches
0.2625 mm. [= 0.010335 in.] from root	0.04125	0.00162
0.8626 mm. [= 0.033961 in.] from root	0.0825	0.00325
Middle of the first spire	0.169	0.00665
End of first spire	0.3	0.01181
Middle of second spire	0.4125	0.01624
End of second spire	0.45	0.01772
At the hamulus	0.495	0.01949

The breadth therefore increases more than twelvefold from the beginning to the end.

Corti's rods also exhibit an increase of size as they approach the vertex of the cochlea, but in a much less degree than the membrana basilaris. The following are Hensen's measurements:—

	At the Round Window		At the Hamulus	
	Mm.	Inch	Mm.	Inch
Length of inner rod	0.048	0.00189	0.0855	0.00337
Length of outer rod	0.048	0.00189	0.098	0.00386
Span of the arch	0.019	0.00075	0.085	0.00335

Hence it follows, as Henle has also proved, that the greatest increase of breadth falls on the outer zone of the basilar membrane, beyond the line of the attachment of the outer rods. This increases from 0.023 mm. [= 0.000905 in.] to 0.41 mm. [= 0.016142 inch] or nearly twentyfold.

In accordance with these measures, the two rows of Corti's rods are almost parallel and upright near to the round window, but they are bent much more strongly towards one another near the vertex of the cochlea.

It has been already mentioned that the membrana basilaris of the cochlea breaks easily in the radial direction, but that its radial fibres have considerable tenacity. This seems to me to furnish a very important mechanical relation, namely, that this membrane in its natural connection admits of being tightly stretched in the transverse direction from the modiolus to the outer wall of the cochlea, but can have only little tension in the direction of its length, because it could not resist a strong pull in this direction.

Now the mathematical theory of the vibration of a membrane with different tensions in different directions shews that it behaves very differently from a membrane which has the same tension in all directions. On the latter, vibrations produced in one part, spread uniformly in all directions, and hence if the tension were uniform it would be impossible to set one part of the basilar membrane in vibration, without producing nearly as strong vibrations (disregarding individual nodal lines) in all other parts of the membrane.

But if the tension in direction of its length is infinitesimally small in comparison with the tension in direction of the breadth, then the radial fibres of the basilar membrane may be approximatively regarded as forming a system of stretched strings, and the membranous connection as only serving to give a fulcrum to the pressure of the fluid against these strings. In that case the laws of their motion would be the same as if every individual string moved independently of all the others, and obeyed, by itself, the influence of the periodically alternating pressure of the fluid of the labyrinth contained in the vestibule gallery. Consequently any exciting tone would set that part of the membrane into sympathetic vibration, for which the proper tone of one of its radial fibres that are stretched and loaded with the various appendages already described, corresponds most nearly with the exciting tone; and thence the vibrations will extend with rapidly diminishing strength on to the adjacent parts of the membrane. . . .

The strongly vibrating parts of the membrane would, as has been explained in respect to all bodies which vibrate sympathetically, be more or less limited, according to the degree of damping power in the adjacent parts, by friction against the fluid in the labyrinth and in the soft gelatinous parts of the nerve fillet.

Under these circumstances the parts of the membrane in unison with higher tones must be looked for near the round window, and those with the deeper, near the vertex of the cochlea, as Hensen also concluded from his measurements. That such short strings should be capable of corresponding with such deep tones, must be explained by their being loaded in the basilar membrane with all kinds of solid formations; the fluid of both galleries in the cochlea must also be considered as weighting the membrane, because it cannot move without a kind of wave motion in that fluid.

The observations of Hasse shew that Corti's arches do not exist in the cochlea of birds and amphibia, although the other essential parts of the cochlea, as the basilar membrane, the ciliated cells in connection with the terminations of the nerves, and Corti's membrane, which stands opposite the ends of these ciliae,

are all present. Hence it becomes very probable that Corti's arches play only a secondary part in the function of the cochlea. Perhaps we might look for the effect of Corti's arches in their power, as relatively firm objects, of transmitting the vibrations of the basilar membrane to small limited regions of the upper part of the relatively thick nervous fillet, better than it could be done by the immediate communication of the vibrations of the basilar membrane through the soft mass of this fillet. Close to the outside of the upper end of the arch, connected with it by the stiffer fibriles of the membrana reticularis, are the ciliated cells of the nervous fillet. . . . In birds, on the other hand, the ciliated cells form a thin stratum upon the basilar membrane, and this stratum can readily receive limited vibrations from the membrane, without communicating them too far sideways.

According to this view Corti's arches, in the last resort, will be the means of transmitting the vibrations received from the basilar membrane to the terminal appendages of the conducting nerve. In this sense the reader is requested hereafter to understand references to the vibrations, proper tone, and intonation of Corti's arches; the intonation meant is that which they receive through their connection with the corresponding part of the basilar membrane.

According to Waldeyer there are about 4500 outer arch fibres in the human cochlea. If we deduct 300 for the simple tones which lie beyond musical limits, and cannot have their pitch perfectly apprehended, there remain 4,200 for the seven octaves of musical instruments, that is, 600 for every Octave, 50 for every Semitone (that is, 1 for every 2 cents); certainly quite enough to explain the power of distinguishing small parts of a Semitone. According to Prof. W. Preyer's investigations, practised musicians can distinguish with certainty a difference of pitch arising from half a vibration in a second, in the doubly accented Octave. This would give 1,000 distinguishable degrees of pitch in the Octave, from 500 to 1,000 vibrations in the second. Towards the limits of the scale the power to distinguish differences diminishes. The 4,200 Corti's arches appear then, in this respect, to be enough to apprehend distinctions of this amount of delicacy. But even if it should be found that many more than 4,200 degrees of pitch could be distinguished in the Octave, it would not prejudice our assumption. For if a simple tone is struck having a pitch between those of two adjacent Corti's arches, it would set them both in sympathetic vibration, and that arch would vibrate the more strongly which was nearest in pitch to the proper tone. The smallness of the interval between the pitches of two fibres still distinguishable, will therefore finally depend upon the delicacy with which the different forces of the vibrations excited can be compared. And we have thus also an explanation of the fact that as the pitch of an external tone rises continuously, our sensations also alter continuously and not by jumps, as must be the case if only one of Corti's arches were set in sympathetic motion at once.

To draw further conclusions from our hypothesis, when a simple tone is presented to the ear, those Corti's arches which are nearly or exactly in unison with it will be strongly excited, and the rest only slightly or not at all. Hence every simple note of determinate pitch will be felt only by certain nerve fibres, and simple tones of different pitch will excite different fibres. When a compound musical tone or chord is presented to the ear, all those elastic bodies will be excited, which have a proper pitch corresponding to the various individual simple tones contained in the whole mass of tones, and hence by properly directing attention, all the individual sensations of the individual simple tones can be perceived. The chord must be resolved into its individual compound tones, and the compound tone into its individual harmonic partial tones.

This also explains how it is that the ear resolves a motion of the air into pendular vibrations and no other. Any particle of air can of course execute only one motion at one time. That we considered such a motion mathematically as a sum of pendular vibrations, was in the first instance merely an arbitrary assumption to facilitate theory, and had no meaning in nature. The first meaning in nature that we found for this resolution came from considering sympathetic vibration, when we discovered that a motion which was not pendular, could produce sympathetic vibrations in bodies of those different pitches, which corresponded to the harmonic upper partial tones. And now our hypothesis has also reduced the phenomenon of hearing to

that of sympathetic vibration, and thus furnished a reason why an originally simple periodic vibration of the air produces a sum of different sensations, and hence also appears as compound to our perceptions.

The sensation of different pitch would consequently be a sensation in different nerve fibres. The sensation of a quality of tone would depend upon the power of a given compound tone to set in vibration not only those of Corti's arches which correspond to its prime tone, but also a series of other arches, and hence to excite sensation in several different groups of nerve fibres.

Physiologically it should be observed that the present assumption reduces sensations which differ qualitatively according to pitch and quality of tone, to a difference in the nerve fibres which are excited. This is a step similar to that taken in a wider field by Johannes Müller in his theory of the specific energies of sense. He has shewn that the difference in the sensations due to various senses, does not depend upon the actions which excite them, but upon the various nervous arrangements which receive them. We can convince ourselves experimentally that in whatever manner the optic nerve and its expansion, the retina of the eye, may be excited, by light, by twitching, by pressure, or by electricity, the result is never anything but a sensation of light, and that the tactual nerves, on the contrary, never give us sensations of light or of hearing or of taste. The same solar rays which are felt as light by the eye, are felt by the nerves of the hand as heat; the same agitations which are felt by the hand as twitterings, are tone to the ear.

Just as the ear apprehends vibrations of different periodic time as tones of different pitch, so does the eye perceive luminiferous vibrations of different periodic time as different colours, the quickest giving violet and blue, the mean green and yellow, the slowest red. The laws of the mixture of colours led Thomas Young to the hypothesis that there were three kinds of nerve fibres in the eye, with different powers of sensation, for feeling red, for feeling green, and for feeling violet. In reality this assumption gives a very simple and perfectly consistent explanation of all the optical phenomena depending on colour. And by this means the qualitative differences of the sensations of sight are reduced to differences in the nerves which receive the sensations. For the sensations of each individual fibre of the optic nerve there remains only the quantitative differences of greater or less irritation.

The same result is obtained for hearing by the hypothesis to which our investigation of quality of tone has led us. The qualitative difference of pitch and quality of tone is reduced to a difference in the fibres of the nerves receiving the sensation, and for each individual fibre of the nerve there remains only the quantitative differences in the amount of excitement.

The processes of irritation within the nerves of the muscles, by which their contraction is determined, have hitherto been more accessible to physiological investigation than those which take place in the nerves of sense. In those of the muscle, indeed, we find only quantitative differences of more or less excitement, and no qualitative differences at all. In them we are able to establish, that during excitement the electrically active particles of the nerves undergo determinate changes, and that these changes ensue in exactly the same way whatever be the excitement which causes them. But precisely the same changes also take place in an excited nerve of sense, although their consequence in this case is a sensation, while in the other it was a motion; and hence we see that the mechanism of the process of irritation in the nerves of sense must be in every respect similar to that in the nerves of motion. The two hypotheses just explained really reduce the processes in the nerves of man's two principal senses, notwithstanding their apparently involved qualitative differences of sensations, to the same simple scheme with which we are familiar in the nerves of motion. Nerves have been often and not unsuitably compared to telegraph wires. Such a wire conducts one kind of electric current and no other; it may be stronger, it may be weaker, it may move in either direction; it has no other qualitative differences. Nevertheless, according to the different kinds of apparatus with which we provide its terminations, we can send telegraphic despatches, ring bells, explode mines, decompose water, move magnets, magnetise iron, develop light, and so on. So with the nerves. The condition of excitement which can be produced in them, and is conducted by them, is, so far as it can be recognised in isolated fibres of a nerve, everywhere the same, but when it is brought to various parts of the brain, or the body, it produces motion, secretions of glands, increase and decrease of the quantity of blood, of redness and of warmth of individual organs, and also sensations of light, of hearing, and so forth. Supposing that every qualitatively different action is produced in an organ of a different kind, to which also separate fibres of never must proceed, then the actual process of irritation in individual nerves may always be precisely the same, just as the electrical current in the telegraph wires remains one and the same notwithstanding the various kinds of effects which it produces at its extremities. On the other hand, if we assume that the same fibre of a nerve is capable of conducting different kinds of sensation, we should have to assume that it admits of various kinds of processes of irritation, and this we have been hitherto unable to establish.

Empirical Theory of Perception and the Theory of Unconscious Inference [6]

When the modes of stimulation of the organs of sense are unusual, incorrect ideas of objects are apt to be formed; which used to be described, therefore, as *illusions of the senses.* Obviously, in these cases there is nothing wrong with the activity of the organ of sense and its corresponding nervous mechanism which produces the illusion. Both of them have to act according to the laws that govern their activity once for all. It is rather simply an illusion in the judgment of the material presented to the senses, resulting in a false idea of it.

The psychic activities that lead us to infer that there in front of us at a certain place there is a certain object of a certain character, are generally not conscious activities, but unconscious ones. In their result they are equivalent to a *conclusion*, to the extent that the observed action on our senses enables us to form an idea as to the possible cause of this action; although, as a matter of fact, it is invariably simply the nervous stimulations

[6] Hermann von Helmholtz, *Handbook of Physiological Optics, op. cit.,* vol. 3, pp. 4–13, 17. Reprinted by permission.

that are perceived directly, that is, the actions, but never the external objects themselves. But what seems to differentiate them from a conclusion, in the ordinary sense of that word, is that a conclusion is an act of conscious thought. An astronomer, for example, comes to real conscious conclusions of this sort, when he computes the positions of the stars in space, their distances, etc., from the perspective images he has had of them at various times and as they are seen from different parts of the orbit of the earth. His conclusions are based on a conscious knowledge of the laws of optics. In the ordinary acts of vision this knowledge of optics is lacking. Still it may be permissible to speak of the psychic acts of ordinary perception as *unconscious conclusions*, thereby making a distinction of some sort between them and the common so-called conscious conclusions. And while it is true that there has been, and probably always will be, a measure of doubt as to the similarity of the psychic activity in the two cases, there can be no doubt as to the similarity between the results of such unconscious conclusions and those of conscious conclusions.

These unconscious conclusions derived from sensation are equivalent in their consequences to the so-called *conclusions from analogy*. Inasmuch as in an overwhelming majority of cases, whenever the parts of the retina in the outer corner of the eye are stimulated, it has been found to be due to external light coming into the eye from the direction of the bridge of the nose, the inference we make is that it is so in every new case whenever this part of the retina is stimulated; just as we assert that every single individual now living will die, because all previous experience has shown that all men who were formerly alive have died.

But, moreover, just because they are not free acts of conscious thought, these unconscious conclusions from analogy are irresistible, and the effect of them cannot be overcome by a better understanding of the real relations. It may be ever so clear how we get an idea of a luminous phenomenon in the field of vision when pressure is exerted on the eye; and yet we cannot get rid of the conviction that this appearance of light is actually there at the given place in the visual field; and we cannot seem to comprehend that there is a luminous phenomenon at the place where the

retina is stimulated. It is the same way in case of all the images that we see in optical instruments.

On the other hand, there are numerous illustrations of fixed and inevitable associations of ideas due to frequent repetition, even when they have no natural connection, but are dependent merely on some conventional arrangement, as, for example, the connection between the written letters of a word and its sound and meaning. Still to many physiologists and psychologists the connection between the sensation and the conception of the object usually appears to be so rigid and obligatory that they are not much disposed to admit that, to a considerable extent at least, it depends on acquired experience, that is, on psychic activity. On the contrary, they have endeavoured to find some mechanical mode of origin for this connection through the agency of imaginary organic structures. With regard to this question, all those experiences are of much significance which show how the judgment of the senses may be modified by experience and by training derived under various circumstances, and may be adapted to the new conditions. Thus, persons may learn in some measure to utilize details of the sensation which otherwise would escape notice and not contribute to obtaining any idea of the object. On the other hand, too, this new habit may acquire such a hold that when the individual in question is back again in the old original normal state, he may be liable to illusions of the senses.

Facts like these show the widespread influence that experience, training and habit have on our perceptions. But how far their influence really does extend, it would perhaps be impossible to say precisely at present. Little enough is definitely known about infants and very young animals, and the interpretation of such observations as have been made on them is extremely doubtful. Besides, no one can say that infants are entirely without experience and practice in tactile sensations and bodily movements. Accordingly, the rule given above has been stated in a form which does not anticipate the decision of this question. It merely expresses what the result is. And so it can be accepted even by those who have entirely different opinions as to the way ideas originate concerning objects in the external world.

Another general characteristic property of our sense-perceptions is, that *we are not in the habit of observing our sensations accurately, except as they are useful in enabling us to recognize external objects. On the contrary, we are wont to disregard all those parts of the sensations that are of no importance so far as external objects are concerned.* Thus in most cases some special assistance and training are needed in order to observe these latter subjective sensations. It might seem that nothing could be easier than to be conscious of one's own sensations; and yet experience shows that for the discovery of subjective sensations some special talent is needed, such as Purkinje [Purkyne] manifested in the highest degree; or else it is the result of accident or of theoretical speculation. For instance, the phenomena of the blind spot were discovered by Mariotte from theoretical considerations. Similarly, in the domain of hearing, I discovered the existence of those combination tones which I have called summation tones. In the great majority of cases, doubtless it was accident that revealed this or that subjective phenomenon to observers who happened to be particularly interested in such matters. It is only when subjective phenomena are so prominent as to interfere with the perception of things, that they attract everybody's attention. Once the phenomena have been discovered, it is generally easier for others to perceive them also, provided the proper precautions are taken for observing them, and the attention is concentrated on them. In many cases, however—for example, in the phenomena of the blind spot, or in the separation of the overtones and combination tones from the fundamental tones of musical sounds, etc.—such an intense concentration of attention is required that, even with the help of convenient external appliances, many persons are unable to perform the experiments. Even the after-images of bright objects are not perceived by most persons at first except under particularly favourable external conditions. It takes much more practice to see the fainter kinds of after-images. A common experience, illustrative of this sort of thing, is for a person who has some ocular trouble that impairs his vision to become suddenly aware of the so-called *mouches volantes* in his visual field, although the causes of this phenomenon have been there in the vitreous humor all his life. Yet now

he will be firmly persuaded that these corpuscles have developed as the result of his ocular ailment, although the truth simply is that, owing to his ailment, the patient has been paying more attention to visual phenomena. No doubt, also, there are cases where one eye has gradually become blind, and yet the patient has continued to go about for an indefinite time without noticing it, until he happened one day to close the good eye without closing the other, and so noticed the blindness of that eye.

When a person's attention is directed for the first time to the double images in binocular vision, he is usually greatly astonished to think that he had never noticed them before, especially when he reflects that the only objects he has ever seen single were those few that happened at the moment to be about as far from his eyes as the point of fixation. The great majority of objects, comprising all those that were farther or nearer than this point, were all seen double.

Accordingly, the first thing we have to learn is to pay heed to our individual sensations. Ordinarily we do so merely in case of those sensations that enable us to find out about the world around us. In the ordinary affairs of life the sensations have no other importance for us. Subjective sensations are of interest chiefly for scientific investigations only. If they happen to be noticed in the ordinary activity of the senses, they merely distract the attention. Thus while we may attain an extraordinary degree of delicacy and precision in objective observation, we not only fail to do so in subjective observations, but indeed we acquire the faculty in large measure of overlooking them and of forming our opinions of objects independently of them, even when they are so pronounced that they might easily be noticed.

The most universal sign by which subjective visual phenomena can be identified appears to be by the way they accompany the movement of the eye over the field of view. Thus, the after-images, the *mouches volantes*, the blind spot, and the "luminous dust" of the dark field all participate in the motions of the eye, and coincide successively with the various stationary objects in the visual field. On the other hand, if the same phenomena recur again invariably at the same places in the visual field, they may be regarded as being objective and as being connected with external bodies. This is the case with contrast phenomena produced by after-images.

The same difficulty that we have in observing subjective sensations, that is, sensations aroused by internal causes, occurs also in trying to analyze the compound sensations, invariably excited in the same connection by any simple object, and to resolve them into their separate components. In such cases experience shows us how to recognize a compound aggregate of sensations as being the sign of a simple object. Accustomed to consider the sensation-complex as a connected whole, generally we are not able to perceive the separate parts of it without external help and support. Many illustrations of this kind will be seen in the following pages. For instance the perception of the apparent direction of an object from the eye depends on the combination of those sensations by which we estimate the adjustment of the eye, and on being able to distinguish those parts of the retina where light falls from those parts where it does not fall. The perception of the solid form of an object of three dimensions is the result of the combination of two different perspective views in the two eyes. The gloss of a surface, which is apparently a simple effect, is due to differences of colouring or brightness in the images of it in the two eyes. These facts were ascertained by theory and may be verified by suitable experiments. But usually it is very difficult, if not impossible, to discover them by direct observation and analysis of the sensations alone. Even with sensations that are much more involved and always associated with frequently recurring complex objects, the oftener the same combination recurs, and the more used we have become to regarding the sensation as the normal sign of the real nature of the object, the more difficult it will be to analyze the sensation by observation alone. By way of illustration, it is a familiar experience that the colours of a landscape come out much more brilliantly and definitely by looking at them with the head on one side or upside down than they do when the head is in the ordinary upright position. In the usual mode of observation all we try to do is to judge correctly the objects as such. We know that at a certain distance green surfaces appear a little different in hue. We get in the habit of

overlooking this difference, and learn to identify the altered green of distant meadows and trees with the corresponding colour of nearer objects. In the case of very distant objects like distant ranges of mountains, little of the colour of the body is left to be seen, because it is mainly shrouded in the colour of the illuminated air. This vague blue-grey colour, bordered above by the clear blue of the sky or the red-yellow of the sunset glow, and below by the vivid green of meadows and forests, is very subject to variations by contrast. To us it is the vague and variable colour of distance. The difference in it may, perhaps, be more noticeable sometimes and with some illuminations than at other times. But we do not determine its true nature, because it is not ascribed to any definite object. We are simply aware of its variable nature. But the instant we take an unusual position, and look at the landscape with the head under one arm, let us say, or between the legs, it all appears like a flat picture; partly on account of the strange position of the image in the eye, and partly because, as we shall see presently, the binocular judgment of distance becomes less accurate. It may even happen that with the head upside down the clouds have the correct perspective, whereas the objects on the earth appear like a painting on a vertical surface, as the clouds in the sky usually do. At the same time the colours lose their associations also with near or far objects, and confront us now purely in their own peculiar differences. Then we have no difficulty in recognizing that the vague blue-grey of the far distance may indeed be a fairly saturated violet, and that the green of the vegetation blends imperceptibly through blue-green and blue into this violet, etc. This whole difference seems to me to be due to the fact that the colours have ceased to be distinctive signs of objects for us, and are considered merely as being different sensations. Consequently, we take in better their peculiar distinctions without being distracted by other considerations.

The connection between the sensations and external objects may interfere very much with the perception of their simplest relations. A good illustration of this is the difficulty about perceiving the double images of binocular vision when they can be regarded as being images of one and the same external object.

In the same way we may have similar experiences with other kinds of sensations. The sensation of the *timbre* of a sound, as I have shown elsewhere, consists of a series of sensations of its partial tones (fundamental and harmonics); but it is exceedingly difficult to analyze the compound sensation of the sound into these elementary components. The tactile sensation of wetness is composed of that of coldness and that of smoothness of surface. Consequently, on inadvertently touching a cold piece of smooth metal, we often get the impression of having touched something wet. Many other illustrations of this sort might be adduced. They all indicate that we are exceedingly well trained in finding out by our sensations the objective nature of the objects around us, but that we are completely unskilled in observing the sensations *per se*; and that the practice of associating them with things outside of us actually prevents us from being distinctly conscious of the pure sensations.

This is true also not merely with respect to qualitative differences of sensation, but it is likewise true with respect to the perception of space-relations. For example, the spectacle of a person in the act of walking is a familiar sight. We think of this motion as a connected whole, possibly taking note of some of its most conspicuous singularities. But it requires minute attention and a special choice of the point of view to distinguish the upward and lateral movements of the body in a person's gait. We have to pick out points or lines of reference in the background with which we can compare the position of his head. But look through an astronomical telescope at a crowd of people in motion far away. Their images are upside down, but what a curious jerking and swaying of the body is produced by those who are walking about! Then there is no trouble whatever in noticing the peculiar motions of the body and many other singularities of gait; and especially differences between individuals and the reasons for them, simply because this is not the everyday sight to which we are accustomed. On the other hand, when the image is inverted in this way, it is not so easy to tell whether the gait is light or awkward, dignified or graceful, as it was when the image was erect.

Consequently, it may often be rather hard to say how much of our apperceptions (*An-schauungen*) as derived by the sense of sight is due directly to sensation, and how much of them, on the other hand, is due to experience and training. The main point of controversy between various investigators in this territory is connected also with this difficulty. Some are disposed to concede to the influence of experience as much scope as possible, and to derive from it especially all notion of space. This view may be called the *empirical theory* (*empiristische Theorie*). Others, of course, are obliged to admit the influence of experience in the case of certain classes of perceptions; still with respect to certain elementary apperceptions that occur uniformly in the case of all observers, they believe it is necessary to assume a system of innate apperceptions that are not based on experience, especially with respect to space-relations. In contradistinction to the former view, this may perhaps be called the *intuition theory* (*nativistische Theorie*) of the sense-perceptions.

In my opinion the following fundamental principles should be kept in mind in this discussion.

Let us restrict the word *idea* (*Vorstellung*) to mean the image of visual objects as retained in the memory, without being accompanied by any present sense-impressions; and use the term *apperception* (*Anschauung*) to mean a perception (*Wahrnehmung*) when it is accompanied by the sense-impressions in question. The term *immediate perception* (*Perzeption*) may then be employed to denote an apperception of this nature in which there is no element whatever that is not the result of direct sensations, that is, an apperception such as might be derived without any recollection of previous experience. Obviously, therefore, one and the same apperception may be accompanied by the corresponding sensations in very different measure. Thus idea and immediate perception may be combined in the apperception in the most different proportions.

A person in a familiar room which is brightly lighted by the sun gets an apperception that is abundantly accompanied by very vivid sensations. In the same room in the evening twilight he will not be able to recognize any objects except the brighter ones, especially the windows. But whatever he does actually recognize will be so intermingled with his recollections of the furniture that he can still move about in the room with safety and locate articles he is trying to find, even when they are only dimly visible. These images would be utterly insufficient to enable him to recognize the objects without some previous acquaintance with them. Finally, he may be in the same room in complete darkness, and still be able to find his way about in it without making mistakes, by virtue of the visual impressions formerly obtained. Thus, by continually reducing the material that appeals to the senses, the perceptual-image (*Anschauungsbild*) can ultimately be traced back to the pure memory-image (*Vorstellungsbild*) and may gradually pass into it. In proportion as there is less and less material appeal to the senses, a person's movements will, of course, become more and more uncertain, and his apperception less and less accurate. Still there will be no peculiar abrupt transition, but sensation and memory will continually supplement each other, only in varying degrees.

But even when we look around a room of this sort flooded with sunshine, a little reflection shows us that under these conditions too a large part of our perceptual-image may be due to factors of memory and experience. The fact that we are accustomed to the perspective distortions of pictures of parallelopipeds and to the form of the shadows they cast has much to do with the estimation of the shape and dimensions of the room, as will be seen hereafter. Looking at the room with one eye shut, we think we see it just as distinctly and definitely as with both eyes. And yet we should get exactly the same view in case every point in the room were shifted arbitrarily to a different distance from the eye, provided they all remained on the same lines of sight.

Thus in a case like this we are really considering an extremely multiplex phenomenon of sense; but still we ascribe a perfectly definite explanation to it, and it is by no means easy to realize that the monocular image of such a familiar object necessarily means a much more meagre perception than would be obtained with both eyes. Thus too it is often hard to tell whether or not untrained observers inspecting stereoscopic views really notice the peculiar illusion produced by the instrument.

We see, therefore, how in a case of this kind reminiscences of previous experiences act in conjunction with present sensations to produce a perceptual image (*Anschauungsbild*) which imposes itself on our faculty of perception with overwhelming power, without our being conscious of how much of it is due to memory and how much to present perception.

Still more remarkable is the influence of the comprehension of the sensations in certain cases, especially with dim illumination, in which a visual impression may be misunderstood at first, by not knowing how to attribute the correct depth-dimensions; as when a distant light, for example, is taken for a near one, or *vice versa*. Suddenly it dawns on us what it is, and immediately, under the influence of the correct comprehension, the correct perceptual image also is developed in its full intensity. Then we are unable to revert to the previous imperfect apperception.

This is very common especially with complicated stereoscopic drawings of forms of crystals and other objects which come out in perfect clearness of perception the moment we once succeed in getting the correct impression.

Similar experiences have happened to everybody, proving that the elements in the sense-perceptions that are derived from experience are just as powerful as those that are derived from present sensations. All observers who have thoroughly investigated the theory of the sense-perceptions, even those who were disposed to allow experience as little scope as possible, have always admitted this.

Hence, at all events it must be conceded that, even in what appears to the adult as being direct apperception of the senses, possibly a number of single factors may be involved which are really the product of experience; although at the time it is difficult to draw the line between them.

Now in my opinion we are justified by our previous experiences in stating that no indubitable present sensation can be abolished and overcome by an act of the intellect; and no matter how clearly we recognize that it has been produced in some anomalous way, still the illusion does not disappear by comprehending the process. The attention may be diverted from sensations, particularly if they are feeble and habitual; but in noting those relations in the external world, that are associated with these sensations, we are obliged to observe the sensations themselves. Thus we may be unmindful of the temperature-sensation of our skin when it is not very keen, or of the contact-sensations produced by our clothing, as long as we are occupied with entirely different matters. But just as soon as we stop to think whether it is warm or cold, we are not in the position to convert the feeling of warmth into that of coldness; maybe because we know that it is due to strenuous exertion and not to the temperature of the surrounding air. In the same way the apparition of light when pressure is exerted on the eyeball cannot be made to vanish simply by comprehending better the nature of the process, supposing the attention is directed to the field of vision and not, say, to the ear or the skin.

On the other hand, it may also be that we are not in the position to isolate an impression of sensation, because it involves the composite sense-symbol of an external object. However, in this case the correct comprehension of the object shows that the sensation in question has been perceived and used by the consciousness.

My conclusion is, that *nothing in our sense-perceptions can be recognized as sensation which can be overcome in the perceptual image and converted into its opposite by factors that are demonstrably due to experience.*

Whatever, therefore, can be overcome by factors of experience, we must consider as being itself the product of experience and training. By observing this rule, we shall find that it is merely the qualities of the sensation that are to be considered as real, pure sensation; the great majority of space-apperceptions, however, being the product of experience and training.

* * * * *

The *empirical theory* attempts to prove that at least no other forces are necessary for their origin beyond the known faculties of the mind, although these forces themselves may remain entirely unexplained. Now generally it is a useful rule in scientific investigation not to make any new hypothesis so long as known facts seem adequate for the explanation, and the necessity of new assumptions has not been demonstrated. That is why I have thought it incumbent to prefer the empirical view essentially. Still less does the *intuition theory* attempt to give any explanation of the origin of our perceptual images; for it simply plunges right into the midst of the matter by assuming that certain perceptual images of space would be produced directly by an innate mechanism, provided certain nerve fibres were stimulated. The earlier forms of this theory implied some sort of self-observation of the retina; inasmuch as we were supposed to know by intuition about the form of this membrane and the positions of the separate nerve terminals in it. In its more recent development, especially as formulated by E. Hering, there is an hypothetical subjective visual space, wherein the sensations of the separate nerve fibres are supposed to be registered according to certain intuitive laws. Thus in this theory not only is Kant's assertion adopted, that the general apperception of space is an original form of our imagination, but certain special apperceptions of space are assumed to be intuitive.

The naturalistic view has been called also a special *theory of identity*, because in it the perfect fusion of the impressions on the corresponding places of the two retinas has to be postulated. On the other hand, the *empirical* theory is spoken of as a *theory of projection*, because according to it the perceptual images of objects are projected in space by means of psychic processes.

WILHELM WUNDT
(1832–1920)

Tridimensional Theory of Feeling [7]

A complete list of simple affective qualities is out of the question, even more than is such

[7] Wilhelm Wundt, *Outlines of Psychology*, trans. Charles Hubbard Judd (New York: Gustav E. Stechert, 1897), pp. 82–85; original German, *Gundriss der Psychologie* (Leipzig, 1896).

a list in the case of simple sensations. Then, too, there are still other reasons why it would be impossible. The feelings, by virtue of the attributes described above, do not form closed systems, as do the sensations of tone, of light, or of taste, but are united in a single manifold, interconnected in all its parts. Furthermore, the union of certain feelings gives rise to feelings which are not only unitary, but even simple in character. In this manifold of feelings, made up, as it is, of a great variety of most delicately shaded qualities, it is nevertheless possible to distinguish certain different *chief directions*, including certain affective opposites of predominant character. Such directions may always be designated by the *two* names that indicate their opposite extremes. Each name is, however, to be looked upon as a collective name including an endless number of feelings differing from one another.

Three such chief directions may be distinguished; we will call them the direction of *pleasurable* and *unpleasurable* feelings, that of *arousing* and *subduing* (exciting and depressing) feelings, and finally that of feelings of *strain* and *relaxation*. Any concrete feeling may belong to all of these directions or only two or even only one of them. The last mentioned possibility is all that makes it possible to distinguish the different directions. The combination of different affective directions which ordinarily takes place, and the above mentioned . . . influences which are due to the overlapping of feelings arising from various causes, all go to explain why we are perhaps never in a state entirely free from feeling, although the general nature of the feelings demands an indifference-zone.

Feelings connected with sensations of the general sense and with impressions of smell and taste, may be regarded as good examples of pure pleasurable and unpleasurable forms. A sensation of pain, for example, is regularly accompanied by an unpleasurable feeling without any admixture of other affective forms. In connection with pure sensations, arousing and subduing feelings may be observed best in the case of color-impressions and clang-impressions. Thus, red is arousing, blue subduing. Feelings of strain and relaxation are always connected with the temporal course of processes. Thus, in expecting a sense-impression, we note a feeling of strain, and on the arrival of the expected event, a feeling of relaxation. Both the expectation and satisfaction may be accompanied at the same time by a feeling of excitement or, under special conditions, by pleasurable or unpleasurable feelings. Still, these other feelings may be entirely absent, and then those of strain and relaxation are recognized as

specific forms which cannot be reduced to others, just as the two directions mentioned before. The presence of more than one direction may be discovered in the case of very many feelings which are, nevertheless, simple in quality, just as much as the feelings mentioned. Thus, the feelings of seriousness and gaiety connected with the sensible impressions of low and high tones or dark and bright colors, are to be regarded as characteristic qualities which are outside the indifference-zone in both the pleasurable and unpleasurable direction and the exciting and depressing direction. We are never to forget here that pleasurable and unpleasurable, exciting and depressing, are not names of single affective qualities, but of *directions*, within which an indefinitely large number of simple qualities appear, so that the unpleasurable quality of seriousness is not only to be distinguished from that of a painful touch, of a dissonance, etc., but even the different cases of seriousness itself may vary in their quality. Again, the direction of pleasurable and unpleasurable feelings, is united with that of feelings of strain and relaxation, in the case of the affective tones of rhythms. The regular succession of strain and relaxation in these cases is attended by pleasure, the disturbance of this regularity by the opposite feeling, as when we are disappointed or surprised. Then, too, under certain circumstances the feeling may, in both cases, be of an exciting or a subduing character.

These examples lead very naturally to the assumption that the three chief directions of simple feelings depend on the relations in which each single feeling stands to the whole *succession of psychical processes*. In this succession every feeling has in general a *threefold* significance. (1) It represents a particular modification of the *state of the present moment;* this modification belongs to the *pleasurable* and *unpleasurable* direction. (2) It exercises a certain definite influence on the *succeeding* state; this influence can be distinguished in its opposite forms as *excitation* and *inhibition*. (3) It is determined in its essential character by the *preceding* state; this determining influence shows itself in the given feeling in the forms of *strain* and *relaxation*. These conditions also render it improbable that other chief directions of feeling exist.

The Mind as Activity
and Psychic Causality [8]

What now is the *nature of mind?* The real answer to this question is contained in all that has been said before. Our mind is nothing else than the sum of our inner experiences, than our ideation, feeling, and willing collected together to a unity in consciousness, and rising in a series of developmental stages to culminate in selfconscious thought and a will that is morally free. At no point in our explanation of the interconnection of these inner experiences have we found occasion to apply this attribute of mentality to anything else than the concrete complex of idea, feeling, and will. The fiction of a trans-cendental substance, of which actual mental content is only the outward manifestation, a fleeting shadow-picture thrown by the still unknown reality of the mind,—such a theory misses the essential difference between the inner and the outer experience, and threatens to turn to mere empty show all that lends solid value and real significance to our mental life. Conscious experience is immediate experience. Being immediate, it can never require that distinction of a substrate, existing independently of our subjective appreciation, which is rendered necessary in natural science by its conception of nature as a sum-total of real things presented to us and persisting independently of us. Our mental experiences are as they are presented to us. The distinction between appearance and reality necessary for the apprehension of the world without, and culminating in the concept of a material substance as a secondary conceptual hypo-thesis which so far seems to do justice to the facts of experience, ceases to have any meaning when applied to the apprehension of the thinking subject by himself. You can under-stand, therefore, that when we are analysing our internal experiences we are never met by the contradictions between particular phe-nomena which in natural science furnish both incentive and means to the gradual developing and perfecting of the concept of matter, a concept which, destined as it is to remain for ever a hypothesis, can still hope to

[8] Wilhelm Wundt, *Lectures on Human and Animal Psychology*, trans. J. E. Creighton and E. B. Titchener (New York: Macmillan, 1894), pp. 451–454; original German, *Vorlesungen über die Menschen und Thierseele* (Leipzig, 1863).

approximate to the truth by an infinite number of efforts towards it.

There is just one single group of empirical facts which have with some show of reason been adduced to prove the necessity of assuming a mental substrate analogous to material substance,—the facts of the *revival of previous experiences.* If we can call up some past idea, it is urged, it surely follows that some trace of that idea has remained in the mind during the meantime, else its reproduction would not be possible. Now we have seen, of course, that no idea, that no mental process whatsoever, can be called up again unchanged. Every remembered idea is really a new formation, composed of numerous elements of various past ideas. Nevertheless, it might be supposed that these very elements were the ideational traces left behind in the mind. But it is evident that even in this form the theory has presuppositions due simply to a transference of the permanent effects observed in the case of physical processes to the hypothetical mental substrate, in other words to an unconscious intermixture of materialistic views. A physical influence acting upon a body produces some more or less permanent alterations in it. Thus we have every right to suppose that a nervous excitation leaves an after-effect in the nervous organs, which is of significance for the physiology of the processes of practice and revival. Now in the theory of "traces" these physical analogies are applied without more ado to the mind. Mind is conceived either as identical with brain, or as a substance localised somewhere in the brain, resembling it and other material substances in every essential attribute. But the physical excitation-process can only leave its after-effect upon the nerve, because it is itself a process of movement in or with a permanent substrate. And if mental processes are not phenomena, but actual immediate experiences, it is very hard to see how their after-effects can be psychologically conceived, except also in the form of directly presented mental processes. If we try to imagine an idea as persisting beneath the limen of consciousness, we can as a matter of fact only think of it as still an idea, *i.e.*, as the same process as that which it was so long as we were conscious of it, with the single difference that it is now no longer conscious. But this implies that psychological explanation has here reached a limit similar to that which confronts it in the question as to the ultimate origin of sensations. It is the limit beyond which one of the two causal series,—the physical,—can be continued, but where the other,—the psychical,—must end; and where the attempt to push this latter farther must inevitably lead to the thinking of the psychical in physical, —*i.e.*, material,—terms.

We conclude, then, that the assumption of a mental substance different from the various manifestations of mental life involves the unjustifiable transference of a mode of thought necessary for the investigation of external nature to a sphere in which it is wholly inapplicable; it implies a kind of unconscious materialism. The consequences of this transference follow at once from its nature; the true value of our mental life is in jeopardy. For this value attaches simply and solely to the actual and concrete processes in mind. What can this "substance" do for us, a substance devoid of will, of feeling, and of thought, and having no part in the constitution of our personality? If you answer, as is sometimes done, that it is these very operations of mind that go to make up its nature, and that therefore mind cannot be thought or conceived without them, why, then the position is granted: the real nature of mind consists in nothing else than our mental life itself. The notion of "operation" as applied to it can only mean, if it has any admissible meaning at all, that we are able to demonstrate how certain mental manifestations follow from, are the effects of the operation of certain other mental manifestations. Physical causality and psychical causality are polar opposites: the former implies always the postulate of a material substance; the latter never transcends the limits of what is immediately given in mental experience. "Substance" is a metaphysical surplusage for which psychology has no use. And this accords with the fundamental character of mental life, which I would have you always bear in mind. It does not consist in the connexion of unalterable objects and varying conditions: in all its phases it is *process;* an *active*, not a passive, existence; *development*, not stagnation. The understanding of the basal laws of this development is the final goal of psychology.

Theory of Apperception [9]

In the simultaneous interconnection of consciousness, for example in a compound clang or in a series of spacial objects, certain *single* components are favored above the others. In both cases we designate the differences in the perception as differences in *clearness* and *distinctness*. Clearness is the relatively favorable comprehension of the object in itself, distinctness the sharp discrimination from other objects, which is generally connected with clearness. The state which accompanies the clear grasp of any psychical content and is characterized by a special feeling, we call *attention*. The process through which any such content is brought to clear comprehension we call *apperception*. In contrast with this, perception which is not accompanied by a state of attention, we designate *apprehension*. Those contents of consciousness upon which the attention is concentrated are spoken of, after the analogy of the external optical fixation-point, as the *fixation-point of consciousness*, or the *inner fixation-point*. On the other hand, the whole content of consciousness at any given moment is called the *field of consciousness*. When a psychical process passes into an unconscious state we speak of its *sinking below the threshold of consciousness* and when such a process arises we say it *appears above the threshold of consciousness*. These are all figurative expressions and must not be understood literally. They are useful, however, because of the brevity and clearness they permit in the description of conscious processes.

If we try to describe the train of psychical compounds in their interconnection with the aid of these figurative expressions, we may say that it is made up of a continual coming and going. At first some compound comes into the field of consciousness and then advances into the inner fixation-point, from which it returns to the field of consciousness before disappearing entirely. Besides this train of psychical compounds which are apperceived, there is also a coming and going of others which are merely apprehended, that is, enter the field of consciousness and pass out again without reaching the inner fixation-

[9] Wilhelm Wundt, *Outlines of Psychology, op. cit.*, pp. 208–211.

point. Both the apperceived and the apprehended compounds may have different grades of clearness. In the case of the first class this appears in the fact that the clearness and distinctness of apperception in general is variable according to the state of consciousness. To illustrate: it can easily be shown that when one and the same impression is apperceived several times in succession, if the other conditions remain the same, the successive apperceptions are usually clearer and more distinct. The different degrees of clearness in the case of compounds that merely apprehended, may be observed most easily when the impressions are composite. It is then found, especially when the impressions last but an instant, that even here, where all the components are obscure from the first, that there are still different gradations. Some seem to rise more above the threshold of consciousness, some less.

These relations cannot be determined through chance introspections, but only by systematic experimental observations. The best kinds of conscious contents to use for such observations are ideas because they can be easily produced at any time through external impressions. Now, in any temporal idea, those components which belong to the *present* moment are in the fixation-point of consciousness. Those of the preceding impressions which were present shortly before, are still in the field of consciousness, while those which were present longer before, have disappeared from consciousness entirely. A spacial idea, on the other hand, when it has only a limited extent, may be apperceived at once in its totality. If it is more composite, then its parts too must pass successively through the inner fixation-point if they are to be clearly apprehended. It follows, therefore, that composite *spacial* ideas (especially momentary visual impressions) are peculiarly well suited to furnish a measure of the amount of content that can be *apperceived* in a single act, or of the *scope of attention;* while composite *temporal* ideas (for example, rhythmical auditory impressions, hammer-strokes) may be used for measuring the amount of all the contents that can enter into consciousness at a given moment, or the *scope of consciousness.* Experiments made in this way give, under different conditions, a scope of from 6 to 12 simple impressions for attention and of 16 to 40 such impressions for consciousness. The smaller figures are for those impressions which do not unite at all to ideational combinations, or at most very incompletely, the larger for those in which the elements combine as far as possible to composite ideas.

HERMANN EBBINGHAUS
(1850–1909)

Nonsense Syllables [10]

In order to test practically ... a way of penetrating more deeply into memory processes ... —I have hit upon the following method.

Out of the simple consonants of the alphabet and our eleven vowels and diphthongs all possible syllables of a certain sort were constructed, a vowel sound being placed between two consonants.

These syllables, about 2,300 in number, were mixed together and then drawn out by chance and used to construct series of different lengths, several of which each time formed the material for a test.

* * * * *

The syllables used each time were carefully laid aside till the whole number had been used, then they were mixed together and used again.

The aim of the tests carried on with these syllable series was, by means of repeated audible perusal of the separate series, to so impress them that immediately afterwards they could voluntarily just be reproduced. This aim was considered attained when, the initial syllable being given, a series could be recited at the first attempt, without hesitation, at a certain rate, and with the consciousness of being correct.

The nonsense material, just described, offers

[10] Reprinted with the permission of the publisher, Hermann Ebbinghaus; *Memory: A Contribution to Experimental Psychology* (New York: Teachers College Press) c. 1913, Teachers College, Columbia University.

many advantages, in part because of this very lack of meaning. First of all, it is relatively simple and relatively homogeneous. In the case of the material nearest at hand, namely poetry or prose, the content is now narrative in style, now descriptive, or now reflective; it contains now a phrase that is pathetic, now one that is humorous; its metaphors are sometimes beautiful, sometimes harsh; its rhythm is sometimes smooth and sometimes rough. There is thus brought into play a multiplicity of influences which change without regularity and are therefore disturbing. Such are associations which dart here and there, different degrees of interest, lines of verse recalled because of their striking quality or their beauty, and the like. All this is avoided with our syllables. Among many thousand combinations there occur scarcely a few dozen that have a meaning and among these there are again only a few whose meaning was realised while they were being memorised.

Experimental Method in Memorization[11]

The following rules were made for the process of memorising.

1. The separate series were always read through completely from beginning to end; they were not learned in separate parts which were then joined together; neither were especially difficult parts detached and repeated more frequently. There was a perfectly free interchange between the reading and the occasionally necessary tests of the capacity to reproduce by heart. For the latter there was an important rule to the effect that upon hesitation the rest of the series was to be read through to the end before beginning it again.

2. The reading and the recitation of the series took place at a constant rate, that of 150 strokes per minute. A clockwork metronome placed at some distance was at first used to regulate the rate; but very soon the ticking of a watch was substituted, that being much simpler and less disturbing to the attention. The mechanism of escapement of most watches swings 300 times per minute.

3. Since it is practically impossible to speak continuously without variation of accent, the following method was adopted to

avoid irregular variations: either three or four syllables were united into a measure, and thus either the 1st, 4th, 7th, or the 1st, 5th, 9th . . . syllables were pronounced with a slight accent. Stressing of the voice was otherwise, as far as possible, avoided.

4. After the learning of each separate series a pause of 15 seconds was made, and used for the tabulation of results. Then the following series of the same test was immediately taken up.

5. During the process of learning, the purpose of reaching the desired goal as soon as possible was kept in mind as much as was feasible. Thus, to the limited degree to which conscious resolve is of influence here, the attempt was made to keep the attention concentrated on the tiresome task and its purpose. It goes without saying that care was taken to keep away all outer disturbances in order to make possible the attainment of this aim. The smaller distractions caused by carrying on the test in various surroundings were also avoided as far as that could be done.

6. There was no attempt to connect the nonsense syllables by the invention of special associations of the mnemotechnik type; learning was carried on solely by the influence of the mere repetitions upon the natural memory. As I do not possess the least practical knowledge of the mnemotechnical devices, the fulfillment of this condition offered no difficulty to me.

7. Finally and chiefly, care was taken that the objective conditions of life during the period of the tests were so controlled as to eliminate too great changes or irregularities. Of course, since the tests extended over many months, this was possible only to a limited extent. But, even so, the attempt was made to conduct, under as similar conditions of life as possible, those tests the results of which were to be directly compared. In particular the activity immediately preceding the test was kept as constant in character as was possible. Since the mental as well as the physical condition of man is subject to an evident periodicity of 24 hours, it was taken for granted that like experimental conditions are obtainable only at like times of day. However, in order to carry out more than one test in a given day, different experiments were occasionally carried on together at different times of day. When too great changes in the

11   *Ibid.*, pp. 24–26.

outer and inner life occurred, the tests were discontinued for a length of time. Their resumption was preceded by some days of renewed training varying according to the length of the interruption.

Length of Lists [12]

It is sufficiently well known that the memorisation of a series of ideas that is to be reproduced at a later time is more difficult, the longer the series is. That is, the memorisation not only requires more time taken by itself, because each repetition lasts longer, but it also requires more time relatively because an increased number of repetitions

becomes necessary. Six verses of a poem require for learning not only three times as much time as two but considerably more than that.

. . . I obtained a few numerical values for it which are worth putting down, although they do not show particularly interesting relations.

The series in question comprised (in the case of the tests of the year 1883–84), 12, 16, 24, or 36 syllables each, and 9, 6, 3, or 2 series were each time combined into a test.

For the number of repetitions necessary in these cases to memorise the series up to the first errorless reproduction (and including it) the following numerical results were found:

X Series	Y Syllables Each	Required Together an Average of Z Repetitions	Probable Error of Average Values	Number of Tests
X =	Y =	Z =		
9	12	158	± 3.4	7
6	16	186	± 0.9	42
3	24	134	± 2.9	7
2	36	112	± 4.0	7

In order to make the number of repetitions comparable it is necessary, so to speak, to reduce them to a common denominator and to divide them each time by the number of the series. In this way it is found out how many repetitions relatively were necessary to learn by heart the single series, which differ from each other only in the number of syllables, and which each time had been taken together with as many others of the same kind as would make the duration of the whole test from fifteen to thirty minutes.

However, a conclusion can be drawn from the figures from the standpoint of decrease in number of syllables. The question can be asked: What number of syllables can be correctly recited after only one reading? For me the number is usually seven. Indeed I have often succeeded in reproducing eight syllables, but this has happened only at the beginning of the tests and in a decided minority of the cases. In the case of six syllables on the other hand a mistake almost never occurs; with them, therefore, a single attentive reading involves an unnecessarily large expenditure of energy for an immediately following reproduction.

If this latter pair of values is added, the

required division made, and the last faultless reproduction subtracted as not necessary for the learning, then the following table results.

Number of Syllables in a Series	Number of Repetitions Necessary for First Errorless Reproduction (Exclusive of It)	Probable Error
7	1	
12	16.6	± 1.1
16	30.0	± 0.4
24	44.0	± 1.7
36	55.0	± 2.8

The longer of the two adjoining curves of Fig. 6 illustrates the regular course of these numbers with approximate accuracy for such a small number of tests. As Fig. 6 shows, in the cases examined, the number of repetitions necessary for the memorisation of series in which the number of syllables progressively increased, itself increases with extraordinary rapidity with the increase in number of the syllables.

At first the ascent of the curve is very steep, but later on it appears to gradually flatten out. For the mastery of five times the number of syllables that can be reproduced after but one reading—i.e., after about 3 seconds—over 50 repetitions were necessary, requiring an uninterrupted and concentrated effort for fifteen minutes.

12   *Ibid.*, pp. 46–48.

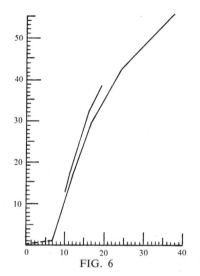

FIG. 6

If it is born in mind that each stanza contains 80 syllables (each syllable, however, consisting on the average of less than three letters) and if the number of repetitions here found is compared with the results presented above, there is obtained an approximate numerical expression for the extraordinary advantage which the combined ties of meaning, rhythm, rhyme, and a common language give to material to be memorised. If the above curve is projected in imagination still further along its present course, then it must be supposed that I would have required 70 to 80 repetitions for the memorisation of a series of 80 to 90 nonsense syllables. When the syllables were objectively and subjectively united by the ties just mentioned this requirement was in my case reduced to about one-tenth of that amount.

Savings Method, Retention, and Repetition [14]

When in repeated cases I memorised series of syllables of a certain length to the point of their first possible reproduction, the times (or number of repetitions) necessary differed greatly from each other, but the mean values derived from them and the character of genuine constants of natural science. Ordinarily, therefore, I learned by heart homogeneous series under similar conditions with, on the average, a similar number of repetitions. The large deviations of the separate values from each other change the total result not at all; but it would require too much time to ascertain with exactness the number necessary for greater precision in detail.

What will happen, it may be asked, if the number of repetitions actually given to a certain series is less than is required for memorisation or if the number exceeds the necessary minimum?

The general nature of what happens has already been described. Naturally the surplus repetitions of the latter alternative do not go to waste. Even though the immediate effect, the smooth and errorless reproduction, is not affected by them, yet they are not without significance in that they serve to make other such reproductions possible at a more or less distant time. The longer a person studies, the longer he retains. And, even in the first case,

The curve has its natural starting point in the zero point of the co-ordinates. The short initial stretch up to the point, $x = 7$, $y = 1$, can be explained thus: in order to recite by heart series of 6, 5, 4, etc., syllables one reading, of course, is all that is necessary. In my case this reading does not require as much attention as does the 7-syllable one, but can become more and more superficial as the number of syllables decreases.

Meaningful Material [13]

In order to keep in mind the similarities and differences between sense and nonsense material, I occasionally made tests with the English original of Byron's "Don Juan." These results do not properly belong here since I did not vary the length of the amount to be learned each time but memorised on each occasion only separate stanzas. Nevertheless, it is interesting to mention the number of repetitions necessary because of their contrast with the numerical results just given.

There are only seven tests (1884) to be considered, each of which comprised six stanzas. When the latter, each by itself, were learned to the point of the first possible reproduction, an average of 52 repetitions (P.E.$_m$ = $\pm$ 0.6) was necessary for all six taken together. Thus, each stanza required hardly nine repetitions; or, if the errorless reproduction is abstracted, scarcely eight repetitions.

[13]   *Ibid.*, pp. 50–51.

[14]   *Ibid.*, pp. 52–57.

something evidently occurs even if the repetitions do not suffice for a free reproduction. By them a way is at least opened for the first errorless reproduction, and the disconnected, hesitating, and faulty reproductions keep approximating more and more to it.

These relations can be described figuratively by speaking of the series as being more or less deeply engraved in some mental substratum. To carry out this figure: as the number of repetitions increases, the series are engraved more and more deeply and indelibly; if the number of repetitions is small, the inscription is but surface deep and only fleeting glimpses of the tracery can be caught; with a somewhat greater number the inscription can, for a time at least, be read at will; as the number of repetitions is still further increased, the deeply cut picture of the series fades out only after ever longer intervals.

* * * * *

I define the inner stability of a series of ideas—the degree of its retainability—by the greater or less readiness with which it is reproduced at some definite time subsequent to its first memorisation. This readiness I measure by the amount of work saved in the relearning of any series as compared with the work necessary for memorising a similar but entirely new series.

The interval of time between the two processes of memorisation is of course a matter of choice. I chose 24 hours.

* * * * *

For ascertaining the relation of dependence between the increase in the number of repetitions of a series and the ever deeper impression of it which results, I have formulated

the problem as follows: If homogeneous series are impressed to different extents as a result of different numbers of repetitions, and then 24 hours later are learned to the point of the first possible reproduction by heart, how are the resulting savings in work related to each other and to the corresponding number of former repetitions?

In order to answer the question just formulated, I have carried out 70 double tests, each of six series of 16 syllables each. Each double test consisted in this, that the separate series —each for itself—were first read attentively a given number of times (after frequently repeated readings they were recited by heart instead of read), and that 24 hours later I relearned up to the point of first possible reproduction the series thus impressed and then in part forgotten. The first reading was repeated 8, 16, 24, 32, 42, 53, or 64 times.

An increase of the readings used for the first learning beyond 64 repetitions proved impracticable, at least for six series of this length. For with this number each test requires about $3/4$ of an hour, and toward the end of this time exhaustion, headache, and other symptoms were often felt which would have complicated the conditions of the test if the number of repetitions had been increased.

The tests were equally divided among the seven numbers of repetitions investigated so that to each of them were allotted 10 double tests. The results were as follows for the six series of a single test taken together and without subtraction of the time used for reciting.

After a preceding study of the series by means of "x" repetitions, they were learned 24 hours later with an expenditure of "y" seconds.

$x = 8$ $y =$	$x = 16$ $y =$	$x = 24$ $y =$	$x = 32$ $y =$	$x = 42$ $y =$	$x = 53$ $y =$	$x = 64$ $y =$
1171	998	1013	736	708	615	530
1070	795	853	764	579	579	483
1204	936	854	863	734	601	499
1180	1124	908	850	660	561	464
1246	1168	1004	892	738	618	412
1113	1160	1068	868	713	582	419
1283	1189	979	913	649	572	417
1141	1186	966	858	634	516	397
1127	1164	1076	914	788	550	391
1139	1059	1033	975	763	660	524
$m = 1167$	1078	975	863	697	585	454
$P.E._m = \pm 14$	± 28	± 17	± 15	± 14	± 9	± 11

The preceding table of numbers gives the times *actually used* in learning by heart the series studied 24 hours previously. Since we are interested not so much in the times used as the times saved, we must know how long it would have taken to learn by heart the same series if no previous study had been made. In the case of the series which were repeated 42, 53, and 64 times, this time can be learned from the tests themselves. For, in their case, the number of repetitions is greater than the average minimum for the first possible reproduction, which in the case of the 16-syllable series amounted to 31 repetitions. In their case, therefore, the point can be determined at which the first errorless reproduction of that series appeared as the number of repetitions kept on increasing. But on account of the continued increase in the number of repetitions and the resulting extension of the time of the test, the conditions were somewhat different from those in the customary learning of series not hitherto studied. In the case of the series to which a smaller number of repetitions than the above were given, the numbers necessary for comparison cannot be derived from their own records, since, as a part of the plan of the experiment, they were not completely learned by heart. I have consequently preferred each time to find the saving of work in question by comparison with the time required for learning by heart not the same but a similar series up to that time unknown. For this I possess a fairly correct numerical value from the time of the tests in question: any six 16-syllable series was learned, as an average of 53 tests, in 1,270 seconds, with the small probable error $\pm$ 7.

If all the mean values are brought together in relation to this last value, the following table results:

I	II		III		IV
After a Preceding Study of the Series by X Repetitions,	They were Just Memorized 24 Hours Later in Y Seconds		The Result Therefore of the Preceding Study Was a Saving of T Seconds,		Or, for Each of the Repetitions, an Average Saving of D Seconds
X =	Y =	P.E.$_m$ =	T =	P.E.$_m$ =	D =
0	1270	7			
8	1167	14	103	16	12.9
16	1078	28	192	29	12.0
24	975	17	295	19	12.3
32	863	15	407	17	12.7
42	697	14	573	16	13.6
53	585	9	685	11	12.9
64	454	11	816	13	12.8
					m = 12.7

The simple relation approximately realised in these numbers is evident: the number of repetitions used to impress the series (Column I) and the saving in work in learning the series 24 hours later as a result of such impression (Col. III) increase in the same fashion. Division of the amount of work saved by the corresponding number of repetitions gives as a quotient a practically constant value (Col. IV).

Consequently the results of the test may be summarised and formulated as follows: When nonsense series of 16 syllables each were impressed in memory to greater and greater degrees by means of attentive repetitions, the inner depth of impression in part resulting from the number of the repetitions increased, within certain limits, approximately proportionally to that number. This increase in depth was measured by the greater readiness with which these series were brought to the point of reproduction after 24 hours. The limits within which this relation was determined were on the one side, zero, and, on the other, about double the number of repetitions that on the average just sufficed for learning the series.

For six series taken together the after-effect of each repetition—*i.e.*, the saving it brought about—amounted on the average to 12.7 seconds, consequently to 2.1 seconds for each single series. As the repetition of a series of 16 syllables in itself takes from 6.6 to 6.8 seconds, its after-effect 24 hours later amounts to a scant third of its own duration. In other words: for each three additional repetitions which I spent on a given day on the study of a series, I saved, in learning that series 24 hours later, on the average, approximately one repetition; and, within the limits stated, it did not matter how many repetitions altogether were spent on the memorisation of a series.

Overlearning and the Savings Method [15]

It would be of interest to know whether the approximate proportionality between the number of repetitions of a series and the saving of the work in relearning the latter made possible thereby, which in my own case seemed to take place within certain limits, continues to exist beyond those limits. If, furthermore, as a result of each repetition a scant third of its own value is saved up to be applied on the reproduction 24 hours later, I should be able to just reproduce spontaneously after 24 hours a series of 16 syllables, the initial syllable being given, provided I had repeated it the first day thrice as many times as were absolutely necessary for its first reproduction. As this requirement is 31–32 repetitions the attainment of the aim in question would necessitate about 100 repetitions. On the supposition of the general

validity of the relation found, the number of repetitions to be made at a given time, in order that errorless reproduction might take place 24 hours later, could be calculated for any kind of series for which, so to say, the "after-effect-coefficient" of the repetitions had been ascertained.

I have not investigated this question by further increasing the number of repetitions of unfamiliar 16 syllable series because, as has been already noted, with any great extension of the tests the increasing fatigue and a certain drowsiness cause complications. However, I have made some trial tests partly with shorter series, and partly with familiar series, all of which confirmed the result that the proportion in question gradually ceases to hold with a further increase of repetitions. Measured by the saving of work after 24 hours the effect of the later repetitions gradually decreases.

Series of 12 syllables (six of the series were each time combined into a test) were studied to the point of first possible reproduction; and immediately after the errorless reproduction each series was repeated three times (in all four times) as often as the memorisation (exclusive of the recital) had required. After 24 hours the same series were relearned to the first possible reproduction. Four tests furnished the following results (the numbers indicate the repetitions):

Repetitions for the Learning and Recital of 6 Series	Immediately Successive Repetitions for the Sake of Greater Surety	Total Number of Repetitions Used for the 6 Series	After 24 Hours the Memorization of the Series Required	Thus the Work Saved by the Total Number of Repetitions Amounted to
104	294	398	41	63
101	285	386	39	62
114	324	438	46	68
109	309	418	38	71
$m = 107$	303	410	41	66
				P.E.$_m$ = 1.4

In my own case—within reasonable limits—the after effect of the repetitions of series of 12 syllables after 24 hours is a little smaller than is the case with 16 syllables; it must be estimated as at least three tenths of the sum total of the repetitions. If this relation were approximately to continue to hold with very numerous repetitions, it would be reasonable

---

[15] *Ibid.*, pp. 59–61.

to expect that, after 24 hours, series on whose impression four times as many repetitions had been expended as were necessary for their first reproduction could be recited without any further expenditure of energy. Instead of this, in the cases examined, the relearning required about 35 per cent of the work required for the first recital. The effect of an average number of 410 repetitions was a saving of only one sixth of this sum. If now the first repetitions were represented by about three tenths of their amount, the effect of the later repetitions must have been very slight.

Investigations of the following kind, which I do not here give in detail, led to the same result. Syllable series of different lengths were gradually memorised by frequent repetitions which, however, did not all take place on one day, but were distributed over several successive days.... When, after several days, only a few repetitions were necessary in order to learn the series by heart, they were repeated three or four times as often as was necessary, at this phase of memorisation, for the first errorless reproduction. But in no single case did I succeed in an errorless reproduction of the series after 24 hours unless I had read them again once or several times. The influence of the frequent repetitions still appeared, indeed, in a certain saving of work, but this became less in proportion to the decreasing amount of work to be saved. It was very hard, by means of repetitions which had taken place 24 hours previously, to eliminate the last remnant of the work of relearning a given series.

To summarise: The effect of increasing the number of repetitions of series of syllables on their inner fixedness in the above defined sense grew at first approximately in proportion to the number of repetitions, then that effect decreased gradually, and finally became very slight when the series were so deeply impressed that they could be repeated after 24 hours, almost spontaneously.

Curve of Retention [16]

1. It will probably be claimed that the fact that forgetting would be very rapid at the beginning of the process and very slow at the end should have been foreseen. However, it would be just as reasonable to be surprised at this initial rapidity and later slowness as they come to light here under the definite conditions of our experiment for a certain individual, and for a series of 13 syllables. One hour after the end of the learning, the forgetting had already progressed so far that one half the amount of the original work had to be expended before the series could be reproduced again; after 8 hours the work to be made up amounted to two thirds of the first

---

[16]   *Ibid.*, pp. 76–77.

effort. Gradually, however, the process became slower so that even for rather long periods the additional loss could be ascertained only with difficulty. After 24 hours about one third was always remembered; after 6 days about one fourth, and after a whole month fully one fifth of the first work persisted in effect. The decrease of this after-effect in the latter intervals of time is evidently so slow that it is easy to predict that a complete vanishing of the effect of the first memorisation of these series would, if they had been left to themselves, have occurred only after an indefinitely long period of time.

2. Least satisfactory in the results is the difference between the third and fourth values, especially when taken in connection with the greater difference between the fourth and fifth numbers. In the period 9–24 hours the decrease of the after-effect would accordingly have been $2\frac{1}{2}$ percent. In the period 24 to 48 hours it would have been 6.1 per cent; in the later 24 hours, then about three times as much as in the earlier 15. Such a condition is not credible, since in the case of all the other numbers the decrease in the after-effect is greatly retarded by an increase in time. It does not become credible even under the plausible assumption that night and sleep, which form a greater part of the 15 hours but a smaller part of the 24, retard considerably the decrease in the after-effect.

Therefore it must be assumed that one of these three values is greatly affected by accidental influences. It would fit in well with the other observations to consider the number 33.7 per cent for the relearning after 24 hours as somewhat too large and to suppose that with a more accurate repetition of the tests it would be 1 to 2 units smaller. However, it is upheld by observations to be stated presently, so that I am in doubt about it.

3. Considering the special, individual, and uncertain character of our numerical results no one will desire at once to know what "law" is revealed in them. However, it is noteworthy that all the seven values which cover intervals of one third of an hour in length to 31 days in length (thus from singlefold to 2,000 fold) may with tolerable approximation be put into a rather simple mathematical formula. I call:

t the time in minutes counting from one minute before the end of the learning,

b the saving of work evident in relearning,

the equivalent of the amount remembered from the first learning expressed in percentage of the time necessary for this first learning, c and k two constants to be defined presently. Then the following formula may be written:

$$b = \{100 \, k/(\log t)^c + k\}$$

By using common logarithms and with merely approximate estimates, not involving exact calculation by the method of least squares,

$$k = 1.84$$

$$c = 1.25.$$

10

German Physiological Psychology

JOHANNES MÜLLER
(1801–1858)

Specific Energy of Nerves [1]

The senses, by virtue of the peculiar properties of their several nerves, make us acquainted with the states of our own body, and they also inform us of the qualities and changes of external nature, as far as these give rise to changes in the condition of the nerves. Sensation is a property common to all the senses; but the kind ("*modus*,") of sensation is different in each: thus we have the sensations of light, of sound, of taste, of smell, and of feeling, or touch. By feeling, or touch, we understand the peculiar kind of sensation of which the ordinary sensitive nerves generally —as, the nervus trigeminus, vagus, glosso-pharyngeus, and the spinal nerves,—are susceptible; the sensations of itching, of pleasure and pain, of heat and cold, and those excited by the act of touch in its more limited sense, are varieties of this mode of sensation. That which through the medium of our senses is actually perceived by the sensorium, is indeed merely a property or change of condition of our nerves; but the imagination and reason are ready to interpret the modifications in the state of the nerves produced by external influences as properties of the external bodies themselves. This mode of regarding sensations

has become so habitual in the case of the senses which are more rarely affected by internal causes, that it is only on reflection that we perceive it to be erroneous. In the case of the sense of feeling or touch, on the contrary, where the peculiar sensations of the nerves perceived by the sensorium are excited as frequently by internal as by external causes, it is easily conceived that the feeling of pain or pleasure, for example, is a condition of the nerves, and not a property of the things which excite it. This leads us to the consideration of some general laws, a knowledge of which is necessary before entering on the physiology of the separate senses.

I. In the first place, it must be kept in mind that *external agencies can give rise to no kind of sensation which cannot also be produced by internal causes, exciting changes in the condition of our nerves.*

In the case of the sense of touch, this is at once evident. The sensations of the nerves of touch (or common sensibility) are those of cold and heat, pain and pleasure, and innumerable modifications of these, which are neither painful nor pleasurable, but yet have the same kind of sensation as their element, though not in an extreme degree. All these sensations are constantly being produced by internal causes in all parts of our body endowed with sensitive nerves; they may also be excited by causes acting from without, but external agencies are not capable of adding any new element to their nature. The sensa-

---
[1] Johannes Müller, *The Physiology of Senses, Voice, and Muscular Motion, with the Mental Faculties*, trans. William Baly (London, 1848), vol. 2, pp. 1059–1087; original German, *Handbuch der Physiologie des Menschen* (Coblenz, 1838).

tions of the nerves of touch are therefore states or qualities proper to themselves, and merely rendered manifest by exciting causes external or internal. The sensation of smell also may be perceived independently of the application of any odorous substance from without, the nerve of smell being thrown by an internal cause into the condition requisite for the production of the sensation. This perception of the sensation of odours without an external exciting cause, though not of frequent occurrence, has been many times observed in persons of an irritable nervous system; and the sense of taste is probably subject to the same affection, although it would always be difficult to determine whether the taste might not be owing to a change in the qualities of the saliva or mucus of the mouth; the sensation of nausea, however, which belongs to the sensations of taste, is certainly very often perceived as the result of a merely internal affection of the nerves. The sensations of the sense of vision, namely, colour, light, and darkness, are also perceived independently of all external exciting cause. In the state of the most perfect freedom from excitement, the optic nerve has no other sensation than that of darkness. The excited condition of the nerve is manifested, even while the eyes are closed, by the appearance of light, or luminous flashes, which are mere sensations of the nerve, and not owing to the presence of any matter of light, and consequently are not capable of illuminating any surrounding objects. Every one is aware how common it is to see bright colours while the eyes are closed, particularly in the morning when the irritability of the nerves is still considerable. These phenomena are very frequent in children after waking from sleep. Through the sense of vision, therefore, we receive from external nature no impressions which we may not also experience from internal excitement of our nerves; and it is evident that a person blind from infancy in consequence of opacity of the transparent media of the eye, must have a perfect internal conception of light and colours, provided the retina and optic nerve be free from lesion. The prevalent notions with regard to the wonderful sensations supposed to be experienced by persons blind from birth when their sight is restored by operation, are exaggerated and incorrect. The elements of the sensation of vision, namely, the sensations of light, colour, and darkness, must have been previously as well known to such persons as to those of whom the sight has always been perfect. If, moreover, we imagine a man to be from his birth surrounded merely by external objects destitute of all variety of colours, so that he could never receive the impressions of colours from without, it is evident that the sense of vision might nevertheless have been no less perfect in him than in other men; for light and colours are innate endowments of his nature, and require merely a stimulus to render them manifest.

The sensations of hearing also are excited as well by internal as by external causes; for, whenever the auditory nerve is in a state of excitement, the sensations peculiar to it, as the sounds of ringing, humming, &c. are perceived. It is by such sensations that the diseases of the auditory nerve manifest themselves; and, even in less grave, transient affections of the nervous system, the sensations of humming and ringing in the ears afford evidence that the sense of hearing participates in the disturbance.

No further proof is wanting to show, that external influences give rise in our senses to no other sensations, than those which may be excited in the corresponding nerves by internal causes.

II. *The same internal cause excites in the different senses different sensations;—in each sense the sensations peculiar to it.*

One uniform internal cause acting on all the nerves of the senses in the same manner, is the accumulation of blood in the capillary vessels of the nerve, as in congestion and inflammation. This uniform cause excites in the retina, while the eyes are closed, the sensation of light and luminous flashes; in the auditory nerve, humming and ringing sounds; and in the nerves of feeling, the sensation of pain. In the same way, also, a narcotic substance introduced into the blood excites in the nerves of each sense peculiar symptoms; in the optic nerves the appearance of luminous sparks before the eyes; in the auditory nerves, "tinnitus aurium;" and in the common sensitive nerves the sensation of ants creeping over the surface.

III. *The same external cause also gives rise to different sensations in each sense, according to the special endowments of its nerve.*

The mechanical influence of a blow, concussion, or pressure excites, for example, in the eye the sensation of light and colours. It is well known that by exerting pressure upon the eye, when the eyelids are closed, we can give rise to the appearance of a luminous circle; by more gentle pressure the appearance of colours may be produced, and one colour may be made to change to another. Children, waking from sleep before daylight, frequently amuse themselves with these phenomena. The light thus produced has no existence external to the optic nerve, it is merely a sensation excited in it. However strongly we press upon the eye in the dark, so as to give rise to the appearance of luminous flashes, these flashes, being merely sensations, are incapable of illuminating external objects. Of this any one may easily convince himself by experiment. I have in repeated trials never been able, by means of these luminous flashes in the eye, to recognise in the dark the nearest objects, or to see them better than before; nor could another person, while I produced by pressure on my eye the appearance of brilliant flashes, perceive in it the slightest trace of real light.

* * * * *

IV. *The peculiar sensations of each nerve of sense can be excited by several distinct causes internal and external.*

The facts on which this statement is founded have been already mentioned; for we have seen that the sensation of light in the eye is excited:

1. By the undulations or emanations which from their action on the eye are called light, although they have many other actions than this; for instance, they effect chemical changes, and are the means of maintaining the organic processes in plants.

2. By mechanical influences; as concussion, or a blow.

3. By electricity.

4. By chemical agents, such as narcotics, digitalis, &c. which, being absorbed into the blood, give rise to the appearance of luminous sparks, &c. before the eyes independently of any external cause.

5. By the stimulus of the blood in the state of congestion.

The sensation of sound may be excited in the auditory nerve:

1. By mechanical influences, namely, by the vibrations of sonorous bodies imparted to the organ of hearing through the intervention of media capable of propagating them.

2. By electricity.

3. By chemical influences taken into the circulation; such as the narcotics, or alterantia nervina.

4. By the stimulus of the blood.

The sensation of odours may be excited in the olfactory nerves:

1. By chemical influences of a volatile nature,—odorous substances.

2. By electricity.

The sensation of taste may be produced:

1. By chemical influences acting on the gustatory nerves either from without or through the medium of the blood; for, according to Magendie, dogs taste milk injected into their blood-vessels, and begin to lap with their tongue.

2. By electricity.

3. By mechanical influences; for we must refer to taste the sensation of nausea produced by mechanically irritating the velum palati, epiglottis, and root of the tongue.

The sensations of the nerves of touch or feeling are excited:

1. By mechanical influences; as sonorous vibrations, and contact of any kind.

2. By chemical influences.

3. By heat.

4. By electricity.

5. By the stimulus of the blood.

V. *Sensation consists in the sensorium receiving through the medium of the nerves, and as the result of the action of an external cause, a knowledge of certain qualities or conditions, not of external bodies, but of the nerves of sense themselves; and these qualities of the nerves of sense are in all different, the nerve of each sense having its own peculiar quality or energy.*

The special susceptibility of the different nerves of sense for certain influences,—as of the optic nerve for light, of the auditory nerve for vibrations, and so on,—was formerly attributed to these nerves having each a specific irritability. But this hypothesis is evidently insufficient to explain all the facts. The nerves of the senses have assuredly a specific irritability for certain influences; for many stimuli, which exert a violent action upon one organ of sense, have little or no effect upon another: for example, light, or vibrations so infinitely rapid as those of light, act only on the nerves of vision and common sensation; slower vibrations, on the nerves of hearing and common sensation, but not upon those of vision; odorous substances only upon the olfactory nerves. The external stimuli must therefore be adapted to the organ of sense—must be "homogeneous:" thus light is the stimulus adapted to the nerve of vision; while vibrations of less rapidity, which act upon the auditory nerve, are not adapted to the optic nerve, or are indifferent to it; for if the eye be touched with a tuning-fork while vibrating, a sensation of tremours is excited in the conjunctiva, but no sensation of light. We have seen, however, that one and the same stimulus, as electricity, will produce different sensations in the different nerves of the senses; all the nerves are susceptible of its action, but the sensations in all are different. The same is the case with other stimuli, as chemical and mechanical influences. The hypothesis of a specific irritability of the nerves of the senses for certain stimuli, is therefore insufficient; and we are compelled to ascribe, with Aristotle, peculiar energies to each nerve,—energies which are vital qualities of the nerve, just as contractility is the vital property of muscle. The truth of this has been rendered more and more evident in recent times by the investigation of the so-called "subjective" phenomena of the senses by Elliot, Darwin, Ritter, Goethe, Purkinje, and Hjort. Those phenomena of the senses, namely, are now styled "subjective," which are produced, not by the usual stimulus adapted to the particular nerve of sense, but by others which do not usually act upon it. These important phenomena were long spoken of as "illusions of the senses," and have been regarded in an erroneous point of view; while they are really true actions of the senses, and must be studied as fundamental phenomena in investigations into their nature.

The sensation of sound, therefore, is the peculiar "energy" or "quality" of the auditory nerve; the sensation of light and colours that of the optic nerve; and so of the other nerves of sense.

* * * * *

VI. *The nerve of each sense seems to be capable of one determinate kind of sensation only, and not of those proper to the other organs of sense; hence one nerve of sense cannot take the place and perform the function of the nerve of another sense.*

The sensation of each organ of sense may be increased in intensity till it becomes pleasurable, or till it becomes disagreeable, without the specific nature of the sensation being altered, or converted into that of another organ of sense. The sensation of dazzling light is an unpleasant sensation of the organ of vision; harmony of colours, an agreeable one. Harmonious and discordant sounds are agreeable and disagreeable sensations of the organ of hearing. The organs of taste and smell have their pleasant and unpleasant tastes and odours; the organ of touch its pleasurable and painful feelings. It appears, therefore, that, even in the most excited condition of an organ of sense, the sensation preserves its specific character. It is an admitted fact that the sensations of light, sound, taste, and odours, can be experienced only in their respective nerves; but in the case of common sensation this is not so evidently the case, for it is a question whether the sensation of pain may not be felt in the nerves of the higher senses,—whether, for example, violent irritation of the optic nerve may not give rise to the sensation of pain. This question is difficult of solution. There are filaments of the nerves of common sensation distributed in the nerves of the other organs of sense: the nostrils are supplied with nerves of common sensation from the second division of the nervus trigeminus in addition to the olfactory nerves; the tongue has common sensibility as well as taste, and may retain the one while it loses the other; the eye and organ of hearing likewise are similarly endowed.

* * * * *

VII. *It is not known whether the essential cause of the peculiar "energy" of each nerve of sense is seated in the nerve itself, or in the parts of the brain and spinal cord with which it is connected; but it is certain that the central portion of the nerves included in the encephalon are susceptible of their peculiar sensations, independently of the more peripheral portion of the nervous cords which form the means of communication with the external organs of sense.*

The specific sensibility of the individual

senses to particular stimuli,—owing to which vibrations of such rapidity or length as to produce sound are perceived, only by the senses of hearing and touch, and mere mechanical influences, scarcely at all by the sense of taste,—must be a property of the nerves themselves; but the peculiar mode of reaction of each sense, after the excitement of its nerve, may be due to either of two conditions. Either the nerves themselves may communicate impressions different in quality to the sensorium, which in every instance remains the same; or the vibrations of the nervous principle may in every nerve be the same and yet give rise to the perception of different sensations in the sensorium, owing to the parts of the latter with which the nerves are connected having different properties. The proof of either of these propositions I regard as at present impossible.

* * * * *

VIII. *The immediate objects of the perception of our senses are merely particular states induced in the nerves, and felt as sensations either by the nerves themselves or by the sensorium; but inasmuch as the nerves of the senses are material bodies, and therefore participate in the properties of matter generally occupying space, being susceptible of vibratory motion, and capable of being changed chemically as well as by the action of heat and electricity, they make known to the sensorium, by virtue of the changes thus produced in them by external causes, not merely their own condition, but also properties and changes of condition of external bodies. The information thus obtained by the senses concerning external nature, varies in each sense, having a relation to the qualities or energies of the nerve.*

Qualities which are to be regarded rather as sensations or modes of reaction of the nerves of sense, are light, colour, the bitter and sweet tastes, pleasant and unpleasant odours, painful and pleasant impressions on the nerves of touch, cold and warmth: properties which may belong wholly to external nature are "extension," progressive and tremulous motion, and chemical change.

All the senses are not equally adapted to impart the idea of "extension" to the sensorium. The nerve of vision and the nerve of touch, being capable of an exact perception of this property in themselves, make

us acquainted with it in external bodies. In the nerves of taste, the sensation of extension is less distinct, but is not altogether deficient; thus we are capable of distinguishing whether the seat of a bitter or sweet taste be the tongue, the palate, or the fauces. In the sense of touch and sight, however, the perception of space is most acute. The retina of the optic nerve has a structure especially adapted for this perception; for the ends of the nervous fibres in the retina are, as Treviranus discovered, so arranged as to be at last perpendicular to its inner surface, and by their papillar extremities form a pavement-like composite membrane. On the great number of these terminal fibrils depends the delicate power of discriminating the position of bodies in space possessed by the sense of vision; for each fibre represents a greater or less field of the visible world, and imparts the impression of it to the sensorium.

* * * * *

IX. *That sensations are referred from their proper seat towards the exterior, is owing, not to anything in the nature of the nerves themselves, but to the accompanying idea derived from experience.*

To know the first independent action of our senses distinct from the results of their education, it would be necessary that we had a full recollection of the first impressions made upon them independently of the ideas obtained through their means. This is impossible. Obscure ideas arise even from the first impressions on the senses of the child. It only remains for us then to analyse the act of sensation and the idea with reference to their real import. Doing this, we find in the act of the mind which accompanies sensation, opposed to each other, *the percipient conscious subject*, or self, of the sentient body whose conditions, whether internal or determined from without, are objects for this "conscious self," and the *external world*, with which the sentient body is brought into collision. To the mental consciousness,—to the "self" of the animal being,—every sensation, every motive from without, every "passion" in the logical sense, is something external. The "self" of the individual opposes itself as a free "subject" to the most intense sensations, —to the most tormenting pains. The limb which gives us pain can be removed without the integrity of the individual spirit being diminished; the "self" of the being may be deprived of most of the limbs (parts) of the organic body, and yet be itself as perfect as before.

* * * * *

X. *The mind not only perceives the sensations and interprets them according to ideas previously obtained, but it has a direct influence upon them, imparting to them intensity. This influence of the mind, in the case of the senses which have the power of distinguishing the property of extension in objects, may be confined to definite parts of the sentient organ; in the sense gifted with the power of distinguishing with delicacy intervals of time, it may be confined to particular acts of sensation. It also has the power of giving to one sense a predominant activity.*

The attention cannot be directed to many impressions at the same time: in proportion as coetaneous impressions on the senses become numerous, the sensations diminish in intensity, or the mind receives one only with distinctness; while the others are only obscurely, or not at all perceived. If the attention be withdrawn from the nerves of sense, and engaged in intellectual contemplation, deep speculations, or an intense passion, the sensations of the nerves make no impression upon the mind; they are not perceived,—that is to say, they are not communicated to the conscious "self," or with so little intensity, that the mind is at the moment, on account of being quite preoccupied by some other idea, unable to retain the impression, or only recollects it some time after, when the equilibrium of the sensorium is restored, and it is freed from the preponderating influence of the idea which had occupied it. The acuteness, which individual senses acquire when others are quite inactive, is therefore readily intelligible; the attention is no longer divided between the several senses, but is wholly engaged in the analysis of the sensations of one.

The blind man acquires such an extraordinary acuteness of touch, as to distinguish with facility the minute elevations on the surface of money, for example; sometimes, indeed, he is able to discriminate between the corpus or grain of one colouring matter and that of another.

By an effort of the mind, however, the detail of a single sensation may be analysed. Since the mind is not capable of directing an equally accurate attention to every part of the cutaneous surface excited to sensation, an acute perception of the state of every part can be attained only by the mind being rapidly directed from the nervous fibres of one part to those of another. By this influence of the mind, an extraordinary degree of troublesome acuteness and permanence may be given to a slight itching sensation at any point of the skin of the face, while it ceases spontaneously when forgotten. The same influence of the mind is evinced in the sense of vision.

* * * * *

In concluding this introduction to the physiology of the senses, the question naturally presents itself: Is the number of the senses limited? may not some animals be endowed with other senses besides those which we possess? The error into which Spallanzani fell, in ascribing a peculiar sense to bats on account of their expertness of flight along the surface of walls when they could not see them, is well known. Many persons again have ascribed to animals a peculiar sense by reason of their foreknowledge of the changes of weather. Since the state of the atmospheric pressure, the quantity of watery vapour in the atmosphere, temperature, and electricity, have so marked an influence on the animal œconomy of our own bodies, that we are sensible of changes which they undergo, the possibility of such and even greater influences on animals may very well be conceived; but even great dependence on the state of the atmosphere with reference to sensation does not require a new sense. On the contrary, the state of the atmosphere may be perceived by its influence on the whole nervous system, and particularly through the sensations of the nerves which are most numerous, and most exposed to the atmosphere, namely, the nerves of touch or common sensation. The supposed existence of a special sense for the perception of electricity in some animals is, *à priori*, not admissible; for electricity acts, as we have already shown, upon all the senses, exciting in each the sensations peculiar to it.

The essential attribute of a new sense is, not the perception of external objects or influences which ordinarily do not act upon the senses, but that external causes should excite in it a new and peculiar kind of sensation different from all the sensations of our five senses. Such peculiar kind of sensation will depend on the powers of the nervous system; and the possibility of the possession of such a faculty by some animals cannot, *à priori*, be denied: no facts, however, are known which establish the existence of such a new mode of sensation, and it is, in fact, quite impossible to have any experience of the nature of a sensation in any other beings than ourselves.

EWALD HERING
(1834–1918)

Theory of Light Sense and Chromatic Sense [2]

Colors can be divided into two main groups. Red, yellow, green, blue, and the transitions between any two of these visual qualities are called hues (*Farbentöne*) by Helmholtz. Regardless of whether a color has a pronounced hue or only a hint of it, we can always distinguish it as a *hued* or *chromatic* color from those colors that reveal no trace of hue. Thus we obtain on the one hand the group of hued or chromatic colors, on the other hand the group of hueless or achromatic colors, which include all the blacks, grays, and whites. In the past these two groups have been distinguished as colored and colorless visual sensations.

The theory of achromatic colors in the narrower sense has been designated the theory of the *light sense*, the theory of the chromatic colors as the theory of the *color sense*.

I shall begin by considering the achromatic colors.

9. *The Series of Achromatic Colors.* All achromatic colors can be thought of as ordered in a series so that the deepest black imaginable is at one extreme and the purest possible white at the other, while in between all possible steps of darkness or brightness— black, grayish black, blackish gray, gray, whitish gray, grayish white, and white—are aligned in a continuous sequence. This achromatic series can also be called the *black-white color series* after its two terminal colors.

* * * * *

12. *The Series of Color Hues.* Every chromatic color of given chromatic quality, which in agreement with Helmholtz I call its hue, can be more or less whitish, grayish, or blackish, that is, can be veiled or masked by white, gray, or black to different degrees. Chromatic colors that do not obviously show such veiling I shall call unmasked chromatic colors (*couleurs franches*); but those which, in addition to their hue, show more or less clear whiteness, grayness, or blackness may be called *veiled*.

Chromatic colors that are as free as possible from masking are usually designated saturated colors. However, since Helmholtz, saturation has also been used as a property of the related light rays, and furthermore, because Helmholtz has taken as the criterion of a saturated color only its lack of definite whiteness or grayness but has not included the absence of blackness, in order to avoid misunderstanding of the word "saturated" I shall not use it at all. We know from experience that the clearest definition of a word is of little use if it is already known to the reader in a different sense; he automatically continues to associate the word with the old ideas.

The chromatic colors, whether masked or not, can be thought of as ordered according to hue in a closed series, a so-called *color circle*, in such a way that the difference in hue of two adjacent colors is minimal, the similarity maximal, and with the hues continuously grading into one another.

If we take any color as starting point on such a color circle, for example, a red similar to that of the long-wavelength end of the spectrum, then we see the red colors lined up in one direction becoming increasingly more yellowish, while simultaneously the redness of the color recedes until passing through orange and gold yellow we reach a yellow with no

---

[2] Ewald Hering, *Outline of a Theory of Light Sense*, trans. Leo M. Hurvich and Dorothea Jameson (Cambridge, Mass.: Harvard University Press, 1964), pp. 26, 41–42, 44–48. Reprinted by permission. See footnote 3.

remaining trace of the redness that was so obvious in the orange. Other yellow colors succeed this yellow, tending more and more toward green (sulfur yellow, canary yellow); further on, the yellow recedes more and more behind the continuously more prominent greenness (as in sap green), and we finally reach a green that looks completely free of yellow. Green colors following this green tend into blue (sea green); further on the blueness becomes continuously stronger and the greenness continuously weaker (sea blue), until we reach a blue that no longer shows any greenness. After this blue come blues of increasing redness and hence decreasing blueness (blue violet, red violet, purple red), until the last trace of blueness vanishes in a true red. Then red hues that begin to show yellowish traces follow this red until we return again to that red from which we started.

This description makes it clear that there are four outstanding loci in the series of hues that make up the closed cirlce: first, the locus of the yellow that shows no remaining trace of redness, and yet reveals no trace of green; second the locus of the blue for which the same is true. These two hues may be called *primary yellow* and *primary blue* [*Urgelb* and *Urblau*]. Likewise we can name, third, the red, and, fourth, the green that are neither bluish nor yellowish *primary red* and *primary green* [*Urrot* and *Urgrün*].

All hues can be arranged in the circle so that these primary hues divide it into its four quadrants.

* * * * *

When we see a color whose hue is very close to one of the four primary hues, there might be some doubt whether or not its hue corresponds exactly to the primary color in question. But if we have a whole sequence of related colors available, for example, red hues of such a sort that at one end of the series there is a quite clearly bluish red, and at the other end a quite clearly yellowish one, and in between all transitional hues that include primary red, then, if we scan the series slowly, say, from the bluish-red end, we always come to a red that constitutes a transition point in the series, for here all blueness ceases and beyond it yellowness begins. If we look through the series starting from the other end, it very commonly happens that the red which

corresponds to the transition point, where yellowness just stops, lies somewhat nearer to the yellowish-red end of the series than the primary red locus found in the first direction of scanning. This is a result of successive color contrast; the eye that has just looked at yellowish red sees because of contrast a bluish red where primary red or even yellowish red would be seen if bluish red had been looked at first. The momentary *chromatic tuning* of the eye, . . . mainly determines which color is elicited by a given radiation, and for that reason it would be impossible to specify for every primary color a precise pigment or a precise radiation as the one that elicits the primary color under all circumstances.

For broad-band distributions, we must also consider differences in the light by which the pigment in question is illuminated, and finally, individual differences in color vision. Every color, including each primary color, is, as we have already seen, not associated with a fixed radiation, but with a specific visual excitation, and only if the tuning of the eye is exactly the same will a given radiation on a different occasion evoke exactly the same kind of activity and hence exactly the same color.

If the series of hues that lie between two primary colors, say primary yellow and primary red, in an ideal color circle were arranged on a straight line (RY, Fig. 3) with the two primary colors at the ends, then we could represent the varying degrees of similarity between individual intermediate hues and the hues of the two primary colors by geometrical means. The quadrangle RR_1Y_1Y is divided by the diagonal RY into a lower red half (RR_1Y), and an upper yellow one (YY_1R_1). For every point on the straight line RY, for instance, the point r, there is an ordinate (ry) that lies partly in the red and partly in the yellow of the color quadrangle; the ratio of these two ordinate segments differs at each point on the line, and expresses the ratio of red to yellow quality that characterizes the hue in question. We see the yellow ordinate segment grow and the red diminish as the similarity of the color to primary yellow increases and its similarity to primary red decreases.

Such a schematic representation of the ratio of hue similarly or relatedness can be applied to the whole color circle. . . . At the same time this schema provides a convenient basis for specifying intermediate hues.   I shall illustrate this for one quadrant of the color circle.

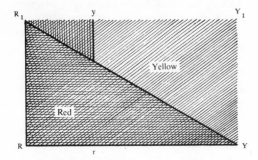

All hues related both to primary red and to primary yellow can be called red yellow or yellow red, which in itself implies nothing about the *proportion* of red to yellow. If these two qualities happen to be equally prominent in the hue, it could be characterized by using signs, red = yellow or yellow = red. If redness obviously exceeds yellowness, then everyday language describes the color as yellow red and in the reverse case as red yellow, which can also be expressed symbolically as yellow < red or red < yellow. Finally, if the predominantly reddish hue has only a perceptible trace of yellow, then it is called yellowish red (yellow ≪ red), and if the hue is quite predominantly yellowish and only tends toward red, then it is called reddish yellow (red ≪ yellow).

One could also proceed as H. Spencer once proposed, and specify the individual hues of the color circle in the way we specify points on the compass if we simply substitute the four primary color hues for the four main compass directions.

But in all these color designations we are concerned only with what is actually *seen* in the color, not with the light mixture or the pigment by which this color was produced and which the color may *bring to mind*.

* * * * *

The fact, . . . that a greenish-looking color is obtained by a mixture of blue and yellow colorants might mislead a person who has not yet learned to distinguish clearly between color as sensory quality and the materials to which the color seems to belong to ascribe both yellow and blue simultaneously to green, even though we know from observation that a completely uniform green field never simultaneously appears clearly yellowish and bluish. There may be some question whether a given green should be accepted as primary green, or whether it may still have a trace of blueness or yellowness. But no one would assert that a green can be clearly both yellowish and bluish, in the way that a violet appears simultaneously bluish and reddish, and no one would call a green blue-yellow or yellow-blue in the same sense as one unhesitatingly designates a violet as red-blue or blue-red.

But whether or not one agrees with the view advocated here, it cannot be disputed that it provides a way of naming the different hues meaningfully. This is possible only because *four* variable properties are assumed in the chromatic colors, namely, red, yellow, green, and blue, and thus these four hues provide the basis for the nomenclature. As soon as one admits only three variable properties, for example, red, green, and violet, and attempts to base a nomenclature on these, one is immediately convinced of the uselessness of such a procedure. One is then forced to describe yellow, for instance, as a red green or green red, blue as a violet green or green violet. That this would be quite incomprehensible to the ordinary person would be disturbing, but of no theoretical consequence. But it would not be immaterial that such a way of assigning names to colors does not at all express in what way and to what extent the colors appear to be interrelated.

Moreover, . . . corresponding to the four hue variables I have assumed, there are four physiological variables. This proposal will then answer the objections to my view on the part of those who want to order colors not according to their own properties, but on the basis of correlated physiological processes.

* * * * *

All [3] sensations of the black-white series of sensations appear related to one another in a twofold manner, and have in common two different kinds of factors, namely, the sensa-

---

[3] Ewald Hering, *Theory of Light Sensation*, trans. Benjamin Rand (Boston: Houghton Mifflin, 1912), pp. 588–591; original German, *Zur Lehre vom Lichtsinne* in *Sitzber. Akad. Wiss. Wien, math-naturw.* (Vienna, 1872–1874; *ibid.*, 1878).

tion of brightness and of darkness, the black and the white. I have also set forth how each member of this sensation series can be characterised by the relation in which both these factors are contained in the given sensation. If now we ask concerning the psychical correlates of those sensations, and concerning the psychophysical or psychochemical processes lying at their basis; not only does the hypothesis, that the physical correlate of the blackest sensation is nothing further than the lowest degree of intensity of the same process which conditions in its highest intensity the clearest or purest white sensation, have nothing in its favor, but even appears to be extravagant and contradictory. For this hypothesis demands one and the same kind of psychophysical process for two clearly fundamentally different qualities of sensation. But our entire psychophysics is based upon the hypothesis, that there exists a certain parallelism between physical and psychical events, and especially that to different qualities of sensation there correspond different qualities or forms of psychophysical phenomena.

If we do not desire, therefore, at the outset to introduce in like manner into this difficult domain an hypothesis which stands in a yet unsolved contradiction to the fundamental presupposition of the entire science of psychophysics, and probably furnishes a bad precedent for other wholly capricious and theoretically improbable hypotheses, we must abandon the present current view. And we can do this the more readily as another hypothesis presents itself which is thoroughly in accord with the aforementioned presupposition of psychophysics, and at the same time satisfies far better than the present theory the demands which must be taken into consideration from the point of view of the general physiology of the nerves. This hypothesis is the following:

To the two qualities of sensation, which we designate as white or bright and as black or dark, correspond two different qualities of chemical activity in the visual substance; and to the different relations of brightness or intensity, with which these two sensations appear in single transitions between pure white and pure black, or to the relations in which they appear mixed, correspond the same relations of intensities of those two psychophysical processes.

It will be readily acknowledged after re-

flection, that this hypothesis is the simplest there is, because it states the simplest formula that can be conceived for the functional connection between physical and psychical phenomena.

But it also satisfies every demand that the general physiology of the nerves can make. We must suppose a substance in the nervous visual apparatus, which suffers change under the influence of the light that falls upon it, and this change, even though it may be characterised as physical, is nevertheless, as the physiology of the nerves must assume, at the same time a chemical process. If the action of the light ceases, the changed (more or less exhausted) substance reverts sooner or later to its original condition. This reversion can in turn be nothing but a chemical change in the opposite direction. If the occurring change of the excitable substance under the direct influence of light is conceived as a partial consumption, the reversion to the former condition must be conceived as a restitution; and if the former is viewed as an analytic process, the latter must be viewed as a synthetic process.

It has also been customary to designate the latter process, by means of which the living organic substance again restores the loss suffered by excitation or activity as *assimilation*, and I will retain this expression. Now every living and excitable organic substance forms in the excitation or activity according to general assumption certain chemical products. The formation of these products I will designate analogously as the process of *dissimilation*.

The propositions concerning assimilation (*A*) and dissimilation (*D*) just set forth are derived from the experiences of general physiology, and particularly of the physiology of the nerves. They have, therefore, been developed wholly independently of our hypothesis. Granted their correctness, it is by no means plausible, that merely the one kind of chemical activity in the visual substance, namely dissimilation, should have a psychophysical significance, but the other, the process of assimilation, none. The common view, that the chemical process taking place under the direct influence of light, namely dissimilation, is alone perceived, is clearly onesided and unjustified. On the contrary, it appears from the outset proper to ascribe an equal value for sensation to both kinds of chemical process. But this leads to none other than the hypothesis above formulated. For we need only to make this hypothesis still more precise, by saying, *that the dissimilation of the visual substance corresponds to the sensation of white or bright, and the assimilation of the visual substance to the sensation of black or dark;* and then the hypothesis . . . satisfies not only the facts of sensation, but also the demands of the general physiology of the nerves.

If my hypothesis is correct we have the means, through the visual sensations, of observing closely the "building up" process of the visual substance, and its two principal factors, assimilation and dissimilation. We do not, therefore, deal hereafter only with the fact, that a complex of sensations is transmitted from the eye to the human soul, which afterwards moulds it into presentations by the aid of correct or false judgments or inferences; but what comes to consciousness as visual sensation is the physical expression or the conscious correlate of the chemical change of the visual substance.

ERNST MACH
(1838–1916)

Analysis of Sensations [4]

Colors, sounds, temperatures, pressures, spaces, times, and so forth, are connected with one another in manifold ways; and with them are associated moods of mind, feelings, and volitions. Out of this fabric, that which is relatively more fixed and permanent stands prominently forth, engraves itself in the memory, and expresses itself in language. Relatively greater permanency exhibit, first, certain *complexes* of colors, sounds, pressures, and so forth, connected in time and space, which therefore receive special names, and are designated *bodies*. Absolutely permanent such complexes are not.

My table is now brightly, now dimly lighted. Its temperature varies. It may receive an ink stain. One of its legs may be broken. It may be repaired, polished, and replaced part for part. But for me, amid all its changes, it remains the table at which I daily write.

* * * * *

Our greater intimacy with this sum-total of permanency, and its preponderance as contrasted with the changeable, impel us to the partly instinctive, partly voluntary and conscious economy of mental representation and

designation, as expressed in ordinary thought and speech. That which is perceptually represented in a single image receives *a single* designation, *a single* name.

As relatively permanent, there is exhibited, further, that complex of memories, moods, and feelings, joined to a particular body (the human body), which is denominated the "I" or "Ego." I may be engaged upon this or that subject, I may be quiet or animated, excited or ill-humored. Yet, pathological cases apart, enough durable features remain to identify the ego. Of course, the ego also is only of relative permanency.

* * * * *

The useful habit of designating such relatively permanent compounds by *single* names, and of apprehending them by *single* thoughts, without going to the trouble each time of an analysis of their component parts, is apt to come into strange conflict with the tendency to isolate the component parts. The vague image which we have of a given permanent complex, being an image which does not perceptibly change when one or another of the component parts is taken away, gradually establishes itself as something which exists *by itself.* Inasmuch as it is possible to take away *singly* every constituent part without destroying the capacity of the image to *stand for* the totality and of being recognised again, it is imagined that it is possible to subtract *all* the parts and to have something still remaining.

[4] Ernst Mach, *Contributions to the Analysis of Sensation,* trans. C. M. Williams (Chicago: Open Court, 1897), ch. 1; original German, *Beitrage aur Analyse der Empfindungen* (Jena, 1886).

Thus arises the monstrous notion of a *thing in itself*, unknowable and different from its "phenomenal" existence.

Thing, body, matter, are nothing apart from their complexes of colors, sounds and so forth—nothing apart from their so-called attributes.

* * * * *

Man possesses, in its highest form, the power of consciously and arbitrarily determining his point of view. He can at one time disregard the most salient features of an object, and immediately thereafter give attention to its smallest details; now consider a stationary current, without a thought of its contents, and then measure the width of a Fraunhofer line in the spectrum; he can rise at will to the most general abstractions or bury himself in the minutest particulars. The animal possesses this capacity in a far less degree. It does not assume a point of view, but is usually forced to it. The babe who does not know its father with his hat on, the dog that is perplexed at the new coat of its master, have both succumbed in this conflict of points of view. Who has not been worsted in similar plights? Even the man of philosophy at times succumbs, as the grotesque problem, above referred to, shows.

* * * * *

We see an object having a point *S*. If we touch *S*, that is, bring it into connexion with our body, we receive a prick. We can see *S*, without feeling the prick. But as soon as we feel the prick we find *S*. The visible point, therefore, is a *permanent fact* or *nucleus,* to which the prick is annexed, according to circumstances, as something accidental. From the frequency of such occurrences we ultimately accustom ourselves to regard *all* properties of bodies as "effects" proceeding from permanent nuclei and conveyed to the ego through the medium of the body; which effects we call *sensations.* By this operation, however, our imagined nuclei are deprived of their entire sensory contents, and converted into mere mental symbols. The assertion, then, is correct that the world consists only of our sensations. In which case we have knowledge *only* of sensations, and the assumption of the nuclei referred to, or of a reciprocal action between them, from which sensations

proceed, turns out to be quite idle and superfluous. Such a view can only suit with a half-hearted realism or a half-hearted philosophical criticism.

* * * * *

That traditional gulf between physical and psychological research, accordingly, exists only for the habitual stereotyped method of observation. A color is a physical object so long as we consider its dependence upon its luminous source, upon other colors, upon heat, upon space, and so forth. Regarding, however, its dependence upon the retina ... it becomes a psychological object, a sensation. Not the subject, but the direction of our investigation, is different in the two domains.

Both in reasoning from the observation of the bodies of other men or animals, to the sensations which they possess, as well as in investigating the influence of our own body upon our own sensations, we must complete observed facts by analogy. This is accomplished with much greater readiness and certainty, when it relates, say, only to nervous processes, which cannot be fully observed in our own bodies—that is, when it is carried out in the more familiar physical domain—than when it is made in connexion with psychical processes. Otherwise there is no essential difference.

* * * * *

Ordinarily pleasure and pain are regarded as different from sensations. Yet not only tactile sensations, but all other kinds of sensations, may pass gradually into pleasure and pain. Pleasure and pain also may be justly termed sensations. Only they are not so well analysed and so familiar as the common sensations. In fact, sensations of pleasure and pain, however faint they may be, really, make up the contents of all so-called emotions. Thus, perceptions, ideas, volition, and emotion, in short the whole inner and outer world, are composed of a small number of homogeneous elements connected in relations of varying evanescence or permanence. Usually, these elements are called sensations. But as vestiges of a one-sided theory inhere in that term, we prefer to speak simply of *elements*, as we have already done. The aim of all research is to ascertain the mode of connexion of these elements.

That in this complex of elements, which fundamentally is *one*, the boundaries of bodies and of the ego do not admit of being established in a manner definite and sufficient for all cases, has already been remarked. The comprehending of the elements that are most intimately connected with pleasure and pain, under one ideal mental-economical unity, the ego, is a work of the highest significance for the intellect in the functions which it performs for the pain-avoiding, pleasure-seeking will. The delimitation of the ego, therefore, is instinctively effected, is rendered familiar, and possibly becomes fixed through heredity. Owing to their high practical value, not only for the individual, but for the entire species, the composites "ego" and "body" assert instinctively their claims, and operate with all the power of natural elements. In special cases, however, in which practical ends are not concerned, but where knowledge is an object in itself, the delimitation in question may prove to be insufficient, obstructive, and untenable.

The primary fact is not the *I*, the ego, but the elements (sensations). The elements *constitute* the *I*. That *I* have the sensation green, signifies that the element green occurs in a given complex of other elements (sensations, memories). When *I* cease to have the sensation green, when *I* die, then the elements no longer occur in their ordinary, familiar way of association. That is all. Only an ideal mental-economical unity, not a real unity, has ceased to exist.

If a knowledge of the connexion of the elements (sensations) does not suffice us, and we ask, *Who* possesses this connexion of sensations, *Who* experiences the sensations? then we have succumbed to the habit of subsuming every element (every sensation) under some *unanalysed* complex, and we are falling back imperceptibly upon an older, lower and more limited point of view.

The so-called unity of consciousness is not an argument in point. Since the apparent antithesis of *real* world and *perceived* world is due entirely to our mode of view, and no actual gulf exists between them, a rich and variously interconnected content of consciousness is in no respect more difficult to understand than a rich and diversified inter-connexion of the world.

If we regard the ego as a *real* unity, we become involved in the following dilemma: either we must set over against the ego a world of unknowable entities (which would be quite idle and purposeless), or we must regard the whole world, the egos of other people included, as comprised in our own ego (a proposition to which it is difficult to yield serious assent).

But if we take the ego simply as a *practical* unity, put together for purposes of provisional survey, or simply as a more strongly coherent group of elements, less strongly connected with other groups of this kind, questions like those above discussed will not arise and research will have an unobstructed future.

* * * * *

Bodies do not produce sensations, but complexes of sensations (complexes of elements) make up bodies. If, to the physicist, bodies appear the real, abiding existences, whilst sensations are regarded merely as their envanescent, transitory show, the physicist forgets, in the assumption of such a view, that all bodies are but thought-symbols for complexes of sensations (complexes of elements). Here, too, the *elements* form the real, immediate, and ultimate foundation, which it is the task of physiological research to investigate. By the recognition of this fact, many points of psychology and physics assume more distinct and more economical forms, and many spurious problems are disposed of.

For us, therefore, the world does not consist of mysterious entities, which by their interaction with another, equally mysterious entity, the ego, produce sensations, which alone are accessible. For us, colors, sounds, spaces, times, ... are the ultimate elements, whose given connexion it is our business to investigate. In this investigation we must not allow ourselves to be impeded by such intellectual abridgments and delimitations, as body, ego, matter, mind, etc., which have been formed for special, practical purposes and with wholly provisional and limited ends in view. On the contrary, the fittest forms of thought must be created in and by that research *itself*, just as is done in every special science. In place of the traditional, instinctive ways of thought, a freer, fresher view, conforming to developed experience, must be substituted.

MAX VON FREY
(1852–1932)

The Four Cutaneous Senses [5]

1. Temperature Sensations

In order to get a clear perspective on these sensations, one must consider what results concerning external objects are gained by skin stimulation alone, without the interference of the other sense organs. To avoid the interference of these other sense organs as factors, one must refrain from moving the sense area itself, and rather, move objects on the surface of the resting skin.

Now although these prescribed conditions are very limited, still the information is very diverse. Included are size, form, volume, absolute and specific weight, texture, general state, elasticity, temperature, and other factors, and, in addition to these sense properties, there are other states that are related to the body itself—tickling, well-being, itching, trembling, etc.

It is easily observable that in objective reports known elements invariably recur, and occur in a variety of situations. It is possible, by means of this fact, to show the elements that are fundamental. The analysis is especially conclusive when successful in bringing out particular elements by experiment and grading them according to intensity. In this way it is possible to establish that in objective reports, one obtains only the sensations of cold, warmth, pressure, pain, as well as their variations in space and time.

Subjective sensory complexes which are not surely drawn up and graded experimentally, and therefore which are not so easily observed, are much more difficult to analyze. Besides those mentioned already, they include many forms of pain sensation. Still, it is possible to show that many sensations of pain are probably not simple sensations of skin, in that stimuli from deeper parts, particularly from the motor-apparatus, interfere with them. This is indeed true of the sensation of lust and can be easily demonstrated to be true of trembling. Above all, the appearance of gooseflesh is associated with peculiar sensations which arise partly from the fixed hair follicles, but in part directly form the contracted smooth muscle cells. Vascular contraction is then a very significant factor in the above-mentioned mixed sensations, and is probably responsible for the painful sensations from the application of cold on large surfaces of the body.

If given the skin as a uniform sensory surface, in contrast to the aforementioned supposition, through which all sorts of sensations might be communicated within one region of sensation by means of various anatomical structures, one would have to expect that those cutaneous surfaces such as the fingertips which have the greatest sensitivity to pressure, would be especially capable of judging temperature. This conclusion contradicts everyday experience. It is obvious to everyone that the skin of the face and trunk have a much stronger sensitivity to temperature than the extremities, particularly of the distal parts. If one were to fill two small flasks with temperatures of 25° C. and 35° C., the touch of the fingertips would hardly pick up the differing temperatures, although the touch of the eyelid or the corner of the mouth is extremely sensitive to the difference. It is obvious that the difference in sensitivity is not an exclusive result of the varying thickness of the epidermis, because the thin skin of the wrist perceives the difference badly. Small metal objects at room temperature can withdraw only a very little amount of heat from the body and are therefore indistinguishable (in temperature) when placed on some surfaces of the skin. However, on the eyelid or upon the lip, they are clearly recognized as cold.

When one uses cold or warm objects having small surfaces for the purpose of thermal skin stimulation, it becomes clear even from the most fleeting examination that coinciding sensations are not released on every surface element of the skin. There are only isolated points upon which sensitivity to temperature appears. Blix, who first discovered this, also observed that cold and warm stimuli are not efficacious on the same areas. Therefore, in regard to thermal stimulation, one must differentiate among three types of surface elements on the skin: (1) insensitive, (2) sensitive to cold, (3) sensitive to warmth, the

[5] Max von Frey, *Vorlesungen über Physiologie* (Berlin: Springer, 1904), pp. 308–326. Translated for the present volume by William S. Annand.

last being always in the minority. Blix named the surface elements of the second type cold spots and those of the third type warm spots. Where the epidermis is thick, stimulation with small-surfaced objects is unsuccessful. But even in the case of thick epidermis, varying sensitivity from spot to spot is noticeable.

When the position and number of the sensitivity spots have been determined for a large skin surface, it becomes obvious that these spots can be relocated again and again after a suitable interval of time. Doubtless, then, these spots are fixed anatomical structures—namely the centripetal nerve endings which allow the skin its sensitivity to temperature and the projections of which on the outer skin are represented by the stationary experimental warm and cold spots. Through interesting research, Thunberg has shown it to be probable that cold spots lie nearer the outer surface than warm ones.

Analyses of the density of these structures have been carried out by Sommer on a large number of skin surfaces. For the cold spots he found an average of 13 per square centimeter totalling 250,000 for the entire body surface. On the other hand the warm spots averaged only 1.5 per square centimeter, totalling 30,000 for the entire body surface.

The distribution of the sensitive spots over the skin is very irregular. Seldom do they appear isolated, and for the most part in groups, so that as large a space as one square centimeter may be present in which sensitivity to warm and cold is lacking.

On many areas of the skin with good or even exceptional sensitivity to cold, there is a lack of sensitivity to warm. To this group belong the connective tissues and cornea of the eye, the penis gland, and the nipples. The membranes of the throat and nose also have a prevailing sensitivity to cold. These same membranes lack in general, like the stomach and intestine, any sensitivity to temperature.

One is now in a position, having established the placement over the skin of the organs sensitive to temperature, to deal with the second theory advanced above, according to which the sensation caused by stimulating certain structural elements within a sensory area should vary in quantity or intensity only, and not in quality. This theory can be completely verified as well with reference to those elements of the skin that have temperature sensitivity. They are, as Blix has shown, capable of being stimulated electrically or mechanically as well as thermally and give only sensations of the quality relative to them. The cold spots react with a cold sensation for temperatures above 45° C., this fact being known as the paradoxical sensation of cold.

Physical and Physiological Scales of Temperature. In physics the series of varying temperatures yields a single extended scale. One can go from temperature (a) to temperature (b) only in one way, through all the temperatures that range between (a) and (b). If the zero mark of the scale and the unit of measurement are clear, then naming the degrees will establish the temperatures. For the physical measurement of temperature, distinguishing between cold and warm temperatures is, therefore, meaningless, and is only a historical residue of the original physiological measurement. This is shown in the arbitrary zero point, which can be set either at the melting temperature of ice or at —17.8° C.

Temperature sensations differ in that they show a much greater variety than instrumental measurement. Warm and cold sensations, separate or combined, can be stimulated in varying intensities, including pain. The best proof of the fact that the sensation of pain does not occur in temperature spots is the use of a shaded convex lens to project sunlight on the skin surface. If the ray hits a warm spot, the sensation of warm occurs. If weak rays hit on one of the surface areas lacking sensitivity to temperature, no sensation of any sort is felt, but if however, the rays are strong, pain will occur. This was first observed by Goldscheider and it is not true of all temperature sensitive spots. As final proof, if sunlight is projected on the surface of a cold spot, amazingly, the sensation of cold appears. Temperatures that stimulate both warm and cold spots are termed hot.

Consequently then, there are three nerve structures in the skin capable of being stimulated by high temperatures. The stimulation of a large surface will activate all three contemporaneously. Low temperatures, the freezing point for instance, can also cause pain. These temperatures are termed severe, biting, or burning cold. In this instance of pain, two nerve structures are brought into action at the same time.

The terms for the sensations show the following relations to the type and number of the structures activated.

	Warm Nerves	Cold Nerves	Pain Nerves
Severe or biting cold	0	+	+
Cold	0	+	0
Cool	0	+	0
Indifferent	0	0	0
Lukewarm	+	0	0
Warm.	+	0	0
Hot.	+	+	0
Burning hot	+	+	+

A plus (+) sign indicates stimulation and zero the absence of stimulation.

The middle point of indifference at which there is no stimulation is arbitrarily set at 33° C. A rise in temperature stimulates the warm nerves, and then the cold nerves, then lastly the pain nerves.

The reaction of temperature on the temperature nerves of the skin is a process which will only be understood with a theory explaining stimulation by temperature. Such a theory is presently lacking. It is safe to say that all changes that lower temperature of an inactive skin surface induce the sensation of cold, and that opposite changes induce warmth. In general, the sharper the changes in temperature, the quicker that the effects are felt; and the larger the area of skin they affect, the clearer the sensations.

2. Pressure Sensations

In addition to the perception by the skin of warm and cold sensations, the sensation of pressure is shown by analysis to be simple and impossible to analyze. Statements of size, form, weight, and texture of objects can be made without consideration of temperature. The statement of E. H. Weber to the effect that when two equal weights are placed upon the skin the colder seems heavier can probably be attributed to an error in judgment, for a weight cooled to less than 0° does lead to the conclusion that a larger volume of metal is present.

It has already been stated that the greatest sensitivity to stimulation by temperature does not occur in the areas of greatest sensitivity to touch. However, quantitative comparison of touch sensitivity in various skin areas is difficult, to say the least. The problem of

distributing weight evenly on the human skin, which is curved in every area, is best coped with by using hydrostatic pressure. Such pressure, however, is known to be not felt. If part of a body is immersed in 1 meter of water or 7.6 cm. of mercury, the resultant pressure, 1/10 that of atmospheric pressure, will not be perceived. But, if one places a hundred gram weight on a skin area which is as level as possible, placing a cork tablet of 1 cm. square under the weight, the pressure, which is again 1/10 that of atmospheric pressure, will no doubt be perceived.

The physiological effect depends not only on the amount of pressure but also on the amount of surface areas on which it is exerted, and the smaller the area pressed, the greater the effect.

The stimulation of a very small surface can be produced by touching a hair or bristle, cut clean across, vertically to the skin.

When using this type of stimulus, it is simple to show that the tip of the tongue, the lip, and the fingertips are exceptional in sensitivity to mechanical stimulation. Even so, these possess a threshold which must be passed if sensation is to take place. The areas where thermal sensitivity is greatest are really not the areas of greatest pressure sensitivity. This would suggest that the two sensations are perceived with different organs.

By stimulating the skin with bristles or hairs in this manner, one realizes that there is a significant difference in single surface elements. When one keeps the level of stimulation near the threshold point when examining skin surfaces, one finds invariably that the majority of the surfaces are insensitive and only single surface elements sensitive. These are termed pressure or touch spots. Their placement is constant and is different from the placement of the warm and cold spots. They are also of greater number. Unlike the temperature spots, their distribution over the surface is even. One touch spot lies near each hair of the hairy areas of the skin. In general the number of hair and touch spots is the same.

When one projects the hair follicle, which slants according to the skin, onto the surface of the skin, the touch spot is located over the projection. Thus we are treating with a nerve apparatus which is related to the hair follicle. On the skin surfaces without hair, (5% of the body), the distribution is not so regular, and often more dense.

3. Sensations of Pain

Pain is among that group of sensations that can be produced from the skin. It should be considered, like the cold, warm, and pressure sensations as a fundamental part of consciousness. Even though it often occurs in the presence of other sensations, it is not dependent on them and appears without them under certain circumstances.

One can distinguish pain from the other skin sensations by its character and also because it is accompanied to a greater extent by feeling, especially feeling of avoidance. Still, it is physiological, since it can occur in a great number of internal organs as well as in the skin. It is also strongly linked to reflex action.

As well as all the layers of the skin, the muscles, both the smooth and striated [mediate pain]. Bruised or torn muscles and pathological changes, such as rheumatic changes, occurring in them, are very painful. Severe contraction of the smooth muscles arouses colic pain or ache. The remainder of the motor apparatus such as tendons, joints, and surface membranes of bones are also subject to pain. Of the glands, the sex glands are most certainly subject to pain, but of the other glands it is not so sure. It is noticeable that significant changes can take place in the lungs without the presence of pain. The brain, and particularly the cortex, is not especially sensitive to pain. However, the meninges can be sensitive. The mucous membranes of the intestine and stomach are insensitive to pain, and, according to Lenander, the visceral peritoneum is also insensitive. The parietal membrane, however, is said to be highly sensitive. The mouth's sensitivity to pain (with the exception of the teeth, the tip of the tongue, and the mucous membrane of the lip) is very small. Kiesow has shown it probable that a large area of the mucous membrane surface of the cheeks is entirely insensitive to pain.

The pain sensations of internal organs probably differ from those of the skin. The weak pain sensations in the skin are called itching, while the stronger ones are termed pricking, burning, biting, and cutting. The temporal course of the pain, its intensity, and other sensations determine in part the description of the sensation. Internal pains are not reinforced by other sensations, are not as pointed, and usually last longer. One terms such pains dull.

Pain sensations can be stimulated in various ways: mechanically, thermally, electrically, and even chemically. In causing pain by mechanical and thermal stimulation, higher intensities of stimulation are required than are needed to induce sensations of touch and temperature. This circumstance has led to the opinion that nerves, when sufficiently stimulated, communicate pain themselves. However, in the case of electrical stimulation, the difference of threshold is not a factor. The use of small electrodes, particularly on the hairy parts of the body, leads to sensations of pain as well as of touch, even though the sensitivity be the same or even less. In chemical stimulation, the placing of droplets of acid on the skin surface has a completely painful effect.... One could theorize that in this instance the nerves sensitive to pain are the ones closest to the surface and so they are the first to be stimulated.... Pure pain sensations may be caused by applying heat over a very small area when one carefully stimulates areas such as the skin on the leg, where the distance between temperature spots is particularly great. When one projects sunlight refracted by a convex lens onto parts of the surface insensitive to temperature, the effect is painful, without any accompanying sensation.

The foregoing experiment proves that pain-sensing organs are present where organs for sensing temperature are lacking, and the same is true of organs for sensing touch. When a small surface of the skin is electrically stimulated it shows the places sensitive to pain to be independent of the placement of the touch spots. It has been attempted to establish that certain spots on the skin are particularly sensitive to pain, and these have been designated pain spots, in line with the terms used for the other sensitive skin areas. In most places, the density of these spots is so much greater than that of the other types of spots that the problem arises of the futility of isolated stimulation. Even so, experiments have shown conclusively that the sensitivity of the skin to pain is not continuous. This fact is brought forth with particular clarity by the existence of large spaces, for example, the Kiesow area in the mucous membrane of the cheek.

The pain-sensing apparatus can be differentiated from the others previously mentioned by its characteristic reactions. With a weak pain stimulation, the sensation takes place afterward, so that perhaps a simultaneous thermal or tactile stimulation can be differentiated from the pain by a short period without sensation.

The Sensory Function of the Skin and the Form of the Nerve Endings. The theory stated at the outset was that in every instance where different types of sensations can be produced in a seemingly uniform area different types of nerves and nerve endings are present. This opinion has been shown to be thoroughly supportable. Now there is to be shown a variety of anatomically traceable types of nerve endings in the skin, with the intent of determining the form of each sensory quality.

The sense of touch is simplest. The relation of touch to the body hair has been proven. There is, as Bonnet first indicated, a characteristic type of nerve ending on every hair which is fully developed on the designated feeling hairs of carniverous animals and whose structure can therefore be fully examined. These nerve endings, to be referred to as the nerve rings of the hair, should therefore be considered the endings of touch nerves in hairy areas of the skin. A large number of different forms can be considered for the touch surfaces of the extremities: the Vater-Pacini and Golgi-Mazzoni corpuscles, Krause's end bulbs, Meissner's corpuscles, Ruffini's nerve bristles, Merkel's touch cells, and simple nerve endings.

In selection, the criterion of sufficient density must be considered, for the density of these touch organs must naturally complement the density of the experimentally known touch spots. There is only one form (of all those just mentioned) that accommodates this demand, that is, Meissner's corpuscles. . . .

In regard to temperature-sensing organs,

the particular forms of nerve endings should be sought after where there is highly developed sensitivity and where the other sensing qualities are excluded to the greatest possible extent. In this instance, the eye is especially interesting. The sense of touch as well as sensitivity to warmth are absent in the connective tissues and the cornea, but sensitivity to cold and pain are well developed there. . . . Only in these areas do we find, as indicated by Dogiel, large numbers of the previously mentioned end bulbs, thus they can be termed as organs for sensing cold. . . .

The middle area of the cornea has sensitivity only to pain, and we find here, as best we know, but one type of nerve ending, the free intraepithelial endings between closely grouped cells, as first described by J. Cohnheim. The existence of this form of ending has been proven not only in the various epithelia but also in structures not ectodermal in their origin. The theory that they are related to the several types of sensitivity is probably because of their extraordinary profusion. The experiments of von Frey and Thunberg further demonstrate that the pain nerves of the skin must have their endings very near to the surface.

The nerve endings for sensing warmth are said to have a deeper location, beneath the surface. The difficulty in locating exactly the placement of the warm spots, and the results of Thunberg's experiments, seem to indicate a deeper location. Thus, the Pacini and Golgi-Mazzoni corpuscles and the recently indicated endings of Ruffini come under consideration. The Pacini and Golgi-Mazzoni corpuscles are uncommonly similar in their structure and thus possible the same in function. The distribution of the Pacini corpuscles does not agree with the specifications of distribution for organs sensitive to warmth. The distribution of the remaining two forms is not sufficiently known so as to allow speculation. Still, Ruffini's endings are found in the eyelid, which being extremely sensitive to warmth, would seem to indicate this quality. . . .

OSWALD KÜLPE
(1862–1915)

Experimental Psychology— Methodology [6]

Psychology as a Science

The business of all science is the description of facts.

* * * * *

The facts with which science in general, apart from philosophy, has to deal we term *facts of experience*. They are the ultimate and original data of our experience: they constitute the subject matter of reflection, although they are not in themselves reflection. Philosophy, on the other hand, has to investigate the description of these facts; our *reflection* upon experience is made the object of a separate inquiry. Now it is evident that the ideas, passions, etc., which psychologists of the most different schools agree in discussing in their treatises, must be considered facts of experience. Hence it follows that psychology belongs not with the philosophical disciplines, but with the special sciences.

* * * * *

Psychology is inductive, for instance, while mathematics is deductive; it stands to pedagogy as theory to practice; it is still in the main descriptive, as compared with the "exact" sciences, which are *par excellence* explanatory. The only principle of delimitation which cannot possibly be employed is that of the subject treated. The reason is, that there is no single fact of experience which cannot be made the subject of psychological investigation. Now since all the other rubrics specify the form and not the matter of the scientific work which they cover, and since the relation of psychology to natural science cannot be subsumed to any one of them in particular, it is clear that we must look for the distinctive character of psychological subject-matter not in the peculiar nature of a definite class of experiential facts, but rather in some property which attaches

to all alike. This property is the *dependency of facts of experience upon experiencing individuals*.

* * * * *

But our definition of psychology as a science of the facts of experience in their dependency upon experiencing individuals is not altogether satisfactory. The term "individual" is used in so many different senses that it itself requires discussion and definition. It might seem at first sight as if we were speaking of a psychical individual, and understanding by the phrase either a transcendent immaterial substance (soul or spirit) or a whole number of experiences and capacities that are ordinarily subjectified (feeling, attention, imagination, etc.). But we cannot, as a matter of fact, accept either of these interpretations. On the first no empirical psychology, on the second no scientific psychology is possible.—The latter statement requires some explanation; the former is self evident.

If psychology is to be scientific, its statements must possess universal validity, and particularly in the second of the two meanings which we attached to this phrase above. Now universal validity can be obtained only by a very complete description of the relations which hold between separate facts, and determine their special character.

Fusion and Colligation [7]

We can, as a matter of fact, distinguish two principal modes: *fusion* and *colligation*. The former is a more close and intimate connection than the latter. Fusion occurs when the connecting qualities are thrust more or less into the background by the total impression which results from their connection,—when, that is, all or sundry of them lose in distinctness by combination. The total impression itself may be, as it were, the resultant of a balance of qualities, or may be dominated by one or more preponderant elements. A simultaneous connection of tones may stand as a typical example of fusion. Colligation

[6] Oswald Külpe, *Outlines of Psychology: Based upon the Results of Experimental Psychology*, trans. Edward Bradford Titchener (New York: Macmillan, 1909, 3rd ed.), pp. 1-3; original German, *Grundriss der Psychologie* (1893).

[7] *Ibid.*, pp. 21, 276–278.

occurs, on the other hand, when the cognisability of the separate qualities is either unaffected by combination, so that they retain their original independence, or is actually increased. The formation of a single qualitative impression is in this case more or less obstructed by the persistent individuality of the elementary constituents. Simultaneous colour contrast (the spatial combination of different colour sensations) may serve as a typical instance of colligation.

It is not necessary at this stage to go further into details of classification. But there is one other point to which attention must be called if we are to avoid misunderstanding of the character of the conscious elements. Just as in nature the various elements never occur alone, absolutely out of connection, but always in physical or chemical combinations with other elements, so the elementary phenomena of mind are never found except in fusion or colligation with their like. And just as natural science obtains its simple substances by analysis, so must we employ the analysis of introspection to make out our elementary qualities. By help of the attention we may, it is true, subject even the less intensive elements to special investigation or observation; but real isolation,—the actual experience of one single sensation, for instance,—can never take place. We may think that we have only heard a tone or seen a colour, but a closer inquiry shows that these were merely parts of a combination upon which the attention was concentrated with peculiar force. "Sensation" and "feeling" are not, therefore, different experiences, in the strict sense, but the results of a qualitative analysis of experience, of which we avail ourselves for scientific purposes. We cannot ascertain the uniformities of complex processes, without this preliminary analysis; and our first task is, accordingly, to examine separately every aspect or attribute which is at all obvious in the concrete mental state.

* * * * *

Our concrete experiences are always made up of connections of the conscious elements. Simple qualities, isolated sensations and feelings, are products of scientific analysis..., and their separate investigation is possible only by the aid of special methods and under favourable general conditions. Even so, the actual experience is practically always complex in character.

We cannot, however, pass at once to the consideration of these actual experiences. Our discussion of conscious connections must also travel, for some time at least, along abstract lines. Psychology (i) has to show that (and how) the connections arise from the elements, and to distinguish between the total impression and its elementary constituents; and (ii) has to inquire whether the connections are all of a single kind, or show characteristic differences, and in the latter case to give the reasons for the divergence. We have, i.e., a further series of problems for analytical treatment, whose solution is necessary for the understanding of the concrete mind.

The elements of consciousness are of two kinds, sensations and feelings. We may, therefore, have connections of sensations with sensations, of feelings with feelings, and of sensations with feelings. It is evident a priori that these three types of connection cannot be of equal importance in consciousness. The qualitative differences of sensation are very numerous..., those of feeling very few...; and the forms and laws of the interconnection of sensations will accordingly be various and complex, while those of the other two categories of connection are correspondingly simple. This is in itself sufficient evidence that we should be ill advised to discuss the subject matter of the second Part of our psychology under three co-ordinate rubrics. But there is another and a more important reason for the rejection of a classification by contents. The doctrine of conscious compounds is mainly occupied with an exact investigation of the formation and attributes of connections. Our task will be very greatly simplified, therefore, if we can discover in these certain general peculiarities (irrespectively of the quality of the connected elements) which may serve as the basis of their broad distinction into definite groups. The best classification of connections, i.e., is a classification in terms of certain distinguishing characteristics of the connections themselves,—provided always that no violence is done by it to the alternative classification in terms of the quality of the connected elements. We have already stated ... that connections, regarded from this point of view, fall into two great classes, and have termed them *fusion* and *colligation*. It is characteristic of the fusion that the elements contained in it are more difficult of analysis, of the colligation that they are easier of analysis, in connection.   Or, to put it in different terms: other things equal (apart, *i.e.*, from the general conditions of sensible discrimination, and its special laws within the given sense department), the character of the connection of compared qualities is of determining influence upon the magnitude and delicacy of sensible discrimination.   In both aspects, it is relatively diminished by fusion and increased by colligation.

A close examination of the conditions under which the two kinds of connection appear in consciousness leads to two important results. We find (*a*) that the quality of sensations or feelings is inessential for fusion and colligation alike; *i.e.*, that the terms really indicate general peculiarities of conscious connection, and are not mere classificatory names, applicable only to definite elements.   And (*b*) we discover a simple rule for the cognition of the particular form of connection in a given case. The rule is couched in terms of the three (or four) attributes of sensations and feelings.   It is plain that we have no right to speak of a connection unless we can, directly or indirectly, analyse it into its elements. If, *e.g.*, two sensations are temporally and spatially indistinguishable and qualitatively identical, we actually have but *one* sensation, though two stimuli may be acting upon consciousness. Nor can we speak in strictness of a connection of two sensations where the two stimuli differ merely in intensity; since stimuli which are identical in all other respects will ordinarily give rise to a single sensation.   Connection, that is, presupposes a noticeable difference in the quality, extension, or duration of its elements.   Our rule now runs as follows: if the connected elements are temporally and spa-

tially identical, but differ in quality, their connection must be termed fusion; if they differ in duration or extension, colligation. Fusion, *i.e.*, may be briefly defined as a qualitative, and colligation as a temporal or spatial connection.   The rule has a further formal value, as transcending the relativity of our general definition of fusion and colligation. This relativity has no practical significance, however: for, given equality of conditions, the different facility of analysis of the two connections is constant and well marked.   The general definition is really relative only in the sense that it restricts the discrimination of fusion and colligation to cases in which their elements are the same.   It tells us that we may compare tonal fusion with tonal colligation, the fusion of colour tone and brightness with their colligation, etc., but that we have no means for the comparison of the fusion of certain elements from one sense with the colligation of certain elements from another.

This limitation is another proof of the dependency of conscious processes upon sensible conditions. . . .   The differences in the sense organs and their adequate stimuli prevent any quantitative comparison of the sensations of different sense departments.   Hence it was impossible to determine the course of the intensive sensible discrimination as between sense and sense. . . .   It follows that we must here treat of fusion and colligation with special reference to the forms which they assume in different sense departments; we must examine separately the fusion of auditory sensations, the fusion of visual sensations, etc. Many of these departments have been but very imperfectly explored, and we shall often be obliged to content ourselves with the demonstration of a few typical cases of the phenomena, while reviewing the rest in more summary fashion.

JOHANNES VON KRIES
(1853–1928)
and
WILIBALD A. NAGEL
(1870–1910)

Duplicity Theory [8]

The theory of the functional difference between the rods and cones was put on a much firmer basis by the researches of Parinaud and von Kries. Independently of each other, and proceeding along different lines, they arrived at a complete confirmation of Max Schultze's hypothesis and shaped it into a reasonable theory. By referring to it as the *duplicity theory* (*Duplizitätstheorie*), which is the name given to it by von Kries, the implication is that there is not simply a morphological duality of the elements of the retinal neuro-epithelium, but a corresponding duality of function as well, and that to a certain extent there are two kinds of vision. One kind is that which is active when the eyes are light-adapted and stimulated by strong light—*Tagessehen* (or *daylight vision, photopia*), as von Kries designates it. Opposed to it is the so-called *Dämmerungssehen* (or *twilight vision, scotopia*), when the eye is dark-adapted and the light stimulus is weak. On the duplicity theory the organ for daylight vision is the "daylight mechanism" or brightness mechanism represented by the totality of the cones; the "twilight mechanism" or darkness-mechanism being constituted by the rods along with the visual purple absorbed in their outer segments.

In agreement with each other and with Schultze, Parinaud and von Kries assumed that only one quality of light sensation can be mediated by the rods. Thus, to a certain extent the twilight mechanism must be considered as being totally colour-blind, whereas the daylight mechanism is *farbentüchtig* or capable of discriminating colours.

The function of the daylight mechanism, pure and simple, is exemplified in vision with the foveal region of the retina where there are

no rods. But the function of the twilight mechanism cannot be isolated so simply. According to the theoretical assumptions, under ordinary circumstances in not too strong light, rods and cones function together simultaneously. But the rods are supposed to have a much greater capacity for dark adaptation. Thus, with low intensity of illumination, the stimulus may be sufficient to excite the rod or twilight mechanism, without being adequate to stimulate the cone mechanism. And hence below a certain limit of intensity, whatever possibility of vision there may be is to be considered as being due entirely to the mediation of the rods. As to whether the rods continue to function along with the cones at high intensities of light, the two kinds of visual epithelium being therefore united for seeing by very bright light, the duplicity theory does not definitely attempt to say. During morning and evening twilight, and in dim light generally, the functions of the two mechanisms are interlinked in a complicated fashion, as will be described in the following sections.

The foundation for the duplicity theory is primarily in the comparison between foveal vision and peripheral rod vision.

* * * * *

On the supposition that the angular diameter of an object which sends out white light is about one degree, and that the eye is thoroughly dark-adapted, the intensity of the light required in order for the object to be just visible when it is fixated directly must be in round numbers one thousand times greater than when the eye views the object with the most sensitive parts of the periphery of the retina; as was stated above. In light adaptation, on the contrary, the sensitivity in the fovea is somewhat greater than in the periphery. The simplest explanation of the superior sensitivity of the dark-adapted periphery of the retina is by assuming that the sensitivity of the rods, which are absent in the fovea but present in the periphery along

---

[8] Wilibald A. Nagel, "Duplicity Theory and Twilight Vision," Johannes von Kries, "Theories of Vision," *Helmholtz' Treatise on Physiological Optics, op. cit.*, pp. 344–350, 430–432. Reprinted by permission.

with the cones, increases in darkness to a much greater degree than that of the cones; and that, therefore, with decreasing illumination, as for example, in the evening twilight, the rods more and more take over the rôle of receptors; until finally, for a certain degree of darkness, the intensity of light is no longer sufficient to stimulate the central part of the retina where there are no rods. Thus the condition is brought about which is characteristic of twilight vision, and in which there is a deficiency of function, a "scotoma," in the centre of the visual field.

* * * * *

Another striking characteristic of twilight vision is the lack of all colour discrimination. The eye is totally colour-blind, as can be verified without difficulty. The observation may be made at night in any room, with a suitable source of light and a device for regulating its intensity, so that it can be made sometimes dark and sometimes bright. As soon as it is possible to distinguish colour, it is a sure sign that the intensity is already above the threshold of the fovea centralis. Suppose, for example, there is a piece of red paper in the dark room, and that at a certain degree of illumination the red colour can be discerned. Under these circumstances, a little bit of this paper subtending an angle of one or two degrees cannot be made to "disappear" in the foveal region of the retina; as can be done so easily with a white object and sufficiently low degree of illumination, by suddenly looking straight at it. . . . The intensity is above the threshold of the foveal sensitivity.

* * * * *

These observations show that the quality of the light sensation in twilight vision is not always colourless, that is, white or grey, but that, at least under certain circumstances, it may be bluish. This is not a contradiction of the existence of total colour blindness in twilight vision; because that expression does not imply the inability of seeing light of any kind of colour at all, but merely the impossibility of distinguishing colours as qualities that are different one from another. When a person looks through a piece of glass which is transparent only to rays of some one particular colour, a dark red ruby glass, for example, he is practically colour blind. Objects

seen through such a glass all appear in various gradations from bright red to black. The colouring in this case is all so intense that there is never any doubt even for a moment as to whether everything is coloured or colourless. It is a different matter when the piece of glass is lightly coloured, and particularly if the glass is blue. Seen through blue goggles everything white looks bright blue at first glance. (Other rays besides the blue rays come through these goggles, and hence red and green objects do not look much changed and often appear almost in their natural colours.) However, after wearing the goggles some hours, the blue disappears more and more from the visual field, and then white objects cease to look blue, and begin to look white. This is particularly the case when the goggles are made like snow-spectacles so as to prevent side light from entering the eye; and consequently comparisons cannot be made with parts of the field that do not radiate blue light.

In a case like this, in large portions of the field in a comparatively short time the specific coloured character of a sensation of blue that is not a very saturated one may disappear and give way to a sensation of colourlessness. And so also in twilight vision something analogous may occur, particularly as the stimulus here is feeble anyhow, and simultaneous contrast between different coloured parts of the field is absent entirely.

On the other hand, it might be supposed that the coloured quality of twilight vision would be particularly manifest when there was a possibility of comparing such a sensation with the sensation aroused in the light-adapted eye under the conditions of daylight vision. The writer has made observations of this sort in the following manner. The observer places his head in front of the open side of a box divided in two parts by a vertical partition, so that each eye looks into one half. The back of the box is made of milk-glass, and behind it there is an annex for holding the contrivances for regulating the illumination of the two halves of the milk-glass plate. There are two iris diaphragms, in which little pieces of milk-glass are inserted. Coloured glasses can be placed over these diaphragms also. In front of each of the apertures a special source of light can be adjusted. By binocular comparison the observer can decide whether the two fields on the inside of the box are equal in luminosity and in colour.

For one of the fields, say, the one on the right, the intensity of the light is so regulated that, although it is below the foveal threshold, it looks as bright as possible to a *thoroughly dark-adapted eye*. (The best way to get this adjustment is by covering the field with black paper with a hole in it subtending an angle of between 3° and 4°. If the piece of milk-glass as seen through this hole when the dark-adapted eye looks straight at it can be made to disappear with certainty, the intensity of the light is far enough below the foveal threshold.)

The observer's right eye is thoroughly dark-adapted by blind-folding it tightly for one hour; the other eye meantime being kept as fully light-adapted as possible. A very bright source of light must be adjusted in front of the left iris diaphragm. Immediately after going into the dark room the luminosity of the two fields is compared, the right field being viewed with the right eye, and the left field with the left eye, the eyes being closed alternately. If the correct intensities of light have been selected, the left field therefore being illuminated about a thousand times more intensely than the right one, the difference of colour in the two fields is manifested in the most striking way. The left field, viewed by the photopic eye, looks generally distinctly yellow-red alongside the greenish blue right half as seen by the scotopic eye. To obtain equality of the fields, a highly coloured blue filter must be interposed in front of the left source of light.

The technical difficulties of this method are so very great that the writer has not yet succeeded in making an accurate determination of the colour of twilight vision in terms of the wave-length of a definite colour of the spectrum. But by a different method von Kries and the writer together have obtained a basis for a determination of this sort. In experiments which will be described below in another connection matches were made, for the eye of a colour-blind person (namely, the writer), between homogeneous lights and a mixture of spectrum red and blue (using a field considerably larger than the foveal region). For reasons that cannot be fully understood until we get further on in the subject, a colour match of this sort does not generally continue valid when the lights in the two halves of the match are reduced in the same proportion (for example, by narrowing the width of the ocular slit) so as to approach the conditions of twilight vision. The colour match previously made under the conditions of full daylight vision is therefore incorrect from two points of view, first with respect to luminosity, and then also with respect to hue. Thus, the nearer the conditions are to those of twilight vision, the more the specific colour of twilight vision, the cyan-blue mentioned above, blends for the observer into the colour of the field; and indeed, as we shall see, this takes place to an unequal extent for the different colours of the spectrum. Thus depending on the wave-length of the homogeneous light used in making the colour match, this homogeneous light, or the red-blue mixture, will change *more* towards blue, when the intensity of the entire field is reduced. If the mixture were made up of red of $670\mu\mu$ and blue-violet of $435\mu\mu$ what was found was, that a homogeneous light of wave-length $495\mu\mu$ (which is colourless to the colour-blind and corresponds therefore to his so-called "neutral point" in the spectrum) appeared brighter and *bluer* than the mixture when the intensity of the whole colour match was reduced. The same behaviour was observed for all kinds of light up to about $485\mu\mu$. But if the wavelength of the homogeneous light is shorter than 480, the mixture was found to be *bluer* than the homogeneous light when the intensity was lowered. Thus between these limits, 480 and $485\mu\mu$, there is a homogeneous light which for the dichromat does not change its hue in the transition from daylight vision to twilight vision. Von Kries and Nagel called this place the "invariable point" in the spectrum and assumed for reasons which will not be discussed here, that it was situated nearer the upper limit, $485\mu\mu$. Accordingly, it may be conjectured that the quality of the sensation in twilight vision is similar to that which is aroused by this light in daylight vision. This, however, is not pure white, but very distinctly blue. Recent researches, which will be taken up later, point to the same conclusion. The statements made here are applicable strictly to colour-blind persons, but they are doubtless true also to a great extent with respect to so-called normal colour vision: because, as numerous observations have shown, the twilight mechanism in the eye of the normal individual and in that of the colour-blind person seem to function in identically the same way.

Incidentally, it is quite conceivable that the light sensations that occur under the conditions of pure twilight vision have a certain range of fluctuation as to their quality, varying from absolute colourlessness to a cyan-blue of no little saturation.

Perhaps this may be connected with a previous colour modulation (*Umstimmung*) of the visual organ. But the writer, judging by his own observations, does not believe this is the case. On the contrary, according to his experience, the blue hue of twilight vision comes out most distinctly right after long dark adaptation, where there cannot be any question of colour adaptation, the indication being rather that the eye must be "neutral" in Hering's use of this term.

The writer would like to guard against what seems to him to be the mistake of using such observations as the above as the origin or basis of any theory as to the rods in the retina being the anatomical substratum of the blue sensation. A conclusive argument against such a view is the fact that, while the peculiar characteristics of twilight vision are lacking entirely in the fovea centralis, still it is undoubtedly capable of mediating the blue sensation. It is only under very special conditions, when the two mechanisms of daylight vision and twilight vision operate together, that it is possible for the blue sensation arising in the twilight mechanism to be blended with colour vision to any noticeable extent.

* * * * *

The phenomena of adaptation are at the basis of the duplicity theory (twilight vision, total colour blindness, the Purkinje phenomenon, etc.). We shall have to see how Helmholtz's theory can be connected with these facts and with the assumptions of the duplicity theory so far as the explanation of these facts is concerned.

At first glance it might indeed seem that the duplicity theory was diametrically opposed to Helmholtz's theory of the sensations of vision. For according to the latter, the sensation of colourless brightness ought to be produced by a combination of processes which of themselves arouse a red-green and a violet sensation; which cannot be considered at all in the case of the activity of the twilight mechanism. However, by imposing some limitations on the Helmholtz theory, as has to be done also for other reasons, this difficulty will be removed. In thus modifying the original theory it is still a question whether this implies something essentially different from what its author had in mind or whether it amounts merely to introducing definite assumptions as to some matters which Helmholtz himself left open to discussion.

In the first place it must be kept in mind here that when Helmholtz made the assumption that the organ of vision was a structure composed of three parts, he did not mean that the *sensation* itself was a combination of three elements (like the three notes of a musical triad). What he meant rather was that, in spite of the composite nature of the physiological process as made up of three independent constituents, the sensation may very well be something perfectly unitary and not capable of psychological sub-division. He regarded the outstanding position of certain sensations (for absence of colour and the so-called pure colours) as the result of psychological relations, connected with the naming of colours, etc. It is this view that stands in such sharp contrast to the one so often entertained nowadays, that the simple investigation of sensations without any auxiliary appliances is sufficient to enable us to find out their "simple elements." In the writer's opinion, from analogy with what is known about other senses, this way of looking at the matter is certainly much less accurate; and Helmholtz's conception is undoubtedly justified to the extent that sensations of complex physiological origin can sometimes convey the impression of being absolutely unitary and typically steadfast.

Thus, while from this point of view there does not seem to be any positive necessity of modifying the Helmholtz theory as proposed above, there are other facts that point in that direction with greater force. We know by experience that the sensation of absence of colour must certainly be exceptionally significant, because in a great many cases colour perceptions cease, and there is nothing left but a colourless sensation. And this is true, indeed, not only under the conditions of twilight vision (where there is a simple explanation for it on the assumptions of the duplicity theory), but also for daylight vision. The variations of vision in passing from the central to the more and more eccentric parts of the retina belong here. Still more important is the fact that by decreasing the size of an object the colour can be made to disappear; as a person with normal vision can very easily verify by using the eccentric parts of his retina, and as can be shown anywhere in the visual field of an anomalous trichromat. Another point in this same connection is that by limiting the time of exposure it can be made impossible for an anomalous trichromat to recognize colour. And, finally, let us allude also to acquired abnormalities of colour vision due to pathological causes, in which likewise colour discrimination is lost. Perhaps, in some of these cases absence of colour can be attributed, as above, to variations of the valence curves; but this explanation is ruled out for the cases of areal and temporal limitations. We are almost bound to make the assumption here that, even when the degrees of activity of the three hypothetical components of the organ of vision are adjusted to correspond to a colour, still in order for the sensation to be really that of a colour, or at least in order for the colour to be recognized as such, some other conditions besides have to be fulfilled; conditions, which by their very nature are in a certain way analogous to the ascent above a threshold value.

On this basis it may be considered as extremely probable that the organization in three components assumed in the Helmholtz theory does not apply to the organ of vision as a whole, but only to those parts that are directly exposed to the action of light and a more or less extended series of parts connected with them; and that, on the other hand, the final results, the immediate substrata of the sensations, are themselves of a different nature; and hence that somewhere along the route the three independent results of stimulus are transformed into processes of a different kind and composition. As to these processes, nothing can be said with certainty, in the writer's opinion, except that in them the colourless sensation has some outstanding physiological significance.

In order to have some short way of referring to this assumption, let us speak of it as a *zonal theory*. From this point of view there seems to be no particular difficulty about supposing that the sensations of vision may be aroused by two different mechanisms more or less independent of each other, only one of which has the tripartite structure in question, whereas the other, being unitary, reacts to its stimulus in a simple monotone.

11

Pioneers of
British Experimental Psychology

ISAAC NEWTON
(1642–1727)

The Color Circle [1]

Prop. V.   Theor. IV

Whiteness and all grey Colours between white and black, may be compounded of Colours, and the whiteness of the Sun's Light is compounded of all the primary Colours mix'd in a due Proportion.

The Proof by Experiments

Exper. 9.   The Sun shining into a dark Chamber through a little round hole in the Window-shut, and his Light being there refracted by a Prism to cast his coloured Image PT [in *Fig.* 5.] upon the opposite Wall: I held a white Paper V to that image in such manner that it might be illuminated by the colour'd Light reflected from thence, and yet not intercept any part of that Light in its passage from the Prism to the Spectrum.   And I found that when the Paper was held nearer to any Colour than to the rest, it appeared of that Colour to which it approached nearest; but when it was equally or almost equally distant from all the Colours, so that it might be equally illuminated by them all it appeared white.   And in this last situation of the Paper, if some Colours were intercepted, the Paper lost its white Colour, and appeared of the Colour of the rest of the Light which was not intercepted.   So then the Paper was illuminated with Lights of various Colours, namely, red, yellow, green, blue and violet, and every part of the Light retained its proper Colour, until it was incident on the Paper, and became reflected thence to the Eye; so that if it had been either alone (the rest of the Light being intercepted) or if it had abounded most, and been predominant in the Light reflected from the Paper, it would have tinged the Paper with its own Colour; and yet being mixed with the rest of the Colours in a due proportion, it made the Paper look white, and therefore by a Composition with the rest produced that Colour.   The several parts of the coloured Light reflected from the Spectrum, whilst they are propagated from thence through the Air, do perpetually retain their proper Colours, because wherever they fall upon the Eyes of any Spectator, they make the several parts of the Spectrum to appear under their proper Colours.   They retain therefore their proper Colours when they fall upon the Paper V, and so by the confusion and perfect mixture of those Colours compound the whiteness of the Light reflected from thence.

* * * * *

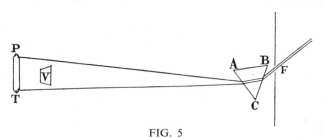

FIG. 5

[1]   Isaac Newton, *Optics or a Treatise of the Reflections, Refractions, Inflections & Colours of Light* (London, 1730, 4th ed.), bk. 1, pt. 2, prop. 5, 6.

Exper. 15. Lastly, In attempting to compound a white, by mixing the coloured Powders which Painters use, I consider'd that all colour'd Powders do suppress and stop in them a very considerable Part of the Light by which they are illuminated. For they become colour'd by reflecting the Light of their own Colours more copiously, and that of all other Colours more sparingly, and yet they do not reflect the Light of their own Colours so copiously as white Bodies do. If red Lead, for instance, and a white Paper, be placed in the red Light of the colour'd Spectrum made in a dark Chamber by the Refraction of a Prism, as is described in the third Experiment of the first Part of this Book; the Paper will appear more lucid than the red Lead, and therefore reflects the red-making Rays more copiously than red Lead doth. And if they be held in the Light of any other Colour, the Light reflected by the Paper will exceed the Light reflected by the red Lead in a much greater Proportion. And the like happens in Powders of other Colours. And therefore by mixing such Powders, we are not to expect a strong and full White, such as is that of Paper, but some dusky obscure one, such as might arise from a Mixture of Light and Darkness, or from white and black, that is, a grey, or dun, or russet brown, such as are the Colours of a Man's Nail, of a Mouse, of Ashes, of ordinary Stones, of Mortar, of Dust and Dirt in Highways, and the like. And such a dark white I have often produced by mixing colour'd Powders. For thus one Part of red Lead, and five Parts of *Viride Æris*, composed a dun Colour like that of a Mouse. For these two Colours were severally so compounded of others, that in both together were a Mixture of all Colours; and there was less red Lead used than *Viride Æris*, because of the Fulness of its Colour. Again, one Part of red Lead, and four Parts of blue Bise, composed a dun Colour verging a little to purple, and by adding to this a certain Mixture of Orpiment and *Viride Æris* in a due Proportion, the Mixture lost its purple Tincture, and became perfectly dun. But the Experiment succeeded best without Minium thus. To Orpiment I added by little and little a certain full bright purple, which Painters use, until the Orpiment ceased to be yellow, and became of a pale red.

Then I diluted that red by adding a little *Viride Æris*, and a little more blue Bise than *Viride Æris*, until it became of such a grey or pale white, as verged to no one of the Colours more than to another. For thus it became of a Colour equal in Whiteness to that of Ashes, or of Wood newly cut, or of a Man's Skin. The Orpiment reflected more Light than did any other of the Powders, and therefore conduced more to the Whiteness of the compounded Colour than they. To assign the Proportions accurately may be difficult, by reason of the different Goodness of Powders of the same kind. Accordingly, as the Colour of any Powder is more or less full and luminous, it ought to be used in a less or greater Proportion.

Now, considering that these grey and dun Colours may be also produced by mixing Whites and Blacks, and by consequence differ from perfect Whites, not in Species of Colours, but only in degree of Luminousness, it is manifest that there is nothing more requisite to make them perfectly white than to increase their Light sufficiently; and, on the contrary, if by increasing their Light they can be brought to perfect Whiteness, it will thence also follow, that they are of the same Species of Colour with the best Whites, and differ from them only in the Quantity of Light. And this I tried as follows. I took the third of the above-mention'd grey Mixtures, (that which was compounded of Orpiment, Purple, Bise, and *Viride Æris*) and rubbed it thickly upon the Floor of my Chamber, where the Sun shone upon it through the opened Casement; and by it, in the shadow, I laid a Piece of white Paper of the same Bigness. Then going from them to the distance of 12 or 18 Feet, so that I could not discern the Unevenness of the Surface of the Powder, nor the little Shadows let fall from the gritty Particles thereof; the Powder appeared intensely white, so as to transcend even the Paper itself in Whiteness, especially if the Paper were a little shaded from the Light of the Clouds, and then the Paper compared with the Powder appeared of such a grey Colour as the Powder had done before. But by laying the Paper where the Sun shines through the Glass of the Window, or by shutting the Window that the Sun might shine through the Glass upon the

Powder, and by such other fit Means of increasing or decreasing the Lights wherewith the Powder and Paper were illuminated, the Light wherewith the Powder is illuminated may be made stronger in such a due Proportion than the Light wherewith the Paper is illuminated, that they shall both appear exactly alike in Whiteness. For when I was trying this, a Friend coming to visit me, I stopp'd him at the Door, and before I told him what the Colours were, or what I was doing; I asked him, Which of the two Whites were the best, and wherein they differed? And after he had at that distance viewed them well, he answer'd, that they were both good Whites, and that he could not say which was best, nor wherein their Colours differed. Now, if you consider, that this White of the Powder in the Sun-shine was compounded of the Colours which the component Powders (Orpiment, Purple, Bise, and *Viride Æris*) have in the same Sun-shine, you must acknowledge by this Experiment, as well as by the former, that perfect Whiteness may be compounded of Colours.

From what has been said it is also evident, that the Whiteness of the Sun's Light is compounded of all the Colours wherewith the several sorts of Rays whereof that Light consists, when by their several Refrangibilities they are separated from one another, do tinge Paper or any other white Body whereon they fall. For those Colours . . . are unchangeable, and whenever all those Rays with those their Colours are mix'd again, they reproduce the same white Light as before.

Prop. VI. Prob. II

In a mixture of Primary Colours, the Quantity and Quality of each being given, to know the Colour of the Compound.

With the Center O [in *Fig.* 11.] and Radius OD describe a Circle ADF, and distinguish its Circumference into seven Parts DE, EF, FG, GA, AB, BC, CD, proportional to the seven Musical Tones or Intervals of the eight Sounds, *Sol, la, fa, sol, la, mi, fa, sol,* contained in an eight, that is, proportional to the Number $\frac{1}{9}, \frac{1}{16}, \frac{1}{10}, \frac{1}{9}, \frac{1}{16}, \frac{1}{16}, \frac{1}{9}$. Let the first Part DE represent a red Colour, the second EF orange, the third FG yellow, the fourth CA green, the fifth AB blue, the sixth BC indigo, and the seventh CD violet. And conceive that these are all the Colours of uncompounded Light gradually passing into one another, as they do when made by Prisms; the Circumference DEFGABCD, representing the whole Series of Colours from one end of the Sun's colour'd Image to the other, so that from D to E be all degrees of red, at E the mean Colour between red and orange, from E to F all degrees of orange, at F the mean between orange and yellow, from F to G all degrees of yellow, and so on. Let *p* be the Center of Gravity of the Arch DE, and *q, r, s, t, u, x,* the Centers of Gravity of the Arches EF, FG, GA, AB, BC, and CD respectively, and about those Centers of Gravity let Circles proportional to the Number of Rays of each Colour in the given Mixture be describ'd: that is, the Circle *p* proportional to the Number of the red-making Rays in the Mixture, the Circle *q* proportional to the Number of the orange-making Rays in the Mixture, and so of the rest. Find the Common Center of Gravity of all those Circles, *p, q, r, s, t, u, x.* Let that Center be Z; and from the Center of the Circle ADF, through Z to the Circumference, drawing the Right Line OY, the Place of the Point Y in the Circumference shall shew the Colour arising from the Composition of all the Colours in the given Mixture, and the Line OZ shall be proportional to the Fulness or Intenseness of the Colour, that is, to its distance from Whiteness. As if Y fall in the middle between F and G, the compounded Colour shall be the best yellow; if Y verge from the middle towards F or G, the compound Colour shall accordingly be a yellow, verging towards orange or green. If Z fall upon the Circumference, the Colour shall be intense and florid in the highest Degree; if it fall in the mid-way

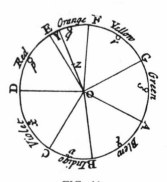

FIG. 11

between the Circumference and Center, it shall be but half so intense, that is, it shall be such a Colour as would be made by diluting the intensest yellow with an equal quantity of whiteness; and if it fall upon the center O, the Colour shall have lost all its intenseness, and become a white. But it is to be noted, That if the point Z fall in or near the line OD, the main ingredients being the red and violet, the Colour compounded shall not be any of the prismatick Colours, but a purple, inclining to red or violet, accordingly as the point Z lieth on the side of the line DO towards E or towards C, and in general the compounded violet is more bright and more fiery than the uncompounded. Also if only two of the primary Colours which in the circle are opposite to one another be mixed in an equal proportion, the point Z shall fall upon the center O, and yet the Colour compounded of those two shall not be perfectly white, but some faint anonymous Colour. For I could never yet by mixing only two primary Colours produce a perfect white. Whether it may be compounded of a mixture of three taken at equal distances in the circumference I do not know, but of four or five I do not much question but it may. But these are Curiosities of little or no moment to the understanding the Phænomena of Nature. For in all whites produced by Nature, there used to be a mixture of all sorts of Rays, and by consequence a composition of all Colours.

THOMAS YOUNG
(1773–1829)

Color Vision [2]

From three simple sensations, with their combinations, we obtain seven primitive distinctions of colours; but the different proportions, in which they may be combined, afford a variety of traits beyond all calculation. The three simple sensations being red, green, and violet, the three binary combinations are yellow, consisting of red and green; crimson, of red and violet; and blue, of green and violet; and the seventh in order is white light, composed by all three united. But the blue thus produced, by combining the whole of the green and violet rays, is not the blue of the spectrum, for four parts of green and one of violet make a blue differing very little from green; while the blue of the spectrum appears to contain as much violet as green: and it is for this reason that red and blue usually make a purple, deriving its hue from the predominance of the violet.

*   *   *   *   *

Now,[3] as it is almost impossible to conceive each sensitive point of the retina to contain an infinite number of particles, each capable of vibrating in perfect unison with every possible undulation, it becomes necessary to suppose the number limited, for instance, to the three principal colours, red, yellow, and blue, of which the undulations are related in magnitude nearly as the numbers 8, 7, and 6; and that each of the particles is capable of being put in motion less or more forcibly, by undulations differing less or more from a perfect unison; for instance, the undulations of green light being nearly in the ratio of $6\frac{1}{2}$, will affect equally the particles in unison with yellow and blue, and produce the same effect as a light composed of those two species: and each sensitive filament of the nerve may consist of three portions, one for each principal colour.

*   *   *   *   *

I had concluded that the rays of light, emitted by objects at a small distance, could only be brought to foci on the retina by a nearer approach of the crystalline to a spherical form; and I could imagine no other power capable of producing this change than a muscularity of a part, or the whole, of its capsule.

But in closely examining, with the naked eye in a strong light, the crystalline from an ox, turned out of its capsule, I discovered a structure which appears to remove all the difficulties with which this branch of optics

[2] Thomas Young, *A Course of Lectures on Natural Philosophy* (London, 1807), vol. 1, p. 40.
[3] Thomas Young, "Observations on vision," *Philosophical Transactions of the Royal Society of London*, 1793, pp. 169–178.

has long been obscured. On viewing it with a magnifier, this structure became more evident.

The crystalline lens of the ox is an orbicular, convex, transparent body, composed of a considerable number of similar coats, of which the exterior closely adhere to the interior. Each of these coats consists of six muscles, intermixed with a gelatinous substance, and attached to six membranous tendons. Three of the tendons are anterior, three posterior; their length is about two thirds of the semi-diameter of the coat; their arrangement is that of three equal and equidistant rays, meeting in the axis of the crystalline; one of the anterior is directed towards the outer angle of the eye, and one of the posterior towards the inner angle, so that the posterior are placed opposite to the middle of the interstices of the anterior; and planes passing through each of the six, and through the axis, would mark on either surface six regular equidistant rays. The muscular fibres arise from both sides of each tendon; they diverge till they reach the greatest circumference of the coat, and, having passed it, they again converge, till they are attached respectively to the sides of the nearest tendons of the opposite surface. The anterior or posterior portion of the six viewed together, exhibits the appearance of three penniformi-radiated muscles. The anterior tendons of all the coats are situated in the same planes, and the posterior ones in the continuations of these planes beyond the axis. Such an arrangement of fibres can be accounted for on no other supposition than that of muscularity. This mass is inclosed in a strong membranous capsule, to which it is loosely connected by minute vessels and nerves; and the connection is more observable near its greatest circumference. Between the mass and its capsule is found a considerable quantity of an aqueous fluid, the liquid of the crystalline.

I conceive, therefore, that when the will is exerted to view an object at a small distance, the influence of the mind is conveyed through the lenticular ganglion, formed from branches of the third and fifth pairs of nerves, by the filaments perforating the sclerotica, to the orbiculus ciliaris, which may be considered as an annular plexus of nerves and vessels; and thence by the ciliary processes to the muscle of the crystalline, which, by the contraction of its fibres, becomes more convex, and collects the diverging rays to a focus on the retina. The disposition of fibres in each coat is admirably adapted to produce this change; for, since the least surface that can contain a given bulk is that of a sphere, ... the contraction of any surface must bring its contents nearer to a spherical form. The liquid of the crystalline seems to serve as a synovia in facilitating the motion, and to admit a sufficient change of the muscular part, with a smaller motion of the capsule.

CHARLES BELL
(1774–1842)

Bell-Magendie Law
of Spinal Nerve Roots [4]

The prevailing doctrine of the anatomical schools is, that the whole brain is a common sensorium; that the extremities of the nerves are organized, so that each is fitted to receive a peculiar impression; or that they are distinguished from each other only by delicacy of structure, and by a corresponding delicacy of sensation, that the nerve of the eye, for example, differs from the nerves of touch only in the degree of its sensibility.

It is imagined that impressions, thus differing in kind, are carried along the nerves to the sensorium, and presented to the mind; and that the mind, by the same nerves which receive sensation, sends out the mandate of the will to the moving parts of the body.

* * * * *

In opposition to these opinions, I have to offer reasons for believing, that the cerebrum and cerebellum are different in function as in form; that the parts of the cerebrum have different functions; and that the nerves which we trace in the body are not single nerves

---

[4] Charles Bell, *Idea of a New Anatomy of the Brain: Submitted for the Observation of His Friends* (London, 1811). Reprinted in *J. Anat. Physiol.,* 1869, **3**, pp. 153–66.

possessing various powers, but bundles of different nerves, whose filaments are united for the convenience of distribution, but which are distinct in office, as they are in origin from the brain:

That the external organs of the senses have the matter of the nerves adapted to receive certain impressions, while the corresponding organs of the brain are put in activity by the external excitement: That the idea of perception is according to the part of the brain to which the nerve is attached, and that each organ has a certain limited number of changes to be wrought upon it by the external impression:

That the nerves of sense, the nerves of motion, and the vital nerves, are distinct through their whole course, though they seem sometimes united in one bundle; and that they depend for their attributes on the organs of the brain to which they are severally attached.

The view which I have to present, will serve to show why there are divisions, and many distinct parts in the brain; why some nerves are simple in their origin and distribution, and others intricate beyond description. It will explain the apparently accidental connection between the twigs of nerves. It will do away with the difficulty of conceiving how sensation and volition should be the operation of the same nerve at the same moment. It will show how a nerve may lose one property, and retain another; and it will give an interest to the labours of the anatomist in tracing the nerves.

* * * * *

There are four kinds of Papillae on the tongue, but with two of those only we have to do at present. Of these, the Papillae of one kind form the seat of the sense of taste; the other Papillae (more numerous and smaller) resemble the extremities of the nerves in the common skin, and are the organs of touch in the tongue. When I take a sharp steel point and touch one of *these* Papillae, I feel the sharpness. The sense of touch informs me of the shape of the instrument. When I touch a Papilla of taste, I have no sensation similar to the former. I do not know that a point touches the tongue, but I am sensible of a metallic taste, and the sensation passes backward on the tongue.

In the operation of couching the cataract,

the pain of piercing the retina with a needle is not so great as that which proceeds from a grain of sand under the eyelid. And although the derangement of the stomach sometimes marks the injury of an organ so delicate, yet the pain is occasioned by piercing the outward coat, not by the affection of the expanded nerve of vision.

If the sensation of light were conveyed to us by the retina, the organ of vision, in consequence of that organ being as much more sensible than the surface of the body as the impression of light is more delicate than that pressure which gives us the sense of touch; what would be the feelings of a man subjected to an operation in which a needle were pushed through the nerve. Life could not bear so great a pain.

This fact is corroborated by experiments made on the eye. When the eyeball is pressed on the side, we perceive various coloured light. Indeed the mere effect of a blow on the head might inform us, that sensation depends on the exercise of the organ affected, not on the impression conveyed to the external organ; for by the vibration caused by the blow, the ears ring, and eye flashes light, while there is neither light nor sound present.

It may be said, that there is here no proof of the sensation being in the brain more than in the external organ of sense. But when the nerve of a stump is touched the pain is as if in the amputated extremity.

* * * * *

If light, pressure, galvanism, or electricity produce vision, we must conclude that the idea in the mind is the result of an action excited in the eye or in the brain, not of anything received, though caused by an impression from without. The operations of the mind are confined not by the limited nature of things created, but by the limited number of our organs of sense. By induction we know that things exist which yet are not brought under the operation of the senses. When we have never known the operation of one of the organs of the five senses, we can never know the ideas pertaining to that sense; and what would be the effect on our minds, even constituted as they now are, with a superadded organ of sense, no man can distinctly imagine.

* * * * *

I shall hereafter shew, that the operations of the mind are seated in the great mass of the cerebrum, while the parts of the brain to which the nerves of sense tend, strictly form the seat of the sensation, being the internal organs of sense. These organs are operated upon in two directions. They receive the impression from without, as from the eye and ear: and as their action influences the operations of the brain producing perception, so are they brought into action and suffer changes similar to that which they experience from external pressure by the operation of the will; or, as I am now treating of the subject anatomically, by the operation of the great mass of the brain upon them.

In all regulated actions of the muscles we must acknowledge that they are influenced through the same nerves, by the same operation of the sensorium.

* * * * *

The operations of the brain may be said to be threefold: (1) The frame of the body is endowed with the characters of life, and the vital parts held together as one system through the operation of the brain and nerves; and the secret operations of the vital organs suffer the control of the brain, though we are unconscious of the thousand delicate operations which are every instant going on in the body. (2) In the second place, the instinctive motions which precede the development of the intellectual faculties are performed through the brain and nerves. (3) In the last place, the operation of the senses in rouzing the faculties of the mind, and the exercise of the mind over the moving parts of the body, is through the brain and nerves. The first of these is perfect in nature, and independent of the mind. The second is a prescribed and limited operation of the instrument of thought and agency. The last begins by imperceptible degrees, and has no limit in extent and variety. It is that to which all the rest is subservient, the end being the calling into activity and the sustaining of an intellectual being.

Thus we see that in as far as is necessary to the great system, the operation of the brain, nerves, and muscles are perfect from the beginning; and we are naturally moved to ask, Might not the operations of the mind have been thus perfect and spontaneous from the beginning as well as slowly excited into action by outward impressions? Then man would have been an insulated being, not only cut off from the inanimate world around him, but from his fellows; he would have been an individual, not a part of a whole.

* * * * *

The brain is a mass of soft matter, in part of a white colour, and generally striated; in part of a grey or cineritous colour having no fibrous appearance. It has grand divisions and subdivisions: and as the forms exist before the solid bone incloses the brain; and as the distinctions of parts are equally observable in animals whose brain is surrounded with fluid, they evidently are not accidental, but are a consequence of internal structure; or in other words they have a correspondence with distinctions in the uses of the parts of the brain.

On examining the grand divisions of the brain we are forced to admit that there are four brains. For the brain is divided longitudinally by a deep fissure; and the line of distinction can even be traced where the sides are united in substance. Whatever we observe on one side has a corresponding part on the other; and an exact resemblance and symmetry is preserved in all the lateral divisions of the brain. And so, if we take the proof of anatomy, we must admit that as the nerves are double, and the organs of sense double, so is the brain double; and every sensation conveyed to the brain is conveyed to the two lateral parts; and the operations performed must be done in both lateral portions at the same moment.

I speak of the lateral divisions of the brain being distinct brains combined in function, in order the more strongly to mark the distinction betwixt the anterior and the posterior grand divisions. Betwixt the lateral parts there is a strict resemblance in form and substance: each principal part is united by transverse tracts of medullary matter; and there is every provision for their acting with perfect sympathy. On the contrary, the cerebrum, the anterior grand division, and the cerebellum the posterior grand division, have slight and indirect connection. In form and division of parts, and arrangement of white and grey matter, there is no resemblance. There is here nothing of that symmetry and correspondence of parts which is so remarkable betwixt the right and left portions.

I have found evidence that the vascular system of the cerebellum may be affected independently of the vessels of the cerebrum. I have seen the whole surface of the cerebellum studded with spots of extravasated blood as small as pin heads, so as to be quite red, while no mark of disease was upon the surface of the cerebrum. The action of vessels it is needless to say is under the influence of the parts to which they go; and in this we have a proof of a distinct state of activity in the cerebrum and cerebellum.

From these factors, were there no others, we are entitled to conclude, that in the operations excited in the brain there cannot be such sympathy or corresponding movement in the cerebrum and cerebellum as there is betwixt the lateral portions of the cerebrum; that the anterior and posterior grand divisions of the brain perform distinct offices.

In examining this subject further, we find, when we compare the relative magnitude of the cerebrum to the other parts of the brain in man and in brutes, that in the latter the cerebrum is much smaller, having nothing of the relative magnitude and importance which in man it bears to the other parts of the nervous system; signifying that the cerebrum is the seat of those qualities of mind which distinguish man. We may observe also that the posterior grand division, or cerebellum remains more permanent in form: while the cerebrum changes in conformity to the organs of sense, or the endowments of the different classes of animals. In the inferior animals, for example, where there are two external organs of the same sense, there is to be found two distinct corresponding portions of cerebrum, while the cerebellum corresponds with the frame of the body . . . .

The medulla spinalis has a central division, and also a distinction into anterior and posterior portions of the brain. Further we can trace down the crura of the cerebellum into the posterior fasciculus. I thought that here I might have an opportunity of touching the cerebellum, as it were, through the posterior portion of the spinal marrow, and the cerebrum by the anterior portion. To this end I made experiments which, though they were not conclusive, encouraged me in the view I had taken.

I found that injury done to the anterior portion of the spinal marrow, convulsed the animal more certainly than injury done to the posterior portion; but I found it difficult to make the experiment without injuring both portions.

Next considering that the spinal nerves have a double root, and being of opinion that the properties of the nerves are derived from their connections with the parts of the brain, I thought that I had an opportunity of putting my opinion to the test of experiment, and of proving at the same time that nerves of different endowments were in the same cord, and held together by the same sheath.

On laying bare the roots of the spinal nerves, I found that I could cut across the posterior fasciculus of nerves, which took its origin from the posterior portion of the spinal marrow without convulsing the muscles of the back; but that on touching the anterior fasciculus with the point of the knife, the muscles of the back were immediately convulsed.

Such were my reasons for concluding that the cerebrum and the cerebellum were parts distinct in function, and that every nerve possessing a double function obtained that by having a double root. I now saw the meaning of the double connection of the nerves with the spinal marrow; and also the cause of that seeming intricacy in the connections of nerves throughout their course, which were not double at their origins.

The spinal nerves being double, and having their roots in the spinal marrow, of which a portion comes from the cerebrum and a portion from the cerebellum, they convey the attributes of both grand divisions of the brain to every part; and therefore the distribution of such nerves is simple, one nerve supplying its destined part. But the nerves which come directly from the brain, come from parts of the brain which vary in operation; and in order to bestow different qualities on the parts to which the nerves are distributed, two or more nerves must be united in their course or at their final destination.

* * * * *

Understanding the origin of the nerves in the brain to be the source of their powers, we look upon the connections formed betwixt distant nerves, and upon the combination of nerves in their passage, with some interest;

but without this the whole is an unmeaning tissue. Seeing the seeming irregularity in one subject, we say it is accident; but finding that the connections never vary, we say only that it is strange, until we come to understand the necessity of nerves being combined in order to bestow distinct qualities on the parts to which they are sent.

The cerebellum when compared with the cerebrum is simple in its form. It has no internal tubercles or masses of cineritious matter in it. The medullary matter comes down from the cineritious cortex, and forms the crus; and the crus runs into union with the same process from the cerebrum; and they together form the medulla spinalis, and are continued down into the spinal marrow; and these crura or processes afford double origin to the double nerves of the spine. The nerves proceeding from the Crus Cerebelli go every-where (in seeming union with those from the Crus Cerebri) they unite the body together, and control the actions of the bodily frame; and especially govern the operation of the viscera necessary to the continuance of life.

* * * * *

The cerebrum I consider as the grand organ by which the mind is united to the body. Into it all the nerves from the external organs of the senses enter; and from it all the nerves which are agents of the will pass out.

If this be not at once obvious, it proceeds only from the circumstance that the nerves take their origin from the different parts of the brain; and while those nerves are con-sidered as simple cords, this circumstance stands opposed to the conclusion which other-ways would be drawn. A nerve having several roots, implies that it propagates its sensation to the brain generally. But when we find that the several roots are distinct in their endowments, and are in respect to office distinct nerves; then the conclusion is un-avoidable, that the portions of the brain are distinct organs of different functions.

To arrive at any understanding of the internal parts of the cerebrum, we must keep in view the relation of the nerves, and must class and distinguish the nerves, and follow them into its substance. If all ideas originate in the mind from external impulse, how can we better investigate the structure of the brain than by following the nerves, which are the

means of communication betwixt the brain and the outward organs of the senses?

The nerves of sense, the olfactory, the optic, the auditory, and the gustatory nerve, are traced backwards into certain tubercles or convex bodies in the base of the brain. And I may say, that the nerves of sense either form tubercles before entering the brain, or they enter into these convexities in the base of the cerebrum. These convexities are the con-stituent parts of the cerebrum, and are in all animals necessary parts of the organs of sense: for as certainly as we discover an animal to have an external organ of sense, we find also a medullary tubercle; whilst the superiority of animals in intelligence is shown by the greater magnitude of the hemispheres or upper parts of the cerebrum.

The convex bodies which are seated in the lower part of the cerebrum, and into which the nerves of sense enter, have extensive connection with the hemisphere, again, there pass down, converging to the crura Striae, which is the medullary matter taking upon it the character of a nerve; for from the Crura Cerebri, or its prolongation in the anterior Fasciculi of the spinal marrow, go off the nerves of motion.

But with these nerves of motion which are passing outward there are nerves going inwards; nerves from the surfaces of the body; nerves of touch; and nerves of peculiar sensibility, having their seat in the body or viscera. It is not improbable that the tracts of cineritious matter which we observe in the course of the medullary matter of the brain, are the seat of such peculiar sensibilities; the organs of certain powers which seem resident in the body.

As we proceed further in the investigation of the function of the brain, the discussion becomes more hypothetical. But surely physiologists have been mistaken in supposing it necessary to prove sensibility in those parts of the brain which they are to suppose the seat of the intellectual operations. We are not to expect the same phenomena to result from the cutting or tearing of the brain as from the injury to the nerves. The function of the one is to transmit sensation; the other has a higher operation. The nature of the organs of sense is different; the sensibilities of the parts of the body are very various. If the needle piercing the retina during the operation of couching gives no remarkable pain, except in touching the common coats of the eye, ought we to imagine that the seat of the higher operations of the mind should, when injured, exhibit the same effects with the irritation of a nerve? So far therefore from thinking the parts of the brain which are insensible, to be parts inferior (as every part has its use), I should even from this be led to imagine that they had a higher office. And if there be certain parts of the brain which are insensible, and other parts which being injured shake the animal with convulsions exhibiting phenomena similar to those of a wounded nerve, it seems to follow that the latter parts which are endowed with sensibility like the nerves are similar to them in function and use, while the parts of the brain which possess no such sensibility are different in function and organization from the nerves, and have a distinct and higher operation to perform.

If in examining the apparent structure of the brain, we find a part consisting of white medullary Striae and fasciculated like a nerve, we should conclude that as the use of a nerve is to transmit sensation, not to perform any more peculiar function, such tracts of matter are media of communication, connecting the parts of the brain; rather than the brain itself performing the more peculiar functions. On the other hand, if masses are found in the brain unlike the matter of the nerve, and which yet occupy a place guarded as an organ of importance, we may presume that such parts have a use different from that of merely conveying sensation; we may rather look upon such parts as the seat of higher powers.

Again, if those parts of the brain which are directly connected with the nerves, and which resemble them in structure, give pain when injured, and occasion convulsion to the animal as the nerves do when they are injured; and if on the contrary such parts as are more remote from the nerves, and of a different structure, produce no such effect when injured, we may conclude, that the office of the latter parts is more allied to the intellectual operations, less to mere sensation.

I have found at different times all the internal parts of the brain diseased without loss of sense; but I have never seen disease general on the surface of the hemispheres without derangement or oppression of the mind during the patient's life. In the case of derangement of mind, falling into lethargy and stupidity, I have constantly found the surface of the hemispheres dry and preternaturally firm, the membrane separating from it with unusual facility.

If I be correct in this view of the subject, then the experiments which have been made upon the brain tend to confirm the conclusions which I should be inclined to draw from strict anatomy; viz. that the cineritious and superficial parts of the brain are the seat of the intellectual functions. For it is found that the surface of the brain is totally insensible, but that the deep and medullary part being wounded the animal is convulsed and pained.

At first it is difficult to comprehend, how the part to which every sensation is referred, and by means of which we become acquainted with the various sensations, can itself be insensible; but the consideration of the wide difference of function betwixt a part destined to receive impressions, and a part which is the seat of intellect, reconciles us to the phenomenon. It would be rather strange to find, that there were no distinction exhibited in experiments on parts evidently so different in function as the organs of the senses, the nerves, and the brain. Whether there be a difference in the matter of the nervous system, or a distinction in organization, is of little importance to our enquiries, when it is proved that their essential properties are different, though their union and co-operation be necessary to the completion of their function—the development of the faculties by impulse from external matter.

* * * * *

From the cineritious matter, which is chiefly external, and forming the surface of the cerebrum; and from the grand center of medullary matter of the cerebrum, what are called the crura descend. These are fasciculated processes of the cerebrum, from which go off the nerves of motion, the nerves governing the muscular frame. Through the nerves of sense, the sensorium receives impressions, but the will is expressed through the medium of the nerves of motion. The secret operations of the bodily frame and the connections which unite the parts of the body into a system, are through the cerebellum and nerves proceeding from it.

CHARLES WHEATSTONE
(1802–1875)

Binocular Parallax and Binocular Vision [5]

§ 1. When an object is viewed at so great a distance that the optic axes of both eyes are sensibly parallel when directed towards it, the perspective projections of it, seen by each eye separately, are similar, and the appearance to the two eyes is precisely the same as when the object is seen by one eye only. There is, in such case, no difference between the visual appearance of an object in relief and its perspective projection on a plane surface; and hence pictorial representations of distant objects, when those circumstances which would prevent or disturb the illusion are carefully excluded, may be rendered such perfect resemblances of the objects they are intended to represent as to be mistaken for them; the Diorama is an instance of this. But this similarity no longer exists when the object is placed so near the eyes that to view it the optic axes must converge: under these conditions a different perspective projection of it is seen by each eye, and these perspectives are more dissimilar as the convergence of the optic axes becomes greater. This fact may be easily verified by placing any figure of three dimensions, an outline cube for instance, at a moderate distance before the eyes, and while the head is kept perfectly steady, viewing it with each eye successively while the other is closed. . . . Fig. 13 represents the two perspective projections of a cube; *b* is that seen by the right eye, and *a* that presented to the left eye, the figure being supposed to be placed about seven inches immediately before the spectator.

The appearances, which are by this simple experiment rendered so obvious, may be easily inferred from the established laws of perspective; for the same object in relief is, when viewed by a different eye, seen from two points of sight at a distance from each other equal to the line joining the two eyes. Yet they seem to have escaped the attention of

every philosopher and artist who has treated of the subjects of vision and perspective. I can ascribe this inattention to a phenomenon leading to the important and curious consequences, which will form the subject of the present communication, only to this circumstance—that the results being contrary to a principle which was very generally maintained by optical writers, viz. that objects can be seen single only when their images fall on corresponding points of the two retinæ, an hypothesis which will be hereafter discussed, if the consideration ever arose in their minds, it was hastily discarded under the conviction that if the pictures presented to the two eyes are under certain circumstances dissimilar, their differences must be so small that they need not be taken into account.

It will now be obvious why it is impossible for the artist to give a faithful representation of any near solid object, that is, to produce a painting which shall not be distinguished in the mind from the object itself. When the painting and the object are seen with both eyes, in the case of the painting two *similar* pictures are projected on the retinæ, in the case of the solid object the pictures are *dissimilar;* there is therefore an essential difference between the impressions on the organs of sensation in the two cases, and consequently between the perceptions formed in the mind; the painting therefore cannot be confounded with the solid object.

After looking over the works of many authors who might be expected to have made some remarks relating to this subject, I have been able to find but one, which is in the "Trattato della Pittura" of Leonardo da Vinci. This great artist and ingenious philosopher observes, "that a painting, though conducted with the greatest art and finished to the last perfection, both with regard to its contours, its lights, its shadows, and its colours, can never show a relievo equal to that of the natural objects, unless these be viewed at a distance and with a single eye. For," says he, "if an object C . . . (fig. 1) be viewed by a single eye at A, all objects in the space behind it, included as it were in a shadow E C F cast by a candle at A, are invisible to the eye at A; but when the other eye at B is opened, part

---

[5] Charles Wheatstone, "Contributions to the physiology of vision. On some remarkable, and hitherto unobserved, phenomena of binocular vision," *Philosophical Transactions of the Royal Society of London* (1838), pp. 371–394.

of these objects become visible to it, those only being hid from both eyes that are included, as it were, in the double shadow C D, cast by two lights at A and B, and terminated in D, the angular space E D G beyond D being always visible to both eyes. And the hidden space C D is so much the shorter as the object C is smaller and nearer to the eyes. Thus the object C seen with both eyes becomes, as it were, transparent, according to the usual definition of a transparent thing—namely, that which hides nothing beyond it. But this cannot happen when an object, whose breadth is bigger than that of the pupil, is viewed by a single eye. The truth of this observation is therefore evident, because a painted figure intercepts all the space behind its apparent place, so as to preclude the eyes from the sight of every part of the imaginary ground behind it."

Had Leonardo da Vinci taken, instead of a sphere, a less simple figure for the purpose of his illustration, a cube for instance, he would not only have observed that the object obscured from each eye a different part of the more distant field of view, but the fact would also perhaps have forced itself upon his attention that the object itself presented a different appearance to each eye. He failed to do this, and no subsequent writer within my knowledge has supplied the omission; the projection of two obviously dissimilar pictures on the two retinæ when a single object is viewed, while the optic axes converge, must therefore be regarded as a new fact in the theory of vision.

§ 2. It being thus established that the mind perceives an object of three dimensions by means of the two dissimilar pictures projected by it on the two retinæ, the following question occurs: What would be the visual effect of simultaneously presenting to each eye, instead of the object itself, its projection on a plane surface as it appears to that eye? To pursue this inquiry it is necessary that means should be contrived to make the two pictures, which must necessarily occupy different places, fall on similar parts of both retinæ. Under the ordinary circumstances of vision the object is seen at the concourse of the optic axes, and its images consequently are projected on similar parts of the two retinæ; but it is also evident that two exactly similar objects may be made to fall on similar parts of the two retinæ, if they are placed one in the direction of each optic axes, at equal distances before or beyond their intersection.

Fig. 2 represents the usual situation of an object at the intersection of the optic axes. In fig. 3 the similar objects are placed in the direction of the optic axes before their intersection, and in fig. 4 beyond it. In all these three cases the mind perceives but a single object, and refers it to the place where the optic axes meet. It will be observed that when the eyes converge beyond the objects, as in fig. 3, the right-hand object is seen by the right eye, and the left-hand object by the left eye; while when the axes converge nearer than the objects, the right-hand object is seen by the left eye, and conversely. As both of these modes of vision are forced and unnatural, eyes unaccustomed to such experiments require some artificial assistance. If the eyes are to converge beyond the objects, this may be afforded by a pair of tubes (fig. 5) capable of being inclined towards each other at various angles, so as to correspond with the different convergences of the optic axes. If the eyes are to converge at a nearer distance than that at which the objects are placed, a box (fig. 6) may be conveniently employed: the objects a a' are placed distant from each other, on a stand capable of being moved nearer the eyes if required, and the optic axes being directed towards them will cross at c, the aperture b b' allowing the visual rays from the right-hand object to reach the left eye, and those from the left-hand object to fall on the right eye; the coincidence of the images may be facilitated by placing the point of a needle at the point of intersection of the optic axes c, and fixing the eyes upon it. In both these instruments (figs. 5 and 6) the lateral images are hidden from view, and much less difficulty occurs in making the images unite than when the naked eyes are employed.

Now if, instead of placing two exactly similar objects to be viewed by the eyes in either of the modes above described, the two perspective projections of the same solid object be so disposed, the mind will still perceive the object to be single, but instead of a representation on a plane surface, as each drawing appears to be when separately viewed by that eye which is directed towards it, the observer will perceive a figure of three dimensions, the exact counterpart of the object from which the drawings were made. To make this matter clear I will mention one or two of the most simple cases.

If two vertical lines near each other, but at different distances from the spectator, be regarded first with one eye and then with the other, the distance between them when referred to the same plane will appear different; if the left-hand line be nearer to the eyes, the distance as seen by the left eye will be less than the distance as seen by the right eye: fig. 7 will render this evident; $a\,a'$ are vertical sections of the two original lines, and $b\,b'$ the plane to which their projections are referred. Now if the two lines be drawn on two pieces of card, at the respective distances at which they appear to each eye, and these cards be afterwards viewed by either of the means above directed, the observer will no longer see two lines on a plane surface, as each card separately shows; but two lines will appear, one nearer to him than the other, precisely as the original vertical lines themselves. Again, if a straight wire be held before the eyes in such a position that one of its ends shall be nearer to the observer than the other is, each eye separately referring it to a plane perpendicular to the common axis, will see a line differently inclined; and then if lines having the same apparent inclinations be drawn on two pieces of card, and be presented to the eyes as before directed, the real position of the original line will be correctly perceived by the mind.

In the same manner the most complex figures of three dimensions may be accurately represented to the mind, by presenting their two perspective projections to the two retinæ. But I shall defer these more perfect experiments until I describe an instrument which will enable any person to observe all the phenomena in question with the greatest ease and certainty.

In the instruments above described the optic axes converge to some point in a plane before or beyond that in which the objects to be seen are situated. The adaptation of the eye, which enables us to see distinctly at different distances, and which habitually accompanies every different degree of convergence of the optic axes, does not immediately adjust itself to the new and unusual condition; and to persons not accustomed to experiments of this kind, the pictures will either not readily unite, or will appear dim and confused. Besides this, no object can be viewed according to either mode when the drawings exceed in breadth the distance of the two points of the optic axes in which their centres are placed.

These inconveniences are removed by the instrument I am about to describe; the two pictures (or rather their reflected images) are placed in it at the true concourse of the optic axes, the focal adaptation of the eye preserves its usual adjustment, the appearance of lateral images is entirely avoided, and a large field of view for each eye is obtained. The frequent reference I shall have occasion to make to this instrument, will render it convenient to give it a specific name; I therefore propose that it be called a Stereoscope, to indicate its property of representing solid figures.

§ 3. The stereoscope is represented by figs. 8 and 9, the former being a front view, and the latter a plan of the instrument. A A' are two plane mirrors, about four inches square, inserted in frames, and so adjusted that their backs form an angle of 90° with each other; these mirrors are fixed by their common edge against an upright B, or, which was less easy to represent in the drawing, against the middle line of a vertical board, cut away in such manner as to allow the eyes to be placed before the two mirrors. C C' are two sliding boards, to which are attached the upright boards D D', which may thus be removed to different distances from the mirrors. In most of the experiments hereafter to be detailed, it is necessary that each upright board shall be at the same distance from the mirror which is opposite to it. To facilitate this double adjustment, I employ a right- and a left-handed wooden screw, $r\,l$; the two ends of this compound screw pass through the nuts $e\,e'$, which are fixed to the lower parts of the upright boards D D', so that by turning the screw pin p one way the two boards will approach, and by turning it the other they will recede from each other, one always preserving the same distance as the other from the middle line f. E E' are pannels, to which the pictures are fixed in such manner that their corresponding horizontal lines shall be on the same level: these pannels are capable of sliding backwards and forwards in grooves on the upright boards D D'. The apparatus having been described, it now remains to explain the manner of using it. The observer must place his eyes as near as possible to the mirrors, the right eye before the right-hand mirror, and the left eye before the left-hand mirror, and he must move the sliding pannels E E' to or from him until the two reflected images coincide at the intersection of the optic axes, and form an image of the same apparent magnitude as each of the component pictures. The pictures will indeed coincide when the sliding pannels are in a variety of different positions, and consequently when viewed under different inclinations of the optic axes; but there is only one position in which the binocular image will be immediately seen single, of its proper magnitude, and without fatigue to the eyes, because in this position only the ordinary relations between the magnitude of the pictures on the retina, the inclination of the optic axes, and the adaptation of the eye to distinct vision at different distances are preserved. The alteration in the apparent magnitude of the binocular images, when these usual relations are disturbed, will be discussed in another paper of this series, with a variety of remarkable phenomena depending thereon. In all the experiments detailed in the present memoir I shall suppose these relations to remain undisturbed, and the optic axes to converge about six or eight inches before the eyes.

If the pictures are all drawn to be seen with the same inclination of the optic axes, the apparatus may be simplified by omitting the screw r l and fixing the upright boards D D' at the proper distances. The sliding pannels may also be dispensed with, and the drawings themselves be made to slide in the grooves.

§ 4. A few pairs of outline figures, calculated to give rise to the perception of objects of three dimensions when placed in the stereoscope in the manner described, are represented from figs. 10 to 20. They are one half the linear size of the figures actually employed. As the drawings are reversed by reflection in the mirrors, I will suppose these figures to be the reflected images to which the eyes are directed in the apparatus—those marked b being seen by the right eye, and those marked a by the left eye. The drawings, it has been already explained, are two different

projections of the same object seen from two points of sight, the distance between which is equal to the interval between the eyes of the observer; this interval is generally about 2½ inches.

a and b, fig. 10, will, when viewed in the stereoscope, present to the mind a line in the vertical plane, with its lower end inclined towards the observer. If the two component lines be caused to turn round their centres equally in opposite directions, the resultant line will, while it appears to assume every degree of inclination to the referent plane, still seem to remain in the same vertical plane.

Fig. 11. A series of points all in the same horizontal plane, but each towards the right hand successively nearer the observer.

Fig. 12. A curved line intersecting the referent plane, and having its convexity towards the observer.

Fig. 13. A cube.

Fig. 14. A cone, having its axis perpendicular to the referent plane and its vertex towards the observer.

Fig. 15. The frustum of a square pyramid; its axis perpendicular to the referent plane, and its base furthest from the eye.

Fig. 16. Two circles at different distances from the eyes, their centres in the same perpendicular, forming the outline of the frustum of a cone.

The other figures require no observation.

For the purposes of illustration I have employed only outline figures, for had either shading or colouring been introduced it might be supposed that the effect was wholly or in part due to these circumstances, whereas by leaving them out of consideration no room is left to doubt that the entire effect of relief is owing to the simultaneous perception of the two monocular projections, one on each retina. But if it be required to obtain the most faithful resemblances of real objects, shadowing and colouring may properly be employed to heighten the effects. Careful attention would enable an artist to draw and paint the two component pictures, so as to present to the mind of the observer, in the resultant perception, perfect identity with the object represented. Flowers, crystals, busts, vases, instruments of various kinds, &c. might thus be represented so as not to be distinguished by sight from the real objects themselves.

It is worthy of remark, that the process by which we thus become acquainted with the real forms of solid objects is precisely

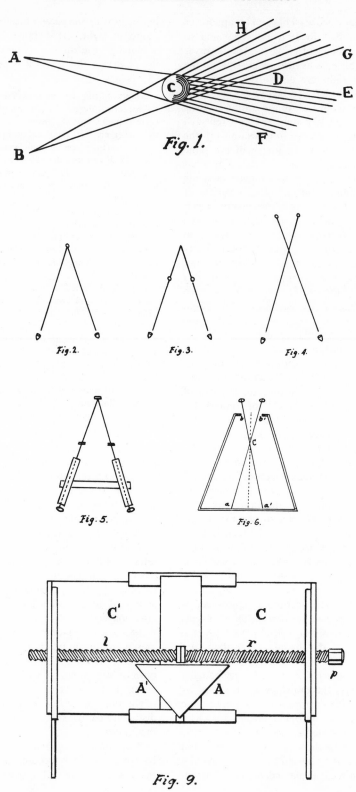

Fig. 1.

Fig. 2.   Fig. 3.   Fig. 4.

Fig. 5.   Fig. 6.

Fig. 9.

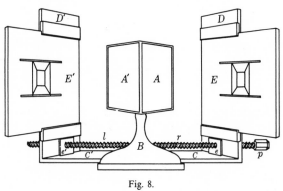

Fig. 8.

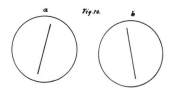

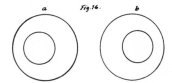

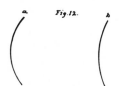

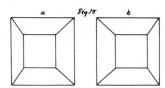

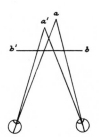

Fig. 7.

Fig. 11.

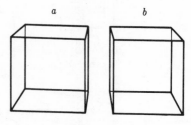

Fig. 13.

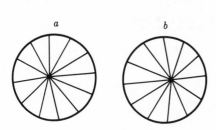

Fig. 14.

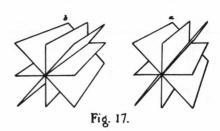

Fig. 17.

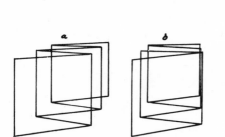

Fig. 19

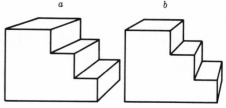

Fig. 18.

Fig. 20.

that which is employed in descriptive geometry, an important science we owe to the genius of Monge, but which is little studied or known in this country. In this science, the position of a point, a right line, or a curve, and consequently of any figure whatever, is completely determined by assigning its projections on two fixed planes, the situations of which are known, and which are not parallel to each other. In the problems of descriptive geometry the two referent planes are generally assumed to be at right angles to each other, but in binocular vision the inclination of these planes is less according as the angle made at the concourse of the optic axes is less; thus the same solid object is represented to the mind by different pairs of monocular pictures, according as they are placed at a different distance before the eyes, and the perception of these differences (though we seem to be unconscious of them) may assist in suggesting to the mind the distance of the object. The more inclined to each other the referent planes are, with the greater accuracy are the various points of the projections referred to their proper places; and it appears to be a useful provision that the real forms of those objects which are nearest to us are thus more determinately apprehended than those which are most distant.

§ 5. A very singular effect is produced when the drawing originally intended to be seen by the right eye is placed at the left-hand side of the stereoscope, and that designed to be seen by the left eye is placed on its right-hand side. A figure of three dimensions, as bold in relief as before, is perceived, but it has a different form from that which is seen when the drawings are in their proper places. There is a certain relation between the proper figure and this, which I shall call its *converse* figure. Those points which are nearest the observer in the proper figure are the most remote from him in the converse figure, and *vice versa*, so that the figure is, as it were, inverted; but it is not an exact inversion, for the near parts of the converse figure appear smaller, and the remote parts larger than the same parts before the inversion. Hence the drawings which, properly placed, occasion a cube to be perceived, when changed in the manner described, represent the frustum of a square pyramid with its base remote from the eye; the cause of this is easy to understand.

This conversion of relief may be shown by all the pairs of drawings from fig. 10 to 19. In the case of simple figures like these the converse figure is as readily apprehended as the original one, because it is generally a figure of as frequent occurrence; but in the case of a more complicated figure, an architectural design, for instance, the mind, unaccustomed to perceive its converse, because it never occurs in nature, can find no meaning in it.

12

British and American Evolutionary Psychology

HERBERT SPENCER
(1820–1903)

Life as a Continuous Adjustment [1]

129. If the doctrine of Evolution is true, the inevitable implication is that Mind can be understood only by observing how Mind is evolved. If creatures of the most elevated kinds have reached those highly integrated, very definite, and extremely heterogeneous organizations they possess, through modifications upon modifications accumulated during an immeas-

[1] Herbert Spencer, *The Principles of Psychology* (London, 1855), vol. 1, sect. 129–131.

urable past—if the developed nervous systems of such creatures have gained their complex structures and functions little by little; then, necessarily, the involved forms of consciousness which are the correlatives of these complex structures and functions must have arisen by degrees. And as it is impossible truly to comprehend the organization of the body in general, or of the nervous system in particular, without tracing its successive stages of complication; so it must be impossible to comprehend mental organization without similarly tracing its stages.

Here, then, we commence the study of Mind as objectively manifested in its ascending gradations through the various types of sentient beings.

130. From what point are we likely to obtain the widest view of this evolution? How shall we guide ourselves towards a conception general enough to include the entire range of mental manifestations, up from creatures that yield but the faintest traces of feeling to creatures having intellects and emotions like our own?

In pursuance of the method of choosing hypotheses, we must compare mental phenomena with the phenomena most like them, and observe what character, presented by no other phenomena, they both present. A generalization uniting two different but allied classes of facts, necessarily unites all the facts contained in either class. Hence, if we find a formula which along with mental evolution includes the evolution nearest akin to it, we shall, by implication, find a formula comprehending the entire process of mental evolution. It may afterwards be needful so to limit this formula that mental evolution alone is expressed by it. But we shall best fulfil the requirements of clear exposition by first exhibiting mental evolution as it may be most generally conceived, and subsequently specializing the conception.

The phenomena which those of Mind resemble in the greatest degree are those of bodily life. While these classes of phenomena are intimately related to one another, they are related to other classes of phenomena in comparatively remote ways. Our question, therefore, becomes—What is it that mental life and bodily life have in common? And this amounts to the question—What distinguishes Life in general?

131. Thus, in looking for a conception of mental evolution sufficiently large to take in all the facts, we are led back to the definition of Life reached at the outset of the *Principles of Biology*.

In Part I., Chap. IV. of that work, the proximate idea we arrived at was that Life is "the definite combination of heterogeneous changes, both simultaneous and successive." In the next chapter it was shown that to develop this proximate idea into a complete idea, it is needful to recognize the connexion between these actions going on within an organism and the actions going on without it. We saw that Life is adequately conceived only when we think of it as "the definite combination of heterogeneous changes, both simultaneous and successive, in correspondence with external co-existences and sequences." Afterwards this definition was found to be reducible to the briefer definition—"The continuous adjustment of internal relations to external relations;" and though, by leaving out the characteristic of heterogeneity, this definition is rendered somewhat too wide, so that it includes a few non-vital phenomena which simulate vitality, yet practically no error is likely to result from its use.

That Life consists in the maintenance of inner actions corresponding with outer actions, was confirmed on further observing how the degree of Life varies as the degree of correspondence. It was pointed out that, beginning with the low life of plants and of rudimentary animals, the progress to life of higher and higher kinds essentially consists in a continual improvement of the adaptation between organic processes and processes which environ the organism. We observed how along with complexity of organization there goes an increase in the number, in the range, in the speciality, in the complexity, of the adjustments of inner relations to outer relations. And in tracing up the increase we found ourselves passing without break from the phenomena of bodily life to the phenomena of mental life.

* * * * *

The [2] reader who recalls certain passages in *First Principles*, in the *Principles of Biology*,

---

[2] Herbert Spencer, *The Principles of Ethics* (London, 1879–1893), vol. 1, sect. 7–9.

and in the *Principles of Psychology*, will perceive above a re-statement, in another form, of generalizations set forth in those works. Especially will he be reminded of the proposition that Life is "the definite combination of heterogeneous changes, both simultaneous and successive, in correspondence with external co-existences and sequences;" and still more of that abridged and less specific formula, in which Life is said to be "the continuous adjustment of internal relations to external relations."

* * * * *

Acts are called good or bad, according as they are well or ill adjusted to ends; and whatever inconsistency there is in our uses of the words, arises from inconsistency of the ends. Here, however, the study of conduct in general, and of the evolution of conduct, have prepared us to harmonize these interpretations. The foregoing exposition shows that the conduct to which we apply the name good, is the relatively more evolved conduct; and that bad is the name we apply to conduct which is relatively less evolved. We saw that evolution, tending ever towards self-preservation, reaches its limit when individual life is the greatest, both in length and breadth;

and now we see that, leaving other ends aside, we regard as good the conduct furthering self-preservation, and as bad the conduct tending to self-destruction. It was shown that along with increasing power of maintaining individual life, which evolution brings, there goes increasing power of perpetuating the species by fostering progeny, and that in this direction evolution reaches its limit when the needful number of young, preserved to maturity, are then fit for a life that is complete in fulness and duration; and here it turns out that parental conduct is called good or bad as it approaches or falls short of this ideal result. Lastly, we inferred that establishment of an associated state, both makes possible and requires a form of conduct such that life may be completed in each and in his offspring, not only without preventing completion of it in others, but with furtherance of it in others; and we have found above, that this is the form of conduct most emphatically termed good. Moreover, just as we there saw that evolution becomes the highest possible when the conduct simultaneously achieves the greatest totality of life in self, in offspring, and in fellow men; so here we see that the conduct called good rises to the conduct conceived as best, when it fulfils all three classes of ends at the same time.

CHARLES DARWIN
(1809–1882)

Emotions as Serviceable Associated Habits [3]

I have now described, to the best of my ability, the chief expressive actions in man, and in some few of the lower animals. I have also attempted to explain the origin or development of these actions through the three principles given in the first chapter. The first of these principles is, that movements which are serviceable in gratifying some desire, or in relieving some sensation, if often repeated, become so habitual that they are performed, whether or not of any service, whenever the same desire or sensation is felt, even in a very weak degree.

[3] Charles Darwin, *The Expression of the Emotions in Man and Animals* (London, 1872), ch. 14.

Our second principle is that of antithesis. The habit of voluntarily performing opposite movements under opposite impulses has become firmly established in us by the practice of our whole lives. Hence, if certain actions have been regularly performed, in accordance with our first principle, under a certain frame of mind, there will be a strong and involuntary tendency to the performance of directly opposite actions, whether or not these are of any use, under the excitement of an opposite frame of mind.

Our third principle is the direct action of the excited nervous system on the body, independently of the will, and independently, in large part, of habit. Experience shows that nerve-force is generated and set free whenever the cerebro-spinal system is excited. The direction which this nerve-force follows is necessarily determined by the lines of connection between the nerve-cells, with each other and with various parts of the body. But the direction is likewise much influenced by habit; inasmuch as nerve-force passes readily along accustomed channels.

The frantic and senseless actions of an enraged man may be attributed in part to the undirected flow of nerve-force, and in part to the effects of habit, for these actions often vaguely represent the act of striking. They thus pass into gestures included under our first principle; as when an indignant man unconsciously throws himself into a fitting attitude for attacking his opponent, though without any intention of making an actual attack. We see also the influence of habit in all the emotions and sensations which are called exciting; for they have assumed this character from having habitually led to energetic action; and action affects, in an indirect manner, the respiratory and circulatory system; and the latter reacts on the brain. Whenever these emotions or sensations are even slightly felt by us, though they may not at the time lead to any exertion, our whole system is nevertheless disturbed through the force of habit and association. Other emotions and sensations are called depressing, because they have not habitually led to energetic action, excepting just at first, as in the case of extreme pain, fear, and grief, and they have ultimately caused complete exhaustion; they are consequently expressed chiefly by negative signs and by prostration. Again, there are other emotions, such as that of affection, which do not commonly lead to action of any kind, and consequently are not exhibited by any strongly marked outward signs. Affection indeed, in as far as it is a pleasurable sensation, excites the ordinary signs of pleasure.

On the other hand, many of the effects due to the excitement of the nervous system seem to be quite independent of the flow of nerve-force along the channels which have been rendered habitual by former exertions of the will. Such effects, which often reveal the state of mind of the person thus affected, cannot at present be explained; for instance, the change of colour in the hair from extreme terror or grief,—the cold sweat and the trembling of the muscles from fear,—the modified secretions of the intestinal canal,—and the failure of certain glands to act.

Notwithstanding that much remains unintelligible in our present subject, so many expressive movements and actions can be explained to a certain extent through the above three principles, that we may hope hereafter to see all explained by these or by closely analogous principles.

Actions of all kinds, if regularly accompanying any state of the mind, are at once recognised as expressive. These may consist of movements of any part of the body, as the wagging of a dog's tail, the shrugging of a man's shoulders, the erection of the hair, the exudation of perspiration, the state of the capillary circulation, laboured breathing, and the use of the vocal or other sound-producing instruments. Even insects express anger, terror, jealousy, and love by their stridulation. With man the respiratory organs are of especial importance in expression, not only in a direct, but in a still higher degree in an indirect manner.

*****

We may confidently believe that laughter, as a sign of pleasure or enjoyment, was practised by our progenitors long before they deserved to be called human; for very many kinds of monkeys, when pleased, utter a reiterated sound, clearly analogous to our laughter, often accompanied by vibratory movements of their jaws or lips, with the corners of the mouth drawn backwards and upwards, by the wrinkling of the cheeks, and even by the brightening of the eyes.

We may likewise infer that fear was expressed from an extremely remote period, in almost the same manner as it now is by man; namely, by trembling, the erection of the hair, cold perspiration, pallor, widely opened eyes, the relaxation of most of the muscles, and by the whole body cowering downwards or held motionless.

Suffering, if great, will from the first have caused screams or groans to be uttered, the body to be contorted, and the teeth to be ground together. But our progenitors will not have exhibited those highly expressive movements of the features which accompany screaming and crying until their circulatory and respiratory organs, and the muscles surrounding the eyes, had acquired their present structure. The shedding of tears appears to have originated through reflex action from the spasmodic contraction of the eyelids, together perhaps with the eyeballs becoming gorged with blood during the act of screaming. Therefore weeping probably came on rather late in the line of our descent; and this conclusion agrees with the fact that our nearest allies, the anthropomorphous apes, do not weep. But we must here exercise some caution, for as certain monkeys, which are not closely related to man, weep, this habit might have been developed long ago in a sub-branch of the group from which man is derived. Our early progenitors, when suffering from grief or anxiety, would not have made their eyebrows oblique, or have drawn down the corners of their mouth, until they had acquired the habit of endeavouring to restrain their screams. The expression, therefore, of grief and anxiety is eminently human.

Rage will have been expressed at a very early period by threatening or frantic gestures, by the reddening of the skin, and by glaring eyes, but not by frowning. For the habit of frowning seems to have been acquired chiefly from the corrugators being the first muscles to contract round the eyes, whenever during infancy pain, anger, or distress is felt, and there consequently is a near approach to screaming; and partly from a frown serving as a shade in difficult and intent vision. It seems probable that this shading action would not have become habitual until man had assumed a completely upright position, for monkeys do not frown when exposed to a glaring light. Our early progenitors, when enraged, would probably have exposed their teeth more freely than does man, even when giving full vent to his rage, as with the insane. We may, also, feel almost certain that they would have protruded their lips, when sulky or disappointed, in a greater degree than is the case with our own children, or even with the children of existing savage races.

Our early progenitors, when indignant or moderately angry, would not have held their heads erect, opened their chests, squared their shoulders, and clenched their fists, until they had acquired the ordinary carriage and upright attitude of man, and had learnt to fight with their fists or clubs. Until this period had arrived the antithetical gesture of shrugging the shoulders, as a sign of impotence or of patience, would not have been developed. From the same reason astonishment would not then have been expressed by raising the arms with open hands and extended fingers. Nor, judging from the actions of monkeys, would astonishment have been exhibited by a widely open mouth; but the eyes would have been opened and the eyebrows arched. Disgust would have been shown at a very early period by movements round the mouth, like those of vomiting,—that is, if the view which I have suggested respecting the source of the expression is correct, namely, that our progenitors had the power, and used it, of voluntarily and quickly rejecting any food from their stomachs which they disliked. But the more refined manner of showing contempt or disdain, by lowering the eyelids, or turning away the eyes and face, as if the despised person were not worth looking at, would not probably have been acquired until a much later period.

Of all expressions, blushing seems to be the most strictly human; yet it is common to all or nearly all the races of man, whether or not any change of colour is visible in their skin. The relaxation of the small arteries of the surface, on which blushing depends, seems to have primarily resulted from earnest attention directed to the appearance of our own persons, especially of our faces, aided by habit, inheritance, and the ready flow of nerve-force along accustomed channels; and afterwards to have been extended by the power of association to self-attention directed to moral conduct. It can hardly be doubted that many animals are capable of appreciating beautiful colours and even forms, as is shown by the pains which the individuals of one sex take in displaying their beauty before those of the opposite sex. But it does not seem possible that any animal, until its mental powers had been developed to an equal or nearly equal degree with those of man, would have closely considered and been sensitive about its own personal appearance. Therefore we may conclude that blushing originated at a very late period in the long line of our descent.

* * * * *

The movements of expression in the face and body, whatever their origin may have been, are in themselves of much importance for our welfare. They serve as the first means of communication between the mother and her infant; she smiles approval, and thus encourages her child on the right path, or frowns disapproval. We readily perceive sympathy in others by their expression; our sufferings are thus mitigated and our pleasures increased; and mutual good feeling is thus strengthened. The movements of expression give vividness and energy to our spoken words. They reveal the thoughts and intentions of others more truly than do words, which may be falsified.

* * * * *

The free expression by outward signs of an emotion intensifies it. On the other hand, the repression, as far as this is possible, of all outward signs softens our emotions. He who gives way to violent gestures will increase his rage; he who does not control the signs of fear will experience fear in a greater degree; and he who remains passive when overwhelmed with grief loses his best chance of recovering elasticity of mind. These results follow partly from the intimate relation which exists between almost all the emotions and their outward manifestations; and partly from the direct influence of exertion on the heart, and consequently on the brain. Even the simulation of an emotion tends to arouse it in our minds.

Instincts and Conscience [4]

The more enduring Social Instincts conquer the less persistent Instincts. We have not, however, as yet considered the main point, on which, from our present point of view, the whole question of the moral sense turns. Why should a man feel that he ought to obey one instinctive desire rather than another? Why is he bitterly regretful, if he has yielded to a strong sense of self-preservation, and has not risked his life to save that of a fellow-creature? Or why does he regret having stolen food from hunger?

It is evident in the first place, that with mankind the instinctive impulses have different degrees of strength: a savage will risk his own life to save that of a member of the same

community, but will be wholly indifferent about a stranger: a young and timid mother urged by the maternal instinct will, without a moment's hesitation, run the greatest danger for her own infant, but not for a mere fellow-creature. Nevertheless many a civilized man, or even boy, who never before risked his life for another, but full of courage and sympathy, has disregarded the instinct of self-preservation, and plunged at once into a torrent to save a drowning man, though a stranger. In this case man is impelled by the same instinctive motive, which made the heroic little American monkey, formerly described, save his keeper, by attacking the great and dreaded baboon. Such actions as the above appear to be the simple result of the greater strength of the social or maternal instincts rather than that of any other instinct or motive; for they are performed too instantaneously for reflection, or for pleasure or pain to be felt at the time; though, if prevented by any cause, distress or even misery might be felt. In a timid man, on the other hand, the instinct of self-preservation might be so strong, that he would be unable to force himself to run any such risk, perhaps not even for his own child.

* * * * *

Although some instincts are more powerful than others, and thus lead to corresponding actions, yet it is untenable, that in man the social instincts (including the love of praise and fear of blame) possess greater strength, or have, through long habit, acquired greater strength than the instincts of self-preservation, hunger, lust, vengeance, &c. Why then does man regret, even though trying to banish such regret, that he has followed the one natural impulse rather than the other; and why does he further feel that he ought to regret his conduct? Man in this respect differs profoundly from the lower animals. Nevertheless we can, I think, see with some degree of clearness the reason of this difference.

Man, from the activity of his mental faculties, cannot avoid reflection: past impressions and images are incessantly and clearly passing through his mind. Now with those animals which live permanently in a body, the social instincts are ever present and persistent. Such animals are always ready to utter the danger-signal, to defend the community, and to give aid to their fellows in accordance with their

---

[4] Charles Darwin, *The Descent of Man and Selection in Relation to Sex* (London, 1871), ch. 4, 5.

habits; they feel at all times, without the stimulus of any special passion or desire, some degree of love and sympathy for them; they are unhappy if long separated from them, and always happy to be again in their company. So it is with ourselves. Even when we are quite alone, how often do we think with pleasure or pain of what others think of us,—of their imagined approbation or disapprobation; and this all follows from sympathy, a fundamental element of the social instincts. A man who possessed no trace of such instincts would be an unnatural monster. On the other hand, the desire to satisfy hunger, or any passion such as vengeance, is in its nature temporary, and can for a time be fully satisfied. Nor is it easy, perhaps hardly possible, to call up with complete vividness the feeling, for instance, of hunger; nor indeed, as has often been remarked, of any suffering. The instinct of self-preservation is not felt except in the presence of danger; and many a coward has thought himself brave until he has met his enemy face to face. The wish for another man's property is perhaps as persistent a desire as any that can be named; but even in this case the satisfaction of actual possession is generally a weaker feeling than the desire: many a thief, if not an habitual one, after success has wondered why he stole some article.

A man cannot prevent past impressions often repassing through his mind; he will thus be driven to make a comparison between the impressions of past hunger, vengeance satisfied, or danger shunned at other men's cost, with the almost ever-present instinct of sympathy, and with his early knowledge of what others consider as praiseworthy or blameable. This knowledge cannot be banished from his mind, and from instinctive sympathy is esteemed of great moment. He will then feel as if he had been baulked in following a present instinct or habit, and this with all animals causes dissatisfaction, or even misery.

The above case of the swallow affords an illustration, though a reversed nature, of a temporary though for the time strongly persistent instinct conquering another instinct, which is usually dominant over all others. At the proper season these birds seem all day long to be impressed with the desire to migrate; their habits change; they become restless, are noisy and congregate in flocks. Whilst the mother-bird is feeding, or brooding over her nestlings, the maternal instinct is probably stronger than the migratory; but the instinct which is the more persistent gains the victory, and at last, at a moment when her young ones are not in sight, she takes flight and deserts them. When arrived at the end of her long journey, and the migratory instinct has ceased to act, what an agony of remorse the bird would feel, if from being endowed with great mental activity, she could not prevent the image constantly passing through her mind, of her young ones perishing in the bleak north from cold and hunger.

At the moment of action, man will no doubt be apt to follow the stronger impulse; and though this may occasionally prompt him to the noblest deeds, it will more commonly lead him to gratify his own desires at the expense of other men. But after their gratification when past and weaker impressions are judged by the ever-enduring social instinct, and by his deep regard for the good opinion of his fellows, retribution will surely come. He will then feel remorse, repentance, regret, or shame; this latter feeling, however, relates almost exclusively to the judgment of others. He will consequently resolve more or less firmly to act differently for the future; and this is conscience; for conscience looks backwards, and serves as a guide for the future.

* * * * *

Concluding Remarks. It was assumed formerly by philosophers of the derivative school of morals that the foundation of morality lay in a form of Selfishness; but more recently the "Greatest happiness principle" has been brought prominently forward. It is, however, more correct to speak of the latter principle as the standard, and not as the motive of conduct. Nevertheless, all the authors whose works I have consulted, with a few exceptions write as if there must be a distinct motive for every action, and that this must be associated with some pleasure or displeasure. But man seems often to act impulsively, that is from instinct or long habit, without any consciousness of pleasure, in the same manner as does probably a bee or ant, when it blindly follows its instincts. Under circumstances of extreme peril, as during a fire, when a man endeavours to save a fellow-creature without a moment's hesitation, he can hardly feel pleasure; and still less has he time to reflect on the dissatisfaction which he might subsequently experience if he did not make the attempt. Should he afterwards reflect over his own conduct, he would feel that there lies within him an impulsive power widely different from a search after pleasure or happiness; and this seems to be the deeply planted social instinct.

In the case of the lower animals it seems much more appropriate to speak of their social instincts, as having been developed for the general good rather than for the general happiness of the species. The term, general good, may be defined as the rearing of the greatest number of individuals in full vigour and health, with all their faculties perfect, under the conditions to which they are subjected. As the social instincts both of man and the lower animals have no doubt been developed by nearly the same steps, it would be advisable, if found practicable, to use the same definition in both cases, and to take as the standard of morality, the general good or welfare of the community, rather than the general happiness; but this definition would perhaps require some limitation on account of political ethics.

When a man risks his life to save that of a fellow-creature, it seems also more correct to say that he acts for the general good, rather than for the general happiness of mankind. No doubt the welfare and the happiness of the individual usually coincide; and a contented, happy tribe will flourish better than one that is discontented and unhappy. We have seen that even at an early period in the history of man, the expressed wishes of the community will have naturally influenced to a large extent the conduct of each member; and as all wish for happiness, the "greatest happiness principle" will have become a most important secondary guide and object; the social instinct, however, together with sympathy (which leads to our regarding the approbation and disapprobation of others), having served as the primary impulse and guide. Thus the reproach is removed of laying the foundation of the noblest part of our nature in the base principle of selfishness; unless, indeed, the satisfaction which every animal feels, when it follows its proper instincts, and the dissatisfaction felt when prevented, be called selfish.

The wishes and opinions of the members of the same community, expressed at first orally, but later by writing also, either form the sole guides of our conduct, or greatly reinforce the social instincts; such opinions, however, have sometimes a tendency directly opposed to these instincts. This latter fact is well exemplified by the *Law of Honour*, that is, the law of the opinion of our equals, and not of all our countrymen. The breach of this law, even when the breach is known to be strictly accordant with true morality, has caused many a man more agony than a real crime. We recognise the same influence in the burning sense of shame which most of us have felt, even after the interval of years, when calling to mind some accidental breach of a trifling, though fixed, rule of etiquette. The judgment of the community will generally be guided by some rude experience of what is best in the long run for all the members; but this judgment will not rarely err from ignorance and weak powers of reasoning. Hence the strangest customs and superstitions, in complete opposition to the true welfare and happiness of mankind, have become all-powerful throughout the world. We see this in the horror felt by a Hindoo who breaks his caste, and in many other such cases. It would be difficult to distinguish between the remorse felt by a Hindoo who has yielded to the temptation of eating unclean food, from that felt after committing a theft; but the former would probably be the more severe.

How so many absurd rules of conduct, as well as so many absurd religious beliefs, have originated, we do not know; nor how it is that they have become, in all quarters of the world, so deeply impressed on the mind of men; but it is worthy of remark that a belief constantly inculcated during the early years of life, whilst the brain is impressible, appears to acquire almost the nature of an instinct; and the very essence of an instinct is that it is followed independently of reason. Neither can we say why certain admirable virtues, such as the love of truth, are much more highly appreciated by some savage tribes than by others; nor, again, why similar differences prevail even amongst highly civilised nations. Knowing how firmly fixed many strange customs and superstitions have become, we need feel no surprise that the self-regarding virtues, supported as they are by reason, should now appear to us so natural as to be thought innate, although they were not valued by man in his early condition.

Notwithstanding many sources of doubt, man can generally and readily distinguish between the higher and lower moral rules. The higher are founded on the social instincts, and relate to the welfare of others. They are supported by the approbation of our fellow-men and by reason. The lower rules, though some of them when implying self-sacrifice hardly deserve to be called lower, relate chiefly to self, and arise from public opinion, matured by experience and cultivation; for they are not practised by rude tribes.

As man advances in civilisation, and small tribes are united into larger communities, the simplest reason would tell each individual that he ought to extend his social instincts and sympathies to all the members of the same nation, though personally unknown to him. This point being once reached, there is only an artificial barrier to prevent his sympathies extending to the men of all nations and races. If, indeed, such men are separated from him by great differences in appearance or habits, experience unfortunately shews us how long it is, before we look at them as our fellow-creatures. Sympathy beyond the confines of man, that is, humanity to the lower animals, seems to be one of the latest moral acquisitions. It is apparently unfelt by savages, except towards their pets. How little the old Romans knew of it is shewn by their abhorrent gladiatorial exhibitions. The very idea of humanity, as far as I could observe, was new to most of the Gauchos of the Pampas. This virtue, one of the noblest with which man is endowed, seems to arise incidentally from our sympathies becoming more tender and more widely diffused, until they are extended to all sentient beings. As soon as this virtue is honoured and practised by some few men, it spreads through instruction and example to the young, and eventually becomes incorporated in public opinion.

The highest possible stage in moral culture is when we recognise that we ought to control our thoughts, and "not even in inmost thought to think again the sins that made the past so pleasant to us." Whatever makes any bad action familiar to the mind, renders its performance by so much the easier. As Marcus Aurelius long ago said, "Such as are thy habitual thoughts, such also will be the character of thy mind; for the soul is dyed by the thoughts."

Our great philosopher, Herbert Spencer, has recently explained his views on the moral sense. He says, "I believe that the experiences of utility organised and consolidated through all past generations of the human race, have been producing corresponding modifications, which, by continued transmission and accumulation, have become in us certain faculties of moral intuition—certain emotions responding to right and wrong conduct, which have no apparent basis in the individual experiences of utility." There is not the least inherent improbability, as it seems to me, in virtuous tendencies being more or less strongly inherited; or, not to mention the various dispositions and habits transmitted by many of our domestic animals to their offspring. I have heard of authentic cases in which a desire to steal and a tendency to lie appeared to run in families of the upper ranks; and as stealing is a rare crime in the wealthy classes, we can hardly account by accidental coincidence for the tendency occurring in two or three members of the same family. If bad tendencies are transmitted, it is probable that good ones are likewise transmitted. That the state of the body by affecting the brain, has great influence on the moral tendencies is known to most of those who have suffered from chronic derangements of the digestion or liver. The same fact is likewise shewn by the "perversion or destruction of the moral sense being often one of the earliest symptoms of mental derangement"; and insanity is notoriously often inherited. Except through the principle of the transmission of moral tendencies, we cannot understand the differences believed to exist in this respect between the various races of mankind.

Even the partial transmission of virtuous tendencies would be an immense assistance to the primary impulse derived directly and indirectly from the social instincts. Admitting for a moment that virtuous tendencies are inherited, it appears probable, at least in such cases as chastity, temperance, humanity to animals, &c., that they become first impressed on the mental organization through habit, instruction and example, continued during several generations in the same family, and in a quite subordinate degree, or not at all, by the individuals possessing such virtues having succeeded best in the struggle for life. My chief source of doubt with respect to any such inheritance, is that senseless customs, superstitions, and tastes, such as the horror of a Hindoo for unclean food, ought on the same principle to be transmitted. I have not met with any evidence in support of the transmission of superstitious customs or senseless habits, although in itself it is perhaps not less probable than that animals should acquire inherited tastes for certain kinds of food or fear of certain foes.

Finally the social instincts, which no doubt were acquired by man as by the lower animals for the good of the community, will from the first have given to him some wish to aid his fellows, some feeling of sympathy, and have compelled him to regard their approbation and disapprobation. Such impulses will have served him at a very early period as a rude rule of right and wrong. But as man gradually advanced in intellectual power, and was enabled to trace the more remote consequences of his actions; as he acquired sufficient knowledge to reject baneful customs and superstitions; as he regarded more and more, not only the welfare, but the happiness of his fellow-men; as from habit, following on beneficial experience, instruction and example, his sympathies became more tender and widely diffused, extending to men of all races, to the imbecile, maimed, and other useless members of society, and finally to the lower animals,—so would the standard of his morality rise higher and higher. And it is admitted by moralists of the derivative school and by some intuitionists, that the standard of morality has risen since an early period in the history of man.

As a struggle may sometimes be seen going on between the various instincts of the lower animals, it is not surprising that there should be a struggle in man between his social instincts, with their derived virtues, and his lower, though momentarily stronger impulses or desires. This, as Mr. Galton has remarked, is all the less surprising, as man has emerged from a state of barbarism within a comparatively recent period. After having yielded to some temptation we feel a sense of dissatisfaction, shame, repentance, or remorse, analogous to the feelings caused by other powerful instincts or desires, when left unsatisfied or baulked. We compare the weakened impression of a past temptation with the ever present social instincts, or with habits, gained in early youth and strengthened during our whole lives, until they have become almost as strong as instincts. If with the temptation still before us we do not yield, it is because either the social instinct or some custom is at the moment predominant, or because we have learnt that it will appear to us hereafter the stronger, when compared with the weakened impression of the temptation, and we realise that its violation would cause us suffering. Looking to future generations, there is no cause to fear that the social instincts will grow weaker, and we may expect that virtuous habits will grow stronger, becoming perhaps fixed by inheritance. In this case the struggle between our higher and lower impulses will be less severe, and virtue will be triumphant.

Summary of the last two Chapters.... There can be no doubt that the difference between the mind of the lowest man and that of the highest animal is immense. An anthropomorphous ape, if he could take a dispassionate view of his own case, would admit that though he could form an artful plan to plunder a garden—though he could use stones for fighting or for breaking open nuts, yet that the thought of fashioning a stone into a tool was quite beyond his scope. Still less, as he would admit, could he follow out a train of metaphysical reasoning, or solve a mathematical problem, or reflect on God, or admire a grand natural scene. Some apes, however, would probably declare that they could and did admire the beauty of the coloured skin and fur of their partners in marriage. They would admit, that though they could make other apes understand by cries some of their perceptions and simpler wants, the notion of expressing definite ideas by definite sounds had never crossed their minds. They might insist that they were ready to aid their fellow-apes of the same troop in many ways, to risk their lives for them, and to take charge of their orphans; but they would be forced to acknowledge that disinterested love for all living creatures, the most noble attribute of man, was quite beyond their comprehension.

Nevertheless the difference in mind between man and the higher animals, great as it is, certainly is one of degree and not of kind. We have seen that the senses and intuitions, the various emotions and faculties, such as love, memory, attention, curiosity, imitation, reason, &c., of which man boasts, may be found in an incipient, or even sometimes in a well-developed condition, in the lower animals. They are also capable of some inherited improvement, as we see in the domestic dog compared with the wolf or jackal. If it could be proved that certain high mental powers, such as the formation of general concepts, self-consciousness, &c., were absolutely peculiar to man, which seems extremely doubtful, it is not improbable that these qualities are merely the incidental results of other highly-advanced intellectual faculties; and these again mainly the result of the continued use of a perfect language. At what age does the new-born infant possess the power of abstraction, or become self-conscious, and reflect on its own existence? We cannot answer; nor can we answer in regard to the ascending organic scale. The half-art, half-instinct of language still bears the stamp of its gradual evolution. The ennobling belief in God is not universal with man; and the belief in spiritual agencies naturally follows from other mental powers. The moral sense perhaps affords the best and highest distinction between man and the lower animals; but I need say nothing on this head, as I have so lately endeavoured to shew that the social instincts,—the prime principle of man's moral constitution—with the aid of active intellectual powers and the effects of habit, naturally lead to the golden rule, "As ye would that men should do to you, do ye to them likewise"; and this lies at the foundation of morality.

* * * * *

Turning now to the social and moral faculties. In order that primeval men, or the ape-like progenitors of man, should become social, they must have acquired the same instinctive feelings, which impel other animals to live in a body; and they no doubt exhibited the same general disposition. They would have felt uneasy when separated from their comrades, for whom they would have felt some degree of love; they would have warned each other of danger, and have given mutual aid in attack or defence. All this implies some degree of sympathy, fidelity, and courage. Such social qualities, the paramount importance of which to the lower animals is disputed by no one, were no doubt acquired by the progenitors of man in a similar manner, namely, through natural selection, aided by inherited habit. When two tribes of primeval man, living in the same country, came into competition, if (other circumstances being equal) the one tribe included a great number of courageous, sympathetic and faithful members, who were always ready to warn each other of danger, to aid and defend each

other, this tribe would succeed better and conquer the other. Let it be borne in mind how all-important in the never-ceasing wars of savages, fidelity and courage must be. The advantage which disciplined soldiers have over undisciplined hordes follows chiefly from the confidence which each man feels in his comrades. Obedience, as Mr. Bagehot has well shewn, is of the highest value, for any form of government is better than none. Selfish and contentious people will not cohere, and without coherence nothing can be effected. A tribe rich in the above qualities would spread and be victorious over other tribes: but in the course of time it would, judging from all past history, be in its turn overcome by some other tribe still more highly endowed. Thus the social and moral qualities would tend slowly to advance and be diffused throughout the world.

But it may be asked, how within the limits of the same tribe did a large number of members first become endowed with these social and moral qualities, and how was the standard of excellence raised? It is extremely doubtful whether the offspring of the more sympathetic and benevolent parents, or of those who were the most faithful to their comrades, would be reared in greater numbers than the children of selfish and treacherous parents belonging to the same tribe. He who was ready to sacrifice his life, as many a savage has been, rather than betray his comrades, would often leave no offspring to inherit his noble nature. The bravest men, who were always willing to come to the front in war, and who freely risked their lives for others, would on an average perish in larger numbers than other men. Therefore it hardly seems probable, that the number of men gifted with such virtues, or that the standard of their excellence, could be increased through natural selection, that is, by the survival of the fittest; for we are not here speaking of one tribe being victorious over another.

Although the circumstances, leading to an increase in the number of those thus endowed within the same tribe, are too complex to be clearly followed out, we can trace some of the probable steps. In the first place, as the reasoning powers and foresight of the members became improved, each man would soon learn that if he aided his fellow-men, he would commonly receive aid in return. From this low motive he might acquire the habit of aiding his fellows; and the habit of performing benevolent actions certainly strengthens the feeling of sympathy which gives the first impulse to benevolent actions. Habits, moreover, followed during many generations probably tend to be inherited.

But another and much more powerful stimulus to the development of the social virtues, is afforded by the praise and the blame of our fellowmen. To the instinct of sympathy, as we have already seen, it is primarily due, that we habitually bestow both praises and blame on others, whilst we love the former and dread the latter when applied to ourselves; and this instinct no doubt was originally acquired, like all the other social instincts, through natural selection. At how early a period the progenitors of man in the course of their development, became capable of feeling and being impelled by, the praise or blame of their fellow-creatures, we cannot of course say. But it appears that even dogs appreciate encouragement, praise, and blame. The rudest savages feel the sentiment of glory, as they clearly show by preserving the trophies of their prowess, by their habit of excessive boasting, and even by the extreme care which they take of their personal appearance and decorations; for unless they regarded the opinion of their comrades, such habits would be senseless.

They certainly feel shame at the breach of some of their lesser rules, and apparently remorse, as shewn by the case of the Australian who grew thin and could not rest from having delayed to murder some other woman, so as to propitiate his dead wife's spirit. Though I have not met with any other recorded case, it is scarcely credible that a savage, who will sacrifice his life rather than betray his tribe, or one who will deliver himself up as a prisoner rather than break his parole, would not feel remorse in his inmost soul, if he had failed in a duty, which he held sacred.

We may therefore conclude that primeval man, at a very remote period, was influenced by the praise and blame of his fellows. It is obvious, that the members of the same tribe would approve of conduct which appeared to them to be for the general good, and would reprobate that which appeared evil. To do good unto others—to do unto others as ye would they should do unto you—is the foundation-stone of morality. It is, therefore, hardly possible to exaggerate the importance during rude times of the love of praise and the dread of blame. A man who was not impelled by any deep, instinctive feeling, to sacrifice his life for the good of others, yet was roused to such actions by a sense of glory, would by his example excite the same wish for glory in other men, and would strengthen by exercise the noble feeling of admiration. He might thus do far more good to his tribe than by begetting offspring with a tendency to inherit his own high character.

With increased experience and reason, man perceives the more remote consequences of his actions, and the self-regarding virtues, such as temperance, chastity, &c., which during early times are, as we have before seen, utterly disregarded, come to be highly esteemed or even held sacred. I need not, however, repeat what I have said on this head in the fourth chapter. Ultimately our moral sense or conscience becomes a highly complex sentiment—originating in the social instincts, largely guided by the approbation of our fellow-men, ruled by reason, self-interest, and in later times by deep religious feelings, and confirmed by instruction and habit.

GEORGE JOHN ROMANES
(1848–1894)

Animal Intelligence and Comparative Psychology [5]

Now, in this mode of procedure what is the kind of activities which may be regarded as indicative of mind? I certainly do not so

5 George J. Romanes, *Animal Intelligence* (London, 1882), pp. 1–10.

regard the flowing of a river or the blowing of the wind. Why? First, because the objects are too remote in kind from my own organism to admit of my drawing any reasonable analogy between them and it; and, secondly, because the activities which they present are of invariably the same kind under the same circumstances; they afford no evidence of feeling or purpose. In other words, two conditions require to be satisfied before we even begin to imagine that observable activities are indicative of mind: first, the activities must be displayed by a living organism; and secondly, they must be of a kind to suggest the presence of two elements which we recognise as the distinctive characteristics of mind as such—consciousness and choice.

* * * * *

Objectively considered, the only distinction between adaptive movements due to reflex action and adaptive movements due to mental perception, consists in the former depending on inherited mechanisms within the nervous system being so constructed as to effect *particular* adaptive movements in response to *particular* stimulations, while the latter are independent of any such inherited adjustment of special mechanisms to the exigencies of special circumstances.

* * * * *

It is, then, adaptive action by a living organism in cases where the inherited machinery of the nervous system does not furnish data for our prevision of what the adaptive action must necessarily be—it is only here that we recognise the objective evidence of mind. The criterion of mind, therefore, which I propose, and to which I shall adhere throughout the present volume, is as follows: —Does the organism learn to make new adjustments, or to modify old ones, in accordance with the results of its own individual experience? If it does so, the fact cannot be due merely to reflex action in the sense above described, for it is impossible that heredity can have provided in advance for innovations upon, or alterations of, its machinery during the lifetime of a particular individual.

* * * * *

And this proof, as I have endeavoured to show, is in all cases and in its last analysis the fact of a living organism showing itself able to learn by its own individual experience.

Wherever we find an animal able to do this, we have the same right to predicate mind as existing in such an animal that we have to predicate it as existing in any human being other than ourselves. For instance, a dog has always been accustomed to eat a piece of meat when his organism requires nourishment, and when his olfactory nerves respond to the particular stimulus occasioned by the proximity of the food. So far, it may be said, there is no evidence of mind; the whole series of events comprised in the stimulations and muscular movements may be due to reflex action alone. But now suppose that by a number of lessons the dog has been taught not to eat the meat when he is hungry until he receives a certain verbal signal: then we have exactly the same kind of evidence that the dog's actions are prompted by mind as we have that the actions of a man are so prompted. Now we find that the lower down we go in the animal kingdom, the more we observe reflex action, or non-mental adjustment, to predominate over volitional action, or mental adjustment. That is to say, the lower down we go in the animal kingdom, the less capacity do we find for changing adjustive movements in correspondence with changed conditions; it becomes more and more hopeless to *teach* animals—that is, to establish associations of ideas; and the reason of this, of course, is that ideas or mental units become fewer and less definite the lower we descend through the structure of mind.

* * * * *

The mental states of an insect may be widely different from those of a man, and yet most probably the nearest conception that we can form of their true nature is that which we form by assimilating them to the pattern of the only mental states with which we are actually acquainted. And this consideration, it is needless to point out, has a special validity to the evolutionist, inasmuch as upon his theory there must be a psychological, no less than a physiological, continuity extending throughout the length and breadth of the animal kingdom.

C. LLOYD MORGAN
(1852–1936)

Canon of Interpretation [6]

For in the study of animal psychology as a branch of scientific inquiry, it is necessary that accurate observation, and a sound knowledge of the biological relationships of animals, should go hand in hand with a thorough appreciation of the methods and results of modern psychology. The only fruitful method of procedure is the interpretation of facts observed with due care in the light of sound psychological principles.

What some of these principles are we have considered, or shall consider, in this work. There is one basal principle, however, the brief exposition of which may fitly bring to a close this chapter. It may be thus stated:—

In no case may we interpret an action as the outcome of the exercise of a higher psychical faculty, if it can be interpreted as the outcome of the exercise of one which stands lower in the psychological scale.

Critique of Animal Intelligence

I contended that a very large percentage of the activities of animals may be fairly explained as due to intelligent adaptation through association founded on sense-experience. I freely admit that there is a small—in my opinion very small—outstanding percentage of cases, the explanation of which seems to involve the attribution to animals of powers of perception and of rational thought. But seeing the smallness of the number of cases of this type, and seeing the anecdotal character of the record, it is my opinion—an opinion which I shall have no hesitation in changing, if the results of systematic investigation and carefully conducted experimental observations warrant my so doing—that, were all the circumstances known, this outstanding percentage would disappear, and that the whole range of animal activities would be explicable as the result of intelligent adaptation. If this be so, then, in comparing the psychology of man and the

[6] C. Lloyd Morgan, *An Introduction to Comparative Psychology* (London, 1894), pp. 53, 358–359.

higher animals, the radical difference lies in the fact that man perceives particular relations among phenomena, and builds the generalized results of these perceptions into the fabric of his conceptual thought; while animals do not perceive the relations, and have no conceptual thought, nor any knowledge—if we use this word to denote the result of such conceptual thought.

* * * * *

I have throughout this work accepted evolution as the basis of explanation of nature, including psychical nature. I have endeavoured to look at the facts, so far as I know them, squarely and fairly, and have not intentionally shirked the many difficulties which are incidental to the inquiry I have undertaken. I have essayed to consider mental evolution in all its aspects, and have thus been led into what some of my scientific friends will term hopelessly metaphysical speculations. But I do not think that the metaphysics of the subject can be avoided in any such inquiry. It is not a question of metaphysics or no metaphysics, but of good metaphysics or bad. In my treatment of questions of zoological psychology some will no doubt accuse me of adopting the *a priori* method; and if by the *a priori* method they mean that based on the application of general principles, I plead guilty to the charge. The question is, Have the general principles themselves been reached by the methods of scientific induction, or have they been assumed without the warranty of inductive study? I have at least done my best to make clear the grounds on which I have been led to adopt the general principles of which I have made use. Again, it may be said that throughout my discussion of zoological psychology, I have fallen into the grave philosophical error of dogmatizing from negative premises. After making some parade of professing my inability, as human chronometer, to learn anything distinctly concerning the working of the animal clock, have I not ended by somewhat dogmatically denying to the clock certain faculties or mental powers? I have throughout been arguing, it may be said, that since I do not find sufficient evidence among animals of reason and the perception of relations, therefore such perceptual and rational powers must be absent, whereas the activities of animals can, it may be urged, be quite as well if not better explained on the assumption that they do perceive relations and exercise the faculty of reason. Such may be the line adopted by certain critics. In reply, let me say, as a last word, first, that in denying to animals the perception of relations and the faculty of reason, I do so in no dogmatic spirit, and not in support of any preconceived theory or opinion, but because the evidence now before us is not, in my opinion, sufficient to justify the hypothesis that any animals have reached that stage of mental evolution at which they are even incipiently rational; and, secondly, that I have all along based my discussion on the canon of interpretation considered in the latter part of the third chapter. If good reason can be shown for the rejection of that canon, the logical foundation of my argument will be destroyed, and the argument itself will fall to the ground.

GRANVILLE STANLEY HALL
(1844–1924)

Adolescent Psychology from a Genetic Standpoint [7]

While inanimate nature and even the lower forms of animal life are relatively stable, some of the latter having persisted from remote geologic ages, man is rapidly changing. His presence on the globe, his dominion over animals, his diffusion, and the historic period, are a series of increasingly recent events. While his bodily form is comparatively stable, his soul is in a transition stage, and all that we call progress is more and more rapid. Old moorings are constantly broken; adaptive plasticity to new environments—somatic, economic, industrial, social, moral and religious —was never so great; and in the changes which we hope are on the whole truly progressive, more and more human traits are too partially acquired to be permanently inherited. All this suggests that man is not a permanent type but an organism in a very active stage of evolution toward a more permanent form. Our consciousness is but a single stage and one type of mind: a late, partial, and perhaps essentially abnormal and remedial outcrop of the great underlying life of man-soul. The animal, savage, and child-soul can never be studied by introspection. Moreover, with missing links and extinct ethnic types, much, perhaps most, soul life has been hopelessly lost. Thus, the adult who seeks self-knowledge by introspection is banausic, and his system is at its best but one human document or return to the eternal but ever unanswered question what man can know, what he should do, and how he most truly feels. From this it follows that we must turn to the larger and far more laborious method of observation, description, and induction. We must collect states of mind, sentiments, phenomena long since lapsed, psychic facts that appear faintly and perhaps but once in a lifetime, and that in only few and rare individuals, impulses that, it may be, never anywhere arise above the threshold, but manifest themselves only in automatisms, acts, behavior, things neglected, trivial and incidental, such as Darwin says are often most vital. We must go to school to the folk-soul, learn of criminals and defectives, animals, and in some sense go back to Aristotle in rebasing psychology on biology, and realize that we know the soul best when we can best write its history in the world, and that there are no finalities save formulæ of development. The soul is thus still in the making, and we may hope for an indefinite further development. Perhaps other racial stocks than ours will later advance the kingdom of man as far beyond our present standpoint as it now is above that of the lowest savage or even animals. There are powers in the soul that slumber like the sleepers in myth, partially aroused, it may be, in great personal or social crises, but sometime to be awakened to dominance. In a word, the view here represents a nascent tendency and is in striking contrast to all those systems that presume to have attained

[7] G. Stanley Hall, *Adolescence: Its Psychology and Its Relations to Physiology, Anthropology, Sociology, Sex, Crime, Religion and Education* (New York: D. Appleton, 1904), vol. 1, pp. vii–xviii.

even an approximate finality. But the twilight is that of dawn and not of evening. It is the morning hours of beginning and not that of completing the day of work, and this can appeal only to those still adolescent in soul.

Holding that the child and the race are each keys to the other, I have constantly suggested phyletic explanations of all degrees of probability. Some of these, I think, have been demonstrated so far as is now possible in this obscure and complicated domain. Realizing the limitations and qualifications of the recapitulation theory in the biologic field, I am now convinced that its psychogenetic applications have a method of their own, and although the time has not yet come when any formulation of these can have much value, I have done the best I could with each instance as it arose. Along with the sense of the immense importance of further coordinating childhood and youth with the development of the race, has grown the conviction that only here can we hope to find true norms against the tendencies to precocity in home, school, church, and civilization generally, and also to establish criteria by which to both diagnose and measure arrest and retardation in the individual and the race. While individuals differ widely in not only the age but the sequence of the stages of repetition of racial history, a knowledge of nascent stages and the aggregate interests of different ages of life is the best safeguard against very many of the prevalent errors of education and of life.

Modern conceptions, which increasingly make all mental processes efferent in their psychophysical nature, suggest a now impending synthesis that may give to our practical age and land the long-hoped-for and long-delayed science of man. To help bring these tendencies to their maturity is the task to which organic thinkers should address themselves. Utilizing to the utmost the lessons of the past, they should free themselves alike from excessive subjectivisms and from the limitations of old systems and methods, and feel it their highest duty to enter upon the less critical and more constructive work of building larger philosophic mansions for the soul. If truth is edification, the highest criterion of pure science is its educative value. The largest possible aspect of all the facts of life and mind is educational,

and the only complete history is the story of the influences that have advanced or retarded the development of man toward his completion, always ideal and forever in the future. Thus psychology and the higher pedagogy are one and inseparable. Not only the beautiful and the good, but the true, can have no other test of validity than that they appeal to and satisfy certain deep needs; and these are many.

* * * * *

The years from about eight to twelve constitute an unique period of human life. The acute stage of teething is passing, the brain has acquired nearly its adult size and weight, health is almost at its best, activity is greater and more varied than ever before or than it ever will be again, and there is peculiar endurance, vitality, and resistance to fatigue. The child develops a life of its own outside the home circle, and its natural interests are never so independent of adult influence. Perception is very acute, and there is great immunity to exposure, danger, accident, as well as to temptation. Reason, true morality, religion, sympathy, love, and esthetic enjoyment are but very slightly developed. Everything, in short, suggests the culmination of one stage of life as if it thus represented what was once, and for a very protracted and relatively stationary period, the age of maturity in some remote, perhaps pigmoid, stage of human evolution, when in a warm climate the young of our species once shifted for themselves independently of further parental aid. The qualities now developed are phyletically vastly older than all the neo-atavistic traits of body and soul, later to be superposed like a new and higher story built on to our primal nature. Heredity is so far both more stable and more secure. The elements of personality are few, but are well organized and on a simple, effective plan. The momentum of the paleopsychic traits is great, and they are often clearly distinguishable from those to be later added. Thus the boy is father of the man in a new sense in that his qualities are indefinitely older and existed well compacted untold ages before the more distinctly human attributes were developed. Indeed, there are a few faint indications set forth in the text of a yet earlier age nodality or meristic segmentation, as if amid the increased instabilities of health at the age of about six we could still detect the ripple-marks of an ancient public beach now lifted high above the tides of a receding shore-line as human infancy has been prolonged. I have also given reasons that lead me to the conclusion that, despite its dominance, the function of sexual maturity and procreative power is peculiarly mobile up and down the ageline independently of many of the qualities usually so closely associated with it, so that much that sex created in the phylum now precedes it in the individual.

Rousseau would leave prepubescent years to nature and to these primal hereditary impulses and allow the fundamental traits of savagery their fling till twelve. Biological psychology finds many and cogent reasons to confirm this view if only a proper environment could be provided. The child revels in savagery, and if its tribal, predatory, hunting, fishing, fighting, roving, idle, playing proclivities could be indulged in the country and under conditions that now, alas! seem hopelessly ideal, they could conceivably be so organized and directed as to be far more truly humanistic and liberal than all that the best modern school can provide. Rudimentary organs of the soul now suppressed, perverted, or delayed, to crop out in menacing forms later, would be developed in their season so that we should be immune to them in maturer years, on the principle of the Aristotelian catharsis for which I have tried to suggest a far broader application than the Stagirite could see in his day.

These nativistic and more or less feral instincts can and should be fed and formed. The deep and strong cravings in the individual to revive the ancestral experiences and occupations of the race can and must be met, at least in a secondary and vicarious way, by tales of the heroic virtues the child can appreciate, and these proxy experiences should make up by variety and extent what they lack in intensity. The teacher art should so vivify all that the resources of literature, tradition, history, can supply which represents the crude, rank virtues of the world's childhood that, with his almost visual imagination, reenforced by psychonomic recapitulatory impulses, the child can enter upon his full heritage, live out each stage of his life to the fullest, and realize in himself all its manifold tendencies. Echoes

only of the vaster, richer life of the remote past of the race they must remain, but just these are the murmurings of the only muse that can save from the omnipresent dangers of precocity. Thus we not only rescue from the danger of loss, but utilize for further psychic growth the results of the higher heredity, which are the most precious and potential things on earth. So, too, in our urbanized hothouse life, that tends to ripen everything before its time, we must teach nature, although the very phrase is ominous. But we must not, in so doing, wean still more from, but perpetually incite to visit field, forest, hill, shore, the water, flowers, animals, the true homes of childhood in this wild, undomesticated stage from which modern conditions have kidnapped and transported him. Books and reading are distasteful, for the very soul and body cry out for a more active, objective life, and to know nature and man at first hand. These two staples, stories and nature, by these informal methods of the home and the environment constitute fundamental education.

* * * * *

Adolescence is a new birth, for the higher and more completely human traits are now born. The qualities of body and soul that now emerge are far newer. The child comes from and harks back to a remoter past; the adolescent is neo-atavistic, and in him the later acquisitions of the race slowly become prepotent. Development is less gradual and more saltatory, suggestive of some ancient period of storm and stress when old moorings were broken and a higher level attained. The annual rate of growth in height, weight, and strength is increased and often doubled, and even more. Important functions previously non-existent arise. Growth of parts and organs loses its former proportions, some permanently and some for a season. Some of these are still growing in old age and others are soon arrested and atrophy. The old moduli of dimensions become obsolete and old harmonies are broken. The range of individual differences and average errors in all physical measurements and all psychic tests increases. Some linger long in the childish stage and advance late or slowly, while others push on with a sudden outburst of impulsion to early maturity. Bones and muscles lead all other tissues, as if they vied with each other, and there is frequent flabbiness or tension as one or the other leads. Nature arms youth for conflict with all the resources at her command—speed, power of shoulder, biceps, back, leg, jaw,—strengthens and enlarges skull, thorax, hips, makes man aggressive and prepares woman's frame for maternity. The power of the diseases peculiar to childhood abates, and liability to the far more diseases of maturity begins, so that with liability to both it is not strange that the dawn of the ephebic day is marked at the same time by increased morbidity but diminished rates of mortality. Some disorders of arrest and defect as well as of excessive unfoldment in some function, part, or organ may now, after long study and controversy, be said to be established as peculiar to this period, and diseases that are distinctly school- and city-bred abound, with apparently increasing frequency. The momentum of heredity often seems insufficient to enable the child to achieve this great revolution and come to complete maturity, so that every step of the upward way is strewn with wreckage of body, mind, and morals. There is not only arrest, but perversion, at every stage, and hoodlumism, juvenile crime, and secret vice seem not only increasing, but develop in earlier years in every civilized land. Modern life is hard, and in many respects increasingly so, on youth. Home, school, church, fail to recognize its nature and needs and, perhaps most of all, its perils. The cohesions between the elements of personality are loosened by the disparities of both somatic and psychic development, and if there is arrest at any stage or in any part before the higher unity is achieved there is almost sure to be degeneration and reunion on a lower level than before. One of the gravest dangers is the persistent ignoring by femininists of the prime importance of establishing normal periodicity in girls, to the needs of which everything else should for a few years be secondary.

The functions of every sense undergo reconstruction, and their relations to other psychic functions change, and new sensations, some of them very intense, arise, and new associations in the sense sphere are formed. Haptic impressions, appetite for food and drink, and smell are most modified. The voice changes, vascular instability, blushing, and flushing are increased. Sex asserts its mastery in field after field, and works its havoc in the form of secret vice, debauch, disease, and enfeebled heredity, cadences the soul to both its normal and abnormal rhythms, and sends many thousand youth a year to quacks, because neither parents, teachers, preachers, or physicians know how to deal with its problems. Thus the foundations of domestic, social, and religious life are oftenest undermined. Between religion and love God and nature have wrought an indissoluble bond so that neither can attain normality without that of the other. Secondary sexual qualities are shown to have an ever-widening range, and parenthood to mean more with every upward step of development. The youth craves more knowledge of body and mind, that can help against besetting temptations, aid in the choice of a profession, and if his intellect is normal he does not vex his soul overmuch about the logical character of the universe or the ultimate sanction of either truth or virtue. He is more objective than subjective, and only if his lust to know nature and life is starved does his mind trouble him by in-growing. There are new repulsions felt toward home and school, and truancy and runaways abound. The social instincts undergo sudden unfoldment and the new life of love awakens. It is the age of sentiment and religion, of rapid fluctuation of mood, and the world seems strange and new. Interest in adult life and in vocations develops. Youth awakes to a new world and understands neither it nor himself. The whole future of life depends on how the new powers now given suddenly and in profusion are husbanded and directed. Character and personality are taking form, but everything is plastic. Self-feeling and ambition are increased, and every trait and faculty is liable to exaggeration and excess. It is all a marvelous new birth, and those who believe that nothing is so worthy of love, reverence, and service as the body and soul of youth, and who hold that the best test of every human institution is how much it contributes to bring youth to the ever fullest possible development, may well review themselves and the civilization in which we live to see how far it satisfies this supreme test.

*   *   *   *   *

We try to impose not only our civilization.

but our religion, upon lower races, even though they are thereby exterminated, and fail to study the nature and needs of even those we try to help.

All this is hard on youth, which was better understood in ancient Greece and Rome than now, for it is profoundly responsive to all these influences. Despite all this I am an optimist root and core, not merely because an evolutionist must hold that the best and not the worst will survive and prevail, but because in most, though not yet in all, of

these fields I see clearly the beginnings of better things. Even in education and religion, the strongholds of conservatism, there are new and better ideals and efforts, and these are less exceptional and are growing in power and influence and are represented by more and better men. In vigor, enthusiasm, and courage we are still young, and our faults are those of youth. Because they have been great our suffering has been also great, and pain is the world's best teacher whose lessons are surest to be laid to heart.

CHRISTINE LADD-FRANKLIN
(1847–1930)

Ladd-Franklin Theory of Color Evolution [8]

In human vision we have, besides the normal colour defects of the non-central retina, many cases (congenital and acquired) of partial colour-blindness; these, in their typical forms, consist in seeing the whole spectrum as yellow in the long-wave end and blue in the short-wave end, with an intermediate point at which vision is achromatic. This colourless point is not at the place where the normal individual gets the pure green colour (the unitary green), but at a place which to him is blue-green. Those who have this yellow and blue vision only are of two distinct types, protanopic and deuteranopic, according as the distribution along the spectrum of their undifferentiated yellow-vision coincides with the normal distribution of the green constituent or of the red constituent. The blue-vision of all these cases coincides with that of normal vision.

* * * * *

Total defect in the chromatic sensations occurs much less frequently; the distribution along the spectrum of the achromatic sensation (which is all that is left in such cases) is sometimes the same as the intensity distribution of normal (tetrachromatic) vision; but more frequently it coincides with that of normal scotopia—the maximum is in the yellow-green. The former cases are doubtless instances of cerebral defect (the fovea is not

blind in these cases); the latter are congenital, typical, and accompanied by total foveal blindness. The defect is plainly, in these latter cases, a non-development of light-sensitive substances in the retina, the cones being doubtless wholly out of function.

This remarkable congruent mass of evidence in regard to the development of the chromatic sensations, which is here briefly summarized, evidently demands a colour theory which takes it into account, and which explains at the same time, by one and the same conception, the facts of complementation. (See the diagrams.) The development colour theory has this for its object, and also the avoidance of the inconsistencies of the theories of Hering and of Helmholtz. It assumes that there occurred, first, a light-sensitive chemical substance in the (low-grade) rods which responded non-specifically to light of any sort within the visible spectrum. The simple cleavage product of this stage of development forms the nerve-excitant which is correlated with the sensation of white. This is the only sensation possible when the rods alone function, i.e. in the cases of (*a*) normal achromatic

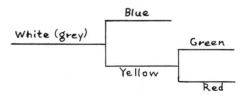

FIG. 15—Development of the Colour-Sense.

[8] Christine Ladd-Franklin, *Colour and Colour Theories* (New York: Harcourt, Brace, 1929), pp. 128–131. Reprinted by permission.

vision in the extreme periphery, and of achromatic vision in (b) the normal eye in a state of darkness-adaptation and with low objective intensities, and in (c) the totally chroma-blind defectives. Development of the colour-sense takes place in the form of the acquiring of greater specificity in that part of the colour-molecule which undergoes cleavage. Instead of responding alike to all parts of the visible spectrum, part of it, S_Y, is synchronous in its electronic vibrations with the longer waves, and part of it, S_B, with the shorter waves; but whenever *both* of these nerve-excitant substances are torn off at the same time, they unite chemically to constitute the former whiteness-excitation. This is the stage of development of the normal mid-periphery, and of the two types of yellow-blue-vision. In Stage III the complete differentiation of the light-sensitive molecule in the way of greater specificity has taken place, and red and green are added as specific sensations. But the nerve-excitant substances, E_G and E_R, when they are both dissociated out together, reconstitute the yellow nerve-excitant, E_Y. Again it is plain that yellow and blue nerve-excitants re-unite to constitute the original nerve-excitant, E_W, whose sensation

effect, when the cortex is reached, is white in quality.

After images are explained as a "residual" phenomenon, due to the completed dissociation of a molecule which in its partially dissociated condition is, like other such substances (Cannon), unstable.

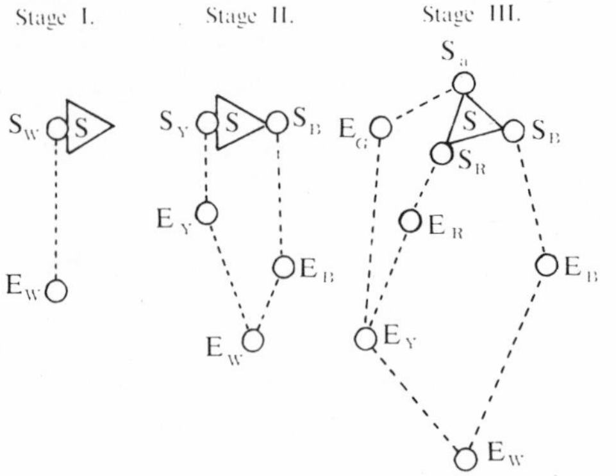

FIG. 16.—The Development Theory of Colour (Ladd-Franklin). S_N, the colour-sensation receptors (resonators, side-chains, light-sensitive electrons, or whatever the current photo-chemical theory may demand), in three successive stages of development. E_N, the several specific nerve-excitant substances for the five specific light-sensations.

JAMES MARK BALDWIN
(1861–1934)

Psychophysical Parallelism in Evolution [9]

I have said that the principle of parallelism is universal, that is, that it is applicable to all instances in which the facts on either side are of the order indicated by the term "psychophysical." The great spheres in which such a truth would have bearings are the two covered by individual life history, from life to death—ontogeny, the sphere of development—and the race history of a species, or of all life upon the earth considered as showing a series of forms connected by links of

progressive descent—phylogeny, or evolution. These two forms of parallelism we may call respectively "individual" and "racial." Earlier discussions of parallelism have had reference largely to the former sphere, and the question has come up for the most part in connection with theoretical discussions of the relation of mind and body. Furthermore, the concomitance of development of mind and body in the individual has had recognition, and its illustrative value for the topic of evolution has been written about—though not at all adequately.

The corresponding racial application of parallelism in the sphere of evolution has not, to the present writer's knowledge, been explicitly made; that is, as going necessarily with an individual parallelism, as part of an

[9] James Mark Baldwin, *Development and Evolution: Including Psychophysical Evolution, Evolution by Orthoplasy, and the Theory of Genetic Modes* (New York: Macmillan, 1902), ch. 1.

intergenetic conception. And yet the two cases must necessarily go together, and no final formulation is possible of the relation of conscious changes to bodily changes which does not have direct application in both these spheres, and indeed the same application in both of them. For in psychology, as in biology, the race series is but a continuous line of individual generations, and to ask the question of the race is but to ask whether parallelism holds for any given number of generations of individuals wherever chosen in the line of descent—this provided we admit that descent is by some form of continuous hereditary transmission.

The questions which arise about heredity, however, do not trouble us, seeing that they are not within the domain of strictly psychophysical inquiry, except in so far as our theory must explain the inheritance of both physical and mental characters to the same degree. For example, the question of the "continuity of germ plasm" may be decided one way or the other—either for or against the actual continuous transmission of an identical substance—without raising the question of a corresponding transmission of anything psychological. For if there be breaks in the psychological series at those nodal points at which generation succeeds generation, there are also, by the principle of equal continuity, discussed above, breaks also in the psychophysical, and we may find the psychological series beginning again at the appropriate point in the development of the organism of the new generation—the point at which the psychophysical again begins. In other words, the advantage gained from the psychophysical point of view is that if there be apparent gaps in one of the series, we may

either assume them filled up by theoretical parallelism with the other series at these points, at which it has no gaps, or we may —if we deny continuity to either—make gaps in the second series in correspondence with the gaps found in the first. We have in any given case, in short, either a psychophysical fact, or we have not: if we have, then either series is sufficient to carry us over the critical point; if we have not, then the break in one series is sufficient evidence of a corresponding break in the other also. The principle of parallelism assumed, we claim once for all the right *to neglect the relation of the two terms, mental and physical, in all circumstances whatsoever.*

* * * * *

We do not have one series of genetic forms, the mental, evolving under shorthand formulas of its own; and another series, the organic, doing the same thing under different formulas. On the contrary, the two sets of facts really go together in the one set of formulas. This is what I am arguing for. We often find it necessary to use the mental facts as antecedents of the physical facts, often the physical as antecedent of the mental, and again, often the psychophysical as antecedent of either or both. . . .

The twofold application of parallelism, considered as an assumption of psychophysical research, may be represented by the accompanying diagram. The two vertical lines (M, B) represent the two series in the evolution of the race-forms of organisms—the dotted line (M, mind) being the mental, and the solid line (B, body) the physical. Across these at any point we may draw similar horizontal lines (*m, b*) representing individual development in any given generation; these are also, of course, dotted (*m*) and solid (*b*). The full theory of parallelism requires, not only that we make the two horizontal lines parallel,— the ordinary application in ontogeny (O); but that having gone so far, we must also draw the two parallel vertical lines—the application in phylogeny (P). At whatever point in the line of descent we apply the principle to individual development, we must perforce raise the corresponding genetic questions about the evolution which has led up to the birth of such individuals at that point. And the series of "shorthand" formulas, laws—in

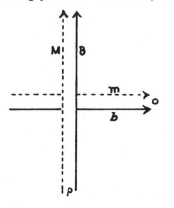

the prosaic equivalent of everyday science, "results"—at which we arrive, must involve the three great problems represented by the four lines: parallel development (the relation of m to b), parallel evolution (the relation of M to B), and intergenetic correlation (the relation of mb to MB). Furthermore, when we recognize in places the absence of the facts we should expect,—apparent breaks in either one of the lines,—we may resort to the resource of using the corresponding facts from the parallel line at the same level, and even those from the analogous line of the other pair of parallels, so far as there are known facts in the particular case which lend themselves to such procedure.

WILLIAM McDOUGALL
(1871–1938)

Hormic Psychology [10]

Anticipating a little the course of history, I shall here assume that the purposive nature of human action is no longer in dispute, and in this article shall endeavor to define and to justify that special form of purposive psychology which is now pretty widely known as *hormic psychology*.

* * * * *

I introduce the term "teleological" early in the exposition because I do not wish to seem to smuggle it in at a later stage after betraying the innocent reader into acceptance of a position which commits him unwittingly to teleology.

* * * * *

The psychologist who can summon enough courage to follow the lead of physicists and biologists and to accept the causal efficacy of psychical activity, of foresight and desire, is confronted with a choice between two theories of the ground of all desire, of all striving or conation, the hedonistic and the hormic.

* * * * *

We are thus driven to the hormic theory as the only alternative teleological theory of action. The essence of it may be stated very simply. To the question—Why does a certain animal or man seek this or that goal?—it replies: Because it is his nature to do so. This answer, simple as it may seem, has deep significance.

Observation of animals of any one species shows that all members of the species seek and strive toward a limited number of goals of certain types, certain kinds of food and of shelter, their mates, the company of their fellows, certain geographical areas at certain seasons, escape to cover in presence of certain definable circumstances, dominance over their fellows, the welfare of their young, and so on. For any one species the kinds of goals sought are characteristic and specific; and all members of the species seek these goals independently of example and of prior experience of attainment of them, though the course of action pursued in the course of striving towards the goal may vary much and may be profoundly modified by experience. We are justified, then, in inferring that each member of the species inherits the tendencies of the species to seek goals of these several types.

Man also is a member of an animal species. And this species also has its natural goals, or its inborn tendencies to seek goals of certain types. This fact is not only indicated very clearly by any comparison of human with animal behavior, but it is so obvious a fact that no psychologist of the least intelligence fails to recognize it, however inadequately, not even if he obstinately reduces their number to a minimum of three and dubs them the "prepotent reflexes" of sex, fear, and rage. Others write of "primary desires," or of "dominant urges," or of "unconditioned reflexes," or of appetites, or of cravings, or of congenital drives, or of motor sets, or of inherited tendencies or propensities; lastly, some, bolder than the rest, write of "so-called instincts." For instincts are out of fashion just now with American psychologists; and to write of instincts without some such qualification as "so-called" betrays a reckless

---

[10] William McDougall, "The hormic psychology," in Carl Murchison (ed.), *Psychologies of 1930* (Worcester, Mass.: Clark University Press, 1930), pp. 3, 5, 11, 12–15. Reprinted by permission.

indifference to fashion amounting almost to indecency. Yet the word "instinct" is too good to be lost to our science. Better than any other word it points to the facts and the problems with which I am here concerned.

The hormic psychology imperatively requires recognition not only of instinctive action but of instincts. Primarily and traditionally the words "instinct" and "instinctive" point to those types of animal action which are complex activities of the whole organism; which lead the creature to the attainment of one or other of the goals natural to the species; which are in their general nature manifested by all members of the species under appropriate circumstances; which exhibit nice adaptation to circumstances; and which, though often suggesting intelligent appreciation of the end to be gained and the means to be adopted, yet owe little or nothing to the individual's prior experience.

The words as thus traditionally used point to a problem. The word "instinctive" describes actions of this type. The word "instinct" implies that unknown something which expresses itself in the train of instinctive action directed towards a particular natural goal. What is the nature of that x to which the word "instinct" points? The problem has provoked much speculation all down the ages; the answers ranging from "the finger of God" to "a rigid bit of reflex nervous mechanism." . . .

Hormic activity is an energy manifestation; but the hormic theory does not presume to say just what form or forms of energy or transformations of energy are involved. It seems to involve liberation of energy potential or latent in chemical form in the tissues; and hormic theory welcomes any information about such transformations that physiological chemistry can furnish. But it refuses to go beyond the facts and to be bound by current hypotheses of physical science; and it refuses to be blinded to the essential facts. And the most essential facts are (a) that the energy manifestation is guided into channels such that the organism approaches its goal; (b) that this guidance is effected through a cognitive activity, an awareness, however vague, of the present situation and of the goal; (c) that the activity, once initiated and set on its path through cognitive activity, tends to continue until the goal is attained; (d) that,

when the goal is attained, the activity terminates; (e) that progress towards and attainment of the goal are pleasurable experiences, and thwarting and failure are painful or disagreeable experiences.

These statements imply that hormic activity is essentially mental activity, involving always cognition or awareness, striving initiated and governed by such cognition, and accruing satisfaction or dissatisfaction. The theory holds that these are three fundamental aspects of all hormic activity, distinguishable by abstraction, but not separable or capable of occurring in nature as separate events. Thus it necessarily holds that hormic activity can be exhibited only by organisms or natural entities that have a certain complexity of organization, such entities as have been traditionally called monads. And it inclines to the view that the simplest form under which such monads appear to us as sensible phenomena is that of the single living cell.

* * * * *

In short, the hormic theory holds that where there is life there is mind; and that, if there has been continuity of evolution of the organic from the inorganic, there must have been something of mind, some trace of mental nature and activity in the inorganic from which such emergence took place.

Social Psychology and Instincts [11]

The Principal Instincts and the Primary Emotions of Man

The instinct of flight and the emotion of fear—The instinct of repulsion and the emotion of disgust—The instinct of curiosity and the emotion of wonder—The instinct of pugnacity and the emotion of anger—The instincts of self-abasement (or subjection) and of self-assertion (or self-display), and the emotions of subjection and elation (or negative and positive self-feeling)—The parental instinct and the tender emotion—The instinct of reproduction—The gregarious instinct—The instinct of acquisition—The instinct of construction.

* * * * *

[11] William McDougall, *An Introduction to Social Psychology* (London: Methuen, 1910), pp. xii, 29–44.

Definition of Instinct

We may, then, define an instinct as an inherited or innate psycho-physical disposition which determines its possessor to perceive, and to pay attention to, objects of a certain class, to experience an emotional excitement of a particular quality upon perceiving such an object, and to act in regard to it in a particular manner, or, at least, to experience an impulse to such action.

It must further be noted that some instincts remain inexcitable except during the prevalence of some temporary bodily state, such as hunger. In these cases we must suppose that the bodily process or state determines the stimulation of sense-organs within the body, and that nervous currents ascending from these to the psycho-physical disposition maintain it in an excitable condition.

The behaviour of some of the lower animals seems to be almost completely determined throughout their lives by instincts modified but very little by experience; they perceive, feel, and act in a perfectly definite and invariable manner whenever a given instinct is excited—i.e., whenever the presence of the appropriate object coincides with the appropriate organic state of the creature. The highest degree of complexity of mental process attained by such creatures is a struggle between two opposed instinctive tendencies simultaneously excited. Such behaviour is relatively easy to understand in the light of the conception of instincts as innate psycho-physical dispositions.

While it is doubtful whether the behaviour of any animal is wholly determined by instincts quite unmodified by experience, it is clear that all the higher animals learn in various and often considerable degrees to adapt their instinctive actions to peculiar circumstances; and in the long course of the development of each human mind, immensely greater complications of the instinctive processes are brought about, complications so great that they have obscured until recent years the essential likeness of the instinctive processes in men and animals. These complications of instinctive processes are of four principal kinds, which we may distinguish as follows:—

(1) The instinctive reactions become capable of being initiated, not only by the perception of objects of the kind which directly excite the innate disposition, the natural or native excitants of the instinct, but also by ideas of such objects, and by perceptions and by ideas of objects of other kinds;

(2) the bodily movements in which the instinct finds expression may be modified and complicated to an indefinitely great degree:

(3) owing to the complexity of the ideas which can bring the human instincts into play, it frequently happens that several instincts are simultaneously excited; when the several processes blend with various degrees of intimacy:

(4) the instinctive tendencies become more or less systematically organised about certain objects or ideas.

* * * * *

It was said above that every instinctive process has the three aspects of all mental process, the cognitive, the affective, and the conative. Now, the innate psycho-physical disposition, which is an instinct, may be regarded as consisting of three corresponding parts, an afferent, a central, and a motor or efferent part, whose activities are the cognitive, the affective, and the conative features respectively of the total instinctive process. The afferent or receptive part of the total disposition is some organised group of nervous elements or neurones that is specially adapted to receive and to elaborate the impulses initiated in the sense-organ by the native object of the instinct; its constitution and activities determine the sensory content of the psycho-physical process.

* * * * *

The excitement of the efferent or motor part reaches it by way of the central part; its constitution determines the distribution of impulses to the muscles of the skeletal system by which the instinctive action is effected, and its nervous activities are the correlates of the conative element of the psychical process, of the felt impulse to action.

Now, the afferent or receptive part and the efferent or motor part are capable of being greatly modified, independently of one another and of the central part, in the course of the life history of the individual; while the central part persists throughout life as the essential unchanging nucleus of the disposition. Hence in man, whose intelligence and adaptability are so great, the afferent and efferent parts of each instinctive disposition are liable to many modifications, while the central part alone remains unmodified: that is to say, the cognitive processes through which any instinctive process may be initiated exhibit a great complication and variety; and the actual bodily movements by which the instinctive process achieves its end may be complicated to an indefinitely great extent; while the emotional excitement, with the accompanying nervous activities of the central part of the disposition, is the only part of the total instinctive process that retains its specific character and remains common to all individuals and all situations in which the instinct is excited.

We may say, then, that directly or indirectly the instincts are the prime movers of all human activity; by the conative or impulsive force of some instinct (or of some habit derived from an instinct), every train of thought, however cold and passionless it may

seem, is borne along towards its end, and every bodily activity is initiated and sustained. The instinctive impulses determine the ends of all activities and supply the driving power by which all mental activities are sustained; and all the complex intellectual apparatus of the most highly developed mind is but a means towards these ends, is but the instrument by which these impulses seek their satisfactions, while pleasure and pain do but serve to guide them in their choice of the means.

Take away these instinctive dispositions with their powerful impulses, and the organism would become incapable of activity of any kind; it would lie inert and motionless like a wonderful clockwork whose mainspring had been removed or a steam-engine whose fires had been drawn. These impulses are the mental forces that maintain and shape all the life of individuals and societies, and in them we are confronted with the central mystery of life and mind and will.

13

British/American
Structural Psychology

EDWARD BRADFORD
TITCHENER
(1867–1927)

Structural Psychology [1]

The point which I wish now to make is this: that, employing the same principle of division, we can represent modern psychology as the exact counterpart of modern biology. There are three ways of approaching the one, as there are the three ways of approaching the other; and the subject matter in every case

may be individual or general. A little consideration will make this clear.

1. We find a parallel to morphology in a very large portion of "experimental" psychology. The primary aim of the experimental psychologist has been to analyze the structure of mind; to ravel out the elemental processes from the tangle of consciousness, or (if we may change the metaphor) to isolate the constituents in the given conscious formation. His task is a vivisection, but a vivisection which shall yield structural, not functional

---

[1] Edward Bradford Titchener, "The postulates of a structural psychology," *Philosophical Review*, 1898, **7**, 449–465.

results. He tries to discover, first of all, what is there and in what quantity, not what it is there for.

* * * * *

2. There is, however, a functional psychology, over and above this psychology of structure. We may regard mind, on the one hand, as a complex of processes, shaped and moulded under the conditions of the physical organism. We may regard it, on the other hand, as the collective name for a system of functions of the psychophysical organism. The two points of view are not seldom confused. The phrase "association of ideas," e.g., may denote either the structural complex, the associated sensation group, or the functional process of recognition and recall, the associating of formation to formation. In the former sense it is morphological material, in the latter it belongs to what I must name (the phrase will not be misunderstood) a physiological psychology.

* * * * *

The remaining four psychologies may be dismissed with a briefer mention. 3. Ontogenetic psychology, the psychology of individual childhood and adolescence, is now a subject of wide interest, and has a large literature of its own. 4. Taxonomic psychology is not yet, and in all likelihood will not be, for some time to come, anything more than an ingredient in "descriptive," and a portion of individual, psychology. It deals with such topics as the classification of emotions, instincts and impulses, temperaments, etc., the hierarchy of psychological "selves," the typical mind of social classes (artists, soldiers, literary men), and so forth. 5. The functional psychology of the collective mind is, as might be expected, in a very rudimentary condition. We can delimit its sphere and indicate its problems; minor contributions to it may be found here and there in the pages of works upon psychology, logic, ethics, æsthetics, sociology, and anthropology; and a few salient points—the question, e.g., of the part played by the æsthetic sentiment in the make-up of a national mind—have been touched upon in essays. But we must have an experimental physiology of the individual mind, before there can be any great progress. 6. Lastly, the labors of the evolutionary school have set phylogenetic psychology upon a

fairly secure foundation, and the number of workers is a guarantee of rapid advance in our understanding of mental development.

The object of the present paper is to set forth the state of current opinion upon the question of the structural elements of mind, their number and nature.

* * * * *

Our appeal will lie, in the first instance, to the experimentalists; but the omission of references to works on descriptive psychology is largely due to considerations of space, and does not by any means necessarily imply that the authors of these works differ from the writers quoted. Some of the "unique" processes still left outstanding will be taken up at the end of this discussion.

We set out from a point of universal agreement. Everyone admits that *sensations* are elementary mental processes. There is, it is true, diversity of opinion as to the range of contents that the term shall cover. Wundt identifies the peripherally excited and the centrally excited processes. "For the psychological attributes of a sensation the circumstance [of external or internal initiation] is entirely irrelevant. . . . It is only the central stimulus that always accompanies sensation." Külpe retains the name "sensation" for both classes, but declares that they "must be treated separately, as they normally present characteristic differences." Ziehen and Ebbinghaus, on the other hand, draw a sharp line of distinction between the "sensation," which is externally aroused, and the "idea" (in Lotze's sense), which is its centrally aroused substitute, and so recognize two elements where Wundt and Külpe see only one. The divergence, however, is not serious. It seems to depend, primarily, upon the admission or exclusion of genetic considerations. If we rule that these are foreign to a strictly morphological examination of mind, the question of one sense element or two becomes a problem set by analysis to analysis, capable of resolution by analytic methods; it is a subject for dispute "inside the ring," and is thus upon a quite different level from the question, e.g., of an elementary will process.—We may note, in passing, that the innervation sensation, while it remains a theoretical possibility, has been generally given up by the experimental school.

Simple *affective* processes, again, are regarded by a large majority as elemental. Both Wundt and Külpe are at some pains to make clear the essential difference between sensation and affection. Lehmann and Ebbinghaus are equally explicit. Ziehen does not give a place to feeling beside sensation and idea; his chapters are entitled "The Affective Tone of Sensation" and "The Affective Tone of Ideas," and his treatment makes affective tone an attribute, coordinate with the intensity and quality of sensation and the clearness and contents (meaning) of idea. Nevertheless, he speaks in one passage of the cortical substrate of this tone as "an entirely new psychophysiological process." Munsterberg, on the other hand, denies the ultimateness of feeling altogether, and seeks to reduce it to the sensations accompanying movements of flexion and extension, reflexively released. There is further, an "inside" controversy as to the number of affective qualities. But analysis will some day settle the question whether there are two of these (Külpe), or two in the sphere of sensation and many more in that of idea (Ziehen), or an inexhaustible variety under the six heads of pleasantness and unpleasantness, tension and relaxation, excitement and tranquilization (Wundt).

It is natural, in view of the intrinsic difficulty of the subject, that the psychology of feeling should be in a less settled state than the psychology of sensation. All the more striking, when we consider the close relation that obtains between "feeling" and "will," is the unanimity with which experimentalists reject the doctrine of a specific will process. "There is no reason," writes Ebbinghaus, "for looking upon acts of will or appetitions as elementary forms of the mental life." And Wundt, Külpe, Ziehen, and Munsterberg are of the same manner of thinking.

No fourth candidate for elemental rank has appeared. No trace has been found, in all the minute analysis of the last twenty years, of a mental krypton or argon. It seems safe, then, to conclude that the ultimate processes are two, and two only, sensations and affections, though we must not forget that the first class, that of sensations, includes the two well-defined sub-species, "sensation" and "idea."

How, now, are these different processes to be distinguished? What is our justification for looking upon them as last things of mind? Disregarding function, and trying to answer the question upon the anatomical plane, we can point at least to three valid criteria. We may refer to experience itself, and note that sensation and affection are irreducible for introspection. The one cannot be derived from, identified with, the other; they "look" different or "feel" different, however far analysis be pushed. Or we may have recourse to physiology. Since the structure of mind is conditioned upon the physical organization, we may differentiate sensation and affection by reference to their physical substrates. Or, again, we may seek a descriptive formula, which shall sum up the essential characteristics of the two processes. It is in this sense that Wundt is speaking, when he says that sensation qualities range between maxima of *difference*, and affective qualities between maxima of *opposition* or antithesis. Any one of these statements is adequate, to the psychological requirements. The last of them, however, as Wundt's exposition shows, implies that we are already familiar with the *attributes* of which sensation and affection are constituted. We must devote a brief space to their consideration.

Once more, we set out from a point of universal agreement. "There are two indispensable determinants of every psychical element, quality and intensity." But discussion is not slow to begin. For these two attributes or determinants are, evidently of different kinds. Quality is specific and individual; it is quality that makes the elemental process a blue or a sweet, a pleasant or a *c* of the third octave. Intensity, on the contrary, is a general attribute, common to all modalities of sensation and qualities of affection. Hence, while some psychologists rank the two determinations together, as coordinate, others set aside quality for itself, and count intensity along with extent and duration as equipollent characteristics, whether of all the mental elements or of certain great groups of qualities. There is also much difference of opinion as to the precise place to be ascribed to the attributes of extent and duration. For Wundt, who holds a genetic theory, psychological space is the resultant of a two-dimensional system of qualitative local signs multiplied into, or fused with, a one-dimensional intensive system of sensations aroused by movement. It is, primarily, tactual or visual. Psychological time, in the same way, is the resultant of qualitatively varied feelings multiplied into, or fused with, the same intensive system of sensations. The affective processes, in abstraction, are timeless; the primary sources of temporal ideas are audition and "internal touch." It follows that space and time, extent and duration, can be predicated only of formations, not of elements. Spatial arrangement (Wundt makes no distinction between "spatial arrangement" and "space" as "absolute contents") cannot "be an original attribute of the elements, analogous to the intensity or quality of sensations;" it "results from the bringing together of these elements," which means the "arising of new psychical conditions;" and the same thing is true of time. Opposed to this genetic theory is the nativistic view, represented for space, e.g., by Stumpf, according to which every sensation has about it something of tridimensionality, a certain bigness or voluminousness, and every elemental process a certain duration.

It is, indeed, hardly possible to keep the psychological problem of space and time clear of epistemology, on the one hand, and of psychogenesis, on the other. It would perhaps, be unwise to make any attempts to do so, in a work meant to serve the purpose of instruction; for the attempt would invoke a total disregard of historical conditions. Nevertheless, there can be little doubt as to the anatomical facts. I am wholly unable to conceive of a sensation or affective process as timeless, as lacking duration; analysis of mind as it is leaves me, always, with a process-lasting-some-time. I am equally unable to conceive of a visual sensation or sensation of pressure as spaceless, punctual; analysis leaves me, always, with a process-spread-out. On the other hand, I feel no constraint to regard the spreading-out as tridimensional. Neither does the surface itself necessarily imply the depth perception, nor need the

relation of the surface to the ideating subject be present in consciousness. And the other sensations, tones, tastes, etc., as well as the affections seem to be entirely devoid of space attributes. In mental morphology, the perfect element (say, a sensation of color) shows us quality, intensity, duration, and superficial extension.

A similar difficulty confronts us with regard to the attribute of clearness. Variation in degree of clearness of the constituent processes in ideas is the anatomical equivalent of what is functionally termed the "distribution of attention." Wundt places degree of clearness on the same level with spatial and temporal arrangement. "As these attributes [clearness and obscurity, distinctness and indistinctness] arise always and only from the interconnection of the various psychical formations, they cannot be considered as determinants of the psychical elements." Yet, on Wundt's own principle of relativity, the same thing would be true of sensation intensity; we cannot say anything of the intensity of a sensation unless a formation—at least two sensations, side by side—be there for "comparison." Moreover, we must exclude genetic arguments here as before. If we make analytic introspection the test, we cannot but admit that the ultimate sensation may be conceived of as clear or obscure.

I conclude, then, that the affective element is constituted of quality, intensity, and duration; the sense element (sensation or idea) of quality, intensity, duration, clearness, and (in some cases) extent. Quality is intrinsic and individual; intensity and clearness are "relative" characteristics; duration and extent are, very probably, extrinsic translations into structure of the lowest terms of a functional series. And the corollary is that the "elements" of the experimentalists, as they themselves have been the first to urge, are artifacts, abstractions, usefully isolated for scientific ends, but not found in experience save as connected with their like.

14

Danish Psychology of Emotions

CARL GEORG LANGE
(1834–1900)

James–Lange Theory of Emotions [1]

If anyone were to dispute it, if, for example, some one attempted to prove to a man who has grown up with the popular conception of this problem that when he is frightened, his fear is only a perception of the changes in his body, he would very probably meet with the following objection first:—"The assumption of this relation is disproved by personal experience, for fear, like every emotion, has a distinct sensation of a peculiar change, a specific condition of the mind, quite independent of the body." I can well understand how this objection may appear very significant to most people, and be difficult to refute, and yet it has obviously no value whatever, in and for itself, since we have absolutely no immediate means of differentiating between a sensation of mental and one of physical nature.   No man, in fact, is capable of differentiating between a sensation of mental and one of physical nature. No man, in fact, is capable of differentiating between psychical and somatic feelings. Whoever attributes a sensation to the mind, does so only on basis of theory, not on basis of immediate perception.   I have no doubt that a mother who mourns the death of her child would resent, yes, be indignant, if any one were to tell her what she feels: the weariness and laxity of her muscles, the coldness of her bloodless skin, the impossibility of her brain to concentrate in clear, quick thought; may be attributed to an image of the cause of these phenomena.   But this is no ground for

indignation, for her feeling is just as strong, just as deep and pure, if attributed to one as to the other cause. It cannot exist, however, without its physical attributes.

Take away the bodily symptoms from a frightened individual; let his pulse beat calmly, his look be firm, his color normal, his movements quick and sure, his speech strong, his thoughts clear; and what remains of his fear?

If, therefore, we cannot rely upon the testimony of personal, subjective experiences in this question because they are incompetent here, nevertheless the question is by no means cleared up. Even if this hypothesis of psychical affections is not made necessary by subjective experiences, it may still be indispensable, since perhaps we cannot understand how the bodily phenomena of the affections arise without it.

And so, next we have to examine whether the physical expressions of affections may arise in a purely physical way; if this be the case, then the necessity of the hypothesis is obviated.

As a matter of fact, it is not difficult to prove now, and by means of the most ordinary and well known experiences, that emotions may be induced by a variety of causes which are utterly independent of disturbances of the mind, and that, on the other hand, they may be suppressed and modified by pure physical means. The fact that our whole manner of living, our daily diet, has developed in the course of generations with this aim in view, to favor the pleasant affections and to modify or entirely remove the unpleasant ones, is very well accepted, even if without clear consciousness of the actual connection of things. I will offer only one example: it will suffice to recall many. It is one of the oldest

[1] Carl Georg Lange, "The emotions," in William James and Carl Georg Lange, *The Emotions* (Baltimore: Williams & Wilkins, 1922), pp. 65–69. Reprinted by permission. Original, *Om Sindsbevaegelser* (Kjöbenhavn, 1885).

experiences of mankind that "wine gladdens the heart" and the power of alcoholic liquors to reduce sorrow and fear and to substitute joy and courage has found application, which is in and for itself natural enough, and would be most wholesome, if the substance did not produce other effects in addition.

We all understand "why Jeppe drinks."[2] He seeks to free himself from his marital troubles and his fear of Master Erich, and he wishes once again to sing and recall the happy past when he was still "with Maliz." Brandy makes him gay and brave, without requiring even a single brightening or enlivening impression, which might act directly upon his mind, and without causing him to forget his cares or his enemies in the least. He wants only to look at them from another point of view, under the influence of brandy; he wants to impress the sexton and to beat his wife again; for alcohol has excited his vasomotor apparatus, has increased the speed and strength of his heart-beats, has dilated his capillaries, thereby increasing his innervation enough to make him chatter loudly, sing and row, instead of dragging himself over the road, moaning and whining. He receives a sensation of warmth, levity and power, instead of his customary laxity and incompetence. His dull brain wakes up under the influence of heightened circulation, thoughts begin to come to him, old memories appear and drive away the habitual feeling of misery, and all for one peg of brandy, whose effect on the circulation we can understand and which requires no intervention of the mind to affect the vasomotor centers.

All those who drink brandy bear a similar relation to it, and we possess this relation to our daily luxuries and comforts, and to our various arrangements which we make to ensure our comfort and convenience. So long as we find ourselves in the easy, accustomed path of our daily life, the relation of our emotions to material influences (for example, to nourishment) is, of course, not so obvious. A different relation obtains when certain substances are partaken of, substances which have such a strong effect on the system that they are used either as medicines or belong to the category of poisons. This is well known

in the case of certain mushrooms, especially of the toad-stool, which call forth violent outbreaks of rage and brutality in whoever partakes of them. Our belligerent ancestors are supposed to have used them to get into the proper spirit for the "Berserk rage," just as we today "take a drink" to "get up" our courage. Attacks of rage may also occur after using Hashish (Indian hemp), which as a rule, only stimulates the system to unrestrained joyfulness in much the same way that alcohol does.

Certain sickening drugs, such as tartar emetic, ipecacuanha, etc., have a depressing effect, which is in some respect comparable to fear and sorrow, and, like these, is accompanied by phenomena of collapse.

If emotional states can be induced by taking certain substances, or in any other purely physical way, it follows that troublesome affections can be counteracted and modified in a similar way. If brandy or opium induces joy, then they will oppose sorrow, etc.

The power of a "cold shower" to dampen violence and wrath sometimes finds practical application, and yet this method can hardly have any direct effect upon the mind, if applied *in natura;* so much the stronger is the effect upon the vasomotor functions. By means of one drug—the well-known potassium bromide—which has a paralyzing effect on the vasomotor apparatus, we have it in our power not only to allay fear and sorrow and other similar unpleasant affections, but also to induce a condition of apathy, which makes it impossible for the subject to be either lively or depressed, fearful or angry, simply because the vasomotor functions have been suspended.

If the conception of the nature of the affections as here represented is established, then we may expect that every influence involving general changes in the vascular nervous system must have an emotional expression. Of course, we cannot expect that these emotions will coincide exactly with the phenomena for which we usually reserve this denotation; the differences in cause will naturally result in various effects. The various psychical causes also have effects which are not at all congruent. Fear of a ghost, for example, does not manifest itself in the same way as the fear of the guns of

[2] Jeppe am Berge.   Character in a classic comedy by Holberg.

the enemy. Nevertheless, the similarity between physically and mentally induced affections has, in many cases, been so conspicuous as to force the immediate conception, as many verbal expressions prove. We have the same expression for mental and physical pain in many languages: their great physiological similarity has been recognized, although the eminent characteristic of physical pain, the subjective sensation resulting from the transference of the peripheral stimulation to the sensory center, is entirely absent in mental pain. The cause of the similarity to emotional pain is the reflexive innervation of the vascular nerves, a regular effect of every strong stimulation of the sensory nerves.

In the same way "shudder" is used in speech for both the effect of sudden cold upon the skin, and for phenomena due to impressions from fright. That this naïve conception knows no difference between emotional and purely physical "shudders" is evident from the story of the boy who set out to "get a thrill," and after he had tried in vain to "thrill" in the presence of dead and of ghosts, finally obtained his wish when he was thrown out of his bed into a tub of cold water. This produced a far stronger effect upon his vasomotor apparatus than did the sight of death-beds or ghosts. To call a man "feverish" who suffers great suspense is another example of how striking is the similarity between the slight symptoms of fever which are induced chiefly by vasomotor disturbances, and those physical conditions which are caused by anxious expectation, etc.

15

American Functional Psychology

WILLIAM JAMES
(1842–1910)

James–Lange Theory of Emotions [1]

The feeling, in the coarser emotions, results from the bodily expression. Our natural way of thinking about these coarser emotions is that the mental perception of some fact excites the mental affection called the emotion, and that this latter state of mind gives rise to the bodily expression. My theory, on the contrary, is that *the bodily changes follow directly the perception of the exciting fact, and that our feeling of the same changes as they occur is the emotion.* Common-sense says, we lose our fortune, are sorry and weep, we meet a bear, are frightened and run; we are insulted by a rival, are angry and strike. The hypothesis here to be defended says that this order of sequence is incorrect, that the one mental state is not immediately induced by the other, that the bodily manifestations must first be interposed between, and that the more rational statement is that we feel sorry because we cry, angry because we strike, afraid because we tremble, and not that we cry, strike, or tremble because we are sorry, angry, or fearful, as the case may be. Without the bodily states following on the perception, the latter would be purely cognitive in form, pale, colorless, destitute of emotional warmth. We might then see the bear and judge it best to run, receive the insult and deem it right to strike, but we should not actually *feel* afraid or angry.

* * * * *

I now proceed to urge the vital point of my whole theory, which is this: *If we fancy some strong emotion, and then try to abstract*

[1] William James, *Psychology* (New York: Henry Holt, 1890), pp. 375–382.

*from our consciousness of it all the feelings
of its bodily symptoms, we find we have
nothing left behind*, no "mind-stuff" out of
which the emotion can be constituted, and
that a cold and neutral state of intellectual
perception is all that remains.

* * * * *

*This view explains the great variability of
emotion.* If such a theory is true, then each
emotion is the resultant of a sum of elements,
and each element is caused by a physiological
process of a sort already well known. The
elements are all organic changes, and each
of them is the reflex effect of the exciting object.

* * * * *

Now the moment an emotion is causally
accounted for, as the arousal by an object
of a lot of reflex acts which are forthwith
felt, *we immediately see why there is no limit
to the number of possible different emotions
which may exist, and why the emotions of
different individuals may vary indefinitely*, both
as to their constitution and as to the objects
which call them forth. For there is nothing
sacramental or eternally fixed in reflex action.
Any sort of reflex effect is possible, and
reflexes actually vary indefinitely, as we know.

Habit [2]

Habit is thus the enormous fly-wheel of
society, its most precious conservative agent.
It alone is what keeps us all within the bounds
of ordinance, and saves the children of
fortune from the envious uprisings of the poor.
It alone prevents the hardest and most
repulsive walks of life from being deserted
by those brought up to tread therein. It keeps
the fisherman and the deck-hand at sea
through the winter; it holds the miner in his
darkness, and nails the countryman to his
log-cabin and his lonely farm through all the
months of snow; it protects us from invasion
by the natives of the desert and the frozen
zone. It dooms us all to fight out the battle
of life upon the lines of our nurture or our
early choice, and to make the best of a
pursuit that disagrees, because there is no
other for which we are fitted, and it is too
late to begin again. It keeps different social
strata from mixing. Already at the age of

[2] *Ibid.*, pp. 143–150.

twenty-five you see the professional mannerism
settling down on the young commercial
traveller, on the young doctor, on the young
minister, on the young counsellor-at-law. You
see the little lines of cleavage running through
the character, the tricks of thought, the
prejudices, the ways of the "shop," in a word,
from which the man can by-and-by no more
escape than his coat-sleeve can suddenly fall
into a new set of folds. On the whole, it is
best he should not escape. It is well for the
world that in most of us, by the age of thirty,
the character has set like plaster, and will
never soften again.

If the period between twenty and thirty is
the critical one in the formation of intellectual
and professional habits, the period below
twenty is more important still for the fixing
of *personal* habits, properly so called, such as
vocalization and pronunciation, gesture, motion, and address. Hardly ever is a language
learned after twenty spoken without a foreign
accent; hardly ever can a youth transferred
to the society of his betters unlearn the
nasality and other vices of speech bred in
him by the associations of his growing years.
Hardly ever, indeed, no matter how much
money there be in his pocket, can he even
learn to *dress* like a gentleman-born. The
merchants offer their wares as eagerly to him
as to the veriest "swell," but he simply *cannot*
buy the right things. An invisible law, as
strong as gravitation, keeps him within his
orbit, arrayed this year as he was the last;
and how his better-clad acquaintances contrive
to get the things they wear will be for him a
mystery till his dying day.

The great thing, then, in all education, is
to *make our nervous system our ally instead
of our enemy.* It is to fund and capitalize our
acquisitions, and live at ease upon the
interest of the fund. *For this we must make
automatic and habitual, as early as possible,
as many useful actions as we can*, and guard
against the growing into ways that are likely
to be disadvantageous to us, as we should
guard against the plague. The more of the
details of our daily life we can hand over
to the effortless custody of automatism, the
more our higher powers of mind will be set
free for their own proper work. There is no
more miserable human being than one in
whom nothing is habitual but indecision, and
for whom the lighting of every cigar, the

drinking of every cup, the time of rising and going to bed every day, and the beginning of every bit of work, are subjects of express volitional deliberation. Full half the time of such a man goes to the deciding, or regretting, of matters which ought to be so ingrained in him as practically not to exist for his consciousness at all. If there be such daily duties not yet ingrained in any one of my readers, let him begin this very hour to set the matter right.

In Professor Bain's chapter on "The Moral Habits" there are some admirable practical remarks laid down. Two great maxims emerge for his treatment. The first is that in the acquisition of a new habit, or the leaving off of an old one, we must take care to *launch ourselves with as strong and decided an initiative as possible.* Accumulate all the possible circumstances which shall re-enforce the right motives; put yourself assiduously in conditions that encourage the new way; make engagements incompatible with the old; take a public pledge, if the case allows; in short, envelop your resolution with every aid you know. This will give your new beginning such a momentum that the temptation to break down will not occur as soon as it otherwise might; and every day during which a breakdown is postponed adds to the chances of its not occurring at all.

The second maxim is: *Never suffer an exception to occur till the new habit is securely rooted in your life.* Each lapse is like the letting fall of a ball of string which one is carefully winding up; a single slip undoes more than a great many turns will wind again. *Continuity* of training is the great means of making the nervous system act infallibly right.

* * * * *

A third maxim may be added to the preceding pair: *Seize the very first possible opportunity to act on every resolution you make, and on every emotional prompting you may experience in the direction of the habits you aspire to gain.* It is not in the moment of their forming, but in the moment of their producing *motor effects*, that resolves and aspirations communicate the new "set" to the brain.

* * * * *

Just as, if we let our emotions evaporate, they get into a way of evaporating; so there is reason to suppose that if we often flinch from making an effort, before we know it the effort-making capacity will be gone; and that, if we suffer the wandering of our attention, presently it will wander all the time. Attention and effort are, as we shall see later, but two names for the same psychic fact. To what brain-processes they correspond we do not know. The strongest reason for believing that they do depend on brain-processes at all, and are not pure acts of the spirit, is just this fact, that they seem in some degree subject to the law of habit, which is a material law. As a final practical maxim, relative to these habits of the will, we may, then, offer something like this: *Keep the faculty of effort alive in you by a little gratuitous exercise every day.* That is, be systematically ascetic or heroic in little unnecessary points, do every day or two something for no other reason than that you would rather not do it, so that when the hour of dire need draws nigh, it may find you not unnerved and untrained to stand the test. Asceticism of this sort is like the insurance which a man pays on his house and goods. The tax does him no good at the time, and possibly may never bring him a return. But if the fire *does* come, his having paid it will be his salvation from ruin. So with the man who has daily inured himself to habits of concentrated attention, energetic volition, and self-denial in unnecessary things. He will stand like a tower when everything rocks around him, and when his softer fellow-mortals are winnowed like chaff in the blast.

The physiological study of mental conditions is thus the most powerful ally of hortatory ethics. The hell to be endured hereafter, of which theology tells, is no worse than the hell we make for ourselves in this world by habitually fashioning our characters in the wrong way. Could the young but realize how soon they will become mere walking bundles of habits, they would give more heed to their conduct while in the plastic state. We are spinning our own fates, good or evil, and never to be undone. Every smallest stroke of virtue or of vice leaves its never so little scar.

The Stream of Consciousness [3]

The Fundamental Fact. The first and foremost concrete fact which every one will affirm to belong to his inner experience is the fact that *consciousness of some sort goes on.* "*States of mind*" *succeed each other in him.* If we could say in English "it thinks," as we say "it rains" or "it blows," we should be stating the fact most simply and with the minimum of assumption. As we cannot, we must simply say that *thought goes on.*

Four Characters in Consciousness. How does it go on? We notice immediately four important characters in the process, of which it shall be the duty of the present chapter to treat in a general way:

1) Every "state" tends to be part of a personal consciousness.

2) Within each personal consciousness states are always changing.

3) Each personal consciousness is sensibly continuous.

4) It is interested in some parts of its object to the exclusion of others, and welcomes or rejects—*chooses* from among them, in a word—all the while.

* * * * *

Consciousness is in constant change. I do not mean by this to say that no one state of mind has any duration—even if true, that would be hard to establish. What I wish to lay stress on is this, that *no state once gone can recur and be identical with what it was before.* Now we are seeing, now hearing; now reasoning, now willing; now recollecting, now expecting; now loving, now hating; and in a hundred other ways we know our minds to be alternately engaged. But all these are complex states, it may be said, produced by combination of simpler ones;—do not the simpler ones follow a different law? Are not the *sensations* which we get from the same object, for example, always the same? Does not the same piano-key, struck with the same force, make us hear in the same way? Does not the same grass give us the same feeling of green, the same sky the same feeling of blue, and do we not get the same olfactory sensation no matter how many times we put our nose to the same flask of cologne? It seems a piece of metaphysical sophistry to

suggest that we do not; and yet a close attention to the matter shows that *there is no proof that an incoming current ever gives us just the same bodily sensation twice.*

* * * * *

Within each personal consciousness, thought is sensibly continuous. I can only define "continuous" as that which is without breach, crack, or division. The only breaches that can well be conceived to occur within the limits of a single mind would either be *interruptions, time-gaps* during which the consciousness went out; or they would be breaks in the content of the thought, so abrupt that what followed had no connection whatever with what went before. The proposition that consciousness feels continuous, means two things:

a. That even where there is a time-gap the consciousness after it feels as if it belonged together with the consciousness before it, as another part of the same self;

b. That the changes from one moment to another in the quality of the consciousness are never absolutely abrupt.

The case of the time-gaps, as the simplest, shall be taken first.

* * * * *

Remembrance is like direct feeling; its object is suffused with a warmth and intimacy to which no object of mere conception ever attains. This quality of warmth and intimacy and immediacy is what Peter's *present* thought also possesses for itself. So sure as this present is me, is mine, it says, so sure is anything else that comes with the same warmth and intimacy and immediacy, me and mine. What the qualities called warmth and intimacy may in themselves be will have to be matter for future consideration. But whatever past states appear with those qualities must be admitted to receive the greeting of the present mental state, to be owned by it, and accepted as belonging together with it in a common self. This community of self is what the time-gap cannot break in twain, and is why a present thought, although not ignorant of the time-gap, can still regard itself as continuous with certain chosen portions of the past.

Consciousness, then, does not appear to itself chopped up in bits. Such words as "chain" or "train" do not describe it fitly as

3   *Ibid.*, pp. 152–159.

it presents itself in the first instance. It is nothing jointed; it flows. A "river" or a "stream" are the metaphors by which it is most naturally described. *In talking of it hereafter, let us call it the stream of thought, of consciousness, or of subjective life.*

The Self [4]

In its widest possible sense, however, *a man's Me is the sum total of all that he* CAN *call his*, not only his body and his psychic powers, but his clothes and his house, his wife and children, his ancestors and friends, his reputation and works, his lands and horses, and yacht and bank-account. All these things give him the same emotions. If they wax and prosper, he feels triumphant; if they dwindle and die away, he feels cast down,—not necessarily in the same degree for each thing, but in much the same way for all. Undertanding the Me in this widest sense, we may begin by dividing the history of it into three parts, relating respectively to—

a. Its constituents;
b. The feelings and emotions they arouse,
—*self-appreciation;*
c. The acts to which they prompt,—*self-seeking and self-preservation.*

a. The constituents of the Me may be divided into two classes, those which make up respectively—

The material me;
The social me; and
The spiritual me.

The Material Me. The *body* is the innermost part of the material me in each of us; and certain parts of the body seem more intimately ours than the rest. The clothes come next. The old saying that the human person is composed of three parts—soul, body and clothes—is more than a joke. We so appropriate our clothes and identify ourselves with them that there are few of us who, if asked to choose between having a beautiful body clad in raiment perpetually shabby and unclean, and having an ugly and blemished form always spotlessly attired, would not hesitate a moment before making a decisive

[4] *Ibid.*, pp. 177–181.

reply. Next, our immediate family is a part of ourselves. Our father and mother, our wife and babes, are bone of our bone and flesh of our flesh. When they die, a part of our very selves is gone. If they do anything wrong, it is our shame. If they are insulted, our anger flashes forth as readily as if we stood in their place. Our home comes next. Its scenes are part of our life; its aspects awaken the tenderest feelings of affection; and we do not easily forgive the stranger who, in visiting it, finds fault with its arrangements or treats it with contempt.

* * * * *

The Social Me. A man's social me is the recognition which he gets from his mates. We are not only gregarious animals, liking to be in sight of our fellows, but we have an innate propensity to get ourselves noticed, and noticed favorably, by our kind. No more fiendish punishment could be devised, were such a thing physically possible, than that one should be turned loose in society and remain absolutely unnoticed by all the members thereof. If no one turned round when we entered, answered when we spoke, or minded what we did, but if every person we met "cut us dead," and acted as if we were non-existing things, a kind of rage and impotent despair would ere long well up in us, from which the cruellest bodily tortures would be a relief; for these would make us feel that, however bad might be our plight, we had not sunk to such a depth as to be unworthy of attention at all.

Properly speaking, *a man has as many social selves as there are individuals who recognize him* and carry an image of him in their mind. To wound any one of these his images is to wound him. But as the individuals who carry the images fall naturally into classes, we may practically say that he has as many different social selves as there are distinct *groups* of persons about whose opinion he cares. He generally shows a different side of himself to each of these different groups. Many a youth who is demure enough before his parents and teachers, swears and swaggers like a pirate among his "tough" young friends. We do not show ourselves to our children as to our club-companions, to our customers as to the laborers we employ, to our own masters and employers as to our intimate friends. From this there results what practically is a division of the man into several selves; and this may be a discordant splitting, as where one is afraid to let one set of his acquaintances know him as he is elsewhere; or it may be a perfectly harmonious division of labor, as where one tender to his children is stern to the soldiers or prisoners under his command.

* * * * *

The Spiritual Me. By the "spiritual me," so far as it belongs to the empirical self, I mean no one of my passing states of consciousness. I mean rather the entire collection of my states of consciousness, my psychic faculties and dispositions taken concretely. This collection can at any moment become an object to my thought at that moment and awaken emotions like those awakened by any of the other portions of the Me. When we *think of ourselves as thinkers*, all the other ingredients of our Me seem relatively external possessions. Even within the spiritual *Me* some ingredients seem more external than others. Our capacities for sensation, for example, are less intimate possessions, so to speak, than our emotions and desires; our intellectual processes are less intimate than our volitional decisions. The more *active-feeling* states of consciousness are thus the more central portions of the spiritual Me. The very core and nucleus of our self, as we know it, the very sanctuary of our life, is the sense of activity which certain inner states possess. This sense of activity is often held to be a direct revelation of the living substance of our Soul. Whether this be so or not is an ulterior question.

Psychological Types [5]

Historically we find the terms "intellectualism" and "sensationalism" used as synonyms of "rationalism" and "empiricism." Well, nature seems to combine most frequently with intellectualism an idealistic and optimistic tendency. Empiricists on the other hand are not uncommonly materialistic, and their optimism is apt to be decidedly con-

___
    [5] William James, *Pragmatism: A New Name for Some Old Ways of Thinking* (New York: Longmans, Green, 1908), pp. 10–13.

ditional and tremulous. Rationalism is always monistic. It starts from wholes and universals, and makes much of the unity of things. Empiricism starts from the parts, and makes of the whole a collection—is not averse therefore to calling itself pluralistic. Rationalism usually considers itself more religious than empiricism, but there is much to say about this claim, so I merely mention it. It is a true claim when the individual rationalist is what is called a man of feeling, and when the individual empiricist prides himself on being hard-headed. In that case the rationalist will usually also be in favor of what is called free-will, and the empiricist will be a fatalist—I use the terms most popularly current. The rationalist finally will be of dogmatic temper in his affirmations, while the empiricist may be more sceptical and open to discussion.

I will write these traits down in two columns. I think you will practically recognize the two types of mental make-up that I mean if I head the columns by the titles "tender-minded" and "tough-minded" respectively.

The Tender-minded	The Tough-minded
Rationalistic (going by "principles")	Empiricist (going by "facts")
Intellectualistic	Sensationalistic
Idealistic	Materialistic
Optimistic	Pessimistic
Religious	Irreligious
Free-willist	Fatalistic
Monistic	Pluralistic
Dogmatical	Sceptical

Pray postpone for a moment the question whether the two contrasted mixtures which I have written down are each inwardly coherent and self-consistent or not—I shall very soon have a good deal to say on that point. It suffices for our immediate purpose that tender-minded and tough-minded people, characterized as I have written them down, do both exist. Each of you probably knows some well-marked example of each type, and you know what each example thinks of the example on the other side of the line. They have a low opinion of each other. Their antagonism, whenever as individuals their temperaments have been intense, has formed in all ages a part of the philosophic atmosphere of the time. It forms a part of the philosophic atmosphere to-day. The tough think of the tender as sentimentalists and soft-heads. The tender feel the tough to be unrefined, callous, or brutal. Their mutual reaction is very much like that that takes place when Bostonian tourists mingle with a population like that of Cripple Creek. Each type believes the other to be inferior to itself; but disdain in the one case is mingled with amusement, in the other it has a dash of fear.

Now, as I have already insisted, few of us are tender-foot Bostonians pure and simple, and few are typical Rocky Mountain toughs.

JAMES ROWLAND ANGELL
(1869–1949)

Functional Psychology [6]

Whatever else it may be, functional psychology is nothing wholly new. In certain of its phases it is plainly discernible in the psychology of Aristotle and in its more modern garb it has been increasingly in evidence since Spencer wrote his *Psychology* and Darwin his *Origin of Species.*

* * * * *

1. There is to be mentioned first the notion which derives most immediately from contrast with the ideals and purposes of structural psychology so-called. This involves the identification of functional psychology with the effort to discern and portray the typical operations of consciousness under actual life conditions, as over against the attempt to analyze and describe its elementary and complex contents. The structural psychology of sensation, e.g., undertakes to determine the number and character of the various un-analyzable sensory materials, such as the varieties of color, tone, taste, etc. The functional psychology of sensation would on the other hand find its appropriate sphere of interest in the determination of the character of the various sense activities as differing in their modus operandi from one another and from other mental processes such as judging, conceiving, willing and the like.

In this its older and more pervasive form functional psychology has until very recent times had no independent existence. . . . But in so far as functional psychology is synonymous with descriptions and theories of mental action as distinct from the materials of mental constitution, so far it is everywhere conspicuous in psychological literature from the earliest times down.

Its fundamental intellectual prepossessions are often revealed by the classifications of mental process adopted from time to time. Witness the Aristotelian bipartite division of intellect and will and the modern tripartite division of mental activities. What are cognition, feeling and will but three basally distinct modes of mental action? To be sure this classification has often carried with it the assertion, or at least the implication, that these fundamental attributes of mental life were based upon the presence in the mind of corresponding and ultimately distinct mental elements. But so far as concerns our momentary interest this fact is irrelevant.

* * * * *

The most essential quarrel which the functionalist has with structuralism in its thoroughgoing and consistent form arises from this fact and touches the feasibility and worth of the effort to get at mental process as it is under the conditions of actual experience rather than as it appears to a merely postmortem analysis. It is of course true that for introspective purposes we must in a sense always work with vicarious representatives of the particular mental processes which we set out to observe. But it makes a great difference even on such terms whether one is engaged simply in teasing apart the fibers of its tissues. The latter occupation is useful and for certain purposes essential, but it often stops short of that which is as a life phenomenon the most essential, i.e., the modus operandi of the phenomenon.

* * * * *

The functionalist is committed *vom Grunde auf* to the avoidance of that special form of the psychologist's fallacy which consists in attributing to mental states without due warrant, as part of their overt constitution in the moment of experience, characteristics

[6] James Rowland Angell, "The province of functional psychology," *Psychol. Rev.*, 1907, **14**, 61–91.

which subsequent reflective analysis leads us to suppose they must have possessed. When this precaution is not scrupulously observed we obtain a sort of *pâté de foie gras* psychology in which the mental conditions portrayed contain more than they ever naturally would or could hold.

* * * * *

The fact that mental contents are evanescent and fleeting marks them off in an important way from the relatively permanent elements of anatomy. No matter how much we may talk of the preservation of psychical dispositions, nor how many metaphors we may summon to characterize the storage of ideas in some hypothetical deposit chamber of memory, the obstinate fact remains that when we are not experiencing a sensation or an idea it is, strictly speaking, non-existent. Moreover, when we manage by one or another device to secure that which we designate the same sensation or the same idea, we not only have no guarantee that our second edition is really a replica of the first, we have a good bit of presumptive evidence that from the content point of view the original never is and never can be literally duplicated.

Functions, on the other hand, persist as well in mental as in physical life. We may never have twice exactly the same idea viewed from the side of sensuous structure and composition. But there seems nothing whatever to prevent our having as often as we will contents of consciousness which mean the same thing. They function in one and the same practical way, however discrepant their momentary texture. The situation is rudely analogous to the biological case where very different structures may under different conditions be called on to perform identical functions; and the matter naturally harks back for its earliest analogy to the instance of protoplasm where functions seem very tentatively and imperfectly differentiated. Not only then are general functions like memory persistent, but special functions such as the memory of particular events are persistent and largely independent of the specific conscious contents called upon from time to time to subserve the functions.

* * * * *

Substantially identical with this first conception of functional psychology, but phrasing itself somewhat differently, is the view which regards the functional problem as concerned with discovering how and why conscious processes are what they are, instead of dwelling as the structuralist is supposed to do upon the problem of determining the irreducible elements of consciousness and their characteristic modes of combination.

* * * * *

Stated briefly the ground on which this position rests is as follows: In so far as you attempt to analyze any particular state of consciousness you find that the mental elements presented to your notice are dependent upon the particular exigencies and conditions which call them forth. Not only does the affective coloring of such a psychical moment depend upon one's temporary condition, mood and aims, but the very sensations themselves are determined in their qualitative texture by the totality of circumstances subjective and objective within which they arise. You cannot get a fixed and definite color sensation, for example, without keeping perfectly constant the external and internal conditions in which it appears. The particular sense quality is in short functionally determined by the necessities of the existing situation which it emerges to meet. If you inquire then deeply enough what particular sensation you have in a given case, you always find it necessary to take account of the manner in which, and the reason why, it was experienced at all. . . . That is to say, the very description itself is functionalistic and must be so.

* * * * *

2. The functional psychologist . . . in his modern attire is interested not alone in the operations of mental process considered merely of and by and for itself, but also and more vigorously in mental activity as part of a larger stream of biological forces which are daily and hourly at work before our eyes and which are constitutive of the most important and most absorbing part of our world. The psychologist of this stripe is wont to take his cue from the basal conception of the evolutionary movement, i.e., that for the most part organic structures and functions possess their present characteristics by virtue of the efficiency with which they fit into the

extant conditions of life broadly designated the environment. With this conception in mind he proceeds to attempt some understanding of the manner in which the psychical contributes to the furtherance of the sum total of organic activities, not alone the psychical in its entirety, but especially the psychical in its particularities—mind as judging, mind as feeling, etc.

* * * * *

3. The third conception which I distinguish is often in practice merged with the second, but it involves stress upon a problem logically prior perhaps to the problem raised there and so warrants separate mention. Functional psychology, it is often alleged, is in reality a form of psychophysics. To be sure, its aims and ideals are not explicitly quantitative in the manner characteristic of that science as commonly understood. But it finds its major interest in determining the relations to one another of the physical and mental portions of the organism.

It is undoubtedly true that many of those who write under functional prepossessions are wont to introduce frequent references to the physiological processes which accompany or condition mental life. Moreover, certain followers of this faith are prone to declare forthwith that psychology is simply a branch of biology and that we are in consequence entitled, if not indeed obliged, to make use where possible of biological materials. But without committing ourselves to so extreme a position as this, a mere glance at one familiar region of psychological procedure will disclose the leanings of psychology in this direction.

The psychology of volition affords an excellent illustration of the necessity with which descriptions of mental process eventuate in physiological or biological considerations. If one takes the conventional analysis of a voluntary act drawn from some one or other of the experiences of adult life, the descriptions offered generally portray ideational activities of an anticipatory and deliberative character which serve to initiate immediately or remotely certain relevant expressive movements. Without the execution of the movements the ideational performances would be as futile as the tinkling cymbals of Scripture. To be sure, many of our psychologists protest themselves

wholly unable to suggest why or how such muscular movements are brought to pass. But the fact of their occurrence or of their fundamental import for any theory of mental life in which consciousness is other than an epiphenomenon, is not questioned.

Moreover, if one considers the usual accounts of the ontogenesis of human volitional acts one is again confronted with intrinsically physiological data in which reflexes, automatic and instinctive acts are much in evidence. Whatever the possibilities, then, of an expurgated edition of the psychology of volition from which should be blotted out all reference to contaminating physiological factors, the actual practice of our representative psychologists is quite otherwise, and upon their showing volition cannot be understood either as regards its origin or its outcome without constant and overt reference to these factors.

* * * * *

Such a functional psychology as I have been presenting would be entirely reconcilable with Miss Calkins' "Psychology of selves" . . . were it not for her extreme scientific conservatism in refusing to allow the self to have a body, save as a kind of conventional biological ornament . . .

It is not clear that the functional psychologist because of his disposition to magnify the significance in practice of the mind-body relationships is thereby committed to any special theory of the character of these relationships, save as was said a moment since, that negatively he must seemingly of necessity set his face against any epiphenomenalist view. He might conceivably be an interactionist, or a parallelist or even an advocate of some wholly outworn creed.

* * * * *

4. If we now bring together the several conceptions of which mention has been made it will be easy to show them converging upon a common point. We have to consider (1) functionalism conceived as the psychology of mental operations in contrast to the psychology of mental elements; or, expressed otherwise, the psychology of the how and why of consciousness as distinguished from the psychology of the what of consciousness. We have (2) the functionalism which deals with

the problem of mind conceived as primàrily engaged in mediating between the environment and the needs of the organism. This is the psychology of the fundamental utilities of consciousness; (3) and lastly we have functionalism described as psychophysical psychology, that is the psychology which constantly recognizes and insists upon the essential significance of the mind-body relationship for any just and comprehensive appreciation of mental life itself.

The second and third delineations of functional psychology are rather obviously correlated with each other. No description of the actual circumstances attending the participation of mind in the accommodatory activities of the organism could be other than a mere empty schematism without making reference to the manner in which mental processes eventuate in motor phenomena of the physiological organism. The overt accommodatory act is, I take it, always sooner or later a muscular movement. But this fact being admitted, there is nothing for it, if one will describe accommodatory processes, but to recognize the mind-body relations and in some way give expression to their practical significance. It is only in this regard, as was indicated a few lines above, that the functionalist departs a trifle in his practice and a trifle more in his theory from the rank and file of his colleagues.

* * * * *

The functionalist's most intimate persuasion leads him to regard consciousness as primarily and intrinsically a control phenomenon. Just as behavior may be regarded as the most

distinctly basic category of general biology in its functional phase so control would perhaps serve as the most fundamental category in functional psychology, the special forms and differentiations of consciousness simply constituting particular phases of the general process of control.

* * * * *

One incidental merit of the functionalist program deserves a passing mention. This is the one method of approach to the problem with which I am acquainted that offers a reasonable and cogent account of the rise of reflective consciousness and its significance as manifested in the various philosophical disciplines. From the vantage point of the functionalist position logic and ethics, for instance, are no longer mere disconnected items in the world of mind. They take their place with all the inevitableness of organic organization in the general system of control, which requires for the expression of its immanent meaning *as psychic* a theoretical vindication of its own inner principles, its modes of procedure and their results. From any other point of view, so far as I am aware, the several divisions of philosophical inquiry sustain to one another relations which are almost purely external and accidental. To the functionalist on the other hand they are and must be in the nature of the case consanguineous and vitally connected. It is at the point, for example, where the good, the beautiful and the true have bearing on the efficacy of accommodatory activity that the issues of the normative philosophical sciences becomes relevant.

GEORGE TRUMBULL LADD
(1842–1921)

Unity of the Active Self [7]

It is by complex synthesis of judgments, based on manifold experiences converging to one conception—the resultant of many acts of memory, imagination, reasoning, and naming—that the Knowledge of the Self as a Unitary Being is attained. The self that

[7] George Trumbull Ladd, *Psychology: Descriptive and Explanatory* (New York: Scribner, 1894), pp. 531–533.

I thus come to know is regarded as the one subject of all the states of consciousness; whether they be states of knowledge, of feeling, or of willing, and whether they be known presentatively, as here and now, objects of self-consciousness, or remembered or imagined as states of the past, or conjectured as possible states to be existent in future time. I thus become known to myself as both real and logical subject of all the states in the ceaselessly flowing stream of consciousness.

This is the final and supreme achievement of self-knowledge. But this knowledge can never, of course, be other than itself a process of conscious mental life, attained as the result of a development. *In one and the same act the mind makes itself the object of its self-knowledge and believes in the real being of that which it creates as its own object;* and then it passes into other states of knowledge that dissolve this unique creation by turning the attention to external things.

It belongs especially to the theory of knowledge and to the philosophy of the mind to discuss the nature and validity of this knowledge of Self as one real being—the subject of all the different states, the subject of a life-history and of a course of development. Psychology can only present this knowledge as being itself the complex resultant of all those activities which enter into the development of knowledge. Such a self-consciousness, however, includes far more than what we are immediately aware of ourselves as being; it is highly abstract and theoretical, so to speak; it is conceptual, as expressive of many trains of reasoning. The foundation on which it rests is the total experience of mind with itself. The fundamental fact here is, as Dr. Ward has said, a "certain objective continuum forming the background or basis to the relatively distinct presentations that are elaborated out of it."

What, we may ask, actually takes place when I try to become conscious of myself as one really existent being? I may come to such self-consciousness in one of two principal ways; but in either case I must *think;* I must by judgment relate, or ascribe, somewhat to that which I call myself. In the most nearly "immediate" acts of developed self-knowledge I find myself endeavoring to grasp together, in an act of judgment, a certain dark and confused complex of ideas and feelings, with points perhaps of more definite lucid mental representation; and meanwhile thinking the proposition that *they are mine.* But what is this "me," whose are the ideas and feelings that constitute the present content of consciousness? The answer to this question can be given only by another similar act of self-knowledge.

Or again the question, What am I to myself, as one real being distinguished from all other beings?—may be answered in a more objective

and historical fashion. I may emphasize in my thinking, not only the conviction that I am *now* one feeling, thinking, willing, being, but that I *have been* one and the same, since I began to be at all. Here, of course, I rely upon memory to inform me as to what I "have been," psychically, in the past. I know myself as one and the same to myself, because I can trace in memory something like the continuity of a life-history. Such self-knowledge, it has truly been said, may be at once the richest and the poorest of all forms of conceptual knowledge—including, as it does, in its varieties, the peculiarities of race, temperament, constitution, social position, and the retreating or advancing bodily basis, differences in stages of intellectual development, and various other like considerations.

Teleology and the Self [8]

It is with no view to provoke metaphysical or theological discussion that we call attention to the fact of the Teleological Import of all mental development. No *science* of the life of the mind is possible without recognizing the presence of final purpose in the collocation and arrangement which the phenomena come to have, as the stream of consciousness flows on. It may be that in saying this we are only enunciating what is the self-conscious and intellectual way of the developed mind for regarding its own development—the way *the Self*, as it were, *seems to itself.* The ultimate nature and ground of the seeming does not now concern us. What does concern us is that, wherever the phenomena of consciousness become objects of knowledge, and so the beginnings of a science of mental life are made possible, there these phenomena appear ordering themselves so as to attain practical ends. *Activity to some purpose is the ruling principle of mental development.* The self-conscious, intelligent, adoption of a plan, and selection of means for its pursuit, is distinctive of the *acme* of man's development. The more comprehensive this plan, and the wiser the selection of means, the higher is the standing of the individual in the scale of intellectual development. But ends suggested by æsthetical and ethical sentiment seem

[8] *Ibid.,* pp. 668–669.

adapted to control large spheres of human activity; and the latter especially, from the very nature of the mandate with which it sanctions the end that promises its own satisfaction, has at least a sort of phenomenal supremacy. But meanwhile the principles of continuity, of relativity, and of conscious and unconscious habit, forbid that any consciously accepted end should be isolated, as it were, from the entire life both bodily and psychical. And when we regard the working of all of these principles, in every detail of mental development, we become aware that the import of final purpose in the mental life extends far beyond the conscious adoption of ends on our own part. In other words, the stream of consciousness appears not so much as a current flowing we know not whence nor whither; but rather as a current designed from the beginning, both as respects its observable surface and its hidden depths— partly self-directed and partly impelled by hidden forces—to the fit performance of a certain work. But what that work most fit is, if any such there be, scientific psychology does not investigate.

In fine, a combination of all these principles, as they appear in their actual operation, secures for every so-called stream of consciousness that continuity, related action, solidarity of character, and that intelligible import as judged by the light of ends and ideals, which are necessary to the history of what we call a Soul, or a Mind.

JOHN DEWEY
(1859–1952)

Critique of the Reflex Arc [9]

The idea of the reflex arc has upon the whole come nearer to meeting this demand for a general working hypothesis than any other single concept. It being admitted that the sensori-motor apparatus represents both the unit of nerve structure and the type of nerve function, the image of this relationship passed over psychology, and became an organizing principle to hold together the multiplicity of fact.

In criticising this conception it is not intended to make a plea for the principles of explanation and classification which the reflex arc idea has replaced; but, on the contrary, to urge that they are not sufficiently displaced, and that in the idea of the sensori-motor circuit, conceptions of the nature of sensation and of action derived from the nominally displaced psychology are still in control.

The older dualism between sensation and idea is repeated in the current dualism of peripheral and central structures and functions; the older dualism of body and soul finds a distinct echo in the current dualism of stimulus and response. Instead of interpreting the character of sensation, idea and action from their place and function in the sensori-motor circuit, we still incline to interpret the latter from our preconceived and preformulated ideas of rigid distinctions between sensations, thoughts and acts. The sensory stimulus is one thing, the central activity, standing for the idea, is another thing, and the motor discharge, standing for the act proper, is a third. As a result, the reflex arc is not a comprehensive, or organic unity, but a patchwork of disjoined parts, a mechanical conjunction or unallied processes. What is needed is that the principle underlying the idea of the reflex are as the fundamental psychical unity shall react into and determine the values of its constitutive factors. More specifically, what is wanted is that sensory stimulus, central connections and motor responses shall be viewed, not as separate and complete entities in themselves, but as divisions of labor, functioning factors, within the single concrete whole, now designated the reflex arc.

What is the reality so designated? What shall we term that which is not sensation-followed-by-idea-followed-by-movement, but which is primary; which is, as it were, the psychical organism of which sensation, idea and movement are the chief organs? Stated on the physiological side, this reality may most conveniently be termed coordination. This is the essence of the facts held together by

[9] John Dewey, "The reflex arc concept in psychology," *Psychol. Rev.*, 1896, **3**, 357-370.

and subsumed under the reflex arc concept. Let us take, for our example, the familiar child-candle instance. (James, *Psychology*, I., 25.) The ordinary interpretation would say the sensation of light is a stimulus to the grasping as a response, the burn resulting is a stimulus to withdrawing the hand as response and so on. There is, of course, no doubt that is a rough practical way of representing the process. But when we ask for its psychological adequacy, the case is quite different. Upon analysis, we find that we begin not with a sensory stimulus, but with a sensori-motor coordination, the optical-ocular, and that in a certain sense it is the movement which is primary, and the sensation which is secondary, the movement of body, head and eye muscles determining the quality of what is experienced. In other words, the real beginning is with the act of seeing; it is looking, and not a sensation of light. The sensory quale gives the value of the act, just as the movement furnishes its mechanism and control, but both sensation and movement lie inside, not outside the act.

Now if this act, the seeing, stimulates another act, the reaching, it is because both of these acts fall within a larger coordination; because seeing and grasping have been so often bound together to reinforce each other, to help each other out, that each may be considered practically a subordinate member of a bigger coordination. More specifically, the ability of the hand to do its work will depend, either directly or indirectly, upon its control, as well as its stimulation, by the act of vision. If the sight did not inhibit as well as excite the reaching, the latter would be purely indeterminate, it would be for anything or nothing, not for the particular object seen. The reaching, in turn, must both stimulate and control the seeing. The eye must be kept upon the candle if the arm is to do its work; let it wander and the arm takes up another task. In other words, we now have an enlarged and transformed coordination; the act is seeing no less than before, but it is now seeing-for-reaching purposes. There is still a sensori-motor circuit, one with more content or value, not a substitution of a motor response for a sensory stimulus.

Now take the affairs at its next stage, that in which the child gets burned. It is hardly

necessary to point out again that this is also a sensori-motor coordination and not a mere sensation. It is worth while, however, to note especially the fact that it is simply the completion, or fulfillment, of the previous eye-arm-hand coordination and not an entirely new occurrence. Only because the heat-pain quale enters into the same circuit of experience with the optical-ocular and muscular quales, does the child learn from the experience and get the ability to avoid the experience in the future.

More technically stated, the so-called response is not merely *to* the stimulus; it is *into* it. The burn is the original seeing, the original optical-ocular experience enlarged and transformed in its value. It is no longer mere seeing; it is seeing-of-a-light-that-means-pain-when-contact-occurs. The ordinary reflex arc theory proceeds upon the more or less tacit assumption that the outcome of the response is a totally new experience; that it is, say, the substitution of a burn sensation for a light sensation through the intervention of motion. The fact is that the sole meaning of the intervening movement is to maintain, reinforce or transform (as the case may be) the original quale; that we do not have the replacing of one sort of experience by another, but the development (or as it seems convenient to term it) the mediation of an experience. The seeing, in a word, remains to control the reaching, and is, in turn, interpreted by the burning.

The discussion up to this point may be summarized by saying that the reflex arc idea, as commonly employed, is defective in that it assumes sensory stimulus and motor response as distinct psychical existences, while in reality they are always inside a coordination and have their significance purely from the part played in maintaining or reconstituting the coordination; and (secondly) in assuming that the quale of experience which precedes the "motor" phase and that which succeeds it are two different states, instead of the last being always the first reconstituted, the motor phase coming in only for the sake of such mediation. The result is that the reflex arc idea leaves us with a disjointed psychology, whether viewed from the standpoint of development in the individual or in the race, or from that of the analysis of the mature consciousness. As to the former, in its failure to see that the arc of which it talks is virtually a circuit, a continual reconstitution, it breaks continuity and leaves us nothing but a series of jerks, the origin of each jerk to be sought outside the process of experience itself, in either an external pressure of "environment," or else in an unaccountable spontaneous variation from within the "soul" or the "organism." As to the latter, failing to see the unity of activity, no matter how much it may prate of unity, it still leaves us with sensation or peripheral stimulus; idea, or central process (the equivalent of attention); and motor response, or act, as three disconnected existences, having to be somehow adjusted to each other, whether through the intervention of an extra-experimental soul, or by mechanical push and pull.

* * * * *

I hope it will not appear that I am introducing needless refinements and distinctions into what, it may be urged, is after all an undoubted fact, that movement as response follows sensation as stimulus. It is not a question of making the account of the process more complicated, though it is always wise to beware of that false simplicity which is reached by leaving out of account a large part of the problem. It is a question of finding out what stimulus or sensation, what movement and response mean; a question of seeing that they mean distinctions of flexible function only, not of fixed existence; that one and the same occurrence plays either or both parts, according to the shift of interest; and that because of this functional distinction and relationship, the supposed problem of the adjustment of one to the other, whether by superior force in the stimulus or an agency *ad hoc* in the center or the soul, is a purely self-created problem.

We may see the disjointed character of the present theory, by calling to mind that it is impossible to apply the phrase "sensorimotor" to the occurrence as a simple phrase of description; it has validity only as a term of interpretation, only, that is, as defining various functions exercised. In terms of description, the whole process may be sensory or it may be motor, but it cannot be sensorimotor. The "stimulus," the excitation of the nerve ending and of the sensory nerve, the central change, are just as much, or just as

little, motion as the events taking place in the motor nerve and the muscles. It is one uninterrupted, continuous redistribution of mass in motion. And there is nothing in the process, from the standpoint of description, which entitles us to call this reflex. It is redistribution pure and simple; as much so as the burning of a log, or the falling of a house or the movement of the wind. In the physical process, as physical, there is nothing which can be set off as stimulus, nothing which reacts, nothing which is response. There is just a change in the system of tensions.

The same sort of thing is true when we describe the process purely from the psychical side. It is now all sensation, all sensory quale; the motion, as physically described, is just as much sensation as is sound or light or burn. Take the withdrawing of the hand from the candle flame as example. What we have is a certain visual-heat-pain-muscular-quale, transformed into another visual-touch-muscular-quale—the flame now being visible only at a distance, or not at all, the touch sensation being altered, etc. If we symbolize the original visual quale by v, the temperature by h, the accompanying muscular sensation by m, the whole experience may be stated as vhm-vh$m$-vhm'; m being the quale of withdrawing, m' the sense of the status after the withdrawal. The motion is not a certain kind of existence; it is a sort of sensory experience interpreted, just as is candle flame, or burn from candle flame. All are on a par.

But, in spite of all this, it will be urged, there is a distinction between stimulus and response, between sensation and motion. Precisely; but we ought now to be in a condition to ask of what nature is the distinction, instead of taking it for granted as a distinction somehow lying in the existence of the facts themselves. We ought to be able to see that the ordinary conception of the reflex arc theory, instead of being a case of plain science, is a survival of the metaphysical dualism, first formulated by Plato, according to which the sensation is an ambiguous dweller on the border land of soul and body, the idea (or central process) is purely psychical, and the act (or movement) purely physical. Thus the reflex arc formulation is neither physical (or physiological) nor psychological; it is a mixed materialistic-spiritualistic assumption.

If the previous descriptive analysis has made

obvious the need of a reconsideration of the reflex arc idea, of the nest of difficulties and assumptions in the apparently simple statement, it is now time to undertake an explanatory analysis. The fact is that stimulus and response are not distinctions of existence, but teleological distinctions, that is, distinctions of function, or part played, with reference to reaching or maintaining an end. With respect to this teleological process, two stages should be discriminated, as their confusion is one cause of the confusion attending the whole matter. In one case, the relation represents an organization of means with reference to a comprehensive end. It represents an accomplished adaptation. Such is the case in all well developed instincts, as when we say that the contact of eggs is a stimulus to the hen to set; or the sight of corn a stimulus to peck; such also is the case with all thoroughly formed habits, as when the contact with the floor stimulates walking. In these instances there is no question of consciousness of stimulus *as* stimulus, of response *as* response. There is simply a continuously ordered sequence of acts, all adapted in themselves and in the order of their sequence, to reach a certain objective end, the reproduction of the species, the preservation of life, locomotion to a certain place. The end has got thoroughly organized into the means. In calling one stimulus, another response we mean nothing more than that such an orderly sequence of acts is taking place. The same sort of statement might be made equally well with reference to the succession of changes in a plant, so far as these are considered with reference to their adaptation to, say, producing seed. It is equally applicable to the series of events in the circulation of the blood, or the sequence of acts occurring in a self-binding reaper.

* * * * *

To sum up: the distinction of sensation and movement as stimulus and response respectively is not a distinction which can be regarded as descriptive of anything which holds of psychical events or existences as such. The only events to which the terms stimulus and response can be descriptively applied are to minor acts serving by their respective positions to the maintenance of some organized coordination. The conscious stimulus or sensation, and the conscious response or motion, have a special genesis or motivation, and a special end or function. The reflex arc theory, by neglecting, by abstracting from, this genesis and this function gives us one disjointed part of a process as if it were the whole. It gives us literally an arc, instead of the circuit; and not giving us the circuit of which it is an arc, does not enable us to place, to center, the arc. This arc, again, falls apart into two separate existences having to be either mechanically or externally adjusted to each other.

The circle is a coordination, some of whose members have come into conflict with each other. It is the temporary disintegration and need of reconstitution which occasions, which affords the genesis of, the conscious distinction into sensory stimulus on one side and motor response on the other. The stimulus is that phase of the forming coordination which represents the conditions which have to be met in bringing it to a successful issue; the response is that phase of one and the same forming coordination which gives the key to meeting these conditions, which serves as instrument in effecting the successful coordination. They are therefore strictly correlative and contemporaneous. The stimulus is something to be discovered; and to be made out; if the activity affords its own adequate stimulation, there is no stimulus save in the objective sense already referred to. As soon as it is adequately determined, then and then only is the response also complete. To attain either, means that the coordination has completed itself. Moreover, it is the motor response which assists in discovering and constituting the stimulus. It is the holding of the movement at a certain stage which creates the sensation, which throws it into relief.

It is the coordination which unifies that which the reflex arc concept gives us only in disjointed fragments. It is the circuit within which fall distinctions of stimulus and response as functional phases of its own mediation or completion. The point of this story is in its application; but the application of it to the question of the nature of psychical evolution, to the distinction between sensational and rational consciousness, and the nature of judgment must be deferred to a more favorable opportunity.

Analysis of a Complete Act of Thought [10]

Five Steps in Reflection

Upon examination, each instance reveals, more or less clearly, five logically distinct steps: (*i*) a felt difficulty; (*ii*) its location and definition; (*iii*) suggestion of possible solution; (*iv*) development by reasoning of the bearings of the suggestion; (*v*) further observation and experiment leading to its acceptance or rejection; that is, the conclusion of belief or disbelief.

Occurrence of a Difficulty

1. The first and second steps frequently fuse into one. The difficulty may be felt with sufficient definiteness as to set the mind at once speculating upon its probable solution, or an undefined uneasiness and shock may come first, leading only later to a definite attempt to find out what is the matter. Whether the two steps are distinct or blended, there is the factor emphasized in our original account of reflection—*viz.* the perplexity or problem.... The problem is *the discovery of intervening terms which when inserted between the remoter end and the given means will harmonize them with each other.*

* * * * *

Definition of the Difficulty

2. As already noted, the first two steps, the feeling of a discrepancy, or difficulty, and the acts of observation that serve to define the character of the difficulty may, in a given instance, telescope together. In cases of striking novelty or unusual perplexity, the difficulty, however, is likely to present itself at first as a shock, as emotional disturbance, as a more or less vague feeling of the unexpected, of something queer, strange, funny, or disconcerting. In such instances, there are necessary observations deliberately calculated to bring to light just what is the trouble, or to make clear the specific character of the problem.

* * * * *

---

[10] John Dewey, *How We Think* (Boston: D. C. Heath, 1910), pp. 72–78.

Occurrence of an Explanation or Solution

3. The third factor is suggestion. The situation in which the perplexity occurs calls up something not present to the senses: the present location, the thought of subway or elevated train; the stick before the eyes, the idea of a flagpole, an ornament, an apparatus for wireless telegraphy; the soap bubbles, the law of expansion of bodies through heat and of their contraction through cold. (*a*) Suggestion is the very heart of inference; it involves going from what is present to something absent....

(*b*) The suggested conclusion so far as it is not accepted but only tentatively entertained constitutes an idea. Synonyms for this are *supposition*, *conjecture*, *guess*, *hypothesis*, and (in elaborate cases) *theory*.

* * * * *

The Rational Elaboration of an Idea

4. The process of developing the bearings —or, as they are more technically termed, the *implications*—of any idea with respect to any problem, is termed *reasoning*. As an idea is inferred from given facts, so reasoning sets out from an idea. The *idea* of elevated road is developed into the idea of difficulty of locating station, length of time occupied on the journey, distance of station at the other end from place to be reached.

* * * * *

Corroboration of Idea and Formation of a Concluding Belief

5. The concluding and conclusive step is some kind of *experimental corroboration*, or verification, of the conjectural idea. Reasoning shows that *if* the idea be adopted, certain consequences follow. So far the conclusion is hypothetical or conditional. If we look and find present all the conditions demanded by the theory, and if we find the characteristic traits called for by rival alternatives to be lacking, the tendency to believe, to accept, is almost irresistible. Sometimes direct observation furnishes corroboration, as in the case of the pole on the boat. In other cases, as in that of the bubbles, experiment is required; that is, *conditions are deliberately arranged in*

accord with the requirements of an idea or hypothesis to see if the results theoretically indicated by the idea actually occur. If it is found that the experimental results agree with the theoretical, or rationally deduced, results, and if there is reason to believe that *only* the conditions in question would yield such results, the confirmation is so strong as to induce a conclusion—at least until contrary facts shall indicate the advisability of its revision.

Observation exists at the beginning and again at the end of the process: at the beginning, to determine more definitely and precisely the nature of the difficulty to be dealt with; at the end, to test the value of some hypothetically entertained conclusion. Between those two termini of observation, we find the more distinctively *mental* aspects of the entire thought-cycle: (*i*) inference, the suggestion of an explanation or solution; and (*ii*) reasoning, the development of the bearings and implications of the suggestion. Reasoning requires some experimental observation to confirm it, while experiment can be economically and fruitfully conducted only on the basis of an idea that has been tentatively developed by reasoning.

16

American Experimental and Physiological Psychology

JAMES McKEEN CATTELL
(1860–1944)

Reaction Time [1]

We undertook to determine the influence of various intensities of the electric shock, and of light on the length of the simple reaction time, and on the reaction time complicated by the addition of simple cerebral operations.

The term "reaction time" is now generally understood. If one lifts one's hand as soon as possible after the sudden appearance of a light, the interval between the application of the stimulus and the beginning of the muscular contraction is a reaction time. In order to investigate the influence of various intensities of light on the length of this time, we used a light produced in a Geissler's tube by an induction current from six Daniell cells. This light we took as normal, and kept constant.

We then arranged five weaker intensities by putting smoked glass before the light. The amount of light transmitted through the smoked glass we determined photometrically. If we set the intensity of the normal light $VI = 1000$, then the intensities of the lights would be

I	II	III	IV	V	VI
1	7	23	123	315	1000

We further obtained two still brighter lights (vii and viii) by means of lenses, but could not determine with our photometer the relation of these to the normal intensity. The observer sat in the dark, and looked through a telescopic tube at the point where the light was to appear. The following table gives the average of 150 reactions made by each of us with the several intensities. No reactions at all were omitted in taking the average. The second line, marked *M*, gives the average of the variation of each from the average of all

[1] James McKeen Cattell, "The influence of the intensity of the stimulus on the length of the reaction time," *Brain*, 1885, **8**, 512–515.

the reactions; that is, if *A* is the average of *n* reactions *a*, *b*, *c*, *d*, then

$$M = \frac{(A-a) + (A-b) + (A-c)\dots}{n}$$

all the differences being taken as positive. *M* shows us how much the reactions differ from one another, and when we know the number of reactions, we can find the probable error of the average. In the table .001 s. is taken as the unit of time.

It will be seen from the table that when the light is taken very weak, just strong enough to be seen, the times are the longest and (with one accidental exception, *B* between V and VI) the greater the intensity of the light, the shorter the time of the reaction. I cannot, however, formulate a general law from the table.

TABLE I

Intensity	I	II	III	IV	V	VI	VII	VIII	Average
					B				
Time	308	235	208	200	192	195	177	168	210
M	26	18	16	15	15	17	18	16	18
					C				
Time	251	175	160	148	147	143	135	128	161
M	30	17	16	14	15	13	16	19	18

In substantially the same manner the relation between the strength of an electric shock and the length of the reaction time was determined. The shock was received on the left forearm, and the reaction made with the right hand. We used four intensities; the strongest IV, somewhat painful, the weakest, I, just enough to be felt. The two intermediate intensities made up, as far as we could judge, four equal steps. The averages of 150 reactions by each observer and on each intensity are given in the table.

TABLE II

Intensity	I	II	III	IV	Average
		B			
Time	182	163	158	160	166
M	17	14	12	11	13
		C			
Time	164	155	132	131	145
M	19	18	14	14	16

It will be noticed that with the electric shock, as with light, the time of the reaction becomes shorter as the stimulus becomes stronger. The differences are not, however, so great, and for the intensities III and IV, the times are about the same; with IV the reaction was probably retarded, because the shock was painful.

In connection with the experiments on the intensity of the light, we made others to determine whether or not the quality of the stimulus, that is, the colour of the light, has any influence on the length of the reaction time. The averages of 180 reactions made by each of the observers, and on each of the six colours used, are given in table III.

The table does not show any decided difference in the times for the several colours. Violet and green, which I have found . . . must work longer on the retina than the other colours, in order that a sensation may be called forth, do not seem to cause a longer reaction time; this is because the reaction is made on the light, without waiting until the colour has been distinguished.

The time is longer when it is necessary to distinguish the colours before the reaction is made. We can determine this time, if instead of always reacting as quickly as possible we use two lights of different colours, say blue

TABLE III

	White	Red	Yellow	Green	Blue	Violet	Average
B	196	203	192	199	199	201	198
C	155	162	160	156	161	153	158

and red, and let the subject react only on one of them. The subject does not know which light is to come, but is to lift his hand as quickly as possible if it is red, but not at all if it is blue. We thus add to the simple reaction the time it takes to see whether the light is blue or red, and complicate somewhat the process of volition in the simple reaction time. We can further let the subject lift his right hand if the light is red, his left hand f it is blue; we then have, besides the time

necessary for the simple reaction and for distinguishing the colour, the time it takes to make a choice between two motions. The results of experiments made with three intensities of light (V, III, and I) are given in table IV.

It seems from the table that the time it takes to see or perceive a colour becomes shorter as the intensity of the light becomes stronger, but that the will time is not a function of the intensity of the stimulus.

TABLE IV

	B			C		
	V	III	I	V	III	I
Reaction time	189	218	273	189	209	303
Reaction with Perception time	238	293	373	274	328	417
Reaction with Perception and Will time	287	320	393	356	388	495
Perception time	49	75	100	85	119	114
Will time	49	27	20	82	60	78

Mental Tests and Measurements [2]

With a view to obtaining agreement among those interested, I venture to suggest the following series of tests and measurements, together with methods of making them.

The first series of ten tests is made in the Psychological Laboratory of the University of Pennsylvania on all who present themselves, and the complete series on students of Experimental Psychology. . . .

The following ten tests are proposed:

    I. Dynamometer Pressure.
   II. Rate of Movement.
  III. Sensation-Areas.
  IV. Pressure Causing Pain.
   V. Least Noticeable Difference in Weight.
  VI. Reaction-Time for Sound.
 VII. Time for Naming Colours.
VIII. Bi-section of a 50 Cm. Line.
  IX. Judgment of 10 Seconds Time.
   X. Number of Letters Remembered on Once Hearing.

* * * * *

Let us now consider the tests in order.

I. *Dynamometer Pressure.* The greatest possible squeeze of the hand may be thought by many to be a purely physiological quantity. It is, however, impossible to separate bodily

from mental energy. The "sense of effort" and the effects of volition on the body are among the questions most discussed in psychology and even in metaphysics. Interesting experiments may be made on the relation between volitional control or emotional excitement and dynamometer pressure. Other determinations of bodily power could be made (in the second series I have included the "archer's pull" and pressure of the thumb and forefinger), but the squeeze of the hand seems the most convenient. It may be readily made, cannot prove injurious, is dependent on mental conditions, and allows comparison of right- and left-handed power. The experimentee should be shown how to hold the dynamometer in order to obtain the maximum pressure. I allow two trials with each hand (the order being right, left, right, left), and record the maximum pressure of each hand.

II. *Rate of Movement.* Such a determination seems to be of considerable interest, especially in connexion with the preceding. Indeed, its physiological importance is such as to make it surprising that careful measurements have not hitherto been made. The rate of movement has the same psychological bearings as the force of movement. . . . I am now making experiments to determine the rate of different movements. As a general test, I suggest the quickest possible movement of the right hand and arm from rest through 50 cm. . . . An electric current is closed by

[2] James McKeen Cattell, "Mental tests and measurements," *Mind*, **15**, 373–381.

the first movement of the hand, and broken when the movement through 50 cm. has been completed. I measure the time the current has been closed with the Hipp chronoscope, but it may be done by any chronographic method. . . .

III. *Sensation-areas.* The distance on the skin by which two points must be separated in order that they may be felt as two is a constant, interesting both to the physiologist and psychologist. Its variation in different parts of the body (from 1 to 68 mm.) was a most important discovery. What the individual variation may be, and what inferences may be drawn from it, cannot be foreseen; but anything which may throw light on the development of the idea of space deserves careful study. Only one part of the body can be tested in a series such as the present. I suggest the back of the closed right hand, between the tendons of the first and second fingers, and in a longitudinal direction. Compasses with rounded wooden or rubber tips should be used, and I suggest that the curvature have a radius of .5 mm. . . . The points must be touched simultaneously, and not too hard. The experimentee must turn away his head. In order to obtain exact results, a large number of experiments would be necessary, and all the tact of the experimenter will be required to determine, without undue expenditure of time, the distance at which the touches may just be distinguished.

IV. *Pressure Causing Pain.* This, like the rate of movement, in a determination not hitherto much considered, and if other more important tests can be devised they might be substituted for these. But the point at which pressure causes pain may be an important constant, and in any case it would be valuable in the diagnosis of nervous diseases and in studying abnormal states of consciousness. . . . To determine the pressure causing pain I use an instrument . . . which measures the pressure applied by a tip of hard rubber 5 mm. in radius. I am now determining the pressure causing pain in different parts of the body; for the present series I recommend the centre of the forehead. The pressure should be gradually increased, and the maximum read from the indicator after the experiment is complete. As a rule, the point at which the experimentee says the pressure is painful should be recorded, but in some

cases it may be necessary to record the point at which signs of pain are shown. I make two trials, and record both.

V. *Least Noticeable Difference in Weight.* The just noticeable sensation and the least noticeable difference in sensation are psychological constants of great interest. Indeed, the measurement of mental intensity is probably the most important question with which experimental psychology has at present to deal. The just noticeable sensation can only be determined with great pains, if at all: the point usually found being in reality the least noticeable difference for faint stimuli. This latter point is itself so difficult to determine that I have postponed it to the second series. The least noticeable difference in sensation for stimuli of a given intensity can be more readily determined, but it requires some time, and consequently not more than one sense and intensity can be tested in a preliminary series. I follow Mr. Galton in selecting "sense of effort" or weight. I use small wooden boxes, the standard one weighing 100 gms. and the others 101, 102, up to 110 gms. The standard weight and another (beginning with 105 gms.) being given to the experimentee, he is asked which is the heavier. I allow him about 10 secs. for decision. I record the point at which he is usually right, being careful to note that he is always right with the next heavier weight.

VI. *Reaction-Time for Sound.* The time elapsing before a stimulus calls forth a movement should certainly be included in a series of psychophysical tests: the question to be decided is what stimulus should be chosen. I prefer sound, on it the reaction-time seems to be the shortest and most regular, and the apparatus is most easily arranged. I measure the time with a Hipp chronoscope, but various chronographic methods have been used.

* * * * *

In measuring the reaction-time, I suggest that three valid reactions be taken, and the minimum recorded. Later, the average and mean variation may be calculated.

VII. *Time for Naming Colours.* A reaction is essentially reflex, and, I think, in addition to it, the time of some process more purely mental should be measured. Several such processes are included in the second series;

for the present series I suggest the time needed to see and name a colour. This time may be readily measured for a single colour by means of suitable apparatus . . ., but for general use sufficient accuracy may be attained by allowing the experimentee to name ten colours and taking the average. I paste coloured papers (red, yellow, green and blue) 2 cm. square, 1 cm. apart, vertically on a strip of black pasteboard. This I suddenly uncover and start a chronoscope, which I stop when the ten colours have been named. I allow two trials (the order of colours being different in each) and record the average time per colour in the quickest trial.

VIII. *Bisection of a 50 Cm. Line.* The accuracy with which space and time are judged may be readily tested, and with interesting results. I follow Mr. Galton in letting the experimentee divide an ebony rule (3 cm. wide) into two equal parts by means of a movable line, but I recommend 50 cm. in place of 1 ft., as with the latter the error is so small that it is difficult to measure, and the metric system seems preferable. The amount of error in mm. (the distance from the true middle) should be recorded, and whether it is to the right or left. One trial would seem to be sufficient.

IX. *Judgment of* 10 *Seconds Time.* This determination is easily made. I strike on the table with the end of a pencil, and again after 10 seconds, and let the experimentee in turn strike when he judges an equal interval to have elapsed. I allow only one trial and record the time, from which the amount and direction of error can be seen.

X. *Number of Letters Repeated on Once Hearing.* Memory and attention may be tested by determining how many letters can be repeated on hearing once. I name distinctly and at the rate of two per second six letters, and if the experimentee can repeat these after me I go on to seven, then eight, &c.; if the six are not correctly repeated after three trials (with different letters), I give five, four, &c. The maximum number of letters which can be grasped and remembered is thus determined. Consonants only should be used in order to avoid syllables.

EDWARD LEE THORNDIKE
(1874–1949)

Laws of Effect and Exercise [3]

The Law of Effect is that: *Of several responses made to the same situation, those which are accompanied or closely followed by satisfaction to the animal will, other things being equal, be more firmly connected with the situation, so that, when it recurs, they will be more likely to recur; those which are accompanied or closely followed by discomfort to the animal will, other things being equal, have their connections with that situation weakened, so that, when it recurs, they will be less likely to occur. The greater the satisfaction or discomfort, the greater the strengthening or weakening of the bond.*

The Law of Exercise is that: *Any response to a situation will, other things being equal, be more strongly connected with the situation in proportion to the number of times it has been connected with that situation and to the*

---

[3] Edward Lee Thorndike, *Animal Intelligence: Experimental Studies* (New York: Macmillan, 1911), pp. 244–246.

average vigor and duration of the connections.

These two laws stand out clearly in every series of experiments on animal learning and in the entire history of the management of human affairs. They give an account of learning that is satisfactory over a wide range of experience, so long as all that is demanded is a rough and general means of prophecy. We can, as a rule, get an animal to learn a given accomplishment by getting him to accomplish it, rewarding him when he does, and punishing him when he does not; or, if reward or punishment are kept indifferent, by getting him to accomplish it much oftener than he does any other response to the situation in question.

For more detailed and perfect prophecy, the phrases "result in satisfaction" and "result in discomfort" need further definition, and the other things that are to be equal need comment.

By a satisfying state of affairs is meant one which the animal does nothing to avoid, often doing such things as attain and preserve it.

By a discomforting or annoying state of affairs is meant one which the animal commonly avoids and abandons.

The satisfiers for any animal in any given condition cannot be determined with precision and surety save by observation. Food when hungry, society when lonesome, sleep when fatigued, relief from pain, are samples of the common occurrence that what favors the life of the species satisfies its individual members. But this does not furnish a completely valid rule.

The satisfying and annoying are not synonymous with favorable and unfavorable to the life of either the individual or the species. Many animals are satisfied by deleterious conditions. Excitement, overeating, and alcoholic intoxication are, for instance, three very common and very potent satisfiers of man. Conditions useful to the life of the species in moderation are often satisfying far beyond their useful point: many conditions of great utility to the life of the species do not satisfy and may even annoy its members.

The annoyers for any animal follow the rough rule that alterations of the animal's "natural" or "normal" structure—as by cuts, bruises, blows, and the like,—and deprivations of or interference with its "natural" or "normal" activities,—as by capture, starvation, solitude, or indigestion,—are intolerable. But interference with the structure and functions by which the species is perpetuated is not a sufficient criterion for discomfort. Nature's adaptations are too crude.

Upon examination it appears that the pernicious states of affairs which an animal welcomes are not pernicious *at the time, to the neurones.* We learn many bad habits, such as morphinism, because there is incomplete adaptation of all the interests of the body-state to the temporary interest of its ruling class, the neurones. So also the unsatisfying goods are not goods to the neurones at the time. We neglect many benefits because the neurones choose their immediate advantage. The neurones must be tricked into permitting the animal to take exercise when freezing or quinine when in a fever, or to free the stomach from certain poisons.

Satisfaction and discomfort, welcoming and avoiding, thus seem to be related to the maintenance and hindrance of the life processes of the neurones rather than of the animal as a whole, and to temporary rather than permanent maintenance and hindrance.

The chief life processes of a neurone concerned in learning are absorption of food, excretion of waste, reception and conduction of the nerve impulse, and modifiability or change of connections.

Animal Intelligence [4]

As a provisional hypothesis to account for what satisfies and what annoys an animal, I suggest the following:

A neurone modifies the intimacy of its synapses so as to keep intimate those by whose intimacy its other life processes are favored and to weaken the intimacy of those whereby its other life processes are hindered. The animal's action-system as a whole consequently does nothing to avoid that response whereby the life processes of the neurones other than connection-changing are maintained, but does cease those responses whereby such life processes of the neurones are hindered.

This hypothesis has two important consequences. First: Learning by the law of effect is then more fully adaptive for the neurones in the changing intimacy of whose synapses learning consists, than for the animal as a whole. It is adaptive for the animal as a whole only in so far as his organization makes the neurones concerned in the learning welcome states of affairs that are favorable to his life and that of his species and reject those that are harmful.

Second: A mechanism in the neurones gives results in the behavior of the animal as a whole that seem beyond mechanism. By their unmodifiable abandonment of certain specific conditions and retention of others, the animal as a whole can modify its behavior. Their one rule of conduct causes in him a countless complexity of habits. The learning of an animal is an instinct of its neurones.

I have limited the discussion to animals in whom the connection-system is a differentiated organ, the neurones. In so far as the law of effect operates in an animal whose connection-system is not anatomically distinguishable and is favored and hindered in its life by the same

---

[4] *Ibid.*, pp. 247–250.

conditions that favor and hinder the life of the animal as a whole, the satisfying and annoying will be those states of affairs which the connection-system, whatever it be, maintains and abandons.

The other things that have to be equal in the case of the law of effect are: First, the frequency, energy and duration of the connection,—that is, the action of the law of exercise; second, the closeness with which the satisfaction is associated with the response; and, third, the readiness of the response to be connected with the situation.

The first of these accessory conditions requires no comment. A slightly satisfying or indifferent response made often may win a closer connection than a more satisfying response made only rarely.

The second is most clearly seen in the effect of increasing the interval between the response and the satisfaction or discomfort. Such an increase diminishes the rate of learning. If, for example, four boxes were arranged so that turning a button caused a door to open (and permit a cat to get freedom and food), in one, five, fifty and five hundred seconds, respectively, a cat would form the habit of prompt escape from the first box most rapidly and would almost certainly never form that habit in the case of the fourth. The electric shock administered just as an animal starts on the wrong path or touches the wrong mechanism, is potent, but the same punishment administered ten or twenty seconds after an act will have little or no effect upon that act.

Close temporal sequence is not the only means of insuring the connection of the satisfaction with the response producing it. What is called attention to the response counts also. If a cat pushes a button around with its nose, while its main occupation, the act to which its general "set" impels it, to which, we say, it is chiefly attentive, is that of clawing at an opening, it will be less aided in the formation of the habit than if it had been chiefly concerned in what its nose was doing. The successful response is as a rule only a part of all that the animal is doing at the time. In proportion as it is an eminent, emphatic part of it, learning is aided. Similarly discomfort eliminates most the eminent, emphatic features of the total response which it accompanies or shortly follows.

The third factor, the susceptibility of the response and situation to connection, is harder to illustrate. But, apparently, of those responses which are equally strongly connected with a situation by nature and equally attended to, some are more susceptible than others to a more intimate connection.

The things which have to be equal in the case of the law of exercise are the force of satisfyingness; that is, the action of the law of effect, and again the readiness of the response to be connected with the situation.

The operation of the laws of instinct, exercise and effect is conditioned further by (1) what may be called the law of assimilation or analogy,—that a situation, especially one to which no particular response is connected by original nature or previous experience, may connect with whatever response is bound to some situation *much like it*,—and (2) by the law of partial activity—that more or less of the total situation may be specially active in determining the response.

The first of these laws is a result of the facts that conduction in the neurones follows the line of least resistance or closest connection, that the action-system is so organized that certain responses tend to be made in their totality if at all, and that slightly different situations may, therefore, produce some one response, the effects of their differences being in the accessories of that response.

The second law is a result of the facts that the situation, itself a compound, produces a compound action in the neurones, and that by reason of inner conditions, the relative intensities of different parts of the compound may vary. The commonest response will be that due to the modal condition of the neural compound, but every condition of the compound will have its response.

ROBERT SESSIONS
WOODWORTH
(1869–1962)

Transfer of Training [5]

The word "function" is used without any rigor to refer to the mental basis of such things as spelling, multiplication, delicacy in discrimination of size, force of movement, marking *a*'s on a printed page, observing the word *boy* in a printed page, quickness, morality, verbal memory, chess playing, reasoning, and so forth. Function is used for all sorts of qualities in all sorts of performances from the narrowest to the widest, e.g., from attention to the word "fire" pronounced in a certain tone, to attention to all sorts of things. By the word "improvement" we shall mean those changes in the workings of functions which psychologists would commonly call by that name. Its use will be clear in each case and the psychological problem will never be different, even if the changes studied be not such as everyone would call improvements. For all purposes "change" may be used instead of "improvement" in the title. By "efficiency" we shall mean the status of a function which we use when comparing individuals or the same individual at different times, the status on which we would grade people in that function. By other function we mean any function differing in any respect whatever from the first. We shall at times use the word "function-group" to mean those cases where most psychologists would say that the same operation occurred with different data. The function *attention*, for instance, is really a vast group of functions.

Our chief method was to test the efficiency of some function or functions, then to give training in some other function or functions until a certain amount of improvement was reached, and then to test the first function or set of functions. Provided no other factors were allowed to affect the tests, the difference between the test before and the test after training measures the influence of the improvement in the trained functions on the functions tested.

[5] E. L. Thorndike and R. S. Woodworth, "The influence of improvement in one mental function upon the efficiency of other functions," *Psychol. Rev.*, 1901, **8**, 247–261, 384–395, 553–564.

It is possible to test the general question in a much neater and more convenient way by using, instead of measures of a function before and after training with another, measures of the correlation between the two functions. If improvement in one function increases the efficiency of another and there has been improvement in one, the other should be correlated with it; the individuals who have high rank in the one should have a higher rank in the other than the general average. Such a result might also be brought about by a correlation of the inborn capacities for those functions. Finding correlation between two functions thus need not mean that improvement in one has brought increased efficiency in the other. But the absence of correlation does mean the opposite.

* * * * *

Perhaps the most striking method of showing the influence or lack of influence of one function on another is that of testing the same function-group, using cases where there are very slightly different data. If, for instance, we test a person's ability to estimate a series of magnitudes differing each from the next very slightly, and find that he estimates one very much more accurately than its neighbors on either side, we can be sure that what he has acquired from his previous experience or from the experience of the test is not improvement in the function-group of estimating magnitudes but a lot of particular improvements in estimating particular magnitudes, improvements which may be to a large extent independent of one another.

The experiments, finally, were all on the influence of the training on efficiency, on ability as measured by a single test, not on the ability *to improve*. It might be that improvement in one function might fail to give in another improved ability, but succeed in giving ability to improve faster than would have occurred had the training been lacking.

The evidence given by our experiments makes the following conclusions seem probable:

It is misleading to speak of sense discrimination, attention, memory, observation, accuracy, quickness, and so forth, as multitudinous separate individual functions are referred to by any one of these words. These functions may have little in common. There is no reason to suppose that any general change occurs corresponding to the words "improvement of the attention," or "of the power of observation," or "of accuracy."

It is even misleading to speak of these functions as exercised within narrow fields as units. For example, "attention to words" or "accurate discrimination of lengths" or "observation of animals" or "quickness of visual perception" are mythological, not real entities. The words do not mean any existing fact with anything like the necessary precision for either theoretical or practical purposes, for, to take a sample case, attention to the meaning of words does not imply equal attention to their spelling, nor attention to their spelling equal attention to their length, nor attention to certain letters in them equal attention to other letters.

The mind is, on the contrary, on its dynamic side a machine for making particular reactions to particular situations. It works in great detail, adapting itself to the special data of which it has had experience. The word *attention*, for example, can properly mean only the sum total of a lot of particular tendencies to attend to particular sorts of data, and ability to attend can properly mean only the sum total of all the particular abilities and inabilities, each of which may have an efficiency largely irrespective of the efficiencies of the rest.

Improvement in any single mental function need not improve the ability in functions commonly called by the same name. It may injure it.

Improvement in any single mental function rarely brings about equal improvement in any other function, no matter how similar, for the working of every mental function-group is conditioned by the nature of the data in each particular case.

The very slight amount of variation in the nature of the data necessary to affect the efficiency of a function-group makes it fair to infer that no change in the data, however slight, is without effect on the function. The loss in the efficiency of a function trained with certain data, as we pass to data more and

more unlike the first, makes it fair to infer that there is always a point where the loss is complete, a point beyond which the influence of the training has not extended. The rapidity of this loss, that is, its amount in the case of data very similar to the data on which the function was trained, makes it fair to infer that this point is nearer than has been supposed.

The general consideration of the cases of retention or of loss of practice effect seems to make it likely that spread of practice occurs only where identical elements are concerned in the influencing and influenced function.

The particular samples of the influence of training in one function on the efficiency of other functions chosen for investigation were as follows:

1. The influence of certain special training in the estimation of magnitudes on the ability to estimate magnitudes of the same general sort, i.e., lengths or areas or weights, differing in amount, in accessory qualities (such as shape, color, form), or in both. The general method was here to test the subject's accuracy of estimating certain magnitudes, e.g., lengths of lines. He would, that is, guess the length of each. Then he would practice estimating lengths within certain limits until he attained a high degree of proficiency. Then he would once more estimate the lengths of the preliminary test series. Similarly with weights, areas, and so forth. This is apparently the sort of thing that happens in the case of a tea-taster, tobacco-buyer, wheat-taster, or carpenter, who attains high proficiency in judging magnitudes or, as we ambiguously say, in delicacy of discriminating certain sense data. It is thus like common cases of sense training in actual life.

2. The influence of training in observing words containing certain combinations of letters (e.g., *s* and *e*) or some other characteristic on the general ability to observe words. The general method here was to test the subject's speed and accuracy in picking out and marking certain letters, words containing certain letters, words of a certain length, geometric figures, misspelled words, and so forth. He then practiced picking out and marking words of some one special sort until he attained a high degree of proficiency. He was then re-tested. The training here corresponds to a fair degree with the training one has in learning to spell, to notice forms and

endings in studying foreign languages, or in fact in learning to attend to any small details.

3. The influence of special training in memorizing on the general ability to memorize.

* * * * *

In all the experiments ... we tested the influence of improvement in a function on *other functions closely allied to it.* We did not in sense-training measure the influence of training one sense on others, nor in the case of training of the attention the influence of training in noticing words on, say, the ability to do mental arithmetic or to listen to a metaphysical discourse.

Situation-and-Goal Set [6]

The eye-voice span in reading aloud affords a well-recorded example of overlapping processes in a behavior sequence. The eyes keep several words ahead of the voice, a variable number, about four or five words on the average in a good reader. The vocal response of pronouncing a word follows the foveal stimulus received from that word by an interval of one or two seconds, which is three to six times the reaction time in reading single familiar words. While one word is being pronounced another word is being seen and intervening words are going through the mill. No real sequence of stimulus-response units can be analyzed out of this behavior; the time-span greatly exceeds that of a single reaction and is evidently determined by a central factor. By holding his voice back in this way, the reader secures more continuity, better phrasing and expression, than if he responded to each word separately with his normal reaction time.

Much simpler two-phase movements, like striking a blow with a hammer, show a smoothness which is very different from a sequence of two separate movements. For a many-phase movement, observe the flight of a bird from a tree to a bit of food on the ground. He hops off, makes a number of strokes of the wings, and passes smoothly into braking with his wings, extending his legs and landing. There is a consistent and persistent steer throughout the performance. If we wish to describe these polyphasic movements as sequences of stimulus-response units we can probably do so, but only on condition that we recognize a persistent steer set up by the original stimulus and continuing till the end of the act. This inner steer can be called a goal set or goal-adjustment.

Just as the concept of situation-set including adjustment to illumination and distance is useful in explaining the perception of objects out there as distinguished from stimuli received, so in describing motor behavior, the notion of goal set is a conceptual means of taking care of the time-span. The goal need be nothing more distant than the outcome of a two-phase movement. Goal seeking in its lowest terms is the following of a consistent temporal pattern under the control of a persisting set.

Situation set and goal set are presumably not separate, especially in the more primitive types of behavior. The situation for which one is adjusted usually includes a goal, since the organism is active and engaged in behavior having a time-span greater than that of a simple reaction. If we conceive of an undifferentiated situation-and-goal-set, we avoid the apparent anthropomorphism of attributing rudimentary cognition and goal seeking to animals. The cognition implied in situation-set is not separated from doing, and the goal seeking does not imply ideational anticipation of the goal since the goal is right there in the presented situation.

* * * * *

A set is a type of implicit response to complexes of stimuli from the environment. The words "set" and "adjustment" are not exactly appropriate since set carries a false suggestion of rigidity and adjustment a false suggestion of quietude. In reality these sets are semifluid, and are revised from moment to moment in conformity with environmental changes. Adjustment to the environment is a readiness for action. Situation-and-goal set is an activity in progress.

* * * * *

I was engaged in a introspective study of the immediate antecedents of a voluntary

---

[6] Robert S. Woodworth, "Situation-and-goal set," *Amer. J. Psychol.*, 1937, **50**, 130–140. Reprinted by permission.

movement.[7] It was, in a sense, a study of the delayed reaction. A short delay was introduced between the decision to make a certain movement and the execution of that movement. Either the subject was told what movement to make or he was given his choice between two or more. He was to report his "condition of mind" in the short interval of delay. There were two types of reports which seemed trustworthy as well as instructive. Both types are included in the report of one subject on his preparation to hit at a mark. First the chosen mark became focal and then retreated to the background, to be succeeded by thought of the chosen hand; this in turn retreated to the background, leaving a rather blank condition of readiness, and the actual movement emerged out of this blank condition. The two points of interest are: (1) that the act was specified in a *series* of perceptions or thoughts, the partial specifications holding over after once being made; and (2) that the act once specified by these perceptions or thoughts remained specified during a blank period immediately preceding the movement. In discussing these reports, I said:

The nervous system may become set or adjusted for a certain act, and remain so for a time without the continuance of clear consciousness of the act. . . . The whole situation, as far as it is known, results in a certain adjustment of the nervous system, so that, for example, acts that would be performed while we are alone are not performed or thought of in public. Each sort of situation produces a corresponding set of the nervous system, and is thus a partial determinant of all the acts that are performed within that situation.

When a man confronted by a novel situation observes this and that feature of it in turn, each new perception leaves behind in the nervous system a temporary adjustment to the feature observed, until the whole situation becomes—not clearly mirrored in any one moment of consciousness—but dynamically represented by the sum or resultant of these partial adjustments. If he then thinks of some change that he can make in the situation and decides to make it, . . . the intention to act adds a new partial adjustment to the existing sum of adjustments.

In revising the above statement today, I should want to say that the partial adjustments resulting from perception of features of the situation are not simply added together but are built into a pre-existing framework of adjustment to the total situation. This adjustment is vague and general at first, and becomes more definite and specific as features of the situation are perceived.

In the well-known experiments on delayed reaction, goal set is often visible in the persistent posture of the animal during the interval of delay. When the animal is able to move about during the interval and still go promptly to the right door or container, we have to suppose some kind of superposture which amounts to a situation-and-goal set. We need not suppose that this set is ideational nor symbolic.

WALTER BRADFORD CANNON
(1871–1945)

Thalamic Theory of Emotions [8]

The relays of sensory channels in the thalamus and the evidence that disturbances in that region are the occasion for intensely affective sensations are all that we need for understanding its relation to the nature of emotions.

Head has cited numerous cases of unilateral lesions in the thalamic region in which there is a marked tendency to react excessively to affective stimuli; pin pricks, painful pressure, excessive heat or cold, all produce more distress on the damaged than on the normal side of the body. Agreeable stimuli also are felt keenly on the damaged side; warmth stimuli may evoke intense pleasure, attended by signs of enjoyment on the face and exclamations of delight. Again, affective stimuli, such as the playing of music and the singing of hymns, may arouse such increased

---

[7] R. S. Woodworth, "The cause of voluntary movement," *Studies in Philosophy and Psychology by Former Students of Charles Edward Garman* (1906), pp. 389 ff.

[8] Walter B. Cannon, *Bodily Changes in Pain, Hunger, Fear and Rage: An Account of Recent Researches into the Function of Emotional Excitement* (New York: D. Appleton, 2nd ed., 1929), pp. 365–376. Reprinted by permission.

emotional feeling on the damaged side that they may be intolerable. Affective conscious states have an influence on the damaged side similar to stimuli from the surface receptors. This extravagant influence of affective stimuli, whether from above or below, Head attributed to release of the thalamus from cortical inhibition. It is not an irritative effect, he argued, because it persists for long periods, well after all the disturbances due to the injury have subsided. And since the affective states are increased when the thalamus is freed from cortical control, Head's conclusion is that the essential thalamic center is mainly occupied with the affective side of sensation.

We are now in a position to consider the evidence that the positions and tensions of skeletal muscle make the differentia of emotion. It will be recalled that, although James belittled this element in his theory, his supporters have stressed it. . . . The thalamic cases provide a means of testing the contribution from skeletal muscles, for the feeling-tone of a sensation is a product of thalamic activity, and the fact that a sensation is devoid of feeling-tone shows that the impulses which underlie its production make no thalamic appeal.

Head found that his patients reported marked differences in the feeling-tone of different sensations. A tuning fork may have no effect, whereas patriotic music is felt intensely on the damaged side. All thermal stimuli make a double appeal, to the cortex and to the thalamus. Unselected tactile stimuli act similarly. On the other hand, *sensations which underlie the appreciation of posture are entirely lacking in feeling-tone.* Precisely those afferent impulses from muscles and joints which James and his supporters have relied upon to provide the extra-visceral part of the felt-emotion are the impulses which lack the necessary quality to serve the purpose! This evidence is supported by human cases in which movement of the facial muscles is made impossible by organic disease. Such patients may be acutely conscious of a particular emotion in spite of lack of expression in the face. In an instance of complete absence of expressional movement because of bilateral facial paralysis the patient testified that "his greatest misfortune was being forced to be joyful or sad without making any demonstration of his feelings to

his fellow creatures." And in another similar instance the patient "retained her good humor and sometimes laughed heartily . . . as if behind a mask, her face being quite immovable and grave whilst the emotion and sound of laughter prevailed." The quality of emotions is to be found, therefore, neither in returns from the viscera nor in returns from the innervated muscles.

* * * * *

The foregoing discussion has disclosed the fact that the neural arrangements for emotional expression reside in subcortical centers, and that these centers are ready for instant and vigorous discharge when they are released from cortical restraint and are properly stimulated. Furthermore, the evidence is clear that when these centers are released the processes aroused in them become a source of vivid affective experience. That this experience is felt on only one side in hemiplegic cases is a peculiarly happy circumstance, for in the same individual the influence of the same affective stimulus can be observed under normal conditions and compared with its influence when given free rein.

The neural organization for an emotion which is suggested by the foregoing observations is as follows: An external situation stimulates receptors and the consequent excitation starts impulses towards the cortex. Arrival of the impulses in the cortex is associated with conditioned processes which determine the direction of the response. Either because the response is initiated in a certain mode or figure and the cortical neurones therefore stimulate the thalamic processes, or because on their inward course the impulses from the receptors excite thalamic processes, they are roused and ready for discharge. That the thalamic neurones act in a special combination in a given emotional expression is proved by the reaction patterns typical of the several affective states. These neurones do not require detailed innervation from above in order to be driven into action. Being *released* for action is a primary condition for their service to the body—they then discharge precipitately and intensely. Within and near the thalamus the neurones concerned in an emotional expression lie close to the relay in the sensory path from periphery to cortex. We may assume that when these neurones discharge in a particular combination, they not only innervate muscles and viscera but also excite afferent paths to the cortex by direct connection or by irradiation. The theory which naturally presents itself is that *the peculiar quality of the emotion is added to simple sensation when the thalamic processes are roused.*

* * * * *

The theory just suggested appears to fit all the known facts. Its service in explaining these facts may be briefly summarized.

When the thalamic discharge occurs, the bodily changes occur almost simultaneously with the emotional experience. This coincidence of disturbances in muscles and viscera with thrills, excitements or depressions was naturally misleading, for, with the rôle of the thalamus omitted from consideration, the obvious inference was that the peculiar quality of the emotion arose from the peripheral changes. Indeed, that inference is the heart of the James-Lange theory. The evidence presented in the foregoing pages shows that the inference is ill-founded; the sensations from the peripheral changes, contrary to James' view, are "pale, colorless and destitute of emotional warmth," whereas the thalamic disturbances contribute glow and color to otherwise simply cognitive states. The theory now proposed explains how James and Lange could reasonably make the suggestion which they made. The lack of factual support for their suggestion requires another account of emotional origins. This is provided by the evidence that thalamic processes can add to sensation an aura of feeling.

One of the strongest arguments advanced for the James-Lange theory is that the assumption of an attitude does in fact help to establish the emotional state which the attitude expresses. "Sit all day in a moping posture, sigh, and reply to everything with a dismal voice, and your melancholy lingers." On the contrary, "smooth the brow, brighten the eye, contract the dorsal rather than the ventral aspect of the frame, and speak in a major key, pass the genial compliment, and your heart must be frigid indeed if you do not gradually thaw!" Persons who have tried this advice have testified to its soundness, and have been convinced, therefore, of the truth of the claim that the moods have followed the assumed attitudes. Not all agree, however, that mimicking the outward appearance of an emotion results in the emotion itself. James suggested that the explanation of the discrepancy lay in variations of involvement of the viscera in the artificial expression. As already shown, however, the visceral changes offer only unreliable support for that idea. Again the processes in the thalamus offer a reasonable and simple explanation. As the cases reported by Head have shown, emotions originating from memories and imagination affect more intensely the half-thalamus that has been released from motor control than they affect the normal half. This shows that cortical processes may start thalamic processes and thus arouse an effective return from that portion of the brain. And if in addition a typical emotional attitude is assumed, the cortical inhibition of the thalamic neurones with reference to that attitude is abolished so that they have complete release. Under such circumstances the enacted emotion would have reality. On the other hand a purely cortical mimicry of emotional expression without thalamic involvement would be as cold and unaffective as some actors have declared it to be. Whether the emotion results or not, the thalamic theory of the source of feeling offers a more satisfactory explanation of the effects of assumed postures than does the James-Lange theory.

The cases of release of the thalamus from cortical control on one side, with accompanying intensification of emotional tone on the same side, present an insurmountable obstacle to the James-Lange theory. Neither the thoracic nor the abdominal viscera can function by halves, the vasomotor center is a unity, and the patients certainly do not engage in right- or left-sided laughter and weeping. The impulses sent back from the disturbed peripheral organs, therefore, must be bilaterally equal. For explanation of the unsymmetrical feeling we are driven to the organ which is functioning unsymmetrically —i.e., the thalamus. It is there that the suggested theory places the source of the emotions.

Another serious difficulty for the James-Lange theory is the evidence that the emotion increases in intensity although the expression is checked. Indeed, there are psychologists who maintain that the emotional state lasts only so long as there is inner conflict between the impulse to act and the hesitant or prudential check on that impulse. So long as the check prevails, however, the organic changes supposed to be the source of the feeling are suppressed. How then can there be felt-emotion? Two answers to this question may be found in James' argument. First he denies the objection. "Refuse to express a passion," he wrote, "and it dies." "Count ten before venting your anger, and its occasion seems ridiculous." On the other hand, he appears to admit that a pent emotion may operate disastrously. "If tears or anger are simply suppressed, whilst the object of grief or rage remains unchanged before the mind, the current which would have invaded the normal channels turns into others, for it must find some outlet of escape. It may then work different and worse effects later on. Thus vengeful brooding may replace a burst of indignation; a dry heat may consume the frame of one who fain would weep, or he may, as Dante says, turn to stone within." There is no intimation that vengeful brooding, being consumed by a dry heat, and turning to stone within are not emotional experiences. Instead of recognizing them as such, however, James stressed the importance of training for repression of emotional display. These rather equivocal and indecisive comments leave untouched the common testimony that intense fear, for example, may be felt, with a pathetic sense of helplessness, before any overt act occurs, and that scarcely does the appropriate behavior start than the inner tumult begins to subside and the bodily forces are directed vigorously and effectively to serviceable ends. The difficulties of the James-Lange theory in meeting this situation are obvious. If there is a double control of behavior, however, both the inner conflict with its keen emotional accompaniment and the later partial subsidence of feeling are readily explicable. The thalamic patterned processes are inherent in the nervous organization, they are like reflexes in being instantly ready to seize control of the motor responses, and when they do so they operate with great power. They can be controlled, however, by the processes in the cerebral cortex, by processes conditioned by all sorts of previous impressions. The cortex also can control all the peripheral machinery except the viscera. The inhibited processes

in the thalamus cannot set the organism in action, except the parts not under voluntary control, but thalamic turmoil can produce emotions in the usual manner, and possibly with greater violence because of the inhibition. And when the cortical check is released, suddenly the conflict is resolved. The two controls formerly in opposition are now coöperative. The thalamic neurones, so long as they continue energetically active, provide the condition for the emotion to persist, as James claimed it does, *during* the manifestation. The new theory, therefore, not only avoids the difficulty of the James-Lange theory, but accounts satisfactorily for the poignancy of feeling in the period of paralyzed inaction.

In relation to the double control of the response there is another point that may be emphasized. McDougall has objected to the James-Lange theory on the ground that it is admittedly concerned with the *sensory* aspect of emotion; it pays little or no attention to the always present and sometimes overwhelming *impulsive* aspect of the experience. The localization of the reaction patterns for emotional expression in the thalamus—in a region which, like the spinal cord, works directly by simple automatisms unless held in check—not only accounts for the sensory side, the "felt emotion," but also for the impulsive side, the tendency of the thalamic neurones to discharge. These powerful impulses originating in a region of the brain not associated with cognitive consciousness and arousing therefore in an *obscure* and *unrelated* manner the strong feelings of emotional excitement, explain the sense of being seized, possessed, of being controlled by an outside force and made to act without weighing of the consequences.

Finally, the view that thalamic processes add feeling-tone to sensation meets satisfactorily a difficulty which the James-Lange theory encountered in explaining the "subtler emotions." James had to assume indefinite and hypothetical bodily reverberations in order to account for mild feelings of pleasure and satisfaction. If a warm test tube, however, is capable of yielding keen delight on the damaged side in a case of thalamic injury, it is clear that almost any object or situation which can rouse thalamic processes can add affective quality to sensation. And just as a stimulus can become conditioned for a certain motor or glandular response, so likewise a stimulus can be conditioned for the patterns of neurone action in the thalamus. When that stimulus recurs the emotion recurs because the pattern is activated. In such manner we may consider that richness and variety of our emotional life are elaborated.

ERNEST GLEN WEVER
(1902–   )

and

CHARLES WILLIAM BRAY
(1904–   )

Wever–Bray Effect [9]

The results of this series of experiments relate to the nature of response in the auditory nerve as a whole during stimulation of the ear by sound, and apply particularly to the response as correlated with the frequency of the sound. A large number of experiments have been made to rule out the possibility of artifact, and to establish definitely whether the responses obtained are due to nerve action currents.

At the date of this writing we have performed these experiments on 18 animals, and have secured auditory nerve responses from every one of these except the first; the first attempt failed, as we now know, because of insufficient amplification. Three animals during the early experiments died very soon after completion of the operation, and permitted observations for only a few minutes. Then, however, we were employing the customary method of decerebration; since our adoption of the method described above this difficulty has disappeared, and the animals have remained in good condition through many hours of experimentation.

* * * * *

1. *The Frequency Correlation.* The fundamental result of these experiments is the discovery that sounds applied to the ear of the animal produce effects in the acoustic nerve which correspond in an essential way to the frequency of these sounds. The electrical changes set up in the nerve in the passage of

the nerve impulses are such as to produce in the receiving apparatus tones of the same nature as those affecting the auditory apparatus of the cat. In other words, the physiological preparation plays the same rôle here as a sound transmitter in an ordinary communication line. A pure tone sounded into the ear of the cat is recognized as that same tone in the receiver. Speech is received readily; and the degree of fidelity can be judged from the fact that under good conditions an observer in the sound-proof room is able to recognize who is speaking into the cat's ear if the person's voice is reasonably familiar to him. Other complex sounds, including noises of all kinds, are received with equal facility, and show further the absence of any great amount of distortion.

The range of tones which we have recorded extends over about five and a half octaves, specifically, from 105 to 5200⁻. The range obtained in any given experiment depends primarily on the amount of amplification used. This is because the sensitivity of the human ear used as the detecting device falls off greatly for low and high frequencies, and grows particularly poor as the frequency is raised beyond 3000⁻. We have no reason to believe that 5200⁻ represents the upper limit of hearing of the animal, and anticipate the demonstration of still higher frequencies.

Throughout the range just mentioned the received frequencies have been shown by direct comparison to correspond to the sound frequencies applied to the ear. For these comparisons a telephone line was set up between operating and sound-proof rooms, and the sound was introduced alternately into the cat's ear and into the transmitter of the telephone system (see the lower diagram of Fig. 1). Under these conditions the

---

[9] Ernest Glen Wever and Charles W. Bray, "The nature of acoustic response: the relations between sound frequency and frequency of impulses in the auditory nerve," *J. exp. Psychol.*, 1930, **13**, 376–380. Reprinted by permission.

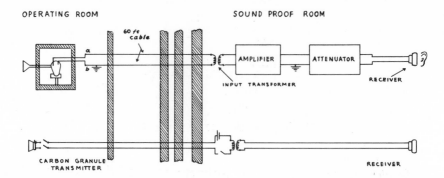

FIGURE 1. *Above*, Apparatus for detection of the nerve currents set up through stimulation of the ear by sound. *Below*, Telephone system used for direct comparison of the nerve currents and the stimulating sounds.

accuracy of a frequency comparison may be very conservatively rated as within 1 or 2 percent. To the observer the tones are of the same pitch.

The degree of tonal discrimination possible through the animal seems as high as can be expected in the presence of the background noise and with the strength of signals available. That is, we consider the discrimination to be limited more by the conditions of observation than by the transmission properties of the cat's auditory apparatus. Tests with the Galton whistle have shown the tones 3433 and 3373 to be discriminated (difference 60⁻) but not the tones 3433 and 3399 (difference 34⁻).

2. *The Intensity Correlation.* The results of this series of experiments apply chiefly to the relation of the nerve response to stimulation frequency, and give less information regarding the relation to intensity. The difference is in part a function of the method of recording; the observer's ear is not very sensitive to small changes of intensity. Indeed, the voltage obtained from the nerve would have to change about 25 percent (2 TU) in order to be detected by this method. Some general results can be reported, however.

Within limits at least, the louder the stimulus the stronger the signal received. We have not observed much difference in the use of medium and strong intensities at high frequencies, but whether we are concerned here with the upper intensive threshold of the animal or with the observational limitation just mentioned we cannot say.

Under good conditions a very weak stimulus is adequate. A faint whisper into the cat's ear is easily audible in the receiver. The observer can hear and often understand ordinary conversation between persons in the operating room. The sounds of walking about and the usual manipulation of apparatus are also audible.

As the condition of the preparation becomes poorer, through injury to the nerve, drying or other impairment of the tissues, or through restriction of the blood-supply, the reception becomes worse, and faint sounds are no longer audible. Loud sounds, however, may still be received. After the death of the animal the responses grow progressively fainter, and finally cease.

This evidence indicates some kind of positive correlation between the voltage established in the nerves as a whole and the

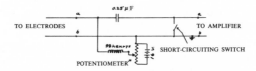

FIGURE 2. Circuit arrangement used in the introduction of a polarizing current into the nerve. This apparatus was introduced into the detecting system at the points *a, b* in Fig. 1.

intensity of the stimulating sound. It does not, however, show the exact functional relationship between these variables.

3. *The Magnitude of the Auditory Response.* Some preliminary information regarding the magnitude of the response from the auditory nerve was secured by a comparison with responses from muscles and other nerves in the same animal.

For observation of muscle currents a small flexor muscle in the foreleg was selected. When the electrode was applied, and the muscle stretched with forceps, the normal tonic discharge increased rapidly in rate and developed into a definite "roar" of sound. For observation of impulses in peripheral nerves the radial nerve in the foreleg was first used. A hook electrode was placed around the nerve. A sharp rap on the paw of this leg gave a short dull sound in the receiver. Pressing on the "quick" of a cut toe-nail for a few seconds gave a slow welling-up and then a decay of impulses. An electrode on the vagus nerve gave a constant bombardment which seemed to increase on hampering the breathing of the animal. All these impulses, including those from the muscle, were of the same general order of intensity as those obtained from the auditory nerve. Their rate, however, probably did not exceed 100 per second (Cat 13).

A rough measurement of the intensity of the action currents was made on one animal by means of the cathode ray oscillograph, and yielded a value of 90 microvolts. We mention this figure only to indicate in a very general way the order of magnitude of the nerve voltage, and hope to report more precise measurements later.

STANLEY SMITH STEVENS
(1906–   )

The Power Law [10]

The prototypes of the two kinds of continua are exemplified by loudness and pitch. Loudness is an aspect of sound that has about it what can best be described as degrees of magnitude or quantity. Pitch does not. Pitch varies from high to low; it has a kind of position, and in a sense it is a qualitative continuum. Loudness may be called a *prothetic* continuum, and pitch a *metathetic* one. The criteria that define these two classes of continua reside wholly in how they behave in psychophysical experiments, but the names themselves are suggested by the nature of the physiological processes that appear to underlie each of them.

Sensory discrimination may be mediated by two processes: the one additive, the other substitutive. Additional excitation may be added to an excitation already present, or new excitation may be substituted for excitation that has been removed. An observer can tell, for example, when a light pressure becomes a strong pressure at a given point on the arm, and he can also tell when the stimulus is moved from that point to another location. Different sets of general laws govern these two types of sensory discrimination.

The metathetic, positional, qualitative continua seem to concern *what* and *where* as opposed to *how much*. They include such things as pitch, apparent position, apparent inclination, and apparent proportion. Perhaps they also include visual saturation and visual hue—at least to whatever extent hue may be made to behave as a continuum. All in all, the metathetic continua do not seem to comprise a neat and orderly class of perceptual variables, and as yet they have not been very thoroughly explored.

The prothetic continua, on the other hand, have lately yielded rich rewards for the systematic efforts made to scale their magnitudes. Some two dozen continua have been examined, always with the same outcome: the sensation magnitude ψ grows as a power function of the stimulus magnitude ϕ. In terms of a formula,

$$\psi = k\phi^n$$

In this equation, the constant k depends on the units of measurement and is not very interesting; but the value of the exponent n

[10] S. S. Stevens, "The quantification of sensation," *Daedalus: J. Acad. Arts Sci.*, 1959, **88**, 613–618. Reprinted by permission of the American Academy of Arts and Sciences.

may vary from one sensory continuum to another. As a matter of fact, perhaps the most interesting thing about a sensory continuum (as we shall see) the value of the exponent *n*.

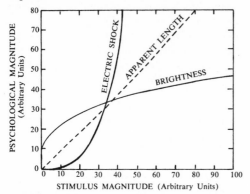

FIGURE 2. The apparent magnitudes of shock, length, and brightness follow different curves of growth. Their exponents are 3.5, 1.1, and 0.33, respectively. The units of the scales have been chosen arbitrarily in order to show the relative form of the curves on a single plot.

So rarely does it happen in psychological studies that a simple quantitative law can be shown to hold under many diverse circumstances, that the widespread invariance of the power law becomes a matter of significant interest. A law of this form seems to govern our reactions to light and sound, taste and smell, warmth and cold, vibration and shock —in fact, every continuum yet explored on which variations in intensity may be said to exist. As a general psychophysical law it provides a new aid to understanding and a new challenge to explanation.

* * * * *

Perhaps the easiest way to elicit the relevant behavior from an observer is to stimulate his eye, say, with a variety of different intensities, and to ask him to assign a number proportional to the apparent magnitude of each brightness, as he sees it. Most observers, once they understand the problem, carry out this process (called magnitude estimation) with reasonable success. Not that all observers make the same estimates, or even feel any great confidence in what they are doing, but the average result for a group of normal observers turns out to be quite stable and reproducible. After all, it is the reaction of the typical (median)

observer that interests us here, for we are not concerned, at the outset at least, with the fact that people differ, or that some are blind and some are photophobic. Psychophysics wants to know, first of all, what the typical input-output operating characteristics of the sensory systems are.

The typical input-output relation for all prothetic continua thus far tested is a power function. To date, the observed values of the exponent in the relation $\psi = k\phi^n$ have ranged from about 0.33 for brightness to about 3.5 for the apparent intensity of electric shock applied to the fingers. The exponent of the power function determines its curvature. If the exponent is exactly 1, the function is a straight line, and the output (reported sensation) varies linearly with the intensity of the stimulus. But when the exponent is greater than 1, the line representing the function ascends in an ever steeper slope. When it is less than 1, the curvature is the other way and the line becomes ever more horizontal.

These relations are illustrated in Figure 2, which shows examples of three perceptual continua, each having a different exponent. Electric current produces a sensation whose intensity grows more and more rapidly as the current increases, whereas brightness seems to grow less and less rapidly with increasing physical intensity. As we might expect, the apparent length of a line seems to grow very nearly in direct proportion to the physical length. One foot looks about half as long as two feet—not quite, it seems, but almost.

A felicitous feature of power functions is

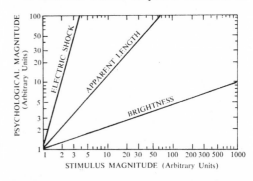

FIGURE 3. When the curves in Figure 2 are plotted against logarithmic coordinates, they become straight lines. The slopes of the line correspond to the exponent of the power function that governs the growth of the sensation.

the form they assume when graphed in log-log coordinates (logarithmic scales on both axes). The plot of a power function then becomes a straight line, and the slope of the line is a direct measure of the exponent. We can see how this works out if we make a log-log plot of the same three functions shown in Figure 2. We find that the differences in curvature in Figure 2 become differences in slope in Figure 3.

The nature of these power functions and the universality of their application testify to the existence of a profoundly simple relation between stimulus and sensory response: equal stimulus ratios produce equal subjective ratios. That is the essence of the psycho-physical law. For example, it requires approximately a ninefold increase in energy to double the apparent brightness of a light, no matter where we start from in the first place. Doubling the apparent intensity of an electric shock requires an increase in current of only about 20 per cent, but this percentage increase is approximately the same all up and down the scale. On all continua governed by the power law, a constant percentage change in the stimulus produces a constant percentage change in the sensed effect.

17

French, Swiss, and Italian Child and Social Psychology

CESARE LOMBROSO
(1835–1909)

Criminal Psychology and the Cephalic Index [1]

I, therefore, began to study criminals in the Italian prisons, and, amongst others, I made the acquaintance of the famous brigand Vilella. This man possessed such extraordinary agility, that he had been known to scale steep mountain heights bearing a sheep on his shoulders. His cynical effrontery was such that he openly boasted of his crimes. On his death one cold grey November morning, I was deputed to make the *post-mortem*, and on laying open the skull I found on the occipital part, exactly on the spot where a spine is found in the normal skull, a distinct

depression which I named *median occipital fossa*, because of its situation precisely in the middle of the occiput as in inferior animals, especially rodents. This depression, as in the case of animals, was correlated with the hypertrophy of the *vermis*, known in birds as the middle cerebellum.

This was not merely an idea, but a revelation. At the sight of that skull, I seemed to see all of a sudden, lighted up as a vast plain under a flaming sky, the problem of the nature of the criminal—an atavistic being who reproduces in his person the ferocious instincts of primitive humanity and the inferior animals. Thus were explained anatomically the enormous jaws, high cheek-bones, prominent superciliary arches, solitary lines in the palms, extreme size of the orbits, handle-shaped or sessile ears found in criminals, savages, and apes, insensibility to pain, extremely acute sight, tattooing, excessive idleness, love of orgies, and the irresistible craving for evil for

---

[1] Cesare Lombroso, "Introduction," in Gina Lombroso Ferrero, *Criminal Man: According to the Classification of Cesare Lombroso Briefly Summarized by His Daughter* (New York: G. P. Putnam's Sons, 1911), pp. xiv–xv. Summary of the original Italian, *L'uomo deliquente* (1876).

its own sake, the desire not only to extinguish life in the victim, but to mutilate the corpse, tear its flesh, and drink its blood.

* * * * *

Criminal Physiognomy [2]

Skin. The skin frequently shows scars and (in the epileptic subject to seizures) lesions on the elbows and temples.

* * * * *

Tattooing. Great care must be taken to ascertain whether the subject is tattooed, and if so, on what parts of his body. Tattooing often reveals obscenity, vindictiveness, cupidity, and other characteristics of the patient, besides furnishing his name or initials, that of his native town or village, and the symbol of the trade he refuses to reveal (sometimes such indications have been blurred or effaced).

* * * * *

Wrinkles. The following are of special importance: the vertical and horizontal lines on the forehead, the oblique and triangular lines of the brows, the horizontal or circumflex lines at the root of the nose and the vertical and horizontal lines on the neck.

* * * * *

Beard. The beard is scanty in born criminals and often altogether absent in epileptics.

* * * * *

Teeth. The greatest percentage of anomalies is found in the incisors; next come the premolars, the molars, and lastly the canines. In criminals, especially if epileptics, the middle incisors of the upper jaw are sometimes missing and their absence is compensated by the excessive development of the lateral incisors.

* * * * *

Ears. The ears of criminals and epileptics exhibit a number of anomalies. They are sometimes of abnormal size or stand out from the face.

* * * * *

---

[2] *Ibid.*, pp. 231–243.

Eyes. The eyebrows are generally bushy in murderers and violators of women. Ptosis, a species of paralysis of the upper lid, which gives the eye a half-closed appearance, is common in all criminals; but more frequently we find strabismus, a want of parallelism in the visual axes, bichromatism of the iris, and rigidity of the pupils.

Nose. In thieves the base of the nose often slants upwards, and this characteristic of rogues is so common in Italy that it has given rise to a number of proverbs. The nose is often twisted in epileptics, flattened and trilobate in cretins.

Jaws. Enormous maxillary development is one of the most frequent anomalies in criminals and is related to the greater size of the zygomæ and teeth.

* * * * *

Chin. This part of the face, which in Europeans is generally prominent, round and proportioned to the size of the face, in degenerates as in apes is frequently receding, flat, too long or too short.

* * * * *

Height. Criminals are rarely tall. Like all degenerates, they are under medium height.

* * * * *

Weight. In proportion to their height, criminals generally weigh less than normal individuals, whose weight in kilogrammes is given by the decimal figures of his height as expressed in metres and centimetres.

Head. The head, or rather the skull, the shape of which is influenced by the cerebral mass it contains, is rarely free from anomalies, and for this reason the careful examination of this part is of the utmost importance. We have no means of studying subtle cranial alterations in the living subject, but we can ascertain the form and capacity of his skull. This is rendered easy and rapid by means of a very convenient craniograph. . . .

In the absence of a craniometer, measurements may be taken with calipers, the arms of which are curved like the ordinary pelvimeters used in obstetrics, and a graduated steel tape.

The following are the principal measurements:

1. Maximum antero-posterior diameter, which is obtained by applying one arm of the instrument above the root of the nose just between the eyebrows and sliding the other arm over the vault of the skull till it reaches the occiput. The distance between the two arms furnishes the maximum longitudinal diameter.

2. The maximum transverse diameter or breadth of the skull is measured by placing the arms of the calipers, one on each side of the head on the most prominent spot.

3. The antero-posterior curve is obtained by fixing the graduated tape at zero on the root of the nose (on the fronto-nasal suture) and passing it over the middle of the forehead, vertex, and occiput to the external occipital protuberance.

4. The transverse, or biauricular curve is obtained by applying the steel tape at zero to a point just above the ear, and carrying it over the head in a vertical direction till it reaches the corresponding point on the other side.

5. The maximum circumference is obtained by encircling the head with the steel tape, touching the forehead immediately above the eyebrows, the occiput at the most prominent point, and the sides of the head more or less at the level, where the external ear joins the head, according to whether the position of the occipital protuberance is more or less elevated.

6. The cranial capacity is obtained by adding together these five measurements, the antero-posterior diameter, maximum transverse diameter, antero-posterior curve, transverse curve, and maximum circumference. For a normal male the capacity is generally 92 inches (1500 c.c.).

7. The cephalic index is obtained by multiplying the maximum width by 100 and dividing the product by the maximum length, according to the following formula:

$$\frac{W \times 100}{L} = X \text{ (cephalic index)}.$$

If the longitudinal diameter is 200 and the transverse diameter 100, the cephalic index is 10,000 divided by 200 = 50.

The cephalic indices of degenerates, like their height, have only a relative importance; that is, when they are compared with the mean cephalic index prevalent in the regions of which the subject is a native. The cephalic index of Italians varies between 77.5 (Sardinians) and 85.9 (Piedmontese).

Skulls are classified according to the cephalic index, in the following manner:

Hyperdolichocephalic	under	66
Dolichocephalic		66–75
Subdolichocephalic		75–77
Mesaticephalic		77–80
Subbrachycephalic		80–83
Brachycephalic		83–90
Hyperbrachycephalic	above	90

We shall find among criminals frequent instances of microcephaly, macrocephaly, and asymmetry, one side of the head being larger than the other. Sometimes the skull is pointed in the bregmatic region (hypsicephaly), sometimes it is narrow in the frontal region in correlation to the insertion of the temporal muscles and the excessive development of the zygomatic arches (stenocrotaphy) . . . or depression of the bregmatic region (cymbocephaly).

Face. We have already remarked on the excessive size of the face compared with the brain-case, owing chiefly to the high cheek-bones, which are one of the most salient characteristics of criminals, and to the enormous development of the jaws, which gives them the appearance of ferocious animals.

* * * * *

Feet. Degenerates and more especially epileptics, frequently have flat or prehensile feet and an elongated big-toe with which, like the Japanese, they are able to grasp objects.

GUSTAVE LE BON
(1841–1931)

Group Psychology: The Crowd [3]

In its ordinary sense the word "crowd" means a gathering of individuals of whatever nationality, profession, or sex, and whatever be the chances that have brought them together. From the psychological point of view the expression "crowd" assumes quite a different signification. Under certain given circumstances, and only under those circumstances, an agglomeration of men presents new characteristics very different from those of the individuals composing it. The sentiments and ideas of all the persons in the gathering take one and the same direction, and their conscious personality vanishes. A collective mind is formed, doubtless transitory, but presenting very clearly defined characteristics. The gathering has thus become what, in the absence of a better expression, I will call an organised crowd, or, if the term is considered preferable, a psychological crowd. It forms a single being, and is subjected to the *law of the mental unity of crowds.*

* * * * *

It being impossible to study here all the successive degrees of organisation of crowds, we shall concern ourselves more especially with such crowds as have attained to the phase of complete organisation. In this way we shall see what crowds may become, but not what they invariably are. It is only in this advanced phase of organisation that certain new and special characteristics are superposed on the unvarying and dominant character of the race; then takes place that turning already alluded to of all the feelings and thoughts of the collectivity in an identical direction. It is only under such circumstances, too, that what I have called above the *psychological law of the mental unity of crowds* comes into play.

* * * * *

The most striking peculiarity presented by a psychological crowd is the following: Whoever be the individuals that compose it,

[3] Gustave Le Bon, *The Crowd: A Study of the Popular Mind* (London: T. Fisher Unwin, 1896), pp. 25–26, 29–38, 159, 194–196; original French, *La psychologie des foules* (1895).

however like or unlike be their mode of life, their occupations, their character, or their intelligence, the fact that they have been transformed into a crowd puts them in possession of a sort of collective mind which makes them feel, think, and act in a manner quite different from that in which each individual of them would feel, think, and act were he in a state of isolation. There are certain ideas and feelings which do not come into being, or do not transform themselves into acts except in the case of individuals forming a crowd. The psychological crowd is a provisional being formed of heterogeneous elements, which for a moment are combined, exactly as the cells which constitute a living body form by their reunion a new being which displays characteristics very different from those possessed by each of the cells singly.

* * * * *

It is more especially with respect to those unconscious elements which constitute the genius of a race that all the individuals belonging to it resemble each other, while it is principally in respect to the conscious elements of their character—the fruit of education, and yet more of exceptional hereditary conditions—that they differ from each other. Men the most unlike in the matter of their intelligence possess instincts, passions, and feelings that are very similar. In the case of everything that belongs to the realm of sentiment—religion, politics, morality, the affections and antipathies, etc.—the most eminent men seldom surpass the standard of the most ordinary individuals. From the intellectual point of view an abyss may exist between a great mathematician and his bootmaker, but from the point of view of character the difference is most often slight or nonexistent.

* * * * *

Different causes determine the appearance of these characteristics peculiar to crowds, and not possessed by isolated individuals. The first is that the individual forming part of a crowd acquires, solely from numerical considerations, a sentiment of invincible power which allows him to yield to instincts which, had he been alone, he would perforce have kept under restraint. He will be the less disposed to check himself from the consideration that, a crowd being anonymous, and in consequence irresponsible, the sentiment of responsibility which always controls individuals disappears entirely.

The second cause, which is contagion, also intervenes to determine the manifestation in crowds of their special characteristics, and at the same time the trend they are to take. Contagion is a phenomenon of which it is easy to establish the presence, but that it is not easy to explain. It must be classed among those phenomena of a hypnotic order, which we shall shortly study. In a crowd every sentiment and act is contagious, and contagious to such a degree that an individual readily sacrifices his personal interest to the collective interest. This is an aptitude very contrary to his nature, and of which a man is scarcely capable, except when he makes part of a crowd.

A third cause, and by far the most important, determines in the individuals of a crowd special characteristics which are quite contrary at times to those presented by the isolated individual. I allude to that suggestibility of which, moreover, the contagion mentioned above is neither more nor less than an effect.

To understand this phenomenon it is necessary to bear in mind certain recent physiological discoveries. We know to-day that by various processes an individual may be brought into such a condition that, having entirely lost his conscious personality, he obeys all the suggestions of the operator who has deprived him of it, and commits acts in utter contradiction with his character and habits. The most careful observations seem to prove that an individual immerged for some length of time in a crowd in action soon finds himself—either in consequence of the magnetic influence given out by the crowd, or from some other cause of which we are ignorant—in a special state, which much resembles the state of fascination in which the hypnotised individual finds himself in the hands of the hypnotiser. The activity of the brain being paralysed in the case of the hypnotised subject, the latter becomes the slave of all the unconscious activities of his spinal cord, which the hypnotiser directs at will. The conscious personality has entirely vanished; will and discernment are lost. All feelings and thoughts are bent in the direction determined by the hypnotiser.

* * * * *

We see, then, that the disappearance of the conscious personality, the predominance of the unconscious personality, the turning by means of suggestion and contagion of feelings and ideas in an identical direction, the tendency to immediately transform the suggested ideas into acts; these we see, are the principal characteristics of the individual forming part of a crowd. He is no longer himself, but has become an automaton who has ceased to be guided by his will.

Moreover, by the mere fact that he forms part of an organised crowd, a man descends several rungs in the ladder of civilisation. Isolated, he may be a cultivated individual; in a crowd, he is a barbarian—that is, a creature acting by instinct. He possesses the spontaneity, the violence, the ferocity, and also the enthusiasm and heroism of primitive beings, whom he further tends to resemble by the facility with which he allows himself to be impressed by words and images—which would be entirely without action on each of the isolated individuals composing the crowd —and to be induced to commit acts contrary to his most obvious interests and his best-known habits. An individual in a crowd is a grain of sand amid other grains of sand, which the wind stirs up at will.

It is for these reasons that juries are seen to deliver verdicts of which each individual juror would disapprove, that parliamentary assemblies adopt laws and measures of which each of their members would disapprove in his own person. Taken separately, the men of the Convention were enlightened citizens of peaceful habits. United in a crowd, they did not hesitate to give their adhesion to the most savage proposals, to guillotine individuals most clearly innocent, and, contrary to their interests; to renounce their inviolability and to decimate themselves.

* * * * *

The conclusion to be drawn from what precedes is, that the crowd is always intellectually inferior to the isolated individual, but that, from the point of view of feelings and of the acts these feelings provoke, the crowd may, according to circumstances, be better or worse than the individual. All depends on the nature of the suggestion to which the crowd is exposed. This is the point that has been completely misunderstood by writers who have only studied crowds from the criminal point of view. Doubtless a crowd is often criminal, but also it is often heroic. It is crowds rather than isolated individuals that may be induced to run the risk of death to secure the triumph of a creed or an idea, that may be fired with enthusiasm for glory and honour, that are led on—almost without bread and without arms, as in the age of the Crusades—to deliver the tomb of Christ from the infidel, or, as in '93, to defend the fatherland. Such heroism is without doubt somewhat unconscious, but it is of such heroism that history is made. Were peoples only to be credited with the great actions performed in cold blood, the annals of the world would register but few of them.

* * * * *

The hero whom the crowd acclaimed yesterday is insulted to-day should he have been overtaken by failure. The reaction, indeed, will be the stronger in proportion as the prestige has been great. The crowd in this case considers the fallen hero as an equal, and takes its revenge for having bowed to a superiority whose existence it no longer admits. While Robespierre was causing the execution of his colleagues and of a great number of his contemporaries, he possessed an immense prestige. When the transposition of a few votes deprived him of power, he immediately lost his prestige, and the crowd followed him to the guillotine with the selfsame imprecations with which shortly before it had pursued his victims. Believers always break the statues of their former gods with every symptom of fury.

Prestige lost by want of success disappears in a brief space of time. It can also be worn away, but more slowly by being subjected to discussion. This latter power, however, is exceedingly sure. From the moment prestige is called in question it ceases to be prestige. The gods and men who have kept their prestige for long have never tolerated discussion. For the crowd to admire, it must be kept at a distance.

* * * * *

Juries, like all crowds, are profoundly impressed by prestige, and President des Glajeux very properly remarks that, very democratic as juries are in their composition, they are very aristocratic in their likes and dislikes: "Name, birth, great wealth, celebrity, the assistance of an illustrious counsel, everything in the nature of distinction or that lends brilliancy to the accused, stands him in extremely good stead."

The chief concern of a good counsel should be to work upon the feelings of the jury, and, as with all crowds, to argue but little, or only to employ rudimentary modes of reasoning. An English barrister, famous for his successes in the assize courts, has well set forth the line of action to be followed:

While pleading he would attentively observe the jury. The most favourable opportunity has been reached. By dint of insight and experience the counsel reads the effect of each phrase on the faces of the jurymen, and draws his conclusions in consequence. His first step is to be sure which members of the jury are already favourable to his cause. It is short work to definitely gain their adhesion, and having done so he turns his attention to the members who seem, on the contrary, illdisposed, and endeavours to discover why they are hostile to the accused. This is the delicate part of his task, for there may be an infinity of reasons for condemning a man, apart from the sentiment of justice.

These few lines resume the entire mechanism of the art of oratory, and we see why the speech prepared in advance has so slight an effect, it being necessary to be able to modify the terms employed from moment to moment in accordance with the impression produced.

The orator does not require to convert to his views all the members of a jury, but only the leading spirits among it who will determine the general opinion. As in all crowds, so in juries there are a small number of individuals who serve as guides to the rest. "I have found by experience," says the counsel cited above, "that one or two energetic men suffice to carry the rest of the jury with them." It is those two or three whom it is necessary to convince by skilful suggestions. First of all, and above all, it is necessary to please them. The man forming part of a crowd whom one has succeeded in pleasing is on the point of being convinced, and is quite disposed to accept as excellent any arguments that may be offered him.

GABRIEL TARDE
(1843–1904)

Social Psychology: Laws of Imitation [4]

By imitation I mean every impression of an inter-psychical photography, so to speak, willed or not willed, passive or active. If we observe that wherever there is a social relation between two living beings, there we have imitation in this sense of the word (either of one by the other or of others by both, when, for example, a man converses with another in a common language, making new verbal *proofs* from very old negatives), we shall have to admit that a sociologist was justified in taking this notion as a look-out post.

I might have been much more justly criticised for having overstretched the meaning of the word *invention*. I have certainly applied this name to all individual *initiatives*, not only without considering the extent in which they are self-conscious—for the individual often innovates unconsciously, and, as a matter of fact, the most imitative man is an innovator on some side or other—but without paying the slightest attention in the world to the degree of difficulty or merit of the innovation in question.

* * * * *

There are two ways of imitating, as a matter of fact, namely, to act exactly like one's model, or to do exactly the contrary. Hence the necessity of those divergences which Spencer points out, without explaining, in his law of progressive differentiation. Nothing can be affirmed without suggesting, no matter how simple the social environment, not only the idea that is affirmed, but the negation of this idea as well. This is the reason why the supernatural, in asserting itself through theologies, suggests naturalism, its negation. . . . This is the reason why the affirmation of idealism gives birth to the idea of materialism; why the establishment of monarchy engenders the idea of republicanism, etc.

Let us say, then, from this wider point of view, that a society is a group of people who display many resemblances produced either by imitation or by *counter-imitation*. For men often counter-imitate one another, particularly when they have neither the modesty to imitate directly nor the power to invent. In counter-imitating one another, that is to say, in doing or saying the exact opposite of what they observe being done or said, they are becoming more and more assimilated, just as much assimilated as if they did or said precisely what was being done or said around them. Next to conforming to custom in the matter of funerals, marriages, visits, and manners, there is nothing more imitative than fighting against one's natural inclination to follow the current of these things, or than pretending to go against it. In the Middle Ages the *black mass* arose from a counter-imitation of the Catholic mass. In his book on the expression of the emotions, Darwin very properly gives a large place to the need of *counter-expression*.

* * * * *

The supreme law of imitation seems to be its tendency towards indefinite progression. This immanent and immense kind of ambition is the soul of the universe. It expresses itself, physically, in the conquest of space by light, vitally, in the claim of even the humblest species to cover the entire globe with its kind. It seems to impel every discovery or innovation, however futile, including the most insignificant individual innovations, to scatter itself through the whole of the indefinitely broadened social field. But unless this tendency be backed up by the coming together of inventions which are logically and teleologically auxiliary, or by the help of the prestige which belongs to alleged superiorities, it is checked by the different obstacles which it has successively to overcome or to turn aside. These obstacles are the logical and teleological contradictions which are opposed to it by other inventions, or the barriers which have been raised up by a thousand causes, by racial pride and prejudice, for the most part, between different families and tribes and peoples and, within each people or tribe, between different classes. Consequently,

[4] Gabriel Tarde, *The Laws of Imitation*, trans. Elsie Clews Parsons (New York: Henry Holt, 1903), pp. 366–370, xiv–xivii; original French, *Lois de l'imitation* (1890).

if a good idea is introduced in one of these groups, it propagates itself without any difficulty until it finds itself stopped short by the group's frontiers. Fortunately, this arrest is only a slowing up. It is true that, at first, in the case of class barriers, a happy innovation which has happened to originate and make its way in a lower class, does not, during periods of hereditary aristocracy and of physiological inequality, so to speak, spread further, unless the advantage of adopting it appear plain to the higher classes; but, on the other hand, innovations which have been made or accepted by the latter classes easily reach down, as I have shown already, to those lower levels which are accustomed to feel their prestige. And it happens that, as a result of this prolonged descent, the lower strata gradually mount up, step by step, to swell the highest ranks with their successive increments. Thus, through assimilating themselves with their models, the copies come to equal them, that is, they become capable of becoming models in their turn, while assuming a superiority which is no longer hereditary, which is no longer centred in the whole person, but which is individual and vicarious. The march of imitation from top to bottom still goes on, but the inequality which it implies has changed in character. Instead of an aristocratic, intrinsically organic inequality, we have a democratic inequality, of an entirely social origin, which we may call inequality if we wish, but which is really a reciprocity of invariably impersonal prestiges, alternating from individual to individual and from profession to profession. In this way, the field of imitation has been constantly growing and freeing itself from heredity.

In the second place, in regard to barriers between families, tribes, or peoples, it is equally true that while the knowledge or institutions or beliefs or industries which belong to any group while it is powerful and triumphant, spread without difficulty to neighbouring groups that have been conquered and brought low; on the other hand, the examples of the weak and vanquished, if we except the case of those whose civilisation is obviously superior, are practically nonexistent for their conquerors. Hence it follows, parenthetically, that war is much more of a civiliser for the conquered than for the conqueror, for the latter does not deign to learn from the former, whereas the former submits himself to the ascendency of victory and borrows from his enemy a number of fruitful ideas to add to his national store. The Egyptians took nothing from the books of the captive Hebrews. They made a great mistake, whereas the Jews gained much inspiration from the hieroglyphics of their masters. But, as I have said, when a people dominates others through its brilliancy, others, who heretofore had imitated none but their forefathers, imitate it. Now, this extra-national propagation of imitation, to which I have given the name of fashion, is, at bottom, merely the application to the relations between states of the law which governs the relations between classes. Thanks to the invasion of fashion, imitation always descends from the state which is for the time being superior to those which are for the time inferior, just as it descends from the highest to the lowest rungs of the social ladder. Consequently, we shall not be surprised to see the rule of fashion producing effects in the former case similar to those produced by it in the matter. In effect, just as the radiation of the examples of the higher classes results in preparing the way for their enlargement, where imitation is facile and reciprocal, through the absorption of the lower classes by them, so the contagious prestige of preponderating states results in preparing the way for their extension, for the extension of states which were originally families, then tribes, and, later, cities and nations, and which have been constantly enlarged through the assimilation of neighbours whom they have annexed, or through the annexation of neighbours whom they have assimilated.

Another analogy. Just as the play of imitation from top to bottom leads, in its continuation, to so-called democratic equality, that is to say, to the fusion of all classes into one, in which reciprocal imitation is admirably practised through the acceptance of one another's respective superiorities, so a prolonged process of fashion-imitation ends by putting pupil-peoples upon the same level, both in their armaments and in their arts and sciences, with their master-people. It creates a kind of federation between them like that which is called in modern times, for example, the European balance of power. By this is meant the reciprocity of every kind of service or exchange which goes on incessantly between the different great centres which divide up European civilisation. In this way, in international relations, the free and unimpeded domain of imitation has been enlarged with scarcely an interruption.

But, at the same time, Tradition and Custom, the conservative forms of imitation, have been fixing and perpetuating its new acquisitions and consolidating its increments in the heart of every class of people that has been raised up through the example of higher classes or of more civilised neighbours. At the same time, too, every germ of imitation which may have been secreted in the brain of any imitator in the form of a new belief or aspiration, of a new idea or faculty, has been steadily developing in outward signs, in words and acts which, according to the law of the march from within to without, have penetrated into his entire nervous and muscular systems.

* * * * *

Every act of imitation, therefore, results in the preparation of conditions that will make possible and that will facilitate new acts of imitation of an increasingly free and rational and, at the same time, precise and definite character. These conditions are the gradual suppression of caste, class, and nationality barriers and, I may add, the lessening of distances through more rapid means of locomotion, as well as through greater density of population.

ALFRED BINET
(1857–1911)
and
THEODORE SIMON
(1873–1962)

Binet–Simon Intelligence Test [5]

The Method

The method here presented is one by which the intelligence of a child may be estimated. The method consists in asking the child some precise questions and having him perform some simple experiments; these questions and experiments are called tests. As much research has revealed which of these tests a normal child passes successfully at a given age, it is easy to ascertain whether the child under examination gives results equal to the normal child of his age, or whether he is advanced or retarded in relation to this norm.

The series of tests used in the method, grouped according to age, are as follows:

---

[5] Alfred Binet and Th. Simon, *A Method of Measuring the Development of the Intelligence of Young Children*, trans. Clara Harrison Town (Chicago: Chicago Medical Book, 3rd ed., 1913), pp. 7–9, 11–14, 18, 20–25, 27, 30–44, 47, 49, 51–61; original French from the *Bulletin de la Société libre pour l'Étude Psychologique de l'Enfant* (April, 1911).

THREE YEARS

Shows nose, eyes and mouth.
Repeats two digits.
Enumerates objects in a picture.
Gives family name.
Repeats a sentence of six syllables.

FOUR YEARS

Gives own sex.
Names key, knife and penny.
Repeats three digits.
Compares two lines.

FIVE YEARS

Compares two weights.
Copies a square.
Repeats a sentence of ten syllables.
Counts four pennies.
Game of patience with two pieces.

SIX YEARS

Distinguishes between morning and afternoon
Defines in terms of use.
Copies a lozenge.
Counts thirteen pennies.
Compares faces from the aesthetic point of view.

SEVEN YEARS

Right hand, left ear.
Describes a picture.
Executes three commissions.
Gives value of 9 sous, three of which are double.
Names four colors.

EIGHT YEARS

Compares two remembered objects.
Counts from 20 to 0.
Indicates omissions in pictures.
Gives the day and date.
Repeats five digits.

NINE YEARS

Gives change from 20 sous.
Defines in terms superior to use.
Recognizes all the pieces of our money.
Enumerates the months.
Understands easy questions.

TEN YEARS

Arranges five weights.
Copies drawings from memory.
Criticises absurd statements.
Understands difficult questions.
Uses three given words in two sentences.

TWELVE YEARS

Resists suggestion (length of lines).
Composes one sentence containing 3 given words.
Says more than sixty words in three minutes.
Defines abstract terms.
Discovers the sense of a sentence the words of
    which are mixed.

FIFTEEN YEARS

Repeats seven digits.
Gives three rhymes.
Repeats a sentence of 26 syllables.
Interprets a picture.
Solves a problem from several facts.

ADULT

Solves the paper cutting test.
Rearranges a triangle.
Gives differences of meanings of abstract terms.
Solves the question of the President.
Gives the resumé of the thought of Hervieu.

* * * * *

Description of Tests

Children of Three Years

I. *Shows Nose, Eyes and Mouth.* To perform the test one should look steadily at the
child, attract his attention, and repeat several
times: "Show me your nose," or "Put your
finger on your nose," and follow this by
repeating the same order for the eyes and
the mouth. Sometimes the child does not
comply because he is distracted, or because
he is timid and too bashful to do that which
is desired, but usually, with a little insistence,
a response is secured. Sometimes a child
shows his nose by thrusting it forward,
without making any hand movement, or
shows his mouth by opening it, as would an
animal. This is, in fact, an animal stage,
when the hand is still a paw, and not an organ
used for significant or expressive movements.

* * * * *

II. *Repeats Two Digits.* The repetition of
numbers requires very nearly the same sort
of effort as the repetition of sentences; however, as numbers have so much less meaning
than sentences, they make little appeal to the
intellect or interest, and therefore require a
greater effort of attention. As a result, a
child of three years who can repeat a sentence
of six syllables can repeat only two digits.
The association of ideas triples the memory
span.

* * * * *

III. *Enumerates Objects in a Picture.*
. . . We reverse the former method, having the
child name the objects which he sees pictured
before him, thus testing his ability to recall
the name of an object which he sees. It is
much more difficult for the child to pass in
thought from an object to its name than from
a name to the corresponding object. Before
the child is placed a picture on which appear
many objects with which he is familiar and
which are interesting to him. He is then asked
to tell us what he sees. He thus has the
opportunity to use what language ability he
may possess in expressing his ideas, and also
the liberty of choosing those objects which
please him most; the response will show us
what interests the child and will also give us
an idea of his mentality, of his manner of
perceiving, interpreting and reasoning. The

test has the remarkable advantage of serving as a diagnostic test of three different intellectual levels. The responses of the subject indicate whether he is at the level of three, seven, or twelve years.

* * * * *

IV. *Gives Family Name.* We now ask for a piece of information which a child of three certainly should possess; its family name. All children of this age know their first names, that goes without saying, or the pet name by which they are usually called; but the family name is not so familiar. However, they are expected to know it at school, and at the "Maternelle" they are habitually called by their family name.

* * * * *

V. *Repeats a Sentence of Six Syllables,* After the comprehension of words, the next step in the development of language is not, as one might think, the verbal expression of thought, the naming of desired objects, but a repetition of words heard. It is easier, apparently, to echo a word than to use it independently—to pass from an idea to a word ... A child of three, if he will make the effort, can easily repeat a word or a phrase.

Children of Four Years

I. *Gives Own Sex.* "Are you a little boy or a little girl?" This is the very simple question which we use. Three-year-old children do not all succeed in answering it. The correct response is: "A little boy" or "A little girl." Sometimes the child merely says yes or no. It is then necessary to ask two distinct questions: "Are you a little boy?" "Are you a little girl?" It takes very little to confuse at this age.

* * * * *

II. *Names Key, Knife, Penny.* Another test of spoken language, but differing from the language suggested by pictures; it is much more difficult. In a picture the child chooses what he wishes to name, and names those objects which he recognizes; here we choose the object; that is, we force him to name some one object and no other.

* * * * *

III. *Repeats Three Digits.* This test is conducted in the same manner as that calling for the repetition of two digits. No further remarks are necessary.

* * * * *

IV. *Compares Two Lines.* Here are some tests which present unexpected difficulties. An imbecile who understands when one says: "Go and open the door," when the words are not supplemented by either a gesture or a glance in the right direction, is unable to compare two lines in regard to their length. Does he see that the two lines are of unequal length? It is quite possible. If it were two biscuits, would he take the longer or the shorter? That is yet to be determined. But he does not comprehend the words: "*the longer;*" he does not understand that he is asked to compare two lines, and, pointing at random, he foolishly puts his finger on the space between the two lines. The child of three years does the same thing. Not until its fourth year does a normal child succeed with this test.

* * * * *

Children of Five Years

I. *Compares Two Weights.* This is a comparison similar to that of the lines; but one judges the lines at a glance, while it is necessary to take the boxes in the hand and heft them; often they are taken in the same hand and compared successively. Conclusion: Very few children younger than five succeed with this test, while those of four succeed in comparing the length of the lines.

* * * * *

II. *Copies a Square.* This is the first time that we have put a penholder into the child's hand.

* * * * *

III. *Repeats Sentences of Ten Syllables.*

* * * * *

IV. *Counts Four Pennies.* The objection is made that enumeration is a test of scholarship which implies instruction rather than intelligence. The objection is just; but where is the being so deprived of tutelage that no one has ever taught him to count? We have studied many imbeciles in the asylums; all those who have sufficient intelligence to count have learned to do so. In spite of the compulsory education laws, there still remain many illiterate people; it is said that there are more than five per cent, among the soldiers, but has one ever met an individual who has never learned to count if his intelligence permitted it? Such an one would be very rare.

* * * * *

V. *Game of Patience with Two Pieces.* This is a game demanding an arrangement, a combining of pieces, which pleases children; they often amuse themselves at school by constructing objects with cubes. It is a game and at the same time a work for the intelligence, operating with the given material, some sensations and some movements. If the operation is analyzed, it is found to consist of the following elements: 1. To keep in mind the end to be attained, that is to say, the figure to be formed; it is necessary to comprehend this end; it is necessary also to think about it, not to lose sight of it. 2. To try different combinations, under the influence of this directing idea, which often guides the efforts of the child, though he be unconscious of the fact. 3. To judge the formed combination, compare it with the model, and decide whether it is the correct one.

* * * * *

Children of Six Years

I. *Distinguishes between Morning and Evening.* The perception of time is a slow development with a child; for a long time yesterday and tomorrow are confused. The distinction of our test is brought out by the following question: "Is it morning or afternoon now?" Some children give a chance answer, others simply say "yes"; not until the age of six is a child absolutely sure whether it is morning or afternoon. Before reaching this age they can often tell, however, whether they have or have not eaten their mid-day meal.

* * * * *

II. *Defines in Terms of Use.* Thus far the verbal responses required from the little ones have all been short; a word or two sufficed. Now we are about to ask for a phrase, for an object can not be defined without forming one. The definition is not solely an exercise and test for language; it serves to show us the idea which a child has formed of an object, the manner in which he has conceived it, the point of view which is to him the most interesting.

* * * * *

III. *Copies a Lozenge.* Hospital experience suggested this test. We were surprised to find imbeciles who could copy a square and yet failed in the attempt to copy a lozenge. These figures are not very different in form, but the direction of the lines of the lozenge is much more difficult to reproduce. We found the same true of the children in the regular schools; at five years of age a child can copy a square; not until six can he copy a lozenge; and even at seven one-fifth of the children fail. At six years one-half fail.

* * * * *

IV. *Counts Thirteen Pennies.* The difficulty of counting is so much increased by the addition of objects that it is necessary to wait until the sixth year before requiring a child to count thirteen pennies.

* * * * *

V. *Compares Faces from the Aesthetic Point of View.* It is incontestable that all young children have the sense of the beautiful, and that it can be brought out by presenting the problem in a simple form; for example, as a comparison, a choice between two faces, one of which is pretty, the other ugly; it is necessary that the contrast between the two faces be very great.

* * * * *

Children of Seven Years

I. *Right Hand, Left Ear.* Another notion gained through instruction, but so easily acquired that the lack of it is conspicuous. The child is asked: "Show your right hand," and this done; "Show your left ear." The last question is almost a trap, for having commenced by asking for the right hand, a tendency is created to show the right ear.

* * * * *

II. *Describes a Picture.* We have seen that at three, four and five years enumeration is the rule and description quite unusual. At six years a very small number of children, scarcely a sixth, try description. At seven years such progress in language has been made that description has become quite general; there are very few exceptions, and this test shows the enormous advance from the point of view of language which takes place between six and seven years.

* * * * *

III. *Executes Three Commissions.* Among the people quite young children are sent on little errands to the stores, to buy milk, bread, to the butcher's more than all, and to bring home a bottle of wine. Physicians who frequent the clinics for retarded children recognize that these children, though they can be trusted to perform one commission, can not be given several at the same time.

* * * * *

IV. *Counts Nine Sous (3 single, 3 double).* On a corner of the table are arranged side by side three single and three double sous. The subject is shown the money and directed: "Count that money and tell me how much is there."

* * * * *

V. *Names Four Colors.* Tests with colors can be indefinitely multiplied. We have chosen the fundamental colors, red, blue, green and yellow, and have omitted those the names of which are less familiar to children; for example, violet and orange. The test is not of the perception and distinction of colors, but the naming of them, which is quite different.

* * * * *

Children of Eight Years

I. *Compares Two Remembered Objects.* This is a valuable test because it does not depend in the least on instruction, and brings into play the natural good sense of the subject. It consists in investigating whether the subject can, in thinking of two objects, distinguish a difference between them; the perception of a difference is in fact the habitual and the most natural result of a comparison. We prepare for the test by talking to the child as follows: "You have seen butterflies, you

know what they are?—Yes.—And flies, you know them also?—Yes.—Are they alike, a fly and a butterfly?—

* * * * *

II. *Counts from 20 to 0.* This is partly a test of school knowledge; one must have learned to count to be able to reverse the process.

* * * * *

III. *Indicates Omissions in Pictures.* Four pictures are shown successively; . . . in one an eye is .lacking, in one the nose, in one the mouth, in one the arms. The child is asked each time: "What is missing in this picture?"

* * * * *

IV. *Gives the Day and Date.* Four facts are required in answer to this question: the day of the week, the month, the day of the month, and the year.

* * * * *

V. *Repeats Five Digits.* The method is described above. Three digits are used at four years; it is necessary to postpone increasing the number to five until we reach seven-year-old children, and still but three-quarters pass the test.

Children of Nine Years

I. *Gives Change from 20 Sous.* This is a test which presupposes some little instruction; but it has so great a practical value that we use it.

* * * * *

II. *Defines in Terms Superior to Use.* This test is explained above. At seven and at eight years one-half of the children give definitions of this kind. At nine years they all do.

* * * * *

III. *Recognizes all the Pieces of Our Money.* These are the following: 0 fr. 05—0 fr. 10—0 fr. 25—0 fr. 50—1 fr.—2 fr.—5 fr.—10 fr.—20 fr.

* * * * *

IV. *Enumerates the Months.* The subject should name the months in 15 seconds without omission or inversion. We, however, allow the error of one omission or one inversion.

* * * * *

V. *Understands Easy Questions.* We give the text of the questions and some good and bad responses.

* * * * *

Children of Ten Years

I. *Arrange Five Weights.* An excellent test which presupposes no schooling or acquired knowledge, and expresses intelligence in its most natural form; but it is a special intelligence, a sensorial intelligence, not at all verbal; and some children who use words easily fail to arrange the weights.

* * * * *

II. *Copies Drawings from Memory.* The child is asked to draw from memory two drawings.

* * * * *

III. *Criticises Absurd Phrases.* This is not the test of which we first thought. Our aim was to test the judgment of the child.

* * * * *

IV. *Understands Difficult Questions.* These questions are similar to the preceding ones, but more subtle, and present in addition some difficulties of vocabulary.

* * * * *

V. *Uses Three Given Words in Two Sentences.* This is the first time that we have asked for an invention. This one is verbal. It presupposes that the child talks, writes, and understands the meaning of the expression "a sentence." Three words are written on a piece of paper—Paris, Fortune, Stream. They are read to the child several times, then he is told: "You make a sentence and use in it these three words."

* * * * *

Children of Twelve Years

I. *Resists Suggestion (Length of Lines).* This test belongs to the twelfth year. A little white paper book of 6 pages is made. On the first page two lines are drawn with ink *a*

and *b;* the first, that is, the one on the left, is four centimeters long, and the second five centimeters; they are placed in line with each other and one centimeter apart; on the second page two similar lines are drawn, the first five centimeters, the second six; on the third page the first line is six centimeters and the second seven. On each of the three following pages two lines are drawn in the same position, but all are of the same length, seven centimeters. We have, then, if we designate the lines by the letters of the alphabet, the following order:

$$a < b$$
$$c < d$$
$$e < j$$
$$g = h$$
$$i = k$$
$$l = m$$

In showing the first three pairs of lines, the experimenter says to the child: "Which is the longer of these two lines?" When the three last pairs are reached, the form of the question is slightly changed, and he limits himself to the words, "And these?" The child succeeds in the test if he judges two of the last three pairs of lines to be equal.

* * * * *

II. *Uses Three Given Words in One Sentence.* This test is explained above. All children succeed at twelve years and scarcely a third at ten.

* * * * *

III. *Says More than Sixty Words in Three Minutes.* The child is told to name in three minutes as many words as he possibly can.

* * * * *

IV. *Defines Abstract Terms.* Definitions are required for three abstract terms—charity, justice and kindness. The formula used is very simple: What is ——————?

* * * * *

V. *Derives the Sense of a Sentence the Words of Which Are Mixed.* This test is suggested by the tests of Ebbinghaus which require the subject to supply missing words in sentences. We use the three following groups of words which we present to the child, saying: "Put those words in their proper order and find the sentence which they make."

1. For—an—the—at—hour—early—we—country—started.

* * * * *

Children of Fifteen Years

I. *Repeats Seven Digits.* This test is made in the same manner as that calling for the repetition of five digits. The child is told in advance that he will have seven numbers to repeat. One success in three trials suffices.

* * * * *

II. *Gives Three Rhymes.* We begin by asking the subject whether he knows the meaning of the word rhyme. Whether he knows it or not (and often he thinks that he knows it when in reality he does not) we give him the following explanation: "Two words which rhyme are two words which end with the same sound. Thus, pumpkin, napkin—*pumpkin! napkin!...*"

* * * * *

III. *Repeats a Sentence of 26 Syllables.* We have composed a series of 22 sentences regularly increasing in length, from 2 to 44 syllables, and each formed of words very easy to understand. By the use of these we can easily measure an individual's ability for verbal repetition.

* * * * *

IV. *Interprets a Picture.* See above.

* * * * *

V. *Solves a Problem from Several Facts.* Another problem, but one which requires good sense rather than insight. We have drawn up two situations each of which presents a problem. Here they are:

1. *A woman walking in the forest of Fontainebleau stopped suddenly dreadfully frightened, hurried to the nearest policeman and told him that she had just seen hanging to the limb of a tree* —————— (after a pause) *what?*

2. *My neighbor has just received some singular visitors. He received one after the other a doctor, a lawyer and a priest. What is going on at my neighbor's?*

* * * * *

Adults

I. *Solves the Paper Cutting Test.* A square sheet of paper folded along both diameters is given to the subject; in the middle of the edge which presents but a single fold, a small triangle (1 cm. in height and having for its base the paper's edge) is drawn. We say to the subject: "Here is a sheet of paper which has been folded in four; suppose that here (pointing to the triangle) I cut away the little triangle of paper which is marked out. Now, if I should unfold the paper, what would I see? Draw the paper, showing how and where it would be cut."

* * * * *

II. *Reconstructs a Triangle.* A visiting card has been cut in two pieces along the diagonal. . . . The pieces are placed on a sheet of paper in their original position. The subject is directed: "Look well at the lower piece. Suppose that I turn it around and place this edge (tracing the edge *a—c* with the finger) on this edge (*a—b* of the upper piece). Suppose further that the point *c* is placed just on the point *b*. Now, I take away the piece; in your imagination, place it as I have described and draw its outline in this position. Commence by following the outline of the upper piece."

* * * * *

III. *Gives Difference in Meaning of Abstract Terms.* "What is the difference between laziness and idleness?—Between event (*événement*) and advent (*avènement*).—Between an evolution and a revolution?" These are the questions that are asked. Correct answers to two suffice.

* * * * *

IV. *Solves the Question concerning the President.* Question: "There are three principal differences between a king and a president of the republic. What are they?" They are the following: Royalty is hereditary, it lasts during the life of the monarch, and it confers very great powers; a president of the republic is elected, his term of office is limited, and his powers are not so great as are those of a king.

* * * * *

V. *Summarizes an Observation Made by*

Hervieu. The following paragraph is read slowly and impressively: . . .

Many opinions have been given on the value of life. Some call it good, others call it bad. It would be more just to say, that it is mediocre,

for on the one hand our happiness is never so great as we would have it, and on the other hand our misfortunes are never so great as others would have them. It is this mediocrity of life which makes it just, or rather which prevents it from being radically unjust.

JEAN PIAGET
(1896–   )

Child Psychology:
Reasoning in Children [6]

Let us suppose that future research is undertaken dealing with a far larger number of children's sentences, and involving a far more thorough examination both personal and collective than that to which we had to limit ourselves. Let us further suppose that these researches eventually demolish the age-limits which we have given, eventually show that difficulties experienced by children with regard to "because" are on the average more or less lasting than we had thought. We believe that in spite of such changes our qualitative analyses would remain of value on a large scale. We would still claim that the child's difficulty in the use of the empirical or logical "because," in the use of "therefore" and "then," or in the use of the terms of discordance are bound up with logical difficulties which in their turn we would still claim to be traceable to social factors such as argument, collaboration between children, and so on.

What further conclusions are to be drawn from this study of reasoning in the child? In the first place we must emphasize the fact that the above enquiries do not bear directly upon reasoning nor, above all, on causality in the child. They bear simply upon his aptitude for inventing sentences, in a word, upon his aptitude for narrative and argument. Now these aptitudes should be neither exaggerated nor underestimated in their importance. The practice of narrative and argument does not lead to invention, but it compels a certain

coherence of thought. A mind incapable of argument and guilty of the verbal confusions which we have been examining in children may be creative, but it is certainly not logical. From this point of view the grammatical study which we have been making leads to certain conclusions, and in particular, to the two that follow. Firstly, that the child, unconscious as he is of his own thought-process, can only reason about isolated or about more or less special cases. Secondly, and this is the most important—that his judgments, being juxtaposed, are lacking in logical necessity.

The study of logical justification showed that if the child is unable to give a local reason for his judgment, even when this judgment is true in itself and correctly introduced in the context, this is because he is not conscious of the motives that have guided his choice. Things happen then more or less as follows. In the presence of certain objects of thought or of certain affirmations the child, in virtue of previous experiences, adopts a certain way of reacting and thinking which is always the same, and which might be called a schema of reasoning. Such schemas are the functional equivalents of general propositions, but since the child is not conscious of these schemas before discussion and a desire for proof have laid them bare and at the same time changed their character, they cannot be said to constitute implicit general propositions. They simply constitute certain unconscious tendencies which live their own life but are submitted to no general systematization and consequently lead to no logical exactitude. To put it in another way, they form a logic of action but not yet a logic of thought.

This absence of conscious realization explains why the child only reasons about particular cases. Since the schema is the only

---

[6] Jean Piaget, *Judgment and Reasoning in the Child*, trans. Marjorie Warden (London: Routledge & Kegan Paul, 1928), pp. 55–57, 130–134; original French, *Le jugement et le raisonnement chez l'enfant* (Neuchâtel and Paris, 1924). Reprinted by permission.

general element in childish ratiocination, and since the schema remains unconscious, the child will become aware only of the discrete objects which occupy his mind. Thus the study of "because" in logical justification showed that even when the child tries ·to prove his statements, he appeals neither to laws nor to general rules, but to singular and specific reasons: "The little cat ate the big dog," "The little cat is little and the big dog is big," "On the way there the road goes up," etc. Furthermore, this was confirmed by an examination of the deductions introduced by the word "then." The deduction moves from one individual case to another: "Then I shall be alone," "Then it is inside out," etc. Finally, our study of discordance indirectly confirms the same law. If children never make use of explicit discordance and do not understand implicit discordance until after the age of 7–8 this is obviously because the notion of an exception to a rule which is presupposed in the notion of discordance between cause and effect is not a primitive notion, and is not one that is familiar to them. For there to be exceptions, there must obviously have been rules, and if the child fails to understand the fact that there are exceptions, it must be because he has never formulated any rules.

The consequence of this fact that the child's formulated thought only takes place in connexion with particular or specific cases is that we cannot speak about deductive thought as such before a very advanced stage of development. For deduction presupposes general propositions, whether these serve to characterize the individual objects with which the reasoning process is concerned, or whether they constitute the aim which the process of deduction has set out to reach. Now the motor schemas of which we were speaking just now cannot do the work of general propositions, and what prevents them is the fact that they do not confront one another in the subject's consciousness and thus give rise to syntheses and oppositions which alone would favour the appearance of logical addition and multiplication.

Provisionally, therefore, we have established three points: absence of conscious realization (*prise de conscience*), absence of general propositions, and absence of deduction.

* * * * *

The child, owing to the difficulty he experienced (a difficulty due to ego-centrism) in becoming aware of his own thought, reasoned only about isolated or particular cases; generalization and consequently any sustained deduction do not come naturally to him. He juxtaposes successive judgments instead of connecting them, so that there is a lack of internal necessity about his thought. Even when the child comes to generalize and deduce with less difficulty, formal deduction is still a closed book to him, because he cannot shake off his personal beliefs nor reason from assumptions suggested from the outside.

* * * * *

The conclusion to which we are finally led is this. The child does not realize that certain ideas, even such as are obviously relative for an adult are relations between at least two terms. Thus he does not realize that a brother must necessarily be the brother of somebody, that an object must necessarily be to the right or left of somebody, or that a part must necessarily be part of a whole, but thinks of all these notions as existing in themselves, absolutely. Or again he defines a family, not by the relation of kinship which unites its members, but by the space they occupy, by the immediate point of view from which he sees them grouped around him in a house. It should be noted that such behaviour is universal, and that the list of examples might have been added to indefinitely. We are indebted, for example, to the kindness of Mme. Passello, a Geneva schoolmistress, for the knowledge of the fact that at the age of 7 the notions of "friend" and "enemy" are still devoid of relativity. An enemy is "*a soldier*," "*someone who fights*," "*a horrid person*," "*someone who is horrid*," "*someone who wants to hurt you*," etc. It is therefore not a person who is an enemy in relation to someone else, but an enemy in himself. Similarly for a friend.

We discovered innumerable examples of the same kind with Mlle. Hahnloser in connexion with the word "foreigner." At the age when children can say that foreigners are people from another country (about 9–10), they are still ignorant of the fact that they are themselves foreigners for these people. All the more reason therefore for their ignorance of the reciprocity of this relation when the term is reserved for people coming from another country but living in Geneva. Such examples could be multiplied indefinitely.

* * * * *

Now such a tendency as this—realistic because it is ego-centric—helps just as much as failure in conscious realization of thought, which is equally the outcome of ego-centrism, to confine the reasoning process of the child to individual or particular cases. For why does the inability to become conscious of thought lead to a form of reasoning that concerns itself only with individual objects? Because, by leaving in the unconscious the motives which guide his thought, and the consciousness of which alone would lead him to general propositions, ego-centrism functioning unconsciously as it inevitably must, leads the child to reason about immediate data only, about such or such an object given without any relation to other objects. And it is obvious that we are led to exactly the same result, from another angle by the childish realism which we have been examining. Just because he fails to grasp the relativity of a notion such as that of brother, or of right and left, the child will be unable to generalize it.

This is why he cannot succeed in finding which is the darkest of the three little girls who are compared to one another by colour relations, nor which is the most to the right of the three objects in a row before him.

Even when he is reasoning about single objects, the child cannot generalize relative notions sufficiently to apply them to all possible cases. Here again we have a spurious generality in place of true generalization. The child unconsciously extends his own immediate point of view to all possible points of view (realism), instead of consciously generalizing a relation which he has conceived clearly as relative and reciprocal (relativism).

Realism is therefore a kind of immediate, illegitimate generalization, while relativism is a generalization that is mediate and legitimate.

With regard to generalization then our study of the logic of relations confirms that of the logic of classes. In both cases the apparent generalization of childish logic comes from a particular and immediate schema being unconsciously applied to all the objects that will more or less fit into it, and in both cases the unconscious and uncontrolled character of the application prevents the actual formula of the reasoning from extending beyond the particular cases. In both cases, in short, the realistic or immediate character of the reasoning process prevents the establishment of relations and stands in the way of generalization. . . .

In addition to this, childish realism, as opposed to adult logic of relations, also leads to a confirmation of the results we reached in studying formal reason. We saw there that until the age of 11–12 children were incapable of entering sufficiently into the point of view of their interlocutors to be able to reason correctly about the latter's beliefs, i.e. that they were incapable of reasoning from pure assumptions, of reasoning correctly from premises which they did not believe in. Now, this age of 11–12 at which such reasoning becomes possible is likewise the age when the relations of brother and of right and left are beginning to be completely mastered. This may be more than a mere coincidence, for the mastery in both cases has the same trait—desubjectivation of thought and the power to see relations as such and handle them in an objective manner.

Our study of the logic of relations thus confirms that of the logic of classes and of more general logical relations. Both of them show that the thought of the child passes from a state of ego-centric immediacy, in which single objects only are known and thought of absolutely, and made to bear no relation to one another, to a state of objective relativism in which the mind extracts from these objects innumerable relations capable of bringing about the generalization of propositions and reciprocity of different points of view.

18

British and German/American Psychology of Individual Differences

FRANCIS GALTON
(1822–1911)

Hereditary Intelligence [1]

I propose to show in this book that a man's natural abilities are derived by inheritance, under exactly the same limitations as are the form and physical features of the whole organic world. Consequently, as it is easy, notwithstanding those limitations, to obtain by careful selection a permanent breed of dogs or horses gifted with peculiar powers of running, or of doing anything else, so it would be quite practicable to produce a highly-gifted race of men by judicious marriages during several consecutive generations. I shall show that social agencies of an ordinary character, whose influences are little suspected, are at this moment working towards the degradation of human nature, and that others are working towards its improvement. I conclude that each generation has enormous power over the natural gifts of those that follow.

* * * * *

The general plan of my argument is to show that high reputation is a pretty accurate test of high ability; next to discuss the relationships of a large body of fairly eminent men— namely, the Judges of England from 1660 to 1868, the Statesmen of the time of George III., and the Premiers during the last 100 years —and to obtain from these a general survey of the laws of heredity in respect to genius. Then I shall examine, in order, the kindred of the most illustrious Commanders, men of Literature and of Science, Poets, Painters, and Musicians, of whom history speaks. I shall also discuss the kindred of a certain

selection of Divines and of modern Scholars. Then will follow a short chapter, by way of comparison, on the hereditary transmission of physical gifts, as deduced from the relationships of certain classes of Oarsmen and Wrestlers. . . .

It will be observed that I deal with more than one grade of ability. Those upon whom the greater part of my volume is occupied, and on whose kinships my argument is most securely based, have been generally reputed as endowed by nature with extraordinary genius. There are so few of these men that, although they are scattered throughout the whole historical period of human existence, their number does not amount to more than 400, and yet a considerable proportion of them will be found to be interrelated.

Another grade of ability with which I deal is that which includes numerous highly eminent, and all the illustrious names of modern English history, whose immediate descendants are living among us, whose histories are popularly known, and whose relationships may readily be traced by the help of biographical dictionaries, peerages, and similar books of reference.

* * * * *

I have no patience with the hypothesis occasionally expressed, and often implied, especially in tales written to teach children, to be good, that babies are born pretty much alike, and that the sole agencies in creating differences between boy and boy, and man and man, are steady application and moral effort. It is in the most unqualified manner that I object to pretensions of natural equality. The experiences of the nursery, the school, the University, and of professional careers,

---

[1] Francis Galton, *Hereditary Genius: An Inquiry into Its Laws and Consequences* (London, 1869), ch. 1, 3.

are a chain of proofs to the contrary. I acknowledge freely the great power of education and social influences in developing the active powers of the mind, just as I acknowledge the effect of use in developing the muscles of a blacksmith's arm, and no further. Let the blacksmith labour as he will, he will find there are certain feats beyond his power that are well within the strength of a man of herculean make, even although the latter may have led a sedentary life.

* * * * *

Everybody who has trained himself to physical exercises discovers the extent of his muscular powers to a nicety. When he begins to walk, to row, to use the dumb bells, or to run, he finds to his great delight that his thews strengthen, and his endurance of fatigue increases day after day. So long as he is a novice, he perhaps flatters himself there is hardly an assignable limit to the education of his muscles; but the daily gain is soon discovered to diminish, and at last it vanishes altogether. His maximum performance becomes a rigidly determinate quantity. He learns to an inch, how high or how far he can jump, when he has attained the highest state of training. He learns to half a pound, the force he can exert on the dynamometer, by compressing it. He can strike a blow against the machine used to measure impact, and drive its index to a certain graduation, but no further. So it is in running, in rowing, in walking, and in every other form of physical exertion. There is a definite limit to the muscular powers of every man, which he cannot by any education or exertion overpass.

This is precisely analogous to the experience that every student has had of the working of his mental powers. The eager boy, when he first goes to school and confronts intellectual difficulties, is astonished at his progress. He glories in his newly-developed mental grip and growing capacity for application, and, it may be, fondly believes it to be within his reach to become one of the heroes who have left their mark upon the history of the world. The years go by; he competes in the examinations of school and college, over and over again with his fellows, and soon finds his place among them. He knows he can beat such and such of his competitors; that there are some with whom he runs on equal terms,

and others whose intellectual feats he cannot even approach. Probably his vanity still continues to tempt him, by whispering in a new strain. It tells him that classics, mathematics, and other subjects taught in universities, are mere scholastic specialities, and no test of the more valuable intellectual powers. It reminds him of numerous instances of persons who had been unsuccessful in the competitions of youth, but who had shown powers in after-life that made them the foremost men of their age. Accordingly, with newly furbished hopes, and with all the ambition of twenty-two years of age, he leaves his University and enters a larger field of competition. The same kind of experience awaits him here that he has already gone through. Opportunities occur—they occur to every man—and he finds himself incapable of grasping them. He tries, and is tried in many things. In a few years more, unless he is incurably blinded by selfconceit, he learns precisely of what performances he is capable, and what other enterprises lie beyond his compass. When he reaches mature life, he is confident only within certain limits, and knows, or ought to know, himself just as he is probably judged of by the world, with all his unmistakeable weakness and all his undeniable strength. He is no longer tormented into hopeless efforts by the fallacious promptings of overweening vanity, but he limits his undertakings to matters below the level of his reach, and finds true moral repose in an honest conviction that he is engaged in as much good work as his nature has rendered him capable of performing.

There can hardly be a surer evidence of the enormous difference between the intellectual capacity of men, than the prodigious differences in the numbers of marks obtained by those who gain mathematical honours at Cambridge. I therefore crave permission to speak at some length upon this subject, although the details are dry and of little general interest. There are between 400 and 450 students who take their degrees in each year, and of these, about 100 succeed in gaining honours in mathematics, and are ranged by the examiners in strict order of merit. About the first forty of those who take mathematical honours are distinguished by the title of wranglers, and it is a decidedly creditable thing to be even a low wrangler;

it will secure a fellowship in a small college. It must be carefully borne in mind that the distinction of being the first in this list of honours, or what is called the senior wrangler of the year, means a vast deal more than being the foremost mathematician of 400 or 450 men taken at hap-hazard. No doubt the large bulk of Cambridge men are taken almost at hap-hazard. A boy is intended by his parents for some profession; if that profession be either the Church or the Bar, it used to be almost requisite, and it is still important, that he should be sent to Cambridge or Oxford. These youths may justly be considered as having been taken at hap-hazard. But there are many others who have fairly won their way to the Universities, and are therefore selected from an enormous area. Fully one-half of the wranglers have been boys of note at their respective schools, and, conversely, almost all boys of note at schools find their way to the Universities. Hence it is that among their comparatively small number of students, the Universities include the highest youthful scholastic ability of all England. The senior wrangler, in each successive year, is the chief of these as regards mathematics, and this, the highest distinction, is, or was, continually won by youths who had no mathematical training of importance before they went to Cambridge. All their instruction had been received during the three years of their residence at the University. Now, I do not say anything here about the merits or demerits of Cambridge mathematical studies having been directed along a too narrow groove, or about the presumed disadvantages of ranging candidates in strict order of merit, instead of grouping them, as at Oxford, in classes, where their names appear alphabetically arranged. All I am concerned with here are the results; and these are most appropriate to my argument. The youths start on their three years' race as fairly as possible. They are then stimulated to run by the most powerful inducements, namely, those of competition, of honour, and of future wealth (for a good fellowship *is* wealth); and at the end of the three years they are examined most rigorously according to a system that they all understand and are equally well prepared for. The examination lasts five and a half hours a day for eight days. All the answers are carefully marked by the examiners, who add up the

marks at the end and range the candidates in strict order of merit. The fairness and thoroughness of Cambridge examinations have never had a breath of suspicion cast upon them.

Unfortunately for my purposes, the marks are not published. They are not even assigned on a uniform system, since each examiner is permitted to employ his own scale of marks; but whatever scale he uses, the results as to proportional merit are the same. I am indebted to a Cambridge examiner for a copy of his marks in respect to two examinations, in which the scales of marks were so alike as to make it easy, by a slight proportional adjustment, to compare the two together. This was, to a certain degree, a confidential communication, so that it would be improper for me to publish anything that would identify the years to which these marks refer. I simply give them as groups of figures, sufficient to show the enormous differences of merit. The lowest man in the list of honours gains less than 300 marks; the lowest wrangler gains about 1,500 marks; and the senior wrangler, in one of the lists now before me, gained more than 7,500 marks. Consequently, the lowest wrangler has more than five times the merit of the lowest junior optime, and less than one-fifth the merit of the senior wrangler.

The precise number of marks obtained by the senior wrangler in the more remarkable of these two years was 7,634; by the second wrangler in the same year, 4,123; and by the lowest man in the list of honours, only 237. Consequently, the senior wrangler obtained nearly twice as many marks as the second wrangler, and more than thirty-two times as many as the lowest man. I have received from another examiner the marks of a year in which the senior wrangler was conspicuously eminent. He obtained 9,422 marks, whilst the second in the same year—whose merits were by no means inferior to those of second wranglers in general—obtained only 5,642. The man at the bottom of the same honour list had only 309 marks, or one-thirtieth the number of the senior wrangler.

* * * * *

In other words, the senior wranglers above mentioned had *more* than thirty, or thirty-two times the ability of the lowest men on the lists of honours. They would be able to

Scale of Merit among the Men Who Obtain Mathematical Honours at Cambridge.

Number of Marks Obtained by Candidates	Number of Candidates in the Two Years, Taken Together, Who Obtained Those Marks
Under 500	24 [1]
500 to 1,000	74
1,000 to 1,500	38
1,500 to 2,000	21
2,000 to 2,500	11
2,500 to 3,000	8
3,000 to 3,500	11
3,500 to 4,000	5
4,000 to 4,500	2
4,500 to 5,000	1
5,000 to 5,500	3
5,500 to 6,000	1
6,000 to 6,500	0
6,500 to 7,000	0
7,000 to 7,500	0
7,500 to 8,000	1
	200

The results of two years are thrown into a single table.
The total number of marks obtainable in each year was 17,000.

I have included in this table only the first 100 men in each year. The omitted residue is too small to be important. I have omitted it lest, if the precise numbers of honour men were stated, those numbers would have served to identify the years. For reasons already given, I desire to afford no data to serve that purpose.

grapple with problems more than thirty-two times as difficult; or when dealing with subjects of the same difficulty, but intelligible to all, would comprehend them more rapidly in perhaps the square root of that proportion.

* * * * *

The mathematical powers of the last man on the list of honours, which are so low when compared with those of a senior wrangler, are mediocre, or even above mediocrity, when compared with the gifts of Englishmen generally. Though the examination places 100 honour men above him, it puts no less than 300 "poll men" below him. Even if we go so far as to allow that 200 out of the 300 refuse to work hard enough to get honours, there will remain 100 who, even if they worked hard, could not get them. Every tutor knows how difficult it is to drive abstract conceptions, even of the simplest kind, into the brains

of most people—how feeble and hesitating is their mental grasp—how easily their brains are mazed—how incapable they are of precision and soundness of knowledge. It often occurs to persons familiar with some scientific subject to hear men and women of mediocre gifts relate to one another what they have picked up about it from some lecture—say at the Royal Institution, where they have sat for an hour listening with delighted attention to an admirably lucid account, illustrated by experiments of the most perfect and beautiful character, in all of which they expressed themselves intensely gratified and highly instructed. It is positively painful to hear what they say. Their recollections seem to be a mere chaos of mist and misapprehension, to which some sort of shape and organization has been given by the action of their own pure fancy, altogether alien to what the lecturer intended to convey. The average mental grasp even of what is called a well-educated audience, will be found to be ludicrously small when rigorously tested.

* * * * *

To conclude, the range of mental power between—I will not say the highest Caucasian and the lowest savage—but between the greatest and least of English intellects, is enormous. There is a continuity of natural ability reaching from one knows not what height, and descending to one can hardly say what depth. I propose in this chapter to range men according to their natural abilities, putting them into classes separated by equal degrees of merit, and to show the relative number of individuals included in the several classes. Perhaps some person might be inclined to make an offhand guess that the number of men included in the several classes would be pretty equal. If he thinks so, I can assure him he is most egregiously mistaken.

The method I shall employ for discovering all this is an application of the very curious theoretical law of "deviation from an average." First, I will explain the law, and then I will show that the production of natural intellectual gifts comes justly within its scope.

* * * * *

Suppose a large island inhabited by a single

race, who intermarried freely, and who had lived for many generations under constant conditions; then the average *height* of the male adults of that population would undoubtedly be the same year after year. Also —still arguing from the experience of modern statistics, which are found to give constant results in far less carefully-guarded examples —we should undoubtedly find, year after year, the same proportion maintained between the number of men of different heights. I mean, if the average stature was found to be sixty-six inches, and if it was also found in any one year that 100 per million exceeded seventy-eight inches, the same proportion of 100 per million would be closely maintained in all other years. An equal constancy of proportion would be maintained between any other limits of height we pleased to specify, as between seventy-one and seventy-two inches; between seventy-two and seventy-three inches; and so on. Statistical experiences are so invariably confirmatory of what I have stated would probably be the case, as to make it unnecessary to describe analogous instances. Now, at this point, the law of deviation from an average steps in. It shows that the number per million whose heights range between seventy-one and seventy-two inches (or between any other limits we please to name) can be *predicted* from the previous datum of the average, and of any one other fact, such as that of 100 per million exceeding seventy-eight inches.

The appended diagram will make this more intelligible. Suppose a million of the men to stand in turns, with their backs against a vertical board of sufficient height, and their heights to be dotted off upon it. The board would then present the appearance shown in the diagram. The line of average height is that which divides the dots into two equal parts, and stands, in the case we have assumed, at the height of sixty-six inches. The dots will be found to be ranged so symmetrically on either side of the line of average, that the lower half of the diagram will be almost a precise reflection of the upper. Next, let a hundred dots be counted from above downwards, and let a line be drawn below them. According to the conditions, this line will stand at the height of seventy-eight inches. Using the data afforded by these two lines, it is possible, by the help of the law of devia-

tion from an average, to reproduce, with extraordinary closeness, the entire system of dots on the board.

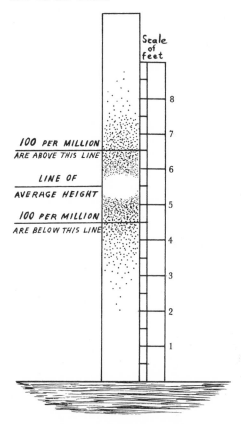

This law of deviation from an average is perfectly general in its application. Thus, if the marks had been made by bullets fired at a horizontal line stretched in front of the target, they would have been distributed according to the same law. Wherever there is a large number of similar events, each due to the resultant influences of the same variable conditions, two effects will follow. First, the average value of those events will be constant; and, secondly, the deviations of the several events from the average, will be governed by this law (which is, in principle, the same as that which governs runs of luck at a gaming-table).

The nature of the conditions affecting the several events must, I say, be the same. It clearly would not be proper to combine the heights of men belonging to two dissimilar races, in the expectation that the compound results would be governed by the same constants. A union of two dissimilar systems of dots would produce the same kind of confusion as if half the bullets fired at a target had been directed to one mark, and the other half to another mark. Nay, an examination of the dots would show to a person, ignorant of what had occurred, that such had been the case, and it would be possible, by aid of the law, to disentangle two or any moderate number of superimposed series of marks. The law may, therefore, be used as a most trustworthy criterion, whether or no the events of which an average has been taken, are due to the same or to dissimilar classes of conditions.

* * * * *

It will, I trust, be clearly understood that the numbers of men in the several classes in my table depend on no uncertain hypothesis. They are determined by the assured law of deviations from an average. It is an absolute fact that if we pick out of each million the one man who is naturally the ablest, and also the one man who is the most stupid, and divide the remaining 999,998 men into fourteen classes, the average ability in each being separated from that of its neighbours by *equal grades*, then the numbers in each of those classes will, on the average of many millions, be as is stated in the table. The table may be applied to special, just as truly as to general ability. It would be true for every examination that brought out natural gifts, whether held in painting, in music, or in statemanship. The proportions between the different classes would be identical in all these cases, although the classes would be made up of different individuals, according

Classification of Men According to Their Natural Gifts

Grades of Natural Ability, Separated by Equal Intervals		Numbers of Men Comprised in the Several Grades of Natural Ability, Whether in Respect to Their General Powers, or to Special Aptitudes							
Below Average	Above Average	Proportionate, viz. One in	In Each Million of the Same Age	In Total Male Population of the United Kingdom, Say 15 Millions, of the Undermentioned Ages					
				20–30	30–40	40–50	50–60	60–70	70–80
a	A	4	256,791	651,000	495,000	391,000	268,000	171,000	77,000
b	B	6	161,279	409,000	312,000	246,000	168,000	107,000	48,000
c	C	16	63,563	161,000	123,000	97,000	66,000	42,000	19,000
d	D	64	15,696	39,800	30,300	23,900	16,400	10,400	4,700
e	E	413	2,423	6,100	4,700	3,700	2,520	1,600	729
f	F	4,300	233	590	450	355	243	155	70
g	G	79,000	14	35	27	21	15	9	4
x all grades below g	X all grades above G	1,000,000	1	3	2	2	2	—	—
On either side of average . . .		500,000	1,268,000	964,000	761,000	521,000	332,000	149,000	
Total, both sides		1,000,000	2,536,000	1,928,000	1,522,000	1,042,000	664,000	298,000	

as the examination differed in its purport.

It will be seen that more than half of each million is contained in the two mediocre classes a and A; the four mediocre classes a, b, A, B, contain more than four-fifths, and the six mediocre classes more than nineteen-twentieths of the entire population. Thus, the rarity of commanding ability, and the vast abundance of mediocrity, is no accident,

but follows of necessity, from the very nature of these things.

The meaning of the word "mediocrity" admits of little doubt. It defines the standard of intellectual power found in most provincial gatherings, because the attractions of a more stirring life in the metropolis and elsewhere, are apt to draw away the abler classes of men, and the silly and the imbecile do not take a part in the gatherings. Hence, the residuum that forms the bulk of the general society of small provincial places, is commonly very pure in its mediocrity.

The class C possesses abilities a trifle higher than those commonly possessed by the foreman of an ordinary jury. D includes the mass of men who obtain the ordinary prizes of life. E is a stage higher. Then we reach F, the lowest of those yet superior classes of intellect, with which this volume is chiefly concerned.

On descending the scale, we find by the time we have reached f, that we are already among the idiots and imbeciles. There are 400 idiots and imbeciles, to every million of persons living in this country; but that 30 per cent of their number, appear to be light cases, to whom the name of idiot is inappropriate. There will remain 280 true idiots and imbeciles, to every million of our population. This ratio coincides very closely with the requirements of class f. No doubt a certain proportion of them are idiotic owing to some fortuitous cause, which may interfere with the working of a naturally good brain, much as a bit of dirt may cause a first-rate chronometer to keep worse time than an ordinary watch. But I presume, from the usual smallness of head and absence of disease among these persons, that the proportion of accidental idiots cannot be very large.

Hence we arrive at the undeniable, but unexpected conclusion, that eminently gifted men are raised as much above mediocrity as idiots are depressed below it, a fact that is calculated to considerably enlarge our ideas of the enormous differences of intellectual gifts between man and man.

I presume the class F of dogs, and others of the more intelligent sort of animals, is nearly commensurate with the f of the human race, in respect to memory and powers of reason. Certainly the class G of such animals is far superior to the g of humankind.

Galton's Whistle [2]

I contrived a small whistle for conveniently ascertaining the upper limits of audible sound

[2] Francis Galton, "Whistles for audibility of shrill notes," *Inquires into Human Faculty and Its Development* (London, 1883).

in different persons, which Dr. Wollaston had shown to vary considerably. He used small pipes, and found much difficulty in making them. I made a very small whistle from a brass tube whose internal diameter was less than one tenth of an inch in diameter. A plug was fitted into the lower end of the tube, which could be pulled out or pushed in as much as desired, thereby causing the length of the bore of the whistle to be varied at will. When the bore is long the note is low; when short, it is high. The plug was graduated, so that the precise note produced by the whistle could be determined by reading off the graduations and referring to a table. . . .

On testing different persons I found there was a remarkable falling off in the power of hearing high notes as age advanced. The persons themselves were quite unconscious of their deficiency so long as their sense of hearing low notes remained unimpaired. It is an only too amusing experiment to test a party of persons of various ages, including some rather elderly and self-satisfied personages. They are indignant at being thought deficient in the power of hearing, yet the experiment quickly shows that they are absolutely deaf to shrill notes which the younger persons hear acutely, and they commonly betray much dislike to the discovery. Every one has his limit, and the limit at which sounds become too shrill to be audible to any particular person can be rapidly determined by this little instrument. Lord Raleigh and others have found that sensitive flames are powerfully affected by the vibrations of whistles that are too rapid to be audible to ordinary ears.

I have tried experiments with all kinds of animals on their powers of hearing shrill notes. I have gone through the whole of the Zoological Gardens, using an apparatus arranged for the purpose. It consists of one of my little whistles at the end of a walking stick—that is, in reality, a long tube; it has a bit of india-rubber pipe under the handle, a sudden squeeze upon which forces a little air into the whistle and causes it to sound. I hold it as near as is safe to the ears of the animals, and when they are quite accustomed to its presence and heedless of it, I make it sound; then if they prick their ears it shows that they hear the whistle; if they do not, it is probably inaudible to them. Still, it is very possible that in some cases they hear but do not heed the sound. Of all creatures, I have found none superior to cats in the power of hearing shrill sounds; it is perfectly remarkable what a faculty they have in this way. Cats, of course, have to deal with mice, and to find them out by their squealing. Many people cannot hear the shrill squeal of a mouse. Some time ago, singing mice were exhibited in London, and of the people who went to hear them, some could hear nothing, whilst others could hear a little, and others again could hear much. Cats are differentiated by natural selection until they have a power of hearing all the high notes made by mice and other little creatures that they have to catch. A cat that is at a very considerable distance, can be made to turn its ear round by sounding a note that is too shrill to be audible by almost any human ear. Small dogs also hear very shrill notes, but large ones do not. I have walked through the streets of a town with an instrument like that which I used in the Zoological Gardens, and made nearly all the little dogs turn round, but not the large ones. At Berne, where there appear to be more large dogs lying idly about the streets than in any other town in Europe, I have tried the whistle for hours together, on a great many large dogs, but could not find one that heard it. Ponies are sometimes able to hear very high notes. I once frightened a pony with one of these whistles in the middle of a large field. My attempts on insect hearing have been failures.

HENRY HERBERT GODDARD
(1866–1957)

The Kallikak Family [3]

The great-great-grandfather of Deborah was Martin Kallikak. That we knew. We had also traced the good family [See Chart II] back to an ancestor belonging to an older generation than this Martin Kallikak, but bearing the same name. He was the father of a large family. His eldest son was named Frederick, but there was no son by the name of Martin. Consequently, no connection could be made. Many months later, a granddaughter of Martin revealed in a burst of confidence the situation. She told us (and this was afterwards fully verified) that Martin had a *half brother* Frederick,—and that Martin never had an own brother "because," as she now naïvely expressed it, "you see, his mother had him before she was married." Deeper scrutiny into the life of Martin Kallikak Sr., which was made possible through well-preserved family records, enabled us to complete the story.

When Martin Sr., of the good family, was a boy of fifteen, his father died, leaving him without parental care or oversight. Just before attaining his majority, the young man joined one of the numerous military companies that were formed to protect the country at the beginning of the Revolution. At one of the taverns frequented by the militia he met a feeble-minded girl by whom he became the father of a feeble-minded son. This child was given, by its mother, the name of the father in full, and thus has been handed down to posterity the father's name and the mother's mental capacity. This illegitimate boy was Martin Kallikak Jr., the great-great-grandfather of our Deborah, and from him have come four hundred and eighty descendants. One hundred and forty-three of these, we have conclusive proof, were or are feeble-minded, while only forty-six have been found normal. The rest are unknown or doubtful.

Among these four hundred and eighty descendants, thirty-six have been illegitimate.

There have been thirty-three sexually immoral persons, mostly prostitutes.

[3] Henry Herbert Goddard, *The Kallikak Family: A Study in the Heredity of Feeble-Mindedness* (New York: Macmillan, 1912), pp. 17–30, 37.

There have been twenty-four confirmed alcoholics.

There have been three epileptics.

Eighty-two died in infancy.

Three were criminal.

Eight kept houses of ill fame.

These people have married into other families, generally of about the same type, so that we now have on record and charted eleven hundred and forty-six individuals.

Of this large group, we have discovered that two hundred and sixty-two were feeble-minded, while one hundred and ninety-seven are considered normal, the remaining five hundred and eighty-one being still undetermined. ("Undetermined," as here employed, often means not that we knew nothing about the person, but that we could not decide. They are people we can scarcely recognize as normal; frequently they are not what we could call good members of society. But it is very difficult to decide without more facts whether the condition that we find or that we learn about, as in the case of older generations, is or was really one of true feeble-mindedness.)

In 1803, Martin Kallikak Jr., otherwise known as the "Old Horror," married Rhoda Zabeth, a normal woman. (See Chart II.) They had ten children, of whom one died in infancy and another died at birth with the mother. Of those who lived, the oldest was Millard, the direct ancestor of our Deborah. He married Althea Haight, and they had fifteen children, of whom more later.

The next born of Martin Jr. was Nathan, known in the community as "Daddy" . . . who died at the advanced age of ninety-three. He was the father of six children. One of his sons was a criminal, a horse thief, who also stole a flock of sheep which the owner all unwittingly helped him to drive away. Three other children of "Daddy" married and themselves had children. These are all families about whose mentality it is difficult to decide. They are all peculiar, but more respectable than some other branches of this family. One is dead. The sixth, a daughter, is feeble-minded and sexually immoral. She married a man who was feeble-minded and alcoholic. Of her six children, two at least are feeble-minded. Whether her husband is the father of all of the children is very doubtful. Sexual immorality and alcoholism are prevalent in this family. One of the sons married a feeble-minded woman who came from feeble-minded stock. They had six children, all of whom were feeble-minded. One of these is of the Mongolian type, an interesting fact, as it shows that this particular form of arrest of development may occur in a defective family.

Martin Jr.'s third child was James (Chart II), who went away, and we know nothing about him.

Martin Jr.'s fourth child, "Old Sal"..., was feeble-minded and she married a feeble-minded man. Two of their children are undetermined, but one of these had at least one feeble-minded grandchild; the other, an alcoholic man, had three feeble-minded grandchildren, one of whom is in the Training School at Vineland. She is thus a cousin of Deborah—a fact not known until this study was made. The two other children of Old Sal were feeble-minded, married feeble-minded wives, and had large families of defective children and grandchildren, as will be seen in the chart.

The fifth child of Martin Jr. was Jemima..., feeble-minded and sexually immoral. She lived with a feeble-minded man named Horser, to whom she was supposed to have been married. Of her five children, three are known to have been feeble-minded, two are undetermined. From these again, have come a large number of feeble-minded children and grandchildren. Jemima had an illegitimate son by a man who was high in the Nation's offices. This son married a feeble-minded girl and they had feeble-minded children, and grandchildren.

The sixth child of Martin Jr., known as "Old Moll"..., was feeble-minded, alcoholic, epileptic, and sexually immoral. She had three illegitimate children who were sent to the almshouse, and from there bound out to neighboring farmers. One of these turned out normal, one was feeble-minded, and the other undetermined. Neither of the two older ones had any children. The third child, a daughter, was tubercular, but nothing is known of her descendants, except that there were several children and grandchildren.

The seventh child of Martin Jr. was a daughter, Sylvia..., who seemed to be a normal woman. She was taken very young by a good family who brought her up carefully. She later married a normal man. Although we have marked her normal, she was always peculiar. All her children and grandchildren were either normal or are undetermined.

The youngest child of Martin Jr. who lived to grow up was Amy Jones, also normal.... She, too, was taken into a good family and married a normal man, and lived to be very old. Two of Amy's children died in infancy. Of two others, one was normal and one feeble-minded. This latter married a normal man and had one feeble-minded and immoral daughter; five other children are undetermined.

We now return to Martin Jr.'s oldest son, Millard..., to take up the story of his descendants, of whom our girl Deborah is one.

Millard married Althea Haight about 1830. They had fifteen children.... The mother died in 1857. This mother, Althea Haight, was feeble-minded. That she came from a feeble-minded family is evidenced by the fact that she had at least one feeble-minded brother, while of her mother it was said that the "devil himself could not live with her." The feeble-minded brother had six children, of whom three are known to have been feeble-minded. He had seven grandchildren who were feeble-minded, and no less than nine feeble-minded great-grandchildren....

The oldest child of Millard and Althea was a daughter who grew up a feeble-minded and immoral woman. She had several husbands, but only one of her children lived to be old enough to marry. This one, a daughter of illegitimate birth, married a man of good family who was a confirmed alcoholic. Their children are all undetermined, except one who was normal.

The second child of Millard, a daughter, was a bad character. We know of one illegitimate and feeble-minded son who married a feeble-minded and immoral girl. They had four children, but all died in infancy. This wife was also the mother of an illegitimate son, who was feeble-minded and sexually immoral.

The third child of Millard was Justin..., the grandfather of our Deborah....

According to Mendelian expectation, all of the children of Millard Kallikak and Althea

Haight should have been feeble-minded, because the parents were such. The facts, so far as known, confirm this expectation, with the exception of the fourth child, a daughter, who was taken into a good family and grew up apparently a normal woman. She married a normal man and they had one son who was normal. He married a normal woman and they have two children, a boy and girl, who are normal and above average intelligence.

The fifth child was Albert, feeble-minded, who died at twenty-five, unmarried.

The sixth child was Warren, who had four children, three of whom were feeble-minded and of very doubtful morality. Each of the three had feeble-minded children. One of these, Guss by name, was specially loose and much mixed in his marital relations.

The seventh child was Lavinia, who died unmarried at the age of thirty-nine. She had been brought up in a good family and never manifested any of those characteristics that indicate feeble-mindedness.

The eighth was Cordelia, who died at nine; condition unknown.

The ninth was Prince, who died at four years.

The tenth was Paula, feeble-minded; married and had four children. Her husband and children are undetermined.

Then comes Gregory, the eleventh, who was feeble-minded and alcoholic. He married an alcoholic and syphilitic woman, mentality difficult to determine. They had seven children, of whom two were feeble-minded, syphilitic, alcoholic, and sexually immoral. One died of delirium tremens, the other of alcoholism, leaving a long line of descendants. The other children died young, except one daughter who has a feeble-minded grandchild who cannot speak.

The twelfth child was Harriet, feeble-minded, twice married, but without children.

The thirteenth, Sanders, who was drowned as a young man, was feeble-minded and sexually immoral.

The fourteenth was Thomas, feeble-minded, alcoholic, and sexually immoral. He died from over self-indulgence. He was married and had a daughter, but her condition as well as her mother's is unknown.

The last child was Joseph, feeble-minded. He married his first cousin, Eva Haight, who was also feeble-minded. They had five children, two dying in infancy, and the rest feeble-minded. Of their nineteen grandchildren, five died in infancy, one is undetermined, and the remaining thirteen are all feeble-minded.

Millard Kallikak married for his second wife a normal woman, a sister of a man of prominence. She was, however, of marked peculiarity. By her, he had three children; two died in infancy. The one who grew to manhood was alcoholic and syphilitic. He ran off with the wife of his nephew, who was about his own age. His mental condition is undetermined. He was killed by an accident a few years later.

We now return to the third born of this family, Justin Kallikak, the grandfather of our Deborah.... He was feeble-minded, alcoholic, and sexually immoral. He married Eunice Barrah, who belonged to a family of dull mentality. Her mother and paternal grandfather were feeble-minded, and the grandfather had a brother that was feeble-minded. That brother had at least six descendants who were feeble-minded. The father, also, had a brother feeble-minded who had eleven children, grandchildren, and great-grandchildren who were feeble-minded....

The children of Deborah's grandparents, Justin and Eunice, were as follows: first, Martha, the mother of our Deborah, whose story has already been partly told. This woman is supposed to have had three illegitimate children before Deborah was born. They died in infancy. The next younger half sister of Deborah was placed out by a charitable organization when very young. From their records we learn that in five years she had been tried in thirteen different families and by all found impossible. In one of these she set the barn on fire. When found by our field worker, she had grown to be a girl of twenty, pretty, graceful, but of low mentality. She had already followed the instinct implanted in her by her mother, and was on the point of giving birth to an illegitimate child. She was sent to a hospital. The child died, and then the girl was placed permanently in a home for feeble-minded. An own brother of this girl was placed out in a private family. When a little under sixteen, his foster mother died and her husband married again. Thus the boy was turned adrift. Having been well trained, and being naturally of an agreeable disposition, he easily found employment. Bad company, however, soon led to his discharge. He has now drifted into one of our big cities. It requires no prophet to predict his future.

The last family of half brothers and sisters of Deborah are, at present, living with the mother and her second husband. The oldest three of these are distinctly feeble-minded. Between them and the two younger children there was a stillbirth and a miscarriage. The little ones appear normal and test normal for their ages, but there is good reason to believe that they will develop the same defect as they grow older.

Besides the mother of Deborah, Justin and Eunice had ten other children, of whom six died in infancy. One of the daughters, Margaret, was taken by a good family when a very small child. When she was about thirteen, she visited her parents for a few weeks. While her mother was away at work, her father, who was a drunken brute, committed incest with her. When the fact became known in her adopted home, she was placed in the almshouse. The child born there soon died, and she was again received into the family where she formerly lived. The care with which she was surrounded prevented her from becoming a vicious woman. Although of dull mentality, she was a good and cheerful worker. When about thirty-five, she married a respectable workingman but has had no children by him.

Another daughter, Abigail, feeble-minded, married a feeble-minded man by whom she had two feeble-minded children, besides a third that died in infancy. She later married a normal man.

The next child of Justin and Eunice was Beede, who is feeble-minded. He married a girl who left him before their child was born. He lives at present with a very low, immoral woman.

The youngest child of Justin and Eunice was a son, Gaston, feeble-minded and a horse thief; he removed to a distant town where he married. He has one child; mentality of both mother and child undetermined.

This is the ghastly story of the descendants of Martin Kallikak Sr., from the nameless feeble-minded girl.

Although Martin himself paid no further attention to the girl nor her child, society has had to pay the heavy price of all the evil he engendered.

Martin Sr., on leaving the Revolutionary Army, straightened up and married a respectable girl of good family, and through that union has come another line of descendants of radically different character. These now number four hundred and ninety-six in direct descent. All of them are normal people. Three men only have been found among them who were somewhat degenerate, but they were not defective. Two of these were alcoholic, and the other sexually loose.

All of the legitimate children of Martin Sr. married into the best families in their state, the descendants of colonial governors, signers of the Declaration of Independence, soldiers and even the founders of a great university. Indeed, in this family and its collateral branches, we find nothing but good representative citizenship. There are doctors, lawyers, judges, educators, traders, landholders, in short, respectable citizens, men and women prominent in every phase of social life. They have scattered over the United States and are prominent in their communities wherever they have gone. Half a dozen towns in New

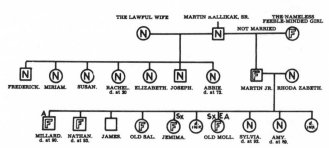

CHART II   N = Normal.   F = Feeble-minded.   Sx = Sexually immoral.   A = Alcoholic.   I = Insane.
Sy = Syphilitic.   C = Criminalistic.   D = Deaf.   d. inf. = died in infancy.   T = Tuberculous.

Jersey are named from the families into which Martin's descendants have married. There have been no feeble-minded among them; no illegitimate children; no immoral women; only one man was sexually loose. There has been no epilepsy, no criminals, no keepers of houses of prostitution. Only fifteen children have died in infancy. There has been one "insane," a case of religious mania, perhaps inherited, but not from the Kallikak side. The appetite for strong drink has been present here and there in this family from the beginning. It was in Martin Sr., and was cultivated at a time when such practices were common everywhere. But while the other branch of the family has had twenty-four victims of habitual drunkenness, this side scores only two.

LEWIS MADISON TERMAN
(1877–1956)

Stanford–Binet Intelligence Scale [4]

Figure 1 shows the distribution of mental ages for 62 adults, including the 30 business men and the 32 high school pupils who were over 16 years of age. It will be noted that the middle section of the graph represents the "mental ages" falling between 15 and 17. This is the range which we have designated as the "average adult" level. Those above 17 are called "superior adults," those between 13 and 15, "inferior adults." Subjects much over 15 years of age who test in the neighborhood of 12 years may ordinarily be considered border-line cases.

The following method was employed for determining the validity of a test. The children of each age level were divided into three groups according to intelligence quotient, those testing below 90, those between 90 and 109, and those with an intelligence quotient of 110 or above. The percentages of passes on each individual test at or near that age level were then ascertained separately for these three groups. If a test fails to show a decidedly higher proportion of passes in the superior IQ group than in the inferior IQ group, it cannot be regarded as a satisfactory test of intelligence. On the other hand, a test which satisfies this criterion must be accepted as valid or the entire scale must be rejected. Henceforth it stands or falls with the scale as a whole.

When tried out by this method, some of the tests which have been most criticized showed a high degree of reliability; certain others which have been considered excellent proved to be so little correlated with intelligence that they had to be discarded.

After making a few necessary eliminations, 90 tests remained, or 36 more than the number included in the Binet 1911 scale. There are 6 at each age level from 3 to 10, 8 at 12, 6 at 14, 6 at "average adult," 6 at "superior adult," and 16 alternative tests. The alternative tests, which are distributed among the different groups, are intended to be used only as substitutes when one or more of the regular tests have been rendered, by coaching or otherwise, undesirable.

Of the 36 new tests, 27 were added and standardized in the various Stanford investigations. Two tests were borrowed from the Healy-Fernald series, one from Kuhlmann, one was adapted from Bonser, and the remaining five were amplifications or adaptations of some of the earlier Binet tests.

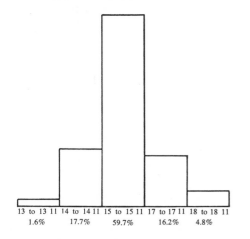

| 13 to 13 11 | 14 to 14 11 | 15 to 15 11 | 17 to 17 11 | 18 to 18 11 |
| 1.6% | 17.7% | 59.7% | 16.2% | 4.8% |

FIG. 1. Distribution of mental ages of 62 normal adults

[4] Lewis M. Terman, *The Measurement of Intelligence* (Boston: Houghton Mifflin, 1916), pp. 54–61, 78–79, 137–141. Reprinted by permission.

Following is a complete list of the tests of the Stanford revision. Those designated *al.* are alternative tests. . . .

The Stanford Revision and Extension

Year III. (6 *tests,* 2 *months each.*)
1. Points to parts of body. (3 of 4.)
   Nose; eyes; mouth; hair.
2. Names familiar objects. (3 of 5.)
   Key, penny, closed knife, watch, pencil.
3. Pictures, enumeration or better. (At least 3 objects enumerated in one picture.)
   (*a*) Dutch Home; (*b*) River Scene; (*c*) Post-Office.
4. Gives sex.
5. Gives last name.
6. Repeats 6 to 7 syllables. (1 of 3.)
Al. Repeats 3 digits. (1 success in 3 trials. Order correct.)

Year IV. (6 *tests,* 2 *months each.*)
1. Compares lines. (3 trials, no error.)
2. Discrimination of forms. (Kuhlmann.) (Not over 3 errors.)
3. Counts 4 pennies. (No error.)
4. Copies square. (Pencil. 1 of 3.)
5. Comprehension, 1st degree. (2 of 3.) (Stanford addition.)
   "What must you do": "When you are sleepy?" "Cold?" "Hungry?"
6. Repeats 4 digits. (1 of 3. Order correct.) (Stanford addition.)
Al. Repeats 12 to 13 syllables. (1 of 3 absolutely correct, or 2 with 1 error each.)

Year V. (6 *tests,* 2 *months each.*)
1. Comparison of weights. (2 of 3.)
   3–15; 15–3; 3–15.
2. Colors. (No error.)
   Red; yellow; blue; green.
3. Æsthetic comparison. (No error.)
4. Definitions, use or better. (4 of 6.)
   Chair; horse; fork; doll; pencil; table.
5. Patience, or divided rectangle. (2 of 3 trials. 1 minute each.)
6. Three commissions. (No error. Order correct.)
Al. Age.

Year VI. (6 *tests,* 2 *months each.*)
1. Right and left. (No error.)
   Right hand; left ear; right eye.
2. Mutilated pictures. (3 of 4 correct.)
3. Counts 13 pennies. (1 of 2 trials, without error.)
4. Comprehension, 2d degree. (2 of 3.) "What's the thing for you to do":

(*a*) "If it is raining when you start to school?"
(*b*) "If you find that your house is on fire?"
(*c*) "If you are going some place and miss your car?"
5. Coins. (3 of 4.)
   Nickel; penny; quarter; dime.
6. Repeats 16 to 18 syllables. (1 of 3 absolutely correct, or 2 with 1 error each.)
Al. Morning or afternoon.

Year VII. (6 *tests,* 2 *months each.*)
1. Fingers. (No error.) Right; left; both.
2. Pictures, description or better. (Over half of performance description:) Dutch Home; River Scene; Post-Office.
3. Repeats 5 digits. (1 of 3. Order correct.)
4. Ties bow-knot. (Model shown. 1 minute.) (Stanford addition.)
5. Gives differences. (2 of 3.)
   Fly and butterfly; stone and egg; wood and glass.
6. Copies diamond. (Pen. 2 of 3.)
Al. Names days of week. (Order correct. 2 of 3 checks correct.)
Al. 2. Repeats 3 digits backwards. (1 of 3.)

Year VIII. (6 *tests,* 2 *months each.*)
1. Ball and field. (Inferior plan or better.) (Stanford addition.)
2. Counts 20 to 1. (40 seconds. 1 error allowed.)
3. Comprehension, 3d degree. (2 of 3.) "What's the thing for you to do":
   (*a*) "When you have broken something which belongs to some one else?"
   (*b*) "When you are on your way to school and notice that you are in danger of being tardy?"
   (*c*) "If a playmate hits you without meaning to do it?"
4. Gives similarities, two things. (2 of 4.) (Stanford addition.) Wood and coal; apple and peach; iron and silver; ship and automobile.
5. Definitions superior to use. (2 of 4.)
   Balloon; tiger; football; soldier.
6. Vocabulary, 20 words. (Stanford addition. For list of words used, see record booklet.)
Al. 1. First six coins. (No error.)
Al. 2. Dictation. ("See the little boy." Easily legible. Pen. 1 minute.)

Year IX. (6 *tests,* 2 *months each.*)
1. Date. (Allow error of 3 days in *c*, no error in *a*, *b*, or *d*.)
   (*a*) day of week; (*b*) month; (*c*) day of month; (*d*) year.
2. Weights. (3, 6, 9, 12, 15. Procedure not illustrated. 2 of 3.)

3. Makes change. (2 of 3. No coins, paper, or pencil.)
   10–4; 15–12; 25–4.
4. Repeats 4 digits backwards. (1 of 3.) (Stanford addition.)
5. Three words. (2 of 3. Oral. 1 sentence or not over 2 coordinate clauses.)
   Boy, river, ball; work, money, men; desert, rivers, lakes.
6. Rhymes. (3 rhymes for two of three words. 1 minute for each part.)
   Day; mill; spring.
Al. 1. Months. (15 seconds and 1 error in naming. 2 checks of 3 correct.)
Al. 2. Stamps, gives total value. (Second trial if individual values are known.)

Year X. (6 *tests*, 2 *months each*.)

1. Vocabulary, 30 words. (Stanford addition.)
2. Absurdities. (4 of 5. Warn. Spontaneous correction allowed.) (Four of Binet's, one Stanford.)
3. Designs. (1 correct, 1 half correct. Expose 10 seconds.)
4. Reading and report. (8 memories. 35 seconds and 2 mistakes in reading.) (Binet's selection.)
5. Comprehension, 4th degree. (2 of 3. Question may be repeated.)
   (a) "What ought you to say when some one asks your opinion about a person you don't know very well?"
   (b) "What ought you to do before undertaking (beginning) something very important?"
   (c) "Why should we judge a person more by his actions than by his words?"
6. Names 60 words. (Illustrate with clouds, dog, chair, happy.)
Al. 1. Repeats 6 digits. (1 of 2. Order correct.) (Stanford addition.)
Al. 2. Repeats 20 to 22 syllables. (1 of 3 correct, or 2 with 1 error each.)
Al. 3. Form board. (Healy-Fernald Puzzle A. 3 times in 5 minutes.)

Year XII. (8 *tests*, 3 *months each*.)

1. Vocabulary, 40 words. (Stanford addition.)
2. Abstract words. (3 of 5.)
   Pity; revenge; charity; envy; justice.
3. Ball and field. (Superior plan.) (Stanford addition.)
4. Dissected sentences. (2 of 3. 1 minute each.)
5. Fables. (Score 4; i.e., two correct or the equivalent in half credits.) (Stanford addition.)
   Hercules and Wagoner; Maid and Eggs; Fox and Crow; Farmer and Stork; Miller, Son, and Donkey.

6. Repeats 5 digits backwards. (1 of 3.) (Stanford addition.)
7. Pictures, interpretation. (3 of 4. "Explain this picture.")
   Dutch Home; River Scene; Post-Office; Colonial Home.
8. Gives similarities, three things. (3 of 5.) (Stanford addition.)
   Snake, cow, sparrow; book, teacher, newspaper; wool, cotton, leather; knife-blade, penny, piece of wire; rose, potato, tree.

Year XIV. (6 *tests*, 4 *months each*.)

1. Vocabulary, 50 words. (Stanford addition.)
2. Induction test. (Gets rule by 6th folding.) (Stanford addition.)
3. President and king. (Power; accession; tenure. 2 of 3.)
4. Problems of fact. (2 of 3.) (Binet's two and one Stanford addition.)
5. Arithmetical reasoning. (1 minute each. 2 of 3.) (Adapted from Bonser.)
6. Clock. (2 of 3. Error must not exceed 3 or 4 minutes.)
   6.22. 8.10. 2.46.
Al. Repeats 7 digits. (1 of 2. Order correct.)

"Average Adult." (6 *tests*, 5 *months each*.)

1. Vocabulary, 65 words. (Stanford addition.)
2. Interpretation of fables. (Score 8.) (Stanford addition.)
3. Difference between abstract words. (3 real contrasts out of 4.)
   Laziness and idleness; evolution and revolution; poverty and misery; character and reputation.
4. Problem of the enclosed boxes. (3 of 4.) (Stanford addition.)
5. Repeats 6 digits backwards. (1 of 3.) (Stanford addition.)
6. Code, writes "Come quickly." (2 errors. Omission of dot counts half error. Illustrate with "war" and "spy.") (From Healy and Fernald.)
Al. 1. Repeats 28 syllables. (1 of 2 absolutely correct.)
Al. 2. Comprehension of physical relations. (2 of 3.) (Stanford addition.)
   Path of cannon ball; weight of fish in water; hitting distant mark.

"Superior Adult." (6 *tests*, 6 *months each*.)

1. Vocabulary, 75 words. (Stanford addition.)
2. Binet's paper-cutting test. (Draws, folds, and locates holes.)
3. Repeats 8 digits. (1 of 3. Order correct.) (Stanford addition.)
4. Repeats thought of passage heard. (1 of 2.) (Binet's and Wissler's selections adapted.)

5. Repeats 7 digits backwards. (1 of 3.) (Stanford addition.)
6. Ingenuity test. (2 of 3. 5 minutes each.) (Stanford addition.)

* * * * *

Frequency of Different Degrees of Intelligence. Before we can interpret the results of an examination it is necessary to know how frequently an IQ of the size found occurs among unselected children. Our tests of 1000 unselected children enable us to answer this question with some degree of definiteness. A study of these 1000 IQ's shows the following significant facts:

The lowest 1   % go to 70 or below,
        the highest 1   % reach 130 or above
The lowest 2   % go to 73 or below,
        the highest 2   % reach 128 or above
The lowest 3   % go to 76 or below,
        the highest 3   % reach 125 or above
The lowest 5   % go to 78 or below,
        the highest 5   % reach 122 or above
The lowest 10   % go to 85 or below,
        the highest 10   % reach 116 or above
The lowest 15   % go to 88 or below,
        the highest 15   % reach 113 or above
The lowest 20   % go to 91 or below,
        the highest 20   % reach 110 or above
The lowest 25   % go to 92 or below,
        the highest 25   % reach 108 or above
The lowest $33^{1}/_{3}$% go to 95 or below,
        the highest $33^{1}/_{3}$% reach 106 or above

Or, to put some of the above facts in another form:

The child reaching   110 is equaled
        or excelled by 20 out of 100
The child reaching (about) 115 is equaled
        or excelled by 10 out of 100
The child reaching (about) 125 is equaled
        or excelled by 3 out of 100
The child reaching (about) 130 is equaled
        or excelled by 1 out of 100

Conversely, we may say regarding the subnormals that:

The child testing at (about) 90 is equaled
        or excelled by 80 out of 100
The child testing at (about) 85 is equaled
        or excelled by 90 out of 100
The child testing at (about) 75 is equaled
        or excelled by 97 out of 100
The child testing at (about) 70 is equaled
        or excelled by 99 out of 100

Classification of Intelligence Quotients. What do the above IQ's imply in such terms as feeble-mindedness, border-line intelligence,

dullness, normality, superior intelligence, genius, etc.? When we use these terms two facts must be borne in mind: (1) That the boundary lines between such groups are absolutely arbitrary, a matter of definition only; and (2) that the individuals comprising one of the groups do not make up a homogeneous type.

Nevertheless, since terms like the above are convenient and will probably continue to be used, it is desirable to give them as much definiteness as possible. On the basis of the tests we have made, including many cases of all grades of intelligence, the following suggestions are offered for the classification of intelligence quotients:

IQ	Classification
Above 140 . . .	"Near" genius or genius.
120–140 . . .	Very superior intelligence.
110–120 . . .	Superior intelligence.
90–110 . . .	Normal, or average, intelligence.
80– 90 . . .	Dullness, rarely classifiable as feeble-mindedness.
70– 80 . . .	Border-line deficiency, sometimes classifiable as dullness, often as feeble-mindedness.
Below 70 . . .	Definite feeble-mindedness.

* * * * *

Finding Mental Age. As there are six tests in each age group from III to X, each test in this part of the scale counts 2 months toward mental age. There are eight tests in group XII, which, because of the omission of the 11-year group, have a combined value of 24 months, or 3 months each. Similarly, each of the six tests in XIV has a value of 4 months ($24 \div 6 = 4$). The tests of the "average adult" group are given a value of 5 months each, and those of the "superior adult" group a value of 6 months each. These values are in a sense arbitrary, but they are justified in the fact that they are such as to cause ordinary adults to test at the "average adult" level.

The calculation of mental age is therefore simplicity itself. The rule is: (1) Credit the subject with all the tests below the point where the examination begins (remembering that the examinations goes back until a year group has been found in which all the tests are passed); and (2) add to this basal credit 2 months for each test passed successfully up to and including year X, 3 months for each test passed in XII, 4 months for each test passed in XIV, 5 months for each success in "average adult," and 6 months for each success in "superior adult."

For example, let us suppose that a child passes all the tests in VI, five of the six tests in VII, three in VIII, two in IX, and one in X. The total credit earned is as follows:

	Years	Months
Credit presupposed, years I to V	5	
Credit earned in VI, 6 tests passed, 2 months each	1	
Credit earned in VII, 5 tests passed, 2 months each . . .		10
Credit earned in VIII, 3 tests passed, 2 months each . . .		6
Credit earned in IX, 2 tests passed, 2 months each		4
Credit earned in X, 1 test passed, 2 months		2
Total credit	7	10

Taking a subject who tests higher, let us suppose the following tests are passed: All in X, six of the eight in XII, two of the six in XIV, and one of the six in "average adult." The total credit is as follows:

	Years	Months
Credit presupposed, years I to IX	9	
Credit earned in X, 6 tests passed, 2 months each	1	
Credit earned in XII, 6 tests passed, 3 months each . . .	1	6
Credit earned in XIV, 2 tests passed, 4 months each . . .	0	8
Credit earned in "average adult," 1 success, 5 months		5
Total credit	12	7

One other point: If one or more tests of a year group have been omitted, as sometimes happens either from oversight or lack of time, the question arises how the tests which were given in such a year group should be evaluated. Suppose, for example, a subject has been given only four of the six tests in a given year, and that he passes two, or half of those given. In such a case the probability would be that had all six tests been given, three would have been passed; that is, one half of all. It is evident, therefore, that when a test has been omitted, a proportionately larger value should be assigned to each of those given.

If all six tests are given in any year group below XII, each has a value of 2 months. If only four are given, each has a value of 3 months ($12 \div 4 = 3$). If five tests only are given, each has a value of 2.4 months ($12 \div 5 = 2.4$). If in year group XII only six of the eight tests are given, each has a value of 4 months ($24 \div 6 = 4$). If in the "average adult" group only five of the six tests are given, each has a value of 6 months instead of the usual 5 months. In this connection it will need to be remembered that the six "average adult" tests have a combined value of 30 months (6 tests, 5 months each); also that the combined value of the six "superior adult" tests is 36 months ($6 \times 6 = 36$). Accordingly, if only five of the six "superior adult" tests are given, the value of each is $35 \div 5 = 7.2$ months.

For example, let us suppose that a subject has been tested as follows: All the six tests in X were given and all were passed; only six of the eight in XII were given and five were passed; five of the six in XIV were given and three were passed; five of the six in "average adult" were given and one was passed; five were given in "superior adult" and no credit earned. The result would be as follows:

	Years	Months
Credit presupposed, years I to IX	9	
Credit earned in X, 6 given, 6 successes	1	
Credit earned in XII, 6 given, 5 passed. Unit value of each test given is $24 \div 6 = 4$. Total value of the 5 tests passed is 5×4 or	1	8
Credit earned in XIV, 5 tests given, 3 passed. Unit value of each of the 5 given $24 \div 5 = 4.8$. Value of the 3 passed is 3×4.8, or	0	14+
Credit earned in "average adult," 5 tests given, 1 passed. Unit value of the 5 tests given is $30 \div 5 = 6$. Value of the 1 success	0	6
Credit earned in "superior adult"	0	0
Total credit	13	4+

The calculation of mental age is really simpler than our verbal illustrations make it appear. After the operation has been performed twenty or thirty times, it can be done in less than a half-minute without danger of error.

The Use of the Intelligence Quotient. As elsewhere explained, the mental age alone does not tell us what we want to know about a child's intelligence status. The significance of a given number of years of retardation or acceleration depends upon the age of the child. A 3-year-old child who is retarded one year is ordinarily feeble-minded; a 10-year-old retarded one year is only a little below normal. The child who at 3 years of age is retarded one year will probably be retarded two years at the age of 6, three years at the age of 9, and four years at the age of 12.

What we want to know, therefore, is the ratio existing between mental age and real age. This is the intelligence quotient, or IQ. To find it we simply divide mental age (expressed in years and months) by real age (also expressed in years and months.) The process is easier if we express each age in terms of months alone before dividing.

* * * * *

How to Find the IQ of Adult Subjects. Native intelligence, in so far as it can be measured by tests now available, appears to improve but little after the age of 15 or 16 years. It follows that in calculating the IQ of an adult subject, it will be necessary to disregard the years he has lived beyond the point where intelligence attains its final development.

Although the location of this point is not exactly known, it will be sufficiently accurate for our purpose to assume its location at 16 years. Accordingly, any person over 16 years of age, however old, is for purposes of calculating IQ considered to be just 16 years old. If a youth of 18 and a man of 60 years both have a mental age of 12 years, the IQ in each case is 12 ÷ 16, or .75.

The significance of various values of the IQ is set forth elsewhere. Here it need only be repeated that 100 IQ means exactly average intelligence; that nearly all who are below 70 or 75 IQ are feeble-minded; and that the child of 125 IQ is about as much above the average as the high-grade feeble-minded individual is below the average. For ordinary purposes all who fall between 95 and 105 IQ may be considered as average in intelligence.

ROBERT MEARNS YERKES
(1876–1956)

Army Alpha and Beta Tests [5]

The psychological examiner is frequently asked this question: "How intelligent is the Army?" There is an inherent difficulty in making an answer, for there are no standards in terms of which the statement can be made. The most familiar measures of intelligence, years of mental age as determined by the Stanford-Binet examination, are the results of investigations of a much smaller group (approximately 1000 cases) than the group studied in the Army. For norms of adult intelligence the results of the Army examinations are undoubtedly the most representative. It is customary to say that the mental age of the average adult is about 16 years. This figure is based, however, upon examinations of only 62 persons; 32 of them high-school pupils from 16 to 20 years of age, and 30 of them "business men of moderate success and of very limited educational advantages." This group is too small to give very reliable results and is furthermore probably not typical. High-school pupils and business men of moderate success presumably do not represent the average American adult with respect to intelligence.... 85 per cent of the men who had been to high school show mental ages above average.

It appears that the intelligence of the principal sample of the white draft, when transmuted from alpha and beta examinations into terms of mental age, is about 13 years (13.08). Here we have a measure of the

[5] Robert M. Yerkes (ed.), "Psychological examining in the United States Army," *Memoirs of the National Academy of Sciences*, Vol. **15** (Washington, D.C.: U.S. Government Printing Office, 1921), pp. 785, 158–166. Reprinted by permission of the National Academy of Sciences.

average intelligence of nearly 100,000 white recruits. We can hardly say, however, with assurance that these recruits are three years mental age below the average. Indeed, it might be argued on extrinsic grounds that the draft itself is more representative of the average intelligence of the country than is a group of high school students and business men. The draft, it is true, is highly selected at the upper end by reason of the fact that men of higher intelligence became officers without being drafted or constituted the greater part of the group of professional and business experts that were exempted from draft because essential to industrial activity in the war. It is impossible to guess the extent of this selection with respect to intelligence. It seems quite impossible that it could have reduced the intelligence level of the draft so much as three years. Considerably less than 15 per cent of the draft . . . lie above 16 years mental age. This discrepancy would mean that a very large number of men in proportion to the draft (considerably more than one man to every three of the draft, perhaps even so great a proportion as two to every three) would have been exempted because of service as an officer or because in some essential industrial occupation. No positive figures of the number of men exempted for these reasons are at present available, but there seems to be no doubt that it was considerably smaller than these indicated proportions. Undoubtedly the intelligence of the draft is somewhat lower than that of the country at large, although it is quite unlikely that the difference should be so great. It must be recalled further that there was also selection at the lower end of the scale on intelligence. The low-grade feeble-minded were not in general included in the draft. This selection tends to offset the selection at the upper end, although presumably it does not completely counterbalance it, and thus to render the average intelligence of the draft more nearly representative of the population at large than would otherwise be the case.

In general, then, we are forced to reply to the question "How intelligent is the Army?" by stating arbitrary figures that refer to the draft itself, and by arguing further that the draft is approximately a representative group which is presumably, however, a little lower in intelligence than is the country at large.

The Army Alpha Tests (for Literates)

Procedure

Examination alpha is to be given to all subjects who remain in the room after the elimination of illiterates. In giving the following directions examiner should speak rather slowly, distinctly, and with proper emphasis. *He should expect and demand perfect order and prompt response to commands.*

When everything is ready examiner proceeds as follows: "Attention! The purpose of this examination is to see how well you can remember, think, and carry out what you are told to do. We are not looking for crazy people. The aim is to help find out what you are best fitted to do in the Army. The grade you make in this examination will be put on your qualification card and will also go to your company commander. Some of the things you are told to do will be very easy. Some you may find hard. You are not expected to make a perfect grade, but do the very best you can.

"Now, in the Army a man often has to listen to commands and then carry them out exactly. I am going to give *you* some commands to see how well you can carry them out. Listen closely. Ask no questions. Do not watch any other man to see what *he* does.

"Look at your papers. Just below where you have been writing, there are several sets of forms—circles, triangles, and so forth. First you will be told to do something with the circles at 1, afterward with the circles at 2, and so on.

"When I call 'Attention,' stop instantly whatever you are doing and hold your pencil up—so. Don't put your pencil down to the paper until I say 'Go.' (Examiner lowers his pencil.) Listen carefully to what I say. Do just what you are told to do. As soon as you are through, pencils up. Remember, wait for the word 'Go'."

* * * * *

Test 1

1. ". . . Look at the circles at 1. When I say 'Go' (but not before) make a cross in the first circle and also a figure 1 in the third circle.—GO!" (Allow not over 5 seconds.)

2. "Attention! Look at 2, where the circles have numbers in them. When I say 'Go' draw a line from circle 1 to circle 4

that will pass *above* circle 2 and *below* circle 3.—GO!" (Allow not over 5 seconds.)

3. "Attention! Look at the square and triangle at 3. When I say 'Go' make a cross in the space which is in the triangle but not in the square, and also make a figure 1 in the space which is in the triangle and in the square.—GO!" (Allow not over 10 seconds.)

4. ... "When I say 'Go' make a figure 1 in the space which is in the circle but not in the triangle or square, and also make a figure 2 in the space which is in the triangle and circle, but not in the sqaure.—GO!" (Allow not over 10 seconds.) ...

5. "... If a machine gun can shoot more bullets a minute than a rifle, then (when I say 'Go') put a cross in the second circle; if not, draw a line *under* the word NO.—GO!" (Allow not over 10 seconds.)

6. "... When I say 'Go' put in the second circle the right answer to the question: 'How many months has a year?' In the third circle do nothing, but in the fourth circle put any number that is a wrong answer to the question that you have just answered correctly.—GO!" (Allow not over 10 seconds.)

7. "... When I say 'Go' *cross out* the letter just before C and also draw a line *under* the second letter before H.—GO!" (Allow not over 10 seconds.)

8. "... Notice the three circles and the three words. When I say 'Go' make in the *first* circle the *first* letter of the *first* word; in the *second* circle the first letter of the *second* word, and in the *third* circle the *last* letter of the *third* word.—GO!" (Allow not over 10 seconds.)

9. "... When I say 'Go' *cross out* each number that is more than 20 but less than 30.—GO!" (Allow not over 15 seconds.)

10. "... Notice that the drawing is divided into five parts. When I say 'Go' put a 3 or a 2 in each of the two largest parts and any number between 4 and 7 in the part next in size to the smallest part.—GO!" (Allow not over 15 seconds.)

11. "... When I say 'Go' draw a line through every even number that is not in a square, and also through every odd number that is in a square with a letter.—GO!" (Allow not over 25 seconds.)

12. "... If 7 is more than 5, then (when I say 'Go') cross out the number 6 unless 6 is more than 8, in which case draw a line

under the number 7.—GO!" (Allow not over 10 seconds.)

13. "Attention! Look at 12. If 3 is more than 1, then (when I say 'Go') cross out the number 2 unless 2 is more than 4, in which case draw a line *under* the number 3.—GO!" (Allow not over 10 seconds.)

* * * * *

Test 3, Practical Judgment

"This is a test of common sense. Below are sixteen questions. Three answers are given to each question. You are to look at the answers carefully; then make a cross in the square before the *best* answer to each question, as in the sample:

"Why do we use stoves? Because
□ they look well
□ they keep us warm
□ they are black."

* * * * *

Test 4, Synonym—Antonym

"If the two words of a pair mean the same or nearly the same, draw a line under *same*. If they mean the opposite or nearly the opposite, draw a line under *opposite*.

* * * * *

Test 5, Disarranged Sentences

... "The words *a eats cow grass* in that order are mixed up and don't make a sentence; but they would make a sentence if put in the right order: *a cow eats grass*, and this statement is true.

"Again, the words *horses feathers have all* would make a sentence if put in the order *all horses have feathers*, but this statement is false.

"Below are 24 mixed sentences. Some of them are true and some are false. When I say 'Go,' take these sentences one at a time. Think what each *would* say if the words were straightened out, but don't write them yourself. Then, if what it *would* say is true draw a line under the word 'true;' if what it would say is false, draw a line under the word 'false.' ..."

Test 6, Number Series Completion

... "Attention! Look at the first sample row of figures at the top of the page—2, 4,

6, 8, 10, 12; the two numbers that should come next are, of course, 14, 16.

"Look at the second sample—9, 8, 7, 6, 5, 4; the two numbers that should come next are 3, 2.

"Look at the third sample—2, 2, 3, 3, 4, 4; the two numbers that should come next are 5, 5.

"Now look at the fourth sample—1, 7, 2, 7, 3, 7; the next two numbers would, of course, be 4, 7.

"Look at each row of numbers below, and on the two dotted lines write the two numbers that should come next.—Ready—GO!" ...

Test 7, Analogies

"Attention! Look at the first sample at the top of the page: Sky—blue : : grass—table, *green*, warm, big.

"Notice the four words in heavy type. One of them—*green*—is underlined. Grass is *green* just as the sky is blue.

"Look at the second sample: Fish—swims : : man—paper, time, *walks*, girl.

"Here the word *walks* is underlined. A man walks and a fish swims.

"Look at the third sample: Day—night : : white—red, *black*, clear, pure.

"Here the word *black* is underlined because black is the opposite of white just as night is the opposite of day.

"In each of the lines below the first two words are related to each other in some way. What you are to do in each line is to see what the relation is between the first two words, and underline the word in heavy type that is related in the same way to the third word. Begin with No. 1 and mark as many sets as you can before time is called.—Ready—GO!"

After 3 minutes, say "STOP! ...

Test 8, Information

... "Notice the sample sentence: People hear with the—eyes—ears—nose—mouth. The correct word is *ears*, because it makes the truest sentence. In each of the sentences below you have four choices for the last word. Only one of them is correct. In each sentence draw a line under the one of these four words which makes the truest sentence."

* * * * *

Total Score and Rating

The result of examination alpha is expressed in a total score which is the sum of the raw scores of the several tests. The raw scores are obtained as follows:

Test	Method of Scoring	Maximum Raw Score
1	R	12
2	R	20
3	R	16
4	R–W	40
5	R–W	24
6	R	20
7	R	40
8	R	40
Total		212

Letter ratings are assigned on examination alpha as follows:

Rating	Score
A	135–212
B	105–134
C+	75–104
C	45– 74
C—	25– 44
D	15– 24
D—[1]	0– 14

[1] Recalled for further examination.

All ratings above D— are entered and reported at once. Men whose scores are below D are recalled for examination beta. Ratings of D— may not be given in alpha, unless recall of the men for beta is impossible.

The Army Beta Test (for Illiterates)

Test 1, Maze

"Now turn your papers over. This is test 1 *here* (pointing to page of record blank). Look." After all have found the page, examiner continues, "Don't make any marks till I say 'Go ahead.' Now *watch*." After touching both arrows, examiner traces through first maze with pointer and then motions the demonstrator to go ahead. Demonstrator traces path through first maze *with crayon*, slowly and hesitatingly. Examiner then traces second maze and motions to demonstrator to go ahead. Demonstrator makes one mistake by going into the blind alley at upper left-hand corner of maze. Examiner apparently does not notice what demonstrator is doing until he crosses line at end of alley; then examiner shakes his head vigorously, says "No—no," takes demonstrator's hand and traces back to the place where he may start right again. Demonstrator traces rest of maze so as to indicate an attempt at haste, hesitating only at ambiguous points. Examiner says "Good." Then holding up blank, "Look here," and draws an imaginary line across the page from left to right for every maze on the page. Then, "All right. Go ahead. Do it (pointing to men and then to books). Hurry up." The idea of working fast must be impressed on the men during the maze test. Examiner and orderlies walk around the room, motioning to men who are not working, and saying, "Do it, do it, hurry up, quick." At the end of 2 minutes examiner says, "Stop!" . . .

Test 2, Cube Analysis

"This is test 2 *here*. Look." After everyone has found the page—"Now watch." The order of procedure is as follows:

(1) Examiner points to the three-cube model on the blackboard, making a rotary movement of the pointer to embrace the entire picture.

(2) With similar motion he points to the three-cube model on shelf.

(3) Examiner points next to picture on blackboard and asks, "How much?"

(4) Examiner turns to cube model and counts aloud, putting up his fingers while so doing, and encouraging the men to count with him.

(5) Examiner tabs each cube on the blackboard and motions to demonstrator, asking him "How much?"

(6) Demonstrator (pointing) counts cubes on blackboard silently and writes the figure 3 in proper place.

In the second sample of this test, when examiner counts cubes of model he

(1) counts the three exposed cubes;

(2) touches the unexposed cube with pointer; and

(3) without removing pointer turns model, so that hidden cube comes into view of group. In other respects procedure with second and third samples is the same as with first.

In counting the 12-cube model, examiner (1) counts the top row of cubes in the model (left to right), (2) counts the exposed bottom row (right to left), (3) taps with pointer the end cube of hidden row, (4) turns the entire model around and completes his counting. Examiner then holds model in same plane as drawing and counts (in the same order as above) the cubes on blackboard, counting lines between front and top row as representing the hidden row. He then asks demonstrator "How much?" Demonstrator counts the cubes on blackboard (pointing but not speaking) and writes the response.

Throughout the demonstration the counting is done deliberately, not more rapidly than one cube per second.

At end of demonstration examiner points to page and says, "All right. Go ahead." At the end of 2½ minutes he says, "Stop!" . . .

Test 3, X–O Series

"This is test 3 *here*. Look." After everyone has found the page—"Now watch." Examiner first points to the blank rectangles at the end, then traces each "O" in chart, then traces outline of "O's" in remaining spaces. Demonstrator, at a gesture, draws them in. Examiner then traces first "X" in next sample, moves to next "X" by tracing the arc of an imaginary semicircle joining the two, and in the same manner traces each "X," moving over an arc to the next. He then traces outlines of "X's" in the proper blank spaces, moving over the imaginary arc in each case, and motions to demonstrator to draw them in. Demonstrator, at a gesture, fills in remaining problems very slowly, standing well to the right of the blackboard and writing with his left hand. Examiner points to page and says, "All right. Go ahead. Hurry up!" At end of 1¾ minutes he says, "Stop!" . . .

Test 4, Digit-Symbol

"This is test 4 *here*. Look." After everyone has found the page—"Now watch." Examiner points to first digit of key on blackboard and then points to the symbol under it. Same for all nine digits in key. Examiner then (1) points to first digit of sample, (2) to the empty space below digit, (3) points to corresponding digit of key, (4) points to proper symbol under digit in key, and (5) traces the outline of the proper symbol in the blank space under the digit in the sample. Same for first five samples. Demonstrator, at a gesture, fills in all the samples, working as follows: (1) Touches the number in the first sample with index finger of right hand; (2) holding finger there, finds with index finger of left hand the corresponding number in key; (3) drops index finger of left hand to symbol for number found; (4) holding left hand in this position writes appropriate symbol in the lower half of the sample.

Similarly with the other samples. While working, demonstrator should stand as far as possible to the left, doing all the samples from this side.

At the end of the demonstration examiner says, "Look here!" and points to key on page, repeating the gestures used in pointing on the blackboard at the beginning of the demonstration. Then, "All right. Go ahead. Hurry up!" Orderlies point out key to men who are at a loss to find it. At the end of two minutes, examiner says, "Stop!" ...

Test 5, Number Checking

"This is test 5 *here*. Look." After everyone has found the page, "Now watch." In this demonstration examiner must try to get "Yes" or "No" responses from the group. If the wrong response is volunteered by the group, examiner points to digits again and gives right response, "Yes" or "No" as the case may be. Examiner points to first digit of first number in left column, then to first digit, first number, in right column, then to second digit, first number, in left column and second digit, first number, in right column, nods head, says "Yes" and makes an imaginary cross at end number in right column. Motions to demonstrator, who makes an "X" there. Examiner does the same for second line of figures, but here he indicates clearly by shaking head and saying "No"—that certain digits are not identical. Examiner repeats for three more sets and after each, looks at group, says, "Yes?" in questioning tone and waits for them to say "Yes" or "No." He repeats correct reply with satisfaction. Demonstrator checks each after group has responded, or at signal from examiner if group does not respond. Demonstrator then works out remaining items,

pointing from column to column and working deliberately. Examiner summarizes demonstrator's work by pointing to the whole numbers in each set and saying "Yes" (indicating X) or "No;" if "No," he shows again where numbers are unlike. Examiner then points to page and says "All right. Go ahead. Hurry up!" At the end of 3 minutes examiner says "Stop." ...

Test 6, Pictorial Completion

"This is test 6 *here*. Look. A lot of pictures." After everyone has found the place, "Now watch." Examiner points to hand and says to demonstrator, "Fix it." Demonstrator does nothing, but looks puzzled. Examiner points to the picture of the hand, and then to the place where the finger is missing and says to demonstrator, "Fix it; fix it." Demonstrator then draws in finger. Examiner says, "That's right." Examiner then points to fish and place for eye and says, "Fix it." After demonstrator has drawn missing eye, examiner points to each of the four remaining drawings and says, "Fix them all." Demonstrator works samples out slowly and with apparent effort. When the samples are finished examiner says, "All right. Go ahead. Hurry up!" During the course of this test the orderlies walk around the room and locate individuals who are doing nothing, point to their pages and say, "Fix it. Fix them," trying to set everyone working. At the end of 3 minutes examiner says, "Stop!" ...

Test 7, Geometrical Construction

"This is test 7 *here*. Look." After everyone has found the page, "Now watch." Examiner points to the first figure on blackboard. He then takes the two pieces of cardboard, fits them on to the similar drawings on blackboard to show that they correspond and puts them together in the square on blackboard to show that they fill it. Then, after running his finger over the line of intersection of the parts, examiner removes the pieces and signals the demonstrator, who draws solution in the square on blackboard. The same procedure is repeated for the second and third sample. Demonstrator works out fourth sample, after much study, pointing from the square to the forms.

Demonstrator first draws two small squares

in the upper half of the large square, then the two triangles in the remaining rectangle. Each small figure is drawn in by tracing its entire circumference, not merely the necessary dividing lines. While drawing each small figure in the large square, demonstrator points with index finger of left hand to the corresponding small figure at left of square, taking care not to obstruct the view. At the end of the demonstration examiner holds up blank, points to each square on the page and says, "All right. Go ahead. Hurry up!" At the end of 2½ minutes, "Stop!" . . .

* * * * *

Total Score and Rating

The result of examination beta is expressed as a "total score," which is the sum of the raw scores of the several tests. The raw scores are obtained as follows:

Test	Method of Scoring	Maximum Score
1 . . .	Half point for each half maze	5
2 . . .	Number right	16
3 . . .	Number right	12
4 . . .	One-third of number right .	30
5 . . .	Right minus wrong	25
6 . . .	Number right	20
7 . . .	Number right	10
Total	. . . .	118

WILLIAM STERN
(1871–1938)

I.Q. [6]

In the systems using age gradation tasks are laid down for every age of childhood corresponding to the normal performance of these ages. If a child is tested with this series the level of accomplishment that he attains (his so-called "mental age" = MA) may be compared with his chronological age (CA). Binet chose as the measure of intelligence the difference between the mental age and the chronological age; nowadays, following my proposal, the ratio of the two values is generally calculated, giving the *intelligence quotient* IQ = MA/CA. For the normal child this value is equal to 100.

Example: An eight-year-old child completes the tests for six-year-olds, but fails at the tasks normal for those from seven to eight years old. CA = 8, MA = 6, the intelligence difference (following Binet) MA — CA = — 2, the intelligence quotient IQ = $^6/_8 \times 100 = 75$. Crudely expressed, the child has "three-quarter intelligence."

The IQ of a child is approximately constant in value over a number of years and may therefore be used as the determined level. To be sure, it furnishes only a very crude characterization, since the bare coefficient leaves out of account the profile schema of

intelligence. The IQ may be regarded only as a first approximation; it takes on significant value only when the bare quantitative statement is completed by a qualitative diagnosis. To base any pedagogical estimate upon the IQ alone for practical purposes (e.g., for assignment to opportunity classes) is indefensible.

This measurement is also of value for the purposes of group statistics. The simple administration of the method permits the testing of very large numbers of children of various ages and of adults as well, and the comparing of the group results.

We may enumerate here some of the results obtained in this way. If a large unselected group of children is tested and classified as to intelligence quotients, a *frequency curve* corresponding to the normal Gaussian curve results. That is, the IQ of 100 and the values nearest to it above and below 100 occur most frequently; beyond this range the curve drops off at both sides, first slowly and then more rapidly; the highest and lowest grades of intelligence are very infrequent.

In comparing experimental intelligence scores with *medical* diagnoses we find inconsistency in the medical terminology of different countries. There is agreement that normality extends down as far as IQ = 90. Between 90 and 80 are the cases bordering on subnormality. But as to express mental deficiency there is much controversy. German investigators ascribe to "debility" a "three-quarters"

---

[6] William Stern, *General Psychology: From the Personalistic Standpoint,* trans. Howard Davis Spoerl (New York: Macmillan, 1938), pp. 310–311; original German, *Allgemeine Psychologie: auf personalistischer Grundlage* (The Hague, 1935).

intelligence centering around an IQ of 75, to imbeciles a "two-thirds" intelligence scattered between 60 and 70. Following American authors there is a much wider range of IQ's. L. S. Hollingworth, for instance, says: "Idiots grade roughly from 0 to 20, imbeciles from 20 to 40, and morons from 40 to 70." Also the mental ages have likewise been related to the different groups as follows: The mental age that can never be exceeded is two years for idiots, seven years for imbeciles, and twelve years for morons.

If the two *sexes* are compared, age, milieu, and school being equal, no noteworthy difference in the group averages of intelligence quotients are revealed. (This result shows clearly the inadequacy of the bare coefficient, for in profiles of female and male intelligence there are differences that are noticeable even in infancy, but which drop out of this kind of calculation.)

Comparisons of children of different racial and national *descent* have revealed significant statistical differences. The racial mixture of the United States has afforded favorable opportunities for investigation in this regard. (As an example, the intelligence cross section of white children and adults is higher than that of colored people.)

Similar results were obtained from children of different *social* strata. The lower level of intelligence of the strata in a poor social position, for example, is plain when public schools in different districts of the city are compared; the average for poorer quarters falls off markedly in contrast with the well-to-do.

Aussage Test [7]

Experiments in "aussage" on little children have so far been made entirely by means of pictures. The test can be carried out principally as follows:

1. The child is asked to describe a picture seen only once either—

   (a) Immediately after looking at the picture ("primary aussage"),

[7] William Stern, *Psychology of Early Childhood up to the Sixth Year of Age*, trans. Anna Barwell (New York: Henry Holt, 2nd ed., 1930), pp. 266–269; original German, *Psychologie der frühen Kindheit bis zum sechsten Lebensjahre* (Leipzig, 1914).

   (b) Again, some time later ("secondary aussage").

2. A "continuous impression" is used as the test for description, i.e. a picture which has been a considerable time before the child's eyes, e.g. hanging on the wall; this continuous impression may be either—

   (a) One that has existed up to the moment of the description, e.g. a picture hanging in the next room;

   (b) One that in the past has existed for a long time, but has been non-existent for some time before the description, e.g. a picture removed from the wall some months before.

The "aussage" can be given in the form of a description (connected narrative) or of a cross-examination (answers to separate questions, a series of which have been drawn up as the result of systematic trials); as a rule both methods are combined. It is valuable, both from a psychological and educational point of view, after the test is over to put the picture before the child once more and let him find out what mistakes he has made (self-correction).

Tests with Pictures Seen Only Once

As an example how such aussage-tests may be carried out at a very early age, we append the result obtained from Eva. . . . A picture she had not seen before, "The Breakfast" . . . was laid before her for two minutes, and she was asked to say all she could see on it; then the picture was taken away and an account and examination followed.

Explanatory

The number of statements given in the "primary aussage" was 35—5 wrong; in the secondary, 37—8 wrong; if the extreme youth be taken into account, the sum-total remembrance was therefore quite excellent. It must be owned by far the greater number of statements were extracted by questions; in the unaided accounts we only find four and five respectively, hence spontaneous remembrance in the three-year-old child is still very small. The effect of the interval between the primary and secondary aussage is not shown by an increase of forgetfulness (for the number of right statements at worst remains the same), but it is an increase of error. The mistakes made are caused in great part by confusion

DURING THE TWO-MINUTE OBSERVATION OF THE PICTURE

A. OBSERVATION AND DESCRIPTION

Gunther eats bread—and here is Tony (the cook)—flower. What is that? (Mother answers: A satchel.) *For the boy—that is a cupboard there and that a room* (pointing to the door). *Where do you go into? And that is the kitchen, What is Gunther eating, I wonder? Bread.*

B. EXAMINATION

Question	Answer
Is the woman standing or sitting?	*Standing—Gunther sits.*
Has she got an apron on?	*Tied round her.*
What colour is it?	*Green.*
What has she got in her hand?	*I don't know without being told.*
Can you see a table?	*Yes.*
What is lying on the table?	*Bread.*
What else?	*Nothing else.*
Isn't there butter as well?	*No.*
Has she got a knife in her hand?	*No.*

AFTER TAKING AWAY THE PICTURE

A. DESCRIPTION

(Mother: Now try and tell me all you have seen.)
Gunther, Tony, Flower in room.
(What else?) Door.
(What more?) Tony. Gunther.

B. EXAMINATION

Question	Answer
How is Gunther dressed?	*Suit, stocking.*
What is he doing?	*Eating.*
How does he hold it?	*In his hand.*
Is there a door in the room?	*Yes.*
Open or shut?	*Open.*
Can you see what is outside?	*No.*
Can you see a box?	*No.*
Can you see a flowerpot?	*No—yes.*
Where was it?	*On the cupboard.*
Can you see a satchel?	*Yes.*
Where?	*Down on the ground.*
What does it look like?	*Like the table.*
Can you see a jug?	*No.*

SECONDARY AUSSAGE, THREE DAYS LATER; THE PICTURE NOT SEEN IN THE INTERVAL

A. DESCRIPTION

(Mother: Do you remember my showing you a picture here on the table? What could you see on it?)

Gunther, Tony, Mother, Door.
(And what else?)
Else (the nurse), Tony.
(You saw Tony and Mother?)
Yes, and Else too.
(Do you remember anything else?)
Door.
(Anything else?)
Hans—nothing else there at all.

B. EXAMINATION

1. Was the mother standing or sitting?
2. What is the woman doing?

3. Had she an apron? What colour?
4. What was she holding?
5. Had she a knife in her hand?
6. Had she got bread in her hand?
7. Can you see a table?
8. What lies on the table?
9. What else was on table?

10. But you said Tony was making soup.
11. No soup then?
12. How was Gunther dressed?
13. Wasn't he barefooted?
14. What is he doing?
15. How does he hold it?
16. Is the door shut or open?
17. Can you see what is outside?
18. Do you not see a window?
19. Do you see a flower-pot?
20. What is standing on the ground?
21. Do you see a jug?

1. *Standing. Gunther was sitting.*
2. *She was cooking soup and the satchel was there too.*
3. *Yes. Green.*
4. *A spoon for the soup.*
5. *No.*
6. *Yes.*
7. *Yes.*
8. *Bread.*
9. *Nothing else at all, but the bread was on the table.*
10. *But it was bread.*
11. *Only bread.*
12. *Suit and stockings.*
13. *No, shoes and stockings.*
14. *Eating bread.*
15. *In his hand.*
16. *Open.*
17. *Yes, nothing but little pots.*
18. *No.*
19. *Yes, there is a flower-pot.*
20. *A school satchei.*
21. *No.*

with impressions arising from other pictures, e.g. this is the cause of the indecision shown in the secondary aussage, when Eva first makes a wrong statement about making soup, but then rightly substitutes bread-cutting. The colour-mistakes are of no importance, since at that time the child was not yet sure of colour-names. In addition, some things really there (jug and knife) were not allowed. On the other hand, exactly the opposite error, the invention of objects not to be seen, does not once occur in the primary aussage and but seldom in the secondary, a proof of the child's good power of observation and her extreme freedom from suggestibility. For in the examination strongly suggestive questions were purposely introduced, e.g. "Isn't the boy barefooted?" "Isn't there butter as well?" But Eva's sure remembrance and great independence of mind prevented their having any effect on her, although they very often have on children of that age or even older.

In such an "aussage"-test, then, in spite of its shortness, we get an insight into the different aspects of childish individuality.

Personality as a Unitas Multiplex [8]

We define the person as follows:

The "person" is a living whole, individual, unique, striving toward goals, self-contained and yet open to the world around him; he is capable of having experience.

Except for the criterion of "experiencing," which was purposely placed at the end, the specifications throughout are *psychophysically neutral*. Into the totality of the person are interwoven both his physical and psychical aspects. Goal-directed activity is manifested in breathing and limb movements as well as in thinking and striving. Independence of and exposure to the environment apply both to bodily functions and to conscious phenomena.

The attribute "capable of having experience" is distinct from all the others in that it is *non-compulsory*. Every person *must* be at all times and in all respects a totality possessing life, individual uniqueness, goal-directed activity, independence of and openness to the world, *but not always consciousness*.

---

[8] William Stern, *General Psychology: From the Personalistic Standpoint, op. cit.*, pp. 70–76.

Even at times when nothing is being "experienced" the person exists, while the loss of any one of the other attributes would suspend existence.

There is a *science* of the human "person," that studies him in his totality and psychophysical neutrality; it is *personalistics*. It furnishes common hypotheses for all specialized scientific studies of the person: for the biology, the physiology, the pathology, the psychology, of the person. *Psychology is the science of the person as having experience or as capable of having experience.* It studies this personal attribute, experience, in regard to the conditions of its appearance, its nature, mode of functioning and regularity, and its significance for personal existence and life considered as a whole. . . .

Only that which lives can have experience. "Life" is the unity of being and acting in a totality open to the environment. A living being is of such character that its total *nature* is constantly being actualized through its activity while likewise remaining a whole in its incessant intercourse with the environment. This "having life" is the basic principle from which any consideration of the person takes its departure. Life comprises the fundament from which all experience develops, that supports all experience, into which all experience discharges. Life is complete, while in comparison experience is fragmentary and intelligible only in terms of life.

The question must here be brought up as to why the term "experience" (*Erleben*) and not the long-established term *consciousness* (*Bewusstsein*) is preferred in characterizing mind. The term "consciousness" originally had a completely intellectualistic meaning; it designated the condition in which the individual is a *knower* (of facts or of himself). Later the word was used more and more loosely (permitting references also to a foggy kind of feeling-consciousness, etc.), but its original purpose was always suggested whenever it was employed. It has become a matter of grave concern for the entire modern conception of mind, that mind came thus to be explained in terms of its latest and most refined characteristic, "knowledge." In the rôle of knower the individual is furthest removed from the estate of continuous and autonomous vital functioning.

* * * * *

The thesis of personalistics, that "experience develops out of and into life," reverses the approach. The primary thing is really conceived as primary, that is, as bearing the stamp of life. But here a fundamental question arises. What do we mean by "life" in reference to the *human* "person"? (Not simply that life which is the subject-matter of current biology.) In human beings life appears in *three modalities*, and in going from one to the other the personal *world* also, to which life is open, takes on diverse aspects.

The first modality was just mentioned as the *biological* in a narrow sense. Human life holds in common with vegetable and animal life those functions which bring the individual naturally and unquestionably into conformity with his environment. Self-maintenance and "self-steering," growth and maturing, reproduction, adaptation, mneme, are such *vital functions*. The "world" is present with respect to these functions as but an extended domain of life, as stimulus or raw material, as shelter or menace; it constitutes the vital world or *biosphere* of the person.

We may skip the second modality for the moment and proceed to describe the third, which contrasts with the first since it deals with the purely *human* sphere in the life of the person. Every trace of this third modality of life is absent in animals and plants. In this sphere every human being constitutes a substrate of value and at the same time the unique, meaningful center of a world that also consists of independent substrata of value, be they other individuals, societies, cultural, historical, or religious facts and ideals.

Modalities of Life

Person	World
I. Vitality	Biosphere
II. Experience (*Erleben*)	World of Objects
III. Introception	World of Values

The aim of human life involves the affirmation by the individual, in his being and acting, both of his own intrinsic significance *and* of the objective significance of the world, so that he acquires reality as a person through the coalescence of the world of objective values with his own substance. This coalescence or incorporation the personalistic theory designates as *introception;* it denotes the activity that gives direction and form to all genuinely human life. The unitary and meaningful pattern of life that introception endeavors to establish is called *personality*. Although the concept of "person" in the sense given above may be applied to any individual animal, *personality* is an uniquely human category.

The concept introception is psychophysically neutral, covering as it does the purposes of life functions and not merely a mode of experience. This is also true of all specific forms of introception: loving, understanding, creating, consecrating, etc.

* * * * *

Between the first modality of life, vitality, and the third, introception, there is another, with which *psychology* is directly concerned: the modality of *experience*. The "world" that belongs to this modality likewise occupies a position between the simple biosphere and the world of values. It is the *world of objects*.

Experience (Erleben)

a. Cleavage. The person is a totality, that is, a *unitas multiplex*. This must be taken literally. All the multiplicity included in the person, the hegemony of elements, events, phases, strata, is *integral* to the totality and not just superficially cemented to it or supported and conditioned by it; it is the *consonance* of multiplicity with the personal whole and of the person with the world, that makes human life possible.

But this consonance is not merely a perpetuated harmony. The more amply a living totality is articulated and the more various the multiplicity integral to it, *the less self-evident* is its life. Whenever the simple modality of vitality is surpassed but the modality of complete introception is not attained, there is tension and dissonance in life, which resist immediate coalescence with the totality; a *dis-living* sets in. But since these cleavages affect the totality, which cannot be abandoned, they become life functions, assuming the special form "experience."

Experience, then, is life under cleavage and tension. Cleavage and tension can never exist as quiescent conditions; they are dynamic processes. Therefore dissonance is constantly being augmented or diminished. All experience consequently tends to become either *salient* against or *embedded* within the totality. Or more accurately, in any experience both tendencies are always simultaneously present, for complete cleavage would destroy the unity of the person while complete embedding would break off the tension and disrupt experience. *The different proportions of salience and embedding* give the process and content of every experience its special character.

* * * * *

The proof that experience has cleavage is expressed first of all in the fact that it has *objects*. Living, with the individual, is absolute and unconditional, but his experience is always *of something*. Experience is transitive; it transfers to and aims at something that is not itself experience.

What *is* this "something" that is experienced? Here we have a new cleavage between the outside world and the person himself. That is, while these two components are one in the immediate vital modality and in the higher totality of introception, in experience they belong to life apart from each other. The individual experiences the outside *world;* external objects, values, laws, that are potential or actual, past, present, future, timeless; or else he experiences *himself;* his own striving, values, dispositions, inarticulate tendencies, former states of being, future possibilities. The scale of *objectified experiences* runs from the first tingle of a touch impression through perceptions, ideas, thoughts, to a complete world-view. The scale of *subjectified experiences* runs from the infant's vague feeling of being alive to the adult's completely formed consciousness of self and sense of his own importance.

* * * * *

b. Appearance. Now although a gap always remains between the experience and its object, on the other hand a *positive* connection obtains between the two; for every experience *points to* some existence (in the external world or in one's own person). This positive relation is suggested by the terms mirroring, *appearing*. (For example, past events appear in a remembrance; the personal weakness of the subject is mirrored in a feeling of inferiority.) In experience the object is given a second time, not, to be sure, actually duplicated, but as a reflection that is both similar and dissimilar to, close to and distant from, that which it reflects. It is *appearance*, but not disembodied appearance; on the contrary it is *authenticated appearance*.

* * * * *

As measured by its objects, then, experience is imperfect and noncongruent; still it deals with appearance and reflection. This raises the question: *What is the significance for the person of this double nature of all experience?*

Experience is fragmentary. The sum total of life processes and contents is not convertible into experience, nor does it need to be. Only such particular occurrences within life as involve *tensions* are at the same time experienced internally. The individual is mirrored in his own experience in so far as he is in a *struggling* state, i.e., in so far as internal resistance and inhibition interrupt the plain current of life. And the world is reflected in his experience in so far as it deviates from the individual and his course of life as something salient, alien, questionable and even hostile.

CHARLES EDWARD SPEARMAN
(1863–1945)

"G" Factor [9]

Correspondence betweem General Discrimination and General Intelligence

Up to now, we have only discussed the correspondence of the various Intelligences with the various sensory activities, Hearing, Sight, Touch, etc. Such isolated facts are

interesting enough, but quite otherwise important is the relation of *any common and essential element in the Intelligences to any common and essential element in the Sensory Functions*. For brevity, we will term these common elements "General Intelligence" and "General Discrimination."

* * * * *

On the whole, then, we reach the profoundly important conclusion that *there really exists*

---

[9] C. Spearman, " 'General intelligence,' objectively determined and measured," *Amer. J. Psychol.*, 1904, **15**, 268–285.

a something that we may provisionally term "General Sensory Discrimination" and similarly a "General Intelligence," and further that the functional correspondence between these two is not appreciably less than absolute.

* * * * *

Universal Unity of the Intellective Function

In view of this community being discovered between such diverse functions as in-school Cleverness, out-of-school Common Sense, Sensory Discrimination, and Musical Talent, we need scarcely be astonished to continually come upon it no less paramount in other forms of intellectual activity. Always in the present experiments, approximately, $\dfrac{r_{pq}}{\sqrt{r_{pp} \cdot r_{qq}}} = 1.$[10]

I have actually tested this relation in twelve pairs of such groups taken at random, and have found the average value to be precisely 1.00 for the first two decimal places with a mean deviation of only 0.05. All examination, therefore, in the different sensory, school, or other specific intellectual faculties, may be regarded as so many independently obtained estimates of the one great common Intellective Function.

Though the range of this central Function appears so universal, and that of the specific functions so vanishingly minute, the latter must not be supposed to be altogether non-existent. We can always come upon them eventually, if we sufficiently narrow our field of view and consider branches of activity closely enough resembling one another. When, for instance, in this same preparatory school we take on the one side Latin translation with Latin grammar and on the other side French prose with French dictation, then our formula gives us a new result; for the two Latin studies correlate with the French ones by an average of 0.59, while the former correlate together by 0.66 and the latter by

---

[10]   Where $r_{pq} =$ the mean of the correlations between the members of the one group p with the members of the other group q,

   $r_{pp} =$ the mean of the inter-correlations of the members of the group p among themselves,

and $r_{qq} =$ the same as regards group q.

0.71; so that the element common to the Latin correlates with the element common to the French by $\dfrac{0.59}{\sqrt{0.66 \times 0.71}} = 0.86$ only.

That is to say, the two common elements by no means coincide completely this time, but only to the extent of 0.86 or 74 %; so that in the remaining 26 %, each pair must possess a community purely specific and unshared by the other pair.

We therefore bring our general theorem to the following form. *Whenever branches of intellectual activity are at all dissimilar, then their correlations with one another appear wholly due to their being all variously saturated with some common fundamental Function (or group of Functions).* This law of the Universal Unity of the Intellective Function is both theoretically and practically so momentous, that it must acquire a much vaster corroborative basis before we can accept it even as a general principle and apart from its inevitable eventual corrections and limitations. Discussion of the *subjective* nature of this great central Function has been excluded from the scope of the present work. But clearly, if it be mental at all, it must inevitably become one of the foundation pillars of any psychological system claiming to accord with actual fact—-and the majority of prevalent theories may have a difficulty in reckoning with it.

Of its objective relations, the principal is its unique universality, seeing that it reappears always the same in all the divers forms of intellectual activity tested; whereas the specific factor seems in every instance new and wholly different from that in all the others. As regards amount, next, there seems to be an immense diversity; already in the present examples, the central factor varies from less than 1/5 to over fifteen times the size of the accompanying specific one. But all cases appear equally susceptible of positive and accurate measurement; thus we are becoming able to give a precise arithmetical limitation to the famous assertion that "at bottom, the Great Man is ever the same kind of thing."

Finally, there is the exceedingly significant fact that this central Function, whatever it may be, is hardly anywhere more prominent than in the simple act of discriminating two nearly identical tones; here we find a correlation exceeding 0.90, indicating the central Function to be more than four times larger than all the other influences upon individual differentiation. Not only the psychical content but also the external relations of Sensory Discrimination offer a most valuable simplicity; for it is a single monotonous act, almost independent of age, previous general education, memory, industry, and many other factors that inextricably complicate the other functions. Moreover, the specific element can to a great extent be readily eliminated by varying and combining the kind of test. For these reasons, Discrimination has unrivalled advantages for investigating and diagnosing the central Function.

The Hierarchy of the Intelligences

The Theorem of Intellective Unity leads us to consider a corollary proceeding from it logically, testing it critically and at once indicating some of its important practical uses. This corollary may be termed that of the Hierarchy of the Specific Intelligences.

For if we consider the correspondences between the four branches of school study, a very remarkable uniformity may be observed. English and French, for instance, agree with one another in having a higher correlation with Classics than with Mathematics. Quite similarly, French and Mathematics agree in both having a higher correlation with Classics than with English. And the same will be found to be the case when any other pair is compared with the remainder. The whole thus forms a *perfectly constant Hierarchy* in the following order: Classics, French, English, and Mathematics. This unbroken regularity becomes especially astonishing when we regard the minuteness of the variations involved, for the four branches have average correlations of 0.77, 0.72, 0.70, and 0.67 respectively.

When in the same experimental series we turn to the Discrimination of Pitch, we find its correlations to be of slightly less magnitude (raw) but in precisely the same relative rank, being: 0.66 with Classics, 0.65 with French, 0.54 with English, and 0.45 with Mathematics. Even in the crude correlations furnished by the whole school without excluding the nonmusicians, exactly the same order is repeated, though with the general diminution caused by the impurity: Classics 0.60, French 0.56, English 0.45, and Mathematics 0.39.

Just the same principle governs even Musical Talent, a faculty that is usually set up on a pedestal entirely apart. For it is not only correlated with all the other functions, but once again in precisely the same order: with Classics 0.63, with French 0.57, with English 0.51, with Mathematics 0.51, and with Discrimination 0.40. Ability for music corresponds substantially with Discrimination of tones, but nevertheless not so much as it does with algebra, irregular verbs, etc.[11]

The actual degree of uniformity in this Hierarchy can be most conveniently and summarily judged from the following table of correlation; the values given are those actually observed (theoretical correction would modify the relative order, but in no degree affect the amount of Hierarchy or otherwise). Each number shows the correlation between the faculty vertically above and that horizontally to the left; except in the oblique line italicized, the value always becomes smaller as the eye travels either to the right or downwards.

Altogether, we have a uniformity that is very nearly perfect and far surpasses the conceivable limits of chance coincidence. When we consider that the probable error varies between about 0.01 for the ordinary studies to about 0.03 for music, it is only surprising that the deviations are not greater. The general Hierarchy becomes even more

[11] Of course, notable instances will easily be found where musical ability is apparently divorced from General Intelligence; in this very school, for example, the best musician is far from standing high intellectually. But not even the most extreme cases necessarily contravene the above rule. A correlation does not state any absolute coincidence between two faculties, but only a limited and precisely measured tendency in this direction; so far from excluding deviations, it proclaims them and even estimates their exact probability. If we may assume the normal law of frequency to approximately hold good and may abstract from further influences, then the proportion of persons with any given amount of musical talent who will attain to any given degree of stupidity (or *vice versa*)

$$= \frac{1}{2} - \frac{1}{\sqrt{\pi}} \int_0^{ah} e^{-t^2} \, dt$$

where h is a measure of the correlation between Musicality and Intelligence, and a = the given inferiority in the latter faculty.

	Classics	French	English	Mathem.	Discrim.	Music
Classics	0.87	0.83	0.78	0.70	0.66	0.63
French	0.83	0.84	0.67	0.67	0.65	0.57
English	0.78	0.67	0.89	0.64	0.54	0.51
Mathem.	0.70	0.67	0.64	0.88	0.45	0.51
Discrim.	0.66	0.65	0.54	0.45		0.40
Music	0.63	0.57	0.51	0.51	0.40	

striking when compared with the oblique line, which is no measure of the central Function and where consequently the gradation abruptly and entirely vanishes.

The above correlations are raw, and therefore do not tell us either the true rank of the respective activities or the full absolute saturation of each with General Intelligence. For the former purpose we must eliminate the observational errors, and for the latter our result must further be *squared*. Thus we get:

Activity	Correlation with Gen. Intell.	Ratio of the Common Factor to the Specific Factor	
Classics	0.99	99 to	1
Common Sense . .	0.98	96	4
Pitch Dis.	0.94	89	11
French.	0.92	84	16
Cleverness	0.90	81	19
English	0.90	81	19
Mathematics . . .	0.86	74	26
Pitch Dis. among the uncultured .	0.72	52	48
Music	0.70	49	51
Light Dis.	0.57	32	68
Weight Dis. . . .	0.44	19	81

It is clear how much the amount of any observable raw correlation depends upon the two very different influences: first, there is the above intellective saturation, or extent to which the considered faculty is functionally identical with General Intelligence; and secondly, there is the accuracy with which we have estimated the faculty. As regards the ordinary school studies, this accuracy is indicated by the oblique italicized line, and therefore appears about equal in all cases (not in the least following the direction of the Hierarchy); but in other cases there is a large divergence on this head, which leads to important practical consequences. Mathematics, for example, has a saturation of 74 and Common Sense has one of about 96; but in actual use the worth of these indications

becomes reversed, so that a subjective impression as to a child's "brightness" is a less reliable sign than the latter's rank in the arithmetic class; almost as good as either appears a few minutes' test with a monochord.

In the above Hierarchy one of the most noticeable features is the high position of languages; to myself, at any rate, it was no small surprise to find Classics and even French placed unequivocally above English (note that this term does not refer to any study of the native tongue, but merely to the aggregate of all the lessons conducted therein, such as History, Geography, Dictation, Scripture, and Repetition).

However it may be with these or any other special facts, here would seem to lie the long wanted general rational basis for public examinations. Instead of continuing ineffectively to protest that high marks in Greek syntax are no test as to the capacity of men to command troops or to administer provinces, we shall at last actually determine the precise accuracy of the various means of measuring General Intelligence, and then we shall in an equally positive objective manner ascertain the exact relative importance of this General Intelligence as compared with the other characteristics desirable for the particular post which the candidate is to assume (such as any required Specific Intelligences, also Instruction, Force of Will, Physical Constitution, Honesty, Zeal, etc.; though some of these factors cannot easily be estimated separately, there is no insuperable obstacle to weighing their *total influence* as compared with General Intelligence). Thus, it is to be hoped, we shall eventually reach our pedagogical conclusions, not by easy subjective theories, nor by the insignificant range of personal experiences, nor yet by some catch-penny exceptional cases, but rather by an adequately representative array of established facts.

LOUIS LEON THURNSTONE
(1887–1955)

A. A. Factor Analysis [12]

For many years psychologists have described a person's mental endowment by a single index of intelligence such as the intelligence quotient—the familiar "I. Q." But it is well known among teachers and employers that two men may have the same general level of mental ability and yet be totally different as to their aptitudes and potentialities, and that therefore the single intelligence index is inadequate for the purpose of describing mental endowment.

It has been found necessary to use, in addition, other indexes of special abilities which cannot be represented by any single index of intelligence. Well known among such abilities, for example, is musical talent, which is really a complex of many abilities. Mechanical aptitude is another well known complex of abilities that cannot be represented by any single index of intelligence. The general use of a single index of intelligence such as the intelligence quotient should be discontinued because of its logical inconsistencies, but it is not the purpose of this article to elaborate on that particular problem.

A better method is to describe each person in terms of a "profile" of abilities in which it is frankly recognized that two men may have the same level of mental endowment and yet be totally different, as shown by the entirely different types of work which they can learn to do and to enjoy. The counseling of young people about their education and life work should be done in terms of this profile of abilities and the temperamental traits which constitute their principal life assets.

If we grant the soundness of this plan, then we must turn to the question: Just what are the fundamental human abilities and traits? Every writer on this subject can set up a list of qualities and their classifications. Hundreds of writers have done this, and there are almost as many lists of abilities and traits as there are writers who attempt to solve this problem by subjective personal judgment.

A better plan is to solve the problem by scientific experiments to discover the differentiable mental functions. The profiles of abilities and traits should then be written in terms of the traits, that have been found to be truly fundamental and independent and not in terms of the trait lists that any author may write on an intuitive basis. When we write Verbal Comprehension and Word Fluency as two traits, it is not just because we have thought up two different trait names. We write them as two distinct abilities in the profile because they have been shown experimentally to be two different mental functions.

Just how should the fundamental human traits be discovered and isolated? That is what "multiple factor analysis" was designed to accomplish. The development of multiple factor analysis was started in 1930 as an extension of the earlier work of the British psychologist, Spearman, whose method of analyzing mental abilities was very suggestive but not quite adequate to cover the complexities of mental organization. The development of multiple factor analysis has been actively pursued by Americans and by some British psychologists and mathematicians for the past fourteen years, and the methods have been applied to a number of experimental studies in this field.

The exploratory studies so far completed have isolated a number of primary mental functions. These include Verbal Comprehension, which is designated by the symbol (V), Word Fluency (W), Number Facility (N), Memory (M), Visualizing or Space Thinking (S), Perceptual Speed (P), Induction (I), Speed of Judgment (J), two factors governing speed and flexibility of closure, an ability which is discussed later in this article, and several others whose existence is indicated but not yet isolated with confidence.

Nobody knows how many of these traits must be isolated before we can describe a person's mental endowment adequately for purposes of educational and vocational counseling. If we knew the fifteen or twenty socially most important of these mental functions we should probably be able to do the counseling quite adequately in most cases.

A brief description of some of the abilities

[12] L. L. Thurstone, "Testing intelligence and aptitudes," *Hygeia: The Health Magazine*, 1945, vol. 23, pp. 32–36, 50–54. Reprinted by permission of the American Medical Association.

that have been identified so far will help the reader to understand methods now in use. The space factor, for example, is the ability to think in terms of two and three dimensions. It is the ability to visualize that was described by Galton in terms of his informal experiments over fifty years ago. Some of the tests for visualizing or space thinking are shown in the accompanying illustrations.

In one of these there are some drawings of hands in different positions. Here the subject, or person whose ability is being tested, is asked to check each drawing to show whether it is a right hand or a left hand. Good visualizers can usually do this task easily whereas poor visualizers have trouble with it. Some people find it necessary to

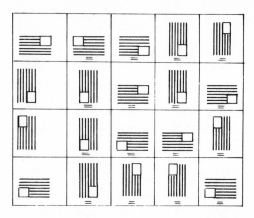

Look at the first flag in each row. Then mark the others in that row which show the same side of flag.

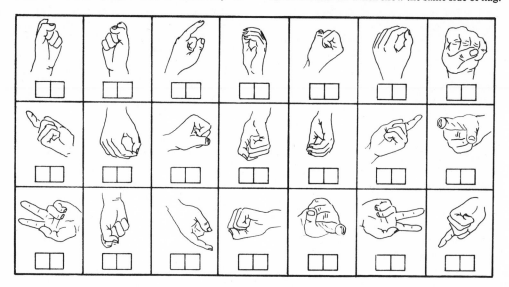

Indicate whether each drawing shows a right or left hand. This tests "space thinking."

twist their own hands into various positions to see which hand is represented by each drawing.

In another illustration one of the simplest and yet one of the most effective tests for the space factor is shown. This illustration shows a few items of the flag test. The subject is asked to look at the first flag in each row and to mark all the others in that row which show the same side of the flag. In the first row, for example, there is only one flag that shows the same side as the first flag. The reason this test is saturated with the space factor is that it requires ordinarily that the figure be turned in

two or three dimensions. Facility in this kind of thinking involves the visualizing or space factor.

Still another of the many different tests for the visualizing factor is shown in one of the accompanying illustrations. Here the subject is asked to indicate how many of the blocks shown touch each block in the group. For example, the block "A" is in contact with five other blocks; hence the subject should record "5" next to the letter "A." The block "B" is in contact with four other blocks, and hence the subject should record "4" next to the letter "B." This again illustrates the ability

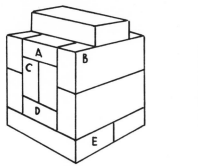

Another test for the visualizing factor: Indicate how many blocks touch each one of the blocks A, B, C, D and E shown in the drawing.

In all these tests you will find great individual differences. Some people keep right on going because they can think readily of words in the required context. Others will think of half a dozen words and then have a "blocking."

The verbal comprehension factor (V) may be tested in many ways. In one test the subject is given sets of five proverbs. Four of these proverbs have essentially the same meaning, and the fifth one has a different meaning. The

to deal readily with two or three dimensional problems.

One of the simplest tests for the word fluency factor (W) requires the subject to write as many words as he can think of which have some specified prefix or suffix such as "end" or "tion." Another test for this same fluency factor is shown here. In the first column the given letters in each row can be rearranged to form the names of well known American cities. A similar test for this factor is to ask the subject to write as many words as he can think of which begin with a specified initial letter, or to ask the subject to think of as many words as he can for things to eat and drink, for example.

PROVERBS

In each group of five proverbs mark the proverb which has a different meaning from the other four proverbs.

☐ A journey of a thousand miles begins with one step.
☐ Tall oaks from little acorns grow.
☐ Great ends from little beginnings.
☐ No grass grows on a beaten road.
☐ Large streams from little fountains flow.

☐ Familiarity breeds contempt.
☐ Every bird likes its own nest best.
☐ Sweets grown common lose their dear delight.
☐ No man is a hero to his valet.
☐ If every day were a sunny day, who would not wish for rain.

☐ There is no smoke without fire.
☐ A spark may start a great fire.
☐ Reputation may be ruined by a word.
☐ A small leak will sink a ship.
☐ Trifles may cause universal disaster.

Vehicles		American Cities	
wango	_____	gochiac	_____
cargiare	_____	tiptsgrub	_____
ract	_____	tooled	_____
nva	_____	velecland	_____
tuao	_____	bulafof	_____
trina	_____	vouislille	_____
gygbu	_____	keemilwau	_____
krcut	_____	ettlsea	_____
elds	_____	sleanpoinim	_____
comolitove	_____	nothingsaw	_____
legsih	_____	orttide	_____
bleiccy	_____	dhomnirc	_____

Word fluency test: Unscramble the words.

subject is asked to check this odd proverb in each set of five. In the first set of those shown in the illustration, the fourth proverb is different from the rest.

A large vocabulary is characteristic of this factor (V), and it is readily apparent that this factor is of fundamental importance in a wide variety of occupations. It should be noticed, however, that these two verbal factors that we have called "verbal comprehension" and "word fluency" are quite distinct. A person may have a large vocabulary and yet not be very fluent. Then again, a person may be quite fluent although his vocabulary is restricted. It is not sufficient merely to name these abilities "verbal." We know that there are several other verbal factors in addition to these two that I have described, and it is our expectation to identify them in experimental work which is about to be undertaken. It may be of passing interest that the word fluency factor (W) has been found to be negatively selective for airplane pilots—that is, men who make good pilots do not score well on tests for this factor. Apparently they are not as a rule a verbally fluent group of young men.

In one of a number of tests for the number factor (N), the subject has the simple task of checking each number in a series which is three higher than the number before it. Every one can do this task, but there are great differences in the speed with which people can do it. The number factor is very restricted. It is concerned with facility in simple numerical operations such as column addition. To be successful in arithmetical reasoning problems, such as those found in accounting, requires much more than this one number factor. Arithmetical reasoning in all its many forms is a complex of factors concerned with verbal thinking, number thinking, visualizing and verbal comprehension. The restricted number factor is simply a part of the complex of arithmetical reasoning.

One of many tests for inductive thinking is presented here to help illustrate what is meant by this factor, which is characterized by the ability to discover the rule or principle that underlies the material presented. The factor transcends the content of the material so that it is independent of the numerical, verbal or spatial nature of the task. In this test, which is called Letter Grouping, the subject is asked to examine the four groups of letters in each row and to discover something which is common to three of them. He is asked to check the odd group. The test shown here starts with the simplest items. In the first row there are three groups that have three letters "A" which are adjacent. The second group should be marked, because it is the odd group. In the last row of letters in this test, we might start with the hypothesis that two letters are identical in each group, but that hypothesis fails because this is true for all four groups. So we try again, and find that the first three letters in each group are in alphabetical order except in the first group. So we mark the first group as the odd one. Each line calls for a new hypothesis.

LETTER GROUPING

In each row, three of the groups of letters are alike in some way. Mark the one that is different.

AAAM	AACA	AAAD	AAAK
ABCD	EFGH	IJKL	OPST
BXYC	FPQG	JXYK	LXYM
DFDF	KLKL	STVW	BCBC
ABCP	CBAQ	ABCR	ABCS
DCCJ	DFFJ	DNNJ	DRSJ
CXYZ	CFGH	DPQR	CLMN
BEFE	HIJI	NOPO	TUVU

Visual closure is a phenomenon which has been investigated by the German gestalt psychologists. By closure we mean the ability to get a synthesis out of a diffuse presentation, so that it becomes unified. Instead of seeing disorganized and discreet parts of the presentation the subject perceives the presentation as a unified whole. This unification frequently happens suddenly, and the phenomenon is called closure. People differ remarkably in the ability with which they can unify the material that they are working with into a complete whole. In the simple test on page 299, the subject is asked to read the words. The first item is evidently the word "bread" and the next is "artist." The next word is "pistol." You might look at this word as though it consisted of a haphazard arrangement of spots. That would mean the absence of closure. When the spots become unified into

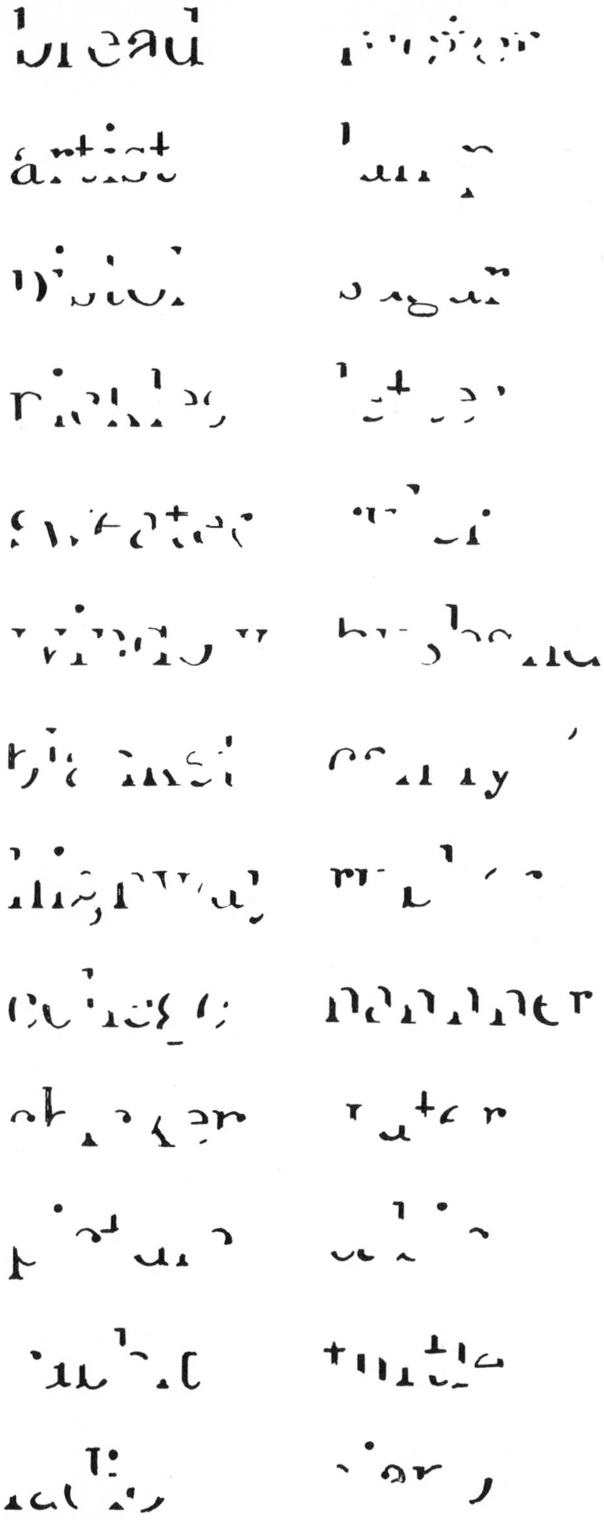

bread

artist

window

pickles

sweater

window

basket

highway

college

officer

picture

child

table

Above: Another test for closure—identify the mutilated pictures. Below: this test measures two abilities—closure and flexibility.

a single perception we have closure. Of course, we are not specially interested in knowing whether the subject can read mutilated words. We are interested, however, in the facility with which the subject can form good closure, and this simple test is one of many in which this ability is revealed. In the next illustration we have a few examples from a test in which the subject is asked to identify each mutilated picture. This is also a test of perceptual closure. The first picture, for example, is a horse and buggy.

In another of the tests shown here we are dealing with two abilities. At the top of the picture are two geometrical figures. The subject is asked to determine which of these two figures is contained in each of the following, more complicated figures and to draw that figure. As you will notice, each of the large figures has a definite configuration of its own. In order to do this task the subject must break up the given figure so that he can

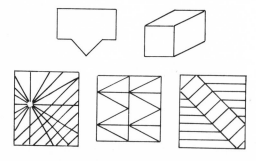

One of these two figures is contained in each of the following drawings. Mark only one figure in each drawing.

see the required figure. This task requires, then, two operations—first, the process of destroying the presented configuration, and, second, the process of seeing a new configuration. The firmness of a configuration is known as "Gestaltbindung." To do this task successfully the subject must not only have the ability to form a closure readily but he must also have an additional ability— namely, flexibility in manipulating the configurations. One authority has described reasoning as the ability to destroy a given configuration so as to think of a better one. These are the abilities that we are trying to appraise by tests of this sort.

It should be emphasized here that these tests are not the conventional kind of intelligence test with which most people are already familiar. Some readers will be glad to know that there is no relation between these closure tests and intelligence as ordinarily estimated! We are dealing here with mental abilities that are not ordinarily represented in the estimates of general intelligence.

A study was completed in our laboratory last year on the auditory aspects of closure. We found that in the field of hearing the same closure effects are operating that have been discussed here in the field of vision. There are great differences among people in the ability to understand speech when it is distorted, for example. This is analogous to the visual closure tests which we have just presented. We are not dealing here with auditory acuity as determined by the audiometer. Two people may be comparable in ordinary hearing tests yet differ tremendously in their ability to understand distorted speech or in their ability to hear something in spite of distracting noises. If you can understand a person across the room in spite of distracting conversation near by, then you have this closure factor.

A simple example of auditory closure is the ability to learn the telegraphic code. About one fourth to one third of the general population finds it very difficult to learn. Two years ago we constructed an aptitude test for code operators. This was a test of code learning and code recognition in which we featured auditory closure. Selection of code operators by their scores on this test can reduce the failures to less than 5 per cent. Tests of this kind are superseding the simpler

MECHANICAL APTITUDES

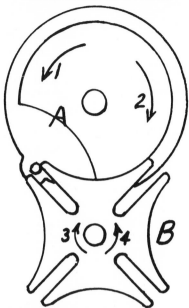

1. If the fan is turning in the direction shown which way does it blow the air? . . . .————
2. If this were a propeller on a boat, which way would the boat move?
3. If this were a propeller on an airplane, which way would the plane move? . . . .————

1. Which part moves only part of the time? . . . .————
2. Which part is the driver? . . . .————
3. Can this mechanism operate when A moves in direction 1? . . . .   Yes   No
4. Can this mechanism operate when A moves in direction 2? . . . .   Yes   No
5. If B moves in the direction 4 which way is A moving? . . . .————
6. How many times does A turn around while B is turning around once? . . . .————

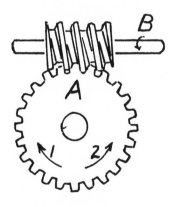

1. If B turns in the direction shown, which way will A turn? . . . . .————
2. Can A be the driver? . . . . . .   Yes   No
3. If the worm were taken off, reversed, and replaced on the same shaft, which way would A turn?————

code aptitude test designed in the last war, which has been in use until the present time.

A few items from a test of mechanical aptitude are also presented in one of our illustrations. This helps explain one aspect of perceptual function that has not yet been adequately explored. In order to answer the simple questions on these figures, the subject must be able to visualize the simple mechanical devices and he must also be able to visualize the movement of these objects. It is probable that mechanical aptitude consists to a large extent of visualizing ability and perceptual closure, together with the ability to imagine constrained movement.

There have been a number of applications of our knowledge of these factors in the selection and training of people for specified jobs. For example, in training people to become draftsmen it has been found that a fairly large proportion of the population has considerable difficulty in learning projection and similar spatial ideas. Most of the failures in such training can be avoided at the start by selecting people who do well on tests involving the space factor and the closure factors. This is a rational procedure, as contrasted with the usual procedure of trying all sorts of tests and determining by crude methods which tests work best. In problems of this kind we can arrive at a solution rationally to the extent that we know something about the mental faculties that are involved.

In this connection I might mention that the problem of mechanical aptitude has not yet been completely solved. We know that the space factor and the closure factors are involved, but we have not yet identified the factors concerned with the visualizing of movement which are undoubtedly involved in mechanical aptitude. It is worth emphasizing also that we should not talk about mechanical aptitude as though it were a single ability. It is much more likely to be a complex of abilities. We have the methods for investigating this problem, and we hope to identify several additional factors which help determine mechanical aptitude.

The final illustration shows what we mean by describing a person's mental endowment as a profile instead of by a single index such as the intelligence quotient. Under each of the profiles on this page we have listed the occupational interests of the subject. The subject in the first profile expressed an interest in modern and classical languages. This profile is high in the two verbal factors and in reasoning. The second profile is high in immediate memory, which is a useful ability necessary in such skills as shorthand and receiving the telegraphic code. The third profile is high in the visualizing or space factor and in induction. This is typical for students of engineering and physical science. The fourth profile is highest in word fluency, which is consistent with this subject's major interest in writing and in commercial interpreting. Musical ability and artistic ability are both complexes of complexes that have not yet been analyzed by the factorial methods.

In counseling young people about their vocational choice we should be careful not to insist on sending them into those occupations in which they would be most typical. Many men are successful in their professions simply because they are not typical. The law student with technical aptitudes might excel in patent law or in dealing with legal problems with technical content. A student with interest in physics might become conspicuously successful in medicine by developing x-ray equipment and other applications of the physical sciences in medicine. We should

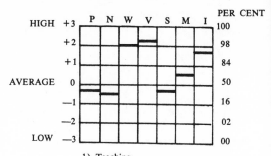

1) Teaching
2) Modern and classical languages

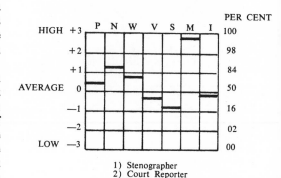

1) Stenographer
2) Court Reporter

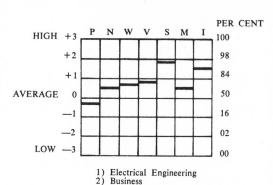

1) Electrical Engineering
2) Business

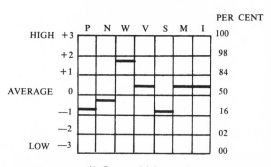

1) Commercial Interpreting
2) Art or Writing

have an explicit policy of encouraging a wide variety of mental types in each profession so as to insure competent talent to deal with the thousands of problems that overlap several professions or sciences. The same principle holds for some of the skilled trades.

In presenting this brief description of the principal or primary factors that have been identified so far it is not my intention to imply that this list is in any sense complete. Many other factors remain to be identified not only in the intellectual realm but also in the description of the dynamic system that constitutes personality. However, even with the present list of primary mental abilities we are able to describe mental endowment for educational and vocational purposes much more adequately than we could a few years ago when such description was dominated by the intelligence quotient. This work is not only consistent with the scientific object of identifying the distinguishable mental functions, but it is also consistent with the desire to recognize every person in terms of the mental and physical assets which make him unique as an individual.

Answers to Problems

Hand Test—Top row (starting at left): L, R, L, L, R, L, L; Middle row: R, R, L, R, R, L, R; Bottom row: L, R, R, L, R, R, L.

Flag Test—Top row: Fourth flag from left is same side as first flag. Second row: Third and fourth flags same as first. Third row: Third, fourth and fifth flags same as first. Bottom row: Second, fourth and fifth flags same as first.

Block Test—A touches 5 other blocks; B, 4; C, 5; D, 6; and E, 4.

Word Fluency—Vehicles: wagon, carriage, cart, van, auto, train, buggy, truck, sled, locomotive, sleigh and bicycle. Cities: Chicago, Pittsburgh, Toledo, Cleveland, Buffalo, Louisville, Milwaukee, Seattle, Minneapolis, Washington, Detroit and Richmond.

Proverbs—First group: The fourth proverb is different from the others. Second group: The second is different. Third group: The first is different.

Letter Grouping—Top row: Second group from left. Second row: Fourth group. Third row: Second group. Fourth row: Third group. Fifth row: Second group. Sixth row: Fourth group. Seventh row: Third group. Bottom row: First group.

Broken Words—First column: bread, artist, pistol, pickles, sweater, window, blanket, highway, college, chicken, picture, rabbit, radio. Second column: motor, lamp or lump, sugar, letter, ruler, husband, candy, rubber, hammer, water, cabin or cubic, turtle, piano.

Mutilated Pictures—Left to right: Horse and buggy, locomotive, woman at laundry tub.

Geometric Figures—The left hand figure in the second row contains the first of the two figures shown at the top; the middle figure below contains the second of the top figures; the right hand figure below contains the first one at the top.

Mechanical Aptitude—First test: (1) B; (2) A; (3) yes; (4) yes; (5) 2; (6) 4. Second test: (1) 2; (2) no; (3) 2. Third test: (1) 1; (2) 2; (3) 2.

DAVID WECHSLER
(1896–   )

WAIS
(Wechsler Adult Intelligence Scale) [13]

The final battery of tests included in the original Wechsler Bellevue Scale and maintained in its present revision consists of six Verbal and five non-verbal or Performance tests as follows: (1) an information test, (2) a general comprehension test, (3) a memory span test (digits forward and backward), (4) an arithmetical reasoning test, (5) a similarities test, (6) a vocabulary test, (7) a picture arrangement test, (8) a picture completion test, (9) a block design test, (10) an object assembly test and (11) a digit symbol test. The grouping of the subtests into Verbal (1–6) and Performance (7–11), while intending to emphasize a dichotomy as regards possible types of ability called for by the individual tests, does not imply that these are the only abilities involved in the tests. Nor does it presume that there are different kinds of intelligence, e.g., verbal, manipulative, etc. It merely implies that these are different ways in which intelligence may manifest itself. The subtests are different measures of intelligence, not measures of different kinds of intelligence, and the dichotomy into Verbal and Performance areas is only one of several ways in which the tests could be grouped.

Apart from technical considerations (suitability for age level, ease of scoring, administration, etc.), final selection of tests was based primarily on 3 considerations: (1) that previous studies should have shown that the tests correlated reasonably well with composite measures of intelligence, (2) that the tests as a group encompassed sufficient diversity of function so as not to favor or penalize subjects with special abilities or disabilities and (3) that the nature and character of subjects' failures on the tests have some diagnostic implications.

* * * * *

[13] David Wechsler, *The Measurement and Appraisal of Adult Intelligence* (Baltimore: Williams & Wilkins, 4th ed., 1958), pp. 63–64, 67–71, 73–75, 77–85. Reprinted by permission.

Information Test

The W–B I Information Test contains 25 questions, the WAIS Information Test 29, each representing a selection from a much larger list. The method employed in choosing the items was to present the questions, generally in sets of 25 to 30, to groups of individuals of known intelligence level. Selection of the items was then made on the basis of the incidence of successes and failures among the various groups. A question was held to be a "good" one if it showed increasing frequency of success with higher intellectual level. Of course, not all questions were equally discriminative at all levels. Thus, the question "Weeks in a year?" discriminates well between mental defectives and the borderline group and not at all between the average and superior. On the other hand, "What is the Koran?" does not discriminate at all the lower levels (since practically every individual there failed it), but showed quite significant differences between the respective percentage of average and superior individuals who passed it. In the restandardization of the WAIS a number of tests items showed up as more difficult, e.g., Capital of Italy, population of the United States, and others less effective, e.g., function of the heart, discoverer of the North Pole, than others that were tried out. Altogether 7 of the original items were omitted from and 13 new ones added to the WAIS.

The order in which the questions are listed approximates roughly their order of difficulty for the sample population at the time of standardization. No doubt, in different localities, the order will be somewhat different; it will also be affected to some extent by the national origin of subjects tested. Thus, "What is the capital of Italy?" is passed almost universally by persons of Italian origin irrespective of their intellectual ability. More interesting than such sources of expected variation are some findings not so easily accounted for on item difficulty. The question "What is the population of the United States?" turns out to be inexplicably hard. It is surprising how many native Americans do not know even the approximate number of inhabitants of their own country. Estimates by college graduates have ranged from 10 to 300 million. On the other hand, more people can tell what a thermometer is than state how many weeks there are in a year; more can give the name of the inventor of the aeroplane than of the author of *Hamlet*.

* * * * *

Comprehension Test

Tests of general comprehension have long been favorites with authors of scales, and our results justify this popularity. General comprehension questions are to be found in the original Binet as well as in all of its revisions. They occur also in many group examinations, such as the Army Alpha and the National Intelligence Tests. The test as it appears on the individual and group examinations, however, cannot be said to be equivalent. One important difference is that on the group test the subject is merely asked to select one of a number of possible answers furnished him by the examiner. On the test given individually, the subject must furnish his own answer to the questions. This way of giving the test not only reduces chance successes, but also enables the examiner to evaluate the subject's response even when it is incorrect. Indeed, one of the most gratifying things about the general comprehension test, when given orally, is the rich clinical data which it furnishes about the subject. It is frequently of value in diagnosing psychopathic personalities, sometimes suggests the presence of schizophrenic trends (as revealed by perverse and bizarre responses) and almost always tells us something about the subject's social and cultural background. The variety of replies one gets to such a question as "What would you do if you found a letter that was already sealed, stamped and addressed?", or "Why does the state require people to get a marriage license?" is far greater than one would suspect, certainly far greater than an examiner could include in a multiple choice questionnaire. The following are sample replies to the first question: "Bring it to the man's house." "Leave it there." "Open it and see if there is any money in it." And here are some answers to the marriage question: "To prevent bigamy." "For census

purposes." "To protect the morals of the community." "To protect the honor of womanhood." "So people will know they are married."

* * * * *

Precisely what function the Comprehension Test involves is difficult to say. Off hand it might be termed a test of common sense, and it is so called on the Army Alpha. Success on the test seemingly depends on the possession of a certain amount of practical information and a general ability to evaluate past experience.

* * * * *

Arithmetical Reasoning Test

The ability to solve arithmetical problems has long been recognized as a sign of mental alertness. Even before the introduction of psychometrics, it was used as a rough and ready measure of intelligence. Now most intelligence scales include items calling for arithmetical reasoning in some form. The inclusion of such items is fully justified; arithmetical reasoning tests correlate highly with global measures of intelligence.

In addition to being a good measure of general intelligence the Arithmetical Reasoning Test enjoys the advantage of being easily devised and standardized. But its merits are lessened by the fact that it is influenced by education and occupational pursuit. Clerks, engineers and businessmen usually do well on arithmetic tests, while housewives, day laborers and illiterates are often penalized by them. Another shortcoming of the test is that individual scores may be affected by fluctuations of attention and transient emotional reactions.

* * * * *

Memory Span for Digits

Perhaps no test has been so widely used in scales of intelligence as that of Memory Span for Digits. It forms part of the original Binet Scale and all the revisions of it. It has been used for a long time by psychiatrists as a test of retentiveness and by psychologists in all sorts of psychological studies. Its popularity is based primarily on the fact that it is easy to administer, easy to score, and specific as to the type of ability it measures. Nevertheless, as a test of general intelligence it is among the poorest. Memory span, whether for digits forward or backward, generally correlates poorly with other tests of intelligence. The ability involved contains little of g and, as Spearman has shown, is more or less independent of this general factor. Our own results confirm these observations. For a long time we considered the desirability of eliminating the test from our battery altogether, but finally decided to retain it for the following reasons: (1) Although Memory Span for Digits backward and forward is on the whole a poor measure of intelligence, it is nevertheless an extremely good test at the lower levels. Except in cases of special defects or organic disease, adults who *cannot* retain 5 digits forward and 3 backward will be found, in 9 cases out of 10, to be feeble-minded or mentally disturbed. (2) Special difficulty with the repetition of digits forward or backward is often of diagnostic significance. Obvious examples are the memory defects which constitute clinical symptoms in certain organic diseases and other types of cases. A marked falling off in memory span is often one of the earliest indications of mental impairment.

Low scores on the Memory Span Test when not associated with organic defect can be due to anxiety or inattention. In either case, difficulty in the reproduction of digits correlates with lack of ability to perform tasks requiring concentrated effort. Individuals with these defects seem to have a special difficulty repeating digits backward.

* * * * *

The words used in each of the standardizations and their order of presentation are given below.

W–B I

Orange	Banana
Coat	Dress
Dog	Lion
Wagon	Bicycle
Daily paper	Radio
Air	Water
Eye	Ear
Egg	Seed
Wood	Alcohol
Poem	Statue
Praise	Punishment
Fly	Tree

WAIS

Orange	Banana
Coat	Dress
Axe	Saw
Dog	Lion
North	West
Eye	Ear
Air	Water
Table	Chair
Egg	Seed
Poem	Statue
Wood	Alcohol
Praise	Punishment
Fly	Tree

The Similarities Test has several merits. It is easy to give and appears to have an interest appeal for the average adult. It is the kind of test which has been recognized by all investigators as containing a great amount of g. Over and above this, the test has certain qualitative features, the most important of which is the light that the type of response sheds upon the logical character of the subject's thinking processes. There is an obvious difference both as to maturity and as to level of thinking between the individual who says that a banana and an orange are alike because they both have a skin, and the individual who says that they are both fruit. As already noted by Terman and others, it is not until the individual approaches adult mentality that he is able to discriminate between essential and superficial likenesses. But it is remarkable how large a percentage of adults never get beyond the superficial type of response. It is for this reason that, unlike previous methods of scoring, the one employed in our scale distinguishes between superior and inferior responses by allowing different credits for each. Thus, when the subject says an orange and banana are alike because "you can eat them," and a bicycle and wagon "because they have wheels," he receives a credit of 1, whereas the responses "both are fruit" and "means of conveyance" are scored 2. This qualitative difference in response is of value not only because it furnishes a more discriminating scoring method, but also because it is often suggestive of the evenness and level of the subject's intellectual functioning. Some subjects' total scores, even when relatively good, are largely made up of 1 credits, whereas the scores of others are of an unpredictable proportion of 0, 1 and 2 credits. The former are likely to bespeak individuals of consistent ability, but of a type from which no high grade of intellectual work may be expected; the latter, while erratic, have many more possibilities.

* * * * *

Picture Arrangement Test

The Picture Arrangement Test consists of a series of pictures which, when placed in the right sequence, tell a little story. The picture series is not unlike the short comic strips found in the daily papers. The pictures are presented to the subject in a disarranged order and he is asked to put them together in the right order so that they make a sensible story. The correct order is the one originally given to the pictures by the artist.

* * * * *

The set of pictures included in our battery represents the final choice from among more than twice that number originally tried out. They were selected on the basis of interest of content, probable appeal to subjects, ease of scoring and discriminating value. Any attempt to satisfy all these conditions was bound to occasion difficulties, and in spite of the considerable labor spent before definitive choices were made, the final selection leaves much to be desired. The fault, however, is not so much with our particular selection as with the limitations inherent in all picture arrangement tests, namely their dependence upon actual content. It is of some importance whether the story told by the pictures is that of a bird building a nest or a policeman pursuing a thief in a radio car. The former is a situation a country boy may grasp at once; the latter may puzzle him a good deal. And what is true for such simple situations plays an even greater role when the story told by the pictures is more complicated. The Picture Arrangement items in both W–B and WAIS represent essentially American situations and sense of humor, and their appreciation may be expected to be influenced by cultural background.

* * * * *

In spite of certain definite limitations, the Picture Arrangement test has some very worthwhile merits. In the first place, it is the type of test which effectively measures a subject's ability to comprehend and size up a total situation. The subject must understand the whole, must get the "idea" of the story, before he is able to set himself effectively to the task. There is, of course, some trial and error experimentation, but the subject is also called upon to attempt appraisal of the total situation more than in most other tests. Secondly, the subject matter of the test nearly always involves some human or practical situation. The understanding of these situations more nearly corresponds to what other writers have referred to as "social intelligence."

* * * * *

Picture Completion Test

The Picture Completion of the W–B and WAIS tests merely require the subject to discover and name the missing part of an incompletely drawn picture. He is shown a picture, e.g., a steamship minus its funnel or a watch with its second hand missing, and asked to indicate the missing part. In its present form the test is very much like that of the Mutilated Pictures of the Binet Scale.

* * * * *

From a purely psychometric point of view the Picture Completion has several assets worth noting. It takes relatively little time to administer, is given *in toto* and may be repeated after short intervals without risk of significant practice effect. The test is particularly good in testing intelligence at the lower levels. Ostensibly it measures the individual's basic perceptual and conceptual abilities in so far as these are involved in the visual recognition and identification of familiar objects and forms. To be able to see what is missing from any particular picture, the subject must first know what that picture represents. But, in addition, he must be able to appreciate that the missing part is in some way essential either to the form or the function of the object or picture. In a broad sense the test measures the ability of the individual to differentiate essential from non-essential details.

* * * * *

Block Design

The Block Design Test was originated by Kohs, who offered it as a comprehensive measure of non-verbal intelligence. The initial enthusiasm for its originator seems fully justified. Adaptations of Kohs Test now appear in a number of intelligence scales, and our own experience shows that it conforms to all criteria of a "good" test. It correlates well with a variety of criterion measures, with total scale score and with most of the subtests of the scale. It also correlates better with Comprehension, Information and Vocabulary than some of the verbal tests themselves.

* * * * *

The Block Design is not only an excellent test of general intelligence, but one that lends itself admirably to qualitative analysis. One can learn much about the subject by watching "how" he takes to the task set him. Already mentioned is the matter of method that may be employed in assembling the designs, by following the figure *versus* breaking it up into its component parts. There is also the difference of attitude and emotional reaction on the part of the subject. One can often distinguish the hasty and impulsive individual from the deliberate and careful type, a subject who gives up easily or becomes disgusted, from the one who persists and keeps on working even after his time is up, and so on. A number of other temperamental traits manifest themselves not infrequently in the course of a subject's performance.

The diagnostic value of the test is particularly worth mentioning. Patients with mental deterioration and seniles have particular difficulty in managing the test and often cannot complete the simplest design, however much they try. This is also true of most cases of brain disease. The difficulty here seems to be due to a lack of synthesizing ability, or loss of the "abstract approach," in K. Goldstein's sense of the term.

* * * * *

Digit Symbol Test

The Digit Symbol or Substitution Test is one of the oldest and best established of all psychological tests. It is to be found in a large variety of intelligence scales, and its wide popularity is fully merited. The subject is required to associate certain symbols with certain other symbols, and the speed and accuracy with which he does it serve as a measure of his intellectual ability. The one concern that presents itself in the use of the Digit Symbol Test for measuring adult intelligence is the possible role which visual acuity, motor co-ordination and speed may play in the performance of the task. Experience with the test shows that, except in cases of individuals with visual defects and specific motor disabilities, the first two are not of significant importance; but the case for motor speed cannot be discounted. We know from general observation and from some experimental studies that older persons do not write or handle objects as fast as younger persons, and what is perhaps equally important, they are not as easily motivated to do so.

* * * * *

Object Assembly Test

The Object Assembly Test consists of three or four figure form-boards (3 on the W–B, 4 on the WAIS). The W–B I "objects" comprise a *Manikin*, a *Feature Profile* and a *Hand*. The Manikin is essentially the same as that devised by Pintner and first used on the Pintner-Paterson scale (399), except that the features have been redrawn to make them more human in appearance. Our Profile resembles that used by the Pintner-Paterson test but differs from the original in several respects. It is a profile of a woman's head instead of a man's, the ear is divided into two instead of four parts, and a piece has been cut out at the base of the skull. The Hand is entirely new and was devised by the author. As presented to the subject, it consists of a mutilated hand from which the fingers and a large section of the palm have been cut away. The *Elephant* has been added to the WAIS series and was also devised by the author. It consists of a side view of a smallish pachyderm which has been cut up asymmetrically into six pieces which the subject is required to put together.... We wanted at least one test which required putting things together into a familiar configuration. Our experience over a long period with the commonly used form-boards had convinced us that whatever their merit when administered to children, they were often ill-adapted for testing adults. Most of the standardized form-boards are much too easy for the average adult, and at the high levels have very little discriminative value. The distribution tables for these form-boards, moreover, have unusually large scatter.

* * * * *

Vocabulary Test

Contrary to lay opinion, the size of a man's vocabulary is not only an index of his schooling, but also an excellent measure of his general intelligence. Its excellence as a test of intelligence may stem from the fact that the number of words a man knows is at once a measure of his learning ability, his fund of verbal information and of the general range of his ideas. The one serious objection that could be raised against it was that a man's vocabulary is necessarily influenced by his educational and cultural opportunities.

* * * * *

A test calling for definition of words is often of value because of its qualitative aspects.

There is an obvious difference in the reasoning ability between two adults, one of whom defines a "donkey" as "an animal" and the other who defines it in such terms as "it has four legs" or that "it looks like a jackass." Sometimes the quality of a subject's definition tells us something about his cultural milieu. The type of word on which a subject passes or fails is always of some significance. Dull subjects from educated homes often get uncommon words like "vesper" and "encumber" but fail on "gamble" and "slice;" the pedant will get "espionage" but fail on "spangle," get "travesty" but fail on "matchless," etc. Perhaps more important from a clinical point of view, is the semantic character of a definition which gives us insight into an individual's thought processes. This is particularly true in the case of schizophrenics, the formal aspects of whose language disturbance is frequently diagnostic.

In estimating the size of a person's vocabulary, items of the kind just discussed do not enter into the quantitative evaluation. What counts is the number of words that he knows. Any recognized meaning is acceptable, and there is no penalty for inelegance of language.

19

French Clinical Psychology

EDME MARIOTTE
(1620–1684)

The Blind Spot [1]

This is my observation concerning the lack of vision that occurs when the image of an object falls right on the optic nerve; I told you that for a long time I was curious to know if the vision is more or less strong at the location of the optic nerve. This causes

---

[1] Edme Mariotte, *Discovery of the Blind Spot.* Translated from the French, *Novvelle découvverte tovchant la veve* (Paris, 1668) by Richard Lewis Sahakian for the present volume.

me to make a curious remark to which I had not paid attention. I hold certain that the vision is made by the reception of rays that make an image of objects at the back of the eye and that this image is situated upside down and backwards to that which the objects represent. I have also observed by the anatomy of both men and animals that the optic nerve never corresponds exactly to the middle of the back of the eye, that is to say, to the place where the image of the objects is made when one looks directly at an object; and that in a man it is a little higher, and on the side toward the nose, to make the rays of an object fall on the optic nerve of my eye and to prove what will happen, I attached on a dark background at the level of my eyes, a small round piece of white paper, to serve as a fixed point of view; and meanwhile I attached another to my right, at a distance of about two feet, but a little lower than the first in order that it would fall on the optic nerve of my right eye, while I would keep the left closed. I stood facing the first paper and moved away little by little, always keeping my right eye fixed on the first; and when I was about ten feet away, the second paper which was nearly four inches, completely disappeared, meanwhile I was not able to attribute this to the obliqueness of this object as much as I could notice other objects that were even further to the side; I would have believed that someone had subtly removed it, if I had not found it in moving my eye a little. But as soon as I looked fixedly at my first paper, this other which was to the right would disappear instantly; and to find it without moving my eye, it was necessary to change its position. I made the same experiment at other distances, moving away or approaching the papers in proportion. I performed it again with the left eye, while keeping the right closed after having moved the paper to the left of my fixed point of view. So by the situation of the parts of the eye, there is no room for doubt that it is the optic nerve that causes this lack of vision.

I communicated this discovery to many of my friends, to whom the same thing occurred; but not always precisely at the same distances; and I attribute this diversity to the different positions of their optic nerves. The R. P. de Billy was one of the first to whom I made part of this experiment—you have done it yourself in the Royal library, where I showed it to gentlemen of your assembly; and you remarked that at a certain distance, there were some, who at the distances I said lost sight of an eight-inch paper and others did not lose sight except when it was a little smaller; this is only able to happen because of the different sizes of the optic nerve in different eyes.

This experiment thus confirmed has given me reason to doubt that the vision is produced in the retina, as I had believed following the most common opinion, and has made me think, that it was rather in this other membrane, that one finds at the back of the eye through the retina, and which is called the chorid. For if it was in the retina, it seems that vision should be produced wherever the retina is to be found; and since it (retina) covers the whole optic nerve, besides the rest of the back of the eye, there would not be any reason why there would be no eyesight at the position of the optic nerve: on the contrary, if it is in the choroid, one can clearly see that the reason for which there is no eyesight at the optic nerve, is because this membrane begins at the edges of this nerve, and does not cover the middle like it covers the rest of the back of the eye.

FRANÇOIS MAGENDIE
(1783–1855)

Bell–Magendie Law on Spinal Nerve Roots [2]

For a long time I had wanted to perform on an animal the experiment of cutting the posterior roots of the nerves which originate

at the spinal cord. I had tried it many times without success, since it is difficult to open the vertebral canal without injury or death to the animal. Last month a litter of eight puppies was brought to my laboratory, about six weeks old. These animals seemed to me particularly suitable for a new attempt at opening the vertebral canal. Using a very sharp scalpel I was able, with a single stroke, so to speak, to lay bare the posterior half of the spinal cord enclosed within its envelopes. All that remained was to cut the surrounding *dura mater*, and this I accomplished without

[2] François Magendie, "Expériences sur les fonctions des racines des nerfs rachidiens," *Journal de Physiologie Expérimentale et Pathologique*, 1822, **2**, 276–279; ¡"Expériences sur les fonctions des racines des nerfs qui naissent de la moëlle épinière," *ibid.*, 366–371. Translated for the present volume by Cleophas W. Boudreau.

difficulty. At this point I had before my eyes the posterior roots of the lumbar and sacral pairs, and, lifting them in turn with the blades of a small pair of scissors, I succeeded in cutting them on one side without injury to the spinal cord. I had no idea what would result from this experiment. I closed the wound with sutures, and observed the animal. At first I believed that the limb corresponding to the cut nerves was completely paralyzed; it was insensitive to pricking and hard pressure, and it also appeared to be immobile. Soon, however, to my surprise, I clearly saw it move, although its sensibility was completely removed. A second and third experiment yielded precisely the same result. I began to consider it probable that the posterior roots of the spinal nerves had different functions from those of the anterior roots, and that they were particularly concerned with sensibility.

It occurred to me, of course, that the next step was to cut the anterior roots while leaving the posterior ones intact. Such an undertaking was easier to conceive than to carry out. How to lay bare the anterior part of the spinal cord without disturbing the posterior roots? The thing appeared impossible; nonetheless I continued to ponder the problem for two days, and I finally decided to try to introduce the blade of a sort of narrow cataract knife under the posterior roots and to cut the anterior roots by pressing them against the posterior surface of the vertebrae. I was obliged to abandon this procedure because of the large veins in the canal on the side that I opened with each progressive movement of the blade. In making these attempts I noted that, by pulling upward the vertebral *dura mater*, I could see the anterior roots bound together into bundles at their entrance into the membrane. Acting immediately I succeeded, in a few moments, in cutting all the pairs I wished to divide. As in previous experiments I performed the section on one side only in order to retain a term of comparison. It is easy to imagine the interest with which I observed the effects of this section. There was no doubt whatsoever: the limb was completely immobilized and flaccid, although there could be no doubt that its sensibility remained unimpaired. Finally, for the sake of thoroughness, I cut both the anterior and the posterior roots;

there was a total loss of feeling and movement.

I repeated with variations these experiments, using different species of animals. The results which I reported previously were abundantly confirmed with regard to both the anterior and posterior limbs.

* * * * *

The facts that I described in the preceding issue are too important to dismiss without further research and discussion.

I wanted first to verify whether the anterior or posterior roots of the spinal nerves could be severed without injury to the spinal cord; since the nervous functions are visibly diminished if the spinal cord is exposed to the air at a low temperature, the desired results can be obtained, though not without difficulty.

The anatomical disposition of the various parts did not rule out the experiment, for each group of spinal roots occupies for some distance its own canal before rejoining and fusing with the other groups. I discovered, in fact, that with the aid of a pair of scissors blunted at the points I could remove enough of the vertebral lamina and lateral parts to lay bare the ganglion of each lumbar pair. With the use of a small probe it is not then too difficult to isolate the canal containing the posterior roots, after which it is very easy to make the section. This method of performing the experiment yielded the same results that I had already observed; but since it is considerably longer and more complicated than the other, I see no reason why it should be preferred.

I next attempted to submit to a further test the results of which I have already spoken. It is common knowledge that the *nux vomica* produces violent tetanic convulsions in men and animals. I was interested in determining whether these convulsions could be produced in a limb in which the motor nerves had been severed, and if so whether they would be as strong as in a limb in which the sensory nerves had been severed. The results agreed perfectly with the earlier ones, that is, in an animal whose posterior roots have been severed the tetanus is as complete and as intense as if the spinal roots were intact. On the other hand, in the case of an animal of which I had severed the motor nerves of one posterior limb, this limb remained supple and motionless while all the other muscles of the body were experiencing the most violent of convulsions under the influence of the poison.

Can contractions be produced by irritating the sensory nerves directly, or by stimulating the posterior spinal roots? Would a direct irritation of motor nerves produce pain? Such were the questions I next confronted, and it was evident that only further experimentation could resolve them.

I began accordingly with an examination of the posterior roots, the sensory nerves. Here is what I observed: the pinching, stretching or pricking of these nerves causes the animal to manifest pain, but this pain is very slight compared to the intense pain produced if one touches, even gently, the spinal cord at the origin of these roots. Almost every time that the posterior roots are stimulated, contractions are produced in the corresponding muscles. However, these contractions are not pronounced, and are much weaker than those produced by touching the spinal cord itself. If an entire bundle of posterior roots is severed, movement is produced throughout the limb that corresponds to that bundle.

I repeated these experiments on the anterior nerve groupings and obtained analogous though opposite results. Here the contractions produced by pinching, pricking, etc. are very strong and even convulsive, whereas the signs of sensibility are hardly visible. These results, then, confirm those that I have already presented; in addition they seem to establish that feeling is not exclusively in the posterior roots, nor movement exclusively in the anterior ones. One difficulty could arise. When, in the preceding experiment, the roots had been cut, they were still continuous with the spinal cord. Could not the stimulus communicated to the cord itself be the true source of the contractions of the pain experienced by the animals? To remove this doubt I repeated the experiments after separating the roots from the cord, and it can be reported that in all cases I observed no appreciable effect of the stimulation of the anterior or posterior roots when separated from the cord, except in the cases of two animals in which I observed contractions when I pinched or pulled the anterior and posterior nerve groupings.

PAUL BROCA
(1824–1880)

Broca's Area [3]

I continue to think until better informed, that true aphasia, that is to say, the loss of speech without the paralysis of the organs of speech, and without the destruction of intelligence, is tied to lesions of the third frontal convolution. But, it is not on this fact that I have come to talk to you. My communication is relative to the singular predilection of the lesions of aphasia, for the left hemisphere of the brain.... The cases where aphasia was found on the right, are only very rare exceptions.

* * * * *

Articulate speech depends then on the part of the encephalon that is assigned to intellectual phenomena and whose cerebral motive

organs are in some way only the ministers. Now, this function of the intellectual order which dominates the dynamic part as well as the mechanical part of articulation seems to be the almost constant endowment of the convolutions of the left hemisphere since the lesions which produce the aphasia occupy almost constantly this hemisphere. It comes down to this, that for language, as for much simpler and more rude acts, of which I was speaking a while back, we are "left-handed" as far as the brain is concerned. Just as we direct the maneuverings of writing, design, embroidering, etc., with the left hemisphere, so we speak with the left hemisphere. It is a habit we get into since our early infancy. Of all the things that we are obliged to learn, articulate speech is perhaps the hardest. The other of our faculties, our other actions, exist at least at a rudimentary state among the animals; but although they certainly have ideas, and although they know how to communicate in a true language, articulate

---

[3] Paul Broca, "Sur le siége de la faculté du langage articulé," *Bulletins et Mémoires Société Anthropologie*, 1865, **6**, 377–393. Translated for the present volume by Raymond Salvagno.

speech is above their grasp. It is this complex and difficult thing that the child has to learn from his youngest age and he gets there after a great deal of groping and a cerebral work of the most complicated order. Till, then, this cerebral work is imposed on him at an epoch very close to these embryonic periods when the development of the left hemisphere is ahead of the development of the right hemisphere. From this, it is not illogical to admit that the more developed and precocious cerebral hemisphere is sooner than the other in a state to direct the execution and coordination of the intellectual as well as muscular acts which constitute articulate speech. In this manner the custom of speaking with the left hemisphere is established and this custom becomes part of our nature to such an extent that when we are deprived of the functions of this hemisphere we lose the faculty of making ourselves understood by means of words. That does not mean that the left hemisphere is the exclusive seat of the general faculty of language which consists in establishing a determinate relation between an idea and a sign, nor of the special faculty of articulate speech which consists in establishing a determinate relation between an idea and an articulated word: the right hemisphere is not more a stranger to this special faculty than the left, and what proves it is that the individual who is rendered aphasic by a deep and extensive lesion of the left hemisphere is in general only deprived of the faculty of reproducing the articulate sounds of language. He continues to understand what is being said to him, and consequently he knows perfectly the relation between words and ideas. In other words,

the faculty of conceiving these relations belong at the same time to the two hemispheres which can, in case of disease, replace each other; but the faculty to express them by coordinated movements, practice which is learned only after a well-established habit, seems to belong to only one hemisphere which is almost always the left one.

* * * * *

The existence of a small number of exceptional individuals who speak with the right hemisphere would explain very well the exceptional cases where aphasia is the consequence of a lesion of this hemisphere. It follows from this that a subject whose third *left* frontal convolution, the ordinary seat of articulate speech, happened to be emaciated since birth will learn to speak and will speak with the third *right* frontal convolution as the child born without a right hand becomes as able with his left hand as one is ordinarily with the other. It is then in this way that one must explain a remarkable fact observed last year at the Salpêtrière.

* * * * *

To summarize, the two halves of the encephalon being perfectly identical, from an anatomical standpoint, cannot have different powers; but the more precocious development of the left hemisphere predisposes us from our first gropings to execute with this half of the brain, the most complicated material and intellectual acts, among which one must certainly include the expressing of ideas by means of language, and more particularly, by means of articulate speech.

JEAN MARTIN CHARCOT
(1825–1893)

Conversion Hysteria, Neurosis, and Hypnosis [4]

The patient, named Pin., aged 18 years, mason by occupation, entered the Salpêtrière

[4] Jean Martin Charcot, *Clinical Lectures on Certain Diseases of the Nervous System*, trans. E. P. Hurd (Detroit: G. S. Davis, 1888), lecture 8; original French, *Leçons sur les maladies du système nerveux* (1873).

March 11, 1885. His mother died at the age of 46 years from the effect of "rheumatism;" his father is a drunkard. One of his sisters, aged 16 years, is subject to frequent nervous attacks. The patient is a young man of robust appearance and vigorous muscles, but the functionment of the nervous system has always left much to be desired. From the age of five to seven years he suffered incontinence of urine. He has always been deficient in intelligence; his memory is weak; and he never learned much at school. Moreover he was timid, and suffered from nightly terrors. From a moral point of view he is ill balanced. From the time that he was nine years old he often left his home and slept under bridges, or in the waiting rooms of railway stations. His father apprenticed him to a fruit dealer, then to a confectioner, and to other tradespeople, but he was always getting into scrapes. One night he was arrested, in company with a band of young vagabonds, and sentenced to the Reformatory of Roquette, where his father left him for a year.

Two years ago, when he was 16 years old, he was taken with an attack of acute articular rheumatism, preceded by an attack of erysipelas of the face, and it is quite probable that from this period we must date the organic alteration of the heart which we note in him to-day.

May 24, 1884, or eighteen months afterward, P., then a mason's apprentice, fell from a height of about two metres, and remained for several minutes without consciousness upon the place where he fell. He was carried to his home, and there several contusions were found on the anterior aspect of the left shoulder, knee, and ankle; these contusions were slight, and did not seriously interfere with the use of the affected parts.

For several days, it was thought that things would remain where they were; but on the 27th of May, i.e., three days after the accident, P. perceived that his left upper limb was becoming feeble. He then went to see a physician, who detected, it would seem, a paresis of all the movements of the left arm, with anæsthesia of this member. On the 8th of June, that is, 15 days after his fall, and 11 days after the commencement of the paresis, he entered the Hotel Dieu. There he was examined with care, and the physicians recognized the well characterized signs of aortic insufficiency. The parts which were bruised were not the seat of any pain, whether spontaneous or provoked by active or passive movements. [Incomplete paralysis of the left superior member.] The patient could still, though incompletely, flex the hand on the forearm, and the latter on the arm, but all movements of the shoulder were impossible. The paralyzed limb was quite flexible in all

its joints; there were no traces of rigidity. The face and the left inferior extremity were absolutely normal; as far as motility was concerned, it was a clear case of monoplegia in the true sense of the word. The study of the sensibility gave the following results: There existed already at this period a generalized left-sided hemi-analgesia; the anæsthesia was complete and confined to the paralyzed limb. At this time there was noted the binocular contraction of the visual field, much more marked, however, on the left side, and which we shall find so existing to-day. In fine, the 25th of June, i.e., 22 days after the onset of the paralysis, the latter had become absolutely complete. The diagnosis remained uncertain, the treatment inefficacious. Faradization, several times applied to the left side, had for its effect only to render the sensibility less obtuse on the trunk, face, and inferior extremity. The anæsthesia and paralysis remained as they were in the left upper limb. The contraction of the visual field had undergone no modification at the time that P. quit the Hotel Dieu.

It was on the eleventh of March of this year, ten months after the fall, and nine months after the complete establishment of the monoplegia, that P. entered the service of the clinic of the Salpêtrière. We then verified the antecedents as I have just stated them, and, moreover, a minute clinical examination disclosed a pronounced aortic insufficiency. There exists a murmur with the second sound and at the base; the arteries of the neck are lifted by beatings which are apparent to the sight; Corrigan pulse; capillary pulse perceptible on forehead.

The motor paralysis of the left upper limb, which is seen to be inert, hangs along the side of the body, and falls heavily when, on being raised, it is abandoned to itself, is complete, absolute. There is no trace of voluntary movement, or of contracture. The muscular masses have preserved their volume; their normal relief and electric reactions, faradic as well as galvanic, are in no respect modified. Very slight relative augmentation of the tendinous reflexes of the elbow and forearm. Cutaneous anæsthesia absolute to contact, to cold, to pricking, to the most intense faradization, along the whole extent of the limb, hand, forearm, arm and shoulder. In its relation to the trunk, this anæsthesia is limited by a circular line producing an almost vertical plane, which, passing by the hollow of the arm-pit, trenches a little on the sub-clavicular hollow in front, the external two-thirds of the shoulder blade behind. The insensibility extends in the same degree to the deep parts; you may, in fact, faradize powerfully the muscles, the nerve trunks themselves, make energetic traction on the articular ligaments, subject the different joints to movements of violent torsion, without the patient having the least consciousness of it. The loss of the different notions attached to the muscular sense is equally complete; the patient is unable to determine, even approximately, the attitude which has been impressed on divers segments of his limb, the place which they occupy in space, the direction and nature of the movements to which they are subjected, etc.

Aside from the left upper member, there does not exist on that half the body any modification of motility, whether of the face, trunk or inferior extremity, but all over this side we find the analgesia already noticed during the sojourn of the patient at the Hotel Dieu. The examination of the visual field gives us on the right side the normal state, while on the left there is an enormous contraction; moreover, the circle of red is transferred outside of that of blue. There has then been produced in the visual field since the sojourn in the Hotel Dieu a modification which it is interesting to note. Moreover, we find that hearing, smell, taste, tested by the ordinary methods, present a very marked diminution of their acuteness on the left side.

It now became our task to determine as far as possible the nature of this singular monoplegia, supervening after a traumatism. The absence of atrophy and of all modification of the electric reactions of the muscles in a case where the paralysis goes back ten months, ought to cause us to reject at once the hypothesis of a lesion of the brachial plexus; while the absence of amyotrophy of itself, as well as the intensity of the troubles of sensibility, compel us to set aside the notion that this may be one of those paralyses so well studied by Lefort and Valtat, which come on in consequence of traumatisms affecting a joint.

A brachial monoplegia may supervene,

though very exceptionally, it is true, as the result of certain lesions of the internal capsule, as is shown by a fact recently published by Drs. Bennett and Campbell in Brain; but in such cases we do not certainly meet with the sensorial and sensitive hemianæsthesia which is sometimes superadded to total hemiplegia of the ordinary kind following lesion of the capsule.

The production in the right hemisphere of a small *foyer* (local lesion), whether from hemorrhage or from softening determined by embolism in consequence of the organic affection of the heart, a disease-focus which we might suppose limited strictly to the motor zone of the arm—such a lesion, I say, might account for the existence of a left brachial monoplegia. But on this supposition, the paralysis would have come on all at once, after a shock, however slight, and not progressively; it would almost certainly, several months after the onset, have been characterized by a certain degree of contracture, and by a well marked exaggeration of the tendon-reflexes; lastly, it would not surely have been accompanied with trouble of the cutaneous and deep sensibility so pronounced as those which we observe in our patient.

We are compelled then to eliminate in our diagnosis this last hypothesis, and that of a spinal lesion will not bear discussion for an instant. On the other hand, our attention has been drawn from the very first to the very significant hereditary antecedents of the subject, to his psychical state and to his habits, to the troubles of sensibility, diffused, though unequally, over all of one side of the body, to the contraction of the visual field so pronounced on the left side, and marked by the transposition of the circle of the red; in fine, to the modifications of activity of the other sensorial apparatuses on the same side; all this has led us almost irresistibly, in the absence of any other hypothesis equally probable, to interpret this case as an example of hysteria. Moreover, the clinical characters of the monoplegia, its traumatic origin even— and in reference to this latter point I must refer you to what I have said before—were not at all at variance with this view. In fact, the limitation of the motor paralysis to one member, without participation at any time of the corresponding side of the face; the absence of marked exaltation of the tendinous reflexes, of muscular atrophy, and of all modification of the electric reactions, the absolute resolution of the limb remaining several months after the onset of the paralysis; the anæsthesia cutaneous and profound, so complete in the paralyzed member, and the utter loss of all notions relative to the muscular sense; all these phenomena, when we find them united and clearly marked as they are in our patient, suffice largely to reveal the hysterical nature of a paralysis.

In consequence, the diagnosis "hysteria" was frankly, resolutely adopted. It was true that the convulsive seizure was wanting; but you well know that this is not at all necessary to the constitution of the disease, and this circumstance ought not, we felt, to stand in the way of a diagnosis. As a result of this view of the case, the prognosis changed completely its character; we were no longer in the presence of an affection of organic cause, perhaps incurable; we could then hope, despite the long duration of the malady, to see supervene spontaneously, or under the influence of certain practices, some one of those sudden modifications which are not rare in the history of hysterical paralyses, and of those in particular which are attended with resolution. At all events we could foresee that sooner or later the patient would get well. A subsequent event was destined soon to justify our previsions and at the same time fully confirm our diagnosis.

The fifteenth of March, four days after the entrance of the patient, we made careful search—a thing which had not been done before—to see if we could find any hystero-genous zones. We found one situated under the left mamma, another over each of the iliac regions; still another over the right testicle. We remarked that even a slight excitation of the infra-mammary zone readily determined the phenomena of the aura: sensation of constriction of the thorax, then of the neck; beatings in the temples, sibilant sounds in the ears, especially in the left ear. On pressing a little harder we saw P. all at once lose consciousness and fall over backwards with stiffening of his members; and we witnessed the first attack of hystero-epilepsy which the patient had ever had. This attack was, moreover, quite typical; to the epileptoid phase soon succeeded that of the great movements. These were of extreme violence, the

patient in his movements of salutation went so far as to smite his face against his knees. A little after, he tore his clothes, his bed curtains, and turning his fury upon himself, he bit his left arm. The phase of passional attitudes then set in; P. seemed a prey to a furious delirium; he reproaches, provokes and excites to violence some imaginary personages. "Hold! take your knife; come, strike!" Lastly he recovers consciousness and affirms that he has no remembrance of anything that has happened.

It is to be remarked that during the entire continuance of the first attack, *the left superior member took no part in the convulsions;* it remained flaccid and completely inert. From this time onward, the fits were repeated every day, spontaneously, several times during the day with precisely the same characters as the provoked attack. During one of these, which took place on the night of the 17th of March, the patient wet his bed. There were two fits on the 19th. On the 21st there was a new crisis *during which the left arm trembled.* On waking, the patient, to his great astonishment found that he could move the divers segments of this member, of the use of which he had been totally deprived during the long period of almost 10 months. The motor paralysis was not completely cured, however, for there remained a certain degree of paresis, but there was a considerable improvement. Only, the troubles of sensibility persisted to the same degree as in the past.

This cure, gentlemen, or more properly speaking, this attempt at a cure, after the diagnosis which we were led to make, did not surprise us. But in our judgment, it supervened prematurely, unseasonably. In fact, it was no longer possible to enable you to witness *de visu*, in all their plenitude (as we had hoped to do), the character of this monoplegia, so excellent a subject for study. The idea then occurred to me that perhaps by acting on the mind of the patient *by way of suggestion in the waking state* (I had previously found that the subject was not hypnotizable) we might reproduce the paralysis, at least for a while. Therefore the next morning, finding P. just coming out of a fit which had in no way modified the state of things, I endeavored to persuade him that he was again paralyzed. "You believe yourself cured," I said to him with assurance, "it is a mistake; you can not raise your arm or bend it; see, you can not move your fingers, you are unable to grasp my hand." The experiment succeeded wonderfully, for after a few minutes, while I was talking, the monoplegia returned just as it was the day before. I was not at all disturbed, I may here say, as to the result of this paralysis artificially reproduced, for I knew by experience that in a matter of hypnotic suggestion, *what one has made one can unmake*. The paralysis, however, did not last longer than 24 hours. The next day a new attack came on, following which, the voluntary movements were definitely reestablished. This time, all the new attempts of suggestion which we made were absolutely powerless. It now remains for me to inform you of the modifications which, as far as voluntary movement is concerned,

have been effected in the limb formerly completely paralyzed.

The patient, as you see, can move at will all the parts of this member. But these movements have but little energy, they yield to the least resistance opposed to them, and while on the right, the dynamometric force expresses itself in the hand by the figure 70, on the left it gives only the figure 10. If then, the motor impotence is not as absolute as formerly, it still persists to a sufficiently high degree. Moreover, the troubles of sensibility are just as they were, not only in the limb which is the subject of paresis, but also on all the left side of the body including the organs of sense; the fits, besides, remain frequent. Truly, as you see, we have here only an improvement in the condition of the arm, and we are far from having attained a cure.

PIERRE JANET
(1859–1947)

L'analyse Psychologique [5]

Psychology of the individual is the necessary consequence of practical psychology which departs from generalities to render service to individuals.

L'analyse psychologique is the indispensable method of psychology of the individual, which has for its object the search for those characteristic behavior traits which distinguish an individual from others. If this is true, it is impossible to indicate in a general way the rules and methods of an *analyse psychologique*. This analysis will vary according to one's proposed aim; it cannot be the same when it is a question of reforming a criminal, educating a child, or curing a neurotic. Above all, this analysis will continue to vary with the progress of science itself as it discovers new functions and new methods for determining the state of each particular function. Today the measurement of basal metabolism enters into the physiological analysis of a patient, whereas several years ago it was

never considered. *L'analyse psychologique* changes every day, and I can survey only very rapidly a few examples to show the high points of a useful analysis today.

* * * * *

A long time ago—for life passes rapidly—I thought that . . . memory . . . was of . . . importance from the psychiatric point of view. Memory of the events of one's own life play a part in the development of personality, and more or less distinct and easily evoked memories of certain emotional situations in one's life are of great importance in certain psychological disorders. In my works published between the years 1886 and 1892, I have shown by numerous illustrations that memories of certain dramatic circumstances to which the subject had not succeeded in adapting himself presented themselves to the mind in the form of unsolved problems, reproduced in a pathological form the original emotion, and by means of various mechanisms gave rise to neurotic symptoms; this I called *traumatic memory of an unassimilated event*. The search for these memories, though difficult, might in some cases give rise to a very useful psychological analysis. I very often resort to this method, which obtains

[5] Pierre Janet, "L'analyse psychologique," in Carl Murchison (ed.), *Psychologies of* 1930 (Worcester, Mass.: Clark University Press, 1930), pp. 369–372. Submitted in French and translated for Clark University Press by Dorothy Olson. Reprinted by permission.

some interesting cures through the modification of this traumatic memory.

However, is it necessary to conclude that this search for traumatic memory constitutes all *l'analyse psychologique* even in the case of a neurotic? Alas! a lengthy experience with patients has disillusioned me on this point. It is often a great mistake to attribute to this or that memory of the patient, even though it be an emotional one, such considerable influence on present disorders. Present exhaustion does not always bear any relation to the more or less conscious persistence of certain memories of this sort. In many cases, the emotional event and its memory have at the start played an important part for a certain period. The disorder to which they have led, the bad thought habits, and the subsequent exhaustion have become independent of the memory itself, and the modifications of the memory do not act upon them. Infectious diseases often terminate in disorders which persist indefinitely even after the disappearance of the microbe, and no tardy and useless disinfection will effect a cure of these remaining disorders. In other cases, constantly repeated slight emotions, which have been quickly forgotten, have made important modifications of the psychological functions. Maladjusted reactions to social situations, so ably pointed out by Adolf Meyer, in speaking of the origin of dementia praecox, faulty education, and many other circumstances, may be more important than this or that memory. Finally, one must not forget hereditary constitutions, and those little understood diseases such as colicbacillary infections so common among neurotics. The psychiatrist must be a well-informed psychologist, but he must also be a doctor. To insist upon pursuing indefinitely an analysis of memories is to misunderstand many other elements which play an important part in mental disorders.

The mind consists of a group of functions which has evolved through the centuries and through the life of the individual as well, and moral equilibrium demands the presence of all these functions. They do not all function at once, but they should be ready to function when circumstances demand. It is always necessary to discover whether some important function or group of functions has been destroyed and whether their failure to function is not the cause of the present disorder. If an individual complains of not being able to read, it is not necessary to search for traumatic memories relative to improper reading, when it would suffice to say that he has a disorder of the eyes.

In fact, phylogenetically older psychological functions have definite organs; those which are less ancient, however, have definite centers in the nervous system. In both these cases, alterations of functions are in accord with discernible modifications of function. *L'analyse psychologique* must understand these studies made upon organs, and upon modifications of reflexes manifesting organic alterations. To limit analysis to non-organic psychological disorders is to raise in vain all kinds of metaphysical problems and to misunderstand the importance of organic difficulties even in a psychosis. *L'analyse psychologique* applies equally well to hemiplegia, aphasia, and delirium. Discovery of a change in function naturally becomes more difficult when it is a question of recent operations whose difficulties do not manifest themselves by means of readily perceptible organic modifications. Above all, it is necessary to guide one's self by the study of the functioning of psychological habits. The method of examination by means of tests is still in its infancy; its great difficulty lies in the fact that it cannot yet indicate to which function of the mind the correct execution of a particular test corresponds. However, it is making progress, and in the future will be of great importance in the distinction between functions which remain intact and those which have undergone modification.

An important characteristic of psychological functions is that they are not all of the same value. They present varying degrees of complexity and efficiency and seem to have been acquired gradually in a certain order. They may be arranged in a *hierarchy* in which the higher functions rule and interfere with the lower ones, thus giving to acts a greater efficiency in both time and space. In the brutal destruction of organs, lesions may by chance destroy functions irregularly. For example, a man may lose the elementary function of vision and still retain the superior function of reflection. This is one of the important characteristics of these so-called organic lesions.

In most cases, it is a case of a general disorder striking all functions, suppressing the superior ones first and descending downward on the psychological hierarchy. The importance of disorders of the higher functions, especially in the field of belief, is shown in various deliria in which lower functions such as assertive belief continue to exist. Determination of the degree to which the disorder has attained is important in the appreciation of the degree of *psychological tension*. *L'analyse psychologique* which is not limited to the notation of ideas and memories acquired by the individual, but which seeks to penetrate more profoundly into the constitution of the mind, should strive to determine the degree of lowering of psychological tension.

Unfortunately, this study is not yet sufficient. It is not alone sufficient to have numerous perfected mechanisms but it is also necessary that these mechanisms function properly under all circumstances. When an automobile stops, it does not necessarily mean that some part is broken; it may simply lack oil. One can sum up briefly by means of the expression *psychological force* those modifications of conduct which are still difficult to measure such as power of movement, number of actions, their undisturbed duration, their rapidity, etc., always keeping in mind their hierarchical values. In fact, it seems that the more elevated an act is in the hierarchy, the more energy it requires.

Diminution of force and modification of the important relationship between tension and psychological force are becoming elements of vast importance to psychological analysis. This diminution of energy is most apparent in certain feelings and deliria. The feeling of pressure, in which effort plays a predominant rôle, indicates a diminution of the functioning of those tendencies for which psychological activity of the whole personality seeks to substitute. Feelings attached to morose inactivity and to melancholy indicate with greater precision a certain general weakness. However, one must suspect these measures of energy as a result of certain feelings and delirium; the latter are regular reactions which may be modified by all sorts of influences and which may easily be mistaken. One of the most important studies of *l'analyse psychologique* will be the appreciation of the degree of psychic energy of an individual and the extent of his weakness; we know nothing of the nature of this psychic energy, but we must study its manifestations and succeed in measuring it as the physicist measures an electric current without understanding the nature of it.

Briefly, *l'analyse psychologique* does not insist upon a pre-established system of study, but consists in the application to definite individuals of all psychological and physiological knowledge; incomplete and difficult, it will doubtless make progress, thanks to the development of psychology proper.

Traumatic Memories [6]

The magnetists had all called especial attention to the memory during the periods of provoked somnambulism. They had frequently described a curious fact, namely, that the subject, during that state, can recount a mass of events from his life to which he never refers during ordinary waking moments, and which seem to be completely forgotten on waking. In examining these modifications of memory, I had occasion to remark in my first studies of 1886-1889 that this amnesia concerned not only events that had taken place during periods of somnambulism, but that it often concerned, in addition to these periods, certain events of normal life when these events had been accompanied by violent emotion. Thus, a young hysteric whom I described at the time under the name of Marie recounted during somnambulism that at the age of thirteen she had been frightened by the appearance of her first menstruation and that she had tried to stop it by getting into a tub of cold water, a measure that had indeed stopped the flow, but that had at the same time brought about great distress, tremors, and delirium. During the same somnambulistic state she also told that she had been frightened on seeing an old woman fall down a staircase and cover the steps with her blood; and that, on another occasion, she had been forced to go to bed with a child whose face was covered with a rash on the left side, and that she had experienced all that night great disgust and great fear. Out-

[6] Pierre Janet, *Principles of Psychotherapy*, trans. H. and E. R. Guthrie (New York: Macmillan, 1924), pp. 37–42; original French, *La médecine psychologique* (Paris, 1923).

side these somnambulistic states she seemed to have no memory of these events. For the rest, this patient showed various neuropathic symptoms, crises of convulsions shortly after the beginning of menstruation with stoppage of the flow, and tremor and delirium, hallucinations in which she saw blood, spasms, and disorders of sensation on the left side of her face, accidents that seemed clearly related to the memories recounted during somnambulism. My writings of this period contain the description of many cases of that sort.

It was not hard to connect these observations with the interpretations that Charcot had given some time before to certain hysterical paralyses. In his studies of 1884-85 he had shown that the physical accident was not the cause of the consequent illness, but that it was necessary to assign a rôle to the memories left by the accident, "to the ideas, and to concern that the invalid maintained in this connection." Many observers, and Moebus (1888) in particular, took up this notion and acknowledged that "certain hysterical accidents were physical changes connected with ideas and memories." I enlarged this conception somewhat by showing that neuropathic troubles of the same sort could develop from a more simple series of events that did not cause any physical wound, but an emotion purely psychic. The memory of the event persisted in the same fashion with its train of various feelings, and it is this memory that determined, directly or indirectly, certain phases of the illness. These disorders may be called traumatic memories.

In the cases I have just mentioned, the traumatic memory presented itself in a special manner; it could not be expressed during waking consciousness, and it reappeared only under special circumstances in a different psychological state. In this we find again a well-known characteristic of hysterical fugues; the subject can recount his fugue and the reasons that have determined it only if he is put into a state of somnambulism, and he seems, during his waking moments, to have forgotten it completely. There is no question here of real failure of memory, of any pretending on the part of the subject; it is a question of a particular modification of consciousness that I tried to describe in 1889 under the name of *subconsciousness through disintegration*. This dissociation, this migra-

tion of certain psychological phenomena into a special group, seemed to me connected with the exhaustion brought on by various causes, and in particular by emotion. I have been led to suppose that in cases of this sort there was a certain relation between this dissociation of memories and the seriousness of the disorders that these memories brought about after they had become subconscious. A fixed idea seemed dangerous because it was apart from the personality, because it belonged to a group of phenomena over which the conscious will of the subject had no longer any control.

This supposition found its justification in some attempts at treatment: all the processes that altered that abnormal form of memory altered in the same degree the hysterical accidents. When one could bring the subject to express his memories, even during waking consciousness, he was freed from his delirium and the disorders connected with these memories.

These observations and these effective treatments led me to formulate some plans of procedure relating to the "psychological treatment of hysteria." When a patient showed certain accidents that might well be related to traumatic memories, it was well to encourage him to describe clearly the memories of various periods of his life, and when gestures, attitudes, disorders or reticences made us suspect a gap, it was necessary to find out whether dreams, somnambulism, automatic writing would not bring to light other memories more deeply hidden. But I had in mind only certain special cases and, although I advised the search for subconscious memories in these cases, I believed it necessary to guard against discovering such memories where they did not exist, and I gave some rules for prudent diagnosis.

At this time a foreign physician, Dr. S. Freud of Vienna, came to Salpétrière and became interested in these studies. He granted the truth of the facts and published some new observations of the same kind. In these publications he changed first of all the terms that I was using; what I had called psychological analysis he called psychoanalysis; what I had called psychological system, in order to designate that totality of facts of consciousness and movement, whether of members or of viscera, whose association constitutes the traumatic memory, he called complex; he considered a repression what I considered a restriction of consciousness; what I referred to as a psychological dissociation, or as a moral fumigation, he baptized with the name of catharsis. But above all he transformed a clinical observation and a therapeutic treatment with a definite and limited field of use into an enormous system of medical philosophy.

20

Austrian, Swiss, and German Clinical Psychology

FRIEDRICH ANTON MESMER
(1734–1815)

Animal Magnetism [1]

1. A responsive influence exists between the heavenly bodies, the earth, and animated bodies.

2. A fluid universally diffused, so continuous as not to admit of a vacuum, incomparably subtle, and naturally susceptible of receiving, propagating, and communicating all motor disturbances, is the means of this influence.

3. This reciprocal action is subject to mechanical laws, with which we are not as yet acquainted.

4. Alternative effects result from this action, which may be considered to be a flux and reflux.

5. This reflux is more or less general, more or less special, more or less compound, according to the nature of the causes which determine it.

6. It is by this action, the most universal which occurs in nature, that the exercise of active relations takes place between the heavenly bodies, the earth, and its constituent parts.

7. The properties of matter and of organic substance depend on this action.

8. The animal body experiences the alternative effects of this agent, and is directly affected by its insinuation into the substance of the nerves.

9. Properties are displayed, analogous to those of the magnet, particularly in the human body, in which diverse and opposite poles are likewise to be distinguished, and these may be communicated, changed, destroyed, and reinforced. Even the phenomenon of declination may be observed.

10. This property of the human body which renders it susceptible of the influence of the heavenly bodies, and of the reciprocal action of those which environ it, manifests its analogy with the magnet, and this has decided me to adopt the term of animal magnetism.

11. The action and virtue of animal magnetism, thus characterized, may be communicated to other animate or inanimate bodies. Both these classes of bodies, however, vary in their susceptibility.

12. This action and virtue may be strengthened and diffused by such bodies.

13. Experiments show that there is a diffusion of matter, subtle enough to penetrate all bodies without any considerable loss of energy.

[1] Friedrich Anton Mesmer, "Propositions concerning animal magnetism," in Alfred Binet and Charles Fere, *Animal Magnetism* (New York: D. Appleton, 1888), pp. 4–8; original French, *Mémoire sur la découverte du magnétisme animal* (1781).

14. Its action takes place at a remote distance, without the aid of any intermediary substance.

15. It is, like light, increased and reflected by mirrors.

16. It is communicated, propagated, and increased by sound.

17. This magnetic virtue may be accumulated, concentrated, and transported.

18. I have said that animated bodies are not all equally susceptible, in a few instances they have such an opposite property that their presence is enough to destroy all the effects of magnetism upon other bodies.

19. This opposite virtue likewise penetrates all bodies: it also may be communicated, propagated, accumulated, concentrated, and transported, reflected by mirrors, and propagated by sound. This does not merely constitute a negative, but a positive opposite virtue.

20. The magnet, whether natural or artificial, is like other bodies susceptible of animal magnetism, and even of the opposite virtue: in neither case does its action on fire and on the needle suffer any change, and this shows that the principle of animal magnetism essentially differs from that of mineral magnetism.

21. This system sheds new light upon the nature of fire and of light, as well as on the theory of attraction, of flux and reflux, of the magnet and of electricity.

22. It teaches us that the magnet and artificial electricity have, with respect to diseases, properties common to a host of other agents presented to us by nature, and that if the use of these has been attended by some useful results, they are due to animal magnetism.

23. These facts show, in accordance with the practical rules I am about to establish, that this principle will cure nervous diseases directly, and other diseases indirectly.

24. By its aid the physician is enlightened as to the use of medicine, and may render its action more perfect, and he can provoke and direct salutary crises, so as completely to control them.

25. In communicating my method, I shall, by a new theory of matter, demonstrate the universal utility of the principle I seek to establish.

26. Possessed of this knowledge, the physician may judge with certainty of the origin, nature, and progress of diseases, however complicated they may be; he may hinder their development and accomplish their cure without exposing the patient to dangerous and troublesome consequences, irrespective of age, temperament, and sex. Even women in a state of pregnancy, and during parturition, may reap the same advantage.

27. This doctrine will finally enable the physician to decide upon the health of every individual, and of the presence of the diseases to which he may be exposed. In this way the art of healing may be brought to absolute perfection.

EMIL KRAEPELIN
(1856–1926)

Nosology of Mental Disease [2]

Classification of Mental Diseases

I. Infection Psychoses

    A. Fever Delirium

    B. Infection Deliria

        Initial deliria of typhoid, of smallpox. Infection delirium of malaria. Delirium of chorea. Deliria of influenza, hydrophobia, and septic states. Acute delirium.

    C. Post-infection Psychoses

        Mild Form. Second group. Severe form. Cerebropathia psychica toxämica.

---

[2] Emil Kraepelin, *Clinical Psychiatry*, trans. A. Ross Diefendorf (New York: Macmillan, 1907), pp. xi–xvi; original German, *Lehrbuch der Psychiatrie* (1883).

II. Exhaustion Psychoses

    A. Collapse Delirium
    B. Acute Confusional Insanity (Amentia)
    C. Acquired Neurasthenia (Chronic Nervous Exhaustion)

III. Intoxication Psychoses

    1. Acute Intoxications
       Ptomaines. Chloroform. Santonin. Hasheesh. Encephalopathia. Saturninia.
    2. Chronic Intoxication
       A. Alcoholism
           Acute Alcoholic Intoxication
           Chronic Alcoholism
           Delirium Tremens
           Korssakow's Psychosis
           Acute Alcoholic Hallucinosis
           Alcoholic Hallucinatory Dementia
           Alcoholic Paranoia
           Alcoholic Paresis
           Alcoholic Pseudoparesis
       B. Morphinism
       C. Cocainism
           Acute Cocain Intoxication. Chronic Cocain Intoxication. Cocain Hallucinosis.

IV. Thyroigenous Psychoses

    A. Myxœdematous Insanity
    B. Cretinism

V. Dementia Præcox

    General Symptomatology: disturbances of apprehension, disturbances of orientation, hallucinations, disturbance of consciousness, disturbance of attention, disturbance of memory, disturbance of the train of thought, disturbance of judgment, disturbance of the emotional field, disturbances in the volitional field
    Hebephrenic Form
    Catatonic Form
    Paranoid Forms:
      Dementia Paranoides
      Second Group

VI. Dementia Paralytica

    General Symptomatology: disturbances of apprehension, disturbances of memory, disturbances of the train of thought, disturbances of judgment, disturbances of the emotions, conduct
    Physical Symptoms: sensory symptoms, paralytic attacks, disturbances of speech, ataxia, reflexes, vasomotor disturbances
    Demented Form
    Expansive Form (megalomania)
    Agitated Form (galloping paresis)
    Depressed Form

VII. Organic Dementias

    Gliosis of Cortex (diffused cerebral sclerosis)
    Huntingdon's Chorea
    Multiple Sclerosis
    Cerebral Syphilis: simple syphilitic dementia, syphilitic pseudoparesis
    Tabetic Psychoses
    Arteriosclerotic Insanity
    Cerebral Tumor
    Brain Abscess
    Cerebral Apoplexy
    Cerebral Trauma: traumatic delirium, traumatic dementia

VIII. Involution Psychoses

    A. Melancholia
        Symptomatology: delusions of self-accusation, hypochondriacal delusions, hallucinations, disturbances of thought, nihilistic delusions.
    B. Presenile Delusional Insanity
    C. Senile Dementia
        Symptomatology. Physical symptoms. Severer grade of senile dementia. Presbyophrenia. Senile Delirium. Senile Delusional Insanity

IX. Manic-depressive Insanity

    Symptomatology: disturbances of apprehension, disturbances of perception, disturbances of memory, disturbances of judgment, disturbances of thought, disturbances of the emotional and volitional fields
    Manic States
        Hypomania
        Mania (Tobsucht)
        Delirious Mania
    Depressive States
        Simple Retardation
        Delusional Form
        Stuporous States
    Mixed States
    Irascible mania. Depressive excitement. Unproductive mania. Manic stupor. Depression with a flight of ideas. Depressive state with flight of ideas and emotional elation.

X. Paranoia

    Querulent Insanity

XI. Epileptic Insanity

    Symptomatology. Physical symptoms. Periodical ill-humor. Befogged states: pre-epileptic insanity, post-epileptic insanity, psychic epilepsy, somnambulism, epileptic stupor, anxious deliria, conscious delirium, dipsomania.

XII. The Psychogenic Neuroses

    A. Hysterical Insanity
        Symptomatology: hysterical personality, changes in character, hypochondriasis. Physical symptoms. Befogged states: delirious states, hysterical lethargy, somnambulism, silly excitement.
    B. Traumatic Neurosis (traumatic hysteria)
    C. Dread Neurosis

XIII. Constitutional Psychopathic States.   (Insanity of Degeneracy.)

   A.   Nervousness
   B.   Constitutional Despondency
   C.   Constitutional Excitement
   D.   Compulsive Insanity
   Tormenting Ideas: onomatomania, arithmomania, Grübelsucht, folie du doute, erythrophobia. Phobias: agoraphobia, mysophobia, délire du toucher. Crises. Impulsions.
   E.   Impulsive Insanity
   The impulse to tramp. Pyromania. Kleptomania. Impulse to kill.
   F.   Contrary Sexual Instincts

XIV. Psychopathic Personalities

   A.   Born criminals (moral insanity, "delinquente nato," moral imbecility)
   B.   The Unstable
   C.   The Morbid Liar and Swindler
   D.   The Pseudoquerulants

XV. Defective Mental Development

   A.   Imbecility: stupid form, lighter grades, energetic type.
   B.   Idiocy
   Symptomatology: severe cases, light cases.

EUGEN BLEULER
(1857–1939)

Autism [3]

Schizophrenia is characterized by a very peculiar alteration of the relation between the patient's inner life and the external world. The inner life assumes pathological predominance (autism). . . .

The most severe schizophrenics, who have no more contact with the outside world, live in a world of their own. They have encased themselves with their desires and wishes (which they consider fulfilled) or occupy themselves with the trials and tribulations of their persecutory ideas; they have cut themselves off as much as possible from any contact with the external world.

This detachment from reality, together with the relative and absolute predominance of the inner life, we term autism.

In less severe cases, the affective and logical significance of reality is only somewhat damaged. The patients are still able to move about in the external world but neither evidence nor logic have any influence on their hopes and delusions. Everything which is in contradiction to their complexes simply does not exist for their thinking or feeling.

An intelligent lady who for many years was mistaken for a neurasthenic "had built a wall around herself so closely confining that she often felt as if she actually were in a chimney." An otherwise socially acceptable woman patient sings at a concert, but unfortunately once started she cannot stop. The audience begins to whistle and hoot and create a disturbance; she does not bother a bit, but continues singing and feels quite satisfied when she finally ends. A well-educated young woman, whose illness is hardly noticeable suddenly moves her bowels before a whole social gathering and cannot comprehend the embarrassment which she causes among her friends. During the course of about ten years, a patient gave me from time to time a note on which the same four

[3] Eugen Bleuler, *Dementia Praecox or the Group of Schizophrenias*, trans. Joseph Zinkin and Nolan D. C. Lewis (New York: International Universities Press, 1950), pp. 63–68; original German, *Dementia Praecox, oder Gruppe der Schizophrenien* (Leipzig and Vienna, 1911). Reprinted by permission.

words were always written and which signified that he had been unjustly incarcerated. It did not make any difference to him if he handed me a half-dozen of these notes at the same time. He did not understand the senselessness of his action when one discussed it with him. Withal, this patient showed good judgment about other patients and worked independently in his ward. Very frequently schizophrenics will give us numerous letters without expecting any answer; or they will ask us a dozen questions one after the other without even giving us time to answer. They predict an event for a certain day, but are so little bothered when the prophecy does not come to pass that they do not even seek to find explanations. Even where reality has apparently become identical with the patient's pathological creations, it will often be ignored.

The wishes and desires of many patients revolve around their release from the hospital. Yet they remain indifferent to the actual discharge. One of our patients who has a marked complex about children made an attempt to murder his wife because she only bore him four children in ten years. Yet he is quite indifferent to the children themselves. Other patients are in love with someone. If this person is actually present, he makes no impression on them at all; if he dies, they do not care. One patient constantly begs to be given the key to the door of his ward. When it is finally given to him, he does not know what to do with it and returns it almost at once. He tries a thousand times each day to open the door. If it is left unlocked, he becomes embarrassed and does not know what to do. He continuously pursues the doctor at each of his visits with the words: "Please, Doctor." Asked what he desires, he appears surprised and has nothing further to say. A woman patient asked to see her doctor. When she was summoned to the interview, she at least was able after a few minutes of perplexity to make her wishes known by pointing to his wedding ring. For weeks on end, a mother exerts every means at her command to see her child. When permission is granted her, she prefers to have a glass of wine. For years a woman longs for a divorce from her husband. When at long last she gets her divorce, she refuses to believe in it at all, and becomes furious if she is not addressed by her husband's name. Many a patient consumes

himself with anxiety over his imminent death but will not take the least precaution for his self preservation and remains totally unmoved in the face of real danger to his life.

Autism is not always to be detected at the very first glance. Initially the behavior of many patients betrays nothing remarkable. It is only on prolonged observation that one sees how much they always seek their own way, and how very little they permit their environment to influence them. Even severe chronic patients show quite good contacts with their environment with regard to indifferent, everyday affairs. They chatter, participate in games, seek out stimulation—but they are always selective. They keep their complexes to themselves, never saying a word about them and not wishing to have them touched upon in any way from the outside.

Thus the indifference of patients toward what would be considered their nearest and dearest interest becomes understandable. Other things are of far greater importance to them. They do not react any more to influences from the outside. They appear "stuporous" even where no other disturbance inhibits their will or actions. The external world must often appear to them as rather hostile since it tends to disturb them in their fantasies. However, there are also cases where the shutting off from the outside world is caused by contrary reasons. Particularly in the beginning of their illness, these patients quite consciously shun any contact with reality because their effects are so powerful that they must avoid everything which might arouse their emotions. The apathy toward the outer world is then a secondary one springing from a hypertrophied sensitivity.

Autism is also manifested by many patients externally. (Naturally, this is, as a rule, unintentional.) Not only do they not concern themselves with anything around them, but they sit around with faces constantly averted, looking at a blank wall; or they shut off their sensory portals by drawing a skirt or bed clothes over their heads. Indeed, formerly, when the patients were mostly abandoned to their own devices, they could often be found in bent-over, squatting positions, an indication that they were trying to restrict as much as possible of the sensory surface area of their skin.

Misunderstandings stemming from the

autistic thought processes can hardly ever, or only with great difficulty, be corrected by the patients.

A hebephrenic lies on a bench in a thoroughly vile mood. As she catches sight of me, she attempts to sit up. I beg her not to disturb herself. She answers in an irritated tone that if she could sit up she would not be lying down, apparently imagining that I was reproaching her for lying on the bench. Several times, using different words, I repeat the suggestion that she remain lying quietly as she was. She merely becomes more and more irritated. Everything I say is interpreted falsely by her in the sense and direction of her autistic train of thought.

The autistic world has as much reality for the patient as the true one, but his is a different kind of reality. Frequently, they cannot keep the two kinds of reality separated from each other even though they can make the distinction in principle. A patient heard us speaking of a certain Dr. N. Immediately afterwards he asks whether it was a hallucination or whether we had spoken of a Dr. N.

The reality of the autistic world may also seem more valid than that of reality itself; the patients then hold their fantasy world for the real, reality for an illusion. They no longer believe in the evidence of their own senses. Schreber described his attendants as "miracled up, changeable individuals." The patient may be very aware that other people judge the environment differently. He also knows that he himself sees it in that form but it is not *real* to him. "They say, that you are the doctor, but I don't know it," or even, "But you are really Minister N." To a considerable extent, reality is transformed through illusions and largely replaced by hallucinations (twilight states, *Dämmerzustande*).

In the usual hallucinatory conditions, more validity is, as a rule, ascribed to the illusions; yet the patients continue to act and orient themselves in accordance with reality. Many of them, however, no longer act at all, not even in accordance with their autistic thinking. This may occur in stuporous conditions, or the autism itself may reach such a high degree of intensity, that the patients' actions lose all relation to the blocked-off reality. The sick person deals with the real world as little as the normal person deals with his dreams. Frequently both disturbances, the stuporous

immobility and the exclusion of reality, occur simultaneously.

Patients who show no clouding of consciousness often appear much less autistic than they really are because they are able to suppress their autistic thoughts or, like certain hysterics, seem to be occupied with them only in a theoretical way, and ordinarily allow them only very little influence upon their actions. These patients rarely remain under our observation for very long because we are inclined to discharge them as improved or cured.

A complete and constant exclusion of the external world appears, if at all, only in the most severe degree of stupor. In milder cases the real and the autistic world exist not only side by side, but often become entangled with one another in the most illogical manner. The doctor is at one moment not only the hospital-physician and at another the shoemaker S., but he is both in the same thought-content of the patient. A patient who was still fairly well-mannered and capable of work, made herself a rag-doll which she considered to be the child of her imaginary lover. When this "lover" of hers made a trip to Berlin, she wanted to send "the child" after him, as a precautionary measure. But she first went to the police, to ask whether it would be considered as illegal to send "the child" as luggage instead of on a passenger ticket.

Wishes and fears constitute the contents of autistic thinking. In those rare cases where the contradictions to reality are not felt at all, it is the wishes alone which are involved; fears appear when the patient senses the obstacles to the fulfillment of his wishes. Even where no true delusions arise autism is demonstrable in the patients' inability to cope with reality, in their inappropriate reactions to outside influences (irritability), and in their lack of resistance to every and any idea and urge.

In the same way as autistic feeling is detached from reality, autistic thinking obeys its own special laws. To be sure, autistic thinking makes use of the customary logical connections insofar as they are suitable but it is in no way bound to such logical laws. Autistic thinking is directed by affective needs; the patient thinks in symbols, in analogies in fragmentary concepts, in accidental connections. Should the same patient turn back to reality he may be able to think sharply and logically.

Thus we have to distinguish between realistic and autistic thinking which exist side by side in the same patient. In realistic thinking the patient orients himself quite well in time and space. He adjusts his actions to reality insofar as they appear normal. The autistic thinking is the source of the delusions, of the crude offenses against logic and propriety, and all the other pathological symptoms. The two forms of thought are often fairly well separated so that the patient is able at times to think completely autistically and at other times completely normally. In other cases the two forms mix, going on to complete fusion, as we saw in the cases cited above.

The patient need not become conscious of the peculiarity, of the deviation of his autistic thinking from his previous realistic type of thinking. However, the more intelligent patients may for years gauge the difference.

They experience the autistic state as painful; only rarely as pleasurable. They complain that reality seems different from what it was before. Things and people are no longer what they are supposed to be. They are changed, strange, no longer have any relationship to the patient. A released patient described it, "as if she were running around in an open grave, so strange did the world appear." Another "had started to think herself into an entirely different life. By comparison, everything was quite different; even her sweetheart was not the way she had imagined him." A still very intelligent woman patient considered it a change for the better that at will, she could transpose herself into a state of the greatest (sexual and religious) bliss. She even wanted to give us instructions to enable us to do likewise.

Autism must not be confused with "the unconscious." Both autistic and realistic thinking can be conscious as well as unconscious.

SIGMUND FREUD
(1856–1939)

Psychoanalysis [4]

Granted that it is a merit to have created psychoanalysis, it is not my merit. I was a student, busy with the passing of my last examinations, when another physician of Vienna, Dr. Joseph Breuer, made the first application of this method to the case of an hysterical girl (1880–82). We must now examine the history of this case and its treatment, which can be found in detail in "Studien über Hysterie," later published by Dr. Breuer and myself.

* * * * *

Dr. Breuer's patient was a girl of twenty-one, of a high degree of intelligence. She had developed in the course of her two years' illness a series of physical and mental disturbances which well deserved to be taken seriously. She had a severe paralysis of both

right extremities, with anæsthesia, and at times the same affection of the members of the left side of the body, disturbance of eye-movements, and much impairment of vision; difficulty in maintaining the position of the head, an intense *Tussis nervosa*, nausea when she attempted to take nourishment, and at one time for several weeks a loss of the power to drink, in spite of tormenting thirst. Her power of speech was also diminished, and this progressed so far that she could neither speak nor understand her mother tongue; and, finally, she was subject to states of "absence," of confusion, delirium, alteration of her whole personality. These states will later claim our attention.

* * * * *

The illness first appeared while the patient was caring for her father, whom she tenderly loved, during the severe illness which led to his death, a task which she was compelled to abandon because she herself fell ill.

* * * * *

His sympathetic observation soon found the means which made the first help possible. It

---

[4] Sigmund Freud, "The origin and development of psychoanalysis," *Amer. J. Psychol.*, 1910, **21**, 181–218. Lectures delivered at the celebration of the twentieth anniversary of the opening of Clark University, September, 1909; translated from the German by Harry W. Chase.

had been noticed that the patient, in her states of "absence," of psychic alteration, usually mumbled over several words to herself. These seemed to spring from associations with which her thoughts were busy. The doctor, who was able to get these words, put her in a sort of hypnosis and repeated them to her over and over, in order to bring up any associations that they might have. The patient yielded to his suggestion and reproduced for him those psychic creations which controlled her thoughts during her "absences," and which betrayed themselves in these single spoken words. These were fancies, deeply sad, often poetically beautiful, day dreams, we might call them, which commonly took as their starting point the situation of a girl beside the sickbed of her father. Whenever she had related a number of such fancies, she was, as it were, freed and restored to her normal mental life. This state of health could last for several hours, and then give place on the next day to a new "absence," which was removed in the same way by relating the newly created fancies. It was impossible not to get the impression that the psychic alteration which was expressed in the "absence" was a consequence of the excitations originating from these intensely emotional fancy-images. The patient herself, who at this time of her illness strangely enough understood and spoke only English, gave this new kind of treatment the name "talking cure," or jokingly designated it as "chimney-sweeping."

The doctor soon hit upon the fact that through such cleansing of the soul more could be accomplished than a temporary removal of the constantly recurring mental "clouds." Symptoms of the disease would disappear when in hypnosis the patient could be made to remember the situation and the associative connections under which they first appeared, provided free vent was given to the emotions which they aroused.

* * * * *

Ladies and Gentlemen, if you will permit me to generalize, as is indispensable in so brief a presentation, we may express our results up to this point in the formula: *Our hysterical patients suffer from reminiscences.* Their symptoms are the remnants and the memory symbols of certain (traumatic) experiences.

* * * * *

Now hystericals and all neurotics behave like these two unpractical Londoners, not only in that they remember the painful experiences of the distant past, but because they are still strongly affected by them. They cannot escape from the past and neglect present reality in its favor. This fixation of the mental life on the pathogenic traumata is an essential, and practically a most significant characteristic of the neurosis. I will willingly concede the objection which you are probably formulating, as you think over the history of Breuer's patient. All her traumata originated at the time when she was caring for her sick father, and her symptoms could only be regarded as memory symbols of his sickness and death. They corresponded to mourning, and a fixation on thoughts of the dead so short a time after death is certainly not pathological, but rather corresponds to normal emotional behavior. I concede this: there is nothing abnormal in the fixation of feeling on the trauma shown by Breuer's patient. But in other cases, like that of the tic that I have mentioned, the occasions for which lay ten and fifteen years back, the characteristic of this abnormal clinging to the past is very clear, and Breuer's patient would probably have developed it, if she had not come under the "cathartic treatment" such a short time after the traumatic experiences and the beginning of the disease.

We have so far only explained the relation of the hysterical symptoms to the life history of the patient; now by considering two further factors which Breuer observed, we may get a hint as to the processes of the beginning of the illness and those of the cure. With regard to the first, it is especially to be noted that Breuer's patient in almost all pathogenic situations had to suppress a strong excitement, instead of giving vent to it by appropriate words and deeds. In the little experience with her governess' dog, she suppressed, through regard for the conventions, all manifestations of her very intense disgust. While she was seated by her father's sick-bed, she was careful to betray nothing of her anxiety and her painful depression to the patient. When, later, she reproduced the same scene before the physician, the emotion which she had suppressed on the occurrence of the scene burst out with especial strength, as though it had been pent up all along. The symptom which had been caused by that scene reached its greatest intensity while the doctor was striving to revive the memory of the scene, and vanished after it had been fully laid bare. On the other hand, experience shows that if the patient is reproducing the traumatic scene to the physician, the process has no curative effect if, by some peculiar chance, there is no development of emotion. It is apparently these emotional processes upon which the illness of the patient and the restoration to health are dependent. We feel justified in regarding "emotion" as a quantity which may become increased, derived and displaced. So we are forced to the conclusion that the patient fell ill because the emotion developed in the pathogenic situation was prevented from escaping normally, and that the essence of the sickness lies in the fact that these "imprisoned" (*eingeklemmt*) emotions undergo a series of abnormal changes. In part they are preserved as a lasting charge and as a source of constant disturbance in psychical life; in part they undergo a change into unusual bodily innervations and inhibitions, which present themselves as the physical symptoms of the case. We have coined the name "hysterical conversion" for the latter process. Part of our mental energy is, under normal conditions, conducted off by way of physical innervation and gives what we call "the expression of emotions." Hysterical conversion exaggerates this part of the course of a mental process which is emotionally colored; it corresponds to a far more intense emotional expression, which finds outlet by new paths. If a stream flows in two channels, an overflow of one will take place as soon as the current in the other meets with an obstacle.

* * * * *

When the patient was hypnotized, it was possible, after considerable difficulty, to recall those scenes to her memory, and by this means of recall the symptoms were removed. It would have been extremely perplexing to know how to interpret this fact, if hypnotic practice and experiments had not pointed out the way. Through the study of hypnotic phenomena, the conception, strange though it was at first, has become familiar, that in one and the same individual several mental groupings are possible, which may remain

relatively independent of each other, "know nothing" of each other, and which may cause a splitting of consciousness along lines which they lay down. Cases of such a sort, known as "double personality" ("*double conscience*"), occasionally appear spontaneously. If in such a division of personality consciousness remains constantly bound up with one of the two states, this is called the *conscious* mental state, and the other the *unconscious*. In the well-known phenomena of so-called post hypnotic suggestion, in which a command given in hypnosis is later executed in the normal state as though by an imperative suggestion, we have an excellent basis for understanding how the unconscious state can influence the conscious, although the latter is ignorant of the existence of the former. In the same way it is quite possible to explain the facts in hysterical cases. Breuer came to the conclusion that the hysterical symptoms originated in such peculiar mental states, which he called "hypnoidal states" (*hypnoide Zustande*). Experiences of an emotional nature, which occur during such hypnoidal states easily become pathogenic, since such states do not present the conditions for a normal draining off of the emotion of the exciting processes. And as a result there arises a peculiar product of this exciting process, that is, the symptom, and this is projected like a foreign body into the normal state. The latter has, then, no conception of the hypnoidal pathogenic situation. Where a symptom arises, we also find an amnesia, a memory gap, and the filling of this gap includes the removal of the conditions under which the symptom originated.

* * * * *

I had substantiated the fact that the forgotten memories were not lost. They were in the possession of the patient, ready to emerge and form associations with his other mental content, but hindered from becoming conscious, and forced to remain in the unconscious by some sort of a force. The existence of this force could be assumed with certainty, for in attempting to drag up the unconscious memories into the consciousness of the patient, in opposition to this force, one got the sensation of his own personal effort striving to overcome it. One could get an idea of this force, which maintained the pathological situation, from the resistance of the patient.

It is on this idea of *resistance* that I based my theory of the psychic processes of hystericals. It had been found that in order to cure the patient it was necessary that this force should be overcome. Now with the mechanism of the cure as a starting point, quite a definite theory could be constructed. These same forces, which in the present situation as resistances opposed the emergence of the forgotten ideas into consciousness, must themselves have caused the forgetting, and repressed from consciousness the pathogenic experiences. I called this hypothetical process "repression" (*Verdrängung*), and considered that it was proved by the undeniable existence of resistance.

But now the question arose: what were those forces, and what were the conditions of this repression, in which we were now able to recognize the pathogenic mechanism of hysteria? A comparative study of the pathogenic situations, which the cathartic treatment has made possible, allows us to answer this question. In all those experiences, it had happened that a wish had been aroused, which was in sharp opposition to the other desires of the individual, and was not capable of being reconciled with the ethical, æsthetic and personal pretensions of the patient's personality. There had been a short conflict, and the end of this inner struggle was the repression of the idea which presented itself to consciousness as the bearer of this irreconcilable wish. This was, then, repressed from consciousness and forgotten. The incompatibility of the idea in question with the "ego" of the patient was the motive of the repression, the ethical and other pretensions of the individual were the repressing forces. The presence of the incompatible wish, or the duration of the conflict, had given rise to a high degree of mental pain; this pain was avoided by the repression. This latter process is evidently in such a case a device for the protection of the personality.

* * * * *

We come to the conclusion, from working with hysterical patients and other neurotics, that they have not fully succeeded in repressing the idea to which the incompatible wish is attached. They have, indeed, driven it out of consciousness and out of memory, and apparently saved themselves a great amount of psychic pain, *but in the unconscious the suppressed wish still exists*, only waiting for its chance to become active, and finally succeeds in sending into consciousness, instead of the repressed idea, a disguised and unrecognizable surrogate-creation (*Ersatzbildung*), to which the same painful sensations associate themselves that the patient thought he was rid of through his repression. This surrogate of the suppressed idea—the symptom—is secure against further attacks from the defenses of the ego, and instead of a short conflict there originates now a permanent suffering. We can observe in the symptom, besides the tokens of its disguise, a remnant of traceable similarity with the originally repressed idea; the way in which the surrogate is built up can be discovered during the psychoanalytic treatment of the patient, and for his cure the symptom must be traced back over the same route to the repressed idea. If this repressed material is once more made part of the conscious mental functions—a process which supposes the overcoming of considerable resistance—the psychic conflict which then arises, the same which the patient wished to avoid, is made capable of a happier termination, under the guidance of the physician, than is offered by repression. There are several possible suitable decisions which can bring conflict and neurosis to a happy end; in particular cases the attempt may be made to combine several of these. Either the personality of the patient may be convinced that he has been wrong in rejecting the pathogenic wish, and he may be made to accept it either wholly or in part; or this wish may itself be directed to a higher goal which is free from objection, by what is called sublimation (*Sublimierung*); or the rejection may be recognized as rightly motivated, and the automatic and therefore insufficient mechanism of repression be reinforced by the higher, more characteristically human mental faculties: one succeeds in mastering his wishes by conscious thought.

* * * * *

I told you how when I gave up using hypnosis I pressed my patients to tell me what came into their minds that had to do with the problem we were working on, I told them that they would remember what they had apparently forgotten, and that the thought which irrupted into consciousness (*Einfall*) would surely embody the memory for which we were seeking. I claimed that I substantiated the fact that the first idea of my patients brought the right clew and could be shown to be the forgotten continuation of the memory. Now this is not always so; I represented it as being so simple only for purposes of abbreviation. In fact, it would only happen the first time that the right forgotten material would emerge through simple pressure on my part. If the experience was continued, ideas emerged in every case which could not be the right ones, for they were not to the purpose, and the patients themselves rejected them as incorrect. Pressure was of no further service here, and one could only regret again having given up hypnosis.

* * * * *

In .the patients whom I treated there were two opposing forces: on the one hand the conscious striving to drag up into consciousness the forgotten experience which was present in the unconscious; and on the other hand the resistance which we have seen, which set itself against the emergence of the suppressed idea or its associates into consciousness. In case this resistance was nonexistent or very slight, the forgotten material could become conscious without disguise (*Entstellung*). It was then a natural supposition that the disguise would be more complete, the greater the resistance to the emergence of the idea. Thoughts which broke into the patient's consciousness instead of the ideas sought for, were accordingly made up just like symptoms; they were new, artificial, ephemeral surrogates for the repressed ideas, and differed from these just in proportion as they had been more completely disguised under the influence of the resistances. These surrogates must, however, show a certain similarity with the ideas which are the object of our search, by virtue of their nature as symptoms; and when the resistance is not too intensive it is possible from the nature of these irruptions to discover the hidden object of our search. This must be related to the repressed thought as a sort of allusion, as a statement of the same thing in *indirect* terms.

* * * * *

Ladies and Gentlemen, it is very useful to designate a group of ideas which belong together and have a common emotive tone, according to the custom of the Zurich school (Bleuler, Jung and others), as a "complex." So we can say that if we set out from the last memories of the patient to look for a repressed complex, we have every prospect of discovering it, if only the patient will communicate to us a sufficient number of the ideas which come into his head. So we let the patient speak along any line that he desires, and cling to the hypothesis that nothing can occur to him except what has some indirect bearing on the complex that we are seeking. If this method of discovering the repressed complexes seems too circumstantial, I can at least assure you that it is the only available one.

In practicing this technique, one is further bothered by the fact that the patient often stops, is at a standstill, and considers that he has nothing to say; nothing occurs to him. If this were really the case and the patient were right, our procedure would again be proven inapplicable. Closer observation shows that such an absence of ideas never really occurs, and that it only appears to when the patient holds back or rejects the idea which he perceives, under the influence of the resistance, which disguises itself as critical judgment of the value of the idea. The patient can be protected from this if he is warned in advance of this circumstance, and told to take no account of the critical attitude. He must say anything that comes into his mind, fully laying aside such critical choice, even though he may think it is unessential, irrelevant, nonsensical, especially when the idea is one which is unpleasant to dwell on. By following this prescription we secure the material which sets us on the track of the repressed complex.

* * * * *

And first, not all dreams are so foreign to the character of the dreamer, are incomprehensible and confused. If you will undertake to consider the dreams of young children from the age of a year and a half on, you will find them quite simple and easy to interpret. The young child always dreams of the fulfillment of wishes which were aroused in him the day before and were not satisfied. You need no art of interpretation to discover this simple solution, you only need to inquire into the experiences of the child on the day before (the "dream day"). Now it would certainly be a most satisfactory solution of the dream-riddle, if the dreams of adults, too, were the same as those of children, fulfillments of wishes which had been aroused in them during the dream day. This is actually the fact; the difficulties which stand in the way of this solution can be removed step by step by a thorough analysis of the dream.

There is, first of all, the most weighty objection, that the dreams of adults generally have an incomprehensible content, which shows wish-fulfillment least of anything. The answer is this: these dreams have undergone a process of disguise, the psychic content which underlies them was originally meant for quite different verbal expression. You must differentiate between the *manifest dream-content*, which we remember in the morning only confusedly, and with difficulty clothe in words which seem arbitrary, and the *latent dream-thoughts*, whose presence in the unconscious we must assume. This distortion of the dream (*Traumentstellung*) is the same process which has been revealed to you in the investigations of the creations (*symptoms*) of hysterical subjects; it points to the fact that the same opposition of psychic forces has its share in the creation of dreams as in the creation of symptoms.

The manifest dream-content is the disguised surrogate for the unconscious dream thoughts, and this disguising is the work of the defensive forces of the ego, of the resistances. These prevent the repressed wishes from entering consciousness during the waking life, and even in the relaxation of sleep they are still strong enough to force them to hide themselves by a sort of masquerading. The dreamer, then, knows just as little the sense of his dream as the hysterical knows the relation and significance of his symptoms. That there are latent dream-thoughts and that between them and the manifest dream-content there exists the relation just described—of this you may convince yourselves by the analysis of dreams, a procedure the technique of which is exactly that of psychoanalysis. You must abstract entirely from the apparent connection of the elements in the manifest dream and seek for the irruptive ideas which arise through free

association, according to the psychoanalytic laws, from each separate dream element. From this material the latent dream thoughts may be discovered, exactly as one divines the concealed complexes of the patient from the fancies connected with his symptoms and memories. From the latent dream thoughts which you will find in this way, you will see at once how thoroughly justified one is in interpreting the dreams of adults by the same rubrics as those of children. What is now substituted for the manifest dream-content is the real sense of the dream, is always clearly comprehensible, associated with the impressions of the day before, and appears as the fulfilling of an unsatisfied wish. The manifest dream, which we remember after waking, may then be described as a *disguised* fulfillment of *repressed* wishes.

It is also possible by a sort of synthesis to get some insight into the process which has brought about the disguise of the unconscious dream thoughts as the manifest dream-content. We call this process "dream-work" (*Traumarbeit*). This deserves our fullest theoretical interest, since here as nowhere else can we study the unsuspected physic processes which are existent in the unconscious, or, to express it more exactly, *between* two such separate systems as the conscious and the unconscious. Among these newly discovered psychic processes, two, condensation (*Verdichtung*) and displacement or transvaluation, change of psychic accent (*Verschiebung*), stand out most prominently. Dream work is a special case of the reaction of different mental groupings on each other, and as such is the consequence of psychic fission. In all essential points it seems identical with the work of disguise, which changes the repressed complex in the case of failing repression into symptoms.

* * * * *

I will also direct your attention to the fact that we have discovered from the analysis of dreams that the unconscious makes use of a sort of symbolism, especially in the presentation of sexual complexes. This symbolism in part varies with the individual, but in part is of a typical nature, and seems to be identical with the symbolism which we suppose to lie behind our myths and legends. It is not impossible that these later creations of the people may find their explanation from the study of dreams.

Finally, I must remind you that you must not be led astray by the objection that the occurrence of anxiety-dreams (*Angsttraüme*), contradicts our idea of the dream as a wish-fulfillment. Apart from the consideration that anxiety-dreams also require interpretation before judgment can be passed on them, one can say quite generally that the anxiety does not depend in such a simple way on the dream content as one might suppose without more knowledge of the facts, and more attention to the conditions of neurotic anxiety. Anxiety is one of the ways in which the ego relieves itself of repressed wishes which have become too strong and so is easy to explain in the dream, if the dream has gone too far towards the fulfilling of the objectionable wish.

* * * * *

From what has been said you can easily understand how the interpretation of dreams, if it is not made too difficult by the resistance of the patient, can lead to a knowledge of the patient's concealed and repressed wishes and the complexes which he is nourishing. I may now pass to that group of everyday mental phenomena whose study has become a technical help for psychoanalysis.

These are the bungling of acts (*Fehl-handlungen*) among normal men as well as among neurotics, to which no significance is ordinarily attached; the forgetting of things which one is supposed to know and at other times really does know (for example the temporary forgetting of proper names); mistakes in speaking (*Versprechen*), which occur so frequently; analogous mistakes in writing (*Verschreiben*) and in reading (*Verlesen*), the automatic execution of purposive acts in wrong situations (*Vergreifen*) and the loss or breaking of objects, etc. These are trifles, for which no one has ever sought a psychological determination, which have passed unchallenged as chance experiences, as consequences of absent-mindedness, inattention and similar conditions. Here, too, are included the acts and gestures executed without being noticed by the subject, to say nothing of the fact that he attaches no psychic importance to them; as playing and trifling with objects, humming melodies, handling one's person and clothing and the like.

These little things, the bungling of acts, like the symptomatic and chance acts (*Symptom-und Zufallshandlungen*) are not so entirely without meaning as is generally supposed by a sort of tacit agreement. They have a meaning, generally easy and sure to interpret from the situation in which they occur, and it can be demonstrated that they either express impulses and purposes which are repressed, hidden if possible from the consciousness of the individual, or that they spring from exactly the same sort of repressed wishes and complexes which we have learned to know already as the creators of symptoms and dreams.

* * * * *

You have already noticed that the psychoanalyst is distinguished by an especially strong belief in the determination of the psychic life. For him there is in the expressions of the psyche nothing trifling, nothing arbitrary and lawless, he expects everywhere a widespread motivation, where customarily such claims are not made; more than that, he is even prepared to find a manifold motivation of these psychic expressions, while our supposedly inborn causal need is satisfied with a single psychic cause.

* * * * *

Now to proceed with the communication of our results. It is true that in another series of cases psychoanalysis at first traces the symptoms back not to the sexual, but to banal traumatic experiences. But the distinction loses its significance through other circumstances. The work of analysis which is necessary for the thorough explanation and complete cure of a case of sickness does not stop in any case with the experience of the time of onset of the disease, but in every case it goes back to the adolescence and the early childhood of the patient. Here only do we hit upon the impressions and circumstances which determine the later sickness. Only the childhood experiences can give the explanation for the sensitivity to later traumata and only when these memory traces, which almost always are forgotten, are discovered and made conscious, is the power developed to banish the symptoms. We arrive here at the same conclusion as in the investigation of dreams—that it is the incompatible, repressed wishes of childhood which lend their power to the creation of symptoms. Without these the reactions upon later traumata discharge normally. But we must consider these mighty wishes of childhood very generally as sexual in nature.

Now I can at any rate be sure of your astonishment. Is there an infantile sexuality? you will ask. Is childhood not rather that period of life which is distinguished by the lack of the sexual impulse? No, gentlemen, it is not at all true that the sexual impulse enters into the child at puberty, as the devils in the gospel entered into the swine. The child has his sexual impulses and activities from the beginning, he brings them with him into the world, and from these the so-called normal sexuality of adults emerges by a significant development through manifold stages. It is not very difficult to observe the expressions of this childish sexual activity; it needs rather a certain art to overlook them or to fail to interpret them.

* * * * *

Lay aside your doubts and let us evaluate the infantile sexuality of the earliest years. The sexual impulse of the child manifests itself as a very complex one, it permits of an analysis into many components, which spring from different sources. It is entirely disconnected from the function of reproduction which it is later to serve. It permits the child to gain different sorts of pleasure sensations, which we include, by the analogues and connections which they show, under the term sexual pleasures. The great source of infantile sexual pleasure is the auto-excitation of certain particularly sensitive parts of the body; besides the genitals are included the rectum and the opening of the urinary canal, and also the skin and other sensory surfaces. Since in the first phase of child sexual life the satisfaction is found on the child's own body and has nothing to do with any other object, we call this phase after a word coined by Havelock Ellis, that of "auto-eroticism." The parts of the body significant in giving sexual pleasure we call "erogenous zones." The thumb-sucking (*Ludeln*) or passionate sucking (*Wonnesaugen*) of very young children is a good example of such an auto-erotic satisfaction of an erogenous zone. The first scientific observer of this phenomenon, a specialist in children's diseases in Budapest by the name of Lindner, interpreted these rightly as sexual satisfaction and described exhaustively their transformation into other and higher forms of sexual gratification. Another sexual satisfaction of this time of life is the excitation of the genitals by masturbation, which has such a great significance for later life and, in the case of many individuals, is never fully overcome. Besides this and other auto-erotic manifestations we see very early in the child the impulse-components of *sexual pleasure*, or, as we may say, of the *libido*, which presupposes a second person as its object. These impulses appear in opposed pairs, as active and passive. The most important representatives of this group are the pleasure in inflicting pain (sadism) and its passive exhibition-pleasure (*Schaulust*). From the first of these later pairs splits off the curiosity for knowledge, as from the latter impulse toward artistic and theatrical representation. Other sexual manifestations of the child can already be regarded from the viewpoint of object-choice, in which the second person plays the prominent part. The significance of this was primarily based upon motives of the impulse of self-preservation. The difference between the sexes plays, however, in the child no very great rôle. One may attribute to every child, without wronging him, a bit of the homosexual disposition.

The sexual life of the child, rich, but dissociated, in which each single impulse goes about the business of arousing pleasure independently of every other, is later correlated and organized in two general directions, so that by the close of puberty the definite sexual character of the individual is practically finally determined. The single impulses subordinate themselves to the overlordship of the genital zone, so that the whole sexual life is taken over into the service of procreation, and their gratification is now significant only so far as they help to prepare and promote the true sexual act. On the other hand, object-choice prevails over auto-eroticism, so that now in the sexual life all components of the sexual impulse are satisfied in the loved person. But not all the original impulse-components are given a share in the final shaping of the sexual life. Even before the advent of puberty certain impulses have undergone the most energetic repression under the impulse of education, and mental forces like shame, disgust and morality are developed, which, like sentinels, keep the repressed wishes in subjection. When there comes, in puberty, the high tide of sexual desire it finds dams in this creation of reactions and resistances. These guide the outflow into the so-called normal channels, and make it impossible to revivify the impulses which have undergone repression.

The most important of these repressed impulses are coprophilism, that is, the pleasure in children connected with the excrements; and further, the tendencies attaching themselves to the persons of the primitive object-choice.

Gentlemen, a sentence of general pathology says that every process of development brings with it the germ of pathological dispositions in so far as it may be inhibited, delayed, or incompletely carried out. This holds for the development of the sexual function, with its many complications. It is not smoothly completed in all individuals, and may leave behind either abnormalities or disposition to later diseases by the way of later falling back or *regression*. It may happen that not all the partial impulses subordinate themselves to the rule of the genital zone. Such an impulse which has remained disconnected brings about what we call a perversion, which may replace the normal sexual goal by one of its own. It may happen, as has been said before, that the auto-eroticism is not fully overcome, as many sorts of disturbances testify. The originally equal value of both sexes as sexual objects may be maintained and an inclination to homosexual activities in adult life result from this, which, under suitable conditions, rises to the level of exclusive homosexuality. This series of disturbances corresponds to the direct inhibition of development of the sexual function, it includes the perversions and the general *infantilism* of the sex life that are not seldom met with.

The disposition to neuroses is to be derived in another way from an injury to the development of the sex life. The neuroses are related to the perversions as the negative to the positive; in them we find the same impulse-components as in perversions, as bearers of the complexes and as creators of the symptoms; but here they work from out the unconscious. They have undergone a re-

pression, but in spite of this they maintain themselves in the unconscious. Psychoanalysis teaches us that overstrong expression of the impulse in very early life leads to a sort of fixation (*Fixirung*), which then offers a weak point in the articulation of the sexual function. If the exercise of the normal sexual function meets with hindrances in later life, this repression, dating from the time of development, is broken through at just that point at which the infantile fixation took place.

* * * * *

Now we turn again to the sexual development of the child. We still have much to say here, since we have given more attention to the somatic than to the mental expressions of the sexual life. The primitive object-choice of the child, which is derived from his need of help, demands our further interest. It first attaches to all persons to whom he is accustomed, but soon these give way in favor of his parents. The relation of the child to his parents is, as both direct observation of the child and later analytic investigation of adults agree, not at all free from elements of sexual accessory-excitation (*Miterregung*). The child takes both parents, and especially one, as an object of his erotic wishes. Usually he follows in this the stimulus given by his parents, whose tenderness has very clearly the character of a sex manifestation, though inhibited so far as its goal is concerned. As a rule, the father prefers the daughter, the mother the son; the child reacts to this situation, since, as son, he wishes himself in the place of his father, as daughter, in the place of the mother. The feelings awakened in these relations between parents and children, and, as a resultant of them, those among the children in relation to each other, are not only positively of a tender, but negatively of an inimical sort. The complex built up in this way is destined to quick repression, but it still exerts a great and lasting effect from the unconscious. We must express the opinion that this with its ramifications presents the *nuclear complex* of every neurosis, and so we are prepared to meet with it in a not less effectual way in the other fields of mental life. The myth of King Oedipus, who kills his father and wins his mother as a wife is only the slightly altered presentation of the infantile wish, rejected later by the opposing barriers of incest. Shakespeare's tale of Hamlet rests on the same basis of an incest complex, though better concealed.

* * * * *

It is unavoidable and quite normal that the child should make his parents the objects of his first object-choice. But his *libido* must not remain fixed on these first chosen objects, but must take them merely as a prototype and transfer from these to other persons in the time of definite object-choice. The breaking loose (*Ablösung*) of the child from his parents is thus a problem impossible to escape if the social virtue of the young individual is not to be impaired. During the time that the repressive activity is making its choice among the partial sexual impulses and later, when the influence of the parents, which in the most essential way has furnished the material for these repressions, is lessened, great problems fall to the work of education, which at present certainly does not always solve them in the most intelligent and economic way.

* * * * *

Ladies and Gentlemen: With the discovery of infantile sexuality and the tracing back of the neurotic symptoms to erotic impulse-components we have arrived at several unexpected formulæ for expressing the nature and tendencies of neurotic diseases. We see that the individual falls ill when in consequence of outer hindrances or inner lack of adaptability the satisfaction of the erotic needs in the sphere of reality is denied. We see that he then flees to sickness, in order to find with its help a surrogate satisfaction for that denied him. We recognize that the symptoms of illness contain fractions of the sexual activity of the individual, or his whole sexual life, and we find in the turning away from reality the chief tendency and also the chief injury of the sickness. We may guess that the resistance of our patients against the cure is not a simple one, but is composed of many motives. Not only does the ego of the patient strive against the giving up of the repression by which it has changed itself from its original constitution into its present form, but also the sexual impulses may not renounce their

surrogate satisfaction so long as it is not certain that they can be offered anything better in the sphere of reality.

The flight from the unsatisfying reality into what we call, on account of its biologically injurious nature, disease, but which is never without an individual gain in pleasure for the patient, takes place over the path of regression, the return to earlier phases of the sexual life, when satisfaction was not lacking. This regression is seemingly a twofold one, a *temporal*, in so far as the *libido* or erotic need falls back to a temporally earlier stage of development, and a *formal*, since the original and primitive psychic means of expression are applied to the expression of this need. Both sorts of regression focus in childhood and have their common point in the production of an infantile condition of sexual life.

The deeper you penetrate into the pathogenic of neurotic diseases, the more the connection of neuroses with other products of human mentality, even the most valuable, will be revealed to you. You will be reminded that we men, with the high claims of our civilization and under the pressure of our repressions, find reality generally quite unsatisfactory and so keep up a life of fancy in which we love to compensate for what is lacking in the sphere of reality by the production of wish-fulfillments. In these phantasies is often contained very much of the particular constitutional essence of personality and of its tendencies, repressed in real life. The energetic and successful man is he who succeeds by dint of labor in transforming his wish fancies into reality. Where this is not successful in consequence of the resistance of the outer world and the weakness of the individual, there begins the turning away from reality. The individual takes refuge in his satisfying world of fancy. Under certain conditions it still remains possible for him to find another connecting link between these fancies and reality, instead of permanently becoming a stranger to it through the regression into the infantile. If the individual who is displeased with reality is in possession of that *artistic talent* which is still a psychological riddle, he can transform his fancies into artistic creations. So he escapes the fate of a neurosis and wins back his connection with reality by this round-about way. Where this opposition to the real world exists, but this valuable talent fails or proves insufficient, it is unavoidable that the *libido*, following the origin of the fancies, succeeds by means of regression in revivifying the infantile wishes and so producing a neurosis. The neurosis takes, in our time, the place of the cloister, in which were accustomed to take refuge all those whom life had undeceived or who felt themselves too weak for life.

* * * * *

Every time that we treat a neurotic psychoanalytically, there occurs in him the so-called phenomenon of *transfer* (*Uebertragung*), that is, he applies to the person of the physician a great amount of tender emotion, often mixed with enmity, which has no foundation in any real relation, and must be derived in every respect from the old wish-fancies of the patient which have become unconscious. Every fragment of his emotive life, which can no longer be called back into memory, is accordingly lived over by the patient in his relations to the physician, and only by such a living of them over in the "transfer" is he convinced of the existence and the power of these unconscious sexual excitations. The symptoms, which, to use a simile from chemistry, are the precipitates of earlier love experiences (in the widest sense), can only be dissolved in the higher temperature of the experience of transfer and transformed into other psychic products. The physician plays in this reaction, to use an excellent expression of S. Ferenczi, the rôle of a *catalytic ferment*, which temporarily attracts to itself the affect which has become free in the course of the process.

The study of transfer can also give you the key to the understanding of hypnotic suggestion, which we at first used with our patients as a technical means of investigation of the unconscious. Hypnosis showed itself at that time to be a therapeutic help, but a hindrance to the scientific knowledge of the real nature of the case, since it cleared away the psychic resistances from a certain field, only to pile them up in an unscalable wall at the boundaries of this field. You must not think that the phenomenon of transfer, about which I can unfortunately say only too little here, is created by the influence of the psychoanalytic treatment. The transfer arises

spontaneously in all human relations and in the relations of the patient to the physician; it is everywhere the especial bearer of therapeutic influences, and it works the stronger the less one knows of its presence. Accordingly psychoanalysis does not create it, it merely discloses it to consciousness, and avails itself of it, in order to direct the psychic processes to the wished-for goal.

* * * * *

The neurotic has lost, by his repressions, many sources of mental energy whose contingents would have been very valuable for his character building and his life activities. We know a far more purposive process of development, to so-called *sublimation* (*Sublimirung*), by which the energy of infantile wish-excitations is not secluded, but remains capable of application, while for the particular excitations, instead of becoming useless, a higher, eventually no longer sexual, goal is set up. The components of the sexual instinct are especially distinguished by such a capacity for the sublimation and exchange of their sexual goal for one more remote and socially more valuable. To the contributions of the energy won in such a way for the functions of our mental life we probably owe the highest cultural consequences. A repression taking place at an early period excludes the sublimation of the repressed impulse; after the removal of the repression the way to sublimation is again free.

... A certain part of the suppressed libidinous excitation has a right to direct satisfaction and ought to find it in life. The claims of our civilization make life too hard for the greater part of humanity, and so further the aversion to reality and the origin of neuroses, without producing an excess of cultural gain by this excess of sexual repression. We ought not to go so far as to fully neglect the original animal part of our nature, we ought not to forget that the happiness of individuals cannot be dispensed with as one of the aims of our culture. The plasticity of the sexual-components, manifest in their capacity for sublimation, may cause a great temptation to accomplish greater culture-effects by a more and more far reaching sublimation. But just as little as with our machines we expect to change more than a certain fraction of the applied heat into useful mechanical work, just as little ought we to strive to separate the sexual impulse in its whole extent of energy from its peculiar goal.

Structure of the Personality: Id, Ego, and Superego [5]

We have arrived at our knowledge of this psychical apparatus by studying the individual development of human beings. To the oldest of these psychical provinces or agencies we give the name of *id*. It contains everything that is inherited, that is present at birth, that is laid down in the constitution—above all, therefore, the instincts, which originate from the somatic organization and which find a first psychical expression here [in the id] in forms unknown to us.

Under the influence of the real external world around us, one portion of the id has undergone a special development. From what was originally a cortical layer, equipped with the organs for receiving stimuli and with arrangements for acting as a protective shield against stimuli, a special organization has arisen which henceforward acts as an intermediary between the id and the external world. To this region of our mind we have given the name of *ego*.

Here are the principal characteristics of the ego. In consequence of the pre-established connection between sense perception and muscular action, the ego has voluntary movement at its command. It has the task of self-preservation. As regards *external* events, it performs that task by becoming aware of stimuli, by storing up experiences about them (in the memory), by avoiding excessively strong stimuli (through flight), by dealing with moderate stimuli (through adaptation) and finally by learning to bring about expedient changes in the external world to its own advantage (through activity). As regards *internal* events, in relation to the id,

it performs that task by gaining control over the demands of the instincts, by deciding whether they are to be allowed satisfaction, by postponing that satisfaction to times and circumstances favourable in the external world or by suppressing their excitations entirely. It is guided in its activity by consideration of the tensions produced by stimuli, whether these tensions are present in it or introduced into it. The raising of these tensions is in general felt as *unpleasure* and their lowering as *pleasure*. It is probable, however, that what is felt as pleasure or unpleasure is not the *absolute* height of this tension but something in the rhythm of the changes in them. The ego strives after pleasure and seeks to avoid unpleasure. An increase in unpleasure that is expected and foreseen is met by a *signal of anxiety;* the occasion of such an increase, whether it threatens from without or within, is known as a *danger*. From time to time the ego gives up its connection with the external world and withdraws into the state of sleep, in which it makes far-reaching changes in its organization. It is to be inferred from the state of sleep that this organization consists in a particular distribution of mental energy.

The long period of childhood, during which the growing human being lives in dependence on his parents, leaves behind it as a precipitate the formation in his ego of a special agency in which this parental influence is prolonged. It has received the name of *super-ego*. In so far as this super-ego is differentiated from the ego or is opposed to it, it constitutes a third power which the ego must take into account.

An action by the ego is as it should be if it satisfies simultaneously the demands of the id, of the super-ego and of reality—that is to say, if it is able to reconcile their demands with one another. The details of the relation between the ego and the super-ego become completely intelligible when they are traced back to the child's attitude to its parents. This parental influence of course includes in its operation not only the personalities of the actual parents but also the family, racial and national traditions handed on through them, as well as the demands of the immediate social *milieu* which they represent. In the same way, the super-ego, in the course of an individual's development, receives contributions from later successors and substitutes of his parents, such as teachers and models in public life of

---

[5] Sigmund Freud, *An Outline of Psycho-Analysis*, trans. James Strachey from *The Standard Edition of The Complete Psychological Works of Sigmund Freud* (London: Hogarth Press, 1964), vol. 23, pp. 145-147; also published in New York by W. W. Norton, 1949), pp. 14–17. Original German, "Abriss der Psychoanalyse," in *Internationale Zeitschrift für Psychoanalyse und Imago;* 1940, **25**. Reprinted by permission.

admired social ideals.   It will be observed that, for all their fundamental difference, the id and the super-ego have one thing in common: they both represent the influences of the past—the id the influence of heredity, the super-ego the influence, essentially, of what is taken over from other people— whereas the ego is principally determined by the individual's own experience, that is by accidental and contemporary events.

ALFRED ADLER
(1870–1937)

Individual Psychology [6]

The point of departure upon this line of research seems to me to be given in a work entitled "Die Aggressionstrieb im Leben und in der Neurose," published in 1906 in a collective volume, *Heilen und Bilden*. . . . Even at that time I was engaged in a lively controversy with the Freudian school, and in opposition to them, I devoted my attention in that paper to the *relation* of the child and the adult to the demands of the external world. I tried to present, howbeit in a very inadequate fashion, the multifarious forms of attack and defense, of modification of the self and of the environment, effected by the human mind, and launched on the momentous departure of repudiating the sexual aetiology of mental phenomena as fallacious.   In a vague way I saw even then that the impulsive life of man suffers variations and contortions, curtailments and exaggerations, *relative to the kind and degree of its aggressive power*. In accordance with the present outlook of individual psychology, I should rather say: relative to the way the power of cooperation has developed in childhood. . . .

I myself was too deeply interested in the problem of what determined the various forms of attack upon the outer world. From my own observations, and supported by those of older authors, also perhaps guided by the concept of a *locus minoris resistentiae*, I arrived at the notion that inferior organs might be responsible for the feeling of psychic inferiority, and in the year 1907 recorded my studies concerning this subject in a volume entitled *Studie über Minderwertigkeit der Organe und die seelische Kompensation*. . . . The purpose of the work was to show that

children born with hereditary organic weaknesses exhibit not only a physical necessity to compensate for the defect, and tend to overcompensate, but that the entire nervous system, too, may take part in this compensation; especially the mind, as a factor of life, may suffer a striking exaggeration in the direction of the defective function (breathing, eating, seeing, hearing, talking, moving, feeling, or even thinking), so that this over-emphasized function may become the mainspring of life, in so far as a *"successful* compensation" occurs.   This compensatory increase, which, as I showed in the above-mentioned book, has originated and continued the development of a human race blessed with inferior organs, may in favorable cases affect also the endocrine glands, as I have pointed out, and is regularly reflected in the condition of the sexual glands, their inferiority and their compensation—a fact which seemed to me to suggest some connection between individual traits and physical heredity.   The link between organic inferiority and psychic effects, which to this day cannot be explained in any other way, but merely assumed, was evident to me in the mind's experience of the inferior organ, by which the former is plunged into a *constant feeling of inferiority*.   Thus I could introduce the body and its degree of excellence as a factor in mental development.

Experts will certainly not fail to see that the whole of our psychiatry has tended in this direction, both in part before that time and quite definitely thereafter. . . .   But they are content to regard the psychic minus quantities as congenital epiphenomena of the physical organic inferiority, without taking account of the fact that it is the *immediate* experience of physical disability which is the key to the failures of performance, as soon as the demands of the outer world and the creative power of the child lead it into "wrong" alleys and force upon it a one-sided interest. What

6 Alfred Adler, "Individual psychology," trans. Susan Langer, in Carl Murchison (ed.), *Psychologies of 1930, op. cit.*, pp. 395–404. Reprinted by permission.

I treated there as failure appeared to me later as a premature curtailment of the cooperative faculty, the social impulse, and a greatly heightened interest for the self.

This work also furnished a test for organic inferiority. As proofs of inferiority it mentions insufficient development of physical form, of reflexes, of functions, or retardation of the latter. Defective development of the nerves in connection with the organ and of the brain-centers involved was also considered. But the sort of compensation which would under favorable circumstances occur in any one of these parts was always insisted upon as a decisive factor.

* * * * *

I repudiated the notion of the hereditary character of psychological traits, in that I referred their origin to the various intensities of organic functions in each individual. Afterwards I added to this the fact that children, in cases of abnormal development, are without any guidance, so that their activity (aggression) may develop in unaccountable ways. The inferior organs offer a temptation but by no means a necessity for neuroses or other mental miscarriages. Herewith I established the problem of the education of such children, with prophylaxis as its aim, on a perfectly sound footing. Thus the family history, with all its plus and minus factors, became an index to the serious difficulties which might be expected and combatted in early childhood. As I said at that time, a hostile attitude toward the world might be the result of excessive stresses which must express themselves somehow in specific characteristics.

In this way I was confronted with the problem of character. There had been a good deal of nebulous speculations on this subject. Character was almost universally regarded as a congenital entity. My conviction that the doctrine of congenital mental traits was erroneous helped me considerably. I came to realize that characters were guiding threads, *ready attitudes* for the solution of the problems of life. The idea of an "arrangement" of all psychical activities became more and more convincing. Therewith I had reached the ground which to this day has been the foundation of individual psychology, the belief that *all psychical phenomena originate*

in the particular creative force of the individual, and are expressions of his personality.

* * * * *

But I had realized the fact that children who were born with defective organs or afflicted by injuries early in life go wrong in the misery of their existence, constantly deprecate themselves, and, usually, to make good this deficiency, behave differently all their lives from what might be expected of normal people. I took another step, and discovered that children may be artificially placed in the same straits as if their organs were defective. If we make their work in very early life so hard that even their relatively normal organs are not equal to it, then they are in the same distress as those with defective physique, and from the same unbearable condition of stress they will give wrong answers as soon as life puts their preparation to any test. Thus I found two further categories of children who are apt to develop an abnormal sense of inferiority—*pampered children and hated children.*

To this period of my complete defection from Freud's point of view, and absolute independence of thought, date such works as *Die seelische Wirzel der Trigeminusneuralgie* . . ., in which I attempted to show how, besides cases of organic origin, there were also certain ones in which excessive partial increase of blood-pressure, caused by emotions such as rage, may under the influence of severe inferiority feelings give rise to physical changes. This was followed by a study, decisive for the development of individual psychology, entitled *Das Problem der Distanz*, wherein I demonstrated, that every individual, by reason of his degree of inferiority feeling, hesitated before the solution of one of the three great problems of life, stops or circumvents, and preserves his attitude in a state of exaggerated tension through psychological symptoms. As the three great problems of life, to which everyone must somehow answer by his attitude, I named: (*a*) society, (*b*) vocation, (*c*) love. Next came a work on *Das Unbewusste*, wherein I tried to prove that upon deeper inspection there appears no contrast between the conscious and the unconscious, that both cooperate for a higher purpose, that our thoughts and feelings become conscious as soon as we are faced with a difficulty, and unconscious as soon as our personality-value requires it. At the same time I tried to set forth the fact that that which other authors had used for their explanations under the name of *conflict, sense of guilt,* or *ambivalence* was to be regarded as symptomatic of a *hesitant attitude,* for the purpose of evading the solution of one of the problems of life. Ambivalence and polarity of emotional or moral traits present themselves as an attempt at a multiple solution or rejection of a problem.

This and some other works dating from the time of the self-emancipation of individual psychology have been published in a volume bearing the title *Praxis und Theorie der Individualpsychologie.* . . .

I have never failed to call attention to the fact that the whole human race is blessed with deficient organs, deficient for coping with nature; that consequently the whole race is constrained ever to seek the way which will bring it into some sort of harmony with the exigencies of life; and that we make mistakes along the way, very much like those we can observe in pampered or neglected children. I have quoted one case especially, where the errors of our civilization may influence the development of an individual, and that is the case of the underestimation of women in our society. From the sense of female inferiority, which most people, men and women alike, possess, both sexes have derived an overstrained desire for masculinity, a superiority complex which is often extremely harmful, a will to conquer all difficulties of life in the masculine fashion, which I have called the *masculine protest.*

Now I began to see clearly in every psychical phenomenon the *striving for superiority.* It runs parallel to physical growth. It is an intrinsic necessity of life itself. It lies at the root of all solutions of life's problems, and is manifested in the way in which we meet these problems. All our functions follow its direction; rightly or wrongly they strive for conquest, surety, increase. The impetus from minus to plus is never-ending. The urge from "below" to "above" never ceases. Whatever premises all our philosophers and psychologists dream of—self-preservation, pleasure principle, equalization—all these are but vague representations, attempts to express the great

upward drive. The history of the human race points in the same direction. Willing, thinking, talking, seeking after rest, after pleasure, learning, understanding, work and love, betoken the essence of this eternal melody. Whether one thinks or acts more wisely or less, one always moves along the lines of that upward tendency. In our right and wrong conceptions of life and its problems, in the successful or the unsuccessful solution of any question, this striving for perfection is uninterruptedly at work. And even where foolishness and imbecility, inexperience, seem to belie the fact of any striving to conquer some defect, or tend to depreciate it, yet the will to conquer is really operative. From this net-work which in the last analysis is simply given with the relationship "man-cosmos," no one may hope to escape. For even if anyone wanted to escape, yes, even if he *could* escape, he would still find himself in the general system, striving "upward," from "below." This does not only fix a fundamental category of thought, the structure of our reason, but what is more, it yields *the fundamental fact of our life.*

The origin of humanity and the ever repeated beginning of infant life rubs it in with every psychic act: "Achieve! Arise! Conquer!" This feeling is never absent, this longing for the abrogation of every imperfection. . . .

The unreluctant search for truth, the ever unsatisfied longing for solution of the problems of life, belongs to this hankering after perfection of some sort.

This, now, appeared to me as the fundamental law of all spiritual expression: that the total melody is to be found again in every one of its parts, as a greatest common measure —in every individual craving for power, for victory over the difficulties of life.

And therewith I recognized a further premise of my scientific proceeding, one which agreed with the formulations of older philosophers, but conflicted with the standpoint of modern psychology: *the unity of the personality.* This, however, was not merely a premise, but could to a certain extent be demonstrated. As Kant has said, we can never understand a person if we do not presuppose his unity. Individual psychology can now add to that: this unity, which we must presuppose, is the work of the individual, which must always continue in the way it once found toward victory.

These were the considerations which led me to the conviction that early in life, in the first four or five years, a *goal* is set for the need and drive of psychical development, a goal toward which all its currents flow. Such a goal has not only the function of determining a direction, of promising security, power, perfection, but it is also of its essence and of the essence of the mind that this portentous goal should awaken feelings and emotions through that which it promises them. Thus the individual mitigates its sense of weakness in the anticipation of its redemption.

Here again we see the meaninglessness of congenital psychic traits. Not that we could deny them. We have no possible way of getting at them. Whoever would draw conclusions from the results is making matters too simple. He overlooks the thousand and one influences after birth, and fails to see the power that lies in the necessity of acquiring a goal.

The staking of a goal compels the unity of the personality in that it draws the stream of all spiritual activity into its definite direction. Itself a product of the common, fundamental sense of inferiority—a sense derived from genuine weakness, not from any comparison with others—the goal of victory in turn forces the direction of all powers and possibilities toward itself. Thus every phase of psychical activity can be seen within one frame, as though it were the end of some earlier phase and the beginning of a succeeding one. This was a further contribution of individual psychology to modern psychology in general—that it insisted absolutely on the indispensability of *finalism* for the understanding of all psychological phenomena. No longer could causes, powers, instincts, impulses, and the like serve as explanatory principles, but the final goal alone. Experiences, traumata, sexual-development mechanisms could not yield us an explanation, but the perspective in which these had been regarded, the individual way of seeing them, which subordinates all life to the ultimate goal.

This final aim, abstract in its purpose of assuring superiority, fictitious in its task of conquering all the difficulties of life, must now appear in concrete form in order to meet its task in actuality. Deity in its widest sense,

it is apperceived by the childish imagination, and under the exigencies of hard reality, as victory over men, over difficult enterprises, over social or natural limitations. It appears in one's attitude toward others, toward one's vocation, toward the opposite sex. Thus we find concrete single purposes, such as: to operate as a member of the community or to dominate it, to attain security and triumph in one's chosen career, to approach the other sex or to avoid it. We may always trace in these special purposes *what sort of meaning the individual has found in his existence*, and how he proposes to realize that meaning.

If, then, the final goal established in early childhood exerts such an influence for better or worse upon the development of the given psychical forces, our next question must be: What are the sources of the individuality which we find in final aims? Could we not quite properly introduce another causal factor here? What brings about the differences of individual attitudes, if one and the same aim of superiority actuates everyone?

Speaking of this last question, let me point out that our human language is incapable of rendering all the qualities within a superiority goal and of expressing its innumerable differences. Certainty, power, perfection, deification, superiority, victory, etc., are but poor attempts to illumine its endless variants. Only after we have comprehended the partial expressions which the final goal effects, are we in any position to determine specific differences.

If there is any causal factor in the psychical mechanism, it is the common and often excessive sense of inferiority. But this continuous mood is only activating a drive and does not reveal the way to compensation and overcompensation. Under the pressure of the first years of life there is no kind of philosophical reflection. There are only impressions, feelings, and a desire to renew the pleasurable ones and exclude those which are painful. For this purpose all energies are mustered, until motion of some sort results. Here, however, training or motion of any sort forces the establishment of an end. There is no motion without an end. And so, in this way, a final goal becomes fixed which promises satisfaction.

* * * * *

From the time of these formulations of individual psychology dates my book, *Ueber den nervösen Charakter* . . ., which introduced *finalism* into psychology with especial emphasis. At the same time I continued to trace the connection between organic inferiority and its psychological consequences, in trying to show how in such cases the goal of life is to be found in the type of overcompensation and consequent errors. As one of these errors I mentioned particularly the *masculine protest*, developed under the pressure of a civilization which has not yet freed itself from its overestimation of the masculine principle nor from an abuse of antithetic points of view. The imperfection of childish modes of realizing the fictitious ideal was also mentioned here as the chief cause for the differences in style of living—the unpredictable character of childish expression, which always moves in the uncontrollable *realm of error*.

By this time, the system of individual psychology was well enough established to be applied to certain special problems. *Zum Problem der Homosexualität* . . . exhibited that perversion as a neurotic construct erroneously made out of early childhood impressions, and recorded researches and findings which are published at greater length in the *Handbuch der normalen und pathologischen Physiologie*. . . . Uncertainty in the sexual rôle, overestimation of the opposite sex, fear of the latter, and a craving for easy, irresponsible successes proved to be the inclining but by no means constraining factors. Uncertainty in the solution of the erotic problem and fear of failure in this direction lead to wrong or abnormal functioning.

More and more clearly I now beheld the way in which the varieties of failure could be understood. In all human failure, in the waywardness of children, in neurosis, and neuropsychosis, in crime, suicide, alcoholism, morphinism, cocainism, in sexual perversion, in fact in all nervous symptoms, we may read lack of the proper degree of *social feeling*. In all my former work I had employed the idea of the individual's attitude toward society as the main consideration. The demands of society, not as of a stable institution but as of a living, striving, victory-seeking mass, were always present in my thoughts. The total accord of this striving and the influence it must exert on each individual had always been one of my main themes. Now I attained somewhat more clarity in the matter. However we may judge people, whatever we try to understand about them, what we aim at when we educate, heal, improve, condemn— we base it always on the same principle: social feeling! cooperation! Anything that we estimate as valuable, good, right, and normal, we estimate simply in so far as it is "virtue" from the point of view of an ideal society. The individual, ranged in a community which can preserve itself only through cooperation as a human society, becomes a part of this great whole through socially enforced division of labor, through association with a member of the opposite sex, and finds his task prescribed by this society. And not only his task, but also his preparation and ability to perform it.

The unequivocally given fact of our organic inferiority on the face of this earth necessitates social solidarity. The need of protection of women during pregnancy and confinement, the prolonged helplessness of childhood, gains the aid of others. The preparation of the child for a complicated, but protective and therefore necessary civilization and labor requires the cooperation of society. The need of security in our personal existence leads automatically to a cultural modification of our impulses and emotions and of our individual attitude of friendship, social intercourse, and love. The social life of man emanates inevitably from the man–cosmos relation, and makes every person a creature and a creator of society.

It is a gratuitous burden to science to ask whether the social instinct is congenital or acquired, as gratuitous as the question of congenital instincts of any sort. We can see only the results of an evolution. And if we are to be permitted a question at all concerning the beginnings of that evolution, it is only this—whether anything can be evolved at all for which no possibilities are in any way given before birth. This possibility exists, as we may see through the results of development, in the case of human beings. The fact that our sense-organs behave the way they do, that through them we may acquire *impressions* of the outer world, may combine these physically and mentally in ourselves, shows our connection with the cosmos. That trait we have in common with all living creatures. What distinguishes man from other organisms, however, is the fact that he must conceive his superiority goal in the social sense as a part of a total achievement. The reasons for this certainly lie in the greater need of the human individual and in the consequent greater mobility of his body and mind, which forces him to find a firm vantage-point in the chaos of life ... !

But because of this enforced sociability, our life presents only such problems which require *ability to cooperate* for their solution. To hear, see, or speak "correctly," means to lose one's self completely in another or in a situation, to become *identified* with him or with it. The capacity for identification, which alone makes us capable of friendship, humane love, pity, vocation, and love, is the basis of the social sense and can be practiced and exercised only in conjunction with others. In this intended assimilation of another person or of a situation not immediately given, lies the whole meaning of comprehension. And in the course of this identification we are able to conjure up all sorts of feelings, emotions, and affects, such as we experience not only in dreams but also in waking life, in neurosis and psychosis. It is always the fixed style of life, the ultimate ideals, that dominates and selects. The style of life is what makes our experiences reasons for our attitude, that calls up these feelings and determines conclusions in accordance with its own purposes. Our very identification with the ultimate ideal makes us optimistic, pessimistic, hesitant, bold, selfish or altruistic.

The tasks which are presented to an individual, as well as the means of their performance, are conceived and formulated within the framework of society. No one, unless he is deprived of his mental capacities, can escape from this frame. *Only within this framework is psychology possible at all.* Even if we add for our own time the aids of civilization and the socially determined pattern of our examples, we still find ourselves confronted with the same unescapable conditions.

From this point of vantage we may look back. As far as we can reasonably determine, it appears that after the fourth or fifth year of life the style of life has been fashioned as a prototype, with its particular way of seizing upon life, its strategy for conquering it, its degree of ability to cooperate. These founda-

tions of every individual development do not alter, unless perchance some harmful errors of construction are recognized by the subject and corrected. Whoever has not acquired in childhood the necessary degree of social sense, will not have it later in life, except under the above-mentioned special conditions. No amount of bitter experience can change his style of life, *as long as he has not gained understanding.* The whole work of education, cure, and human progress can be furthered only along lines of better comprehension.

There remains only one question: What influences are harmful and what beneficial in determining differences in the style of life, i.e., in the capacity for cooperation?

Here, in short, we touch upon the matter of preparation for cooperation. It is evident, of course, that deficiencies of the latter become most clearly visible when the individual's capacity to cooperate is put to the test. As I have shown above, life does not spare us these tests and preliminary trials. We are always on trial, in the development of our sense-organs, in our attitude toward others, our understanding of others, in our morals, our philosophy of life, our political position, our attitude toward the welfare of others, toward love and marriage, in our aesthetic judgments, in our whole behavior. As long as one is not put to any test, as long as one is without any trials or problems, one may doubt one's own status as a fellow of the community. But as soon as a person is beset by any problem of existence, which, as I have demonstrated, always involves cooperative ability, then it will unfailingly become apparent—as in a geographical examination—how far his preparation for cooperation extends.

The first social situation that confronts a child is its relation to its mother, from the very first day. By her educational skill the child's interest in another person is first awakened. If she understands how to train this interest in the direction of cooperation, all the congenital and acquired capacities of the child will converge in the direction of social sense. If she binds the child to herself exclusively, life will bear for it the meaning that all other persons are to be excluded as much as possible. Its position in the world is thereby rendered difficult, as difficult as that of defective or neglected children. All these grow up in a hostile world and develop a low degree of cooperative sense. Often in such cases there results utter failure to adjust to the father, brothers and sisters, or more distant persons. If the father fails to penetrate the circle of the child's interest, or if by reason of exaggerated rivalry the brothers and sisters are excluded, or if because of some social short-coming or prejudice the remoter environment is ruled out of its sphere, then the child will encounter serious trouble in acquiring a healthy social sense. In all cases of failure later in life it will be quite observable that they are rooted in this early period of infancy. The question of responsibility will naturally have to be waived there, since the debtor is unable to pay what is required of him.

Our findings in regard to these errors and erroneous deductions of early childhood, which have been gathered from a contemplation of this relation complex which individual psychology reveals, are exceedingly full. They are recorded in many articles in the *Internationalen Zeitschrift für Individualpsychologie*, in my *Understanding Human Nature . . .*, in *Individualpsychologie in der Schule . . .*, and in *Science of Living. . . .* These works deal with problems of waywardness, neurosis and psychosis, criminality, suicide, drunkenness, and sexual perversion. Problems of society, vocation, and love have been included in the scope of these studies. In *Die Technik der Individualpsychologie . . .* I have published a detailed account of a case of fear and compulsion neurosis.

Individual psychology considers the essence of therapy to lie in making the patient aware of his lack of cooperative power, and to convince him of the origin of this lack in early childhood maladjustments. What passes

during this process is no small matter; his power of cooperation is enhanced by collaboration with the doctor. His "inferiority complex" is revealed as erroneous. Courage and optimism are awakened. And the "meaning of life" dawns upon him as the fact that proper meaning must be given to life.

This sort of treatment may be begun at any point in the spiritual life. The following three points of departure have recommended themselves to me, among others: (*a*) to infer some of the patient's situation from his place in the order of births, since each successive child usually has a somewhat different position from the others; (*b*) to infer from his earliest childhood recollections some dominant interest of the individual, since the creative tendency of the imagination always produces fragments of the life ideal (*Lebensstyl*); (*c*) to apply the individualistic interpretation to the dream-life of the patient, through which one may discover in what particular way the patient, guided by the style-of-life ideal, conjures up emotions and sensations contrary to common sense, in order to be able to carry out his style of life more successfully.

If one seems to have discovered the guiding thread of the patient's life, it remains to test this discovery through a great number of expressive gestures on his part. Only a perfect coincidence of the whole and all the parts gives one the right to say: I understand. And then the examiner himself will always have the feeling that, if he had grown up under the same misapprehensions, if he had harbored the same ideal, had the same notions concerning the meaning of life, if he had acquired an equally low degree of social sense, he would have acted and lived in an "almost" similar manner.

CARL GUSTAV JUNG
(1875–1961)

Analytical Psychology

The Personal and Collective Unconscious [7]

A more or less superficial layer of the unconscious is undoubtedly personal. I call it

the *personal unconscious*. But this personal unconscious rests upon a deeper layer, which does not derive from personal experience and is not a personal acquisition but is inborn. This deeper layer I call the *collective un-*

[7] *The Collected Works of C. G. Jung*, trans. by R. F. C. Hull. Volume 9, part i, *The Archtypes and the Collective Unconscious*, pp. 3–4, 275–277; Volume 9, part ii, *Aion: Researches into the Phenomenology of the Self*, pp. 5–6. Copyright 1959 by Bollingen Foundation, New York. Bollingen Series XX. 9, i and XX. 9, ii; original German, *Von den Wurzeln des Bewusstseins* (Zurich: 1954). Distributed by Princeton University Press. Reprinted by permission.

conscious. I have chosen the term "collective" because this part of the unconscious is not individual but universal; in contrast to the personal psyche, it has contents and modes of behaviour that are more or less the same everywhere and in all individuals. It is, in other words, identical in all men and thus constitutes a common psychic substrate of a suprapersonal nature which is present in every one of us.

Psychic existence can be recognized only by the presence of contents that are *capable of consciousness*. We can therefore speak of an unconscious only in so far as we are able to demonstrate its contents. The contents of the personal unconscious are chiefly the *feeling-toned complexes*, as they are called; they constitute the personal and private side of psychic life. The contents of the collective unconscious, on the other hand, are known as *archetypes*.

* * * * *

I[8] have suggested calling the total personality which, though present, cannot be fully known, the self. The ego is, by definition, subordinate to the self and is related to it like a part to the whole.... Since it is the point of reference for the field of consciousness, the ego is the subject of all successful attempts at adaptation so far as these are achieved by the will. The ego therefore has a significant part to play in the psychic economy. Its position there is so important that there are good grounds for the prejudice that the ego is the centre of the personality, and that the field of consciousness is the psyche *per se*.

* * * * *

This[9] brief consideration will show that, even in the normal individual, character-splitting is by no means an impossibility. We are, therefore, perfectly justified in treating the question of dissociation of personality

also as a problem of normal psychology. According to my view then—to pursue the discussion—the above question should be met with a frank avowal that such a man has no real character at all, i.e. he is not *individual* but *collective*, i.e. he corresponds with general circumstance and expectations. Were he an individual, he would have but one and the same character with every variation of attitude. It would not be identical with the momentary attitude, neither could it nor would it prevent his individuality from finding expression in one state just as clearly as in another. He is an individual, of course, like every being; but an unconscious one. Through his more or less complete identification with the attitude of the moment, he at least deceives others, and also often himself, as to his real character. He puts on a *mask*, which he knows corresponds with his conscious intentions, while it also meets with the requirements and opinions of his environment, so that first one motive then the other is in the ascendant. The mask, viz. the ad hoc adopted attitude, I have called the *persona*, which was the designation given to the mask worn by actors of antiquity. A man who is identified with this mask I would call "personal" (as opposed to "individual").

Two Psychological Types:

Extraversion and Introversion

Extraversion[10] means an outward-turning of the libido. With this concept I denote a manifest relatedness of subject to object in the sense of a positive movement of subjective interest towards the object. Everyone in the state of extraversion thinks, feels, and acts in relation to the object, and moreover in a direct and clearly observable fashion, so that no doubt can exist about his positive dependence upon the object. In a sense, therefore, extraversion is an outgoing transference of interest from the subject to the object. If it is an intellectual extraversion, the subject thinks himself into the object; if a feeling extraversion, then the subject feels himself into the object. The state of extraversion means a strong, if not exclusive, determination by the object. One should speak of an *active* extraversion when deliberately willed, and of

---

[8] Carl Jung, "The ego," in *Aion: Researches into the Phenomenology of the Self*, trans. R. F. C. Hull (New York: Bolingen Foundation, 1959), vol. 9, pt. 2, p. 6; original German, *Aion: Untersuchungen zur Symbolgeschichte* (Zürich, 1951). Reprinted by permission.

[9] Carl G. Jung, *Psychological Types or the Psychology of Individuation*, trans. H. Godwin Baynes (New York: Random House, Inc., 1924), p. 590; original German, *Psychologische Typen* (Zürich, 1921). Reprinted by permission.

[10] *Ibid.*, pp. 542–543.

a *passive* extraversion when the object compels it, i.e. attracts the interest of the subject of its own accord, even against the latter's intention. Should the state of extraversion become habitual, the *extraverted type* appears.

Introversion[11] means a turning inwards of the libido whereby a negative relation of subject to object is expressed. Interest does not move towards the object, but recedes towards the subject. Everyone whose attitude is introverted thinks, feels, and acts in a way that clearly demonstrates that the subject is the chief factor of movitation while the object at most receives only a secondary value. Introversion may possess either a more intellectual or more emotional character, just as it can be characterized by either intuition or sensation. Introversion is *active*, when the subject *wills* a certain seclusion in face of the object; it is *passive* when the subject is unable to restore again to the object the libido which is streaming back from it. When introversion is habitual, one speaks of an *introverted type*.

The Four Functions [12]

By psychological function I understand a certain form of psychic activity that remains theoretically the same under varying circumstances. From the energic standpoint a function is a phenomenal form of libido which theoretically remains constant, in much the same way as physical force can be considered as the form or momentary manifestation of physical energy. I distinguish four basic functions in all, two rational and two irrational—viz. *thinking* and *feeling*, *sensation* and *intuition*.

The Individuation Process [13]

I use the term "individuation" to denote the process by which a person becomes a

psychological "in-dividual," that is, a separate, indivisible unity of "whole." It is generally assumed that consciousness is the whole of the psychological individual. But knowledge of the phenomena that can only be explained on the hypothesis of unconscious psychic processes makes it doubtful whether the ego and its contents are in fact identical with the "whole." If unconscious processes exist at all, they must surely belong to the totality of the individual, even though they are not components of the conscious ego.

* * * * *

I am convinced that such evidence exists. Unfortunately, the material to prove this belongs to the subtleties of psychological analysis. . . . I shall begin with a brief statement: in the unconscious of every man there is hidden a feminine personality, and in that of every woman a masculine personality.

It is a well-known fact that sex is determined by a majority of male or female genes, as the case may be. But the minority of genes belonging to the other sex does not simply disappear. A man therefore has in him a feminine side, an unconscious feminine figure —a fact of which he is generally quite unaware. I may take it as known that I have called this figure the "anima," and its counterpart in a woman the "animus." . . .

Another, no less important and clearly defined figure is the "shadow." Like the anima, it appears either in projection on suitable persons, or personified as such in dreams. The shadow coincides with the "personal" unconscious (which corresponds to Freud's conception of the unconscious). . . . The shadow personifies everything that the subject refuses to acknowledge about himself and yet is always thrusting itself upon him directly or indirectly—for instance, inferior traits of character and other incompatible tendencies.

The Hundred Word Association Test [14]

The history of the association method in vogue in psychology, as well as the method

11   *Ibid.*, p. 567.

12   *Ibid.*, p. 547.

13   Carl G. Jung, "Conscious, unconscious, and individuation," in *The Archetypes and the Collective Unconscious, op. cit.*, vol. 9, part 1, pp. 275–276. Originally written in English as "The meaning of individuation," in *The Integration of Personality* (New York: Farrar and Rinehart, 1939); it is here revised according to the German version, "Bewusstein, Unbewusstes und Individuation," *Zentralblatt für Psychotherapie und ihre Grenzgebiete* (Leipzig, 1939). Reprinted by permission.

14   Carl G. Jung, "The association method," *Amer. J. Psychol.*, 1910, **21**, 219–269. Lectures delivered at the celebration of the twentieth anniversary of the opening of Clark University, September, 1909; trans. A. A. Brill.

itself, is, of course, so familiar to you that there is no need to enlarge upon it. For practical purposes I make use of the following formula:

1. head	51. frog
2. green	52. to part
3. water	53. hunger
4. to sing	54. white
5. dead	55. child
6. long	56. to take care
7. ship	57. lead pencil
8. to pay	58. sad
9. window	59. plum
10. friendly	60. to marry
11. to cook	61. house
12. to ask	62. dear
13. cold	63. glass
14. stem	64. to quarrel
15. to dance	65. fur
16. village	66. big
17. lake	67. carrot
18. sick	68. to paint
19. pride	69. part
20. to cook	70. old
21. ink	71. flower
22. angry	72. to beat
23. needle	73. box
24. to swim	74. wild
25. voyage	75. family
26. blue	76. to wash
27. lamp	77. cow
28. to sin	78. friend
29. bread	79. luck
30. rich	80. lie
31. tree	81. deportment
32. to prick	82. narrow
33. pity	83. brother
34. yellow	84. to fear
35. mountain	85. stork
36. to die	86. false
37. salt	87. anxiety
38. new	88. to kiss
39. custom	89. bride
40. to pray	90. pure
41. money	91. door
42. foolish	92. to choose
43. pamphlet	93. hay
44. despise	94. contented
45. finger	95. ridicule
46. expensive	96. to sleep
47. bird	97. month
48. to fall	98. nice
49. book	99. woman
50. unjust	100. to abuse

This formula has been constructed after many years of experience. The words are chosen and partially arranged in such a manner as to strike easily almost all complexes which occur in practice. As shown above, there is a regulated mixing of the grammatical qualities of the words. For this there are definite reasons.

Before the experiment begins the test person receives the following instruction: "Answer as quickly as possible with the first word that occurs to your mind."

* * * * *

The first thing that strikes us is the fact that many test-persons show a marked prolongation of the reaction time. This would seem to be suggestive of intellectual difficulties, —wrongly however, for we are often dealing with very intelligent persons of fluent speech. The explanation lies rather in the emotions.

* * * * *

Let us, in the first place, continue the discussion concerning the prolonged reaction time. It often happens that the test-person actually does *not* know what to answer to the stimulus word. He waives any reaction, and for the moment he totally fails to obey the original instructions, and shows himself incapable of adapting himself to the experimenter. If this phenomenon occurs frequently in an experiment, it signifies a high degree of disturbance in adjustment. I would call attention to the fact that it is quite indifferent what reason the test-person gives for the refusal. Some find that too many ideas suddenly occur to them; others, that they suffer from a deficiency of ideas. In most cases, however, the difficulties first perceived are so deterrent that they actually give up the whole reaction.

* * * * *

Yet another sign of impeded adaptation is the often occurring *repetitions of the stimulus words*. The test-persons repeat the stimulus word as if they had not heard or understood it distinctly. They repeat it just as we repeat a difficult question in order to grasp it better before answering. This same tendency is shown in the experiment. The questions are repeated because the stimulus words act on hysterical individuals in much the same way as difficult personal questions. In principle it is the same phenomenon as the subsequent completion of the reaction.

HERMANN RORSCHACH
(1884–1922)

The Rorschach Ink Blot Test [15]

The experiment consists in the *interpretation of accidental forms*, that is, of non-specific forms. . . .

The production of such accidental forms is very simple: a few large ink blots are thrown on a piece of paper, the paper folded, and the ink spread between the two halves of the sheet. Not all figures so obtained can be used, for those used must fulfill certain conditions. In the first place, the forms must be relatively simple; complicated pictures make the computations of the factors of the experiment too difficult. Furthermore, the distribution of the blots on the plate must fulfill certain requirements of composition or they will not be suggestive, with the result that many subjects will reject them as "simply an ink-blot" without consideration of other possible interpretations.

Every figure in the series has to fulfill certain special requirements as well as these general ones, and each, as well as any whole series, must be thoroughly tried out before it can be used as apparatus for the test. . . . The construction of a suitable series of ten figures is not so simple as might appear at first glance.

From the method of preparation it will be apparent that the figures will be symmetrical, with very little difference between the two halves. Asymmetrical figures are rejected by many subjects; symmetry supplies part of the necessary artistic composition. It has a disadvantage in that it tends to make the answers somewhat stereotyped. On the other hand, symmetry makes conditions the same for right- and left-handed subjects: furthermore, it facilitates interpretation in certain inhibited and blocked subjects. Finally, symmetry makes possible the interpretation of whole scenes.

* * * * *

Procedure

The subject is given one plate after the other

and asked, "What might this be?" He holds the plate in his hand and may turn it about as much as he likes. The subject is free to hold the plate near his eyes or far away as he chooses; however, it should not be viewed from a distance. The length of the extended arm is the maximum permissible distance. Care must be taken that the subject does not catch a glimpse of the plate from a distance, since this would alter the conditions of the experiment. For instance, Plate I is frequently interpreted "the head of a fox" when seen at a distance of several meters; at a closer range this answer is almost never given. Once the subject has interpreted the plate as the head of a fox it becomes very difficult for him to see anything else when it is brought nearer.

An attempt is made to get at least one answer to every plate, though suggestion in any form is, of course, avoided. Answers are taken down as long as they are produced by the subject. It has proved unwise to set a fixed time for exposure of the card. Coercion should be avoided as much as possible.

Occasionally it becomes necessary to show a suspicious subject how the figures are prepared, ad oculos. In general, however, rejection of the test is relatively rare, even among suspicious and inhibited patients.

Interpretation of the Figures as Perception

Almost all subjects regard the experiment as a test of imagination. This conception is so general that it becomes, practically, a condition of the experiment. Nevertheless, the interpretation of the figures actually has little to do with imagination, and it is unnecessary to consider imagination a prerequisite. It is true, however, that those gifted with imagination react differently from those not so gifted. On the other hand, it makes little difference whether one encourages the subject to give free rein to his imagination or not; the results will be little changed. Those who have imagination show it, those who do not have it may apologize for the lack, but the results may be compared without taking richness or poverty of imagination into account.

The interpretation of the chance forms falls

[15] Hermann Rorschach, *Psychodiagnostics*, trans. Paul Lemkau and Bernard Kronenberg; W. Morgenthaler (ed.), (Berne: Hans Huber; and New York: Grune & Stratton, 4th ed., 1942), pp. 14, 16–18; original German, *Psychodiagnostik: Methodik und Ergebnisse eines wahrnehmungs-diagnostischen* (1921). Reprinted by permission.

*in the field of perception and apperception
rather than imagination.*

* * * * *

If perception can also be called an associative integration of available engrams (memory-pictures) with recent complexes of sensations, then the interpretation of chance forms can be called a perception in which the effort of integration is so great that it is realized consciously as an effort. This intrapsychic realization that the complex of sensations and the engrams are not perfectly identical gives the perception the character of an interpretation.

All answers given by the subjects are not interpretations in this sense, however. Most organic cases (senile dements, paretics), epileptics, many schizophrenics, most manics, almost all the feebleminded subjects, and even many normals are not aware of the assimilative effort. These subjects do not interpret the pictures, they name them. They may even be astonished that someone else is able to see something different in them. We deal in these cases not with an interpretation but with a perception in the strict sense of the word. They are as unconscious of the associative-assimilative performance as a normal person is of the process of seeing a familiar face or in perceiving a tree. From the above discussion, we conclude that there must be a kind of threshold beyond which perception (assimilation without consciousness of assimilative effort) becomes interpretation (perception with consciousness of assimilative effort). This threshold must be very high in cases of senile dementia, in manic states, in feeblemindedness, etc.

Where this threshold is low, it is to be expected that even the simplest, most commonplace perception brings with it the consciousness of assimilative effort. This is the case in certain pedants who demand an absolutely exact correspondence between sensation complex and engrams for their perceptions. It is even more apparent in some depressed subjects. Here the assimilative effort may have become so great that it can no longer be overcome and everything they perceive seems "changed" and "strange." Pedantic and depressed subjects show just this in the test; they search for those details in the figures that happen to have distinct counterparts in nature, frequently going on to say: "I know that I am interpreting and that actually it must be something else."

Normal subjects frequently speak of the "interpretation" of the figures spontaneously.

Cases showing congenital or acquired defects of intelligence want to "recognize" the pictures.

These different ways of handling the figures indicate that the difference between interpretation and perception lies in associative factors. Furthermore, reactions of subjects in elated moods show more of a perceptive character, while in depressed moods the reaction is more interpretative. Finally, it is apparent that the difference cannot be said to be due only to associative processes; emotional factors may also shift the boundary between perception and interpretation.

In summary, we may conclude that *the differences between perception and interpretation are dependent on individual factors, not on general ones; that there is no sharp delineation, but a gradual shifting of emphasis; and that interpretation may be called a special kind of perception.* There is, therefore, no doubt that this experiment can be called a test of the perceptive power of the subject.

* * * * *

Interpretation of the Rorschach Test [16]

I. The "Form Interpretation Test" consists in the interpretation of indeterminate figures by the subject. The results of this procedure allow computation because the same series of ten plates is used in every case.

Interpretation of the figures differs from actual perception only in some, not all, of the subjects. In these cases, the difference is due to that fact that the perception is carried out with more or less awareness of the process of assimilation of recent impressions and engrams. This is not a general but an individual difference; it is not an absolute difference, but one which shows gradual differentiation.

II. The problems of the experiment deal primarily with the formal principles (pattern) of the perceptive process. The actual content

---

[16]   *Ibid.*, pp. 181–183.

of the interpretations comes into consideration only secondarily. The clarity of form visualization, the relationships between kinaesthetic and color factors, the manner in which the plates are apperceived, whether as wholes or as parts, and also a number of other factors which may be computed from the protocol of the experiment; all these show typical relationships which are characteristic of the various categories of normal individuals and of the psychoses.

III. The experiment leaves room for completion by further work with standardized parallel series of plates and appropriate control experiments.

IV. Results of the experiment:

Certain relationships of the factors of the test express certain components of "intelligence" of subjects. In particular, the establishment of the mode of apperception of the plates allows the setting up of "apperceptive types" and intelligence types (abstract, theoretical, imaginative, grumbling, pedantic, etc.).

The relationship between movement and color factors represents the relation between introversion, the faculty of doing "inner work," and extratension, the faculty of turning to the outer world, in the subject. This relationship expresses a condition in the subject, or the form of a psychosis when one is present. This relationship may be formulated in terms of the "experience type." The following types may be distinguished:

1. *Introversive Experience Type*. Predominance of kinaesthetic responses. (Example: Imaginative subjects.)

2. *Extratensive Experience Type*. Predominance of color responses. (Example: Practical subjects.)

3. *Coartated (Narrowed) Experience Type*. Marked submergence of movement and color factors to the extent that the subject reacts with form responses exclusively. (Examples: Pedants, subjects in depressive mood or actually psychotically depressed, subjects with dementia simplex.)

4. *Ambiequal Experience Type*. Many kinaesthetic and equally many color responses. (Examples: Talented individuals, compulsion neurotics, manics, catatonics.)

The results frequently show suppression of either introversive or extratensive factors, or both.

Color responses represent lability of affect. The more color responses predominate over kinaesthetic responses the more unstable the affectivity of the subject; the more predominant the kinaesthetic responses, the more stable the affectivity. Neurotic subjects suffer "color shock" on encountering the colored plates. (This is evidence of emotional suppression.)

There is a correlation between the experience type and certain groups of functions and phenomena; certain definite experience types are correlated with certain definite components of intelligence, with definite situations of affective dynamics, also with definite types of character, with definite perceptive and, apparently, imagery types, with certain potentialities for the development of talents, with the sense hallucinated, and finally, with the form of neurosis or psychosis present in the subject. (Problem of the determinants of neuroses and psychoses.)

The experience type has an habitual status. It is narrowed by depressive moods, dilated by the lighter moods. Fatigue and similar factors influence the experience type. In the course of the life of an individual it undergoes a number of shifts which are probably characteristic of all subjects. Variations in the experience type affect all the groups of functions and phenomena mentioned above; this is simply an expression of the correlations noted between experience type and the functions. Studies of the variations of the experience type include researches into variation at different times and under various conditions. Comparative studies of experience type include researches into the types in men and women and the development of the type in these groups, into comparisons of types in the same and different families, and finally comparison of types in different peoples and races. Such studies must include the study of variations and similarities of certain components of intelligence, personality, talents and imagery types as a part of the research.

The experience type indicates form or pattern, not content; it represents apparatus with which to act, not action itself. Content and action are determined by instinct and by disciplined thinking.

Disciplined thinking narrows the experience type. The capacity to experience is in some general way opposed by disciplined thinking.

V. The test has proved to be of diagnostic value. In normals it makes possible differential diagnosis of personality; in patients, the diagnosis of the illness. Furthermore, it presents an intelligence test almost completely independent of previous knowledge, memory, practice, and degree of education. It is possible by means of the test to draw conclusions concerning many affective relationships. The test has the advantage of almost unlimited applicability making possible without further data comparison of the results in the most heterogeneous subjects.

ERNST KRETSCHMER
(1888–1964)

Constitutional Types [17]

With the methods we have described, three ever-recurring principal types of physique have emerged from our clinical material, which we will call "asthenic," "athletic," and "pyknic."

* * * * *

Asthenic Type

The essential characteristic of the type of the male asthenic is, in a few words, taking the general total impression, *a deficiency in thickness combined with an average unlessened length.* This deficiency in the thickness development is present in all parts of the body—face, neck, trunk, extremities—and in all the tissues—skin, fat, muscle, bone, and vascular system throughout. On this account we find the average weight, as well as the total circumference and breadth measurements, below the general value for males.

We have, therefore, in the clearest cases, the following general impression . . .: a lean narrowly-built man, who looks taller than he is, with a skin poor in secretion and blood, with narrow shoulders, from which hang lean arms with thin muscles, and delicately boned hands; a long, narrow, flat chest, on which we can count the ribs, with a sharp rib-angle; a thin stomach, devoid of fat, and lower limbs which are just like the upper ones in character. In the average values for the measurements in males, the way the weight of the body lags behind the length (50.5 : 168.4), and the chest measurement behind the hip measurement (84.1 : 84.7) stands out clearly.

* * * * *

Athletic Type

The male athletic type is recognized by the strong development of the skeleton, the musculature and also the skin.

The rough impression of the best example of this species is as follows:

A middle-sized to tall man, with particularly wide projecting shoulders, a superb chest, a firm stomach, and a trunk which tapers in its lower region, so that the pelvis, and the magnificent legs, sometimes seem almost graceful compared with the size of the upper limbs and particularly the hypertrophied shoulders.

The solid long head is carried upright on a free neck, so that the sloping linear contour of the firm trapezius, looked at from in front, gives that part of the shoulder which is nearest the neck its peculiar shape.

The outlines and shadings of the body are determined by the swelling of the muscles of the good or hypertrophied musculature which stands out plastically as muscle-relief. The bone-relief is specially prominent in the shape of the face. The coarse boning throughout is to be seen particularly in the collar-bones, the hand and foot joints, and the hands. Next to the shoulders the trophic accent often lies on the extremities, which in some cases are reminiscent of acromegaly. The largest hand circumference among our material reached the very remarkable figure of 25 cms., that is to say, a measurement which oversteps the male average value of about 20 cms. by

[17] Ernst Kretschmer, *Physique and Character: An Investigation of the Nature of Constitution and the Theory of Temperament,* trans. W. J. H. Sprott (New York: Harcourt, Brace & World, 2nd ed., 1936), pp. 20, 22–23, 25–27, 30–31, 214–215; original German, *Körperbau und Charakter* (Berlin, 1921). Reprinted by permission.

5 cms. Hand circumferences of 23 cms. are quite common. Besides the hand circumference, the width of the shoulders is with this type specially remarkable, which, in two cases, reached the astonishingly high figure of 42.5 cms., which defeats the average figure of our people of roughly 37.5 to 38 cms. by about 5 cms. The length of the extremities is rather long than short. Together with bone and muscle the skin has its share of the general hypertrophy. It has a very good, firm, elastic turgor, and, particularly in the face, it looks solid, thick, and often pasty. In contradistinction to all this tissue, the fat is relatively only moderately developed, and, speaking absolutely, is more or less normal. It is on this account, above all, that the distinctive muscle-relief is conditioned, since the overdeveloped musculature stands out through only a thin sheath of fat.

The height lies above the average; length measurements of over 180 cms. are not rare, the tallest athletic of our material measured 186 cms. At the other end of the scale the boundary cannot be fixed, because the morphological transition stages between the athletic type and the type of hypoplastic broad shoulders (see below) cannot be defined. At the tall end we must notice transitions to certain gigantic types which are to be described later.

* * * * *

Pyknic Type

The pyknic type, in the height of its perfection in middle-age, is characterized by the pronounced peripheral development of the body cavities (head, breast, and stomach), and a tendency to a distribution of fat about the trunk, with a more graceful construction of the motor apparatus (shoulders and extremities).

The rough impression in well-developed cases is very distinctive: middle height, rounded figure, a soft broad face on a short massive neck, sitting between the shoulders; the magnificent fat paunch protrudes from the deep *vaulted* chest which broadens out towards the lower part of the body.

If we look at the limbs, we find them soft, rounded, and displaying little muscle-relief, or bone-relief, often quite delicate, the hands soft, rather short and wide. In particular the joints of the hands and the clavicle are often slim and almost elegantly formed. The shoulders are not broad and projecting as with the athletics, but (especially among older people) are rounded, rather high, and pushed forwards together, and they are often set down against the breast with a characteristically sharp depression on the inner deltoid curve. It seems then as if the whole mass of the shoulders were slipping downwards and inwards over the swelling chest; and the head also plays a part in this static displacement: it sinks forward between the shoulders, so that the short thick neck seems almost to disappear, and the upper portion of the spinal column takes on a slight kyphotic bend. In profile the neck no longer seems, as is the case with the other types, a slim round column, which carries the chin like a sharply cut-off, widely projecting capital, but in well-developed cases of middle-age and over, the point of the chin is directly joined with the upper forehead, without any definite bends, by a sloping line. . . .

The breast-shoulder-neck proportion is, apart from the shape of the head and face, and the manner of the disposition of the fat, the most characteristic mark of the pyknic character. The ratio of the moderate-sized breadth of shoulder to the large-sized breast circumference—36.9 : 94.5—stands out strongly by the side of the characteristic proportions of the athletic, where the chest circumference is completely dominated by the huge breadth of the shoulders—(39.1 : 91.7). While the athletic torso seems especially broad, the pyknic appears deep; in the former the trophic accent lies on the shoulders and extremities, in the latter on the width of the trunk, or the bowl-shaped chest which widens towards the lower region of the body, and on the fat abdomen. The extremities are on an average rather short than long.

* * * * *

For this reason it is advisable to change the nomenclature also. We call the members of that large constitution-class from which the schizophrenes are recruited, "*schizothymes*," and those corresponding to the circular psychotics are called "*cyclothymes*." One may for convenience call the transitional stages between illness and health, or the abortive pathological forms, "schizoid" and "cycloid," as we have already done. We must, accordingly, make it clear from the outset, that the notions "schizothyme" and "cyclothyme" have nothing to do with the question: pathological or healthy; but that they are inclusive terms for large general bio-types, which include the great mass of healthy individuals with the few cases of corresponding psychoses which are scattered among them. The words do not indicate that the majority of schizothymes must have psychic clefts, and that the majority of cyclothymes must have periodical emotional disturbances; we are only using for the sake of convenience a designation for the healthy corresponding to that which is already applied to psychopaths of the same type.

The method employed for the following investigation was as follows: Out of a few hundred healthy persons, who were very well known to me as regards both their bodily and psychic natures, I picked out about 150 whose physique was characterized by significant and unmistakable marks of the asthenic, athletic, or pyknic types. Of the majority I possess photographs. Corresponding, then, to the schizophrene group, were found people with long noses, angular profiles, abnormally high middle faces, long-oval and egg-shaped, narrow facial contours, and figures which were either thin and slender, or wiry and lanky, or having marked muscular and bony relief; over against these we have in the circular group the well-known pyknic figures, with their full smooth faces, having broad, shield-shaped or five-cornered contours and a harmonious construction of the profile, their short necks, rounded limbs, and characteristic tendency to fatness.

Thus there emerged two large classes of temperament, of which the one is encased in all essentials in the pyknic form, while the other has a physique corresponding to the schizophrene group; here, again, there is also a small number of partial or complete crossings.

VIKTOR FRANKL
(1905–   )

Logotherapy [18]

Paradoxical Intention

In the frame of Logotherapy of Existential Analysis (*Existenzanalyse*), a specific technique has been developed to handle obsessive, compulsive, and phobic conditions. This procedure, called Paradoxical Intention, is based on the fact that a certain amount of pathogenesis in phobias and obsessive-compulsive neuroses is due to the increase of anxieties and compulsions that is caused by the endeavor to avoid or fight them. Paradoxical Intention consists in a reversal of the patient's attitude toward his symptom, and enables him to detach himself from his neurosis. This technique mobilizes what is called in Logotherapeutic terms the Psychonoetic Antagonism, i.e., the specifically human capacity for self-detachment. Paradoxical Intention lends itself particularly as a useful tool in short-term therapy, especially in cases

with an underlying anticipatory anxiety mechanism.

* * * * *

In order to understand fully what takes place when this technique is utilized, we shall use as a starting point a phenomenon which is known to every clinically trained psychiatrist, namely anticipatory anxiety. It is commonly observed that such anxiety often produces precisely that situation of which the patient is afraid. The erythrophobic individual, for example, who is afraid of blushing when he enters a room and faces a group of people, will actually blush at precisely that moment.

In case histories which display anticipatory anxiety, the fear of some pathologic event (thus, ironically, precipitating it), one may frequently observe an analogous phenomenon. This is the compulsion to self-observation. For instance, in cases of insomnia, the patients often report in the anamnesis that they become especially aware of the problem of falling asleep when they go to bed. Of course this very attention inhibits the sleeping process.

---

[18] Viktor E. Frankl, "Paradoxical intention: a logotherapeutic technique," *Amer. J. Psychother.*, 1960, **14**, 520–535. Reprinted by permission.

In addition to the fact that excessive *attention* proves to be an intrinsically pathogenic factor with regard to the etiology of neuroses, we also observe in many neurotic patients that excessive *intention* may also be pathogenic. Many sexual neuroses, at least according to the findings and teachings of Logotherapy, may be traced back to the forced intention of attaining the goal of sexual intercourse—be it the male seeking to demonstrate his potency, or the female her ability to experience orgasm. The author has discussed this subject at length in various papers . . ., pointing out that as a rule the patient seeks pleasure intentionally (one might say that he takes the "pleasure principle" literally). However, pleasure belongs to that category of events which cannot be brought about by direct intention, but, on the contrary, is a mere side-effect or by-product. Therefore, the more one strives for pleasure, the less one is able to attain it. Thus we see an interesting parallel in which anticipatory anxiety brings about precisely what the patient had feared, while excessive intention, as well as excessive self-observation with regard to one's own functioning makes this functioning impossible.

It is this twofold fact upon which Logotherapy bases the technique known as "paradoxical intention." For instance, when a phobic patient is afraid that something will happen to him, the logotherapist encourages him to intend or wish, even if only for a second, precisely what he fears.

The following clinical reports will indicate what I mean:

A young physician came to our clinic because of a severe hidrophobia. He had for a long time been troubled by disturbances of the autonomic nervous system. One day he happened to meet his chief on the street and, as the young man extended his hand in greeting, he noticed that he was perspiring more than usually. The next time he was in a similar situation he expected to perspire again and this anticipatory anxiety precipitated excessive sweating. It was a vicious circle; hyperhidrosis provoked hidrophobia and hidrophobia, in turn, produced hyperhidrosis. We advised our patient, in the event that his anticipatory anxiety should recur, to resolve deliberately to show the people whom he confronted at the time how much he could really sweat. A week later he returned to report that whenever he met anyone who triggered his anticipatory anxiety, he

said to himself, "I only sweated out a liter before, but now I'm going to pour out at least 10 liters!" What was the result of this paradoxical resolution? After suffering from his phobia for four years, he was quickly able, after only one session, to free himself of it for good by this new procedure.

The reader will note that this treatment consists not only in a reversal of the patient's attitude toward his phobia—inasmuch as the usual "avoidance" response is replaced by an intentional effort—but also, that it is carried out in as humorous a setting as possible. This brings about a change of attitude toward the symptom which enables the patient to place himself at a distance from the symptom, to detach himself from his neurosis. This procedure is based on the fact that, according to logotherapeutic teaching, the pathogenesis in phobias and obsessive-compulsive neuroses is partially due to the increase of anxieties and compulsions that is caused by the endeavor to avoid or fight them. A phobic person usually tries to avoid the situation in which his anxiety arises, while the obsessive-compulsive tries to suppress, and thus to fight, his threatening ideas. In either case the result is a strengthening of the symptom. Conversely, if we succeed in bringing the patient to the point where he ceases to flee from or to fight his symptoms, but on the contrary, even exaggerates them, then we may observe that the symptom diminishes and that the patient is no longer haunted by it.

Such a procedure must make use of the unique potentiality for self-detachment inherent in a sense of humor. . . . I would venture to say that humor also deserves to be mentioned among the basic human capacities. No animal is able to laugh.

As a matter of fact, when paradoxical intention is used, the purpose is to enable the patient to develop a sense of detachment toward his neurosis by laughing at it, to put it simply. . . .

A few more case reports may serve to develop and clarify this method further:

I once received a letter from a young medical student who had in the past listened to my clinical lectures on Logotherapy. She reminded me of a demonstration of paradoxical intention that she had attended, and continued: "I tried to apply the method which you had used in the classroom demonstration to myself. I, too, suffered continually from the fear that, while dissecting at the

Institute of Anatomy, I would begin to tremble when the anatomy instructor entered the room. Soon this fear actually did cause a tremor. Then, remembering what you had told us in the lecture that dealt with this very situation, I said to myself whenever the instructor entered the dissecting room 'Oh, here is the instructor! Now I'll show him what a good trembler I am—I'll really show him how to tremble!' But whenever I deliberately tried to tremble, I was unable to do so!' " [19]

Another case, which was treated by one of my assistants, Dr. Kurt Kocourek, concerned a woman, Mary B., who had been undergoing various treatment methods for 11 years, yet her complaints, rather than being alleviated, had increased. She suffered from attacks of palpitation accompanied by marked anxiety and anticipatory fears of a sudden collapse. After the first attack she began to fear that it would recur and, consequently, it did. The patient reported that whenever she had this fear, it was followed by palpitations. Her chief concern was, however, that she might collapse in the street. Dr. Kocourek advised her to tell herself at such a moment: "My heart shall beat still faster! I will collapse right here on the sidewalk!" Furthermore, the patient was advised to seek out deliberately places which she had experienced as disagreeable, or even dangerous, instead of avoiding them. Two weeks later, the patient reported: "I am quite well now and feel scarcely any palpitations. The fear has completely disappeared." Some weeks after her discharge, she reported: "Occasionally mild palpitations occur, but when they do, I say to myself, 'My heart should beat even faster,' and at that moment the palpitations cease."

Paradoxical intention may even be used therapeutically in cases which have an underlying somatic basis:

The patient was suffering from a coronary infarct. Subsequently he developed anxiety as a psychic response to his somatic illness, and this anxiety became so intense that it became his main complaint. He began to withdraw from his professional and social contacts and finally could not bear to leave the hospital where he had been a patient for six months and where a heart specialist

was at hand. Finally the patient was transferred to our clinic and logotherapeutic treatment was begun by Dr. Gerda Becker. The following is a brief summary of tape-recorded comments of the patient:

"I felt very anxious and the pain in my heart region began to trouble me again. Then I asked the nurse to call the doctor. She stopped in for a moment and told me to try to make my heart beat faster and to *increase* the pain and fear until she could return a little later. I tried this and when she came back after about a quarter of an hour, I had to confess to her that, to my great surprise, my endeavors had been in vain—I could increase neither the pain nor the palpitations but, as a matter of fact, both had disappeared! . . . Encouraged by this turn of events, I left the clinic for an hour or so and went for a walk through the streets—something that I had not attempted for more than six months. Upon entering a store I felt a slight palpitation but, as the doctor had suggested, I immediately started saying to myself, 'Try to feel even more anxiety!' Again it was in vain, I simply could not do it! I returned to the clinic happy over my achievement of leaving the hospital and strolling around alone." We invited the patient to visit us six months later and he reported that he was free of any complaints and had, meanwhile, resumed his professional work.

Now let us turn to the following case:

Mrs. H. R. had been suffering for 14 years when she came to the clinic. She was severely handicapped by a counting compulsion as well as the compulsion to check whether her dresser drawers were in order and securely locked. She did this by continually checking the contents of the drawers, closing them by a sharp rapping of her knuckles, and finally by attempting to turn the key in the lock several times. Eventually this condition became so chronic that her knuckles were often bruised and bleeding and the keys and locks on the bureau were ruined.

On the day of her admission, Dr. Eva Niebauer demonstrated to the patient how to practice paradoxical intention. She was shown how to throw things carelessly into her dresser and closet, to try to create as much disorder as possible. She was to say to herself, "These drawers should be as messy as possible!" The result was that two days after admission her counting compulsion disappeared and, after the fourth day, she felt no need to recheck her dresser. She even forgot to lock it—something that she had not failed to do for decades! Sixteen days after hospitalization she felt free of any complaints or symptoms, was very proud of her achievement, and was able to do her daily chores without compulsive repetition. She admitted that obsessive-compulsive ideas occa-

---

[19] Once I encountered the most severe case of stuttering that I have seen in my many years of practice: I met a man who had stuttered severely all his life—except once. This happened when he was twelve years old, and had hitched a ride on a street car. When he was caught by the conductor, he thought that the only way of escape would be to evoke his sympathy, and so he tried to demonstrate that he was just a "poor, stuttering boy." But when he tried to stutter, he was utterly unable to do it!

sionally recurred but reported that she was able to ignore them, or, to make light of them. Thus she overcame her compulsion not by frantically fighting it (which only strengthens it) but, on the contrary, by "making a joke of it;" in other words, by applying paradoxical intention.

A remarkable fact about this case is that after her symptoms had cleared up, the patient spontaneously, during a psychotherapeutic interview, revived some significant memories. She remembered that when she was five years old, her brother had destroyed a favorite doll and thereafter she began locking her toys in her dresser drawer. When she was sixteen, she caught her sister in the act of putting on some of the patient's best party clothes without her permission. From that time on she always carefully locked up her clothes. Thus, even if we take it for granted that her compulsions were rooted in these traumatic experiences, it is, nevertheless, the radical *change of attitude* toward her symptoms which was therapeutically effective. The bringing to consciousness of such psychic traumata cannot, at any rate, *in itself* be the appropriate treatment, inasmuch as a method which does not include such a procedure proved to be so efficient.

* * * * *

Thus we see that paradoxical intention works even in cases in which either the actual *somatic* basis (the patient with the coronary infarct) or the presumed *psychic* cause (the case of H. R.) were not touched upon. Paradoxical intention is effective irrespective of the underlying etiologic basis; in other words, it is an intrinsically nonspecific method. According to the author's opinion, based upon clinical experience, in every severe case involving phobic symptoms, one has to reckon with an autonomic-endocrine or an anankastic substructure. This does not entail a fatalistic viewpoint, however, for a full-fledged neurosis is nothing but a superstructure built upon these constitutional elements; it may well be that it can be psychotherapeutically alleviated without necessarily removing, or even taking into account, the underlying basis. Such a therapy is palliative rather than causal. This is not to say that it is a symptomatic therapy, however, for the logotherapist, when applying paradoxical intention, is concerned not so much with the symptom in itself but, rather,

the patient's *attitude* toward his neurosis and its symptomatic manifestations. It is the very act of changing this attitude that is involved whenever an improvement is obtained.

This nonspecificity helps to clarify why paradoxical intention is sometimes effective in severe cases. I wish to emphasize "sometimes;" for I do not wish to convey the impression that beneficial results were *always* obtained, nor that paradoxical intention is an universal panacea or a miracle method. On the other hand, however, I feel obliged to present the range of its applicability and the degree of its effectiveness accurately. I should like to add parenthetically that the percentage of cures or cases improved to a degree that has made further treatment unnecessary, is somewhat higher (75.7 %) than the figures reported in the literature. . . .

* * * * *

Paradoxical intention can also be applied to cases of sleep disturbance, as mentioned before. The fear of sleeplessness increases sleep disturbance because anticipatory anxiety completes and perpetuates the vicious circle. In addition, it results in a forced intention to sleep which incapacitates the patient to do so. Dubois, the famous French psychiatrist, once compared sleep with a dove which has landed near one's hand and stays there as long as one does not pay any attention to it; if one attempts to grab it, it quickly flies away. But how can one remove the anticipatory anxiety which is the pathologic basis of forced intention? In order to take the wind out of the sails of this specific fearful expection, we advise the patient not to try to force sleep, since the necessary amount of sleep will be automatically secured by the organism. Therefore, he can safely try to do just the opposite, to stay awake as long as possible. In other words, the forced intention to fall asleep, arising from the anticipatory anxiety of not being able to fall asleep, should be replaced by the paradoxical intention of not falling asleep at all! (Which in turn will be followed very rapidly by sleep.)

* * * * *

De-Reflection

In reference to this phenomenon, Logotherapy includes a therapeutic device known as *"de-reflection."* Just as paradoxical intention is designed to counteract anticipatory anxiety, de-reflection is intended to counteract the impulsive inclination to self-observation. In other words, what has to be achieved in such cases is more than trying to "ironize" the trouble by using paradoxical intention and its humorous formulation; one should also be able to *ignore* the trouble to some degree. Such ignoring, or de-reflection, however, can only be attained to the degree in which the patient's awareness is directed toward positive aspects. De-reflection, in itself, contains both a negative and a positive aspect. The patient must be de-reflected *from* his anticipatory anxiety *to* something else.

* * * * *

Let us, in conclusion, review the indications of paradoxical intention from the perspective of what Logotherapy presents as the four characteristic patterns of response toward neurotic problems:

I.   *Wrong Passivity.* By this is meant the behavioral pattern which may be observed in cases of anxiety neurosis or phobic conditions, or both. It is the withdrawal from those situations in which the patient, because of his anticipatory anxiety, expects his fears to recur. What we have to deal with in this case is the "*flight* from fear"—most commonly fear of collapsing on the street or having a heart attack.

II.   *Wrong Activity.* This behavioral pattern is characteristic, in the first place, of obsessive-compulsive neurosis. 1. The individual, rather than trying to avoid conflict situations, *fights* against his obsessive ideas and neurotic compulsions and thus reinforces them. This struggle is motivated by two basic fears: (a) that the obsessive ideas indicate an imminent, or actual, psychotic condition, and (b) that the compulsions will someday result in a homicidal or suicidal attempt. 2. Another

aspect of "wrong activity" may be observed in sexual neurosis, namely a struggle *for* something, rather than *against* something: a striving for orgasm and potency. The underlying motivation is usually as follows: the patient feels that competent sexual performance is "demanded" of him either by the partner, by the situation, or by himself, in the event that he may have, so to speak, "scheduled" it for that moment. Due to this very "pursuit of happiness" the sexually neurotic individual founders, like the obsessive-compulsive neurotic, by responses that are inappropriate to the situation: pressure precipitates counterpressure.

In contrast to these negative, neurotic, "wrong" behavorial patterns, there are two positive, normal ones:

III.   *Right Passivity.* This is the case when the patient, by means of paradoxical intention, "ironizes" his symptoms rather than trying to either run away from them (phobias) or to fight them (obsessive-compulsions).

IV.   *Right Activity.* Through de-reflection, the patient is enabled to ignore his neurosis by focusing his attention away from himself. He will be directed to *a life full of potential meanings and values with a specific appeal to his personal potentialities.*

In addition to this personal aspect, a social factor is involved as well. More and more we meet individuals who are suffering from what Logotherapy calls man's "existential vacuum".... Such patients complain of a feeling of a *total and ultimate meaninglessness* in their lives. They display an inner void or emptiness in which neurotic symptoms may abound. Filling this vacuum may thus assist the patient in overcoming his neurosis by helping him become aware of the full spectrum of his concrete and personal meaning and value possibilities, or, in other words, by confronting him with *the "logos" of his existence.*

21

Continental European and American Neurophysiological Psychotherapy

JULIUS RITTER
WAGNER–JAUREGG
(1857–1940)

Malarial Treatment of General Paresis [1]

Although progressive paralysis was considered not so long ago a disease against which physicians were practically powerless (see for instance the discussion by Kraft-Ebbing in Nothnagel's *Handbook*, 1894, and most of the psychiatric textbooks of that day), there has been a reversal of opinion in the last few years, reports having come in from various sources concerning successful attempts at improving this condition.

Two kinds of treatment are used, the specific and the non-specific.

Specific methods of treatment are based on the fact that progressive paralysis is the result of syphilitic infection, and they therefore use the same means as in other manifestations of syphilis, namely, salvarsan, mercury and iodine in different forms.

The non-specific methods are empiric in origin, based on the observation that cases of progressive paralysis have often been improved by acute attacks of infectious disease, and they attempt to reproduce artifically the elements of these diseases, to which the improvement is ascribed, such as fever or leucocytosis, by the use of tuberculin and other bacterial products, sodium nucleinate, milk injections, etc.

The correct procedure is undoubtedly a combination of specific and non-specific treatment, as I first stated in my report on the tuberculin-mercury treatment.

[1] J. Wagner–Jauregg, "The effect of malaria on progressive paralysis," *Psychiat. Neuro. Wochenschr.*, 1918, **20**, 132–134, 251–255. Original typed transcript in the New York Academy of Medicine Library: Dated, 11/4/25, but without a translator's name. Reprinted by permission.

We do not, however, limit ourselves, in our Vienna clinic, to a single course of tuberculin-mercury injections, but repeat it after six months in favorable cases in order to prevent relapses as much as possible, and also fill in the time between the two courses of treatment with other therapeutic measures, such as single or repeated series of neosalvarsan injections, intravenous staphyloccocus vaccine, and iodine cures.

I distinguish between three groups of non-specific methods: those using material that is not the result of bacterial activity (milk, proteins, sodium nucleinate); those that do result from such activity (tuberculin and different kinds of vaccines); and finally the infectious diseases themselves.

I include the last group for the reason that I observed, in the numerous cases of paralysis that I have treated in the past twelve years, that it happened comparatively often that remissions were especially long-continued and complete when some kind of infectious disease happened to attack the patient during the course of his treatment.

I am also inclined to consider these three non-specific treatment groups of unequal value in their effects, the first being the least intensive in its effects, the second more so, and the last-named, the infectious disease itself, the most valuable. This conviction induced me to try an experiment that I had long ago suggested (*Psychiatrische Jahrbücher*, 1888, volume 7), and bring on, in a patient suffering from such a disease as progressive paralysis, some infection that was quite safe, on account of its own slight danger and because it could be successfully treated.

In July, 1917, I inoculated three paralytics with the blood of a patient with tertian malaria who had already had several typical attacks and in whose blood the presence of tertian plasmodia had been microscopically proved. The inoculation was made by taking blood from a vein in the arm during an attack of fever and spreading it on small scarifications in the arm of the paralytic.

In order to prevent any danger to the environment, I had numerous mosquitoes caught in the gardens around the clinic, and convinced myself that there were no Anopheles, only Culex, in that neighborhood.

Two of the three patients first inoculated showed a reaction, the third did not.

Blood was again drawn twice from the arm of the same malaria patient, during attacks of fever and 1 cc. of it injected subcutaneously into the back of the paralytic patients. The results were the same as before.

Other paralytics were then inoculated at three different times with blood from the paralytics that had acquired malaria, and one of the former supplied blood for still two more, the plasmodia in this last case having thus passed through three persons. All these later inoculations were successful.

In all these patients tertian plasmodia were microscopically demonstrated in the blood during attacks of fever.

One fact of interest was that the period of incubation was gradually decreased by this passage through several human bodies. The period lasted about 17.5 days in the original cases, infected by mosquitoes; 12.3 days in those whose plasmodia has already passed through two persons; and 9.5 days in those whose plasmodia had passed through three persons.

It was further observed that most of the patients inoculated had repeated rises in temperature, up to 37.5 and 38, during the incubation period, and that these were of the tertian type, before they had any distinctly malaria attacks with chills, fever and perspiration.

Furthermore, only one of the cases of fever in the paralysis patients remained strictly of the tertian type, the others going over very soon into the quotidian type, one of them remaining permanently altered after the fourth attack, while the others only at times changed back into the tertian.

In all but one case, in which the patient died of a paralytic attack during his malaria, bisulphate of quinine was given in 1 gram doses daily, for three days, after from seven to twelve attacks, then in 0.5 doses daily, for fourteen consecutive days. After that the patients were given at intervals of one week three doses of 0.3, 1.45 and 0.6 grams of neosalvarsan intravenously.

The fever ceased in every case after the first dose of quinine; no malaria relapse has occurred in any of them since then, that is to say, during a whole year.

During the attacks of fever the patients were very low, with anemia and edema of the face and legs. The body weight was peculiarly altered, falling at first, then rising on account of the edema, then falling again at the beginning of convalescence, and finally rising as the physical condition improved, which happened rather quickly under the quinine and salvarsan treatment. In almost all cases the final weight was above the original one. Psychic improvement was much slower, so slow, in fact, that in most cases doubts arose, that later proved to be unfounded, as to whether the treatment would really do any good. In five cases another series of seven injections of polyvalent staphylococcus vaccine were therefore given a few weeks after the salvarsan treatment, at two-day intervals and in doses of 10 to 1,000 bacilli.

Full remission occurred so early and definitely in three of the nine cases that there was no further question of treatment. These patients were discharged as able to take up their regular occupations from two to six months after the beginning of the treatment, and are yet, after about a year, still satisfactorily carrying on.

A fourth patient was also discharged after about four months, but relapsed after a few weeks into paralytic melancholia. This case is also otherwise peculiar, as the history will show.

In two other cases improvement was very slow, but did progress to such an extent that the patients could be discharged after about a year. One, a soldier, could be used as a helper, while the other, a railway employee, was at least able to take care of himself, whether at his old occupation remains to be seen.

In only two cases was there no trace whatever of remission; the patients had to be placed in insane asylums.

UGO CERLETTI
(1877–1963)

Electroshock Therapy (EST or ECT) [2]

The idea of inducing convulsions with electric current for therapeutic purposes in man instead of using convulsing drugs was the logical, I might say unavoidable, result of the study of changes in nervous structures following experimental epileptiform convulsions in animals.

* * * * *

The Preparatory Period

The preparatory period includes a series of researches, in which I—first in Genoa and later in Rome—set out to provoke experimental epileptic fits in dogs. The problem was whether the sclerotic alterations of Ammon's horn (particularly of Sommer's sector), which are so frequent in the brains of epileptics, should be regarded as previous injuries which might be involved in the production of fits or were themselves consequences of repeated fits. I wished experimentally to provoke various types of series of convulsions in dogs, and to examine the brains from a histopathological standpoint, studying Ammon's horn particularly. It was already known to physiologists at that time that, in addition to injecting various toxic substances, convulsions in animals could be induced by applying a strong electric current across the head. But I wished to subject the brain to the direct action of the current as little as possible, in order to avoid adding anything to changes that would, by other possibility, remain definitely chargeable to the fit itself. Upon the advice of the physiologist Viale, I therefore adopted a mouth-rectum circuit rather than one across the head. Viale had already carried out experiments in America with this type of circuit in medicolegal researches upon death by lightning.

I arranged experiments of this kind in Genoa (1933), with the assistance of Professor Balduzzi, of his assistant, Dr. Laz-

seri, and of Chiauzzi, an undergraduate. A 125-volt alternating current from the lighting plant was sent through a mouth-rectum circuit in dogs.

Having had some deaths with this method at first, I set out to determine what conditions were the most favorable for survival. I was able to establish that the dangerous factor was not so much the height of the *voltage* as the *duration* of the current's passage. In some cases, in fact, the 210-volt industrial plant took the place of the 125-volt lighting plant and no differences of any note were to be observed in results. By reducing the length of time of application to a minimum, the usual convulsion was obtained without any further trouble ensuing. I therefore replaced the knife-switch, which had proved insufficiently quick in response, with a button-switch; thus, with the aid of a metronome, fixing the length of time best suited for this purpose at from 0.1 to 0.5 second.

With this technique, I prepared a certain number of dogs in which fits had been induced at various frequencies and for various lengths of time and was on the point of the histological examination of their brains.

* * * * *

The fact is that no one at the clinic seriously thought of applying electric convulsions to *man*, even though experiments continued upon dogs, both with electricity and with Cardiazol. So, over a year went by.

Nevertheless I, who had gone to such lengths in striving to preserve dogs from death when given electrically induced convulsions, had now come to the conviction that a discharge of electricity must prove equally harmless to a man if the duration of the current's passage were reduced to a minimum interval. Continually turning the problem over in my mind, I felt that I would sooner or later be able to solve it; so much so that in 1937, not being able to go to the Munsingen Congress, I allowed Bini to hint at these vague hopes, and I, myself, at the 1937 Milan Assembly concerning the therapeutics of schizophrenia, announced these hopes that I had been nourishing.

[2] Ugo Cerletti, "Old and new information about electroshock," *Amer. J. Psychiat.*, 1950, **107**, 87–91. Reprinted by permission of the American Psychiatric Association.

This inactivity in the face of so momentous a question greatly depressed me, so that I immediately jumped at the information, given me by my colleague, Professor Vanni, that "at the Rome slaughterhouse pigs are killed by electricity." As though to justify my passiveness and to settle my hopes by facing a real fact, I decided to see this electric slaughtering with my own eyes, and immediately went to the slaughterhouse.

There I was told that the application of a current across the pigs' heads had been in use for some years. The butchers took hold of the pigs near their ears with a large scissor-shaped pair of pincers. The pincers were connected to the lighting plant with wires, and terminated in two teethed disc-electrodes enclosing a sponge wet with water. As they were seized, the pigs fell on their sides and were soon taken by fits (convulsed). Then the butcher, taking advantage of the unconscious state of the animal, gave its neck a deep slash, thus bleeding it to death.

I at once saw that the fits were the same as those I had been producing in dogs, and that these pigs were not being "killed by electricity," but were bled to death during their epileptic coma.

* * * * *

These clear proofs, certain and oft repeated, caused all my doubts to vanish, and without more ado I gave instructions in the clinic to undertake, next day, the experiment upon man. Very likely, except for this fortuitous and fortunate circumstance of pigs' pseudo-electrical butchery, electroshock would not yet have been born.

A schizophrenic of about 40, whose condition was organically sound, was chosen for the first test. He expressed himself exclusively in an incomprehensible gibberish made up of odd neologisms, and, since his arrival from Milan by train without a ticket, not a thing had been ascertainable about his identity.

Preparations for the experiment were carried out in an atmosphere of fearful silence bordering on disapproval in the presence of various assistants belonging to the clinic and some outside doctors.

As was our custom with dogs, Bini and I fixed the 2 electrodes, well wetted in salt solution, by an elastic band to the patient's temples. As a precaution, for our first test, we used a reduced tension (70 volts) with a duration of 0.2 second. Upon closing the circuit, there was a sudden jump of the patient on his bed with a very short tensing of all his muscles; then he immediately collapsed onto the bed without loss of consciousness. The patient presently started to sing at the top of his voice, then fell silent. It was evident from our long experience with dogs that the voltage had been held too low.

I, bearing in mind the observations with repeated applications of the day before upon pigs, made arrangements for a repetition of the test.

Someone got nervous and suggested whisperingly that the subject be allowed to rest; others advised a new application to be put off to the morrow. Our patient sat quietly in bed, looking about him. Then, of a sudden hearing the low-toned converation around him, he exclaimed—no longer in his incomprehensible jargon, but in so many clear words and in a solemn tone—"Not *a second. Deadly!*"

The situation was such, weighted as it was with responsibility, that this warning, explicit and unequivocal, shook the persons present to the extent that some began to insist upon suspension of the proceedings. Anxiety lest something that amounted to superstition should interfere with my decision urged me on to action. I had the electrodes reapplied, and a 110-volt discharge was sent through for 0.5 second. The immediate, very brief cramping of all the muscles was again seen; after a slight pause, the most typical epileptic fit began to take place. True it is that all had their hearts in their mouths and were truly oppressed during the tonic phase with apnea, ashy paleness, and cadaverous facial cyanosis—an apnea which, if it be awe-inspiring in a spontaneous epileptic fit, now seemed painfully never-ending —until at the first deep, stertorous inhalation, and first clonic shudders, the blood ran more freely in the bystanders' veins as well; and, lastly, to the immense relief of all concerned, was witnessed a characteristic, gradual awakening "by steps." The patient sat up of his own accord, looked about him calmly with a vague smile, as though asking what was expected of him. I asked him: "What has been happening to you?" He answered with no more gibberish: "I don't know; perhaps I have been asleep."

That is how the first epileptic fit experimentally induced in man through the electric stimulus took place. So electroshock was born; for such was the name I forthwith gave it....

Our schizophrenic went on getting better rapidly. Having entirely abandoned his jargon, he was able to supply all the data for his identification and anamnesis. He began to take an interest in his surroundings, and share in the life of his ward. After 11 complete ECTs and 3 incomplete ones (over about 2 months) he was discharged from the clinic in a "complete remission." It may be of interest to note that the patient said upon leaving that he was well satisfied because a very tiresome whistling in his ears that had troubled him for years had also disappeared.

MANFRED SAKEL
(1900–1957)

Insulin Shock Treatment of Schizophrenia [3]

Theoretical considerations led me to use insulin in the treatment of drug addicts. In the course of the practical application of this procedure I produced hypoglycemic states of a certain intensity by means of borderline doses of insulin. At that time, however, it sometimes unavoidably happened in the course of this borderline treatment that severe hypoglycemic shocks unintentionally occurred either because of an overdose of insulin or because the patient was given insufficient nourishment after insulin was administered. The observations which I made on these occasions encouraged me to use hypoglycemia as such as a therapy—at first for excited states.

The successful results which ensued, as well as the observation of remarkable mental and characterological changes which followed severe hypoglycemic shock in certain cases, led me to seek a way to use severe hypoglycemic states as an etiologically non-specific (though clinically specific) treatment for psychoses, regardless of their possibly toxic origin. The treatment was regarded as etiologically non-specific because the causative agent of the schizophrenic symptom complex was unknown, and I thought that the schizophrenic disorder might be caused by several

[3] Manfred Sakel, *The Pharmacological Shock Treatment of Schizophrenia*, trans. Joseph Wortis (New York: Nervous and Mental Disease Publishing, 1938), pp. 1–13. Enlarged version of a series of articles from *Wiener medizinische Wochenschrift* (1934–1935). Reprinted by permission of the Association for Research in Nervous and Mental Disease.

different types of injury all of which might attack a common point such as perhaps, for example, the vegetative nervous system. We could not assume that the pharmacological shock acted directly upon the noxae but rather supposed it served to restore the balance of certain vegetative centers, and as a result restored the balance of the total physiological function.

* * * * *

Although the results of the treatment at that time (1929–1933) were clearly positive, it was only after Professor Pötzl kindly gave me the opportunity to treat a large series of cases at the University Psychiatric Clinic in Vienna, that I could undertake to describe the difficult method.

* * * * *

The method may be divided roughly into four phases:

Phase I. Progressively larger doses of insulin are given once a day by deep intramuscular injection. The doses start with about 10 to 30 units and are increased by 5 to 10 units daily until they reach 40 units or more. The first injection is given in the morning fasting, and food is withheld for approximately 4 to 4½ hours thereafter. There is usually no marked reaction at first, but as the doses grow larger, there may be a more pronounced physical reaction. Treatment even at this stage produces quantitative mental changes, particularly in excited patients, consisting of a more or less marked pacification of the patient.

* * * * *

Phase II consists of the production of severe hypoglycemic shocks. These develop when the doses in Phase I have become sufficiently high or when the hypoglycemic period is sufficiently prolonged to produce a severe reaction.

The shock may consist either of *coma* or of an *epileptic seizure*. In the former case, the shock starts with profuse perspiration and progressive somnolence and may be interrupted by psychotic excitement but ends typically in coma. This usually occurs in the fourth hour following the injection of insulin.

This coma may attain a varying depth. If the patient is merely somnolent he can be awakened but contact is no longer possible. All the reflexes at this stage are still intact and energetic commands can rouse the patient's swallowing reflexes to the point where the patient will swallow food. But as the coma deepens the reflexes become pathological and finally disappear.

* * * * *

In the course of such a "wet" shock, brief transitory muscular spasms of one or more of the extremities may appear at intervals, or else fine or coarse myoclonic twitchings, or an intense tremor of the entire body may intervene. Where the course of such a shock is smooth and without complication a marked bradycardia develops and the pulse rate may drop to as low as 34 beats a minute in some cases. The temperature may drop to as low as 30° C. (89.6° F.).

Less commonly than this type of shock a "dry shock" may develop. This consists of a sudden severe and typical epileptic seizure with tonic and clonic spasms, tongue bite, and sometimes a bad pulse. The convulsion may appear without any easily ascertainable premonitory signs.

The epileptic type of hypoglycemic reaction cannot always be predicted in advance. The depth and severity of the first type of reaction, which I call "wet" shock, can be regulated at will, as necessary, by postponing sugar administration. In other words when the proper dose of insulin is found with which "wet" shock is produced in any particular patient, the depth of coma may then be regulated by shortening or lengthening the hypoglycemic period.

The typical dry shock, or epileptic seizure, which, like coma, represents the maximum therapeutic reaction, occurs in the second or third hour after the injection, in contrast to the coma, which occurs in the fourth hour. It is self-evident that when the epileptic seizure occurs, the therapeutic effect of that particular hypoglycemic state has been achieved, and the hypoglycemia should be terminated soon after the convulsion has occurred. The patient should be given an adequate amount of carbohydrates, in spite of the fact that he may be roused from somnolence by the convulsion itself, and the hypoglycemic state should not be allowed to progress much further.

To avoid complications it should be made clear at this point that there are two varieties of epileptic convulsion during hypoglycemia: the "dry" shock or early epileptic seizure, which occurs in the second or third hour, and which is in some cases therapeutically especially desired and encouraged; and the late epileptic seizure which occurs in the fourth or fifth hour of hypoglycemia and not infrequently in the course of a wet shock.

The late epileptic convulsion must be regarded as a danger signal and is an indication for immediate interruption with intravenous glucose, and should be regarded as a sign of an excessively protracted hypoglycemic state. The patient in this case does not ordinarily rouse from somnolence, but may develop a status epilepticus, since the original state of irritation of the cell, due to the protracted hypoglycemia, persists. The distinction between the threatening late epileptic convulsion and the therapeutically effective and relatively harmless early convulsion must be kept clearly in mind.

* * * * *

Phase III. After a series of severe shocks I introduce one or more rest days for recuperation and observation, as the patient's condition requires. During this phase the patient is given no insulin or small doses of insulin, but in any case never more than is essential to pacify the patient.

Phase IV, the terminal or polarization phase. This is short and may last for example 5 to 8 days, during which 30 to 40 units of insulin are administered once a day. These moderate doses of insulin are again given to produce borderline physical signs of hypoglycemia. Due consideration must be given to any hypersensitivity or diminished sensitivity to insulin which has appeared in the meantime. In any case carbohydrates should not be administered later than two hours after the injection in this phase. In some cases this phase may be entirely omitted.

* * * * *

Patients who have gone through the complete course of treatment show the following course: In Phase I they are pacified (in the case of excited patients) and physically adapted to the impending shocks. The pacification is particularly marked in cases of catatonic excitement. This phase varies in duration, and may serve to diminish the dangers of Phase II. Phase II constitutes the actual assault on the illness. It should be emphasized that this phase, even more than Phase I, has no fixed duration. It has to be continued for a varying period of time or repeated several times. Within this phase doses must be varied from time to time in accordance with the changing reaction of the patient, and in accordance with the shock type that is desired. Phase III allows the patient to recuperate and affords the physician an opportunity to register the effect of the shocks. It should be decided at this time which type of shock is best suited for the particular state the patient is in, so that in cases that have not been making satisfactory progress the shock type can be changed in accordance with the patient's needs. Thus we see for example insulin-resistant patients, especially chronic ones, who do not respond with adequately severe shocks in spite of high insulin doses but who respond to a sudden drop of the dose, to one-half or one-third of the original dose, with severe comatose or epileptic reactions. This is attributable to the fact that the endogenous self-regulating activity of the adrenal system is not called into action by the smaller dose since it has

been habituated to higher doses. . . . The shocks can sometimes also be more readily induced after the provocation of several epileptic seizures (every second day) in about the third hour of hypoglycemia by means of metrazol (Georgi) so that the following shocks, both dry and wet, occur after much smaller doses of insulin. After a severe shock the patient should have a rest day and receive little or no insulin at all, so that the behavior of the patient can be observed and the decision made as to further procedure. In Phase IV the insulin doses are only allowed to produce a "prehypoglycemic" reaction, which is the term I use to roughly describe that phase of hypoglycemia where obvious physical reactions are barely about to appear. Phase IV should stabilize and compose the patient's mental condition. When the patient seems and feels both lucid and adequate the doses are then gradually diminished, or treatment may sometimes be advantageously ended without a terminal phase.

* * * * *

I now use the nasal tube almost exclusively to terminate shock if the patient is in no immediate danger. In those cases where there is reason to prolong shock so far that the patient can no longer swallow, the tube may be introduced as soon as coma intervenes, as a precautionary measure, and kept in place ready for use throughout the period of coma. Its position is checked by the aspiration of stomach fluid (preferably with a large 200 c.c. syringe) and a test for its acidity with litmus. This is usually possible in most cases. The hypoglycemic period is terminated by pouring a water or milk solution of glucose or ordinary sucrose into the funnel. If deep coma has not developed and the patient can still swallow, sugar solution is simply administered by mouth.

LAZLO JOSEPH MEDUNA
(1896–1964)

Metrazol Convulsive Shock Therapy [4]

Ignorance of the pathobiologic processes underlying schizophrenia renders therapy of

[4] L. J. Meduna, "New methods of medical treatment of schizophrenia," *Arch. Neurol. Psychiat.*, 1936, **35**, 361–363. Reprinted by permission of the American Medical Association.

the etiologic factors as yet impossible. There are, however, accidentally discovered correlations which may form the starting point of therapeutic efforts, as in the case of dementia paralytica, in which remissions coinciding with accidental fevers led to the establishment of a biologic antagonism between the disease process and the febrile condition and thus to malarial therapy. Fever therapy has been applied also in cases of schizophrenia, but without results worth mentioning, owing, according to my conception, to the absence of a biologic antagonism between fevers and schizophrenia. My task was, then, to look for probable biologic antagonists of schizophrenia. Observations in this direction had been made before, without, however, being systematized and utilized for conclusions regarding therapy.

In 1929 Nyirö and Jablonszky published observations made on the epileptic patients of the Budapest-Lipótmezö Mental Hospital. They were struck by the fact that in cases of epilepsy combined with schizophrenia the epileptic convulsions ceased or became rare. In a case of epilepsy in which schizophrenia developed years after the onset, the epileptic convulsions became conspicuously rare and later ceased. The schizophrenic process itself subsided in this case in one year. Nyirö and Jablonszky reached the conclusion that the condition was cured in 1.05 per cent of cases of simple epilepsy, as compared with 16.05 per cent of cases of epilepsy complicated with schizophrenia—a statistical result proving the existence of a biologic antagonism between schizophrenia and epilepsy. This was recognized by these authors, who also made an attempt to utilize it therapeutically by treating epileptic patients with transfusions of blood from schizophrenic patients. The presence of this antagonism was stated later by G. Steiner and A. Strauss in a report on six thousand cases of schizophrenia. According to these authors, "typical epileptic convulsions are so rare in schizophrenia, if they occur at all, as to throw doubt upon the correctness of the psychiatric diagnosis." In 1930 G. Müller published reports of two cases of catatonia in which recovery ensued after spontaneous epileptic convulsions.

Summing up these observations, it is possible to establish the existence of a biologic antagonism between the schizophrenic and the epileptic process. I shall now report my experiments regarding the therapeutic applicability of this antagonism.

Observations

As already reported, I endeavored to produce epileptiform convulsions in patients with schizophrenia and to observe the effect on the schizophrenic process. There are several ways of producing epileptiform convulsions. First, I used a 25 per cent oily solution of camphor in intramuscular injections, raising the dose from 8 to 30 cc. Later I used metrazol in a 10 per cent solution, injecting it intravenously in doses of from 3 to 6 or 7 cc. The difference between the ways in which these substances act is that after the administration of camphor the epileptiform convulsions appear in from one to two hours, while after the administration of metrazol they appear immediately. Of the two, metrazol is the more suitable for the production of epileptic convulsions. The convulsions caused by the two substances are similar. As yet, however, I am in no position to judge whether the remissions caused by these substances are of equal value.

In my first publication I reported on twenty-six patients treated in this way. Of these twenty-six patients, ten were cured and three improved to the extent of being able to return to their normal surroundings; in thirteen the condition remained unaltered. The number of cases has since risen to forty-three, in which nineteen patients were cured, seven showed improvement and the condition of seventeen remained unchanged. In the wards for female patients (medical superintendent, Dr. A. Z. Rath) similar experiments have been carried out with camphor only. Of thirty-one patients there, ten were cured, four showed improvement and the condition of seventeen remained unchanged. Summing up, Dr. Rath and I have treated altogether seventy-four patients, of whom twenty-nine (39 per cent) were cured, 11 (15 per cent) showed improvement and the condition of thirty-four (46 per cent) remained unchanged.

Comment and Conclusions

During the experiments I observed that the likelihood of cure is proportionate to the patient's liability to convulsions, as shown by the fact that the first ten male patients cured had, on an average, six convulsions after receiving altogether on an average 70 Gm. of pure camphor, while the first ten patients whose condition remained unchanged required a total dose of 129 Gm. on an average to produce an average of two convulsions. For a full valuation of the number of cures it is necessary to keep in mind that the material consisted mostly of patients with chronic conditions, chiefly of two to three years' duration. I am convinced that experiments carried out in a larger number of recent cases of conditions of not more than six months' duration would lead to considerably better results. These results do not affect the theory of the endogenous nature of schizophrenia. The number of cures—39 per cent—is rendered even more considerable when it is remembered that the condition in from 20 to 25 per cent of the seventy-four patients treated first, can be considered to be of hereditary nature, in which case the possibility of cure is out of the question.

The short duration of the experiments (one year) has prevented me from drawing far-reaching conclusions. Some of the cures may be due to an incidental spontaneous remission coinciding with the treatment. There are, however, two points to be emphasized:

1. The percentage of cures far exceeds the number of spontaneous remissions recorded in the literature.

2. There were relapses in which the prompt application of convulsive therapy led to a remission on the day following the convulsion.

The manner in which the convulsions may lead to therapeutic effects may be explained in different ways: First, I thought of the known detoxicating effect of camphor. This possibility, however, is excluded by the similar results achieved with the chemically entirely different metrazol. The shock effect of the convulsion may serve as an explanation. Easy as it may be to conceive that a catatonic stupor may be ended by a sudden shock, it is not plausible to imagine a cure of delusions and hallucinations in this way.

The only possibility left to explain the effect of the epileptic convulsions is that they change the chemical constitution of the organism in a way suitable for the cure of schizophrenia. Similar remissions of schizophrenia are not unknown, e.g., remissions preceding death, explainable by nothing but a preagonal change in the chemical milieu of the organism at the beginning of dissolution.

Far from considering the convulsion therapy as the only possible way of curing schizophrenia, I think that it is only a first step on the as yet unaccustomed biologic road of influencing the schizophrenic process. It is necessary to try other substances, as well as to search for the factor mobilized by the convulsion and causing its beneficial effect. In this way it will perhaps become possible to eliminate the convulsion and apply only its secondary effects.

Carbon Dioxide Psychotherapy [5]

One of the basic tenets of modern psychiatry has been that psychoneurotic aspects of behavior are symbolic in nature. The symbolic nature and the real meaning of symbolic manifestations have been assumed to be hidden from the patient in some levels of the function of the brain for which the name "subconscious" has been coined. It also has been assumed that, if desymbolization of the psychoneurotic manifestations were achieved, the patient, by recognizing the true or real meaning of his manifestations, will be enabled to control or do away with the symptoms, not having further need for symbolical expressions of heretofore unknown trends or desires, etc. To effect the desymbolization, several methods have been developed. But the fallacy in any of these methods can be easily discerned if we consider that desymbolization can be accomplished only by using symbols or symbolical references. The use of any symbol to divest the patient of his fictitious symbols apparently creates a need in him to produce new symbols. This need is easily recognized during analysis by the fact that a symbolic pathological manifestation is rarely the expression of a basic disturbance but is merely a representation of another symbol which is, in turn, the expression of symbols lying even deeper. So the procedure of desymbolization, by whatever method, may become a semantic nightmare which necessitates an extension of the procedure for three, four or more years. The basic error in the procedure is not so much the assumption that most of the pathological manifestations are symbolic in nature as it is the presumption that by recognizing the meaning of the symbolical expression the individual must be capable of dealing with the basic drives which, unrecognized, have forced him

[5] L. J. Meduna, "Alteration of neurotic pattern by use of CO_2 inhalations," *J. nerv. ment. Dis.*, 1948, **108**, 373–379. Reprinted by permission.

to travestied expressions. This error has been easily recognized by many psychoanalysts, who in turn have attributed the failure of any given psychotherapeutic procedure to lack of developing a "transference" between doctor and patient. Thus a physiological element, i.e., an emotion, has been brought into the presumably purely intellectual procedure. There can be no doubt that psychoneurotic manifestations are basically emotional troubles of some sort. Therefore, any procedure capable of influencing the emotional mode of the patient may influence the neurotic problem. By utilizing this possibility a number of psychotherapies have been developed, for each of which has been claimed—and, I believe, rightly claimed—a measure of success. This success becomes understandable in terms of physiology if we consider that the human brain is capable of conceiving and understanding only a very few symbols void of emotional value, such as the mathematical and the scientific concepts. The everyday life is channeled, directed, inhibited, or promoted by symbols having greater or lesser emotional charge; and the degree of power of these symbols depends on the dynamic force attributed to them by their emotional charge.

The basic biochemical and physiological processes which actuate one group or system of nerve cells to produce emotions and another system to create symbols must be essentially the same. Therefore, it is conceivable that any interference with the biochemical function of the one group of nerve cells must be capable of influencing the other group of nerve cells.

If we ask ourselves what differentiates the psychoneurotic person from the normal person, the answer will be not that the psychoneurotic produces manifestations of symbolic nature and the normal does not, for almost any expression of any change in the human apparatus, if it is recognized and conceived by the apparatus, will be conceived in symbols. Another identity in the functions of the normal and the psychoneurotic brains is that the meanings of manifestations are essentially the same, provided that the patterns of language, culture and education are the same. This identity, in fact, is the logical basis of the evolution of a culture belonging to a group of human beings. The difference between normal and pathological persons

cannot be defined on the assumption that the pathological persons do not know the meanings of their symbols while normal people do, for not knowing the meaning of a symbolic expression does not brand the expression as pathological.

Any difference, therefore, between the normal and the psychoneurotic persons cannot be of kind, but only of gradation. Life in itself is suffering, suffering by anything affecting the living organism which tends to restore its homeostatic balance on every level of manifestations after this balance has been disturbed. The ratio between the degree of the disturbance of this homeostatic balance and the ability to restore the balance will be the decisive factors in producing a psychoneurotic condition. Therefore, if we want to give a definition of a psychoneurotic state, we have to start from an understanding of what we may call a normal state.

* * * * *

Thus the basic difference between a psychoneurotic and a normal person is to be sought for and found in a "disproportion between excitement and excitability." If this disproportion exists, the afflicted individual will develop a low threshold even to subnormal stimulation or an unduly strong reaction to normal stimulation. The suffering of this person must be greater than that of a normal person; and his endeavor to re-establish his homeostatic balance may be delayed, inhibited or prevented.

If this conclusion be correct, then any procedure which is capable of increasing the threshold of stimulation of the brain must facilitate re-establishing the homeostatic balance and finally change behavior as the expression of the balance achieved by the procedure. We know a number of procedures which tend to increase the threshold of stimulation of the brain by direct or indirect means; it is sufficient to mention here the desensitization method of Cameron, that of using adrenalin injections. Also, as a means of increasing the threshold of stimulation of the brain against inside and outside stimuli, I have evolved a treatment for different psychoneurotic conditions, which eliminates the necessity of using symbolical approach to the psychoneurotic person.

This treatment consists of inducing anesthesia through repeated inhalations of carbon dioxide. The carbon dioxide increases the threshold of stimulation of every single nerve cell in direct proportion to the logarithm of the concentration of the carbon dioxide inside and outside the cell membrane. After a very few respirations of a mixture of 30% carbon dioxide and 70% oxygen, the increment in the threshold of stimulation is so great as to produce anesthesia. And, after the anesthesia had been terminated, its residuum is effective long enough to give to the whole brain adequate time to have an increased threshold for inside stimuli, time sufficiently long to permit the normal homeostatic balance of the brain to begin to function. By repeating the inhalations for a protracted period of time, the patient regains a normal homeostatic balance; and his excitability to old and new pathogenic influences becomes so lowered that the particular influences cease to be pathogenic.

Procedure

For the inhalations, a mixture of 30% carbon dioxide and 70% oxygen is used. This mixture—which is obtained, already prepared, in tanks—is administered by means of a reducing valve and an inhalation mask with a central valve. During the administration of the gas the patient is lying on a bed or on a comfortably padded treatment table. One nurse is necessary to handle the patient during the treatment. The same nurse counts the number of respirations taken by the patient, in a loud tone in order that the patient can hear and remember the last count that he has heard before the full anesthesia is achieved.

At the first treatment it is advisable not to give more than 20 to 25 respirations. The patient is usually able to remember 8 to 16, sometimes even 20 respirations. If the patient does not lose consciousness with about 25 respirations, an increase of 3 to 5 respirations should be made on the next day. Further increase in the number of respirations should be determined by the patient's reaction to the gas during the administration and afterward on that or on the following day.

Preparation of the Patient

The patient is told that his disease or trouble is considered nervous in nature and that the gas will act upon the highest central organ of the nervous system, the brain. He is told that the gas to be inhaled will produce a particular kind of anesthesia during which he may experience unusual dreams, emotions, or thoughts; that old memories may come back to him; or that he may not experience anything strange but a dreamless sleep. He is told, furthermore, that his experiences during the anesthesia may or may not be important for the doctor to know; but he is encouraged to tell anything he remembers upon awakening. A timid patient may have to be reassured as to the safety of the treatment. In order to minimize the suggestive element present in any kind of medical procedure, I always tell my patients that the whole procedure is experimental and that I haven't the slightest idea as to whether or not the treatment will help him.

Physiological Reactions

The 30% carbon dioxide produces a remarkable alteration of almost every nervous activity. It may produce simple rudimentary sensory phenomena, complicated dreams, with or without emotional discharge, or emotional discharge without any dream whatsoever, complicated conditions of temporary confusion, hypnagogic hallucinations and complicated cortical and subcortical motor discharges.

After the patient has inhaled the gas his respiration becomes somewhat increased and forced, his pulse rate and blood pressure increase and flushing and perspiration may appear. Some patients lose consciousness at the third or fourth respiration; some do not lose it in 15 to 20 or more respirations. Between the tenth and the fortieth respiration, indications of psychomotor excitement may be seen. The psychomotor excitement can take almost any form, such as a struggle to escape discomfort or, in some cases, a repetition of some struggle the patient has gone through in his life. For example, a female patient who had previously been exposed to an attempted rape re-enacted her experience several times while going under carbon dioxide.

During the first 10 to 40 respirations, the lower extremities are flexed at the hip and knee joints and slightly abducted. This position may be, in a number of cases, of sexual context. There is also a slight flexor hypertonus in the upper extremities and, very frequently, carpal spasm of both hands.

If the administration of carbon dioxide is continued beyond this phase—let us say between 30 and 50 respirations—adversive seizures lasting a few seconds may appear. During these seizures the pupils react to light. The movements of the patient during this phase resemble bicycling or sometimes imitate quadrupedal locomotion.   At 50 to 60 inhalations plantar responses disappear, and sometimes Babinski's sign can be elicited. If, in some cases, the treatment has been prolonged beyond this phase to the next stage, say from 60 to 90 or more respirations, the pupils become rigid and the picture of decerebrate rigidity develops.

The sensory phenomena are mostly optical in nature and consist of the appearance of a vague reddish light or small spots in the visual field. These spots, or points or dots, arrange themselves in geometrical patterns or, quite often, into elaborate figures with a straightforward or gyrating movement; or they may develop a perspective and become an actual dream. These dreams, in some cases, appear to be open symbolic interpretation. In some other cases, they are so weird and fantastic that they may even defy any description; in these cases, the patient becomes the subject of an ecstatic condition such as that of some epileptic auras or of some religious experiences.

During this whole procedure the patient is free from any danger. Although I have administered more than 20,000 carbon dioxide treatments, I have seen no complications other than one tongue biting and three or four spontaneous urinations. It must be understood, however, that before the patient is submitted to the carbon dioxide treatment a thorough physical examination should be made, one which includes the tracing of an electrocardiogram.

Duration of the Treatment and Mode of Action

There is no set rule to determine the duration of the treatment. I usually give the treatment three to six times a week, depending upon the patient's need and the time available. Each treatment takes about six minutes; about two minutes before the administration of the gas, during which time I orient myself by asking the patient whether he has felt

any kind of change since the previous treatment; about 30 to 120 seconds for the administering of the gas; and two or three minutes in which I question the patient regarding the experiences he has had during his inhalation of the gas.

The patient can leave the hospital or the office immediately after the treatment. The number of treatments necessary to achieve improvement in my group have varied from 20 to 150. If the patient does not experience considerable improvement during the first 20 or 30 treatments, I have found there is little hope that further treatment will be of any help to him. In many cases it is necessary to experiment with various depths of anesthesia in order to determine the dosage of gas therapeutically most useful for the individual patient. This I usually do in the following way: On the first occasion I administer the gas, giving the patient 25 respirations. On the next day, I question the patient as to whether he has felt differently since the treatment. If he does not report any change in his condition, I repeat the treatment, with the same number of respirations, two or three times on consecutive days. Then, if there is still no change, I increase the number of respirations to 30.   After repeating the procedure a number of times—in any case, in about 10 to 15 treatments—I am able to establish the necessary degree of saturation with carbon dioxide.

The improvement of patients may follow different patterns. In a number of patients the symptoms slowly diminish and finally disappear without my ever having received from them any psychological material which would enable me to understand why or how the neuroses developed and how these have been cured. In another group of patients, the improvement occurs because of what seems to be a direct abreaction of pathogenic emotions. The reaction of these patients is extremely dramatic. They live through the pathogenic experiences again and again and discharge their emotions sometimes with great force.   In still other patients these abreactions of emotions occur in connection with dreams which have no bearing on reality, i.e., they are not a revival of old experiences, but they may be subjected to symbolic interpretations.   There is a fourth group of patients which does not show any considerable emotional discharge during the treatment or does not have any dream recollections of past experiences, but which later, on the day of the treatment, recollects forgotten or supressed pathogenic experiences and dis-

covers the causal relation of these experiences to the actual symptoms. As the treatment proceeds, more and more of this material is revived by these patients, and the pathological symptoms correspondingly disappear.

TABLE I

Statistical Material

Descriptive Diagnosis	No. of Cases	Number Improved	Number not Improved
Obsessive-compulsive neurosis	11	None	11
Stuttering	32	16	16
Spastic colitis.	13	10	3
Anxiety neurosis	8	5	3
Feeling of inferiority ⎫ Irritability ⎬ . . . . Neurotic fatigue ⎭	13	8	5
Alcoholism ⎫ Homosexuality ⎬ . . . . Character neurosis ⎭	16	8	8
	93	47	46

Contraindications

The only contraindications to this treatment that I know of at present are active tuberculosis of the lungs, high blood pressure and organic heart disease.

Indications for the Treatment

This treatment is ineffective in the anankastic reactions, such as the obsessive and compulsive neuroses and the classic form of hypochondria. And—as has been established by Loevenhart, Lorenz and Waters, who have studied the effect of carbon dioxide on psychotic patients

—this treatment is of no permanent help in any psychosis. On the other hand, carbon dioxide inhalations make easily manageable a great percentage of patients with conversion symptoms, such as those who create physical symptoms without underlying organic pathology. Also susceptible to this treatment are two other groups of patients: those with faulty control of emergency reactions, such as anxiety neuroses with symptoms of sense of guilt or of inadequacy and irritability, and those with personality maladjustments manifested by social and unconventional behavior and emotional instability.

EGAS MONIZ
(1874–1955)

Prefrontal Leukotomy [6]

My decision to perform the surgical operation which I named the "prefrontal leukotomy" did not come about as the result of some sudden burst of inspiration. This I made clear in my first publication on the subject (1936) and subsequently in the monograph first published in Turin (1937).

Considerably influenced by the doctrines

of Ramon y Cajal, and basing my views on the concept of connected nerve cells, I had frequently reflected upon the genesis of normal and pathological psychic activity in its interdependence with neuronal activity. The impulses pass through the neurons via the fibrils, and in the synapses alterations are produced which, in turn, are projected into many other cells.

All this passed through my mind in the course of solitary cogitations on the subject.

Besides the functioning of the brain in connection with normal mental activity, there were also the disturbances characteristic of a

[6] Egas Moniz, "How I succeeded in performing the prefrontal leukotomy, *J. clin. exp. Psychopath.*, 1954, **15**, 373–379. Reprinted by permission.

large number of psychoses for which, up to that time, there was still no valid anatomico-pathological explanation. My attention was particularly struck by the circumstance that certain mental patients—as a type, I had in mind obsessive and melancholiac cases—have a circumscribed mental existence confined to a limited cycle of ideas which, dominating all others, constantly revolve in the patient's diseased brain. And I sought to arrive at an explanation of this fact.

Nerve impulses come from everywhere: from the exterior world, via the nerve termini; from the chemical reactions and metabolic processes, which take place within the intimate confines of the nerve tissue; and from stimuli from diverse sources, many originating from the cellular activity of the intracranial neuronal complexes. Currents are formed which, at a high rate of speed, pass through the nerve conductors, ascending from the sensitive and sensory peripheral nerves and the great sympathetic nerve to the brain and the complex of tissue interconnecting the encephalic areas. The neurons are distributed chain-fashion, and the fibrils of the axis-cylinders are not directly linked to other cells; they form contacts through the Held's bundles, in various forms. The latter are the terminal organs of the fibrils which rest upon the dendrites and cell bodies without penetrating them. In the normal individual, these contacts do not become permanently and adhesively fixed.

On the basis of this anatomical concept, which we owe to Ramon y Cajal, I arrived at the conclusion that these synapses, repeated in countless cells, constitute the organic basis of thought.

Normal psychic activity depends upon proper synaptic functioning, while mental disturbances derive from derangement of the synapses.

Mental activity is interconnected in direct ratio to the functioning and interplay of these fibrillary activities.

The Held's bundles, at their point of contact with the nerve cell, rest upon an intercalary, separating substance, a membrane—or more probably, a colloidal substance—in which chemical and electrical phenomena take place, and possibly other phenomena of an unknown nature. These factors give the impulse current new qualities, or they contribute to the modifications which take place within the cell body. In this manner, the impulse passes on to other cells, where again new alterations occur.

When these fibrils cease to be healthy, or the intercalary substance undergoes alteration, due to exogenous or endogenous modification, the more or less complete discontinuity which ensues has the effect of interrupting the passage of the impulses. In still other cases, the Held's bundles, through abnormal adhesion, become affixed to the cells, and the impulses then keep following the same path and constantly giving rise to the same psychic manifestations. It is thus that I explain the persistence of the same morbid ideas, which are reproduced over and over again.

Even under normal conditions, there appears to be a certain tendency toward a relative fixity of the fibrils at the level of the synapses. When we are first learning to typewrite, for example, the operations performed are of necessity directly imitative. Practice makes this imitation easier, and when the operations have been executed many times, then automatism develops, in a greater or lesser degree.

This leads me to the conviction that a simplification of the path has been established in the succession of neuronal fibrils. Many of the side branches of the path, originally traversed, have ceased to be used. The course of the nerve impulses is so simplified in such cases that they no longer reach the synaptic complex which provides the notion of consciousness, for the act has been performed without its involvement, i.e., automatically.

In this manner a series of synaptic links is established, always the same, through which the impulses pass without hindrance and always arrive at the same destination.

The neurons are of organic origin and do not increase in number during one's lifetime, whereas the neuronal prolongations and the fibrils and arborizations are highly variable. They vary in number from individual to individual, from the uneducated man to the educated. In the latter they are more abundant, and it is supposed that they present different characteristics, according to the person's degree of culture, as well as in different parts of the brain. The fibrils, on the other hand, vary in volume and shape: they grow thicker, more ramified and arborescent.

The terminal points at the level of the

synapses do not function with the same intensity at the same time. We are still unable to prove this, and even less able to explain the intimate mechanism which conditions them.

The nutrition of the tissue doubtless plays an important role in the vitality of these minuscule but important organs, and the functioning of the synapses is affected both by exogenous intoxicants (alcohol, morphine, etc.) and endogenous ones, such as those of digestive, hepatic, and renal origin, and also alterations in the products of the internal glands, the various tissues of the organism, etc. All these intoxicants exert an ultimate effect on the synapses.

It is there that the anatomical and physiological substratum of many psychoses must be sought.

The actual passage of impulses has been demonstrated through the use of the galvanometer, which has shown the presence of electrical phenomena. This does not prove, however, that the impulses we have been referring to are solely of an electrical nature. They are doubtlessly much more complex, produced by the release of chemical energy and possibly other factors as yet unknown.

These nerve impulse currents are not immutable, nor are they haphazard in their movement. For this, evidence is provided by Pavlov's experiments on dogs. It has been incontrovertibly shown, through conditioned reflexes, that new paths for impulses or stimuli can be established in the brain, which lead to the same destination and have their origin in highly diverse fibrillary complexes.

If we place in the mouth of a dog food which it likes, as for example a piece of meat, abundant salivation results, which can be measured in terms of drops. The next time, just before the meat is placed in the animal's mouth, a definite sound is produced. This experiment is repeated a number of times.

Subsequently, when the meat is withheld, the sound alone has the effect of causing the saliva to flow in the same quantity and at the same juncture previously observed. The sound, contrary to what one might suppose, has acquired the property of producing an abundant salivary secretion in the animal.

New synaptic paths have been established in response to a sonorous excitation, wholly different from the gustatory excitation produced by the meat.

Although some reservations are essential when it comes to transferring to man phenomena established with regard to animals, conditioned reflexes nevertheless correspond closely to a number of facts observed in connection with the human brain.

The prefrontal lobe—a designation which does not seem to have met with the most favorable reception—is to us that part of the frontal lobe which is located directly in front of the motor region, and which has long been considered to be the part most closely linked with psychic activity. The premotor and motor cerebral areas, 4 and 6, lie outside the prefrontal lobe. Also excluded from it are the 8 areas and the 44 zones of aphasia.

This prefrontal lobe, as we have defined it, appears in mammals, and in man it is much larger than in the primates. It reaches practically twice the size of the anterior portion of the frontal lobe of the chimpanzee, and its cytoarchitectonic fields are, in turn, much more complex.

On the other hand, the prefrontal lobe is the most important brain mass in which it has thus far not been possible to discover localizations comparable to those we are familiar with in the occipital, parietal, and temporal lobes. Everything tends to indicate that the functions of these lobes must be of a different character.

The cytoarchitectonic structure of the areas of the prefrontal lobe present certain common characteristics which are considerably different from the motor areas. The granular layers are more developed in this region, while the layers of pyramidal cells, compared to those of the motor zone, are more reduced. Over and above this, its structure is not constant in all individuals. It varies in its degree of extension and even, it would appear, in the quantitative correlation of its cells. The cytoarchitectonic charts of this region do not provide an exact coverage of all individual cases. From this fact the inference has also been drawn by some that the zone in question constitutes the base of all psychic functions. That it is a highly important region, there can be no doubt; but there is no center or centers which correspond to given mental activities. The entire brain and the entire nervous system are involved in the psychic activity of each individual, although there are some regions in which these higher functions are more concentrated than in others. Amongst these, the regions belonging to the prefrontal lobes must certainly occupy a position of prime importance. Also apparently correlated with these latter zones are certain diencephalic and mesencephalic areas, which in turn have a special function of their own. There can be no question, however, of any "centers" in the layman's sense of the term, and comparable, for example, to those of the motor zone. These, too, are not independent, but have a quite marked individuality.

The zones which are especially associated with psychic phenomena are less autonomous in their functioning than the brain centers mentioned. Their activity depends upon the increased quantity of synapses of highly varied neurons which play a part in the production of psychic phenomena.

The functions of the prefrontal lobes are known as the result of data gathered in connection with experiments on the higher animals and clinical data on man.

The experiments conducted long ago by Bechterew and Luzaro must first be considered. Having removed the frontal lobes from dogs, they found that the animals became aggressive, irritable, and impulsive. Their adaptive faculties were reduced. These findings were confirmed by experiments reported by other authors.

The work performed by Fulton and Jacobsen on previously trained chimpanzees is of especial value. They found that the unilateral excision of the frontal areas did not produce noteworthy modifications, whereas the extirpation of bilateral areas always produced alterations in the behavior of the animal. After extensive lesions, the re-education of the animal was no longer possible.

The same mutilations performed on the parietal and temporal lobes did not produce similar phenomena, which led these authors to conclude that the frontal lobes are associated with higher functions.

These findings are in agreement with what has been ascertained in the case of man. Clinical reports have provided useful data which throw light on this important problem.

In cases of lesions of the frontal lobe due to wounds, many cases of which were provided by the war of 1914 to 1918, disturbances in equilibrium, incoordination of movements, facial tics, and apraxia were found, all of which are more or less associated with mental activity.

Other observers have noted loss of attention and of mental synthesis, decrease in memory power and disappearance of the association of ideas. Some have also found changes in character and personality.

This apparent disagreement in the symptomatology observed reflects the varying extent of the lesions, whether one or both lobes had been affected, and in some cases the association of other brain lesions.

A tremendous amount of literature exists on the subject of psychic disturbances in their relation to lesions of the frontal lobes, of which a special study was made by Karl Kleist of Frankfurt. Even more vast, however, is that pertaining to the study of mental disturbances in connection with certain tumors of these lobes. These latter cases are of less interest than the former, for they are almost always accompanied by intracranial hypertension with general symptoms which cannot be connected with the frontal localization of the neoplasia.

Such cases nevertheless offer new elements worthy of consideration. Baruk's opinion in this regard sums up the thinking of the majority of neurologists on the subject: It is tumors of the frontal lobes and of the corpus callosum which, of all the various types of intracranial tumors, are most frequently accompanied by psychic disturbances. According to my own observations, it is the tumors of the corpus callosum which most consistently result in psychic alterations.

Mental disturbances are highly accentuated when both frontal lobes are invaded by the neoplasia, to which tumors of the corpus callosum more or less correspond, anatomically, and with the same psychic symptoms.

Still another series of observations exists, of greater importance than those mentioned, namely, the literature on surgical ablations of the frontal lobes. It is known that one of these lobes can be excised without disagreeable effects on the patient's psychic existence. At most, there is a reaction of confusion and disorientation in time and space for the first few days; these disturbances, however, gradually recede (Penfield).

The case reported by Richard Brickner is of genuine importance. This author made a painstaking and persevering study of a patient from whom Dandy was obliged to excise substantial portions of both frontal lobes in order to be able to extract a large meningioma of the sphenoid. At first the patient lost some of his acquired knowledge; nevertheless, he continued to regress to his normal state, though not without noticeable shortcomings in the nature of change of character, suppression of his higher qualities of intelligence, etc. In the end, according to Brickner, the patient became essentially the same as he had been before the operation; he had preserved his "personal type."

The prefrontal leukotomy contributed better data with which to judge the functions of the frontal lobe. But I am going back into the history of it all here and speaking of the period before that in which I performed the operation which brings us together here at the moment. I am still on the other side of the river, outlining the reasons which led me to cross it.

If we consider, for example, melancholic patients, we find that they suffer from permanent afflictive ideas which are inaccessible to treatment, whether medical treatment, shock therapy, or psychotherapy. They live in a state of anxious torment from a continual thought to which all their normal life preoccupations are enslaved.

Unlike automatic acts, these morbid ideas are deeply submerged in the synaptic complex which conditions the notion of consciousness. They stimulate the synaptic complex and keep it in a continual state of live activity.

All these considerations led me to the following conclusion: These synaptic relations must be altered, and the paths in which the impulses revolve in constant passage must be modified, so that the ideas which are connected with them will be modified and the thought will take another course.

Guided by this reasoning, and having for over two years spent my every spare moment in reflection upon the matter, at the same time weighing my responsibilities, I came to the decision that I would undertake to cut the fibers joining the active neurons. Inasmuch as I was convinced of the importance of the prefrontal lobes in mental activity, I chose this region for the experiments. The choice appears to have been a propitious one. By breaking up these relationships and bringing other fibrillo-synaptic complexes into action, I could not help but transform the patient's psychic

reactions and bring him benefit. Since my objective was to inactivate an advantageous number of associations, we decided in favor of attacking en masse the fibers of the cellular connections of the anterior portion of both frontal lobes. I wished to discover if this would achieve positive results. Pursuant to the destructive process, alcohol injections were first given, and immediately thereafter incisions were made with the leukotome, a small apparatus we devised especially for this purpose. Inasmuch as the white substance of the brain has a very limited circulation, our surgical operation had to be free of danger. The entire operation was carried out with the greatest of care, in order to safeguard the patients' lives.

Allow me, if you will, to quote at this point a passage from my volume *Tentatives opératoires* (*Surgical Experiments*) which marks a decisive moment in my career:

> In the disquietude I justifiably felt on the eve of the first operation to be attempted, all trepidations were overcome by my hope of obtaining favorable results. If, indeed, it was to prove possible to bring about the disappearance of certain symptomatic complexes of a psychic nature by destroying certain cell-connecting structures, we would have established in a definitive manner that psychic functions and the parts of the brain involved in producing them stood in intimate relationship with one another. This would represent a great step forward, as a piece of knowledge of fundamental importance in the study of psychic functions on an organic basis.

And in conclusion I stated:

> We do not doubt that what we have undertaken here will provoke a great deal of lively discussion, in the fields of medicine, psychiatry, psychology, philosophy and sociology alike. This we expect, but we continue to hope that any such discussion will contribute to the progress of science, and above all, to the welfare of mental patients.

Together with Professor Almeida Lima, my worthy collaborator, to whom a great part of the initial work is due, I set to work. The first alcoholization of the white substance of the prefrontal lobe was carried out on November 12, 1935. The first operation with the "leukotome" was performed on December 27, of the same year. Both cures and improvements resulted. No adverse effects that would have forced us to suspend our undertaking were observed.

As soon as we achieved positive results, we released an account of our work to the public.

Those who gave it a friendly welcome were few. Nevertheless, leukotomies were performed in other psychiatric centers, notably in Raconigi, in Italy, and finally, on the other side of the Atlantic, came the achievements of Professors Freeman and Watts which definitely established the new operation as a beneficial treatment for psychoses. Their work was furthered by the availability of new cases and their development of a different surgical technique involving a more extensive incision of the white substance of the anterior part of the frontal lobe. They called their operation a "lobotomy."

WALTER FREEMAN
(1895–   )

and

JAMES W. WATTS
(1904–   )

Prefrontal Lobotomy [7]

In 1936 a bilateral operation upon the frontal lobes was reported by Egas Moniz for the treatment of certain mental disorders. He considered the symptoms in the functional psychoses due to the development of stereotyped patterns in cortical association centers, and thought that by forcibly breaking up the connections over a large area an opportunity would be given for reintegration of cortical activity along different lines. He first injected small amounts of alcohol into the white matter of the prefrontal region but soon substituted the leucotome, which was found to be more effective. The Moniz leucotome consists of a cannula, and a trocar armed with a cutting blade near its tip. The tip of the cannula is closed, but there is a slit over its distal end, through which, when a stilet is pressed, the cutting blade protrudes to a distance of 5 mm. By rotating the leucotome with the blade extruded, Almeida Lima, his surgical colleague, made a half dozen spherical cuts or cores in the upper half of each frontal lobe. As psychosurgery was taken up in various parts of the world many other methods of cutting the pathways were developed.

Numerous special leucotomes have been devised for operating through burr holes or trephine openings. Lyerly developed an open method through which he sections the white matter under direct vision. Fiamberti used the transorbital approach. We have developed several instruments but have emphasized the necessity for precision-and roentgenographic verification of the plane of section.

We had so many failures with the original Egas Moniz technic that we tried to obtain better results by making the core-like incisions close to the base. However, this proved to be dangerous because of lacerated blood vessels, and had the additional disadvantage that it left behind devitalized tissue. We then devised subcortical section of the frontal lobes, choosing the plane of the coronal suture as a guide. Though this was fairly reliable, and we still adhere to it in a fairly large percentage of the cases, the number of failures was considerable. These failures sometimes appeared as relapses after the patient had improved for a longer or shorter period. It seemed to us that an insufficient number of fibers had been sectioned.

Secondary operations were undertaken in many of these cases. Sometimes the incisions were made posterior to the original incisions, sometimes they were extended toward the midline but still in the plane of the coronal suture. When the results of posterior operations were assessed it was found that inertia, incontinence, and other indications of severe damage to the frontal lobe were enduring residuals. So we learned by experience that the incisions should not be made too far behind the coronal suture, at least in the upper quadrants. We have somewhat more

[7] From Walter Freeman and James W. Watts, *Psychosurgery: In the Treatment of Mental Disorders and Intractable Pain*, rev. ed., 1950. Courtesy of Charles C. Thomas, Publisher, Springfield, Illinois. Reprinted by permission.

leeway at the base, and we believe that this area is of much greater importance in the eventual results of operation.

The problem in psychosurgery is to place the incisions so that the affective charge of the psychosis or neurosis shall be reduced to the point where the ideas no longer disable the patient. At the same time it is desirable to preserve those parts of the brain that are requisite for adequate social adjustment. The problem becomes, then, one of locating incisions as precisely as possible in a plane decided upon for each case before the skin incisions are made. The decision as to where to make the incisions depends upon a number of factors such as age, personality disorganization, and degree of emotional deterioration. A young person with prolonged psychosis, much disorganization, and some emotional deterioration requires a radical operation reaching the base of the frontal lobes as much as 12 to 15 mm. posterior to the sphenoidal ridge. Lobotomy fails in markedly deteriorated cases because the incisions cannot be made sufficiently far back to relieve the psychosis without, at the same time, extinguishing the personality factors that will be needed in reorganization of the individual in the social environment. The deteriorated schizophrenic is unchanged by prefrontal lobotomy.

In contrast to the type of patient described above is the patient with involutional depression. Here it is usually not necessary to trespass upon the structures behind the sphenoidal ridge. In fact, an older person is much more disabled by such incisions than is a younger one. Sometimes in a long-standing case a radical operation is required, but a considerable sacrifice of personality organization. In prefrontal lobotomy we would rather err on the conservative side, taking a chance that a standard or even a minimal operation will be effective, and, later on, if the effects are not sufficiently good, we may reoperate.

While there are various modifications to suit individual cases we classify the lobotomies in current use as (1) standard, (2) radical, (3) minimal, (4) transorbital.

The precision method that has been developed at the George Washington University Hospital and the Doctors Hospital will be described. In subsequent chapters the choice of the plane of section will be discussed, the preoperative

and the postoperative care outlined, and the complications analyzed. Before entering into details which may concern only the neurosurgeon, it seems desirable to present the fundamental steps in a lobotomy, as this is necessary for a proper understanding of the problem. . . .

The white matter in the frontal lobes is cut approximately in the plane of the coronal suture. A burr hole is made through or near the suture line and with a long cannula the sphenoidal ridge is identified. With the coronal suture and the sphenoidal ridge as landmarks, the nerve pathways can be sectioned in the desired plane. The lobotomy may be performed with a blunt knife-like instrument or with a special leucotome—this is a matter of individual preference. However, accuracy in the placement of the incisions in the frontal lobes is of paramount importance if one is to compare clinical results and draw conclusions about frontal lobe function.

Frontal Lobes and the Psychoses

The foregoing parts of this book have dealt with factual material—historical, experimental, observational—and with interpretations based upon the fact observed. Obviously the interpretations are subject to review and revision when new facts and more penetrating study are brought to bear. It is by no means intended to be the last word to be said upon the subject of the frontal lobes. Nevertheless, the authors may perhaps be pardoned for their temerity in discussing their own theories as to the relationship of the frontal lobes to the psychoses, it being understood that these theories are their responsibility alone. Hence this chapter is of all the most subjective, and is not to be considered as contributing to the factual material of the work, but rather as an exercise in logical interpretation of observed phenomena in terms of psychobiologic activity.

We propose first to review briefly the defects in personality integration consequent upon the operation upon the frontal lobes, both those in the intellectual and those in the emotional domain, realizing all the time that the two are inseparable, and that personality is to be considered the sum of the intellectual-emotional-energetic components of the individual. Then we shall take up the question of the functioning of those parts of the brain that are inactivated, either by removal or by separation from the rest of the brain; and, finally, we shall attempt some explanation of the way in which those inactivated portions, in conjunction with the rest of the hemispheres may bring about personality deviations that are inconsistent with health. The reader is cautioned against accepting the theories at their face value, and the authors caution themselves against attempting to rewrite the subject of psychobiology on the basis of a few sick individuals and a few damaged brains.

The person whose frontal areas have been partially inactivated by prefrontal lobotomy presents a number of peculiarities that distinguish him from his preoperative self. He is freed from anxiety and from feelings of inferiority; he loses interest in himself, both as to his body and as to his relation with his environment, no longer caring whether his heart beats or his stomach churns, or whether his remarks embarrass his associates. His interests turn outward, and obsessive thinking is abolished. He responds immediately and sometimes vividly to external impressions, showing something of an emotional incontinence that makes for ready laughter or petulance. The emotional responses may be vivid but they are lacking in depth and quickly evaporate. His mood is, on the whole, elevated, and the extraversion and ready response make for an apparently quick-witted enthusiastic individual who gets along superficially with everybody. There is something child-like in the cheerful and unselfconscious behavior of the operated patient.

The intellectual equipment, in the sense of past experience, is undamaged, but close examination discloses certain defects that become more obvious in the cases of extensive incisions. Whether there is a substantial difference between lobotomy and lobectomy is still open to question. These intellectual defects immediately following prefrontal lobotomy consist in a certain rigidity of categorical attitude, in an inability to find new or different methods of solution for difficult problems; an inability to retain in consciousness a number of concepts presented simultaneously; a disturbance of the temporal patterning of activity; a certain lack of ability to synthesize and to arrive at a correct solution after considering all the factors involved. In the ensuing months these defects become attenuated or disappear entirely. More important than all the rest, there is an apparent inability to foresee accurately the results of a series of planned acts as they relate to the individual himself. Patients can often solve complicated problems in the intellectual field where multiple choices are offered, but their inability to foresee the effect upon themselves in their relation to their environment is particularly outstanding. Contract, checkers, designing, inventing, law—all these require a capacity to visualize the future in terms of the goal sought, but they are, nevertheless, relatively impersonal. Patients whose frontal lobes have been extensively incised may advance distinctly in their strategy during a period of training and experience, and may regain considerable ability to foresee results and to modify their attacks upon difficult problems.

22

Contemporary
American Clinical Psychology and
Personality Theory

ARNOLD GESELL
(1880–1961)

Infant Development [1]

There are three major brands of philosophy which deal with the principles and practices of child care: (1) authoritarian; (2) laissez-faire; (3) developmental. The authoritarian approach insists on the priority of the culture. It also holds that children are habit-forming creatures, who should be molded to the patterns of the culture, through training, learning, and conditioned reflexes. Behaviorism as a social theory concedes little to the child's heredity and magnifies the influence vested in the environment. In its extreme form it leads to totalitarian trends of thought in home, school, and government.

Laissez-faire doctrine, on the contrary, imposes no constraint on the child or on the culture. Let things take their own wise course: the child will know and select what is best for him if he is not confused and restricted by unnatural requirements. This outlook leads to the policy of noninterference. It encourages great freedom of action for the child, and demands a corresponding indulgence on the part of the adult.

A developmental philosophy in temper and in principle lies between the two foregoing extremes. In matters of child care a developmental outlook is suspicious of authoritarian absolutes and it does not favor license. It is sensitive to the relativities of growth and is concerned with the changing needs of the child. A developmental philosophy acknowledges the profound forces of racial and familial inheritance which determine the growth sequences and the distinctive growth pattern of each individual child.

It is easy to see how these three contrastive and rival brands of philosophy affect all human relationships, especially those between adult and child. The conflicts in point of view have by no means been resolved. Many current ideas about child behavior are essentially pre-Darwinian in their absoluteness. The concept of evolution as it applies to the race is much more widely appreciated and accepted than the corollary concept of growth as it applies to infant and child. We still tend to approach the problems of child care, child discipline, and even of child education in terms of flat absolutes without awareness of the depth-dimension of development. Our culture at present is more rational about the physical universe than it is about children. The lawfulness of nuclear energy, of light and gravity, is freely granted. It is becoming apparent that the human life cycle is equally governed by natural laws.

In surety and precision the laws of development are comparable to those of gravitation. This fact gives ground for faith. It means that the remarkable advances of the life sciences and the physical sciences can ultimately lead to a greater comprehension and control of the forces of life and growth.

Meanwhile, a developmental philosophy favors a better understanding of the child, besieged as he is by a highly technological culture. This philosophy enables us to see the child as an everchanging organism in a long but lawful cycle of growth. His behavior as a member of the species and as an individual thus takes on more meaning and truer

[1] From pp. 82–85, *Infant Development* by Arnold Gesell, M.D. Copyright 1952 by Arnold Gesell. Reprinted by permission of Harper & Row, Publishers.

proportions. His distinctive growth characteristics prove to be the essence of his individuality and by the same token a key to his educability.

The dynamics of development are by no means limited to the early embryology of behavior. Our studies have demonstrated that the higher psychical manifestations of the child life also are profoundly subject to the laws of development. Psychically, the child inherits nothing fully formed. Each and every part of his nature has to grow—his sense of self; his fears, his affections and his curiosities; his feelings toward mother, father, playmates, and sex; his judgments of good and bad, of ugly and beautiful; his respect for truth and property; his sense of humor; his ideas about life and death, crime, war, nature, and deity. All his sentiments, concepts, and attitudes are products of growth and experience. For all these diverse areas of behavior it is possible to formulate gradients of growth which represent the natural maturational stages by which the child assimilates the complex culture into which he is born.

He manifests his individuality from the very beginning in his natural rhythms of feeding, sleep, and self-activity. Given wisely managed opportunity, he seems to know when to sleep, when to be hungry, and how much to sleep and eat. His educability is not so bland and undifferentiated that he responds neatly to an iron-clad feeding schedule. Things work out better if his own self-regulation mechanisms, which are really growth mechanisms, are given a reasonable scope. The discerning physician makes no arbitrary distinctions between physical and mental factors; he gives conjoint consideration to the infant's nutritional status, to his immunities, allergies, and behavior traits. The child grows as a unit.

The task of the culture, likewise, is to watch for signs and symptoms of the child's total well-being with a special concern for psychological health. We must go along with the infant far enough to give him a sense of security. But self-dependence is fully as important. Step by step it is possible to build up his self-reliance and a self-confidence based upon confidence in his caretakers. Gradually he gains in morale and social insights, not through sheer indulgence, but through perceptive guidance on the part of his elders. And the more these elders know about the processes of growth, the more they will respect the truly remarkable progress which normal children make even in the first five years of life.

The intrinsic badness of children has been vastly exaggerated by distorting interpretations of their misbehavior. Well-constituted children with healthy inheritance have an intrinsic charm—a charm which betokens intrinsic goodness. The growth potentials for good far outweigh those for evil, unless the cultural odds are too heavily weighted against the child.

It is too freely said that science is indifferent to human values. Science by implication is always concerned with values, and the life sciences which deal with the physiology and the pathologies of growth are profoundly coming to grips with the deepmost determiners of human values. The race evolved; the child grows. And we shall not have the requisite self-knowledge to manage our culture until we make a more sedulous effort to understand the ways of all growth and the potentials of child growth, which are the culminating evidences and products of organic evolution.

This evolution has not ceased, and to that degree man still remains educable. He seems to have reached the very acme of mass cruelty, confusion, conflict, and destructiveness. Therein lies a tithe of hope. It would seem that on sheer evolutionary grounds of survival, man must and can shift to a higher cerebral plane of attitude and action. Among other things he surely needs a science of behavior, a systematically prosecuted science, which will not only probe the lingering wickedness of Old Adam, but which will explore with unrelenting penetration the rich repository of potentials for good, which are revealed with awesome mystery in the sequences of child development.

JACOB L. MORENO
(1892–)

Group Psychotherapy [2]

The cornerstones of sociometric conceptualization are the universal concepts of spontaneity and creativity. . . .

Spontaneity and creativity are not identical or similar processes. They are different categories, although strategically linked. In the case of Man his s may be diametrically opposite to his c; an individual may have a high degree of spontaneity but be entirely uncreative, a spontaneous idiot. Another individual may have a high degree of creativity but be entirely without spontaneity, a creator "without arms."

* * * * *

Creativity without spontaneity becomes lifeless; its living intensity increases and decreases in proportion to the amount of spontaneity in which it partakes. Spontaneity without creativity is empty and runs abortive. *Spontaneity and creativity are thus categories of a different order; creativity belongs to the categories of substance—it is the arch substance —spontaneity to the categories of catalyzer— it is the arch catalyzer.*

Psychodrama

Drama is a transliteration of the Greek δϱᾶμα which means action, or a thing done. Psychodrama can be defined, therefore, as the science which explores the "truth" by dramatic methods. It deals with inter-personal relations and private worlds.

The psychodramatic method uses mainly five instruments—the stage, the subject or actor, the director, the staff of therapeutic aides or auxiliary egos, and the audience. The first instrument is the stage. Why a stage? It provides the actor with a living space which is multi-dimensional and flexible to the maximum. The living space of reality is often narrow and restraining, he may easily lose his equilibrium. On the stage he may find

it again due to its methodology of freedom— freedom from unbearable stress and freedom for experience and expression.

* * * * *

The second instrument is the subject or actor. He is asked to be himself on the stage, to portray his own private world. He is told to be himself, not an actor, as the actor is compelled to sacrifice his own private self to the rôle imposed upon him by a playwright. Once he is warmed up to the task it is comparatively easy for the subject to give an account of his daily life in action, as no one is as much of an authority on himself as himself. He has to act freely, as things rise up in his mind; that is why he has to be given freedom of expression, spontaneity.

* * * * *

The third instrument is the director. He has three functions: producer, counsellor and analyst. As producer he has to be on the alert to turn every clue which the subject offers into dramatic action, to make the line of production one with the life line of the subject, and never to let the production lose rapport with the audience. As director attacking and shocking the subject is at times just as permissible as laughing and joking with him; at times he may become indirect and passive and for all practical purposes the session seems to be run by the subject. As analyst he may complement his own interpretation by responses coming from informants in the audience, husband, parents, children, friends or neighbors.

The fourth instrument is a staff of auxiliary egos. These auxiliary egos or participant actors have a double significance. They are extensions of the director, exploratory and guiding, but they are also extensions of the subject, portraying the actual or imagined personae of their life drama. The functions of the auxiliary ego are threefold: the function of the actor, portraying roles required by the subject's world; the function of the counsellor, guiding the subject; and the function of the social investigator.

---

[2] J. L. Moreno, *Who Shall Survive? Foundations of Sociometry, Group Psychotherapy and Sociodrama* (Beacon, N.Y.: Beacon House, 1953), pp. 39–40, 81–92. Reprinted by permission.

The fifth instrument is the audience. The audience itself has a double purpose. It may serve to help the subject or, being itself helped by the subject on the stage, the audience becomes the problem. In helping the subject it is a sounding board of public opinion. Its responses and comments are as extemporaneous as those of the subject, they may vary from laughter to violent protest. The more isolated the subject is, for instance, because his drama on the stage is shaped by delusions and hallucinations, the more important becomes, to him, the presence of an audience which is willing to accept and understand him. When the audience is helped by the subject, thus becoming the subject itself, the situation is reversed. The audience sees itself, that is, one of its collective syndromes portrayed on the stage.

* * * * *

Sociodrama

Sociodrama has been defined as a deep action method dealing with inter-group relations and collective ideologies.

The procedure in the development of a sociodrama differs in many ways from the procedure which I have described as psychodramatic. In a psychodramatic session, the attention of the director and his staff are centered upon the individual and his private problems. As these are unfolded before a group, the spectators are affected by the psychodramatic acts in proportion to the affinities existing between their own context of roles, and the role context of the central subject. Even the so-called group approach in psychodrama is in the deeper sense individual-centered. The audience is organized in accord with a mental syndrome which all participating individuals have in common, and the aim of the director is to reach every individual in his own sphere, separated from the other. He is using the group approach only to reach actively more than one individual in the same session. The group approach in psychodrama is concerned with a group of *private* individuals, which makes the group itself, in a sense, private. Careful planning and organizing the audience is here indispensable because there is no outward sign indicating which individual suffers from the same mental syndrome and can share the same treatment situation.

The true subject of a sociodrama is the *group*. It is not limited by a special number of individuals, it can consist of as many persons as there are human beings living anywhere, or at least of as many as belong to the same culture. Sociodrama is based upon the tacit assumption that the group formed by the audience is already organized by the social and cultural rôles which in some degree all the carriers of the culture share. It is therefore incidental who the individuals are, or of whom the group is composed, or how large their number is. It is the group as a whole which has to be put upon the stage to work out its problem, because the group in sociodrama corresponds to the individual in psychodrama. Sociodrama, therefore, in order to become effective, has to assay the difficult task of developing deep action methods, in which the working tools are representative types within a given culture and not private individuals. Catharsis in the sociodrama differs from catharsis in the psychodrama. The psychodramatic approach deals with personal problems principally and aims at personal catharsis; the sociodramatic approach deals with social problems and aims at social catharsis.

The concept underlying this approach is the recognition that *man is a rôleplayer*, that every individual is characterized by a certain range of rôles which dominate his behavior, and that every culture is characterized by a certain set of rôles which it imposes with a varying degree of success upon its membership.

* * * * *

Group Psychotherapy

The late arrival of group psychotherapy has a plausible explanation when we consider the development of modern psychiatry out of somatic medicine. The premise of scientific medicine has been since its origin that the *locus of physical ailment is within an individual organism*. Therefore, treatment is applied to the locus of the ailment as designated by diagnosis. The physical disease with which an individual A is afflicted does not require the collateral treatment of A's wife, his children and friends. If A suffers from an appendicitis and an appendectomy is indicated, only the appendix of A is removed, no one thinks of the removal of the appendix of A's wife and children too. When in budding psychiatry scientific methods began to be used, axioms gained from physical diagnosis and treatment were *automatically* applied to mental disorders as well. The premise prevailed that there is no locus of ailment beyond the individual, that there is, for instance, no group situation which requires special diagnosis and treatment.

BASIC CATEGORIES OF GROUP PSYCHOTHERAPY

Subject of Therapy

1. As to the *Constitution* of the Group

Amorphous	vs.	Structured (organized) Group
Without considering the organization of the group in the prescription of therapy.		Determining the dynamic organization of the group and prescribing therapy upon diagnosis.

2. As to *Locus* of Treatment

Treatment of Group in *Loco Nascendi, in Situ*	vs.	Treatment Deferred to Secondary Situations
Situational, for instance within the home itself, the workshop itself, etc.		Derivative, for instance in especially arranged situations, in clinics, etc.

3. As to *Aim* of Treatment

Causal	vs.	Symptomatic
Going back to the situations and individuals associated with the syndrome and including them *in vivo* in the treatment situation.		Treating each individual as a separate unit. Treatment may be deep, in the psychoanalytic sense, individually, but it may not be deep groupally.

Agent of Therapy

1. As to *Source* or *Transfer* of Influence

Therapist Centered	vs.	Group Centered Methods
Either chief therapist alone or chief therapist aided by a few auxiliary therapists. Therapist treating every member of the group individually or together, but the patients themselves are not used systematically to help one another.		Every member of the group is a therapeutic agent to one or another member, one patient helping the other. The group is treated as an interactional whole.

2. As to *Form* of Influence

Spontaneous and Free	vs.	Rehearsed and Prepared Form
Freedom of experience and expression. Therapist or speaker (from inside the group) is extemporaneous, the audience unrestrained.		Suppressed experience and expression. Therapist memorizes lecture or rehearses production. The audience is prepared and governed by fixed rules.

Medium of Therapy

1. As to *Mode* of Influence

Lecture or Verbal	vs.	Dramatic or Action Methods
Lectures, interviews, discussion, reading, reciting.		Dance, music, drama, motion pictures.

2. As to *Type* of Medium

Conserved, Mechanical or Unspontaneous	vs.	Creative Media
Motion pictures, rehearsed doll drama, rehearsed dance step, conserved music, rehearsed drama.		Therapeutic motion pictures as preparatory steps for an actual group session, extemporaneous doll drama with the aid of auxiliary egos behind each doll, psychomusic, psychodrama and sociodrama.

3. As to *Origin* of Medium

Face to Face	vs.	From-a-Distance Presentations
Any drama, lecture, discussion, etc.		Radio and television.

Although, during the first quarter of our century, there was occasional disapproval of this exclusive, individualistic point of view, it was more silent than vocal, coming from anthropologists and sociologists particularly. The decisive turn came with the development of sociometric and psychodramatic methodology.

When the locus of therapy changes from the individual to the group, the group becomes the new subject (first step). When the group is broken up into its individual little therapists and they become the agents of therapy, the chief therapist becomes a part of the group (second step) and finally, the medium of therapy is separated from the healer as well as the group therapeutic agents

(third step). Due to the transition from individual psychotherapy to group psychotherapy, group psychotherapy includes individual psychotherapy.

The three principles, *subject*, *agent* and *medium* of therapy can be used as points of reference for constructing a table of polar categories of group psychotherapies. Here follow eight pairs of categories: amorphous vs. structured, *loco nascendi* vs. secondary situations, causal vs. symptomatic, therapist vs. group centered, spontaneous vs. rehearsed, lectural vs. dramatic, conserved vs. creative, and face to face vs. from a distance. With these eight sets of pairs, a classification of every type of group psychotherapy can be made.

HENRY A. MURRAY
(1893–   )

and

CHRISTIANA MORGAN
(1893–1967)

Thematic Apperception Test [3]

The method which is to be described is based on the well recognized fact that when some one attempts to interpret a complex social situation he is apt to tell as much about himself as he is about the phenomena on which attention is focused. At such times the person is off his guard, since he believes that he is merely explaining objective occurrences. To one with "double hearing," however, he is exposing certain inner forces and arrangements—wishes, fears and traces of past experience. Another fact which was relied on in devising the present method is that a great deal of written fiction is the conscious or unconscious expression of the author's experiences or fantasies. The process involved is that of projection—something well known to analysts. It is utilized in the Rorschach test.

Procedure

The procedure which suggested itself was this: to present subjects with a series of pictures, each

of which depicts a different dramatic event, with the instructions to interpret the action in each picture and give an imaginary reconstruction of the preceding events and the final outcome. It was anticipated that in the performance of this task a subject would necessarily be forced to project some of his own fantasies into the material and so reveal some of his more pressing underlying needs.

Since for purposes of comparison it is desirable to make such a procedure as uniform as possible, that is, to present every subject with similar stimuli and similar instructions for response, the attempt was made to find a standard set of pictures. Each picture should suggest some critical situation and be effective in evoking a fantasy relating to it. The set should also be comprehensive. Ideally, there should be a picture which would act as a trellis to support the growth and unfolding of every root fantasy. It was considered, and the idea was later confirmed by experience, that there should be at least one person in each picture with whom the subject could easily identify himself. Such an object may be termed an evoker, that is, one who evokes empathy in another. Thus, there should be a separate set of pictures for males and females, and also for children, young adults and elderly persons. Since in the present experiments the subjects were all young men between the ages of 20 and 30, most of the pictures to be described included at least one figure of that sex and age.

[3] Christiana D. Morgan and Henry A. Murray, "A method for investigating fantasies: the thematic apperception test," *Arch. Neur. Psychiat.*, 1935, **34**, 289–306. Reprinted by permission.

After a preliminary selection from several hundred pictures and an elimination of those which on repeated trials proved unproductive, we found a set of twenty which gave good results. This test was one of many to which fifty subjects were exposed. It formed a part of a comprehensive study of personality in which about twenty experimenters participated.

The subject was seated in a comfortable chair with his back to the experimenter, and the following directions were read to him:

"This is a test of creative imagination. I am going to show you a picture, and I want you to make up a plot or story for which it might be used as an illustration. What is the relation of the individuals in the picture? What has happened to them? What are their present thoughts and feelings? What will be the outcome? I want you to do your very best. As this is a test of literary imagination you may make your story as long and as detailed as you wish."

The subject was then handed picture 1, and the experimenter wrote down everything that he said. If, in giving his story, the subject omitted the antecedent circumstances or the outcome, he was reminded of it by such remarks as, "What led up to this situation?" "How will it end" etc. When the subject finished his story he was handed picture 2 and asked to proceed as before. There were twenty pictures in the series, but as the test was stopped after an hour most of the subjects did not have time to make up stories for more than two thirds of them.

The test was given once to forty subjects as a group test, the stories being written. The time saved by this method was considerable, but the results were less satisfactory.

After a few days had elapsed each subject was interviewed. This time the experimenter explained that he was studying the imaginative process in the construction of literary plots and that he wished to know if what professional writers had told about their creative experiences was true for every one. The subject was then asked if he would cooperate by trying to remember whether his story had come from something which he had seen or read; whether it had come out of the experience of friends or relatives, or whether it had come out of his own private experience. The subject was then reminded of the plot of each story in turn and encouraged to speak freely and openly.

Results

An examination of the stories concocted by our subjects in conjunction with material obtained from introspections, autobiographies, hours of free association, interviews, etc., reveals the fact that there were four chief sources from which the plots and the items of the plots were drawn: (1) books and moving pictures, (2) actual events in which a friend or a member of the family participated, (3) experiences (subjective or objective) in the subject's own life and (4) the subject's conscious and unconscious fantasies.

Although the material from the first two of these four sources may seem at first blush to be of little importance, it was discovered that even here much of significance was revealed. This, it seems, may be explained by referring to the tendency exhibited by most subjects to enjoy observing most and to remember best the external events which resemble their underlying fantasies. Thus, when a subject gives a vivid account of an occurrence one may profitably consider whether or not the theme of the event is a clue to his latent personality.

That every subject almost immediately projects his own circumstances, experiences or preoccupations into the evoker was only too obvious. For instance, in one experiment six of the eleven college men who took the test said that the youth in picture 4 was a student, whereas none of the twelve noncollege men who acted as subjects described him as such. One subject, whose father had been a ship's carpenter, wanted to go to sea himself, to travel and see the world. This was his dominant fantasy. Three of the scenes in his stories were laid on board a ship and two were in the Orient. In regard to picture 17, which illustrates a middle-aged man talking to a younger man, the subject said: "The older man is educated and has traveled a lot. He convinces the other to travel, to take a job that will take him to different places." In commenting on a picture which illustrates a young man sitting in a chair brooding rather disconsolately, this subject said: "This is a business man who runs quite a business in town. He is weighing the possibility of a European trip. He has been arguing with his wife on the subject. She got angry because he would not go and finally took up her hat and left. He is thinking it over. He changes his opinion, goes out and buys tickets." In interpreting another picture, illustrating two laborers engaged in conversation, the same subject said: "These two fellows are a pair of adventurers. They always manage to meet in out of the way places. They are now in India. They have heard of a new revolution in South America, and they are planning how they can get there. . . . In the end they work their way in a freighter."

Many other examples of this sort of thing could be cited. No subject failed to exemplify it. Some of them, in fact, gave stories which were frank and unabashed autobiographies.

* * * * *

What we have to show is that subjects project their deepest fantasies into such dramatic pictures and thereby reveal directional tensions of which they are quite unconscious. Though some of their stories are elaborations of conscious fantasies, others are not recognized by the subjects as having any personal reference. It is these—in which the personal reference is suggested by other data—that have been ascribed to unconscious fantasies. Of course, the stories as given are conscious fantasies. Like dreams, they must be interpreted if one is to arrive at the unconscious trends which determine them. Before presenting typical case histories to support this assumption, however, it will be necessary to outline the conceptual scheme which we have adopted for the classification of fantasies.

* * * * *

Our own reflections have led us to the conclusion that every fantasy may be analyzed into a series of events, each event, in turn, being an occurrence which is usually analyzable into: (1) a driving force (or fusion of forces in the subject), (2) an object (or group of objects) toward which or away from which the force is directed, and (3) the outcome of their interaction expressed in terms of subjective feeling—satisfaction or dissatisfaction. This mode of analysis is applicable not only to a fantasy but to an actual event as well. Sometimes it is preferable to speak first of the object, i.e., the environmental press or stimulus situation, and second of the subjective trend, i.e., the response. Stated in this way, our mode of representation resembles the familiar S-R formula of the behaviorists, except that with us the stimulus is more than a single sensation or perception. It is a temporal *Gestalt* of stimuli which bear the same dynamic meaning—the press. And with us the response is ordinarily represented not as a particular muscular movement or reflex but as a need or general course of action, the tendency of which is to produce a certain effect.

To incorporate fantasies into a scientific system of psychology, then, we propose to classify them according to the single events which compose them, every event, as we have pointed out, being classified according to its essential structure. To refer to the dynamic structure or plot of a fantasied event—or, for that matter, of an actual event—we have found it convenient to use the term thema (th.). A simple thema we shall define as the abstract formula for a single event. It consists of a particular press-need combination. The term complex thema may be used to describe a commonly encountered temporal association of simple themas, some of which may be dominant and some subsidiary.

In some events only the press is known or the press is of primary importance (something happens or an object does something and the subject merely experiences it or adapts to it), whereas in other events nothing is known of the press or the press is merely the usual environment and it is the subject's action which is significant. In the former case the press alone will constitute the thema, and in the latter case, the need alone. For instance, "p punishment" will describe an event in which the subject is punished by an object, and "n punishment" or just "punishment" will describe an event in which the subject punishes an object. Strictly speaking, a thema is the structure of a momentary event, but the term may also be used to describe a long continued press followed by a long continued response, provided the intervening events are more or less irrelevant. For instance, "p family discord" may be used to describe the fact that a child is frequently exposed to quarrels between his father and his mother, and "revenge" may be used to describe a subject's long enduring resentment and a series of retaliative actions. . . .

Since the subjects who take this test are asked to interpret each picture, that is, to apperceive the plot or dramatic structure exhibited by each picture, we have named it the "thematic apperception test."

* * * * *

Conclusions

We have been able to present only a small fraction of the evidence which supports our general conclusion that the thematic apperception test is an effective means of disclosing a subject's regnant preoccupations and some of the unconscious trends which underlie them. The advantages of the test are that it is a simple procedure which may be completed in two hours or in an abbreviated form in half that time, and that it may be performed in a casual and informal fashion. Since the subject is led to believe that it is a test of creative imagination, even when it is given in a clinic, he is unaware of the fact that he is revealing his innermost thoughts. The subject's attention is not on himself, and so in many instances he indirectly confesses to things which he would not be willing to mention directly. But, more than this, he exposes latent tendencies of the existence of which he is entirely unconscious. For the fantasies by being projected may be inwardly disclaimed and thus avoid complete repression.

Of all the short procedures and tests which we have tried, the results of this one have given us the best understanding of the deeper layers of personality. It is undoubtedly a useful method for the investigation of fantasy production under various conditions. Whether it is of any value as a preanalytic measure

remains to be seen. It may, perhaps, aid a physician in deciding whether a given patient had better be analyzed by a man or by a woman, or it may give some clue to the probable course or length of an analysis.

Our results suggest, however, that the present test will be most helpful when used by trained analysts in cases in which the patient does not need or cannot afford a complete analysis. Undoubtedly many neuroses may be avoided and many spiritual dilemmas solved by proper guidance at the right time. This is particularly true for young persons. In our experience the minimum amount of preliminary information which a therapeutist should possess for such guidance may be supplied by a ten page autobiography, an hour of relaxed reminiscing about childhood experiences and fantasies, the thematic apperception test and an hour of direct questioning. Of these, the thematic apperception test is frequently the most helpful, for it brings to the forefront just those underlying issues which are of immediate consequence.

WILLIAM H. SHELDON
(1899–   )

Constitutional Psychology [4]

The Basic Components of Morphology. The procedures employed in the morphological analyses of human beings have already been described (*The Varieties of Human Physique*, 1940). Having failed to arrive at useful results with anthropometric techniques alone, we came to the conclusion that in order to set up the framework of a morphological taxonomy *ab initio*, it would first be necessary to *scrutinize* a large collection of physiques, and if possible to see them all at one time. Photography not only would make this possible, but also would permit us to see each physique from as many directions at once as we might desire. Accordingly, a procedure was adopted in which the individual is photographed in a

standardized posture from the frontal, lateral, and dorsal positions on a single film.

Four thousand college students were photographed in this manner, and later many more who were not college students. When the four thousand cases were assembled so that they could be studied in one place, and could be arranged experimentally in series, it was found that a certain orderliness of nature could be made out by the unaided eye. Certainly there were no "types," but only dimensions of variation.

The first problem was to determine how many dimensions or components of structural variation could be recognized by inspectional examination. The criteria we employed in seeking to discover "primary structural components" were two: (1) Could the entire collection of photographs be arranged in an ascending (or descending) progression of strength of the characteristic under consideration, with agreement between experimenters working independently? (2) In the case of a

From William H. Sheldon, "Constitutional Factors in Personality" in *Personality and the Behavior Disorders*, edited by J. McV. Hunt, copyright 1944, The Ronald Press Company, New York. Reprinted by permission.

suspected new component of structural variation, is it, upon examination of the photographs, found to be impossible to define this apparently new component in terms of mixtures, regular or dysplastic, of the other already accepted components?

Application of these two criteria revealed the presence of three primary components of structural variation, and although a set of photographs was virtually worn out by experimental sortings and rearrangements, we were unable to find a fourth structural variant which was not obviously the result of a mixture of these three.

To arrange the entire series of four thousand along each of the three accepted axes of variation was relatively easy, not only for the body as a whole, but also for different regions of the body separately (thus providing a method for the ultimate measurement of dysplasia). The distributions for the body as a whole were then scaled tentatively by the method of equal-appearing intervals, and we had at hand a rough approximation to the general patterning of a continuous tridimensional distribution. This was not yet an objectively defined distribution, but the first step toward meaningful objectification had been taken. We now had a fairly good idea of what it was that needed to be measured, and were ready to make use of anthropometry.

The second problem was to find such anthropometric measurements as would, (1) most reliably reflect those obvious differences in physique that our anthroposcopic inspection had already shown to be present, and (2) refine and objectify these differences so that precise allocations of physiques on the tridimensional distribution could be made. Such measurements were selected by trial and error. We found by experiment that the measurements most valuable for the purpose were certain diameters expressed as ratios to stature, and that most of these diameters could be taken with needle point dividers from the film more accurately (more reliably) than from the living subjects, provided the photographs were perfectly posed.

The question of how many such diameters to use is simply the question of how precisely accurate an allocation is desired. In dealing with groups statistically, we scale the strength of each of the primary components on a 7-point scale. For this purpose a minimum of seventeen diameter measurements is adequate for determining what is called the somatotype. In the detailed analysis of an individual, more precise differentiation may be made by using a greater number of measurements.

In order more readily to determine the somatotype from a series of seventeen measurements, a machine has been constructed into which the measurements may be entered. The manipulation of switches then discloses the correct somatotype. This machine, as at present constructed, may be used for the somatotyping of any male individual in the age range of 16 to 21.

The somatotype is a series of three numerals, each expressing the approximate strength of one of the primary components in a physique. The first numeral always refers to *endomorphy* (see below), the second to *mesomorphy*, and the third to *ectomorphy*. Thus when a 7-point scale is used, a 7-1-1 is the most extreme endomorph, a 1-7-1 is the most extreme mesomorph, and a 1-1-7 the most extreme ectomorph. The 4-4-4 falls at the mid-point (of the scale, not the frequency distribution) with respect to all three components. Seventy-six different somatotypes have been described, and photographic illustrations of most of them are presented in *The Varieties of Human Physique* (Sheldon, Stevens, and Tucker, 1940).

As these components occur in nature they are complex, continuous variables. The somatotype is an oversimplification which merely serves the purpose of bracketing a physique within certain defined boundaries. When the somatotype is determined, analysis of the physique is of course only begun, but the somatotype provides the basis for a morphological taxonomy which is both comprehensive and statistically manipulable. The bugaboo of types thus disappears in a continuous distribution in which every physique has a place, and the establishment of norms becomes a routine.

When *endomorphy* predominates, the digestive viscera are massive and highly developed, while the somatic structures are relatively weak and undeveloped. Endomorphs are of low specific gravity. They float high in the water. Nutrition may of course vary to some degree independently of the primary components. Endomorphs are usually fat but they are sometimes seen emaciated. In the latter event they do not change into mesomorphs or ectomorphs any more than a starved spaniel will change into a mastiff or a collie. They become simply emaciated endomorphs.

When *mesomorphy* predominates, the somatic structures (bone, muscle, and connective tissue) are in the ascendancy. The mesomorphic physique is high in specific gravity and is hard, firm, upright, and relatively strong and tough. Blood vessels are large, especially the arteries. The skin is relatively thick with large pores, and it is heavily reinforced with underlying connective tissue. The hallmark of mesomorphy is uprightness and sturdiness of structure, as the hallmark of endomorphy is softness and sphericity.

Ectomorphy means fragility, linearity, flatness of the chest, and delicacy throughout the body. There is relatively slight development of both the visceral and somatic structures. The ectomorph has long, slender, poorly muscled extremities with delicate, pipestem bones, and he has, relative to his mass, the greatest surface area and hence the greatest sensory exposure to the outside world. He is thus in one sense overly exposed and naked to his world. His nervous system and sensory tissue have relatively poor protection. It might be said that the ectomorph is biologically "extraverted," as the endomorph is biologically "introverted." Psychologically, as we shall see later, these characteristics are usually reversed—the ectomorph is the introvert, the endomorph is *one type* of extravert. The hallmark of ectomorphy is the stooped posture and hesitant restraint of movement.

The digestive viscera (dominant in endomorphy) are derived principally from the endodermal embryonic layer. The somatic tissues (dominant in mesomorphy) are derived from the mesodermal layer, while the skin and nervous system, which are relatively predominant in ectomorphy, come from the ectodermal embryonic layer.

The anthropometric measurements are standardized for normal or average nutrition, within a particular age range. Therefore those measurements which change with nutritional changes readily detect the under- or over-nourished individual. But apparently no nutritional change can cause the measurements of a person of one somatotype to stimulate those of another somatotype. Nutritional changes are recognized as such by the somatotyping process. When an individual's measurements are posted in the somatotyping machine, the machine indicates where the somatotype lies. If a severe nutritional disturbance is present, the machine does not indicate a false somatotype, but indicates only an unusual aberration from the normal pattern. We have as yet seen no case in which metabolic or nutritional changes led us to the assignment of two different somatotypes for the same individual, although we have somatotyped people from photographs taken at different periods in their (adult) lives when a weight change of as much as 100 pounds had taken place.

When the relative strength of the three primary components of morphology has been determined, the physical analysis may be said to be anchored. But identification of the somatotype is only a beginning. So many secondary variables still remain to be described that the horizon of individuality seems only to broaden and to recede to greater distance as the techniques of physical description mature to usefulness.

Some of the important secondary variables are dysplasia, gynandromorphy (bisexuality), texture (fineness or coarseness of tissue), aesthetic harmony of structure, secondary local dysplasias or hereditary local patternings of the primary components (often called racial characteristics), pigmentation, distribution of secondary sexual characteristics (gynandromorphic dysplasias and characteristic patterns), hair and hair distribution, and so on. We have tried to standardize the scaling of most of these characteristics just mentioned, but many other important physical variables lie on beyond these. Furthermore the work on secondary factors is for the most part new and incomplete, since none of this work could be done in a meaningful frame of reference until the somatotyping techniques and the norms for the primary components were well established.

The Basic Components of Temperament. As in the studies of physique, the first problem at this more complex level of personality was to discover and define criteria for a useful basic taxonomy. It was necessary at the beginning to determine what first-order components are present in temperament. The method which has finally yielded fruitful results is a variation on the technique of factor analysis applied to quantitative ratings on a group of traits.

The literature on temperament and especially on the measurement of extraversion and introversion, contains many hundreds of references to alleged traits of temperamental differentiation. This literature was first combed for differentiate behavioral traits. The trait definitions were then modified and rewritten until they appeared to embrace or to imply all of the specific characteristics mentioned in the literature. A number of trait definitions were added which were drawn from our own clinical and general observation of people, and finally the list was boiled down to exactly 50 traits.

A group of 33 young men, mostly graduate students and instructors, were then studied by the writer through the course of a series of weekly analytic interviews extending through a period of one year. These men were finally rated on each of the 50 experimental traits, a 7-point scale being used. The intercorrelations for the 50 traits were then run, and were posted on a correlation chart. . . . That is to say, the basic procedure of what is now called factor analysis was carried out. The purpose was to discover whether or not there were any "nuclear clusters" of traits showing positive correlation among themselves and also negative correlation with other nuclear clusters which might be present.

The result was clear-cut. Clusters of the sort just indicated were present, and clearly defined. After some statistical experimenting had been done, two criteria were adopted for qualification of a trait within a nuclear cluster. (1) The trait must show a positive correlation of at least $+.60$ with each of the other traits already accepted in the cluster, and (2) it must shown a negative correlation of at least $-.30$ with every trait found in any of the other clusters. When the criteria of positive intracorrelation and negative intercorrelation were applied, it was found that three clusters of traits were present in the material. Six traits then defined what was designated as group 1, seven defined group 2, and nine defined group 3. Twenty-two of the original 50 traits had qualified. These 22 appear in Table I.

TABLE 1

Twenty-two Traits Originally Defining the Three Primary Temperamental Components

Group 1	*Group* 2	*Group* 3
V– 1[1] Relaxation	S– 1 Assertive Posture	C– 1 Restraint in Posture
V– 2 Love of Comfort	S– 3 Energetic Characteristic	C– 3 Overly Fast Reaction
V– 6 Pleasure in Digestion	S– 4 Need of Exercise	C– 8 Sociophobia
V–10 Dependence on Social Approval	S– 7 Directness of Manner	C– 9 Inhibited Social Address
V–15 Deep Sleep	S–13 Unrestrained Voice	C–10 Resistance to Habit
V–19 Need of People when Troubled	S–16 Quality of Seeming Older	C–13 Vocal Restraint
	S–19 Need of Action when Troubled	C–15 Poor Sleep Habits
		C–16 Youthful Intentness
		C–19 Need of Solitude when Troubled

[1] The number before each trait refers to its position in Table II.

This was the beginning of what is called the Scale for Temperament. It now consists of 60 traits, 20 in each group. The additional 38 items were added as rapidly as traits meeting the criteria could be discovered and tested—a tedious process, since each individual used as a subject was analyzed through a period of at least one year. The scale in its present form is shown in Table II.

TABLE II

The Scale for Temperament

Name   *Date*   *Photo No.*   *Scored by*

I VISCEROTONIA . . .	II SOMATOTONIA . . .	III CEREBROTONIA . . .
( ) 1. Relaxation in Posture and Movement	( ) 1. Assertiveness of Posture and Movement	( ) 1. Restraint in Posture and Movement, Tightness
( ) 2. Love of Physical Comfort	( ) 2. Love of Physical Adventure	— 2. Physiological Overresponse
( ) 3. Slow Reaction	( ) 3. The Energetic Characteristic	( ) 3. Overly Fast Reactions
— 4. Love of Eating	( ) 4. Need and Enjoyment of Exercise	( ) 4. Love of Privacy
— 5. Socialization of Eating	— 5. Love of Dominating, Lust for Power	( ) 5. Mental Overintensity, Hyperattentionality, Apprehensiveness
— 6. Pleasure in Digestion	( ) 6. Love of Risk and Chance	( ) 6. Secretiveness of Feeling, Emotional Restraint
( ) 7. Love of Polite Ceremony	( ) 7. Bold Directness of Manner	( ) 7. Self-conscious Motility of the Eyes and Face
( ) 8. Sociophilia	( ) 8. Physical Courage for Combat	( ) 8. Sociophobia
— 9. Indiscriminate Amiability	( ) 9. Competitive Aggressiveness	( ) 9. Inhibited Social Address
— 10. Greed for Affection and Approval	— 10. Psychological Callousness ·	— 10. Resistance to Habit, and Poor Routinizing
— 11. Orientation to People	— 11. Claustrophobia	— 11. Agoraphobia
( ) 12. Evenness of Emotional Flow	— 12. Ruthlessness, Freedom from Squeamishness	— 12. Unpredictability of Attitude
( ) 13. Tolerance	( ) 13. The Unrestrained Voice	( ) 13. Vocal Restraint, and General Restraint of Noise
( ) 14. Complacency	— 14. Spartan Indifference to Pain	— 14. Hypersensitivity to Pain
— 15. Deep Sleep	— 15. General Noisiness	— 15. Poor Sleep Habits, Chronic Fatigue
( ) 16. The Untempered Characteristic	( ) 16. Overmaturity of Appearance	( ) 16. Youthful Intentness of Manner and Appearance
( ) 17. Smooth, Easy Communication of Feeling, Extraversion of Viscerotonia	— 17. Horizontal Mental Cleavage, Extraversion of Somatotonia	— 17. Vertical Mental Cleavage, Introversion
— 18. Relaxation and Sociophilia under Alcohol	— 18. Assertiveness and Aggression under Alcohol	— 18. Resistance to Alcohol, and to other Depressant Drugs
— 19. Need of People when Troubled	— 19. Need of Action when Troubled	— 19. Need of Solitude when Troubled
— 20. Orientation toward Childhood and Family Relationships	— 20. Orientation toward Goals and Activities of Youth	— 20. Orientation toward the Later Periods of Life

NOTE: The thirty traits with brackets constitute collectively the short form of the scale.

Names have been given to the three correlated groups of traits. *Viscerotonia*, the first component, in its extreme manifestation is characterized by general relaxation, love of comfort, sociability, conviviality, gluttony for food, for people, and for affection. The viscerotonic extremes are people who "suck hard at the breast of mother earth" and love physical proximity with others. The motivational organization is dominated by the gut and by the function of anabolism. The personality seems to center around the viscera. The digestive tract is king, and its welfare appears to define the primary purpose of life.

Somatotonia, the second component, is roughly a predominance of muscular activity and of vigorous bodily assertiveness. The motivational organization seems dominated by the soma. These people have vigor and push. The executive department of their internal economy is strongly vested in their somatic muscular systems. Action and power define life's primary purpose.

Cerebrotonia, the third component, is roughly a predominance of the element of restraint, inhibition, and of the desire for concealment. These people shrink away from sociality as from too strong a light. They "repress" somatic and visceral expression, are hyperattentional, and sedulously avoid attracting attention to themselves. Their behavior seems dominated by the inhibitory and attentional functions of the cerebrum, and their motivational hierarchy appears to define an antithesis to both of the other extremes.

Concerning the Relationship between Physique and Temperament. We have been less interested in the statistical relationship between physique and temperament than in the problem of standardizing a procedure for the general (physical and temperamental) analysis of the individual. The project may be regarded as in one sense an effort to make a contribution to the theory and technique of psychoanalysis. Constitutional psychology and Freudian analysis are, as we see it, something like upward and downward extensions, respectively, of a continuum. The Freudians start with consciousness and go as far (down) as they can. We start with the solid bone and flesh of the individual and go as far (up) as we can. The two procedures need to be carried on conjointly, and indeed in certain cases where the two analyses have been so conducted, excellent results have obtained.

The correlation between physique and temperament is, however, an interesting by-product of constitutional analysis. In a study extending over a period of five years we have been able to analyze 200 cases, both morphologically and temperamentally. The intra-correlations among the three primary components at each level, and the intercorrelations between the two levels are shown in Table III.

TABLE III

Intracorrelations and Intercorrelations among the Primary Components

	Viscero-tonia	Meso-morphy	Somato-tonia	Ecto-morphy	Cerebro-tonia
Endomorphy	+ .79	— .29	— .29	— .41	— .32
Viscerotonia		— .23	— .34	— .41	— .37
Mesomorphy			+ .82	— .63	— .58
Somatotonia				— .53	— .62
Ectomorphy					+ .83

The correlations between the same components at the two levels, morphological and temperamental, are seen to be of the order of +.81 (endomorphy-viscerotonia, +.79; mesomorphy-somatotonia, +.82; and ecto-morphy-cerebrotonia, +.83). These correlations are higher than we had previously expected, and they contradict the current academic supposition that physical constitution plays only a small part in motivation and temperament. However, this common supposition can hardly be regarded as founded upon any convincing evidence, since there have been no previous studies which attempted to break down both physical and temperamental factors into comparable component elements.

In any event the correlation between the two levels is by no means perfect, and we have found that from the point of view of individual analysis, it is the disagreements or inconsistencies between the physical and temperamental patterns that are most valuable in throwing light on motivation.

Roughly, we find at least four general factors at work in the development of a personality: (1) The amount of the endowment; (2) the quality of the endowment; (3) the mixture of the components, or their order of predominance; and (4) the dyscrasias or incompatibilities between morphology and manifest temperament. Of the latter, there are several subvarieties, the most important being those cases in which the temperamental manifestation reverses a relationship of dominance between two of the morphological components. Beyond these general factors

there are many secondary variables which can be measured with a greater or less degree of reliability, once the analysis of the primary components is made secure. Such factors as peripheral and central concentration of strength, endowment of sexuality, and gynandrophrenia (mental bisexuality) appear to play an important part, and these factors are closely related to the primary morphological components.

CARL R. ROGERS
(1902–   )

Client-Centered Therapy [5]

The Predictable Process of Client-Centered Therapy

The first of the three distinctive elements of client-centered therapy to which I wish to call your attention is the predictability of the therapeutic process in this approach. We find, both clinically and statistically, that a predictable pattern of therapeutic development takes place. The assurance which we feel about this was brought home to me recently when I played a recorded first interview for the graduate students in our practicum immediately after it was recorded, pointing out the characteristic aspects, and agreeing to play later interviews for them to let them see the later phases of the counseling process. The fact that I knew with assurance what the later pattern would be before it had occurred only struck me as I thought about the incident. We have become clinically so accustomed to this predictable quality that we take it for granted. Perhaps a brief summarized description of this therapeutic process will indicate those elements of which we feel sure.

It may be said that we know how to initiate a complex and predictable chain of events in dealing with the maladjusted individual, a chain of events which is therapeutic, and which operates effectively in problem situations of the most diverse type. This predictable chain of events may come about through the use of language, as in counseling, through

symbolic language, as in play therapy, through disguised language as in drama or puppet therapy. It is effective in dealing with individual stations, and also in small group situations.

It is possible to state with some exactness the conditions which must be met in order to initiate and carry through this releasing therapeutic experience. Below are listed in brief form the conditions which seem to be necessary, and the therapeutic results which occur.

This experience which releases the growth forces within the individual will come about in most cases if the following elements are present:

1. If the counselor operates on the principle that the individual is basically responsible for himself, and is willing for the individual to keep that responsibility.

2. If the counselor operates on the principle that the client has a strong drive to become mature, socially adjusted, independent, productive, and relies on this force, not on his own powers, for therapeutic change.

3. If the counselor creates a warm and permissive atmosphere in which the individual is free to bring out any attitudes and feelings which he may have, no matter how unconventional, absurd, or contradictory these attitudes may be. The client is as free to withhold expression as he is to give expression to his feelings.

4. If the limits which are set are simple limits set on behavior, and not limits set on attitudes. (This applies mostly to children. The child may not be permitted to break a window or leave the room, but he is free to feel like breaking a window, and the feeling

5 Carl R. Rogers, "Significant aspects of client-centered therapy," *Amer. Psychologist*, 1946, **1**, 415–422. Reprinted by permission of the American Psychological Association and of the author.

is fully accepted. The adult client may not be permitted more than an hour for an interview, but there is full acceptance of his desire to claim more time.)

5. If the therapist uses only those procedures and techniques in the interview which convey his deep understanding of the emotionalized attitudes expressed and his acceptance of them. This understanding is perhaps best conveyed by a sensitive reflection and clarification of the client's attitudes. The counselor's acceptance involves neither approval nor disapproval.

6. If the counselor refrains from any expression or action which is contrary to the preceding principles. This means refraining from questioning, probing, blame, interpretation, advice, suggestion, persuasion, reassurance.

If these conditions are met, then it may be said with assurance that in the great majority of cases the following results will take place.

1. The client will express deep and motivating attitudes.

2. The client will explore his own attitudes and reactions more fully than he has previously done and will come to be aware of aspects of his attitudes which he has previously denied.

3. He will arrive at a clearer conscious realization of his motivating attitudes and will accept himself more completely. This realization and this acceptance will include attitudes previously denied. He may or may not verbalize this clearer conscious understanding of himself and his behavior.

4. In the light of his clearer perception of himself he will choose, on his own initiative and on his own responsibility, new goals which are more satisfying than his maladjusted goals.

5. He will choose to behave in a different fashion in order to reach these goals, and this new behavior will be in the direction of greater psychological growth and maturity. It will also be more spontaneous, and less tense, more in harmony with social needs of others, will represent a more realistic and more comfortable adjustment to life. It will be more integrated than his former behavior. It will be a step forward in the life of the individual.

The best scientific description of this process is that supplied by Snyder. Analyzing a number of cases with strictly objective research techniques, Snyder has discovered that the development in these cases is roughly parallel, that the initial phase of catharsis is replaced by a phase in which insight becomes the most significant element, and this in turn by a phase marked by the increase in positive choice and action.

Clinically we know that sometimes this process is relatively shallow, involving primarily a fresh reorientation to an immediate problem, and in other instances so deep as to involve a complete reorientation of personality. It is recognizably the same process whether it involves a girl who is unhappy in a dormitory and is able in three interviews to see something of her childishness and dependence, and to take steps in a mature direction, or whether it involves a young man who is on the edge of a schizophrenic break, and who in thirty interviews works out deep insights in relation to his desire for his father's death, and his possessive and incestuous impulses toward his mother, and who not only takes new steps but rebuilds his whole personality in the process. Whether shallow or deep, it is basically the same.

We are coming to recognize with assurance characteristic aspects of each phase of the process. We know that the catharsis involves a gradual and more complete expression of emotionalized attitudes. We know that characteristically the conversation goes from superficial problems and attitudes to deeper problems and attitudes. We know that this process of exploration gradually unearths relevant attitudes which have been denied to consciousness.

We recognize too that the process of achieving insight is likely to involve more adequate facing of reality as it exists within the self, as well as external reality; that it involves the relating of problems to each other, the perception of patterns of behavior; that it involves the acceptance of hitherto denied elements of the self, and a reformulating of the self-concept; and that it involves the making of new plans.

In the final phase we know that the choice of new ways of behaving will be in conformity with the newly organized concept of the self; that first steps in putting these plans into action will be small but symbolic; that the individual will feel only a minimum degree of confidence that he can put his plans into effect; that later steps implement more and more completely the new concept of self, and that this process continues beyond the conclusion of the therapeutic interviews.

If these statements seem to contain too much assurance, to sound "too good to be true," I can only say that for many of them we now have research backing, and that as rapidly as possible we are developing our research to bring all phases of the process under objective scrutiny. Those of us working clinically with client-centered therapy regard this predictability as a settled characteristic, even though we recognize that additional research will be necessary to fill out the picture more completely.

* * * * *

The Discovery of the Capacity of the Client

Naturally, the question is raised, What is the reason for this predictability in a type of therapeutic procedure in which the therapist serves only a catalytic function? Basically the reason for the predictability of the therapeutic process lies in the discovery—and I use that word intentionally—that within the client reside constructive forces whose strength and uniformity have been either entirely unrecognized or grossly underestimated. It is the clearcut and disciplined reliance by the therapist upon those forces within the client which seems to account for the orderliness of the therapeutic process and its consistency from one client to the next.

I mentioned that I regarded this as a discovery. I would like to amplify that statement. We have known for centuries that catharsis and emotional release were helpful. Many new methods have been and are being developed to bring about release, but the principle is not new. Likewise, we have known since Freud's time that insight, if it is accepted and assimilated by the client, is therapeutic. The principle is not new. Likewise we have realized that revised action patterns, new ways of behaving, may come about as a result of insight. The principle is not new.

But we have not known or recognized that in most if not all individuals there exist growth forces, tendencies toward self-actualization, which may act as the sole motivation for therapy. We have not realized that under suitable psychological conditions these forces bring about emotional release in those areas and at those rates which are most beneficial to the individual. These forces drive the individual to explore his own attitudes and his relationship to reality, and to explore these areas effectively. We have not realized that the individual is capable of exploring his attitudes and feelings, including those which have been denied to consciousness, at a rate which does not cause panic, and to the depth required for comfortable adjustment. The individual is capable of discovering and perceiving, truly and spontaneously, the interrelationships between his own attitudes, and the relationship of himself to reality. The individual has the capacity and the strength to devise, quite unguided, the steps which will lead him to a more mature and more comfortable relationship to his reality. It is the gradual and increasing recognition of these capacities within the individual by the client-centered therapist that rates, I believe, the term "discovery." All of these capacities I have described are released in the individual if a suitable psychological atmosphere is provided.

There has, of course, been lip service paid to the strength of the client, and the need of utilizing the urge toward independence which exists in the client. Psychiatrists, analysts, and especially social caseworkers have stressed this point. Yet it is clear from what is said, and even more clear from the case material cited, that this confidence is a very limited confidence. It is a confidence that the client can take over, if guided by the expert; a confidence that the client can assimilate insight if it is first given to him by the expert, can make choices providing guidance is given at crucial points. It is, in short, the same sort of attitude which the mother has toward the adolescent, that she believes in his capacity to make his own decisions and guide his own life, providing he takes the directions of which she approves.

This is very evident in the latest book on psychoanalysis by Alexander and French. Although many of the former views and practices of psychoanalysis are discarded, and the procedures are far more nearly in line with those of nondirective therapy, it is still the therapist who is definitely in control. He gives the insights; he is ready to guide at crucial points. Thus while the authors state that the aim of the therapist is to free the patient to develop his capacities, and to increase his ability to satisfy his needs in ways acceptable to himself and society; and while they speak of the basic conflict between competition and cooperation as one which the individual must settle for himself; and speak of the integration of new insight as a normal function of the ego, it is clear when they speak of procedures that they have no confidence that the client has the capacity to do any of these things. For in practice:

As soon as the therapist takes the more active role we advocate, systematic planning becomes imperative. In addition to the original decision as to the particular sort of strategy to be employed in the treatment of any case, we recommend the conscious use of various techniques in a flexible manner, shifting tactics to fit the particular needs of the moment. Among these modifications of the standard technique are: using not only the method of free association but interviews of a more direct character, manipulating the frequency of the interviews, giving directives to the patient concerning his daily life, employing interruptions of long or short duration in preparation for ending the treatment, regulating the transference relationship to meet the specific needs of the case, and making use of real-life experiences as an integral part of therapy.

At least this leaves no doubt as to whether it is the client's or the therapist's hour; it is clearly the latter. The capacities which the client is to develop are clearly not to be developed in the therapeutic sessions.

The client-centered therapist stands at an opposite pole, both theoretically and practically. He has learned that the constructive forces in the individual can be trusted, and that the more deeply they are relied upon, the more deeply they are released. He has come to build his procedures upon these hypotheses, which are rapidly becoming established as facts: that the client knows the areas of concern which he is ready to explore; that the client is the best judge as to the most desirable frequency of interviews; that the client can lead the way more efficiently than the therapist into deeper concerns; that the client will protect himself from panic by ceasing to explore an area which is becoming too painful; that the client can and will uncover all the repressed elements which it

is necessary to uncover in order to build a comfortable adjustment; that the client can achieve for himself far truer and more sensitive and accurate insights than can possibly be given to him; that the client is capable of translating these insights into constructive behavior which weighs his own needs and desires realistically against the demands of society; that the client knows when therapy is completed and he is ready to cope with life independently. Only one condition is necessary for all these forces to be released, and that is the proper psychological atmosphere between client and therapist.

Our case records and increasingly our research bear out these statements. One might suppose that there would be a generally favorable reaction to this discovery, since it amounts in effect to tapping great reservoirs of hitherto little-used energy. Quite the contrary is true, however, in professional groups. There is no other aspect of client-centered therapy which comes under such vigorous attack. It seems to be genuinely disturbing to many professional people to entertain the thought that this client upon whom they have been exercising their professional skill actually knows more about his inner psychological self than they can possibly know, and that he possesses constructive strengths which make the constructive push by the therapist seem puny indeed by comparison. The willingness fully to accept this strength of the client, with all the reorientation of therapeutic procedure which it implies, is one of the ways in which client-centered therapy differs most sharply from other therapeutic approaches.

The Client-Centered Nature of the Therapeutic Relationship

The third distinctive feature of this type of therapy is the character of the relationship between therapist and client. Unlike other therapies in which the skills of the therapist are to be exercised upon the client, in this approach the skills of the therapist are focused upon creating a psychological atmosphere in which the client can work. If the counselor can create a relationship permeated by warmth, understanding, safety from any type of attack, no matter how trivial, and basic acceptance of the person as he is, then the client will drop his natural defensiveness and use the situation. As we have puzzled over the characteristics of a successful therapeutic relationship, we have come to feel that the sense of communication is very important. If the client feels that he is actually communi-cating his present attitudes, superficial, con-fused, or conflicted as they may be, and that his communication is understood rather than evaluated in any way, then he is freed to communicate more deeply. A relationship in which the client thus feels that he is com-municating is almost certain to be fruitful.

JOHN DOLLARD
(1900–   )

and

NEAL E. MILLER
(1909–   )

S-R Learning Theory of Personality [6]

Fundamental Principles

1. The principle of reinforcement has been substituted for Freud's pleasure principle. The concept of "pleasure" has proved a difficult and slippery notion in the history of psychology. The same is true of the idea that the behavior that occurs is "adaptive," be-cause it is awkward to have to explain maladaptive behavior on the basis of a prin-ciple of adaptiveness. The principle of rein-forcement is more exact and rigorous than either the pleasure principle or the adaptive-ness principle. Since the effect of immediate reinforcement is greater than that of reinforce-ment after a delay, the investigator is forced to examine the exact temporal relationships between responses, stimuli, and reinforcement. He is thus provided with a better basis for predicting whether or not adaptive behavior will be learned. Where reinforcement is delayed, some account must be given of the means by which the temporal gap is bridged.

2. The relatively neglected and catchall concept of Ego strength has been elaborated in two directions: first is the beginning of a careful account of higher mental processes; second is the description of the culturally valuable, learned drives and skills. The importance of the foregoing factors in human behavior can hardly be overemphasized. The functioning of higher mental processes and

learned drives is not limited to neuroses or psychotherapy. It is an essential part of the science of human personality.

3. A naturalistic amount is given of the immensely important mechanism of repres-sion. Repression is explained as the inhibition of the cue-producing responses which mediate thinking and reasoning. Just what is lost by repression and gained by therapy is much clearer in the light of this account.

4. Transference is seen as a special case of a wider concept, generalization. This explanation draws attention to the fact that many humdrum habits which facilitate therapy are transferred along with those that obstruct it. The analysis shows also why such intense emotional responses should be directed toward the therapist in the transference situation.

5. The dynamics of conflict behavior are systematically deduced from more basic principles. Thus, a fundamental fact of neurosis —that of conflict—is tied in with general learning theory. A clear understanding of the nature of conflict serves to provide a more rational framework for therapeutic practice.

6. We have been obliged to put great stress on the fact that the patient gets well in real life. Only part of the work essential to therapy is done in the therapeutic situation. Reinforcement theory supplies logical reasons why this should be expected.

7. The somewhat vague concept of "reali-ty" is elaborated in terms of the physical and social conditions of learning, especially the conditions provided by the social structure of a society. In order to predict behavior we must know these conditions as well as the

---

[6] From *Personality and Psychotherapy* by John Dollard and Neal E. Miller. Copyright, 1950, by McGraw-Hill, Inc. Used with per-mission of McGraw-Hill Book Company.

psychological principles involved. Psychology supplies the principles while sociology and social anthropology supply the systematic treatment of the crucial social conditions.

8. The concepts of repression and suppression are supplemented by the parallel ones of inhibition and restraint. The idea that it is important to suppress and restrain tendencies to unconventional thoughts and acts is not a novelty with us.

* * * * *

Four Fundamentals of Learning

Four factors are exceedingly important in learning. These are: drive, cue, response, and reinforcement. The drive impels responses which are usually channelized by cues from other stimuli not strong enough to act as drives but more specifically distinctive than the drive. If the first response is not rewarded, this creates a dilemma in which the extinction of successive nonreinforced responses leads to so-called random behavior. If some one response is followed by reinforcement, the connection between the stimulus pattern and this response is strengthened, so that the next time the same drive and other cues are present this reponse is more likely to occur. Since reinforcements presumably produce their effect by reducing the strength of the drive stimulus, events cannot be rewarding in the absence of an appropriate drive. After the drive has been satiated by sufficient reward, the tendency to make the rewarded response is weakened so that other responses occur until the drive reappears.

* * * * *

Three "Levels" of Generalization and Discrimination

Three "levels" of generalization and discrimination may be distinguished:

1. *Those based solely on innate similarities and differences.* After the subject learns a response to one cue, this response will tend to generalize to other similar cues, with more generalization occurring to cues that are more similar. This is called a *gradient of innate stimulus generalization.* For example, a child who is burned by one object will tend to fear other similar objects, showing more fear of objects that are more similar.

If the response to the original cue is repeatedly reinforced and that to the dissimilar cue is repeatedly nonreinforced, the response to the former will tend to be strengthened while that to the latter will be weakened until a *discrimination* is established. With further experience of being burned by one object but not by others, the child's fear will tend to become restricted to the hot object. Because of generalization, the difficulty in establishing a discrimination will be a function of the similarity of the cues, and if the cues are too similar, it will be impossible to establish a discrimination.

2. *Those in which innate similarities or differences are enhanced by appropriate labels or other cue-producing responses.* Attaching the same label to different cues increases the amount of generalization. Attaching different labels to similar cues decreases the amount of generalization and thus makes subsequent discriminations easier to learn. For example, if a child has already learned to apply the words "hot" and "cold" to the right objects but has had no experience with being burned, he will be more likely to generalize the fear caused by his first serious burn to other objects labeled "hot," and it will be somewhat easier for him to learn to discriminate these from ones labeled "cold."

3. *Those in which labels or other cue-producing responses mediate the transfer of already learned responses.* If the correct instrumental or emotional responses have already been learned to the appropriate labels, these responses can be immediately transferred to a new cue by learning to label it correctly. For example, if the child has already learned to respond appropriately to objects labeled "hot" and "cold" it is possible to transfer this discrimination to the new objects by teaching him to label one "hot" and the other "cold."

It can be seen that the first "level" differs from the other two in that no labeling or other cue-producing response is involved. In the second, the label is already learned but the appropriate response to the label still has to be learned. In the third, the appropriate response to the label has already been learned and is thus available for immediate transfer as soon as new objects are given the correct labels.

Actually the three "levels" blend into one another, as when a child tends to fear a new object because it has been labeled "hot" but is overcome by curiosity, touches it, and is burned, so that fear is reinforced as a response to the label and also as a direct response to the new object. Furthermore, if the label elicits strong enough responses, it may serve as a learned reinforcement. Then the responses that it elicits may become conditioned to the new stimulus object, so that by repeated labeling (without any primary reinforcement such as a burn) the new object becomes able to elicit the responses directly without the need for the continued intervention of the label.

* * * * *

Conditions for Successful Reasoning and Planning

One can see that a number of different conditions have to be met before reasoning and planning can produce adaptive behavior in a given dilemma. First, the direct instrumental responses to the internal drives and external cues must be inhibited in order to give the cue-producing responses time to occur; the subject must stop and think before rushing precipitately into action. Then, the proper thoughts must occur. These can fail to occur either because they are not in the individual's repertory of learned responses or because they are inhibited by competing thoughts. If the cue-producing responses that have been learned do not parallel objects and events in the environment, the solution or plan will be unrealistic. Finally, it is necessary for the thoughts to be carried over into action. In other words, the instrumental responses elicited indirectly via the cue-producing sequence must be stronger than the direct responses to internal drives and external cues. As we shall see, the likelihood of these conditions being met is enormously increased by specific kinds of training that the child receives in the process of socialization.

* * * * *

Social Training in Thinking

The various "levels" of adjustment may now be recapitulated.

At the lower level are direct responses to cues. These may be innate reflexes (like a blink to a cinder in the eye), responses that are originally learned as direct responses (like the blink to a sudden motion toward the eye), or ones that were originally learned as responses to verbal instructions and later so strongly associated with the external cues that they are out of verbal control (like pressing on the floorboards when a child runs in front of a car in which one is a passenger).

On a higher level are responses mediated by one or more intervening cue-producing responses. Because these responses are not limited by the mechanical and social possibilities of the immediate environment, they can become anticipatory or work backward from the goal step by step. This enables them to mediate adaptive, new combinations of responses that would be unlikely to occur otherwise. Thought is obviously highly creative and vastly superior to instrumental trial and error.

Attaching the same label (or other cue-producing response) to two distinctive stimulus objects increases the generalization of emotional and instrumental responses from one to the other. Attaching different labels (or other distinctive cue-producing responses) to two similar stimulus situations increases the discrimination between the two. If the proper habits have been learned, words can arouse strong learned drives or give powerful reward and reassurance. In this way, verbal responses play an especially important role in mediating the foresightful response to remote rewards or punishments.

Cue-producing responses, such as imagery, that are not socially observable are not subject to direct, intensive social training. The use of these private cue-producing responses thus tends to be relatively unsophisticated. On the other hand, the public cue-producing responses, like words and sentences, that are used in social communication receive an enormous amount of social training. The accumulated cultural heritage of generations of trial and error is represented in the categories, common-sense rules of logic, standards of reasonableness, and sequences of orderly narration of language. This greatly increases the usefulness of verbal responses and their derivatives, such as mathematics, in the solution of social, emotional, and instrumental problems.

In our society, there seems to be much more emphasis on formal training in special techniques for solving problems in the physical environment than on ones for solving emotional problems.

Only a modest and uncertain start has been made toward understanding the marvelous intricacies of language and the higher mental processes. In this extremely important area there is a great need for more detailed observations of patients in therapy and of the socialization of children in the home, for a more rigorous theoretical formulation and a more penetrating experimental analysis.

As we increase our scientific knowledge in this area, we may be able to improve our social training in the use of the higher mental processes.

* * * * *

Neurosis as Learned

Conflict itself is no novelty. Emotional conflicts are the constant accompaniment of life at every age and social level. Conflicts differ also in strength, some producing strong and some weak stimuli. Where conflicts are strong and unconscious, the individuals afflicted keep on making the same old mistakes and getting punished in the same old way. To the degree that the conflict can be made conscious, the ingenuity and inventiveness of higher mental life can aid in finding new ways out of the conflict situation. This applies to all emotional dilemmas, to those which survive from early childhood and to those which are created in the course of later life.

High drives produced during the nursing period can have disturbing side-effects. The child first faces severe cultural pressure in the cleanliness-training situation. At this time intense anger-anxiety conflicts can arise. Similarly, in the discipline of the masturbation habit and of heterosexual approach tendencies, the sex-anxiety conflict is regularly created in all of us. In some it has traumatic intensity. When the elements of this conflict are unconscious, they can have an abiding effect on life adjustment in the marital sphere. The culture takes a harsh attitude toward the angry and hostile behavior of children and regularly attaches anxiety to it, usually by direct punishment. Anger can be aroused in any of the situations of childhood where frustrating conditions are created. Conflicts centering around social class and mobility are known, especially in families where the parents have different social aspirations for the child.

Not all conflict arises through the pitting of primary drives one against the other, as in the case of hunger vs. pain. It is possible to have severe conflict based on one primary and one strong learned drive. This is exemplified by the sex-anxiety conflict. It is further possible to have severe conflict when two strong learned drives are involved—as in the case of anger-anxiety. In later life many of the strong learned drives, some quite remote from their primitive sources of reinforcement, can produce painful conflicts. "Ambition" can be pitted against "loyalty." The wish to be truthful can be arrayed against "tact." Wishes for social advancement may be deterred by the fear of appearing vulgar and "pushy." Many of these complex learned drives have never been effectively described in terms of the reinforcing circumstances. We do know, however, that when they compete they can plunge the individual into a painful state.

We must admit that we do not know the exact conditions under which the common conflict-producing circumstances of life generate severe conflicts in some and not-so-severe conflicts in others. We know that the conditions and factors described here *do* occur in those who later turn out to show neurotic behavior. It may be that the circumstances of life are not really "the same for normals and neurotics," that this sameness is an illusion based on poor discrimination of the actual circumstances. Therefore it may actually be that some individuals have much stronger conflicts than others. It may be that some are less well able to use higher mental processes than others and are therefore less well able to resolve traumatic tension. It may be that some are more "predisposed" than others in that they have stronger primary drives, or stronger tendencies to inhibition, or in other unknown respects. It is quite likely that the provocative circumstances of later life which precipitate neuroses are more severe in some cases than others; or that some are exposed to just those circumstances which for them excite neurotic behavior but that others are luckier and do not come into contact with just those adverse conditions which would set them off.

We must also say that the data available are subject to several severe faults. Much of the data is from clinical case histories and may be damaged by various flaws in reporting and by inability to report. There may also be, and probably are, various kinds of sampling errors. Neurotic people may come from "a different basket." We have not been able to study the matter experimentally to see just which factors differentiate neurotic persons from their normal controls.

Transference as a Generalized Response

Strong emotions occur during the course of therapeutic work. They are directed at the therapist and are felt by the patient to be real. They occur because the permissive conditions of therapy weaken repression and inhibition and thus increase the net strength of inhibited tendencies. These tendencies generalize more strongly to the therapist than to others just because the avoidance responses to him are less strong. These responses are ones which, having been long inhibited, have frequently never been labeled. By labeling these emotions while they are occurring, the therapist makes it possible for them to be represented in the patient's reasoning and planning activity. Frequently these responses block therapeutic progress. By identifying them and showing that they are generalized, the therapist mobilizes the learned drives to be reasonable and healthy, thus helping the patient to return to his project of self-understanding. Generalization of emotional response is not only

useful but inevitable; it is not purposive and should not be thought of as a duel.

* * * * *

Therapeutic Learning

Much of therapy consists of teaching the patient new discriminations. Some of these are achieved by directing the patient's attention toward relevant aspects of his environment or behavior. Some are achieved by contrasting the patient's present inhibitions with the lack of punishment in his present environment. Others are achieved by reviving memories of traumatic conditions of childhood, so that they can be contrasted with the different conditions of adult status. When the contrast is clear and immediate, the effect can be direct and automatic. Verbal responses play an important role in discriminations. They can help to revive memories of the past and to direct attention toward relevant details. They can function to make past neurotic habits seem similar to present ones but to make past conditions of reinforcement seem highly different from those of the present. They can also be the means of contrasting neurotic inhibitions of the present with real-life possibilities of gratification. Verbal cues can prevent generalization of anxiety from past to present. They can mediate responses inhibitory of anxiety. They can excite acquired drives which impel the patient to view the world realistically and to act intelligently. As anxiety is reduced by discrimination, reassurance, and extinction, new responses occur. When they reduce neurotic drives, these responses can be the basis of new habits which will permanently resolve the neurotic conflict.

RAYMOND B. CATTELL
(1905–)

Multivariate Experimental Psychology [7]

The Galton-Spearman experimental tradition has been multivariate and non-manipulative, and has developed more directly as a

[7] Raymond B. Cattell (ed.), *Handbook of Multivariate Experimental Psychology* (Chicago: Rand McNally, 1966), p. 18. Reprinted by permission.

response to the inherent needs of the behavorial sciences, whence it has spread to other life sciences. It enables wholistic real-life action to be analyzed without manipulative control. For too long, it was regarded and used as a method for psychometrics and the study of abilities, but it actually admits of manipulative experimental control and has been the main contributor more recently to personality and dynamics, and, potentially, to learning.

* * * * *

The[8] Russian development of psychology out of physiology, by Ivan Pavlov (1849–1936) and his followers is properly called the *reflexological* development because it takes a reflex (initially an actual nerve reflex arc) from stimulus to response as its 'model.' Actually it is a sub-section of that larger, controlled, laboratory, "brass instrument" methodology, which includes the work of Wilhelm Wundt (1832–1920) and many others, and which for reasons soon to be explained we shall call the *univariate experimental* approach (or sometimes the "bivariate," because there is one variable manipulated and one variable watched).

The successes of classical "univariate" experiments in building a clear-cut body of theory and experiment have been very great, notably in perception and learning, though the repeated attempts to bring it fruitfully into contact with personality and psychotherapy have not been considered so successful—except in Russia. There the tradition fits political assumptions, e.g. of materialistic, physiological emphasis, and the notion that heredity is unimportant compared to environmental conditioning. It may become evident as we study the complexity of personality why this univariate approach—this concentration on a single stimulus with a single response—has had only limited success in dealing with individual differences and the behaviour of the functionally unitary organism. Yet personality and learning theory must be brought together.

The second main confluent stream, which has been called *multivariate experiment* (experiment handling many variables at once) had a very different beginning. Sir Francis Galton (1822–1911), a cousin of Darwin, an African explorer, and the discoverer of the cyclone-anticyclone structure in meteorology, was also an indefatigable and very resourceful student of human nature. In connexion with his studies of abilities, he invented (with Karl Pearson, a rather austere mathematical statistician of London University) the correlation coefficient and began to show how the structure and development

of individual personality differences could be elucidated by statistical analyses of natural behaviour outside the laboratory, as well as in it. Close to the laboratory which he founded at University College, London, Charles Spearman (1863–1945) and Sir Cyril Burt continued his multivariate development, and the ball was soon picked up abroad by Thurstone. . . .

Whereas the univariate method follows the older sciences in bringing the man into the laboratory chair, surrounded by brass instruments, the multivariate method says that with sufficient analytical subtlety we can tease out the connexions from the behaviour of the man in his actual life situation—without the false situation of controlling and manipulating. (Multivariate experiment *can* control but it has no *need* to do so.) Consequently, whereas the Wundt-Pavlov methods and interests took their beginnings close to physiology—indeed Pavlov was researching on stomach physiology when he noticed the conditioned reflex, and many of the German psychologists were investigating the physiology of the special senses—the Galton-Spearman developments began broadly with life behaviour as such and especially social behaviour.

Sir Francis Galton gathered statistics on personality and ability wherever it was available, but principally in regard to high cultural performance, while Karl Pearson was especially interested in what the *average* man is like, anthropologically and psychologically. In its break from the classical univariate experiment theirs was a more bold and imaginative step in studying human psychology than Wundt's, and it has led to tremendous developments in mathematical statistical use of the electronic computer in analysing human behaviour. Wundt's clinging more closely to established sciences may have been oriented to giving to the new science of psychology more standing, whereas Galton had the sublime indifference to appearances which one sees in a fox terrier with his nose in a rabbit burrow.

When Spearman, from 1900 to 1930, followed up this early quantitative study of individual differences by setting up controlled "tests," his approach was still not that of "taking a bit of a man into the laboratory" but rather of studying the whole man in virtually natural surroundings, and finding

---

[8] Raymond B. Cattell, *The Scientific Analysis of Personality* (Baltimore: Penguin Books, 1965), pp. 19–23. Reprinted by permission.

out by statistical analysis how various kinds of behaviour are connected. Notably Spearman asked the question, "Is there one general ability, which we may call general intelligence, or are people's minds made up of *a lot of distinct and independent* abilities?" To answer this, he took a few hundred people and gave them thirty to forty different kinds of tests. He then, by a precise computation of correlation coefficients..., found out if people tended to keep the same rank order in different tests. In answering his question (Yes, there *is* a single general intelligence structure), he gave birth to the method of factor analysis....

One can get a more sympathetic understanding of many disagreements over theory, and a wider view of why personality study is developing the way it is, if one keeps in mind the difference between those two traditions, which we have called the univariate and the multivariate. They still remain to some extent distinct, though equally important parts of the true science of experimental psychology now going forward so vigorously in this century. The persisting feature of the Galton–Spearman approach is that it is multivariate, i.e. it studies many measurements on the same person, instead of only one variable or process at a time, as in the Wundt–Pavlov tradition, and that it studies behaviour with less artificial control or interference. The univariate, laboratory method, with its isolation of the single process, has worked well in the older sciences, but where total organisms have to be studied, the theoretical possibility must be faced that one can sometimes hope to find a law only if *the total organism* is included in the observations and experiences —not just a bit of its behaviour. In this respect, the emphasis on "wholeness" in the multivariate method is actually the same as in the clinical method, but it is quantitative and follows explicit calculations of laws and general conclusions. For the clinician appraises the total pattern "by eye," and tries to make generalizations from a good memory, whereas the multivariate experimenter actually *measures* all the variables and may then set an electronic computer to abstract the regularities which exist, instead of depending on human powers of memory and generalization. The clinical approach to personality is thus really that of a multivariate experimenter without benefit of apparatus—and has had

the additional drawback that it produces its personality theories from data gathered from abnormal, diseased processes rather than normal ranges.

There is one other respect in which the psychologist studying personality by multivariate methods has advantages over the classical univariate experimenter who clamps his subject in place in the laboratory. The fact that he can study behaviour in its natural setting means that he can deal with emotionally important matters and real personality learning. Neither our ethics, nor the self-protectiveness of people themselves, will stand for psychologists giving subjects major emotional shocks or altering their whole personalities for a laboratory thesis!

An experimenter exactly following the classical experimental design, but who happened to be a moral imbecile, might with cold logic and force of habit set out to find the effect upon the personality of a mother of losing a child. Furthermore, he would need to "out-Herod Herod" by removing the child in half the cases, and continuing with the child in the other half of his "controlled experiment." Since life itself inevitably makes these tragic "experiments," a researcher in the tradition of the Galton–Spearman statistical tradition will simply compare mothers who have and have not suffered such bereavement and make his analysis of the results "balancing" for the things he cannot manipulate. In short, the method everywhere seeks to get out by subtle statistical analysis of natural data what in the physical sciences would be done by manipulative control.

To follow the classical univariate controlled experiment in personality study would, therefore, mean to be confined to emotionally trivial, superficial matters or else to be forced to experiment on animals—where major frustration and emotional upsets can be applied. But then one encounters the defect that the "personality" of an animal is pretty remote from human personality and culture. On the other hand, the development of beautiful and complex mathematico-statistical methods like factor analysis has enabled us to take natural data, much as the clinician has long done—except that normals are now included—and to find laws and build sound theories about the structure and functioning of personality.

Factor Theory of Personality [9]

Personality Defined

Personality may be defined as that which tells what a man will do when placed in a given situation. This statement can be formulated:

$$R = f(S.P)$$

which says that R, the nature and magnitude of a person's behavioural response, i.e. what he says, thinks, or does, is some function of the S, the stimulus situation in which he is placed and of P, the nature of his personality. For the moment, we do not attempt to say more precisely what f, the function, is. That is something to be found by research. Nor shall we bother too much at this stage about how the stimulus is to be measured. But we can be reasonably certain that we shall want to describe and measure the personality by a number of *traits*, and perhaps also by mood states at the time.

For example, the situation could be a pretty girl sitting on the next seat in a bus. The response of the young man in whose personality we are interested might be to take surreptitious sidelong glances, or to speak to her, or perhaps to attempt to kiss her. If we know even one trait in his personality, namely, his degree of shyness, we might make a tolerable prediction of how long he would remain silent before attempting conversation. If we watched fifty young men in this situation, we might even find a numerical value for f, which relates the score on shyness (say on a ten-point scale) to the length of time in seconds (measured on a stop watch) before he thinks of something to say. Perhaps it would be:

$$\text{Response Time} = 23.5 \times P_s$$

where P_s is the shyness score in personality. It will be noticed that S, the situation, is left out here, because it is a constant, the same for everyone, but essentially we are using the formula $R = f(S.P)$.

* * * * *

Factor Analysis

The trouble with measuring traits is that there are too many of them!

* * * * *

[9] *Ibid.*, pp. 25–26, 55–57, 78–81, 365, 372–373.

The studies showed almost as many different shades of meaning and ways of measuring it, so that the studies could not be integrated. What a tower of Babel would arise in chemistry if every chemist had a different test for the presence of, say, chlorine, and, indeed, no really common conception of what chlorine is!

The answer to this problem, though it has technical complications which are still not fully straightened out by many of its users, is a statistical method called *factor analysis*. Prior to factor analysis some psychologists reached such a stage of desperation that they were ready to fix traits if necessary by fiat, by setting up a commission to say what the important traits are and how they should be defined. Factor analysis, on the other hand, believes that there are natural, unitary structures in personality and that it is these traits, rather than the endless labels in the dictionary, on which we should concentrate. In other words, if there are natural elements in the form of functional unities, logically equivalent to an element in the physical world, then it would be far better to begin our studies —our comparisons and developmental understandings—on measures of such traits.

The problem which baffled psychologists for many years was to find a method which would tease out these functionally unitary influences in the chaotic jungle of human behaviour. But let us ask how, in the literal tropical jungle, the hunter decides whether the dark blobs which he sees are two or three rotting logs or a single alligator? He watches for movement. If they move together—come and disappear together—he infers a single structure. Just so, as John Stuart Mill pointed out in his philosophy of science, the scientist should look for "concomitant variation" in seeking unitary concepts.

When it came to putting this philosophical notion into practice, psychologists were for a while baffled, until the statisticians came to their help. For it is rare for two manifestations literally to go together *every* time they are observed. They become "by chance or nature's changing course untrimmed." How *much* observed going together does there have to be for us to conclude that, but for other interfering circumstances, these two (or more) behavioural manifestations would always constitute a single trait?

The answer to this appeared in the form of

the correlation coefficient, which Sir Francis Galton conceived when he was sheltering, on his daily walk, from a passing shower. The English statistician Pearson and the French mathematician Bravais polished it up, and it became known as the Bravais–Pearson correlation coefficient. The way it works can be seen by looking at Diagram 5.

If a school teacher asks whether skill in English and in arithmetic are quite different traits or expressions of a single trait of general intelligence, he would administer tests of both to, say, a hundred children and plot the results as shown opposite. Each point represents a person, his position being defined by his score on the English axis and his score on the arithmetic axis. If there is a tendency for abilities to 'go together,' the persons will scatter in a long ellipse as shown at (*a*), i.e. when a person's score on English is above average his arithmetic score will tend to be above average, and vice versa. On the other hand, if they are unrelated a random circular mass will appear as at (*b*). If they are negatively related the ellipse will slope backwards as in (*c*). The correlation coefficient is a value derived from these plots, by a calculation shown in Diagram 5.

Behaviour Equation and Specification Equation

It has sometimes been critically remarked about the trait approach that it takes the personality to pieces into recognizable unitary sources but that, like the small boy with the parts of the grandfather clock, it is unable to assemble them again. This has been true of some verbal dialectics, but not of the factor analytic approach, which presents a "mathematical model"—that is to say a set of precise rules for handling and combining the measurements involved. Any such model in science is the very heart of a theory. By it the theory is tested quantitatively, and on the "fit" of the experimental results to the quantities predicted the theory stands or falls. By this test the factor theory of personality does very well, which is not to say, however, that like the Newtonian model for the solar system it may not later need smaller adjustments, based on more comprehensive theory.

To illustrate the integration of traits by the three source traits *A*, *B*, and *C* so far described let us consider people playing tennis. Imagine

fifty young people placed in order of effectiveness as the result of a long series of matches. Obviously, general intelligence, *B*, will enter into success because intelligent planning is necessary in match tennis. Possibly also trait *A* will produce effects because the easy-going affectothymes will not follow up with the tenacity and precision of the sizothymes. Finally, ego strength, *C*, will also play a part because a low *C* person, who loses his temper easily or easily becomes discouraged, will not use his abilities to best advantage.

Presumably, by adding each person's scores on these three traits (*A* and *C* negatively) we should obtain a first approximation to the relative goodness of each, thus:

$$R_i = -A_i + B_i - C_i$$

where R_i is the tennis "response" or performance of any individual and the others are his trait scores. However, probably intelligence is decidedly more important than sizothymia, and in fact we can find this out by working out the correlation between the performance rank, *R*, and *A*, *B*, etc. If intelligence is in fact involved more it will have a higher correlation with tennis success. By putting in these correlation "weights," which might be as follows, we get a better estimate, thus:

$$R_i = -0.1A_i + 0.6B_i - 0.4C_i$$

These values (−0.1, +0.6, and −0.4) are also called *loadings*, showing the degree of involvement of each source trait in the given performance, and they can be alternatively reached by the factor analytic process itself.

At this point it will occur to the commonsense observer that the sheer amount of practice each person has had at tennis is also important, and we ought to add a term *T* for tennis practice to this, the weight for which can also be found by correlation. Then we should have:

$$R_i = -0.1\,A_i + 0.6\,B_i - 0.4\,C_i + 0.7\,T$$

Traits *A*, *B*, and *C* are called *common* traits, because they enter and are common to a lot of things besides tennis. But *T* is called a specific, because it is a set of dexterities quite specific to practice in this one thing, tennis.

The equation just set out is a very important one with many implications for personality testing, and it is called the *specification equation*, because it specifies the way in which

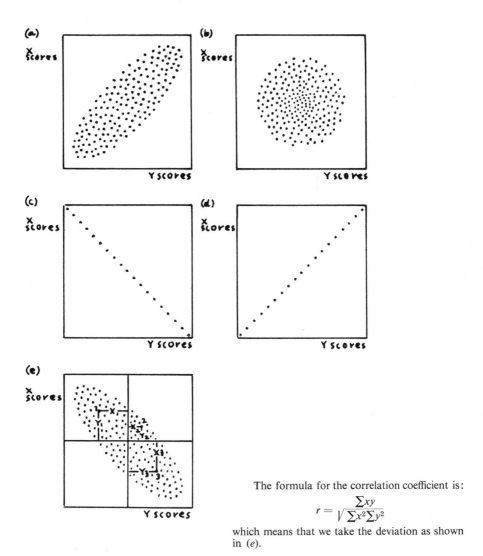

The formula for the correlation coefficient is:

$$r = \frac{\sum xy}{\sqrt{\sum x^2 \sum y^2}}$$

which means that we take the deviation as shown in (e).

DIAGRAM 5. Correspondences of measurement on people in various sizes of correlation coefficient.

traits are to be combined to predict and understand any particular performance or response. For instance, having obtained the correlations on our fifty tennis players we could take a fifty-first person, whose play has never been seen, and, from his scores on traits A, B, and C, and the specific, T, weighted and added as in the equation, we might get a pretty good estimate of how well he will actually perform.

Normally, of course, one would consider more than three source traits, and the specification equation can be put in perfectly general form up to any number (K) of factors

$$R_{ij} = b_{jA}A_i + b_{jB}B_i + ... b_{jK}K_i + b_{jS}S_j$$

where j is *any* behavioural response, S_j is the specific to it, and the b's are weights, peculiar to j and to each factor. These b's are mathematically weights but are best psychologically called *situational indices*, or *behavioural situation indices* (hence "*b*"), because they show how much each personality factor is involved in the situation *j*. To the geometrically inclined, it may be helpful to see these *b*'s as tangents, showing how rapidly the performance R_j increases as endowment in the given personality factor increases.

At this point the reader may feel like the modern philosopher who, looking at the work of the physicists, has said, "If you follow their analysis of matter you will not get anything like common sense has always supposed matter to be. You will get mathematics." Perhaps the best thing would be to go to arithmetic examples and show, in known persons, that if you insert their "standard scores" (a device to bring all factors to the same units) on traits you in fact get good predictions from these weights. Such illustration is best deferred, however, to the "applied" Chapter 11. Here we are concerned

only with the principle of combining, and it will be noticed that we have used the simplest way of integrating, namely *adding* (or subtracting) the effect of one trait to that of another. One can imagine that traits might get together in some more complex way, such as by one multiplying the effect of another, or by one catalysing another, and in advanced work these possibilities are being investigated. But science starts with the simplest hypothesis or model and gives it up only if and when some less likely arrangement is required by new facts. At present the additive action of traits in the specification equation fits the date quite well.

If one thinks back now to our general behaviour equation

$$R_{ij} = f(S_j P_i)$$

and the occasion when we put a numerical weight for the situation *S*, he will recognize that we have at last settled on a form for the function *f*. We are now saying that the

Technical and popular labels for personality factors A to Q_i

Low Score Description	Factor		Factor	High Score Description
Reserved (Sizothymia)	$A-$	vs	$A+$	Outgoing (Affectothymia)
Less intelligent (Low 'g')	$B-$	vs	$B+$	More intelligent (High 'g')
Emotional (Low ego strength)	$C-$	vs	$C+$	Stable (High ego strength)
Humble (Submissiveness)	$E-$	vs	$E+$	Assertive (Dominance)
Sober (Desurgency)	$F-$	vs	$F+$	Happy-go-lucky (Surgency)
Expedient (Lower super-ego)	$G-$	vs	$G+$	Conscientious (High super-ego)
Shy (Threctia)	$H-$	vs	$H+$	Venturesome (Parmia)
Tough-minded (Harria)	$I-$	vs	$I+$	Tender-minded (Premsia)
Trusting (Alaxia)	$L-$	vs	$L+$	Suspicious (Protension)
Practical (Praxernia)	$M-$	vs	$M+$	Imaginative (Autia)
Forthright (Artlessness)	$N-$	vs	$N+$	Shrewd (Shrewdness)
Placid (Assurance)	$O-$	vs	$O+$	Apprehensive (Guilt-proneness)
Conservative (Conservatism)	Q_1-	vs	Q_1+	Experimenting (Radicalism)
Group-tied (Group adherence)	Q_2-	vs	Q_2+	Self-sufficient (Self-sufficiency)
Casual (Low integration)	Q_3-	vs	Q_3+	Controlled (High self-concept)
Relaxed (Low ergic tension)	Q_4-	vs	Q_4+	Tense (Ergic tension)

stimulation S_j is represented by a lot of situational indices, b_{jA}, b_{jB}, etc., thus:

$$S_j = b_{jA}, b_{jB} \ldots b_{jK} \qquad (1)$$

and that the person, P_i, is represented by a lot of dimensions thus:

$$P_i = A_i, B_i \ldots K_i \qquad (2)$$

When we link these into a single equation we have:

$$R_{ij} = b_{jA}A_i + b_{jB}B_i \ldots + b_{jK}K_i, \text{ etc.} \qquad (3)$$

A multidimensional person comes into contact with a multidimensional situation, and the result is a response of magnitude peculiar to that individual i.

Glossary

Multivariate experiment. An experimental design in which many variables are allowed to vary simultaneously, and in which all possible relations among them are worked out.

* * * * *

P-technique. A factor analytic design which measures a single person on the same set of variables repeatedly over a number of different occasions. Correlations between the variables are computed over these occasions as entries, then factor analysed. P-technique and incremental factor analysis are the two main methods for determining dimensions of personality change-over-time (or states).

* * * * *

Q-data. Evidence on personality from self-evaluative, introspective report, as in the consulting room or filling out a questionnaire.

Q'-technique. A method in which one correlates people over tests (instead of conversely as in *R-technique*) to see how alike they are. It is not a method of factor analysis (as in Q-technique) but only of searching for clusters of people as shown by the correlations.

* * * * *

R-technique. Ordinary factor analysis in which tests are given to people and correlated over people.

GORDON W. ALLPORT
(1897–1967)

Personalistic Theory of Personality [10]

PERSONALITY IS THE DYNAMIC OR-GANIZATION WITHIN THE INDIVI-DUAL OF THOSE PSYCHOPHYSICAL SYSTEMS THAT DETERMINE HIS UNIQUE ADJUSTMENTS TO HIS EN-VIRONMENT

This formulation contains the seeds of the hierarchical, integrative, adjustive, and distinctive classes of definitions described above. In a sense, therefore, *it represents a synthesis of contemporary psychological usage.* But each portion of the definition is to be accurately understood.

Dynamic Organization. To escape from the sterile enumerations of the omnibus definitions it is necessary to stress active organization. The crucial problem of psychology has always

been mental organization (association)....
Hence "organization" must appear in the definition. Yet this organization must be regarded as constantly evolving and changing as motivational and as self-regulating: hence the qualification "dynamic." Organization must also imply at times the correlative process of *disorganization*, especially in those personalities that we are wont to regard as "abnormal."

Psychophysical Systems. Habits, specific and general attitudes, sentiments, and dispositions of other orders are all psychophysical systems. In later chapters these dispositions will be ordered within a theory of *traits.* The term "system" refers to traits or groups of traits in a latent or active condition. The term "psychophysical" reminds us that personality is neither exclusively mental nor exclusively neural. The organization entails the operation of both body and mind, inextricably fused into a personal unity.

Determine. This term is a natural consequence of the biophysical view. Personality

[10] From *Personality: A Psychological Interpretation* by Gordon W. Allport. Copyright 1937 by Holt, Rinehart and Winston, Inc. Copyright © 1965 by Gordon W. Allport, pp. 48-50, 194, 196, 341. Reprinted by permission of Holt, Rinehart and Winston, Inc.

is something and *does* something. It is not synonymous with behavior or activity; least of all is it merely the impression that this activity makes on others. It is what lies *behind* specific acts and *within* the individual. The systems that constitute personality are in every sense *determining tendencies*, and when aroused by suitable stimuli provoke those adjustive and expressive acts by which the personality comes to be known.

Unique. Strictly speaking every adjustment of every person is unique, in time and place, and in quality. In a sense, therefore, this criterion seems redundant. It becomes important, however, in our later discussions of the problem of *quantitative* variation among individuals in respect to the so-called "common" traits and is therefore emphasized in the definition.

Adjustments to His Environment. This phase has a functional and evolutionary significance. Personality is a mode of survival. "Adjustments," however, must be interpreted broadly enough to include maladjustments, and "environment" to include the behavioral environment (meaningful to the individual) as well as the surrounding geographical environment.

Above all, adjustments must not be considered as merely reactive adaptation such as plants and animals are capable of. The adjustments of men contain a great amount of spontaneous, creative behavior toward the environment. Adjustment to the physical world as well as to the imagined or ideal world—both being factors in the "behavioral environment"—involves *mastery* as well as passive adaptation.

* * * * *

Traits

Variable though they are, still in every mature personality certain *central* traits can normally be identified. So too can *secondary* traits, though these are less distinctive, less prominent, and more circumscribed in their operation. Whenever a disposition is so little generalized that it is aroused by only a narrow range of stimulus situations, it is more properly called an *attitude* than a trait. Somewhat rarely a personality is dominated by one outstanding *cardinal* trait, to which other

dispositions serve as merely subsidiary, congruent foci.

* * * * *

Functional Autonomy

Let us begin in a common sense way. An ex-sailor has a craving for the sea, a musician longs to return to his instrument after an enforced absence, a city-dweller yearns for his native hills, and a miser continues to amass his useless horde. Now, the sailor may have first acquired his love for the sea as an incident in his struggle to earn a living. The sea was merely a conditioned stimulus associated with satisfaction of his "nutritional craving." But now the ex-sailor is perhaps a wealthy banker; the original motive is destroyed; and yet the hunger for the sea persists unabated, even increases in intensity as it becomes more remote from the "nutritional segment."

* * * * *

Science must generalize.... Perhaps it must, but what the objectors forget is that *a general law may be a law that tells how uniqueness comes about.* It is manifest error to assume that a general principle of motivation must involve the postulation of abstract or general motives. The principle of functional autonomy, here described, is general enough to meet the needs of science, but particularized enough in its operation to account for the uniqueness of personal conduct.

The dynamic psychology proposed here regards adult motives as infinitely varied and, as self-sustaining, *contemporary* systems, growing out of antecedent systems, but functionally independent of them. Just a as child gradually repudiates his dependence on his parents, develops a will of his own, becomes self-active and self-determining, and outlives his parents, so it is with motives. Each motive has a definite point of origin which may lie in the hypothetical instincts, or, more likely, in the organic tensions and diffuse irritability.

The Nature of Prejudice [11]

In all cases of intense character-conditioned prejudice a common factor emerges which

[11] Gordon W. Allport, *The Nature of Prejudice* (Reading, Mass.: Addison-Wesley Publishing, 1954), pp. 396–397. Reprinted by permission.

Newcomb has called "threat orientation." Underlying insecurity seems to lie at the root of the personality. The individual cannot face the world unflinchingly and in a forthright manner. He seems fearful of himself, of his own instincts, of his own consciousness, of change, and of his social environment. Since he can live in comfort neither with himself nor with others, he is forced to organize his whole style of living, including his social attitudes, to fit his crippled condition. It is not his specific social attitudes that are malformed to start with; it is rather his own ego that is crippled.

The crutch he needs must perform several functions. It must give reassurance for past failures, safe guidance for present conduct, and ensure confidence in facing the future. While prejudice by itself does not do all these things, it develops as an important incident in the total protective adjustment.

To be sure, not all character-conditioned prejudice serves precisely the same purposes in every prejudiced personality, for "threat orientation" differs in nature from person to person. In some, for example, it may be particularly related to unresolved infantile conflicts with parents or siblings, in others to persistent failure in later years. But in any case, we are likely to find a picture of ego-alienation, longing for definiteness, for safety, for authority. Personalities which for any reason feel threatened are likely to evolve similar patterns of accommodation to life in general.

An essential feature of this pattern is *repression.* Since the person cannot in his conscious life face and master the conflicts presented to him, he represses them in whole or in part. They are fragmented, forgotten, not faced. The ego simply fails to integrate the myriad of impulses that arise within the personality and the myriad of environmental presses without. This failure engenders feelings of insecurity, and these feelings engender, in turn, repression.

Thus an outstanding result of studies of bigoted personalities seems to be the discovery of a sharp cleavage between conscious and unconscious layers. In a study of anti-Semitic college girls they appeared on the surface to be charming, happy, well-adjusted, and entirely normal girls. They were polite, moral, and seemed devoted to parents and friends. This was what an ordinary observer would see. But probing deeper (with the aid of projective tests, interviews, case histories), these girls were found to be very different. Underneath the conventional exterior there lurked intense anxiety, much buried hatred toward parents, destructive and cruel impulses. For tolerant college students, however, the same cleavage did not exist. Their lives were more of a piece. Repressions were fewer and milder. The *persona* they presented to the world was not a mask but was their true personality. Having few repressions, they suffered no ego-alienation, and facing their own calamities frankly, they needed no projection screen.

ABRAHAM H. MASLOW
(1908–   )

Self-Actualizationism [12]

I think it is finally possible to begin to delineate this view of human nature as a total, single, comprehensive system of psychology.... Finding a single label for it is still a difficult task, perhaps a premature one. I have called it the "holistic-dynamic" psychology to express my conviction about its major

roots. Some have called it "organismic" following Goldstein.

* * * * *

Because of the limited space I have, I will present only some of the major propositions of this point of view....

1. We have, each one of us, an essential inner nature which is intrinsic, given, "natural" and usually, very resistant to change.

* * * * *

I include in this essential inner nature instinctoid needs, capacities, talents, anatomi-

---

[12] Reprinted with permission of the Association for Supervision and Curriculum Development and A. H. Maslow. Copyright © 1962 by the Association for Supervision and Curriculum Development.

cal equipment, physiological balances, pre-natal and natal injuries, and traumata to the neonate.

* * * * *

2. Each person's inner nature has some characteristics which all other selves have (species-wide) and some which are unique to the person (idiosyncratic). The need for love characterizes every human being that is born (although it can disappear later under certain circumstances). Musical genius, however, is given to very few and these differ markedly from each other in style, e.g., Mozart and Debussy.

3. It is possible to study this inner nature scientifically and objectively (that is, with the right kind of "science") and to discover what it is like (*discover*, not invent or construct). It is also possible to do this subjectively, by inner search and by psychotherapy, and the two enterprises supplement and support each other.

4. Even though weak, this inner nature rarely disappears or dies, in the usual person, in the U.S. (such disappearance or dying is possible however). It persists underground, unconsciously, even though denied and re-pressed. Like the voice of the intellect, it speaks softly but it *will* be heard, even if in a distorted form. That is, it has a dynamic force of its own, pressing always for open, uninhibited expression. Effort must be used in its suppression or repression from which fatigue can result. This force is one main aspect of the "will to health," the urge to grow, the pressure to self-actualization, the quest for one's identity. It is this that makes psychotherapy, education and self-improve-ment possible in principle.

5. However, this inner core, or self, grows into adulthood only partly by (objective or subjective) discovery, uncovering and ac-ceptance of what is "there" beforehand. Partly it is also a creation of the person himself. Life is a continual series of choices for the individual in which a main determinant of choice is the person as he already is (including his goals for himself, his courage or fear, his feeling of responsibility, his ego-strength or "will power," etc.). We can no longer think of the person as "fully determined" where this phrase implies "determined only by forces external to the person." The person,

insofar as he *is* a real person, is his own main determinant. Every person is, in part, "his own project" and makes himself.

6. No psychological health is possible unless this essential core of the person is fundamentally accepted, loved and respected by others and by himself, (the converse is not necessarily true, i.e., that if the core is re-spected, etc., then psychological health must result, since other prerequisite conditions must also be satisfied).

The psychological health of the chrono-logically immature is called healthy growth. The psychological health of the adult is called variously, self-fulfillment, emotional maturity, individuation, productiveness, self-actualiza-tion, etc.

Healthy growth is conceptually subordinate, for it is usually defined now as "growth toward self-actualization," etc. . . .

Self-actualization is defined in various ways but a solid core of agreement is perceptible. All definitions accept or imply, (*a*) acceptance and expression of the inner core or self, i.e., actualization of these latent capacities, and potentialities, "full functioning," availability of the human and personal essence. (*b*) They all imply minimal presence of ill health, neurosis, psychosis, of loss or diminution of the basic human and personal capacities.

7. If this essential core (inner nature) of the person is frustrated, denied or suppressed, sickness results, sometimes in obvious forms, sometimes in subtle and devious forms, some-times immediately, sometimes later.

* * * * *

That is, general-illness of the personality is seen as any falling short of growth, or of self-actualization. And the main source of illness although (not the only one) is seen as frustration (of the basic needs, of idio-syncratic potentials, of expression of the self, and of the tendency of the person to grow in his own style) especially in the early years of life.

8. This inner nature, as much as we know of it so far, is definitely not "evil," but is either what we adults in our culture call "good," or else it is neutral. The most accu-rate way to express this is to say that it is "prior to good and evil." There is little question about this if we speak of the inner nature of the infant and child. The statement

is much more complex if we speak of the "infant" as he still exists in the adult.

9. "Evil" behavior has mostly referred to unwarranted hostility, cruelty, destructiveness, "mean" aggressiveness. This we do not know enough about. To the degree that this quality of hostility is instinctoid, mankind has one kind of future. To the degree that it is reactive (a response to bad treatment), mankind has a very different kind of future. My opinion is that the weight of the evidence so far indicates that *destructive* hostility is reactive, because uncovering therapy reduces it, and changes its quality into "healthy" self-affirmation, forcefulness, righteous indignation, etc. In any case, the *ability* to be aggressive and angry is found in all self-actualizing people, who are able to let it flow forth freely when the external situation "calls for" it.

* * * * *

10. This inner core, even though it is biologically based and "instinctoid," is weak rather than strong. It is easily overcome, suppressed or repressed. It may even be killed off permanently. Humans no longer have instincts in the animal sense, powerful, unmistakable inner voices which tell them unequivocally what to do, when, where, how and with whom. All that we have left are instinct-remnants. And furthermore, these are weak, subtle and delicate, very easily drowned out by learning, by cultural expectations, by fear, by disapproval, etc. They are *hard* to know, rather than easy. Authentic selfhood can be defined in part as being able to hear these impulse-voices within oneself, i.e., to know what one really wants or doesn't want, what one is fit for and what one is *not* fit for, etc.

11. For all these reasons, it is at this time best to bring out and encourage, or at the very least, to recognize this inner nature, rather than to suppress or repress it. Pure spontaneity consists of free, uninhibited, uncontrolled, trusting, unpremeditated expression of the self, i.e., of the psychic forces, with minimal interference by consciousness.

* * * * *

12. Coordinate with this "acceptance" of the self, of fate, of one's call, is the conclusion that the main path to health and self-fulfill-

ment for the masses is via basic need gratification rather than via frustration.

* * * * *

13. In the normal development of the normal child, it is now known that *most* of the time, if he is given a really free choice, he will choose what is good for his growth. This he does because it tastes good, feels good, gives pleasure or *delight*. This implies that *he* "knows" better than anyone else what is good for him. A permissive regime means not that adults gratify his needs directly but make it possible for *him* to gratify his needs, and make his own choices, i.e., let him *be*.

* * * * *

14. But we know also that the *complete absence* of frustration is dangerous. To be strong, a person must acquire frustration-tolerence, the ability to perceive physical reality as essentially indifferent to human wishes, the ability to love others and to enjoy their need-gratification as well as one's own (not to use other people only as means). The child with a good basis of safety, love and respect-need-gratification, is able to profit from nicely graded frustrations and become stronger thereby. If they are more than he can bear, if they overwhelm him, we call them traumatic, and consider them dangerous rather than profitable.

* * * * *

15. To make growth and self-actualization possible, it is necessary to understand that capacities, organs and organ systems press to function and express themselves and to be used and exercised, and that such use is satisfying, and disuse irritating. The muscular person likes to use his muscles, indeed, *has* to use them in order to "feel good" and to achieve the subjective feeling of harmonious, successful, uninhibited functioning (spontaneity) which is so important an aspect of good growth and psychological health. So also for intelligence, for the uterus, the eyes, the capacity to love. Capacities clamor to be used, and cease their clamor only when they *are* well used. That is, capacities are also needs. Not only it is fun to use our capacities, but it is also necessary. The unused capacity or organ can become a disease center or else atrophy, thus diminishing the person.

16. The psychologist proceeds on the assumption that for his purposes there are two kinds of worlds, two kinds of reality, the natural world and the psychic world, the world of unyielding facts and the world of wishes, hopes, fears, emotions, the world which runs by non-psychic rules and the world which runs by psychic laws. This differentiation is not very clear except at its extremes, where there is no doubt that delusions, dreams and free associations are lawful and yet utterly different from the lawfulness of logic and from the lawfulness of the world which would remain if the human species died out. This assumption does not deny that these worlds are related and may even fuse.

* * * * *

17. Immaturity can be contrasted with maturity from the motivational point of view, as the process of gratifying the deficiency-needs in their proper order. Maturity, or self-actualization, from this point of view, means to transcend the deficiency-needs. This state can be described then as a meta-motivated, or unmotivated (if deficiencies are seen as the only motivations). It can also be described as self-actualizing, Being, expressing, rather than coping. This state of Being, rather than of striving, is suspected to be synonymous with selfhood, with being "authentic," with being a person, with being fully human. The process of growth is the process of *becoming* a person. *Being* a person is different.

18. Immaturity can also be differentiated from maturity in terms of the cognitive capacities (and also in terms of the emotional capacities). Immature and mature cognition have been best described by Werner and Piaget. I wish to add another differentiation, that between D-cognition and B-cognition (D = Deficiency; B = Being). D-cognition can be defined as the cognitions which are organized from the point of view of basic needs or deficiency-needs and their gratification and frustration. That is, D-cognition could be called selfish cognition, in which the world is organized into gratifiers and frustrators of our own needs, with other characteristics being ignored or slurred. The cognition of the object, in its own right and its own Being, without reference to its need-gratifying or need-frustrating qualities, that is, without primary reference to its value for the observer or its effects upon him, can be called B-cognition (or self-transcending, or unselfish, or objective cognition). The parallel with maturity is by no means perfect, (children can also cognize in a selfless way) but in general, it is mostly true that with increasing selfhood or firmness of personal identity (or acceptance of one's own inner nature) B-cognition becomes easier and more frequent. (This is true even though D-cognition remains for *all* human beings, including the mature ones, the main tool for living-in-the-world).

* * * * *

19. A by-product of this aspect of cognition is a better understanding of the higher and lower levels of love. D-love can be differentiated from B-love on approximately the same basis as D-cognition and B-cognition, or D-motivation and B-motivation. No ideally good relation to another human being, especially a child, is possible without B-love.

* * * * *

20. Though, in principle, growth towards self-actualization is easy, in practice it rarely happens (by my criteria, certainly in less than 1 % of the adult population).

* * * * *

21. Growth has not only rewards and pleasures but also many intrinsic pains and always will have. Each step forward is a step into the unfamiliar and is possibly dangerous. It also means giving up something familiar and good and satisfying. It frequently means a parting and a separation, with consequent nostalgia, loneliness and mourning. It also often means giving up a simpler and easier and less effortful life, in exchange for a more demanding, more difficult life. Growth forward *is in spite* of these losses and therefore requires courage and strength in the individual, as well as protection, permission and encouragement from the environment, especially for the child.

22. It is therefore useful to think of growth or lack of it as the resultant of a dialectic between growth-fostering forces and growth-discouraging forces (regression, fear, pains of growth, ignorance, etc.).

23. All this implies a naturalistic system of values, a by-product of the empirical description of the deepest tendencies of the human species and of specific individuals.

* * * * *

24. The state of being without a system of values is psychopathogenic, we are learning. The human being needs a framework of values, a philosophy of life, a religion or religion-surrogate to live by and understand by, in about the same sense that he needs sunlight, calcium or love. This I have called the "cognitive need to understand." The value-illnesses which result from valuelessness are called variously anhedonia, anomie, apathy, amorality, hopelessness, cynicism, etc., and can become somatic illness as well.

25. At the level of self-actualizing, many dichotomies become resolved, opposites are seen to be unities and the whole dichotomous way of thinking is recognized to be immature. For self-actualizing people, there is a strong tendency for selfishness and unselfishness to fuse into a higher, superordinate unity. Work tends to be the same as play, vocation and avocation become the same thing. When duty is pleasant and pleasure is fulfillment of duty, then they lose their separateness and oppositeness. The highest maturity is discovered to include a childlike quality, and we discover healthy children to have some of the qualities of mature self-actualization. . . .

26. One especially important finding in self-actualizing people is that they tend to integrate the Freudian dichotomies and trichotomies, i.e., the conscious, preconscious and the unconscious, (as well as id, ego, superego). The Freudian "instincts" and the defenses are less sharply set off against each other. The impulses are more expressed and less controlled; the controls are less rigid, inflexible, anxiety-determined. The superego is less harsh and punishing and less set off against the ego. The primary and secondary cognitive processes are more equally available and more equally valued, (instead of the primary processes being stigmatized as pathological). Indeed in the "peak-experience" the walls between them tend to fall together.

* * * * *

27. Healthy people are more integrated in another way. In them the conative, the cognitive, the affective and the motor are less separated from each other, and are more synergic, i.e., working collaboratively without conflict to the same ends.

* * * * *

28. This development toward the concept of a healthy unconscious, and of a healthy irrationality, sharpens our awareness of the limitations of purely abstract thinking, of verbal thinking and of analytic thinking.

* * * * *

29. This ability of healthier people to dip into the unconscious and preconscious, to use and value their primary processes instead of fearing them, to accept their impulses instead of always controlling them, to be able to regress voluntarily without fear, turns out to be one of the main conditions of creativity. We can then understand why psychological health is so closely tied up with certain universal forms of creativeness (aside from special-talent), as to lead some writers to make them almost synonymous.

* * * * *

30. Esthetic perceiving and creating and esthetic peak-experiences are seen to be a central aspect of human life and of psychology and education rather than a peripheral one. This is true for several reasons. (1) All the peak-experiences are (among other characteristics) integrative of the splits within the person, between persons, within the world, and between the person and the world. Since one aspect of health is integration, the peak-experiences are moves toward health and are themselves, momentary healths. (2) These experiences are life-validating, i.e., they make life worthwhile. . . .

31. Self-actualization does not mean a transcendence of all human problems. Conflict, anxiety, frustration, sadness, hurt, and guilt can all be found in healthy human beings. In general, the movement, with increasing maturity, is from neurotic pseudo-problems to the real, unavoidable, existential problems, inherent in the nature of man (even at his best) living in a particular kind of world. Even though he is not neurotic he may be troubled by real, desirable and necessary guilt rather than neurotic guilt, (which isn't desirable or necessary), by an intrinsic conscience

(rather than the Freudian superego). Even though he has transcended the problems of Becoming, there remain the problems of Being. To be untroubled when one *should* be troubled can be a sign of sickness. Sometimes, smug people have to be scared "*into* their wits."

32. Self-actualization is not altogether general. It takes place via femaleness *or* maleness, which are prepotent to general-humanness. That is, one must first be a healthy, femaleness-fulfilled woman before general-human self-actualization becomes possible.

There is also a little evidence that different constitutional types actualize themselves in somewhat different ways (because they have different inner selves to actualize).

33. Another crucial aspect of healthy growth to selfhood is dropping away the techniques used by the child, in his weakness and smallness for adapting himself to the strong, large, all-powerful, omniscient, god-like adults. He must replace these with the techniques of being strong and independent and of being a parent himself.

* * * * *

34. From this point of view, a society or a culture can be either growth-fostering or growth-inhibiting. The sources of growth and of humanness are essentially within the human person and are not created or invented by society, which can only help or hinder the development of humanness, just as a gardener can help or hinder the growth of a rosebush, but cannot determine that it shall be an oak tree. This is true even though we know that a culture is a sine qua non for the actualization of humanness itself, e.g., language, abstract thought, ability to love; but these exist as potentialities in human germ plasm prior to culture.

This makes theoretically possible a comparative sociology, transcending and including cultural relativity. The "better" culture gratifies all basic human needs and permits self-actualization. The "poorer" cultures do not. The same is true for education. To the extent that it fosters growth toward self-actualization, it is "good" education.

* * * * *

35. The achievement of self-actualization

(in the sense of autonomy) paradoxically makes *more* possible the transcendance of self, and of self-consciousness and of selfishness. It makes it *easier* for the person to be homonomous, i.e., to merge himself as a part in a larger whole than himself.

* * * * *

36. An important existential problem is posed by the fact that self-actualized persons (and *all* people in their peak-experiences) occasionally live out-of-time and out-of-the-world, (atemporal and aspatial) even though mostly they *must* live in the outer world. Living in the inner psychic world (which is ruled by psychic laws and not by the laws of outer-reality), i.e., the world of experience, of emotion, of wishes and fears and hopes, of love, of poetry, art, and fantasy, is different from living in and adapting to the non-psychic reality which runs by laws he never made and which are not essential to his nature even though he has to live by them. The person who is not afraid of this inner, psychic world, can enjoy it to such an extent that it may be called Heaven by contrast with the more effortful, fatiguing, externally responsible, world of "reality," of striving and coping, of right and wrong, of truth and falsehood.

* * * * *

37. The foregoing propositions generate a different understanding of the role of action in psychology. Goal-directed, motivated, coping, striving, purposeful action is an aspect or by-product of the necessary transactions between a psyche and a non-psychic world.

* * * * *

38. From Freud we learned that the past exists *now* in the person. Now we must learn, from growth theory and self-actualization theory that the future also *now* exists in the person in the form of ideals, hopes, goals, unrealized potentials, mission, fate, destiny, etc. One for whom no future exists is reduced to the concrete, to hopelessness, to emptiness. For him, time must be endlessly "filled." Striving, the usual organizer of most activity, when lost, leaves the person unorganized and unintegrated.

23

German Gestalt Psychology

MAX WERTHEIMER
(1880–1943)

Gestalt Psychology [1]

The fundamental "formula" of Gestalt theory might be expressed in this way: There are wholes, the behaviour of which is not determined by that of their individual elements, but where the part-processes are themselves determined by the intrinsic nature of the whole. It is the hope of Gestalt theory to determine the nature of such wholes.

* * * * *

Gestalt theory has to do with concrete research; it is not only an *outcome* but a *device:* not only a theory *about* results but a means toward further discoveries. This is not merely the proposal of one or more problems but an attempt to *see* what is really taking place in science. This problem cannot be solved by listing possibilities for systematization, classification, and arrangement. If it is to be attacked at all, we must be guided by the spirit of the new method and by the concrete nature of the things themselves which we are studying, and set ourselves to penetrate to that which is really given by nature.

There is another difficulty that may be illustrated by the following example. Suppose a mathematician shows you a proposition and you begin to "classify" it. This proposition, you say, is of such and such type, belongs in this or that historical category, and so on. Is that how the mathematician works?

"Why, you haven't grasped the thing at all," the mathematician will exclaim. "See here, this formula is not an independent,

closed fact that can be dealt with for itself alone. You must see its dynamic *functional* relationship to the whole from which it was lifted or you will never understand it."

What holds for the mathematical formula applies also to the "formula" of Gestalt theory. The attempt of Gestalt theory to disclose the functional meaning of its own formula is no less strict than is the mathematician's. The attempt to explain Gestalt theory in a short essay is the more difficult because of the terms which are used: part, whole, intrinsic determination. All of them have in the past been the topic of endless discussions where each disputant has understood them differently. And even worse has been the cataloguing attitude adopted toward them. What they *lacked* has been actual research. Like many another "philosophic" problem they have been withheld from contact with reality and scientific work.

About all I can hope for in so short a discussion is to suggest a few of the problems which at present occupy the attention of Gestalt theory and something of the way they are being attacked.

To repeat: the *problem* has not merely to do with scientific work—it is a fundamental problem of our times. Gestalt theory is not something suddenly and unexpectedly dropped upon us from above; it is, rather, a palpable convergence of problems ranging throughout the sciences and the various philosophic standpoints of modern times.

Let us take, for example, an event in the history of psychology. One turned from a living experience to science and asked what it had to say about this experience, and one found an assortment of elements, sensations, images, feelings, acts of will and laws governing these elements—and was told, "Take your choice, reconstruct from them the experience you had." Such procedure led to difficulties in concrete psychological research and to the

---
[1] Max Wertheimer, "Gestalt theory," in Willis D. Ellis (ed.), *A Source Book of Gestalt Psychology* (London: Kegan Paul, Trench, Trubner, 1938), pp. 2–5; original German, *Über Gestalttheorie*, an address delivered before the Kant Society, Berlin, December 17, 1924. Reprinted by permission.

emergence of problems which defied solution by the traditional analytic methods. Historically the most important impulse came from von Ehrenfels who raised the following problem. Psychology had said that experience is a compound of elements: we hear a melody and then, upon hearing it again, memory enables us to recognize it. But what is it that enables us to recognize the melody when it is played in a new key? The sum of the elements is different, yet the melody is the same; indeed, one is often not even aware that a transposition has been made.

When in retrospect we consider the prevailing situation we are struck by two aspects of von Ehrenfels's thesis; on the one hand one is surprised at the essentially summative character of his theory, on the other one admires his courage in propounding and defending his proposition. Strictly interpreted von Ehrenfels's position was this: I play a familiar melody of six tones and employ six *new* tones, yet you recognize the melody despite the change. There must be a something *more* than the sum of six tones, viz. a seventh something, which is the form-quality, the *Gestaltqualität*, of the original six. It is this *seventh* factor or element which enabled you to recognize the melody despite its transposition.

However strange this view may seem, it shares with many another subsequently abandoned hypothesis the honour of having clearly seen and emphasized a fundamental problem.

But other explanations were also proposed. One maintained that in addition to the six tones there were intervals—relations—and that *these* were what remained constant. In other words we are asked to assume not only elements but "relations-between-elements" as additional components of the total complex. But this view failed to account for the phenomenon because in some cases the relations *too* may be altered without destroying the original melody.

Another type of explanation, also designed to bolster the elementaristic hypothesis, was that *to* this total of six or more tones there come certain "higher processes" which operate upon the given material to "*produce*" unity.

This was the situation until Gestalt theory raised the radical question: Is it really true that when I hear a melody I have a *sum* of individual tones (pieces) which constitute the primary foundation of my experience? Is not perhaps the reverse of this true? What I really have, what I hear of each individual note, what I experience at each place in the melody is a *part* which is itself determined by the character of the whole. What is given me by the melody does not arise (through the agency of any auxiliary factor) as a *secondary* process from the sum of the pieces as such. Instead, what takes place in each single part already depends upon what the whole is. The flesh and blood of a tone depends from the start upon its role in the melody: a *b* as leading tone to *c* is something radically different from the *b* as tonic. It belongs to the flesh and blood of the things given in experience [*Gegebenheiten*], how, in what role, in what function they are in their whole.

The Phi Phenomenon [2]

One sees motion: an object has moved from one position to another. One describes the physical circumstances: up to the time t_1 the object was in the position p_1 (in the location l_1); from the time t_n onwards, it has been in position p_n (in the location l_n). In the interval between t_1 and t_n, the object was situated successively in the intermediate positions between p_1 and p_n, and, with spatial and temporal continuity, has reached p_n through them.

One sees this motion. One does not merely see that the object is now some place else than before, and so knows that it has moved (as one knows that a slowly moving clock hand is in motion), rather one [actually] sees the motion. What is psychically given?

One is tempted to say, in a simple analogy to the physical circumstances, that the seeing of motion occurs when the seen-thing, the psychic visual object, also arrives at p_n from the seen-position p_1, through continuous intermediate spatial positions: hence, as such a sequence of intermediate positions is psychically given, so the seeing of motion is given.

[2] Max Wertheimer, "Experimental Studies on the Seeing of Motion," in Thorne Shipley (ed.), *Classics in Psychology* (New York: Philosophical Library, 1961), pp. 1032–1033, 1057–1065; original German, "Experimentelle Studien über das Sehen von Bewegug," *Z. Psychol.*, 1912, **61**, 161–265. Reprinted by permission.

If this seeing of motion were achieved as an "illusion." i.e. if physically, first really only one stationary [*ruhende*] position was given, and afterwards, another stationary position was presented at a definite distance from the first, then some subjective supplementation [*Ergänzung*] would have taken place on the basis of the sensations of the two stationary objects, and in conjunction with them: namely, the passage, the perception of the intermediate positions, was somehow supplied subjectively.

The following investigation deals with impressions of motion which can be achieved even when two such successive positions are presented at a considerable spatial distance from one another.

* * * * *

On the Phenomenon of Pure Motion

What is psychically given in the field of motion? The thesis previously quoted . . . said that the intermediate positions of the object are subjectively supplied. (One could also quote the *à priori* argument, that motion is unthinkable unless an object, a thing, a seen-thing moves.)

If only fully optimal motion occurred, in the sense that the object moved or rotated clearly and distinctly (from the initial position, through the field, to the final position), then this assertion could be demonstrated easily.

But it appears that the essence of the passage across or of the rotation, has nothing to do with subjective intermediate positions. There are cases where ϕ, the motion across, the rotation, is clearly given, without a line being present in the field of motion in any way. The initial and final positions were present, and between them the motion, but in the field of motion, no optical supplementation, no seeing or imagining of the intermediate positions of the rod. This occurred spontaneously with all the observers; in the experimental arrangement . . . (below) this "pure" ϕ (without any supplementation of intermediate positions) could be demonstrated in a simple way.

During the impression of unitary whole motion, the following appeared many times, with more acute observation of what was actually present in the field of motion: if, for example, in the angle- or in the parallel-experiments, *a* and *b* were white stripes and the ground was black, and if there existed unitary motion from *a* to *b*, it [the motion] was present, although clearly, in no sense was there a stripe in passage through the intermediate positions in the field of motion, not even the color of the stripe, except in the positions, *a,b* themselves and perhaps on the borders of the field of motion.

For example: angle arrangement, *a* horizontal, *b* vertical, red stripe on black ground: "very clear unitary rotation, sensibly clear to describe the horizontal stripe visibly rotates part of the way, the vertical [rotates] somewhat into its final position; but the whole is a unity, not a disjointed motion, but a whole rotation clearly seen from *a* to *b*; concerning the center, it can be said that, optically, there was nothing of a stripe, nothing of red." And, similarly, for example, with white stripes: "it is curious that I don't see the white bar anywhere during the motion; true, in the last part of the motion, about 15°, where the white is already present, it makes the final part of the motion; but before that it is not there, I could never see the white bar anywhere in the region of 45°." Or, further: *a* vertical: "a kind of clear, compelling motion occurs, a rotation of about 90°, it is impossible to think of it as a succession; it is not the white vertical that moves, but there simply is a process, a transition; one sees the horizontal 'lie down'; earlier positions of the stripe, or of white, e.g. in the region of 45°, were certainly not apparent, not as such; nevertheless, though nothing white rotates, and though no object rotates, motion is still clearly given and, separately, even the final part of the motion [is given] in the 'lying down' of the horizontal." And, in many cases, spontaneously: "the stripes *a* and *b* are seen, clear motion between them, between *a* and *b* nothing of intermediate positions; the stripe (its color, or the object itself) has not passed through the field, the ground remained quite blank—but the motion goes across." And, finally, similarly in some cases where the two stripes, *a* and *b*, were completely at rest—and between them nothing other than motion. (Particularly convincing were all those cases, with greater distances between *a* and *b*, in which the observation gave unitary clear motion through the field while optically there was nothing of *ab* present at all.)

Thus, these cases showed that not even the thought that "an object has moved across" was present. What was apparent, of the objects, was given in the two positions. Neither one or the other of them, or anything similar, embodied the motion; but motion was given between them; not an object-motion. Nor was it: "that the object moves across, only I don't see it." But there was, simply, motion; without reference to an object.

In this field, where there was nothing to be seen of other optical qualities (except for the blank ground); where no conception was supplied of a stripe passing through the places; and where there was no thought that the stripe was passing across—what, then, was it that was psychically given?

Wherever the attention was concentrated, the impression [of motion] occurred there even more strongly. . . . Nothing else optical was present; in no sense was there anything of a passage of the stripe through the intermediate positions; nevertheless there was "a strong unitary motion here in this field; a specific, compelling 'passage across' or 'rotation'."

I presented the 90° angle arrangement, in an optimal-identity rotation; and added on the exposure field, B, in the region of 45°, a shorter stripe, c, of the same color, which did not reach the vertex (Fig. 14), that is, in a place where any stripe supplemented in the intermediate positions would have to pass over. For example, if a and b were white stripes of 1/2 or 1 cm. by 6 or 8 cm., then c was just as wide but shorter, 1 or 2 cm,. etc., (something like a piece of a central stripe). Attention would be focused on c or on its inner end, or on the distance between it and

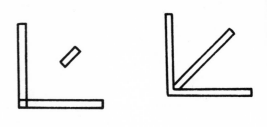

FIG. 14

the vertex. The motion ab, whole rotation by 90°, remained optimal. Was the white stripe c supplemented in any way? Does c appear somewhat lengthened for a moment, by the passage of a supplemented moving stripe or does a shimmer glide by in the place between c and the vertex? Numerous observations always yielded this characteristic result: there was a clear, compelling motion of about 90°, the specific "across" could be observed clearly; nothing of white glides through the place between c and the vertex, the ground remains quite black in this place, no supplementation occurred there, even for a moment; but there was an "across" in that place—not the "across" of the stripe, but simply an "across," a "rotation."

I have also arranged this experiment with a slide (Fig. 15). Analogous results occurred with an arrangement in the tachistoscopic experiments, in which c was affixed identically to both exposure fields of the tachistoscope. . . .

But it is even simpler to demonstrate. One places a slide before oneself (in a manner described above . . .), for example Fig. 16.

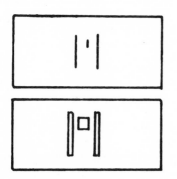
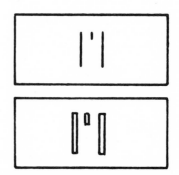

FIG. 15

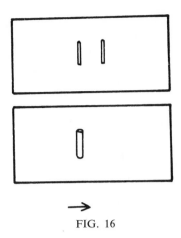

FIG. 16

Then one places an object between the two slits, e.g. a visible little rod or something similar, and fixates it. Or, analogously, on a larger scale: the slide slits may be projected in optimal motion in a not quite darkened room, onto a white wall. Between the two projected images (the distance from each other being, say, 60 cm. or 30 cm.), stands a light brown wooden support about 10 cm. wide. Several times the subjects exclaimed immediately: "I see the movement across! Also where the support stands—but the brown support is quite still and clear, no stripe passes over it, it seems at first as if I saw the motion going through a tunnel!" Then again: "The exact situation is this: the passage across, the compelling motion from a to b, is there clear and distinct, strong and entirely continuous, but nothing of white passes across and no stripe passes across."

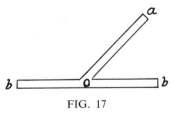

FIG. 17

And also: "the ground remains entirely clear on the right and on the left of the support, nothing slips across it"; "I see whiteness only in the stripes in the initial and in the final positions of the back and forth motion, in between there is only this curious passage across given in the space between a and b." "But there is no passage across of the stripe itself! Only the passage across, a strong motion in itself — —!"

In this separation of the phenomenon from the visual objects a and b, there were also cases where two pure ϕ-motions (rotations) appeared from a *single a*, and in such a way that it did not seem in any sense as if a was being split into two parts. In the arrangement of Fig. 17, (the shorter vertical a in the center of the longer horizontal b) it often happened (as long as one direction was not favored . . .) that the phenomenon of rotation clearly appeared, both to the left and to the right at the same time (rotation by 90° towards the right and towards the left). But it did not at all appear as if the vertical itself turned, let alone as if two lines were turning in opposite directions. Rather, both the vertical and horizontal lines were seen, and the two ϕ-rotations. Eventually, the horizontal (b) participated in the very last part of the rotations; but, as with the clear immobility of the lines, the ϕ-phenomenon was between them. Occasionally [these rotations appeared] in different strength; thus, when the right side was favored . . .: "two rotations, a strong one to the right and at the same time a weaker and a less compelling one to the left." This occurred not only with the right-angle arrangement, but also with the a line in the diagonal position (e.g. on the right, motion in an arc of 135°; on the left, motion in one of 45°), and so forth.

This ϕ-phenomenon, this "across" or "rotation," was present several times so strongly in the tachistoscopic experiments, especially with novel arrangements or reversals from ab into ba, that the observer could report nothing about the objects themselves . . .: "I can say nothing about what kind of objects there were; I have seen a strong motion (showing the correct direction) but I know nothing of the objects, and to my knowledge I have seen nothing of the objects." Similarly, with the arrangement in Fig. 14b where, in the naive procedure, a right-angle was exposed as b and a stripe (in the 45° position of this b-angle) was exposed as a: "a motion was there, at its conclusion there stood a right-angle; there was a rotating motion about the vertex downwards to the horizontal in the lower part of the right angle; I don't know what has turned—the horizontal was lying still, so was the vertical, and it was not as if the horizontal had rotated in its position."

By virtue of these experiments, we must contend not only with a theoretical argument, namely that ϕ may also occur without any supplementation of the intermediate positions of the objects and that the characteristics of the ϕ-process do not appear at all to be influenced by the absence of a supplementation of the intermediate positions, but [we must also contend] with a crucial experiment in the literal sense [*Demonstrations experiment in pragnantem Sinn*], in which the pure ϕ-process appears.

Apart from the color of the ground, nothing of the ordinary optical qualities appears in the field of motion; there is nothing in the process of color or of contour; in the ordinary optical sense, nothing has changed in the region of the intermediate field, the ground. The observer, here, does not say that the line moves across, nor does he believe that the line moves across (from a to b), or even that it seems to move across. But, rather: "I see a, I see b, I see motion between the two, I see the 'across,' the 'rotation'—not that of the line or lines, which are in their locations a and b—but a relatively stronger or a weaker 'across' in itself." "I see motion; thus (illustrating) not an across of something." And this occurs with the fullest concentration of attention on the field and with the most critical observation; the stronger the attention, the more centrally it is concentrated in the field, the better.

One might think, that, where nothing of a supplementation appeared, nothing of a thought-motion [*gedachter Bewegung*] (that an object itself moved across), nothing of intermediate positions of the object, the "illusion" of motion would disappear. But, on the contra-

ry, the motion is present compellingly and characteristically in its specific nature; it is given clearly and distinctly and is always observable.

These motion phenomena may appear in stronger or weaker intensity. They are given in the extremes as two simultaneous appearances; for example, as in Fig. 17, where the arrangement is adjusted for the right to be the greater angle: to the right, a colossally strong [motion occurs], while to the left, a weak ϕ-phenomenon occurs at the same time.

They also vary characteristically with the nature of the experiment: a "rapid across," a "lazy, slow rotation," a "quiet rotation',' a "rotation with a jerky beginning and end," etc.

They also show specific motion-curves . . . , and appear with definite spatial localization.[3]

These are psychic phenomena, which are directed in the same way as the actual sensed form and color contents (appearing objectively, not subjectively). Contrary to other psychic data they are dynamic, not static in nature; they have their psychological flesh and blood in the specific characteristic "across," etc., and this cannot be composed from the usual optical content.

[3]   In the experiments considered here, this localization was in one spatial section of the field plane. In order to see whether a ϕ-phenomenon is present under complicated circumstances in a definite plane, I projected two slide slits, each one on a wall at different distances in space (Fig. 18a—view of the arrangement from above). The observer stood on the side, and a distinct motion phenomenon occurred (Fig. 18b).

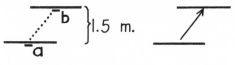

FIG, 18a, b

WOLFGANG KÖHLER
(1887–1967)

Mentality of Apes [4]

(Chimpanzees, whose behaviour is in-

[4]   Wolfgang Köhler, *The Mentality of Apes*, trans. Ella Winter (New York: Humanities Press, and London: Kegan Paul, 1927), pp. 169–174, 177–180, 236–238; original German, "Intelligenzprüfungen an Anthropoiden," *Abhandlungen der königlich preussischen Akademie der Wissenschaften*, 1917, **1**.

comparably more expressive than that of hens, show by their careful looking around that they really begin with something very like an inventory of the situation. And this survey then gives rise to the behaviour required for the solution.)

We can, in our own experience, distinguish sharply between the kind of behaviour which from the very beginning arises out of a consideration of the structure of a situation, and one that does not. Only in the former case do we speak of insight, and only that behaviour of animals definitely appears to us intelligent which takes account from the beginning of the lay of the land, and proceeds to deal with it in a single, continuous, and definite course. Hence follows this criterion of insight: *the appearance of a complete solution with reference to the whole lay-out of the field.*

* * * * *

In the description of these experiments it should have been apparent enough that what is lacking for this explanation is that most necessary thing, a composition of the solutions out of chance parts. It is certainly not a characteristic of the chimpanzee, when he is brought into an experimental situation, to make any chance movements, out of which, among other things, a non-genuine solution could arise. He is very seldom seen to attempt anything which would have to be considered accidental in relation to the situation (excepting, of course, if his interest is turned away from the objective to other things). As long as his efforts are directed to the objective, all distinguishable stages of his behaviour (as with human beings in similar situations), tend to appear as complete attempts at solutions, *none* of which appears as the product of accidentally arrayed parts. This is true, most of all, of the solution which is finally successful. Certainly, it often follows upon a period of perplexity or quiet (often a period of survey), but in real and convincing cases, the solution never appears in a disorder of blind impulses. It is one continuous smooth action, which can be resolved into parts *only by abstract thinking* by the onlooker; in *reality* they do *not* appear independently. But that in so many "genuine" cases as have been described, these solutions *as wholes* should have arisen from mere chance, is an entirely inadmissible supposition, which the theory cannot allow without renouncing what is considered its chief merit.

* * * * *

It may happen that the animal will attempt a solution which, while it may not result in success, yet has some meaning in regard to the situation. "Trying around" then consists in attempts at solution in the *half-understood* situation; and the real solution may easily arise by some chance outcome of it, i.e. it will not arise from chance impulses, but from actions, which, because they are *au fond* sensible, are great aids to chance. Secondly, a lucky accident may occur in some action, which has nothing to do with the objective. Here again, there is no question of a meaningless impulse—the chimpanzee only gives way to these, as already remarked, when driven to it—but of some kind of intelligent activity, even if with no reference to the objective. This is what probably occurs, when Sultan[5] discovers the way to combine two sticks; only a Philistine would call his playing with these sticks "meaningless impulses," because it follows no practical purpose. That an accident helped him is not the most important fact in either case; the important thing is how the experiment then proceeds. For we know from Man that even an accident may lead to *intelligent* further work (or intelligent repetition), especially in scientific discoveries (compare Oersted: *Current and Magnet*). Thus Sultan's behaviour, when he has once carried out his usual play, "put stick in hole," with both the bamboo rods, is exactly the same as if he had discovered the new procedure in a genuine solution. After this there is no doubt that he makes use of the double-stick technique intelligently, and the accident seems merely to have acted as an aid—fairly strong it is true—which led at once to "insight."

If one does not watch attentively, the crude stupidities of the animals, already referred to several times, might be taken as proofs that the chimpanzee does, after all, perform senseless actions, a sequence of which may, by chance, give rise to apparent solutions.

The chimpanzee commits three kinds of errors:

1. "*Good errors,*" of which more will be said later. In these, the animal does not make a stupid, but rather an almost favourable impression, if only the observer can get right away from preoccupation with human achievements, and concentrate only on the nature of the behaviour observed.

2. *Errors caused by complete lack of comprehension of the conditions of the task.*

---

5 A chimpanzee.

This can be seen when the animals, in putting a box higher up, will take it from a statically good position and put it into a bad once. The impression one gets in such cases is that of a certain innocent limitation.

3. *Crude stupidities arising from habit* in situations which the animal ought to be able to survey (e.g. dragging the box to the railings—Sultan). Such behaviour is extremely annoying—it almost makes one angry.

Here we are dealing with the third class, and it is easily seen that these mistakes are not at all liable to confirm the chance theory. This kind of behaviour never arises unless a similar procedure often took place beforehand as a real and genuine solution. The stupidities are not accidental "natural" fractions, from which *primarily* apparent solutions can arise —I know of no case in which such an interpretation is even possible—they are the *after-effects* of former genuine solutions, which were often repeated, and so developed a tendency to appear *secondarily* in later experiments, without much consideration for the special situation. The preceding conditions for such mistakes seem to be drowsiness, exhaustion, colds, or even excitement. For instance, a chimpanzee, when he performs an experiment for the first time and cannot reach the objective lying outside the bars without an implement, will never have the "accidental impulse" to drag a box to the bars, and even get up on it. On the other hand, one may see that actually, after frequent repetition of a solution originally arrived at genuinely, and in the consequent mechanization of the proceeding, such stupidities are easily committed. Not infrequently have I demonstrated

an experiment to interested observers, and, for the sake of simplicity, usually chose the opening of a door, in front of the hinge side of which the objective was hanging. After the animal had done this about twenty times since the first solution, and always at the same place, there began to appear a tendency to fetch down objectives hung high up with the help of a door, even when other methods were more obvious, and the use of a door had been made very difficult, in fact, almost impossible. And if attempts at other solutions developed, they were more or less under the influence, or magnetic power, of the door. Chica, for instance, made out of the jumping-stick method, which she had in its simple form completely mastered, a combination of this and the door-method; and quite unnecessarily, because it was by no means an improvement. Before the door had come into intelligent use for the first time, the chimpanzees had paid no attention to it in any experiment, not even when the experiment took place opposite to it.

* * * * *

For one who has actually watched the experiments, discussions like the above have something comic about them. For instance, when one has seen for oneself, how in the first experiment of her life . . ., it did not dawn on Tschego for hours to push the obstructing box out of the way, how she merely stretched out her arm uselessly, or else sat down quietly, but then, fearing the loss of her food, suddenly seized the obstacle, and pushed it to one side, thus solving the task in a second —when one has watched that, then to "secure

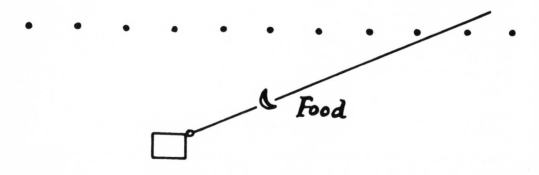

FIG. 14

these facts against misinterpretation" seems almost pedantic. But the living impression will not be reproduced, and many a question can be raised on the words of a report, which would not even occur to anyone after some observation. Nevertheless, it may be that after these discussions, the description of a further experiment carried out as a model will be particularly instructive; an experiment which is characterized both by its simplicity and its unequivocal relation to several theories.

A heavy box is standing upright at some distance on the other side of the oft-mentioned bars; one end of a stout string is affixed to it, and the string itself is laid down obliquely so that its free end lies between the vertical bars of the railings. Half-way between the box and the bars fruit is tied to the string (cf. Fig. 14); it cannot be reached from the bars as it is, but only if the string is laid straight. (19.6.1914) First of all, Chica pulls in the direction in which the string is lying, and so hard that the board of the box breaks, the string is freed, and the objective can be pulled to her. The box is then replaced by a heavy stone and the string tied round it. As the simple solution by pulling is no longer possible, Chica takes the string in one hand, passes it round the bar to her other, which she puts through the next space, and so on, passing it thus until the string is at right angles to the bars, and the objective can be seized.

Grande seems at first not to see the string

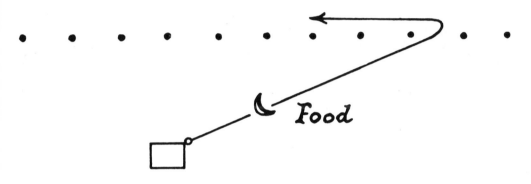

FIG. 15

which is grey and lying on a grey ground She drags stones about senselessly . . .—an after-effect of earlier experiments—tries to detach an iron rod from the wall, which she presumably wants to use as a stick, and at last sees the string. After this the experiment runs as with Chica, a solution without any hesitations.

Rana first pulls twice in the direction of the string, then suddenly changes the direction completely, while trying to pull the string to a spot just opposite the one at which it is tied (cf. Fig. 15); at the same time she stands opposite this point herself and keeps on looking at the objective and pulling the string parallel to the bars. This vain attempt is made twice in succession, in separate stages, and then is replaced by the proper solution, as in Grande's and Chica's cases. This experiment shows that the task consists of two parts: one, crude in its geometric and dynamic properties, "turn string at right angles to bars so that the objective comes nearer," and the more refined special problem, arising from the structure of the bars. Chica and Grande solve both parts at once; Rana solves the first one quickly, and the second one only later.

Sultan pulls for a moment like Rana (cf. Fig. 15) and immediately afterwards solves the problem completely, like the others. It becomes quite clear through this that the crude dynamic problem can be solved without any regard for the special one (the second problem), which in this case only seems to be noticed through non-success. Similar effects were encountered in the building with boxes.

Tercera cannot be cajoled into taking part. Tschego and Konsul show—in case it is not already realized—that the solution is not obvious; for neither gets any further than pulling the thread in the direction in which it is lying.

(21.6) The experiment is repeated with Chica, but this time the thread lies on the floor *turned in the other direction.* The animal does not pull at all in the direction of the thread, but starts the hand-over-hand process straight away, in the *opposite* direction from the previous experiment, till the goal can be reached. After this I did not think it necessary to make the same experiment with the other animals.

After the foregoing explanations, it need hardly be pointed out again that experiments like the one just described give *better* information about the chimpanzee than the usual animal tests with complicated locked doors, etc. Also it should be realized that an experiment so simple and clear as this contains the whole problem to be considered.

If anyone should still be of the opinion that such simple solutions are obvious and have nothing to do with intelligence, I can only invite him to show definitely and exactly

the way in which the procedure comes into being. I am afraid no psychologist is able to accomplish this at present.

I separated the two parts of the problem, which, as we saw, are independent, and I shall now consider only the crude one and its solution. This can be characterized simply by the sketch (cf. Fig. 16), leaving out of consideration how the animal, at the first moment of the solution, actually performs the arrow movement in detail (taking the bars into consideration or not).

Do the animals arrive at the solution in accordance with the theory we have discussed? If so, we should expect to find in all cases the appearance of a large number of impulses which might, in some of the chimpanzees, perhaps, accidentally contain the right "fragments" in the right succession. In reality Grande is the only animal that does anything senseless, and that in the form of a habit stupidity, when she had not yet thoroughly surveyed the possibilities of the problem; when she sees the string, a new stage of behaviour sets in, and immediately afterwards

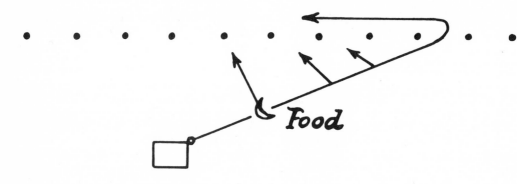

FIG. 16

a perfectly clear solution is achieved. Altogether only two movements ("impulses" may occur in lizards, but rarely in chimpanzees) really take place with regard to the objective. These two movements are:

1. *Pulling in the direction of the string,* i.e. a sensible proceeding, the practicability of which Chica once proves. No man, still less a chimpanzee, can otherwise find out if the string will not really come loose from box or stone.

2. Pulling at the string, or continuous passing of the rope hand-over-hand—in both cases in the *right direction for a solution* (see arrows in the diagram).

Not in a single animal was anything approaching a direction midway between these two observed, much less a third quite new one, etc. Where the more primitive tendency appeared first (in the direction of the string), the jump to the other one was yet made quite abruptly.

Conclusion

The chimpanzees manifest intelligent behaviour of the general kind familiar in human beings. Not all their intelligent acts are externally similar to human acts, but under well-chosen experimental conditions, the type of intelligent conduct can always be traced. This applies, in spite of very important differences between one animal and another, even to the least gifted specimens of the species that have been observed here, and, therefore, must hold good for every member of the species, as long as it is not mentally deficient, in the pathological sense of the word. With this exception, which is presumably rare, the success of the intelligence tests in general will be more likely endangered by the person making the experiment than by the animal. One must learn and, if necessary, establish by preliminary observation, within what limits of difficulty and in what functions the chimpanzee *can possibly* show insight.

* * * * *

At any rate, this remains true: Chimpanzees not only stand out against the rest of the animal world by several morphological and, in the narrower sense, physiological, characteristics, but they also show a type of behaviour which counts as specifically human. As yet we know little of their neighbours on the other side, but according to the little we do know, with the results of this report, it is not impossible that, in this region of experimental tasks, the anthropoid is nearer to man *in intelligence too*, than to many of the lower monkey-species. So far, observations agree well with the theories of evolution; in particular, the correlation between intelligence, and the development of the brain, is confirmed.

* * * * *

In the method adopted so far we have not been able to tell how far back and forward stretches the time "in which the chimpanzee lives"; for we know that, though one can prove some effects of recognition and reproduction after considerable lapses of time—as is actually the case in anthropoids—this is not the same as "life for a longer space of time." A great many years spent with chimpanzees lead me to venture the opinion that, besides in the lack of speech, it is in the extremely narrow limits in *this* direction that the chief difference is to be found between anthropoids and even the most primitive human beings. The lack of an invaluable technical aid (speech) and a great limitation of those very important components of thought, so-called "images," would thus constitute the causes that prevent the chimpanzee from attaining even the smallest beginnings of cultural development. With special reference to the second fact, the chimpanzee, who is easily puzzled by the simplest optical complications, will indeed fare badly in "image-life," where even man has continually to be fighting against the running into one another, and melting together, of certain processes.

In the field of the experiments carried out here the insight of the chimpanzee shows itself to be principally determined by his optical apprehension of the situation; at times he even starts solving problems from a too visual point of view, and in many cases in which the chimpanzee *stops* acting with insight, it may have been simply that the structure of the situation was too much for his visual grasp (relative "weakness of form perception"). It is therefore difficult to give a satisfactory explanation of all his performances, so long as no detailed theory of form (*Gestalt*) has been laid as a foundation. The need for such a theory will be felt the more, when one remembers that, in this field of intelligence, *solutions* showing insight necessarily are of the same nature as the structure of the situations, in so far as they arise in dynamic processes *co-ordinated with the situation*.

KURT KOFFKA
(1886–1941)

Prägnanz, Isomorphism, Closure, and Figure-Ground [6]

For we can at least select psychological organizations which occur under simple conditions and can then predict that they must possess regularity, symmetry, simplicity. This conclusion is based on the principle of isomorphism, according to which characteristic aspects of the physiological processes are also characteristic aspects of the corresponding conscious processes.

* * * * *

Law of Prägnanz. Thus we have gained a general, though admittedly somewhat vague, principle to guide us in our investigation of psychophysical organization. In the process of our research we shall make this principle more concrete; we shall learn more about simplicity and regularity itself. The principle was introduced by Wertheimer, who called it the *Law of Prägnanz.* It can briefly be formulated like this: psychological organization will always be as "good" as the prevailing conditions allow. In this definition the term "good" is undefined. It embraces such properties as regularity, symmetry, simplicity and others which we shall meet in the course of our discussion.

* * * * *

Closed Contour Figures. If a line forms a closed, or almost closed, figure, we see no longer merely a line on a homogeneous background, but a surface figure bounded by the line. This fact is so familiar that unfortunately it has, to my knowledge, never been made the subject of a special investigation. And yet it is a very startling fact, once we strip it of its familiarity. Therefore, we want a functional proof for our claim that a figure surrounded by contours is an entity different from the field outside the contours, which in all other respects produces the same stimulation. We possess methods by which

a difference between a contour figure and its surroundings could be established, but these methods have not been applied to our problem. We might measure the threshold of a small figure produced either inside or outside the contour of our original figure, e.g., by projecting such a figure on the contoured surface and having an episcotister between the lantern and the surface, an apparatus like that employed by Hempstead. . . . If then the little figure required a greater episcotister opening in order to become visible inside than outside the contour, we should have proved a greater cohesiveness of the enclosed area as compared with its surroundings, which would make it more difficult to produce a new figure on it. Unfortunately this experiment has never been made, although from two similar experiments, one by Gelb and Granit and the other by Granit, our assumed result seems predictable.

The Dynamic Causes of Contour Figures. But our main problem appears when we accept this difference as a real one. For we want to know the causes which separate not only the contour from the rest of the field, but at the same time the enclosed figure from its surroundings. Our principle of discontinuity certainly does not explain it. For the discontinuity between the contour and the surface on which it is drawn is the same in either direction, towards the inside and the outside. From our old principle we can only explain why we see lines as lines, i.e., as units segregated from the rest, but not the case which concerns us now, viz., when we see the area enclosed by a line, or a pattern of lines, segregated from the rest of the field and not in the same way segregated from the contour. Although discontinuity of stimulation still has a segregating effect and in so far is in harmony with our law, this segregation is asymmetrical. What is the reason of this asymmetry?

Factor of Closure. Unfortunately this question has not been treated. But since a mere profession of ignorance might raise some doubt in the minds of the readers as to the validity of our general principle, we shall try to point out some factors which might possibly explain the phenomenon. The first point we would raise is the fact that closed, or almost closed, lines or patterns of lines have this peculiarity, whereas it is lacking in unclosed ones. This seems to indicate that the process of organization depends upon the properties of its result, in strict accordance with the general law of prägnanz. Closed areas seem to be selfsustaining, stable organizations.

*　*　*　*　*

Closure. Let us now turn to closure. We averred in a previous discussion ... that closed areas were more stable and therefore more readily produced than unclosed ones. We shall prove this by producing closed organization against the factors of proximity and of good continuation. Fig. 45, taken from Köhler ... exemplifies the first. Predominantly not those vertical lines which are in closer proximity form the groups but those which enclose space, although in Fig. 45 their

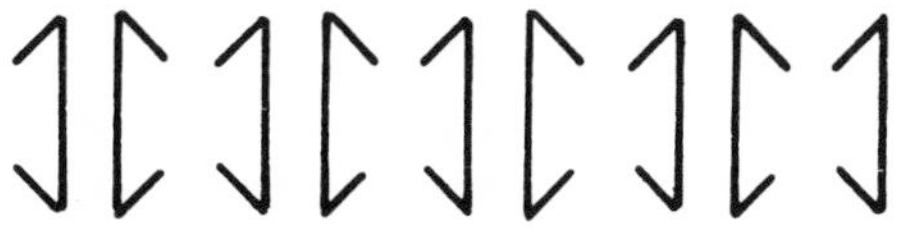

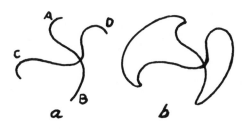

FIG. 45

distance is three times as great as that of the nearer ones, the distance between the ends of the short oblique lines being equal to that of the nearer vertical ones. And in Fig. 46*b* the parts A B C D of Fig. 46*a* are

FIG. 46

contained, but whereas in *a*, according to good continuation, B is the continuation of A, D of C, in *b* the two closed areas appear as subwholes, so that A is no longer continued by B, nor C by D. That closure does not always win out over good continuation is shown by several patterns in Wertheimer's paper which I shall omit here, where I want to demonstrate the effectiveness of the closure principle.

*　*　*　*　*

Law of Prägnanz.
Minimum and Maximum Simplicity

It is meet to compare our accomplishments with the introduction of this chapter in which we formulated a guiding principle for our investigation, the law of pragnänz, which related the resulting stationary organizations to certain maximum-minimum principles. As a matter of fact this law has pervaded our whole discussion; we have encountered it in various forms, as unity, uniformity, good continuation, simple shape, and closure. But there remains one point which was mentioned in the beginning and not followed up in the later discussion, viz., the difference between what we called the simplicity of a maximum and a minimum event. We must now envisage our discussion from this point of view and add some more evidence in order to give more substance to our distinction.

Roughly speaking, a minimum simplicity will be the simplicity of uniformity, a maximum simplicity that of perfect articulation. In our examples both kinds have figured; the first kind in after-image experiments and in the other effects of reduced external forces of organization; the second in examples of good shape and continuation. Can we derive a hint as to the causes or conditions which make for either of these two effects? Unfortunately we lack a special systematic investigation of our problem, but we may tentatively derive some conclusions from the facts familiar to us, if we supplement them by a few others. When we look at a portrait photograph, we see a face with its form and expression; but if we try to develop an after-image of it, all we see is a blurred patch. The after-image is much less articulated, much more uniform than the perception, the former shows simplification of the minimum, the latter of the maximum kind. It is, however, not impossible to produce an after-image of a face, but then the original must possess much stronger contrasts than any ordinary photograph.

*   *   *   *   *

Secondly, look at the pattern of Fig. 50. At a casual glance you will see it as a chaotic jumble of lines. But when you are told that this pattern is a real picture and make an effort to discover it, you will find the face of a good-humoured portly gentleman.

FIG. 50   *   *   *   *   *

These examples suggest the following kind of conclusion: when the organism is active, at a high degree of vigilance, to use Sir Henry Head's term, it will produce good articulation; when it is passive, in a state of low vigilance, it will produce uniformity. In our interpretation of vigilance we suggested that high vigilance means that the organism has much energy at its disposal. And if we apply this interpretation to our last cases it means that simplicity of the maximum kind, high articulation, will occur when the disposable energy of the organism is great, and simplicity of the minimum kind, uniformity, when it is small. All our three examples fit into this explanation. That fatigue, low vigilance, is a condition of lowered energy has been our starting point. The second case, where the attitude of searching for a meaningful picture produced articulation, is also clearly a case of greater disposable energy, since here the Ego-system with its store of energy is brought to bear on the organization. The first case is the most difficult to understand. But the comparison between the negative effect of an ordinary portrait and the positive effect of the Hindenburg pattern clears up the difficulty. The external organizing forces are much stronger in the second case than in the first, owing to the greater jumps of stimulation between the different field parts, and the greater articulation is due to these greater forces. Therefore, if greater articulation implies that more energy is consumed in the process, then these greater forces must have

liberated more energy, just as an electromotor doing work against forces uses up more energy than an idling motor.

*   *   *   *   *

Figure-Ground. If things are shaped may we conclude that the framework is not? And if it be not, whence comes this difference? For systematic and historic reasons it is expedient to study our problem in two dimensions before we include the third. For the same distinction holds with regard to surfaces, where, since the pioneer work of Rubin (1915), it is called the distinction between figure and ground.

*   *   *   *   *

Figure-Ground in Normal Behavioural Environments. We now apply the figure-ground category to the normal behavioural environment. It is created by retinal stimulation which is *in kind* the same as that operative in the cases discussed so far, but ever so much more complex in its distribution. Furthermore, new factors of organization are usually introduced by binocular parallax. However, since the main features of the behavioural environment are not essentially different in one-eyed persons from those with binocular vision, we shall disregard this factor for the moment. All normal fields of vision have a great amount of depth detail apart from the detail of form. At the same time in all normal fields the contours have the one-sided function. We see, to use von Hornbostel's phrase, the things and not the holes between them.

Why We See Things and Not the Holes Between Them. We can now attempt an answer to the question why we do so. Two of the factors of organization which we have so far discussed seem to me to be the most important causes of this effect. In the first place, the segregation and unification which occurs will separate areas of different degrees of internal articulation, and according to our law, the more highly articulated ones will become figures, the rest fusing together to form the ground. Look at any landscape photograph. You see the shape of the things, the mountains, and trees and buildings, but not of the sky. The second factor, equally important, is that of good continuation and good shape. The things which we see have a better shape, are bounded by better contours, than the holes which we might see but do not. Therefore, when in exceptional circumstances these conditions are reversed, we see the hole and not the things, as the shape of a gap between two projecting rocks with sharp profiles, which may look like a face, an animal, or some other object, while the shape of the rock disappears.

KURT GOLDSTEIN
(1878–1965)

Organismic Psychology [7]

The fact that the organism represents, so to speak, a historical being, makes it imperative to consider the time factor in dealing with any detail. All performances must be determined not only according to quality and spatial conditions, but also according to their temporal index. A performance is normal or "adequate," if it shows an adequate temporal structure.... If, in a statically minded approach, we arrest for a moment *in abstracto* the development in the course of time, then the organism may possibly appear perfectly embedded in a world which it fits like a statue in its mold. But we may also strike another moment in which a grave discrepancy exists between the organism and the world. In the first instance, our impression of the organism seems to correspond completely to the prototype—it is from such static impressions that the prototype forms itself for us. In the second instance, a strange organism appears before us, showing at best only a distorted semblance of the prototype. On this basis, we would never be able to obtain a prototype. These two moments represent, on the one hand, Being-in-order, in adequate stimulus evaluation, and on the other hand, Being-in-disorder, in adequate stimulus evaluation, in "catastrophe." If the organism is "to be," it always has to pass again from moments of catastrophe to states of ordered behavior. Catastrophic shocks, that is, traumas of existence, arise when the organism clashes with the world in the productive coming to terms with it. They really signify as much a concussion of the world as of the organism itself. They represent a disequilibrium which must be overcome, if the organism is not to lose its existence. This balancing process occurs through mutual adjustment of the organism and the world, and is realized because the organism is able to find its "milieu" in the world.

If it is true that these catastrophes are the expression of a clash of the individuality of the organism with the "otherness" of the world, then the organism must proceed from catastrophe to catastrophe. But this is not its intrinsic Being, rather only the transition to its true realization. The clash, so to speak, provides only a shake-up from which the re-patterning, that is, the real pattern, the real performance, the revelation of the organism and the world, emerges. Indeed there is no performance without a new region of the world becoming manifest.

In these moments of performance, we find the organism in an ordered state and specific Gestalt, on the basis of which we form our conception of the organism. Such are the situations of preferred behavior, towards which the organism, changed and shaken by the outer world, repeatedly strives. Such are the phenomena from which we derive the constants of the organism; such are the moments of its real existence, when the organism is its real self, as compared to states of deterioration and enslavement to the world which must always be overcome to make performances possible. From this point of view, "being in order and existence," "meaning and being," are the same; and "being" signifies nothing other than a self-realization which keeps in step with the conquest of the world, i.e. inclusion and transformation. This leads on the one hand to what, in terms of the individual, is Experience, on the other hand, to what in terms of the world is organization and patterning. Thus organism and world realize themselves simultaneously, and grow from the sphere of potentiality into that of actuality.

Life has always a positive character; it never *manifests itself in negative terms*. All attempts at an explanation which necessitates the assumption of negative factors, e.g. such concepts as inhibition, antagonism, struggle between opposing lower and higher forces, and, finally, such concepts as "negation" of the "vital forces" through the mind, are unproductive. Wherever negative factors seem to operate, this is either due to false theoretical presuppositions which demand an amendment through the introduction of such negative factors, or it is due to the erroneous hypostatization of processes as absolute, which actually belong to performances, occurring in antagonistic phases so far as they are considered in a state of isolation.

This criticism is as valid for the theory of "antagonistic" movements, as for the so-called "antagonism" between the mind and the "vital sphere." The phenomena which have occasioned the doctrine of such interpretations are only an expression of the process of coming to terms with the world under continual tension. Although individual phenomena become really intelligible to us only if we regard them positively as pertaining to a unitary, holistic being, still we have had to restrict this view to a certain degree. We have seen that a certain amount of *fluctuation in antagonistic phases is evidently part and parcel of the normal process*. We had to admit that we can volitionally impede processes in the organism . . . that it belongs to human nature to oppose, in some measure, the drive-impulse by means of the mind. We even had to admit more: in reality the self-realization of the organism by no means exhibits consistency throughout. Every creature is easily drawn back and forth. In man, especially, consistency, perfect centering, and integration are almost the exception. Man seems to oscillate between passion and reason, between drives and intellect. One might argue: What right do we have to minimize these more frequently observed phenomena, to subordinate them to the unitary whole which neither is consistently nor completely realized throughout? Why do we not proceed in the opposite manner, starting with the variety of the individual phenomena, with the existence of reflex and inhibition-mechanisms with drives and intellect, and attempt to explain life on the basis of these phenomena through their counterplay and interplay? Why do we not take offense at the incompleteness of knowledge in determining the whole? And

why do we take offense at the inadequacy of regulating principles which one is compelled to introduce, in order to maintain consistency, if one makes the single phenomenon the starting point?

One may reply to this that the difference between the two views is the following: In the atomistic approach, advancement of knowledge hinges upon theory, while in the view which we have advocated, it clings to empiric data. To be sure, the former also aims to scrutinize and revise its theoretical views through experience, and it amends the theory on proof of new observations. But these corrections are done rather with hesitation. No matter what field we may consider, we shall always see that an old theory is given up only very reluctantly even if new data challenge it; that one rather takes recourse to all possible amendments and auxiliaries, before the theory is entirely rejected. Usually, experiences which do not fit are at first simply left "outside," and one does not refrain from granting validity to two or more theories at the same time.

Such procedures are impossible for us in principle. Since every new additional experience is never simply one more, standing apart from the others, it forces us rather to reconsider the entire theory, if for no other reason than because an experience becomes a "fact" only if it fits into the whole. In this respect we cannot accept compromise, and have to uphold unceasingly the cause of the scientific attitude. Yet ultimately our procedure is rooted in a more profound conviction: this is *the conviction that a state of greater perfection can never be understood from that of less perfection, and that only the converse is possible*. It is very feasible to isolate parts from a whole, but a perfect whole can never be composed by synthesizing it from the less perfect parts. True, the reflex can be understood as a manifestation of the whole, as a special condition during isolation of a part, but the whole can never be comprehended from the reflexes.

When centering is defective, when parts are split off from the whole, it is certainly possible that the outcome is antagonism, for example, a contest in the field of perceptions or drives, or something in the nature of a struggle between "mind" and "drives." Then it is even possible that a so-called "drive" may become so pathologically dominant that it is mistaken for a true, essential characteristic of the normal organism, as in the anthropology of Freud. But from such partitive phenomena, it will never be possible to understand, even approximately, the inner coherence and unity of holistic behavior. From no single phenomenon does a path lead to the whole; yet it can be comprenended as a privation of the whole. The possibility of such privations is no objection to the holistic organization; rather, they express the imperfection in self-realization resulting from a lack in potency of "essential nature." This lack is either innate, through defective genesis—or as one may say, through a deprivation of the grace of endowments—or it is acquired through disease, or is a sequel of overpowering demands by the environment.

It is well worth noting that we meet this imperfection in disease, and among all creatures, especially in man. The first is easily understood because disease means reduction of centering. The second would indicate that for man, of the creatures, ideal centering is most difficult to achieve; and this in turn points to the specific intricacy of his organization. This finds expression in individuality, the one factor which may be regarded as the ultimate reason why no being can ever attain a realization completely corresponding to its nature. Individuality in no way means simply that "I" exist, but that there are, simultaneously with me "other" creatures; and that fact necessarily implies incomplete realization of every individual, it means impact, catastrophic reactions, antagonism, competition between creatures, and struggle between "mind" and "life". . . . The higher the organization, the more differentiated and the more individual the creature, the greater is the inner imperfection, together with the relative perfection. Therefore, we find in man, along with the most pronounced and developed individuality and the greatest relative perfection, forces adverse to both. This opposition may go so far that the "mind" can "say no" to "life." Evidently such a creature must meet with great obstacles and conflicts in order to realize its nature.

Realization is determined by its structural organization as much as by its capacity to tolerate or overcome catastrophes. Every defect destroys structure; and this is the cause for frequent occurrence of inadequate stimulus-reactions, i.e. catastrophes, in a milieu which would formerly have been adequate. Such occurrences can be obviated through nothing but performances, which one can achieve only if he finds the adequate milieu. That achievement implies limitation of his world, corresponding to the limitation of the premorbid performance capacities. At this stage, the organism is really and solely striving for "preservation." The manner in which an organism copes with a defect is always characteristic of its individual nature. This reveals itself not only in the quality of the performance—that is, in the scope and differentiation of his world—but equally as much in the strength with which shocks can be resisted without breaking the organism. . . .

At this point the analysis made it indispensable to include the intellectual power the "mind," as an intrinsic characteristic of human nature. In man alone, the privation of essential performances and limitation of world can be mitigated, because he has the capacity to bear insufficiency, i.e. suffering. This capability is *the* characteristic of human nature, and reveals the very highest form of life in the phenomenon of freedom.

In deliberate limitation of our textual scope, we have regarded the organism primarily as individual Being. Here we halt, and confine ourselves to an understanding which, of course, is only preliminary. Many phenomena of the organism point beyond the individual. First of all, any attempt to regard the essential peculiarities of an organism, or of the kingdom of living creatures in its entirety, as forming a hierarchy, is oriented upon the presupposition of a prototype of the entirety of living creation. Two criteria seemed to us suitable as guiding principles for determining the "level" of a living creature. One is its degree of perfect centering, and the other is its richness or abundance. However, we were not definite as to the justification of such an attempt, which may already constitute an artificial separation.

Depending upon how we regard it, every organism appears to us as relatively perfect or relatively imperfect. It is relatively perfect, if considered as an ordered entity commensurate with its individual nature. It is more or less imperfect in comparison with the nature of its class or species, and more so, in comparison with the whole of nature.

The individualization, which always means an emancipation from the superordinated whole, be it species, group, etc., involves a necessary contrast between the individual and his fellow men, and so brings about that *imperfection* which manifests itself in the catastrophic form of all coming to terms of the organism with the world. In that fact is given the transitoriness of all living beings bearing a specific individuality. This may well be the only genuine, real imperfection by the very nature of life, the imperfection which is inherent in life as such. It shows itself in the incompleteness of the individual's participation in that reality to which it belongs according to its nature. All the minor catastrophic reactions to which the organism is continually exposed thus appear as inevitable waystations in the process of its actualization, so to speak, as the expression of its

inescapable participation in the general imperfections of the living world. . . . This is a different imperfection from that which is due to defective genesis (changes) caused through extraneous influences which impair the individual in its centering so much that it is no longer capable of realizing its individuality even proximately. In such cases, imperfection becomes "disease," i.e. existence in "transition" becomes existence in "decay," and is destined for death. That such a privation in essential nature is at all possible—especially when we meet it in our fellow men, and thus when it comes so close to us—this is the most stirring experience which the biologist can have. However, this perturbing shock is transfigured into admiration for nature and veneration for its benignity. One realizes that, simultaneously with the privation in essence, the awareness of this privation may be lost, and thus the victim is spared the catastrophic shock which such awareness must necessarily carry with it.

KURT LEWIN
(1890–1947)

Topology and Field Theory [8]

Psychological Behavior and the Person

To understand or predict the psychological behavior (B) one has to determine for every kind of psychological event (actions, emotions, expressions, etc.) the momentary whole situation, that is, the momentary structure and state of the person (P) and of the psychological environment (E). $B = f(PE)$. Every fact which exists psychobiologically must have a position in this field and only facts which have such position have dynamic effects (are causes of events). The environment is, for all of its properties (directions, distances, etc.), to be defined not physically but *psychobiologically*, that is, according to its quasi-physical, and quasi-social, and quasi-mental structure.

It is possible to represent the dynamic structure of the person and of the environment by means of mathematical concepts. The coordination between the mathematical rep-

resentation and its psychodynamic meaning has to be strict and without exception.

We shall first describe the psychological field forces and their mode of operation, without consideration of the question whether the object in any particular case has acquired its valence through some previous "experience" or in some other way.

Psychological Regions, Boundaries, Field Forces, Vectors, Valence, and Locomotion

The first presupposition for the understanding of the child is the determination of the psychological "place" at which the child concerned is, and of his region of freedom of movement, i.e., of the regions that are accessible to him and of those regions that psychologically exist for the child but which are inaccessible to him by reason of the social situation (prohibition by the adult, limitation by other children, etc.) or because of the limitations of his own social, physical, and intellectual abilities. Whether his region of freedom of movement is large or small is

[8] Murchison, Carl Allanmore (ed.), *A Handbook of Child Psychology*, second edition, revised (1933). New York: Russell & Russell, 1967. Reprinted by permission.

of decisive significance for the whole behavior of the child. . . .

One can characterize these possible and not possible psychodynamic locomotions (quasi-bodily, quasi-social, quasi-mental locomotions) at every point of the environment with the help of the concept of *topology*, which is a non-quantitative discipline about the possible kinds of connections between "spaces" and their parts.

The basis for the coordination between mathematical and *psychodynamic* concepts so far as environmental questions are concerned is the coordination of topological *path* and psychodynamic *locomotion*. The topological description determines which points the different paths lead to and which regions these paths cross. One can characterize the region which a child cannot reach by means of *barriers* between these regions and their neighboring regions. The barrier corresponds as a dynamic concept to the mathematical concept of boundary. One must distinguish between different strengths of barriers. . . .

To determine not only which locomotions (paths) are possible but which of the possible locomotions will occur at a given moment one has to use the concept of *force*.

A force is defined through three properties: (1) direction, (2) strength, (3) point of application. The first and second properties are to be represented through the mathematical concept *vector*. The point of application is indicated in the figures (as is the custom in physics) by the point of the arrow.

Dynamically the force is correlated with psychobiological locomotions in a one-to-one correspondence. "The real locomotion must occur in every case according to the direction and the strength of the resultant of the momentary forces" and "in any case of locomotion there exists a resultant of forces in its direction."

The direction which the valence imparts to the child's behavior varies extremely, according to the content of the wants and needs. Nevertheless, one may distinguish two large groups of valences according to the sort of initial behavior they elicit: the *positive* valences (+), those effecting approach; and the *negative* (—), or those producing withdrawal or retreat.

The *actions* in the direction of the valence may have the form of uncontrolled impulsive

behavior or of directed voluntary activity; they may be "appropriate" or "inappropriate."

Those processes which make an especially "goal striving" impression are usually characterized dynamically by a reference to a *positive* valence. . . .

One has to distinguish between *driving* forces (which correspond to positive or to

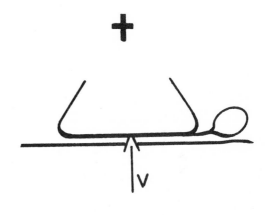

FIGURE 2

negative valences) and *restraining* forces which correspond to barriers.

. . . That the valence is not associated merely with a subjective experience of direction, but that a directed force, determinative of the behavior, must be ascribed to it, may be seen in the fact that a change in the position of the attractive object brings about (*ceteris paribus*) a change in the direction of the child's movements.

An especially simple example of an action in the direction of a positive valence is illustrated in Figure 2. A six-months-old infant stretches arms, legs, and head toward a rattle or a spoonful of porridge in accordance with the direction of the vector (*V*).

The direction of the field forces plays an important part in such intelligent behavior as has to do with detour (*Umweg*) problems. The child perhaps wants to get a piece of chocolate on the other side of a bench. (See Figure 3, *C* = child, *Ch* = chocolate, *B* = bench.) The difficulty of such a problem consists primarily, not in the *length* of the detour (*D*), but in the fact that the initial direction of the appropriate route does not agree with that of the vector from the valence. The detour is more difficult, *ceteris paribus*, the more the barrier makes it necessary for the child in making the detour to start off in a direction opposed to the direction of the valence (Figure 4).

The situation is similar when the child wants to take a ring off a stick, while the

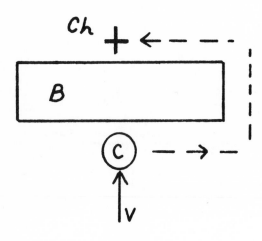

FIGURE 3

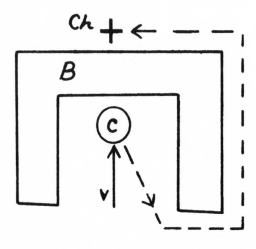

FIGURE 4

stick stands in such a way that the ring cannot be pulled directly toward the child, but must first be moved upward, or away from himself. Similar factors are operative when a child at a certain age may have difficulties in sitting

down on a chair or a stone. The child approaches with its face toward the stone (*S*). In order to sit down it must turn around, i.e., execute a movement opposed to the direction of the field force (Figure 5)....

FIGURE 5

When the child finds the solution of such a detour problem, it happens by reason of a restructuring of the field.... There occurs a perception of the total situation of such a kind that the *path to the goal* becomes a unitary whole. The initial part of the route, which "objectively" is still a moment away from the goal (cf., e.g., Figure 4), thereby loses psychologically that character and becomes the *first phase* of a general movement *toward* the goal.

How critically important the question of *direction* is in this case is indicated by the fact that one cannot force a solution of the detour by increasing the *strength* of the valence. If the attraction is much too weak, it is, to be sure, unfavorable, because the child does not concern himself sufficiently with the affair. But if we continue to strengthen the valence, the solution of the task ceases to be facilitated and instead becomes more difficult. The strength of the attraction then makes it doubly difficult for the child to start in a direction opposed to the field force. Instead, the child will execute, with all its energy, affective meaningless actions in the direction of the valence (cf. *infra*). Above all, that relative detachment and inward "retirement" from the valence which is so favorable to perception of the whole situation and hence to be transformation (*Umstrukturierung*) of the total field, which occurs in the act of insight, is made much more difficult (cf. *infra*). For the same reason, the prospect of an especially intense reward or punishment may impede the solution of intellectual tasks.

To older children of normal intelligence the preceding examples of detour problems offer no difficulty, because they already have a sufficient survey of such situations or corresponding experiences. For them, it no longer requires a special act of intelligence in order that, instead of the spatial directions, the *functional* directions become decisive for the movement.

We may at this point remark a circumstance of general importance: direction in the psychological field is not necessarily to be identified with physical direction, but must be defined primarily in psychological terms. The difference between psychobiological and physical direction appears more prominently in older children. When the child fetches a tool or applies to the experimenter for help, that does not mean, even when it involves physical movement in a direction opposite to the goal, a turning-away from the goal, but an approach to it. Such indirect approaches are more rare among babies. This is due to the slighter functional differentiation of their environment and to the fact that *social* structure has not yet the overwhelming significance for them that it has for older children.

* * * * *

In the cases mentioned, the direction of the field forces is determined by objects which, by reason of visual or auditory distance perceptions, have a definite place in the environment. In the case of newborn children one can speak of such precisely directed field forces only in so far as the psychological environment has sufficient structure and solidity.

Directed action in response to certain forms of *tactile* stimulation may be observed very early. Touching the child's cheek with the nipple may elicit a turning of the head in the corresponding direction.

Also among older children the (psychological) *separation of the self from the valence* remains in many respects a necessary condition for the action upon the valence. Fairly often the action does not proceed immediately to the use of the object, but the field force disappears (or is at least very much weakened) as soon as the object comes into the "possession" of the individual involved. An example from our films: a nine-months-old child before which two rattles are laid does not begin to play after getting one of them, but is interested only in the rattle that he does *not* have. The close relationship between directed field forces and the separation of the self from the goal object can also be demonstrated in various ways with older children.

. . . For the strength of the valences, internal factors, especially the actual momentary state of the child's needs, are of crucial significance. . . . In addition, the strength of the field force going out from a valence depends also upon the *position* of the valence relative to the individual and upon the presence or absence of other valences.

Fajans . . . has shown that, *ceteris paribus*, at least in certain cases, the strength of a valence increases with its apparent *proximity*. This is expressed by both the duration and the intensity of the efforts toward the goal.

* * * * *

Again one may not, to be sure, simply assume that psychological distance corresponds to physical distance. In the first place, a difference in apparent distance is significant only within a rather narrowly limited range, in accordance with the smallness of the child's life-space; and this range, as the work of Fajans shows, is considerably smaller for the one-year-old than for the three-year-old child. Just as visual extent in perceptual space (for example, with reference to the law of apparent size) increases with age . . . the life-space of the child increases and differentiates in dynamic respects as well. Difference in distance cannot be purely physically defined also because the range in which the child "almost" gets the desired object has qualitatively a special character. This *"almost" situation* has an especially marked significance, e.g., with reference to experiences of success and failure, and cannot be reckoned simply as a smaller distance. . . .

An obvious discrepancy between spatial and psychological distance was observed in a group of four-year-old children who experienced the situation less as an "objective task" than as a *social* relationship with the experimenter. They were simply faced by an adult who would not give them a doll. For these children the kind and duration of approach remained independent of the distance of the valence. Indeed, for the social route to the valence (by way of the experimenter) the psychological distance is the same in any case.

With older children the intellectual appreciation of the functional and particularly the sociological relations (perhaps of their dependence upon the might of other children and of adults) is so far developed that physical distance usually plays a much smaller part in such situations.

* * * * *

With increasing age *temporally* distant events also acquire increasing significance. To the psychological situation belong not only those facts that are actually perceptible and "objectively" present, but also a range of past and future events. A censure or a commendation may long remain a *present* psychological fact for the child, and an expected event may have psychological reality in advance of its occurrence.

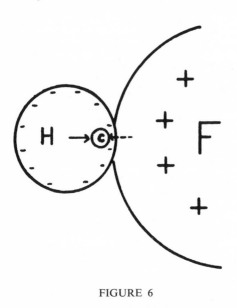

FIGURE 6

As an example of the increase in the strength of the valence with *temporal proximity*, it may be pointed out that, among the inmates of homes for delinquent children, reform

schools, and similar institutions, it is not infrequently observed that they become especially difficult just before their discharge. We noted this paradoxical behavior, so sharply opposed to their own interests, especially in previously well-behaved individuals. The essential reason was found to be the following: Even for the youth who is at first well-behaved in the home the wish for freedom is an important motive of his behavior. But at first this freedom is a distant half-imaginary goal and, most important, good conduct in the home is the way that shall ultimately lead him there. Now that his discharge is approaching, the longed-for, but until now uncertain, world of freedom is just ahead (Figure 6). The boundary of the home thereby acquires in much greater degree the character of a marked barrier (*B*) which separates the youth from his almost-attained goal. Hence the home acquires a pronounced negative valence. Emotional and rebellious actions are further facilitated by the very high *state of tension* . . . and by the fact that the youth already feels half free. In a topologically similar experimental situation with infants an increase of affectivity occurred in 85 per cent of the cases when the field forces in the direction of the goal behind the barrier were strengthened and the general state of tension thereby raised. . . . In many cases the impatience of children can be explained by a similar structure of the environment.

The experiments of Fajans show that the restraining forces corresponding to the barrier increase when the strength of the valence behind the barrier is increased. . . .

Conflict is defined psychologically as the opposition of approximately equally strong field forces. There are three basic cases of conflicts as far as driving forces are concerned.

1. The child stands between two positive valences (Figure 7). He has to choose perhaps

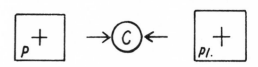

FIGURE 7

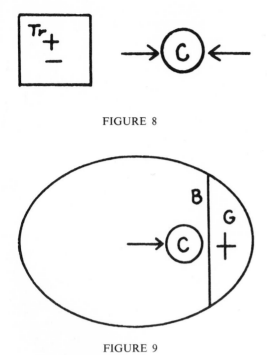

FIGURE 8

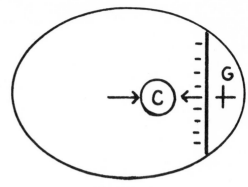

FIGURE 9

FIGURE 10

General Topology of the Situation with a Barrier between the Child and His Goal.

valence (Figure 10). Besides the positive, there comes into existence a negative vector, and we have the Type 2 conflict situation. The negative vector usually increases gradually in strength and finally becomes stronger than the positive. Accordingly, the child *goes out of the field.*

This withdrawal (*Aus-dem-Felde-Gehen*) may be either physical, as when the child retreats, turns away, or possibly leaves the room or place, or it may be an *inward* going out of the field, as when the child begins to play or to occupy itself with something else. It not infrequently occurs, for example in embarrassment, that the child makes certain bodily movements toward the goal but at the same time is mentally occupied with something else. In such cases the bodily act has the character of a more or less set "gesture". . . .

In such situations the withdrawal is at first almost always merely temporary. The child turns away, only to return after a while for another try at the barrier. . . . A final and permanent withdrawal usually occurs only after several temporary withdrawals, the *duration* of which increases until finally the child does not return.

Unusual persistence in such a situation is not necessarily an indication of *activity*. On the contrary, active children usually "go out of the field" earlier than passive children. It is not the duration but the *kind* of approach that is significant for activity. . . . Related to this is the fact that under certain circumstances the single actions in such a conflict

between going along on a picnic (*P*) and playing (*Pl*) with his comrades. In this type of conflict situation decision is usually relatively easy. As a result of the fact that after the choice the goal chosen often seems inferior . . ., oscillation does sometimes occur.

2. The child faces something that has simultaneously both a positive *and* a negative valence (Figure 8). He wants, for example, to climb a tree (*Tr*), but is afraid.

This constellation of forces plays an important part in cases in which a reward is offered for an activity (e.g., a school task) which the child does not want to execute.

Conflict situations of this type usually develop rather quickly also in the detour experiments mentioned above, in the experiments of Fajans, or in similar situations in which the attainment of a goal is impeded by some barrier. At first the child sees a difficult way through a barrier (*B*) between himself and his goal (*G*), which hinders the completion of actions in the direction of the field forces (Figure 9). But after the child has run against the barrier several times, and perhaps hurt himself, or had the wounding experience of failure, the barrier itself acquires a negative situation are longer with the infant than with the young child . . ., although in general the duration of action unities increases with the age of the child. . . .

3. The third type of conflict situation occurs when the child stands *between* two *negative* valences, for example, when it is sought by threat of punishment (*P*) to move a child to do a task (*T*) it does not want to do (Figure 11).

There is an essential difference between this and the conflict situation described under 1. This becomes clear when one proceeds to represent the total distribution of forces in the field of force.

Field of Force. The field of force indicates

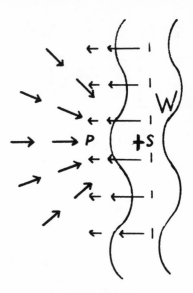

FIGURE 13

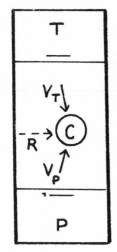

FIGURE 11

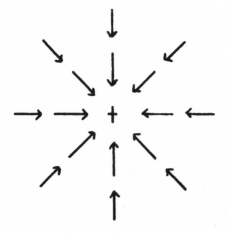

FIGURE 12

which forces would exist at each point in the field if the individual involved were at that point. To a positive valence there corresponds a central field (Figure 12).

As a simple example of the structure of the field of force in a conflict situation of Type 2, a case from one of my films may be adduced: A three-year-old boy wants to fetch a rubber swan out of the water to the beach, but is afraid of the water. To the swan (*S*) as positive valence there corresponds a central field. This field is overlaid by a second field which corresponds to the negative valence of the waves (Figure 13). It is important that here, as frequently in such cases, the *strength* of the field forces which correspond to the negative valence diminishes much more rapidly with increasing spatial *distance* than do the field forces corresponding to the positive valence. From the direction and strength of the field forces at the various points of the field it can be deduced that the child must move to the point *P* where *equilibrium* occurs. (At all other points there exists a resultant which finally leads to *P*.) Corresponding to the momentary oscillations of the situation, above all to the more or less threatening aspect of the waves, this point of equilibrium approaches and retreats from the water. Indeed, this oscillation is reflected in the child's approaches to and retreats from the water.

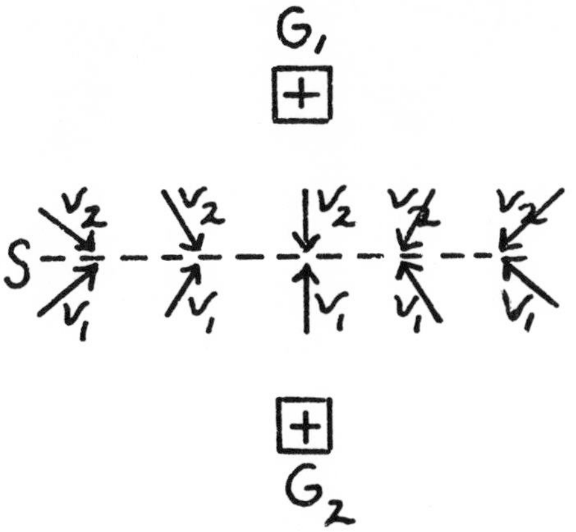

FIGURE 14
(Situation A)

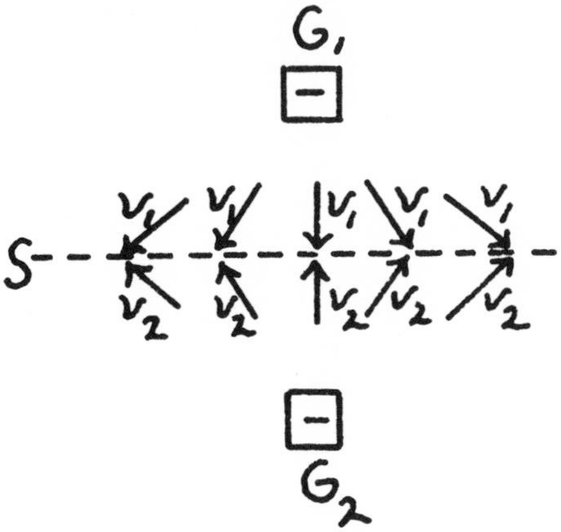

FIGURE 15
(Situation B)

(From K. Lewin's "Vectors, Cognitive Processes, and Mr. Tolman's Criticism," *J. Gen. Psychol.*, 1933, **8**, 341.)

BLUMA WULFORMNA ZEIGARNIK
(1900–   )
(Russian)

Zeigarnik Effect [9]

An intention implies not so much a predetermined opportunity for its realization as it does a need or quasi-need whose dynamic state of tension *makes* opportunities. Therefore it may be asked whether such a need functions only to accomplish this task or whether the state of tension also influences other aspects of the person's behaviour. In the present study we shall investigate the influence of such tensions upon an achievement of *memory*. Specifically we shall seek to answer the question: *What is the relation between the status in memory of an activity which has been interrupted before it could be completed and of one which has not been interrupted?* We suspect that an unsatisfied quasi-need probably does influence even purely memorial retention.

The experiments reported here were con-

[9] Bluma Zeigarnik, "On finished and unfinished tasks," in Willis D. Ellis (ed.), *A Source Book of Gestalt Psychology, op. cit.*, 300–302, 312–314; original German, "Über das Behalten von erledigten und unerledigten Handlungen," *Psychol. Forsch.*, 1927, **9**, 1–85. Reprinted by permission.

ducted with 164 individual subjects (students, teachers, children), and in addition there were two group experiments (47 adults, 45 children).

Procedure. The instructions were: "I shall give you a series of tasks which you are to complete as rapidly and correctly as possible." The subject was then given from 18 to 22 tasks one at a time—but half of these were *interrupted* before he could complete them. The order and type of interruption was such that no one could suspect the reason. For example, two tasks would be interrupted, then two allowed to reach completion, one interrupted followed by two completed, etc.

Following the last task the experimenter asked, "Please tell me what the tasks were upon which you worked during this experiment." No time limit was imposed during the subject's report. A record was kept noting the *order* of recall. Very often a number of tasks would be mentioned, and then a pause would occur during which the subject tried to remember what other tasks he had had. The quantitative results given below refer to the number of tasks recalled *before* this pause.

After the experiment was over, introspective

reports were requested. Following this the subjects were asked to tell which tasks had been the most and which the least interesting, pleasant, etc. In addition to these data the experimenter also made notes of all spontaneous remarks occurring during the work period.

The tasks themselves consisted of manual work (constructing a box of cardboard, making clay figures, etc.) and of mental problems such as puzzles, arithmetic, and the like. The time required for most of these was 3–5 minutes. The tasks were divided by the experimenter (without the subject's knowledge) into two groups, a and b, and half of the total number of subjects completed all of the a and none of the b tasks; the other half completed all of the b and none of the a tasks. Hence our data refer to memory for each task both as completed and as interrupted.

Results. Let us designate those tasks which were *interrupted and recalled* as IR, those which were *completed and recalled* as CR. If the memory for both types was in any given case the same, then IR/CR would equal 1. Should there be a case in which IR/CR = 1.5, this would mean that the interrupted tasks were recalled 50 per cent better than the completed ones. If IR/CR = 3, the superiority of interrupted over completed tasks would be 200 per cent. If IR/CR = 0.8, then recall of the interrupted tasks was 20 per cent worse than that of the completed ones.

The results obtained from our first 32 subjects indicate an average memory advantage of 90 per cent enjoyed by *interrupted* tasks (i.e. IR/CR = 1.9). The extremes extend from a 500 per cent advantage with one subject to a 25 per cent *dis*advantage with another. Summarizing, we find that of the 32 subjects, 26 remembered interrupted tasks best; 3 remembered the completed and interrupted ones equally well; 3 remembered the completed better than the interrupted. That interruption of a task greatly improves its chances of being remembered can be seen from this survey: of the 22 tasks used, 17 were remembered best when interrupted, 2 were equally well recalled regardless of interruption or completion, 3 were better recalled when completed.

So far as amount of time is concerned, the advantage *should* lie with completed tasks

since a subject who completed a task naturally spent a longer time with it than one who did not. That, however, completed tasks were not the best recalled can be seen from the foregoing figures.

As regards the order of recall we find that the interrupted tasks were mentioned first three times as often as were the completed ones. The same holds almost as decisively for the second task to be mentioned. (Somewhat later in the recall there is a reversal of this: completed tasks are then mentioned more frequently than the interrupted ones). This shows that the memory advantage of interrupted tasks is also apparent as regards priority of recall.

The foregoing experiment was repeated with a *new* set of tasks and 15 *new* subjects. The results were an almost exact duplicate of those already reported. In this case the recall advantage of interrupted tasks was 100 per cent (i.e. IR/CR = 2).

Group Experiments. The next two experiments were given to groups of 47 adults and 45 school children (average age of the latter, 14 years). There were 18 tasks; the material for each was presented in a separate envelope. An additional envelope contained a questionnaire for the report. At the word "Begin" each subject opened the first envelope, noted the instructions for that task and began work. As soon as he had finished, or immediately upon being told to stop, the entire contents were returned to the envelope. All subjects began each new task at the same time. Because some worked faster than others the instructions to stop (interruption) were given when approximately half of the group had completed a given task.

The results show a memory advantage enjoyed by interrupted tasks of 90 per cent (IR/CR = 1.9) for adults and of 110 per cent (IR/CR = 2.1) for children. Of the 47 adults, 37 remembered the interrupted task best, 3 remembered both equally well, 7 recalled the completed ones best. Among the 45 children, 36 were best in recalling unfinished tasks, 4 were equal, and 5 remembered the finished tasks best.

* * * * *

Individual Differences. The range of values obtained in the main experiment extended from 500 to —25 per cent memorial advantage for unfinished tasks. The question naturally arises: Was this spread due to chance or did it depend upon genuine individual differences between the subjects themselves? To study this more closely the experiment was repeated (new tasks being used) with 14 subjects after an interval of 3–6 months. The correlation between results from the earlier and later experiments was 0.9— which, as an answer to our question, clearly shows that the spread of results in the main experiment was due almost entirely to consistent individual differences between the persons acting as subjects.

Further insight into the matter of individual differences may be gotten by comparing the results obtained from children (average memorial advantage of unfinished tasks 150 per cent) with those of the adult subjects (average 90 per cent). It was characteristic of children, for example, that they sometimes recalled *only* the unfinished tasks. They took the experiment much more seriously than did the adults. By comparison with older subjects, the children's attitude towards these tasks was far more *natural*. In consequence, each task assumed for them decided lineaments of its own. If an adult could not recall the name of a task he would perhaps content himself with some such designation as, "Well, and then there was that folding task." Not so with the child. If he could not recall its name, he would reproduce the task in pantomime, describing it in detail as he proceeded. And the tone of voice was also noticeably different. Never did any child speak in a "superior" manner about the tasks. One could see that with children there had been a genuine *need* to complete the tasks given them and not infrequently they would beg to continue the interrupted tasks even two or three days after the experiment was over.

This attitude of earnest concern for the work given them was not, however, wholly confined to children. Adult subjects who let themselves go were also to be found among the members of our principal group. Comparing the results of these subjects with those of the very staid adults one finds that whereas with the latter unfinished tasks had a memorial advantage of only 10 per cent (IR/CR = 1.1), its value for the "child-like" subjects was 190 per cent (IR/CR = 2.9).

Summary. The experiments reported here have shown that *unfinished* tasks are remembered approximately twice as well as completed ones. Neither affective colouring nor other special characteristics of the tasks themselves will account for this. Nor will reference to the "shock"-effect accompanying interruption provide grounds for an explanation of this finding. Instead the recall-value of unfinished tasks is high because at the time of report there still exists an unsatisfied quasi-need.

This quasi-need corresponds to a state of tension whose expression may be seen not only in desire to finish the interrupted work but also in memorial prominence as regards that work. Prominence of the quasi-need to recall unfinished tasks depends upon the intensity and structure of the tension system, and also upon the strength and kind of quasi-need set up by the experimenter's instructions to report all tasks. If the subject considers the request a test of his memory, interrupted tasks will enjoy no particular recall-value. If he makes a free and untrammelled report, these tasks will be far better recalled than the others.

A quasi-need persists if the task has not been completed *to the subject's own* satisfaction regardless of whether this is equivalent to what may seem from another's inspection to constitute "finished" or "unfinished." Tasks with whose solution the subject is not content will function in his memory as "unfinished" even though the experimenter may have classified them as completed tasks, and vice versa.

With ambitious subjects inner spheres of the person himself are more involved than is ordinarily the case. In consequence the recall-value of interrupted tasks is higher than the general average.

It is essential for the memorial advantage of unfinished tasks that the tension systems be sufficiently isolated from one another. When the individual tasks lack separate lineaments for the subject, there develops only one large tension system in place of several. This was the case with subjects who had been told beforehand what the tasks were to be; it held also for others who considered the tasks merely incidental to some hidden meaning lying behind them.

When fatigue diminishes firmness in the total field, the development and maintenance of tension systems is greatly impaired. Excitement or some radical change of situation will also weaken or destroy the walls separating these systems.

The strength with which such tension systems arise and persist evidently varies greatly between different individuals but remains very nearly constant with the same individual. Strong needs, impatience to gratify them, a child-like and natural approach —the more there is of these, the more will unfinished tasks enjoy in memory a special advantage over those which have been completed.

24

Russian Behaviorism

IVAN PETROVICH PAVLOV
(1849–1936)

Conditioned Reflex [1]

In studying over a period of years the normal working of the digestive glands, and analysing the constant conditions of this work, I came upon conditions of a psychical character, which, incidentally, had been observed by others before me. There were no grounds for neglecting these conditions, since they participated constantly and prominently in the normal physiological process. I was obliged to investigate them if I wanted to make a really thorough study of my subject. But how? All that follows in my exposition supplies the answer to this question.

From all our material I shall select only the experiments with the salivary glands— organs which apparently play a very insignificant physiological role; however, I am convinced that they will become classical objects for the new type of research about which I shall have the honour of telling you today; part of this research has already been carried out and part is in the planning stage.

In observing the normal working of the salivary glands one cannot but be amazed by the high degree of their adaptability.

Give the animal dry, hard food substances and there will be an abundant salivary secretion—give it liquid food and the secretion will be much smaller.

It is obvious that for the chemical testing of the food, for mixing it and converting it into a lump to be swallowed, water is required—and the salivary glands supply it. From the mucous salivary glands there flows for every kind of food, saliva rich in mucin— a lubricating saliva, which facilitates the smooth passage of the food into the stomach. All highly irritant substances, such as acids, salts, etc., also produce a salivary secretion which varies in accordance with the strength of their stimulating action; clearly, as we know from everyday experience, the purpose of this secretion is to neutralize or dilute the substances and to cleanse the mouth. In this case the mucous glands secrete fluid saliva containing little mucin. For what would be the purpose of the mucin here? If pure insoluble quartz pebbles are placed in the mouth of a dog it will move them around, try to chew them, and finally, it will drop them. There is either no secretion of saliva at all, or at most two or three drops flow out. Again, what purpose would the saliva serve here? The pebbles are easily ejected by the animal and nothing remains in the mouth. But if sand is placed in the dog's mouth, i.e., the same pebbles but in pulverized form, there will be an abundant flow of saliva. It is clear

[1] Ivan Petrovitch Pavlov, *Lectures on Conditioned Reflexes*, trans. S. Belsky (Moscow: Foreign Languages Publishing House, 1955), pp. 151–163. Lecture entitled: "Experimental Psychology and Psychopathology in Animals," read before the International Congress of Medicine, Madrid, April, 1903.

that without saliva, without fluid in the oral cavity, the sand could neither be ejected, nor forwarded to the stomach.

Here we have exact and constant facts—facts which seem to imply intelligence. But the entire mechanism of this intelligence is absolutely plain. On the one hand, physiology has long known about the centrifugal nerves of the salivary glands, which now chiefly cause water to enter into the saliva, and now accumulate in the saliva special organic substances. On the other hand, the internal lining of the oral cavity consists of separate areas which act as receptors of different special stimuli—mechanical, chemical, thermal. Moreover, these stimuli may be further subdivided, the chemical, for example, into salts, acids, etc. There are grounds for assuming that the same thing is true of the mechanical stimuli. It is in the areas acting as receptors of special stimuli that the specific centripetal nerves have their origin.

Thus, the reactions of adaptation are based on a simple reflex originated by definite external conditions acting only on certain kinds of centripetal nerve endings; from here the excitation passes along a definite nervous path to the centre, and thence, also along a definite path, to the salivary gland, evoking its specific function.

* * * * *

All the foregoing objects, which, after being placed in the mouth, influenced the salivary glands in different and at the same time definite ways, exert on these glands exactly the same action, at least qualitatively, when placed at a certain distance from the dog. Dry food produces much saliva—moist food only a little. A thick, lubricating saliva flows from the mucous glands to the food substances. Various inedible irritants also produce secretion from all the glands, including the mucous glands. But it is fluid and contains but a small amount of mucin. Pebbles, when shown to the animal, have no effect on the glands, while sand evokes profuse salivation. These facts were partly obtained and partly systematized in my laboratory by Dr. S. G. Wolfson. The dog sees, hears, and smells all these substances, pays attention to them, rushes to them if edible or agreeable, but turns away from them and resists their introduction into the mouth when disagree-

able. Everybody would say that this is a psychical reaction, psychical stimulation of the animal's salivary glands.

* * * * *

In our psychical experiments we have before us definite external objects, exciting the animal and evoking in it a definite reaction, in the given case—secretion of the salivary glands. As has been said, the effect of these objects is substantially the same as in the physiological experiments, when they come into contact with the oral cavity. Consequently, we have before us simply further adaptation—the object acts on the salivary glands the moment it is being brought close to the mouth.

What are the specific features of these new phenomena compared with the physiological ones? Above all, the difference seems to be that in the physiological form of the experiment the substance comes into direct contact with the organism, while in the psychical form it acts from a distance. But this circumstance in itself, if we reflect on it, does not, obviously, signify any essential difference between these, in a way specific, experiments, and the purely physiological ones. The point is that in these cases the substances act on other special receiving surfaces of the body—nose, eye, ear—through the medium in which both the organism and the stimulating substances exist (air, ether). How many simple physiological reflexes are transmitted by the nose, eye and ear, that is, originate at a distance! Hence, the essential difference between the new phenomena and the purely physiological does not lie here.

It lies much deeper, and should be sought, in my view, in a comparison of the following facts. In the physiological case the activity of the salivary glands is connected with the properties of the substance on which the effect of the saliva is directed. The saliva moistens dry substances and any ingested material; it neutralizes the chemical effect of the substances. These properties constitute the special stimuli of the specific mouth surface. Consequently, in the physiological experiments the animal is stimulated by the essential, unconditioned properties of the object in relation to the physiological role of the saliva.

In the psychical experiments the animal is excited by the properties of the external object, which are unessential for the activity of the salivary glands, or even entirely accidental. The visual, acoustic and even purely olfactory properties of our objects, when they are present in other objects, do not of themselves exert any influence on the salivary glands which, in their turn, so to speak, have no business relations with these properties. In the psychical experiments the salivary glands are stimulated not only by the properties of the objects unessential for the work of the glands, but absolutely by all the conditions surrounding these objects, or with which they are connected one way or another—for example, the dish in which they are contained, the article on which they are placed, the room, the people who usually bring the objects, even the noises produced by these people, though the latter may not be seen at the given moment—their voices, even the sound of their steps. Thus, in psychical experiments, the connection of the objects acting as stimuli on the salivary glands becomes more and more distant and delicate. Here, undoubtedly, we have a phenomenon of further adaptation. We can admit in this case that such a distant and delicate connection as that between the step of the person who usually feeds the animal and the working of the salivary glands has no specific physiological significance other than its delicacy. But we need only recall those animals whose saliva contains protective poison, to appreciate the great vital significance of this timely provision of a protective means against an approaching enemy. The significance of the distant signs of objects producing a motor reaction in the organism, is, of course, easily recognized. By means of distant and even accidental characteristics of objects the animal seeks its food, evades enemies, etc.

If that is so, then the following questions are of decisive significance for our subject: can this seemingly chaos of relations be included in a definite scheme? Is it possible to make the phenomena constant, to disclose the laws governing their development and their mechanism? It seems to me that the examples which I shall now present entitle me to give an emphatically positive answer to these questions, to find at the basis of all psychical experiments the one and same special reflex as the chief and most general mechanism. True, in its physiological form, our experiment, excluding, of course, all extraordinary conditions, always yields one and the same result; it is the unconditioned reflex. But the main feature of the psychical experiment is its impermanence, its obvious capriciousness. However, the results of a psychical experiment undoubtedly recur too, otherwise we would not speak of them at all. Consequently, the point is in the greater number of factors which influence the results of a psychical experiment, compared with a physiological one. This, then, is a conditioned reflex. Here are facts which show that our psychical material may also be included in a definite scheme and that it is subject to certain laws. These facts were obtained in my laboratory by Dr. I. F. Tolochinov.

It is not difficult to recognize during the first psychical experiments the chief conditions guaranteeing their success, i.e., their constancy. If an animal is stimulated (i.e., its salivary glands) by food placed at a distance, the result of the experiment depends solely on whether the animal has been prepared for it by a certain period of fasting. An animal experiencing keen hunger yields positive results; on the contrary, the most voracious and least fastidious animal, if it has just had a good meal, fails to respond to food placed at a distance. Thinking in terms of physiology we can say that we have here a different degree of excitability of the salivarx centre—greatly increased in the first case, and greatly decreased in the second. We may rightly assume that just as the carbonic acid contained in the blood determines the energy of the respiratory centre, so the different composition of the blood in a hungry animal and in one that is sated determines the above-mentioned fluctuations in the excitability and reactivity of the salivary centres. From the subjective point of view this could be designated as attention. When the stomach is empty, the sight of food easily causes the mouth to water; in sated animals the same reaction is either very weak or entirely lacking.

Let us proceed. If the animal is shown food or certain disagreeable substances, and if this is repeated several times, then with each repetition the experiment will produce a weaker result, and in the end there will be no reaction whatever. There is, however, a sure method of restoring the reaction; it can be achieved by giving the dog food or by introducing into its mouth substances which ceased to act as stimuli. This, of course, produces the usual strong reflex, and the object begins to act from a distance again. For the subsequent result it is immaterial whether food is placed in the mouth or any disagreeable substance. For example, if meat powder no longer stimulates the animal from a distance, its effect can be restored either by letting it eat the powder or by introducing into the mouth an undesired substance, e.g., acid. We can say that thanks to the direct reflex the excitability of the salivary centre has been heightened, and the weak stimulus —the object at a distance—has become sufficiently strong. Do we not experience the same thing ourselves when appetite comes with eating, or when, after unpleasant, powerful excitation, we begin to have the appetite that we previously lacked?

Here is a number of other facts of a constant character. The object placed at a distance stimulates the salivary glands not only by the entire complex of its properties, but also by its individual properties. If a hand smelling of meat or meat powder, is brought into proximity with the dog, it often proves sufficient to induce a salivary reaction. Similarly the sight of food placed at a distance, and consequently the mere optical effect of the object, may also stimulate the activity of the salivary glands. But the combined, simultaneous action of all these properties of the object always produces a better and greater effect, i.e., the action of the sum of the stimuli is more powerful than each individual stimulus.

* * * * *

The above-mentioned facts, on the one hand, provide certain, and in my view, important conclusions about the processes taking place in the central nervous system; on the other hand, they make possible further successful analysis. Let us consider from the standpoint of physiology some of our facts, and first of all our fundamental fact. When a given object—a certain food or chemical irritant—is brought into contact with the special surface of the oral cavity and stimulates it by means of those of its properties on which the activity of the salivary glands is specially directed, then the other properties of the object that have nothing to do with the working of the salivary glands or even with the entire environment of the object, but simultaneously stimulating other sensory surfaces of the body, become connected, apparently, with the same nervous centre of the salivary glands to which the stimulation emanating from the essential properties of the object is conducted through a fixed centripetal path. It can be assumed in this case that the salivary centre acts in the central nervous system as a point of attraction for stimuli coming from other sensory surfaces. Thus, a certain path is opened from the other excited areas of the body to the salivary centre. But this connection of the centre with accidental points is very fragile and tends to disappear of itself. Constant repetition of simultaneous stimulation by means of the essential and unessential properties of the object is required to make this connection increasingly durable. In this way a temporary relation is established between the activity of a certain organ and the external objects. The temporary relation and its law—to become stronger as a result of repetition and to disappear when not repeated—play a big role in the well-being and integrity of the organism; by means of it the adaptability of the organism and the conformity of its activity to the surroundings become more perfect and delicate. The two parts of this law are equally important: if the temporary relation to the object is of great significance for the organism, then the rupture of this relation is essential when it is no longer justified by reality. Otherwise the relations of the animal, instead of being delicate, would assume a chaotic character.

VLADIMIR MICHAILOVITCH
BECHTEREV
(1867–1927)

Reflexology [2]

After all that has been said, it is obvious that that science which I have duly called reflexology consists in the study of the organism's correlative activity in the wide sense of the word, and by correlative activity we mean all the organism's inherited and individually acquired reactions, beginning from innate and complex-organic reflexes up to, and including, the most complex acquired reflexes, which in man go by the name of actions and conduct and comprise his characteristic behaviour.

Comparative reflexology embraces the correlative functions of all living beings, but in what follows we are interested mainly in problems of human reflexology, and chiefly in those of the higher manifestations of man's correlative activity characterised by association reflexes.

As we know, every external influence acting on the organism is capable of producing, in addition to physico-chemical reactions, local reflexes in the form of simple or ordinary reflexes. Moreover, external influences produce general reactions of an inherited character, in other words, racial reactions in the form of urges or the so-called instincts, or, synonymously, complex-organic reflexes, but they also produce acquired or association reflexes based on past experience. The aim of reflexology as a scientific study is the explication and investigation of response reactions in general, and, in particular, of association reflexes, the study of which must be made in relation to current, past, and, also, hereditary influences.

It must be noted that ordinary reflexes in the animal world, not excluding man, have been comparatively well investigated, and continue to be studied, and, therefore, we shall not dilate on this subject. Recently, as we have seen, acquired reactions, too, in the animal world have been submitted to objective investigation in various directions. But, as

we have already said, the centre of interest in the following exposition is human reflexology, which has as its aim to study not only man's constitutional conditions, but also his external reactions of an inherited, complex-organic, and also acquired character—reactions which develop under the influence of external or internal stimuli either present or past. In this direction reflexology may achieve its aim in the following ways:

1. By the objective, bio-social study of all the external manifestations of a human being, and by the noting of their correlations with the external and internal influences, present and past, and also by the study of the consecutive development of the correlative, and particularly the association-reflex, activity from the day of birth.

2. By the experimental and observational investigation of the conformity to law of the development of association-reflex activity under various conditions.

3. By the study of that mechanism through the mediation of which is established the correlation of certain association and other reflexes with the external and internal stimuli, present and past; this study is prosecuted by experiments in which areas of the brain of the animal are destroyed and by the observation of pathological conditions in men.

4. By the study of the ontogenesis and the phylogenesis of the correlative, and particularly the association-reflex, activity in relation to the purely genetic development of the cerebral hemispheres.

5. By the study of the correlation of the objective processes of the association-reflex activity with man's verbal account of the experiences connected with them.

The first aim is difficult to achieve in the case of an adult. Anyhow, it may be achieved only by means of a detailed and elaborate scheme in which all possible external reactions are set down under the categories of their external manifestations (speech, actions, facial expressions, gestures, organic or instinctive manifestations) and in which are, at the same time, set down the external stimuli which have produced them. Besides, there is required a careful collection and objective analysis of

---

[2] Vladimir Michailovitch Bechterev, *General Principles of Human Reflexology: An Introduction to the Objective Study of Personality*, trans. Emma and William Murphy (London: Jarrolds Publishers, 1933), pp. 116–119, 171–173.

material concerning the human individual in the past and the present. This aim is much more easily achieved in the case of new-born infants, if trouble is taken to record, in strictly objective fashion and according to a definite scheme, all the infant's external manifestations in relation to the past and present influences, external and internal, acting on him.

The second aim naturally follows from the analysis of the material mentioned, but it is also achieved by present-day laboratory methods of artificially inculcating association reflexes, methods through which both the development of these reflexes, as well as certain alien influences acting on them, may be studied in strictly objective fashion. Nevertheless, observation of the behaviour of man and animals under various conditions also provides much pertinent material.

The third aim is achieved mainly by experimentally investigating association reflexes in animals when various areas of the nervous system have been destroyed, and in man in cases of affection of the brain and of the nervous system in general.

The fourth aim is concerned with genetic and comparative reflexology.

The fifth aim is achieved through comparison of the objective investigation of external reaction with the verbal account of the unexpressed or latent reflexes which are studied chiefly on oneself.

Let us note in conclusion that man is an agent whose mechanism is set in motion by external and internal stimuli, for he is a product both of the past life of his ancestors (racial experience) and of his own past individual experience. In accordance with this, and in dependence on it, he develops reactions to certain external and internal influences, and these reactions take the form of various—sometimes complex, sometimes more simple—concatenated reflexes produced by external, as well as internal, stimuli not only present, but also past. Thus, for reflexology, man is not distinguishable into subject and object, but is a unitary being, both object and subject at once, in the form of an agent, whose external aspect alone is accessible to scientific investigation by an external observer. This external aspect is comprised of the totality of the various reflexes, and primarily appertains to objective study, while the

subjective aspect does not appertain to direct observation, and, consequently, cannot be studied directly; but what we can study is the objectively given verbal account of the inner or latent reflexes, an account which has to be taken into consideration, but must be invariably checked and tested against objective data.

* * * * *

The fundamental activities of all living beings are acts of aggression and defence; in other words, they are aggressive and defensive reflexes, which are to be found not only in the lower animals, but even in plants which are tied by nature to a definite spot and get food from the environment.

In general, the concept of reflex has been recently regarded from two points of view: On the one hand, we have begun to understand by reflex not only such mechanical acts as writing, reading, etc., but also tropisms in the vegetable world, as, for instance, the turning of a plant and its blossoms to the sun, etc., and the responses of bacteria to increased stimulation. On the other hand, reflexology regards all the organism's more complex correlations with its environment as higher reflexes, which we call "association" reflexes. In reflexology, we go further than biology, and reduce to reflexes, on the one hand, such phenomena as morphogenesis and propagation, and, on the other, the social interrelations between human beings.

In the animal kingdom, even the simple cell exhibits an aggressive, as well as a defensive, reflex, for every cell contracts under the activity of unfavourable external conditions, and expands again under favourable nutritional conditions. All of this applies not only to the cell body, but also to the protoplasmic projections or dendrites of the neuron, for these projections shorten in the first case, and become elongated in the second.

It is obvious that the concentration of the cell and its projections is an act of self-defence or protection, because by this very activity the cellular surface is decreased, and so, simultaneously, becomes, on the one hand, more dense and less permeable, and, on the other, is withdrawn to a certain extent from the unfavourable stimulus, while, in the case of cellular expansion, we have the activity of aggression and absorption, for the absorptive surface of the cell and its projections becomes, under favourable conditions, more extensive and permeable, approaches the favourable stimulus to some extent, and finally absorbs it.

* * * * *

Along with defence reflexes, there develop everywhere in the animal kingdom reflexes of aggression or attack and of seizing, the former of which often serve simultaneously for active defence, although the fundamental aim of the reflex of attack is both the finding and seizing of food as a stimulus, and the satisfaction of other demands.

It is scarcely necessary to say that aggression and defence, inasmuch as they are fundamental functions of the organism, must represent the earliest reflexes in animal phylogenesis, and, consequently, as we have seen, we find these reflexes in the simplest unicellular organisms, beginning from the amœba, and even in plants. Besides, the organs of movement serve simultaneously for both functions on the most divergent planes of the development of animal life. Thus, the octopus both catches its prey and propels itself by means of its arms.

In many animals, organs used in feeding, for instance, jaws, which in arthropoda are transformed legs, serve for defence and aggression. But there are also more specialised organs of defence and aggression, such as the chelæ of the cray-fish, the sting of bees (ovipositor), the poisonous sting of the scorpion, the stinking fluid of the skunk, the horns of some mammals, and even the horny bristles (as in the porcupine and the hedgehog), which, by the way, serve rather for defence than aggression.

* * * * *

In conclusion, let us remark that, on the ground of reflex activity, plants must be classified with animals, and this is comprehensible, for "the kingdom of living beings forms one harmonious, coherent whole, which in its primitive stages can only artificially be divided into animals and plants" (Strasburger). But also, on the highest planes of both kingdoms, we find processes which are, in many respects, identical in character, especially when there is question of such fundamental vital functions as feeding, metabolism, respiration.

25

American Behaviorism and Neobehaviorism

JOHN BROADUS WATSON
(1878–1958)

Behaviorism [1]

Psychology as the behaviorist views it is a purely objective experimental branch of natural science. Its theoretical goal is the prediction and control of behavior. Introspection forms no essential part of its methods, nor is the scientific value of its data dependent upon the readiness with which they lend themselves to interpretation in terms of

consciousness. The behaviorist, in his efforts to get a unitary scheme of animal response, recognizes no dividing line between man and brute. The behavior of man, with all of its refinement and complexity, forms only a part of the behaviorist's total scheme of investigation.

It has been maintained by its followers generally that psychology is a study of the science of the phenomena of consciousness.

* * * * *

It is agreed that introspection is the method *par excellence* by means of which mental

[1] John B. Watson, "Psychology as the behaviorist views it," *Psychol. Rev.*, 1913, **20**, 158–177. Reprinted by permission of the American Psychological Association.

states may be manipulated for purposes of psychology. On this assumption, behavior data (including under this term everything which goes under the name of comparative psychology) have no value *per se*. They possess significance only in so far as they may throw light upon conscious states. Such data must have at least an analogical or indirect reference to belong to the realm of psychology.

Indeed, at times, one finds psychologists who are sceptical of even this analogical reference. Such scepticism is often shown by the question which is put to the student of behavior, "What is the bearing of animal work upon human psychology?" I used to have to study over this question. Indeed it always embarrassed me somewhat. I was interested in my own work and felt that it was important, and yet I could not trace any close connection between it and psychology as my questioner understood psychology. I hope that such a confession will clear the atmosphere to such an extent that we will no longer have to work under false pretenses. We must frankly admit that the facts so important to us which we have been able to glean from extended work upon the senses of animals by the behavior method have contributed only in a fragmentary way to the general theory of human sense organ processes, nor have they suggested new points of experimental attack. The enormous number of experiments which we have carried out upon learning have likewise contributed little to human psychology. It seems reasonably clear that some kind of compromise must be effected: either psychology must change its viewpoint so as to take in facts of behavior, whether or not they have bearings upon the problems of "consciousness"; or else behavior must stand alone as a wholly separate and independent science. Should human psychologists fail to look with favor upon our overtures and refuse to modify their position, the behaviorists will be driven to using human beings as subjects and to employ methods of investigation which are exactly comparable to those now employed in the animal work.

Any other hypothesis than that which admits the independent value of behavior material, regardless of any bearing such material may have upon consciousness, will inevitably force us to the absurd position of attempting to *construct* the conscious content of the animal whose behavior we have been studying. On this view, after having determined our animal's ability to learn, the simplicity or complexity of its methods of learning, the effect of past habit upon present response, the range of stimuli to which it ordinarily responds, the widened range to which it can respond under experimental conditions,—in more general terms, its various problems and its various ways of solving them,—we should still feel that the task is unfinished and that the results are worthless, until we can interpret them by analogy in the light of consciousness. Although we have solved our problem we feel uneasy and unrestful because of our definition of psychology: we feel forced to say something about the possible mental processes of our animal. We say that, having no eyes, its stream of consciousness cannot contain brightness and color sensations as we know them,—having no taste buds this stream can contain no sensations of sweet, sour, salt and bitter. But on the other hand, since it does respond to thermal, tactual and organic stimuli, its conscious content must be made up largely of these sensations; and we usually add, to protect ourselves against the reproach of being anthropomorphic, "if it has any consciousness." Surely this doctrine which calls for an analogical interpretation of all behavior data may be shown to be false: the position that the standing of an observation upon behavior is determined by its fruitfulness in yielding results which are interpretable only in the narrow realm of (really human) consciousness.

This emphasis upon analogy in psychology has led the behaviorist somewhat afield. Not being willing to throw off the yoke of consciousness he feels impelled to make a place in the scheme of behavior where the rise of consciousness can be determined. This point has been a shifting one. A few years ago certain animals were supposed to possess "associative memory," while certain others were supposed to lack it. One meets this search for the origin of consciousness under a good many disguises. Some of our texts state that consciousness arises at the moment when reflex and instinctive activities fail properly to conserve the organism. A perfectly adjusted organism would be lacking in consciousness. On the other hand whenever we find the presence of diffuse activity which results in habit formation, we are justified in assuming consciousness. I must confess that these arguments had weight with me when I began the study of behavior. I fear that a good many of us are still viewing behavior problems with something like this in mind. More than one student in behavior has attempted to frame criteria of the psychic— to devise a set of objective, structural and functional criteria which, when applied in the particular instance, will enable us to decide whether such and such responses are positively conscious, merely indicative of consciousness, or whether they are purely "psychological." Such problems as these can no longer satisfy behavior men. It would be better to give up the province altogether and admit frankly that the study of the behavior of animals has no justification, than to admit that our search is of such a "will o' the wisp" character. One can assume either the presence or the absence of consciousness anywhere in the phylogenetic scale without affecting the problems of behavior by one jot or one tittle; and without influencing in any way the mode of experimental attack upon them. On the other hand, I cannot for one moment assume that the paramecium responds to light; that the rat learns a problem more quickly by working at the task five times a day than once a day, or that the human child exhibits plateaux in his learning curves. These are questions which vitally concern behavior and which must be decided by direct observation under experimental conditions.

This attempt to reason by analogy from human conscious processes to the conscious processes in animals, and *vice versa:* to make consciousness, as the human being knows it, the center of reference of all behavior, forces us into a situation similar to that which existed in biology in Darwin's time.

* * * * *

In psychology we are still in that stage of development where we feel that we must select our material. We have a general place of discard for processes, which we anathematize so far as their value for psychology is concerned by saying, "this is a reflex"; "that is a purely physiological fact which has nothing to do with psychology." We are not interested (as psychologists) in getting all

of the processes of adjustment which the animal as a whole employs, and in finding how these various responses are associated, and how they fall apart, thus working out a systematic scheme for the prediction and control of response in general. Unless our observed facts are indicative of consciousness, we have no use for them, and unless our apparatus and method are designed to throw such facts into relief, they are thought of in just as disparaging a way. I shall always remember the remark one distinguished psychologist made as he looked over the color apparatus designed for testing the responses of animals to monochromatic light in the attic at Johns Hopkins. It was this: "And they call this psychology!"

* * * * *

The time seems to have come when psychology must discard all reference to consciousness; when it need no longer delude itself into thinking that it is making mental states the object of observation. We have become so enmeshed in speculative questions concerning the elements of mind, the nature of conscious content (for example, imageless thought, attitudes and Bewusstseinslage, etc.) that I, as an experimental student, feel that something is wrong with our premises and the types of problems which develop from them. There is no longer any guarantee that we all mean the same thing when we use the terms now current in psychology. Take the case of sensation. A sensation is defined in terms of its attributes. One psychologist will state with readiness that the attributes of a visual sensation are *quality*, *extension*, *duration*, and *intensity*. Another will add *clearness*. Still another that of *order*. I doubt if any one psychologist can draw up a set of statements describing what he means by sensation which will be agreed to by three other psychologists of different training. Turn for a moment to the question of the number of isolable sensations. Is there an extremely large number of color sensations—or only four, red, green, yellow and blue? Again, yellow, while psychologically simple, can be obtained by superimposing red and green spectral rays upon the same diffusing surface! If, on the other hand, we say that every just noticeable difference in the spectrum is a simple sensation, and that every just noticeable increase in the white value of a given color gives simple sensations, we are forced to admit that the number is so large and the conditions for obtaining them so complex that the concept of sensation is unusable, either for the purpose of analysis or that of synthesis.

* * * * *

The condition in regard to other mental processes is just as chaotic. Can image type be experimentally tested and verified? Are recondite thought processes dependent mechanically upon imagery at all? Are psychologists agreed upon what feeling is? One states that feelings are attitudes. Another finds them to be groups of organic sensations possessing a certain solidarity. Still another and larger group finds them to be new elements correlative with and ranking equally with sensations.

My psychological quarrel is not with the systematic and structural psychologist alone. The last fifteen years have seen the growth of what is called functional psychology. This type of psychology decries the use of elements in the static sense of the structuralists. It throws emphasis upon the biological significance of conscious processes instead of upon the analysis of conscious states into introspectively isolable elements. I have done my best to understand the difference between functional psychology and structural psychology. Instead of clarity, confusion grows upon me. The terms sensation, perception, affection, emotion, volition are used as much by the functionalist as by the structuralist. The addition of the word "process" ("mental act as a whole," and like terms are frequently met) after each serves in some way to remove the corpse of "content" and to leave "function" in its stead. Surely if these concepts are elusive when looked at from a content standpoint, they are still more deceptive when viewed from the angle of function, and especially so when function is obtained by the introspection method. It is rather interesting that no functional psychologist has carefully distinguished between "perception" (and this is true of the other psychological terms as well) as employed by the systematist, and "perceptual process" as used in functional psychology. It seems illogical and hardly fair to criticize the psychology which the system-

atist gives us, and then to utilize his terms without carefully showing the changes in meaning which are to be attached to them. I was greatly surprised some time ago when I opened Pillsbury's book and saw psychology defined as the "science of behavior." A still more recent text states that psychology is the "science of mental behavior." When I saw these promising statements I thought, now surely we will have texts based upon different lines. After a few pages the science of behavior is dropped and one finds the conventional treatment of sensation, perception, imagery, etc., along with certain shifts in emphasis and additional facts which serve to give the author's personal imprint.

One of the difficulties in the way of a consistent functional psychology is the parallelistic hypothesis. If the functionalist attempts to express his formulations in terms which make mental states really appear to function, to play some active role in the world of adjustment, he almost inevitably lapses into terms which are connotative of interaction. When taxed with this he replies that it is more convenient to do so and that he does it to avoid the circumlocution and clumsiness which are inherent in any thoroughgoing parallelism. As a matter of fact I believe the functionalist actually thinks in terms of interaction and resorts to parallelism only when forced to give expression to his views. I feel that *behaviorism* is the only consistent and logical functionalism. In it one avoids both the Scylla of parallelism and the Charybdis of interaction. Those time-honored relics of philosophical speculation need trouble the student of behavior as little as they trouble the student of physics. The consideration of the mind-body problem affects neither the type of problem selected nor the formulation of the solution of that problem. I can state my position here no better than by saying that I should like to bring my students up in the same ignorance of such hypotheses as one finds among the students of other branches of science.

This leads me to the point where I should like to make the argument constructive. I believe we can write a psychology, define it as Pillsbury, and never go back upon our definition: never use the terms consciousness, mental states, mind, content, introspectively verifiable, imagery, and the life. I believe that

454

we can do it in a few years without running into the absurd terminology of Beer, Bethe, Von Uexkull, Nuel, and that of the so-called objective schools generally. It can be done in terms of stimulus and response, in terms of habit formation, habit integrations and the like. Furthermore, I believe that it is really worth while to make this attempt now.

The psychology which I should attempt to build up would take as a starting point, first, the observable fact that organisms, man and animal alike, do adjust themselves to their environment by means of hereditary and habit equipments. These adjustments may be very adequate or they may be so inadequate that the organism barely maintains its existence; secondly, that certain stimuli lead the organisms to make the responses. In a system of psychology completely worked out, given the response the stimuli can be predicted; given the stimuli the response can be predicted. Such a set of statements is crass and raw in the extreme, as all such generalizations must be. Yet they are hardly more raw and less realizable than the ones which appear in the psychology texts of the day. I possibly might illustrate my point better by choosing an everyday problem which anyone is likely to meet in the course of his work. Some time ago I was called upon to make a study of certain species of birds. Until I went to Tortugas I had never seen these birds alive. When I reached there I found the animals doing certain things: some of the acts seemed to work peculiarly well in such an environment, while others seemed to be unsuited to their type of life. I first studied the responses of the group as a whole and later those of individuals. In order to understand more thoroughly the relation between what was habit and what was hereditary in these responses, I took the young birds and reared them. In this way I was able to study the order of appearance of hereditary adjustments and their complexity, and later the beginnings of habit formation. My efforts in determining the stimuli which called forth such adjustments were crude indeed. Consequently my attempts to control behavior and to produce responses at will did not meet with much success. Their food and water, sex and other social relations, light and temperature conditions were all beyond control in a field study. I did find it possible to control their reactions in a measure

by using the nest and egg (or young) as stimuli. It is not necessary in this paper to develop further how such a study should be carried out and how work of this kind must be supplemented by carefully controlled laboratory experiments. Had I been called upon to examine the natives of some of the Australian tribes, I should have gone about my task in the same way. I should have found the problem more difficult: the types of responses called forth by physical stimuli would have been more varied, and the number of effective stimuli larger. I should have had to determine the social setting of their lives in a far more careful way. These savages would be more influenced by the responses of each other than was the case with the birds. Furthermore, habits would have been more complex and the influences of past habits upon the present responses would have appeared more clearly. Finally, if I had been called upon to work out the psychology of the educated Europeans, my problem would have required several lifetimes. But in the one I have at my disposal I should have followed the same general line of attack. In the main, my desire in all such work is to gain an accurate knowledge of adjustments and the stimuli calling them forth. My final reason for this is to learn general and particular methods by which I may control behavior. My goal is not "the description and explanation of states of consciousness as such," nor that of obtaining such proficiency in mental gymnastics that I can immediately lay hold of a state of consciousness and say, "this, as a whole, consists of gray sensation number 350, of such and such extent, occurring in conjunction with the sensation of cold of a certain intensity; one of pressure of a certain intensity and extent," and so on *ad infinitum*.

* * * * *

What gives me hope that the behaviorist's position is a defensible one is the fact that those branches of psychology which have already partially withdrawn from the parent, experimental psychology, and which are consequently less dependent upon introspection are today in a most flourishing condition. Experimental pedagogy, the psychology of drugs, the psychology of advertising, legal psychology, the psychology of tests, and psychopathology are all vigorous growths.

* * * * *

I am more interested at the present moment in trying to show the necessity for maintaining uniformity in experimental procedure and in the method of stating results in both human and animal work, than in developing any ideas I may have upon the changes which are certain to come in the scope of human psychology. Let us consider for a moment the subject of the range of stimuli to which animals respond. I shall speak first of the work upon vision in animals. We put our animal in a situation where he will respond (or learn to respond) to one of two mono-chromatic lights. We feed him at the one (positive) and punish him at the other (negative). In a short time the animal learns to go to the light at which he is fed. At this point questions arise which I may phrase in two ways: I may choose the psychological way and say "does the animal see these two lights as I do, *i.e.*, as two distinct colors, or does he see them as two grays differing in brightness, as does the totally color blind?" Phrased by the behaviorist, it would read as follows: "Is my animal responding upon the basis of the difference in intensity between the two stimuli, or upon the difference in wave-lengths?" He nowhere thinks of the animal's response in terms of his own experiences of colors and grays. He wishes to establish the fact whether wave-length is a factor in that animal's adjustment. If so, what wave-lengths are effective and what differences in wave-length must be maintained in the different regions to afford bases for differential re-responses? If wave-length is not a factor in adjustment he wishes to know what difference in intensity will serve as a basis for response, and whether that same difference will suffice throughout the spectrum. Furthermore, he wishes to test whether the animal can respond to wave-lengths which do not affect the human eye. He is as much interested in comparing the rat's spectrum with that of the chick as in comparing it with man's. The point of view when the various sets of comparisons are made does not change in the slightest. However we phrase the question to our-selves, we take our animal after the association has been formed and then introduce certain control experiments which enable us to return answers to the questions just raised. But there is just as keen a desire on our part to test man under the same conditions, and to state the results in both cases in common terms.

The man and the animal should be placed as nearly as possible under the same experi-mental conditions. Instead of feeding or punishing the human subject, we should ask him to respond by setting a second apparatus until standard and control offered no basis for a differential response. Do I lay myself open to the charge here that I am using introspection? My reply is not at all; that while I might very well feed my human subject for a right choice and punish him for a wrong one and thus produce the response if the subject could give it, there is no need of going to extremes even on the platform I suggest. But be it understood that I am merely using this second method as an abridged behavior method.

* * * * *

What we need to do is to start work upon psychology, making *behavior*, not *conscious-ness*, the objective point of our attack. Certainly there are enough problems in the control of behavior to keep us all working many lifetimes without ever allowing us time to think of consciousness *an sich*. Once launched in the undertaking, we will find ourselves in a short time as far divorced from an introspective psychology as the psychology of the present time is divorced from faculty psychology.

Summary

1. Human psychology has failed to make good its claim as a natural science. Due to a mistaken notion that its fields of facts are conscious phenomena and that introspection is the only direct method of ascertaining these facts, it has enmeshed itself in a series of speculative questions which, while funda-mental to its present tenets, are not open to experimental treatment. In the pursuit of answers to these questions, it has become further and further divorced from contact with problems which vitally concern human interest.

2. Psychology, as the behaviorist views it, is a purely objective, experimental branch of natural science which needs introspection as

little as do the sciences of chemistry and physics. It is granted that the behavior of animals can be investigated without appeal to consciousness. Heretofore the viewpoint has been that such data have value only in so far as they can be interpreted by analogy in terms of consciousness. The position is taken here that the behavior of man and the behavior of animals must be considered on the same plane; as being equally essential to a general understanding of behavior. It can dispense with consciousness in a psychological sense. The separate observation of "states of consciousness" is, on this assumption, no more a part of the task of the psychologist than of the physicist. We might call this the return to a non-reflective and naive use of consciousness. In this sense consciousness may be said to be the instrument or tool with which all scientists work. Whether or not the tool is properly used at present by scientists is a problem for philosophy and not for psychology.

3. From the viewpoint here suggested the facts on the behavior of amœbæ have value in and for themselves without reference to the behavior of man. In biology studies on race differentiation and inheritance in amœbæ form a separate division of study which must be evaluated in terms of the laws found there.

The conclusions so reached may not hold in any other form. Regardless of the possible lack of generality, such studies must be made if evolution as a whole is ever to be regulated and controlled. Similarly the laws of behavior in amœbæ, the range of responses, and the determination of effective stimuli, of habit formation, persistency of habits, interference and reinforcement of habits, must be determined and evaluated in and for themselves, regardless of their generality, or of their bearing upon such laws in other forms, if the phenomena of behavior are ever to be brought within the sphere of scientific control.

4. This suggested elimination of states of consciousness as proper objects of investigation in themselves will remove the barrier from psychology which exists between it and the other sciences. The findings of psychology become the functional correlates of structure and lend themselves to explanation in physico-chemical terms.

5. Psychology as behavior will, after all, have to neglect but few of the really essential problems with which psychology as an introspective science now concerns itself. In all probability even this residue of problems may be phrased in such a way that refined methods in behavior (which certainly must come) will lead to their solution.

CLARK L. HULL
(1884–1952)

A Behavior System [2]

Behavior Theory

Scientific theories are mainly concerned with dynamic situations, i.e., with the consequent events of conditions which, with the passage of time, will follow from a given set of antecedent events or conditions. The concrete activity of theorizing consists in the manipulation of a limited set of symbols according to the rules expressed in the postulates (together with certain additional rules which make up the main substance of logic) in such a way as to span the gap separating the antecedent conditions or states

from the subsequent ones. Some of the symbols represent observable and measurable elements or aggregates of the situation, whereas others represent presumptive intervening processes not directly subject to observation. The latter are theoretical constructs. All well-developed sciences freely employ theoretical constructs wherever they prove useful, sometimes even sequences or chains of them. The scientific utility of logical constructs consists in the mediation of valid deductions; this in turn is absolutely dependent upon every construct, or construct chain, being securely anchored both on the antedecent and on the consequent side to conditions or events which are directly observable. If possible, they should also be measurable.

The theory of behavior seems to require the use of a number of symbolic constructs,

[2] Clark L. Hull, *Principles of Behavior: An Introduction to Behavior Theory* (New York: Appleton-Century-Crofts, 1943), pp. 381–398. Reprinted by permission.

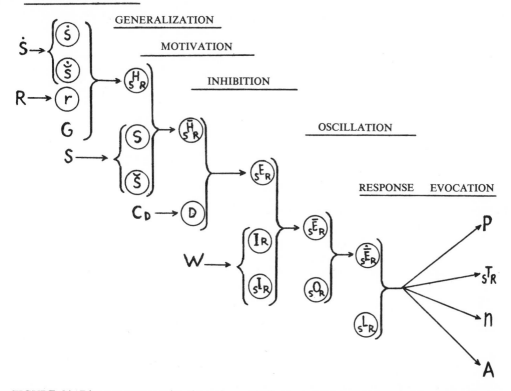

FIGURE 84. Diagram summarizing the major symbolic constructs (encircled symbols) employed in the present system of behavior theory, together with the symbols of the supporting objectively observable conditions and events. In this diagram S represents the physical stimulus energy involved in learning; R, the organism's reaction; $\dot{s}$, the neural result of the stimulus; $\overset{\circ}{s}$, the neural interaction arising from the impact of two or more stimulus components; r, the efferent impulse leading to reaction; G, the occurrence of a reinforcing state of affairs; sH_R, habit strength; S, evocation stimulus on the same stimulus continuum as $\dot{S}$; $s\bar{H}_R$, the generalized habit strength; C_D, the objectively observable phenomena determining the drive; D, the physiological strength of the drive to motivate action; sE_R, the reaction potential; W, work involved in an evoked reaction; I_R, reactive inhibition; sI_R, conditioned inhibition; $s\bar{E}_R$, effective reaction potential; sO_R, oscillation; $s\dot{\bar{E}}_R$, momentary effective reaction potential; sL_R, reaction threshold; p, probability of reaction evocation; st_R, latency of reaction evocation; n, number of unreinforced reactions to produce experimental extinction; and A, amplitude of reaction. Above the symbols the lines beneath the words *reinforcement, generalization, motivation, inhibition, oscillation,* and *response evocation* indicate roughly the segments of the chain of symbolic constructs with which each process is especially concerned.

arranged for the most part in a single chain. The main links of this chain are represented in Figure 84. In the interest of clarity, the symbolic constructs are accompanied by the more important and relevant symbols representing the objectively anchoring conditions or events. In order that the two types of symbols shall be easily distinguishable, circles have been drawn around the symbolic constructs. It will be noticed that the symbols representing observables, while scattered throughout the sequence, are conspicuously clustered at the beginning and at the end of the chain, where they must be in order to make validation of the constructs possible. . . .

Organisms as Self-Maintaining Mechanisms

From the point of view of biological evolution, organisms are more or less successfully self-maintaining mechanisms. In the present context a *mechanism is defined as a physical aggregate whose behavior occurs under ascertainable conditions according to definitely statable rules or laws.* In biology, the nature of these aggregates is such that for individuals and species to survive, certain optimal conditions must be approximated. When conditions deviate from the optimum, equilibrium may as a rule be restored by some sort of action on the part of the organism; such activity is described as "adaptive." The organs effecting the adaptive activity of animals are for the most part glands and muscles.

In higher organisms the number, variety, and complexity of the acts required for protracted survival is exceedingly great. The nature of the act or action sequence necessary to bring about optimal conditions in a given situation depends jointly (1) upon the state of disequilibrium or need of the organism and (2) upon the characteristics of the environment, external and internal. For this reason a prerequisite of truly adaptive action is that both the condition of the organism and that of all relevant portions of the environment must somehow be brought simultaneously to bear on the reactive organs. The first link of this necessary functional *rapport* of the effector organs with organismic needs and environmental conditions is constituted by receptors which convert the biologically more important of the environmental energies (S) into neural impulses (s). For the most part these neural impulses flow to the brain, which acts as a kind of automatic switchboard mediating their efferent flow (r) to the effectors in such a way as to evoke response (R). In this connection there are two important neural principles to be noted.

The first of these principles to be observed is that after the stimulus (S) has ceased to act upon the receptor, the afferent impulse (s) continues its activity for some seconds, or possibly minutes under certain circumstances, though with gradually decreasing intensity. This *perseverative stimulus trace* is biologically important because it brings the effector organ *en rapport* not only with environmental events which are occurring at the time but with events which have occurred in the recent past, a matter frequently critical for survival. Thus is effected a short-range temporal integration (Postulate 1)....

The second neural principle is that the receptor discharges and their perseverative traces (s) generated on the different occasions of the impact of a given stimulus energy (S) upon the receptor, while usually very similar, are believed almost never to be exactly the same. This lack of uniformity is postulated as due (1) to the fact that many receptors are activated by stimulus energies simultaneously and (2) to "afferent neural interaction." The latter hypothesis states that the receptor discharges interact, while passing through the nervous system to the point where newly acquired receptor-effector connections have their locus, in such a way that each receptor discharge changes all the others to a greater or less extent; i.e., s is changed to $š_1$, $š_2$, or $š_3$, etc., in accordance with the particular combination of other stimulus energies which is acting on the sensorium at the time (see Figure 84). This type of action is particularly important because the mediation of the responses of organisms to distinctive combinations or patterns of stimuli, rather than to the components of the patterns, is presumably dependent upon it (Postulate 2)....

The detailed physiological principles whereby the nervous system mediates the behavioral adaptation of the organism are as yet far from completely known. As a result we are forced for the most part to get along as best we can with relatively coarse molar formulations derived from conditioned-reflex and other behavior experiments. From this point of view it appears that the processes of organic evolution have yielded two distinct but closely related means of effective behavioral adaptation. One of these is the laying down of unlearned receptor-effector connections (sU_R) within the neural tissue which will directly mediate at least approximate behavioral adjustments to urgent situations which are of frequent occurrence but which require relatively simple responses (Postulate 3).... The second means of effecting behavioral adjustment is probably evolution's most impressive achievement; this is the capacity of organisms themselves to acquire automatically adaptive receptor-effector connections. Such acquisition is *learning*.

Learning and Reinforcement

The substance of the elementary learning

process as revealed by much experimentation seems to be this: A condition of need exists in a more or less complex setting of receptor discharges initiated by the action of environmental stimulus energies. This combination of circumstances activates numerous vaguely adaptive reaction potentials mediated by the unlearned receptor-effector organization ($_sU_R$) laid down by organic evolution. The relative strengths of these various reaction potentials are varied from instant to instant by the oscillation factors ($_sO_R$). The resulting spontaneous variability of the momentary unlearned reaction potential ($_s\dot{U}_R$) produces the randomness and variability of the unlearned behavior evoked under given conditions. In case one of these random responses, or a sequence of them, results in the reduction of a need dominant at the time, there follows as an indirect effect what is known as reinforcement (G, of Figure 84). This consists in (1) a strengthening of the particular receptor-effector connections which originally mediated the reaction and (2) a tendency for all receptor discharges ($\dot{s}$) occurring at about the same time to acquire new connections with the effectors mediating the response in question. The first effect is known as primitive trial-and-error learning; the second is known as conditioned-reflex learning. In most adaptive situations both processes occur concurrently; indeed, *very likely they are at bottom the same process, differing only in the accidental circumstance that the first begins with an appreciable strength, whereas the second sets out from zero.* As a result, when the same need again arises in this or a similar situation, the stimuli will activate the same effectors more certainly, more promptly, and more vigorously than on the first occasion. Such action, while by no means adaptively infallible, in the long run will reduce the need more surely than would a chance sampling of the unlearned response tendencies ($_sU_R$) at the command of other need and stimulating situations, and more quickly and completely than did that particular need and stimulating situation on the first occasion. Thus the acquisition of such receptor-effector connections will, as a rule, make for survival; i.e., it will be adaptive.

Careful observation and experiment reveal, particularly with the higher organisms, large numbers of situations in which learning occurs with no associated primary need reduction. When these cases are carefully studied it is found that the reinforcing agent is a situation or event involving a stimulus aggregate or compound which has been closely and consistently associated with the need reduction. Such a situation is called a secondary reinforcing agent, and the strengthening of the receptor-effector connections which results from its action is known as secondary reinforcement. This principle is of immense importance in the behavior of the higher species.

The organization within the nervous system brought about by a particular reinforcement is known as a habit; since it is not directly observable, habit has the status of a symbolic construct. Strictly speaking, habit is a functional connection between s and r; it is accordingly represented by the symbol $_sH_r$. Owing, however, to the close functional relationship between S and s on the one hand, and between r and R on the other, the symbol $_sH_R$ will serve for most expository purposes; the latter symbol has the advantage that S and R both refer to conditions or events normally open to public observation. The position of $_sH_R$ in the chain of constructs of the present system is shown in Figure 84.

While it is difficult to determine the quantitative value of an unobservable, various indirect considerations combine to indicate as a first approximation that habit strength is a simple increasing growth function of the number of reinforcements. The unit chosen for the expression of habit strength is called the *hab*, a shortened form of the word "habit"; a hab is 1 per cent of the physiological limit of habit strength under completely optimal conditions.

Conditions Influencing the Magnitude of Habit Increment per Reinforcement

A more careful scrutiny of the conditions of reinforcement reveals a number which are subject to variation, and experiments have shown that the magnitude of the habit increment (Δ_sH_R) per reinforcement is dependent in one way or another upon the quantitative variation of these conditions. One such factor concerns the primary reinforcing agent. It has been found that, quality remaining constant, the magnitude of the increment of habit strength per reinforcement is a negatively accelerated increasing function of the quantity of the reinforcing agent employed per reinforcement.

A second factor of considerable importance in determining the magnitude of $\Delta_S H_R$ is the degree of asynchronism between the onset of the stimulus and of the response to which it is being conditioned. This situation is complicated by whether or not the stimulus terminates its action on the receptor before the response occurs. In general the experimental evidence indicates that in case both the stimulus and the response are of very brief duration, the increment of habit strength per reinforcement is maximal when the reaction (and the reinforcement) occurs a short half second after the stimulus, and that it is a negatively accelerated decreasing function of the extent to which asynchronisms in either direction depart from this optimum. In case the reaction synchronizes with the continued action of the stimulus on the receptor, the increment of habit strength per reinforcement is a simple negative growth function of the length of time that the stimulus has acted on the receptor when the reaction occurs.

A third important factor in the reinforcing situation is the length of time elapsing between the occurrence of the reaction and of the reinforcing state of affairs (G, Figure 84). Experiments indicate that this "gradient of reinforcement" is a negatively accelerated decreasing growth function of the length of time that reinforcement follows the reaction. The principle of secondary reinforcement, combined with that of the gradient of reinforcement, explains the extremely numerous cases of learning in which the primary reinforcement is indefinitely remote from the act reinforced. A considerable mass of experimental evidence indicates that a kind of blending of the action of these two principles generates a secondary phenomenon called the "goal gradient." Upon empirical investigation this turns out to be a decreasing exponential or negative growth function of the time (t) separating the reaction from the primary reinforcement for delays ranging from ten seconds to five or six minutes; delays greater than six minutes have not yet been sufficiently explored to make possible a quantitative statement concerning them.

There are doubtless other conditions which influence the magnitude of the increment of habit strength resulting from each reinforcement. Those listed above certainly are typical and probably comprise the more important of them. An adequate statement of the primary law or laws of learning would accordingly take the form of an equation in which $_S H_R$ would be expressed as a joint function not only of N but of the quantity and quality of the reinforcing agent, and of the temporal relationships of S to R and of R to G. . . .

Stimulus Generalization

With the primary laws of learning formally disposed of, we proceed on to the consideration of certain dynamical principles according to which habits, in conjunction with adequate stimulation (S) and drive (D), mediate overt behavior. In this connection we note the fact that a stimulus (S, Figure 84), through its afferent impulses (s, represented in Figure 84) will often evoke the reaction (R) even though s may be rather different from $\acute{s}$ or $\widetilde{s}$, the receptor impulse originally conditioned to R. This means that when a stimulus ($\dot{S}$) and a reaction (R) are conjoined in a reinforcement situation, there is set up a connection not only to the stimulus involved in the reinforcement but to a whole zone of other potential stimuli lying on the same stimulus continuum, such as S_1, S_2, S_3, and so forth. This fact, known as stimulus generalization, is of immense adaptive significance; since stimuli are rarely if ever exactly repeated, habits could scarcely function adaptively without it.

Stimulus generalization has the characteristic that in general the greater the physical deviation of S from $\acute{S}$, the weaker will be the habit strength which is mobilized. More precisely, the strength of a generalized habit $_S\bar{H}_R$) is a linear increasing function of the strength of the habit at the point of reinforcement and a negatively accelerated decreasing function of the difference (d) between $\acute{S}$ and S as measured in discrimination thresholds (j.n.d.'s). Thus $_S\bar{H}_R$ is a theoretical construct anchored to the construct $_S H_R$ and to the observables $\acute{S}$ and S (see Figure 84).

Stimulus generalization appears to take two forms—(1) qualitative stimulus generalization and (2) stimulus intensity generalization; another way of stating the same thing is to say that each stimulus has two generalization dimensions, quality and intensity.

Both dimensions display the negatively accelerated falling generalization gradient, but the qualitative gradient is markedly steeper than is that of stimulus intensity (Postulate 5)....

Primary Motivation

The condition of need in organisms not only is an important factor in habit formation, through the need reduction and reinforcement relationship; it also plays an important rôle in determining the occasions when habits shall function in the evocations of action, the vigor of such evocations, and their persistence in the absence of reinforcement. This is, of course, in the highest degree adaptive, since activity such as would lead to the reduction of a need is a sheer waste of energy when the need either does not exist or impend.

It is a fact that the dynamic actions of many, if not all, of the primary needs of organisms are associated with the presence or absence in the blood of small amounts of certain potent conditions or substances such as hormones. In one way or another there are also associated with most needs certain characteristic stimuli (S_D) whose intensity varies with the intensity of the need in question (Postulate 6)....

In this connection it must be pointed out that drive (D) is a logical construct, since it cannot be observed directly any more than can effective habit strength ($s\bar{H}_R$). Fortunately, the more carefully studied drives, such as hunger, thirst, and so on, have a clear possibility of being expressed as functions of objectively observable conditions or events; these are represented by the symbol C_D in Figure 84. Since $s\bar{H}_R$ is also thus anchored, the result (sE_R, Figure 84) of the combination of definite functions of these two antecedently anchored values is itself securely anchored on the antecedent side.

When the numerous facts of primary motivation are examined in quantitative detail, they yield the conclusion that the potentiality of response evocation (sE_R) is the product of a function of drive intensity multiplied by a function of habit strength (Postulate 7).... Drive stimuli (S_D) naturally become conditioned to the reaction which is associated with reduction of the need, and so they become an integral component of the habit (sH_R) involved. The drive substance (or condition) in the blood appears in some

way to sensitize the action of all habits, regardless of what drives have been involved in their formation, in a manner which enhances their power of mediating reaction. The characteristic stimuli associated with each need, through the action of stimulus patterning, suffice to effect reactions likely to reduce whatever need is dominant at the moment, rather than those appropriate to other needs which at the time stand at or near zero.

Extinction, Inhibition, and Effective Reaction Potential

When a reaction is evoked repeatedly without a closely associated drive reduction, the power of the stimulus-motivational combination to evoke the response in question gradually diminishes; this diminution is called experimental extinction. Such a cessation of futile activity is in the highest degree adaptive because it tends to prevent waste of the organism's energy reserve.

That experimental extinction does not concern merely habit strength is shown by the fact that an increase in the drive alone will serve to reinstate the power of stimuli to evoke a reaction which has been extinguished to zero. A careful survey of the numerous well-authenticated phenomena of experimental extinction in connection with presumably related phenomena in primary motivation has led to the hypothesis that experimental extinction is to a considerable extent motivational in nature. It is supposed that each response evocation produces in the organism a certain increment of a fatigue-like substance or condition which constitutes a need for rest. The mean net amount deposited at each response appears to be a positively accelerated increasing function of work or energy expenditure (W) consumed in the execution of the act (see Figure 84). It is assumed, further, that this substance or condition has the capacity directly to inhibit the power of S to evoke R; for this reason it is called reactive inhibition (I_R). Its accumulation would therefore produce experimental extinction, and its progressive removal from the tissues by the blood stream (on the fatigue analogy) would produce spontaneous recovery.

In case the response evocations are accompanied by reinforcement and occur at relatively long intervals, and ordinary motivation remains fairly high, the increase in habit strength will usually keep the reaction potential above the reaction threshold. The spontaneous dissipation of the inhibitory state is known to be much more rapid than is the ordinary loss of learning effects. This would produce the phenomenon of reminiscence which has been especially studied in rote learning.

Since the presence of I_R constitutes a need, the cessation of the activity which generated the need would initiate the need-reduction process; but since need reduction is the critical element in reinforcement, there follows with fair plausibility the molar principle that cessation of the activity would be conditioned to any stimuli which are consistently associated with such cessation (Postulate 9). . . . But a tendency to the cessation of an act would be directly inhibitory to the performance of that act. Therefore the inclusion of such an inhibitory stimulus in a stimulus compound, the remainder of which is positively conditioned to the response, would tend to prevent the evocation of the response in question; this is, in fact, the ordinary empirical test for conditioned inhibition (sI_R, Figure 84).

On the above view that sI_R is a negative habit, the injection of alien stimuli into the stimulus compound would, through the principle of afferent interaction, produce disinhibition, i.e., a temporary reduction or total abolition of sI_R. But on the assumption that sI_R is being set up during the process of accumulating I_R, it follows that the total inhibition ($\dot{I}_R$) at the conclusion of experimental extinction must be in part I_R and in part sI_R. For this reason disinhibition will take place only in so far as $\dot{I}_R$ is composed of sI_R, and spontaneous recovery will take place only in so far as $\dot{I}_R$ is composed of I_R; this means that neither disinhibition nor spontaneous recovery can ever restore an extinguished reaction potential to its full original strength. Other implications which flow from the above assumptions are that there is greater economy in distributed than in massed repetitions in rote learning, and that, other things equal, organisms receiving the same reinforcement following two responses which require different energy expenditures will, as practice continues, gradually come to choose the less laborious response. This is the "law of less work."

Implicit in the preceding discussion has been the assumption that the reaction potential actually available for reaction evocation, i.e., the effective reaction potential ($s\bar{E}_R$, Figure 84), is what remains of the reaction potential (sE_R) after the subtraction of the total inhibition, $\dot{I}_R$; i.e.,

$$s\bar{E}_R = sE_R - \dot{I}_R.$$

Since both sE_R and $\dot{I}_R$ are anchored to objectively observable antecedent conditions, it follows that $s\bar{E}_R$ is also thus anchored.

Oscillation of Effective Reaction Potential

At this point it must be noted at once that the full value of $s\bar{E}_R$ is rarely brought to bear in the evocation of action. Instead it is subject to random or chance downward variability. These fluctuations are believed to be due to a little-understood physiological process which has the power of neutralizing reaction potentials to degrees varying from moment to moment. Because of this latter characteristic, the process is called "oscillation"; it is represented by the symbol sO_R. Effective reaction potential as modified by oscillation is called "momentary effective reaction potential"; this is represented by the symbol $s\dot{\bar{E}}_R$.

Since sO_R is not directly observable, it has something of the status of a symbolic construct; on the other hand, owing to its presumably constant value, it has less elusiveness than an ordinary construct; it is therefore not placed in a circle in Figure 84. The hypothetical characteristics of sO_R may be listed as follows:

1. It is active at all times.
2. It exerts an absolute depressing action against any and all reaction potentials, whether great or small.
3. The magnitude of this potentiality varies from instant to instant according to the normal probability distribution.
4. The magnitude of its action on different reaction potentials at a given instant is uncorrelated (Postulate 10).

Since oscillation is continuously active on all reaction potentials, it plays a very great rôle in adaptive behavior. It presumably is responsible for many of the phenomena grouped by the classical psychologists under the head of "attention." It is in large measure responsible for the fact that the social sciences must pool many observations before ordinary empirical laws may become manifest. Thus natural laws in the social sciences must always be based on statistical indices of one kind or another. This in its turn has induced much preoccupation with statistical methods on the part of the various behavior sciences. The necessity of pooling large numbers of observations in order to isolate empirical laws has greatly increased the labor associated with empirical investigations and has doubtless appreciably retarded the development of the behavior sciences.

Reaction Threshold and Response Evocation

The anchoring on the posterior or consequent side of our chain of behavioral constructs culminating in $s\bar{E}_R$, as shown in Figure 84, lies in the evocation of observable reactions. In the determination of the functional relationship of $s\bar{E}_R$ to the various measurable phenomena of responses, we encounter special difficulties owing to the fact that $s\bar{E}_R$ is itself not directly observable. If we were quite sure of the quantitative functional relationship of $s\bar{E}_R$ to its combination of antecedent anchors, the value of $s\bar{E}_R$ could be calculated in empirical situations and equations could then be fitted to the relationship of these numbers to the corresponding response values; these equations are what we seek. Unfortunately the necessary antecedent functional relationships are not yet known with sufficient certainty.

It happens, however, that in typical sets of simple learning results, employing the four measurable response phenomena, the fitted equations in all cases are easily and naturally expressible by equations involving the simple positive growth (exponential) function of the number of reinforcements (N). This tends somewhat to confirm the soundness of the general growth hypothesis of the relation of N to $s H_R$ and so of N to $s\bar{E}_R$. Further independent confirmation of the soundness of the growth hypothesis of the relation of $s\bar{E}_R$ to N, lies in the following fact: when the probability-of-reaction-evocation type of learning curve is analyzed theoretically, it turns out to be yielded in a degree of detail scarcely attributable to chance on the above assumption of the relation of $s\bar{E}_R$ to N coupled with two additional assumptions, each well supported by independent evidence —that of the oscillation function ($s O_R$) and

that of the reaction threshold ($s L_R$) (see Figure 84). The characteristics of the oscillation function have been summarized above. Moreover, the concept of the reaction threshold is well established, since notions fairly comparable to it have long been current in classical psychophysics and in physiology. As here employed, the reaction threshold ($s L_R$) is the minimal amount of momentary effective reaction potential ($s\bar{E}_R$) which is necessary to mediate reaction evocation when the situation is uncomplicated by competing reaction potentials (Postulate 11). . . .

Acting, then, on the fairly well-authenticated growth hypothesis of the relation of $s\bar{E}_R$ to N, it is a relatively simple matter, by inspecting the equations fitted to concrete examples of the three remaining types of learning curves and utilizing the method of residues, to determine the functional relationship of $s\bar{E}_R$ to the particular behavior phenomena employed. As a result of this procedure it is concluded that probability of reaction evocation stands in an ogival relationship to effective reaction potential (Postulate 12); that reaction latency stands in a negatively accelerated inverse relationship (Postulate 13); . . . and that both resistance to experimental extinction and reaction amplitude (of autonomically mediated responses) are increasing linear functions of $s\bar{E}_R$ (Postulates 14 and 15). . . .

A final complication concerning reaction evocation arises from the fact that often the stimulus elements impinging on the receptors at a given instant may mobilize superthreshold reaction potentials to several different reactions, some or all of which may be mutually incompatible. In such cases all but the strongest will necessarily suffer associative inhibition (Postulate 16). . . . There are also some indications that the dominant potential itself may suffer a certain amount of blocking; indeed, this is the basis of the most plausible theory of "forgetting" now available.

This concludes our summary of primary principles. All of these principles are also statable in the form of quantitative equations. This means that if the antecedent conditions $\dot{S}$, $\check{s}$, R, G, t, t', S, $\check{s}$, C_D, W, $s O_R$, and $s L_R$ were known, it would be possible to compute p, st_R, n, or A by substituting appropriately in a succession of these equations beginning on the left-hand side of Figure 84 and proceeding toward the right. For example, the calculation of $_st_R$ would employ equations 16, 34, 44, 45, and 48.

Dynamics of Stimulus Compounds and Patterns

For the most part the molar principles outlined in the preceding chapters are presumably primary in nature, though occasional secondary principles have been presented. Because of their relatively primitive status in the logical hierarchy of the system and of their especially intimate relation to survival, a few secondary principles or mechanisms have been given special consideration and have been listed as "major corollaries." One of these concerns the quantitative summation of the reaction potentials mobilized by the several stimulus components of a stimulus compound, and the other concerns the matter of stimulus patterning. We shall first take up the matter of the summation of reaction potentials.

In spite of the presumptive fact of afferent neural interaction, the afferent discharge of each receptor contains a large amount of similarity regardless of the influence of other stimulus elements (and receptors) which may be active at the time. This means that any stimulus component conditioned to a reaction will ordinarily command an appreciable potentiality to that reaction regardless of the other stimuli accompanying it. Now, according to the primary law of learning, each individual receptor discharge bears its load of habit strength, and so of reaction potential. The reaction-potential loadings thus borne by the several receptor discharges initiated by the different stimulus elements of a stimulus compound presumably combine quantitatively in the same way as do the different increments of habit strength, i.e., not by a simple addition but according to a kind of diminishing-returns principle. Thus if two stimulus aggregates bearing equal loads of reaction potential to the evocation of the same response are acting simultaneously as a stimulus compound, their physiological summation, quite apart from afferent interaction effects, will be less than the arithmetical sum of the two reaction potentials; similarly, if one of the two equally loaded stimulus aggregates making up a stimulus compound should be withdrawn from the compound,

more than half of the total reaction potential would remain. As a result (except for afferent neural interaction effects), the more completely a reinforced stimulus compound is repeated on a subsequent occasion, the more likely it will be to evoke the reaction in question.

This mode of action has special adaptive significance, because the more completely the stimulus compound is repeated, the more similar will be the environmental situation in general to the situation in which need reduction originally occurred, and therefore the more probably will the response in question lead again to a reduction in the need. Here we have a primitive automatic mechanism which in effect roughly gauges the probability of a given stimulus situation's yielding need reduction in case a given response is evoked. This adaptive mechanism has the great advantage of being instantly available at the presentation of any stimulus situation, novel or otherwise.

The other secondary principle mediating the response of organisms to stimulus compounds, which we have included in the present work, is that known as patterning. This operates concurrently with the summation principle just discussed but is much slower in its action. However, given sufficient time for the rather difficult learning process to take place, stimulus patterning may be very precisely adaptive. It is a fact that in very large numbers of situations the question of whether or not a given response will be followed by reinforcement depends upon the presence or absence of a particular combination of physical circumstances and so, for the organism, upon a particular combination or pattern of stimulus elements, rather than upon the presence or absence of any of the components. Since each combination of stimulus elements will modify to some extent the afferent impulses produced by each stimulus component, any change in the stimulus compound will also modify to some extent the afferent responses initiated by all the remaining stimulus components. In the process of the irregular alternation of reinforcement and extinction called differential reinforcement, which is characteristic of the form of trial and error known as discrimination learning, higher organisms are able to emerge with one response successfully conditioned to one combination of stimuli and with a quite different response successfully conditioned to another combination of stimuli containing many of the components of the first, provided some of the elements are different.   At bottom this discrimination is possible because the afferent impulse $\check{s}_1$ which arises from the stimulus element S_1 when occurring concurrently with the stimulus element S_2, is to some extent different from $\check{s}_3$, which arises from the same stimulus element, S_1, when occurring concurrently with a different stimulus element, S_3. The physiological summation of the several component reaction potentials characteristic of various stimulus patterns which have many, and even most, of their stimulus elements in common, accordingly may result in the evocation without confusion of the distinctive reaction conditioned to each. Thus each of the forty or so elementary speech sounds is a fairly distinctive pattern made up of a "fundamental" physical vibration rate and a particular combination of higher partials.   Each of the thousands of words of the better-developed languages consists of a temporally patterned sequence of these elementary speech sounds, stops, and so forth. In reading, each letter is a complex visual pattern, each word is a complex pattern of these letter patterns, and each sentence is a temporally patterned sequence of printed word patterns. Indeed, it is impossible to think of a life situation which is not patterned to a considerable extent. The limiting case of this kind of learning is that in which a stimulus compound is conditioned to evoke a reaction while the several components when acting alone are consistently extinguished.

Behavior Postulates [3]

Here follow the behavior postulates and major corollaries, set up in bold-faced type and italics, respectively, to distinguish them clearly from the body of the text.

Postulate I.

Unlearned Stimulus-response Connections ($_sU_R$)

Organisms at birth possess receptor-effector connections ($_sU_R$) which under combined stimu-

---

[3] Clark L. Hull, *A Behavior System: An Introduction to Behavior Theory concerning the Individual Organism* (New Haven, Conn.: Yale University Press, 1952), pp. 5–14. Reprinted by permission.

lation (S) and drive (D) have the potentiality of evoking a hierarchy of responses that either individually or in combination are more likely to terminate a need than would be a random selection from the reactions resulting from other stimulus and drive combinations.**

Postulate II.

Stimulus Reception (S and s)

A.   When a brief stimulus (S) impinges upon a suitable receptor there is initiated the recruitment phase of a self-propagating molar afferent trace impulse ($\dot{s}'$), the molar stimulus equivalent ($\dot{S}'$) of which rises as a power function of time (t) since the beginning of the stimulus, i.e.,

$$\dot{S}' = 465{,}190 \times t^{7.6936} + 1.0, \qquad (1)$$

$\dot{S}'$ reaching its maximum (and termination) when t equals about 0.450″.

B.   Following the maximum of the recruitment phase of the molar stimulus trace, there supervenes a more lengthy subsident phase (s′), the stimulus equivalent of which descends as a power function of time (t′), i.e.,

$$\dot{S}' = 6.9310(t' + .01)^{-1.0796}, \qquad (2)$$

where $t' = t - 0.450″$.

C.   The intensity of the molar stimulus trace (s′) is a logarithmic function of the molar stimulus equivalent of the trace, i.e.,

$$s' = \log S'. \qquad (3)$$

Postulate III.

Primary Reinforcement

Whenever an effector activity (R) is closely associated with a stimulus afferent impulse or trace (s) and the conjunction is closely associated with the rapid diminution in the motivational stimulus (S_D or s_G), there will result an increment (Δ) to a tendency for that stimulus to evoke that response.

Corollary i. Secondary Motivation

When neutral stimuli are repeatedly and consistently associated with the evocation of a primary or secondary drive and this drive stimulus undergoes an abrupt diminution, the hitherto neutral stimuli acquire the capacity to bring about the drive stimuli (S_D), which thereby become the condition (C_D) of a secondary drive or motivation.

Corollary ii. Secondary Reinforcement

A neutral receptor impulse which occurs repeatedly and consistently in close conjunction with a reinforcing state of affairs, whether primary or secondary, will itself acquire the power of acting as a reinforcing agent.

Postulate IV.

The Law of Habit Formation ($_sH_R$)

If reinforcements follow each other at evenly distributed intervals, everything else constant, the resulting habit will increase in strength as a positive growth function of the number of trials according to the equation,

$$_sH_R = 1 - 10^{-.0305\,\dot{N}}, \qquad (4)$$

where $\dot{N}$ is the total number of reinforcements from Z.

Postulate V.

Primary Motivation or Drive (D)

A. Primary motivation (D), at least that resulting from food privation, consists of two multiplicative components: (1) the drive proper (D′) which is an increasing monotonic sigmoid function of h, the number of hours of food privation; and (2) a negative or inanition component (ϵ) which is a positively accelerated monotonic function of h decreasing from 1.0 to zero, i.e.,

$$D = D' \times \epsilon. \qquad (5)$$

where

$$D' = 37.824 \times 10^{-27.496\frac{1}{h}} + 4.001,$$

and

$$\epsilon = 1 - .00001045h^{2.486}.$$

B. The functional relationship of drive (D) to one drive condition (food privation) is: during the time from h = 0 to about h = 3, drive rises in a linear manner until the function abruptly shifts to a near horizontal, then to a concave-upward course, gradually changing to a convex-upward course reaching a maximum of 12.3σ at about h = 59, after which it gradually falls to the reaction threshold ($_sL_R$) at around h = 100.

C. Each drive condition (C_D) generates a characteristic drive stimulus (S_D) which is a monotonic increasing function of this state.

D. At least some drive conditions tend

partially to motivate into action habits which have been set up on the basis of different drive conditions.

Postulate VI.

Stimulus-intensity Dynamism (V)

Other things constant, the magnitude of the stimulus-intensity component (V) of reaction potential ($_sE_R$) is a monotonic increasing logarithmic function of S, i.e.,

$$V = 1 - 10^{-.44\,\log S}. \qquad (6)$$

Postulate VII.

Incentive Motivation (K)

The incentive component (K) of reaction potential ($_sE_R$) is a negatively accelerated increasing monotonic function of the weight (w) of food or quantity of other incentive (K′) given as reinforcement, i.e.,

$$K = 1 - 10^{-a\sqrt{w}}. \qquad (7)$$

Postulate VIII.

The Constitution of Reaction Potential ($_sE_R$)

The reaction potential ($_sE_R$) of a bit of learned behavior at any given stage of learning, where conditions are constant throughout learning and response-evocation, is determined (1) by the drive (D) operating during the learning process multiplied (2) by the dynamism of the signaling stimulus trace (V_1), (3) by the incentive reinforcement (K), and (4) by the habit strength ($_sH_R$), i.e.,

$$_sE_R = D \times V_1 \times K \times {}_sH_R. \qquad (8)$$

Corollary iii. Delay in Reinforcement (J)

A. *The greater the delay in reinforcement of a link within a given behavior chain, learning and response-evocation conditions remaining constant, the weaker will be the resulting reaction potential of the link in question to the stimulus traces present at the time.*

B. *The greater the delay in the receipt of the incentive by groups of learning subjects, learning and response-evocation conditions remaining constant, the weaker will be the resulting learned reaction potentials ($_sE_{R_d}$), the shape of the gradient as a function of the respective delays being roughly that of decay* *with the lower limit of the extended gradient passing beneath the reaction threshold, i.e.,*

$$J = {_s}\underline{E}R_d = D \times V_2 \times K \times {_s}H_R \times 10^{-.15d} \times V_1 ,$$
(9)

where,

$$d = \log \dot{S}' \text{ of } V_1 - \log \dot{S}' \text{ of } V_2.$$

Corollary iv. The Summation ($\dot{+}$) of Habit Strengths

If two stimuli, S' and S, are reinforced separately to a response (R) by $\dot{N}'$ and $\dot{N}$ reinforcements respectively, and the ${_{s'}}H_R$ generalizes to S in the amount of ${_s}H'_R$, the summation ($\dot{+}$) of the two habit strengths at S will be the same as would result from the equivalent number of reinforcement at S, i.e.,

$$_sH_R \dot{+} {_s}H'_R = {_s}H_R + {_s}H'_R - {_s}H_R \times {_s}H'_R. \quad (10)$$

Corollary v. The Summation ($\dot{+}$) of Reaction Potentials

If two stimuli, S' and S, are reinforced separately to a response (R) and ${_{s'}}E_R$ generalizes to S in the amount of ${_s}E'_R$, the two reaction potentials will summate at S as would the equivalent number of reinforcements in an original learning, i.e.,

$${_s}E_R \dot{+} {_s}E'_R = {_s}E_R + {_s}E'_R - \frac{{_s}E_R \times {_s}E'_R}{M}, \quad (11)$$

where M is the asymptote of ${_s}E_R$ by distributed trials.

Corollary vi. The Withdrawal ($\dot{-}$) of Habit Strength

If a smaller habit strength (${_s}H'_R$) is to be withdrawn ($\dot{-}$) from a larger habit strength (C), the result will be:

$$C \dot{-} {_s}H'_R = {_s}H_R = \frac{C - {_s}H'_R}{1 - {_s}H'_R} \quad (12)$$

Corollary vii. The Withdrawal ($\dot{-}$) of Reaction Potential

If a smaller reaction potential (${_s}\underline{E}'_R$) is to be withdrawn ($\dot{-}$) from a larger reaction potential (C), the result will be:

$$C \dot{-} {_s}\underline{E}'_R = {_s}E_R = \frac{M(C - {_s}E'_R)}{M - {_s}\underline{E}'_R}. \quad (13)$$

Corollary viii. The Problem of the Behavioral Summation ($\dot{+}$) of Incentive Substances (K)

If two incentive substances, f and a, have $A \sqrt{w}$ and $B \sqrt{m}$ as the exponential components of their respective functional equations, the second substance will combine ($\dot{+}$) with the first in the production of the total K according to the following equation:

$$K_{f+a} = 1 - 10^{-A\sqrt{w + m \times \frac{B^2}{A^2}}}. \quad (14)$$

Postulate IX.

Inhibitory Potential

A. Whenever a reaction (R) is evoked from an organism there is left an increment of primary negative drive (I_R) which inhibits to a degree according to its magnitude the reaction potential (${_s}E_R$) to that response.

B. With the passage of time since its formation, I_R spontaneously dissipates approximately as a simple decay function of the time (t) elapsed, i.e.,

$$I'_R = I_R \times 10^{-.018t}. \quad (15)$$

C. If responses (R) occur in close succession without further reinforcement, the successive increments of inhibition (ΔI_R) to these responses summate to attain appreciable amounts of I_R. These also summate with ${_s}I_R$ to make up an inhibitory aggregate ($\dot{I}_R$), i.e.,

$$\dot{I}_R = I_R \dot{+} {_s}I_R. \quad (16)$$

D. When experimental extinction occurs by massed practice, the $\dot{I}_R$ present at once after the successive reaction evocations is a positive growth function of the order of those responses ($\dot{n}$), i.e.,

$$\dot{I}_R = 1.84 (1 - 10^{-.0434\dot{n}}). \quad (17)$$

E. For constant values of superthreshold reaction potential (${_s}E_R$) set up by massed practice, the number of unreinforced responses (n) producible by massed extinction procedure is a linear decreasing function of the magnitude of the work (W) involved in operating the manipulanda, i.e.,

$$n = 3.25 (1.1476 - .00984W). \quad (18)$$

Corollary ix. Conditioned Inhibition

Stimuli and stimulus traces closely associated with the cessation of a given activity, and in the presence of appreciable I_R from that *response, become conditioned to this particular non-activity, yielding conditioned inhibition ($_s\dot{I}_R$) which will oppose $_sE_R$'s involving that response, the amount of $\triangle_s\dot{I}_R$ generated being an increasing function of the I_R present.*

Corollary x. Inhibitory Potential ($\dot{I}_R$) as a Function of Work

For a constant value of n, the inhibitory potential ($\dot{I}_R$) generated by the total massed extinction of reaction potential set up by massed practice begins as a positively accelerated increasing function of the work (W) involved in operating the manipulandum, which gradually changes to a negative acceleration at around 80 grams, finally becoming asymptotic at around 110 grams.

Corollary xi. Inhibitory Potential ($\dot{I}_R$) as a Function of the Number of Responses

For a constant value of the work (W) involved in operating the manipulandum, the inhibitory potential ($\dot{I}_R$) generated by the total massed extinction of reaction potential set up by massed practice is a negatively accelerated increasing function of the total number of reactions (n) required.

Postulate X.

Stimulus Generalization ($_s\bar{H}_R$, $_s\underline{E}_R$, and $_s\dot{I}_R$)

A. In the case of qualitative stimuli, S_1 and S_2, the effective habit strength ($_s\bar{H}_R$) generates a stimulus generalization gradient on the qualitative continuum from the simple learned attachment of S_1 to R:

$$_{S_2}\bar{H}_R = {_{S_1}H_R} \times 10^{-.0135d}, \qquad (19)$$

where d represents the difference between S_1 and S_2 in j.n.d.'s, and

$$_{S_2}\underline{E}_R = D \times K \times V_2 \times {_{S_2}\bar{H}_R}, \qquad (20)$$

and where $D \times K \times V_2$ is constant.

B. A stimulus intensity (S_1) generalizes to a second stimulus intensity (S_2) according to the equation,

$$_{S_2}\bar{H}_R = {_{S_1}H_R} \times 10^{-bd} \times V_1, \qquad (21)$$

where d represents the difference between S_1 and S_2 in log units and

$$_{S_2}\underline{E}_R = D \times K \times V_2 \times {_{S_2}\bar{H}_R}, \qquad (22)$$

and where ($D \times K$) is constant and V_2 is the stimulus-intensity dynamism at S_2.

C. In the case of qualitative stimulus

differences, ordinary conditioning and extinction spontaneously generate a gradient of inhibitory potential ($_s\dot{I}_R$) which is a negative growth function of $_s\dot{I}_R$ and d, i.e.,

$$_{S_2}\dot{I}_R = {_{S_1}\dot{I}_R} \times 10^{-ad}, \qquad (23)$$

and in the case of stimulus-intensity differences,

$$_{S_2}\dot{I}_R = {_{S_1}\dot{I}_R} \times 10^{-bd} \times V_2. \qquad (24)$$

Corollary xii. The Generalization of $_s\bar{H}_R$ and $_s\underline{E}_R$ on S_D as a Continuum

When a habit is set up in association with a given drive intensity (S_D) and its strength is tested under a different drive intensity, there will result a falling gradient of $_s\bar{H}_R$ and $_s\underline{E}_R$.

Postulate XI.

Afferent Stimulus Interaction

All afferent impulses (s's) active at any given instant, mutually interact converting each other into š's which differ qualitatively from the original s's so that a reaction potential ($_sE_R$) set up on the basis of one afferent impulse (s) will show a generalization fall to $_{\check{s}}E_R$ when the reaction (R) is evoked by the other afferent impulse (š), the amount of the change in the afferent impulses being shown by the number of j.n.d.'s separating the $_sE_R$'s involved according to the principle,

$$d = \frac{\log \dfrac{_sE_R}{_{\check{s}}E_R}}{\bar{I}} \qquad (25)$$

Postulate XII.

Behaviorial Oscillation ($_sO_R$)

A. A reaction potential ($_sE_R$) oscillates from moment to moment, the distribution of behaviorial oscillation ($_sO_R$) deviating slightly from the Gaussian probability form in being leptokurtic with β_2 at about 4.0; i.e., the distribution is represented by the equation,

$$y = y_0 \frac{1}{\left(1 + \dfrac{x^2}{a^2}\right)^m}.$$

B. The oscillation of $_sE_R$ begins with the dispersion of approximately zero at the absolute zero (Z) of $_sH_R$, this at first rising as a positive growth function of the number of subthreshold reinforcements to an unsteady maximum, after which it remains relatively constant though with increasing variabliity.

C. The oscillations of competing reaction potentials at any given instant are asynchronous.

Corollary xiii. Response Generalization

A. *The contraction of each muscle involved in a habitual act varies its $_SE_R$ from instant to instant ($_SO_R$) about a central reinforced region of intensity which is approximately normal (leptokurtic) in distribution; this constitutes* response-intensity generalization.

B. *Where several muscles jointly contract to produce a given habitual act, the contraction of each muscle varies more or less ($_SO_R$) independently of the others, producing a qualitative deviation from the central tendency of the joint result of the muscular contractions originally reinforced; this constitutes* qualitative response generalization.

Postulate XIII.

Absolute Zero of Reaction Potential (Z) and the Reaction Threshold ($_SL_R$)

A. The reaction threshold ($_SL_R$) stands at an appreciable distance (B) above the absolute zero (Z) of reaction potential ($_SE_R$), i.e.,

$$_SL_R = Z + B. \tag{26}$$

B. No reaction evocation (R) will occur unless the momentary reaction potential at the time exceeds the reaction threshold, i.e., unless,

$$_S\dot{E}_R > _SL_R. \tag{27}$$

Corollary xiv. The Competition of Incompatible Reaction Potential ($_S\bar{E}_R$)

When the net reaction potentials ($_S\bar{E}_R$) to two or more incompatible reactions (R) occur in an organism at the same instant, each in a magnitude greater than $_SL_R$, only that reaction whose momentary reaction potential ($_S\dot{\bar{E}}_R$) is greatest will be evoked.

Postulate XIV.

Reaction Potential ($_SE_R$) as a Function of Reaction Latency ($_St_R$)

Reaction potential ($_SE_R$) is a negatively accelerated decreasing function of the median reaction latency ($_St_R$), i.e.,

$$_SE_R = 2.845 \, (_St_R)^{-.483}. \tag{28}$$

Postulate XV.

Reaction Potential ($_SE_R$) as a Function of Reaction Amplitude (A)

Reaction potential ($_SE_R$) is an increasing linear function of the Tarchanoff galvanic skin reaction amplitude (A), i.e.,

$$_SE_R = .02492 \, A. \tag{29}$$

Postulate XVI.

Complete Experimental Extinction (n) as a Function of Reaction Potential ($_SE_R$)

A. The reaction potentials ($_SE_R$) acquired by massed reinforcements are a negatively accelerated monotonic increasing function of the median number of massed unreinforced reaction evocations (n) required to produce their experimental extinction, the work (W) involved in each operation of the manipulandum remaining constant, i.e.,

$$_SE_R = 4.0 \, (1 - 10^{-.0110n}) + .46. \tag{30}$$

B. The reaction potentials ($_SE_R$) acquired by quasi-distributed reinforcements are a positively accelerated monotonic increasing function of the median number of massed unreinforced reaction evocations (n) required to produce their experimental extinction, the work (W) involved in each operation of the manipulandum remaining constant, i.e.,

$$_SE_R = .1225 \times 10^{.0647n} + 2.114. \tag{31}$$

Postulate XVII.

Individual Differences

The "constant" numerical values appearing in equations representing primary molar behavioral laws vary from species to species, from individual to individual, and from some physiological states to others in the same individual at different times, all quite apart from the factor of behavioral oscillation ($_SO_R$).

Corollary xv. Secondary Reinforcement by Fractional Antedating Goal Reaction ($r_G \rightarrow s_G$)

When a stimulus (S) or a stimulus trace (s) acts at the same time that a hitherto unrelated response (R) occurs and this coincidence is accompanied by an antedating goal reaction (r_G), the secondary reinforcing powers of the stimulus evoked by the latter (s_G) will reinforce S to R, giving rise to a new S → R dynamic connection.

EDWARD CHASE TOLMAN
(1886–1961)

Purposive Behaviorism [4]

Surely any "tough-minded" reader will . . . be up in arms. For it is clear that . . . to identify behaviors in terms of goal-objects, and patterns of commerces with means-objects as selected short ways to get to 'or from the goal-objects, is to imply something perilously like purposes and cognitions. And this surely will be offensive to any hard-headed, well-brought-up psychologist of the present day.

And yet, there seems to be no other way out. Behavior as behavior, that is, as molar, *is* purposive and *is* cognitive. These purposes and cognitions are of its immediate descriptive warp and woof. It, no doubt, is strictly and completely dependent upon an underlying manifold of physics and chemistry, but initially and as a matter of first identification, behavior as behavior reeks of purpose and of cognition. And such purposes and such cognitions are just as evident, as we shall see later, if this behavior be that of a rat as if it be that of a human being.

Finally, however, it must nonetheless be emphasized that purposes and cognitions which are thus immediately, immanently, in behavior are wholly objective as to definition. They are defined by characters and relationships which we observe out there in the behavior. We, the observers, watch the behavior of the rat, the cat, or the man, and note its character as a getting to such and such by means of such and such a selected pattern of commerces-with. It is we, the independent neutral observers, who note these perfectly objective characters as immanent in the behavior and have happened to choose the terms *purpose* and *cognition* as generic names for such characters.

* * * * *

The first initiating causes of behavior are environmental stimuli and initiating physiological states. These operate on or through the behavior-determinants. The behavior-determinants are, it appears further, subdivisible into three classes: (a) immediately "in-lying" objectively defined purposes and cognitions—i.e., the "immanent determinants"; (b) the purposive and cognitive "capacities" of the given individual or species, which mediate the specific immanent determinants as a result of the given stimuli and the given initiating states; (c) "behavior-adjustments," which, under certain special conditions, are produced by the immanent determinants in place of actual overt behavior and which serve to act back upon such immanent determinants, to remould and "correct" the latter and thus finally to produce a new and different overt behavior from that which would otherwise have occurred.

Behavior, as such, is a molar phenomenon as contrasted with the molecular phenomena which constitute its underlying physiology. And, as a molar phenomenon, behavior's immediate descriptive properties appear to be those of: getting to or from goal-objects by selecting certain means-objects-routes as against others and by exhibiting specific patterns of commerces with these selected means-objects. But these descriptions in terms of gettings to or from, selections of routes and patterns of commerces-with imply and define immediate, immanent purpose and cognition aspects in the behavior. These two aspects of behavior are, however, but objectively and functionally defined entities. They are implicit in the facts of behavior docility. They are defined neither in the last analysis, nor in the first instance, by introspection. They are envisaged as readily in the behavior-acts of the cat and of the rat as in the more refined speech reactions of man. Such purposes and cognitions, such docility, are, obviously, functions of the organism as a whole. Lastly, it has also been pointed out that there are two other classes of behavior-determinants in addition to the immanent determinants, viz., capacities and behavior-adjustments. These also intervene in the equation between stimuli and initiating physiological states on the one side and behavior on the other.

In FIGURE 72 we have drawn a diagram for Purposive Behaviorism, which is analogous to that for Spearmanism, and should now, therefore, be fairly easily understood. There are, however, several new features in it, which need elucidation.

First, it will be observed that in the upper right-hand side of the diagram we have introduced a new independent variable P (initiating physiological state). And, descending from this through a succession of innate or acquired means-end-readinesses, we have indicated a succession of D's (demanded types of goal-object). In Purposive Behaviorism there is, in short, a fourth type of independent cause of behavior. According to it the final behavior is a function, not only of S and of H and T, but also of the initiating physiological state, P, which may happen to be active at the moment. The

organism responds to the given stimuli only, by virtue of an initiating physiological state which, given his innate or acquired means-end-readinesses, gives rise to demands, D (superordinate or subordinate)—one or more of which leads him to respond to the given S as presenting an appropriate means-object. These depending demands control the whole line of the S → R process.

It appears, in short, that whereas Structuralism and Gestalt Psychology seemed to assume but one final type of cause underlying behavior, viz., S; and Spearmanism added but two more, viz., H and T; Purposive Behaviorism finds, in all, four such ultimately independent causes of behavior, viz., S. H. T and P.[5]

Consider, next, the nature of the stimulus-

[5] S (stimulus), H (Hereditary endowment), T (previous training), P (purpose).

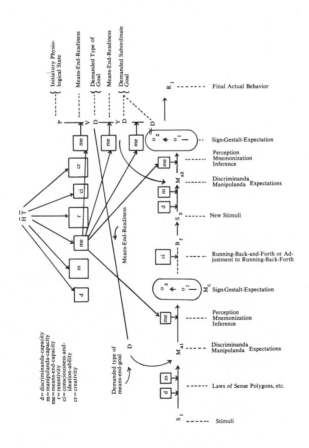

FIGURE 72

response sequence as shown in the diagram. From what has gone before in the preceding chapter this $S_1 \rightarrow R_1$ sequence, as here drawn, should be readily understood. The principal point to note is that for the purposes of this illustration we have taken a case in which the first sign-gestalt-expectation arrived at is relatively uncertain. The uncertainty leads the organism to break out into either an actual running-back-and-forth or a "behavior-adjustment" to such a running-back-and-forth. And these actual or adjustmental "back-and-forths" we have symbolized by B_f. As a result of this B_f the organism reinforces its stimuli. In the place of the original S_1 he achieves an improved S_2. And he thereby arrives at a new sign-gestalt-expectation. And it appears then, finally, that the O_2 of this latter is such as to be accepted as goal-object by one of the super-ordinately, or sub-ordinately, released demands. The final actual behavior thereupon results. Purposive Behaviorism thus explains, in terms of such demands, the final going off of the R—a matter that was left largely unconsidered by either Structuralism, Gestalt Psychology or Spearmanism.

Next, consider the matter of capacities. It will be observed that, to avoid confusion, we have not attempted for the most part to draw the interconnecting arrows from the innate or acquired "funds" represented at the top of the diagram and the actual operations of such factors indicated below in connection with the actual S – R performance. The one exception is in the case of *me* (means-end-capacity). It will be observed, further, that this drawing for the capacity-features of Purposive Behaviorism is somewhat analogous to that for Spearmanism. That is, he and we both seem to accept about the same number of factors. And a discriminating reader will observe a certain likeness between our *d* (discriminanda-capacity) and *m* (manipulanda-capacity) and Spearman's *s*'s (specific factors). Further our *me* (means-end-capacity), *r* (retentivity), *ci* (consciousness-ability and ideation-ability) and *cr* (creativity) seem somewhat analogous to his *g* and other general factors (*c*, *o* and *w*). At any rate, our *me*, *r*, *ci* and *cr* are, like his *g* (*c*, *o*, and *w*), relatively general and operative in some degree in all types of performance. Accepting this similarity it must next be pointed

out, however, that we would now wish to raise a criticism against both the Spearman doctrine of capacities and our own, as thus far outlined.

* * * * *

Conclusion

Finally, we can now, on a basis of all the above, summarize the causal and explanatory variables and their interrelations as assumed by Purposive Behaviorism in the following statements:

(1) The ultimately independent causes of behavior are four, viz., stimuli, heredity, past training, and momentary initiating physiological states (S, H, T, and P).

(2) Intervening between these "ultimate causes" of behavior and behavior itself there are a set of intermediate variables which, for convenience, may be called the behavior-determinants.

(3) These behavior-determinants are to be subdivided into four sub-groups:

(a) Capacities considered as ultimate genetic and training factors in the individual. These are of the nature of innate and acquired "funds" and are, it would seem, "very many" in number, and each relatively minor in character.

(b) Capacities considered as the "immediate response requirements," or needs, of actual S → R sequences. These, it would seem, probably vary from occasion to occasion, and hence can be only roughly identified and sorted out under such general headings as such-and-such discriminanda-capacity, such-and-such manipulanda-capacity, such-and-such a means-end-capacity, such-and-such retentivity, such-and-such consciousness- and ideation-ability, such-and-such creativity.

(c) The immanent purposive and cognitive determinants, which lie in the very warp and woof of the S → R sequence, viz., demands, means-end-readinesses, discriminanda- and manipulanda-expectations, means-end-expectations, (sign-gestalt-expectations).

(d) A unique sort of substitute for, or rather interregnum, in ordinary "practical" behaviors, viz., the back-and-forth behaviors, and the back-and-forth-behavior-adjustments.

Our system has been presented. It conceives mental processes as functional variables intervening between stimuli, initiating physiological states, and the general heredity and past training of the organism, on the one hand, and final resulting responses, on the other. These intervening variables it defines as behavior-determinants. And these behavior-determinants it subdivides further into (1) immanent purposive and cognitive determinants, (2) capacities and (3) behavior-adjustments. All three of these types of determinant are to be discovered, in the last analysis, by behavior experiments. They have to be inferred "back" from behavior. They are precipitated out from the empirical correlations which can be observed between specific stimuli and initiating physiological states, on the one hand, and specific resultant acts, on the other. They are to behavior as electrons, waves, or whatever it may be, are to the happenings in inorganic matter. There is nothing private or "mentalistic" about them. They are pragmatically conceived, objective variables the concepts of which can be altered and changed as proves most useful. They are not the dictates of any incontrovertible moments of immediacy.

BURRHUS FREDERIC SKINNER
(1904–   )

Operant Behavior [6]

Definition of Behavior

By behavior, then, I mean simply the movement of an organism or of its parts in a frame of reference provided by the organism itself or by various external objects or fields of force. It is convenient to speak of this as the action of the organism upon the outside world, and it is often desirable to deal with an effect rather than with the movement itself, as in the case of the production of sounds.

* * * * *

Static Laws of the Reflex

The Law of Threshold. The intensity of the stimulus must reach or exceed a certain critical value (called the threshold) in order to elicit a response.

* * * * *

The Law of Latency. An interval of time (called the latency) elapses between the beginning of the stimulus and the beginning of the response.

* * * * *

The Law of the Magnitude of the Response. The magnitude of the response is a function of the intensity of the stimulus.

* * * * *

The Law of After-Discharge. The response may persist for some time after the cessation of the stimulus.

* * * * *

The preceding statements regard the intensity of the stimulus as the only property of which the response is a function, but the duration must not be ignored. The laws are subject to the following elaboration:

The Law of Temporal Summation. Prolongation of a stimulus or repetitive presentation within certain limiting rates has the same effect as increasing the intensity.

* * * * *

Dynamic Laws of Reflex Strength

The Law of the Refractory Phase. Immediately after elicitation the strength of some reflexes exists at a low, perhaps zero, value. It returns to its former state during subsequent inactivity.

* * * * *

The Law of Reflex Fatigue. The strength of a reflex declines during repeated elicitation and returns to its former value during subsequent inactivity.

* * * * *

The Law of Facilitation. The strength of a reflex may be increased through presentation of a second stimulus which does not itself elicit the response.

* * * * *

The Law of Inhibition. The strength of a reflex may be decreased through presentation of a second stimulus which has no other relation to the effector involved.

* * * * *

The Law of Conditioning of Type S. The approximately simultaneous presentation of two stimuli, one of which (the 'reinforcing' stimulus) belongs to a reflex existing at the moment at some strength, may produce an increase in the strength of a third reflex composed of the response of the reinforcing reflex and the other stimulus.

The Law of Extinction of Type S. If the reflex strengthened through conditioning of Type S is elicited without presentation of the reinforcing stimulus, its strength decreases.

* * * * *

Operant Behavior

With the discovery of the stimulus and the collection of a large number of specific relationships of stimulus and response, it came to be assumed by many writers that all behavior would be accounted for in this way as soon as the appropriate stimuli could be identified. Many elaborate attempts have been made to establish the plausibility of this assumption, but they have not, I believe, proved convincing. There is a large body of behavior that does not seem to be *elicited*, in the sense in which a cinder in the eye elicits closure of the lid, although it may eventually stand in a different kind of relation to external stimuli. The original "spontaneous" activity of the organism is chiefly of this sort, as is the greater part of the conditioned behavior of the adult organism, as I hope to show later. Merely to assert that there *must* be eliciting stimuli is an unsatisfactory appeal to ignorance. The brightest hope of establishing the generality of the eliciting stimulus was provided by Pavlov's demonstration that part of the behavior of the adult organism could be shown to be under the control of stimuli which had *acquired* their power to elicit. But a formulation of this process will show that in every case the response to the conditioned stimulus must first be elicited by an unconditioned stimulus. I do not believe that the "stimulus" leading to the elaborate

responses of singing a song or of painting a picture can be regarded as the mere substitute for a stimulus or a group of stimuli which originally elicited these responses or their component parts.

Most of the pressure behind the search for eliciting stimuli has been derived from a fear of "spontaneity" and its implication of freedom. When spontaneity cannot be avoided, the attempt is made to define it in terms of unknown stimuli. . . .

But an event may occur without any observed antecedent event and still be dealt with adequately in a descriptive science. I do not mean that there are no originating forces in spontaneous behavior but simply that they are not located in the environment. We are not in a position to see them, and we have no need to. This kind of behavior might be said to be *emitted* by the organism, and there are appropriate techniques for dealing with it in that form. One important independent variable is time. In making use of it I am simply recognizing that the observed datum is the appearance of a given identifiable sample of behavior at some more or less orderly rate. The use of a rate is perhaps the outstanding characteristic of the general method to be outlined in the following pages, where we shall be concerned very largely with behavior of this sort.

The attempt to force behavior into the simple stimulus-response formula has delayed the adequate treatment of that large part of behavior which cannot be shown to be under the control of eliciting stimuli. It will be highly important to recognize the existence of this separate field in the present work. Differences between the two kinds of behavior will accumulate throughout the book, and I shall not argue the distinction here at any length. The kind of behavior that is correlated with specific eliciting stimuli may be called *respondent* behavior and a given correlation *a respondent*. The term is intended to carry the sense of a relation to a prior event. Such behavior as is not under this kind of control I shall call *operant* and any specific example *an operant*. The term refers to a posterior event, to be noted shortly. The term reflex will be used to include both respondent and operant even though in its original meaning it applied to respondents only. A single term for both is convenient beause both are topographical units of behavior and because an operant may and usually does acquire a relation to prior stimulation. In general, the notion of a reflex is to be emptied of any connotation of the active "push" of the stimulus. The terms refer here to correlated entities, and to nothing more. All implications of dynamism and all metaphorical and figurative definitions should be avoided as far as possible.

An operant is an identifiable part of behavior of which it may be said, not that no stimulus can be found that will elicit it (there may be a respondent the response of which has the same topography), but that no correlated stimulus can be detected upon occasions when it is observed to occur. It is studied as an event appearing spontaneously with a given frequency. It has no static laws comparable with those of a respondent since in the absence of a stimulus the concepts of threshold, latency, after-discharge, and the R/S ratio are meaningless. Instead, appeal must be made to frequency of occurrence in order to establish the notion of strength. The strength of an operant is proportional to its frequency of occurrence, and the dynamic laws describe the changes in the rate of occurrence that are brought about by various operations performed upon the organism.

Other Dynamic Laws

Three of the operations already described in relation to respondent behavior involve the elicitation of the reflex and hence are inapplicable to operants. They are the refractory phase, fatigue, and conditioning of Type S. The refractory phase has a curious parallel in the rate itself, as I shall note later, and a phenomenon comparable with fatigue may also appear in an operant. The conditioning of an operant differs from that of a respondent by involving the correlation of a reinforcing stimulus with a *response*. For this reason the process may be referred to as of Type R. Its two laws are as follows.

The Law of Conditioning of Type R. If the occurrence of an operant is followed by presentation of a reinforcing stimulus, the strength is increased.

The Law of Extinction of Type R. If the occurrence of an operant already strengthened through conditioning is not followed by the reinforcing stimulus, the strength is decreased.

Interaction of Reflexes

The Law of Compatibility. Two or more responses which do not overlap topographically may occur simultaneously without interference.

* * * * *

The Law of Prepotency. When two reflexes overlap topographically and the responses are incompatible, one response may occur to the exclusion of the other.

* * * * *

The Law of Algebraic Summation. The simultaneous elicitation of two responses utilizing the same effectors but in opposite directions produces a response the extent of which is an algebraic resultant.

* * * * *

The Law of Blending. Two responses showing some topographical overlap may be elicited together but in necessarily modified forms.

* * * * *

The Law of Spatial Summation. When two reflexes have the same form of response, the response to both stimuli in combination has a greater magnitude and a shorter latency.

* * * * *

The Law of Chaining. The response of one reflex may constitute or produce the eliciting or discriminative stimulus of another.

* * * * *

The Law of Induction. A dynamic change in the strength of a reflex may be accompanied by a similar but not so extensive change in a related reflex, where the relation is due to the possession of common properties of stimulus or response.

* * * * *

The Reflex Reserve

It has already been noted that one kind of operation (for example, that involved in fatigue and conditioning) is unique in its effect and changes the strength of a single reflex, while another kind (for example, that of drive or emotion) has an effect that is common to other operations and is felt by a group of reflexes. In the latter case the notion of a middle term (such as a "state" of drive or emotion) is convenient, but in the former a different conception is suggested. An operation affecting the strength of a single reflex always involves elicitation. In reflex fatigue, for example, the strength is a function of repeated elicitation. And this relation between strength and previous elicitation is such that we may speak of a certain amount of *available activity*, which is exhausted during the process of repeated elicitation and of which the strength of the reflex is at any moment a function.

I shall speak of the total available activity as the *reflex reserve*.

* * * * *

The Organism

The rats used in the following experiments were in part members of a long inbred strain of albinos and an inbred hooded strain, and in part commercial albinos of unidentified stock. With a very few exceptions all were males. Experimentation was usually begun at about 100 days of age. Experimental groups were practically always made up of litter mates. The rats were healthy at the beginning of the experiments and were discarded if any illness developed.

* * * * *

The Operant and the Skinner Box

The operant that I have used is the behavior of pressing downward a small lever. A typical lever is made of 1/8-inch brass rod and is shown in its place in the apparatus in Figure 1. The part available to the rat is a horizontal section 8 cm. long parallel to and approximately 1 cm. from the wall of the experimental box and 8 to 10 cm. above the floor. In order to press the lever down the rat must lift its forelegs from the floor, put one or both of them on the bar, and press downward with about 10 grams of pressure. The vertical movement of the bar is through a distance of about 1.5 cm.

The selection of this sample of operant behavior is based upon the following considerations.

(a) Either it is a practically universal unconditioned response (if it is to be regarded as unconditioned investigatory behavior) or it does not presuppose conditioned manipulatory behavior that is at all extraordinary for the species. Less than one per cent of the rats I have used have failed to make the response at some time or other.

(b) It has a convenient frequency of occurrence before conditioning takes place. An untrained rat placed in a small box with the lever will press it from one to ten or more times per hour, depending upon hunger, the presence of other stimuli, and so on. This is an adequate amount of "spontaneous" activity for the conditioning of an operant.

(c) At the same time it does not occur so frequently without conditioning that the effect of reinforcement is obscured. In this respect it may be contrasted with running, lifting the fore part of the body into the air, and so on.

(d) It is not included in any other significant behavior. The response of flexing a foreleg, for example, might be a component part in the responses of scratching, eating, cleaning the face, running, climbing, and so on. A description of its changes in strength would need to take all these various behaviors into account. Two difficulties of this sort arise in the case of pressing a lever, but they may be eliminated in the following way. (1) The lever may be pressed when the rat is exploring the wall space above the lever, but this may be corrected by projecting the wall or a screen forward for a short distance above the lever (see the figure). (2) In certain types of experiments (involving an emotional reaction) the rat may gnaw the lever and incidentally move it up and down. When necessary this may be avoided by using a lever of larger diameter (say, 1.5 cm.) so that gnawing is either impossible or quickly discouraged.

(e) The response is relatively unambiguous. There is no difficulty in deciding whether or not a given movement is to be counted as an elicitation, as would be the case if the response were defined as a given movement of a leg, for example.

(f) It is made in approximately the same way upon each occasion. The differences actually observed will be discussed later.

(g) Lastly, the response requires external discriminative stimulation (provided by the lever). . . . Its presence is necessary for two reasons. If the response did not need . . .

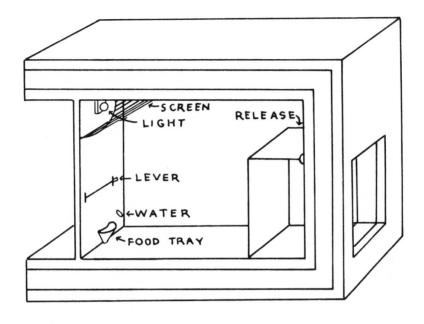

FIGURE 1

A TYPICAL EXPERIMENTAL BOX [THE SKINNER BOX]

One side has been cut away to show the part occupied by the animal. The space behind the panel at the left contains the rest of the lever, the food magazine, and other pieces of apparatus.

external support, it might be made by the organism outside the experimental situation, but no record would be taken and no reinforcement provided. Experiments which extended over a number of experimental periods would be seriously disturbed. Secondly, the sample must be discriminative in order to be typical. It would be quite possible experimentally to use such an "unsupported" response as flexing a leg or flicking the tail, but it is only in verbal behavior that such non-mechanically effective responses are reinforced (*i.e.*, when they become gestures). In general, a response must act upon the environment to produce its own reinforcement. Although the connection between the movement of the lever and reinforcement is in one sense artificial, it closely parallels the typical discriminated operant in the normal behavior of the rat.

The response of pressing a lever meets these several requirements with reasonable success

and is perhaps nearly optimal in this respect. It does not follow that the laws arrived at in this case cannot be demonstrated with other kinds of responses. The analysis necessary for the demonstration would simply be more difficult. For example, if the response were part of many different kinds of conditioned and unconditioned behavior . . ., the curves obtained during various changes in strength would be composite and highly complex but not for that reason less lawful.

The reinforcement of the response is accomplished automatically with a food magazine which discharges pellets of food of uniform size into a tray immediately beneath the lever. The pellets are made with a device similar to a druggist's "pill-machine" and are composed of the standard food with which the rats are normally fed. When the lever has been pressed and a pellet eaten, the rat is left in approximately the same position relative to the lever as at the beginning.

The entire behavior of lifting up the fore part of the body, pressing and releasing the lever, reaching into the tray, seizing the pellet of food, withdrawing from the tray, and eating the pellet is, of course, an extremely complex act. It is a chain of reflexes, which for experimental purposes must be analyzed into its component parts.

* * * * *

Conclusion

One outstanding aspect of the present book, which can hardly be overlooked, is the shift in emphasis from respondent to operant behavior. The definition of behavior as a whole ... may not be altogether acceptable to the reader. By appealing to what the organism is doing to the environment a great deal of what is often called behavior is minimized or even excluded. Most of the responses of glands and smooth-muscle fail to act upon the environment in such a way as to yield the *conspicuousness* which is offered as a defining characteristic. Any definition of a scientific field is to a considerable extent arbitrary, but it is worth pointing out that, were we to make operant behavior a subject matter in itself, we should avoid many of these problems. Operant behavior clearly satisfies a definition based upon what the organism is doing to the environment, and the question arises whether it is not properly the main concern of a student of behavior and whether respondent behavior, which is chiefly involved in the internal economy of the organism, may not reasonably be left to the physiologist. Operant behavior with its unique relation to the environment presents a separate important field of investigation. The facts of respondent behavior which have been regarded as fundamental data in a science of behavior (Sherrington, Pavlov, and others) are, as we have seen, not to be extrapolated usefully to behavior as a whole nor do they constitute any very large body of information that is of value in the study of operant behavior.

Although a distinction may be drawn between the operant and the respondent field, there is also a certain continuity, which I have tried to indicate by beginning with respondent laws and by comparing conditioning of Type S (which is largely, if not wholly, respondent) with Type R (which is apparently wholly operant). A more important sort of continuity is manifested by the use of the term "reflex" in both fields. This is to some extent a matter of controversy. In operant behavior the original figurative meaning of reflex is lost, since there is no stimulus to be "reflected" in the form of a response. It is also true that from its being applied first to respondent examples the term has acquired incidental connotations (especially in its neurological use) which are opposed to the general use made of it here. But I have tried to show elsewhere (2) from a consideration of the history of the term that many of its connotations have sprung, not from the discovery of additional information, but from prejudices and preconceptions concerning the behavior of organisms. The simple positive fact of a correlation of stimulus and response has unnecessarily given rise to an elaborated negative definition of an action "unlearned, unconscious, and involuntary." Pavlov has extended the term into the field of "learning" by showing that one can obtain the same kind of relation of stimulus and response in acquired behavior. The property of "consciousness" is either irrelevant or ineffective in differentiating between two kinds of behavior. The remaining distinction between voluntary and involuntary ... is probably closely paralleled by the operant-respondent distinction, but its traditional use in defining a reflex is more closely related to the question of predictability or freedom, which is of no significance here. A definition which respects the actual data may be derived from the simple observation of the correlation of stimulus and response. Somewhat more generally, the term applies to a way of predicting behavior or to a predictable unit. In this broad sense the concept of the reflex is useful and applicable wherever predictability may be achieved. Its range has steadily increased as more and more behavior has submitted to experimental control, and its ultimate extension to behavior as a whole is a natural consequence of an increasing demonstration of lawfulness.

One important practice has been observed in the traditional study of reflexes which is of paramount importance in the kind of system here set up and which supports the extended use of the term. The practice is that of referring to specific movements of parts of the organism. In spite of the generic nature of the term, the topographical reference has always been relatively narrow and precise. One reason why this is important is that the phenomena are then in a better position to be reduced to neurological terms. Such an argument may strike the reader as strange in view of the preceding chapter, but I agree with Carmichael . . . that "those concepts which do not make physiological formulation impossible and which are amenable to growing physiological knowledge are preferable, other things being equal, to those not so amenable." The principal significance of a sharp reference to behavior, however, is not that a neurological investigation is facilitated but that the descriptive value of the term is kept at a maximum.

This characteristic may be better understood by comparing a reflex or a law of reflex strength with a law or principle which describes the "adaptive" or "adjustive" nature of behavior or some other equally general property. Suppose, for example, that a principle is demonstrated from which it may be deduced that an organism facing a barrier in the path toward a goal will remain active until some response is made by virtue of which the barrier is surmounted. Granted the validity of the principle, we are still unable to say what the precise behavior will be. Similarly, a principle that enables one to predict that in a given situation behavior will have "survival value" or will require "least effort" may be valid enough so far as it goes, but it lacks the specificity of reference which the concept of the reflex presupposes. So far as I am aware, the reflex is the only important historical concept that has closely respected the actual movements of the organism, and the term may justifiably be preserved in a field in which that kind of reference is of first importance.

* * * * *

The reader will have noticed that almost no extension to human behavior is made or suggested. This does not mean that he is expected to be interested in the behavior of the rat for its own sake. The importance of a science of behavior derives largely from the possibility of an eventual extension to human affairs.

26

German & French Phenomenological and Existential Psychology

FRANZ BRENTANO
(1838–1917)

Act Psychology [1]

Our object is the elucidation of the two terms: physical phenomenon—mental phenomenon. We wish to exclude misunderstanding and confusion in connection with them. And for this we needn't be concerned about the means used, if only they really serve to produce clarity.

Giving more general, superordinate definitions is not the only useful means that can be employed for such an end. Just as induction is contrasted with deduction in the sphere of demonstration, here definition by way of the specific, i.e., by way of an example, is contrasted with definition by means of the more general. And the former method will be more appropriate as long as the particular term is more intelligible than the general.

---

[1] Franz Brentano, *Psychology from an Empirical Standpoint*, translated for the present volume from the German, *Psychologie vom empirischen Standpunkte* (Leipzig, 1874), Vol. 1., bk. 2, ch. 1, by D. B. Terrell.

Hence, it may be a more effective procedure to define the term "color" by saying that it designates the general class for red, blue, green, and yellow, than to choose to give an account of red—following the opposite procedure—as a particular species of color. Definition by way of particular cases will perform still more useful service in connection with terms, such as those involved in our case, which are not at all common in ordinary life, while the names of the particular phenomena comprehended under them are familiar enough. So let us start with an attempt to make our concepts clear by way of examples.

Every presentation (*Vorstellung*) of sensation or imagination offers an example of the mental phenomenon; and here I understand by presentation not that which is presented, but the act of presentation. Thus, hearing a sound, seeing a colored object, sensing warm or cold, and the comparable states of imagination as well, are examples of what I mean; but thinking of a general concept, provided such a thing does actually occur, is equally so. Furthermore, every judgment, every recollection, every expectation, every inference, every conviction or opinion, every doubt, is a mental phenomenon. And again, every emotion, joy, sorrow, fear, hope, pride, despair, anger, love, hate, desire, choice, intention, astonishment, wonder, contempt, etc., is such a phenomenon.

Examples of physical phenomena, on the other hand, are a color, a shape, a landscape, which I see; a musical chord, which I hear; heat, cold, odor, which I sense; as well as comparable images, which appear to me in my imagination.

These examples may suffice as concrete illustrations of the distinction between the two classes.

Nevertheless, we will attempt to give a definition of the mental phenomenon in another, more unified way. For this, there is available a definition we have used before, when we said that by the term, mental phenomena, we designate presentations and, likewise, all those phenomena which are based on presentations. It scarcely requires notice that, once again, by presentation we understand here not what is presented but the presenting of it. This presentation forms the basis not merely of judgments, but also of desires, as well as of every other mental act.

We cannot judge of anything, cannot desire anything, cannot hope for anything, or fear anything, if it is not presented. Hence, the definition which we gave embraces all of the examples just introduced and, in general, all of the phenomena belonging to this domain.

It is a sign of the immature state in which psychology finds itself that one can scarcely utter a single sentence about mental phenomena which would not be disputed by many. Still, the great majority agree with what we just said; presentations are the basis for the other mental phenomena. Thus, Herbart is quite correct in saying: "In every case of emotion, something, no matter how diversified and complicated, must be in consciousness as something presented; so that this particular presentation is included in this particular feeling. And every time we have a desire . . . [we] also have in our thoughts that which we desire."

* * * * *

From several of his expressions it seems to me to follow that Meyer understands the concept of presentation more narrowly than we have understood it, while he broadens the concept of feeling to an equal extent. "Presentation," he says, "first enters in when the sensed change in one's own state can be understood as the result of an outer stimulus, even if this expresses itself, at first, only in the unconscious looking or feeling around for an external object which results from it." If Meyer were to understand the same thing under presentation as we do, then it would be impossible for him to speak in this way. He would see that a state like the one which he describes as the origin of presentation would already include an abundant number of presentations: for example, presentations of temporal proximity, of spatial proximity, and of cause and effect. If all of this must already be present in the soul in order that a presentation in J. B. Meyer's sense might be formed, it is surely clear that such a thing cannot be the basis of every other mental phenomenon. On the contrary, the very state of being present (*Gegenwartig-sein*) which belongs to each of the things named is precisely a state of being presented (*Vorgestelltsein*) in our sense. And such is the case generally, wherever something appears in consciousness: whether it be hated or loved or regarded indifferently;

whether it be affirmed or rejected, or, in the case of complete withholding of judgment— I cannot express myself better than by saying —presented. As we use the word "to present," "to be presented" comes to the same thing as "to appear."

Even J. B. Meyer recognizes that a presentation in this sense is presupposed by every feeling, even the most lowly feelings of pleasure and displeasure; but deviating from us in his terminology he calls *it* a feeling and not a presentation.

*   *   *   *   *

We see clearly that what is, in our opinion, the only thing to deserve the name "feeling," also arises, in J. B. Meyer's opinion, as a successor [to something else. Its predecessor] falls under the concept of presentation, as we understand it, and forms the indispensable presupposition of the other. Hence it appears that if Meyer's viewpoint is translated into our language, the contradiction disappears of its own accord.

Perhaps the same is also true of others who express themselves similarly to Meyer. Still, we may surely find that, as regards some kinds of sensual feelings of pleasure and displeasure, someone does actually hold the opinion that there is no presentation, even in our sense, on which they are based. We cannot deny a certain temptation in that direction, at least. This holds, for example, in regard to feelings which are caused by a cut or a burn. If someone is cut, then for the most part he has no further perception of touch; if he is burned, no further perception of heat; but pain alone seems to be present in the one case and the other.

Nonetheless, there is no doubt that even here the feeling is based on a presentation. In such cases we always have the presentation of a definite spatial location, which we ordinarily specify in relation to one or the other of the visible and palpable parts of our body. We say that our foot hurts, or our hand hurts, this or the other place on our body is in pain. In the first place, then, those who look on such a spatial presentation as something originally given by means of the neural stimulation itself will therefore be unable to deny that a presentation is the basis of this feeling. But others, too, cannot avoid making

the same assumption. For we have within us not merely the presentation of a definite spatial location, but also that of a particular sensory quality, analogous to color, sound, and other so-called sensory qualities, a quality which belongs among the physical phenomena and which is definitely to be distinguished from the accompanying feeling. If we hear a pleasant, mild sound or a shrill one, a harmonious chord or a discord, it will occur to no one to identify the sound with accompanying feeling of pleasure or pain. But, likewise, when a cut, a burn, or a tickle arouses a feeling of pain or pleasure in us, we must maintain in a similar manner the distinction between a physical phenomenon, which enters in as the object of outer perception, and a mental phenomenon of feeling, which accompanies its appearance, even though the superficial observer is rather inclined to confusion here.

The principal basis of the illusion is probably the following. It is well known that our sensations are mediated by the so-called afferent (*sensibeln*) nerves. It was believed earlier that specialized nerves served exclusively as conductors for each class of sensory qualities, color, sound, and so on. Recently, physiology has inclined more and more to the opposite point of view. Particularly, it teaches almost universally that the nerves for tactile sensations, when stimulated in one way, produce in us the sensations of heat and cold, and when stimulated in another way, produce the so-called sensations of pain and pleasure. In fact, however, something similar holds for all nerves, insofar as a sensory phenomenon of the kind just mentioned can be aroused in us by way of every nerve. If they are very strongly stimulated, all nerves arouse painful phenomena, which are not distinguished in kind one from another. If a nerve serves as the medium of diverse classes of sensations, it often happens that it serves as the medium of several at the same time, as, for example, looking at an electric light results simultaneously in a "beautiful" sensation of color, i.e., one that is pleasant to us, and a painful phenomenon of another class. The nerves of the tactile sense frequently communicate at the same time a so-called sensation of touch, a sensation of heat or cold, and a so-called sensation of pain or pleasure. Now it is manifest that when several sensory phenomena appear together, it is not seldom the case that they are regarded as being *one*. This has been demonstrated in a striking way in connection with the sensations of taste and smell. It is established that almost all of the differences which we are accustomed to look upon as differences of taste are, in fact, only differences in simultaneously occurring phenomena of smell. It is a similar matter when we eat a food cold or warm: we often believe ourselves to have differences in taste which are in fact only differences in phenomena of temperature. It is not to be wondered at, then, if we do not always maintain a strict distinction between what is a phenomenon of temperature and what is a tactile phenomenon. Indeed, we would perhaps not distinguish them at all if they did not ordinarily appear independently of each other. But if now we consider the sensations of feeling (*Gefühlsempfindungen*) we find that for the most part they are bound up with sensations of another class and that when the excitation is very strong these other sensations sink into insignificance beside them. It is very easy, then, to account for the fact that we should be deceived about the occurrence of a particular class of sensory qualities and believe ourselves to have a single sensation instead of two. Since the supervening presentation was accompanied by a relatively very strong feeling, incomparably stronger than the one which followed upon the first kind of quality, this mental phenomenon was regarded as the only one which had newly been experienced. And if the first kind of quality disappeared entirely, then we would believe that we possessed nothing besides a feeling, without any presentation on which it was based.

A further basis of the illusion is that the quality on which the feeling ensues, and the feeling itself, do not bear two distinct names. We call the physical phenomenon, which occurs along with the feeling of pain, itself pain in this case. We do not say that this or that phenomenon in the foot is experienced with pain so much as we say that pain is experienced in the foot. To be sure, this is an equivocation such as we find elsewhere, whenever things stand in a close relationship to each other. We call the body healthy, and in connection with it, the air, food, facial color, and so on, but plainly in different senses. In our case, a physical phenomenon itself is called pleasure or pain, after the feeling of pleasure or pain which accompanies its appearance, and here too the sense is modified. It is as if we should say of a harmonious sound that it is a pleasure to us, because we experience a feeling of pleasure on its occurrence; or that the loss of a friend is a great sorrow to us. Experience shows that equivocation is one of the foremost hindrances to our knowledge of distinctions. It must necessarily be very much so here, where a danger of being deluded exists in and of itself, and the transference of the term was perhaps itself the result of a confusion. Hence, many psychologists were deceived, and further errors were tied up with this one. Many arrived at the false conclusion that the experiencing subject must be present at the place of the injured limb in which a painful phenomenon is localized in perception. For, insofar as they identified the phenomenon with the accompanying feeling of pain, they regarded it as a mental, not as a physical, phenomenon. And for just that reason, they believed its perception in the limb to be an inner, and consequently, an evident and infallible perception. But their opinion is contradicted by the fact that the same phenomena often appear in the same way after the limb has been amputated. Others accordingly argued rather to the opposite effect, skeptically opposing the self-evidence (*Evidenz*) of inner perception. This is all resolved, if one has learned to distinguish between the pain in the sense in which the term designates the apparent property of a part of our body and the feeling of pain which is tied up with sensing it. But if one has done this, then one is no longer inclined to hold that the feeling of sensory pain which one experiences on being injured, is not based on any presentation.

We may, accordingly, regard it as an indubitably correct definition of mental phenomena that they are either presentations or (in the sense which has been explained) rest on presentations as their basis. In this we would thus have a second definition of the concept [of mental phenomena] which breaks down into fewer terms. Yet it is not entirely unified, since it presents mental phenomena as divided into two groups.

* * * * *

What positive attribute will we now be able to advance? Or is there, perhaps, no positive definition at all which holds true of all mental phenomena generally?

A. Bain says that in fact there is none. Nonetheless, psychologists of an earlier period have already directed attention to a particular affinity and analogy which exists among all mental phenomena, while the physical do not share in it. Every mental phenomenon is characterized by what the scholastics of the Middle Ages called the intentional (and also mental) inexistence (*Inexistenz*) of an object (*Gegenstand*), and what we could call, although in not entirely unambiguous terms, the reference to a content, a direction upon an object (by which we are not to understand a reality in this case), or an immanent objectivity. Each one includes something as object within itself, although not always in the same way. In presentation something is presented, in judgment something is affirmed or denied, in love [something is] loved, in hate [something] hated, in desire [something] desired, etc.

This intentional inexistence is exclusively characteristic of mental phenomena. No physical phenomenon manifests anything similar. Consequently, we can define mental phenomena by saying that they are such phenomena as include an object intentionally within themselves.

But here, too, we come up against conflict and contradiction. And it is Hamilton in particular who denies the alleged property of a whole broad class of mental phenomena, namely, of all those which he designates as feelings, of pleasure and pain in their most diverse shades and varieties. He is in agreement with us concerning the phenomena of thinking and desire. Obviously, there would be no thinking without an object which is thought, no desire without an object which is desired.

* * * * *

In the first case, there would be something there which, according to Hamilton's way of expression, is "objective"; in the second, something which is "objectively subjective," as in self-knowledge, whose object Hamilton therefore calls subject-object; Hamilton, in denying both with regard to feeling, most definitely denies any intentional inexistence to it.

However, what Hamilton says is surely not entirely correct. Certain feelings are unmistakably referred to objects, and language itself indicates these through the expressions it uses. We say that a person rejoices in or about something, that a person sorrows or grieves about something. And once again: that delights me, that pains me, that hurts me, and so on. Joy and sorrow, like affirmation and denial, love and hate, desire and aversion, distinctly ensue upon a presentation and are referred to what is presented in it.

At the utmost, one could be inclined to agree with Hamilton in *those* cases in which one succumbs most easily, as we saw before, to the illusion that feeling is not based on any presentation: the case of the pain which is aroused by a cut or burn, for example. But its basis is none other than the very temptation toward this hypothesis, which, as we saw, is erroneous. Moreover, even Hamilton recognizes with us the fact that, without exception, presentations form the basis of feelings, and consequently [do so] in these cases as well. Therefore, his denial that feelings have an object seems so much the more striking.

To be sure, one thing is to be granted. The object to which a feeling refers is not always an external object. Even when I hear a harmonious chord, the pleasure which I feel is not really a pleasure in the sound, but a pleasure in the hearing [of it]. Indeed, one might not be mistaken in saying that it even refers to itself in a certain way and, therefore, that what Hamilton asserts, namely, that the feeling is "fused into one" with its object, *does* occur more or less. But this is nothing which does not likewise hold true of many phenomena of presentation and knowledge, as we shall see in our study of inner consciousness. Nevertheless, in them there is still a mental inexistence, a subject-object, to speak Hamilton's language; and the same will therefore hold true of these feelings as well. Hamilton is mistaken when he says that, in them, everything is "subjectively subjective," an expression which is indeed really self-contradictory; for where we can no longer speak of an object, we can no longer speak of a subject either. Even when Hamilton spoke of a fusion-into-one of the feeling with the mental modification, he gave witness against himself if we consider the matter exactly. Every fusion is a unification of several things; and consequently the pictorial expression, which is intended to make us concretely aware of the distinctive character of feeling, still indicates a certain duality in the unity.

We may thus take it to be valid that the intentional inexistence of an object is a general distinguishing characteristic of mental phenomena, which differentiates this class of phenomena from the class of physical phenomena.

* * * * *

We said that mental phenomena are the only ones of which a perception in the strict sense is possible. We could just as well say that they are the only phenomena to which actual, as well as intentional, existence pertains. Knowledge, joy, desire, exist actually; color, sound, heat, only phenomenally and intentionally.

There are philosophers who go so far as to say that it is selfevident that no actuality *could* correspond to a phenomenon such as we call a physical one. They maintain that anyone who assumes this and ascribes to physical phenomena any existence other than mental holds a view which is self-contradictory in itself.

* * * * *

I must confess that I am not in a position to be convinced of the correctness of this argument. As certain as it is that a color only appears to us when it is an object of our presentation [*wenn wir sie vorstellen*], it is nevertheless not to be inferred from this that a color could not exist without being presented. Only if being presented were included as one factor in the color, just as a certain quality and intensity is included in it, would a color which is not presented signify a contradiction, since a whole without one of its parts is truly a contradiction. This, however, is obviously not the case. Otherwise it would be strictly inconceivable how the belief in the actual existence of the physical phenomenon outside of our presentation of it could have, not to say originated, but achieved the most general dissemination, been maintained with the utmost tenacity, and, indeed, even long been shared by thinkers of the first rank. If what Bain says were correct: "We can think of [a tree] as perceived, but not as unperceived. There is manifest contradiction

in the supposition," then his further conclusion would surely no longer be subject to objection. But it is precisely this which is not to be granted. Bain explains his dictum by saying: "We are required at the same moment to perceive the thing and not to perceive it." But it is not true that this is required: For, in the first place, not every case of thinking is a perception; and further, even if this were the case, it would only follow that a person could only think of trees perceived by him, but not that he could only think of trees *as perceived by him*. To taste a white piece of sugar does not mean to taste a piece of sugar *as white*. The fallacy reveals itself quite distinctly when it is applied to mental phenomena. If one should say: "I cannot think of a mental phenomenon without thinking of it; and so I can only think of mental phenomena as thought by me; hence no mental phenomena exists outside of my thinking," this mode of inference would be exactly like the one Bain uses. Nonetheless, Bain himself will not deny that his individual mental life is not the only thing to which actual existence belongs. When Bain adds, "We know the touch of iron, but it is not possible that we should know the touch apart from the touch," he uses the word "touch," in the first place, obviously, in the sense of what is felt, and then in the sense of the feeling of it. These are different concepts even if they have the same name. Accordingly, only someone who permits himself to be deceived by the equivocation could make the concession of immediate evidence required by Bain.

It is not true, then, that the hypothesis that a physical phenomenon like those which exist intentionally in us exists outside of the mind in actuality includes a contradiction. It is only that, when we compare one with the other, conflicts are revealed, which show clearly that there is no actual existence corresponding to the intentional existence in this case. And even though this holds true in the first instance only as far as our experience extends, we will, nevertheless, make no mistake if we quite generally deny to physical phenomena any existence other than intentional existence.

* * * * *

Others have chosen to see a peculiarity of

mental life in the fact that only *one* obejct can ever be grasped in consciousness, and never several at the same time. They point to the noteworthy case of error in time-determination which regularly occurs in astronomical observations, in that the simultaneous swing of the pendulum does not enter into consciousness simultaneously with, but earlier or later than, the moment when the observed star touches the hairline in the telescope. Thus, mental phenomena always merely follow one another in a simple series. But certainly a person would be mistaken to generalize on the basis of what such a case (involving the utmost concentration of attention) shows, without any further evidence.

* * * * *

But if it were assumed to be correct that all cases of perception are like the astronomer's, would we not always have to grant at least that we often have a presentation of something and simultaneously make a judgment about it or desire it? So there would still be several simultaneous mental phenomena. Indeed, one could more correctly advance the opposite contention, that, often enough, several mental phenomena are present but never more than one physical phenomenon.

What is the only sense, then, in which we might say that invariably only one mental phenomenon is apparent but, on the other hand, that many physical phenomena appear simultaneously? We can say this insofar as the entire multiplicity of mental phenomena which appear to someone in inner perception always manifests itself to him as a unity, while this does not hold true of the physical phenomena which he simultaneously grasps by means of so-called outer perception. As is commonly the case elsewhere, many persons have confused unity with simplicity here and therefore maintain that they perceive themselves in inner consciousness as something simple. Others, in contradicting the simplicity of the phenomenon, at the same time denied its unity. But just as the former group could not maintain a consistent position, since, as soon as they described what was within them, a great number of different factors came to be mentioned, so the latter could also not prevent themselves from testifying involuntarily to the unity of the mental phenomenon.

They speak, as do others, of an "I" and not a "we," and sometimes call this entity a "bundle" of perceptions, sometimes by other names which describe a state of hanging-together in an internal unity. When we perceive simultaneously color, sound, heat, smell, nothing hinders us from ascribing each to a particular thing. On the other hand, we are obliged to take the diverse set of corresponding acts of sensation, seeing, hearing, sensing heat, and smelling, and with them the willing and feeling and considering going on at the same time, and the inner perception by which we are aware of all of them as well, to be partial phenomena of a unified phenomenon which includes them, and to take them to be a single, unified thing.

* * * * *

In conclusion, let us summarize the results of our comments on the distinction between physical and mental phenomena. First of all, we made ourselves concretely aware of the distinctive nature of the two classes by means of *examples*. We then defined mental phenomena as *presentations* and such phenomena which are *based upon presentations;* all the rest belong to the physical. We next spoke of the attribute of *extension*, which was taken by psychologists to be a distinctive characteristic of all physical phenomena; all mental phenomena were supposed to lack it. The contention had not remained uncontested, however, and only later investigations could decide the issue; that in fact mental phenomena do invariably appear unextended was all that could be confirmed now. We next found *intentional inexistence*, the reference to something as an object, to be a distinguishing feature of all mental phenomena; no physical phenomenon manifests anything similar. We further defined mental phenomena as the exclusive *object of inner perception;* they alone are therefore perceived with immediate evidence; indeed, they alone are perceived in the strict sense of the word. And with this there was bound up the further definition, that they alone are phenomena which possess *actual* existence besides their intentional existence. Finally, we advanced it as a distinguishing [feature] that the mental phenomena which someone perceives *always* appear *as a unity* despite their variety, while the physical phenomena which he may perceive simultaneously are not all presented in the same way as partial phenomena within a single phenomenon.

* * * * *

With respect to the definition of psychology, it may be apparent in the first place that the concept of mental phenomena is to be broadened rather than narrowed. For the physical phenomena of imagination, at least, fall completely within its scope just as much as do mental phenomena, in the sense defined earlier; and those which appear in sensation can also not remain unconsidered in the theory of sensation. But it is obvious that they come into consideration only as the content of mental phenomena, when the characteristics of those phenomena are being described. And the same holds true of all mental phenomena which possess exclusively phenomenal existence. It is only mental phenomena in the sense of actual states which we shall have to regard as the true object of psychology. And it is exclusively with reference to them that we say psychology is the science of mental phenomena.

CARL STUMPF
(1848–1936)

Tonal Fusion [2]

We term fusion that relation of two contents, especially sensation-contents, in which they form not a mere sum, but a whole. The consequence of this relation is, that in its higher degrees the total impression under otherwise like conditions approaches more and more that of a single unified sensation, and becomes more and more difficult to analyze. These results can also be employed for a definition, and we can say: fusion is that relation of two sensations as a consequence of which, etc. But in either way, the matter would remain an empty concept for everyone to whom the phenomena in question, and especially the phenomena of tones, were foreign. The real truth of the assertion, that sensations form a whole and approximate more or less the impression of a single unified sensation, can after all be learned only by means of examples.

Nevertheless, I remark, that the inclusion of the concept of tonal fusion under that more general quality of simultaneous as opposed to successive sensations, of which we have elsewhere spoken, is not indispensable for what follows.

* * * * *

It suffices perfectly for the attainment of the concept here necessary, to perceive and in perceiving to contrast, the differences of the cases which exist already within the tonal domain, and which will be more accurately described in what follows. We must hear and compare tonal fusions, just as we must hear and contrast tones, in order to know what a tone is.

* * * * *

It is above all, therefore, not meant by fusion, that two simultaneous tones coalesce in a certain unity in consciousness only by degrees, however quickly. Fusion signifies to us here not a process, but a present relation. I would, therefore, rather use "blend" (Schmelz), or "coalescence" (Schmalz), if this had also not its objections. Such expressions also as "to separate" (auseinandertreten) etc., are to be understood in this sense of an already existent being; just as they are likewise used in the sense of rest in the description of architectonic forms.

That fusion is not to be viewed as originating a third tonal quality in addition to or instead of the other two, needs no farther amplification.

* * * * *

Finally it is to be remarked, that the expression and concept of fusion stands here in no relation, either essentially or historically, with the general psychological doctrine of Herbart, in which "fusion" plays such a prominent part; and which for the sake of clearness everyone, who has knowledge of it, is asked for the present to banish from his mind.

[2] Carl Stumpf, The Psychology of Tone in Benjamin Rand (ed.), The Classical Psychologists, op. cit., pp. 620–630; original German, Tonpsychologie (Leipzig, 1883).

The Degrees of Fusion

If in the first place we confine ourselves to a tonal domain, which is limited by the ratio of vibrations 1 : 2, I remark the following degrees of different tones, from the highest to the lowest.

First the fusion of the octave (1 : 2).

Secondly that of the fifth (2 : 3).

Thirdly that of the fourth (3 : 4).

Fourthly that of the so-called natural thirds and sixths (4 : 5, 5 : 6, 3 : 5, 5 : 8), between which I find in this respect no clear distinctions.

Fifthly that of all the remaining musical and unmusical tonal combinations, which, for my hearing at least, offer no discernible differences of fusion, but on the contrary all the least degree of it. At most the so-called natural seventh (4 : 7) could indeed fuse somewhat more than the others.

If we employ here the modern names of the intervals, and the general expression *interval* itself, we do so not in any musical sense at all, but only to have a known and short term for the numerical relations of vibrations with which we are here concerned.

When we speak of *degrees* of fusion, we mean that we are dealing with the degrees of differences, which, as is well known, constantly pass over into one another, from the highest to the lowest degree. Further we make use of the general expression *degrees of fusion*.

The Laws of Fusion

The dependence of the degrees of fusion upon the so-called ratio of vibrations is the principal law of tonal fusion. In addition to it stand the following:

(*a*) The degree of fusion is independent of the tonal region. In the lowest pitch, where analysis meets with difficulties, the recognition and comparison of degrees of fusion become naturally difficult and impossible. But where it is possible, we find the fusion unchanged with the change of pitch, so long only as the ratio of vibrations of the two tones remain the same.

Only in the very highest pitch, approximating about 4000 vibrations, that is, from the octave five tones about the staff upward, do the differences of fusion appear to me, so far as I have yet been able to observe, to vanish. With tuning-forks 2000 : 3000 I still discern with full clearness the fusion of the fifth, whereas with 3000 : 5000, 5000 : 10000, etc., I can discern only the slightest degree of fusion at all.

(*b*) The degree of fusion is also independent of the strength, whether indeed it be the absolute or the relative strength. That it is not changed by the mere change of the absolute strength of the two tones is at once clear. With the change of relative strength it is again noteworthy, that ultimately analysis becomes impossible with great difference of strength, since the softer is suppressed by the stronger tone, so far as perception or even sensation is concerned. But so long as they remain distinguishable, I cannot notice any change of the degree of fusion. For example, if I make *c* and *g* at first of equal strength, then *c* noticeable stronger than *g*, or the reverse.

(*c*) The degree of fusion of two given tones is in no way influenced by the addition at pleasure of a third and fourth tone. Indeed, a consonance is so much the less easily analyzed, the more tones it contains, and becomes at last wholly confused and not analysable. But so long as two tones are at all distinguishable in a composite sound, their fusion also is recognised as the same as if the two alone were sounded.

In this proposition together with (*b*), there is also expressed the fact, that the overtones especially, and thereby the timbre, make no change in the ratio of two fundamental tones of musical sounds, as is also confirmed by direct observation.

(*d*) As in general the changes of stimulus below a certain degree effect no perceptible changes of sensation, so likewise very minute deviations of the number of vibrations from the abovementioned ratios create no perceptible change of the degree of fusion. If the deviation is increased, the fusion in all pairs of tones which do not belong to the very lowest degree of fusion, passes into this degree without running through the intermediate degrees, if any. And this transition occurs the more rapidly, (with the smaller relative differences of vibrations), the greater was the initial fusion.

* * * * *

(*e*) The fusion remains and retains its degree when both tones do not affect the same ear, but one is presented exclusively to the right, the other exclusively to the left. A tuningfork of medium pitch, that is not sounded too loud, held before one ear is not perceived by the other, as we discover from the fact, that if the first is stopped up nothing is heard. If now we apply two forks which for example form a fifth, one to each ear, no difference is observable between this fusion, and the perception by one and the same ear. On the contrary, the analysis can be facilitated by this process.

(*f*) Fusion remains also in the mere representation of the imagination. If I merely represent *c* and *g* as sounding at the same time, I can conceive them only as fusing, and indeed with the definite degree of fusion which they possess in the actual hearing. The same is true of any other two tones. *A priori* this is not necessarily to be expected, even if we recognise sensations and representations of the imagination in general as similar. Not all properties of simultaneous sensations pass over of necessity to the representation of the imagination: *c* and *c* sharp in actual hearing (upon the same ear) necessarily make vibrations, but in the imagination I can represent them perfectly without vibrations. Moreover, if I represent them as vibrating, I can represent them with slow or quick, strong or weak vibrations; whilst the choice of the degree of fusion is not free to me.

In regard to the representation of the imagination we must accordingly complete the fundamental law as follows: Tones represented as simultaneous fuse in the degree which corresponds to the ratio of vibrations of tones of the same pitch created objectively.

(*g*) If we proceed above an octave, the same degrees of fusion recur with the rates of vibration increased one or more octaves. The ninths have the same fusion as the seconds, the tenths as the thirds, the double and triple octave as the octave; and in general $m : n.2^x$, the same as $m : n$, if $m < n$ and x a small whole number.

We must not be misled here by the greater ease of the analysis. *C* and c^4 sounding together are more easily and certainly analyzed by the unmusical than *C* and *c*, even than *C* and *G;* although these two tones fuse less with one another than the former. The analysis depends upon very different conditions; it is peculiarly difficult especially in the lowest register; it is further facilitated by increase in the difference of pitch of the two tones. But if analysis takes place in both cases, we shall also further find, that *C* and c^4 are nevertheless in sensuous impression less perfectly sundered than *C* and *G*, and not more perfectly than *C* and *c*.

If I compare the sounds of the tuning-fork *CG* with *Cg*, *CA* with *Ca*, etc., it is evident to me, that detection of difference between every second combination is always easier, but the fusion is the same as in the first.

If I play upon the d^1 string of the violin the octave d^1, and then the double octave d^2 (on the a^1 string), I have in both cases the same impression of homogeneity and of approximation to a real tonal unity. We can always for sake of contrast play the *d* in question with the free e^2 string; the difference of the fusion is always the same, that of the highest and of the lowest degree.

If an orchestra plays the entire 7 octave tones from *C* up to c^5, we still designate the impression as *unison*. The seven tones are more homogeneous than the two tones *c* and *a*, to say nothing of *c* and *b*. We cannot here assume as true, that only the two neighboring members of the series always fuse with one another, *C* with *c*, *c* with c^1, etc., and that the farther removed do so only by means of the intermediate; for if *C* and c^5 fuse by themselves less than *C* and *c*, or even *c* and *g*, this could not be changed by means of the intervening octaves, according to (*c*).

* * * * *

In general it will also be well first to take tones of the same sensation-strength, because then the danger is best avoided that any one of them should remain totally imperceptible or obscure. In order to produce similar strength of sensation in large intervals of tone, one must frequently—according to the instrument—give the higher tone with less physical strength. Further the greatest possible similarity in the initial utterance and duration of tone is naturally preferable, since inequalities of every kind divert the attention. Likewise, similar tone color is desirable, although this is of no influence in the fusion of the keynotes. Purity of interval, that is, exact harmony with the respective numbers of vibrations, is so much the more necessary, the more acute the hearing; although minimal variations, which can never be avoided, do no important injury to the fusion particularly in the lower grades. The piano with its tempered pitch permits the differences of the higher degrees still to appear (the octave is even here pure); but not between the last two degrees. It is even here $c:d$ sharp $=$ $c:e$ flat, and $c:g$ sharp $=c:a$ flat.

* * * * *

Confirmation through Unmusical Persons

For the guidance of my own judgment I have pursued still another method. As the question is here put, it can only be addressed to those who are sufficiently endowed with power of tonal observations to analyze the fifths and octaves easily and directly. With such there exists only the difficulty last mentioned, and many times previously touched upon, as to the dominating consciousness of the harmonious character and sensation-value of the interval. But we can obtain information also in an indirect way through unmusical persons, and those unpractised in the judgment of tones: by means of the use of the aforementioned difficulty of analysis. The different degrees of fusion must reveal themselves in the different degrees of difficulty of analysis, if all the remaining circumstances upon which the latter depend are taken precisely equal. We shall recognise them in the results. In this way we can even obtain figures, by the enumeration of correct and false judgments, upon the question, whether one or more tones are present in each interval. The combinations of more strongly fusing tones under otherwise similar conditions will more rarely be judged to be two tones than those fusing less strongly.

* * * * *

The Cause of Fusion is Physiological

That also within the organ, especially of the labyrinth in the ear, the physical processes do not yet possess that characteristic which corresponds to the fusion of the tones in sensation, appears not merely from the just-mentioned isolated transmission but also from the fact, that the fusion is perceptible in the same way when the two tones are divided between the two ears, as well as when they are merely imagined. At least it would be

a violent and improbable assumption, that the process creating fusion in the case of simultaneous hearing occurs in the ear itself, but in the division of the tones occurs first in the brain.

Certain differences in the last processes of the centre of hearing must therefore correspond to the differences in the degrees of fusion as a physical correlate, or as a cause, (according as one thinks in a monistic or a dualistic way). But we know nothing of what nature these differences are, for this reason, if for no other, that in general we know nothing concerning the nature of the last processes. Indeed I must say, that although up to a certain point we can express in physical or chemical terms the occurrence of vibrations, competition, contrast, and other phenomena, in respect to the processes of the brain, which might lie at the basis of the phenomena of fusion, such a hypothetical image does not even occur to me.

* * * * *

If we are willing in the lack of adequate apprehension to content ourselves with an abstract notion (which after all is nothing but a word), we might once more speak of specific energies. The specific energies, which lie at the foundation of fusion, have only this peculiarity, that they are not aroused by means of isolated stimuli, but by the concurrence of two stimuli. For this reason, we can call them specific energies of a higher rank, or still better, *specific synergies*. By such specific synergy we should therefore understand a determinate mode of coöperation of two nervous formations, having its ground in the structure of the brain, of such a kind that whenever these two formations produce their corresponding sensations, there arises at the same time a determinate degree of fusion of these sensations. As adequate and inadequate stimuli are distinguished in the production of sensations, by means of both of which nevertheless one and the same quality of sensation is produced; so likewise a determinate degree of fusion is here not united as such exclusively and unconditionally to the "adequate" stimulus-relation, (e.g., $1:2$), but the same specific synergy can also, by way of exception, be aroused by another objective relation of vibration, and the octave relation, etc., be established in the sensation. On the other hand, these specific energies of higher rank are, to be sure, inseparably united with those of the first rank: for the fusion reveals itself constantly as the same between two determinate qualities of tone.

That fusion remains preserved in imagination, is not opposed to what has been said, but is only a new example in proof of the fact, that the mere ideas of the imagination have themselves a physical basis, and indeed in general the same as the sensations.

ERICH R. JAENSCH
(1883–1940)

Eidetic Imagery [3]

The most important aspect of *Eidetics*— the theory of eidetic or perceptual images (*Anschauungsbilder*)—is that its development represents the first systematic application of typological methods of investigation.

* * * * *

Optical perceptual (or eidetic) images are phenomena that take up an intermediate position between sensations and images. Like ordinary physiological after-images, they are always *seen* in the literal sense. They have this property of necessity and under all conditions, and share it with sensations. In other respects they can also exhibit the properties of images (*Vorstellungen*). In those cases in which the imagination has little influence, they are merely modified after-images, deviating from the norm in a definite way, and when that influence is nearly, or completely zero, we can look upon them as slightly intensified after-images. In the other limiting case, when the influence of the imagination is at its maximum, they are ideas that, like after-images, are projected outward and literally *seen*. Just as there are different shades of orange, which all lie somewhere between pure red and pure yellow, so, too, the slightly intensified after-image and the projected, literally visible, memory image are the limiting cases between which the eidetic images lie. It was found that the point between these extremes at which the phenomenon of eidetic images manifests itself, whether it approximates to, or coincides with one or other pole, depends on the psycho-

physical constitution. We can therefore make use of a similar symbolic representation, as is usual in colour theories. We may imagine a line drawn between the two "end-points" red and yellow, so that the various shades of yellow are represented by points on this line. Similarly, we may imagine a line drawn between the "end-points," pure physiological after-images, and outwardly projected, literally visible, memory images. The points on this line would then represent different types of eidetic images, sometimes approaching after-images, sometimes memory images. Because of the fluctuations in the personality, however, we cannot assign one definite point to the eidetic image, but must assign to it a finite range within which the phenomenon can fluctuate according to the momentarily operative functional circumstances (experimental conditions), now approaching the one pole, now the other. The localization of the phenomenon on our symbolic line depends in the first place, therefore, on a permanent factor, the constitution of the personality. But since the personality often changes in the course of development, it would be better to say that localization depends on a *relatively permanent, constitutionally determined factor*. In the second place, it depends to a lesser degree on a *momentary, functionally determined factor*. This can be introduced at any moment and depends on the particular circumstances or experimental conditions in which we happen to place the person to be investigated.

It must be especially emphasized that this schema has not been evolved by *a priori* construction: we have been led to it by rigorously empirical procedure.

* * * * *

For the great majority of adults there is an unbridgeable gulf between sensations and

---

[3] Erich R. Jaensch, *Eidetic Imagery*, trans. Oscar Oeser (London: Kegan Paul, Trench, Trubner, 1930), pp. 1–15; original German, *Die Eidetik und die typologische Forschungmethode* (Leipzig, 1925). Reprinted by permission.

images. It has always been known that for a few individuals this is not true. Some people have peculiar "intermediate experiences" between sensations and images. From the description that such people have given of these experiences, and from the characterization we have just given of eidetic images, we must conclude that their "experiences" are due to eidetic images. These phenomena, it is true, are rare among average adults.

* * * * *

First of all we have to take care that the individuals to be investigated understand us correctly when we talk about phenomena that can literally be *seen*. Otherwise children might understand us to be referring merely to visual *memory images*. We must therefore demonstrate to them exactly what it means to *see* something, although no object is actually present. This will have to be done for some case that is realizable whether the subject has eidetic images or not. The only case where this is possible is in physiological after-images, which are obtained when a simple object of intense colour is fixated for some time. We therefore begin each investigation by showing the subject some after-images.

* * * * *

Eidetic images proper, which we wish to bring forth, are usually best seen on a homogeneous dark grey (not black) background of 50° white and 310° cloth-black on the colour disc. We therefore use such a screen from the very beginning, as well as in the later experiments.

* * * * *

For mass investigations we can therefore begin by presenting some object that is suitable for generating after-images to a whole class, or to the group to be investigated. Those who have intensified after-images can then be singled out for more detailed individual investigation, which is necessary in *every* case. Here we pay special attention to those whose after-images are not in the complementary, but in the original colour, as this points to a relatively high degree of eidetic faculty.

The cases of eidetic imagery that are related to the A.I., and that reveal themselves at this preliminary test, are verified by a second test. A complicated object, *e.g.* a silhouette picture with numerous details, is *fixated* for 15 seconds. When the picture is removed, a non-eidetic will see at most a few details on the screen, as experience has shown. If the subject sees the whole picture, or the majority of the details sharply defined, this points with even greater certainty to the presence of the eidetic faculty. If the colour of this "after-image" corresponds to that of the original, we have a certain proof.

* * * * *

After a sufficiently long interval, the coloured square that was used in the first test is presented for non-fixating inspection for a shorter time (10–15 secs.). If this results in a picture with sharp contours, not merely in an irregular blot, we may look upon this as indicating even more conclusively the presence of the eidetic faculty, particularly if the colour is pronounced as well. We may be absolutely certain, if the colour of the image is the same as that of the original square.

* * * * *

As a rule the E.Is. are best seen on a dark gray background of the type mentioned above. If the result is negative, however, one should also try the experiment when head and background are in deep shadow, e.g. thrown by a piece of cloth, or let the subject try with his eyes closed. It sometimes happens that the E.I. is only visible under these conditions. In the latter case one should particularly note whether there is any colour contrast along the edges. One also finds that in rare cases the E.I. is best seen on a light background. Finally, one should always note whether E.Is. occur spontaneously under special circumstances, particularly in emotionally toned situations. Even in the weak cases that have the conceptual component, such occasional, spontaneous images are hardly ever entirely lacking, since emotional participation is an important factor in this component.

* * * * *

Although the disposition for E.Is., even in their more pronounced forms, is widely prevalent up to puberty, we must not expect to find the same, or even approximately the same percentage of eidetics everywhere. In this respect the greatest differences exist between one locality and the next, and in the same place between different classes in a school. The eidetic disposition is correlated with certain constitutional types, whose distribution varies from locality to locality, and this explains the variation in the frequency of pronounced eidetic cases. Far more fundamental, apparently, is its dependence on the type of education, in particular on the difference between the so-called *Lernschule* in the old sense and the *Arbeitsschule* in the new. The latter takes far more account of the idiosyncrasies of the child, in particular its natural attention to the world of the senses. This type of school, by continually reinforcing abstract thought with concrete particulars ("object lessons"), takes into account the desire of the child for activity, and in so doing combats "school passivity" and the lowering of intellectual activity, which otherwise manifest themselves soon after the child's entrance into school. This is probably the reason why statistical enquiries in schools of this type, in many different German towns, have hitherto always yielded an incomparably larger percentage of eidetics than others.

* * * * *

But the most conclusive and most general proof that E.Is. are literally *seen*, is that E.Is. are within wide limits subject to the same laws as sensations and perceptions. Our subjects do not know anything about these laws, and the fact that they are obeyed cannot therefore be the result of suggestion.

EDMUND HUSSERL
(1859–1938)

Phenomenological Psychology [4]

Phenomenology denotes a new, descriptive, philosophical method, which, since the concluding years of the last century, has established (1) an *a priori* psychological discipline, able to provide the only secure basis on which a strong empirical psychology can be built, and (2) a universal philosophy, which can supply an organum for the methodical revision of all the sciences.

Present-day psychology, as the science of the "psychical" in its concrete connection with spatio-temporal reality, regards as its material whatever is present in the world as "ego-istic"; *i.e.*, "living," perceiving, thinking, willing, etc., actual, potential and habitual. And as the psychical is known as a certain stratum of existence, proper to men and beasts, psychology may be considered as a branch of anthropology and zoology. But animal nature is a part of physical reality, and that which is concerned with physical reality is natural science. Is it, then, possible to separate the psychical cleanly enough from the physical to establish a pure psychology parallel to natural science? That a purely psychological investigation is practicable

within limits is shown by our obligation to it for our fundamental conceptions of the psychical, and most of those of the psychophysical.

But before determining the question of an unlimited psychology, we must be sure of the characteristics of psychological experience and the psychical data it provides. We turn naturally to our immediate experiences. But we cannot discover the psychical in any experience, except by a "reflection," or perversion of the ordinary attitude. We are accustomed to concentrate upon the matters, thoughts, and values of the moment, and not upon the psychical "act of experience" in which these are apprehended. This "act" is revealed by a "reflection"; and a reflection can be practised on every experience. Instead of the matters themselves, the values, goals, utilities, etc., we regard the subjective experiences in which these "appear." These "appearances" are phenomena, whose nature is to be a "consciousness-of" their object, real or unreal as it be. Common language catches this sense of "relativity," saying, I was thinking *of* something, I was frightened *of* something, etc. Phenomenological psychology takes its name from the "phenomena," with the psychological aspect of which it is concerned: and the word "intentional" has been borrowed from the scholastic to denote the essential

[4] Edmund Husserl, "Phenomenology," trans. C. V. Solomon, in *Encyclopædia Britannica* (1929). Reprinted by permission.

"reference" character of the phenomena. All consciousness is "intentional."

In unreflective consciousness we are "directed" upon objects, we "intend" them; and reflection reveals this to be an immanent process characteristic of all experience, though infinitely varied in form. To be conscious of something is no empty having of that something in consciousness. Each phenomenon has its own intentional structure, which analysis shows to be an ever-widening system of individually intentional and intentionally related components. The perception of a cube, for example, reveals a multiple and synthesized intention: a continuous variety in the "appearance" of the cube, according to differences in the points of view from which it is seen, and corresponding differences in "perspective," and all the difference between the "front side" actually seen at the moment and the "backside" which is not seen, and which remains, therefore, relatively "indeterminate," and yet is supposed equally to be existent. Observation of this "stream" of "appearance-aspects" and of the manner of their synthesis, shows that every phase and interval is already in itself a "consciousness-of" something, yet in such a way that with the constant entry of new phases the total consciousness, at any moment, lacks not synthetic unity, and is, in fact, a consciousness of one and the same object. The intentional structure of the train of a perception must conform to a certain type, if any physical object is to be perceived as there! And if the same object be intuited in other modes, if it be imagined, or remembered, or copied, all its intentional forms recur, though modified in character from what they were in the perception, to correspond to their new modes. The same is true of every kind of psychical experience. Judgment, valuation, pursuit, these also are no empty experiences having in consciousness of judgments, values, goals and means, but are likewise experiences compounded of an intentional stream, each conforming to its own fast type.

Phenomenological psychology's comprehensive task is the systematic examination of the types and forms of intentional experience, and the reduction of their structures to the prime intentions, learning thus what is the nature of the psychical, and comprehending the being of the soul.

The validity of these investigations will obviously extend beyond the particularity of the psychologist's own soul. For psychical life may be revealed to us not only in self-consciousness but equally in our consciousness of other selves, and this latter source of experience offers us more than a reduplication of what we find in our self-consciousness, for it establishes the differences between "own" and "other" which we experience, and presents us with the characteristics of the "social life." And hence the further task accrues to psychology of revealing the intentions of which the "social life" consists.

Phenomenological-Psychological and Eidetic-Reductions. The Phenomenological psychology must examine the self's experience of itself and its derivative experience of other selves and of society, but whether, in so doing, it can be free of all psycho-physical admixture, is not yet clear. Can one reach a really pure self-experience and purely psychical data? This difficulty, ever since Brentano's discovery of intentionality, as the fundamental character of the psychical, has blinded psychologists to the possibilities of phenomenological psychology. The psychologist finds his self-consciousness mixed everywhere with "external" experience, and non-psychical realities. For what is experienced as external belongs not to the intentional "internal," though our experience of it belongs there as an experience of the external. The phenomenologist, who will only notice phenomena, and know purely his own "life," must practice an ἐποχή [*epoche:* a suspension of judgment]. He must inhibit every ordinary objective "position," and partake in no judgment concerning the objective world. The experience itself will remain what it was, an experience of this house, of this body, of this world in general, in its particular mode. For one cannot describe any intentional experience, even though it be "illusory," a self-contradicting judgment and the like, without describing what in the experience is, as such, the object of consciousness.

Our comprehensive ἐποχή puts, as we say, the world between brackets, excludes the world which is simply there! from the subject's field, presenting in its stead the so-and-so-experienced - perceived - remembered - judged - thought-valued-etc., world, as such, the "bracketed" world. Not the world or any part of it appears, but the "sense" of the world. To enjoy phenomenological experience we must retreat from the objects posited in the natural attitude to the multiple modes of their "appearance," to the "bracketed" objects.

The phenomenological reduction to phenomena, to the purely psychical, advances by two steps: (1) systematic and radical ἐποχή of every objectifying "position" in an experience, practised both upon the regard of particular objects and upon the entire attitude of mind, and (2) expert recognition, comprehension and description of the manifold "appearances" of what are no longer "objects" but "unities" of sense. So that the phenomenological description will comprise two parts, description of the "noetic" (νόεω) or "experiencing" and description of the "noematic" (νόημα) or the "experienced." Phenomenological experience is the only experience which may properly be called "internal" and there is no limit to its practice. And as a similar "bracketing" of objective, and description of what then "appears" ("noema" in "noesis"), can be performed upon the "life" of another self which we represent to ourselves, the "reductive" method can be extended from one's own self-experience to one's experience of other selves. And, further, that society, which we experience in a common consciousness, may be reduced not only to the intentional fields of the individual consciousness, but also by the means of an inter-subjective reduction, to that which unites these, namely the phenomenological unity of the social life. Thus enlarged, the psychological concept of internal experience reaches its full extent.

But it takes more than the unity of a manifold "intentional life," with its inseparable complement of "sense-unities," to make a "soul." For from the individual life that "ego-subject" cannot be disjoined, which persists as an identical ego or "pole," to the particular intentions, and the "habits" growing out of these. Thus the "inter-subjective," phenomenologically reduced and concretely apprehended, is seen to be a "society" of "persons," who share a conscious life.

Phenomenological psychology can be purged of every empirical and psycho-physical element, but, being so purged, it cannot deal with "matters of fact." Any closed field may be considered as regards its "*essence*," its εἶδος, and we may disregard the factual side of our phenomena, and use them as "examples" merely. We shall ignore individual souls and societies, to learn their *a priori*, their "possible" forms. Our thesis will be "theoretical," observing the invariable through variation, disclosing a typical realm of *a priori*. There will be no psychical existence whose "style" we shall not know. Psychological phenomenology must rest upon eidetic phenomenology.

The phenomenology of the perception of bodies, for example, will not be an account of actually occurring perceptions, or those which may be expected to occur, but of that invariable "structure," apart from which no perception of a body, single or prolonged, can be conceived. The phenomenological reduction reveals the phenomena of actual internal experience; the eidetic reduction, the essential forms constraining psychical existence.

Men now demand that empirical psychology shall conform to the exactness required by modern natural science. Natural science, which was once a vague, inductive empiric, owes its modern character to the *a priori* system of forms, nature as it is "conceivable," which its separate disciplines, pure geometry, laws of motion, time, etc., have contributed. The methods of natural science and psychology are quite distinct, but the latter, like the former, can only reach "exactness" by a rationalization of the "essential."

The psycho-physical has an *a priori* which must be learned by any complete psychology; this *a priori* is not phenomenological, for it depends no less upon the essence of physical, or more particularly organic nature.

MARTIN HEIDEGGER
(1889–   )

Dasein Analysis [5]

We are ourselves the entities to be analysed. The Being of any such entity is *in each case mine*. These entities, in their Being, comport themselves towards their Being. As entities with such Being, they are delivered over to their own Being. *Being* is that which is an issue for every such entity. This way of characterizing Dasein has a double consequence:

1. The "essence" ["Wesen"] of this entity lies in its "to be" [Zu-sein]. Its Being-what-it-is [Was-sein] (*essentia*) must, so far as we can speak of it at all, be conceived in terms of its Being (*existentia*). But here our ontological task is to show that when we choose to designate the Being of this entity as "existence" [Existenz], this term does not and cannot have the ontological signification of the traditional term "*existentia*"; ontologically, *existentia* is tantamount to *Being-present-at-hand*, a kind of Being which is essentially inappropriate to entities of Dasein's character. To avoid getting bewildered, we shall always use the Interpretative expression "*presence-at-hand*" for the term "*existentia*," while the term "existence," as a designation of Being, will be allotted solely to Dasein.

The "essence" of Dasein lies in its existence. Accordingly those characteristics which can be exhibited in this entity are not "properties" present-at-hand of some entity which "looks" so and so and is itself present-at-hand; they are in each case possible ways for it to be, and no more than that. All the Being-as-it-is [So-sein] which this entity possesses is primarily Being. So when we designate this entity with the term "Dasein," we are expressing not its "what" (as if it were a table, house or tree) but its Being.

2. That Being which is an *issue* for this entity in its very Being, is in each case mine. Thus Dasein is never to be taken ontologically as an instance or special case of some genus of entities as things that are present-at-hand. To entities such as these, their Being is "a

matter of indifference"; or more precisely, they "are" such that their Being can be neither a matter of indifference to them, nor the opposite. Because Dasein has *in each case mineness* [*Jemeinigkeit*], one must always use a *personal* pronoun when one addresses it: "I am," "you are."

Furthermore, in each case Dasein is mine to be in one way or another. Dasein has always made some sort of decision as to the way in which it is in each case mine [je meines]. That entity which in its Being has this very Being as an issue, comports itself towards its Being as its ownmost possibility. In each case Dasein *is* its possibility, and it "has" this possibility, but not just as a property [eigenschaftlich], as something present-at-hand would. And because Dasein is in each case essentially its own possibility, it *can*, in its very Being, "choose" itself and win itself; it can also lose itself and never win itself; or only "seem" to do so. But only in so far as it is essentially something which can be *authentic*—that is, something of its own—can it have lost itself and not yet won itself. As modes of Being, *authenticity* and *inauthenticity* (these expressions have been chosen terminologically in a strict sense) are both grounded in the fact that any Dasein whatsoever is characterized by mineness. But the inauthenticity of Dasein does not signify any "less" Being or any "lower" degree of Being. Rather it is the case that even in its fullest concretion Dasein can be characterized by inauthenticity—when busy, when excited, when interested, when ready for enjoyment.

The two characteristics of Dasein which we have sketched—the priority of "*existentia*" over *essentia*, and the fact that Dasein is in each case mine [die Jemeinigkeit]—have already indicated that in the analytic of this entity we are facing a peculiar phenomenal domain. Dasein does not have the kind of Being which belongs to something merely present-at-hand within the world, nor does it ever have it. So neither is it to be presented thematically as something we come across in the same way as we come across what is present-at-hand. The right way of presenting it is so far from self-evident that to determine what form it shall take is itself an essential

[5] From pp. 67–69, 78–85, *Being and Time* by Martin Heidegger. Translated by John Macavarrie and Edward Robinson. Copyright © 1962 by SCM Press Ltd. Reprinted by permission of Harper & Row, Publishers.

part of the ontological analytic of this entity. Only by presenting this entity in the right way can we have any understanding of its Being. No matter how provisional our analysis may be, it always requires the assurance that we have started correctly.

In determining itself as an entity, Dasein always does so in the light of a possibility which it *is* itself and which, in its very Being, it somehow understands. This is the formal meaning of Dasein's existential constitution. But this tells us that if we are to Interpret this entity *ontologically*, the problematic of its Being must be developed from the existentiality of its existence. This cannot mean, however, that "Dasein" is to be construed in terms of some concrete possible idea of existence. At the outset of our analysis it is particularly important that Dasein should not be Interpreted with the differentiated character [Differenz] of some definite way of existing, but that it should be uncovered [aufgedeckt] in the undifferentiated character which it has proximally and for the most part. This undifferentiated character of Dasein's everydayness is *not nothing*, but a positive phenomenal characteristic of this entity. Out of this kind of Being—and back into it again— is all existing, such as it is. We call this everyday undifferentiated character of Dasein "*averageness*."

* * * * *

Being-in-the-World [6]

We have brought out some characteristics of Being which will provide us with a steady light for our further investigation, but which will at the same time become structurally concrete as that investigation continues. Dasein is an entity which, in its very Being, comports itself understandingly towards that Being. In saying this, we are calling attention to the formal concept of existence. Dasein exists. Furthermore, Dasein is an entity which in each case I myself am. Mineness belongs to any existent Dasein, and belongs to it as the condition which makes authenticity and inauthenticity possible. In each case Dasein exists in one or the other of these two modes, or else it is modally undifferentiated.

---

[6] *Ibid.*, pp. 78–85.

But these are both ways in which Dasein's Being takes on a definite character, and they must be seen and understood *a priori* as grounded upon that state of Being which we have called "*Being-in-the-world*." An interpretation of this constitutive state is needed if we are to set up our analytic of Dasein correctly.

The compound expression "Being-in-the-world" indicates in the very way we have coined it, that it stands for a *unitary* phenomenon. This primary datum must be seen as a whole. But while Being-in-the-world cannot be broken up into contents which may be pieced together, this does not prevent it from having several constitutive items in its structure. Indeed the phenomenal datum which our expression indicates is one which may, in fact, be looked at in three ways. If we study it, keeping the whole phenomenon firmly in mind beforehand, the following items may be brought out for emphasis:

First, the "*in-the-world*." With regard to this there arises the task of inquiring into the ontological structure of the "world" and defining the idea of *worldhood* as such. . . .

Second, that *entity* which in every case has Being-in-the-world as the way in which it is. Here we are seeking that which one inquires into when one asks the question "Who?" By a phenomenological demonstration we shall determine who is in the mode of Dasein's average everydayness. . . .

Third, *Being-in* [*In-sein*] as such. We must set forth the ontological Constitution of inhood [Inheit] itself. . . . Emphasis upon any one of these constitutive items signifies that the others are emphasized along with it; this means that in any such case the whole phenomenon gets seen. Of course Being-in-the-world is a state of Dasein which is necessary *a priori*, but it is far from sufficient for completely determining Dasein's Being. Before making these three phenomena the themes for special analyses, we shall attempt by way of orientation to characterize the third of these factors.

What is meant by "*Being-in*"? Our proximal reaction is to round out this expression to "Being-in 'in the world' ", and we are inclined to understand this Being-in as "Being in something" ["Sein in . . ."]. This latter term designates the kind of Being which an entity has when it is "in" another one, as the water is "in" the glass, or the garment is "in" the cupboard. By this "in" we mean the relationship of Being which two entities extended "in" space have to each other with regard to their location in that space. Both water and glass, garment and cupboard, are "in" space and "at" a location, and both in the same way. This relationship of Being can be expanded: for instance, the bench is in the lecture-room, the lecture-room is in the university, the university is in the city, and so on, until we can say that the bench is "in world-space." All entities whose Being "in" one another can thus be described have the same kind of Being—that of Being-present-at-hand—as Things occurring "within" the world. Being-present-at-hand "in" something which is likewise present-at-hand, and Being-present-at-hand-along-with [Mit-vorhandensein] in the sense of a definite location-relationship with something else which has the same kind of Being, are ontological characteristics which we call "categorial": they are of such a sort as to belong to entities whose kind of Being is not of the character of Dasein.

Being-in, on the other hand, is a state of Dasein's Being; it is an existentiale. So one cannot think of it as the Being-present-at-hand of some corporeal Thing (such as a human body) "in" an entity which is present-at-hand. Nor does the term "Being-in" mean a spatial "in-one-another-ness" of things present-at-hand, any more than the word "in" primordially signifies a spatial relationship of this kind. "In" is derived from "innan"—"to reside," "habitare," "to dwell" [sich auf halten]. "An" signifies "I am accustomed," "I am familiar with," "I look after something." It has the signification of "colo" in the senses of "habito" and "diligo." The entity to which Being-in in this signification belongs is one which we have characterized as that entity which in each case I myself am [bin]. The expression "bin" is connected with "bei," and so "ich bin" ["I am"] means in its turn "I reside" or "dwell alongside" the world, as that which is familiar to me in such and such a way. "Being" [Sein], as the infinitive of "ich bin" (that is to say, when it is understood as an existentiale), signifies "to reside alongside . . . ," "to be familiar with. . . ." "Being-in" is thus the formal existential expression for the Being of

Dasein, which has Being-in-the-world as its essential state.

"Being alongside" the world in the sense of being absorbed in the world (a sense which calls for still closer interpretation) is an existentiale founded upon Being-in. In these analyses the issue is one of seeing a primordial structure of Dasein's Being—a structure in accordance with whose phenomenal content the concepts of Being must be Articulated; because of this, and because this structure is in principle one which cannot be grasped by the traditional ontological categories, this "Being-alongside" must be examined still more closely. We shall again choose the method of contrasting it with a relationship of Being which is essentially different onto-logically—viz. categorial—but which we express by the same linguistic means. Fundamental ontological distinctions are easily obliterated; and if they are to be envisaged phenomenally in this way, this must be done explicitly, even at the risk of discussing the "obvious." The status of the ontological analytic shows, however, that we have been far from interpreting these obvious matters with an adequate "grasp," still less with regard for the meaning of their Being; and we are even farther from possessing a stable coinage for the appropriate structural concepts.

As an existentiale, "Being alongside" the world never means anything like the Being-present-at-hand-together of Things that occur. There is no such thing as the "side-by-side-ness" of an entity called "Dasein" with another entity called "world." Of course when two things are present-at-hand together alongside one another, we are accustomed to express this occasionally by something like "The table stands 'by' ['bei'] the door" or "The chair 'touches' ['berührt'] the wall." Taken strictly, "touching" is never what we are talking about in such cases, not because accurate re-examination will always eventually establish that there is a space between the chair and the wall, but because in principle the chair can never touch the wall, even if the space between them should be equal to zero. If the chair could touch the wall, this would presuppose that the wall is the sort of thing "for" which a chair would be encounterable. An entity present-at-hand within the world can be touched by another entity only if by its very nature the latter entity has Being-in as its own kind of Being —only if, with its Being-there [Da-sein], something like the world is already revealed to it, so that from out of that world another entity can manifest itself in touching, and thus become accessible in its Being-present-at-hand. When two entities are present-at-hand within the world, and furthermore are *worldless* in themselves, they can never "touch" each other, nor can either of them "*be*" "*alongside*" the other. The clause "furthermore are worldless" must not be left out; for even entities which are not worldless —Dasein itself, for example—are present-at-hand "in" the world, or, more exactly, *can* with some right and within certain limits be *taken* as merely present-at-hand. To do this, one must completely disregard or just not see the existential state of Being-in. But the fact that "Dasein" can be taken as something which is present-at-hand and just present-at-hand, is not to be confused with a certain way of "presence-at-hand" which is Dasein's *own*. This latter kind of presence-at-hand becomes accessible not by disregarding Dasein's specific structures but only by understanding them in advance. Dasein understands its ownmost Being in the sense of a certain "factual Being-present-at-hand." And yet the "factuality" of the fact [Tatsache] of one's own Dasein is at bottom quite different ontologically from the factual occurrence of some kind of mineral, for example. Whenever Dasein is, it is as a Fact; and the factuality of such a Fact is what we shall call Dasein's "*facticity*." This is a definite way of Being [Seinsbestimmtheit], and it has a complicated structure which cannot even be grasped *as a problem* until Dasein's basic existential states have been worked out. The concept of "facticity" implies that an entity "within-the-world" has Being-in-the-world in such a way that it can understand itself as bound up in its "destiny" with the Being of those entities which it encounters within its own world.

In the first instance it is enough to see the ontological difference between Being-in as an *existentiale* and the category of the "insideness" which things present-at-hand can have with regard to one another. By thus delimiting Being-in, we are not denying every kind of "spatiality" to Dasein. On the contrary, Dasein itself has a "**Being-in-space**"

of its own; but this in turn is possible only *on the basis of Being-in-the-world in general.* Hence Being-in is not to be explained ontologically by some ontical characterization, as if one were to say, for instance, that Being-in in a world is a spiritual property, and that man's "spatiality" is a result of his bodily nature (which, at the same time, always gets "founded" upon corporeality). Here again we are faced with the Being-present-at-hand-together of some such spiritual Thing along with a corporeal Thing, while the Being of the entity thus compounded remains more obscure than ever. Not until we understand Being-in-the-world as an essential structure of Dasein can we have any insight into Dasein's *existential spatiality*. Such an insight will keep us from failing to see this structure or from previously cancelling it out—a procedure motivated not ontologically but rather "metaphysically" by the naïve supposition that man is, in the first instance, a spiritual Thing which subsequently gets misplaced "into" a space.

Dasein's facticity is such that its Being-in-the-world has always dispersed [zerstreut] itself or even split itself up into definite ways of Being-in. The multiplicity of these is indicated by the following examples: having to do with something, producing something, attending to something and looking after it, making use of something, giving something up and letting it go, undertaking, accomplishing, evincing, interrogating, considering, discussing, determining. . . . All these ways of Being-in have *concern* as their kind of Being—a kind of Being which we have yet to characterize in detail. Leaving undone, neglecting, renouncing, taking a rest—these too are ways of concern; but these are all *deficient* modes, in which the possibilities of concern are kept to a "bare minimum." The term "concern" has, in the first instance, its colloquial [vorwissenschaftliche] signification, and can mean to carry out something, to get it done [erledigen], to "straighten it out." It can also mean to "provide oneself with something." We use the expression with still another characteristic turn of phrase when we say "I am concerned for the success of the undertaking." Here "concern" means something like apprehensiveness. In contrast to these colloquial ontical significations, the expression "concern" will be used in this investigation as an ontological term for an *existentiale*, and will designate the Being of a possible way of Being-in-the-world. This term has been chosen not because Dasein happens to be proximally and to a large extent "practical" and economic, but because the Being of Dasein itself is to be made visible as *care*. This expression too is to be taken as an ontological structural concept. It has nothing to do with "tribulation," "melancholy," or the "cares of life," though ontically one can come across these in every Dasein. These—like their opposites, "gaiety" and "freedom from care" —are ontically possible only because Dasein, when understood *ontologically*, is care. Because Being-in-the-world belongs essentially to Dasein, its Being towards the world [Sein zur Welt] is essentially concern.

From what we have been saying, it follows that Being-in is not a "property" which Dasein sometimes has and sometimes does not have, and *without* which it could *be* just as well as it could with it. It is not the case that man "is" and then has, by way of an extra, a relationship-of-Being towards the "world"— a world with which he provides himself occasionally. Dasein is never "proximally" an entity which is, so to speak, free from Being-in, but which sometimes has the inclination to take up a "relationship" towards the world. Taking up relationships towards the world is possible only *because* Dasein, as Being-in-the-world, is as it is. This state of Being does not arise just because some other entity is present-at-hand outside of Dasein and meets up with it. Such an entity can "meet up with" Dasein only in so

far as it can, of its own accord, show itself within a *world*.

Nowadays there is much talk about "man's having an environment [Umwelt]"; but this says nothing ontologically as long as this "having" is left indefinite. In its very possibility this "having" is founded upon the existential state of Being-in. Because Dasein is essentially an entity with Being-in, it can explicitly discover those entities which it encounters environmentally, it can know them, it can avail itself of them, it can *have* the "world." To talk about "having an environment" is ontically trivial, but ontologically it presents a problem. To solve it requires nothing else than defining the Being of Dasein, and doing so in a way which is ontologically adequate. Although this state of Being is one of which use has made in biology, especially since K. von Baer, one must not conclude that its philosophical use implies "biologism." For the environment is a structure which even biology as a positive science can never find and can never define, but must presuppose and constantly employ. Yet, even as an *a priori* condition for the objects which biology takes for its theme, this structure itself can be explained philosophically only if it has been conceived beforehand as a structure of Dasein. Only in terms of an orientation towards the ontological structure thus conceived can "life" as a state of Being be defined *a priori*, and this must be done in a privative manner. Ontically as well as ontologically, the priority belongs to Being-in-the-world as concern. In the analytic of Dasein this structure undergoes a basic Interpretation.

LUDWIG BINSWANGER
(1881–1966)

Existential Psychotherapy [7]

Martin Heidegger's analytic of existence is doubly significant for psychiatry. It affords empirical psychopathological research a new methodological and material basis that goes beyond its previous framework, and its treatment of the existential concept of science places *psychiatry in general* in a position to

account for the actuality, possibility, and limits of its own scientific world-design or, as we may also call it, transcendental horizon of understanding. . . .

The purpose of *Sein und Zeit* was the "concrete" working out of the question as to the meaning of *Being*. Its preliminary goal was to interpret time as the possible horizon of any understanding of Being. To this end, Heidegger, as we know, gives us the "concrete" working out of the *ontological structure* of the Dasein as being-in-the-world or trans-

[7] From *Being-In-The-World, Selected Papers of Ludwig Binswanger*, translated by Jacob Needleman, © 1963 by Basic Books, Inc., Publishers, New York, pp. 206–218.

cendence. In thus indicating the basic structure of the Dasein as being-in-the-world, Heidegger places in the psychiatrist's hands a key by means of which he can, free of the prejudice of any scientific *theory*, ascertain and describe the *phenomena* he investigates in their full phenomenal content and intrinsic context. It was Edmund Husserl's great achievement to have shown, after Brentano, just what this "phenomenological" method is, and to have indicated what enormous vistas it opened for research in the various sciences. Husserl's doctrine, however, concerns itself solely with the sphere of *intentionality*, considered as the unitary relation between transcendental subjectivity and transcendental objectivity. The shift from the "theoretical" ascertainment and description of psychic processes or events in a "subject" to the ascertainment and description of the forms and structures of "intentional consciousness," consciousness of something or directedness toward something, was a quite decisive shift for psychopathological research. Nevertheless, this consciousness was still suspended in the air, in the thin air of the transcendental ego. The—in the full sense of the word— "fundamental" accomplishment of Heidegger consisted not only in stating the problematic nature of the transcendental possibility of intentional acts. What he did, in addition, was to solve this problem by showing how the intentionality of consciousness is grounded in the temporality of human existence, in the Dasein. Intentionality in general is only possible on the basis of "transcendence" and is thus neither identical with it nor, conversely, does it make transcendence possible. Only by referring intentionality back to the Dasein as transcendence or being-in-the-world and only, therefore, with the inclusion of the transcendental ego in the actual Dasein, was the ("objective-transcendental") question posed as to the *what-ness* of the beings that we ourselves are.

* * * * *

2. We turn our attention now to the second aspect of Heidegger's dual significance for psychiatry—namely, the question as to the actuality, possibility, and limits of the horizon of understanding, or world-design of psychiatry in general.

* * * * *

In its clinical setting, psychiatry views its object, the "mentally ill human being" from the aspect of nature, and, thus, within the natural-scientific—mainly biological—horizon of understanding. Here psychiatry's object is—as it is in all of medicine—the "sick" organism. But in psychotherapy, it views its object from the aspect of "the human being," and thus within an (either prescientific or systematic) anthropological horizon of understanding. Here the object of psychiatry is the "mentally ill" Other, the fellow man. The incompatibility of these two conceptual horizons or reality-conceptions is not resolvable within science and leads not only to endless scientific controversy, but, also, as the present situation in psychiatry shows, to a split into two separate psychiatric camps. This fact alone shows how important it is for psychiatry to concern itself with the question as to what we human beings *are*.

In actual practice, these two conceptual orientations of psychiatry usually overlap— as one quick glance at its "praxis" tells us. The clinician, too, first "relates himself to" his patient or seeks "an understanding with him." And precisely from this relating or understanding he attains his initial perspective from which to ascertain the *symptoms* of the disease. It was, in fact, Hönigswald who expressed the view that psychiatric symptoms are primarily disturbances of communication and thus refer to a "meaning given to human intercourse." One of the basic demands of medical psychotherapy, on the other hand, is to view the prospective patient *also* as an organism, the demand, namely, that what must first be ascertained is whether the patient is intact "as" an organism—especially as regards the central nervous system—and whether the possibility of such a disturbance of intactness sets up certain therapeutic limitations from the outset.

* * * * *

3. *Scientific* understanding is oriented toward fact and factuality, i.e., toward reality and objectivity. Such a project (or design) separates areas of fact and places the various entities in a factual, real, objective, and systematic interconnection. Heidegger has shown that such a project is not simply a demarcation of regions, but is also the establishing of a ground. That is, in such a

project a particular sphere "of being" (beings) are "thematized" and thereby rendered accessible to objective inquiry and determination.

* * * * *

Heidegger's phenomenological-philosophical analytic of existence is important for psychiatry. This is so because it does not inquire merely into particular regions of phenomena and fact to be found "in human beings," but, rather, inquires into the *being* of *man as a whole*. Such a question is not answerable by scientific methods alone. The conception of man as a physical-psychological-spiritual unity does not say enough. For, as Heidegger says, the being of man cannot be ascertained by the "summative enumeration" of the rather ambiguous ontological modes of body, mind, and soul. What is needed is the return to (subjective) transcendence, to the Dasein as being-in-the-world, even while constant attention is being accorded its objective transcendence.

* * * * *

In practice, whenever the psychiatrist himself tries to look beyond the limitations of his science and seeks to know the ontological grounds of his understanding and treatment of those placed in his care, it is Heidegger's analytic of existence that can broaden his horizon. For it offers the possibility of understanding man as both a creature of nature, and a socially determined or historical being—and this by means of *one* ontological insight, which thus obviates the separation of body, mind, and spirit. Man as a creature of nature is revealed in the thrownness of the Dasein, its "that-it-is," its *facticity*. "Has the Dasein, as such, ever freely decided and will it ever be able to decide as to whether it wants to come into 'existence' or not?" The Dasein, although it exists essentially for its own sake (*umwillen seiner*), has nevertheless not itself laid the ground of its *being*. And also, as a creature "come into existence," it is and remains, *thrown*, determined, i.e., enclosed, possessed, and compelled by beings in general. Consequently it is not "completely free" in its world-design either. The "powerlessness" of the Dasein here shows itself in that certain of its possibilities of being-in-the-world are *withdrawn* because of commitment to and by beings, because of its facticity. But

it is also just this withdrawal that lends the Dasein its *power:* for it is this that first brings *before* the Dasein the "real," graspable possibilities of world-design.

Transcendence is thus not only a striding or swinging of the Dasein toward the world, but is, at the same time, withdrawal, limitation—and only *in* this limiting does transcendence gain power "over the world." All this, however, is but a "transcendental document" of the Dasein's *finitude*. The thrownness of the Dasein, its facticity, is the transcendental horizon of all that scientific systematic psychiatry delimits as reality under the name of organism, body (and heredity, climate, milieu, etc.), and also for all that which is delimited, investigated, and researched as psychic *determinateness:* namely, as mood and ill humor, as craziness, compulsive or insane "possessedness," as addiction, instinctuality, as confusion, phantasy determination, as, in general, unconsciousness. Now, whereas the science of psychiatry not only observes and establishes connections *between* these two spheres, but also erects the theoretical bridge of the psychophysical—*Daseinsanalyse*, on the other hand, shows that it is the scientific dichotomization of man's ontological wholeness that gives rise to this postulate in the first place. It shows that this dichotomization results from projecting the whole of human being upon the screen of that which is merely objectively present [*vorhanden*]. It also indicates the general world-design of science as stemming from one and the same Dasein, from, namely, the Dasein's ontological potentiality of scientific being-in-the-world. Here, too, it is true to say that what lends the world-design its (limited) scientific power is obtained only through its powerlessness to understand the being of human existence [Dasein] as a whole.

It is to Heidegger's great credit that he summed up the being of the Dasein under the all too easily misunderstood title of Care (= caring for), and to have phenomenologically explored its basic structures and make-up. Thrownness, in the sense of the facticity of the Dasein's answerability to its that-it-is, is only *one* component ("existential") of this structure, the others, as we know, being existence (project) and fallenness. Thus what in psychiatry is irreversibly separated into discrete realities of fields of study, namely, the finite human Dasein, is presented here in its basic structural unity. (It cannot be emphasized too often that this presentation signifies something quite different from the approach to man under the aegis of one particular *idea*, such as the idea of the will to power, libido, or any idea involving man as, in general, a creature of nature, or even, indeed, the idea of man as a child of God, as *homo aeternus*, etc.) But where there is structure there can be no dissociation of one structural member from the structural whole. Each, rather, remains implicated in the others, and a change in one structural element involves a change in the others. The Dasein can thus never get "behind" its thrownness and can only project those possibilities into which it is thrown. Only, therefore, as surrendered to its *that*, as thrown, does the Dasein *exist* within the ground of its power-to-be. The self of existence, although it has to lay its own ground, can therefore never have power over this ground. As a being, it has to be "as it is and can be." Its being is a projection of its own power-to-be, and to this extent it is always already in *advance* of itself. This being in advance of itself also concerns the whole of the Dasein's structure. Corresponding to all that we know of its thrownness (as already-being-in-the-world), the being-in-advance-of itself of the Dasein, its futurity, is through and through implicated with its past. Out of both these temporal "ecstasies" the authentic present temporalizes itself. This is what was referred to in the opening pages as the "way" of *Sein und Zeit:* the attempt to understand the basic structure of the Dasein *via* the unitariness of temporality and its ecstasies.

* * * * *

The insight into the temporal essence of the Dasein, or transcendence, not only instructs psychiatry as to its "object"—the various modes of "abnormal" human existence—but also instructs it in its understanding of itself in that it compels it to realize that its dissection of human being into various factual regions with their corresponding conceptualizations cannot be the last word. For, as I have already mentioned, it thereby takes *one* level, that of things objectively present [*vorhanden*] "in time and space," here and now, and projects upon that level what makes

the understanding of spatialization and temporalization possible in the first place: the Dasein.

* * * * *

4. I have already cited Hönigswald's essay on philosophy and psychiatry. In it, he also remarks that it must essentially be expected of the organism "that it call itself *I*." The analytic of existence indicates the root of this "expectation," namely, the basic anthropological fact that the Dasein is, in its being, concerned essentially with this being itself, in other words, that its whereto and wherefore is always directed toward itself. This being for itself by no means signifies an attitude of the I to itself that gives it the possibility of calling itself *I*. If this potentiality is to be "expected" also of the organism, it is because we realize that if this power to say *I* (and *me* and *mine*) is lost sight of in the reality-conception wherein man is projected, then the splitting of man into organism and Ego, body and soul, physical and psychic, *res extensa* and *res cogitans*, will never be set aright, and that what will be lost sight of is man as he really is.

* * * * *

And *we too*, from the perspective of Heidegger's analytic of existence, must conceive of both mental disease (Häberlin's somatosis) and neurosis (Häberlin's psychosis) as a disturbance of *koinonia*, of the functional *unity* of the Dasein's ontological potentialities. On this basis it is, for example, understandable that the mental disease called melancholia can be conceived as a disturbance of the *koinonia* between the bodily and mental being of the Dasein, which manifests itself on the one hand as a "vegetative" disturbance of the organism, and on the other hand as an "isolated," heightened, and distorted form of the finite Dasein's inherent guilt. It is not surprising, therefore, that melancholia can arise because of family tragedy, loss of power, or concrete guilt on the one hand, or on the other hand, in connection with intestinal diseases or even "for no reason at all." Nor is it surprising, then, that we can "cure" the melancholic with electroshock, or calm him with opium, or comfort him with assurances about his recovery and thus spur him on toward a steadfast endurance of his suffering.

In each instance, we seek to restore the *koinonia* of body and mind. That in this case success is easier when the patient is treated from the "physical" side only indicates the nature of the melancholic form of existence that involves the *dominant power* of thrownness as already-being-in-the-world (mood), i.e., pastness (*Gewesenheit*) over existence as being-in-advance-of-itself in the future. It in no way argues against the notion that the mental illness known as melancholia involves the Dasein as a whole. The same, in turn, is true of the "neuroses." No matter how well psychopathology may understand neurosis (in strictly Freudian terms) as "psychic conflict," from the point of view of existential analysis, the neuroses must not *merely* be understood within the perspective of existence. That human beings *can* become "neurotic" at all is *also* a sign of the thrownness of the Dasein and a sign of its potentiality of fallenness—a sign, in short, of its finitude, its transcendental limitedness or unfreedom.

Only he who scorns these limits, who—in Kierkegaard's terms—is at odds with the fundamental conditions of existence, can become "neurotic," whereas only he who "knows" of the unfreedom of finite human existence and who obtains "power" over his existence within this very powerlessness is unneurotic or "free." The *sole task* of "psychotherapy" lies in assisting man toward this "power." It is only the *ways* to this goal that are *various*.

JEAN-PAUL SARTRE
(1905–   )

Existential Psychoanalysis [8]

Freedom is existence, and in it existence precedes essence. The upsurge of freedom is immediate and concrete and is not to be distinguished from its choice; that is, from the person himself. But the structure under consideration can be called the *truth* of freedom; that is, it is the human meaning of freedom.

It should be possible to establish the human truth of the person, as we have attempted to do by an ontological phenomenology. The catalogue of empirical desires ought to be made the object of appropriate psychological investigations, observation and induction and, as needed, experience can serve to draw up this list. They will indicate to the philosopher the comprehensible relations which can unite to each other various desires and various patterns of behaviors, and will bring to light certain concrete connections between the subject of experience and "situations" experientally defined (which at bottom originate only from limitations applied in the name of positivity to the fundamental situation of the subject in the world). But in establishing and classifying fundamental desires of *individual persons* neither of these methods is appropriate. Actually there can be no question of determining *a priori* and ontologically what appears in all the unpredictability of a free act. This is why we shall limit ourselves here to indicating very summarily the possibilities of such a quest and its perspectives. The very fact that we can subject any man whatsoever to such an investigation—that is what belongs to human reality in general. Or, if you prefer, this is what can be established by an ontology. But the inquiry itself and its results are on principle wholly outside the possibilities of an ontology.

On the other hand, pure, simple empirical description can only give us catalogues and put us in the presence of pseudo-irreducibles (the desire to write, to swim, a taste for adventure, jealousy, etc.). It is not enough in fact to draw up a list of behavior patterns, of drives and inclinations, it is necessary also to *decipher* them; that is, it is necessary to know how to *question* them. This research can be conducted only according to the rules of a specific method. It is this method which we call existential psychoanalysis.

The *principle* of this psychoanalysis is that man is a totality and not a collection. Consequently he expresses himself as a whole in even his most insignificant and his most superficial behavior. In other words there

[8] Jean-Paul Sartre, *Being and Nothingness: An Essay on Phenomenological Ontology*, trans. Hazel E. Barnes (New York: Philosophical Library, 1956), pp. 567–575; original French, *L'Être et le Néant* (1943). Reprinted by permission.

is not a taste, a mannerism, or an human act which is not *revealing*.

The *goal* of psychoanalysis is to *decipher* the empirical behavior patterns of man; that is to bring out in the open the revelations which each one of them contains and to fix them conceptually.

Its *point of departure* is *experience;* its pillar of support is the fundamental, pre-ontological comprehension which man has of the human person. Although the majority of people can well ignore the indications contained in a gesture, a word, a sign and can look with scorn on the revelation which they carry, each human individual nevertheless possesses *a priori* the *meaning* of the revelatory value of these manifestations and is capable of deciphering them, at least if he is aided and guided by a helping hand. Here as elsewhere, truth is not encountered by chance; it does not belong to a domain where one must seek it without ever having any presentiment of its location, as one can go to look for the source of the Nile or of the Niger. It belongs *a priori* to human comprehension and the essential task is an hermeneutic; that is, a deciphering, a determination, and a conceptualization.

Its *method* is comparative. Since each example of human conduct symbolizes in its own manner the fundamental choice which must be brought to light, and since at the same time each one disguises this choice under its occasional character and its historical opportunity, only the comparison of these acts of conduct can effect the emergence of the unique revelation which they all express in a different way. The first outline of this method has been furnished for us by the psychoanalysis of Freud and his disciples. For this reason it will be profitable here to indicate more specifically the points where existential psychoanalysis will be inspired by psychoanalysis proper and those where it will radically differ from it.

Both kinds of psychoanalysis consider all objectively discernible manifestations of "psychic life" as symbols maintaining symbolic relations to the fundamental, total structures which constitute the individual person. Both consider that there are no primary givens such as hereditary dispositions, character, *etc.* Existential psychoanalysis recognizes nothing *before* the original upsurge of human freedom; empirical psychoanalysis holds that the original affectivity of the individual is virgin wax *before* its history. The libido is nothing besides its concrete fixations, save for a permanent possibility of fixing anything whatsoever upon anything whatsoever. Both consider the human being as a perpetual, searching, historization. Rather than uncovering static, constant givens they discover the meaning, orientation, and adventures of this history. Due to this fact both consider man in the world and do not imagine that one can question the being of a man without taking into account all his *situation*. Psychological investigations aim at reconstituting the life of the subject from birth to the moment of the cure; they utilize all the objective documentation which they can find; letters, witnesses, intimate diaries, "social" information of every kind. What they aim at restoring is less a pure psychic event than a twofold structure: the crucial event of infancy and the psychic crystallization around this event. Here again we have to do with a *situation*. Each "historical" fact from this point of view will be considered at once as a *factor* of the psychic evolution and as a *symbol* of that evolution. For it is nothing in itself. It operates only according to the way in which it is taken and this very manner of taking it expresses symbolically the internal disposition of the individual.

Empirical psychoanalysis and existential psychoanalysis both search within an existing situation for a fundamental attitude which can not be expressed by simple, logical definitions because it is prior to all logic, and which requires reconstruction according to the laws of specific syntheses. Empirical psychoanalysis seeks to determine the *complex*, the very name of which indicates the polyvalence of all the meanings which are referred back to it. Existential psychoanalysis seeks to determine the *original choice*. This original choice operating in the face of the world and being a choice of position in the world is total like the complex; it is prior to logic like the complex. It is this which decides the attitude of the person when confronted with logic and principles; therefore there can be no possibility of questioning it in conformance to logic. It brings together in a prelogical synthesis the totality of the existent, and as such it is the center of reference for an infinity of polyvalent meanings.

Both our psychoanalyses refuse to admit that the subject is in a privileged position to proceed in these inquiries concerning himself. They equally insist on a strictly objective method, using as documentary evidence the data of reflection as well as the testimony of others. Of course the subject *can* undertake a psychoanalytic investigation of himself. But in this case he must renounce at the outset all benefit stemming from his peculiar position and must question himself exactly as if he were someone else. Empirical psychoanalysis in fact is based on the hypothesis of the existence of an unconscious psyche, which on principle escapes the intuition of the subject. Existential psychoanalysis rejects the hypothesis of the unconscious; it makes the psychic act coextensive with consciousness. But if the fundamental project is fully experienced by the subject and hence wholly conscious, that certainly does not mean that it must by the same token be *known* by him; quite the contrary. The reader will perhaps recall the care we took in the Introduction to distinguish between consciousness and knowledge. To be sure, as we have seen earlier, reflection can be considered as a quasi-knowledge. But what it grasps at each moment is not the pure project of the for-itself as it is symbolically expressed—often in several ways at once—by the concrete behavior which it apprehends. It grasps the concrete behavior itself; that is, the specific dated desire in all its characteristic network. It grasps at once symbol and symbolization. This apprehension, to be sure, is entirely constituted by a pre-ontological comprehension of the fundamental project; better yet, in so far as reflection is almost a non-thetic consciousness of itself as reflection, it *is* this same project, as well as the non-reflective consciousness. But it does not follow that it commands the instruments and techniques necessary to isolate the choice symbolized, to fix it by concepts, and to bring it forth into the full light of day. It is penetrated by a great light without being able to express what this light is illuminating. We are not dealing with an unsolved riddle as the Freudians believe; all is there, luminous; reflection is in full possession of it, apprehends all. But this "mystery in broad daylight" is due to the fact that this possession is deprived of the means which would ordinarily permit *analysis* and *conceptualization*. It grasps every-

thing, all at once, without shading, without relief, without connections of grandeur—not that these shades, these values, these reliefs exist somewhere and are hidden from it, but rather because they must be established by another human attitude and because they can exist only *by means of* and *for* knowledge. Reflection, unable to serve as the basis for existential psychoanalysis, will then simply furnish us with the brute materials toward which the psychoanalyst must take an objective attitude. Thus only will he be able to *know* what he *already understands*. The result is that complexes uprooted from the depths of the unconscious, like projects revealed by existential psychoanalysis, will be apprehended *from the point of view of the Other.* Consequently the *object* thus brought into the light will be articulated according to the structures of the transcended-transcendence; that is, its being will be the being-for-others even if the psychoanalyst and the subject of the psychoanalysis are actually the same person. Thus the project which is brought to light by either kind of psychoanalysis can be only the totality of the individual human being, the irreducible element of the transcendence with the structure of *being-for-others.* What always escapes these methods of investigation is the project as it is for itself, the complex in its own being. This project-for-itself can be experienced only as a living possession; there is an incompatibility between existence for-itself and objective existence. But the object of the two psychoanalyses has in it nonetheless the *reality of a being;* the subject's knowledge of it can in addition contribute to *clarify* reflection, and that reflection can then become a possession which will be a quasi-knowing.

At this point the similarity between the two kinds of psychoanalysis ceases. They differ fundamentally in that empirical psychoanalysis has decided upon its own irreducible instead of allowing this to make itself known in a self-evident intuition. The libido or the will to power in actuality constitutes a psychobiological residue which is not clear in itself and which does not appear to us as *being beforehand* the irreducible limit of the investigation. Finally it is experience which establishes that the foundation of complexes is this libido or this will to power; and these results of empirical inquiry are perfectly contingent, they are not convincing. Nothing prevents our conceiving *a priori* of a "human reality" which would not be expressed by the will to power, for which the libido would not constitute the original, undifferentiated project.

On the other hand, the choice to which existential psychoanalysis will lead us, precisely because it is a choice, accounts for its original contingency, for the contingency of the choice is the reverse side of its freedom. Furthermore, inasmuch as it is established on the *lack of being*, conceived as a fundamental characteristic of being, it receives its legitimacy *as a choice*, and we know that we do not have to push further. Each result then will be at once fully contingent and legitimately irreducible. Moreover it will always remain *particular;* that is, we will not achieve as the ultimate goal of our investigation and the foundation of all behavior an abstract, general term, libido for example, which would be differentiated and made concrete first in complexes and then in detailed acts of conduct, due to the action of external facts and the history of the subject. On the contrary, it will be a choice which remains unique and which is from the start absolute concreteness. Details of behavior can express or *particularize* this choice, but they can not make it more concrete than it already is. That is because the choice is nothing other than the being of each human reality; this amounts to saying that a particular partial behavior *is* or expresses the original choice of this human reality since for human reality there is no difference between existing and choosing for itself. From this fact we understand that existential psychoanalysis does not have to proceed from the fundamental "complex," which is exactly the choice of being, to an abstraction like the libido which would explain it. The complex is the ultimate choice, it is the choice of being and *makes itself such.* Bringing it into the light will reveal it each time as evidently irreducible. It follows necessarily that the libido and the will to power will appear to existential psychoanalysis neither as general characteristics common to all mankind nor as irreducibles. At most it will be possible after the investigation to establish that they express by virtue of particular ensembles in certain subjects a fundamental choice which can not be reduced

to either one of them. We have seen in fact that desire and sexuality in general express an original effort of the for-itself to recover its being which has become estranged through contact with the Other. The will to power also originally supposes being-for-others, the comprehension of the Other, and the choice of winning its own salvation by means of the Other. The foundation of this attitude must be an original choice which would make us understand the radical identification of being-in-itself-for-itself with being-for-others.

The fact that the ultimate term of this existential inquiry must be a *choice*, distinguishes even better the psychoanalysis for which we have outlined the method and principal features. It thereby abandons the supposition that the environment acts mechanically on the subject under consideration. The environment can act on the subject only to the exact extent that he comprehends it; that is, transforms it into a situation. Hence no objective description of this environment could be of any use to us. From the start the environment conceived as a situation refers to the for-itself which is choosing, just as the for-itself refers to the environment by the very fact that the for-itself is in the world. By renouncing all mechanical causation, we renounce at the same time all *general* interpretation of the symbolization confronted. Our goal could not be to establish empirical laws of succession, nor could we constitute a universal symbolism. Rather the psychoanalyst will have to rediscover at each step a symbol functioning in the particular case which he is considering. If each being is a totality, it is not conceivable that there can exist elementary symbolic relationships (e.g.; the faeces = gold, or a pincushion = the breast) which preserve a constant meaning in all cases; that is, which remain unaltered when they pass from one meaningful ensemble to another ensemble. Furthermore the psychoanalyst will never lose sight of the fact that the choice is living and consequently can be *revoked* by the subject who is being studied. We have shown in the preceding chapter the importance of the *instant*, which represents abrupt changes in orientation and the assuming of a new position in the face of an unalterable past. From this moment on, we must always be ready to consider that symbols change meaning and to abandon the symbol used hitherto. Thus existential psycho-analysis will have to be completely flexible and adapt itself to the slightest observable changes in the subject. Our concern here is to understand what is *individual* and often even instantaneous. The method which has served for one subject will not necessarily be suitable to use for another subject or for the same subject at a later period.

Precisely because the goal of the inquiry must be to discover a *choice* and not a *state*, the investigator must recall on every occasion that his object is not a datum buried in the darkness of the unconscious but a free, conscious determination—which is not even resident in consciousness, but which is one with this consciousness itself. Empirical psychoanalysis, to the extent that its method is better than its principles, is often in sight of an existential discovery, but it always stops part way. When it thus approaches the fundamental choice, the resistance of the subject collapses suddenly and he *recognizes* the image of himself which is presented to him as if he were seeing himself in a mirror. This involuntary testimony of the subject is precious for the psychoanalyst; he sees there the sign that he has reached his goal; he can pass on from the investigation proper to the cure. But nothing in this principles or in his initial postulates permits him to understand or to utilize this testimony. Where could he get any such right? If the complex is really unconscious—that is, if there is a barrier separating the sign from the thing signified—how could the subject *recognize* it? Does the unconscious complex recognize itself? But haven't we been told that it lacks *under-standing?* And if of necessity we granted to it the faculty of understanding the signs, would this not be to make of it by the same token a conscious unconscious? What is understanding if not to be conscious of what is understood? Shall we say on the other hand that it is the subject as conscious who recognizes the image presented? But how could he compare it with his true state since that is out of reach and since he has never had any knowledge of it? At most he will be able to judge that the psychoanalytic explanation of his case is a *probable* hypothesis, which derives its probability from the number of behavior patterns which it explains. His relation to this interpretation is that of a

third party, that of the psychoanalyst himself; he has no privileged position. And if he *believes* in the probability of the psycho-analytic hypothesis, is this simple belief, which lives in the limits of his consciousness, able to effect the breakdown of the barriers which dam up the unconscious tendencies? The psychoanalyst doubtless has some obscure picture of an abrupt coincidence of conscious and unconscious. But he has removed all methods of conceiving of this coincidence in any positive sense.

Still, the enlightenment of the subject is a fact. There is an intuition here which is accompanied by evidence. The subject guided by the psychoanalyst does more and better than to give his agreement to an hypothesis; he touches it, he sees what it is. This is truly understandable only if the subject has never ceased being conscious of his deep tendencies; better yet, only if these drives are not dis-tinguished from his conscious self. In this case as we have seen, the traditional psycho-analytic interpretation does not cause him to attain *consciousness* of what he is; it causes him to attain *knowledge* of what he is. It is existential psychoanalysis then which claims the final intuition of the subject as deci-sive.

This comparison allows us to understand better what an existential psychoanalysis must be if it is entitled to exist. It is a method destined to bring to light, in a strictly ob-jective form, the subjective choice by which each living person makes himself a person; that is, makes known to himself what he is. Since what the method seeks is a *choice of being* at the same time as a *being*, it must reduce particular behavior patterns to funda-mental relations—not of sexuality or of the will to power, but *of being*—which are expressed in this behavior. It is then guided from the start toward a comprehension of being and must not assign itself any other goal than to discover being and the mode of being of the being confronting this being. It is forbidden to stop before attaining this goal. It will utilize the comprehension of being which characterizes the investigator in-asmuch as he is himself a human reality; and as it seeks to detach being from its symbolic expressions, it will have to rediscover each time on the basis of a comparative study of acts and attitudes, a symbol destined to decipher them. Its criterion of success will be the number of facts which its hypothesis permits it to explain and to unify as well as the self-evident intuition of the irreducibility of the end attained. To this criterion will be added in all cases where it is possible, the decisive testimony of the subject. The results thus achieved—that is, the ultimate ends of the individual—can then become the object of a classification, and it is by the comparison of these results that we will be able to establish general considerations about human reality as an empirical choice of its own ends. The behavior studied by this psychoanalysis will include not only dreams, failures, obsessions, and neuroses, but also and especially the thoughts of waking life, successfully adjusted acts, style, *etc.*

Landmarks in the History of Psychology

c. 1950 B.C. Code of Hammurabi recommending opium and olive oil as cure for demonism

499–428 The introduction of the concept *nous* (mind) by Anaxagoras of Clazomene (499–428)

460–367 Hippocrates' presentation of the humoral theory of personality and behavior, the theory that mental (and physical) illness is grounded in natural causes, Hippocratic division of mental illness: mania, melancholia, dementia. Publication of 87 treatises by Hippocrates, the father of medicine

460–370 Founding of materialistic psychology (atomistic psychology) and the study of sensation and perception by Democritus of Abdera (460–370)

427–347 Founding of idealistic psychology and self-realizationism by Plato of Athens (427–347)

384–322 Localization of the mind in the heart; founding of functionalism and psychological science by Aristotle of Athens (384–322)

c. 350 B.C. Development of Aristotle's theory of five senses

c. 300 B.C. Theory of representative images of perception by Epicurus (341–270)

25 B.C.–A.D. 50 Publication of *De Medicina* by Aulus Cornelius Celsus, coiner of the term "insanity" (*insania*) and designer of a therapy for phrenitus or delirium

A.D.

23–29 Pliny the Elder's use of the torpedo fish to relieve labor pains in pregnant women

43–48 Scribinio Largo's treatment of head ache by the application of the torpedo-fish (with its 25–30 volts) to the region of the ache

c. 129–199 The localization of the mind in the brain

c. 130–200 Development of the humoral theory of psychopathology by the Greek physician, Galen

c. 180 Publication of *On the Soul* by Tertullian, the first Christian psychologist

201 Galen's use of the electrified torpedo fish to cure headaches

203–249 Caelius Aurelianus' recommendation of using "irritant injections in the ear" as a treatment of the mentally ill; also his opposition to the use of violence, chains, and starvation (a common practice in his day in dealing with the mentally ill)

323 Birth of Oribasius (d. 400), author of *Collecta Medicinalia*

354–430 The introduction of St. Augustine's (354–430) influential doctrine of the will

429 The prohibition of magic as an evil by the *Codex Theodosianus*

786–809 The curing of Harun-al-Rashid's wife of mental illness with fear and shame as the psychotherapeutic technique

800 Publication of *De Natura Hominis* by Meletios of Tiberiopolis

950 Publication of *Compendium Totius Artis Medicinae* by Theophanes

980–1037 Avicenna's theory that the various mental illnesses are caused by anomalies in different parts of the brain

1060 Compilation of a list of Arabian therapeutic remedies by Simeon Seth

1135 Birth of Maimonides (d. 1204), author of *Hygiene of the Soul*

c. 1150 Development of "trephination" (psychosurgery by opening the skull) for the treatment of mania and melancholia by Roger Frugardi of Salerno

1215–1277 The first medieval treatise devoted to psychology by Peter of Spain (*c.* 1215–1277)

1225 Birth of St. Thomas Aquinas (d. 1274) who theorized the soul to be an intellective principle

c. 1235–1311 Analdo de Villanova's theory that manic and melancholic states are related to menstrual disorders

1250 Establishment of the University of Paris and with it the first of the medical schools for the training of "doctors"

—— Publication of *Antidotarium* by Nicholas Myrepsos

1410 Establishment of the world's first institution for the mentally ill at Valencia, Spain

1435 Establishment of the world's second asylum for the mentally ill at Sargossa, Spain

1452 Establishment of the Granada asylum in Spain by King Ferdinand and Queen Isabella

1484 A papal edict to eradicate witchcraft

1492 Birth of the Spanish psychologist Juan Luis Vives (d. 1540), author of *De Anima et Vita*, and precursor of modern psychology

1496 The writing of the first thesis on syphilis by Pollich von Mellerstadt

1497 Birth of Philipp Melanchthon (d. 1560), coiner of the term "psychology"

1511 Passing of England's medical act as one of the first laws controlling the abuse of medical practice

1515 Birth of Johann Weyer (d. 1588), "father of modern psychiatry" and author of *De Praestigiis*

1525 Publication by Heinrich Cornelius Agripp of Nettesheim's (1486–1535) *Occult Philosophy*, an attack on the occult sciences

c. 1530 Birth of Juan Huarte (d. 1589), forerunner of testing theory and differential psychology

1537 Dissection of a human body and lectures on its anatomy by Andreas Vesalius (1514–1564), author of *Concerning the Fabric of the Human Body* (1543)

1538 Publication of *De Anima et Vita* by Juan Luis Vives (1492–1540) of Valencia

1540 Publication of Philipp Melanchthon's *Commentarius de Anima*, a commentary on Aristotle's *De Anima*

1543 Publication of Andreas Vesalius' (1514–1564) *De Humani Corporis Fabrica*, ideas that revolutionized anatomy

1547 Birth of Goeckel (d. 1628), author of *Psychologia Anthropologica*

—— Establishment of the Bethlehem Royal Hospital in London for the mentally ill (nicknamed "Bedlam"), its founding by Simon Fitzmary 300 years earlier as a priory (also accepted mental patients)

1548 Establishment of Italy's first hospital for psychiatric care, the Santa Maria della Pieta at Rome

1563 Birth of Charles Lepois (d. 1633), theorized the cause of hysteria to reside in the brain rather than the uterus

—— Publication of Johann Weyer's (1515–1588) *On the Delusions about Demons*, treating medicopsychology

1566 Establishment of the first hospital for the mentally ill in the Americas by Bernardino Alvares in Mexico

1567 Publication by Theophrastus Bombastus von Hohenheim (Paracelsus; 1493–1541) of *The Diseases That Deprive Man of His Reason*, written in 1526

1574 Birth of Bartolommeo Estachio (b., *c.* 1524), a founder of modern anatomy; described the Eustachian tube in the ear, uterus, etc.

1590 Publication of Rudolf Goeckel's *Psychology, or on the Improvement of Man*

1600 Beginnings of electrotherapy with the queen's physician, William Gilbert, as recorded in his *Tractatus de Magnete*, containing his doctrine of magnetism

1604 Theory of the inversion of retinal images by Johannes Kepler (1571–1630)

1612 Publication of Ferrand's *La maladie d'amour ou melancolie erotique*, tracing melancholic depression to frustrations of romance

1613 Publication of Pierre de Lancre's *Tableau de l'inconstance des mauvais anges et demons*, a description of psychotic syndromes

1621 Publication of Robert Burton's *Anatomy of Melancholy*

1622 Introduction of the technique of assessing personality from the nature of one's handwriting (graphology) by Camillo Baldo in his *A Method to Recognize the Nature and Quality of a Writer from His Letters*

1623 Publication of Francesco Torreblanca's *Demonologia*, containing clinical descriptions of psychotic illness

1632 Founding in Paris of the Maison de St. Lazare for the mentally ill by St. Vincent de Paul (1576–1660)

1638 Theory of visual perception of distance, shape, and size by secondary psychological cues by René Descartes (1596–1650) in his *The Dioptrics*

1645 Oldest institution for the insane, Florence, Italy

1650 The starting point of modern psychology—with René Descartes. The introduction of psychophysical interactionism by Descartes. Publication of Descartes' *The Passions of the Soul*

1651 Publication of Thomas Hobbes' (1588–1679) *Leviathan*

1657 Founding of the Accademia del Cimento at Florence

1660 Founding of the Royal Society of London (chartered in 1662)

1665 Founding of *Philosophical Transactions* of the Royal Society

—— Initial publication of the *Journal des Savants*

1666 Founding of the *Academie des Sciences* at Paris, and the establishment of its organ, *Mémoires*

1668 Construction of the first reflecting telescope by Isaac Newton (1642–1727)

1672 Isaac Newton's discovery of white as the mixture of colored light

1674 Publication of Malebranche's *Recherche de la vérité*

1675 Isaac Newton's theory of seven colors of the spectrum

1677 Posthumous publication of Benedict Spinoza's (1632–1677) *Ethics*, containing his psychological theories, including the doctrine of psychophysical parallelism

1679 Beginnings of "magnetism" or mesmerism with the publication of *De Medicina Magnetica* by William Maxwell, an Englishman

1681 Establishment of an institution for the mentally ill at Avignon, France

—— Publication of Thomas Willis' *Opera Omnia*, containing a section devoted to mental disease

1687 Publication of Isaac Newton's *Principia*

1690 The ushering in of the period of the Enlightenment by the publication of John Locke's (1632–1704) *Essay concerning the Human Understanding*. Locke's coining of the phrase "association of ideas" and the founding of systematic empiricism

1691 Publication of a study involving animal behavior, *The Wisdom of God as Manifested in the Works of the Creation* by John Ray (1628–1705), father of British naturalism

1692 Founding of the Academia Naturae Curiosi by a group of German physicians

1698 The advocating of a psychotherapy of beating by Karl F. Paullini in his *Flagellum Salutis*

1700 Hermann Boerhaave's use of sleep therapy in treating melancholy

—— Founding of the Berlin Akademie through the efforts of Gottfried Wilhelm Leibniz (1646–1716)

1702 Publication of Georg Ernst Stahl's (1660–1734) *De Medicina Necessaria*, a forerunner of psychosomatic medicine, dream psychology, and unconscious perception. First to divide mental illness into psychic and organic

1704 Isaac Newton's development of the color circle in his *Opticks*

—— Leibniz' development of the unconscious as "petites perceptions"

1707 Publication of G. E. Stahl's *Theoria Medica Vera*, containing a discussion on mental illness

1709 Publication of George Berkeley's (1685–1753) *An Essay towards a New Theory of Vision*, enunciating his theory of visual space perception entailing secondary psychological cues

1710 Publication of Berkeley's *A Treatise concerning the Principles of Human Knowledge*, explicating idealism's theory of reality as being of the nature of experience

1714 Publication of Leibniz' *The Principles of Nature and Grace*, introducing his principle of "pre-established harmony" and the theory of psychophysical parallelism

1728 Establishment of Poland's first institution for the mentally ill

1729 Publication of *Essai d'optique*, enunciating the theory of the differential threshold of illumination by Pierre Bouquer (1698–1758), author of *Traite d'optique sur la gradation de la lumière*

1732 The drawing of a distinction between "empirical" and "rational" psychology and one of the earliest uses of the word "psychology" by Christian Wolff (1679–1754), author of *Psychologia Empirica*

1733 Publication of Berkeley's *The Theory of Vision, or Visual Language, Showing the Immediate Presence and Providence of a Deity*, containing his doctrine of divine arbitrariness as an explanation of causation

——— Publication of George Cheyne's *The English Malady: Or, a Treatise of Nervous Diseases of All Kinds, as Spleen, Vapours, Lowness of Spirits, Hypochondriacal, and Hysterical Distempers*

1734 Publication of Christian Wolff's *Rational Psychology*, a treatise on faculty psychology and the unity of the soul

1735 Recommendation of "sleep therapy" in treating schizophrenics by Hermann Boerhaave in his *Aphorisms: Concerning the Knowledge and Care of Diseases*, published in London

1736 Coining of the term "reflex" by Jean Astruc (1684–1766), a French physician

1739 Publication of David Hume's (1711–1776) *A Treatise of Human Nature*, containing his associationism, phenomenalism, and the theory of scientific causation as the regularity of natural phenomena

1741 Establishment of an institution for the mentally ill in Springfield, England

1744 Initial annual report on electrotherapy by the French Royal Academy of Science

——— Publication of *Theoretical Doctrine of the Emotions* by Georg Friedrich Meier (1718–1777)

1745 Birth of the Frenchman, Philippe Pinel (d. 1826), founder of modern psychiatry and author of *Traite medio-philosophique sur l'alienation mentale*

1746 Publication of Jonathan Edwards' (1703–1758) *A Treatise concerning Religious Affections*

1748 Introduction of behavioristic psychological thought in France by Julien Offray de la Mettrie (1709–1751) through his *Man a Machine*

1749 Publication of David Hartley's (1705–1757) *Observations on Man, His Frame, His Duty, and His Expectation*, marking the start of British associationism in modern psychology, and offering a neurological theory of memory, association, and learning

1751 Development of a stimulus response theory by Robert Whytt (1714–1766) in his *An Essay on the Vital and Other Involutionary Motions of Animals*

——— Classification of olfactory odors by the Swedish botanist Carl Linné (1707–1778), author of *Philosophia Botanica*

1752 First treatment of mental patients in an American hospital, the Pennsylvania Hospital (not exclusively for mental illness)

——— Publication of Samuel Johnson's (1696–1772) *Elementa Philosophica*, considered the first American text in psychology

1754 Introduction of sensationalism in France by the publication of Étienne Bonnot de Condillac's (1715–1780) *Treatise on Sensations*, an attempt to prove mental life as comprised of sensations

——— Publication of Bonnet's (Swiss) *Essai de psychologie*

——— Publication of Jonathan Edwards' *Freedom of the Will*

1756 Electroshock therapy in treating the mentally ill by Richard Lovett

1757 Birth of Karl Philipp Moritz (d. 1793), founder of the first journal of psychology, *Magazin zur Erfahrungsseelenkunde*

1757–1766 Publication of the 8 volume *Elementia Physiologiae Corporis Humani*, (containing the theory of the irritability of living tissue and physiological muscle excitation) by Albrecht von Haller (1708–1777)

1758 Publication of *De l'esprit* by Claude Adrien Helvetius (1715–1771) presenting a doctrine of sensationalism and sharing ideas of La Mettrie

1759 Publication of Adam Smith's (1723–1790) *Theory of Moral Sentiments*, containing a psychological discussion of the place of human motives in the social structure

1760 Publication of Bonnet's *Essai analytique sur les facultés de l'âme*, treating memory in terms of nerve fibers and experimentation on the span of attention

1766 Founding of Sweden's first institution for the mentally ill at Uppsala

—— Founding of Denmark's first institution for the mentally ill at Copenhagen

1771 Notation of a distinction between voluntary and involuntary movements by Johann August Unzer (1727–1799) in his first *Principles of the Physiology, etc. of Animated Bodies*

1772 Establishment of Austria's first mental institution at Salzburg

1773 Establishment of the first public hospital for treating mental illness at Williamsburg, Virginia

1774 Enactment (in Italy) through the efforts of Valsalva and Chiarugi of the "Law of the Insane," a law calling for humane treatment of the mentally ill

—— Publication of Zückert's *Von den Leidenschaften*, a treatise on the passions

1775 The invention of the electrophorus by Alessandro Volta (1745–1827), also the inventor of the voltaic pile

—— Publication of Johann Kasper Lavater's *Physiognomische Fragmente*, theorizing facial expressions as the key to character; founder of physiognomy

1777 Publication of *Philosophical Essay on Human Nature* by J. Nicolas Tetens (1736–1807)

1779 The introduction of animal magnetism or mesmerism (hypnotism) by Anton

Mesmer (1734–1815), a Viennese physician

1780 Discovery of the electrical nature of nerve impulses by Luigi Galvan (1737–1798), Italian physicist, physician, and founder of galvanism

1781 Publication of Immanuel Kant's (1724–1804) *Critique of Pure Reason*, containing his theory of the *a priori* intuition of space and time

1783 Origin of professional psychiatry in America by Benjamin Rush (1745–1813) of the Pennsylvania Hospital and author of *Medical Inquiries and Observations upon Diseases of the Mind* (1812)

1784 Discovery of autonomatic nerve responses by George Prochaska (1749–1820)

1785 The founding of the Scottish school of empiricism under the leadership of Thomas Reid (1710–1796), an advocate of faculty psychology and author of *Essays on the Intellectual Powers of Man*, an attack on human skepticism

1786 Publication of *De Structura Nervorum* by Johann C. Reil (1759–1813), founder of *Archiv für Physiologie* and *Magazin für psychische Heilkunde* (the first psychiatric journal)

1787 Liberation of mental patients from their chains in Geneva by Abraham Joly

—— Publication of Scheidemantel's *Von den Leidenschaften als Heilmittel betrachtet*, the utilization of the passions as a means of cure

1788 Reform in the care of the mentally ill by Vincenzo Chiarugi (1759–1820), Asylum of St. Boniface, Florence

1789 Publication of Jeremy Bentham's (1748–1832) *An Introduction to the Principles of Morals and Legislation*, a defense of psychological hedonism as ethical

1790 Establishment of psychiatry as an independent discipline in France

—— Publication of James Beattie's (1735–1803) *Elements of Moral Science*, the first portion of which is entitled: "Psychology"

1791 Construction of wet cell batteries from frogs' legs and the discovery of nerve responses (galvanism or galvanic current) by Luigi Galvani (1737–1798), author of *Commentary on the Power of Electricity on Muscular Motion*

1792 Publication of Joseph Daquin's (1757–1815) *The Philosophy of Insanity: A Philosophical Essay on Persons Afflicted by Insanity*

1793 Birth of modern psychiatry in France by the appointment of Philippe Pinel (1745–1826) as physician-in-chief at Bicêtre Hospital for the Insane, Paris. Removal of chains from mental patients at Bicêtre by Pinel

1794 Discovery of color blindness by John Dalton (1766–1844) as recorded in a paper (delivered before the Manchester Literary and Philosophical Society) entitled *Extraordinary Facts Relating to the Vision of Colours*

1796 Founding of the York Retreat, a Quaker hospital for the mentally ill, by William Hack Tuke (1732–1822), an Englishman

—— Founding of the *Archiv für die Physiologie* by Johann Christian Reil (1759–1813)

1797 Publication of Johann Gottfried Langermann's (1768–1832) *On the Method of Diagnosing and Treating Chronic Mental Diseases*, the first doctoral dissertation in the field of psychiatry

1798 Publication of Clement Joseph Tissot's (1750–1826) *De l'influence des passions de l'âme dans les maladies, et des moyens d'en corriger les mauvais effects*, utilizing emotions as an instrument in cure

—— Publication of Thomas Robert Malthus' (1766–1834) "An Essay on the Principle of Population" (*Linnean Society J.*) hypothesizing a struggle owing to growing population and limited food supplies

1800 The invention of the voltaic pile by Alessandro Volta (1745–1827), Italian physicist for whom the volt was named

1801 Publication of Ruhland's *Medicophilosophical Treatises on the Concept of Mental Disorders*

1802 Publication of Thomas Young's (1773–1829) "On the Theory of Light and Colours," in *Philosophical Transactions of the Royal Society of London*, enunciating his three component theo-

ry of color and the undulatory theory of light

—— Publication of *Relation between the Physical System and the Mental Faculties of Man*, treating physiological psychology and S-R acts by Pierre Jean George Cabanis (1757–1808) regarded by some as the founder of physiological psychology

1803 Publication of Johann Christian Reil's (1759–1813) *Rhapsodieen über die Anwendung der psychischen Curmethode auf Geisteszerruttungen*, presenting a rhapsodic psychotherapy

1804 Enactment of French psychiatric laws dating from the Napoleonic Code

—— Publication of Mason Cox's *Practical Observations on Insanity*, theorizing excessive blood in the brain as the cause of mental illness

1805 Initial publication of the German journal, *Magazin für psychische Heilkunde*, founded by Christian Reil and Kayssler

—— Initial publication of the German periodical devoted to mental illness, *Archiv für Genüths und Nervenkrankheiten*, founded by A. S. Winkelman

—— Publication of Jean Étienne Dominique Esquirol's (1772–1840) *Les passions considerées comme causes, symptomes, et moyens curatifs de l'alienation mentale*, tracing mental illness to emotional sources

1808 Publication of the first *History of Psychology* by Friedrich August Carus (1770–1807), professor of philosophy at the University of Leipzig

—— Publication of Franz Joseph Gall's (1758–1828) *Researches into the Nervous System in General and the Brain in Particular: With Observations upon the Possibility of Ascertaining Several Intellectual and Moral Dispositions of Man and Animals, by the Configuration of Their Heads*, marking the founding of phrenology

1809 Discovery of the Gaussian law, normal curve of errors, or Gaussian distribution by Karl Friedrich Gauss (1777–1855), author of *Theoria Motus Corporum Coelestrium*

—— Presentation of the theory of inherited acquired characteristics by Jean Baptiste Lamarck (1744–1829) in his *Philosophie zoologique*

1810 Johann Wolfgang Goethe's (1749–1832) publication of his two volume *Theory of Colors*, containing his color theory

—— Publication of Thomas Brown's (1778–1820) *Lectures on the Philosophy of the Human Mind*, a treatment of his associational psychology

—— Publication of F. J. Gall's *The Anatomy and Physiology of the Nervous System in General, and of the Brain in Particular* (4 vols. completed in 1819)

1811 Publication of Charles Bell's (1774–1842) *A New Idea of the Anatomy of the Brain*, containing his theory of separate sensory and motor nerves, thereby forecasting the doctrine of specific nerve energy

—— Publication of Johannes Friedreich's *Insania*, an early doctoral dissertation on the subject of mental illness

1812 Publication of Benjamin Rush's *Medical Inquiries and Observations upon the Diseases of the Mind*, the first American psychiatric textbook

—— Founding of the theory of probability by Pierre Laplace (1749–1827)

1813–1814 Development of the "environmentalist" point of view by the coiner of the term "socialism," Robert Owen (1771–1858), British industrialist and author of *A New View of Society: Essays on the Formation of Character*

1816 Publication of the first textbook on psychology, *A Textbook of Psychology*, by Johann Friedrich Herbart (1776–1841), the father of experimental pedagogy and the founder of mathematical psychology

1817 Establishment of the Friends' Asylum in Frankford, Pennsylvania, one of the first institutions in America for mental illness

1818 Establishment of McLean Asylum (renamed McLean Hospital) in Belmont, Mass.

—— Awareness of moral factors in the etiology of mental illness by Johann C. C. A. Heinroth (1773–1843), initial occupant of the chair of psychical medicine at the University of Leipzig

1819 Establishment of the Bloomingdale

Asylum (New York) for mental illness

1820 Introduction of British associationism into Scotland by the publication of Thomas Brown's (1778–1820) *Lectures on the Philosophy of the Human Mind*

—— Publication of Jakob Friedrich Fries' (1773–1843) *Handbook of Psychical Anthropology*, presenting man's mental constitution on a Kantian basis

c. 1820 The introduction of the concept "personal equation" by Friedrich Wilhelm Bessel (1784–1846)

1821 The independent discovery by Francois Magendie (1783–1855) of the Bell-Magendie law of spinal nerve roots

1823 Appointment as professor at Breslau, of the "father of histology," Jan Evangilista Purkinje [Purkyne] (1787–1869), known for the "Purkinje phenomenon," "Purkinje network," and coiner of the term "protoplasm"

—— Founding in Edinburgh of the *Phrenological Journal* (terminated in 1847, but continuing once again in Philadelphia until 1911)

1824 Theory of the localization of specific functions of the brain resulting from experiments on the brains of pigeons as espoused by Pierre J. M. Flourens (1794–1867) and recorded in his *Researches on the Properties and Functions of the Nervous System in Vertebrate Animals*, also author of *Comparative Psychology* (1864)

—— Establishment of the Lexington Asylum (Kentucky) for mental illness

1826 The discovery of a sixth sense, a muscle sense, by Charles Bell

—— Presentation of a theory of the retinal image size by Johannes Müller (1801–1858)

—— First lectures in psychiatry by the head of Charenton Asylum, Jean E. D. Esquirol (1772–1840), author of *Mental Illness* (1838)

—— Discovery of the bromides as an anticonvulsant in treating epilepsy and allied maladies

1827 Publication of Charles E. J. Delezenn's (1776–1866) *Recueil des traveau de la Société des Sciences de Lille*, presenting the theory of the differential threshold for the pitch of tones

—— Publication of *Elements of Intellectual*

Philosophy (the first comprehensive treatment of psychology in America) by Thomas C. Upham (1789–1872) of Bowdoin College

—— Publication of *The Philosophy of the Human Voice* (a forerunner of the psychology of speech) by James Rush (1786–1869)

—— Introduction of mesmerism into England by Richard Chevenix, an Irishman

1829 Reduction of all laws of association to the one law of contiguity in *Analysis of the Phenomena of the Human Mind* by James Mill (1773–1836)

—— Initial publication of the German periodical, *Magazin für die philolosophische, medizinische und gerichtliche Seelenkunde* (renamed the *Archiv für Psychologie für Arzte und Juristen* in 1883)

1830 Publication of *An Inquiry concerning the Indication of Insanity; with Suggestions for the Better Protection and Cure of the Insane* by John Conolly (1794–1866), originator of the "non-restraint movement"

—— Publication of Johannes Friedrich's *Synopsis Librorum de Pathologie et Therapia Morborum Psychicorum*

1831 Founding of the British Association for the Advancement of Science, with psychology being added in 1913 as a subsection of physiology, and as an independent section in 1921

1832 Discovering of the hypnodrug, "chloral hydrate"

—— The appearance of 29 British Societies of phrenology

1833 Discovery of reflex action by Marshall Hall (1790–1857), a British physician and author of *Reflex Function of the Medulla Oblongata and Medulla Spinalis*

—— Publication of Eduard Beneke's (1798–1854) *A Textbook of Psychology as Natural Science*, a presentation of his doctrine of "traces"

—— Establishment of Massachusetts State Hospital (Worcester, Mass.) for the mentally ill

1834 The discovery of "Weber's law" by Ernst Heinrich Weber (1795–1878), recorded in *De Tactu*

1835 Publication of James Cowles Prichard's *Treatise on Insanity*, a standard text of

that time; also author of *Treatise on Diseases of the Nervous System* (1822)

1836 Establishment of the Vermont State Asylum for the mentally ill

1837 Development of the cell theory of life by J. E. Purkinje

1838 Publication of Johannes Müller's (1801–1858) *Handbuch der Physiologie des Menschen*, containing his doctrine of the specific energies of nerves

—— Publication of the two volume *Mental Illness* by Jean Étienne Dominique Esquirol (1772–1840), founder of French psychiatry

—— Publication of Isaac Ray's (1807–1881) *A Treatise on the Medical Jurisprudence of Insanity*, an early treatise on social psychology and legal questions pertaining to human motivation

—— Publication of Charles Wheatstone's (1802–1875) "Contributions to the Physiology of Vision," *Philos. Trans. Royal Society*, containing his theory of binocular parallax and stereoscopic depth perception

—— Founding of the *American Phrenological Journal* by O. S. Fowler (1809–1887) and L. N. Fowler (1811–1896)

—— Passage of the "Law of 1838" in France, requiring the establishment of a psychiatric hospital in each of France's 90 *departments*

—— Establishment of the Ohio State Asylum for the mentally ill

—— Publication of *An Inquiry Respecting the Self-Determining Power of the Will* by Jeremiah Day (1773–1867), president of Yale University

1840 The undertaking of a reform movement for more humane treatment of the mentally ill by Dorothea Lynde Dix (1802–1887) of Boston

—— Publication of the first psychology textbook in English, entitled: *Psychology, or a View of the Human Soul: Including Anthropology* by Frederick Rauch (1806–1841), president of Marshall College

—— Publication of Moreau de Tours' *Études physiologiques sur la folie*, containing an early psychological explanation of mental disorder

1841 Organization in England of the Association of Medical Officers of Asylums and Hospital for the Insane; renamed the Medico-Psychological Association in 1865; renamed again in 1926, the Royal Medico-Psychological Association

—— Establishment in Paris by Jean Pierre Falret (1794–1870) of the "aftercare movement" for the concern of patients released from hospital for mental illness

1842   Initial publication of the French periodical, *Annales Medico-Legales*

—— Publication of *Psychology* by Samuel Simon Schmucker (1799–1873), founder of Gettysburg College (1832–1834)

1843   Introduction of the term "mental hygiene" in Sweetser's *Mental Hygiene, an Examination of the Intellect and Passions, Designed to Illustrate Their Influence on Health and Duration of Life*

—— Initial use of the word "hypnotism" in James Braid's (1795–1860) *Neurypnology, or, the Rationale of Nervous Sleep Considered in Relation with Animal Magnetism*, emphasizing subjective factors on the patient's part, e.g., belief, suggestibility, and hypnotism

—— Initial publication of *Zooist* (edited by Elliotson), a periodical devoted to the study of mesmerism and cerebral physiology

—— Discovery of the "principle of associative similarity" by John Stuart Mill (1806–1873), enunciated in his *System of Logic*

1844   Founding of the *American Journal of Insanity*, renamed *American Journal of Psychiatry*

—— Founding of the Association of Medical Superintendents of American Institutions for the Insane (with Samuel B. Woodward of Worcester State Hospital, Mass., its first president); later renamed the American Medico-Psychological Association, and today known as the American Psychiatric Association

1845   Origin of psychiatry in Germany with the publication of *Pathologie und Therapie der Psychischen Krankheiten* by Wilhelm Griesinger (1817–1868), founder of *Archiv für Psychiatrie und Nervenkrankheiten*

—— The Britisher, John Frederick William Herschel (1792–1871), the first to offer the theory of "dichromism" in explaining color blindness

1846   Publication of *Concluding Unscientific Postscript*, the basis of contemporary existentialism, by Sören Kierkegaard (1813–1855), the father of existentialism

—— Publication of Ernst Heinrich Weber's (1795–1878) *Der Tastsinn und das Gemeingefühl*, containing his theory of touch

—— Development of the "product moment" formula in statistics by Auguste Bravais (1811–1863), the first to offer a theory correlation

1847   Founding of the Société Medico-Psychologique by Guillaume Ferrus (1784–1861) and others

—— Founding of Park House, Highgate, England (for the mentally ill) by Andrew Reed (1787–1862)

1848   Birth of M. Toyama (d. 1900) of the University of Tokyo, first Japanese to give lectures in psychology

—— Founding in England of the *Journal of Psychological Medicine and Mental Pathology* by Forbes Winslow (1810–1874); terminating publication in 1883

—— Publication by the American, Martyn Paine (1794–1877), of *Physiology of the Soul and Instinct as Distinguished from Materialism*, a forerunner of psychosomatic medicine

—— Publication of *Rational Psychology* by the American, Laurens P. Hickok (1798–1888), who later published *Empirical Psychology* (1854)

—— Birth of spiritualism in America by the Fox family

1848–1849   Discovery of animal electricity by Emil du Bois-Reymond (1818–1896), pioneer in German experimental psychology

1849   Founding of a mesmeric hospital by John Elliotson (1791–1868), founder of the Phenological Society

1850   Initiation of psychophysical experimentation by Gustav T. Fechner (1801–1887)

—— Measurement of the rate of nerve impulse by Hermann von Helmholtz (1821–1894)

c. 1851   Founding of the Ghost Society in

England by a group interested in psychical phenomena

1852 Employment of the modern use of the term "evolution" by Herbert Spencer (1820–1903)

—— The theory of local signs by Rudolf H. Lotze (1817–1881) as introduced in his *Medical Psychology or the Physiology of the Soul*

—— Presentation of E. H. Weber's theory of cutaneous space perception

—— Development of "secondary degeneration" or the Wallerian method of identifying tracts of nerve fibers by Augustus Volney Waller (1816–1870)

1853 First British publication with the term "psychology" in its title: *Elements of Psychology* by J. D. Morell (1816–1891)

—— Founding of the *American Psychological Journal*

—— Initial publication (in England) of the *Journal of Mental Science*

—— Publication of *Juvenile Deliquency* by Mary Carpenter (1807–1877), sister of W. B. Carpenter of England

1854 Initial publication of the *American Journal of Insanity* (renamed the *American Journal of Psychiatry*)

—— Publication of *Psychological Enquiries* (a dialogue published posthumously) by Benjamin Brodie (1783–1862), president of the Royal Society

—— Publication of L. P. Hickok's *Empirical Psychology or the Human Mind as Given in Consciousness*, written in the German tradition but nonphysiological

1855 The transition from associationism to scientific psychology in Great Britain by Alexander Bain (1818–1903) with the publication of his *The Senses and the Intellect*

—— Discovery of the "law of the succession of psychical changes" by Herbert Spencer (1820–1903) in his *Principles of Psychology*

—— Initial publication of the British periodical, *Asylum Journal of Mental Science;* renamed in 1858 to *Journal of Mental Science;* and in 1963 to the *British Journal of Psychiatry*, organ of the Royal Medico-Psychological Association

—— Publication of Dietrich Georg Kieser's (1711–1799) *Elements of Psychiatry*,

written from a nonempirical or from a philosophical position

—— Publication of *Elements of Psychological Medicine* by D. Noble (1810–1885), an Englishman

—— Publication of *Researches on Colour Blindness* by George Wilson (1818–1859) of Edinburgh

—— Publication of *Grammatik, Logik, und Psychologie* by Hayim Steinthal (1823–1899), a forerunner in social psychology

1856–1866 Publication of Hermann Ludwig Ferdinand von Helmholtz' (1821–1894) *Physiological Optics*, containing the Young-Helmholtz theory of color vision, theory of unconscious inference, and empirical theory of perception

1856 Introduction of the theory of nonrestraint in the treatment of the mentally ill by John Conolly (1794–1866) in his *The Treatment of the Insane without Mechanical Restraints*

1857 Publication of *Mental Philosophy* by Joseph Haven (1816–1874) of Amherst College

1858 Publication by J. C. Bucknoll (1817–1897) and Daniel Hack Tuke (1827–1895) of *Manual of Psychological Medicine*, a standard in Britain for half a century

—— Publication of R. Dunn's (1799–1877) *An Essay on Physiological Psychology*

1859 Theory of internal environment (*milieu intérieur*) by Claude Bernard (1813–1878), a French physiologist

—— Publication of Alexander Bain's *The Emotions and the Will*, a companion volume to his *The Senses and the Intellect*

—— Publication of *The Origin of Species by Means of Natural Selection or the Preservation of Favored Races in the Struggle for Life* by Charles Darwin (1809–1882), a presentation of his theory of evolution, survival of the fittest, and the doctrine of instincts

—— Posthumous publication of William Hamilton's (1788–1856) *Lectures on Metaphysics*, enunciating his doctrine of "Redintegration" (a theory of memory and association)

—— Publication of John Stuart Mill's (1806–1873) *On Liberty*, introducing social instinct theory

—— Publication of Karl Marx' (1818–1883) *A Contribution to the Critique of Political Economy*, containing the doctrine that social being determines consciousness

—— William James' attendance (in Geneva) at the lectures of Edouard Claparede (1873–1940), co-editor of *Archives de Psychologie*

1860 Formulation of "Fechner's law," founding of experimental psychology and psychophysics by Gustav Theodor Fechner (1801–1887), author of *Elements of Psychophysics*

—— Publication of *Traite des maladies mentales* by Benedict A. Morel (1809–1873), coiner of the term "dementia praecox" (*demence precoce*)

—— Noting of a relationship of cretinism to thyroid abnormality by Cesare Lombroso in *A Diagnosis of Cretinism Implies a Diagnosis of Goiter*

—— Declaration of the Criminal Lunatics Act in England, segregating the mentally ill from criminals

1861 Discovery of "Broca's area" of the "speech area" in the brain by Paul Broca (1824–1880) as reported in "Remarques sur siège de las faculté du language articule, suives d'une observation d'aphemie" (*Bulletin de la Société Anatomique de Paris*)

1863 Introduction of the "simple reaction time experiment" by Frans Cornelis Donders (1818–1889) as recorded in his *Oven den physiologischen Tijd der psychische Processen* (1865)

—— Publication of *Reflexes of the Brain* by Ivan M. Sechenov (1829–1905), founder of Russian behavioristic or reflex psychology, and of "Sechenov's center" (the inhibitory center of the brain)

—— Publication of Helmholtz' *On the Sensations of Tone as a Physiological Basis for the Theory of Music*, containing his resonance theory of hearing and his doctrine of specific nerve energies

—— Publication of *Man's Place in Nature* by Thomas H. Huxley (1825–1895), coiner of the term "epiphenomenalism"

—— Publication of Eduard von Hartmann's (1842–1906) *The Philosophy of the Unconscious*, containing his doctrine of "panpneumatism"

—— Publication of Isaac Ray's (1807–1881) *Mental Hygiene*, an early study by a New Englander; also authored *Medical Jurisprudence of Insanity* (1838)

1864 Publication of Ewald Hering's (1834–1918) *Beiträge zur Physiologie*, containing his nativistic theory of space perception

1865 Publication of *Sir William Hamilton's Philosophy* by John Stuart Mill, enunciating his theory of the "permanent possibilities of sensation"

—— Introduction of experimental psychology in France with the appearance of Claude Bernard's (1813–1878) *Introduction to the Study of Experimental Medicine*

—— Publication by the Scot, J. F. McLennan (1827–1881) of *Primitive Marriage*, introducing the term "totemism"

1866 First description of mongolian idiocy by J. Langdon-Down in *Clinical Lectures and Reports*, London Hospital, III

—— Nerve impulse theorized as a "wave of negativity" by Julius Bernstein

—— Presentation of the duplicity (or duplexity) theory of vision by Schultze

—— Publication of A. A. Liebault's *Du someil et des états analogues*, presenting his theory of "suggestion" therapy or hypnosis

1867 Founding of the *Quarterly Journal of Psychological Medicine and Medical Jurisprudence*

—— Publication in English of the first modern text in psychiatry, *Mental Pathology and Therapeutics* by Wilhelm Griesinger (1817–1868) of Germany

—— Publication of *The Physiology and Pathology of Mind* by Henry Maudsley (1835–1918), for whom Maudsley Hospital, London, is named

1867 Publication in England of J. S. Watson's *The Reasoning Power of Animals*

1868 The introduction of Scottish psychology into the U.S. by Noah Porter (1811–1882), author of the *Human Intellect with an Introduction upon Psychology and the Soul*, a milestone in American psychology

1869 Francis Galton's (1822–1911) claim of intelligence as hereditary in *Hereditary Genius*

—— Publication of the social psychological work, *Physics and Politics*, by Walter Bagehot (1826–1877)

1870 Localization of motor centers in the brain through electrical stimulation by Gustav Fritsch (1838–1927) and Eduard Hitzig (1838–1907), "Ueber die elektrische Erregbarkeit des Grosshirns," (*Archiv für Anatomie, Physiologie, und wissenschaftliche Medicin*)

—— Publication of *Contemporary English Psychology* by Theodule Armand Ribot (1839–1916), founder of *Revue Philosophique*, pioneer in French experimental psychology, and founder of French psychology

1871 Publication of C. Darwin's *Descent of Man*, differentiating man from the animal in degree only—not in kind

1872 Publication of Darwin's *Expression of the Emotions in Man and Animals*, an evolutionary theory of emotions

—— Development of the power law of sense intensities by Joseph A. F. Plateau (1801–1883), originator of the stroboscopic method of investigating vibratory motion

—— Publication of Daniel Hack Tuke's *Illustrations of the Influence of the Mind upon the Body in Health and Disease*, an early treatise on psychosomatic medicine

—— D. A. Spaulding's conclusion that birds fly by instinct (by maturation rather than by learning)

1872–1874 Publication of Ewald Hering's (1834–1918) *Theory of Light Sensation*, expounding his six component theory of color vision

1873 Publication of Carl Stumpf's *Ueber den psychologischen Ursprung der Raumvorstellung*, discussing his nativistic theory of space perception

1873 Publication of *Principles of Psychology* by Guiseppe Sergi (1841–1936), Italy's pioneer in psychology

1873–1874 Publication of the first textbook in physiological psychology—Wilhelm Wundt's (1832–1920) *Principles of Physiological Psychology*

1874 Birth of "act psychology" with the

publication of *Psychology from an Empirical Standpoint* by Franz Brentano (1838–1917)

—— William James' (1842–1910) contention of having opened the first psychological laboratory in America (at Harvard University)

—— Publication of *Sensation and Intuition* by James Sulley (1843–1923), a British evolutionist

—— Introduction of Western psychology into Japan through the translations of A. Nishi (1829–1898)

1875 Discovery of modern graphology by Jean Hippolyte Michon (1806–1881), author of *System of Graphology*

—— Discovery of mental deficiency as hereditary by Richard Lewis Dugdale (1841–1883) as reported in his *The Jukes, a Study in Crime, Pauperism, Disease, and Heredity*

1876 Publication of David Ferrier's (1843–1928) *Functions of the Brain*, containing his studies in localization of cerebral functions, and researches in frontal lobotomy of monkeys

—— Introduction by Francis Galton of "nature and nuture" as synonyms for "heredity and environment" in "The History of Twins, as a Criterion of the Relative Powers of Nature and Nurture" (*J. Anthropol. Inst.*)

—— Founding of the British journal, *Mind*, by Alexander Bain (1818–1903) of the University of Aberdeen

—— Publication of the first study in criminal psychology, *The Delinquent Man*, by Cesare Lombroso (1835–1909), Italian psychologist known for Lombrosian theory; precursor of constitutional psychology

1877 The first working out of "statistical correlation" by Francis Galton

—— The theory of tracing hysteria to sex suppression by Andrew J. Ingersoll (*Health*, 1892)

—— Publication of W. W. Ireland's *Idiocy and Imbecility*, citing ten forms

1878 Experimentation on fatigue by Étienne Jules Marey (1804–1904), inventor of the sphygmograph (1863), and experimenter with electrical phenomena in animals

—— Publication of *An Outline Study of*

Man: Or the Body and Mind in One System (anticipating organismic or holistic psychology) by the American, Mark Hopkins (1802–1887)

—— Publication of Alexander Bain's *Education as a Science*, marking the beginnings of educational psychology

—— Founding of the *Journal of Physiology* in England, with M. Foster as its first editor

1879   Coining of the term "comparative psychology" by George John Romanes (1848–1894)

—— The founding of Neo-Thomistic psychology under the leadership of Désiré Mercier (1851–1926) of Belgium

—— The establishment of the world's first psychological laboratory by Wilhelm Wundt of Leipzig University, thus marking the birth of psychology as a science

—— Establishment of the "After-Care Association" in England for the assistance of mental patients on their release from the hospital

1880   The "cure of Anna O. of her neurotic symptoms" by Josef Breuer (1842–1925) and his "talking out" psychotherapy

—— Founding of the Aristotelian Society in England

—— Publication of *American Nervousness with Its Causes and Consequences* by George Miller Beard (1839–1883), coiner of the term "neurasthenia"

—— Publication of *Emotions* by James McCosh, president of Princeton University (named College of New Jersey at that time)

1881   G. Stanley Hall's (1844–1924) contention of instituting the first psychological laboratory in the United States (at Johns Hopkins), two years following the world's first—that of W. Wundt in Leipzig

—— Founding of a psychological laboratory in Göttingen University by G. E. Müller

—— Establishment of a chair in clinical neurology at the University of Paris with Jean Martin Charcot (1825–1893) as its first occupant

—— Birth of Ludwig Binswanger (d. 1966),

coiner of the term "dasein analysis" as a system of psychotherapy

—— Publication of T. A. Ribot's *Diseases of Memory*

1882   Publication in Germany of Wilhelm Theirry Preyer's (1841–1897) *The Mind of the Child*, marking the opening of serious study in child psychology

—— Publication of *Animal Intelligence* by George Romanes, founder of comparative psychology

—— Founding in England of the Society for Psychical Research, with Henry Sidgwick (1838–1888) of Cambridge University as its first president

—— Publication of *The Nerve Currents in Brain and Spinal Cord* by Vladimir M. Bechterev (1857–1927), founder of reflexology

—— Removal of an ovary as a cure of hysteria by Jules Emile Pean (1830–1898), founder of gynecological surgery

—— Publication of D. H. Tuke's chapters in the *History of the Insane* in the British Isles

—— Publication of the two-volume *History of Philosophy* (including psychology) by Harold Höffding (1843–1931) of Denmark

—— Publication of John Lubbock's (1834–1913) *Ants, Bees, and Wasps*, a study of social instincts in animals

1883   W. Wundt's founding of the first journal in experimental psychology, the *Philosophische Studien* (terminated in 1903)

—— Publication of the first edition of Emil Kraepelin's (1856–1926) *Psychiatry*, containing his nosology, and division of (and coining of) "neuroses and psychoses"

—— Publication of the two-volume *Psychology of Tone* by Carl Stumpf (1848–1936)

—— Publication of Francis Galton's *Inquiries into Human Faculty and Its Development*, a comparative study of various human races showing their evolvement as the result of adaptation to specific environmental conditions

—— Publication of G. Stanley Hall's *Methods of Teaching History*, an early study in pedagogical psychology

—— Theory of the subjective equality of

just noticeable differences in sense by the Belgian, Joseph Remi Leopold Delboeuf (1831–1896)

—— Gautier's doctoral dissertation on dementia praecox (*demence precoce*)

1884 Development of the James-Lange theory of emotions by William James (1842–1910) and the following year by Carl George Lange (1834–1900)

—— The first complete textbook of psychology published in Great Britain, *Outlines of Psychology* by James Sully (1843–1923)

—— Doctrine of dissolution (forerunner of Freudian regression) by John Hughlings Jackson (1835–1911) in *The Croonian Lectures on the Evolution and Dissolution of the Nervous System*

—— Publication of *La paura*, an experimental study of fear and emotion with its physiological relationship by Angelo Mosso (1846–1910), developer of an ergograph and sphygmomanometer

1885 Publication of Carl Lange's *Om Sindsbevaegelser*, containing his formulation of the James-Lange theory of emotions

—— Publication of Hermann Ebbinghaus' (1850–1909) *Memory: A Contribution to Experimental Psychology*, containing his study of completion tests, nonsense syllables, and the application of the law of error

—— James McKeen Cattell's (1860–1944) invention of the millisecond (sigma) measurement

—— The founding of a psychological laboratory at the University of Rome by Giuseppe Sergi (1841–1936)

—— Publication of T. A. Ribot's *Diseases of Personality*

1886 F. Galton's development of the "index of corelation" with J. D. H. Dickson's assistance; termed "Galton's function," and today known as "coefficient of correlation"

—— The founding of psychological laboratories at: (1) the University of Berlin by H. Ebbinghaus, (2) the University of Copenhagen by A. Lehmann, and (3) Kazan University, Russia, by V. Bechterev.

—— Granting of the world's first Ph.D. in psychology to Joseph Jastrow (1863–

1944) at Johns Hopkins University

—— James McKeen Cattell (1860–1944) the first American to receive the doctorate in the new psychology at Leipzig

—— Publication of Ernst Mach's (1838–1916) *Contributions to the Analysis of Sensations*, marking the founding of the philosophy of "empiriocriticism"

—— Publication of *Psychopathia Sexualis* by Richard von Krafft-Ebing (1840–1902), specialist in forensic psychiatry

—— Publication of Hippolyte Bernheim's *De la suggestion et de ses applications à la therapeutique*

1887 Publication of the first psychology textbook in America, George Trumbull Ladd's (1842–1921) *Elements of Physiological Psychology*

—— Founding of the first psychological journal in the United States, the *American Journal of Psychology*, by G. Stanley Hall

—— First lectureship in psychology in America (as an independent department) at the University of Pennsylvania; and in 1888, a professorship with the appointment of J. McK. Cattell

—— Establishment of a psychological laboratory at the University of Iowa through the efforts of G. T. W. Patrick

—— Founding of the *Revue de l'Hypnotisme et de la Psychologie Physiologique*, a French journal devoted to hypnotism (terminated in 1902)

—— Publication of Auguste Florel's (1848–1931) *Experiences et remarques critiques sur les sensations des insects*, a study on social instincts in animals

—— Publication of Alfred Binet and C. Fere's *Animal Magnetism*, a study in hypnosis

1888 Conferring of the Ph.D. (Johns Hopkins) on Yujiro Motora (1858–1912), the University of Tokyo's first professor of psychology

—— Discovery of the secretory nerves in the pancreas by the Russian, Ivan P. Pavlov (1849–1936)

—— Publication of P. J. Moebius' (1853–1907) *The Concept of Hysteria*, theorizing hysteria as a mental illness in which ideas produce physical symptoms

—— The University of Wisconsin as the second college in the United States to treat psychology as an independent discipline, under the professorship of Joseph H. Jastrow

—— Publication of John Lubbock's *Senses, Instincts, and Intelligence of Animals*, a study in social instincts in animals

1889 The 1st International Congress of Psychology, Paris; T. Ribot, President, J. M. Charcot, Honorary President

—— Establishment of psychological laboratories at: the Sorbonne (France's first laboratory) by A. Binet and H. Beaunis, the University of Toronto (first in the British Empire) by James Mark Baldwin (1861–1934), and at the University of Munich by Carl Stumpf (1848–1936)

—— Publication of *Animal Magnetism* by Joseph Remy Leopold Delboeuf (1831–1896), author of *Étude psychophysique* (1873)

—— Publication of A. Florel's *Hypnotism*

—— Discovery of the Müller-Lyer illusion by F. C. Müller-Lyer, founder of Müller-Lyer rectangles (an illusion)

1890 Founding of psychosurgery by Gottlieb Burckhardt, a Swiss psychiatrist

—— Christian von Ehrenfel's (1859–1932) development of form-quality or "Gestaltqualität" (*Vierteljahrsschr. f. wiss. Philos.*)

—— First psychological tests of individual differences and the coining of the term "mental test" by J. McK. Cattell

—— Publication by the Scot, James George Frazer (1854–1941), of the 12-volume *The Golden Bough* (completed in 1936), a social psychological treatment of primitive culture from an intellectualist slant

—— Publication of Gabriel Tarde's (1843–1904) *The Laws of Imitation*, theorizing that the inferiors copy their superiors and the lower classes imitate the upper

—— William James' publication of *The Principles of Psychology* together with the development of his doctrine of the stream of consciousness

—— Publication of Felkin's *Hypnotism, or Psychotherapeutics*

—— Founding of the German periodical, *Journal of Psychology and Physiology*

of the Sense Organs by Hermann Ebbinghaus (1850–1909) and Arthur König (1856–1901)

—— Discovery of the membrane theory of nerve conduction by Wilhelm Ostwald (1853–1932), discoverer of Ostwald's dilution law

1891 Formulation of Wilhelm Waldeyer's (1836–1921) theory of neurones and synaptic connections (*Deutsch. Med. Wochenschr.*)

—— Life defined as a "continuous adjustment of internal relations to external relations" by Herbert Spencer (1820–1903)

—— Invention of the "ergograph" by the Italian, Angelo Mosso (1846–1910), a device for measuring fatigue and efficiency as explained in his *Fatigue*

—— The founding of psychological laboratories at: Columbia University by James McK. Cattell, Wellesley College by Mary Calkins, Cornell University by Frank Angell, Catholic University of America, and Louvain University (Belgium) by D. Mercier, J. F. Heymans, and A. Thiery

—— Founding of the *Journal of Genetic Psychology*, (originally named *Pedagogical Seminary* until 1927) by G. Stanley Hall, America's second journal in psychology

—— Publication of C. Lloyd Morgan's *Animal Life and Intelligence*

—— Publication of Theordor Ziehen's (1862–1950) *Introduction to the Study of Physiological Psychology*

1891–1893 Publication of J. L. A. Koch's (1841–1908) *Die psychopathischen Minderwertigkeiten*, an early treatment of psychological inferiority

1892 Formation of the American Psychological Association with 26 members (at Clark University); its first meeting at the University of Pennsylvania with G. Stanley Hall as its first president

—— Coining of Galton's function as the "coefficient of correlation" by F. Y. Edgeworth (represented by the symbol r)

—— Publication of D. H. Tuke's *A Dictionary of Psychological Medicine*

—— Publication of Pierre Janet's (1859–1947) *The Mental State of Hystericals*, studies in personality dissociation

—— German translation of *Fundamental Laws of Human Affective Life* by Alfred Lehmann (1858–1921), the first Danish psychologist

—— Experimentation with psychomimetic drugs by Emil Kraepelin

—— Founding of the *Zeitschrift für Hypnotismus, Psychotherapie so wie andere psychophysiologische und psychopathologische Forschungen* (terminated in 1902)

—— Founding of psychological laboratories at: Yale University by G. T. Ladd, with E. W. Scripture in charge; Brown University by E. B. Delabarre; the University of Geneva by Theodore Flournoy (1854–1920); and H. Münsterberg's undertaking of the psychological laboratory at Harvard

—— Publication of Adolf Strümpell's (1853–1925) *Ueber die Entstehung und die Heilung von Krankheiten durch Vorstellung*, theorizing ideas as the cause of physical ailments in hysterical cases

—— Second International Congress of Psychology, London; H. Sidgwick, president

—— Birth of Harry Stack Sullivan (d. 1949), founder of the "interpersonal theory of psychiatry"

1892–1893 First use of the statistical terms "standard deviation" and "normal curve" by Carl Pearson (1857–1936)

1893 First psychological demonstrations with apparatus at a world's fair (Chicago), under the supervision of H. Münsterberg and J. Jastrow

—— Publication of Oswald Külpe's (1862–1915) *Outlines of Psychology*, containing his definition of psychology as the science of the facts of experience, his study of "imageless thought," and precursory ideas on "mental set"

—— Coining of the term "proprioceptive" by Charles Sherrington (1857–1952) of Liverpool and Oxford

—— Founding of psychological laboratories at: Princeton University by J. M. Baldwin; University of Chicago by J. Dewey and J. R. Angell; and Stanford University by F. Angell

1894 Formulation of the "duplicity theory" of vision by Johannes von Kries (1853–1928)

—— Development of Max von Frey's (1852–1932) theory of cutaneous sensibility

—— Development of Morgan's canon in *An Introduction to Comparative Psychology* by Conwy Lloyd Morgan (1852–1936)

—— Publication of *The Factors of Insanities* by Hughlings Jackson (1835–1911), Britain's foremost 19th-century neurologist, specializing in aphasia

—— The founding of the following journals by J. McK. Cattell and J. M. Baldwin: (1) *Psychological Review*, (2) *Psychological Monographs*, and (3) *Psychological Index*

—— Founding of psychological laboratories at: University of Breslau by H. Ebbinghaus, and Austria's first at University of Graz by Alexius Meinong (1853–1920)

—— Publication of Alfred Binet's *Introduction to Experimental Psychology*

1895 The tracing of paresis to syphilis by the research of Frederick Mott (1853–1926)

—— Publication of Josef Breuer's (1842–1925) and Sigmund Freud's (1856–1939) *Studies on Hysteria*, marking the birth of psychoanalysis

—— Founding of psychological laboratories at: Leningrad University (St. Petersburg at that time) by V. Bechterev, and at the University of Turin by F. Kiesow

—— Development of the first objective educational achievement test by Rice

—— Development of graphology in Germany with the publication of Wilhelm Thierry Preyer's (1841–1897) *Psychology of Handwriting*

—— Founding of the French journal *L'Année Psychologique* by Alfred Binet

—— Publication of Gustav LeBon's (1841–1931) *The Crowd*, offering a theory of group mind and group suggestion

—— The first British publication devoted to child psychology, *Studies in Psychology* by James Sully (1842–1923)

—— Mary Whiton Calkins' (1863–1930) study of association between pairs of items in "Association," *Psychol. Rev., Monogr. Suppl.*

1896 Karl Pearson's (1857–1936) development of the mathematical procedure for determining the "correlation coefficient" (Pearson *r*), and the coining of the term "product moment," *Philos. Trans.*

—— Development of Wilhelm Wundt's (1832–1920) "tridimensional theory of feeling" in his *Outline of Psychology*

—— Discovery of "decerebrate rigidity" and "reciprocal innervations" by Charles Scott Sherrington (1857–1952), author of *The Integrative Action of the Nervous System* (1906)

—— Publication of John Dewey's (1859–1952) "The Reflex Arc Concept in Psychology," *Psychol. Rev.*, a critique of reflexology

—— Publication of *An Outline of Psychology* by Edward Bradford Titchener (1867–1927)

—— The study of "imageless thoughts" by George Frederick Stout (1860–1944) in his *Analytic Psychology*

—— The initiation of clinical psychology at the University of Pennsylvania, under Lightner Witmer (1867–1956)

—— Formulation of psychophysical axioms by Georg Elias Müller (1850–1934) "Zur Psychophysik der Gesichtsempfindungen," *Zsch. Psychol.*

—— Third International Congress of Psychology, Munich; C. Stumpf, president

—— Establishment of psychological laboratories at: University of Würzburg by O. Külpe; and Reggio Emilia by C. G. Ferrari and Augusto Tamburini, cofounders of the Italian journal *Rivista di Psicologia*

—— Founding in Germany of the Graphological Society by Ludwig Klages (1872–1956), author of *The Problems of Graphology* (1910), *Handwriting and Character* (1928), and *Introduction to the Psychology of Handwriting* (1928)

—— Establishment of the Russian Society of Normal and Abnormal Psychology by V. Bechterev

1897   Development of Jost's law (concerning two associations of equal strength, the older one maintains its strength better than the earlier) by Adolph Jost in "Die Associationsfestigkeit in ihrer Abhängigkeit von der Verteilung der Wiederholungen," *Zsch. Psychol.*

—— Publication of Edward Wheeler Scrip-

ture's (1864–1945) *The New Psychology*, containing the first treatment of statistics for psychology

—— Publication of Havelock Ellis' (1859–1939) *Studies in the Psychology of Sex* (seven volumes appearing from 1897–1928)

—— Publication of Bernard Bosanquet's (1848–1923) *Psychology of the Moral Self*, presented from the standpoint of philosophical idealism

—— Publication of Herbert Spencer Jennings' (1868–1947) *Behavior of the Lower Organisms*, viewing life as consciousness

—— Publication of Hermann Ebbinghaus' (1850–1909) *Grundzüge der Psychologie* (first part); experimentation on the effects of fatigue and completion tests

—— Publication of *Raumaesthetik* by Theodor Lipps (1851–1914), known for his theory of "empathy"

—— Establishment of psychological laboratories at: Cambridge University under Rivers; University College, London, by J. Sully; University of Brussels by G. Dwelshauvers; and the University of Cracow, Poland, by W. Heinrich

1898   Publication of Edward Lee Thorndike's (1874–1949) *Animal Intelligence: An Experimental Study of the Associative Processes in Animals*, republished in 1911, containing his study of the laws of effect and of exercise, and the "puzzle box"

—— Development of the statistical formula for the probable error of a correlation coefficient by Karl Pearson

—— Coining of the terms "autonomic" in reference to the involuntary nervous system, and (in 1903) "parasympathetic" by John Newport Langley (1852–1925), author of *The Autonomic Nervous System* (1921)

—— Discovery of "mescaline," a psychomimetic drug producing schizophrenoid states

—— Publication of G. F. Stout's *Manual of Psychology*, the ruling text in Britain for approximately a quarter of a century (a functionalist's approach to psychology)

—— Publication of E. B. Titchener's "The

Postulates of a Structural Psychology," *Philos. Rev.*

—— Publication of *Treatise of Aphasia* by H. Charton Bastian (1837–1915), the neurologist who coined the term "*kinaesthesis*"

1899 Discovery of nervous impulses as separated by "refractory phases" by Francis Gotch (1853–1913)

—— Publication by the Italian psychologist, Sante De Santis (1863–1935), of *Dreams*, the first extended work devoted to the subject

—— Founding of the *Archives of Neurology and Psychiatry* by its first editor, Frederick Mott

—— Publication of E. L. Thorndike's "The Mental Life of the Monkey," *Psychol. Rev., Monogr. Suppl.*

—— Publication of E. B. Titchener's "Structural and Functional Psychology," *Philos. Rev.*

1900 The introduction (into statistics) of the chi-square test of "goodness of fit" by Karl Pearson

—— Publication of the first volume of W. Wundt's *Folk Psychology*, a 10-volume work on social psychology completed in 1920

—— Publication of Edmund Husserl's (1859–1938) *Logical Investigations* from 1900 to 1901

—— Publication of Edwin Diller Starbuck's *Psychology of Religion*, an early treatment of the subject

—— Publication of S. Freud's *The Interpretation of Dreams;* for some, the marking of psychoanalysis

—— Publication of A. Binet's *La suggestibilité*, his theory on the psychology of suggestion

—— Publication of Hugo Münsterberg's (1863–1916) *Grundzüge de Psychologie* (Vol. 1), presenting his "action" theory and stressing "process" rather than structure

—— The employment of psychodynamic techniques in psychiatry by August Hoch at McLean Hospital, Belmont, Mass.

—— Publication of Hugo de Vries' (1848–1935) mutation theory in evolution prompted from researches on osmosis and plasmolysis as recorded in his *Die Mutationstheorie* (1900–1903), 2 vols.

—— Publication of C. Lloyd Morgan's *Animal Behaviour*

—— Fourth International Congress of Psychology, Paris: T. Ribot, president

—— Founding of the first psychological laboratory in South America, at the University of Buenos Aires by H. G. Pinero

1901 Discovery of the conditioned (conditional) reflex by Ivan P. Pavlov (1849–1936), a Russian physiologist

—— Discovery of the principle of the "transfer of training" by Edward Lee Thorndike (1874–1949) and Robert Sessions Woodworth (1869–1962)

—— Development of the maze for the study of animal behavior by Robert Mearns Yerkes (1876–1956) in the United States, and Williard Stanton Small (1870–1943) in England

—— Establishment of the British Psychological Society, with Charles S. Myers (1873–1946) as its first president and cofounder

—— Development of Külpe's Würzburg School

—— Establishment of the *Archives of Psychology* at Geneva by Theodore Flourney (1854–1920) and Edouard Claparede (1873–1940)

—— Publication of *Mind in Evolution* by Leonard Trelawney (1864–1929), the first professor of sociology

—— Publication of the first English language *Dictionary of Psychology and Philosophy* (1901–1906), 2 vols., under the editorship of James Mark Baldwin (1861–1934)

—— Publication of *Experimental Psychology: A Manual of Laboratory Practice* (in 4 volumes from 1901 to 1905) by Edward Bradford Titchener (1867-1927)

—— Founding of the journal, *Biometrika*, by F. Galton, K. Pearson, and W. F. R. Weldon, at the University College, London (a journal for mathematical research in psychology, statistics, and the life science)

1902 Initiation of the neuropsychological mode of investigation and the discovery of the relearning of habits lost through brain tissue damage, by Shepherd Ivory Franz (1874–1933)

—— Introduction of electronarcosis (sleep induced electrically) as a technique of sleep psychotherapy by Stephane Leduc

—— Development of the "order-of-merit" method by James McK. Cattell

—— A pioneer study of learning curves by E. Kraepelin

—— Publication of William James' *The Varieties of Religious Experience*, a study in the psychology of religion

—— Publication of Alfred Binet's *La psychologie des grands calculateurs et joueurs d'échec*, a study of mental brilliance and defectives

1903 Discovery of the sedative effects of barbiturates and their use in treating mental illness by E. Fischer and Joseph von Mering

—— Initial recording of experiments on the salivary reflex by I. Pavlov

—— Founding of the *Archiv für die gesamte Psychologie* by Ernst Meumann (1862–1915), and the publication of his *Oekonomie und Technik des Lernen*, an early classic in educational psychology

—— Founding of the first psychological laboratory in Japan by Matataro Matsumoto (1865–1943) at Tokyo University; of another at the University of Florence by F. de Sarlo

—— Birth of the German Psychological Society

—— Publication of Frederic William Henry Myers' (1843–1901) *Human Personality and Its Survival of Bodily Death*, a psychical study entailing the subliminal self

—— Publication of A. Binet's *L'étude expérimentale de l'intelligence*, a study of thought processes with his two daughters as his subjects

1904 Publication of S. Freud's *Psychopathology of Everyday Life*, treating "Freudian slips" and unconscious mistakes

—— Publication of *Les psychoneuroses et leur traitement moral* by Paul Dubois (1848–1918)

—— Introduction by Charles Edward Spearman (1863–1945) of general intelligence ("G" factor or "two-factor theory"); later to become "factor analysis"; found in "General Intelligence Ob-

jectively Determined and Measured," *Amer. J. Psychol.*

—— Publication of Max von Frey's (1852–1932) *Vorlesungen über Physiologie*, containing his theory of the four cutaneous senses: warmth, cold, pressure, and pain

—— Publication of *Adolescence: Its Psychology and Its Relations to Physiology, Anthropology, Sociology, Sex, Crime, Religion, and Education* by G. Stanley Hall

—— Development of Carl Gustav Jung's (1875–1961) "100-word association test," reported later in "The Association Method," *Amer. J. Psychol.*, 1910

—— Discovery of "bulbocapnine," a cataleptic-producing drug

—— Development of the contingency coefficient by Karl Pearson

—— Founding of the journals: (1) *Journal of Philosophy, Psychology, and Scientific Method;* (2) *Journal of Religious Psychology* by G. Stanley Hall (terminated in 1914); (3) *Psychological Bulletin* by J. McK. Cattell and J. M. Baldwin; and (4) *British Journal of Psychology* by J. Ward, W. H. R. Rivers, and C. S. Myers

—— Founding of the Society of Experimental Psychologists

—— First Congress of Experimental Psychology

—— The experimental study of thought by H. J. Watt (1879–1925)

—— Founding of a psychological laboratory in a mental hospital by Shepherd Ivory Franz at McLean Hospital at Belmont, Mass.

1905 Formulation of the Binet-Simon scale, the first intelligence test, by Alfred Binet (1857–1911) and Theodore Simon (1873–1962) in "Méthodes nouvelles pour le diagnostic du niveau intellectuel des anormaux," *Ann. Psychol.*

—— The study of thought, volition, and awareness through systematic experimental introspection by Narziss Ach (1871–1946) of the Würzburg School

—— First psychoanalytic treatment of a patient in England by the psychoanalyst, Ernest Jones (1879–1958) author of *Papers on Psychoanalysis* (1912)

—— Development of the theory of multiple personality in *Dissociation of a Personality* by Morton Prince (1854–1929)

—— Fifth International Congress of Psychology, Rome; G. Sergi, president; L. Bianchi, honorary president

—— Study of the relation of the unconscious to handwriting in neurotics by Rogues de Fursac in *Les écrits et les dessins dans les maladies nerveuses et mentales*

—— Publication of *Histological Studies on the Localization of Cerebral Function* by A. W. Campbell (1868–1937)

1906 The initial appearance of the term "psychoanalysis," found in an article in the *Journal of Abnormal Psychology* by James Jackson Putnam (1846–1918), founder of one of the first neurological clinics in the United States

—— Founding of the journals: *Archives of Psychology;* and the *Journal of Abnormal Psychology* (renamed *Journal of Abnormal and Social Psychology*) by Morton Prince

—— Initial introduction of psychology in India, at the University of Calcutta

—— Publication of Alfred Binet's *Les révélations de l'écriture d'après un controle scientifique*, a study of abnormality through handwriting

—— Establishment of three chairs of psychology in Italy: University of Rome, occupied by Sante De Sanctis (1863–1935); University of Turin, occupied by Friedrich Kiesow (1858–1940); and one at the University of Naples to Cesare Colucci

—— Founding of the first psychological laboratory in Scotland, at the University of Edinburgh by W. G. Smith

—— Founding of the Vineland Training School for the Feebleminded by Henry Herbert Goddard (1866–1957), author of *The Kallikak Family* (1912)

1907 Publication of V. M. Bechterev's *Objective Psychology*, containing his development of "reflexology" or "associated reflex" and the founding of the Psychoneurological Institute at St. Petersburg by him during the same year

—— Publication of *A Study of Organ Inferiority and Its Psychical Compensation* by Alfred Adler (1870–1937), founder of the school of "individual psychology" and developer of the concept of the "inferiority complex"

—— Erich R. Jaensch's (1883–1940) introduction of "eidetic imagery" in his book by the same title

—— Discovery of the anticonvulsant value of the barbituate "phenylethyl-barbituric acid" (phenobarbital) by Alfred Hauptman in "Luminal bei Epilepsie," *Müchen med. Wschr.*

—— Discovery of pure word blindness by Otto Pötzl, Austrian neuropathologist

—— Publication of *The Major Symptoms of Hysteria* (lectures delivered at Harvard Medical School on neurosis, suggestion, hysteria, somnambulism, etc.) by Pierre Marie Felix Janet (1859–1947), formulator of the concept of the dissociation of personality

—— Founding of the journals: *The Psychological Clinic* by Lightner Witmer (1867–1956); *Journal of Applied Psychology* (German) by William Stern (1871–1938)

—— The development of the "Ausfragemethode" and the study of "nonsensory thought processes" by K. Bühler in "Tatsachen und Probleme zu einer Psychologie der Denkvorgänge," *Arch. ges. Psychol.*

—— Publication of Charles Hubbard Judd's (1873–1946) *Psychology*, written from the standpoint of functionalism

—— Establishment of the first laboratory course in psychology in France by Henri Pieron at the École des Hautes Études, Paris

1908 First Congress of International Psychoanalytic Association, Salzburg, Austria; with Sandor Ferenzi credited as its founder

—— Manhattan State Hospital, the first in the United States to employ psychoanalysis regularly

—— Founding of the journal: *Jahrbuch für psychoanalytische und psychopathologische Forschungen* (terminated in 1912 when Jung, Adler, and Stekel severed with Freud)

—— Creation of the first chair in psychology and a psychological laboratory at Kyoto University, Japan, with Matataro Matsumoto (1865–1943) as professor of psychology and director of the laboratory

—— Development of the Binet-Simon scale of general intelligence on the basis of mental age

—— Experimentation with avoidance conditioning by V. Bechterev

—— Publication of Walter Dill Scott's (1869–1955) *Psychology of Advertising*, a pioneer work in advertising

—— Publication of *Introduction to Social Psychology* by William McDougall (1871–1938); sharing the honor with Edward Alsworth Ross (1866–1951; author of *Social Psychology*) as the first to publish books entitled "Social Psychology"

—— Publication of H. Mübsterberg's *On the Witness Stand*, a pioneer publication in the psychology of law

—— Publication of A. F. Tredgold's (1870–1952) *Mental Deficiency* (9th ed., 1956), a standard text for many years

—— Publication of *Human Nature and Politics* by Graham Wallas (1858–1932), considered by some as the first British social psychologist

—— Introduction of the "t" statistic for the distribution of sample variance by W. S. Gossett

—— Publication of *A Mind That Found Itself* (a plea by a once mentally ill patient for humane treatment of mental patients) by Clifford Whittingham Beers (1876–1943), founder of: Connecticut Society for Mental Hygiene (1908), first group of its kind; National Commission for Mental Hygiene (1909); American Foundation for Mental Hygiene (1928); International Foundation for Mental Hygiene (1931)

1909   Publication of Charles Parsons' *Choosing a Vocation*, the first book on vocational guidance

—— Freud's visit to the United States, at Clark University, Worcester, Mass., where he delivered a series of five lectures

—— The organization in Chicago by William Healy of the Juvenile Psychopathic Institute, a psychological clinic for delinquents

—— Publication of E. B. Titchener's *A Textbook of Psychology*, written from a structuralist's point of view

—— Publication of *Treasury of Human Inheritance* (1909–1933), and the development of the biserial correlation method by Karl Pearson

—— Establishment in New York of the National Committee for Mental Hygiene, with its organ, *Mental Hygiene*, founded in 1917

—— Initial publications of: *Monographs on Nervous and Mental Disease;* and G. Stanley Hall's founding of the *Journal of Race Development* (lasted until 1919)

—— Publication of the *Psychological Origin and Nature of Religion* by James Henri Leuba (b. 1868), the first psychologist devoted to the study of religion

—— Sixth International Congress of Psychology, Geneva; T. Flournoy, president

1909–1910   Publication of Friedrich Wilhelm Nietzsche's (1844–1900) *Will to Power*, containing ideas that influenced the psychology of Freud and Adler

1910   Second Congress of International Psychoanalytic Association, Nuremburg, Germany, with C. G. Jung as its first president

—— Introduction of "dynamic psychology" by Robert S. Woodworth, author of *Dynamic Psychology* (1918)

—— Publication of *Grammar of Science* by Karl Pearson (1857–1936), founder of statistics as a science

—— Development of industrial psychology in Japan through the efforts of Yoichi Ueno (1833–1957) and K. Suzuki

—— Establishment of a psychological clinic at the University of Iowa by Carl Emil Seashore (1866–1949), author of *Psychology of Music* (1938)

—— Development of the Kent-Rosanoff word association test by Grace H. Kent (b. 1875) and Aaron J. Rosanoff (b. 1878) as recorded in "A Study of Associations in Insanity," *Amer. J. Insanity*

—— Publication of John Dewey's *How We Think*, containing his psychology of the thinking process

—— Initial publication of the *Journal of Educational Psychology*

—— Founding of a psychological laboratory at McGill University by William Dunlop Tait (b. 1879)

—— Publication of *The Evolution of Memory* by Henri Pieron (1881–1964), author of *Thought and the Brain* (1927), and editor of *L'Année Psychologique* (from 1913 to 1964)

1911 Founding of the journals: (1) *Zentralblatt für Psychoanalyse* by Freud, with Stekel as editor; (2) the Japanese publication, *Experimental Psychology* by K. Ohtsuki; (3) *Journal of Animal Behavior* lasting until 1921, when it merged with *Psychobiology* to become the *Journal of Comparative Psychology*; (4) *The Journal of Experimental Pedagogy*, later siring the *British Journal of Educational Psychology*; and (5) *Psychic Study*, a Japanese journal

—— Founding of the American Psychoanalytic Association, by Ernest Jones, with J. J. Putnam as its first president (a few months after the founding of the New York Psychoanalytic Society by A. A. Brill)

—— Founding of the school of "individual psychology" by Alfred Adler, on severing relations with Freud

—— Introduction of psychoanalysis into France by Morichau-Beauchant

—— Recording of the law of exercise and the law of effect by E. L. Thorndike in *Animal Intelligence: Experimental Studies*

—— The offering of a diploma of Psychological Medicine at Edinburgh, Durham, and London universities (for the first time in Great Britain)

—— Publication by A. Binet and T. Simon of "A Method for Measuring the Development of the Intelligence of Young Children," *Bull. Soc. Libre pour L'Étude Psychologique de l'Enfant*, containing the Binet-Simon intelligence scale

—— Opening of the psychological institute at the University of Moscow under the direction of G. I. Chelpanov (1862-1936)

—— Third Congress of International Psychoanalytic Association, Weimar, Germany; Jung's reelection as president

—— Carl Jung's lecture series at Fordham University Medical School

—— Publication of Eugen Bleuler's *Dementia Praecox or the Group of Schizophrenias*

—— Publication of *Elements of Physiological Psychology* by G. T. Ladd and R. S. Woodworth

1912 Development of the I.Q. (intelligence quotient) by William Stern (1871–1938) and the publication of his *The Psychological Methods of Testing Intelligence*

—— H. H. Goddard's argument of mental deficiency as hereditary in *The Kallikak Family: A Study in the Heredity of Feeble-Mindedness*

—— Development of the Montessori system by Maria Montessori (1870–1952) author of *The Montessori Method*, founder of the House of Children, and Italy's first female recipient of the M.D. degree

—— The birth of "gestalt psychology" and the discovery of the "phi phenomenon" by Max Wertheimer (1880–1943) of the University of Frankfort

—— Publication of the first Japanese treatise on personality: *Prosopology: The Study of Personality* by T. Watanabe

—— The introduction of psychoanalysis into Japanese psychological thought

—— Development of the Coué method of autosuggestion in *La maîtrise de soi-même par l'autosuggestion consciente* by Émile Coué (1857–1926)

—— First English work on psychoanalysis, *Papers on Psychoanalysis*, by Ernest Jones (1879–1958)

—— Publication of Bernard Hart's (b. (1879) *The Psychology of Insanity*

—— Establishment of a psychoeducational clinic by J. E. Wallace Wallin (b. 1876) at the University of Pittsburgh

—— Establishment of a laboratory of educational psychology at Moray House, Edinburgh, under the direction of James Drever

—— Publication of *The Mechanistic Conception of Life* by Jacques Loeb (1858–1924), a leader in the mechanistic movement

—— Establishment of the American Association for the Study of Feeble-mindedness, together with its organ, *The Journal of Psychoaesthenics*

—— Organization of the National Committee for Mental Hygiene

1913 Publication of Freud's *Totem and Taboo*, treating similarities between the psychology of savages and neurotics

—— Creation of the first internships for psychologists at the Boston Psychopathic Hospital under the direction of Robert Mearns Yerkes (1876–1956)

—— Publication of John Watson's (1878–1958) "Psychology as the Behaviorist Views It," *Psychol. Rev.*, introducing behaviorism to America and the substitution of behavior for consciousness

—— Publication of J. M. Baldwin's *History of Psychology* in two small volumes

—— Founding of the English language *Psychoanalytic Review* by William Alanson White (1870–1937) and Smith Ely Jelliffe (1866–1945), founder of psychosomatic medicine of the U.S.

—— Founding of the journal, *Internationale Zeitschrift für Psychoanalyse* under Freud's organization (terminated in 1941)

—— Fourth Congress of International Psychoanalytic Association, Munich, with Jung as its president

—— Founding of the London Society of Psycho-analysts by Ernest Jones

—— Founding of the "analytical school" of psychology by Carl G. Jung, on his severance from psychoanalysis

—— Publication of Karl Jaspers' (b. 1883) *General Psychopathology*, a comprehensive treatment of the subject (7th ed., 1959)

—— Establishment by Jessie Murray of the Medico-Psychological Clinic of London, England's first psychotherapeutic clinic

—— Publication of E. L. Thorndike's *Educational Psychology*, the first complete text in the field

—— Publication of *Psychology and Industrial Efficiency* by Hugo Münsterberg, the first applied psychologist

1914 Tachistoscopic experimentation by Otto Pötzl, leading to *déjà vu* illusions and dream psychology

—— Development of "reactology" by K. H. Korniloff (1879–1957) of the University of Moscow, and director of the Institute of Experimental Psychology

—— The introduction of behaviorism into Japanese psychology by Asataro Narasaki (b. 1882) and Hiroshi Hayami (b. 1876)

—— Origin of the "psychology of structure" under the leadership of Eduard Spranger

—— Publication of C. E. Spearman's "The Theory of Two Factors," *Psychol. Rev.*

—— Publication of Edwin Bissell Holt's (1873–1945) *The Concept of Consciousness*, viewing consciousness as the organism's adjustment

—— Publication of H. H. Goddard's *Feeble-mindedness: Its Causes and Consequences*

—— A social psychological study of primitive religion, *The Threshold of Religion* by R. R. Marrett (1866–1943), coiner of the term "animatism"

—— Founding of the Boston Psychoanalytic Society with James J. Putnam as its president

—— Jung's resignation as president of the International Psychoanalytic Association, with Karl Abraham serving as interim president

1915 First exposition of Freudianism in an American book, *Freudian Wish and Its Place in Ethics*, by Edwin B. Holt, a discussion from the standpoint of neorealism

—— The birth of "totality psychology" (school of *Ganzheitspsychologie*) by Felix Krueger (1874–1948) of Leipzig

—— Development of the emergency or thalamic theory of emotions by Walter Bradford Cannon (1871–1945) in his *Bodily Changes in Pain, Hunger, Fear and Rage*

—— Development of the block design performance test by Samuel Calmin Kohs (b. 1890) as explained in his *Intelligence Measurement: Psychological and Statistical Study Based upon the Block Design Tests* (1923)

—— Development of the maze performance test by S. D. Porteus as explained in his *The Porteus Maze Test and Intelligence* (1950)

—— Establishment in England of the Society of Orthopsychics, with T. Percy Nunn (1870–1941) as its first president

1916 Appointment of America's first professor of applied psychology, Walter Dill Scott (1869–1955) of Carnegie Institute, author of *The Theory of Advertising* (1903) and *The Psychology of Advertising* (1910)

—— Founding of a psychological laboratory at the University of Calcutta by Narendra Nath Sen-Gupta, editor of the *Indian Journal of Psychology*

—— Establishment of the Child Study Institute in Japan by Yoshihide Kubo (1883–1942)

—— Establishment in Berlin of the *Institute für Arbeitspsychologie*

—— Development of the Stanford-Binet Test by Louis Madison Terman (1877–1956) as explained in his *The Measurement of Intelligence*

—— Publication of C. G. Jung's *The Psychology of the Unconscious*

—— Initial publication of the *Journal of Experimental Psychology*

1917 Establishment of the American Association of Clinical Psychologists, with Leta S. Hollingworth (b. 1886) as its first president

—— Administration of the Army Alpha tests to 2 million American soldiers, and (in 1918) the Army Beta tests to 100,000 illiterates

—— Discovery of malaria treatment of general paresis by Julius Wagner-Jauregg (1857–1940), a Viennese psychiatrist

—— Discovery of learning by insight in animals by Wolfgang Köhler (1887–1967), as explained in his *The Mentality of Apes*

—— Development of the Woodworth Personal Data Sheet for screening disturbed army recruits by Robert S. Woodworth in Personal Data Sheet

—— Publication of the Pintner-Paterson Performance Test in *A Scale of Performance Tests* by Rudolf Pintner (b: 1884) and Donald Gildersleeve Paterson (b. 1892)

—— Introduction of the *Psychoneurotic Inventory* by Woodworth and Wells

—— Publication of *General Principles of Human Reflexology* by V. M. Bechterev

—— Founding of the Russian journal, *Psychological Review*, by G. I. Chelpanov (1862–1936)

—— Publication of James Ward's (1843–1925) *Psychological Principles*, a philosophical psychology based on his classic article in the *Encyclopædia Britannica* (9th ed., 1885)

—— G. Stanley Hall's founding of the *Journal of Applied Psychology*

—— Introduction of August Hoch's "open-door policy" for treating mentally ill patients

—— Posthumous publication of *The Conduction of the Nervous Impulse* by Keith Lucas (1879–1916)

—— Founding of the journal, *Mental Hygiene*

1918 Fifth Congress of International Psychoanalytic Association, Budapest, Hungary

—— Organization (by the British) of the National Institute of Industrial Psychology

1919 Publication of *Psychology; From the Standpoint of a Behaviorist* by John Watson

—— Founding of the *Spontaneity Theatre* (*Das Stegreiftheater*) by Jacob L. Moreno (b. 1892)

—— Designing of a musical aptitude test by Carl Emil Seashore (b. 1866) of the University of Iowa, author of *The Psychology of Musical Talent*

—— Founding of the International Association of Applied Psychology under the leadership of Edouard Claparede (b. 1873), its first president

—— Establishment of the first U.S. consulting firm in the area of industrial psychology, The Scott Company, by Walter Dill Scott

—— Founding of the *Japanese Journal of Psychology* by Genji Kuroda (b. 1886)

—— Establishment of the University of Rome Clinic for nervous and mental diseases

—— Establishment of England's first chair of psychology, at the University of Manchester

1920 Establishment of the Institute of Psychology at the University of Paris

—— Introduction of Gestalt psychology into Japanese thought

—— Founding in Geneva of the International Congress of Psychotechnology

—— Establishment of the Don Neuropsychiatric Clinic (renamed Soloviev Hospital) in the Soviet Union

—— First International Conference on Psychology as Applied to Vocational Guidance, under the organization of Edouard Claparede

—— Founding of the English language *International Journal of Psycho-Analysis* by Ernest Jones in London

—— Sixth Congress of International Psychoanalytic Association, The Hague, Holland

—— Development of the first Interest Inventory by Bruce V. Moore (b. 1891) of Carnegie Institute

—— Publication of C. G. Jung's *Psychological Types*, treating introversion and extraversion

—— Publication of S. Freud's *Beyond the Pleasure Principle*, introducing his doctrine of "thanatos" or death instinct and "eros" or life (sex) instinct

—— Publication of W. McDougall's *Group Psychology*

—— Publication of W. Köhler's *Physical Gestalten in Rest and in Stationary State*

—— Publication of Walther Moede's (b. 1888) *Experimentelle Massenpsychologie*, studies in experimental group psychology

—— Establishment of a certification committee of the A.P.A.

—— Publication of Henry Head's (1861–1940) *Studies in Neurology*, containing his doctrine of "the schema" in reference to cortical functions

—— Development of experimental catalepsy or catatonia through the use of bulbocapnine by Herman de Jong, in his *Experimental Catatonia and Its Implications for Human Pathology*

1921 Development by the Swiss, Hermann Rorschach (1884–1922), of the "ink blot" test, a projective technique for diagnosing personality disorders as recorded in his *Psychodiagnostik*

—— Theory regarding constitutional types and characterology by Ernst Kretschmer (1888–1964) in his *Physique and Character*

—— Publication of the U.S. Army "Alpha and Beta Tests" under the supervision of Robert Mearns Yerkes (1876–1956)

in the *Memoirs of the National Academy of Sciences*

—— Founding of the *Psychologische Forschung* by the Gestalt psychologists: Wertheimer, Köhler, Koffka, Goldstein, and Hans Gruhle

—— Establishment of the Psychological Corporation by J. McK. Cattell in New York

—— Publication of the *Autonomic Nervous System* by J. N. Langley

—— Publication of G. S. Brett's *A History of Psychology*

—— Founding in England of the National Institute of Industrial Psychology (N.I.I.P.) with the following organs: *Journal of the N.I.I.P.* (from 1922 to 1931); *The Human Factor* (from 1932 to 1937); and *Occupational Psychology* since 1938

—— Establishment of the New York State Association of Consulting Psychologists, with David Mitchell as its first president

—— John Augustus Larson's (b. 1892) devising of a "lie detector," followed a few years later by Leonarde Keeler's (b. 1903), *Lying and Its Detection*, authored by Larson

1922 Founding of the *Chinese Journal of Psychology*, the organ of the Chinese Psychological Society

—— Organization of the Indian Psychoanalytic Society

—— Publication of G. Stanley Hall's *Senescence*, the world's first geriatric psychology

—— Utilization of "prolonged narcosis" (sleep therapy) in treating schizophrenics by Jacob Klaesi of Zürich's Burgholzli Hospital

—— Publication of *Mentalité primitive* by Lucien Levy-Bruhl (1857–1938), a French social psychologist

—— Institution of a postgraduate diploma in psychology (industrial) at the University of London

—— Seventh Congress of International Psychoanalytic Association, Berlin; Ernest Jones, presiding

—— Didactic analysis required of those becoming psychoanalysts in New York

—— Establishment of the Laboratory of Industrial Psychology, Moscow

—— Publication of an early or first book on *The Psychology of Women* by Hiroshi Chiwa (b. 1891) of Tokyo Imperial University

—— The renaming of the *Journal of Abnormal Psychology* to the *Journal of Abnormal and Social Psychology*

—— Publication by Arthur Sinton Otis (b. 1886) of the *Otis-Self-Administering Tests of Mental Ability*, forms A and B, a verbal group test

1923 Pavlov's discovery of "experimental neuroses," as discussed in *Relation between Excitation and Inhibition and Their Delimitations; Experimental Neuroses in Dogs*, and in 1931 in *Experimental Neuroses*

—— Publication of *The Language and Thought of the Child* by Jean Piaget (b. 1896), professor of experimental psychology and director of the psychological laboratory at the University of Geneva

—— L. L. Thurstone's designing of a vocational test for engineers, "Intelligence Tests for Engineering Students," *Eng. Educ.*

—— Publication of C. Lloyd Morgan's *Emergent Evolution*, a term coined by G. H. Lewes

—— Publication of Robert Henry Thouless' (b. 1894) *Introduction to the Psychology of Religion*, the first work by a Britisher

—— Publication of Freud's *The Ego and the Id*, containing a discussion of his structure of the personality: id, ego, and superego

—— Development of the Graphic Rating Scale by Max Freyd (b. 1896); "The Graphic Rating Scale," *J. Educ. Psychol.*

—— Publication of Frederic Charles Bartlett's (b. 1886) *Psychology and Primitive Culture*, theorizing the knowledge of primitive culture as the best way of understanding contemporary social psychology

—— Publication of James Arthur Hadfield's *Psychology and Morals*, an early study linking the moral life and neurosis

—— Seventh International Congress of Psychology, Oxford; C. S. Myers, president

1923–1924 Publication of *Nouveau traité de psychologie* edited by Georges Dumas (1866–1946), cofounder of the *Journal de Psychologie*

1924 Publication of Otto Rank's (1884–1939) *The Trauma of Birth* theorizing an unconscious significance of the birth trauma

—— Discovery of the "stretch reflex" by C. Sherrington

—— Analysis of personality through finger-painting initiated by R. F. Shaw in *Finger Painting*

—— Hans Berger's recording of electrical potentials in the brain (forerunner of electroencephalography), and the discovery of Berger rhythms; "Uber das Elektrenkephalogramm des Menschen," *Arch. Psychiat.* (1929)

—— Eighth Congress of International Psychoanalytic Association, Salzburg, Austria; Ernest Jones, presiding

—— Establishment of a psychology department at Mysore University, India

—— Appointment of a lecturer (not a chair) of psychology at St. Andrews University

—— Publication of A. Adler's *Practice and Theory of Individual Psychology*, containing the fundamental tenets of the "individual school of psychology"

—— Publication of *The Psychology of Religion* by W. B. Selbie of Oxford

—— Publication of Jean Piaget's *Judgment and Reasoning in the Child*, citing the child's thought as egocentric, less deductive than adults, and deficient in causal and logical relations

—— Publication of Floyd H. Allport's (b. 1890) *Social Psychology*

1925 Initial publication of a multivolume work by L. M. Terman, *Genetic Studies of Genius*

—— The founding of a dialectical materialistic psychology by Konstantin N. Kornilov (1879–1957) Director of the Institute of Experimental Psychology, Moscow

—— Introduction of the Rorschach Ink Blot Test into Japan by Y. Uchida

—— Development of the "z" statistic and the "analysis of variance" method by the Cambridge mathematician, R. A. Fisher (1890–1962) in *Methods for Research Workers*

—— Publication of the CAVD test by E. L. Thorndike in *I.E.R. Intelligence Scale CAVD;* and in *The Measurement of Intelligence* (1926)

—— Founding of the *Genetic Psychology Monographs*

—— Ninth Congress of International Psychoanalytic Association, Bad Homburg, Germany; Karl Abraham, presiding

—— Publication of August Aichorn's (b. 1878) *Wayward Youth*, an early application of psychoanalysis to juvenile deliquency

—— The study of handwriting as a psychiatric diagnostic technique in Robert Saudek's *The Psychology of Handwriting*

—— A psychological study of the causes of crime in Great Britain by Cyril L. Burt (b. 1883) in *The Young Delinquent*

1926 Theory of vigilance (the manner in which lower neural levels are activated by higher ones) by Henry Head (1861–1940), author of *Aphasia and Kindred Disorders of Speech*

—— Introduction into Japan of William Stern's "personalistic psychology"; and the undertaking of original research in Gestalt psychology by Kanae Sakuma (b. 1888) of Kyushu Imperial University and Usao Onoshima (b. 1894) of Tokyo Imperial University

—— Founding of the *Japanese Journal of Educational Psychology* and the *Indian Journal of Psychology*

—— Founding of the *Indian Psychological Association*

—— Eighth International Congress of Psychology, Groningen; Gergardus Heymans, president

—— Publication of Florence Laura Goodenough's (b. 1886) "draw-a-man test," discussed in *Measurement of Intelligence by Drawings*

—— Publication of Bronislaw Kasper Malinowski's (1884–1942) *Sex and Repression in Savage Society*, ideas obtained from an expedition to New Guinea

—— Publication of Jean Piaget's *The Child's Conception of the World*, treating the child's problem of distinguishing between the objective and subjective

world as well as his difficulty in coping with the notions of cause and law

1927 Discovery of insulin hypoglycemic shock treatment for schizophrenics by Manfred Sakel (1900–1957), a Viennese who migrated to the United States in 1938

—— Development of the law of comparative judgment by L. L. Thurstone in "A Law of Comparative Judgment," *Psych. Rev.*

—— Development in Japan of the Uchida-Kraepelin Psychodiagnostic Test, a personality test

—— Publication of Bluma Wulformna Zeigarnik's (b. 1900) "On Finished and Unfinished Tasks," *Psychol. Forsch.*

—— Publication of Martin Heidegger's (b. 1889) *Being and Time*, containing the basis of existential psychology and "dasein analysis"

—— Establishment of the Japanese Psychological Association, with its two organs: *Japanese Journal of Psychology* and *Japanese Psychological Research*

—— Founding of the Harvard Psychological Clinic by Morton Prince (1854–1929)

—— Establishment of the International Association of Applied Psychology

—— Founding of a psychobiological laboratory for child study by Henri Wallon (1879–1962)

—— Founding of the journals: *Psychological Abstracts* and the *Journal of General Psychology*

—— Tenth Congress of International Psychoanalytic Association, Innsbruck, Austria

—— Publication of S. Freud's *Inhibition, Symptom, and Anxiety*, a presentation of his latest theory on anxiety

—— Publication of *Textbook of Psychology from the Standpoint of Dialectical Materialism* by N. Kornilov, first of its kind

—— Publication of C. E. Spearman's *The Abilities of Man: Their Nature and Measurement*

—— Publication of Wilhelm Reich's *The Function of the Orgasm: Sex-Economic Problems of Biological Energy*, theorizing that psychic health is contingent upon orgastic potency, a form of Freudianism

1928 Founding of the journal, *Psychology*, the first genuinely psychological journal of the Soviets (under the editorship of K. N. Kornilov)

—— Introduction of metrazol shock treatment for schizophrenia by Lazlo Joseph Meduna (1896–1964)

—— Establishment of Psi Chi, an honor society in psychology

—— Discovery of mescaline psychosis (pseudoschizophrenia) through mescaline intoxication by Heinrich Klüver, recorded in his *Mescal*

—— Development of Zen psychotherapy and theory of neurosis by S. Morita

—— The use of "laughing gas" (nitrous oxide) as a treatment of mental illness as reported by J. Zador in "Tausch in seiner Bedeutung für Psychiatrie und Neurologie," *Arch. Psychiat.*

1929 Development of a system of psychotherapy termed "fate analysis" by Lipot Szondi

—— Founding of the Impromptu Theatre by Jacob L. Moreno

—— Discovery of carbon dioxide psychotherapy by A. S. Loevenhart (and others), "Cerebral Stimulation," *J. Amer. Med. Ass.*

—— Report on the research of EEG (electroencephalography) by Hans Berger, "Uber das Elektrenkephalogramm des Menschen," *Arch. Psychiat.*

—— Publication of Carl Murchison's (ed.) *The Psychological Register*, an international listing with bibliographical and biographical data covering over 27 nations (first work of its kind)

—— Publication of "Phenomenology" (including phenomenological psychology) in the 14th edition of the *Encyclopædia Britannica* by Edmund Husserl (1859–1938), the founder of the phenomenological movement and its journal, *Jahrbuch für Philosophie und phänomenologische Forschung* (initial publication in 1913)

—— Founding of the journals: *Die psychoanalytische Bewegung*, under the editorship of A. J. Storfer (terminating publication in 1933); and the *Journal of Social Psychology*

—— Publication of Otto Rank's *Technik der Psychoanalyse*, a presentation of Rank-ian "will psychotherapy," translated into English as *Will Therapy*

—— Ninth International Congress of Psychology, New Haven, Conn., J. McK. Cattell, president; with Pavlov in attendance

—— Eleventh Congress of International Psychoanalytic Association, Oxford, England; Max Eitington presiding

—— Publication of Edwin Garrigues Boring's (b. 1886) *A History of Experimental Psychology*, first and only text of its kind

—— Publication of Karl Spencer Lashley's (1890–1958) *Brain Mechanisms and Intelligence: A Quantitative Study of Injuries to the Brain*

—— Publication of B. K. Malinowski's *The Sexual Life of Savages in N.W. Melanesia*

—— Publication of Bruno Lasker's *Race Attitudes in Children*, first of the studies of childhood race attitudes

1930 Establishment of an official classification of 21 psychic illnesses by the German Psychiatric Association; adoption of the list by the Austrians in 1940

—— First of the volumes on *A History of Psychology in Autobiography* by Carl Murchison (ed.)

—— First International Congress for Mental Hygiene, Washington, D.C.

—— Theory of equipotentiality of cerebral action by Karl S. Lashley (1890–1958)

—— Development of the Babcock Test of Mental Deterioration by Harriet Babcock, "An Experiment in the Measurement of Mental Deterioration," *Arch. Psychol.* (revisions in 1933 and 1940)

—— Publication by Donald Gildersleeve Paterson (b. 1892), and others of, "The Minnesota Mechanical Ability Test," a battery of tests for mechanical ability

—— Publication of David Katz's (1884–1953) *Der Aufbau der Farbwelt*, a phenomenological study of color by a professor in Sweden

—— Founding of the journals *Child Development* and the Japanese psychological journal, *Acta Psychologica Keijo*

—— Founding (in Nanking) of the Chinese Association of Psychological Testing

1931 Establishment of the New York

Psychoanalytic Institute under the direction of Sandor Rado

—— Founding of the Japanese Society of Applied Psychology by T. Wantanabe, K. Tanaka, and Y. Awaji

—— Establishment of China's first child study laboratory at Fu Jen University, Peiping

—— Publication of H. E. Burtt's *Legal Psychology*, an early interest in the psychology of law

—— Development in Japan of the Awaji-Okabe introversion-extraversion inventory

—— Development of psychopharmacology with the publication of Louis Lewin's *Phantastica: Narcotic and Stimulating Drugs: Their Use and Abuse*

—— Development of the Allport-Vernon scale for measuring values in *A Study of Values*

—— Development of the Henmon-Nelson Self-Scoring Tests, a verbal group test

—— Founding of the *Japanese Journal of Experimental Psychology*

—— Publication of *A Handbook of Child Psychology* by C. Murchison

—— Publication of *Contemporary Schools of Psychology* by R. S. Woodworth

1932 Coining of the term "homeostasis" for the self-regulation of the internal environment by Walter B. Cannon

—— Development of "experimental neurosis" in animals, conducted by W. Horsley Gantt of Johns Hopkins, as recorded in *Experimental Basis for Neurotic Behavior* (1944)

—— Establishment at Amsterdam University of the first professorship of psychology with the appointment of Geza Revesz (1878–1955), cofounder of the journal *Acta Psychologia*

—— Establishment of the *Psychoanalytic Quarterly*, with Dorian Feigenbaum as its editor

—— Tenth International Congress of Psychology, Copenhagen; Harold Höffding, president (E. Rubin presiding owing to Höffding's death)

—— Twelfth Congress of International Psychoanalytic Association, Wiesbaden, Germany; Max Eitington presiding

—— Publication of Edward Chase Tolman's

(1886–1961) *Purposive Behavior in Animals and Men*, containing the development of his purposive behaviorism

—— Publication of S. Zuchermann's *The Social Life of Monkeys and Apes*, a study at the London Zoo

1933 Development of a "social distance scale" for the study of racial prejudice by Emory S. Bogardus

—— Adoption by the American Psychiatric Association of a classification of mental illness comprising 22 major groups and 36 minor ones

—— Establishment of the Institute of Human Relations at Yale University

—— Establishment of the Psychological Corporation of Psychological Barometers, among the first for the study of public opinion

—— Development of the Arthur Point Scale of Performance, a performance test

—— Development of the method of "thinking aloud" or *reflexion parlée* for the study of thought processes, by the functionalist Edouard Claparede (1873–1940) of Switzerland

—— First elaborate experimental treatment of hypnosis by Clark L. Hull (1884–1952) in *Hypnosis and Suggestibility*

—— Publication of Wilhelm Reich's *Character Analysis*, psychotherapy through the removal of "character resistances" and the alteration of character attitude

—— Founding of the British journal, *The Psychologist;* and the Japanese journal, *Tokohu Psychologica Folia*

—— Founding of the British Union of Practical Psychologists

—— Publication of C. G. Jung's *Modern Man in Search of a Soul*, psychology of religion from the standpoint of analytical psychology

—— Publication of *One Hundred Years of Psychology*, a treatment of predominantly European psychology by John Carl Flugel (1884–1955) of University College, London

—— Publication of *The Brain and Its Mechanisms* by C. Sherrington, president of the Royal Society

1934 Use of the drug "amphetamine sulphate" (benzedrine) in psychiatry as a stimulant narcolepsy and an anti-depressant for neurotics and psychotics

—— Development of the Cornell-Coxe Ability Scale, a performance test

—— Organization of the American Institute of Public Opinion

—— Publication of Jacob L. Moreno's *Who Shall Survive? A New Approach to the Problem of Human Relations*, containing his theory of group psycho-therapy, and his doctrine of spontan-eity-creiveity

—— Publication of Arnold Gesell's (1880–1961) *Atlas of Infant Behavior*

—— Publication of *Dictionary of Psychology* under the editorship of Howard C. Warren

—— Publication of the *Handbook of General Experimental Psychology*, Carl Murchison (ed.)

—— Publication of J. B. Rhine's *Extra-Sensory Perception*, an experimental investigation of the subject

—— Establishment of the University of London Council for Psychical Investigation by Harry Price

—— Thirteenth Congress of International Psychoanalytic Association, Lucerne, Switzerland; Ernest Jones presiding

1935 Suspension of all journals in the field of psychology by Soviet Russia

—— Introduction of lobotomy as a control of emotional behavior by John F. Fulton and Carlyle F. Jacobson

—— Development of the Thematic Apperception Test (TAT), a test for the assessment of personality by Christiana Morgan (1893–1967) and Henry A. Murray (b. 1893), "A Method for Investigating Fantasies," *Arch. Neurol. Psychiat.*

—— Publication of Manfred Sakel's *A New Treatment Method in Schizophrenia*, a discussion of his insulin shock treatment in schizophrenia

—— Formation of the Psychometric Society, with L. L. Thurstone as its president

—— Founding of the *Journal of Psychology*

—— Publication of *Sex and Temperament in Three Primitive Societies* by Margaret Mead (b. 1901)

—— Publication of Kurt Lewin's (1890–1947) *A Dynamic Theory of Personality*,

a presentation of his field theory of personality

—— Publication of L. L. Thurstone's *The Vectors of Mind*

—— Publication of Kurt Koffka's (1886–1941) *Principles of Gestalt Psychology*, a systematic survey of the experimental investigations of the members of the Gestalt school

—— Publication of Anna Freud's (b. 1895) *Ego and the Mechanisms of Defence*, a description of the ego's defense mechanisms

1936 Discovery of "bilateral prefrontal leucotomy" by Egas Moniz (1874–1955), a Portuguese psychiatrist; recorded in *Tentatives operatoires dans le traitement des certaines psychoses*

—— Establishment of psychology as an independent department at Harvard University

—— Founding of the "therapeutic theatre" by Jacob L. Moreno

—— Founding of a psychological laboratory at Oxford University by W. Brown

—— Founding of three public opinion polls: Gallup, Roper, and Crossley

—— Formation of the Society for the Psychological Study of Social Issues

—— Establishment of the Institute for the Study of Animal Behaviour (in England) through the efforts of Julian Huxley and F. B. Kirkman

—— Founding of the journal, *Psychometrika*

—— Development of the Progressive Matrices Test by J. C. Raven as explained in "A New Series of Perceptual Tests," *B. J. med. Psychol.;* and in 1838, *Progressive Matrices*

—— Publication of Kurt Lewin's *Principles of Topological Psychology*, containing his topological theory of personality

—— Fourteenth Congress of International Psychoanalytical Association, Marienbad, Czechoslovakia; Ernest Jones, presiding

1937 Development of electroshock therapy (EST or ECT) in treating mental illness by Ugo Cerletti and Lucio Bini of Rome

—— Development of "transorbital lobotomy," a form of psychosurgery introduced by A. M. Fiamberti, an Italian

—— Discovery of "sodium diphenyl hydantoinate" as an anticonvulsant drug in the control of epileptic seizures (*grand mal*) by T. J. Putnam and H. H. Merritt, "Experimental Determination of the Anticonvulsant Properties of Some Phenyl Derivatives," *Science*

—— Revision of the Stanford-Binet, termed the Terman-Merrill Revision in *Measuring Intelligence: A Guide to the Administration of the New Revised Stanford-Binet Tests of Intelligence*

—— Founding of the journals: *Psychological Record; Journal of Consulting Psychology*, the organ of the American Association of Applied Psychology; *Sociometry: A Journal of Interpersonal Relations*, founded by L. Moreno; and *Psychology* (Cheshire, England)

—— Establishment of the following associations: Chinese Psychological Association; Chinese Association for Mental Hygiene; Institute for Propaganda Analysis; and the American Association for Applied Psychology

—— Eleventh International Congress of Psychology, Paris: Henri Pieron, President; Pierre Janet, Honorary President

—— Publication of Gordon W. Allport's *Personality: A Psychological Interpretation*, a presentation of his personalistic or trait approach to personality

—— Publication of Karen Horney's (1885–1952) *The Neurotic Personality of Our Time*, a presentation of her cultural theory of neurosis

—— Publication of H. H. Newman, F. N. Feeman, and K. J. Holzinger's *Twins: A Study of Heredity and Environment*, depicting striking resemblances in intelligence between identical twins

—— Publication of Charles Spearman's two-volume *Psychology down the Ages*

1938 Development of the Bender-Gestalt Test (perceptual-motor test) by Lauretta Bender in "A Visual Motor Gestalt Test and Its Clinical Use"

—— Publication of B. F. Skinner's *The Behavior of Organisms*, an account of "operant conditioning"

—— Introduction of the concept of "overinclusive thinking" in schizophrenics by N. Cameron (*Psychol. Monogr.* and *Amer. J. Psychol.*)

—— Publication of Henry A. Murray's *Explorations of Personality*, a presentation of his personology or need press theory of personality

—— Development of cybernetics by Norbert Wiener

—— Fifteenth Congress of International Psychoanalytic Association, Paris; Ernest Jones presiding

—— Publication of the first edition of *Mental Measurements Year Book* under the editorship of O. K. Buros

—— Publication of R. S. Woodworth's *Experimental Psychology*, long a standard in its field (revised in 1954 with Harold Schlosberg)

1939 Introduction of the Wechsler-Bellevue Adult Intelligence Scale (WAIS) in *The Measurement of Adult Intelligence* by David Wechsler (b. 1896)

—— Publication of Kurt Goldstein's (1878–1965) *The Organism*, an account of his organismic theory of personality

—— Publication of Karen Horney's *New Ways in Psychoanalysis*, a presentation of her character analysis, environmentalism in neurosis, and self-realization as the psychotherapeutic goal

—— Development in France by R. Desoille of the "directed daydream," a psychotherapeutic technic

—— Publication of Kurt Kolle's *Psychiatry*, a leading German text

1940 Experimental mescaline psychosis reported by G. T. Stockings in "A Clinical Study of the Mescaline Psychosis with Special Reference to the Mechanism of the Genesis of Schizophrenia and Other Psychotic States," *J. ment. Sci.*

—— The use of "conditioned aversion" through the use of nauseants as a psychotherapeutic technique in treating alcoholism as reported by W. L. Voegthlin in "Treatment of Alcoholism by Establishing a Conditioned Reflex," *Amer. J. med. Sci.*

—— Development of a sentence completion test for assessing personality by Amanda Rohde and Gertrude Hildreth as contained in the former's *The Sentence Completion Method*

—— Development of the Shipley-Hartford scale for deriving a "conceptual quotient (CQ) by Walter C. Shipley and C. C. A. Burlingame in "A Convenient Self-Administering Scale for Measuring Intellectual Impairment in Psychotics," *J. Psychol.*

—— Publication of William H. Sheldon's (b. 1899) *The Varieties of Human Physique*, the basis of his "constitution psychology"

—— Introduction of the "interpersonal theory of psychiatry" by Harry Stack Sullivan (1892–1949) in *Conceptions of Modern Psychiatry (Psychiat.)*

—— Founding of the National Institute of Psychology in Rome by Ferruccio Banissoni (1888–1952)

—— Founding of the Psychodramatic Institute in New York by J. L. Moreno

—— Publication of *Factors of the Mind* by Cyril Burt (b. 1883), editor of the *British Journal of Psychology* and author of "Experimental Tests of General Intelligence," *B. J. Psychol.* (1909)

—— Publication of Kurt Goldstein's *Human Nature in the Light of Psychopathology*, an account of his holistic or Gestalt theory of personality

1941 Development of a diagnostic test for assessing organicity by Kurt Goldstein and Martin Scheerer in "Abstract and Concrete Behavior: An Experimental Study with Special Tests," *Psychol. Monogr.*

—— First institute for psychoanalytic training by a recognized medical school, the New York Medical College

—— Publication of Andras Angyal's (1902–1960) *Foundations for a Science of Personality*, an account of his holistic theory of personality

—— Publication of Erich Fromm's (b. 1900) *Escape from Freedom*, an account of "humanistic psychoanalysis" applied to individuals and society

1942 Development of prefrontal lobotomy by Walter Freeman (b. 1895) and James W. Watts (b. 1904) of George Washington University Hospital, authors of *Psychosurgery: Intelligence, Emotion, and Social Behavior following Prefrontal Lobotomy for Mental Disorders*

—— Development of the Gardner behavior chart for rating emotional behavior by

P. H. Wilcox in "The Gardner Behavior Chart," *Amer. J. Psychiat.*

—— Publication of William H. Sheldon's *The Varieties of Temperament*, an account of a theory of personality based on "constitutional psychology"

—— Development of "client-centered" or nondirective psychotherapy by Carl R. Rogers (b. 1902) as recorded in his *Counseling and Psychotherapy*

1943 Discovery of the hallucinogenic effects of LSD-25 (lysergic acid diethylamide) by Albert Hoffman, a Swiss chemist

—— Development of "existential psychoanalysis" by Jean-Paul Sartre (b. 1905) in *Being and Nothingness*

—— Publication of John Stephen Horsley's *Narco-Analysis*, a study of drug psychotherapy and narcotic hypnosis

—— Initial appearance of the *Minnesota Multiphase Personality Inventory: Manual* (1951)

—— Development of the Strong Vocational Interest Test by E. K. Strong in *Vocational Interests of Men and Women*

—— Publication of Samuel R. Slavson's *An Introduction to Group Therapy*, a theory of analytic group therapy

—— Publication of Clark L. Hull's (1884–1952) *Principles of Behavior*, enunciating his system of behaviorism

—— Publication of Werner Wolff's *The Expression of Personality*, a synthesis of Gestalt and psychoanalytic ideas applied to personality study

—— Initial publication of the *Japanese Annual of Animal Psychology*

1944 Establishment of the first chair of psychology at Birkbeck College, University of London (occupant of chair, C. A. Mace; b. 1894)

—— Publication of the two-volume *Personality and Behavior Disorders* under the editorship of J. McV. Hunt

—— Development of the "psychological deficit" theory of schizophrenia by J. McV. Hunt in his two-volume edited work *Personality and the Behavior Disorders*

1945 Establishment of the Department of Social Relations at Harvard University (separating clinical psychology from experimental physiological psychology)

—— Incorporation of the Association for

Applied Psychology with the American Psychological Association

—— Columbia University's establishment of a psychoanalytic institute

—— Establishment of the Research Center for Group Dynamics at the Massachusetts Institute of Technology under the supervision of Kurt Lewin

—— Development of a word association test by David Rapaport and others in *Diagnostic Psychological Testing*, a work accenting the role of experimental psychology in the clinical field

—— Initial publication of the *Journal of Clinical Psychology*, an independent journal under the editorship of its founder, F. C. Thorne

—— Publication of Maurice Merleau-Ponty's (1907–1961) *Phenomenology of Perception*, a phenomenological and existential account

1946 Introduction of "logotherapy" with the publication of Viktor E. Frankl's (b. 1905) *Doctor and the Soul* (enlarged English revision containing his doctrine of "paradoxical intention" in 1966); also *Man's Search for Meaning: An Introduction to Logotherapy* (1946)

—— Introduction of a four-year clinical program for psychologists by the Veterans Administration (with the approval of the A.P.A.)

—— Establishment of the American Board of Examiners in Professional Psychology

—— A.P.A.'s publication of the *American Psychologist*, a journal of newsworthy items and articles for the profession

—— Organization in Germany of *Berufsverband*, an association of applied psychologists

—— Publication of *Psychoanalytic Therapy* by F. Alexander and T. M. French

—— Publication of *Encyclopedia of Psychology* by Philip L. Harriman (b. 1894), (ed.)

—— Development of pioneer work in human factors psychology with the publication of Ross Armstrong McFarland's (b. 1901) *Human Factors in Air Transport Design*

—— Development of a trait theory and factor analysis of personality in *Description and Measurement of Personality* by Raymond B. Cattell (b. 1905)

1947 Oxford University's acceptance of psychology as an independent department and its establishment of a psychological laboratory and chair in psychology

—— Establishment of a department of psychology at the universities of Moscow, Kiev, Leningrad, and Tblisi

—— Introduction (in France) of "amphetamine shock" to encourage verbalization in mute schizophrenics (*Weckanalyse*) by J. Delay and P. Pichot

—— Development of a "biosocial theory of personality" by Gardner Murphy (b. 1895) in his *Personality: A Biosocial Approach to Origins and Structure*

—— Offering of a factor theory or "dimensional approach" to personality by Hans J. Eysenck (b. 1916) in *Dimensions of Personality*

—— Publication of L. L. Thurstone's *Multiple Factor Analysis: A Development and Expansion of the Vectors of the Mind*

—— Studies of civilian morale in World War II in *The Psychology of Rumor* by G. W. Allport and L. Postman

—— Publication of Italy's most complete text in psychology, *Introduction to Psychology* by Agostine Gemelli (1878–1959), cofounder (with Friedrich Kiesow, 1858–1940) of the Italian periodical, *Archives of Psychology, Neurology, and Psychiatry*

—— Publication of F. Morel's *Introduction to Neurological Psychiatry*, neurologically oriented psychiatric theories by the director of the University of Geneva Psychiatric Hospital

1948 The utilization of tetraethylthiuramdisulfide (antabuse) in "conditioned aversion psychotherapy" as reported by J. Hald, "The Sensitizing Effect of Tetraethylthiuramdisulfide (Antabuse) to Ethyl Alcohol," *Acta Pharmacol. Toxicol.*

—— Moral theory of neurosis and the "neurotic paradox" developed by O. H. Mowrer in "Learning theory and the neurotic paradox" (*Amer. J. Orthopsychiat.*)

—— Development of the House-Tree-Person test (H-T-P) by J. N. Buck in *House-Tree-Person Projective Technique*

—— First knighthood for a psychologist, Frederic Charles Bartlett (b. 1886), Cambridge University's first Professor of Psychology, and editor of the *British Journal of Psychology*

—— The utilization of hypnosis as a psychotherapeutic measure in the cure of neuroses, character disorders, and psychosomatic conditions by Lewis R. Wolberg (b. 1905) in *Medical Hypnosis*

—— Publication of *Sexual Behavior in the Human Male* by A. C. Kinsey, W. B. Pomeroy, and C. E. Martin; citing sexual practices in the American male

—— Publication of *The Commonsense Psychiatry of Dr. Adolf Meyer*, posthumously published papers of Meyer's (1866–1950) psychobiologic psychology and psychotherapy

—— Twelfth International Congress of Psychology, Edinburgh; J. Drever, President (G. Thomson presiding, owing to Drever's illness)

—— Establishment of the World Federation for Mental Health, with its organ, *World Mental Health*

—— The International Congress on Mental Health, London

1949 Introduction of the Wechsler Intelligence Scale for Children (WISC) in David Wechsler's book by the same name

—— Development of the frustration theory of animal neurosis by N. R. F. Maier

—— "Marital schism and skew" hypothesis of schizophrenia developed by R. W. and T. Lidz (*Amer. J. Psychiat.*)

—— Use of "phenylacetyl urea (phenurone) as an anticonvulsant, reported by M. Zeifert in "Phenurone in Epilepsy," *Dis. nerv. System*

—— Development of the figure drawing test by Karen Machover in *Personality Projection in the Drawing of the Human Figure*

—— Establishment of the Foundation of Ergonomics Research Society

—— Reorganization, in Taiwan, of the Chinese Association of Mental Hygiene

—— Establishment of a psychology department at National Taiwan University, through the efforts of H. Y. Su

—— Establishment in all departments of France of "open services" (psychiatric care for all voluntary patients)

—— The founding (in Germany) of the *Psychological Review* (*Psychologische Rundschau*) by Johannes Allesch (b. 1882)

—— Development of a Pavlovian form of "behavior psychotherapy" by Andrew Salter as discussed in his *Conditioned Reflex Therapy: The Direct Approach to the Reconstruction of Personality*

—— Publication of Gilbert Ryle's (b. 1900) *The Concept of Mind*, a treatise on philosophical psychology containing an introduction of the "category mistake," and a discussion of a philosophical behaviorism

—— Introduction of a neobehaviorism of a moderate type in *The Organization of Behavior: A Neuropsychological Theory* by Donald O. Hebb (b. 1904) of McGill University

—— Sixteenth Congress of International Psychoanalytic Association, Zurich; Ernest Jones, presiding

1950 Development in the early fifties of the tranquilizers (e.g., phenothiazine) for treatment of mental illness

—— Use in the 1950's of psychomimetic drugs or hallucinogens, such as, mescaline and lysergic acid diethylamide (LSD-25), in psychotherapy

—— Awarding of degrees in psychology at St. Andrews, but without a chair in the department of psychology even to the present time

—— The Ph.D. as a mandatory requirement by the VA for clinical psychologists in its employ

—— Development of the theory of "stress" as the prototype of mental illness by Hans Selye (b. 1907) as recorded in *The Physiology and Pathology of Exposure to Stress*

—— Development of brain localization and memory mechanisms by Wilder Penfield as reported in *The Cerebral Cortex of Man* (with T. Rasmussen) and in *Arch. Neurol. Psychiat.* (1952)

—— First International Congress of Psychiatry

—— The application of the learning theory to human behavior by Q. Hobart Mowrer (b. 1907) in *Learning Theory and Personality Dynamics*

—— Presentation of a learning theory of

personality and an S-R approach to psychotherapy in *Personality and Psychotherapy: An Analysis in Terms of Learning, Thinking and Culture* by John Dollard (b. 1900) and Neal E. Miller (b. 1909)

—— A factor or statistical theory of personality by Raymond B. Cattell (b. 1905) in *Personality: A Systematic, Theoretical and Factual Study*

—— An almost exhaustive account of Meyer's "psychobiologic" psychology and psychiatry in the four-volume *Collected Papers of Adolf Meyer*

—— Publication of a description of psychopathic personalities in *Clinical Psychology* by Kurt Schneider, Germany's principal formulator of ideas in clinical psychiatry

—— Development of a psychotherapeutic system synthesizing Freudian psychoanalysis and Sullivan's interpersonal theory in the *Principles of Intensive Psychotherapy* by Frieda Fromm-Reichmann

—— Founding of the British *Journal of Medical Hypnotism*

1951 Introduction of MAO-inhibitors (iproniazed and isocarboxazid) as antidepressants in treating psychotics

—— Reestablishment (in Taiwan) of the Chinese Association of Psychological Testing, accompanied by its Chinese language journal, *Psychological Testing*

—— Institution of the Psychological Research Bureau in Taiwan

—— Thirteenth International Congress of Psychology, Stockholm; D. Katz, president

—— Seventeenth Congress of International Psychoanalytic Association, Amsterdam, Holland; Leo Bartemeier, presiding

—— Founding of the Interamerican Society of Psychology

—— Founding of the International Union of Scientific Psychology, with Henri Pieron as its first president

—— Publication of Stanley Smith Stevens' (b. 1906) edited book, *Handbook of Experimental Psychology*, an appraisal of the status of experimental psychology at mid-century

—— Publication of Carl R. Rogers' *Client-Centered Therapy*, updating his nondirective psychotherapy

—— Publication of Kurt Lewin's *Field Theory in Social Science*, a collection of his papers in topological or field theory

—— Publication of *Gestalt Therapy: Excitment and Growth in the Human Personality* by Frederick Pearls, Ralph E. Hefferline, and Paul Goodman; Gestalt principles applied to psychotherapy

—— Publication of H. Schultz-Henke's *Manual of Analytic Therapy*, a system of evolutional functional analysis of a new German school of neoanalytic psychotherapy

1952 Discovery of the "general adaptation syndrome" by Hans Selye (b. 1907) as reported in *The Story of the Adaptation Syndrome*

—— Cerebral localization discoveries by Wilder Penfield of the Montreal Neurological Institute, "Memory Mechanisms," *Arch. Neurol. Psychiat.*

—— Discovery in Switzerland of the tranquilizing effect of reserpine, chrysalline alkaloid from rauwolfia (a derivative of the plant *rauwolfia serpentina*)

—— Discovery of chlorpromazine (thorazine) and its use as a tranquilizer in treating psychoses by Jean Delay (University of Paris), P. Deniker, and Harl; as recorded in J. Delay, and P. Deniker, "Le traitement des psychoses par une méthode neurolytique derivée de l'hibernotherapie (le 4560 R.P. utilisé seul en cure prolongée et continué)," *C.R. Congr. Médecins Alienistes Neurol.*

—— Development of a chemical theory of schizophrenia by H. Osmond and Smythies

—— Publication of Clark L. Hull's *A Behavior System: An Introduction to Behavior Theory concerning the Individual Organism*, containing his neobehavioristic theory

—— Publication by the Tufts College Institute of Applied Experimental Psychology of the *Handbook of Human Engineering Data*, a handbook of human factors psychology

—— Publication of Solomon Asch's (b.

1907) *Social Psychology*, study of group behavior from the standpoint of Gestalt psychology

—— Posthumous publication of Paul Federn's *Ego Psychology and the Psychoses*, a theory of "ego-psychology" psychotherapy

—— Publication of H. J. Eysenck's *The Scientific Study of Personality*, a factor theory of personality

—— Publication of *A Dictionary of Psychology*, compiled by James Drever; revised by Harvey Wallerstein (a British orientation)

—— Publication of *History of American Psychology* by Abraham A. Roback, lecturer extension courses of the Massachusetts Department of Education

—— Founding of the *Bulletin*, journal of the International Association of Applied Psychology

—— Founding of the *Japanese Journal of Educational Psychology*

1953 Illegalization of the practice of psychoanalysis by laymen in France

—— Pioneer experimental work in the psychology of meaning by Charles E. Osgood (b. 1916) in his *Method and Theory in Experimental Psychology* (1953) and *The Measurement of Meaning* (1957; with others)

—— Kinsey's report on the *Sexual Behavior of the Human Female*

—— The introduction of "largactil psychotherapy" in treating schizophrenics by J. E. Staehelin, recorded in "General Remarks on Largactil Therapy in the University of Basel Psychiatric Clinic," *Schweizer Archiv. f. Neurol. Psychiat.* (1954); and "Largactil Therapy with Schizophrenics and Other Psychotic States.; From the Largactil Symposium at the University of Basel Psychiatric Clinic on November 28, 1953," *Ibid.*, 1954

—— Development of an "experiential" theory of psychotherapy by Carl A. Whitaker and Thomas P. Malone in *The Roots of Psychotherapy*

—— Two factor-learning theories applied to personality and psychotherapy by O. Hobart Mowrer in *Psychotherapy: Theory and Research*

—— A theory of "milieu psychotherapy" offered by Maxwell Jones in *The Therapeutic Community*

—— The major tenets of the "interpersonal theory of psychology" by Harry Stack Sullivan in his posthumous work, *The Interpersonal Theory of Psychiatry*

—— Publication of B. H. Skinner's *Science and Human Behavior*, a restatement of his pioneering work, *Behavior of Organisms*

—— Development of the "process-reactive" hypothesis of schizophrenia by Robert E. Kantor, Julius M. Wallner, and C. L. Winder (*J. consult. Psychol*)

—— Development of the "Taylor manifest anxiety scale" by Janet Taylor Spence (*J. abnorm. soc. Psychol.*)

—— Publication of the first professional code of ethics for psychologists

—— Eighteenth Congress of International Psychoanalytic Association, London; Heinz Hartmann presiding

—— Founding of the journals: *Psychological Contributions* (German) (*Psychologische Beiträge*); *The British Journal of Animal Behavior; Journal of Clinical and Experimental Hypnosis;* and *The Journal of the American Psychoanalytic Association*

1954 "Focused ultrasound," an ultrasonic radiation substitute for prefrontal lobotomy as introduced by P. Lindstrom in his "Prefrontal Ultrasonic Radiation—A Substitute for Lobotomy," *Arch. neurol. Psychiat.*

—— Development of Abram Hoffer's "Adrenochrome" theory of psychoses as recorded in "Adrenalin Metabolites and Schizophrenia," *Dis. nerv. Syst.*

—— Social learning theory with a psychotherapeutic application developed by Julian B. Rotter in *Social Learning and Clinical Psychology* (later in *Clinical Psychology*, 1964)

—— Publication of Abraham H. Maslow's (b. 1908) *Motivation and Personality*, an account of his self-actualizationism or his "meta motivational" theory of personality

—— Publication of Lewis R. Wolberg's two-volume *The Technique of Psychotherapy*, a comprehensive treatment of hypnotherapy (2nd rev. ed., 1967)

—— Publication of *Psychiatry* by the Soviet psychiatrist, V. A. Gilyarovsky (1878–1959)

—— Fourteenth International Congress of Psychology, Montreal; E. A. Bott and E. C. Tolman, co-presidents

—— Founding of the Psychoanalytic Institute in Paris by the Psychoanalytic Society of Paris, under the direction of S. Nacht

—— Founding of two Japanese journals: *Tokohu Journal of Experimental Psychology;* and the *Japanese Psychological Research*

1955 Publication of Ludwig Binswanger's (1881–1966) *Ausgewählte Vortrage und Aufsatze*, containing his "dasein analysis" psychiatry (portions translated in *Being-in-the-World*, 1963)

—— Development of a "construct" theory of personality and psychotherapy entailing "constructive alternativism" in George A. Kelly's (b. 1905) *The Psychology of Personal Constructs*

—— Publication of Kurt Kolle's *The Image of Man in Psychiatry*, a study of endogenous psychoses by a leading German psychiatrist

—— A "progressive teleological regression" hypothesis of schizophrenia developed by Silvano Arieti in *Interpretation of Schizophrenia*

—— Glasgow University's establishment of a chair in psychology

—— Founding of the journals: *Problems of Psychology* (in the Soviet Union); and *International Journal of Social Psychiatry*

1956 Development of the "interference" theory and "assertion-structured" psychotherapy by E. Lakin Phillips' (b. 1915) in *Psychotherapy: A Modern Theory and Practice*, and continued in his (with Daniel N. Wiener) *Short-term Psychotherapy and Behavior Change* (1966)

—— Development of the "double-bind" hypothesis in schizophrenia by Gregory Bateson, Don D. Jackson, Jay Haley, and John Weakland (*Behav. Sci.*)

—— Formation of a section on "animal psychology" by the International Union of Biologists

—— Founding of the journals: *Contempo-*

rary Psychology, the A.P.A.'s journal for reviews of books in psychology; and the *Translation Journal of Psychology* (consisting of Soviet articles translated into Chinese)

1957 Establishment by the human factors psychologists of the Human Factors Society, with its monthly journal, *Human Factors*

—— Development of nicotinic acid treatment of psychosis by A. Hoffer and others in "Treatment of Schizophrenia with Nicotinic Acid and Nicotinamide," *J. clin. exp. Psychopath.*

—— Fifteenth International Congress of Psychology, Brussels; A. Michotte, president

—— Organization of the Society of Psychologists in the Soviet Union with A. A. Smirnov (b. 1894) as its first president

—— Founding of the journals: *Japanese Psychological Review;* and the English language journal, *Psychologia*, an international Oriental publication edited by Koji Sato of Kyoto University

—— Publication of E. J. McCormick's *Human Engineering*, marking the established position of human factors psychology

—— Publication of the first systematic critical treatment of major personality theories, *Theories of Personality* by Calvin S. Hall (b. 1909) and Gardner Lindzey (b. 1920)

—— Development of a psychology of time by Paul Fraisse (b. 1911), (director of the psychological laboratory at the Sorbonne) in his *The Psychology of Time*

—— Initial publication of the *American Psychological Association Directory*

1958 Development of "reciprocal inhibition" as a psychotherapeutic principle by Joseph Wolpe (b. 1915) in *Psychotherapy by Reciprocal Inhibition*

—— Development (at Longview State Hospital, Ohio) of a sentence completion test for psychodiagnostic purposes as recorded in *Sentence Completion D-Scale* by G. W. Kisker

—— A presentation of existential psychology and its application to psychotherapy in *Existence: A New Dimension in Psy-*

chiatry and Psychology, edited by Rollo May (b. 1909)

—— Development of a learning theory of schizophrenia by Sarnoff A. Mednick (*Psychol. Bull.*)

—— A presentation of contemporary work in Soviet psychology of education in *Thinking and Methods of Its Study* by S. L. Rubinstein (Rubinshtein)

—— Founding of the journals: *Acta Psychologica Taiwanica*, a Chinese journal with English abstracts; and the *Journal of the Experimental Analysis of Behavior*, based on a Skinner-behavioristic point of view

—— Publication of *A Comprehensive Dictionary of Psychological and Psychoanalytical Terms* by H. B. English and A. C. English

1959 Formulation of the "power law" by Stanley Smith Stevens (b. 1906) in "The Quantification of Sensation," *Daedalus*

—— Brain localization discoveries by W. Penfield and L. Roberts in *Speech and Brain-Mechanisms*

—— Development of a psychotherapy consisting of a synthesis of "progressive relaxation" with hypnosis and suggestion by J. H. Schultz in *Autogenic Training*

—— Extension of S-R concepts to conflict behavior and social learning by Neal E. Miller (*Psychology: A Study of a Science*, vol. 2, Sigmund Koch, ed.)

—— Initial publication of: (1) *International Directory of Psychologists;* (2) *Psychopharmacologia;* and *Psychology: A Study of a Science* under the editorship of Sigmund Koch (b. 1917)

—— Organization of the Psychonomic Society

—— Development of Harry F. Harlow's (b. 1905) learning set theory (LS) and error factor theory (EF)

—— Publication of Alphonse Chapanis' (b. 1917) *Research Techniques in Human Engineering*, emphasizing the established position of human factors psychology

1960 Development of "paradoxical intention" by Viktor E. Frankl, "Paradoxical Intention: A Logotherapeutic Technique," *Amer. J. Psychother.*

—— Presentation of chemical theories of psychoses by A. Hoffer and H. Osmond in *The Chemical Basis of Clinical Psychiatry*

—— Establishment of "milieu" theory or the "therapeutic community" of psychotherapy in *Community as Doctor: New Perspectives on a Therapeutic Community* by R. N. Rapoport

—— Development of an "interactional psychotherapeutic technique" by Benjamin B. Wolman (b. 1908), author of *Contemporary Theories and Systems of Psychology*

—— Development of the theory of "over-inclusive thinking" in schizophrenics by R. W. Payne (*Handbook of Abnormal Psychology*, edited by H. J. Eysenck, and *Brit. J. soc. clin. Psychol.*, 1962)

—— Third revision of the Stanford-Binet scale (called the L-M form) in *The Stanford-Binet Intelligence Scale*

—— Establishment of the International Brain Research Organization (IBRO), affiliate of the United Nations

—— First Congress of the International Ergonomics Association

—— Sixteenth Congress of Psychology, Bonn; W. Metzger, President; Karl Bühler (b. 1879), honorary president

—— Founding of the journals: *Japanese Annals of Social Psychology; Japanese Journal of Educational and Social Psychology; Journal of Child Psychology and Psychiatry;* and the *Journal of Existential Psychiatry* (renamed *Journal of Existentialism*)

—— Institution of a department of psychology at the University of Indonesia at Jakarta

1961 Development of a form of group therapy through self-knowledge by Eric Berne in *Transactional Analysis in Psychotherapy: A Systematic Individual and Social Psychiatry*

—— Development of a Zen Buddhistic form of psychotherapy by Alan W. Watts in *Psychotherapy East and West*

—— Development of a "repression-sensitization" scale by Donn Byrne (*J. Personality*)

—— Study of the psychology of law in *Legal*

and Criminal Psychology, H. Toch (ed.)

—— Compilation of seven main divisions of mental illness by the American Medical Association in the *Standard Nomenclature of Diseases and Operations* (5th ed.)

—— Publication of H. J. Eysenck's *Handbook of Abnormal Psychology*

—— Founding of the journals: *Review of Existential Psychology and Psychiatry; Journal of Psychiatric Research; Journal of Humanistic Psychology*

—— Founding of the American Association for Humanistic Psychology

1962 Development of a theory of "rational psychotherapy" by Albert Ellis in *Reason and Emotion in Psychotherapy*

—— Development of niacin psychotherapy by Abram Hoffer in *Niacin Therapy in Psychiatry*

—— Establishment of the Psychological Association of the Philippines with S. Padilla as its first president

—— Founding of the journals: *British Journal of Social and Clinical Psychology; Journal of Verbal Learning and Verbal Behavior; Behavior Research and Therapy* (edited by H. J. Eysenck)

—— Development of an "interference" (segmental set) theory of schizophrenia by David Shakow (*Arch. gen Psychiat.*)

1963 Organization of a national psychological association in Taiwan

—— Publication of *Human Brain and Psychological Processes* by Alexander R. Luria (b. 1902), professor of psychology, State Institute of Psychology, Moscow

—— Seventeenth Congress of Psychology, Washington, D.C.; E. G. Boring, president

1964 The story of the development of British psychology in *A Short History of British Psychology* by L. S. Hearn-

shaw, past president of the British Psychological Society

—— Founding of *The Existential Analyst*

1965 Severing of the *Journal of Abnormal and Social Psychology* into (1) the *Journal of Abnormal Psychology* and (2) the *Journal of Personality and Social Psychology*

—— Publication of the *Handbook of Clinical Psychology* under the editorship of Benjamin Wolman

—— Publication of Raymond B. Cattell's *The Scientific Analysis of Personality*, a multivariate approach to personality, utilizing factor theory

1966 Eighteenth International Congress of Psychology, Moscow; A. N. Lenotiev, president

—— Publication of the *Handbook of Multivariate Experimental Psychology* under the editorship of Raymond B. Cattell

—— Publication of the third volume of the *American Handbook of Psychiatry* under the editorship of Silvano Arieti (appearance of volume one in 1959)

—— Publication of a psychopathology text from an experimentalist's orientation by Brendan A. Maher (*Principles of Psychopathology: An Experimental Approach*)

—— Publication of *History of Psychology: An Overview* by Henryk Misiak (b. 1911) and Virginia S. Sexton (b. 1916)

1967 Publication of Viktor E. Frankl's *Psychotherapy and Existentialism*, containing the later developments of "logotherapy" and the psychology of will-to-meaning

—— Initial publication of *Psychology Today*, the first magazine designed for intelligent laymen

—— Development of the theory of "existential neurosis" by Salvatore R. Maddi (*J. abnorm. soc. Psychol.*)

Bibliography of Works in English Relating to the History of Psychology

Ackerknecht, E. H., *A short history of psychiatry*. New York: Hafner, 1959.

Akhilananda, S., *Hindu psychology*. New York: Harper, 1946.

Alexander, F. G., and Selesnick, S. T., *Psychoanalytic pioneers*. New York: Basic, 1965.

Alexander, F. G., and Selesnick, S. T., *The history of psychiatry; an evaluation of psychiatric thought and practice from prehistoric times to the present*. New York: Harper, 1966.

Altschule, M. D., and Hegedus, E. R., *Roots of modern psychiatry*. (2nd rev.) New York: Grune and Stratton, 1965.

Anderson, O., *Studies in the prehistory of psychoanalysis*. Boston: Universitesforlaget, 1962.

Atkinson, W. J., Walker, A. E., and Green, E. G., (eds.), *A history of neurological surgery*. Baltimore: Williams, 1951.

Baldwin, J. M., *History of psychology*. New York: G. P. Putnam, 1913. 2 vols.

Bamborough, John Bernard, *The little world of man*. Longmans, Green, 1952.

Bauer, R. A., *A new man in Soviet psychology*. Cambridge, Mass.: Harvard University Press, 1952.

Bauer, R. A. (ed.), *Some views on Soviet psychology*. Washington, D.C.: American Psychological Assoc., 1962.

Beare, J. I., *Greek theories of elementary cognition from Alcmaeon to Aristotle*. Oxford: Clarendon, 1906.

Bellak, Leopold (ed.), *Contemporary European psychiatry*. New York: Grove Press, 1961.

Blakey, Robert, *History of the philosophy of mind: embracing the opinion of all writers on mental science from the earliest period to the present time*. London: Longman, Brown, Green, and Longmans, 1850.

Boring, E. G., *Sensation and perception in the history of experimental psychology*. New York: Appleton-Century-Crofts, 1942.

Boring, E. G., *A history of experimental psychology*. 2nd ed. New York: Appleton-Century-Crofts, 1950.

Boring, E. G., *History, psychology, and science: selected papers*. (Edited by R. I. Watson and D. T. Campbell) New York: Wiley, 1963.

Boring, E. G., and Annin, E. L., (eds.), *Harvard list of books in psychology*. 3rd ed. Cambridge, Mass.: Harvard University Press, 1964.

Brain, W. R., (ed.), *Recent advances in neurology and neuropsychiatry*. 7th ed. Boston: Little, Brown, 1962.

Brennan, R. E., *History of psychology from the standpoint of a Thomist*. New York: Macmillan, 1945.

Brett, G. S., *A history of psychology*. London: G. Allen & Co., 1912–1921. 3 vols.

Brett, G. S., *Psychology, ancient and modern*. New York: Longmans, Green, 1928.

Brett, G. S., *A history of psychology*. (Edited and abridged by R. S. Peters) London: Allen & Unwin, 1953. 2nd rev. ed. Cambridge, Mass.: M.I.T. Press, 1965.

Bromberg, W., *Man above humanity: a history of psychological therapy and psychoanalysis*. New York: Lippincott, 1954. Revision of *Mind of man*. New York: Harper, 1937.

Brooks, C. McC., and Cranefield, P. F., *The historical development of physiological thought*. New York: Hafner, 1959.

Cattell, J. McK., *Psychology in America*. New York: Science, 1929.

Chaplin, J., and Krawiec, T. S., *Systems and theories in psychology*. New York: Holt, Rinehart & Winston, 1960.

Clark, K. E., *America's psychologists: a survey of a growing profession*. Washington, D.C.: American Psychological Assoc., 1957.

Copleston, F., *A history of philosophy*. Westminister, Md.: Newman Press, 1946.

Crafts, L. W., *Recent experiments in psychology*. New York: McGraw Hill, 1938.

Dennis, W., *Readings in the history of psychology*. New York: Appleton-Century-Crofts, 1948.

Dessoir, M., *Outlines of the history of psychology*. New York: Macmillan, 1912.

Deutsch, A., *The history of mental hygiene*. New York: Columbia University Press, 1944.

Drever, J. (ed.), *Sourcebook in psychology.* New York: Philosophical Library, 1960.

Durbray, C. A., *The theory of psychical dispositions.* Washington, D.C.: Ph.D. thesis, Catholic University of America, 1905. (also published in monograph supplement no. 30 of the *Psychol. Rev.*)

Ehrenwald, J. (ed.), *From medicine man to Freud; an anthology.* New York: Dell, 1956.

Ellis, W. D., *A source book of gestalt psychology.* New York: Harcourt, Brace & World, 1938.

Esper, E. A., *A history of psychology.* Philadelphia: W. B. Saunders, 1964.

Fay, J. W., *American psychology before William James.* New Brunswick, N.J.: Rutgers University Press, 1939.

Fearing, F., *Reflex action: a study in the history of physiological psychology.* Baltimore: Williams & Wilkins, 1930.

Fink, M., *Selected bibliography of EEG in human psychophamacology,* 1951–1962. New York: American Elsevier, 1964.

Flugel, J. C., *A hundred years of psychology, 1833–1933.* Part V: *1933–1963,* revised by D. J. West. London: Duckworth, 1964.

Foster, M., *Lectures on the history of physiology during the sixteenth, seventeenth, and eighteenth centuries.* Cambridge: Cambridge University Press, 1901.

Foucault, M. J. P., *Madness and civilization, a history of insanity in the age of reason.* New York: Pantheon, 1965.

Freeman, L. and Small, M., *Story of psychoanalysis.* New York: Pocket Books, 1960.

Freud, S., "History of the psychoanalytic movement." *Amer. J. Psychol.* 1910, *21.*

Fulton, J. F., *Selected readings in the history of physiology.* (Completed by Leonard G. Wilson). 2nd rev. ed. Springfield, Ill.: Charles C. Thomas, 1966.

Garrett, H. E., *Great experiments in psychology.* 3rd ed. New York: Appleton-Century-Crofts, 1951.

Goshen, C. E., *Documentary history of psychiatry: a source book on historical principles.* New York: Philosophical Library, 1967.

Hall, G. S., *Founders of modern psychology.* New York: Appleton-Century-Crofts, 1912.

Hartmann, G. W., *Gestalt psychology.* New York: Ronald, 1935.

Havemann, Ernest, *Age of psychology.* New York: Simon & Shuster, 1957.

Hearnshaw, L. S., *A short history of British psychology 1840–1940.* London and New York: Barnes & Noble, 1964.

Heidbreder, Edna, *Seven psychologies.* New York: Appleton-Century-Crofts, 1933, 1961.

Henle, Mary (ed.), *Documents of gestalt psychology.* Berkeley, Calif.: California University Press, 1961.

Herrnstein, R. J., and Boring, E. G. (eds.), *A source book in the history of psychology.* Cambridge, Mass.: Harvard University Press, 1965.

Höffding, H., *A history of modern philosophy.* London: Macmillan, 1920, 1924. 2 vols.

Hulin, W. S., *A short history of psychology.* New York: Holt, 1934.

Hunter, R. A., and Macalpine, Ida (eds.), *Three hundred years of psychiatry, 1535–1860.* Oxford: Oxford University Press, 1963.

Kanner, L., *A history of the care and study of the mentally retarded.* Springfield, Ill.: Thomas, 1964.

Kantor, J. R.: *The scientific evolution of psychology.* Vol. 1. Chicago: Principia, 1963.

Keller, F. S., *The definition of psychology: an introduction to psychological systems.* New York, London: D. Appleton-Century, 1937.

Klemm, O., *History of psychology.* New York: Scribner, 1914.

Kraepelin, E., *One hundred years of psychiatry.* New York: Philosophical Library, 1962.

Lachman, S. J., *History and methods of physiological psychology: a brief overview.* Detroit: Hamilton, 1963.

Leigh, D., *The historical development of British psychiatry.* Oxford: Pergamon Press, 1961.

Levine, A. J., *Current psychologies.* Cambridge: Sci-Art, 1940.

Lowrey, L. G. (ed.), *Orthopsychiatry 1923–1948 retrospect and prospect.* New York: American Orthopsychiatric Assoc., 1948.

Mandler, Jean M., and Mandler, G., *Thinking: from association to gestalt.* New York: Wiley, 1964.

Marx, M. H. (ed.), *Psychological theory.* New York: Macmillan, 1951.

Marx, M. H. (ed.), *Theories in contemporary psychology.* New York: Macmillan, 1963.

Marx, M. H., and Hillix, W. A., *Systems and theories in psychology*. New York: McGraw-Hill, 1963.

Mercier, D., *The origins of contemporary psychology*. New York: P. J. Kenedy & Sons, 1918.

Meyer, D. B., *Positive thinkers*. New York: Doubleday, 1965.

Miller, G. A., *Psychology: the science of mental life*. New York: Harper & Row, 1962.

Misiak, H., *The philosophical roots of scientific psychology*. New York: Fordham University Press, 1961.

Misiak, H., and Staudt, Virginia M., *Catholics in psychology: a historical survey*. New York: McGraw-Hill, 1954.

Misiak, H., and Sexton, V. S., *History of psychology: an overview*. New York: Greene & Stratton, 1966.

Moore, J. S., *The foundations of psychology*. Princeton, N.J.: Princeton University Press, 1933.

Muller-Freienfels, R., *The evolution of modern psychology*. New Haven, Conn.: Yale University Press, 1935.

Murchison, C. (ed.), *Psychologies of 1925*. Worcester, Mass.: Clark University Press, 1926.

Murchison, C. (ed.), *Psychological register*. Worcester, Mass.: Clark University Press, 1929–1932. 3 vols.

Murchison, C. (ed.), *A history of psychology in autobigraphy*. Worcester, Mass.: Clark University Press, 1930–1936. Volume 4 edited by E. G. Boring *et al.;* New York: Russell and Russell, 1952. Volume 5 edited by E. G. Boring and G. Lindzey, New York: Appleton-Century-Crofts, 1967.

Murchison, C. (ed.), *Psychologies of 1930*. Worcester, Mass.: Clark University Press, 1930.

Murphy, G., *Historical introduction to modern psychology*. Rev. ed. New York: Harcourt, Brace, 1949.

Nuttin, J., *Psychology in Belgium*. Louvain: Publications Universitaires, 1961.

Oberndorf, C. P., *A history of psychoanalysis in America*. New York: Grune & Stratton, 1953.

Pillsbury, W. B., *The history of psychology*. New York: Norton, 1929.

Postman, L. (ed.), *Psychology in the making*. New York: Knopf, 1962.

Poynter, F. L. N. (ed.), *The history and philosophy of knowledge of the brain and its functions*. Oxford: Blackwell, 1958.

Rand, B. (ed.)., *The classical psychologists*. New York: Houghton Mifflin, 1912.

Rao, S. K., *Development of psychological thought in India*. Mysore, India: Kavyalaya Publishers, 1962.

Ray, M. B., *Doctors of the mind*. Indianapolis: Bobbs-Merrill, 1963.

Reeves, J. W., *Body and mind in western thought: an introduction to some origins of modern psychology*. Harmondsworth, Middlesex: Penguin Books, 1958.

Ribot, T., *English psychology*. New York: D. Appleton, 1874.

Ribot, T., *German psychology of today: the empirical school*. New York: Scribner, 1899.

Riese, W., *A history of neurology*. New York: MD Publications, 1959.

Roback, A. A., *History of psychology and psychiatry*. New York: Philosophical Library, 1961.

Roback, A. A., *A history of American psychology*. Rev. ed. New York: Collier, 1964.

Roe, A., *A psychological study of eminent psychologists and anthropologists*. Washington, D.C.: American Psychological Assoc., 1953.

Schneck, J. M., *A history of psychiatry*. Springfield, Ill.: Thomas, 1960.

Shakow, D., and Rapaport, D., *The influence of Freud on American psychology*. New York: International University Press, 1964.

Shipley, T. (ed.), *Classics in psychology*. New York: Philosophical Library, 1961.

Sinka, J., *Indian psychology*. London: Kegan Paul, Trench, Trubner, 1934.

Singer, C., *A short history of anatomy and physiology from the Greeks to Harvey*. New York: Dover, 1957.

Spearman, C. E., *Psychology down the ages*. London: Macmillan, 1937. 2 vols.

Stratton, G. M., *Theophrastus and the Greek physiological psychology before Aristotle*. New York: Macmillan, 1917.

Titchener, E. B., *Systematic psychology: prolegomena*. New York: Macmillan, 1929.

Ueberweg, F., *History of philosophy*. New York: Scribner, 1891.

Villa, G., *Contemporary psychology*. New York: Macmillan, 1903.

Walker, Helen M., *Studies in the history of statistical method*. Baltimore: Williams & Wilkins, 1931.

Walker, Nigel, *A short history of psychotherapy*. London: Routledge & Kegan Paul, 1957.

Wangh, M. (ed.), *Fruition of an idea: fifty years of psychoanalysis in New York*. New York: International Universities, 1962.

Wann, T. (ed.), *Behaviorism and phenomenology*. Chicago: Chicago University Press, 1964.

Warren, H. C., *A history of association psychology*. New York: Scribner, 1921.

Watson, R. I., *The great psychologists from Aristotle to Freud*. New York: Lippincott, 1963.

Westerhof, A. C., *Representative psychologists*. Union Bridge, Md.: Pilot Pub., 1938.

Williams, R. D., and Bellows, R. W., *Background of contemporary psychology*. Columbus: Hedrick, 1935.

Windelband, W., *A history of philosophy*. New York: Macmillan, 1893, 1901.

Windelband, W., *History of ancient philosophy*. New York: Dover, 1956.

Winkler, J. K., *Mind explorers*. New York: Reynal & Hitchock, 1939.

Winn, R. B., *Soviet psychology*. New York: Philosophical Library, 1961.

Wolman, B. B., *Contemporary theories and systems in psychology*. New York: Harper, 1960.

Wolman, B. B. (ed.), *Historical Roots of Contemporary Psychology*. New York: Harper & Row, 1968.

Woodworth, R. S., and Sheehan, Mary R., *Contemporary schools of psychology*. 3rd ed. New York: Ronald, 1964.

Wortis, J., *Soviet psychiatry*. Baltimore: Williams and Wilkins, 1950.

Wortis, J. (ed.), *Recent advances in biological psychiatry*. New York: Grune, 1960–1961. 3 vols.

Zeller, E., *Outlines of the history of Greek philosophy*. New York: Henry Holt, 1890.

Zilboorg, G., and Henry G. W., *A history of medical psychology*. New York: Norton, 1951.

Index of Names

Names of contributing authors are followed by their dates, and the first page numbers given refer to that writer's selections. All other page numbers refer to brief discussions in the text.

Index of Subjects

THE BOOK MANUFACTURE

History of Psychology was typeset by Holland-Breumelhof N.V. Printers and Publishers in Amsterdam. Offset printing and binding was done by Kingsport Press, Kingsport, Tennessee. The paper is Perkins & Squire Company's Glatfelter Old Forge. Internal design and case design was by John Goetz. The type in this book is Times Roman with Bulmer headings.